The Legal
Environment
of Business

The Legal Environment of Business

A CRITICAL THINKING APPROACH

Fourth Edition

Nancy K. Kubasek

Bartley A. Brennan

M. Neil Browne

Bowling Green University

PEARSON
Prentice Hall

Prentice Hall
Upper Saddle River, NJ 07458

Library of Congress Cataloging-in-Publication Data

Kubasek, Nancy.
   The legal environment of business : a critical thinking approach / Nancy K. Kubasek,
Bartley A. Brennan, M. Neil Browne. — 4th ed.
      p. cm.
   includes bibliographical references and index
   ISBN 0-13-149856-8 (alk. paper)
   1. Industrial laws and legislation—United States. 2. Trade regulation—United States. 3.
Business law—United States. 4. Critical thinking. I. Brennan, Bartley A. II. Browne, M.
Neil, 1944–   III. Title.
   KF1600 .K83 2005
   346.8307—dc22

                                                                2004061122

Acquisitions Editor: Bill Larkin
Editorial Director: Jeff Shelstad
Assistant Editor: Sam Goffinet
Editorial Assistant: Joanna Doxey
Media Project Manager: Nancy Welcher
Director of Marketing: Eric Frank
Marketing Assistant: Tina Panagioutou
Managing Editor (Production): Cynthia Regan
Production Editor: Melissa Owens
Permissions Supervisor: Charles Morris
Manufacturing Buyer: Diane Peirano

Design Manager: Maria Lange
Designer: Steve Frim
Cover Design: Steve Frim
Cover Image: Art Resource, N.
Director, Image Resource Center: Melinda Reo
Manager, Rights and Permissions: Zina Arabia
Manager: Visual Research: Beth Brenzel
Manager, Cover Visual Research & Permissions: Karen Sanatar
Manager, Print Production: Christy Mahon
Composition/Full-Service Project Management: Preparé, Inc.
Printer/Binder: Courier Kendalville

Pearson Education LTD.
Pearson Education Australia PTY, Limited
Pearson Education Singapore, Pte. Ltd
Pearson Education North Asia Ltd
Pearson Education, Canada, Ltd
Pearson Educación de Mexico, S.A. de C.V.
Pearson Education–Japan
Pearson Education Malaysia, Pte. Ltd

10 9 8 7 6 5 4 3 2 1

ISBN 0-13-149856-8

To the numerous students who appreciate the importance of developing their critical thinking skills for their personal growth and development.

NANCY K. KUBASEK AND M. NEIL BROWNE

To Sandra for everything.

BARTLEY A. BRENNAN

BRIEF CONTENTS

Part Three
PUBLIC LAW AND THE LEGAL ENVIRONMENT OF BUSINESS   469

CONTENTS

Part Two
Private Law and the Legal Environment of Business   261

Part Three
Public Law and the Legal Environment of Business   469

17 THE LAW OF ADMINISTRATIVE AGENCIES   470

PREFACE

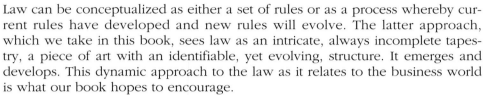

Law can be conceptualized as either a set of rules or as a process whereby current rules have developed and new rules will evolve. The latter approach, which we take in this book, sees law as an intricate, always incomplete tapestry, a piece of art with an identifiable, yet evolving, structure. It emerges and develops. This dynamic approach to the law as it relates to the business world is what our book hopes to encourage.

This book also does something that no other textbook has tried to do; that is, it helps students clearly see the links between the legal environment and all of the other core disciplines in business. Many of us have discussed the role of the legal environment with our colleagues in other disciplines, and we have talked about the need for an integrated curriculum. We believe this book, with its linking law and business approach, is an important first step in creating a truly integrated curriculum.

The readers of this book will typically be prospective managers of public and private enterprises. How can a text best prepare these future managers for functioning in the global and ever-changing legal environment of business? Critical thinking skills are the essential ingredient for understanding current legal rules and making future business decisions that both comply with and contribute to emergent law. The importance of these skills for contemporary organizations has been recognized not only by educators but also by those in the business community.

The initial motivation for this book was the authors' perception that there was no legal environment book available that explicitly and adequately facilitated the development of students' critical thinking skills. Teaching students in a systematic manner that developed their critical thinking skills required the use of an additional supplemental critical thinking textbook.

Some people may argue that merely using the traditional method of case analysis allows them to develop their students' critical thinking skills. The problem with such an approach, however, is that the case method focuses only on the students' analytical skills, ignoring the evaluative component that is really the essence of critical thinking. Another problem with the traditional method of case analysis is that it does not include an ethical component. To engage in critical thinking necessarily includes consideration of the impact of values on the outcome being considered.

The use of cases in the legal environment of business classroom, however, can provide an excellent opportunity for the development of students' critical thinking abilities when the traditional case method is modified to emphasize the development of critical thinking skills. So, the initial two authors of this text contacted M. Neil Browne, one of the authors of the best-selling critical thinking textbook, *Asking the Right Questions* (Prentice Hall, Seventh Edition, 2005), and asked him whether he would be interested in collaborating on a legal environment of business textbook that incorporated the teaching of critical thinking skills. Because he has a law degree, and in fact, has written articles about the relationship between critical thinking and traditional case analysis, he was most interested in the project.

The result of this collaboration is a textbook that explicitly lays out in the first chapter the critical thinking skills that students are to acquire. It provides a modified approach to case analysis that gives students the opportunity to practice these skills throughout the semester, whenever they read either a case or an article containing legal analysis. Case questions that focus on various critical thinking skills appear after several cases throughout the book. Critical thinking questions also open up each chapter and get students thinking critically about each new area of the law.

Those who wish to devote even more attention to their students' critical thinking skills can do so by using the paperback guide to critical thinking, *Asking the Right Questions About the Legal Environment of Business*, which can be shrink-wrapped with our text. Each chapter of the supplement, which draws heavily on the best-selling textbook *Asking the Right Questions*, explains in detail and models a different critical thinking skill. Development of the skills can be further encouraged through the use of the student study guide. Both of these supplements are described later.

As we think about the value of this book to the faculty and students who use it, there are really ten features that we think make the book valuable. In the following sections, we explain each of them.

(1) CONTAINS AN EXPLICIT CRITICAL THINKING MODEL THAT IS CLEARLY SUPPORTED BY THE SUPPLEMENTS PACKAGE

This is the first legal environment of business textbook that defines critical thinking for students and gives them opportunities to explicitly work on developing those critical thinking skills. The critical thinking materials were developed by M. Neil Browne, a recognized authority in the field of critical thinking, who also has a law degree.

The model of critical thinking provided in the book is one that can also be easily adapted to essays, so that students can internalize the kinds of questions they ask when analyzing cases or editorials in the newspaper.

The book was written in a manner that will give instructors maximum flexibility in terms of the degree to which they want to emphasize the development of their students' critical thinking skills. Faculty members who do not wish to emphasize critical thinking with their students may simply instruct the students to think about their responses to questions in the critical thinking boxes when they read the material but then concentrate class discussions on the substantive material in the text.

Those who want to maximize the development of students' critical thinking skills have a plethora of options available with this text. Some of these options include the following:

- **An explicit critical thinking model explained in Chapter 1.** The authors have modified the traditional approach to case analysis to incorporate some of the fundamental critical thinking questions. Chapter 1 explains this model in detail, and those emphasizing critical thinking skills may find it helpful to spend a significant amount of time discussing Chapter 1 and having students apply the model it develops to cases in subsequent chapters.

- **Critical thinking boxes at the beginning of each chapter and following selected cases.** The beginning-of-chapter critical thinking boxes serve a dual function of introducing chapter material in a more thoughtful and challenging way, while also providing another opportunity for students to practice one of their critical thinking skills. Some of the cases are written in a manner that makes them an especially good vehicle for practicing one or two specific critical thinking skills. We have tried to take advantage of those cases by following them with appropriate critical thinking questions. Any of these questions may provide the basis for classroom discussion or may be used for a written assignment.

- **Newly revised critical thinking student study guide.** In addition to providing the traditional kinds of questions that test students' mastery of the subject matter, this study guide, written by M. Neil Browne, also provides additional opportunities for students to practice their critical thinking skills.

- **Revised Instructor's Manual.** The new Instructor's Manual is written by Professor Andrea Giampetro-Meyer, recipient of Loyola College's top teaching award and author of numerous articles on critical thinking and teaching. This manual offers supplemental study questions that instructors who wish to emphasize critical thinking may distribute to their students as a further guide for classroom discussion. She also provides editorials on topics relevant to each chapter for professors interested in having their students apply the critical thinking approach not just to cases but also to prescriptive articles. Many instructors who have said they never use instructor's manuals have found Professor Giampetro-Meyer's instructor's manual to be the rare exception that is extremely useful.

- **Revised Test Item File.** The test item file has been completely revised with this edition to incorporate essay questions that explicitly test students' critical thinking abilities. Students often will primarily study the subject matter on which they will be tested; with this test item file as a source for exam questions, they will work harder to develop their critical thinking skills knowing that these skills are going to be essential for doing well on exams! The *TestGen* testing software, a computerized test bank developed by Tamarack Software, Inc., is also available to assist instructors in creating tests for their classes. The versatility of this program allows for a range of functions to suit instructors' needs and individualize their tests. The process of test creation is accelerated and expanded with the *TestGen's* drag-and-drop feature, randomized test option, and other various easy-to-use features.

With all of these options, every instructor should be able to tailor this text and its accompanying supplements to incorporate the level of critical thinking emphasis that is desirable for his or her own situation. What some of our long-term users have found is that after trying to do just a little critical thinking at first, their emphasis on these critical thinking skills grows from year to year. And what they have found is that as they increase their focus on developing students' critical thinking skills, their students' understanding of the substance of the law also seems to improve.

(2) EXPLICITLY LINKS LAW TO OTHER BUSINESS DISCIPLINES

The Linking Law and Business feature that follows (shown in context) is designed to respond to a call for more *integration* among the courses in colleges of business. This call is coming from deans, who want to have more cohesive programs, as well as faculty members teaching legal environment of business courses, who want to be able to respond to questions from colleagues from other disciplines who are not all that certain that there is a real need for students to have a law course.

This feature provides small boxed discussions of concepts from other disciplines that are directly related to the material in the legal environment chapter. In addition to showing students how integrally law is related to other business disciplines, these boxes can be pointed out to faculty members of other disciplines who might question how the law fits into the business curriculum.

Following is an illustration of this feature from Chapter 13 on product liability:

Linking Law & Business

Management

In your management class, you learned about total quality management (TQM), a process by which all members within an organization function to achieve goals associated with product quality. TQM places a strong emphasis on the importance of high-quality products for three reasons: (1) to promote a positive image for the organization; (2) to lower costs and increase market share; and (3) to decrease liability costs associated with defective products. By improving quality, an organization is less likely to manufacture potentially dangerous products. Thus, it is probable that the organization will be faced with fewer strict liability charges.

Source: S. Certo, *Modern Management* (Upper Saddle River, N.J.: Prentice Hall, 2000), pp. 504–505.

(3) FEATURES AN EMPHASIS ON TECHNOLOGY

No one can ignore the sweeping changes that technology is bringing to many areas of the law. If our students are to thrive in the new workplace, they are going to have to understand the changes technology is bringing to the legal environment of business. Realizing the growing importance of technology-induced changes in the law, we considered both adding a separate chapter on cyberlaw, as well as the primary alternative, introducing these changes in the other substantive areas of the law where they would be relevant (e.g., antitrust law and the *Microsoft* case in Chapter 23). To ensure that our students are up to date on how technology is affecting the law, we decided to do both in the previous edition, adding a new chapter on cyberlaw (Chapter 7) and inserting Technology and the Legal Environment boxes in other chapters, where we feel these changes need to be highlighted. The technology materials have been substantially updated in this edition.

Following is an example of a typical technology box from Chapter 5:

Technology and the Legal Environment

Taxation of the Internet?

The rapid rise in Internet commerce has many states wondering how they will collect their fair share of sales taxes. According to the U.S. Department of Commerce, Internet retail sales have continued to increase from $28 billion in 2000 to $44 billion in 2002. Although Internet sales comprise only 1.4 percent of overall retail sales in the United States, advocates of taxes on Internet sales insist that states are losing a considerable amount of revenue each year.[1]

Currently, states are only allowed to require business to submit sales tax payments if the business has a store or distribution center in the state. Otherwise, states are prohibited from collecting sales taxes, although residents are supposed to report the taxes on personal income tax returns. In addition to the e-commerce business, increased access to the Internet has some clamoring for a use tax on Internet access, in addition to a sales tax on Internet purchases.

In 1998, Congress approved the Internet Tax Freedom Act, which established a moratorium on Internet taxes until November 2001. The 1998 bill provided a grandfather clause that allowed several states to continue levying taxes on Internet access established before the Internet Tax Freedom Act was passed. In November 2001, Congress extended the moratorium for two more years to allow for more discussion and research on the effects of the ban on state governments.

In September 2003, the House of Representatives passed the Internet Tax Nondiscrimination Act (H.R. 49), a bill designed to replace the Internet Tax Freedom Act that would have expired in November 2003 with a permanent ban on taxes on Internet access and a permanent extension of the moratorium on multiple and discriminatory taxes on electronic commerce. The House bill also eliminated all grandfather clauses of the 1998 bill. H.R. 49 was sent to the Senate for consideration in late September 2003.

On April 29, 2004, the Senate passed a different version of the Internet Tax Nondiscrimination Act (S.150) that extends the moratorium on Internet taxes until November 2007. The Senate bill was a compromise between supporters of a permanent Internet tax ban and a group of senators who questioned how a permanent ban would affect state and local budgets.

In addition to the four-year moratorium, the Senate version of the bill allows a handful of states that began taxing Internet access before the 1998 moratorium to continue levying those taxes until the moratorium expires in November 2007. The bill also allows 17 states that now tax DSL Internet access to continue those taxes until November 2005. The Senate sent the bill back to the House of Representatives for consideration. At the time the book went to press final action by both houses had not yet been taken.

---

[1] U.S. Department of Commerce, Electronic Commerce Statistics, April 15, 2004; access to statistics can be found at **www.census.gov/estats**.

(4) EMPHASIZES THE ROLE OF ETHICS

One of the issues professors continually grapple with is how to integrate ethics into the legal environment of business course. The critical thinking model introduced in Chapter 1 incorporates ethics into the case analysis. Questioning how a person's ethics influences his or her decision making, therefore, becomes a routine part of a student's evaluative behavior. For those who want to emphasize this approach to ethics, Chapter 5 in the new shrink-wrapped supplement will be essential.

The book also contains a chapter on ethics and social responsibility (Chapter 9) for those who prefer a more traditional approach to ethics or who would like to spend additional time discussing ethics.

(5) CONTAINS CURRENT AND CLASSIC CASES

The textbook contains many of the most significant contemporary cases, including important United States Supreme Court decisions handed down as recently as 2004. Yet it also retains many classic cases whose holdings have continued to have a significant impact on the legal environment of business for years after they were decided. Some of the more recent cases excerpted or discussed in the new edition of this text include:

United States v. Martha Stewart and Peter Bacanivic, 323 F.Supp.2d 606 (S.D.N.Y. 2004) (excerpted in Chapter 1)

Snowey's v. Harrah's Entertainment, Inc., 11 Ca1.Rptr.3d 35 (Ct. App., Calif, 2004) (discussed in Chapter 3)

Ashcroft v. ACLU, 124 S. Ct. 2783 (2004) (discussed in Chapter 4)

Thornton v. United States, 124 S. Ct. 2127 (2004) (discussed in Chapter 5)

Pierce County v. Guillen, 537 U.S. 129 (2003) (discussed in Chapter 5)

United States v. American Library Association, Ashcroft v. ACLU, 124 S. Ct. 2783 (2004) (discussed in Chapter 5)

Illinois v. Lidster, 124 S. Ct. 885 (2004) (discussed in Chapter 5)

United States v. Gray, Eleventh Circuit Court of Appeals 367 F. 3D 1263 (2004) (excerpted in Chapter 7)

Optinrealbig.com v. Ironport Systems (SpamCop.net), 323 F. Supp. 1037 (2004) (discussed in Chapter 12)

Campbell v. State Farm, 123 S. Ct. 1513 (2002) (discussed in Chapter 12)

Traffix Devices, Inc. v. Marketing Displays, Inc., 121 S. Ct. 1225 (2001) (discussed in Chapter 14)

County of Wayne v. Hathcock, 684 N.W.2d 765 (2004) (excerpted in Chapter 14)

Brown University and International Union, United Automobile, Aerospace and Agricultural Implement Workers of America, UAW AFL-CIO, Case I-RC-21368 (July 13, 2004) (discussed in Chapter 19)

General Dynamics Land Systems, Inc. v. Dennis Cline et al., 540 U.S. 581 (2004) (discussed in Chapter 20)

Department of Transportation v. Public Citizen, 124 S. Ct. 2204 (2004) (excerpted in Chapter 21)

United States v. Microsoft Corporation, 253 F.3d 34 (D.C. Cir. June 28, 2001) (excerpted in Chapter 23)

(6) EMPHASIZES THE IMPORTANCE OF THE GLOBAL ENVIRONMENT

In recognition of the growing importance of the global environment, we have introduced the international environment of business to the students in the third chapter of the text. Of course, individual instructors may always choose to have the students read this chapter later, but its placement reflects the importance the authors place on international considerations, an importance also stressed recently by the AACSB.

We have also incorporated into every chapter a section that focuses on the global dimensions of the subject matter of each chapter. In this way, international issues may be discussed throughout the semester.

(7) STRESSES VOCABULARY DEVELOPMENT

We all recognize the importance of being able to use the "language of the law." Our text recognizes the importance of students acquiring the necessary vocabulary to discuss legal issues by providing a running glossary in the margin.

(8) CONTAINS NUMEROUS CHARTS, TABLES, AND EXHIBITS

Student learning is facilitated by the use of charts, tables, and exhibits. These matters convey the material to the students in a slightly different form, sometimes making concepts easier to comprehend.

We have, therefore, incorporated them wherever possible. The publisher has carefully designed these elements in full color for effective comprehension by the student.

(9) CONTAINS WEB SITES FOR EACH CHAPTER

We cannot ignore the fact that many of our students feel more comfortable on the Web than in the library. Therefore, at the end of each chapter, we have provided numerous Web sites to which they can go to learn more about the topics covered in the chapter.

(10) COVERAGE THAT SATISFIES THE AACSB STANDARDS

The AACSB mandates coverage of global and ethical issues; the influence of political, social, legal and regulatory, and environmental and technological issues; and the impact of demographic diversity on organizations. This book covers every one of the topics listed in the AACSB mandate and is especially strong in its emphasis on ethics and international issues. The critical thinking approach of the book makes students recognize that ethics plays a significant role in every business decision they make.

Most of the changes made to this edition have been described in detail in the foregoing section on unique features of the text, but for those current users of the text who just want a quick rundown of how the text has changed, the following list highlights the most significant changes:

- Reorganized the first part of the text to better reflect the order in which a number of adopters use the chapters.
- Integrated discussions of the varied implications of Sarbanes-Oxley throughout the text.
- Added a number of more recent cases, as noted previously.
- Added numerous new business examples throughout the text.
- Revised and updated many of the case problems at the end of each chapter.
- Added an "Assignment on the Internet" to the end of each chapter.

Many of the supplements that have been described previously are crucial to the flexible approach to critical thinking that distinguishes this text from the others in the field. Following is a convenient listing of all the supplements for instructors to review when deciding which supplements to select.

ASKING THE RIGHT QUESTIONS ABOUT THE LEGAL ENVIRONMENT OF BUSINESS

This supplement, which may be shrink-wrapped with the text, is the most exciting addition to our list of resource materials designed to help you develop your students' critical thinking skills while developing a better understanding of the legal environment of business. A number of professors already use *Asking the Right Questions*, on which this supplement is based, as a second text in their law-related courses. This supplement has the advantage of being tailored specifically to the legal environment of business classroom. You can think of it as your students' private critical thinking tutor.

INSTRUCTOR'S RESOURCE MANUAL

Once again, our instructor's resource manual has been expertly prepared by Andrea Giampetro-Meyer of Loyola College, a recipient of teaching awards from the ALSB, her college, and Beta Gamma Sigma. Because she uses the textbook, she is able to incorporate ideas into the manual that have actually been tested in her classroom. The author is also someone who has expertise in the area of critical thinking, having written numerous articles on the topic. The manual includes the following features:

- Discussion outlines for each chapter, with references to other supplements when appropriate.
- Answers to questions in the Critical Thinking About the Law boxes.
- Answers to end-of-chapter questions.
- Additional critical thinking questions and assignments.
- Editorials from the *Wall Street Journal* that are related to the substance of the chapters, which can be used to apply students' critical thinking skills to the kinds of reading materials they are likely to encounter in the business world.
- General teaching tips and teaching-related research that professors can use to improve their teaching.

STUDENT STUDY GUIDE/CRITICAL THINKING SUPPLEMENT

M. Neil Browne, who authored the critical thinking materials in the text, has once again written the student study guide for the fourth edition. This study guide provides significant opportunities for students to practice and improve their critical thinking skills, in addition to providing them with exercises to test their knowledge of the substantive materials provided in the text. The idea for this supplement grew out of users' requests that we provide more opportunities for students to focus on developing their critical thinking skills.

POWERPOINT SLIDES

Enhance your classroom presentations with this well-developed PowerPoint presentation set. More than 500 text-specific PowerPoints highlight fundamental concepts and integrate key figures and illustrations from the text.

PRENTICE HALL CUSTOM TEST

The test item file was revised this year by Professor Nancy Kubasek. The test item file incorporates essay questions that test students' critical thinking skills in addition to their knowledge of the substance of the chapters. The test item file also includes objective questions that are designated as easy, moderate, and difficult to allow the instructor maximum flexibility in constructing exams.

WEB SITE SUPPORT

Introducing the Companion Web Site for *The Legal Environment of Business: A Critical Thinking Approach*, Fourth Edition

The Companion Web Site is a guide to the free online resources for your book and is located at www.prenhall.com/kubasek.

Instructor's Resources are available electronically via Prentice Hall's Instructor Resource Center. Ask your local Prentice Hall sales representative for details.

CASE UPDATES

Adopters of the book may subscribe to a list that will provide regular case updates via e-mail, consisting of edited versions of newly decided cases and accompanying critical thinking questions that may be used to stimulate discussions about these cases. To take advantage of this opportunity, just send an e-mail to Nancy Kubasek, at nkubase@cba.bgsu.edu and ask to be added to the CTLEB list, and you will be subscribed to the list.

ACKNOWLEDGMENTS

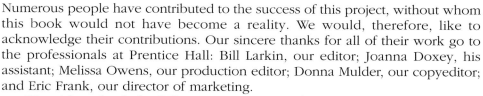

Numerous people have contributed to the success of this project, without whom this book would not have become a reality. We would, therefore, like to acknowledge their contributions. Our sincere thanks for all of their work go to the professionals at Prentice Hall: Bill Larkin, our editor; Joanna Doxey, his assistant; Melissa Owens, our production editor; Donna Mulder, our copyeditor; and Eric Frank, our director of marketing.

We wish to thank the following reviewers and users whose numerous comments, suggestions, and criticisms significantly improved the content of this edition: Lisa A. Hubasek, Texas A&M; Paul J. Graf, San Diego State University; Kenneth R. Taurman, Jr.; Indiana University Southeast; Craig R. Stilwell, Michigan State; Teri Elkins, University of Houston; Linda Christiansen, Indiana University Southeast; Linda Axelrod, Metropolitan State University, Normandale and Anoka-Ramsey Community Colleges; Robert McOmber; Bowling Green State University; Wm. Dennis Ames, Indiana University of Pennsylvania.

We also want to thank again the reviewers of previous editions of this text, as the current edition is based on the foundation that these reviewers influenced: Louis Aranda, Arizona State University; Roy J. Girasa, Pace University; Jane A. Malloy, Delaware Valley Community College; Ernest W. King, University of Southern Mississippi; James Marshall, Michigan State University; John McGee, Southwest Texas State University; Royce Barondes, Louisiana State University; Debra Burke, Western Carolina University; James Marshall, Michigan State University; Paulette Stenzel, Michigan State University; Frank Chong, Southeast Missouri State University; Daphyne Sounders Thomas, James Madison University; John McGee, Southwest Texas State University; Kurt Saunders, California State University; Lauren Ross, California State, Northridge, and UCLA extension.

One other important group of dedicated individuals we wish to thank for their assistance on this project is our research assistants: Alex Frondorf, currently a law student at St. Louis University School of Law, and Steve Weigand and Sara Mercier, both students at Bowling Green State University. And we do not want to forget the work done on previous editions of this text by our former assistants Anne Hardenbaugh, Wesley J. Hires, Carrie Williamson, and Michael Meuti.

We also thank the word-processing staff at Bowling Green State University who retyped numerous versions of this manuscript without complaint: Karen Masters and Tami Thomas. They have worked on as many editions of this text as the authors!

And, finally, we thank the numerous students who have used the book and made suggestions for improving it.

The authors hope that this book will help fulfill its purpose of providing a useful tool for students who wish to develop their critical thinking skills while gaining a better understanding of the legal environment of business. Toward that end, the authors would be happy to correspond with any readers via e-mail. If you have any questions while reading the text, please feel free to contact Nancy Kubasek at nkubase@cba.bgsu.edu or Neil Browne at nbrown2@cba.bgsu.edu

ABOUT THE AUTHORS

Nancy Kubasek is a Professor of Legal Studies at Bowling Green State University, where she teaches the Legal Environment of Business, Environmental Law, and an Honors Seminar on Moral Principles. For eight years she team-taught a freshman honors seminar on critical thinking and values analysis. She has published an undergraduate textbook titled *Environmental Law*, Fourth Edition (Prentice Hall, 2002) and more than 50 articles. Professor Kubasek's articles have appeared in such journals as the *American Business Law Journal*, the *Journal of Legal Studies Education*, the *Harvard Women's Law Journal*, the *Georgetown Journal of Legal Ethics*, and the *Harvard Journal on Legislation*. She received her J.D. from the University of Toledo College of Law and her B.A. from Bowling Green State University.

Active in her professional associations, Professor Kubasek has served as president of the TriState Regional Academy of Legal Studies in Business, and is currently the vice president of her national professional association, the Academy of Legal Studies in Business (ALSB). Committed to helping students become excited about legal research, she organized the first Undergraduate Student Paper Competition of the ALSB's Annual Meeting, an event that now provides an annual opportunity for students to present their original legal research at a national convention. She has also published several articles with students and has received her university's highest award for faculty–student research. She states:

> The most important thing that a teacher can do is to help his or her students develop the skills and attitudes necessary to become lifelong learners. Professors should help their students learn the types of questions to ask to analyze complex legal issues, and to develop a set of criteria to apply when evaluating reasons. If we are successful, students will leave our legal environment of business classroom with a basic understanding of important legal concepts, a set of evaluative criteria to apply when evaluating arguments that includes an ethical component, and a desire to continue learning.
>
> To attain these goals, the classroom must be an interactive one, where students learn to ask important questions, define contexts, generate sound reasons, point out the flaws in erroneous reasoning, recognize alternative perspectives, and consider the impacts that their decisions (both now and in the future) have on the broader community beyond themselves.

Bartley A. Brennan is an Emeritus Professor of Legal Studies at Bowling Green State University. He is a graduate of the School of Foreign Service, Georgetown University (B.S. International Economics); the College of Law, State University of New York at Buffalo (J.D.); and Memphis State University (M.A. Economics). He was a volunteer in the United States Peace Corps, was employed by the Office of Opinions and Review of the Federal Communications Commission, and worked in the general counsel's office of a private international corporation. Professor Brennan has received appointments as a visiting associate professor, the Wharton School, University of Pennsylvania, and as a Research Fellow, Ethics Resource Center, Washington, D.C. He is the author of articles dealing with the Foreign Corrupt Practices Act of 1977, as amended; the business judgment rule; law and economics; and business ethics. He has published numerous articles in such journals as the *American Business Law Journal*, *University of North Carolina Journal of International Law*, and the *Notre Dame University Journal of Legislation*. He is a coauthor of *Modern Business Law* (third edition). He has testified on amending the Foreign Corrupt Practices Act before the Sub-Committee on International Economics and Finance of the House Commerce, Energy, and Telecommunications Committee.

M. Neil Browne is a Distinguished Teaching Professor of Economics and director of IMPACT, an Honors Residential Learning Community Centered Around the Principles of Intellectual Discovery and Moral Commitment, at Bowling Green State University. He received a J.D. from the University of Toledo and a Ph.D. from the University of Texas. He is the coauthor of seven books and more than a hundred research articles in professional journals. One of his books, *Asking the Right Questions: A Guide to Critical Thinking*, Sixth Edition, is a leading text in the field of critical thinking. His most recent book, *Striving for Excellence in College: Tips for Active Learning*, provides learners with practical ideas for expanding the power and effectiveness of their thinking. Professor Browne has been asked by dozens of colleges and universities to aid their faculty in developing critical thinking skills on their respective campuses. He also serves on the editorial board of the *Korean Journal of Critical Thinking*. In 1989, he was a silver medalist in the Council for the Advancement and Support of Education's National Professor of the Year award. Also, in 1989, he was named the Ohio Professor of the Year. He has won numerous teaching awards on both a local and national level. He states:

> When students come into contact with conflicting claims, they can react in several fashions; my task is to enable them to evaluate these persuasive attempts. I try to provide them with a broad range of criteria and attitudes that reasonable people tend to use as they think their way through a conversation. In addition, I urge them to use productive questions as a stimulus to deep discussion, a looking below the surface of an argument for the assumptions underlying the visible component of the reasoning. The eventual objectives are to enable them to be highly selective in their choice of beliefs and to provide them with the greater sense of meaning that stems from knowing that they have used their own minds to separate sense from relative nonsense.

Part One

AN INTRODUCTION TO THE LAW AND THE LEGAL ENVIRONMENT OF BUSINESS

Part One introduces the concept of critical thinking that provides the framework for our study of the legal environment of business. It also gives an overview of this legal environment through our exploration of alternative philosophies of law, alternative philosophies of ethics, how the constitutional foundations of our legal system work to resolve both criminal and civil disputes, how the American system works, and alternative methods of resolving disputes. It concludes with a discussion of that corrosion of the legal environment of business known as white-collar crime.

1

CRITICAL THINKING AND LEGAL REASONING

THE IMPORTANCE OF CRITICAL THINKING

Success in the modern business firm requires the development of **critical thinking skills**: the ability to understand what someone is saying and then to apply evaluative criteria to assess the quality of the reasoning offered to support the conclusion. Because they are under increasing competitive pressure, business and industry need managers with advanced thinking skills.[1] Highlighting this need, a report by the secretary of education states that because "one of the major goals of business education is preparing students for the workforce, students and their professors must respond to this need for enhancing critical thinking skills."[2]

Calls for improvements in critical thinking skills also come from persons concerned about business ethics: "Managers stand in need of sharp critical thinking skills that will serve them well [in tackling] ethical issues," according to an editorial in *Management Accounting*.[3] As a future business manager, you will experience many ethical dilemmas. Where should our facilities be located? Whom should we hire? What are the boundaries of fair competition? What responsibilities do firms owe various stakeholders? All such questions require legal analysis and ethical understanding, guided by critical thinking.

The message is clear: Success in business today requires critical thinking skills, and there is no better context in which to develop them than in the study of the laws that affect business. Critical thinking skills learned in the legal environment of business course will be easily transferred to your eventual role as a manager, entrepreneur, or other business professional.

Remember, as you learn about our legal system and how its evolution affects the legal environment of business, you will also be developing your critical thinking skills. You will find that, as your critical thinking skills develop, your understanding of the law will be enhanced. The skills are mutually beneficial.

Legal reasoning is like other reasoning in some ways and different in others. When people, including lawyers and judges, reason, they do so for a purpose. Some problem or dilemma bothers them. The stimulus that gets them thinking is the issue. It is stated as a question because it is a call for action. It requires them to do something, to think about answers.

For instance, in our legal environment of business course we are interested in such issues as the following:

1. When are union organizers permitted under the National Labor Relations Act to trespass on an employer's property?

2. Do tobacco manufacturers have liability for the deaths of smokers?

3. Must a business fulfill a contract when the contract is made with an unlicensed contractor in a state requiring that all contractors be licensed?

These questions have several different answers. Which one should you choose as your answer? Critical thinking moves us toward better choices. Some of your answers could get you into trouble; others could advance your purpose. Each answer is called a conclusion. The **conclusion** is a position or stance on an issue.

critical thinking skills The ability to understand the structure of an argument and apply a set of evaluative criteria to assess its merits.

conclusion A position or stance on an issue; the goal toward which reasoning moves.

---

[1] C. Sormunen and M. Chalupa, *Critical Thinking Skills Research: Developing Evaluation Techniques*, 69 J. Educ. Bus. 172 (1994).

[2] *Id.*

[3] P. Madsen, *Moral Mazes in Management*, Mgmt. Acct., July 1990, at 56.

Business firms encounter legal conclusions in the form of laws or court decisions. Business managers are, therefore, both consumers of and contributors to legal conclusions. As businesses learn about and react to decisions or conclusions made by courts, they have two primary methods of response:

1. Memorize the conclusions or rules of law as a guide for future business decisions

2. Make judgments about the quality of the conclusions

This book encourages you to do both. What is unique about this text is its practical approach to evaluating legal reasoning. This approach is based on using critical thinking skills to understand and evaluate the law as it affects business.

There are many forms of critical thinking, but they all share one characteristic: They focus on the quality of someone's reasoning. Critical thinking is active; it challenges each of us to form judgments about the quality of the link between someone's reasons and conclusions. In particular, we will be focusing on the link between a court's reasons and conclusions.

You will be interested in the legal environment of business not just to understand the current rules governing your business decisions but also to help you evaluate the rules you will encounter as a business manager.

A CRITICAL THINKING MODEL

You will learn critical thinking by practicing it. The text will tutor you. But your efforts are the key to your skill as a critical thinker. Because people often learn best by example, we will introduce you to critical thinking by demonstrating it in a model that you can easily follow.

We now turn to a sample of critical thinking in practice. The eight critical thinking questions listed in Exhibit 1–1 and applied in the sample case that follows illustrate the approach you should use when reading cases to develop your critical thinking abilities.

As a citizen, entrepreneur, or manager, you will encounter cases like the one that follows. How would you respond? What do you think about the quality of Judge Cedarbaum's reasoning?

CASE 1-1

United States of America v. Martha Stewart and Peter Bacanovic
United States District Court for the Southern District of New York 2004 U.S. Dist. LEXIS 12538

Defendants Martha Stewart and Peter Bacanovic were both convicted of conspiracy, making false statements, and obstruction of an agency proceeding, following Stewart's sale of 3,928 shares of ImClone stock on December 27, 2001. Stewart sold all of her ImClone stock after Bacanovic,

Stewart's stockbroker at Merrill Lynch, informed Stewart that the CEO of ImClone, Samuel Waksal, was trying to sell his company stock. On December 28, 2001, ImClone announced that the FDA did not approve the company's cancer-fighting drug Erbitux, after which the Securities and Exchange

Commission and the United States Attorney's Office for the Southern District of New York began investigations into the trading of ImClone stock, including investigations of Stewart and Bacanovic. Following Stewart and Bacanovic's criminal convictions, the defendants filed a motion for a new trial, alleging that expert witness Lawrence F. Stewart, director of the Forensic Services Division of the United States Secret Service, had committed perjury in his testimony on behalf of the prosecution. As the "national expert for ink analysis," Lawrence Stewart testified about the reliability of Defendant Bacanovic's personal documents that contained information about Martha Stewart's investments in ImClone.

Judge Cedarbaum

Rule 33 provides: "Upon the defendant's motion, the court may vacate any judgment and grant a new trial if the interest of justice so requires." However, "in the interest of according finality to a jury's verdict, a motion for a new trial based on previously-undiscovered evidence is ordinarily 'not favored and should be granted only with great caution.' " In most situations, therefore, "relief is justified under Rule 33 only if the newly-discovered evidence could not have been discovered, exercising due diligence, before or during trial, and that evidence 'is so material and non-cumulative that its admission would probably lead to an acquittal.' "

But the mere fact that a witness committed perjury is insufficient, standing alone, to warrant relief under Rule 33. "Whether the introduction of perjured testimony requires a new trial initially depends on the extent to which the prosecution was aware of the alleged perjury. To prevent prosecutorial misconduct, a conviction obtained when the prosecution's case includes testimony that was known or should have been known to be perjured must be reversed if there is any reasonable likelihood that the perjured testimony influenced the jury." When the Government is unaware of the perjury at the time of trial, "a new trial is warranted only if the testimony was material and 'the court [is left] with a firm belief that but for the perjured testimony, the defendant would most likely not have been convicted.' "

Since [*United States v.*] *Wallach*, the Second Circuit has noted that even when the prosecution knew a witness was committing perjury, "where independent evidence supports a defendant's conviction, the subsequent discovery that a witness's testimony at trial was perjured will not warrant a new trial."

Defendants have failed to demonstrate that the prosecution knew or should have known of Lawrence's perjury. However, even under the stricter prejudice standard applicable when the Government is aware of a witness's perjury, defendants' motions fail. There is no reasonable likelihood that knowledge by the jury that Lawrence lied about his participation in the ink tests and whether he was aware of a book proposal could have affected the verdict.

The verdict, the nature of Lawrence's perjury, and the corroboration that Lawrence's substantive testimony received from the defense's expert demonstrate that Lawrence's misrepresentations could have had no effect on defendants' convictions.

First, the jury found that the Government did not satisfy its burden of proof on the charges to which Lawrence's testimony was relevant. Defendants do not dispute that Bacanovic was acquitted of the charge of making and using a false document, and that none of the false statement and perjury specifications concerning the existence of the $60 agreement were found by the jury to have been proved beyond a reasonable doubt. ... In other words, the jury convicted defendants of lies that had nothing to do with the $60 agreement. The outcome would have been no different had Lawrence's entire testimony been rejected by the jury, or had Lawrence not testified at all.

Defendants argue that acquittal on some charges does not establish that the jury completely disregarded Lawrence's testimony. They contend that the $60 agreement constituted Stewart and Bacanovic's core defense and that the "@60" notation was evidence which supported that defense; thus, to the extent that awareness of Lawrence's perjury could have caused the jury to discredit his testimony and have greater confidence in the existence of the agreement and the validity of the notation, the jury would have been more willing to believe defendants' version of the events.

This argument is wholly speculative and logically flawed. The existence of the $60 agreement would not have exonerated defendants. It would not have been inconsistent for the jury to find that defendants did make the $60 agreement, but that the agreement was not the reason for the sale. Defendants do not persuasively explain how knowledge of Lawrence's lies could have made the jury more likely to believe that the agreement was the reason for the sale.

Second, Lawrence's false statements were entirely collateral to the substance of his testimony and to defendants' culpability for the crimes charged. Courts have consistently held that no new trial is warranted under Rule 33 when the allegedly perjured testimony comes from a witness who is not key to the prosecution's case or when the perjury touches on matters collateral to the facts in dispute or to the defendants' guilt or innocence.

As an initial matter, defendants overstate the importance of the $60 agreement to this prosecution. That a $60 agreement was the reason for Stewart's sale was only one of many lies defendants were charged with telling investigators to conceal that Stewart sold her stock because of Bacanovic's tip.

Third, in the words of Bacanovic's lawyer, the prosecution and defense experts "really agreed on almost everything about the main important points." Lyter agreed that the "@60" notation was made with ink which was different from the rest of the ink the Government had tested and that it was not possible to tell whether the "@60" notation was made at the same time as the other notations. Accordingly, even putting aside indications that the jury did not give credence to Lawrence's testimony, it is clear that the impeachment value of Lawrence's perjury would be severely limited since the most critical aspects of his scientific analysis were corroborated by the defense.

In addition to the substantial basis for concluding that the jury's decision could not have been affected by the revelation of Lawrence's misrepresentations, ample evidence unrelated to the $60 agreement or to Lawrence's testimony supports defendants' convictions.

The testimony of Faneuil, Perret, and Pasternak supports the jury's determinations that Stewart lied when she told investigators that she did not recall being informed of Waksal's trading on December 27 …

Finally, Faneuil's testimony supports the jury's determination that Stewart lied when she claimed not to have spoken with Bacanovic about the Government investigation into ImClone trading or Stewart's ImClone trade (Specifications Six and Seven of Count Three). Faneuil stated that Bacanovic repeatedly told him in January 2002 and afterward that Bacanovic had spoken to Stewart and that everyone was "on the same page."

But defendants fail to explain how the revelation of this perjury—if in fact it is perjury—could have affected the verdict. Defendants cannot escape the fact that the jury acquitted Bacanovic of Count Five and both defendants of making false statements relating to the existence of the $60 agreement, and the fact that ample evidence supports the charges of which the jury convicted defendants.

Motion for a new trial *Denied*.

First, review the eight steps of a critical thinking approach to legal reasoning in Exhibit 1-1. We will call these the critical thinking questions throughout the book. Notice the primary importance of the first four steps; their purpose is to discover the vital elements in the case and the reasoning behind the decision. Failure to consider these four foundational steps might result in our reacting too quickly to what a court or legislature has said.

The answers to these four questions enable us to understand how the court's argument fits together and to make intelligent use of legal decisions. These answers are the necessary first step in a critical thinking approach to legal analysis. The final four questions are the critical thinking component of legal reasoning. We ask them to form our reaction to what the court decided.

Our reactions to legal arguments shape our efforts to either support the status quo in the legal environment of business or support the institution of particular changes. Without the last four questions, legal reasoning would be sterile. Why are we even curious about the legal environment? The answer is we want it to be the best we can create. But improvement requires our very best critical thinking.

You will develop your own workable strategies for legal reasoning, but we urge you to start by following our structure. Every time you read a case, ask yourself these eight questions. Then improve upon this set of questions as you become comfortable with the questions.

The remainder of this section will demonstrate the use of each of the eight steps in order. Notice that the order makes sense. The first four follow the path that best allows you to discover the basis of a particular legal decision; the next four assist you in deciding what you think about the worth of that decision.

EXHIBIT 1-1

THE EIGHT STEPS TO LEGAL REASONING

> **8.** Is there relevant missing information?
>   **7.** How appropriate are the legal analogies?
>   **6.** What ethical norms are fundamental to the court's reasoning?
>   **5.** Does the legal argument contain significant ambiguity?
>   **4.** What are the relevant rules of law?
>   **3.** What are the reasons and conclusion?
>   **2.** What is the issue?
>   **1.** What are the facts?

THE CRITICAL THINKING STEPS

FACTS

First we look for the most basic building blocks in a legal decision or argument. These building blocks, or facts, provide the environment or context in which the legal issue is to be resolved. Certain events occurred; certain actions were or were not taken; particular persons behaved or failed to behave in specific ways. All of these and many more possibilities together make up the intricate setting for the playing out of the issue in question. We always wonder: What happened in this case? Let's now turn our attention to the *Stewart* case:

1. Martha Stewart sold 3,928 shares of her ImClone stock on December 27, 2001.
2. On December 28, 2001, ImClone announced the FDA's rejection of its new cancer-fighting drug, causing the company's stock to lose value.
3. Stewart and Bacanovic were convicted of conspiracy, making false statements, and obstruction of an agency proceeding.
4. Expert witness Lawrence Stewart was accused of perjuring himself in the testimony he gave prior to the defendants' conviction.
5. According to a federal rule and case law, perjury of a witness could constitute grounds for a new trial.

ISSUE

In almost any legal conflict, finding and expressing the issue is an important step in forming our reaction. The issue is the question that caused the lawyers and their clients to enter the legal system. Usually there are several reasonable perspectives concerning the correct way to word the issue in dispute.

1. In what instances may a court grant a new trial?
2. Does perjury of a witness mean that defendants should have a new trial?
3. Do the regulations associated with Rule 33 and relevant case law permit the defendants to have a new trial?

Do not let the possibility of multiple useful ways to word the issue cause you any confusion. The issue is certainly not just anything that we say it is. If we claim something is an issue, our suggestion must fulfill the definition of an issue in this particular factual situation.

REASONS AND CONCLUSION

Judge Cedarbaum held that the defendants should not have a new trial. This finding by Judge Cedarbaum is her conclusion; it serves as her answer to the legal issue. Why did she answer this way? Here we are calling for the **reasons**, explanations or justifications provided as support for a conclusion.

reason An explanation or justification provided as support for a conclusion.

1. Under Rule 33 and relevant case law, perjury is not sufficient to warrant a new trial, unless (a) the government knew about the perjury or (b) the perjured testimony was so material that the verdict would probably result in acquittal of the defendants.

2. The defendants did not demonstrate that the government knew or should have known about the perjured testimony.

3. The jury would have still convicted the defendants apart from Lawrence's testimony.

4. Defense experts agreed with Lawrence on the "most critical aspects of his scientific analysis."

Let's not pass too quickly over this very important critical thinking step. When we ask "why" of any opinion, we are showing our respect for reasons as the proper basis for any assertion. We want a world rich with opinions so we can have a broad field of choice. But we should agree with only those legal opinions that have convincing reasons supporting the conclusion. So to ask "why" is our way of saying, "I want to believe you, but you have an obligation to help me by sharing the reasons for your conclusion."

RULES OF LAW

Judges cannot offer just any reasoning that they please. They must always look back over their shoulders at the laws and previous court decisions that together provide an anchor for current and future decisions.

This particular case is an attempt to match the words of the Federal Rules of Criminal Procedure, specifically Rule 33, and its regulations with the facts in this instance. The court also references case law, specifically the Second Circuit's ruling in *United States v. Wallach*. What makes legal reasoning so complex is that statutes and findings are never crystal clear. They may be clear, but judges and businesspeople have room for interpretive flexibility in their reasoning.

AMBIGUITY

ambiguous Susceptible to two or more possible interpretations.

The court's reasoning leans on its implied assumptions about the meaning of several ambiguous words or phrases. (An **ambiguous** word is one capable of having more than one meaning in the context of these facts.) For instance, Judge Cedarbaum stated that Rule 33 permits the court's granting a new trial if the "interest of justice so requires." But what is the "interest of justice"?

Does the interest of justice entail strict conformity to legal precedents? Or could the court's reliance on certain precedents result in some form of injustice in the *Stewart* case? To assume the former definition, we would be more inclined to conclude that the judge's denying the defendants' motion for a new trial was consistent with the "interest of justice." However, if the legislators who created Rule 33 intended a definition of justice that placed a stronger emphasis on judicial fairness, for example, in that defendants should be entitled to a fair trial in which perjury does not taint the verdict, perhaps we would be less supportive of Judge Cedarbaum's decision. The kind of justice that we assume is relevant to the amount of support we have for the judge's decision.

Another illustration of important ambiguity in the decision is the court's use of the term *reasonable likelihood*, referring to the probability that Lawrence's alleged perjury could not have affected the jury's verdict. But what degree of probability is a "reasonable likelihood"? Does this level of probability suggest that knowledge of Lawrence's testimony *could* have affected the jury's verdict? If we interpret "reasonable likelihood" as still including the possibility that knowledge of Lawrence's perjury *could* have affected the jury, we might reach a conclusion that differs from the court's decision. However, if we assume a definition of "reasonable likelihood" similar to the "beyond a reasonable doubt" standard (more than 99 percent certain), we would be more inclined to agree with the judge's decision. Hence, until we know what "reasonable likelihood" means, we cannot fairly decide whether the judge made the appropriate decision.

ETHICAL NORMS

The primary ethical norms that influence judges' decisions are justice, stability, freedom, and efficiency. Judge Cedarbaum expresses herself as a defender of efficiency. (Here is a good place to turn to Exhibit 1-2 to check alternative definitions

EXHIBIT 1-2

CLARIFYING THE PRIMARY ETHICAL NORMS

A judge's claiming or implying allegiance to a particular ethical norm focuses our attention on a specific category of desired conduct. We have or think we have an understanding of what is meant by freedom and other ethical norms.

But do we? Ethical norms are, without exception, complex and subject to multiple interpretations. Consequently, to identify the importance of one of the ethical norms in a piece of legal reasoning, we must look at the context to figure out which form of the ethical norm is being used. The types of conduct called for by the term *freedom* not only differ depending on the form of freedom being assumed, but at times they can contradict each other.

As a future business manager, your task is to be aware that there are alternative forms of each ethical norm. Then a natural next step is to search for the form used by the legal reasoning so you can understand and later evaluate that reasoning.

The following alternative forms of the four primary ethical norms can aid you in that search.

ETHICAL NORM	*FORMS*
1. Freedom	To act without restriction from rules imposed by others.
	To possess the capacity or resources to act as one wishes.
2. Security	To possess a large enough supply of goods and services that basic needs are met.
	To be safe from those wishing to interfere with your property rights.
	To achieve the psychological condition of self-confidence such that risks are welcomed.
3. Justice	To receive the product of your labor.
	To treat all humans identically, regardless of class, race, gender, age, and so on.
	To provide resources in proportion to need.
	To possess anything that someone else was willing to grant you.
4. Efficiency	To maximize the amount of wealth in our society.
	To get the most from a particular input.
	To minimize costs.

of efficiency.) She is unwilling to grant a new trial simply on the grounds that one of the witnesses allegedly committed perjury. Instead of granting the defendants' motion, Judge Cedarbaum elevates the "interest of according finality to a jury's verdict," even if the prosecution knew or should have known about the alleged perjury. Citing previous case law, she holds to those precedents that grant new trials only in rare instances.

Although the court does not explicitly address its feelings about stability, that ethical norm is assigned low priority by the reasoning. The court rejects the possibility of deviating from certain restrictions of previous case law in its argument, acting more consistently with a judge's belief in judicial restraint than judicial activism. (See Chapter 5 for a discussion of these two judicial philosophies.)

We certainly cannot say as a result that Judge Cedarbaum does not value stability. Surely she does! But for this fact pattern, stability has a lower ethical pull on the reasoning than is provided by the ethical norm of efficiency.

ANALOGIES

Ordinarily, our examination of legal analogies will require us to compare legal precedents cited by the parties with the facts of the case we are examining. Those precedents are the analogies on which legal decision making depends. In this case, Judge Cedarbaum relies on several legal precedents as analogies for her ruling, including *United States v. Wallach*.

In this particular precedent, the Second Circuit held that even if the prosecution knew of a witness's perjury, the court should not grant a new trial when independent evidence is sufficient to convict a defendant. The worth of this analogy depends on a greater understanding of independent evidence. In other words, what constitutes independent evidence? And is the strength of independent evidence in the *Stewart* case comparable to the independent evidence in *Wallach*? Or are there significant differences between the two cases such that the court's reliance on *Wallach* is unwarranted in this case?

To feel comfortable with the analogy, we would need to be persuaded that, like *United States v. Wallach*, the independent evidence in the *Stewart* case is similar to the independent evidence in the precedent.

MISSING INFORMATION

In the search for relevant missing information, it is important not to say just anything that comes to mind. For example, where did the defendants last eat Thanksgiving dinner? Anyone hearing that question would understandably wonder why it was asked. Ask only questions that would be helpful in understanding the reasoning in this particular case.

To focus on only relevant missing information, we should include with a request for additional information an explanation for why we want it. We have listed a few examples here for the *Stewart* case. You can probably identify others.

1. How well informed is Judge Cedarbaum with respect to the deliberations of the jury? If her understanding of the jurors' preverdict discussions is very limited, the defendants' request for a new trial might be more con-

vincing because Judge Cedarbaum repeatedly contends that jurors' knowledge of Lawrence's alleged perjury would not have affected the jurors' decision.

2. Congress, as it does with any legislation, discussed the Rules of Criminal Procedure before passing them. Does that discussion contain any clues as to Congress's intent with respect to the various conditions required for a defendant to receive a new trial? The answer would conceivably clarify the manner in which the court should apply Rule 33.

3. Are there examples of cases in which courts have examined similar fact patterns as the *Stewart* case but reached different conclusions about a new trial? The answer to this question would provide greater clarity about the appropriateness of using certain case precedents, thereby corroborating or undermining Judge Cedarbaum's decision.

Many other critical thinking skills could be applied to this and other cases. In this book we are focusing on the ones especially valuable for legal reasoning. Consistently applying this critical thinking approach will enable you to understand the reasoning in the cases and to increase your awareness of alternative approaches our laws could take to many problems you will encounter in the legal environment of business. The remaining portion of this chapter examines each of the critical thinking questions in greater depth to help you better understand the function of each.

You will have plenty of practice opportunities in this text to apply this set of critical thinking questions to the cases you read. You should also answer the questions contained in the "Critical Thinking About the Law" boxes that follow many of the cases.

USING CRITICAL THINKING TO MAKE LEGAL REASONING COME ALIVE

Our response to an issue is a conclusion. It is what we want others to believe about the issue. For example, a court might conclude that an employee, allegedly fired for her political views, was actually a victim of employment discrimination and is entitled to a damage award. Conclusions are reached by following a path that is produced by reasoning. Hence, examining reasoning is especially important when we are trying to understand and evaluate a conclusion.

There are many paths by which we may reach conclusions. For instance, I might settle all issues in my life by listening to voices in the night, asking my uncle, studying astrological signs, or just playing hunches. Each method could produce conclusions. Each could yield results.

But our intellectual and legal tradition demands a different type of support for conclusions. In this tradition, the basis for our conclusions is supposed to consist of reasons. When someone has no apparent reasons or the reasons don't match the conclusion, we feel entitled to say, "But that makes no sense." We aren't impressed by claims that we should accept someone's conclusion "just because."

This requirement that we all provide reasons for conclusions is what we mean in large part when we say we are going to think. We will ponder what the reasons and conclusion are and whether they mesh. This intense study of how a certain conclusion follows from a particular set of reasons occupies much of the time involved in careful decision making.

Persons trained to reason about court cases have a great appreciation for the unique facts that provoked a legal action. Those facts and no others provide the context for our reasoning. If an issue arises because environmentalists want to prevent an interstate highway from extending through a wilderness area, we want to know right away—What are the facts?

Doesn't everyone want to know about the context for an event? Unfortunately, the answer is no. Many people rush to judgment once they know the issue. One valuable lesson you can take with you as you practice legal analysis is the fundamental importance of the unique set of facts that provides the setting for the legal dispute.

Legal reasoning encourages unusual and necessary respect for the particular factual situation that stimulated disagreement between parties. These fact patterns, as we call them, bring the issue to our attention and limit the extent to which the court's conclusion can be applied to other situations. Small wonder that the first step in legal reasoning is to ask and answer the question: What are the facts?

LEGAL REASONING

STEP 1: What Are the Facts? The call for the facts is not a request for all facts but only those that have a bearing on the dispute at hand. That dispute tells us whether a certain fact is pertinent. In some cases the plaintiff's age may be a key point; in another it may be irrelevant.

Only after we have familiarized ourselves with the relevant legal facts do we begin the familiar pattern of reasoning that thoughtful people use. We then ask and answer the following question: What is the issue?

STEP 2: What Is the Issue? The issue is the question that the court is being asked to answer. For example, courts face groups of facts relevant to issues such as the following:

1. Does Title VII apply to sexual harassment situations when the accused and the alleged victim are members of the same sex?

2. Does a particular merger between two companies violate the Sherman Act?

3. When does a governmental regulation require compensation to the property owner affected by the regulation?

As we pointed out earlier, the way we express the issue guides the legal reasoning in the case. Hence, forming an issue in a very broad or a highly narrow manner has implications for the scope of the effect stemming from the eventual decision. You can appreciate now why parties to a dispute work very hard to get the court to see the issue in a particular way.

You will read many legal decisions in this book. No element of your analysis of those cases is more important than careful consideration of the issue at hand. The key to issue spotting is asking yourself what question do the parties want to be answered by the court. The next logical step in legal analysis is to ask: What are the reasons and conclusion?

STEP 3: What Are the Reasons and Conclusion? The issue is the stimulus for thought. The facts and the issue in a particular case get us started thinking critically about legal reasoning. But the conclusion and the reasons for that conclusion provide flesh to the court's reaction to the legal issue. They tell us how the court has responded to the issue.

To find the conclusion, use the issue as a helper. Ask yourself: How did the court react to the issue? The answer is the conclusion. The reasons for that conclusion provide the answer to the question: Why did the court prefer this response to the issue rather than any alternative? One part of the answer to that question is the answer to another question: What are the relevant rules of law?

STEP 4: What Are the Relevant Rules of Law? The fourth step in legal reasoning reveals another difference from general nonlegal reasoning. The issue arises in a context of existing legal rules. We do not treat each legal dispute as if it were the first such dispute in human history. On the contrary, society has already addressed similar disputes in its laws and court findings. It has already responded to situations much like the ones now before the court. The historical record of pertinent judicial decisions provides a rich source of reasons on which to base the conclusion of courts. These prior decisions, or legal precedents, provide legal rules to which those in a legal dispute must defer. Thus, the fourth step in legal reasoning requires a focus on those rules. These legal rules are what the parties to a dispute must use as the framework for their legal claims. How those rules and the reasoning and conclusions built on them are expressed, however, is not always crystal clear. So another question—one that starts the critical thinking evaluation of the conclusion—is: Does the legal argument contain significant ambiguity?

STEP 5: Does the Legal Argument Contain Significant Ambiguity? Legal arguments are expressed in words, and words rarely have the clarity we presume. Whenever we are tempted to think that our words speak for themselves, we should remind ourselves of Emerson's observation that "to be understood is a rare luxury." Hence, legal reasoning possesses elasticity. It can be stretched and reduced to fit the purpose of the attorney or judge.

As an illustration, a rule of law may contain the phrase "public safety." At first glance, as with any term, some interpretation arises in our mind. But as we continue to consider the extent and limits of "public safety," we realize it is not so clear. To be more certain about the meaning we must study the intent of the person making the legal argument. Just how safe must the public be before an action provides sufficient threat to public safety to justify public intervention?

As a strategy for critical thinking, the request for clarification is a form of evaluation. The point of the question is that we cannot make the reasoning our own until we have determined what we are being asked to embrace.

What we are being asked to embrace and the reasoning behind it usually involve an ethical component. So an important question to ask is: What ethical norms are fundamental to the court's reasoning?

STEP 6: What Ethical Norms Are Fundamental to the Court's Reasoning? The legal environment of business is established and modified according to ethical norms. A **norm** is a standard of conduct, a set of expectations that we bring to social encounters. For example, one norm we collectively understand and obey is that our departures are ordinarily punctuated by "good-bye." We may presume rudeness or preoccupation on the part of someone who leaves our presence without bidding us some form of farewell.

Ethical norms are special because they are steps toward achieving what we consider good or virtuous. Goodness and virtue are universally preferred to their opposites, but the preference has little meaning until we look more deeply into the meaning of these noble aims. As you are well aware, there are dozens of alternative visions about what it means to be good or to have a good society.

Conversations about ethics explore these alternative visions. They do so by comparing the relative merit of human behavior that is guided by one ethical norm or another. Ethical norms represent the abstractions we hold out to others as the most fundamental standards defining our self-worth and value to others.

For example, any of us would be proud to know that others see us as meeting the ethical norms we know as honesty, dependability, and compassion. Ethical norms are the standards of conduct we most want to see observed by our children and our neighbors.

The legal environment of business has received ethical guidance from many norms. Certain norms, however, play a particularly large role in legal reasoning. Consequently, we highlight what we will refer to as the four **primary ethical norms**: freedom, stability, justice, and efficiency. (See Exhibit 1–2 for clarification of these norms.) The interplay among these four provides the major ethical direction for the laws governing business behavior. As you examine the cases in this text, you may identify other ethical norms that influence judicial opinions.

As critical thinkers we will want to always search for the relevant ethical norms. To do so requires us to infer their identity from the court's reasoning.

norm A standard of conduct.

ethical norms Standards of conduct that we consider good or virtuous.

primary ethical norms The four norms that provide the major ethical direction for the laws governing business behavior: freedom, stability, justice, and efficiency.

Courts often do not announce their preferred pattern of ethical norms, but the norms are there anyway, having their way with the legal reasoning. As critical thinkers, we want to use the ethical norms, once we find them, as a basis for evaluating the reasoning. Another element used in arriving at legal conclusions is the device of reasoning by analogy. Part of the critical thinking process in the evaluation of a legal conclusion is another question: How appropriate are the legal analogies?

STEP 7: How Appropriate Are the Legal Analogies? A major difference between legal reasoning and other forms of analysis is the heavy reliance on analogies. Our legal system places great emphasis on the law as it has evolved in previous decisions. This evolutionary process is our heritage, the collective judgments of our historical mothers and fathers. We give them and their intellects our respect by using legal precedents as the major support structure for judicial decisions. By doing so, we do not have to approach each fact pattern with new eyes; instead, we are guided by similar experiences that our predecessors have already studied.

The use of precedent to reach legal conclusions is so common that legal reasoning can be characterized as little but analogical reasoning. An **analogy** is a verbal device for transferring meaning from something we understand quite well to something we have just discovered and have, as yet, not understood satisfactorily. What we already understand in the case of legal reasoning is the precedent; what we hope to understand better is the current legal dispute. We call on precedent for enlightenment.

analogy A comparison based on the assumption that if two things are alike in some respect, they must be alike in other respects.

To visualize the choice of legal analogy, imagine that we are trying to decide whether a waitress or waiter can be required to smile for hours as a condition of employment. (What is artificial about such an illustration, as we hope you already recognize, is the absence of a more complete factual picture to provide context.) The employer in question asks the legal staff to find appropriate legal precedents. They discover the following list of prior decisions:

1. Professional cheerleaders can be required to smile within reason, if that activity is clearly specified at the time of employment.

2. Employees who interact regularly with customers can be required as a condition of employment to wear clothing consistent with practice in the trade.

3. Employers may not require employees to lift boxes over 120 pounds without the aid of a mechanical device under the guidelines of the Employee Health Act.

Notice that each precedent has similarities to, but each has major differences from, the situation of the waiter or waitress. To mention only a few:

- Is a smile more natural to what we can expect from a cheerleader than from a waiter or waitress?

- Were the restaurant employees told in advance that smiling is an integral part of the job?

- Is a smile more personal than clothing? Are smiles private, as opposed to clothing, which is more external to who we are?

- Is a plastered-on smile, held in place for hours, a serious risk to mental health?

- Is a potential risk from smiling as real a danger as the one resulting from physically hoisting huge objects?

The actual selection of precedent and, consequently, the search for appropriate analogies are channeled by the theory of logic we find most revealing in this case. For example, if you see the requirement to smile as an invasion of privacy, you will likely see the second precedent as especially appropriate. Both the precedent and the case in question have employment situations with close customer contact.

However, the differences could be significant enough to reject that analogy. Do you see your clothing as part of your essence in the same fashion as you surely see the facial form you decide to show us at any given moment? Furthermore, the second precedent contains the phrase "consistent with practice in the trade." Would not a simple field trip to restaurants demonstrate that a broad smile is a pleasant exception?

As you practice looking for similarities and differences in legal precedents and the legal problem you are studying, you will experience some of the fun and frustration of legal reasoning within a business context. The excitement comes when you stumble on just the perfect, matching fact pattern; then, after taking a closer look, you are brought back to earth by those annoying analogical differences that your experience warns you are always present.

Ambiguity, ethical norms, and legal analogies are all areas in which legal arguments may be deficient. But even if you are satisfied that all those considerations meet your standards, there is a final question that must not be overlooked in your critical analysis of a conclusion: Is there relevant missing information?

STEP 8: Is There Relevant Missing Information? When we ask about the facts of a case, we mean the information presented in the legal proceedings. However, we are all quite aware that the stated facts are just a subset of the complete factual picture responsible for the dispute. How could any of us expect to ever have all the facts about a situation? We know we could use more facts than we have, but at some point we have to stop gathering information and settle the dispute.

You might not be convinced that the facts we know about a situation are inevitably incomplete. But consider how we acquire facts. If we gather them ourselves, we know the limits on our own experience and perceptions. We often see what we want to see, and we consequently select certain facts to file in our consciousness. Other facts may be highly relevant, but we ignore them. We can neither see nor process all the facts.

Our other major source of information is other people. We implicitly trust their intentions, abilities, and perspective when we take the facts they give us and make them our own. But no one gives us a complete version of the facts. For several reasons, we can be sure that the facts shared with us are only partial.

Armed with your awareness of the incompleteness of facts, what can you do as a future businessperson or employee to effectively resolve disagreements and apply legal precedents?

You can seek a more complete portrayal of the facts. Keep asking for detail and context to aid your thinking. For example, once you learn that a statute requires a firm to use the standard of conduct in the industry, you should not be satisfied with the following fact:

> *On 14 occasions, our firm attempted to contact other firms to determine the industry standards. We have bent over backwards to comply with the ethical norms of our direct competitors.*

Instead, you will persist in asking probing questions designed to generate a more revealing pattern of facts. Among the missing information you might ask for would be the extent and content of actual conversations about industry standards, as well as some convincing evidence that "direct" competitors are an adequate voice, representing "the industry."

APPLYING THE CRITICAL THINKING APPROACH

Now that you have an understanding of the critical thinking approach, you are ready to begin your study of the legal environment of business. Remember to apply each of the questions to the cases as you read them.

After you become proficient at asking these questions of every case you read, you may find that you start asking these evaluative questions in other contexts. For example, you might find that, when you read an editorial in the *Wall Street Journal*, you start asking whether the writer has used ambiguous terms that affect the quality of the reasoning, or you start noticing when important relevant information is missing. Once you reach this point, you are well on your way to becoming a critical thinker whose thinking skills will be extremely helpful for functioning in the legal environment of business.

ASSIGNMENT ON THE INTERNET

You have now been introduced to the critical thinking steps that create a working strategy to evaluate legal reasoning. In the same manner that you evaluated *United States of America v. Martha Stewart and Peter Bacanovic*, practice evaluating the legal reasoning on a case of your choosing.

Go to **www.law.cornell.edu** for current legal issues and cases. Find a case of interest to you and evaluate the reasoning using the critical thinking steps outlined in the chapter. The following Web sites on critical thinking may assist you in evaluating legal reasoning.

 ## ON THE INTERNET

www.palgrave.com/skills4study/html/studyskills/critical.htm This site provides helpful studying tips that utilize the critical thinking skills discussed in this chapter.

commhum.mccneb.edu/argument/summary.htm Use this site for practice identifying reasons and conclusions in arguments.

www.austhink.org/critical

pegasus.cc.ucf.edu/~janzb/reasoning Both sites contain numerous links for those wishing additional reading and practice with the critical thinking skills learned in this chapter.

2

INTRODUCTION TO LAW AND THE LEGAL ENVIRONMENT OF BUSINESS

- **DEFINITION OF THE LEGAL ENVIRONMENT OF BUSINESS**
- **DEFINITION OF LAW AND JURISPRUDENCE**
- **SOURCES OF LAW**
- **CLASSIFICATIONS OF LAW**
- **GLOBAL DIMENSIONS OF THE LEGAL ENVIRONMENT OF BUSINESS**

This book is about the legal environment in which the business community operates today. Although we concentrate on law and the legal variables that help shape business decisions, we have not overlooked the ethical, political, and economic questions that often arise in business decision making. In this chapter, we are especially concerned with legal variables in the context of critical thinking, as outlined in Chapter 1. In addition, we examine the international dimensions of several areas of law. In an age of sophisticated telecommunication systems and computer networking it would be naive for readers to believe that, as citizens of a prosperous, powerful nation situated between two oceans, they can afford to ignore the rest of the world. Just as foreign multinational companies must interact with U.S. companies and government agencies, so must U.S. entities interact with regional and international trade groups.

The United States, Canada, and Mexico created the North American Free Trade Agreement (NAFTA) to lower trade barriers among themselves. In the Asian-Pacific Economic Cooperation (APEC) forum, the United States

Critical Thinking About the Law

This chapter serves as an introduction to the legal and ethical components in the environment of business. You will learn about different schools of jurisprudence and about sources and classifications of law. In addition, this chapter offers the opportunity to practice the critical thinking skills you just learned in Chapter 1. The following critical thinking questions will help you better understand the introductory topics discussed in this chapter.

1. Why should we be concerned with the ethical components of the legal environment of business? Why shouldn't we just learn the relevant laws regarding businesses?

    Clue: Which critical thinking questions address the ethical components of the legal environment of business?

2. As you will soon discover, judges and lawyers often subscribe to a particular school of legal thought. However, judges and lawyers will probably not explicitly tell us which school of thought they prefer. Why do you think this knowledge might be beneficial when critically evaluating a judge's reasoning?

    Clue: Think about why we look for missing information. Furthermore, why do we want to identify the ethical norms fundamental to a court's reasoning?

3. You tell your landlord that your front door lock is broken, but he doesn't repair the lock. A week later, you are robbed. You decide to sue the landlord, and you begin to search for an attorney. As a legal studies student, you ask the potential lawyers what school of jurisprudence they prefer. Although you find a lawyer who prefers the same school of jurisprudence you prefer, your decision is not complete. What else might you want to ask the lawyer?

    Clue: Think about the other factors that might affect a lawyer's performance.

and 17 Pacific Rim nations are discussing easing barriers to trade and investments among themselves and creating a Pacific free trade zone extending from Chile to China. In 2004 the European Union added 10 new member nations, bringing its total to 25. The General Agreement on Trade and Tariffs/World Trade Organization continues to lower trade barriers among the 144 nations that have joined it. No nation is an island unto itself today, and economic globalization is sure to continue—even accelerate— in the twenty-first century. (See Chapter 9 for discussion of the global legal environment of business.)

DEFINITION OF THE LEGAL ENVIRONMENT OF BUSINESS

Scholars define the "legal environment of business" in various ways, according to the purposes of their studies. For our purposes, the study of the legal environment of business shall include:

• The study of legal reasoning, critical thinking skills, ethical norms, and schools of ethical thought that interact with the law.

- The study of the legal process and our present legal system, as well as alternative dispute resolution systems, such as private courts, mediation, arbitration, and negotiations.
- The study of the administrative law process and the role of businesspeople in that process.
- The study of selected areas of public and private law, such as securities regulation, antitrust, labor, product liability, contracts, and consumer and environmental law. In each of these areas, we emphasize the processes by which business managers relate to individuals and government regulators.
- The examination of the international dimensions of the legal environment of law.

Our study of the legal environment of business is characterized by five features:

1. *Critical thinking skills.*

2. *Legal literacy.* A survey by the Hearst Corporation found that 50 percent of Americans believe that it is up to the criminally accused to prove their innocence, despite our common-law heritage that a person is presumed innocent until proven guilty. Only 41 percent were able to identify the then chief justice (Warren Burger) and the first woman Supreme Court justice (Sandra Day O'Connor). Of those responding to the survey, 49.9 percent had served on a jury, and 31 percent were college graduates.

3. *An understanding that the law is dynamic, not static.* The chapters on discrimination law, securities regulation, antitrust law, and labor law, especially, have had to be constantly updated during the writing of this book because federal regulatory agencies issue new regulations, rules, and guidelines almost daily.

4. *Real-world problems.* You will be confronted with real, not theoretical, legal and ethical problems. As the great American jurist Oliver Wendell Holmes once pointed out, the law is grounded in "experience." In reading the cases excerpted in this book, you will see how business leaders and others either were ignorant of the legal and ethical variables they faced or failed to consider them in making important decisions.

5. *Interdisciplinary nature.* Into our discussions of the legal environment of business we interweave materials from other disciplines that you either are studying now or have studied in the past, especially economics, management, finance, marketing, and ethics. You may be surprised to learn how often officers of the court (judges and attorneys) are obliged to consider material from several disciplines in making decisions. Your own knowledge of these other disciplines will be extremely helpful to understanding the court decisions set out in this book.

The connections to other areas of business are so significant that we have chosen to highlight many of them in subsequent chapters of the book. As you are reading, you will encounter boxes entitled "Linking Law and Business." These boxes contain material from other business disciplines that is related to the business law material you are studying. By highlighting these connections, we hope to provide greater cohesiveness to your education as a future business manager.

As listed in Exhibit 2–1, there are a number of benefits to be gained by studying the legal environment of business.

EXHIBIT 2-1

TOP TEN REASONS FOR STUDYING THE LEGAL ENVIRONMENT OF BUSINESS

1. Becoming aware of the rules of doing business.
2. Familiarizing yourself with the legal limits on business freedom.
3. Forming an alertness to potential misconduct of competitors.
4. Appreciating the limits of entrepreneurship.
5. Being able to communicate with your lawyer.
6. Making you a more fully informed citizen.
7. Developing an employment-related skill.
8. Exploring the fascinating complexity of business decisions.
9. Providing a heightened awareness of business ethics.
10. Opening your eyes to the excitement of the law and business.

EXHIBIT 2-1

TOP TEN REASONS FOR STUDYING THE LEGAL ENVIRONMENT OF BUSINESS

DEFINITION OF LAW AND JURISPRUDENCE

Jurisprudence is the science or philosophy of law, or law in its most generalized form. Law has been defined in different ways by scholarly thinkers. Some idea of the range of definitions can be gained from the following quote from a distinguished legal philosopher:

> *We have been told by Plato that law is a form of social control; by Aristotle that it is a rule of conduct, a contract, an ideal of reason; by Cicero that it is the agreement of reason and nature, the distinction between the just and the unjust; by Aquinas that it is an ordinance of reason for the common good; by Bacon that certainty is the prime necessity of law; by Hobbes that law is the command of the sovereign; by Hegel that it is an unfolding or realizing of the idea of right.*[1]

The various ideas of law expressed in that passage represent different schools of jurisprudence. To give you some sense of the diversity of meaning the term *law* has, we will examine seven accepted schools of legal thought: (1) natural law, (2) positivist, (3) sociological, (4) American realist, (5) critical legal theory, (6) feminist, and (7) law and economics. Table 2–1 summarizes the outstanding characteristics of each of these schools of jurisprudence.

jurisprudence The science or philosophy of law; law in its most generalized form.

NATURAL LAW SCHOOL

For adherents of the natural law school, which has existed since 300 B.C., law consists of the following concepts: (1) There exist certain legal values or value judgments (e.g., a presumption of innocence until guilt is proved); (2) these values or value judgments are unchanging because their source is absolute (e.g., nature, God, or reason); (3) these values or value judgments can be determined by human reason; and (4) once determined, they supersede any form of human law. Perhaps the most memorable statement of the natural law school of thought in this century was made by Martin Luther King, Jr., in his famous letter from a Birmingham, Alabama, city jail. Here is how he explained to a group of ministers why he had violated human laws that discriminated against his people:

> *There are just laws and there are unjust laws. I would be the first to advocate obeying just laws. One has not only a legal but moral responsibility to obey just*

[1] See H. Cairns, *Legal Philosophy from Plato to Hegel* (Baltimore: Johns Hopkins University Press, 1949).

TABLE 2-1

SCHOOLS OF JURISPRUDENCE

School	Characteristics
Natural Law School	Source of law is absolute (nature, God, or reason).
Positivist School	Source of law is the sovereign.
Sociological School	Source of law is contemporary community opinion and customs.
American Realist School	Source of law is actors in the legal system and scientific analysis of their actions.
Critical Legal Theory School	Source of law is a cluster of legal and nonlegal beliefs that must be critiqued to bring about social and political change.
Feminist School	Jurisprudence reflects a male-dominated executive, legislative, and judicial system in which women's perspectives are ignored and women are victimized.
Law and Economics School	Classical economic theory and empirical methods are applied to all areas of law in order to arrive at decisions.

laws. Conversely, one has a moral responsibility to disobey unjust laws. I would agree with Saint Augustine that "an unjust law is no law at all."

Now what is the difference between the two? How does one determine when a law is just or unjust? A just law is a man-made code that squares with the moral law or the law of God. An unjust law is a code that is out of harmony with the moral law. To put it in the terms of Saint Thomas Aquinas, an unjust law is a human law that is not rooted in eternal and natural law. Any law that uplifts human personality is just. Any law that degrades human personality is unjust. All segregation statutes are unjust because segregation distorts the soul and damages the personality ...

Let us turn to a more concrete example of just and unjust law. An unjust law is a code that a majority inflicts on a minority that is not binding on itself. This is difference made legal. On the other hand, a just law is a code that a majority compels a minority to follow that it is willing to follow itself. This is sameness made legal.

Let me give another explanation. An unjust law is a code inflicted upon a minority which that minority had no part in enacting or creating because they did not have the unhampered right to vote.[2]

Adherents of other schools of legal thought view King's general definition of law as overly subjective. For example, they ask, "Who is to determine whether a man-made law is unjust because it is 'out of harmony with the moral law'?" Or: "Whose moral precepts or values are to be included in the 'moral law'?" The United States is a country of differing cultures, races, ethnic groups, and religions, each of which may reflect unique moral values.

POSITIVIST SCHOOL

Early in the 1800s, followers of positivism developed a school of thought in opposition to the natural law school. Its chief tenets are (1) law is the expression of the will of the legislator or sovereign, which must be followed; (2) morals are separate from law and should not be considered in making legal decisions (thus, judges should not take into consideration extralegal factors such as contemporary community values in determining what constitutes a violation of law); and (3) law is a "closed logical system" in which correct legal

---

[2]See M. L. King, Jr., "Letters from a Birmingham Jail" (April 16, 1963), reprinted in M. McGuaigan, *Jurisprudence* (New York: Free Press, 1979), p. 63.

decisions are reached solely by logic and the use of precedents (previous cases decided by the courts).

Disciples of the positivist school would argue that when the Congress of the United States has not acted on a matter, the United States Supreme Court has no power to act on that matter. They would argue, for example, that morality has no part in determining whether discrimination exists when a business pays workers differently on the basis of their sex, race, religion, or ethnic origin. Only civil rights legislation passed by Congress, and previous cases interpreting that legislation, should be considered.

Positivism has been criticized by adherents of other schools of thought as too narrow and literal minded. Critics argue that the refusal to consider social, ethical, and other factors makes for a static jurisprudence that ill serves society.

SOCIOLOGICAL SCHOOL

Followers of the sociological school propose three steps in determining law:

1. A legislator or a judge should make an inventory of community interests.
2. Judges and legislators should use this inventory to familiarize themselves with the community's standards and mores.
3. They should rule or legislate in conformity with those standards and mores.

For those associated with this school of legal thought, human behavior or contemporary community values are the most important factors in determining the direction the law should take. This philosophy is in sharp contrast to that of the positivist school, which relies on case precedents and statutory law. Adherents of the sociological school seek to change the law by surveying human behavior and determining present community standards. For example, after a famous U.S. Supreme Court decision stating that material could be judged "obscene" on the basis of "contemporary community standards,"[3] one mayor of a large city immediately went out and polled his community on what books and movies they thought were obscene. (He failed to get a consensus).

Critics of the sociological school argue that this school would make the law too unpredictable for both individuals and businesses. They note that contemporary community standards change over time and, thus, the law itself would be changing all the time and the effects could harm the community. For example, if a state or local legislature offered a corporation certain tax breaks as an incentive to move to a community and then revoked those tax breaks a few years later because community opinion on such matters had changed, other corporations would be reluctant to locate in that community.

AMERICAN REALIST SCHOOL

The American realist school, though close to the sociological school in its emphasis on people, focuses on the actors in the judicial system instead of on the larger community to determine the meaning of law. This school sees law as a part of society and a means of enforcing political and social values. In a book entitled *The Bramble Bush*, Karl Llewellyn wrote: "This doing of something about

---

[3]*Roth v. United States*, 354 U.S. 476, 479 (1957).

disputes, this doing it reasonably, is the business of the law. And the people who have the doing of it are in charge, whether they be judges, or clerks, or jailers, or lawyers, they are officials of the law. What these officials do about disputes is, to my mind, the law itself."[4] For Llewellyn and other American realists, anyone who wants to know about law should study the judicial process and the actors in that process. This means regular attendance at courthouses and jails, as well as scientific study of the problems associated with the legal process (e.g., plea bargaining in the courtroom).

Positivists argue that if the American realist definition of law were accepted, there would be a dangerous unpredictability to the law.

CRITICAL LEGAL STUDIES SCHOOL

As a contemporary extension of American legal realism, critical legal studies seeks to connect what happens in the legal system to the political-economic context within which it operates. Adherents of critical legal jurisprudence believe that law reflects a cluster of beliefs that convinces human beings that the hierarchical relations that they live and work under are natural and must be accommodated. According to this school, this cluster of beliefs has been constructed by elitists to rationalize their dominant power. Using economics, mass communications, religion, and, most of all, law, members of society's elite have constructed an interlocking system of beliefs that reinforces established wealth and privilege. Only by critiquing these belief structures, critical legal theorists believe, will people be able to break out of a hierarchical system and bring about democratic social and political change.

Traditional critics argue that the critical legal theorists have not developed concrete strategies to bring about the social and political changes they desire but have constructed an essentially negative position.

FEMINIST SCHOOL

There is a range of views as to what constitutes feminist jurisprudence. Most adherents of this school, believing that significant rights have been denied to women, advocate lobbying legislatures and litigating in courts for changes in laws to accommodate women's views. They argue that our traditional common law reflects a male emphasis on individual rights, which at times is at odds with women's views that the law should be more reflective of a "culture of caring." To other adherents of this school of jurisprudence, the law is a means of male oppression. For example, some feminists have argued that the First Amendment, forbidding Congress from making any laws abridging the freedom of speech, was authored by men and is presently interpreted by male-dominated U.S. courts to allow pornographers to make large profits by exploiting and degrading women.

Traditional critics of feminist jurisprudence argue that it is too narrow in scope and that it fails to account for changes taking place in U.S. society such as the increasing number of women students in professional and graduate schools and their movement into higher-ranking positions in both the public and private sectors.

---

[4]K. Llewellyn, *The Bramble Bush* (Dobbs Ferry, N.Y.: Oceana Publications, 1950), p. 12.

LAW AND ECONOMICS SCHOOL

The law and economics school of jurisprudence started to evolve in the 1950s, but it has been applied with some rigor for the last 20 years. It advocates using classical economic theory and empirical methods of economics to explain and predict judges' decisions in such areas as torts, contracts, property, criminal administrative law, and law enforcement. The proponents of the law and economics school argue that most court decisions, and the legal doctrines they depend on, are best understood as efforts to promote an efficient allocation of resources in society.

Critics of the school of law and economics argue that there are many schools of economic thoughts and, thus, no single body of principles governs economics. For example, neo-Keynesians and classical market theorists have very different views of the proper role of the state in the allocation of resources. A related criticism is that this school takes a politically conservative approach to the legal solution of economic or political problems. Liberals and others argue that it is a captive of conservative thinkers.

SOURCES OF LAW

The founders of this country created in the United States Constitution three direct sources of law and one indirect source. The legislative branch (Article I) is the maker or creator of laws; the executive branch (Article II), the enforcer of laws; and the judicial branch (Article III), the interpreter of laws. Each branch represents a separate source of law while performing its functions (Table 2–2). The fourth (indirect) source of law is administrative agencies, which will be briefly discussed in this chapter and examined in detail in Chapter 17.

THE LEGISLATURE AS A SOURCE OF STATUTORY LAW

Article I, Section 1, of the U.S. Constitution states, "All legislative Powers herein granted shall be vested in a Congress of the United States which shall consist of a House and Senate." It is important to understand the process by which a law (called a statute) is made by the Congress, because this process and its results have an impact on such diverse groups as consumers, businesspeople, taxpayers, and unions. It should be emphasized that at every stage of the process, each of the groups potentially affected seeks to influence the proposed piece of legislation through lobbying. The federal legislative process described here (Exhibit 2–2) is similar in most respects to the processes used by state legislatures, though state constitutions may prescribe some differences.

Steps in the Legislative Process

STEP 1 A bill is introduced into the U.S. House of Representatives or Senate by a single member or by several members. It is generally referred to the committee of the House or Senate that has jurisdiction over the subject matter of the bill. (In most cases, a bill is simultaneously introduced into the Senate and House. Within each body, committees may vie with each other for jurisdictional priority.)

STEP 2 Let's briefly follow through the House of Representatives a bill proposing to deregulate the trucking industry by doing away

TABLE 2-2 WHERE TO FIND THE LAW

Level of Government	Legislative Law	Executive Orders	Common Law/Judicial Interpretations	Administrative Regulations
Federal	• United States Code (U.S.C.) • United States Code Annotated (U.S.C.A.) • United States Statutes at Large (Stat.)	• Title 3 of the Code of Federal Regulations • Codification of Presidential Proclamations and Executive Orders	• United States Reports (U.S.) • Supreme Court Reporter (S. Ct.) • Federal Reporter (F., F.2d) • Federal Supplement (F.Supp.) • Federal agency reports (titled by agency; e.g., F.C.C. Reports) • Regional reporters • State reporters	• Code of Federal Regulations (C.F.R.) • Federal Register (Fed. Reg.)
State	• State code or state statutes (e.g., Ohio Revised Code Annotated, Baldwin's)	• Executive Orders of Governors and Proclamations		• State administrative code or state administrative regulations
Local	• Municipal ordinances		• Varies; often difficult to find. Many municipalities do not publish case decisions but do preserve them on microfilm. Interested parties usually must contact the clerk's office at the local courthouse.	• Municipality administrative regulations

with the rate-making power of the Interstate Commerce Commission (ICC). This bill would be referred to the House Committee on Energy and Commerce, which, in turn, would refer it to the appropriate subcommittee.

STEP 3   The House subcommittee holds hearings on the bill, listening to testimony from all concerned parties and establishing a hearing record.

STEP 4   After hearings, the bill is "marked up" (drafted in precise form) and then referred to the subcommittee for a vote.

STEP 5   If the vote is affirmative, the subcommittee forwards the bill to the full House Energy and Commerce committee, which either accepts the subcommittee's recommendation, puts a hold on the bill,

This graphic shows the typical way in which proposed legislation is enacted into law. There are more complicated, as well as simpler, routes, and most bills fall by the wayside and never become law. The process is illustrated with two hypothetical separate bills covering the same subject matter: House bill No. 1 (HR 1) and Senate bill No. 2 (S 2). (In practice, most legislation begins as similar proposals in both houses.) Each bill must be passed by both houses of Congress in identical form before it can become law. The path of HR 1 is traced by a blue line, that of S 2 by a red line

EXHIBIT 2-2

HOW A BILL BECOMES A LAW

Source: Reprinted with permission of Congressional Quarterly, Inc.

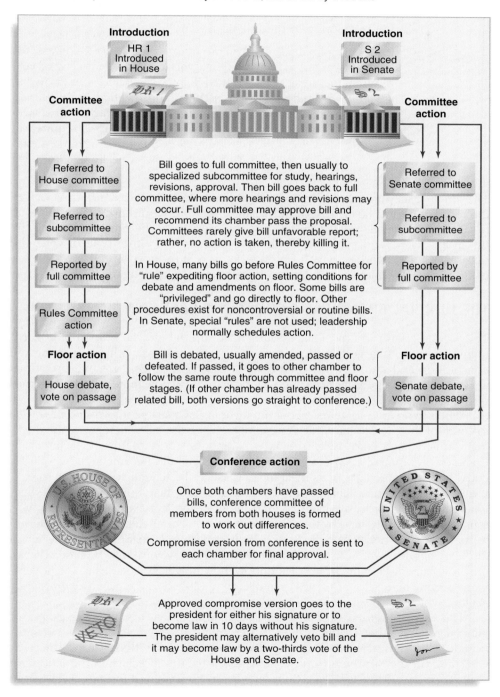

or rejects it. If the House committee votes to accept the bill, it reports it to the full House of Representatives for a vote by all members.

STEP 6 If the bill is passed by the House of Representatives and a similar bill is passed by the Senate, the bills go to a Senate–House Conference Committee to reconcile any differences in content. After compromise and reconciliation of the two bills, a single bill is reported to the full House and Senate for a vote.

STEP 7 If there is a final affirmative vote by both houses of Congress, the bill is forwarded to the president, who may sign it into law or veto it. When the president signs the bill into law, it becomes known as a statute, meaning it is written down and codified in the *United States Code Annotated*. In the event of a presidential veto, a two-thirds vote of the Senate and House membership is required to override the veto. If the president takes no action within ten days of receiving the bill from Congress, it automatically becomes law without the president's signature.

The single exception to this procedure occurs when Congress adjourns before the ten-day period has elapsed: In that case, the bill would not become law. It is said to have been "pocket-vetoed" by the president: The president "stuck the bill in a pocket" and vetoed it by doing nothing. With either type of veto, the bill is dead and can be revived only by being reintroduced in the next session of Congress, in which case the procedure begins all over again.

THE JUDICIAL BRANCH AS A SOURCE OF CASE LAW

The federal courts and most state courts make up the judicial branch of government. They are charged by their respective constitutions with interpreting the constitution and statutory law on a case-by-case basis. Most case interpretations are reported in large volumes called reporters. These constitute a compilation of our federal and state case law.

When two parties disagree about the meaning of a statute, they bring their case to court for the court to interpret. For example, when the bill to deregulate the trucking industry and take away the rate-making function of the ICC (Interstate Commerce Commission) was signed by the president and became law, two parties could have disagreed about its meaning and asked the federal courts to interpret it. If the law had been challenged, the court would have first looked at the law's legislative history in order to determine the intent of the legislature. This history was found in the hearings held by the subcommittees and committees previously referred to, as well as any debates on the Senate and House floors. Hearings are published in the *U.S. Congressional News and Administrative Reports*, which may be ordered from the Government Printing Office or found in most university libraries in the government documents section. Debates on a bill are published in the daily *Congressional Record*, which may also be found in most university libraries.

The U.S. Supreme Court and most state supreme courts have the power of judicial review—that is, the power to determine whether a statute is constitutional. Although this power was not expressly provided for in the U.S. Constitution, the Supreme Court established it for the judiciary in the landmark case *Marbury v. Madison*[5] (see Chapter 3 for a discussion of this case). The right of judicial review gives the U.S. Supreme Court the ultimate power to check the excesses of either the legislative or the executive branch.

Furthermore, this decision establishes case law precedents, which are followed by all federal and state courts. Thus, through its case-by-case interpretation of the Constitution and statutes, the U.S. Supreme Court establishes a line of authoritative cases on a particular subject that has to be followed by the lower courts, both federal and state. Similarly, state supreme courts establish precedents that must be followed by lower courts in their particular state systems.

THE EXECUTIVE BRANCH AS A SOURCE OF LAW

The executive branch is composed of the president, the president's staff, and the cabinet, which is made up of the heads of each of the executive departments (e.g., the secretary of state, the secretary of labor, the secretary of defense, and the secretary of the treasury) and the counselor to the president. The Executive Office is composed of various offices, such as the Office of Management and Budget (OMB) and the Office of Personnel Management (OPM). The executive branch is a source of law in two ways.

Treaty Making. The president has the power, subject to the advice and consent of the Senate, to make treaties. These treaties become the law of the land, on the basis of the Supremacy Clause of the United State Constitution (Article VI), and supersede any state law. When President Carter entered into a treaty returning the Panama Canal Zone to the nation of Panama under certain conditions, it became the law of the land, and the treaty provisions superseded any federal or state laws inconsistent with the treaty.

Executive Orders. Throughout history, the president has made laws by issuing executive orders. For example, as we shall see in Chapter 17, President Reagan, by virtue of an executive order, ruled that all executive federal agencies must do a cost–benefit analysis before setting forth a proposed regulation for comment by interested parties. President Truman, by executive order, directed the secretary of commerce to seize all the nation's steel mills to prevent a strike in this essential industry during the Korean War. President Johnson issued Executive Order No. 11246 requiring government contractors to set out an affirmative action plan for hiring and promoting minorities and women. (This executive order is discussed in Chapter 20.)

The executive order as a source of law is also used by state governors to deal with emergencies and with budget functions. Often a governor will call out the national guard or, in some states, implement particular aspects of the budget by executive order. For example, a governor may order a freeze on the hiring of employees in the state university system or order an across-the-board cut in budgets in all state departments.

ADMINISTRATIVE AGENCIES AS A SOURCE OF LAW

Less well known as a source of law are the federal regulatory agencies, among which are the Securities and Exchange Commission (SEC), the Federal Trade Commission (FTC), the Equal Employment Opportunity Commission (EEOC), and the Occupational Safety and Health Administration (OSHA). Congress has delegated to these agencies the authority to make rules governing the conduct

---

[5]5 U.S. (1 Branch) 137 (1803).

of business and labor in certain areas. This authority was delegated because it was thought to be in the public interest, convenience, and necessity. Because each of the agencies must notify the public of proposed rule making and set out a cost–benefit analysis, all proposed and final rules can be found in the *Federal Register*. Administrative agencies constitute what many have called a fourth branch of government. They exist at the state and local levels as well.

CLASSIFICATIONS OF LAW

statutory law Law made by the legislative branch of government.

case law Law resulting from judicial interpretations of constitutions and statutes.

criminal law Composed of federal and state statutes prohibiting wrongful conduct ranging from murder to fraud.

Besides **statutory law** made by the legislative branch and **case law** resulting from judicial interpretation of constitutions and statutes, there are several other classifications of law that are necessary to know about in order to understand the legal environment of business.

CRIMINAL LAW AND CIVIL LAW

Criminal law comprises those federal and state statutes that prohibit wrongful conduct such as arson, rape, murder, extortion, forgery, and fraud. The purpose of criminal law is to punish offenders by imprisonment or fines as well as rehabilitation. The plaintiff in a criminal case is the United States, State X, County X, or City X, representing society and the victim against the defendant, who is most likely to be an individual but may also be a corporation, partnership, or a single proprietorship. The plaintiff must prove beyond a reasonable doubt that the defendant committed a crime.

Crimes are generally divided into felonies and misdemeanors. In most states, felonies are serious crimes (e.g., rape, arson, and criminal fraud) that are punishable by incarceration in a state penitentiary. Misdemeanors are less serious crimes (e.g., driving while intoxicated) that are usually punishable by shorter periods of imprisonment in a county or city jail or by fines. An act that is a misdemeanor in one state could be a felony in another state. White-collar felonies and misdemeanors are discussed in Chapter 7.

civil law Law governing litigation between two private parties.

Civil law comprises federal and state statutes governing litigation between two private parties. Neither the state nor the federal government is represented in most civil cases (exceptions will be pointed out in future chapters). Rather than prosecutors, there are plaintiffs, who are usually individuals or businesses suing other individuals or businesses (the defendants) to obtain compensation for an alleged breach of a private duty. For example, *A*, a retailer, enters into a contract with *B*, a manufacturer, who agrees to supply *A* with all the bicycles of a certain brand that the retailer can sell. *A* advertises and sales exceed all expectations. *B* refuses to ship any more bicycles, and *A*'s customers sue him for reneging on the raincheck he gave them. In turn, *A* sues *B* for breach of contract. *A* must show by a **preponderance of evidence** (a lower standard of proof than the "beyond a reasonable doubt" standard that prevails in criminal cases) that *B* is liable (legally obligated) to fulfill the contract. Note that *A* is not seeking to put *B* in prison or to fine *B*. *A* is seeking only to be compensated for his advertising costs, his lost sales, and what it may cost him in lawyers' fees, court costs, and damage to settle with his customers. (See Table 2–3.)

	Civil Law	*Criminal Law*
Parties	Individual or Corporate Plaintiff (in most cases) versus Individual or Corporate Defendant (in most cases)	County, City, State, or Federal Prosecutor versus Individual or Corporate Defendant (in most cases)
Purpose	Compensation Deference-deterrence	Punishment Deference-deterrence Rehabilitation
Burden of proof and sanctions	Preponderance of Evidence Monetary Damages Equitable Terms	Beyond a Reasonable Doubt Imprisonment Fines

TABLE 2-3

COMPARISON OF CIVIL AND CRIMINAL LAW

PUBLIC AND PRIVATE LAW

Public law deals with the relationship of government to individual citizens. Constitutional law, criminal law, and administrative law fit this classification. Constitutional law (discussed in Chapter 4) comprises the basic principles and laws of the nation as set forth in the U.S. Constitution. It determines the powers and obligations of the government and guarantees certain rights to citizens. Examples of questions that fall under constitutional law: Does an individual citizen have a Sixth Amendment right to counsel when stopped by a police officer, taken into custody, and interrogated? Is it cruel and unusual punishment under the Eighth Amendment to electrocute a person when that person has been found guilty of certain crimes, such as first-degree murder or killing a police officer in the line of duty? We have already touched on criminal law (which is discussed more fully in Chapter 7). Administrative law (examined in Chapter 17) covers the process by which individuals or businesses can redress grievances against regulatory agencies such as the Federal Trade Commission (FTC) and the Securities and Exchange Commission (SEC). It prevents the agencies from acting in an arbitrary or capricious manner and from extending their power beyond the scope that Congress has given them. For example, when the Federal Communications Commission (FCC) ruled that cable television corporations had to set aside so many channels for access by any public group that requested time, the courts reversed this FCC rule, deciding that it was beyond the agency's authority and in violation of a provision of the Federal Communications Act. Administrative law also covers the process whereby government agencies represent individuals or classes of individuals against business entities—for example, when the Equal Employment Opportunity Commission (EEOC) represents individuals alleging discrimination in pay under the provisions of the Civil Rights Act of 1964.

private law Law dealing with the enforcement of private duties.

public law Law dealing with the relationship of government to individual citizens.

Private law is generally concerned with the enforcement of private duties between individuals, between an individual and a business, and between two businesses. Contracts, torts, and property law fall under this classification. Note that the government is not a concerned party in most private law cases.

SUBSTANTIVE AND PROCEDURAL LAW

Substantive Law. Substantive law creates and regulates legal rights. For example, the rules of contract law (set out for your study in Chapters 10 and 11 of this text) determine whether an agreement between two parties is binding and, thus, an enforceable contract.

Procedural Law. Procedural law sets forth the rules of enforcing substantive rights in a court of law. In effect, procedural law defines the manner by which to obtain a remedy in a court of law. When there is a possible breach of contract, the plaintiff will have to file a complaint indicating the basis for the suit, and the defendant will set forth an answer responding to the complaint, indicating why the defendant should not have to compensate the plaintiff.

GLOBAL DIMENSIONS OF THE LEGAL ENVIRONMENT OF BUSINESS

At the beginning of this chapter, we stated that managers need to be aware of the impact of international variables on their business. As of the year 2004, approximately 30 percent of all jobs in the United States depended on exports and, in the view of many experts, that percentage will soon rise to 50 percent. Additionally, many jobs are being outsourced to other countries by American corporations for cost purposes. Trade treaties will make the international dimensions of the legal environment of business increasingly important to U.S. firms. Throughout this book, therefore, we discuss the international dimensions of product liability, tort, contracts, labor, securities and antitrust law, as well as ethics whenever appropriate. For example, current U.S. securities laws include the Foreign Corrupt Practices Act of 1977 (FCPA), as amended in 1988. If the laws of Country X do not forbid bribery in order to obtain a $10 million contract to build an oil pipeline, should U.S. companies be constrained by the FCPA prohibitions against such bribery? Ethical and cultural relativists would say no; "When in Rome do as the Romans do." Normative ethical theorists, such as rule utilitarians, would say yes, arguing that rules agreed upon by the world community, or a preponderance of it, cannot be compromised by a particular situation. They would point out that both the United Nations' Multinational Code and the laws of most of the UN's member states prohibit bribery.

SUMMARY

The study of the legal environment of business includes the study of legal reasoning, critical thinking skills, and ethical norms; the legal and administrative law processes; selected areas of public and private law; and relevant international law. Jurisprudence is the science or philosophy of law, or law in its most generalized form. The major schools of jurisprudence are natural law, positivism, sociological, American realism, critical legal theory, feminism, and law and economics.

The three direct sources of law are the legislative (statutory), judicial (case law), and executive (executive orders) branches of government. Administrative agencies, which promulgate regulations and rules, constitute the fourth (indirect) source of law. The international dimensions of law include legal, financial, economic, and ethical variables that have an impact on business decision making.

REVIEW QUESTIONS

2-1 Contrast the natural law school's definition of law with that of the positivist school.

2-2 Explain how the critical legal theory and the feminist school of jurisprudence are similar.

2-3 Describe how the executive branch of government is a source of law.

2-4 What is the difference between statutory law and case law? Explain.

2-5 If the president vetoes a bill passed by Congress, is there any way that the bill can become law? Explain.

2-6 Distinguish between the pairs of terms in each of these three classifications of law:

a. public law, private law

b. civil law, criminal law

c. felonies, misdemeanors

REVIEW PROBLEMS

2-7 Three men are trapped in a cave with no hope of rescue and no food. They roll dice to determine who will be killed and eaten by the others in order to survive. The two survivors are rescued ten days later and tried for murder. Judge A finds them guilty, saying that the unjustifiable killing of another is against the homicide laws of State X. He bases his decision solely on statutory law and case precedents interpreting the law. To which school of legal thought does Judge A belong? Explain.

2-8 Basing his decision on the same set of facts as given in Problem 2–7, Judge B rules that the survivors are not guilty because they were cut off from all civilized life and, in such a situation, the laws of nature apply, not man-made laws. To which school of legal thought does Judge B belong? Explain.

2-9 Basing her decision on the same set of facts as given in Problem 2–7, Judge C rules that the two survivors are not guilty because, according to a scientific survey of the community by a professional polling organization, the public believes that the survivors' actions were defensible. To which school of legal thought does Judge C belong? Explain.

2-10 Imagine that you were a judge in the case set forth in Problem 2–7. How would you decide the case? On the basis of the reasons for your decision, explain which legal philosophy you think you hold.

2-11 Madison and his adult son lived in a house owned by Madison. At the request of the son, Marshall painted the house. Madison did not authorize the work, but he knew that it was being done and raised no objection. Madison refused to pay Marshall, arguing that he had not contracted to have the house painted. Marshall asked his attorney if Madison was legally liable to pay him. The attorney told Marshall that in their state several appellate court opinions had established that when a homeowner allows work to be done on his home by a person who would ordinarily expect to be paid a duty to pay exists. The attorney stated that, on the basis of these precedents, it was advisable for Marshall to bring a suit to collect the reasonable value of the work he had done. Explain what the attorney meant by precedent and why the fact that precedent existed was significant.

2-12 Smith was involved in litigation in California. She lost her case in the trial court. She appealed to the California appellate court, arguing that the trial court judge had incorrectly excluded certain evidence. To support her argument, she cited rulings by the supreme court of North Dakota and the supreme court of Ohio. Both the North Dakota and Ohio cases involved facts that were similar to those in Smith's case. Does the California court have to follow the decisions from North Dakota and Ohio? Support your answer.

CASE PROBLEMS

2-13 Walt Disney Company entered into a contract with Irving Berlin, Inc., assigning musical copyrights in exchange for a share of Berlin revenues. The agreement exempted from copyright protection Disney's use of the assigned music in motion pictures. The music was used in several Disney feature-length cartoons that were later made available for sale on videocassette. Berlin's heirs brought suit, alleging infringement. Was this new technology an infringement? How would a judge's legal philosophy affect how he or she would rule in this case? *Bourne v. Walt Disney Co.*, 68 F. 3d 621 (2d Cir. 1995).

2-14 Three same-sex couples who are residents of Vermont have lived together in committed relationships for a period. Two of the couples have raised children together. All three couples applied for marriage licenses and were refused a license on the grounds that they were ineligible under the state marriage laws. Plaintiffs sought a declaratory judgment that the refusal to issue them a license violated the marriage statutes and the Vermont constitution. They argued that it violated the Common Benefits Clause of the Vermont constitution, which provides "[t]hat government is, or ought to be instituted for the common benefit, protection, and security of the people, nation, or community, and not for the particular emolument or advantage of a single person, family, or set of persons, who are part of that community. ..." They argued that in not having access to a civil marriage license, they are denied many legal benefits and protections, including coverage under a spouse's medical, life, and disability insurance, hospital visitation and other medical decision-making privileges, and spousal support. Argue whether Vermont's marriage license law violates the same-sex couples' rights under the Vermont constitution.

2-15 Beattie was seriously injured in an automobile accident in Delaware and was a quadriplegic following the accident. She filed suit against her husband for damages, alleging that his negligence was the cause of her injuries. Because the Beatties had substantial liability insurance, Margaret Beattie would have received a large sum in damages if she were able to establish her case. Unfortunately for her, Delaware follows the precedent of not allowing one spouse to sue the other spouse in tort. Should this precedent prevent Margaret from being allowed to sue her husband for damages in this case? *Beattie v. Beattie*, 630 A.2d 1096 (Del. 1993).

2-16 The federal Equal Employment Opportunity Commission (EEOC) brought suit against the Commonwealth of Massachusetts, challenging a statute mandating that state police must retire at 50 as a violation of the Age Discrimination Act. In an earlier suit brought by a state policeman named Mahoney, who held a desk job, the federal courts upheld the Massachusetts law on the grounds that being under 50 was a bona fide occupational requirement. The district court rejected the EEOC's challenge to the law on the basis of the ruling in Mahoney's case. The EEOC appealed, arguing that Mahoney's case should not be considered binding precedent for all members of the state police force. How did the EEOC appeal this case? Did it represent the agency or individuals or both? Who won? *EEOC v. Trabucco*, 791 F.2d 283 (1986).

2-17 A&M Records, plaintiffs, are in the business of the commercial recording, distribution, and sale of copyrighted musical compositions and sound recordings. It filed suit against Napster, Inc. (Napster) as a contributory and vicarious copyright infringer. Napster operates an online service for "peer-to-peer file sharing" (www.Napster.com) so that users can, free of charge, download recordings via the Internet through a process known as "ripping," which is the downloading of digital MP3 files. *MP3* is the abbreviated term for audio recordings in a digital format known as MPEG-3. Napster's online service provides a search vehicle for files stored on others' computers and permits the downloading of the recordings from the hard drives of other Napster users. Napster provides technical support as well as a chat room for users to exchange information. The result is that users, who register and have a password through Napster, could download single songs and complete CDs or albums, via the peer-to-peer file sharing. The district court granted a preliminary injunction to the plaintiffs enjoining Napster from "engaging in, or facilitating others in copying, downloading, uploading, transmitting, or distributing plaintiffs' copyrighted musical compositions and sound recordings, protected by either federal or state law, without express permission of the rights owner." Who won? *A&M Records v. Napster*, 239 F3d. 1004 (9th Cir., 2001).

2-18 A short time after the bombing of the federal building in Oklahoma City in April 1995, a message was posted anonymously on an America Online (AOL) bulletin board advertising "Naughty Oklahoma

T-Shirts." The posting advertised the sale of shirts featuring offensive and tasteless slogans celebrating the tragic bomb blast, which killed 168 people. The ad stated that interested buyers should call "Ken" at a phone number in Seattle. The phone number given was the actual number of Mr. Kenneth Zeran, who had nothing to do with the posting and most definitely had no such T-shirts for sale.

During the following few weeks, Mr. Zeran received hundreds of phone calls and voice mail messages. These calls caused him a great deal of distress. He notified AOL by telephone, letters, and e-mail about the bogus posting and harassment and asked AOL to immediately remove it and issue a public retraction. Although AOL did remove the original posting (the parties dispute how quickly this occurred), soon thereafter the unknown prankster posted another message advertising new T-shirts with more offensive slogans related to the Oklahoma City bombing, again giving

Mr. Zeran's phone number and also stating, "Please call back if busy."

For the next few days, Mr. Zeran's phone rang almost every two minutes with irate messages. Meanwhile the perpetrator of the hoax continued to post new messages on AOL, advertising several new distasteful items (fictitious) such as bumper stickers and key chains celebrating the Oklahoma City massacre and again giving Mr. Zeran's phone number. An Oklahoma City radio station read the messages on the air and encouraged listeners to express their outrage. Mr. Zeran sued AOL for its slowness in removing the posting. The federal district court dismissed the suit, holding the Communications Decency Act prevented the suit. The Fourth Circuit Court of Appeals affirmed. Explain how the legal philosophy one adheres to would make one more or less supportive of the court's ruling in favor of the AOL. *Zeran v. AOL*, 129 F.3d 327 4th Cir. (1997).

ASSIGNMENT ON THE INTERNET

This chapter introduces you to seven different schools of jurisprudence, each with distinct elements. Yet, the various schools also share a number of similarities that often blur the lines separating one from the other. Using the Internet, research at least two of the schools of jurisprudence discussed here to go beyond the information provided in this chapter. Then apply the critical thinking skills highlighted in Chapter 1 to compare the two schools you researched. How are they similar? How are they different?

For example, if you wanted to compare critical legal theory to the feminist school, you could begin by visiting this page on critical legal theory: www.law.cornell.edu/topics/critical_theory.html. Then visit a site exploring the feminist school. One such site can be found at www.law.cornell.edu/topics/feminist_jurisprudence.html. The following sites may also be of use in better understanding theories of jurisprudence.

 ## ON THE INTERNET

gsulaw.gsu.edu/pwiseman/home_pages/Jurisprudence/readings.html This site contains numerous links to readings on the philosophical foundation for the various schools of jurisprudence.

www.seanet.com/~rod/marbury.html Learn about the jurisprudence of access to justice from this page.

www.iep.utm.edu/j/jurisfem.htm The various components of feminist jurisprudence, discussed in greater detail, can be found at this site along with reading recommendations for further study.

www.fact-index.com/v/vi/virtue_jurisprudence.html Seven schools of legal thought or jurisprudence are discussed in this chapter, yet other theories of jurisprudence exist. This site provides an overview to Virtue Jurisprudence.

www.archives.gov/federal_register/executive_orders/executive_orders.html This is the Web site of the *Federal Register*, which allows you to search and read executive orders.

thomas.loc.gov Search, read, and follow the legislative progress of bills through both houses of Congress by using this research site.

3

THE AMERICAN LEGAL SYSTEM

- **JURISDICTION**
- **VENUE**
- **THE STRUCTURE OF THE COURT SYSTEM**
- **THE ACTORS IN THE LEGAL SYSTEM AND THEIR RELATIONSHIP TO THE BUSINESS COMMUNITY**
- **THE ADVERSARY PROCESS**
- **STEPS IN CIVIL LITIGATION AND THE ROLE OF BUSINESSPERSONS**
- **GLOBAL DIMENSIONS OF THE AMERICAN LEGAL SYSTEM**

We are all subject to both state and federal laws. Under our dual court system, all lawsuits must be brought in either the federal or the state court system. In some cases, an action may be brought in either. Thus, it is important that those in the business community understand how the decisions are made as to which court system can resolve their grievances. This chapter first considers the principles that determine which court system has the power to hear various types of cases and then examines in greater detail the structure of the two basic divisions of our dual court system. Next, it focuses on the primary actors who play major roles in our litigation process. Finally, it examines the philosophy behind our American legal system and traces the procedures that must be followed when using one of our courts.

Critical Thinking About the Law

Our American legal system can seem confusing at first. Using your critical thinking skills to answer the following questions as you read this chapter will help you understand how our legal system operates.

1. Critical thinkers recognize that ambiguous words—words that have multiple possible meanings—can cause confusion. Sam boldly asserts that the court of common pleas has jurisdiction over *Jones v. Smith*, while Clara asserts equally strongly that the court of common pleas does not have jurisdiction over the case. Explain the ambiguity that allows these two apparently contradictory statements to both be true.

   Clue: Is it possible for a court to have one type of jurisdiction and not another?

2. Our legal system contains numerous procedural requirements. Which of the primary values is furthered by these requirements?

   Clue: Review the four primary values described in Chapter 1.

3. Many say that the adversary system is consistent with the American culture. What value that is furthered by our adversary system is important to our culture?

   Clue: Can you go beyond the four primary values described in Chapter 1 and think of any other important values?

JURISDICTION

The concept of jurisdiction is exceedingly simple, yet at the same time, exceedingly complex. At its most simple level, **jurisdiction** is the power of the courts to hear a case and render a decision that is binding on the parties. Jurisdiction is complex, however, because there are several types of jurisdiction that a court must have in order to hear a case.

jurisdiction The power of a court to hear a case and render a binding decision.

ORIGINAL VERSUS APPELLATE JURISDICTION

Perhaps the simplest type of jurisdiction to understand is the distinction between original and appellate jurisdiction, which refers to the role the court plays in the judicial hierarchy. A court of **original jurisdiction**, usually referred to as a trial court, has the power to initially hear and decide a case. It is in the court of original jurisdiction that a case originates; hence, its name.

A court with **appellate jurisdiction** has the power to review a previously made decision to determine whether the trial court erred in making its initial decision.

original jurisdiction The power to initially hear and decide (try) a case.

appellate jurisdiction The power to review a previously made decision by the trial court.

JURISDICTION OVER PERSONS AND PROPERTY

Before the court can render a decision affecting a person, the court must have **in personam jurisdiction**, or **jurisdiction over the person**. In personam jurisdiction is the power to render a decision affecting the specific persons before the court. When a person files a lawsuit, that person, called the **plaintiff**, gives the court

in personam jurisdiction (jurisdiction over the person) The power of a court to render a decision that affects the legal rights of a specific person.

plaintiff Party on whose behalf the complaint is filed.

defendant Party against whom an action is being brought.

complaint The initial pleading in a case that states the names of the parties to the action, the basis for the court's subject matter jurisdiction, the facts on which the party's claim is based, and the relief that the party is seeking.

summons Order by a court to appear before it at a certain time and place.

service Providing the defendant with a summons and a copy of the complaint.

long-arm statute A statute authorizing a court to obtain jurisdiction over an out-of-state defendant when that party has sufficient minimum contacts with a state.

in personam jurisdiction over him or her. By filing a case, the plaintiff is asking the court to make a ruling affecting his or her rights. The court must acquire jurisdiction over the party being sued, the **defendant**, by serving him or her with a copy of the plaintiff's complaint and a summons. The **complaint**, discussed in more detail later in this chapter, is a detailed statement of the basis for the plaintiff's lawsuit and the relief being sought. The **summons** is an order of the court notifying the defendant of the pending case and telling him or her how and when to respond to the complaint.

Personal **service**, whereby a sheriff or other person appointed by the court hands the summons and complaint to the defendant, has been the traditional method of service. Today, other types of service are more common. Residential service may be used, whereby the summons and complaint are left by the representative of the court with a responsible adult at the home of the defendant. Certified mail or, in some cases, ordinary mail is also used to serve defendants. Once the defendant has been properly served, the court has in personam jurisdiction over him or her and may render a decision affecting his or her legal rights, regardless of whether the defendant responds to the complaint.

When one thinks about how the rules of service would apply to a suit against a corporation, the question arises: How do you serve a corporation? The legal system has solved that question. Most states require that corporations appoint an agent for service when they are incorporated. This agent is a person who has been given the legal authority to receive service for the corporation. Once the agent has been served, the corporation is served. In most states, service on the president of the corporation also constitutes service on the corporation.

A court's power is generally limited to the borders of the state in which it is located. So, traditionally, a defendant had to be served within the state in which the court was located in order for the court to acquire jurisdiction over the person of the defendant. This restriction imposed severe hardships when a defendant who lived in one state entered another state and injured the plaintiff. If the defendant never again entered the plaintiff's state, the plaintiff could bring an action against the defendant only in the state in which the defendant lived. Obviously, this restriction would prevent many legitimate actions from being filed.

To alleviate this problem, most states enacted **long-arm statutes**. These statutes enable the court to serve the defendant outside the state as long as the defendant has engaged in certain acts within the state. Those acts vary from state to state, but most statutes include such acts as committing a tort within the state or doing business within the state. The following case demonstrates the application of such a statute.

CASE 3-1

World-Wide Volkswagen Corporation v. Woodson, District Judge of Cook County
United States Supreme Court
444 U.S. 286 (1980)

Mr. and Mrs. Robinson, the plaintiffs in the original case, filed a product liability action against defendant World-Wide Volkswagen in a state court in Oklahoma to collect compensation for damages they incurred as a result of an accident involving an automobile they had purchased in New York. The defendants in that case, the retailer and wholesaler of the car, were both New York corporations.

Defendants claimed that the Oklahoma court could not exercise jurisdiction over them because they were nonresidents and they lacked sufficient "minimum contacts" with the state to be subject to its in personam jurisdiction.

The trial court rejected defendant-petitioner's claims. The Oklahoma Supreme Court likewise rejected their claims, and so they petitioned the U.S. Supreme Court. Note that the case that went to the Supreme Court is against the trial court, because the issue on appeal is whether the trial court acted properly in asserting jurisdiction.

Justice White

The issue before us is whether, consistently with the Due Process Clause of the Fourteenth Amendment, an Oklahoma court may exercise in personam jurisdiction over a nonresident automobile retailer and its wholesale distributor in a products liability action, when the defendants' only connection with Oklahoma is the fact that an automobile sold in New York to New York residents became involved in an accident in Oklahoma.

As has long been settled, and as we reaffirm today, a state court may exercise personal jurisdiction over a nonresident defendant only so long as there exist "minimum contacts" between the defendant and the forum State. The concept of minimum contacts, in turn, can be seen to perform two related, but distinguishable, functions. It protects the defendant against the burdens of litigating in a distant or inconvenient forum. And it acts to ensure that the States, through their courts, do not reach out beyond the limits imposed on them by their status as coequal sovereigns in a federal system.

The protection against inconvenient litigation is typically described in terms of "reasonableness" or "fairness." We have said that the defendant's contacts with the forum State must be such that maintenance of the suit "does not offend 'traditional notions of fair play and substantial justice.'"

The limits imposed on state jurisdiction by the Due Process Clause, in its role as a guarantor against inconvenient litigation, have been substantially relaxed over the years. This trend is largely attributable to a fundamental transformation in the American economy:

Today many commercial transactions touch two or more States and may involve parties separated by the full continent. With this increasing nationalization of commerce has come a great increase in the amount of business conducted by mail across state lines. At the same time modern transportation and communication have made it much less burdensome for a party sued to defend himself in a State where he engages in economic activity.

Nevertheless, we have never accepted the proposition that state lines are irrelevant for jurisdictional purposes, nor could we, and remain faithful to the principles of interstate federalism embodied in the Constitution.

Applying these principles to the case at hand, we find in the record before us a total absence of those affiliating circumstances that are a necessary predicate to any exercise of state court jurisdiction. Petitioners carry on no activity whatsoever in Oklahoma. They close no sales and perform no services there. They avail themselves of none of the privileges and benefits of Oklahoma law. They solicit no business there either through salespersons or through advertising reasonably calculated to reach the State. Nor does the record show that they regularly sell cars at wholesale or retail to Oklahoma customers or residents or that they indirectly, through others, serve or seek to serve the Oklahoma market. In short, respondents seek to base jurisdiction on one isolated occurrence and whatever inferences can be drawn therefrom: the fortuitous circumstance that a single Audi automobile sold in New York to New York residents happened to suffer an accident while passing through Oklahoma.

It is argued, however, that because an automobile is mobile by its very design and purpose it was "foreseeable" that the Robinsons' Audi would cause injury in Oklahoma. Yet "foreseeability" alone has never been a sufficient benchmark for personal jurisdiction under the Due Process Clause.

If foreseeability were the criterion, a local California tire retailer could be forced to defend in Pennsylvania when a blowout occurs there, a Wisconsin seller of a defective automobile jack could be hauled before a distant court for damage caused in New Jersey, or a Florida soft-drink concessionaire could be summoned to Alaska to account for injuries happening there.

This is not to say, of course, that foreseeability is wholly irrelevant. But the foreseeability that is critical to due process analysis is not the mere likelihood that a product will find its way into the forum State. Rather, it is that the defendant's conduct and connection with the forum State are such that he should reasonably anticipate being hauled into court there. When a corporation "purposefully avails itself of the privilege of conducting activities within the forum State," it has clear notice that it is subject to suit there, and can act to alleviate the risk of burdensome litigation by procuring insurance, passing the expected costs on to customers, or, if the risks are too great, severing its connection with the State. Hence, if the sale of a product of a manufacturer or distributor such as Audi or Volkswagen is not simply an isolated occurrence, but arises from the efforts of the manufacturer or distributor to serve directly or indirectly the market for its product in other States, it is not unreasonable to subject it to suit in one of those States if its allegedly defective merchandise has there been the source of injury to its owner or to others.

But there is no such or similar basis for Oklahoma jurisdiction over World-Wide or Seaway in this case. Seaway's sales are made in Massena, New York. World-Wide's market, although substantially larger, is limited to dealers in New York, New Jersey, and Connecticut. There is no evidence of record that any automobiles distributed by World-Wide are sold to retail customers outside this tristate area. It is foreseeable that the purchasers of automobiles sold by World-Wide and Seaway may take them to Oklahoma. But the mere "unilateral activity of those who claim some relationship with a nonresident defendant cannot satisfy the requirement of contact with the forum State."

Reversed in favor of World-Wide Volkswagen Corporation.

Contrast the facts in the foregoing case with those in the 2004 case of *Snowney v. Harrah's Entertainment, Inc.*,[1] in which the court came to a contrary decision. In *Snowney*, the defendant, a California resident, filed a class action suit against Harrah's and other Nevada casino operators, in a California state court, alleging unfair competition, breach of contract, and false advertising. The trial court dismissed the suit for lack for personal jurisdiction. The California Court of Appeals overturned the dismissal, explaining that when the court was deciding whether it could exercise its jurisdiction over a nonresident, it must consider (1) the burden on the defendant of defending an action in the forum; (2) the forum state's interest in adjudicating the dispute; (3) the plaintiff's interest in obtaining relief; (4) judicial economy; and (5) the states' shared interest in furthering fundamental substantive social policies. In finding that there were sufficient minimum contacts with the state to justify exercising jurisdiction, the court cited the facts that the hotels and casinos (1) purposefully directed advertising at California residents; (2) conducted business with some residents by an interactive Web site, and (3) solicited and received the patronage of California residents.

In Rem Jurisdiction. If a defendant has property within a state, the plaintiff may seek to bring the action directly against the property rather than against the owner. For example, if a Michigan defendant owned land in Idaho on which taxes had not been paid for ten years, the state could bring an action to recover those taxes. The Idaho court would have **in rem jurisdiction** over the property and, in an in rem proceeding, could order the property sold to pay the taxes. Such proceedings are often used when the owner of the property cannot be located for personal service.

in rem jurisdiction The power of a court to render a decision that affects property directly rather than the owner of the property.

SUBJECT MATTER JURISDICTION

subject matter jurisdiction The power of a court to render a decision in a particular type of case.

One of the most important types of jurisdiction is **subject matter jurisdiction**, the power of the court to hear certain kinds of cases. Subject matter jurisdiction is extremely important because if a judge renders a decision in a case over which the court does not have subject matter jurisdiction, the decision is void or meaningless. The parties cannot give the court subject matter jurisdiction. It is granted by law as described in the subsequent sections.

At the beginning of the chapter, you learned that we have a dual court system, comprised of both a state and a federal system. The choice of the system in which to file a case is not purely a matter of deciding which forum is most convenient or which judge would be most sympathetic. Subject matter jurisdiction determines what court may hear the case. When you think about the concept of subject matter jurisdiction, it is easiest to think of it in two steps. First, which court system does the case fall within? Once you know which court system has jurisdiction over the

---

[1] 11 Cal.Rptr.3d 35 (Ct. App., Calif., 2004).

Technology and the Legal Environment

The Internet and In Personam Jurisdiction

Is the sponsor of a Web site that can be visited from every state subject to in personam jurisdiction in every state? As long as the sponsor is not conducting any business or trying to reach customers in a state, many courts have held that mere access to the Web site is not sufficient to grant in personam jurisdiction.

One case that illustrates this point involved two organizations that both used the name Carefirst. Carefirst of Maryland, a nonprofit insurance company, accused Carefirst Pregnancy Center (CPC), a Chicago-based non-profit organization, of trademark infringement.[a] Carefirst of Maryland operated a Web site from which the company promoted its products to consumers who are located primarily in the Mid-Atlantic region, with the majority of its consumers living in Maryland. CPC also operated a Web site, which was accessible anywhere in the world, for the purpose of promoting its services for women with pregnancy-related crisis and to generate donations for the organization. CPC's operations were confined almost entirely to the state of Illinois.

Since CPC began using the name Carefirst, the Chicago-based organization has received only one donation from a Maryland resident via the company's Web site. From 1991 to 2001, CPC claimed that only 0.0174 percent of its donations came from Maryland residents. The only means through which CPC has contact with Maryland residents is CPC's Web site. Therefore, a district court in Maryland and the appellate court both dismissed the case for lack of personal jurisdiction, concluding that even though CPC's Web site could be contacted from anywhere, its purpose was to provide information about the organization and solicit donations primarily from Illinois residents. While the court noted that the donations received from Maryland residents were negligible, the court also held that CPC made no effort to target Maryland donors. Furthermore, the court observed that CPC had no agents, employees, or offices located in Maryland. Hence, there was not sufficient contact with Maryland to support personal jurisdiction.

If the potential defendant, however, is actively trying to do business in other states via a Web site, the outcome of a case may be different. For example, in *Gator.com Corp v. L.L. Bean, Inc.*[b] the Ninth Circuit Court of Appeals held that L.L. Bean was subject to in personam jurisdiction in California. Gator.com, a company that develops software for consumers who make online purchases, also created pop-up coupons that would appear on L.L. Bean's Web site for L.L. Bean's competitors, like Eddie Bauer. In response to its receiving a cease-and-desist letter from L.L. Bean, Gator.com sought a declaratory judgment that its actions were not illegal according to state and federal laws. L.L. Bean filed a motion to dismiss, after which a district court in California ruled that the court did not have in personam jurisdiction. The Ninth Circuit reversed on appeal, noting that 6 percent of L.L. Bean's $1 billion in annual sales is attributable to California customers. The court also observed that L.L. Bean "targets" California consumers with its direct e-mail solicitations, while also maintaining a highly interactive Web site, from which numerous California customers make online purchases and interact with L.L Bean sales representatives. Hence, the Ninth Circuit found these e-mail solicitations and Web site services to California consumers to be sufficient minimum contacts for in personam jurisdiction.

You will learn more about the impact of the Internet on jurisdictional issues when you read Chapter 6.

Sources: [a]*Carefirst of Maryland, Inc. v. Carefirst Pregnancy Centers, Inc.*, 334 F.3d 390 (2003).
[b]*Gator.com, Inc. v. L.L. Bean*, 341 F.3d 1072 (2002).

---

case, you then need to ask whether there is a special court within that system that hears that specific type of case. When asking which court system has subject matter jurisdiction, there are three possible answers: state jurisdiction, exclusive federal jurisdiction, or concurrent federal jurisdiction (Exhibit 3–1).

State Jurisdiction. The **state court** system has subject matter jurisdiction over all cases not within the exclusive jurisdiction of the federal court system. Only a very limited number of cases fall within the exclusive jurisdiction of the federal courts. Consequently, almost all cases fall within the state court's jurisdiction.

state court jurisdiction
Applies to cases that may be heard only in the state court system.

EXHIBIT 3-1

SUBJECT MATTER JURISDICTION

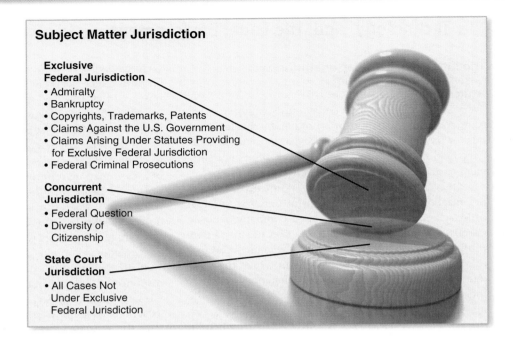

Subject Matter Jurisdiction

Exclusive Federal Jurisdiction
• Admiralty
• Bankruptcy
• Copyrights, Trademarks, Patents
• Claims Against the U.S. Government
• Claims Arising Under Statutes Providing for Exclusive Federal Jurisdiction
• Federal Criminal Prosecutions

Concurrent Jurisdiction
• Federal Question
• Diversity of Citizenship

State Court Jurisdiction
• All Cases Not Under Exclusive Federal Jurisdiction

Suits for breach of contract, products liability actions, and divorces are just a few of the types of cases falling within the state court system's jurisdiction.

Exclusive Federal Jurisdiction. A few types of cases may be heard only in the federal courts. Such cases are within the exclusive jurisdiction of the federal court system. If these cases were tried in a state court, any decision rendered by the judge would be void. Cases that fall within the exclusive jurisdiction of the federal courts include such matters as admiralty, bankruptcy, federal criminal prosecutions, claims against the United States, and claims arising under those federal statutes that include a provision for **exclusive federal jurisdiction**. Many of these last cases are of particular concern to those in business. For example, one statute that gives exclusive jurisdiction to the federal court system is the National Environmental Policy Act, discussed in Chapter 21. Cases brought under this act must be filed in a federal district court.

Concurrent Federal Jurisdiction. Many cases may be heard in either the federal or the state court. These cases are said to fall within the federal court's **concurrent jurisdiction**, meaning that both court systems have jurisdiction, so the plaintiff may file in the trial court of either system. There are two types of such cases. The first are federal question cases. If a case requires an interpretation of the U.S. Constitution, a federal statute, or a federal treaty, it is said to involve a federal question and may be heard in either state or federal court. Many people make the mistake of thinking that when a person believes his or her rights under the federal Constitution have been violated, the case must go to the federal courts. They are wrong. Such a case involves a federal question and is, therefore, within the concurrent jurisdiction of both court systems.

The second means by which a case may fall within the federal court's concurrent jurisdiction is through diversity of citizenship. If the opponents in a case are from different states, there is said to be diversity of citizenship. The diversity must be complete. If any two parties on opposing sides reside in the same state, diversity

exclusive federal jurisdiction Applies to cases that may be heard only in the federal court system.

concurrent jurisdiction Applies to cases that may be heard in either the federal or the state court system.

is lost. For example, if the plaintiff is an Ohio resident and one of the defendants lives in Michigan and the other in Indiana, diversity exists. However, if an Ohio plaintiff is bringing an action against a Michigan defendant and an Ohio defendant, there is not complete diversity and, therefore, no concurrent federal jurisdiction. When the basis for federal jurisdiction is diversity of citizenship, there must be an amount in excess of $75,000 in controversy (increased from $50,000 in 1996).

When a case falls within the federal court's concurrent jurisdiction because of either a federal question or diversity of citizenship, the suit may be filed in either state or federal court. If the case is filed in state court, the defendant has a right of removal, which means that he or she may have the case transferred to federal court. All the defendant has to do is file a motion with the court asking to exercise his or her right of removal and the case must be transferred to federal court; the judge has no discretion but must comply with the request.

The right of removal arises only when the case is filed in state court; there is no right of removal to state court. As a result, whenever there is a case under concurrent jurisdiction, if either party wants the case heard in federal court, that is where it will be heard.

Why should both parties have the right to have such a case heard in federal court? In certain cases, a party may fear local prejudice in a state court. Juries for a state court are generally drawn from the county in which the court is located. The juries for federal district courts are drawn from the entire district, which encompasses many counties. Juries in state court are, therefore, usually more homogeneous than those of a district court. One problem that this homogeneity may present to the out-of-state corporate defendant occurs when the county in which the court is located is predominantly rural. If the case involves an injury to a member of this rural community, the defendant may feel that the rural jurors would be more sympathetic to the local injured party, whereas jurors drawn from a broader area, including cities, may be more likely to view the victim less sympathetically. City residents are also more likely to work for a corporation and, thus, may not regard corporations as unfavorably as might rural residents.

When a case involves a federal question, some people believe federal judges are better qualified to hear such cases because they have more experience in resolving questions that require an interpretation of federal statutes. Finally, if a party anticipates that it may be necessary to appeal the case to the U.S. Supreme Court, bringing the case first in a federal district court may save one step in the appeals process.

When one party wishes to have the case tried in federal court and the other prefers state court, the issue of whether the case is within the concurrent jurisdiction of the federal courts sometimes arises. The following case provides an illustration of such a situation.

CASE 3-2

Gafford v. General Electric Company
United States Court of Appeals for the Sixth Circuit
997 F.2d 150 (1993)

Plaintiff Carol Gafford filed an action against defendant General Electric Company for violating the Kentucky Civil Rights Statute by discriminating against her on grounds of gender. She filed the case in the state court. The defendant filed a motion to exercise his right of removal, and the case was accordingly transferred to the federal district court over the plaintiff's objection. The trial was held and the plaintiff lost. She appealed on the grounds that the case should never have been tried in federal court because there was not sufficient evidence of complete diversity of citizenship.

Judge Jones

Gafford takes issue with the district court's determination that diversity of citizenship among the parties was complete. Gafford is a citizen of Kentucky. For purposes of determining diversity jurisdiction, a corporation can be a citizen of two states: (1) its state of incorporation; and (2) the state of its principal place of business. GE is incorporated in New York.

What is disputed is whether GE's principal place of business is in Kentucky. Gafford basically argues that, given the size of the GE facility in Kentucky, which encompasses over 9,000 employees, "[i]t would be reasonable to conclude that Jefferson County, Kentucky is a principal place of business for General Electric."

Gafford maintains that GE did not make a sufficient showing of workforce distribution and the like in order to meet its burden of proof, which we take to be a preponderance of the evidence.

By common sense and by law, a corporation can have only one principal place of business for purposes of establishing its state of citizenship. GE submitted evidence to the court that Schenectady, New York, is its principal place of business, where basic corporate and personnel records are maintained. At the hearing, Earl F. Jones produced a copy of the 10-K form GE had filed with the United States Securities and Exchange Commission for the fiscal year ended December 31, 1990.

In the affidavit submitted by GE, Jones also noted:

There are many states in the United States in which General Electric has extensive manufacturing operations. Several of those states contain General Electric business operations that generate more revenue for General Electric than Appliance Park in Kentucky.

Gafford presented no evidence to rebut the affidavit or the testimony put forth by Jones at the jurisdiction hearing.

"The question of a corporation's principal place of business is essentially one of fact, to be determined on a case-by-case basis, taking into account such factors as the character of the corporation, its purposes, the kind of business in which it is engaged, and the situs of its operations."

In making this determination, courts have followed various approaches, or "tests." The "nerve center" test emphasizes the situs of corporate decision-making authority and overall control. The "corporate activities"/"place of activity" test emphasizes the location of production activities or service activities. These tests are not mutually exclusive.

Where a corporation carries on its business in a number of states and no one state is clearly the state in which its business is principally conducted, the state in which the substantial part of its business is transacted and from which centralized general supervision of its business is exercised is the state in which it has its principal place of business.

Since GE is neither incorporated nor has its principle [sic] place of business in Kentucky, it is not a citizen of the state for the purposes of diversity.

Given GE's basic corporate structure, it was not clearly erroneous to conclude that the significant administrative activity in New York justified finding New York to be GE's principal place of business.

Affirmed in favor of defendant.

Critical Thinking About the Law

Legal reasoning has two basic elements: a conclusion and some reasons. The reasons provide a basis whereby we are urged to have confidence in the conclusion. For reasons to do their job, they must provide support, something reliable that moves our understanding in the direction of the conclusion.

Some courts provide reasons that restate in different words the conclusion they have chosen. These so-called reasons are disappointing because they do not do the job we expect from reasons.

1. Case 3-2 has an unusually large amount of these pseudo or false reasons. Locate an instance where the court writes as if it is providing a reason but is actually simply rewording its conclusion.

Clue: Words such as *since* often signal us that the writer believes she or he is about to provide a reason.

VENUE

Subject matter jurisdiction should not be confused with venue. Once it is determined which court system has the power to hear the case, **venue** determines which of the many trial courts in that system is appropriate. Venue, clearly prescribed by statute in each state, is a matter of geographic location. It is usually based on the residence of the defendant, the location of the property in dispute, or the location in which the incident out of which the dispute arose occurred. When there are multiple defendants who reside in various geographic locations, the party filing the lawsuit may usually choose from among the various locales. If the location of the court in which the case is filed presents a hardship or inconvenience to one of the parties, that person may request that the case be moved under the doctrine of forum non conveniens, which simply means that the location of the trial court is inconvenient. The judge in the case will consider the party's request and decide whether to grant the party's request. Unlike the right of removal, the request for change of venue is granted at the judge's discretion. There will usually be a hearing on the issue of whether the judge should grant the motion, because the plaintiff generally filed the case in a particular court for a reason and will, therefore, be opposed to the defendant's motion.

venue County of the trial court; prescribed by state statute.

THE STRUCTURE OF THE COURT SYSTEM

As noted previously, our system has two parallel court structures, one federal and one state system. Because of subject matter jurisdiction limitations, one often does not have a choice as to the system in which to file the case. Once a case is filed in a system, it will stay within that system, except for appeals to the U.S. Supreme Court. The following sections set forth the structure of the two systems. As you will see, they are indeed very similar. Their relationship is illustrated in Exhibit 3–2.

THE FEDERAL COURT SYSTEM

Federal Trial Courts. As you already know, trial courts are the courts of original jurisdiction. In the federal court system, the trial courts are the U.S. district courts. The United States is divided into 96 districts, and each district has at least one trial court of general jurisdiction. General jurisdiction means that the court has the power to hear cases involving a wide variety of subject matter and that it is not limited in the types of remedies that it can grant. All cases to be heard in the federal system are filed in these courts, except those cases for which Congress has established special trial courts of limited jurisdiction.

Trial courts of limited jurisdiction in the federal system are limited in the type of cases they have the power to hear. Special federal trial courts of limited jurisdiction have been established for bankruptcy cases; claims against the U.S. government; and copyright, patent, and trademark cases. In an extremely limited number of cases, the U.S. Supreme Court also functions as a trial court of limited jurisdiction. Such cases include controversies between two or more states and suits against foreign ambassadors.

Intermediate Courts of Appeal. The second level of courts in the federal system is made up of the U.S. circuit courts of appeal. The United States is divided into 12 geographic areas, including the District of Columbia, each of which has a circuit court of appeals. Exhibit 3–2 illustrates this division. There is also a federal circuit court of appeals and a recently established United States Veterans' Court of Appeals. Each circuit court of appeals hears appeals from all of the district courts located within its geographic area. These courts also hear appeals from administrative agencies located within their respective circuits. In some cases, appeals from administrative agencies are heard by the Federal Circuit Court of Appeals. The Veterans' Court of Appeals hears appeals of benefits decisions made by the Veterans Administration.

Court of Last Resort. The U.S. Supreme Court is the final appellate court in the federal system. In a limited number of instances, discussed in the last section of this chapter, the U.S. Supreme Court also hears cases from the court of last resort in a state system. As previously noted, the U.S. Supreme Court also functions as a trial court in a limited number of cases. The federal court system is illustrated in Exhibit 3–3.

STATE COURT SYSTEMS

There is no uniform state court structure because each state has devised its own court system. Most states, however, follow a general structure similar to that of the federal court system.

State Trial Courts. In state court systems, most cases are originally filed in the trial court of general jurisdiction. As in the federal system, state trial courts of general jurisdiction are those that have the power to hear all the cases that would be tried in the state court system, except those cases for which special trial courts of limited jurisdiction have been established. These trial courts of general jurisdiction are distributed throughout each state, usually by county. The names of these courts vary from state to state but are usually called courts of common pleas or county courts. New York uniquely calls its trial courts of general jurisdiction supreme courts. In some states, these courts may have specialized divisions, such as domestic relations or probate.

Most states also have trial courts of limited jurisdiction. These courts are usually limited in the remedies that they may grant. Some may not issue injunctions or orders for specific performance. A common court of limited jurisdiction in most states is the small claims court, which may not grant damage awards in excess of specified amounts. Some courts of limited jurisdiction are limited to certain types of cases, such as traffic cases. Some criminal courts of limited jurisdiction may be limited to hearing misdemeanors. It is difficult to generalize about these courts because they vary so much from state to state. The main distinction between trial courts of general and limited jurisdiction, however, is that the former hear almost all types of cases that are filed in the state system and are unlimited in the remedies they can provide, whereas the latter hear only a particular type of case or may award only limited remedies.

Intermediate Courts of Appeal. Intermediate courts of appeal, analogous to the federal circuit courts of appeal, exist in approximately half the states. These courts usually have broad jurisdiction, hearing appeals from courts of general

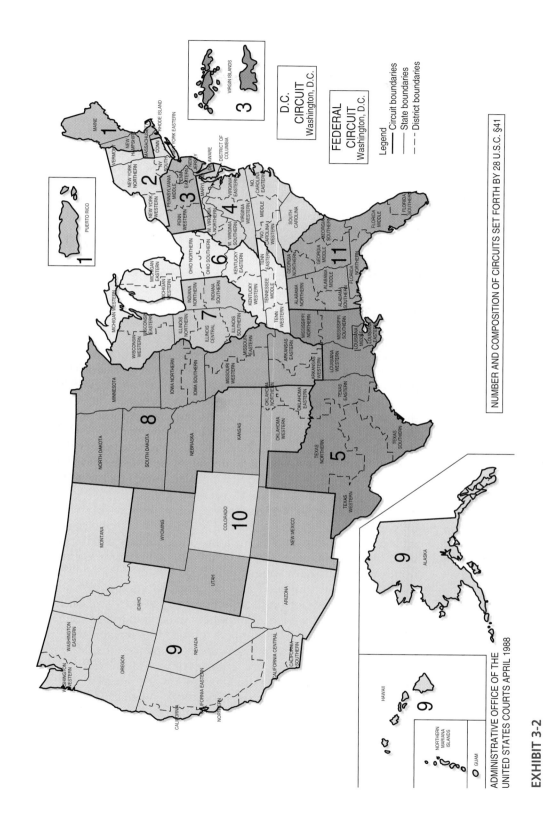

Legend

— Circuit boundaries
— State boundaries
--- District boundaries

NUMBER AND COMPOSITION OF CIRCUITS SET FORTH BY 28 U.S.C. §41

ADMINISTRATIVE OFFICE OF THE
UNITED STATES COURTS APRIL 1988

EXHIBIT 3-2

GEOGRAPHIC BOUNDARIES OF UNITED STATES COURTS OF APPEALS AND UNITED STATES DISTRICT COURTS and limited jurisdictions, as well as from state administrative agencies. The names of these courts also vary by state. They may be called courts of appeal or superior courts.

COURTS OF LAST RESORT

In almost all cases filed in the state court system, the last appeal is to the state court of last resort. This court is frequently called the supreme court. In some states, it is known as the court of appeals. In approximately half of the states, it is the second court to which an appeal can be made; in the remaining states, it is the only appellate court.

THE ACTORS IN THE LEGAL SYSTEM AND THEIR RELATIONSHIP TO THE BUSINESS COMMUNITY

THE ATTORNEY

An understanding of the structure of the legal system would be incomplete without an awareness of the primary actors within the system. The party with whom businesspersons usually have the most frequent contact is the attorney. Although the exact qualifications for being an attorney vary from state to state, most require that an attorney have a law degree, have passed the state's bar examination, and be of high moral character. Attorneys are the legal representatives of the parties before the court. Some corporations have full-time attorneys, referred to as in-house counsel. Other corporations send all their legal work to an outside law firm. Many larger businesses have in-house counsel and also use outside counsel when a problem arises that requires a specialist.

attorney–client privilege
Provides that information furnished by a client to an attorney in confidence, in conjunction with a legal matter, may not be revealed by the attorney without the client's permission.

Attorney–Client Privilege. The attorney can provide effective representation only when he or she knows all the pertinent facts of the case. The businessperson who withholds information from his or her attorney may cause irreparable harm if the hidden facts are revealed by the opposing side in court. To encourage client honesty, the **attorney–client privilege** was established. This privilege provides that information furnished in confidence to an attorney, in conjunction with a legal matter, may not be revealed by that attorney without permission from the client. There is, however, an important exception to this rule. If the lawyer knows the client is about to commit a crime, the lawyer may reveal confidential information in order to prevent the commission of that crime. Revealing such information, however, is not required of the attorney; it is simply allowed. This protection also extends to the attorney's work product under what is known as the **work-product doctrine**. The work product includes those formal and informal documents prepared by the attorney in conjunction with a client's case.

work-product doctrine
Provides that formal and informal documents prepared by an attorney in conjunction with a client's case are privileged and may not be revealed by the attorney without the client's permission.

One of the problems arising out of the use of the attorney–client privilege in the corporate setting is the definition of the client. The client is the corporation, but the communication sought to be protected is that between the attorney and upper-, middle-, or lower-level employees of the corporation. In such cases, the corporate attorney usually tries to rely on the work-product doctrine

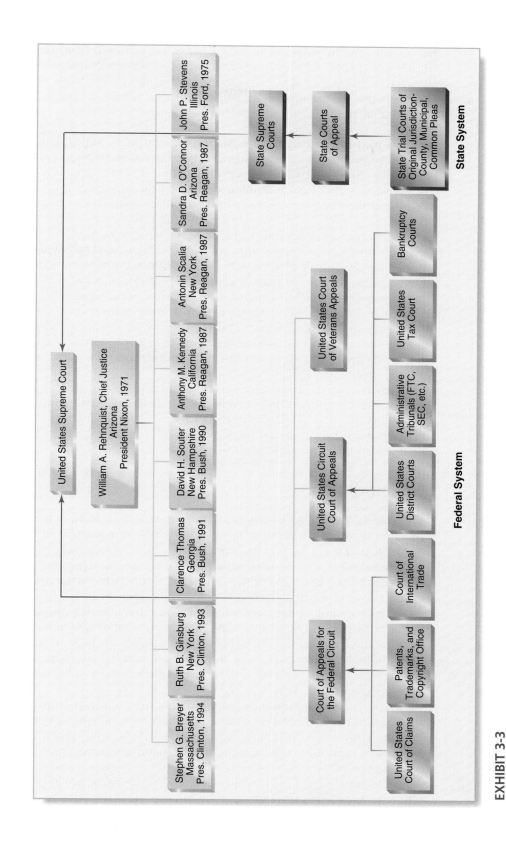

EXHIBIT 3-3

THE STRUCTURE OF THE COURT SYSTEM

49

to protect the information that he or she has gathered from employees, especially when such information is in the form of written communications. Such an approach has generally been successful, but the courts have not yet precisely defined the parameters of the attorney–client privilege and the work-product doctrine as they apply to the corporate setting.

Additional Functions of the Attorney. Attorneys are probably best known for representing clients in litigation, but they also provide other services for business clients. Attorneys represent their clients not only in courtroom litigation but also before administrative boards. Attorneys may be called on to represent their corporate clients in negotiations with labor unions or with other firms.

Corporate attorneys also serve as advisors or counselors, reviewing proposed corporate activities and advising management of legal problems that may arise as a result of such activities. In-house counsel familiar with the various activities of the firm are often in the best position to fulfill this role. Thus, businesspersons should attempt to establish a good working relationship with in-house counsel, using them as a resource whenever legal issues arise. Managers should not assume that they know all the legal ramifications of all the business activities in which they engage. Most in-house counsel would prefer to be consulted before an activity is undertaken rather than after it results in a legal problem.

Finally, the attorney may serve as a draftsperson, drawing up contracts, deeds, the corporate charter, securities registration statements, and all other legal documents needed by the corporation. Thus, is it clear that the attorney is one actor in the American legal system who is of special importance to the business manager.

THE JUDGE

The role of the judge is especially important in our legal system. The judge's function changes, depending on whether he or she is a trial or appellate court judge. A trial court judge presides over the trial, making sure the case is heard with reasonable speed; rules on all motions made in the case; and decides all questions of the law. One of the most crucial functions of the trial court judge is ruling on whether or not certain pieces of evidence are admissible. Failure of the judge to admit certain items into evidence may be determinative of the outcome of a case, and a judge's ruling on any piece of evidence may subsequently become the basis for the appeal of an unfavorable decision. If the parties waive their rights to a jury trial, or if they are not entitled to a jury, the judge also decides the facts in the case and renders a decision accordingly. A single judge presides over each case.

Appellate judges serve on panels. They review lower-court cases to determine whether errors of law were committed by the lower courts. Their review consists primarily of reading the transcript of the trial, reading written arguments by counsel for both parties, and sometimes hearing oral arguments from both parties' attorneys.

State court judges are usually elected, although some are appointed, whereas federal court judges are appointed by the president with the advice and consent of the Senate. This appointment process is a good example of how the legislative and executive branches serve as checks on each other. The president has the greatest role because he makes the nomination, but he cannot choose just any-one. The president will usually select a list of potential nominees that will then be rated by a committee of the American Bar Association. The Bar Association will look at the nominees' legal experience and read their written opinions and published articles in an attempt to ensure that only the most qualified candidates will be named to the federal bench. The Senate will also scrutinize the list and give the president an idea in advance of whether or not the various potential nominees will have a high likelihood of being confirmed. Once the president makes a nomination, the Senate Judiciary Subcommittee will hold formal hearings on the nominees' fitness for office. After the hearings, the full Senate will vote on the nomination. While the president will generally try to nominate some-one with a similar ideological background, if the Senate is dominated by the opposite political party, a nominee who has too strong an ideology is not likely to be confirmed. In recent years, the appointment process has become familiar to most Americans as the hearings on Supreme Court nominees have been tele-vised. Federal court judges serve for life, whereas state court judges generally serve definite terms, the length of which varies from state to state.

There is a lot of debate over whether judges should be appointed for life or elected for specific terms. The rationale behind appointment for life is that it takes the politics out of the judicial process. A judge will be selected based on his or her credentials as opposed to the quality of his or her campaign skills. Once in office, the judge is free to make honest decisions without having to worry about the impact of any decision on reelection.

Of course, that independence is just what makes some people prefer elected judges. They argue that the members of every other branch of govern-ment are elected and are, therefore, forced to represent the will of the people, and judges should represent the people no less than members of the other branches.

The Power of Judicial Review. One very important power that the judges have is the power of judicial review, that is, the power to determine whether a law passed by the legislature violates the Constitution. Any law that violates the Constitution must be struck down as null and void. The justices of the Supreme Court are the final arbiters of the constitutionality of our statutory laws.

This power of judicial review was not explicitly stated in the Constitution. This power was established in the classic 1803 case of *Marbury v. Madison*,[2] wherein the Supreme Court stated, "It is emphatically the province and duty of the judicial department to say what the law is. Those who apply the rule to par-ticular cases must of necessity expound and interpret that rule. If two laws con-flict with each other, the courts must decide which of these conflicting rules governs the case. This is of the very essence of judicial duty."

When individual justices exercise this power of judicial review, they do so with different philosophies and attitudes. Their philosophies can have a power-ful effect on how they make decisions.

One distinction that is frequently made with respect to judicial philosophies is the difference between a judge who believes in judicial activism and one who believes in judicial restraint.

A judge who believes in **judicial restraint** believes that the three branches are coequal, and the judiciary should refrain from determining the constitution-ality of an act of Congress unless absolutely necessary to keep from interfering

> **judicial restraint** A judicial philosophy that says courts should refrain from determining the constitutionality of a legislative act unless absolutely necessary and that social, political, and economic change should come out of the political process.

---

[2] 5 U.S. 137 (1803).

in the congressional sphere of power. These justices tend to believe that social, economic, and political change should result from the political process, not from judicial action. They consequently give great deference to actions of the state and federal legislatures.

Those who believe in judicial restraint will be much less likely to overturn an existing precedent. They tend to focus much more on the facts than on questioning whether the law needs to be changed. They tend to uphold lower-court decisions unless these decisions are clearly wrong on the facts.

Judicial activists tend to see a need for the court to take an active role in encouraging political, economic, and social change because the political process is often too slow to bring about necessary changes. They believe that constitutional issues must be decided within the context of today's society and that the framers meant for the Constitution to be an evolving document.

Judicial activists are much less wedded to precedent and are result oriented. They are much more likely to listen to arguments about what result is good for society. Activist judges are responsible for many social changes, especially in the civil rights area.

judicial activism A judicial philosophy that says the courts need to take an active role in encouraging political, economic, and social change.

THE JURY

The jury is the means by which citizens participate in our judicial system. It had its roots in ancient Greek civilization, and it is often seen as the hallmark of democracy. A jury is a group of individuals, selected randomly from the geographic area in which the court is located, who will determine questions of fact. There are two types of juries: petit and grand.

PETIT JURIES

petit jury A jury of 12 citizens impaneled to decide on the facts at issue in a criminal case and to pronounce the defendant guilty or not guilty.

Businesspersons are primarily concerned with **petit juries**. These juries serve as the finders of fact for trial courts. Originally composed of 12 members, most juries in civil cases are allowed to have fewer members in many jurisdictions. Traditionally, jury decisions had to be unanimous. Today, however, more than half the jurisdictions no longer require unanimity in civil cases. This change in the jury system has been made primarily to speed up trial procedures.

An important decision to be made by any corporate client and her or his attorney is whether to have a jury. In any civil action in which the plaintiff is seeking a remedy at law (money damages), a jury may hear the case. If both parties to the case agree, however, the jury may be waived and a judge decides the facts of the case. There is no rule about when a jury should be chosen, but a few factors should frequently be considered. One is the technical nature of the case. If it is a case that is highly technical, it may be a case that can be more fairly decided by a judge, especially one with expertise in the area in dispute. Another factor is the emotional appeal of the case. If the case is one for which the opponent's arguments may have strong emotional appeal, a judge may render a fairer decision.

indictment A formal written accusation in a felony case.

Grand Juries. Grand juries are used only in criminal matters. The Fifth Amendment requires that all federal prosecutions for "infamous" crimes (including all federal offenses that carry a term of imprisonment in excess of one year) be commenced with an **indictment** (a formal accusation of the commission of a crime, which must be made before a defendant can be tried for the crime) by a **grand jury**. This jury hears evidence presented by the prosecutor and determines whether there is enough evidence to justify charging a defendant. The prudent business manager who carefully heeds the advice of an attorney should not be faced with a potential indictment by a grand jury. Increasingly, however, corporate managers are facing criminal charges for actions taken to benefit their corporate employers. Such cases are discussed in Chapter 8.

grand jury A group of 12 to 23 citizens convened in private to decide whether enough evidence exists to try the defendant for a felony.

THE ADVERSARY PROCESS

Our system of litigation is accurately described as an adversary system. In an **adversarial system**, a neutral fact finder, a judge, hears evidence and arguments presented by both sides and then makes an objective decision based on the facts and the law as presented by the proponents of each side. Strict rules govern the types of evidence that the fact finder may consider.

Theoretically, the adversary system is the best way to bring out the truth, for each side will aggressively seek all the evidence that supports its position. Each side will attempt to make the strongest possible argument for its position.

adversarial system System of litigation in which the judge hears evidence and arguments presented by both sides in a case and then makes an objective decision based on the facts and the law as presented by each side.

CRITICISMS OF THE ADVERSARY SYSTEM

Many people criticize this system. They argue that because each side is searching for only that evidence that supports its position, a proponent who discovers evidence helpful to the other side will not bring such evidence to the attention of the court. This tendency to ignore contrary evidence prevents a fair decision, one based on all the available evidence, from being rendered.

Another argument of the critics is that the adversary process is extremely time-consuming and costly. Two groups of "investigators" are seeking the same evidence. Thus, there is a duplication of effort that lengthens the process and increases the cost unnecessarily.

Others argue that the adversary system, as it functions in this country, is unfair. Each party in the adversarial process is represented by an attorney. Having the most skillful attorney is a tremendous advantage. As the wealthier a party is, the better the attorney she or he can afford to hire, the system unjustifiably favors the wealthy.

Law professor Marc Galanter has written an interesting critique of our adversary system that has generated a lot of discussion.[3] He argues that given the structure of our system, certain parties tend to have a distinct advantage in our system.

Galanter divides litigants into two groups: the repeat players (RPs), those who are engaged in similar litigations over time, and the one-shotters (OSs), those who have only occasional recourse to the courts. Repeat players would typically be large corporations, financial institutions, landlords, developers, government agencies, and prosecutors. Typical OSs would be debtors, employees with grievances against their employers, tenants, and victims of accidents.

---

[3] Marc Galanter, Why the Haves Come Out Ahead: Speculation on the Limits of Legal Change, 9 J. L. & Soc. Rev. 96 (1974).

According to Galanter, the RPs have a distinct advantage over the OSs in litigation. Because of their experience, RPs are better prepared for trial; they know what kinds of records to keep and how to structure transactions so they will have an advantage in court. RPs will have developed expertise in the area and will have access to specialists. They will have low "start-up costs" for a case because they have been through it before. RPs will have developed helpful informal relationships with those at the courthouse. The RP knows the odds of success better because of his or her experience and can use that knowledge to calculate whether to settle. Finally, RPs can litigate for rules or for an immediate outcome.

Thus, in a typical case involving an RP and an OS, the RP has a distinct advantage. Some people believe this advantage is significant enough to prevent our current system from dispensing justice in these cases.

STEPS IN CIVIL LITIGATION AND THE ROLE OF BUSINESSPERSONS

THE PRETRIAL STAGE

Every lawsuit is the result of a dispute. Business disputes may result from a breach of contract, the protested firing of an employee, or the injury of a consumer who uses the corporation's product. This section focuses on dispute resolution in this country under the adversary system. It examines the procedure used in a civil case, the stages of which are outlined in Exhibit 3–4. The rules that govern such proceedings are called the **rules of civil procedure**. There are federal rules of civil procedure, which apply in all federal courts, as well as state rules, which apply in the state courts. Most of the state rules are based on the federal rules.

rules of civil procedure
The rules governing proceedings in a civil case; federal rules of procedure apply in all federal courts, and state rules apply in state courts.

Informal Negotiations. For the businessperson involved in a dispute, the first step is probably going to be to discuss the dispute directly with the other disputing party. When it appears that the parties are not going to be able to resolve the problem themselves, the businessperson will then discuss the dispute with an attorney. It is important that the attorney be given all relevant information, even if it does not make the businessperson look good. The more relevant facts the attorney has, the better the attorney's advice will be. Together, the attorney and the client may be able to resolve the dispute informally with the other party.

Initiation of a Legal Action. Once a party decides that an informal resolution is not possible, the parties enter what is often called the pleading stage of the lawsuit. **Pleadings** are papers filed by a party in court and then served on the opponent. The basic pleadings are the complaint, the answer, the counterclaim, and the motion to dismiss. Exhibit 3–5 provides an illustration of a typical complaint. The attorney of the businessperson who feels he or she has been wronged initiates a lawsuit by filing a complaint in the appropriate court. A complaint is a document that states the names of the parties to the action, the basis for the court's subject matter jurisdiction, the facts on which the party's claim is based, and the relief that the party is seeking. Remember that the party on whose behalf the complaint is filed is the plaintiff, and the defendant is the party against whom the action is being brought.

pleadings Papers filed by a party in court and then served on the opponent in a civil lawsuit.

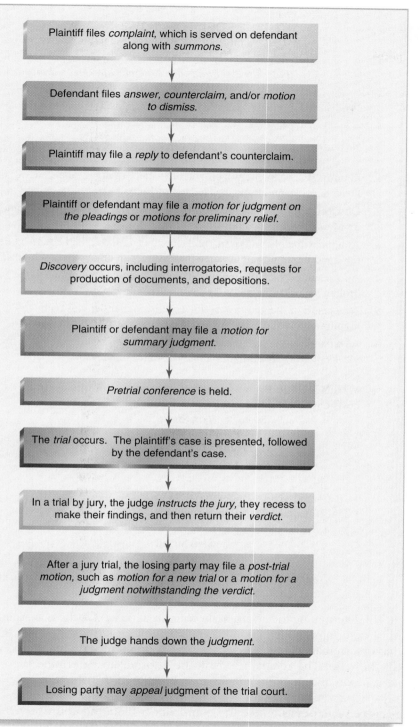

EXHIBIT 3-4

ANATOMY OF A CIVIL LAWSUIT

Plaintiff files *complaint*, which is served on defendant along with *summons*.

Defendant files *answer, counterclaim,* and/or *motion to dismiss.*

Plaintiff may file a *reply* to defendant's counterclaim.

Plaintiff or defendant may file a *motion for judgment on the pleadings* or *motions for preliminary relief.*

Discovery occurs, including interrogatories, requests for production of documents, and depositions.

Plaintiff or defendant may file a *motion for summary judgment.*

Pretrial conference is held.

The *trial* occurs. The plaintiff's case is presented, followed by the defendant's case.

In a trial by jury, the judge *instructs the jury,* they recess to make their findings, and then return their *verdict.*

After a jury trial, the losing party may file a *post-trial motion,* such as *motion for a new trial* or a *motion for a judgment notwithstanding the verdict.*

The judge hands down the *judgment.*

Losing party may *appeal* judgment of the trial court.

EXHIBIT 3-5

COMPLAINT

THE COURT OF COMMON PLEAS
OF LUCAS COUNTY, OHIO

Pam Streets, Plaintiff v. Daniel Lane, Defendant
COMPLAINT FOR NEGLIGENCE
Case No. _____

Now comes the plaintiff, Pam Street, and, for her complaint, alleges as follows:

1. Plaintiff, Pam Streets, is a citizen of Lucas County, in the state of Ohio, and Defendant, Daniel Lane, is a citizen of Lucas County in the state of Ohio.
2. On December 1, 1987, the Plaintiff was lawfully driving her automobile south on Main Street in Toledo, Ohio.
3. At approximately 4:00 p.m., on December 1, 1987, the Defendant negligently ran a red light on Starr Avenue, and as a result crashed into Plaintiff's car.
4. As a result of the collision, the Plaintiff suffered lacerations to the face and a broken leg, incurring $10,000 in medical expenses.
5. As a result of the above described collision, her car was damaged in the amount of $12,000.
6. As a result of the foregoing injuries, the Plaintiff was required to miss eight weeks of work, resulting in a loss of wages of $2,400.

WHEREFORE, Plaintiff demands judgment in the amount of $24,400, plus costs of this action.

> Sam Snead
> Attorney for Plaintiff
> 124 East Broadway
> Toledo, OH 43605

JURY DEMAND
Plaintiff demands a trial by jury in this matter.

> Sam Snead
> Attorney for Plaintiff

In determining the appropriate court in which to file the complaint, the attorney must determine which court has subject matter jurisdiction over the case. Once that determination has been made, the attorney must ascertain the proper venue for the case. The means used by the attorney to determine the subject matter jurisdiction and venue were discussed earlier in this chapter.

Service of Process. Once the complaint is filed, the court serves a copy of the complaint and a summons on the defendant. The reader should remember that service is the procedure used by the court to ensure that the defendant actually receives a copy of the summons and the complaint. Service of process gives the court in personam jurisdiction over the defendant and provides his or her due process right of notice of the charges filed against him or her.

Defendant's Response. Once the defendant has been properly served, he or she files an answer and possibly a counterclaim. The answer is a response to the allegations in the plaintiff's complaint. The answer must admit, deny, or state that the defendant has no knowledge about the truth of each of the plaintiff's allegations. The answer may also contain affirmative defenses, which consist of facts that were not stated in the complaint that would provide justification for the defendant's actions and a legally sound reason to deny relief to the plaintiff. These defenses must be stated in the answer. If they are not raised in the answer, the court may not allow these defenses to be raised later. The defendant is required to plead his or her affirmative defenses in the answer in order to give the plaintiff notice of all the issues that will be raised at the trial.

As an illustration, two affirmative defenses to a breach-of-contract action might be that the plaintiff procured the defendant's signature on the contract through fraud and that the contract was illegal because its enforcement would result in a violation of the antitrust laws. Another example would be, if a manufacturer were being sued because the plaintiff was injured by the manufacturer's negligently produced defective product, the defendant might raise the affirmative defense of contributory negligence, arguing that the plaintiff's injury would not have occurred if the plaintiff had not also been negligent. Notice the use of an affirmative defense in the sample answer in Exhibit 3–6. It is important that the businessperson who is being sued try immediately to think of any potential affirmative defenses that might excuse his or her actions.

When a defendant, upon receiving the complaint, believes that even if all of the plaintiff's factual allegations were true the plaintiff would not be entitled to a favorable judgment, the defendant may file a **motion to dismiss**. There are no factual issues being debated, so the judge accepts the facts as stated by the plaintiff and makes a ruling on the legal questions in the case. Judges are generally not receptive to such motions, granting them only when it appears beyond doubt that the plaintiff can prove no set of facts in support of his claim, which would entitle him to relief.

If the defendant believes that he or she has a cause of action against the plaintiff, this will be included as a **counterclaim**. The form of a counterclaim is just like that of a complaint. The defendant states the facts supporting his or her claim and asks for the relief to which he or she feels entitled. Exhibit 3–6 also contains a counterclaim.

If the defendant files a counterclaim, the plaintiff generally files a reply. A reply is simply an answer to a counterclaim. In the reply, the plaintiff admits, denies, or states that he or she is without knowledge of the truth of the facts asserted by the defendant in the counterclaim. Any affirmative defenses that are appropriate must be raised in the reply.

Pretrial Motions. The early pleadings just described serve to establish the legal and factual issues of the case. Once these issues have been established, either the plaintiff or the defendant may file a motion designed to bring the case to an early conclusion or to gain some advantage for the party filing the motion. A motion is simply a request by a party for the court to do something. A party may request, or move, that the court do almost anything pertaining to the case, such as a motion for some form of temporary relief until a decision has been rendered. For example, if a suit is brought over the right to a piece of property, the court may grant a motion prohibiting the current possessor of that property from selling it.

motion to dismiss Defendant's application to the court to put the case out of judicial consideration because even if the plaintiff's factual allegations are true, the plaintiff is not entitled to relief.

counterclaim Defendant's statement of facts showing cause for action against the plaintiff and a request for appropriate relief.

EXHIBIT 3-6

AFFIRMATIVE DEFENSES AND COUNTERCLAIM

> ### THE COURT OF COMMON PLEAS OF LUCAS COUNTY, OHIO
>
> *Pam Streets, Plaintiff v. Daniel Lane, Defendant*
> ### ANSWER AND COUNTERCLAIM
> Case No. _____
>
> ---
>
> Now comes the Defendant, Daniel Lane, and answers the complaint of Plaintiff herein as follows:
>
> **FIRST DEFENSE**
>
> 1. Admits the allegations in paragraphs 1 and 2.
> 2. Denies the allegation in paragraph 3.
> 3. Is without knowledge as to the truth or falsity of the allegations contained in paragraphs 4, 5, and 6.
>
> **SECOND DEFENSE**
>
> 4. If the court believes the allegations contained in paragraph 3, which the Defendant expressly denies, Plaintiff should still be denied recovery because she was negligently driving in excess of the speed limit and without her glasses, both of which contributed to the cause of the accident.
>
> **COUNTERCLAIM**
>
> 5. Defendant lawfully drove his automobile in an eastbound direction on Starr Avenue on December 1, 1987.
> 6. At approximately 4:00 p.m., on December 1, 1987, Plaintiff negligently drove her automobile at an excessive speed through a red light on Main Street where Said Street crosses Starr Avenue, colliding into Defendant's automobile.
> 7. As a result of the collision, Defendant suffered bruises and a concussion, resulting in $5,000 in medical bills.
> 8. Defendant further suffered $6,000 in property damage to his automobile.
>
> WHEREFORE, Defendant prays for a judgment dismissing the Plaintiff's complaint, granting the Defendant a judgment against Plaintiff in the amount of $11,000 plus costs of this action.
>
> > Shelly Shaker
> > Attorney for Defendant
> > 216 Nevada
> > Toledo, OH 43605

When a party files any motion with the court, a copy is always sent to the opposing attorney. That attorney may respond to the motion, usually requesting that the judge deny the motion. In many cases the judge will simply rule on the motion, either granting or denying it. In some cases, the judge may hold a hearing at which the two sides orally present their arguments.

discovery The pretrial gathering of information from each other by the parties.

Discovery. Once the initial pleadings and motions have been filed, the parties gather information from each other through **discovery**. At this stage, the businessperson is frequently asked by her or his attorney to respond to the opponent's discovery requests. There are a number of tools of discovery. One of the most common is interrogatories, which are a series of written questions that are sent to the opposing party, who must truthfully answer them under oath. The interrogatories are frequently accompanied by a request to admit certain facts. The attorney and the client work together to answer these interrogatories and requests for admission of facts.

A request to produce documents or other items is another tool of discovery. Unless the information requested is privileged or is irrelevant to the case, it must be produced. Photographs, contracts, written estimates, and forms that must be filed with governmental agencies are among the items that may be requested. One party may also request that the other party submit to a mental or physical examination. This motion will be approved only when the party's mental or physical health is at issue in the case.

Finally, testimony before trial may be obtained by the taking of a **deposition**. At a deposition, a witness is examined under oath by attorneys. A court reporter (stenographer) records every word spoken by the attorneys and witnesses. The testimony is usually transcribed so that both parties have a written copy. If a businessperson is to be deposed in a case, it is very important that he or she and the attorney talk extensively about what kinds of questions may come up at the deposition and how such questions are to be answered. The party who requested the deposition is not only seeking information but is also laying the groundwork for identifying any inconsistencies that may arise between a person's testimony at the deposition and in court. If such inconsistencies exist, they will be brought to the attention of the fact finder and may result in a loss of credibility for the courtroom testimony.

deposition Pretrial testimony by witnesses who are examined under oath.

Depositions may also be used when a potential witness is old or ill and may die before the trial. They are useful if witnesses may be moving or for some other reason may not be available at the time of the trial.

As a result of discovery, each party should have knowledge of most of the facts surrounding the case. This process is supposed to prevent surprises from occurring in the courtroom.

Parties must comply with requests for discovery, or the court may order that the facts sought to be discovered be deemed to be admitted. Thus, it is important that the businessperson involved in litigation produce for the attorney all requested discovery material. An attorney who feels that certain material should not be discovered makes arguments about its lack of relevance to the case, but if the court disagrees, the information must be supplied.

Pretrial Conference. If the judge finds that questions of fact do exist, he or she usually holds a pretrial conference. This is an informal meeting of the judge with the lawyers representing the parties. At this meeting, they try to narrow the legal and factual issues and to work out a settlement if possible. When the lawsuit begins, there are many conflicting assertions as to what events actually led up to the lawsuit. Questions about what actually happened are referred to as questions of fact. Many times, as a result of discovery, parties come to agree on most of the facts. Remaining factual disputes may often be resolved at the conference. Then the only questions left are how to apply the law to the facts and what damages, if any, to award.

By the time of the pretrial conference, the businessperson should have determined the limits on any settlement to which he or she is willing to agree and should have communicated those limits to his or her attorney, who may be able to reach a settlement at the conference. Judges frequently try very hard to help the parties reach agreement before trial. If no settlement can be reached, the attorneys and the judge discuss the administrative details of the trial, its length, the witnesses, and any pretrial stipulations of fact or law to which the parties can agree.

THE TRIAL

Once the pretrial stage has concluded, the next step is the trial. As stated previously, if the plaintiff is seeking a legal remedy (money damages), he or she is usually entitled to a jury trial. The judge is the fact finder when an equitable remedy (an injunction or other court order) is being sought or the parties have waived their right to a jury. For example, when a plaintiff in a product liability action requests a judgment for $10,000 in medical expenses, he or she would be seeking a legal remedy and would be entitled to a jury trial. But a plaintiff seeking an injunction, under the antitrust laws, to prohibit two defendant corporations from merging would be requesting an equitable remedy and would not be entitled to a jury. It is important for the business manager to determine at the outset whether a jury is desirable, because a jury must be demanded in the complaint.

The stages of the trial are (1) jury selection, (2) the opening statements, (3) the plaintiff's case, (4) the defendant's case, (5) the conference on jury instructions, (6) closing arguments, and (7) post-trial motions.

Jury Selection. An important part of a jury trial is the selection of the jury. A panel of potential jurors is selected randomly from a list of citizens. In the federal court system, voter lists are used. In a process known as **voir dire**, the judge or the attorneys, or both, question potential jurors to determine whether they could render an unbiased opinion in the case.

When a juror's response to a question causes an attorney to believe that this potential juror cannot be unbiased, the attorney will ask that the potential juror be removed "for cause." For example, in an accident case, a potential juror might reveal that he had been in a similar accident. Or the potential juror may have filed a similar lawsuit against one of the defendant's competitors five years ago. Attorneys are given an unlimited number of challenges for cause. In most states, each attorney is allowed to reject a minimal number of potential jurors without giving a reason. These rejections are called peremptory challenges.

While the legitimate rationale for peremptories is that they recognize a lawyer's "gut reaction" to a potential juror who does not say anything that technically reveals a bias, there has been some abuse of peremptories in the past. One potential source of abuse was to use peremptories to discriminate against certain classes, such as race or gender.

In 1986, in the case of *Batson v. Kentucky*,[4] the U.S. Supreme Court ruled that prosecutors could not use race-based peremptory challenges in criminal cases. Subsequently, the Supreme Court extended the ban to the use of race-based challenges by either party in civil cases. Several unsuccessful attempts were made to extend the prohibition to challenges based on gender. Finally, in 1994, the Court in the following case extended the equal protection guarantee to cover gender.

voir dire Process whereby the judge and/or the attorneys question potential jurors to determine whether they will be able to render an unbiased opinion in the case.

---
[4] 476 U.S. 79 (1986).

CASE 3-3

J.E.B. v. Alabama, EX REL. T.B.
United States Supreme Court
511 U.S. 127 (1994)

On behalf of T.B., the unwed mother of a minor child, the State of Alabama filed a complaint for paternity and child support against J.E.B. A panel of 12 males and 24 females was called by the court as potential jurors. After the court removed 3 individuals for cause, only 10 males remained. The state used its peremptory challenges to remove 9 male jurors, J.E.B. removed the tenth, resulting in an all-female jury. The court rejected J.E.B.'s objection to the gender-based challenges, and the jury found J.E.B. to be the father.

J.E.B. appealed to the court of appeals, who affirmed the trial court's decision that the Equal Protection Clause does not prohibit gender-based challenges. The Alabama Supreme Court denied certiorari, and J.E.B. then appealed to the U.S. Supreme Court.

Justice Blackmun

Today we reaffirm what should be axiomatic: Intentional discrimination on the basis of gender by state actors violates the Equal Protection Clause, particularly where, as here, the discrimination serves to ratify and perpetuate invidious, archaic, and overbroad stereotypes about the relative abilities of men and women.

Discrimination on the basis of gender in the exercise of peremptory challenges is a relatively recent phenomenon. Gender-based peremptory strikes were hardly practicable for most of our country's existence, since, until the 19th century, women were completely excluded from jury service.

Many States continued to exclude women from jury service well into the present century, despite the fact that women attained suffrage upon ratification of the Nineteenth Amendment in 1920.

Despite the heightened scrutiny afforded distinctions based on gender, respondent argues that gender discrimination in the selection of the petit jury should be permitted, though discrimination on the basis of race is not. Respondent suggests that "gender discrimination in this country ... has never reached the level of discrimination" against African-Americans, and therefore gender discrimination, unlike racial discrimination, is tolerable in the courtroom.

While the prejudicial attitudes toward women in this country have not been identical to those held toward racial minorities, the similarities between the experiences of racial minorities and women, in some contexts, "overpower those differences." Certainly, with respect to jury service, African-Americans and women share a history of total exclusion.

Discrimination in jury selection, whether based on race or on gender, causes harm to the litigants, the community, and the individual jurors who are wrongfully excluded from participation in the judicial process. The litigants are harmed by the risk that the prejudice which motivated the discriminatory selection of the jury will infect the entire proceedings. The community is harmed by the State's participation in the perpetuation of invidious group stereotypes and the inevitable loss of confidence in our judicial system that state-sanctioned discrimination in the courtroom engenders.

When state actors exercise peremptory challenges in reliance on gender stereotypes, they ratify and reinforce prejudicial views of the relative abilities of men and women. Because these stereotypes have wreaked injustice in so many other spheres of our country's public life, active discrimination by litigants on the basis of gender during jury selection "invites cynicism respecting the jury's neutrality and its obligation to adhere to the law."

In recent cases we have emphasized that individual jurors themselves have a right to nondiscriminatory jury selection procedures.

As with race-based *Batson* claims, a party alleging gender discrimination must make a prima facie showing of intentional discrimination before the party exercising the challenge is required to explain the basis for the strike. When an explanation is required, it need not rise to the level of a "for cause" challenge; rather, it merely must be based on a juror characteristic other than gender and the proffered explanation may not be pretextual.

Equal opportunity to participate in the fair administration of justice is fundamental to our democratic system. It reaffirms the promise of equality under the law—that all citizens, regardless of race, ethnicity, or gender, have the chance to take part directly in our democracy. When persons are excluded from participation in our democratic processes solely because of race or gender, this promise of equality dims, and the integrity of our judicial system is jeopardized.

In view of these concerns, the Equal Protection Clause prohibits discrimination in jury selection on the basis of gender, or on the assumption that an individual will be biased in a particular case for no reason other than the fact that the person happens to be a woman or happens to be a man. As with race, the "core guarantee of equal protection, ensuring citizens that their State will not discriminate ..., would be meaningless were we to approve the exclusion of jurors on the basis of such assumptions, which arise solely from the jurors' [gender]."

Reversed and remanded. In favor of Defendant, J.E.B.

Justice Scalia, Dissenting

Today's opinion is an inspiring demonstration of how thoroughly up-to-date and right-thinking we Justices are in matters pertaining to the sexes, and how sternly we disapprove the male chauvinist attitudes of our predecessors. The price to be paid for this display—a modest price, surely—is that most of the opinion is quite irrelevant to the case at hand. The hasty reader will be surprised to learn, for example, that this lawsuit involves a complaint about the use of peremptory challenges to exclude men from a petit jury. To be sure, petitioner, a man, used all but one of his peremptory strikes to remove women from the jury (he used his last challenge to strike the sole remaining male from the pool), but the validity of his strikes is not before us. Nonetheless, the Court treats itself to an extended discussion of the historic exclusion of women not only from jury service, but also from service at the bar (which is rather like jury service, in that it involves going to the courthouse a lot). All this, as I say, is irrelevant since the case involves state action that allegedly discriminates against men.

The Court also spends time establishing that the use of sex as a proxy for particular views or sympathies is unwise and perhaps irrational. The opinion stresses the lack of statistical evidence to support the widely held belief that, at least in certain types of cases, a juror's sex has some statistically significant predictive value as to how the juror will behave. This assertion seems to place the Court in opposition to its earlier Sixth Amendment "fair cross-section" cases. ("Controlled studies … have concluded that women bring to juries their own perspectives and values that influence both jury deliberation and result.")

Of course the relationship of sex to partiality would have been relevant if the Court had demanded in this case what it ordinarily demands: that the complaining party have suffered some injury. Leaving aside for the moment the reality that the defendant himself had the opportunity to strike women from the jury, the defendant would have some cause to complain about the prosecutor's striking male jurors if male jurors tend to be more favorable towards defendants in paternity suits. But if men and women jurors are (as the Court thinks) fungible, then the only arguable injury from the prosecutor's "impermissible" use of male sex as the basis for his peremptories is injury to the stricken juror, not to the defendant. Indeed, far from having suffered harm, petitioner, a state actor under precedents, has himself actually inflicted harm on female jurors. The Court today presumably supplies petitioner with a cause of action by applying the uniquely expansive third-party standing analysis of according petitioner a remedy because of the wrong done to male jurors. Insofar as petitioner is concerned, this is a case of harmless error if there ever was

one; a retrial will do nothing but divert the State's judicial and prosecutorial resources, allowing either petitioner or some other malefactor to go free.

The core of the Court's reasoning is that peremptory challenges on the basis of any group characteristic subject to heightened scrutiny are inconsistent with the guarantee of the Equal Protection Clause. That conclusion can be reached only by focusing unrealistically upon individual exercises of the peremptory challenge, and ignoring the totality of the practice. Since all groups are subject to the peremptory challenge (and will be made the object of it, depending upon the nature of the particular case) it is hard to see how any group is denied equal protection.

Even if the line of our later cases guaranteed by today's decision limits the theoretically boundless *Batson* principle to race, sex, and perhaps other classifications subject to heightened scrutiny, much damage has been done. It has been done, first and foremost, to the peremptory challenge system, which loses its whole character when (in order to defend against "impermissible stereotyping" claims) "reasons" for strikes must be given. The right of peremptory challenge "is," as Blackstone says, "an arbitrary and capricious right; and it must be exercised with full freedom, or it fails of its full purpose."

And damage has been done, secondarily, to the entire justice system, which will bear the burden of the expanded quest for "reasoned peremptories" that the Court demands. The extension of **Batson** to sex, and almost certainly beyond, will provide the basis for extensive collateral litigation. … Another consequence, as I have mentioned, is a lengthening of the voir dire process that already burdens trial courts.

The irrationality of today's strike-by-strike approach to equal protection is evident from the consequences of extending it to its logical conclusion. If a fair and impartial trial is a prosecutor's only legitimate goal; if adversarial trial stratagems must be tested against that goal in abstraction from their role within the system as a whole; and if, so tested, sex-based stratagems do not survive heightened scrutiny—then the prosecutor presumably violates the Constitution when he selects a male or female police officer to testify because he believes one or the other sex might be more convincing in the context of the particular case, or because he believes one or the other might be more appealing to a predominantly male or female jury. A decision to stress one line of argument or present certain witnesses before a mostly female jury—for example, to stress that the defendant victimized women—becomes, under the Court's reasoning, intentional discrimination by a state actor on the basis of gender.

I dissent.

Critical Thinking About the Law

The reasoning in Case 3-3 is played out with *Batson v. Kentucky* standing tall and visible in the background. The legal system reinforces our ethical preference for order. The resulting dependability of our legal rules serves as a guide for business decisions, facilitating the many transactions required by modern business.

Yet the courts recognize that rules must evolve as our social needs and understandings change. Hence, the courts must struggle with achieving a balance between order and flexibility. *J.E.B.* provides an opportunity to use our critical thinking to see this tension in action.

1. What facts in our society have become more visible such that Justice Blackmun feels it appropriate to expand the application of *Batson*?

   Clue: What about our history makes Blackmun's reasoning less likely to have been the basis for a Supreme Court decision in 1950?

2. Justice Blackmun disagrees with the respondent concerning the comparative "level of discrimination" experienced by nonwhites and women. Our reasoning frequently contains phrases like "level of discrimination" that require some numerical determination. Recognize that *clear* numbers measuring such a level are hard to come by. As critical thinkers, you can often see soft spots in reasoning by asking: Now how are they measuring that concept? Could you help Justice Blackmun measure "level of discrimination" by suggesting what data might be useful for this determination?

   Clue: Start with the number of people affected, the probability they would be affected, and the extent of the harm.

3. Justice Scalia does not categorically disagree with extension of *Batson*. What facts would have had to be different for Scalia to have concurred with the majority?

   Clue: Find the section in his dissent in which he explains the inadequacies in the majority's reasoning.

The voir dire process has changed significantly over the years, and to many lawyers, a successful voir dire is the essential element in winning a case. Jury selection today has become a "science," and in most cases involving large potential judgments, at least one side, and often both, use a professional jury selection service. An example of one such service is Litigation Sciences, a firm established in 1979. By 1989, ten years later, the firm claimed to have handled over 900 cases, with a win figure of 90 to 95 percent. It employed a full-time staff of over 100, and the average cost of its services was approximately $200,000, although some cases ran into the millions.[5] Its clients include both major law firms and corporations.

Some of the services include identifying demographic data to help lawyers build a profile of the ideal juror, helping design questions for the lawyers to ask during voir dire, and providing such post–voir dire services as mock juries and shadow juries.

A **mock jury** is a body of individuals whose demographic makeup matches that of the actual jury. The lawyers practice their case before the mock jury to

mock jury Group of individuals, demographically matched to the actual jurors in a case, in front of whom lawyers practice their arguments before presenting their case to the actual jury.

---

[5]Maureen E. Lane, *Twelve Carefully Selected Not So Angry Men: Are Jury Consultants Destroying the American Legal System?* 32 Suffolk University Law Review 463 (1999).

find out how receptive the "jurors" are to the arguments and how the mock jurors relate to the witnesses. Lawyers can gain valuable information about what they need to change before presenting the case. Depending on how much money a client has, lawyers may go through multiple "trials" before a mock jury.

shadow jury Group of individuals, demographically matched to the actual jurors in a case, that sits in the courtroom during a trial and then "deliberates" at the end of each day so that lawyers have continuous feedback of how their case is going.

A **shadow jury** again matches the demographics of the real jury, but the shadow jury actually sits in the courtroom during the trial. They "deliberate" at the end of each day, so the lawyer has an ongoing idea of how the case is going. The shadow jury's deliberations may let a lawyer know when damage has been done to the case that needs to be repaired. After the trial is finished, the shadow jury deliberates for a predetermined, brief period of time. Their "verdict" then helps the lawyer decide whether to try to settle the case before the jury comes back with a verdict. (Remember, the parties can agree to settle at any time until the judge hands down the final decision in the case.)

You can see from this brief discussion how valuable a jury selection service can be. You can also see why many argue that such services should not be allowed. After all, they give a tremendous advantage to the client with more money to spend on the trial.

Opening Statements. Once a jury has been impaneled, or selected, the case begins with the opening statements. Each party's attorney explains to the judge and the jury what facts he or she intends to prove, the legal conclusions to which these facts will lead, and how the case should be decided.

Plaintiff's Case. The plaintiff then presents his or her case, which consists of examining witnesses and presenting evidence. The procedure for each witness is the same. First, the plaintiff's attorney questions the witness in what is called direct examination. The plaintiff's lawyer asks questions designed to elicit from the witnesses facts that support the plaintiff's case. Then the opposing counsel may cross-examine the witness; only questions pertaining to the witness's direct examination may be asked. The purpose of cross-examination is often to "poke holes" in the witness's testimony or to reduce the credibility of the witness. The plaintiff's attorney then has the opportunity for redirect examination to repair any damage done by the cross-examination. The opposing counsel then has a last opportunity to cross-examine the witness to address facts brought out in redirect examination. This procedure is followed for each of the plaintiff's witnesses.

Immediately following the plaintiff's case, the defendant may make a motion for a directed verdict. In making such a motion, the defendant is stating to the court that even if all the plaintiff's factual allegations are true, the plaintiff has not proved his or her case. For example, as will be discussed in Chapter 12, to prove a case of negligence, the plaintiff must prove that the defendant breached his or her duty to the plaintiff, causing compensable injury. If the plaintiff offers no evidence of any compensable injury, then there can be no judgment for the plaintiff. In such a case, a motion for a directed verdict would be granted, and the case would be dismissed. Such motions are rarely granted, because the plaintiff will usually introduce some evidence of every element necessary to establish the existence of his or her case.

A motion for a directed verdict also may be made by either party after the presentation of the defendant's case. The party filing the motion (the moving party) is saying that even if the judge looks at all the evidence in the light most favorable to the other party, it is overwhelmingly clear that the only decision the jury could come to is that the moving party is entitled to judgment in his or her favor.

Defendant's Case. If the defendant's motion for a directed verdict is denied, the trial proceeds with the defendant's case in chief. The defendant's witnesses are questioned in the same manner as were the plaintiff's, except that it is the defendant's attorney who does the direct and redirect examination, and the plaintiff's attorney is entitled to cross-examine the witnesses.

Conference on Jury Instructions. If the case is being heard by a jury, the attorneys and the judge then retire for a conference on jury instructions. Jury instructions are the court's explanation to the jury of what legal decision they must make if they find certain facts to be true. Each attorney presents to the judge the set of jury instructions he or she feels will enable the jury to accurately apply the law to the facts. Obviously, each attorney tries to state the law in the manner most favorable to his or her client. The judge confers with the attorneys regarding their proposed instructions and then draws up the instructions for the jury.

Closing Arguments. The attorneys' last contact with the jury then follows. The attorneys present their closing arguments. The party who has the burden of proof, the plaintiff, presents the first closing argument; the defendant's closing argument follows. Finally, the plaintiff is entitled to a rebuttal. The judge then reads the instructions to the jury, and the jurors retire to the jury room to deliberate. When they reach a decision, the jurors return to the courtroom, where their verdict is read.

Post-Trial Motions. The party who loses has a number of options. A motion for a judgment notwithstanding the verdict may be made. This motion is a request for the judge to enter a judgment contrary to that handed down by the jury on the grounds that as a matter of law the decision could only have been different from that reached by the jury. For example, if a plaintiff requests damages of $500 but introduces evidence of only $100 in damages, the jury cannot award the plaintiff the $400 for unsubstantiated damages. If they do so, the defendant would file a motion for a judgment notwithstanding the verdict. Alternatively, the dissatisfied party may file a motion for a new trial on the grounds that the verdict is clearly against the weight of the evidence. If neither of these motions is granted and the judge enters a judgment in accordance with the verdict, the losing party may appeal the decision.

APPELLATE PROCEDURE

As explained earlier, the court to which the case is appealed depends on the court in which the case was originally heard. If a case was heard in a federal district court, it is appealed to the U.S. circuit court of appeals for the geographic region in which the district court is located. If heard in a state trial court, the case is appealed to that state's intermediate appellate court or, if none exists, to the state's final appellate court.

To appeal a case, the losing party must allege that a prejudicial error of law occurred during the trial. A prejudicial error is one that is so substantial that it could have affected the outcome of the case. For example, the judge may have ruled as admissible in court certain evidence that had a major impact on the decision, when that evidence was legally inadmissible. Or the party may argue that the instructions that the judge read to the jury were inaccurate and resulted in a misapplication of the law to the facts.

affirm Term used for an appellate court's decision to uphold the decision of a lower court in a case that has been appealed.

modify Term used for an appellate court's decision that, although the lower court's decision was correct, it granted an inappropriate remedy that needs to be changed.

reverse Term used for an appellate court's decision that the lower court's decision was incorrect and cannot be allowed to stand.

remand Term used for an appellate court's decision that an error was committed that may have affected the outcome of the case and that therefore the case must be returned to the lower court.

When a case is appealed, there is not a new trial. The attorney for the appealing party (the appellant) and the attorney for the party who won in the lower court (the appellee) file briefs, or written arguments, with the court of appeals. They also generally present oral arguments before the appeals court. The court considers these arguments, reviews the record of the case, and renders a decision. The decisions of the appellate court can take a number of forms. The court may accept the decision of the lower court and **affirm** that decision. Alternatively, the appellate court may conclude that the lower court was correct in its decision, except for granting an inappropriate remedy, and so it will **modify** the remedy. If the appellate court decides that the lower court was incorrect in its decision, that decision will be **reversed**. Finally, the appeals court may feel that an error was committed, but it does not know how that error would have affected the outcome of the case, so it will **remand** the case to the lower court for a new trial.

Although the appeals procedure may sound relatively simple compared to the initial trial procedure, appeals require a great deal of work on the part of the attorneys. They are consequently expensive. Thus, when deciding whether to appeal, the businessperson must consider how much money he or she wishes to spend. If a judgment is rendered against a businessperson, it may be less expensive to pay the judgment than to appeal.

Another factor to consider when one is deciding whether to appeal is the precedential value of the case. The case may involve an important issue of law that a party hopes may be decided in her or his favor by an appeals court. If she or he anticipates similar suits arising in the future, it may be important to get a favorable ruling, and if the case appears to be strong, an appeal may be desirable.

Appellate courts, unlike trial courts, are usually composed of a bench of at least three judges. There are no juries. The decision of the court is determined by the majority of the judges. One of the judges who votes with the majority records the court's decision and their reasons in what is called the majority opinion. These have precedential value and are used by judges to make future decisions and by attorneys in advising their clients as to the appropriate course of behavior in similar situations. If any of the judges in a case agrees with the ultimate decision of the majority but for different reasons, he or she may write a concurring opinion, stating how this conclusion was reached. Finally, the judge or judges disagreeing with the majority may write their dissenting opinion, giving their reasons for reaching a contrary conclusion. Dissenting opinions may be cited in briefs by attorneys arguing that the law should be changed. Dissents may also be cited by an appellate judge who decides to change the law.

For most cases, only one appeal is possible. In some states, where there is both an intermediate and a superior court of appeals, a losing party may appeal from the intermediate appellate court to the state supreme court. In a limited number of cases, a losing party may be able to appeal from a state supreme court or a federal circuit court of appeals to the U.S. Supreme Court.

Appeal to the U.S. Supreme Court. Every year thousands of individuals attempt to have their appeals heard by the U.S. Supreme Court. But the Court hears, on average, only about 80 cases every year. When a party wishes to have his or her case heard by the highest court in the nation, he or she files a petition with the Court, asking it to issue a writ of certiorari, which is an order to the lower court to send to the Supreme Court the record of the case.

As you may guess from the number of cases heard by the Supreme Court, very few writs are issued. The justices review the petitions they receive and will

Linking Law & Business

Management

In your management class, you may have learned about a concept known as cost-benefit analysis. This idea is defined as the process by which managers weigh the benefits or revenues of a particular activity in comparison to the costs of performing the action. Usually, managers will decide to pursue an action if the benefits outweigh the costs.

Managers or other decision makers can effectively come to a conclusion as to which alternative to pursue after the options have been evaluated. There are three basic steps in this evaluation that decision makers should follow: (1) estimate, as accurately as possible, the potential effects of each of the possible actions; (2) assign probabilities to each of the expected effects of each decision if the idea was implemented; and (3) compare the possible effects of each alternative decision and the probabilities of each. Meanwhile, consideration should be given to organizational objectives. After these three steps have been followed, managers will have a better understanding about the benefits of alternative decisions. Therefore, a choice can be made that will hopefully be most advantageous to the organization.

This concept of cost-benefit analysis can also be applied when a businessperson is faced with the decision of whether to appeal a court decision. The businessperson should examine the costs of the appellate procedures, the probability of the outcome in the appeals court, and the time involved with the appeals process. Thereafter, a decision can be made by the businessperson that will potentially be most beneficial.

Source: S. Certo, *Modern Management* (Upper Saddle River, N.J.: Prentice Hall, 2000), pp. 152, 432.

issue a writ only when at least four justices vote to hear the case. The Court is most likely to issue a writ when (1) the case presents a substantial federal question that has not yet been addressed by the Supreme Court; (2) the case involves a matter that has produced conflicting decisions from the various circuit courts of appeal and is, therefore, in need of resolution; (3) a state court of last resort holds that a federal law is invalid or upholds a state law that has been challenged as violating federal law; or (4) a federal court has ruled that an act of Congress is unconstitutional.

It is often difficult to project whether the Court will hear a case. In the first instance described above, for example, a federal question is simply an issue arising under the federal Constitution, treaties, or statutes. Substantiality is a more difficult issue to define. If the decision would affect a large number of people or is likely to arise again if not decided, it may be considered substantial. But sometimes a case may in fact involve a very important federal question of statutory interpretation, yet the Supreme Court may believe that the problem was unclear drafting by Congress, and so it may choose to not hear the case in anticipation of an amendment of the federal statute whose interpretation is at issue. If the Supreme Court refuses to hear a case, this refusal has no precedential effect.

CLASS ACTIONS

In discussing the stages of civil litigation, we have been talking as if there is only one plaintiff and one defendant, but remember, there can be multiple parties joined as plaintiffs and multiple parties joined as defendants. For example, if a person gets injured using a defective product, he or she would probably sue both the manufacturer and the retailer.

There is a special kind of case, however, in which the plaintiff is not a single party, or even a few parties, but rather a large group of individuals who may not even know each other but whom all share a common complaint against the defendant. This kind of case is referred to as a class action. For example, all of the shareholders of a corporation may want to sue a member of the board of directors. One of the most common class actions involves product liability cases, situations in which numerous people injured by the same product join together to sue that product's manufacturer. Other kinds of cases that may give rise to class action suits include discrimination claims and antitrust claims. Sometimes people will come together to bring a class action because their individual claims may be so small that separate litigation really is not feasible, but when all the claims are combined, the amount is large enough that it will be profitable for a lawyer to take the case.

Class actions are seen by some as efficient because instead of all the individuals filing and trying individual cases based on the same issue, all of the claims can be brought in one action. This efficiency seems even more significant when there are complex issues involved and high costs of trial preparation. When a class action is brought, the case is usually filed in the name of one or two of the parties and all others who are similarly situated. The named plaintiffs in the case have to pay all of the court costs, including the costs of finding the names and addresses of everyone in the class and notifying them.

The first step in a class action suit, which differentiates it from other suits, is certification of the class. The court will review the claims to ensure that all the named plaintiffs indeed share a common interest that can be adequately raised by the named plaintiffs. If the class action is being filed in a federal court because of diversity of citizenship, each of the named plaintiffs' claims must meet the jurisdictional amount of $75,000. Defendants will often challenge the certification of the class, knowing that if the class does not get certified, the named plaintiffs may not have the resources to bring the case as an individual action.

Once the class has been certified, the parties will often enter into settlement negotiations. The court will approve the classwide settlement only if it is fair and equitable and benefits the entire class, not just the named plaintiffs and their lawyers. Once a settlement has been approved by the court, it legally satisfies the claims of all the class members.

GLOBAL DIMENSIONS OF THE AMERICAN LEGAL SYSTEM

This chapter has focused on the American legal system. With the growth of multinationals and increasing trade among nations, Americans will increasingly become involved in disputes in foreign nations, and foreigners will increasingly become involved in disputes with Americans and American corporations.

When parties make international agreements, they can incorporate as a term of the agreement their choice of which nation's court will hear any disputes arising under the agreement. Because of differences between our litigation system and others, it is important to compare the procedures in each country before choosing a forum. For example, in Japan, there is no procedure comparable to discovery, and so parties go to trial not knowing what evidence the other side has.

With the increase in trade, many foreigners now purchase American goods. Because of some differences between court systems, many citizens of foreign countries injured by U.S. corporations will prefer to sue in the United States. In Japan, for example, there are no contingency fees, and an injured plaintiff must pay his or her lawyer's fees up front, at a cost of 8 percent of the proposed recovery plus nonrefundable court costs. Also, in Japan, there are no class actions.

SUMMARY

Our American legal system is really two systems: a federal system and a state system. When one has a legal dispute, subject matter jurisdiction determines which court system will hear the case. Almost all cases fall within the state court's jurisdiction. Only the limited number of cases within the exclusive jurisdiction of the federal courts do not. A case may be heard in either court when there is concurrent jurisdiction. Concurrent jurisdiction exists when (1) the case involves a federal question, or (2) there is diversity of citizenship between the plaintiff and defendant. Besides having subject matter jurisdiction, a court must also have in personam jurisdiction and proper venue to hear a case.

Cases are filed in courts of original jurisdiction. In the state system, these courts are usually called the courts of common pleas or county courts. In the federal system, the courts of original jurisdiction are called the district courts. In the state system, state courts of appeals and state supreme courts have appellate jurisdiction. Depending on the state, there may be either one or two levels of appeal. In the federal system, cases are appealed to the circuit court of appeals and then to the U.S. Supreme Court.

Cases are guided through the courts by attorneys. Juries act as finders of fact in trials. Judges resolve questions of law and, in bench trials, also serve as finders of fact.

There are four basic stages in a lawsuit. In the pretrial stage, there are (1) informal negotiations, (2) pleadings, (3) pretrial motions, (4) discovery, and (5) a pretrial conference. Next comes the trial, with (1) jury selection, (2) opening statements, (3) the plaintiff's case, (4) the defendant's case, (5) jury instructions, and (6) closing arguments. Third are the post-trial motions, which may include a motion for a judgment notwithstanding the verdict and a motion for a new trial. The final stage is the appellate stage, during which the party who lost at the trial appeals his or her case.

REVIEW QUESTIONS

3-1 Identify the different types of jurisdiction and explain why each is important.

3-2 Explain the two situations that cause the state and federal courts to have concurrent jurisdiction.

3-3 What is venue?

3-4 What is the relationship between federal district courts and courts of common pleas?

3-5 What is the attorney–client privilege and what is the rationale for its existence?

3-6 Explain the importance of the work-product doctrine.

REVIEW PROBLEMS

3-7 Jacobson, a Michigan resident, sued Hasbro Corporation for negligence after one of Hasbro's truck drivers fell asleep and ran his semi off the road and into Jacobson's house, causing structural damage of approximately $80,000. Hasbro has small plants in Michigan, Ohio, and Indiana. The company is incorporated in Illinois and has its central offices there. Jacobson files his case in the state court in Michigan. Hasbro files a motion for removal, which Jacobson contests, arguing that the case does not fall within the concurrent jurisdiction of the federal courts. Should the case be transferred? Why or why not?

3-8 Bill, a white male, is charged with spousal abuse. His attorney uses his peremptory challenges to remove all white females from the jury. The prosecution objects. Was there any impropriety in the jury selection process?

3-9 Marx Corporation is incorporated in the state of Delaware, but all of the firm's business is conducted within the state of New York. Sanders, a Delaware resident, is injured by one of Marx Corporation's products and subsequently files suit against Marx Corporation in Delaware State Court. Marx files a motion to dismiss the case on grounds that Delaware cannot assert jurisdiction over the corporation because it does not conduct business in Delaware and only incorporated there because it gained certain legal advantages from incorporating in that state. Explain why the Delaware state court system does or does not have jurisdiction over this case.

3-10 Carson is a resident of Clark County, Nevada. He sued Stevens, a resident of Washoe County, Nevada, for injuries he received in an accident that took place in Washoe County. Carson filed the case in Clark County. Can Stevens get the case moved to Washoe County? How would he try to do so?

3-11 Attorney Fox represented Davis in a number of drunk driving cases. Davis shows up at Fox's office to discuss having the attorney draw up a will for him. The attorney recognizes that Davis is clearly intoxicated. The attorney offers to pay for a cab to take Davis home, but he refuses the offer. Fox's secretary suggests that he call the state highway patrol. If Fox calls the highway patrol, is he violating the attorney–client privilege? Why or why not?

3-12 Watson brought a negligence case against the Hasbro Drug Store to recover damages for injuries he received from falling on the wet floor of the store. He thought the store was negligent for marking the floor with only a small sign that said "Slippery When Wet." The trial court refused to let Watson introduce evidence that after his fall the store started marking wet floors with cones and a large sign saying, "Caution—Floor Is Wet and Slippery." Watson lost in the trial court and lost his appeals to the state appeals court and state supreme court. Will he be able to appeal to the U.S. Supreme Court? Why or why not?

CASE PROBLEMS

3-13 International Shoe Corporation, which had its principal place of business in Missouri, employed from 11 to 13 salespersons in the state of Washington, who exhibited samples and solicited orders for shoes from prospective buyers within that state. International Shoe Corporation was assessed by the state of Washington for contributions to a state unemployment fund. The assessment was served on one of the defendant's sales representatives within the state, and a copy was sent by registered mail to the company's headquarters in Missouri. International Shoe's representative showed up at court to challenge the assessment on numerous grounds, including the ground that the corporation had not been properly served. Is the corporation's defense valid? Why or why not? *International Shoe Company v. Washington*, 326 U.S. 310 (1945)

3-14 Atlas Global Group, a Texas-based partnership, filed a state law suit against Grupo Dataflux, a Mexican corporation, in federal court on the grounds that there was diversity jurisdiction. The federal district court ruled in favor of Atlas, but before judgment was entered, the Mexican corporation moved to dismiss, claiming that even though two Mexican members of the partnership left the Texas partnership, they were still partners when Atlas filed suit. Hence, the Mexican corporation claimed the court did not have subject matter jurisication because the parties were not diverse when the suit was filed. The magistrate judge agreed with the Mexican corporation and dismissed the case because diversity did not exist when the case was filed, even though the Mexican partners left Atlas before the trial. The appellate court reversed, claiming that because the jurisdictional error was not initially identified, the change of partnership after the filing cured the jurisdictional error. Explain how you think the United States Supreme Court ruled on appeal. *The Grupo Dataflux v. Atlas Global Group*, 124 S. Ct. 1920 (2004)

3-15 Prior to his becoming governor of California, Arnold Schwarzenegger resided as a citizen of California. Schwarzenegger brought suit against Fred Martin Motors, an Ohio-based car dealer, in a California district court. Schwarzenegger claimed that Fred Martin advertised his used cars in the *Akron Beacon Journal*, a locally owned Ohio newspaper, while inappropriately using Schwarzenegger's photograph as the "Terminator," thereby constituting an alleged violation of Schwarzenegger's right to publicity. Fred Martin regularly purchased imported automobiles from California, but he dealt only with their representatives in Illinois and New Jersey. In addition, Fred Martin relied on the services of a California-based marketing company to implement direct-mail advertisments. Explain why the state court in California can or cannot exercise personal jurisdiction over the defendant. *Arnold Schwarzenegger v. Fred Martin Motors*, 374 F.3d 797 (2004)

3-16 Plaintiff, a Virginia resident, sued the defendants, residents of Texas and New Mexico, in the Eastern District Court of Virginia for defamation and intentional infliction of emotional distress from comments they posted on AOL's Usenet groups. The defendants have never been to Virginia, and they posted their comments using a service provider from California. Defendants sought to dismiss the case on the grounds that Virginia lacked jurisdiction. Plaintiff argued that there was jurisdiction under the state long-arm statute that provides jurisdiction over a defendant who com-

mits a tort in the state. Plaintiff alleged that the defamatory action occurred in Virginia because the defendants posted their statements using their AOL account, and AOL's server is located in Virginia. Thus, the defamatory messages would have been temporarily stored in Virginia and then would have been transmitted worldwide from Virginia. With which party do you believe the court sided? Why? *Bochan v. LaFontaine*, 68 F. Supp.2d 692 (1999)

3-17 From 1989 to 1991, Brandt, a German attorney, did legal work for Wien Air, a corporation that was located in Texas, when Tjontveit bought the company. Brandt visited Texas in 1989 and then did other work from Germany, communicating with employees at the Texas office by mail, telephone, and fax. Wien Air sued Brandt for fraud, breach of contract, and breach of fiduciary duties over some of the work he did for Tjontveit, the sole owner of Wien Air. The suit was filed in Texas state court and then removed to the federal district court. Brandt filed a motion to dismiss on the grounds that he did not have sufficient minimum contacts with Texas to allow the state to assert in personam jurisdiction over him. The district court agreed and dismissed the suit. Wien appealed. How do you believe the appellate court ruled? Why? *Wien Air Alaska, Inc. v. Brandt*, 195 F.3d 208 (5th Cir, 1999)

3-18 Arnold Holloway was convicted of first-degree murder and sentenced to death. During the voir dire for the case, the prosecutor used 12 peremptory strikes, 11 of which were used to remove African Americans. Holloway, an African American, challenged the prosecutor's use of the peremptory challenges as being purposeful discrimination on the basis of race. Did the court of appeals overturn Holloway's conviction? Why or why not? *Arnold Holloway v. Martin Horn*, 355 F.3d 707 (2004)

ASSIGNMENT ON THE INTERNET

As you learned in this chapter, the question of jurisdiction determines whether a court has the power to render a meaningful decision. The growth of Internet commerce, however, brings additional jurisdictional questions and concerns that have yet to be resolved. Use the Web site **profs.lp.findlaw.com/netjuris**, to familiarize yourself with the interactive and passive use distinctions made in cases of Internet jurisdiction.

Next, apply this distinction to the case of *Barton Southern Company, Inc.* v. Manhole Barrier Systems, Inc. and JFC Company, 318 F.Supp. 1174 (2004), which can be found using findlaw.com or through the Lexis-Nexis database. Does the interactive/passive distinction help resolve the issue of jurisdiction in this case? Why or why not?

ON THE INTERNET

www.kentlaw.edu/cyberlaw/resources/guide.html Questions of in personam jurisdiction are becoming more complex with the increased growth and use of the Internet. This site provides several articles on the issue of Internet jurisdiction. If this issue is of interest to you, see Chapter 7 for more information on cyberlaw.

www.jurydynamics.com Jury Dynamics is a company that specializes in litigation services, including consultation with the jury selection process and providing mock and shadow juries.

www.law.com/index.shtml This site provides a collection of litigation resources, including judicial news, decisions, employment listings, and information about federal practices and trial technology.

www.martindale.com This is the site of the Martindale-Hubble Law Directory, which provides information about lawyers and law firms. Typical entries include area of special expertise, address, and telephone number.

www.lexisone.com/legalresearch/legalguide/codes_statutes/federal_rules_of_civil_procedure.htm
This site will lead you to a number of sites that contain the federal rules of civil procedure in a variety of formats.

www.lawresearch.com/v2/statute/statstat.htm Go to this page to find a link to your state's constitution, statutes, and rules of civil procedure.

www.uscourts.gov This site provides information about the federal court system and links to all federal courts.

www.supremecourtus.gov/about/about.html This site provides a wealth of information about the United States Supreme Court.

ALTERNATIVE TOOLS
OF DISPUTE RESOLUTION

NEGOTIATION AND SETTLEMENT

ARBITRATION

MEDIATION

MINITRIALS

EARLY NEUTRAL CASE EVALUATION

PRIVATE TRIALS

SUMMARY JURY TRIALS

COURT-ANNEXED ALTERNATIVE DISPUTE RESOLUTION

THE FUTURE OF ALTERNATIVE DISPUTE RESOLUTION

GLOBAL DIMENSIONS OF ALTERNATIVE DISPUTE RESOLUTION

Pacific Gas and Electric Company (PG & E) was faced with six disputes stemming from the crash of a helicopter that hit one of its electrical lines. Officials at PG & E knew that they were facing the expensive and time-consuming litigation process described in Chapter 3. They were aware that a trial would take about two years to wind its way through the court system, with litigation costs of $300,000 if the matter was settled before the trial and double that amount if the case was tried through to a verdict. Instead, the case was resolved within ten months, and legal fees and administrative costs were kept to around $20,000.[1] How?

---

[1] E. J. Pollock, "Mediation Firms Alter the Legal Landscape," *Wall Street Journal*, March 22, 1993, p. 1.

alternative dispute resolution (ADR) Resolving legal disputes through methods other than litigation, such as negotiation and settlement, arbitration, mediation, private trials, minitrials, summary jury trials, and early neutral case evaluation.

Like a growing number of would-be litigants who see the trial process as unwieldy, time-consuming, and expensive, PG & E decided to consider resolving its dispute outside the court, through what is often referred to as **alternative dispute resolution**, or **ADR**. Many judges now encourage the increased use of these alternatives to litigation, which include (1) negotiation and settlement, (2) arbitration, (3) mediation, (4) minitrials, (5) private trials, (6) summary jury trials, and (7) early neutral case evaluation. The ADR method that PG & E successfully opted for was mediation.

These options are becoming so common that many law and some business schools now offer courses covering alternative dispute-resolution methods. In the business world, 600 of the nation's largest corporations have signed a pledge to not sue another corporation before first trying to resolve the conflict out of court.[2] Nearly every state court has some ADR program in place.

Almost all of these alternative methods share certain advantages over litigation. First, they are generally less expensive. For example, PG & E shifted toward an aggressive litigation alternative approach in 1988, and, by 1993, its legal department's operation costs, including legal fees, had fallen by 9 percent. The amount it paid out in judgments and settlements during that time fell by 25 percent.[3] Second, most ADR methods are more convenient for the participants: They are less time-consuming, and the formal hearing times and places can be set to accommodate the parties. Admittedly, it is difficult to estimate the time required by a given ADR case. However, studies of private commercial arbitration cases have shown that the average time lag from filing date to the decision date is 145 days. Third, the persons presiding over the resolution process can be chosen by the parties, and, in many cases, they are chosen because they would be more familiar with the subject matter of the dispute than a randomly assigned judge would be.

These alternatives may also prevent adverse publicity, which could be ruinous to a business. Imagine how much better Denny's image might be, for example, if it had not received the adverse publicity as a result of litigation over charges of discrimination! Similarly, these alternatives preserve confidentiality, which may be extremely important when a company's trade secrets are involved. A lot of information that a firm might wish to keep from its competitors could come out in a lawsuit but would not be subject to public disclosure if the matter was settled through an ADR method. Another related potential advantage might be that the immediate case could be resolved through ADR without a precedent being set. Finally, the less adversarial of these methods might also help to preserve the relationship between the parties, who often desire to continue doing business with one another. In the following sections, we will examine the most important

---

[2] M. Chambers, "Sua Sponte," *National Law Journal*, September 27, 1993, p. 21.

[3] Pollock, *supra* note 1.

Critical Thinking About the Law

Why would one want to use an alternative method for dispute resolution? Alternative dispute resolution seems to be advantageous compared with the traditional method of litigation for several reasons. For example, ADR methods are less time-consuming than litigation. The following questions will help you learn to think critically about alternative dispute resolution.

1. What are the reasons offered to suggest that ADR is advantageous compared with litigation?

   Clue: Reread the introductory section.

2. What primary ethical norms are behind the reasons given to suggest that ADR is advantageous?

   Clue: Examine the reasons given in response to Question 1. Consider the list of ethical norms given in Chapter 1. For example, ADR methods are less time-consuming. Which ethical norm is being upheld in this reason?

ADR methods in greater detail. From these discussions, future businesspersons should gain some awareness of typical situations in which each of these alternatives may be preferable to litigation.

NEGOTIATION AND SETTLEMENT

The oldest, and perhaps the simplest, alternative to litigation is negotiation and settlement. **Negotiation and settlement** is the process by which the parties to a dispute come together informally, either with or without their lawyers, and attempt to resolve their dispute. No independent or neutral third party is involved.

> **negotiation and settlement** An alternative dispute-resolution method in which the disputant parties come together informally to try to resolve their differences.

To successfully negotiate a settlement, each party must, in most cases, give up something in exchange for getting something from the other side. Almost all lawyers will attempt to negotiate a settlement before taking a case to trial or going to some other more formal type of dispute-resolution method. Attempts at negotiation and settlement are so common that we often do not even consider negotiation as an alternative to litigation.

ARBITRATION

One of the most well-known alternatives to litigation, **arbitration**, is the resolution of a dispute by a neutral third party outside the judicial setting. According to a 2003 study by the nonprofit American Arbitration Association, 85% of Fortune 1000 companies chose this form of ADR for resolving their commercial disputes.[4] The arbitration hearing is similar to a trial, but there is no prehearing

> **arbitration** A dispute-resolution method whereby the disputing parties submit their disagreement to a mutually agreed-upon neutral decision maker or one provided for by statute.

---

[4] Groundbreaking Study Finds Companies that Use ADR to Manage conflicts Excel in Controlling Costs, Preserving Relationships, American Arbitration Association <org/index2.1.jsp?JSPssid= 15780&JSPsrc-upload\LIVESITE\About\..News And Events\Press\Dispute 9020 wise.htm

discovery process. In addition, the stringent rules of evidence applicable in a trial are generally relaxed. Each side presents its witnesses and evidence and has the opportunity to cross-examine its opponent's witnesses. The arbitrator frequently takes a much more active role in questioning the witness than would a judge. If the arbitrator needs to know more information, he or she generally does not hesitate to ask for that information from witnesses.

As a general rule, no official record of the arbitration hearing is made. Rather, the arbitrator and each of the parties usually take their own notes of what happens. However, the parties and the arbitrator may agree to have a stenographer record the proceedings at the expense of the parties. Although attorneys may represent parties in arbitration, legal counsel is not required. Individuals may represent themselves or have nonlawyers represent them. For example, in a labor dispute, as discussed in Chapter 19, the union may be represented by one of its officers. In addition to the oral presentation, in some cases, the arbitrator may request written arguments from the parties. These documents are called arbitration briefs.

award The arbitrator's decision.

The arbitrator usually provides a decision for the parties within 30 days of the hearing. In many states, this deadline is mandated by statute. The arbitrator's decision is called the **award**, even if no monetary compensation is ordered. The award does not have to state any findings of fact or conclusions of law. Nor must the arbitrator cite any precedent for the decision or give any reasons. He or she must only resolve the dispute. If the arbitrator, however, hopes to continue to be selected by parties, he or she should provide reasons for the decision.

For a number of reasons, the arbitrator's decision is much more likely to be a compromise than a decision handed down by a court. First, the arbitrator is not as constrained by precedent as are judges. An arbitrator is interested in resolving a factual dispute, not in establishing or strictly applying a rule of law. Second, the arbitrator may be more interested than a judge in preserving an ongoing relationship with the parties. A compromise is much more likely to achieve this result than is a clear win-or-lose decision. Finally, because an arbitrator frequently decides cases in a particular area, he or she wants to maintain a reputation of being fair to both sides. For example, a person who focuses on labor arbitrations would not want to gain a reputation as being prolabor or promanagement.

The decision rendered by the arbitrator is legally binding. In some cases, such as labor cases, a decision may be appealed to the district court, but there are few such appeals. Of the more than 25,000 labor cases decided by arbitrators each year, fewer than 200 are challenged. The following recent circuit court opinion demonstrates the deference the courts give to arbitrators' decisions.

CASE 4-1

Trailmobile Trailer, LLC v. International Union of Electronic, Electrical, Salaried, Machine and Furniture Workers, AFL-CIO, Local Union No. 1149
United States Court of Appeals for the Eighth Circuit
223 F.3d 744 (Eighth Cir. 2000)

Gwen Wigginton, a painter for Trailmobile, was discharged for an altercation with coworker Joe Garcia. His discharge was in accordance with rules in the employee handbook that provide that an employee may be discharged without notice for (1) any act that may endanger the safety of others or (2) fighting on the company premises.

Wigginton was a member of the union that had entered into a collective bargaining agreement with Trailmobile. After Wigginton's termination, the union filed a grievance on his behalf. The process failed to achieve a successful resolution, and the parties then submitted the matter to an arbitrator, stipulating the following issue: "Did the Company have just cause for terminating Gwen Wigginton? If not, what should the remedy be?"

The collective bargaining agreement between Trailmobile and the union contained four sections that were relevant to his discharge: (1) "[T]his Agreement does not affect and shall not be deemed or construed to impair or limit in any way the Employer's right in its sole discretion and judgment, to … hire, promote, demote, and transfer, to suspend, discipline and discharge for just cause"; (2) "The Employer shall also have the right … to make and enforce … reasonable rules"; (3) "In the event an employee is discharged and he believes there is no just cause, he … shall grieve the matter"; and (4) "In any case in which the discharge or discipline of an employee is at issue, the Arbitrator shall determine whether the discharge or discipline was for just cause."

The arbitrator found that Wigginton's discharge was not justified and ordered his reinstatement with retroactive benefits. The company sought to vacate the arbitrator's award in the district court, and the union counterclaimed for enforcement. The court concluded that the arbitrator's decision was within his authority and entered judgment in favor of the union. Trailmobile appealed, arguing that the arbitrator imposed his own brand of industrial justice and ignored the plain language of the contract.

Chief Judge Wollman

Although concluding that Wigginton "[p]robably … could have turned his cheek one more time," the arbitrator found that Garcia had provoked and pushed Wigginton to start the fight, and that Wigginton had responded in self-protection. For two years or more Garcia had harassed and played nasty tricks on Wigginton, who had rarely retaliated, instead requesting transfers from management. The arbitrator noted that although Wigginton "got in some blows" during the altercation, both men testified that machinery and parts caused some of Garcia's injuries. The arbitrator determined that Garcia was "wholly at fault in provoking" the altercation, and noted that although several employees had been discharged for fighting, there was also testimony that others had received lesser penalties for such conduct. …

Our review of an arbitration award generally involves two inquiries: (1) Did the parties agree to arbitrate? and (2) Did the arbitrator have the power to make the award that he made? … Only the answer to the second question is disputed.

Judicial review of a final arbitration decision is extremely narrow. "[A]s long as the arbitrator is even arguably construing or applying the contract and acting within the scope of his authority, that a court is convinced he committed serious error does not suffice to overturn his decision." … We will vacate an arbitration award as beyond the power of the arbitrator only in certain circumstances;

if, for example, it exceeds the arbitrator's power, or if the award fails to "draw its essence" from the contract between the disputants. … Although the arbitrator's authority is broad, it is not unlimited. For example, the arbitrator may not disregard or modify unambiguous contract provisions.

Trailmobile contends that the arbitrator ignored the plain language of the management rights clause, which grants to it "sole discretion" in employment decisions. Trailmobile concedes, however, that its authority to discipline is limited by the requirement that such discipline be for "just cause," a term that is not defined in the contract. Notwithstanding this concession, Trailmobile argues that the arbitrator's finding that Wigginton was involved in a fight constituted an implicit finding of just cause for discharge, inasmuch as discharge is the default penalty fixed by the employee handbook for that infraction. Trailmobile asserts that because the plain language of the contract gives to it the authority in its sole discretion to determine appropriate punishment, the arbitrator's decision was not drawn from the essence of the contract. We disagree.

Whether Wigginton was discharged for just cause was a matter of contract interpretation within the arbitrator's domain. The parties' request gave the arbitrator the authority to decide the issue of whether just cause existed for termination. … Having requested that the arbitrator determine whether Wigginton was discharged for just cause, Trailmobile will not now be heard to complain that the arbitrator performed the analysis that it requested instead of making a purely factual finding. It was for the arbitrator to harmonize any discordant provisions within the contract relating to the discretionary authority granted management and the just-cause requirements limiting that authority.

Moreover, the arbitrator did not ignore the plain language of the agreement when he interpreted the contract. … [W]hen an agreement does not define just cause and does not include an explicit provision for offenses that will lead to termination, a reviewing court must defer to an arbitrator's interpretation of the just cause provisions.

Our case law similarly differentiates between explicit contractual language and rules or policies promulgated under a general management rights clause like the one in the present case. …

Trailmobile's handbook rules were not expressly written into the contract, which specifically provided for arbitration of disputes regarding discharge, and Trailmobile cites to no contract limitation on the arbitrator's power of remedy other than the provisions for employer discretion previously discussed. Furthermore, the handbook rule provides that an employee "may" be discharged, suggesting a case-by-case analysis that further supports the arbitrator's decision to review the choice of a disciplinary measure. Accordingly, we conclude that the arbitrator did not violate the plain language of the contract when he determined that Wigginton had engaged in fighting and yet should not have been discharged.

Trailmobile's final contention is that the arbitrator should have considered the union's failure to object to or grieve past discharges as a "common law of the shop" that gives to Trailmobile the discretion to determine whether discharge is appropriate. We find this argument to be without merit. Whatever the union's passivity in the past, the contract provides that past practices shall not "be considered as a waiver or lessening of any Union, employee or Company right provided in this Agreement." In any event, we note that the arbitrator did in fact consider testimony on the subject of what penalties employees had received for fighting in the past.

In sum, it was the arbitrator's task to reconcile the contract provisions to determine whether there was just cause for Trailmobile to discharge Wigginton. The arbitrator brought his experience to bear and "entered an award in accordance with [his] understanding of the meaning of the contract provisions. That was [his] prerogative and duty, and we see no justification for setting aside" the award.

Affirmed, in favor of Union.

The policy of deferring to the arbitrator's decision applies to disputes in areas other than labor contracts. Unless there is a clear showing that the arbitrator's decision is contrary to law or there was some defect in the arbitration process, the decision will be upheld. Section 10 of the Federal Arbitration Act, the federal law enacted to encourage the use of arbitration, sets forth the four grounds on which the arbitrator's award may be set aside:

1. The award was the result of corruption, fraud, or other "undue means."
2. The arbitrator exhibited bias or corruption.
3. The arbitrator refused to postpone the hearing despite sufficient cause, refused to hear evidence pertinent and material to the dispute, or otherwise acted to substantially prejudice the rights of one of the parties.
4. The arbitrator exceeded his or her authority or failed to use such authority to make a mutual, final, and definite award.

METHODS OF SECURING ARBITRATION

binding arbitration clause
A provision in a contract mandating that all disputes arising under the contract be settled by arbitration.

submission agreement
Separate agreement providing that a specific dispute be resolved through arbitration.

Arbitration may be secured voluntarily, or it may be imposed on the parties. The first voluntary means of securing arbitration is by including a **binding arbitration clause** in a contract. Such a clause provides that all or certain disputes arising under the contract are to be settled by arbitration. The clause should also include the means by which the arbitrator is to be selected. More than 95 percent of the collective bargaining agreements in force today have some provision for arbitration.[5] Exhibit 4-1 contains a sample binding arbitration clause that could be included in almost any business contract.

If their contract contains no binding arbitration clause, the parties may secure arbitration by entering into a **submission agreement**, an example of

EXHIBIT 4-1

SAMPLE BINDING ARBITRATION CLAUSE

Any controversy, dispute, or claim of whatever nature arising out of, in connection with, or in relation to the interpretation, performance, or breach of this agreement, including any claim based on contract, tort, or statute, shall be resolved, at the request of any party to this agreement, by final and binding arbitration conducted at a location determined by the arbitrator in (City), (State), administered by and in accordance with the existing rules of Practice and Procedure of Judical Arbitration & Mediation Services, Inc. (J.A.M.S.), and judgment upon any award rendered by the arbitrator may be entered by any state of federal court having jurisdition thereof.

---

[5] M. Jacobs, "Required Job Arbitration Stirs Critics," *Wall Street Journal*, June 22, 1993, p. B3.

American Arbitration Association

SUBMISSION TO DISPUTE RESOLUTION

Date: _____

The named parties hereby submit the following dispute for resolution under the _____
_____ Rules* of the American Arbitration Association:

Procedure Selected: ❏ Binding Arbitration ❏ Mediation Settlement
❏ Other _____
(Describe)

FOR INSURANCE CASES ONLY:

_____ to _____
Policy Number   Effective Dates   Applicable Policy Limits

Date of Incident _____ Location _____
Insured: _____ Claim Number: _____

Name(s) of Claimant(s)	**Check if a Minor**	**Amount Claimed**
_____	❏	_____
_____	❏	_____

Nature of Dispute and/or Injuries Alleged (attach additional sheets if necessary): _____

Place of Hearing: _____

We agree that, if binding arbitration is selected, we will abide by and perform any award rendered hereunder and that a judgement may be entered on the award.

To Be Completed by the Parties

Name of Party	Name of Party
Address	Address
City, State, and ZIP Code	City, State, and ZIP Code
( )	( )
Telephone Fax	Telephone Fax
Signature†	Signature†
Name of Party's Attorney or Representative	Name of Party's Attorney or Representative
Address	Address
City, State, and ZIP Code	City, State, and ZIP Code
( )	( )
Telephone Fax	Telephone Fax
Signature†	Signature†

Please file three copies with the AAA.

* If you have a question as to which rules apply, please contact the AAA.
† Signatures of all parties are required for arbitration.   Form G1 - 6/91

EXHIBIT 4-2

SAMPLE SUBMISSION AGREEMENT

Source: Reproduced with permission of the American Arbitration Association, 140 West 51st Street, New York, NY 10020.

which is provided in Exhibit 4-2. This contract can be entered into at any time. It is a written contract that states that the parties wish to settle their dispute by arbitration. Usually, it specifies the following conditions:

- How the arbitrator will be selected
- The nature of the dispute
- Any constraints on the arbitrator's authority to remedy the dispute
- The place where the arbitration will take place
- A time by which the arbitration must be scheduled

Usually, both parties will declare their intent to be bound by the arbitrator's award.

If the parties have entered into a submission agreement or have included a binding arbitration clause in their contract, they will be required to resolve their disputes through arbitration. Both federal and state courts must defer to arbitration if the contract in dispute contains a binding arbitration clause. This constraint was mandated by the U.S. Supreme Court in the following case.

CASE 4-2

Southland Corporation v. Keating
Supreme Court of the United States
465 U.S.1 (1984)

Plaintiffs, a group of individuals who ran 7-Eleven stores franchised by the Southland Corporation, sued the defendant corporation for breach of contract, fraud, and violation of the California Franchise Investment Law. The defendant responded by filing a motion to compel arbitration because their contract included a clause stating that any claim or controversy related to the agreement would be settled by arbitration in accordance with the rules of the American Arbitration Association. The trial court held that the fraud and breach-of-contract claims should be arbitrated but that the cause of action (or claim) filed under the state franchise law should be litigated. The California Court of Appeals held that all claims should be subject to arbitration. The court stated that to allow the state franchise law claim to be litigated would be to contravene the Federal Arbitration Act, which withdraws from the courts claims covered by an arbitration clause. The California Supreme Court reversed the decision of the court of appeals and reinstated the trial court's decision. The defendant corporation appealed to the U.S. Supreme Court.

Chief Justice Burger

The California Franchise Investment Law provides:

> *Any condition, stipulation or provision purporting to bind any person acquiring any franchise to waive compliance with any provision of the law or any rule or order hereunder is void.*

The California Supreme Court interpreted this statute to require judicial consideration of claims brought under the State statute and accordingly refused to enforce the parties' contract to arbitrate such claims. So interpreted, the California Franchise Investment Law directly conflicts with Section 2 of the Federal Arbitration Act and violates the Supremacy Clause.

In enacting Section 2 of the Federal Act, Congress declared a national policy favoring arbitration and withdrew the power of the states to require a judicial forum for the resolution of claims which the contracting parties agreed to resolve by arbitration. The Federal Arbitration Act provides:

> *A written provision in any maritime transaction or a contract evidencing a transaction involving commerce to settle by arbitration a controversy thereafter arising out of such contract or transaction, or the refusal to perform the whole or any part thereof, or an agreement in writing to submit to arbitration an existing controversy arising out of such a contract, transaction, or refusal, shall be valid, irrevocable, and enforceable, save upon such grounds as exist at law or in equity for the revocation of any contract.*

Congress has thus mandated the enforcement of arbitration agreements.

We discern only two limitations on the enforceability of arbitration provisions governed by the Federal Arbitration Act: they must be part of a written maritime contract or a contract "evidencing a transaction involving commerce" and such clauses may be revoked upon "grounds as exist at law or in equity for the revocation of any contract." We see nothing in the Act indicating that the broad principle of enforceability is subject to any additional limitations under State law.

The Federal Arbitration Act rests on the authority of Congress to enact substantive rules under the Commerce Clause. The Court examined the legislative history of the Act and concluded that the statue "is based upon … the incontestable federal foundations of 'control over interstate commerce and over admiralty.'"

We reaffirmed our view that the Arbitration Act "creates a body of federal substantive law" and expressly stated what was implicit, the substantive law the Act created was applicable in state and federal court.

Although the legislative history is not without ambiguities, there are strong indications that Congress had in mind something more than making arbitration agreements enforceable only in the federal courts. The House Report plainly suggests the more comprehensive objectives:

> *The purpose of this bill is to make valid and enforceable agreements for arbitration contained in contracts involving interstate commerce or within the jurisdiction or admiralty, or which may be the subject of litigation in the Federal courts.*

The broader purpose can also be inferred from the reality that Congress would be less likely to address a problem whose impact was confined to federal courts than a problem of large significance in the field of commerce. The Arbitration Act sought to "overcome the rule of equity, that equity will not specifically enforce any arbitration agreement."

And since the overwhelming proportion of all civil litigation in this country is in the state courts, we cannot believe Congress intended to limit the Arbitration Act to disputes subject only to federal court jurisdiction. Such an interpretation would frustrate Congressional intent to place "an arbitration agreement … upon the same footing as other contracts, where it belongs."

In creating a substantive rule applicable in state as well as federal courts, Congress intended to foreclose state legislative attempts to undercut the enforceability of arbitration agreements. We hold that Section 31512 of the California Franchise Investment Law violates the Supremacy Clause.

Reversed in favor of Defendant, Southland Corporation.

Critical Thinking About the Law

By now, you realize that legal reasons have degrees of quality, reliability, and acceptability. A claim is not valid simply because reasons are given for its truth or merit.

The following questions, pertaining to Case 4-2, will refresh your appreciation of this point.

1. Crucial to the Court's reasoning is its claim that Congress intended the Federal Arbitration Act's authority to extend to the state courts. What evidence does the Court provide for this claim?

    Clue: Reread the section that begins with this claim.

2. Having answered Question 1, you now know that the Court relies to some extent on the legislative history of the act to support its position. What are the dangers with this type of evidence?

    Clue: Think about your own personal history. Have your intentions always been expressed in a form that everyone who knew you could interpret accurately?

The U.S. Supreme Court had the opportunity to reexamine its holding in *Southerland v. Keating* in 1995 when it agreed to hear the case of *Allied-Bruce-Termix Companies v. Dobson.*[6] In that case, Mr. Gibbs and a termite exterminator had entered into a termite control contract that included a clause providing that all disputes under the contract would be settled exclusively by arbitration. Dobson had purchased Gibbs's house and took over the contract. When Allied-Bruce-Termix was unable to fulfill the terms of the contract, Dobson filed suit in court, asking the state to uphold a state law invalidating predispute arbitration clauses. The state's highest court upheld the state law, saying that the Federal Arbitration Act (FAA) did not apply to this case because the parties did not contemplate any interstate transaction under the contract. On the appeal before the U.S. Supreme Court, 20 state attorneys general signed an amicus curiae (friend of the court) brief arguing in favor of overruling Southerland and upholding the Alabama court's decision. The Court, however, overruled the Alabama court and upheld Southerland, saying that the contract clearly involved interstate commerce because Termix was a multistate operation, and, furthermore, the materials used by the company were purchased in another state. The Court thereby reinforced its intent to interpret the statute broadly.

The most recent opportunity the U.S. Supreme Court had to uphold, and perhaps some would say expand, this broad interpretation of the application of

---

[6] 513 U.S. 265 (1995).

the FAA was in the 2001 case of *Circuit City Stores, Inc. v. Saint Clair Adams*.[7] A provision of the work application that Adams filled out when he went to work for Circuit City required all employment disputes to be settled by arbitration. He subsequently wanted to file a state discrimination action against his employer. When the employer attempted to enforce the arbitration clause, Adams argued that the language of the FAA excludes from that act's coverage "contracts of employment of seamen, railroad employees, or any other class of workers engaged in foreign or interstate commerce." Adams contended that this language meant that the FAA was not intended to apply to his contract of employment. The district court issued an order compelling arbitration, but the Ninth Circuit Court of Appeals reversed, finding that the language of the act exempted all employment contracts from the FAA's reach. The Supreme Court, however, reversed the appellate court's decision, relying on Termix and finding that Congress was exercising its full Commerce Clause power in the coverage provision, and was excluding only transportation workers by the clause at issue.

The drafters of either a submission agreement or a binding arbitration clause must be precise because courts will enforce the agreements as written. And parties who decide to specify that a certain state's laws govern an agreement should be familiar with all of the laws that might be applicable, including the state laws governing the arbitration procedures themselves.

Drafters must also be sure that the binding arbitration clause is fair to both sides. Courts are now starting to scrutinize binding arbitration clauses and submission agreements to make sure that they are not so extraordinarily one-sided as to make them "unconscionable" and, therefore, unenforceable. In the following case, the Supreme Court of California explains unconscionability in the context of an arbitration agreement and explains what impact a finding of unconscionability will have on the contract.

CASE 4-3

Marybeth Armendariz et al. v. Foundation Health Psychcare Services, Inc.
Supreme Court of California
6 P.3d 669 (2000)

In the summer of 1995, defendant Foundation Health Psychcare Services, Inc., hired the plaintiffs, Marybeth Armendariz and Dolores Olague-Rodgers; they were subsequently given supervisory positions. On June 20, 1996, they were informed that they were being terminated because their positions were being eliminated. They sued their former employer for wrongful termination, alleging that they had been subject to sexually based harassment and discrimination during their employment, and that they were "terminated … because of their perceived and/or actual sexual orientation (heterosexual)." They sought to recover general damages, punitive damages, injunctive relief, and attorney fees and costs of suit.

Both plaintiffs had executed an employment arbitration agreement containing an arbitration clause that read,

"In the event my employment is terminated, and I contend that such termination was wrongful or otherwise in violation of the conditions of employment or was in violation of any express or implied condition, term or covenant of employment, whether founded in fact or in law, including but not limited to the covenant of good faith and fair dealing, or otherwise in violation of any of my rights, I and Employer agree to submit any such matter to binding arbitration pursuant to. … the California Code of Civil Procedure. … I and Employer further expressly agree that in any such arbitration, my exclusive remedies for violation of the terms, conditions or covenants of employment shall be limited to a sum equal to the wages I would have earned from the date of any discharge until the date of the arbitration award. I understand that I shall not be entitled

---

[7] 532 U.S. 105 (2001).

to any other remedy, at law or in equity, including but not limited to reinstatement and/or injunctive relief."

The employer filed a motion for an order to compel arbitration. The trial court denied the motion on the ground that the arbitration provision in question was an unconscionable contract. The trial court first found that the arbitration agreement was an "adhesion contract." It also found that several of the provisions of the contract are "so one-sided as to 'shock the conscience.'" In particular, it singled out the fact that only employees who file claims against an employer are required to arbitrate their claims, but not vice versa. Second, the agreement limited damages to back pay, precluding damages available for statutory antidiscrimination claims and tort damages, such as punitive damages. The trial court also mentioned the supposed lack of discovery under the arbitration agreement. It concluded: "Given the overall unfairness of the provision," this was not an appropriate case for striking the unlawful provisions of the arbitration agreement; instead it invalidated the entire agreement.

The employer appealed, and the court of appeals reversed, concluding that the contract was indeed one of adhesion and that the damages provision was unconscionable and contrary to public policy, but held that the rest of the arbitration agreement should be enforced. The plaintiffs appealed to the California Supreme Court.

Justice Mosk

D. Unconscionability of the Arbitration Agreement

1. General Principles of Unconscionability

… Unconscionability analysis begins with an inquiry into whether the contract is one of adhesion. … "The term signifies a standardized contract, which, imposed and drafted by the party of superior bargaining strength, relegates to the subscribing party only the opportunity to adhere to the contract or reject it." … If the contract is adhesive, the court must then determine whether "other factors are present which, under established legal rules—legislative or judicial—operate to render it [unenforceable]." … "Generally speaking, there are two judicially imposed limitations on the enforcement of adhesion contracts or provisions thereof. The first is that such a contract or provision which does not fall within the reasonable expectations of the weaker or 'adhering' party will not be enforced against him. The second—a principle of equity applicable to all contracts generally—is that a contract or provision, even if consistent with the reasonable expectations of the parties, will be denied enforcement if, considered in its context, it is unduly oppressive or 'unconscionable.'"

… [The California Civil Code] states: "If the court as a matter of law finds the contract or any clause of the contract to have been unconscionable at the time it was

made, the court may refuse to enforce the contract, or it may enforce the remainder of the contract without the unconscionable clause, or it may so limit the application of any unconscionable clause as to avoid any unconscionable result." Because unconscionability is a reason for refusing to enforce contracts generally, it is also a valid reason for refusing to enforce an arbitration agreement. … The United States Supreme Court, in interpreting the same language found in section 2 of the FAA, recognized that "generally applicable contract defenses, such as fraud, duress, or unconscionability, may be applied to invalidate arbitration agreements. …"

As explained in *A & M Produce Company*, "unconscionability has both a 'procedural' and a 'substantive' element," the former focusing on "oppression" or "surprise" due to unequal bargaining power, the latter on "overly harsh" or "one-sided" results. "The prevailing view is that [procedural and substantive unconscionability] must both be present in order for a court to exercise its discretion to refuse to enforce a contract or clause under the doctrine of unconscionability."

2. Unconscionability and Mandatory Employment Arbitration

Applying the above principles to this case, we first determine whether the arbitration agreement is adhesive. There is little dispute that it is. It was imposed on employees as a condition of employment and there was no opportunity to negotiate.

Moreover, in the case of preemployment arbitration contracts, the economic pressure exerted by employers on all but the most sought-after employees may be particularly acute, for the arbitration agreement stands between the employee and necessary employment, and few employees are in a position to refuse a job because of an arbitration requirement.

… [T]he employees contend that the agreement is substantively unconscionable because it requires only employees to arbitrate their wrongful termination claims against the employer, but does not require the employer to arbitrate claims it may have against the employees. … The court relied in part on *Saika v. Gold*, in which the court had refused to enforce a provision in an arbitration agreement between a doctor and a patient that would allow a "trial de novo" if the arbitrator's award was $25,000 or greater. The *Saika* court reasoned that such a clause was tantamount to making arbitration binding when the patient lost the arbitration but not binding if the patient won a significant money judgment.

We conclude that [previous cases] are correct in requiring this "modicum of bilaterality" in an arbitration agreement. Given the disadvantages that may exist for plaintiffs arbitrating disputes, it is unfairly one-sided for an employer with superior bargaining power to impose arbitration on the employee as plaintiff but not to accept such limitations when it seeks to prosecute a claim against the employee, without at least some reasonable justification for such one-sidedness based on "business realities." As has been recognized, "unconscionability turns not only on a 'one-sided' result, but also on an absence of 'justification' for it." ... If the arbitration system established by the employer is indeed fair, then the employer as well as the employee should be willing to submit claims to arbitration. Without reasonable justification for this lack of mutuality, arbitration appears less as a forum for neutral dispute resolution and more as a means of maximizing employer advantage.

... We conclude, rather, that in the context of an arbitration agreement imposed by the employer on the employee, such a one-sided term is unconscionable. Although parties are free to contract for asymmetrical remedies and arbitration clauses of varying scope, [prior cases] are correct that the doctrine of unconscionability limits the extent to which a stronger party may, through a contract of adhesion, impose the arbitration forum on the weaker party without accepting that forum for itself.

Applying these principles to the present case, we note the arbitration agreement was limited in scope to employee claims regarding wrongful termination. Although it did not expressly authorize litigation of the employer's claims against the employee, such was the clear implication of the agreement.

This is not to say that an arbitration clause must mandate the arbitration of all claims between employer and employee in order to avoid invalidation on grounds of unconscionability. ... But an arbitration agreement imposed in an adhesive context lacks basic fairness and mutuality if it requires one contracting party, but not the other, to arbitrate all claims arising out of the same transaction or occurrence or series of transactions or occurrences. The arbitration agreement in this case lacks mutuality in this sense because it requires the arbitration of employee—but not employer—claims arising out of a wrongful termination. An employee terminated for stealing trade secrets, for example, must arbitrate his or her wrongful termination claim under the agreement, while the employer has no corresponding obligation to arbitrate its trade secrets claim against the employee.

The unconscionable one-sidedness of the arbitration agreement is compounded in this case by the fact that it does not permit the full recovery of damages for employees, while placing no such restriction on the employer. Even if the limitation on FEHA damages is severed as con-

trary to public policy, the arbitration clause in the present case still does not permit full recovery of ordinary contract damages. The arbitration agreement specifies that damages are to be limited to the amount of back pay lost up until the time of arbitration. This provision excludes damages for prospective future earnings, so-called "front pay," a common and often substantial component of contractual damages in a wrongful termination case. ... The employer, on the other hand, is bound by no comparable limitation should it pursue a claim against its employees.

E. Severability of Unconscionable Provisions

The employees contend that the presence of various unconscionable provisions or provisions contrary to public policy leads to the conclusion that the arbitration agreement as a whole cannot be enforced. The employer contends that, insofar as there are unconscionable provisions, they should be severed and the rest of the agreement enforced.

The basic principles of severability ... [require courts] to look to the various purposes of the contract. If the central purpose of the contract is tainted with illegality, then the contract as a whole cannot be enforced. If the illegality is collateral to the main purpose of the contract, and the illegal provision can be extirpated from the contract by means of severance or restriction, then such severance and restriction are appropriate. ...

In this case, two factors weigh against severance of the unlawful provisions. First, the arbitration agreement contains more than one unlawful provision; it has both an unlawful damages provision and an unconscionably unilateral arbitration clause. Such multiple defects indicate a systematic effort to impose arbitration on an employee not simply as an alternative to litigation, but as an inferior forum that works to the employer's advantage. In other words, given the multiple unlawful provisions, the trial court did not abuse its discretion in concluding that the arbitration agreement is permeated by an unlawful purpose. Second, in the case of the agreement's lack of mutuality, such permeation is indicated by the fact that there is no single provision a court can strike or restrict in order to remove the unconscionable taint from the agreement. Rather, the court would have to, in effect, reform the contract, not through severance or restriction, but by augmenting it with additional terms.

Reversed in favor of Plaintiffs.

While the foregoing case was decided by a state court, federal courts have likewise begun to closely scrutinize arbitration agreements. For example, the Fourth Circuit Court of Appeals refused to enforce an agreement between Hooters Restaurant and one of its waitresses to settle all employment disputes through arbitration, because the court found that the rules for arbitration under the agreement were "so one-sided that their only possible purpose is to undermine the neutrality of the proceeding."[8] Some of the more objectionable rules incorporated in the agreement included:

- The employee had to provide notice of the specifics of the claim, but Hooters did not need to file any type of response to these specifics or notify the claimant of what kinds of defenses the company planned to raise.

- Only the employee had to provide a list of all fact witnesses and a brief summary of the facts known to each.

- Although the employee and Hooters could each choose an arbitrator from a list and those arbitrators would then select a third to create the arbitration panel that would hear the dispute, Hooters alone selected the arbitrators on the list.

- Only Hooters had the right to widen the scope of arbitration to include any matter, whereas the employee was limited to those raised in its notice.

- Only Hooters had the right to record the arbitration.

- Only Hooters had the right to sue to vacate or modify an arbitration award because the arbitration panel exceeded its authority.

- Only Hooters could cancel the agreement to arbitrate or change the arbitration rules.[9]

If you think about these conditions, each of them individually seems inherently unfair. When you consider their impact as a group, it is easy to see why the court refused to uphold the agreement.

As increasing numbers of employers began incorporating mandatory, binding arbitration clauses in their employment contracts, a question that arose was whether certain statutory rights, such as the right to not be discriminated against based on age, sex, race, religion, color, or national origin, were so important that one could not contract away his or her ability to protect those rights through litigation. The U.S. Supreme Court addressed that issue in the case of *Gilmer v. Interstate/Johnson Lane Corporation*.[10] Gilmer was a 62-year-old securities broker who sued his employer under the Age Discrimination in Employment Act (ADEA) when he was terminated. The employer argued that Gilmer had to submit his age discrimination claim to arbitration because as part of his application to be a securities representative with the New York Stock Exchange, he signed an agreement to arbitrate "any claim, dispute, or controversy" arising between himself and Interstate.

The High Court upheld the binding arbitration clause, noting that the employee was not agreeing to give up any statutory rights; instead, the employee was simply agreeing to resolve disputes involving those rights through arbitration. The Court had no problem with such a waiver of the employee's right to sue to enforce his statutory rights, as long as the employee understood that the binding arbitration clause also encompassed statutory rights.

---

[8] *Hooters of America, Inc. v. Phillips*, 173 F.3d 933 (4th Cir. 1999).

[9] *Id.* For further discussion of the implications of this case, see Carmine A. Iannaccone, Gerald F. Spada, Ronald K. Silversten, *Arbitration and Employment Disputes: Drafting to Maximize Employer Protection*, 18 No. 2 ACCADKT 17 (February 2000).

[10] 500 U.S. 20 (1991).

The initial impact of this ruling was to increase the use of mandatory arbitration agreements in employment contracts in all industries. In fact, about 100 large companies soon moved to follow the securities industry's policy. However, some courts and the Equal Employment Opportunity Commission (EEOC) became increasingly concerned about whether arbitration agreements that had to be accepted as a condition of employment were really voluntary. On July 10, 1997, the EEOC issued a policy statement saying that the mandatory "arbitration of discrimination claims as a condition of employment are [sic] contrary to the fundamental principles of employment discrimination laws." The EEOC chairman stated that the agency strongly supported agreements to arbitrate once a dispute had arisen but did not believe that a prospective employee could make a voluntary agreement to arbitrate future disputes as part of a "take it or leave it" contract of employment. In 2003, however, in the case of EEOC v. Luce, Forward, Hamilton & Scripps, the Ninth Circuit,[11] cleared the way for the inclusion of mandatory arbitration clauses in employment agreements. The court held that federal civil rights claims can be the subject of mandatory arbitration agreements, and an employer can require all employees to sign such an agreement as a condition of employment.

But even if an employer does not provide its employees with a choice in statutory discrimination disputes, the Supreme Court recently upheld the EEOC's right to seek remedies in discrimination cases, even when a binding arbitration agreement exists to settle all employment-related disputes. In EEOC v. Waffle House, Inc.,[12] an employee brought suit against his employer, claiming that he was unlawfully discharged following a seizure he had at work. With regard to the defendant's allegations that this discharge violated the Americans with Disabilities Act, the Supreme Court ruled that the EEOC could seek statutory remedies, including "victim-specific" relief, back pay, compensatory, and punitive damages. In the year after this case was handed down, the EEOC settled a case by agreeing to allow an employer to require employees to sign a mandatory arbitration agreement as long as the employee was notified of his right to still file a charge with the EEOC that the agency might wish to pursue.

While in 1997, the National Association of Securities Dealers changed their policy to allow employees to choose between entering into private arbitration agreements with their employer or reserving the right to file a claim in state or federal court, the trend in many industries is toward an increasing use of binding arbitration clauses in their employment agreements. After all, the EEOC files suit in less than 1 percent of the charges it receives each year. Hence, even if an employee wants to litigate for statutory discrimination, the likelihood that the EEOC will represent him or her is very small. To avoid any chance of an arbitration clause being challenged by an employee wishing to bring a lawsuit under a civil rights statute, the binding arbitration clause should be drafted in such a way as to make it clear that the employee knew that he or she was agreeing to arbitrate all disputes arising out of the employment situation, including statutory rights.

If the binding arbitration clause is contained in an agreement between the employer and the union, and individuals under the agreement are giving up their rights to sue for statutory violations, the agreement to arbitrate statutory

---

[11] 345 F3d 742 (2003).

[12] 534 U.S. 279 (2002).

disputes must be even more explicit; it must be clear and unmistakable. In *Wright v. Universal Maritime Service*,[13] the U.S. Supreme Court said that the "right to a federal judicial forum is of sufficient importance to be protected against a less-than-explicit union waiver in a CBA [collective bargaining agreement]. The CBA in this case does not meet that standard. Its arbitration clause is very general, providing for arbitration of '[m]atters under dispute'—which could be understood to mean matters in dispute under the contract. And the remainder of the contract contains no explicit incorporation of statutory antidiscrimination requirements." Thus, an employer wishing to avoid litigation of allegations of civil rights violations must be even more careful in crafting the binding arbitration clause when it is the union that is waiving its members' rights.

However, binding arbitration clauses are not only included in employment agreements, but also these clauses are sometimes included in consumer and business-to-business contracts. For instance, in *Eagle v. Fred Martin Motor Co.*[14] plaintiff Lisa Eagle sued Fred Martin Motors, alleging that the defendant violated the Consumer Sales Practices Act, after the plaintiff's new car repeatedly stalled and experienced other mechanical problems that the dealer failed to fix. After Eagle filed suit, Fred Martin Motors motioned to compel arbitration in accordance with a binding arbitration clause that was included in the sales agreement. The common pleas court granted the defendant's motion, and Eagle appealed, claiming that the arbitration agreement was unconscionable.

The appellate court reversed the common pleas court's decision. Explaining that consumer transactions should be subject to closer scrutiny, the judge claimed that the agreement was substantively unconscionable because the agreement included excessive filing fees, especially for the plaintiff, who earned only about $14,000 per year. The judge stated that the binding arbitration clause was procedurally unconscionable because the preprinted purchase contract was an adhesion contract, in the sense that the plaintiff had no actual choice about the terms of arbitration. Furthermore, the judge cited several additional factors relating to procedural unconscionability, including allegations that the dealer's sales representative hurried through the purchasing papers with the plaintiff, the plaintiff was not made aware of the binding arbitration clause during the purchase nor did the plaintiff know what arbitration meant, and the arbitration clause did not mention the excessive costs. Considering the plaintiff's limited educational and economic background, the judge agreed that these two factors were also relevant in his concluding that the arbitration clause was procedurally unconscionable. Hence, the court ruled that the binding arbitration clause was substantively and procedurally unconscionable and therefore, unenforceable. See Exhibit 4-3 for a list of points to consider to insure that any mandatory arbitration clause you draft will not be struck down as unconscionable.

In addition to the two voluntary means of securing arbitration, state law may mandate the process for certain types of conflicts. For instance, in some states, public employees must submit collective bargaining disputes to binding arbitration. In other states, disputes involving less than a certain amount of money automatically go to arbitration.

---

[13] 525 U.S. 70 (1998).

[14] 157 Ohio App. 3d 150 (2004).

EXHIBIT 4-3

DRAFTER'S CHECKLIST

Checklist for Insuring that a Mandatory Arbitration Clause Is Not Unconscionable

- The contract is not a contract of adhesion, that is, one where the consumer could not meaningfully negotiate the inclusion and terms of the mandatory arbitration clause.
- The mandatory arbitration clause and its provisions are not buried in fine print.
- The provisions of the clause do not unduly favor the interests of drafter of the contract.
- The provisions of the clause do not impose significant costs on the consumer.
- The provisions of the clause do not include a confidentiality requirement (which may make it difficult for consumers to share information).
- The provisions do not limit the ability of the consumer to obtain punitive damages.

SELECTION OF AN ARBITRATOR

Once the decision to arbitrate has been made, an arbitrator must be selected. Arbitrators are generally lawyers, professors, or other professionals. They are frequently selected on the basis of their special expertise in some area. If the parties have not agreed on an arbitrator before a dispute, they generally use one of two sources for selecting one: the Federal Mediation and Conciliation Services (FMCS), a government agency discussed further in Chapter 15, or the American Arbitration Association (AAA), a private, nonprofit organization founded in 1926, whose stated purpose is "to foster the study of arbitration in all of its aspects, to perfect its techniques under arbitration law, and to advance generally the science of arbitration for the prompt and economical settlement of disputes." Its slogan is "Speed, Economy, and Justice." It currently employs over 8,000 arbitrators and mediators worldwide, over 1,100 of whom are bilingual or multilingual—with over 40 languages collectively spoken. The parties may also turn to one of the private arbitration services.

When the disputants contact one of these agencies, they receive a list of potential arbitrators along with a biographical sketch of each. The parties will jointly select an arbitrator from the list. Once the arbitrator has been selected, the parties and the arbitrator agree on the time, the date, and the location of the arbitration. They also agree on the substantive and procedural rules to be followed in the arbitration. Regardless of whether the arbitrator is selected through the AAA, the FMCS, or some private association, he or she will be subject to the Arbitrator's Code of Ethics. Organized by canons of ethics, the code is designed to ensure that arbitrators perform their duties diligently and in good faith, thereby maintaining public confidence in the arbitration process. Exhibit 4-4 contains the seven canons of the Arbitrator's Code of Ethics.

COMMON USES OF ARBITRATION

As noted earlier, arbitration is frequently used to resolve grievances under collective bargaining agreements. It is so frequently used in these cases that it is sometimes identified primarily as a means for resolving labor disputes, but it is also used to resolve a much broader range of issues—such as insurance and

EXHIBIT 4-4

THE ARBITRATOR'S CODE OF ETHICS

CANON 1

• An arbitrator will uphold the integrity and fairness of the arbitration process.

CANON 2

• If the arbitrator has an interest or relationship that is likely to affect his or her impartiality or that might create an appearance of partiality or bias, it must be disclosed.

CANON 3

• An arbitrator, in communicating with the parties, should avoid impropriety or the appearance of it.

CANON 4

• The arbitrator should conduct the proceedings fairly and diligently.

CANON 5

• The arbitrator should make decisions in a just, independent, and deliberate manner.

CANON 6

• The arbitrator should be faithful to the relationship of trust and confidentiality inherent in that office.

CANON 7

• In a case where there is a board of arbitrators, each party may select an arbitrator. That arbitrator must ensure that he or she follows all the ethical considerations in this type of situation.

uninsured motorists claims, construction disputes, and securities, real estate, intellectual property, and other commercial disputes illustrates. For example, many consumer complaints are now being handled by arbitration sponsored by Better Business Bureaus (BBBs) in more than 100 cities. Under the BBBs' National Consumer Arbitration Program, which has been in effect since 1972, the consumer first files a complaint with the BBB, whose representative attempts to negotiate a solution between the consumer and the business. If negotiation fails, the consumer and the business representative sign a submission agreement specifying the disputed issues. Then they select an arbitrator from a panel of five trained volunteers from the local community. After the hearing (at which the parties are usually not represented by counsel), the arbitrator has ten days to render a decision.

Another area where we are seeing an increasing use of arbitration is in technology disputes. In 2003, the AAA handled technology-related claims that totalled over 1 billion. The average claim was $1.2 million, and the average counterclaim $2.3 million.

The National Consumer Arbitration Program is limited in that arbitrators cannot award damages beyond the value of the product in question. They cannot, for example, award punitive damages or damages for personal injuries suffered as a result of a defective product. Despite these limitations, this program provides an excellent forum for disputes that often would not be resolved in court, because the cost of litigation would probably exceed or come close to the amount of the damage award. The use of arbitration in consumer cases is further discussed in Chapter 24.

Linking Law & Business

Management

Your management professor may have taught you about the concept of perceptions, the psychological process of selecting stimuli, gathering data from observation, and interpreting the organized information. From the perspective of an employee, one of the most important perceptions about the workplace is procedural justice, which is the apparent fairness of processes used to determine outcomes. Examples of these processes include performance appraisals, interviews, payment systems, methods of making decisions, and ADR. Procedural justice evaluates the fairness of these methods, with an employee's expectation that the managers will make fair decisions as leaders in these processes. Despite the difficulty of determining the consequences of unfair behavior, some research suggests that there is often an increased amount of job absenteeism and turnover, less production efficiency, lower employee morale, and a lack of employee self-confidence. If there is some truth in this research, it is in the best interest of managers to continually examine the attitudes of employees as a means of understanding the perceived fairness of the organization from their perspective. Thereafter, measures can be taken to remedy unfair processes, which may lead to greater organizational productivity. Additionally, a greater perception of fairness from the employees' point of view may act as a preventative measure for disputes within the organization. As a result, managers can focus more of their time and finances on attaining organizational objectives.

Source: S. Certo, *Modern Management* (Upper Saddle River, N.J.: Prentice Hall, 2000), pp. 409, 412–413.

As mentioned in the previous section, an area in which arbitration is increasingly being used is in employment disputes. Other areas in which arbitration is prevalent include malpractice cases, environmental disputes, community disputes and elections, and commercial contract conflicts. It is also being increasingly used to handle insurance liability claims arising from accidents.

PROBLEMS WITH ARBITRATION

Despite the growing use of arbitration, the process is not free of criticism, especially in the securities industry. From 1991, when the U.S. Supreme Court affirmed the authority of the securities industry to do so, until 1997, securities firms required that employees who execute, buy, or sell orders at brokerages or investment banks take all their employment disputes—including allegations of race, sex, and age discrimination—to arbitration instead of to court.

According to a study by the General Accounting Office (GAO), those disputes are most likely to be filed by women and minorities. They are also the cases most likely to be heard by white males over age 60. Only 11 percent of the arbitrators are female, and fewer than 1 percent are Asian or black. Arbitrators in the securities industry come from the New York Stock Exchange and the National Association of Securities Dealers. Most are retired or semiretired executives or professionals, so they frequently lack subject matter expertise in the discrimination matters.

Although not criticizing the fairness of the outcomes in any particular cases, the GAO did recommend that the industry appoint as arbitrators in discrimination cases people who had some knowledge about discrimination. They also recommended that the industry track the outcome of discrimination cases and establish criteria to keep individuals with records of regulatory violations or other disciplinary actions from becoming arbitrators. Finally, the report expressed concern over the lack of regularized SEC oversight of the arbitration process in general, including the thousands of broker–customer disputes arbitrated each year. The GAO asked the SEC to establish a regular cycle of reasonably frequent reviews of all securities arbitrations, which the SEC has agreed to do.

The trend toward greater use of compulsory arbitration in employment and termination cases concerns some lawyers and legal scholars. They are concerned that such a requirement erodes workers' rights. Thus, an employee who is subject to mandatory arbitration gives up the right to a public trial, the ability to get an injunction to stop unlawful practices, and the right to bring a class action suit.

Another potential problem is the arbitrator's background. For example, although about half of the AAA's arbitrators are lawyers, often an arbitrator is merely someone with expertise in the area in which the dispute arose. He or she may be solving a legal dispute without any real understanding of the applicable law.

A related problem is that if more employers (and other institutions) turn to mandatory arbitration, arbitration may start to become more and more like litigation. Those forced to give up their day in court may start pressing for their "due process" rights in arbitration. They may also argue that arbitrators should be allowed to grant the same remedies as courts. Ultimately, arbitration proceedings could be burdened with the same kinds of formalities that plague litigation—that is, the same disadvantages that have given rise to ADR in the first place.

Some also question the absence of written opinions. Without such opinions, legal precedents cannot develop to reflect changing circumstances. Finally, there is a question of whether the public interest is harmed by allowing an industry to use arbitration to "hide" its disputes from the public. If, for example, a bank required all billing disputes to be handled by arbitration, the public

Linking Law & Business

Marketing

In your marketing class, you may have learned about public relations. This department plays a major role in the promotion of an organization's products and services. In addition, public relations is responsible for improving the firm's image in the eyes of the various publics and with its stakeholders. The public relations department uses several tools to reach interest groups, including the news, special events, speeches, and written and audiovisual materials. One advantageous feature of public relations is that it can increase public awareness about the company through cheaper means than advertising. An interesting story involving the company may be passed along to the public through the media with no advertising costs to the firm. The story may have the same impact on the public that a million-dollar advertising campaign would, with more credibility than advertising. Some disputes may provide an interesting story for the public without harming the image of an organization, especially when the company can choose what information it wishes to release about the dispute. Therefore, public relations could circulate selected information through several different media, hoping that their efforts would increase the public's interest in the company.

Source: P. Kotler and G. Armstrong, *Principles of Marketing* (Upper Saddle River, N.J.: Prentice Hall, 2001), pp. 565–570.

would never know if that bank was continually making overbilling errors. If such cases went to court, the public would be informed about the bank practices and inefficiencies. In addition, of course, firms that are secure in the knowledge that their operations will not be publicized are more likely to be lax than are firms that know they are subject to public scrutiny.

MEDIATION

mediation An alternative dispute-resolution method in which the disputant parties select a neutral party to help them reconcile their differences by facilitating communication and suggesting ways to solve their problems.

Another method of dispute resolution is mediation. Mediation primarily differs from arbitration and litigation in that the mediator makes no final decision. She or he is simply a facilitator of communication between disputing parties.

Mediation is an informal process in which the two disputants select a party, usually one with expertise in the disputed area, to help them reconcile their differences. It is sometimes characterized as a creative and collaborative process involving joint efforts of the mediator and the disputants.

Even though different mediators use different techniques, their overall goals are the same. They try to get the disputants to listen to each other's concerns and understand each other's arguments with the hope of eventually getting the two parties communicating. Once the parties are talking, the mediator attempts to help them decide how to solve their problem. The agreed upon resolution should be "fair, equitable," and "based upon sufficient information."

Although there is no guarantee that a decision will be reached through mediation, once a decision is reached the parties generally enter into a contract that embodies the terms of their settlement. Skilled mediators will attempt to help the parties to draft agreements that reflect the principles that underlie mediation; that is, the agreement should not attempt to assess blame either implicitly or explicitly but should reflect mutual problem solving and consensual agreement. If one party does not live up to the terms of the settlement, he or she can then be sued for breach of contract. Often, however, the parties are more likely to live up to the terms of the agreement than they are to obey a court order, because they were the ones who reached the agreement. The agreement is their idea of how to solve the dispute, not some outsider's solution.

If the mediation is not successful and the parties subsequently take their dispute to arbitration or litigation, nothing that was said during mediation can be used by either party at a later proceeding. Whatever transpires during the mediation is confidential.

SELECTION OF A MEDIATOR

Mediators are available from several sources. In addition to the nonprofit AAA and the Federal Mediation and Concilliation Service (FMCS), described earlier, private companies providing mediators are thriving. One of the most well known private services is JAMS Resolution Services, which has locations across the country. A person in need of mediation services can find a mediator by going to the Web site of one of the aforementioned provided or by going to a site such as Mediate.com, which contains a mediator directory.

One factor to consider when selecting a mediator is what type of background he or she has. Some companies use only former judges, whereas others use judges, lawyers, and nonlawyers as mediators. There is, not surprisingly, a lot of contention over who makes the best mediator. Many people prefer judges because of their legal knowledge, but others say that judges are too ready to make a decision because they spend most of their careers making decisions.

COMMON USES OF MEDIATION

Perhaps the best-known use of mediation is in collective bargaining disputes. Under the National Labor Relations Act, before engaging in an economic strike to achieve better wages, hours, or working conditions under a new collective bargaining agreement, a union must first contact the Federal Mediation and Conciliation Services and attempt to mediate contract demands.

Mediation is also used increasingly to resolve insurance claim disputes and commercial contract problems. More and more frequently a mediation clause is being included in commercial contracts in conjunction with a standard arbitration clause. Under such clauses, if mediation is unsuccessful, the parties would then submit the dispute to arbitration. Going through both of these processes is still generally less time-consuming and expensive than litigation, especially when one considers the drawn-out discovery process.

Some argue that mediation should play a greater role in employment disputes. Often such disputes arise out of miscommunication, and mediation helps to open the lines of communication. There is a wide variety of creative remedies that might be applicable to the employment situation. In fact, JAMS/Endispute offers three basic employment dispute options: standard mediation, streamlined mediation, and a mediation–arbitration combination.

A growing area for mediation is in the resolution of environmental disputes. Many advocate the use of mediation for environmental matters because the traditional dispute-resolution methods are designed to handle a problem between two parties, whereas environmental disputes often involve multiple parties. Mediation can easily accommodate multiple parties. Environmental matters are often likely to involve parties who will have to deal with one another in the future, so preservation of their relationship is of utmost importance. For example, you might have a dispute over a new development in which a local citizen group, a developer, the municipality, and an environmental interest group might all have concerns. Mediation could theoretically resolve their problems in a way that would prevent greater problems in the future. Mediation also offers the potential for creative solutions, which are often needed for environmental disputes.

ADVANTAGES OF MEDIATION

The primary advantage of mediation is that, because of its nonadversarial nature, it tends to preserve the relationship between the parties to a greater extent than would a trial or any of the other alternatives to litigation. Because the parties are talking *to* each other, not talking *about* each other and trying to make the other look bad, there is less of the bitterness that often results from a trial. Parties will almost always come away from a trial with increased hostility toward the other side, whereas even if the parties cannot resolve their differences completely, they almost always leave mediation with a little better understanding of each other's position. Thus, it is used more and more frequently in cases in which the parties will have an ongoing relationship once the immediate dispute is settled.

Another important advantage to mediation is its ability to result in creative solutions. Because the parties are not searching for a decision in their favor or an award of money damages, they are more open to finding some sort of creative solution that may allow both parties to receive some benefit from the situation. Finally, as with other ADR methods, mediation is usually less expensive and less time-consuming than litigation. It's difficult to measure precisely how successful mediation is, however, because settlements are not made public.

CRITICISMS OF MEDIATION

The process of mediation has its critics. They argue that the informal nature of the process represses and denies certain irreconcilable structural conflicts, such as the inherent strife between labor and management. They also argue that this informal process tends to create the impression of equality between the disputants when no such equality exists. The resultant compromise between unequals is an unequal compromise, but it is clothed in the appearance of equal influence.

The mediation process can also arguably be abused. A party who believes that he or she will ultimately lose a dispute may enter the mediation process in bad faith, dragging the process out as long as possible.

Technology and the Legal Environment

Resolving Disputes Online

Today, dispute resolution can be as convenient as sitting at your desktop and going online, thanks to a burgeoning number of online dispute resolution service providers. One place you can go to solve commercial disputes online is The Electronic Courthouse, located at http://www.electroniccourthouse.com/. Parties interested in using the Electronic Courthouse complete their submissions online, using point and click forms, search the online legal data base for answers to their legal questions, use their translation services, and meet with the other party and their resolution professional in a secure Web-based meeting facility supported by voice conferencing. Parties are often able to complete the process in a matter of days. According to the sites operators, the process also has the advantage of being a less expensive form of dispute resolution.

Alternative Resolution Services, located at http://www.arc4adr.com/specialties/123settle.html, offers the following three different online programs:

1. **Online Offer and Demand Exchanges.** Parties log on and submit case information and three blind offers or demands. ARS will compare the numbers and, if they are within set parameters, notify the parties of a settlement.

2. **Arc Mediator or Arbitrator Online Access.** Users submit case information to 123Settle.com. An ARC mediator will contact parties by email, phone or fax.

3. **Neutral Opinion Online.** Users submit facts, evidence, arguments, and other confidential information to an ARC arbitrator for an evaluation of liability and/or damages.

Many online dispute resolution providers specialize in resolving particular kinds of disputes. For example, Cybersettle, located at http://www.cybersettle.com/, specializes in solving insurance claims. Coming online in 1998, the firm claims to have settled over $600,000,000 in claims by mid-2004, with most claims settled within 6 months, and a number within 72 hours. Another provider, Mediations Arbitration Services (MARS) offers consumers and merchants the opportunity for the online resolution of disputes that resulted from online transactions. This service can be found at http://www.resolvemydispute.com/

To find out more about the wide range of online dispute resolution options available, go to http://www.odr.info/providers-php, where you will find a list of online dispute resolution providers.

MINITRIALS

A relatively new means of resolving commercial disputes, probably first used in the United States in 1977 to resolve a dispute between TRW and Telecredit, is the minitrial. A **minitrial** is presided over by a neutral adviser, but the settlement authority resides with senior executives of the disputing corporations. Lawyers for each side make a presentation of the strengths and weaknesses of their respective positions. The adviser may be asked to give his or her opinion as to what the result would be if the case went to trial. Then the corporate executives meet, without their attorneys, to discuss settlement options. Once they reach a settlement, they can make it binding by entering into a contract that encompasses the terms of the settlement.

The use of a minitrial before resorting to arbitration or litigation may be provided for in a clause in the contract. One modification of the minitrial is to give the neutral adviser the authority to settle the case if the corporate executives cannot agree on a means of resolving the dispute within a given period of time.

The minitrial is seen by some as more desirable than arbitration because the disputes involve complex matters that may be better understood by parties directly involved in the contract than by an outside arbitrator. The process also requires intensive, direct communication between the disputants, which may help them better understand the other party's position and may ultimately help their relationship. Minitrials, in some cases, also have the advantage of being less costly than arbitration. For example, the Army Corps of Engineers settled several cases through the use of minitrials, including one trial that involved a $105 million claim that was lowered to a $7 million settlement.[15] Another Army Corp of Engineers case was settled in two and a half days, reducing a complex $515,213 claim to $155,000.[16]

minitrial An alternative dispute-resolution method in which lawyers for each side present the case for their side at a proceeding referred by a neutral adviser, but settlement authority usually resides with senior executives of the disputing corporations.

early neutral case evaluation When parties explain their respective positions to a neutral third party who then evaluates the strengths and weaknesses of the case. This evaluation then guides the parties in reaching a settlement.

EARLY NEUTRAL CASE EVALUATION

Early neutral case evaluation is similar to a minitrial. In **early neutral case evaluation**, parties select a neutral third party and explain their respective positions to this neutral party, who then evaluates the strengths and weaknesses of the case. This evaluation guides the parties in reaching a settlement.

PRIVATE TRIALS

In several states, legislation now permits **private trials** in which cases are tried by a referee selected and paid by the disputants. These referees are empowered by statute to enter legally binding judgments. Referees usually need not have any special training, but they are frequently retired judges, hence, the disparaging reference to this ADR method as "rent-a-judge." The time and place of the trial are set by the parties at their convenience. Cases may be tried in private, a provision that ensures confidentiality.

private trial An alternative dispute-resolution method in which cases are tried, usually in private, by a referee who is selected by the disputants and empowered by statute to enter a binding judgment.

---

[15] Eldon H. Crowell and Charles Pou, Jr., *Appealing Government Contract Decisions: Reducing the Cost and Delay of Procurement Litigation with Alternative Dispute Resolution Techniques*, 49 Md. L. Rev. 183 (1990).

[16] *Id.*

On hearing the case, the referee states findings of facts and conclusions of law in a report with the trial court. The referee's final judgment is entered with the clerk when the report is filed. Any party who is dissatisfied with the decision can move for a new trial before the trial court judge. If this motion is denied, the party can appeal the final judgment.

Until recently, private trials did not involve juries. But private jury trials are now offered by a small number of private firms, most notably JAMS/Endispute. Jurors in these cases tend to be slightly better educated than the typical jury, and many will have served on several previous private juries. Whether having "semiprofessional" jurors serving on many cases perverts the idea of a "jury of one's peers" is currently being debated.

Like other forms of ADR, private trials are subject to criticisms. Many people, for example, are concerned that the use of private trials may lead to the development of a two-tier system of justice. Disputants with sufficient resources will be able to channel their disputes through an efficient, private system; everyone else will have to resolve their complaints through a slower, less efficient public system. Similarly, critics suggest that as wealthier individuals and corporations opt for the private courts, they will be less willing to channel their tax dollars into the public system. With less funding, the public system would then become even less effective. Finally, there is the same question that was raised with respect to arbitration of whether the public interest is harmed by allowing an industry to use private trials to "hide" its disputes from the public.

SUMMARY JURY TRIALS

summary jury trial An alternative dispute-resolution method that consists of an abbreviated trial, a nonbinding jury verdict, and a settlement conference.

Originating in a federal district court in Cleveland, Ohio, in 1983 as a way to clean up an overcrowded docket, **summary jury trials** are today used in many state and federal courts across the nation for that purpose. The primary advantage of a summary jury trial is that it lasts one day. The judge first instructs a jury on the law. Each side then has a limited amount of time to make an opening statement and to present a summary of the evidence it would have presented at a regular trial.

The jury, which is usually composed of no more than six people, then retires to reach a verdict. The verdict, however, is only advisory, although jurors are usually not aware that their decision does not have a binding effect.

Immediately after receiving the verdict, the parties retire to a settlement conference. Roughly 95 percent of all cases settle at this point. If the parties do not settle, the case is then set for trial. If a case goes to trial, nothing from the summary trial is admissible as evidence.

COURT-ANNEXED ALTERNATIVE DISPUTE RESOLUTION

USE OF COURT-ANNEXED ADR IN THE STATE AND FEDERAL SYSTEMS

In an attempt to relieve the overburdened court systems and in partial recognition of the success of voluntary ADR, many state and federal jurisdictions are mandating that disputants go through some formal ADR process before certain types of cases may be brought to trial. It is difficult to generalize about the use of ADR in the court system, however, because practices vary from jurisdiction to jurisdiction, and even from court to court, as courts experiment with a broad range of programs and approaches. Some courts mandate ADR; others make it voluntary. Some refer almost all civil cases to ADR; others target certain cases by subject matter or by amount in controversy.

In the federal system, for example, in 1984, some federal district courts began adopting programs for mandatory, nonbinding arbitration of disputes involving amounts of less than $100,000. The subsequent passage of the Alternative Dispute Resolution Act of 1998 required all federal district courts to have an ADR program along with a set of rules regarding this program. Under these mandatory programs, less than 10 percent of the cases referred to arbitration end up going to trial. When Congress enacted the ADR Act of 1998, Congress did not create any programs for appellate courts, because all federal circuit courts had already implemented ADR programs. The one exception is the Federal Circuit, which involves cases of more specific and complex subject matter and, therefore, only suggests that parties discuss settlements before a trial. Nevertheless, ADR programs appear to be successful at the appellate level. For example, the Court of Appeals in the Ninth Circuit, similar to most courts at the appellate level, offers opposing parties an opportunity to reach a settlement during the appeals process. Relying primarily on mediation, the Ninth Circuit settled 739 cases in 2000, returning only 98 for additional litigation.

More than half of the states have enacted legislation authorizing ADR in the courts or have established statewide task forces to develop ADR programs. And probably every state has at least one court that has experimented with some form of ADR. Mediation is the most common form of ADR used, due in part to the informality of proceedings, the greater emphasis on cooperation over competition, and the larger amount of control that lawyers and parties have over their cases.

The aggressiveness with which a state encourages the use of ADR methods varies a great deal. For instance, Florida courts mandate the highest degree of ADR, as the courts referred about 113,000 claims to ADR proceedings in 2001. However, in some states, such as Missouri, a completely voluntary approach is used. Courts are simply required to provide all parties with a notice of the availability of ADR services and names and addresses of persons or agencies able to provide such services. Although such a casual approach is criticized on grounds that few people will voluntarily use such services, defenders point out that if people choose ADR, their commitment to the process will be stronger than if they are forced into it and, therefore, it is more likely to work. Many states have adopted programs that require parties to take certain types of cases either to mandatory nonbinding arbitration or to mediation. In fact, at least 28 states require arbitration or mediation for certain kinds of cases or for cases under a particular monetary amount. It is only when the parties cannot reach an agreement through mediation or when one party disagrees with the arbitrator's decision that the court will hear the case.

New Jersey provides one example of a state that requires nonbinding arbitration. For two decades, New Jersey courts have required all civil suits involving vehicular accidents to be sent to arbitration. In 2000, the requirements were extended to include most claims involving personal injury, contracts, and commercial disputes. Consequently, New Jersey experienced a 75 percent increase in the number of arbitration claims filed each year. In Minnesota, parties must consult with each other and decide within 45 days of filing a case which form of ADR they would like to use. Their decision is reported to the court. If the parties cannot agree, or the judge disagrees with their selection, a conference with the judge is held and the judge then orders participants to use a particular ADR method.

Similarly, in the Western District of Missouri, approximately one-third of litigants must select a form of ADR to use. If the litigants cannot decide, an administrator of the court will meet with the parties and their lawyers and make a decision for them.

Some state systems also use ADR at the appellate level. South Carolina was the first state to do so. Under its system, arbitration at the appellate level is optional, but once arbitration has been selected, the decision of the arbitrator is binding.

DIFFERENCES BETWEEN COURT-ANNEXED AND VOLUNTARY ADR

Arbitration. Probably the major difference between court-annexed arbitration and voluntary arbitration is that, in most cases, the court-mandated arbitration is not binding on the parties. If either party objects to the outcome, the case will go to court for a full trial. As you remember from earlier sections of this chapter, the outcome of voluntary arbitration is binding. The right of a dissatisfied party to reject a court-mandated arbitration decision is really necessary, however, in order to preserve the disputants' due process rights. In the interests of streamlining the justice system, the government cannot take away a person's right to his or her day in court.

Of course, a person who chooses to go forward with a trial after rejecting an arbitrator's decision may still be penalized to some extent in a number of states. In some systems, a party who rejects an arbitrator's decision and does not receive a more favorable decision from the trial court may be forced to pay the opposing counsel's court fees. In other systems, that party may be required to pay the costs of the arbitration or other court fees.

Another difference between court-mandated and voluntary arbitration lies in the rules of evidence, which are generally more relaxed in arbitration than in litigation. A few states do treat evidence in court-mandated arbitration in this same relaxed fashion, either allowing almost any evidence to be admitted regardless of whether it would be admissible in court or allowing the arbitrator to decide what evidence is admissible. However, in most states, the same rules of evidence apply to court-annexed arbitration that apply to trials.

Mediation. The primary difference between court-mandated mediation and voluntary mediation is in the attitudes of the parties toward the process. In voluntary mediation, the parties are likely to enter the mediation process with a desire to work out an agreement; in court-ordered mediation, they are much more likely to view mediation as simply a hurdle to go through before the trial. While some have tried to challenge the power of the courts to mandate some form of ADR, the courts have generally upheld this power. For example, in 2002, the First Circuit Court of Appeals, in the case of Re Atlanta Pipe Corporation, held that the district court had inherent power to require the parties to participate in nonbinding mediation and to share the costs.[17]

---

[17] 304 F3d 135 (1st Cir. 2002).

THE FUTURE OF ALTERNATIVE DISPUTE RESOLUTION

You are already familiar with some of the problems associated with each of the ADR methods. You should also be aware of some of the concerns raised about the overall increase in the use of ADR.

First, some legal scholars are concerned about whether a dispute resolution firm can be truly unbiased when one of the parties to the dispute is a major client of the dispute-resolution provider. For example, if a major insurance company includes a binding arbitration clause in all its contracts and specifies that JAMS/Endispute will provide the arbitrator, it may be tempting for JAMS/Endispute to favor the insurance company to try to ensure that it will continue to benefit from the firm's business in the future. The more intense the competition among ADR providers, the more tempted the providers may be to favor large firms. Another issue raised by some critics is whether it is fair for consumers to be coerced into an ADR forum and thereby forced to give up their right to a trial, especially when (1) they may be much more likely to get a higher award from a jury than from an arbitrator and (2) they may find themselves having "agreed" to arbitration not really voluntarily but because of a clause stuck in a purchase agreement that they failed to read. Despite these concerns, however, interest in ADR continues to grow, and there is no reason to think this growth will end in the near future. During 2000, the AAA handled nearly 200,000 cases through ADR, more than double the number of cases handled in 1998.

GLOBAL DIMENSIONS OF ALTERNATIVE DISPUTE RESOLUTION

Internationally, alternative dispute-resolution methods are highly favored. Seventy-three countries currently belong to the United Nations Convention on the Recognition and Enforcement of Foreign Arbitral Awards, commonly referred to as the New York Convention. The primary function of this treaty is to ensure that an arbitration award made in any of the signatory countries is enforceable in the losing party's country. Defenses to enforcement that are allowed under the treaty include one of the parties to the contract lacked the legal capacity to enter into a contract, the losing party did not receive proper notice of the arbitration, and the arbitrator was acting outside the scope of his or her authority when making the awards.

Organizations exist to provide alternative dispute-resolution services for firms of different nations. The most commonly known to U.S. businesspersons is probably the American Arbitration Association. Others include the United Nations Commission of International Trade Law, the London Court of International Arbitration, the Euro-Arab Chamber of Commerce, and the International Chamber of Commerce.

The U.S. policy favors arbitration of international disputes. The following case demonstrates this policy.

CASE 4-4

Mitsubishi Motors Corporation v. Soler Chrysler-Plymouth
United States Supreme Court
473 U.S. 614 (1985)

Plaintiff Mitsubishi, a Japanese corporation, and Chrysler International, a Swiss corporation, formed a joint venture company, Mitsubishi Motors, to distribute worldwide motor vehicles manufactured in the United States and bearing Mitsubishi and Chrysler trademarks. Defendant Soler Chrysler-Plymouth, a dealership incorporated in Puerto Rico, entered into a distributorship agreement with Mitsubishi that included a binding arbitration clause. When Soler began having difficulty selling the requisite number of cars, it first asked Mitsubishi to delay shipment of several orders and then subsequently refused to accept liability for its failure to sell vehicles under the contract.

Plaintiff Mitsubishi filed an action to compel arbitration. The district court ordered arbitration of all claims, including defendants' allegations of antitrust violations. The court of appeals reversed in favor of the defendant. The plaintiff, Mitsubishi, appealed to the U.S. Supreme Court.

Justice Blackmun

We granted certiorari primarily to consider whether an American court could enforce an agreement to resolve antitrust claims by arbitration when that agreement arises from an international transaction. Soler reasons that because it falls within a class of whose benefit the federal and local antitrust laws were passed, the clause cannot be read to contemplate arbitration of these statutory claims.

We do not agree, for we find no warrant in the Arbitration Act for implying in every contract a presumption against arbitration of statutory claims. The "liberal federal policy favoring arbitration agreements," manifested by the Act as a whole, is at bottom a policy guaranteeing the enforcement of private contractual arrangements: the Act simply "creates a body of federal substantive law establishing and regulating the duty to honor an agreement to arbitrate."

There is no reason to depart from these guidelines where a party bound by an arbitration agreement raises claims founded on statutory rights. Of course, courts should remain attuned to well-supported claims that the agreement to arbitrate resulted from the sort of fraud or overwhelming economic power that would provide grounds "for the revocation of any contract." But, absent such compelling considerations, the Act itself provides no basis for disfavoring agreements to arbitrate statutory claims.

By agreeing to arbitrate a statutory claim, a party does not forgo the substantive rights afforded by the statute, it only submits to their resolution in an arbitral, rather than a judicial, forum. It trades the procedures and opportunity for review of the courtroom for the simplicity, informality, and expedition of arbitration.

We now turn to consider whether Soler's antitrust claims are nonarbitrable even though it agreed to arbitrate them. ... [W]e conclude that concerns of international comity, respect for the capacities of foreign and transnational tribunals, and sensitivity to the need of the international commercial system for predictability in the resolution of disputes require that we enforce the parties' agreement, even assuming that a contrary result would be forthcoming in a domestic context.

There is no reason to assume at the outset of the dispute that international arbitration will not provide an adequate mechanism. To be sure, the international arbitral tribunal owes no prior allegiance to the legal norms of particular states; hence, it has no direct obligation to vindicate their statutory dictates. The tribunal, however, is bound to effectuate the intentions of the parties. Where the parties have agreed that the arbitral body is to decide a defined set of claims that includes, as in these cases, those arising from the application of American antitrust law, the tribunal therefore should be bound to decide that dispute in accord with the national law giving rise to the claim.

As international trade has expanded in recent decades, so too has the use of international arbitration to resolve disputes arising in the course of that trade. The controversies that international arbitral institutions are called upon to resolve have increased in diversity as well as in complexity. Yet the potential of these tribunals for efficient disposition of legal disagreements arising from commercial relations has not yet been tested. If they are to take a central place in the international legal order, national courts will need to "shake off the old judicial hostility to arbitration," and also their customary and understandable unwillingness to cede jurisdiction of a claim arising under domestic law to a foreign or transnational tribunal. To this extent, at least, it will be necessary for national courts to subordinate domestic notions of arbitrability to the international policy favoring commercial arbitration.

Accordingly, we "require this representative of the American business community to honor its bargain," ... by holding this agreement to arbitrate "enforce[able] in accord with the explicit provisions of the Arbitration Act."

[As to the issue of arbitrability] *Reversed and remanded* in favor of the Plaintiff, Mitsubishi.

SUMMARY

As the burden on our court system increases, many disputants are turning to alternative ways of resolving disputes. These alternatives include (1) negotiation and settlement, (2) arbitration, (3) mediation, (4) minitrials, (5) early neutral case evaluation, (6) private trials, and (7) summary jury trials.

Which, if any, alternative is best for an individual depends on the situation. The primary benefits that come from these alternatives, in varying degrees, include (1) less publicity, (2) less time, (3) less expense, (4) more convenient proceedings, and (5) a better chance to have a reasonable relationship with the other disputant in the future.

Alternative dispute resolution (ADR) also has its critics. Some of their concerns are that compulsory ADR may force parties to give up their "day in court," that a party who consistently procures ADR services from one firm will end up with a "neutral" that is biased toward that party, and that we will end up with a two-tier system of justice—an efficient private system and an overburdened public one.

REVIEW QUESTIONS

4-1 Explain why the use of ADR is increasing.

4-2 When will a judge overturn an arbitrator's decision?

4-3 Explain how to secure arbitration as a means of resolving a dispute.

4-4 Why are some people opposed to the growing use of arbitration?

4-5 What are the basic obligations of an arbitrator according to the Arbitrator's Code of Ethics?

4-6 Identify the factors that would lead a disputant to favor mediation as a dispute-resolution method.

REVIEW PROBLEMS

4-7 McGraw and Duffy have a contract that includes a binding arbitration clause. The clause provides for arbitration of any dispute arising out of the contract. The clause also provides that the arbitrator is authorized to award damages of up to $100,000 in any dispute arising out of the contract. McGraw allegedly breaches the contract. Duffy seeks arbitration, and the arbitrator, given the willfulness of the breach and the magnitude of its consequences, awards Duffy $150,000 in damages. Would a court uphold the award? Why or why not?

4-8 Sam and Mary enter into a contract that does not include a provision for arbitration. Mary wants to arbitrate the dispute, but Sam believes that arbitration is not possible because there is no binding arbitration clause in the contract. How can the parties secure arbitration?

4-9 Howard and Hannah decide to resolve a contract dispute through arbitration. They select their arbitrator through a private service. The arbitrator returns a significant award for Howard. The weekend after receiving a notice of the award, Hannah finds out from one of Howard's coworkers that, although the arbitrator and Howard acted as if they did not know each other, they actually had been college roommates. Does Hannah have any basis for getting the award set aside?

4-10 Eloise is hired as a pharmacist and signs an employment agreement that includes a provision that she will submit any employment disputes to arbitration. After being on the job for three years, she is denied a promotion that she feels she deserved. She files a sex discrimination charge with the EEOC and a lawsuit in the federal district court. The employer files a motion to compel arbitration. Will she be forced to arbitrate her claims? Why or why not?

4-11 Boxley Corporation and Eberly Corporation have a contract dispute before an arbitrator. Eberly wants to present evidence of prior contract disputes the two have had, but the arbitrator refuses to receive that evidence, saying it is not relevant to the alleged breach of contract at issue before him. When Boxley receives an award from the arbitrator that entitles it to significant damages from Eberly, the latter appeals the arbitrator's decision on the grounds that the excluded evidence would have changed the outcome. Why is Eberly likely or unlikely to have the award overturned?

4-12 Marshall files a complaint against S.A. & E., a brokerage firm registered with the Securities and Exchange Commission. The complaint alleges a violation of the Securities Exchange Act by engaging in fraudulent excessive trading. S.A. & E. files a motion to dismiss the case because Marshall had signed a customer agreement that included in its terms a promise to submit all disputes arising under their accounts to arbitration. Marshall argues that, owing to the egregious nature of S.A. & E.'s conduct, Marshall should be entitled to his "day in court" and the binding arbitration clause should be nullified. Why will the court grant or deny S.A. & E's motion?

CASE PROBLEMS

4-13 Saturn adopted a "Mission and Philosophy" of manufacturing and selling cars. As part of this mission, all Saturn dealer agreements contained a binding alternative dispute-resolution clause. This clause provides for a mandatory two-step process that includes mediation and binding arbitration, which provides for document discovery and a hearing. The decision of the arbitration panel is final and unappealable, except as provided by the Federal Arbitration Act. Saturn refuses to contract with anyone who refuses to agree to this provision.

Virginia passed a law that prohibited automobile manufacturers and dealers from entering into agreements that contain mandatory alternative dispute-resolution provisions, such as Saturn's contracts include. Saturn challenged the law as being preempted by the Federal Arbitration Act. Was Saturn's challenge successful? Why or why not? *Saturn Distributing Corporation v. Williams,* 498 U.S. 983 (1990)

4-14 Terry Rogers and Larry Mays are the sole shareholders of MRM, which owns and operates several Kentucky Fried Chicken/Taco Bell ("KFC") franchises. From January 3 through August 2000, Tonya Cooper worked as an assistant manager of MRM's KFC store in Waverly, Tennessee, at $400–450 per week, plus possible bonuses. On January 5, 2000, MRM required her to sign a document entitled "Arbitration of Employee Rights," which provided: "Because of the delay and expense of the court systems, KFC and I agree to use confidential binding arbitration for any claims that arise between me and KFC, its related companies, and/or their current or former employees. Such claims would include any concerning compensation, employment (including, but not limited to any claims concerning sexual harassment), or termination of

employment. Before arbitration, I agree: (i) first, to present any such claims in full written detail to KFC; (ii) next, to complete any KFC internal review process; and (iii) finally, to complete any external administrative remedy (such as with the Equal Employment Opportunity Commission). In any arbitration, the then prevailing rules of the American Arbitration Association (and, to the extent not inconsistent, the then prevailing rules of the [FAA]) will apply."

The parties agree that MRM did not separately advise Cooper that she was giving up her right to a jury trial, nor did they provide her with a copy of the AAA's rules. Cooper alleges that she was forced to quit in August 2000 as a result of sexual harassment. She found a job at another restaurant, where she earned $7,200 in 2001, and tended bar part-time, earning an additional $300 to $500 per week as of early 2002. In January 2001, Cooper filed a Charge of Discrimination with the EEOC, which issued a Dismissal and Notice of Rights in September 2001.

Cooper then filed a lawsuit against MRM in December 2001. MRM filed a motion to compel arbitration. Following oral argument, the district court denied MRM's motion on May 1, 2002, on the grounds that the binding arbitration clause constituted an unconscionable adhesion contract. The district court based its ruling on its findings that MRM prepared the agreement, a standardized form, with no negotiation or input from Cooper. MRM appealed on May 28, 2002. What do you believe the outcome of the appeal was? Why? *Tonya Cooper v. MRM Investment Company, Term Rogers and Larry Mays,* 367 F.3d 493 (2004)

4-15 Plaintiffs-Appellants were twenty-three individuals who were employees of Seagull Energy. The Plaintiffs comprised virtually all of the employees of the

Operations and Construction Group ("O&C Group"), a division of Seagull. Seagull had adopted a Management Stability Plan (the "Plan") in 1995 which provided that employees involuntarily terminated within two years after a "change in control," such as a merger, would receive specified severance benefits. It provided that disputes under the Plan should be submitted to arbitration.

After a merger, Plaintiffs did not timely receive severance benefits pursuant to the terms of the Plan, so they each filed a claim with the Ocean Organization and Compensation Committee (the "Committee"), which was also the named fiduciary with the power to administer the Plan and to review claims. It was primarily composed of outside Directors and Senior Ocean executives. The Committee based its decision on a packet of information, including a denial letter drafted by the company's general counsel. The Committee met for one hour and decided to deny benefits.

The plaintiffs filed suit in Texas state district court. Ocean removed to federal court and then moved the district court to compel arbitration. The district court ordered "plaintiffs' claims" to be arbitrated. The parties agreed on an arbitrator and submitted the case. The arbitrator entered a forty-two-page opinion awarding the Plaintiffs benefits under the Plan totaling some $1.5 million plus $75,000 attorney fees and 6% pre-award interest and 10% post-award interest.

Ocean then filed an application to vacate the award in the district court, arguing that the arbitrator had exceeded his authority by reviewing the merits of the Plan and its amendments. Plaintiffs' Statement of Claim had clearly presented to the arbitrator all of the issues decided by the arbitrator. The defendant never objected to any of the issues submitted to arbitration by plaintiffs until after the arbitrator decided against defendant. The district court vacated the award, finding that the arbitrator had "exceeded his powers, misunderstood the law, and misread the documents."

Plaintiffs appealed, asserting that the district court improperly applied a de novo standard of review ignoring the considerable deference due arbitration awards. Ocean argued that the arbitrator exceeded his powers by reviewing the merits of the Plan and its amendments. On appeal, was the district court order to vacate the arbitration award upheld? Why or why not? *Harold A. Kergosien, et al. v. Ocean Energy, Inc.*, 2004 WL 2451351 (5th Cir.(Tex.)).

4-16 AutoNation ran a chain of used-car lots. Its "Purchase Agreements," or sales contracts, contained a general arbitration clause requiring all disputes to go to the American Arbitration Association. Customers who financed their vehicles also signed a "Retail Installment Contract." It did not have an arbitration provision. The Purchase Agreements noted that AutoNation charged a documentary fee of $50, the highest amount allowed under Texas law. For two months, due to a computer error, AutoNation had a $95 documentary fee on the Retail Installment Contract. Leroy, suing on behalf of herself and all other members of a proposed class of buyers who paid $95, sought class action status. AutoNation opposed the class certification and moved to compel the enforcement of the arbitration clause. The district court held that the Retail Installment Contract did not have an arbitration clause, so allowed the litigation, and certified the class. AutoNation appealed. How do you think the appellate court ruled? Why? *AutoNation USA Corp. v. Leroy*, 105 S.W.3d 190 (Ct.App.,Tex., 2003).

4-17 David McCrory had worked as a law clerk for approximately three and a half years when he was terminated. He believed he was fired because of an impending two-week leave of absence for annual military training and filed a wrongful termination action against the firm. The firm moved to compel arbitration, citing an agreement signed by McCrory.

In opposing the motion, McCrory argued that he had signed the agreement because he "was told that if I did not sign the agreement, that I would be fired. I was given no choice but to do it." He also declared the cost of the arbitration "will be a severe hardship to me."

The agreement provided: "Because of the mutual benefits ... which private binding arbitration can provide both Employer and myself, I voluntarily agree that any claim, dispute, and/or controversy ... arising from, related to, or having any relationship or connection whatsoever with my ... employment ... whether based on tort, contract, statutory, or equitable law, or otherwise ... shall be submitted to and determined exclusively by binding arbitration under the Federal Arbitration Act." The agreement added the requirement that the arbitrator "shall be a retired California Superior Court Judge." Such arbitrators charge a minimum of $400 per hour and typically require deposits of $8,000 before proceedings begin.

The agreement also requires appellate-type review by a second arbitrator at either party's request. The sentence at the end of the arbitration provisions reads: "I understand by voluntarily agreeing to this binding arbitration provision, both I and Employer give up our rights to trial by jury." The agreement provides for the signature of the employee only.

The trial court granted the motion, and McCrory appealed. The state supreme court used a two-part analysis to determine whether to enforce or vacate the lower court's order. Explain how you believe the court would analyze this case, and what the consequent outcome would be. *McCrory v. Superior Court*, 104 Cal. Rptr. 2d 504 (2001)

4-18 Scott Folb was fired from his position as administrative director at the Motion Picture Industry Pension and Health Plans (the "Plans"). Folb argued that the directors at the Plans fired him in retaliation for various whistleblowing activities in which he was involved. Folb had objected to and reported various misbehaviors by the Plans. The Plans argued that Folb was fired for sexually harassing another employee, Vivian Vasquez.

Vasquez had filed a sexual harassment complaint against Folb, her manager. In February 1997, Vasquez and the Plans engaged in formal mediation to settle Vasquez's sexual harassment claims. Vasquez and the Plans signed an agreement ensuring the confidentiality of the mediation. Vasquez's counsel prepared a mediation brief and provided copies of this brief to the Plans' attorney as well as the mediator. Vasquez and the Plans did not reach an agreement during the mediation; however, they settled the claim during later negotiations.

Earlier, the Plans had hired Deborah Saxe, an outside attorney, to investigate Vasquez's sexual harassment claim. At some point, the counsel for the Plans gave Saxe a copy of the mediation brief prepared by Vasquez's attorney, who did not authorize the Plans to give this brief to Saxe.

Folb, in his own claim against the Plans, wanted the Plans to produce (1) Vasquez's mediation brief, (2) correspondence between Vasquez's attorney and counsel for the Plans regarding mediation or other settlement discussions, and (3) notes prepared by Vasquez's attorney regarding settlement communications. Folb argued that the Plans claimed that it legitimately fired Folb because of the sexual harassment. Yet, Folb argues, in the mediation and negotions, the Plans may have argued that Vasquez was never sexually harassed at all. The Plans refused to produce the information because it asserted that the documents were confidential. Magistrate Judge Woehrle denied Folb's motion to compel production of the documents, and Folb objected. Did the court require the Plans to produce the documents? Why or why not? *Folb v. Motion Picture Industry Pension and Health Plans et al.*, 16 F.Supp. 2d 1164 (C.D. Cal. 1998)

ASSIGNMENT ON THE INTERNET

After reading this chapter you should have an understanding about the advantages and disadvantages of ADR. Using the Internet, find a private mediation and arbitration firm, such as National Arbitration and Mediation. Visit its Web site (www.namadr.com) and create a list of questions you would want to ask before hiring its services by applying the information in this chapter and your critical thinking skills.

What kind of problems might be associated with this company's process? Where do its mediators or arbitrators come from? What qualities would you look for in choosing a mediator or arbitrator? What are the advantages of using this company? What are the disadvantages?

Now that you have evaluated one ADR firm, make a comparison to another firm that you found on the Internet (for example, www.resolvemydispute.com). What distinguishes one firm from the other? Why would you choose one and not the other? What factors affect your answer? When would you forgo ADR and use the court system?

 ## ON THE INTERNET

www.adrr.com This ADR site contains substantial online materials for ADR and particularly for mediation.
www.cybersettle.com This site is another online dispute-resolution service.
www.pon.harvard.edu/main/home/index.php3 This Harvard Law School page is dedicated to improving the theory and practice of negotiation and dispute resolution.
www.adr.org This is the home page of the American Arbitration Association.
www.sixthform.info/law/02_cases/mod2/11_2_adr.htm For examples of cases that have been resolved by ADR, visit this Web site. The names of recent disputes and a brief summary are provided for each case. Links to other pages on the site may also be of use in exploring ADR methods.
www4.law.cornell.edu/uscode/9 The Federal Arbitration Act can be found at this Web site.

5

CONSTITUTIONAL PRINCIPLES

- **THE CONSTITUTION**
- **FEDERALISM**
- **SEPARATION OF POWERS**
- **THE IMPACT OF THE COMMERCE CLAUSE ON BUSINESS**
- **THE TAXING AND SPENDING POWERS OF THE FEDERAL GOVERNMENT**
- **THE IMPACT OF THE AMENDMENTS ON BUSINESS**

Fiercely independent, highly individualistic, and very proud of their country would be a good characterization of Americans. Many say there is no place they would rather live than the United States. Much of their pride stems from a belief that we have a strong Constitution, which secures for all individuals their most fundamental rights. Most people, however, are not aware of precisely what their constitutional rights are or of how to go about enforcing those rights. This chapter provides the future business manager with basic knowledge of the constitutional framework of our country as well as an overview of how some of the constitutional provisions have a significant impact on the legal environment of business.

Critical Thinking About the Law

The Constitution secures numerous rights for U.S. citizens. If we did not have these rights, our lives would be very different. Furthermore, businesses would be forced to alter their practices because they would not enjoy the various constitutional protections. As you will soon learn, various components of the Constitution, such as the Commerce Clause and the Bill of Rights, offer guidance and protection for businesses. The following questions will help sharpen your critical thinking about the protection and guidance for businesses offered by the Constitution.

1. One of the basic elements in the Constitution is the separation of powers in the government. What ethical norm would guide the framers' thinking in creating a system with a separation of powers and a system of checks and balances?

   Clue: Consider what might happen if one branch of government became too strong.

2. If the framers of the Constitution wanted to offer the protection of unrestricted speech for citizens and businesses, what ethical norm would they view as most important?

   Clue: Return to the list of ethical norms in Chapter 1. Which ethical norm might the framers view as least important in protecting unrestricted speech?

3. Why should you, as a future business manager, be knowledgeable about the basic protections offered by the Constitution?

   Clue: If you were ignorant of the constitutional protections, how might your business suffer?

THE CONSTITUTION

The Constitution provides the legal framework for our nation. The articles of the Constitution set out the basic structure of our government and the respective roles of the state and federal governments. The Amendments to the Constitution, especially the first ten, were primarily designed to establish and protect individual rights.

FEDERALISM

federalism A system of government in which power is divided between a central authority and constituent political units.

Underlying the system of government established by the Constitution is the principle of **federalism**, which means that the authority to govern is divided between two sovereigns, or supreme lawmakers. In the United States, these two sovereigns are the state and federal governments. Federalism allocates the power to control local matters to local governments. This allocation is embodied in the U.S. Constitution. Under the Constitution, all powers that are neither given exclusively to the federal government nor taken from the states are reserved to the states. The federal government has only those powers granted to it in the Constitution. Therefore, whenever federal legislation that affects business is passed, the question of the source of authority for that regulation always arises. The Commerce Clause is the predominant source of authority for the federal regulation of business, as we will see later.

In some areas, the state and federal governments have concurrent authority; that is, both governments have the power to regulate the matter in question. This situation arises when authority to regulate in an area has been expressly given to the federal government by the Constitution. In such cases, a state may regulate in the area as long as its regulation does not conflict with any federal regulation of the same subject matter. A conflict arises when a regulated party cannot comply with both the state and the federal laws at the same time. When the state law is more restrictive, such that compliance with the state law is automatically compliance with the federal law, the state law will usually be valid. For example, as discussed in Chapter 21, in many areas of environmental regulation, states may impose much more stringent pollution-control standards than those imposed by federal law.

SUPREMACY CLAUSE

The outcome of conflicts between state and federal laws is dictated by the **Supremacy Clause**. This clause, found in Article V of the Constitution, provides that the Constitution, laws, and treaties of the United States constitute the supreme law of the land, "any Thing in the Constitution or Laws of any State to the Contrary notwithstanding." This principle is known as the principle of **federal supremacy**: Any state or local law that directly conflicts with the federal Constitution, laws, or treaties is void. Federal laws include rules promulgated by federal administrative agencies. Exhibit 5-1 illustrates the application of the Supremacy Clause to state regulation.

Supremacy Clause Provides that the U.S. Constitution and all laws and treaties of the United States constitute the supreme law of the land; found in Article V.

federal supremacy Principle that states that any state or local law that directly conflicts with the federal Constitution, laws, or treaties is void.

FEDERAL PREEMPTION

The Supremacy Clause is also the basis for the doctrine of **federal preemption**. This doctrine is used to strike down a state law that, although it does not directly conflict with a federal law, attempts to regulate an area in which federal legislation is so pervasive that it is evident that the U.S. Congress wanted only federal regulation in that general area. It is often said in these cases that federal law "preempts the field." Cases of federal preemption are especially likely to arise in matters pertaining to interstate commerce, in which a local regulation

federal preemption In an area in which federal regulation is pervasive, state legislation cannot stand.

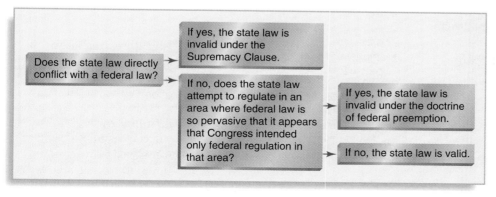

EXHIBIT 5-1

APPLICATION OF THE SUPREMACY CLAUSE TO STATE REGULATION

imposes a substantial burden on the flow of interstate commerce through a particular state. This situation is discussed in some detail in the section on the Commerce Clause.

SEPARATION OF POWERS

The U.S. Constitution, in its first three articles, establishes three independent branches of the federal government, each with its own predominant and independent power. These three are the legislative, executive, and judicial branches. Each branch was made independent of the others and was given a separate sphere of power to prevent any one source from obtaining too much power and consequently dominating the government.

The doctrine of **separation of powers** calls for Congress, the legislative branch, to enact legislation and appropriate funds. The president is commander in chief of the armed forces and is also charged with ensuring that the laws are faithfully executed. The judicial branch is charged with interpreting the laws in the course of applying them to particular disputes. No member of one branch owes his or her tenure in that position to a member of any other branch; no branch can encroach on the power of another. This system is often referred to as being a system of checks and balances; that is, the powers given to each branch operate to keep the other branches from being able to seize enough power to dominate the government. Exhibit 5-2 provides a portrait of this system.

separation of powers
Constitutional doctrine whereby the legislative branch enacts laws and appropriates funds, the executive branch sees that the laws are faithfully executed, and the judicial branch interprets the laws.

EXHIBIT 5-2 SYSTEM OF CHECKS AND BALANCES

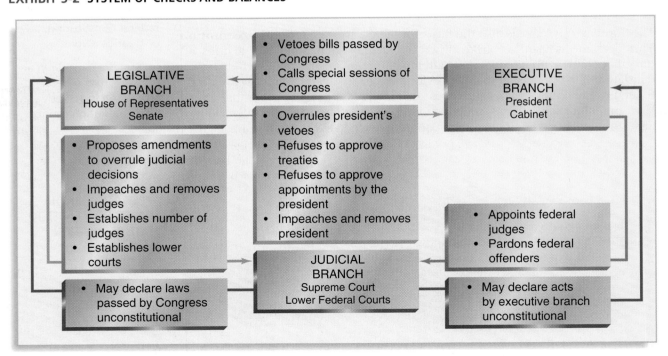

Despite this delicate system of checks and balances, there have been numerous occasions when a question arose as to whether one branch was attempting to encroach on the domain of another. This situation most recently arose in an unusual context: a sexual harassment charge against President Bill Clinton.

CASE 5-1

William Jefferson Clinton v. Paula Corbin Jones
Supreme Court of the United States
520 U.S. 681, 117 S.Ct. 1636 (1997)

Plaintiff Paula Jones filed a civil action against defendant President Bill Clinton, alleging that he made "abhorrent" sexual advances. She sought $75,000 in actual damages and $100,000 in punitive damages.

Defendant Clinton sought to dismiss the claim on the grounds of presidential immunity, or, alternatively, to delay the proceedings until his term of office had expired.

The district court denied the motion to dismiss and ordered discovery to proceed, but it also ordered that the trial be stayed until the end of the president's term. The court of appeals affirmed the denial of the motion to dismiss and reversed the stay of the trial. President Clinton appealed to the U.S. Supreme Court.

Justice Stevens

Petitioner's principal submission—that "in all but the most exceptional cases," the Constitution affords the President temporary immunity from civil damages litigation arising out of events that occurred before he took office—cannot be sustained on the basis of precedent.

Only three sitting presidents have been defendants in civil litigation involving their actions prior to taking office. Complaints against Theodore Roosevelt and Harry Truman had been dismissed before they took office; the dismissals were affirmed after their respective inaugurations. Two companion cases arising out of an automobile accident were filed against John F. Kennedy in 1960 during the Presidential campaign. After taking office, he unsuccessfully argued that his status as Commander in Chief gave him a right to a stay. The motion for a stay was denied by the District Court, and the matter was settled out of court. Thus, none of those cases sheds any light on the constitutional issue before us.

The principal rationale for affording certain public servants immunity from suits for money damages arising out of their official acts is inapplicable to unofficial conduct. In cases involving prosecutors, legislators, and judges we have repeatedly explained that the immunity serves the public interest in enabling such officials to perform their designated functions effectively without fear that a particular decision may give rise to personal liability.

That rationale provided the principal basis for our holding that a former president of the United States was "enti-

tled to absolute immunity from damages liability predicated on his official acts." Our central concern was to avoid rendering the President "unduly cautious in the discharge of his official duties."

This reasoning provides no support for an immunity for unofficial conduct. ... "[T]he sphere of protected action must be related closely to the immunity's justifying purposes." But we have never suggested that the President, or any other official, has an immunity that extends beyond the scope of any action taken in an official capacity.

Moreover, when defining the scope of an immunity for acts clearly taken within an official capacity, we have applied a functional approach. "Frequently our decisions have held that an official's absolute immunity should extend only to acts in performance of particular functions of his office." Petitioner's strongest argument supporting his immunity claim is based on the text and structure of the Constitution. The President argues for a postponement of the judicial proceedings that will determine whether he violated any law. His argument is grounded in the character of the office that was created by Article II of the Constitution, and relies on separation-of-powers principles.

As a starting premise, petitioner contends that he occupies a unique office with powers and responsibilities so vast and important that the public interest demands that he devote his undivided time and attention to his public duties. He submits that—given the nature of the office—the doctrine of separation of powers places limits on the authority of the Federal Judiciary to interfere with the Executive Branch that would be transgressed by allowing this action to proceed.

We have no dispute with the initial premise of the argument. We have long recognized the "unique position in the constitutional scheme" that this office occupies.

It does not follow, however, that separation-of-powers principles would be violated by allowing this action to proceed. The doctrine of separation of powers is concerned with the allocation of official power among the three co-equal branches of our Government. The Framers "built into the tripartite Federal Government ... a self-executing safeguard against the encroachment or aggrandizement of one branch at the expense of the other." Thus, for example, the

Congress may not exercise the judicial power to revise final judgments, or the executive power to manage an airport.

… [I]n this case there is no suggestion that the Federal Judiciary is being asked to perform any function that might in some way be described as "executive." Respondent is merely asking the courts to exercise their core Article III jurisdiction to decide cases and controversies. Whatever the outcome of this case, there is no possibility that the decision will curtail the scope of the official powers of the Executive Branch. The litigation of questions that relate entirely to the unofficial conduct of the individual who happens to be the President poses no perceptible risk of misallocation of either judicial power or executive power.

Rather than arguing that the decision of the case will produce either an aggrandizement of judicial power or a narrowing of executive power, petitioner contends that— as a by-product of an otherwise traditional exercise of judicial power—burdens will be placed on the President that will hamper the performance of his official duties. We have recognized that "[e]ven when a branch does not arrogate power to itself … the separation-of-powers doctrine requires that a branch not impair another in the performance of its constitutional duties." As a factual matter, petitioner contends that this particular case—as well as the potential additional litigation that an affirmance of the Court of Appeals judgment might spawn—may impose an unacceptable burden on the President's time and energy, and thereby impair the effective performance of his office.

Petitioner's predictive judgment finds little support in either history or the relatively narrow compass of the issues raised in this particular case. If the past is any indicator, it seems unlikely that a deluge of such litigation will ever engulf the presidency. As for the case at hand, if properly managed by the District Court, it appears to us highly unlikely to occupy any substantial amount of petitioner's time.

Of greater significance, petitioner errs by presuming that interactions between the Judicial Branch and the Executive, even quite burdensome interactions, necessarily rise to the level of constitutionally forbidden impairment of the Executive's ability to perform its constitutionally mandated functions. Separation of powers does not mean that the branches "ought to have no partial agency in, or no control over the acts of each other." The fact that a federal court's exercise of its traditional Article III jurisdiction may significantly burden the time and attention of the Chief Executive is not sufficient to establish a violation of the Constitution. Two long-settled propositions … support that conclusion.

First, we have long held that when the President takes official action, the Court has the authority to determine whether he has acted within the law. Perhaps the most dramatic example of such a case is our holding that President Truman exceeded his constitutional authority when he issued an order directing the Secretary of Commerce to take possession of and operate most of the Nation's steel mills, in order to avert a national catastrophe. *Youngstown Sheet & Tube Co. v. Sawyer*, 343 U.S. 579 (1952).

Second, it is also settled that the President is subject to judicial process in appropriate circumstances. We … held that President Nixon was obligated to comply with a subpoena commanding him to produce certain tape recordings of his conversations with his aides. As we explained, "neither the doctrine of separation of powers, nor the need for confidentiality of high-level communications, without more, can sustain an absolute, unqualified presidential privilege of immunity from judicial process under all circumstances."

Sitting Presidents have responded to court orders to provide testimony and other information with sufficient frequency that such interactions between the Judicial and Executive Branches can scarcely be thought a novelty. President Ford complied with an order to give a deposition in a criminal trial, and President Clinton has twice given videotaped testimony in criminal proceedings.

In sum, "[i]t is settled law that the separation-of-powers doctrine does not bar every exercise of jurisdiction over the President of the United States." If the Judiciary may severely burden the Executive Branch by reviewing the legality of the President's official conduct, and if it may direct appropriate process to the President himself, it must follow that the federal courts have power to determine the legality of his unofficial conduct. The burden on the President's time and energy that is a mere by-product of such review surely cannot be considered as onerous as the direct burden imposed by judicial review and the occasional invalidation of his official actions. We therefore hold that the doctrine of separation of powers does not require federal courts to stay all private actions against the President until he leaves office.

In all events, the question whether a specific case should receive exceptional treatment is more appropriately the subject of the exercise of judicial discretion than an interpretation of the Constitution.

Reversed in part. *Affirmed* in part in favor of
Respondent, Jones.

COMMENT: After this case was sent back for trial on the merits, the case was ultimately dismissed on April 1, 1998, on a motion for summary judgment on grounds that the plaintiff's allegations, even if true, failed to state a claim of criminal sexual assault or sexual harassment. It is ironic that despite the high court's claim that the case would be "highly unlikely to occupy any substantial amount of the petitioner's time," matters arising out of this case managed to occupy so much of the president's time and become such a focus of a media frenzy that many people were calling for the media to reduce coverage of the issues so the president could do his job.[1]

---

[1] *Paula Corbin Jones v. William Jefferson Clinton and Danny Ferguson*, 12 F.Supp.2d 931 (E.D. Ark 1998).

Linking Law & Business

Finance

The principle behind the separation of powers in government is also modeled in another realm of business. In your accounting class, you learned that internal controls are the policies and procedures used to create a greater assurance that the objectives of an organization will be met. One feature of internal controls is the separation of duties. This feature calls for the functions of authorization, recording, and custody to be exercised by different individuals. The likelihood of illegal acts by employees is reduced when the responsibility of completing a task is dependent on more than one person. If there are three people responsible for carrying out a particular task, then each person acts as a deterrent to the other two in regard to the possibility of embezzlement by one or more employees. Therefore, the chance of dishonest behavior is minimized when employees act as a check on the other employees involved in striving to meet organizational objectives.

Source: T. Edmonds, F. McNair, E. Milam, and P. Olds, *Fundamental Financial Accounting Concepts* (New York: McGraw-Hill, 2000), pp. 259–260.

Cases like Jones v. Clinton are not common. The reason is not that each branch generally operates carefully within its own sphere of power. Rather, the explanation lies in the fact that because it is difficult to determine where one branch's authority ends and another's begins, each branch rarely challenges the power of its competing branches. The powers of each branch were established so that, although the branches are separate, each branch still influences the actions of the others. And, although the branches are independent and have their own separate functions, there is still a substantial amount of interaction among the three.

THE IMPACT OF THE COMMERCE CLAUSE ON BUSINESS

THE COMMERCE CLAUSE AS A SOURCE OF FEDERAL AUTHORITY

The primary powers of Congress are listed in Article I of the Constitution. It is important to remember that Congress has only limited legislative power. Congress possesses only that legislative power granted to it by the Constitution. Thus, all acts of Congress not specifically authorized by the Constitution or necessary to accomplish an authorized end are invalid.

The **Commerce Clause** provides the basis for most of the federal regulation of business today. This clause empowers the legislature to "regulate Commerce with foreign Nations, and among the several States, and with the Indian Tribes." Early in our history, the Supreme Court was committed to a laissez-faire ideology, an ideology that was grounded in individualism. A narrow

Commerce Clause
Empowers Congress to regulate commerce with foreign nations, with Indian tribes, and among the states; found in Article I.

interpretation of the Commerce Clause means that only a limited amount of trade or exchange can be regulated by Congress.

Under the Court's initial narrow interpretation, the Commerce Clause was interpreted to apply to only the transportation of goods. Manufacturing of goods, even of goods that were going to be sold in another state, did not have a direct effect on interstate commerce and, thus, was not subject to federal regulation. Businesses conducted solely in one state were similarly excluded from the authority of Congress. Under this restrictive interpretation, numerous federal regulations, such as laws attempting to regulate the use of child labor in manufacturing plants,[2] were struck down.

During the 1930s, the Supreme Court's interpretation of the Commerce Clause was broadened to allow a greater scope for federal regulations. In *NLRB v. Jones & Laughlin Steel Corp.*,[3] for example, the Court said that "[a]lthough activities may be intrastate in character when separately considered, if they have such a close and substantial relationship to interstate commerce that their control is essential or appropriate to protect that commerce from burdens or obstructions, Congress cannot be denied the power to exercise that control." Exhibit 5-3 lists additional cases demonstrating the range of activities that courts have interpreted to be subject to federal regulation under the Commerce Clause.

As the cases in Exhibit 5-3 illustrate, during most of the twentieth century, almost any activity, even if purely intrastate, could be regulated by the federal government if it substantially affected interstate commerce. The effect may be direct or indirect, as the U.S. Supreme Court demonstrated in the 1942 case of *Wickard v. Filburn*,[4] when it upheld federal regulation of the production of wheat on a farm in Ohio that produced only 239 bushels of wheat solely for consumption on the farm. The Court's rationale was that even though one wheat farmer's activities might not matter, the combination of a lot of small farmers' activities could have a substantial impact on the national wheat market. This broad interpretation of the Commerce Clause has made possible much of the legislation covered in other sections of this book.

More recently, however, the Supreme Court has appeared to be scrutinizing congressional attempts to regulate based on the Commerce Clause a little more closely. In the 1995 case of *United States v. Lopez*,[5] the U.S. Supreme Court found that Congress had exceeded its authority under the Commerce Clause when it passed the Gun-Free School Zone Act, a law that banned the possession of guns within 1,000 feet of any school. The Court found the statute to be unconstitutional because Congress was attempting to regulate in an area that had "nothing to do with commerce, or any sort of economic enterprise." At first, commentators did not see this case, decided in a 5-4 vote, as a major shift in the Supreme Court's Commerce Clause interpretation. However, as the following case demonstrates, *Lopez* may have indeed indicated that the courts are going to look more closely at congressional attempts to regulate interstate commerce, an action that seems consistent with the high court's increasing tendency to support greater power for states in conflicts between the state and federal governments.

---

[2] *Hammer v. Dagenhart*, 247 U.S. 251 (1918).

[3] 301 U.S. 1 (1937).

[4] 317 U.S. 111 (1942).

[5] 514 U.S. 549 (1995).

Case	Federal Statute	Activity and Rationale for Decision
United States v. Lake, 985 F.2d 265 (1995)	Federal Mine Safety and Health Act	Defendant operated a mine whose coal was sold locally, and he purchased miningsupplies from local dealers and consumed commercially produced electricity. "Even if coal production at the mine was small and sales of coal were entirely local . . . such small-scale efforts, when combined with others, could influence interstate coal pricing and demand."
International House of Pancakes v. Theodore Pinnock, 844 F. Supp. 574 (1993)	Americans with Disabilities Act	Although defendant's restaurant was located in a single state, it was located within two miles of two interstate highways and there were three hotels within walking distance. The restaurant was also a franchise of a large, international, publicly held corporation that had 547 franchises in 35 states, Japan, and Canada. These facts were sufficient evidence that the restaurant's activities affected interstate commerce.
Perez, Petitioner v. United States, 402 U.S. 146 (1971)	Consumer Credit Protection Act	Loansharking activities, whereby criminals use extortion to collect loan payments, is a local activity, "but in its national setting it is one way that organized interstate crime holds its guns to the heads of the poor . . . and syphons funds from numerous locations to finance its national operations" and thereby affects interstate commerce.

EXHIBIT 5-3

INTRASTATE ACTIVITIES THAT AFFECTED INTERSTATE COMMERCE

CASE 5-2

Christy Brzonkala v. Antonio J. Morrison et al.
United States Supreme Court
529 U.S. 598, 120 S.Ct. 1740 (2000)

Petitioner Christy Brzonkala, Antonio Morrison, and James Crawford were students at Virginia Polytechnic Institute (Virginia Tech). Brzonkala alleged that, within 30 minutes of meeting Morrison and Crawford, they assaulted and repeatedly raped her. After the attack, Morrison allegedly told Brzonkala, "You better not have any … diseases." In the months following the rape, in the dormitory's dining room, Morrison also allegedly made boasting, debasing, and vulgar remarks about what he would do to women. Brzonkala alleges that this attack,

and Morrison's subsequent behavior, caused her to become severely emotionally disturbed and depressed. She sought assistance from a university psychiatrist, who prescribed antidepressant medication. Shortly after the rape, Brzonkala stopped attending classes and withdrew from the university.

Brzonkala filed a complaint against respondents under Virginia Tech's Sexual Assault Policy. While Morrison was initially found guilty and suspended for two semesters, his punishment was ultimately set aside.

Brzonkala subsequently sued Morrison, Crawford, and Virginia Tech in federal court, alleging, among other claims, that Morrison's and Crawford's attack violated the Violence Against Women Act. Morrison and Crawford moved to dismiss this complaint on the grounds that it failed to state a claim and that the Act's (Section 13981's) civil remedy was unconstitutional.

The district court held that Brzonkala's complaint stated a claim against Morrison and Crawford under Section 13981 but dismissed the complaint because it concluded that Congress lacked authority to enact the section. The United States Court of Appeals, by a divided vote, affirmed the district court's conclusion that Congress lacked constitutional authority to enact Section 13981's civil remedy.

Chief Justice Rehnquist

In these cases we consider the constitutionality of 42 U.S.C. Section 13981. ... Section 13981 was part of the Violence Against Women Act of 1994. ... It states that "[a]ll persons within the United States shall have the right to be free from crimes of violence motivated by gender." To enforce that right, subsection (c) declares:

"A person ... who commits a crime of violence motivated by gender and thus deprives another of the right declared in subsection (b) of this section shall be liable to the party injured, in an action for the recovery of compensatory and punitive damages, injunctive and declaratory relief, and such other relief as a court may deem appropriate."

Every law enacted by Congress must be based on one or more of its powers enumerated in the Constitution. ... [W]e turn to the question whether Section 13981 falls within Congress's power under Article I, Section 8, of the Constitution. Brzonkala and the United States rely upon the third clause of the Article, which gives Congress power "[t]o regulate Commerce with foreign Nations, and among the several States, and with the Indian Tribes."

As we discussed at length in *Lopez*, our interpretation of the Commerce Clause has changed as our Nation has developed. ... *Lopez* emphasized, however, that even under our modern, expansive interpretation of the Commerce Clause, Congress's regulatory authority is not without effective bounds. ... [M]odern Commerce Clause jurisprudence has "identified three broad categories of activity that Congress may regulate under its commerce power. ... First, Congress may regulate the use of the channels of interstate commerce. ... "Second, Congress is empowered to regulate and protect the instrumentalities of interstate commerce, or persons or things in interstate commerce, even though the threat may come only from intrastate activities. ... Finally, Congress's commerce authority includes the power to regulate those activities having a substantial relation to interstate commerce, ... i.e., those activities that substantially affect interstate commerce."

Petitioners ... seek to sustain Section 13981 as a regulation of activity that substantially affects interstate commerce. Given Section 13981's focus on gender-motivated violence wherever it occurs ... we agree that this is the proper inquiry.

Since *Lopez* most recently canvassed and clarified our case law governing this third category of Commerce Clause regulation, it provides the proper framework for conducting the required analysis of Section 13981. In *Lopez*, we held that the Gun-Free School Zones Act of 1990, which made it a federal crime to knowingly possess a firearm in a school zone, exceeded Congress's authority under the Commerce Clause. Several significant considerations contributed to our decision.

First, we observed that Section 922(q) was "a criminal statute that by its terms has nothing to do with 'commerce' or any sort of economic enterprise, however broadly one might define those terms." ... [T]he pattern of analysis is clear. "Where economic activity substantially affects interstate commerce, legislation regulating that activity will be sustained."

Both petitioners and Justice Souter's dissent downplay the role that the economic nature of the regulated activity plays in our Commerce Clause analysis. But a fair reading of *Lopez* shows that the noneconomic, criminal nature of the conduct at issue was central to our decision in that case. ... *Lopez*'s review of Commerce Clause case law demonstrates that in those cases where we have sustained federal regulation of intrastate activity based upon the activity's substantial effects on interstate commerce, the activity in question has been some sort of economic endeavor.

The second consideration that we found important in analyzing Section 922(q) was that the statute contained "no express jurisdictional element which might limit its reach to a discrete set of firearm possessions that additionally have an explicit connection with or effect on interstate commerce." Such a jurisdictional element may establish that the enactment is in pursuance of Congress's regulation of interstate commerce.

Third, we noted that neither Section 922(q) "nor its legislative history contain[s] express congressional findings regarding the effects upon interstate commerce of gun possession in a school zone." ... While "Congress normally is not required to make formal findings as to the substantial burdens that an activity has on interstate commerce," the existence of such findings may "enable us to evaluate the legislative judgment that the activity in question substantially affect[s] interstate commerce, even though no such substantial effect [is] visible to the naked eye."

Finally, our decision in *Lopez* rested in part on the fact that the link between gun possession and a substantial effect on interstate commerce was attenuated. ... The United States argued that the possession of guns may lead to violent crime, and that violent crime "can be expected to affect the functioning of the national economy in two ways. First, the costs of violent crime are substantial, and, through the mechanism of insurance, those costs are spread throughout the population."

"Second, violent crime reduces the willingness of individuals to travel to areas within the country that are perceived to be unsafe." The Government also argued that the presence of guns at schools poses a threat to the educational process, which in turn threatens to produce a less efficient and productive workforce, which will negatively affect national productivity and thus interstate commerce. We rejected these "costs of crime" and "national productivity" arguments because they would permit Congress to "regulate not only all violent crime, but all activities that might lead to violent crime, regardless of how tenuously they relate to interstate commerce." We noted that, under this but-for reasoning: "Congress could regulate any activity that it found was related to the economic productivity of individual citizens: family law (including marriage, divorce, and child custody), for example. Under the[se] theories…, it is difficult to perceive any limitation on federal power, even in areas such as criminal law enforcement or education where States historically have been sovereign. Thus, if we were to accept the Government's arguments, we are hard pressed to posit any activity by an individual that Congress is without power to regulate."

With these principles underlying our Commerce Clause jurisprudence as reference points, the proper resolution of the present cases is clear. Gender-motivated crimes of violence are not, in any sense of the phrase, economic activity. While we need not adopt a categorical rule against aggregating the effects of any noneconomic activity in order to decide these cases, thus far in our Nation's history our cases have upheld Commerce Clause regulation of intrastate activity only where that activity is economic in nature.

Like the Gun-Free School Zones Act at issue in *Lopez*, Section 13981 contains no jurisdictional element establishing that the federal cause of action is in pursuance of Congress's power to regulate interstate commerce.

In contrast with the lack of congressional findings that we faced in *Lopez*, Section 13981 is supported by numerous findings regarding the serious impact that gender-motivated violence has on victims and their families. … But the existence of congressional findings is not sufficient, by itself, to sustain the constitutionality of Commerce Clause legislation. As we stated in *Lopez*, "'[S]imply because Congress may conclude that a particular activity substantially affects interstate commerce does not necessarily make it so.'" … Rather, "'[w]hether particular operations affect interstate commerce sufficiently to come under the constitutional power of Congress to regulate them is ultimately a judicial rather than a legislative question, and can be settled finally only by this Court.'"

In these cases, Congress's findings are substantially weakened by the fact that they rely so heavily on a method of reasoning that we have already rejected as unworkable if we are to maintain the Constitution's enumeration of powers. Congress found that gender-motivated violence affects interstate commerce "by deterring potential victims from traveling interstate, from engaging

in employment in interstate business, and from transacting with business, and in places involved in interstate commerce; … by diminishing national productivity, increasing medical and other costs, and decreasing the supply of and the demand for interstate products." Given these findings and petitioners' arguments, the concern that we expressed in *Lopez* that Congress might use the Commerce Clause to completely obliterate the Constitution's distinction between national and local authority seems well founded.

The reasoning that petitioners advance seeks to follow the but-for causal chain from the initial occurrence of violent crime (the suppression of which has always been the prime object of the States' police power) to every attenuated effect upon interstate commerce. If accepted, petitioners' reasoning would allow Congress to regulate any crime as long as the nationwide, aggregated impact of that crime has substantial effects on employment, production, transit, or consumption. Indeed, if Congress may regulate gender-motivated violence, it would be able to regulate murder or any other type of violence since gender-motivated violence, as a subset of all violent crime, is certain to have lesser economic impacts than the larger class of which it is a part.

Petitioners' reasoning, moreover, will not limit Congress to regulating violence but may, as we suggested in *Lopez*, be applied equally as well to family law and other areas of traditional state regulation since the aggregate effect of marriage, divorce, and childrearing on the national economy is undoubtedly significant.

We accordingly reject the argument that Congress may regulate noneconomic, violent criminal conduct based solely on that conduct's aggregate effect on interstate commerce. The Constitution requires a distinction between what is truly national and what is truly local. … In recognizing this fact we preserve one of the few principles that has been consistent since the Clause was adopted. The regulation and punishment of intrastate violence that is not directed at the instrumentalities, channels, or goods involved in interstate commerce has always been the province of the States.

Affirmed.

Dissent
Justice Souter, with whom Justice Stevens, Justice Ginsberg, and Justice Breyer join

… Congress has the power to legislate with regard to activity that, in the aggregate, has a substantial effect on interstate commerce. The fact of such a substantial effect is not an issue for the courts in the first instance, but for the Congress, whose institutional capacity for gathering evidence and taking testimony far exceeds ours. By passing legislation, Congress indicates its conclusion, whether explicitly or not, that facts support its exercise of the commerce power. The business of the courts is to review the congressional assessment, not for soundness but simply for the rationality of concluding that a jurisdictional basis exists in fact. Any explicit findings that Congress chooses to make, though not dispositive of the question of rationality, may advance judicial review by identifying factual authority on which Congress relied.

One obvious difference from *United States v. Lopez* is the mountain of data assembled by Congress, here showing the effects of violence against women on interstate commerce. Passage of the Act in 1994 was preceded by four years of hearings, which included testimony from physicians and law professors; from survivors of rape and domestic violence; and from representatives of state law enforcement and private business. The record includes reports on gender bias from task forces in 21 States, and we have the benefit of specific factual findings of the eight separate Reports issued by Congress and its committees over the long course leading to enactment.

Having identified the problem of violence against women, Congress may address what it sees as the most threatening manifestation. ... Congress found that "crimes of violence motivated by gender have a substantial adverse effect on interstate commerce, by deterring potential victims from traveling interstate, from engaging in employment in interstate business, and from transacting with business, and in places involved, in interstate commerce ... [,] by diminishing national productivity, increasing medical and other costs, and decreasing the supply of and the demand for interstate products. ..."

Congress thereby explicitly stated the predicate for the exercise of its Commerce Clause power. Is its conclusion irrational in view of the data amassed? True, the methodology of particular studies may be challenged, and some of the figures arrived at may be disputed. But the sufficiency of the evidence before Congress to provide a rational basis for the finding cannot seriously be questioned. ... Indeed, the legislative record here is far more voluminous than the record compiled by Congress and found sufficient in two prior cases upholding Title II of the Civil Rights Act of 1964 against Commerce Clause challenges.

The fact that the Act does not pass muster before the Court today is therefore proof, to a degree that *Lopez* was not, that the Court's nominal adherence to the substantial effects test is merely that. Although a new jurisprudence has not emerged with any distinctness, it is clear that some congressional conclusions about obviously substantial, cumulative effects on commerce are being assigned lesser values than the once-stable doctrine would assign them. These devaluations are accomplished not by any express repudiation of the substantial effects test or its application through the aggregation of individual conduct, but by supplanting rational basis scrutiny with a new criterion of review.

Thus the elusive heart of the majority's analysis in these cases is its statement that Congress's findings of fact are "weakened" by the presence of a disfavored "method of reasoning." This seems to suggest that the "substantial effects" analysis is not a factual enquiry, for Congress in the first instance with subsequent judicial review looking only to the rationality of the congressional conclusion, but one of a rather different sort, dependent upon a uniquely judicial competence.

This new characterization of substantial effects has no support in our cases (the self-fulfilling prophecies of *Lopez* aside), least of all those the majority cites. ... All of this convinces me that today's ebb of the commerce power rests on error, and at the same time, leads me to doubt that the majority's view will prove to be enduring law.

Although the current Supreme Court seems to prefer greater regulatory power for states, a recent case provides one example in which the Supreme Court upheld a congressional act on the basis of the Commerce Clause. In *Pierce County v. Guillen*,[6] the Supreme Court held that the Hazard Elimination Program was a valid exercise of congressional authority under the Commerce Clause. This program provided funding to state and local governments to improve conditions of some of their most unsafe roads. To receive federal funding, however, state and local governments were required to regularly acquire information about potential road hazards. The state and local governments were relectant to avail themselves of the progam for fear that the information they acquired to receive funding would be used against them in lawsuits based on negligence. To alleviate these fears, Congress amended the program, allowing state and local governments to conduct engineering surveys without publicly disseminating the acquired information, even for discovery purposes in trials.

Following his spouse's death in an automobile accident, Ignacio Guillen brought suit against Pierce County, after the county refused to provide Guillen

---

[6] 537 U.S. 129 (2003).

with information related to previous accidents at the intersection where his wife died. The county argued that such information was protected under the provisions of the Hazard Elimination Program. Reversing the appellate court's holding that Congress exceeded its powers when amending the act, the Supreme Court concluded that the amended act was valid under the Commerce Clause. The Supreme Court reasoned that Congress had a significant interest in maintaining and promoting the safety of public roadways, including interstate highways. The Court validated Congress's belief that state and local governments would be more likely to collect relevant and accurate information about potential road hazards if those governments would not be required to provide such information in discovery. Hence, the Supreme Court held that the amended act of Congress was valid on the basis of the Commerce Clause.

THE COMMERCE CLAUSE AS A RESTRICTION ON STATE AUTHORITY

Because the Commerce Clause grants authority to regulate commerce to the federal government, a conflict arises over the extent to which granting such authority to the federal government restricts the states' authority to regulate commerce. The courts have attempted to resolve the conflict over the impact of the Commerce Clause on state regulation by distinguishing between regulations of commerce and regulations under the state police power. **Police power** means the residual powers retained by the state to enact legislation to safeguard the health and welfare of its citizenry. When the courts perceived state laws to be attempts to regulate interstate commerce, these laws would be struck down. But when the courts found state laws to be based on the exercise of the state police power, the laws were upheld.

police power The state's retained authority to pass laws to protect the health, safety, and welfare of the community.

Since the mid-1930s, whenever states have enacted legislation that affects interstate commerce, the courts have applied a two-pronged test. First, they ask: Is the regulation rationally related to a legitimate state end? If it is, then they ask: Is the regulatory burden imposed on interstate commerce outweighed by the state interest in enforcing the legislation? If it is, the state's regulation is upheld. The following case provides an illustration of the court's examination of a state law that was ultimately found to be an unconstitutional interference with interstate commerce.

CASE **5-3**

Oregon Waste Systems, Inc. v. Department of Environmental Quality of the State of Oregon
Supreme Court of the United States, 511 U.S. 93 (1994)

The state of Oregon passed legislation imposing an $.85 per ton fee on in-state disposal of solid wastes generated within Oregon and a $2.25 per ton disposal charge on wastes generated outside the state. Plaintiffs brought an action alleging that the surcharge violated the Commerce Clause by favoring in-state economic interests over those out-of-state parties who would have to pay the higher surcharge. The state court of appeals upheld the Oregon legislation, and the Oregon Supreme Court affirmed. The case was appealed to the U.S. Supreme Court.

Justice Thomas

Though phrased as a grant of regulatory power to Congress, the Commerce Clause has long been understood to have a "negative" aspect that denies the States the power unjustifiably to discriminate against or burden the interstate flow of articles of commerce. ...

[W]e have held that the first step in analyzing any law subject to judicial scrutiny under the negative Commerce Clause is to determine whether it "regulates evenhandedly with only 'incidental' effect on interstate commerce, or discriminates against interstate commerce." ... As we use the term here, "discrimination" simply means differential treatment of in-state and out-of-state economic interests that benefits the former and burdens the later.

In *Chemical Waste Management, Inc. v. Hunt*, we easily found Alabama's surcharge on hazardous waste from other States to be facially discriminatory because it imposed a higher fee on the disposal of out-of-state waste than on the disposal of identical in-state waste. We deem it equally obvious here that Oregon's $2.25 per ton surcharge is discriminatory on its face. The surcharge subjects waste from other States to a fee almost three times greater than the $.85 per ton charge imposed on solid in-state waste. It is well-established that a law is discriminatory if it "tax[es] a transaction or incident more heavily when it crosses state lines than when it occurs entirely within the state."

Respondents argue, and the Oregon Supreme Court held, that the statutory nexus between the surcharge and "the [otherwise uncompensated] costs to the State of Oregon and its political subdivisions of disposing of solid waste generated out-of-state," necessarily precludes a finding that the surcharge is discriminatory. We find respondents' narrow focus on Oregon's compensatory aim to be foreclosed by our precedents. Even if the surcharge merely recoups the costs of disposing of out-of-state waste in Oregon, the fact remains that the differential charge favors shippers of Oregon waste over their counterparts handling waste generated in other States. In making that geographic distinction, the surcharge patently discriminates against interstate commerce.

Because the Oregon surcharge is discriminatory, the surcharge must be invalidated unless respondents can "sho[w] that it advances a legitimate local purpose that cannot be adequately served by reasonable nondiscriminatory alternatives." Our cases require that justifications for discriminatory restrictions on commerce pass the "strictest scrutiny."

No claim has been made that the disposal of waste from other States imposes higher costs on Oregon and its political subdivisions than the disposal of in-state waste. Also, respondents have not offered any safety or health reason unique to nonhazardous waste from other States for discouraging the flow of such waste into Oregon.

Respondents' principal defense of the higher surcharge on out-of-state waste is that it is a "compensatory tax" necessary to make shippers of such waste pay their "fair share" of the costs imposed on Oregon by the disposal of their waste in the State. In *Chemical Waste* we noted the possibility that such an argument might justify a discriminatory surcharge or tax on out-of-state waste. In making that

observation, we implicitly recognized the settled principle that interstate commerce may be made to "pay its way."

Although it is often no mean feat to determine whether a challenged tax is a compensatory tax, we have little difficulty concluding that the Oregon surcharge is not such a tax. Oregon does not impose a specific charge of at least $2.25 per ton on shippers of waste generated in Oregon, for which the out-of-state surcharge might be considered compensatory. Respondents' failure to identify a specific charge on intrastate commerce equal to or exceeding the surcharge is fatal to their claim.

Respondents argue that, despite the absence of a specific $2.25 per ton charge on in-state waste, intrastate commerce does pay its share of the costs underlying the surcharge through general taxation. Whether or not that is true is difficult to determine, as "[general] tax payments are received for the general purposes of the [government], and are, upon proper receipt, lost in the general revenues." Even assuming, however, that various other means of general taxation, such as income taxes, could serve as an identifiable intrastate burden roughly equivalent to the out-of-state surcharge, respondents' compensatory tax argument fails because the in-state and out-of-state levies are not imposed on substantially equivalent events.

We conclude that, far from being substantially equivalent, taxes on earning income and utilizing Oregon landfills are "entirely different kind[s] of tax[es]."

Respondents' final argument is that Oregon has an interest in spreading the costs of the in-state disposal of Oregon waste to all Oregonians. That is, because all citizens of Oregon benefit from the proper in-state disposal of waste from Oregon, respondents claim it is only proper for Oregon to require them to bear more of the costs of disposing of such waste in the State through a higher general tax burden. At the same time, however, Oregon citizens should not be required to bear the costs of disposing of out-of-state waste, respondents claim. The necessary result of that limited cost-shifting is to require shippers of out-of-state waste to bear the full costs of in-state disposal, but to permit shippers of Oregon waste to bear less than the full cost.

We fail to perceive any distinction between respondents' contention and a claim that the State has an interest in reducing the costs of handling in-state waste. Our cases condemn as illegitimate, however, any governmental interest that is not "unrelated to economic protectionism," and regulating interstate commerce in such a way as to give those who handle domestic articles of commerce a cost advantage over their competitors handling similar items produced elsewhere constitutes such protectionism.

Because respondents have offered no legitimate reason to subject waste generated in other States to a discriminatory surcharge approximately three times as high as that imposed on waste generated in Oregon, the surcharge is facially invalid under the negative Commerce Clause.

Reversed in favor of Plaintiff, Oregon Waste Systems.

Critical Thinking About the Law

1. Once a surcharge is found to be discriminatory under the Commerce Clause, it can still be upheld. The Court has a standard, however, that such a discriminatory surcharge must meet if it is to be permitted. Locate that standard in the decision. What aspect of that standard is especially ambiguous and, thus, needs clarification?

   Clue: Imagine that you were an attorney trying to meet this standard. On which words in the standard would you focus your analysis? What characteristic of those words causes you to answer as you did?

2. What ethical norm is responsible both for Justice Thomas's reasoning and for the respondents' "final argument"?

   Clue: Look at the list of ethical norms and determine which of the four is underlying the reasoning in both instances.

Numerous state statutes, however, are challenged but upheld. One such example is Chicago's ban on the use of spray paint in the city. Paint retailers challenged the statute, arguing that it could have caused $55 million in lost sales over the next six years for spray paint retailers. The U.S. Court of Appeals eventually found the law to be constitutional. The state had a legitimate interest in trying to clean up graffiti, and it did not "discriminate against interstate commerce" nor violate the Commerce Clause. The appeals court reversed the previous ruling and allowed Chicago's enactment of this ordinance to remain intact.[7]

THE TAXING AND SPENDING POWERS OF THE FEDERAL GOVERNMENT

Article I, Section 8, of the Constitution gives the federal government the "Power to lay and collect Taxes, Duties, Imports and Excises." The taxes laid by Congress, however, must be uniform across the states. In other words, the U.S. government cannot impose higher taxes on residents of one state than another.

Although the collection of taxes is essential for the generation of revenue needed to provide essential government services, taxes can be used to serve additional functions. For example, the government may wish to encourage the development of certain industries and discourage the development of others, so it may provide tax credits for firms entering the favored industries. As long as the "motive of Congress and the effect of its legislative action are to secure revenue for the benefit of the general government,"[8] the tax will be upheld as constitutional. The fact that it also has what might be described as a regulatory impact will not affect the validity of the tax.

Article I, Section 8, also gives Congress its spending power, by authorizing it to "pay the Debts and provide for the common Defence and general Welfare of the United States." Just as Congress can indirectly use its power to tax to achieve certain social welfare objectives, it can do the same with its spending power. For example, the U.S. Supreme Court in 1987 upheld the right of

---

[7] *National Paint & Coatings Association et al. v. City of Chicago*, 45 F.3d 1124 (7th Cir. 1995).

[8] *J. W. Hampton Company v. United States*, 276 U.S. 394 (1928).

Congress to condition the states' receipt of federal highway funds on their passing state legislation making 21 the legal drinking age.

THE IMPACT OF THE AMENDMENTS ON BUSINESS

The first ten amendments to the U.S. Constitution, known as the Bill of Rights, have a substantial impact on governmental regulation of the legal environment of business. These amendments prohibit the federal government from infringing on certain freedoms that are guaranteed to individuals living in our society. The Fourteenth Amendment extends most of the provisions in the Bill of Rights to the behavior of states, prohibiting their interference in the exercise of those rights. Many of the first ten amendments have also been held to apply to corporations because corporations are treated, in most cases, as "artificial persons." The activities protected by the Bill of Rights and the Fourteenth Amendment are not only those that occur in one's private life but also those that take place in a commercial setting. Several of these amendments have a significant impact on the regulatory environment of business, and they are discussed in the remainder of this chapter.

THE FIRST AMENDMENT

First Amendment
Guarantees freedom of speech, press, and religion and the right to peacefully assemble and to petition the government for redress of grievances.

The **First Amendment** guarantees freedom of speech and of the press. It also prohibits the abridgment of the right to assemble peacefully and to petition for redress of grievances. Finally, it prohibits the government from aiding the establishment of a religion and from interfering with the free exercise of religion.

Although we say these rights are guaranteed, they obviously cannot be absolute. Most people would agree that a person does not have the right to yell "Fire!" in a crowded theater. Nor does one's right of free speech extend to making false statements about another that would be injurious to that person's reputation. Because of the difficulty of determining the boundaries of individual rights, a large number of First Amendment cases have been decided by the courts. Attempts to regulate new technologies also raise First Amendment issues. For example, Congress passed the Communications Decency Act of 1996 (CDA) to protect minors from harmful material on the Internet. But the United States Supreme Court found that provisions of the CDA that criminalized and prohibited the "knowing" transmission of "obscene or indecent" messages to any recipient under age 18 by means of telecommunications devices or through the use of interactive computer services were content-based blanket restrictions on freedom of speech. Because these provisions of the statute were too vague and overly broad, repressing speech that adults have the right to make, these provisions were found to be unconstitutional.[9]

After the Supreme Court held that the CDA was unconstitutional, Congress responded by passing the Child Online Protection Act (COPA), which imposed a $50,000 fine and six months' imprisonment on individuals who posted material for commercial purposes that was harmful to minors. However, Web sites that required individuals to submit a credit card number or some other form of age verification were not in violation of the act. Nevertheless, the Supreme Court

---

[9]*Janet Reno v. American Civil Liberties Union*, 521 U.S. 844 (1997).

Technology and the Legal Environment

Taxation of the Internet?

The rapid rise in Internet commerce has many states wondering how they will collect their fair share of sales taxes. According to the U.S. Department of Commerce, Internet retail sales have continued to increase from $28 billion in 2000 to $44 billion in 2002. Although Internet sales comprise only 1.4 percent of overall retail sales in the United States, advocates of taxes on Internet sales insist that states are losing a considerable amount of revenue each year.[1]

Currently, states are only allowed to require business to submit sales tax payments if the business has a store or distribution center in the state. Otherwise, states are prohibited from collecting sales taxes, although residents are supposed to report the taxes on personal income tax returns. In addition to the e-commerce business, increased access to the Internet has some clamoring for a use tax on Internet access, in addition to a sales tax on Internet purchases.

In 1998, Congress approved the Internet Tax Freedom Act, which established a moratorium on Internet taxes until November 2001. The 1998 bill provided a grandfather clause that allowed several states to continue levying taxes on Internet access established before the Internet Tax Freedom Act was passed. In November 2001, Congress extended the moratorium for two more years to allow for more discussion and research on the effects of the ban on state governments.

In September 2003, the House of Representatives passed the Internet Tax Nondiscrimination Act (H.R. 49), a bill designed to replace the Internet Tax Freedom Act that would have expired in November 2003 with a permanent ban on taxes on Internet access and a permanent extension of the moratorium on multiple and discriminatory taxes on electronic commerce. The House bill also eliminated all grandfather clauses of the 1998 bill. H.R. 49 was sent to the Senate for consideration in late September 2003.

On April 29, 2004, the Senate passed a different version of the Internet Tax Nondiscrimination Act (S.150) that extends the moratorium on Internet taxes until November 2007. The Senate bill was a compromise between supporters of a permanent Internet tax ban and a group of senators who questioned how a permanent ban would affect state and local budgets.

In addition to the four-year moratorium, the Senate version of the bill allows a handful of states that began taxing Internet access before the 1998 moratorium to continue levying those taxes until the moratorium expires in November 2007. The bill also allows 17 states that now tax DSL Internet access to continue those taxes until November 2005. The Senate sent the bill back to the House of Representatives for consideration. At the time the book went to press final action by both houses had not yet been taken.

[1] U.S. Department of Commerce, Electronic Commerce Statistics, April 15, 2004; access to statistics can be found at **www.census.gov/estats**.

---

ruled that this act was also unconstitutional, as the provisions of the act likely violated the First Amendment.[10] The Court reasoned that COPA was not narrowly tailored to a compelling governmental interest, and the regulations were not the least restrictive methods of regulating in this area, as filtering programs could more easily restrict minors' access to obscene material than criminal penalties.

Congress also passed the Child Internet Protection Act (CIPA), requiring libraries to implement filtering software to prevent minors from accessing pornography or other obscene and potentially harmful material. Libraries that did not comply with the provisions of CIPA would not receive federal funding for Internet access. In *U.S. v. American Library Association*,[11] numerous libraries and Web site publishers brought suit, claiming that the CIPA was unconstitutional. Reversing the district court's decision that the act was unconstitutional as it violated the First Amendment,

---

[10] *Ashcroft v. ACLU*, 124 S.Ct. 2783 (2004).

[11] 539 U.S. 194 (2003).

the Supreme Court ruled in a split decision that the act was constitutional. Although six justices ruled that the act was not unconstitutional, there was greater disagreement about the Court's opinion. The majority reasoned that the act did not violate an individual's First Amendment rights, as libraries are afforded broad discretion about the kinds of materials that they may include in their collections. In other words, a library is not a public forum in the traditional sense.

An interesting issue that has arisen on many campuses is whether so-called "hate speech," derogatory speech directed at members of another group, such as another race, is unprotected speech that can be banned. Thus far, hate-speech codes on campuses that were challenged as unconstitutional have been struck down by state courts or federal appeals courts, although the issue has not yet reached the Supreme Court. Hate speech is a serious issue that affects more than 1 million students every year, prompting 60 percent of universities to ban verbal abuse and verbal harassment and 28 percent of universities to ban advocacy of an offensive viewpoint.[12] Because universities are often viewed as breeding grounds for ideas and citizen development, courts have not looked favorably on limits to speech on campuses. The international community has been more willing to call hate speech unprotected speech, with a declaration from the United Nations and laws in several countries.[13]

Corporate Commercial Speech. Numerous cases have arisen over the extent to which First Amendment guarantees are applicable to corporate commercial speech. The doctrine currently used to analyze commercial speech is discussed in the following case.

CASE 5-4

Central Hudson Gas & Electric Corporation v. Public Service Commission of New York
United States Supreme Court 447 U.S. 557, 100 S.Ct. 2343 (1980)

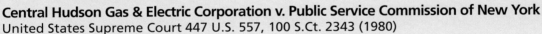

Plaintiff Central Hudson Gas and Electric Corporation filed an action against Public Service Commission of New York to challenge the constitutionality of a regulation that completely banned promotional advertising by the utility but permitted "informational" ads—those designed to encourage shifting consumption from peak to nonpeak times. The regulation was upheld by the trial court. On appeal by the utility, the New York Court of Appeals sustained the regulation, concluding that governmental interests outweighed the limited constitutional value of the commercial speech at issue. The utility appealed.

Justice Powell

The Commission's order [enforcing the regulation's advertising ban] restricts only commercial speech, that is, expression related solely to the economic interests of the

speaker and its audience. The First Amendment, as applied to the States through the Fourteenth Amendment, protects commercial speech from unwarranted governmental regulation. Commercial expression not only serves the economic interest of the speaker, but also assists consumers and furthers the societal interest in the fullest possible dissemination of information. In applying the First Amendment to this area, we have rejected the "highly paternalistic" view that government has complete power to suppress or regulate commercial speech. Even when advertising communicates only an incomplete version of the relevant facts, the First Amendment presumes that some accurate information is better than no information at all. Nevertheless, our decisions have recognized "the 'common sense' distinction between speech proposing a commercial transaction, which occurs in an area tradi-

---

[12] Timothy C. Shiell, *Campus Hate Speech on Trial* (Lawrence: University Press of Kansas, 1998), pp. 2, 49.

[13] *Ibid.* at 32.

tionally subject to government regulation, and other varieties of speech."

The Constitution therefore accords a lesser protection to commercial speech than to other constitutionally guaranteed expression. The protection available for particular commercial expression turns on the nature both of the expression and of the governmental interests served by its regulation. Two features of commercial speech permit regulation of its content. First, commercial speakers have extensive knowledge of both the market and their products. Thus, they are well situated to evaluate the accuracy of their messages and the lawfulness of the underlying activity. In addition, commercial speech, the offspring of economic self-interest, is a hardy breed of expression that is not "particularly susceptible to being crushed by overbroad regulation."

If the communication is neither misleading nor related to unlawful activity, the government's power is more circumscribed. The State must assert a substantial interest to be achieved by restrictions on commercial speech. Moreover, the regulatory technique must be in proportion to that interest. The limitation on expression must be designed carefully to achieve the State's goal. Compliance with this requirement may be measured by two criteria. First, the restriction must directly advance the state interest involved; the regulation may not be sustained if it provides only ineffective or remote support for the government's purpose. Second, if the governmental interest could be served as well by a more limited restriction on commercial speech, the excessive restrictions cannot survive.

The second criterion recognizes that the First Amendment mandates that speech restrictions be "narrowly drawn." The regulatory technique may extend only as far as the interest it serves. The State cannot regulate speech that poses no danger to the asserted state interest, nor can it completely suppress information when narrower restrictions on expression would serve its interest as well. In commercial speech cases, then, a four-part analysis has developed. At the outset, we must determine whether the expression is protected by the First Amendment. For commercial speech to come within that provision, it at least must concern lawful activity and not be misleading. Next, we ask whether the asserted governmental interest is substantial. If both inquiries yield positive answers, we must determine whether the regulation directly advances the governmental interest asserted, and whether it is not more extensive than is necessary to serve that interest.

The Commission does not claim that the expression at issue is inaccurate or relates to unlawful activity. Yet the New York Court of Appeals questioned whether Central Hudson's advertising is protected commercial speech. Because appellant holds a monopoly over the sale of electricity in its service area, the state court suggested that the Commission's order restricts no commercial speech of any worth.

In the absence of factors that would distort the decision to advertise, we may assume that the willingness of a business to promote its products justifies belief that consumers are interested in the advertising. Since no such extraordinary conditions have been identified in this case, appellant's monopoly position does not alter the First Amendment's protection for its commercial speech.

The Commission offers two state interests as justifications for the ban on promotional advertising. The first concerns energy conservation. Any increase in demand for electricity—during peak or off-peak periods—means greater consumption of energy. The Commission argues that the State's interest in conserving energy is sufficient to support suppression of advertising designed to increase consumption of electricity. In view of our country's dependence on energy resources beyond our control, no one can doubt the importance of energy conservation. Plainly, therefore, the state interest asserted is substantial.

We come finally to the critical inquiry in this case: whether the Commission's complete suppression of speech ordinarily protected by the First Amendment is no more extensive than necessary to further the State's interest in energy conservation. The Commission's order reaches all promotional advertising, regardless of the impact of the touted service on overall energy use. But the energy conservation rationale, as important as it is, cannot justify suppressing information about electric devices or services that would cause no net increase in total energy use. In addition, no showing has been made that a more limited restriction on the content of promotional advertising would not serve adequately the State's interests.

Appellant insists that but for the ban, it would advertise products and services that use energy efficiently. These include the "heat pump," which both parties acknowledge to be a major improvement in electric heating, and the use of electric heat as a "backup" to solar and other heat sources. Although the Commission has questioned the efficiency of electric heating before this Court, neither the Commission's Policy Statement nor its order denying rehearing made findings on this issue. The Commission's order prevents appellant from promoting electric services that would reduce energy use by diverting demand from less efficient sources, or that would consume roughly the same amount of energy as do alternative sources. In neither situation would the utility's advertising endanger conservation or mislead the public. To the extent that the Commission's order suppresses speech that in no way impairs the State's interest in energy conservation, the Commission's order violates the First and Fourteenth Amendments and must be invalidated.

The Commission also has not demonstrated that its interest in conservation cannot be protected adequately by more limited regulation of appellant's commercial expression. To further its policy of conservation, the Commission could attempt to restrict the format and content of Central Hudson's advertising. It might, for example, require that the advertisements include information about the relative efficiency and expense of the offered service, both under current conditions and for the foreseeable future.

Reversed in favor of Plaintiff, Central Hudson.

Critical Thinking About the Law

In Case 5-4, the Court had to balance government interests in energy efficiency as well as fair and efficient pricing with the conflicting constitutional value of Central Hudson's right to free commercial speech. Having affirmed the validity of government's substantial interests in regulating the utility company, the Court sought to determine whether these interests could have been sufficiently served with more limited restrictions. Because this determination is of central importance to the Court's reversal of the earlier court's judgment, it will be the focus of the questions that follow.

1. What primary ethical norm is implicit in the legal requirement that regulations on commercial speech must be of the most limited nature possible in carrying out the desired end of advancing the state's substantial interest?

    Clue: Review the four primary ethical norms. You want to focus not on the government regulation but on the rationale for limits on that regulation.

2. What information missing from the Court's opinion must you, as a critical thinker, know before being satisfied entirely with the decision?

    Clue: You want to focus on the issue about which the Public Service Commission and Central Hudson have conflicting viewpoints. What information would you want to know before accepting the soundness of the Court's judgment in resolving this conflict?

The test set forth in *Central Hudson* was reaffirmed by the U.S. Supreme Court in two decisions handed down in the summer of 1995, when it applied the test in *Rubin v. Coors Brewing Co.*[14] and *Florida Bar v. Went for It and John T. Blakely.*[15] In the first case, Coors challenged a regulation of the Federal Alcohol Administration Act that prohibited beer labels from disclosing the beer's alcohol content. The Court found that the government's interest in suppressing "strength wars" among beer producers was "substantial" under the *Central Hudson* test, but the ban failed to meet the asserted government interest and is no more extensive than necessary to serve that interest.

A restriction that passed the *Central Hudson* test was the Florida ethics rule upheld in the latter case. The rule requires lawyers to wait 30 days before sending targeted direct-mail solicitation letters to victims of accidents or disasters. The high court found a substantial interest both in protecting the privacy and tranquility of victims and their loved ones against invasive and unsolicited contact by lawyers and in preventing the erosion of confidence in the profession that such repeated invasions have caused. The bar association had established, by unrebutted survey data, that Floridians considered immediate postaccident direct-mail solicitation to be an invasion of victims' privacy that reflects poorly on lawyers. The Court also found that the ban's scope is reasonably well tailored to meet the stated objectives. It is limited in duration, and there are other ways for injured Floridians to learn about the availability of legal services during the ban. Thus, the ban was upheld as directly advancing the asserted legitimate interest in a manner no more extensive than necessary to serve that interest.

The U.S. Supreme Court once again reaffirmed and applied the four-part test of *Central Hudson* in the case of *Lorillard Tobacco Company et al., v. Thomas F. Reilly,*[16] a case challenging Massachusetts's comprehensive set of reg-

---

[14] 514 U.S. 476, 115 S.Ct. 1585 (1995).
[15] 515 U.S. 618, 115 S.Ct. 2371 (1995).
[16] 533 U.S. 525 (2001).

ulations of cigarette, cigar, and smokeless tobacco advertising and distribution. The high court found that Massachusetts's outdoor advertising regulations that prohibited smokeless tobacco or cigar advertising within 1,000 feet of a school or playground violated the First Amendment because they failed the fourth part of the *Central Hudson* test. The Court reasoned as follows:

> Their broad sweep indicates that the Attorney General did not "carefully calcu-lat[e] the costs and benefits associated with the burden on speech imposed." ... The record indicates that the regulations prohibit advertising in a substantial portion of Massachusetts' major metropolitan areas; in some areas, they would constitute nearly a complete ban on the communication of truthful information. This substantial geographical reach is compounded by other factors. "Outdoor" advertising includes not only advertising located outside an establishment, but also advertising inside a store if visible from outside. Moreover, the regulations restrict advertisements of any size, and the term advertisement also includes oral statements. The uniformly broad sweep of the geographical limitation and the range of communications restricted demonstrate a lack of tailoring. The govern-mental interest in preventing underage tobacco use is substantial, and even com-pelling, but it is no less true that the sale and use of tobacco products by adults is a legal activity. A speech regulation cannot unduly impinge on the speaker's abil-ity to propose a commercial transaction and the adult listener's opportunity to obtain information about products. The Attorney General has failed to show that the regulations at issue are not more extensive than necessary.[17]

In that same case, the high court also struck down regulations prohibiting indoor, point-of-sale advertising of smokeless tobacco and cigars lower than 5 feet from the floor of a retail establishment located within 1,000 feet of a school or playground because they failed both the third and fourth steps of the *Central Hudson* analysis. The Court found that the 5-foot rule did not seem to advance the goals of preventing minors from using tobacco products and curbing demand for that activity by limiting youth exposure to advertising because not all children are less than 5 feet tall, and those who are can look up and take in their surroundings. In the case, the Court overruled the circuit court's finding that the regulations met the four-part test of *Central Hudson*, so it clearly is not always easy to know how the test is going to be applied.[18]

Corporate Political Speech. Not all corporate speech is considered commercial speech. Sometimes, for example, corporations might spend funds to support political candidates or referenda. At one time, states restricted the amount of advertising firms could engage in because of a fear that, with their huge assets, corporations' speech on behalf of a particular candidate or issue would drown out other voices. But in the 1978 case of *First National Bank of Boston v. Bellotti*,[19] the U.S. Supreme Court struck down a state law that prohibited certain corporations from making contributions or expenditures influencing voters on any issues that would not materially affect the corporate assets or business. Stating that "the concept that the government may restrict speech of some elements of our society in order to enhance the relative voice of others is wholly foreign to the First Amendment," the high court ruled that corporate political speech should be protected to the same extent as the ordinary citizen's political speech.

---

[17] *Id.*

[18] *Id.*

[19] 435 U.S. 765 (1978).

Our discussion of the First Amendment has focused on its effect on people's ability to speak, but just as the First Amendment may also prevent the government from prohibiting speech, the Amendment may also prevent the government from compelling individuals to express certain views, or from compelling certain individuals to pay subsidies for speech to which they object. This protection is illustrated by the 2001 case of *United States and Department of Agriculture, v. United Foods, Inc.*,[20] in which the Court struck down a governmental assessment against mushroom growers that was used primarily for generic advertising to promote mushroom sales. The mushroom producer who challenged the assessment wanted to be able to promote his mushrooms as different from other producers' mushrooms and, hence, did not want to be forced to help fund generic advertising that promoted the idea that all mushrooms were good. The Supreme Court agreed, stating that "First Amendment values are at serious risk if the government can compel a citizen or group of citizens to subsidize speech on the side that it favors. ..."[21]

THE FOURTH AMENDMENT

Fourth Amendment
Protects the right of individuals to be secure in their persons, homes, and personal property by prohibiting the government from conducting unreasonable searches of individuals and seizing their property.

The **Fourth Amendment** protects the right of individuals to be secure in their persons, their homes, and their personal property. It prohibits the government from conducting unreasonable searches of individuals and seizing their property to use as evidence against them. If such an unreasonable search and seizure occurs, the evidence obtained from it cannot be used in a trial.

An unreasonable search and seizure is basically one conducted without the government official's having first obtained a warrant from the court. The warrant must specify the items sought, and this requirement is strictly enforced, as a recent Supreme Court case illustrates. In *Groh v. Ramizez*[22], the high court ruled that a search warrant was invalid on its face when it utterly failed to describe the persons or things to be seized, despite the fact that the requisite particularized description was contained in the search warrant application. The residential search that was conducted pursuant to this facially invalid warrant was therefore unreasonable, despite the fact that the officers conducting the search exercised restraint in limiting the scope of the search to materials listed in the application.[23]

Government officials are able to obtain such a warrant only when they can show probable cause to believe that the search will turn up the specified evidence of criminal activity. Supreme Court decisions, however, have recently narrowed the protection of the Fourth Amendment by providing for circumstances in which no search warrant is needed. For example, warrantless searches of automobiles, under certain circumstances, are allowed. And the Supreme Court even held in a recent case that an out-of-car arrest and subsequent warrantless search of the individual's car did not violate the individual's Fourth Amendment rights.[24] The Supreme Court decided in another recent case that police highway checkpoints, whereby police officers questioned drivers on a particular highway for information about a recent incident, did not violate dri-

---

[20] 533 U.S. 405, 121 S.Ct. 2334 (2001).

[21] *Id.* at 411.

[22] Groh v. Ramirez, 450 U.S. 551, 124 S.Ct. 1284. (2004)

[23] *Id.*

[24] *Thornton v. United States*, 124 S.Ct. 2127 (2004).

vers' Fourth Amendment rights, even though the police arrested one of the passing drivers for drunk driving.[25]

In Ohio, the state ACLU and a college professor challenged an interesting law that the state passed, which the plaintiffs claim is an attempt to restrict some people's Fourth Amendment rights.[26] The law at issue requires buyers of five or more beer kegs to provide the address of the party to the beer distributor and sign a form permitting police and liquor agents to enter their property to enforce the state liquor laws. In June 2003, the state dropped the law, but as of late 2004, the professor had still refused to withdraw his suit on grounds that if the law is not declared unconstitutional, the state can reinstate it at any time.[27]

Improvements in technology have also caused problems in the application of the Fourth Amendment because it is now simpler to eavesdrop on people and to engage in other covert activities. One such case was decided by the United States Supreme Court in mid-2001.[28] In that case, the police had information from informants that led them to believe that Danny Kyllo was growing marijuana in his home. Kyllo also had unusually high electricity bills, common when you are using heat lamps to grow the plant indoors. The police used a thermal imager, an instrument that can detect unusually high levels of heat emissions and translate them into an image, to provide them with the evidence necessary to get a warrant to physically search his house. The question the Court had to address was whether the use of the thermal imaging instrument on the property constituted a "search." Or, if we think of the case the way judges do, by comparing it to past precedents, it is a question of whether thermal imaging is more like going through someone's garbage or more like using a high-powered telescope to look through someone's window. If the former situation is more analogous, then the behavior does not constitute a search. But if the case is more analogous to the latter scenario, then using thermal imaging on a home is a search that requires a warrant. The Ninth Circuit, in a case of first impression (the first time an issue is ruled on by the court), found that using thermal imaging was not a search that was prohibited by the Fourth Amendment without a warrant.

The United States Supreme Court, however, in a 5–4 decision, ruled that the use by the police of a thermal imaging device to detect patterns of heat coming from a private home is a search that requires a warrant. The Court said further that the warrant requirement would apply not only to the relatively crude device at issue but also to any "more sophisticated systems" in use or in development that let the police gain knowledge that in the past would have been impossible without a physical entry into the home. In explaining the decision, Justice Scalia wrote that in the home, "all details are intimate details, because the entire area is held safe from prying government eyes." He went on to add that the Court's precedents "draw a firm line at the entrance to one's house."[29]

Although many were happy with the Supreme Court's decision in this case, some were quick to point out that this case is not necessarily the final word

[25] *Illinois v. Lidster*, 124 S.Ct. 885 (2004).

[26] Liz Sidotti, "Ohio Law Challenged as Intrusive; Key Buyers Get Grilled," Cincinnati Enquirer, on-line edition, **http://www.enqirer.com/edition/2001/05/25/10c_ohio_law_challenged.html**.

[27] "OU Professor Refused to Drop '5-Keg Rule' Lawsuit," **www.wcpo.com/news/2003/local/07/13/5kegrule.html**, July 13, 2003.

[28] *Kyllo v. U.S.*, 533 U.S. 27, 121 S.Ct. 2038 (2001).

[29] *Id.*

when it comes to the use of technology. They noted that Scalia seemed to rely heavily on the fact that the thermal imaging was used to see inside one's home. It is, therefore, not clear whether thermal imaging of some other locale would be upheld.

The Fourth Amendment protects corporations as well as individuals. This protection is generally applicable, as noted earlier, in criminal cases. However, Fourth Amendment issues also arise when government regulations authorize, or even require, warrantless searches by administrative agencies.

Although administrative searches are presumed to require a search warrant, an exception has been carved out. If an industry has been subject to pervasive regulation, a warrantless search is considered reasonable under the Fourth Amendment. In such industries, warrantless searches are required in order to make sure that regulations are being upheld, and a warrantless search would not be unreasonable because the owner has a reduced expectation of privacy. When a warrantless search is challenged, and the state argues that the "pervasively regulated" exception should apply, before the court will find that the search was reasonable, the agency will have to demonstrate:

1. there is "a substantial government interest that informs the regulatory scheme pursuant to which the inspection is made";[30]

2. the warrantless inspections must be "necessary to further the regulatory scheme";[31] and

3. "the statute's inspection program, in terms of the certainty and regularity of its application, must provide a constitutionally adequate substitute for a warrant,"[32] that is, it advises the business owner that "the search is being made pursuant to the law and has a properly defined scope," and limits the discretion of the inspecting officers.[33]

> **Fifth Amendment** Protects individuals against self-incrimination and double jeopardy and guarantees them the right to trial by jury; protects both individuals and businesses through the Due Process Clause and the Takings Clause.

As the Fourth Amendment is currently interpreted, a warrantless search authorized by the Gun Control Act or the Federal Mine Safety and Health Act would be legal. A warrantless search under the Occupational Safety and Health Act, however, would violate the Fourth Amendment because there is no history of pervasive legislation on working conditions before the act's passage.

THE FIFTH AMENDMENT

> **Due Process Clause** Provides that no one can be deprived of life, liberty, or property without "due process of law"; found in Fifth Amendment.

The **Fifth Amendment** provides many significant protections to individuals. For instance, it protects against self-incrimination and double jeopardy, that is, being tried twice for the same crime. Of more importance to businesspersons, however, is the **Due Process Clause** of the Fifth Amendment. This provision provides that one cannot be deprived of life, liberty, or property without due process of law.

> **procedural due process** Procedural steps to which individuals are entitled before losing their life, liberty, or property.

There are two types of due process: procedural and substantive. Originally, due process was interpreted only procedurally. **Procedural due process** requires that a criminal whose life, liberty, or property would be taken by a conviction be given a fair trial; that is, that he or she is entitled to notice of the alleged criminal action and the opportunity to confront his or her accusers

---

[30] *New York v. Burger*, 482 U.S. 691, 107 S.Ct. 2636 (1987).

[31] *Id.*

[32] *Id.*

[33] *Id.*

before an impartial tribunal. The application of procedural due process soon spread beyond criminal matters, especially after passage of the Fourteenth Amendment, discussed in the next section, which made the requirement of due process applicable to state governments.

Today, the Due Process Clause has been applied to such diverse situations as the termination of welfare benefits,[34] the discharge of a public employee from his or her job, and the suspension of a student from school. It should be noted, however, that the types of takings to which the Due Process Clause applies are not being continually increased. In fact, after a broad expansion of the takings to which this clause applied, the courts began restricting the application of this clause during the 1970s and have continued to do so since then. The courts restrict the clause's application by narrowing the interpretation of property and liberty. This narrowing is especially common in interpreting the Due Process Clause as it applies to state governments under the Fourteenth Amendment.

What procedural safeguards does procedural due process require? The question is not easily answered. The procedures that the government must follow when there may be a taking of an individual's life, liberty, or property vary according to the nature of the taking. In general, as the magnitude of the potential deprivation increases, the extent of the procedures required also increases.

The second type of due process is substantive due process. The concept of **substantive due process** refers to the basic fairness of laws that may deprive an individual of his or her liberty or property. In other words, when a law is passed that will restrict individuals' liberty or their use of their property, the government must have a proper purpose for the restriction or it violates substantive due process.

substantive due process Requirement that laws depriving individuals of liberty or property be fair.

During the late nineteenth and early twentieth centuries, this concept was referred to as economic substantive due process and was used to strike down a number of pieces of social legislation, including laws that established minimum wages and hours. Business managers successfully argued that such laws interfered with the liberty of employer and employee to enter into whatever type of employment contract they might choose. Analogous arguments were used to defeat many laws that would have allegedly helped the less fortunate at the expense of business interests. Economic substantive due process flourished only until the late 1930s. Today, many pieces of social legislation are in force that would have been held unconstitutional under the old concept of economic substantive due process.

The concept of substantive due process is not dead. However, its use today protects not economic interests, but personal rights, such as the still evolving right to privacy. The right to privacy is a liberty now deemed to be protected under the Constitution. In order for a law restricting one's right to privacy to conform to substantive due process, the restriction in question must bear a substantial relationship to a compelling governmental purpose.

The Fifth Amendment further provides that if the government takes private property for public use, it must pay the owner just compensation. This provision is referred to as the **Takings Clause**. Unlike the protection against self-incrimination, which does not apply to corporations, both the Due Process

Takings Clause Provides that if the government takes private property for public use, it must pay the owner just compensation; found in Fifth Amendment.

---

[34] *Goldberg v. Kelly*, 90 U.S. 101 (1970). In this case, the U.S. Supreme Court stated that the termination of a welfare recipient's welfare benefits by a state agency without affording him or her the opportunity for an evidentiary hearing before termination violates the recipient's procedural due process rights.

Clause and the provision for just compensation are applicable to corporations. This provision for just compensation has caused considerable litigation recently. One significant issue that has arisen is the question of what constitutes a "public use," for which the government can take property. This issue is discussed in greater detail in Chapter 14.

A second issue under this takings provision is the question of when a government regulation can become so onerous as to constitute a taking for which just compensation is required. Environmental regulations, because they often have an impact on the way landowners may use their property, have been increasingly challenged as unconstitutionally violative of the takings provision. In the following case, the Supreme Court examined a state regulation challenged as violating the Fifth Amendment, as applied to the state by the Fourteenth Amendment.

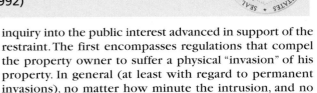

CASE 5-5

David Lucas v. South Carolina Coastal Commission
Supreme Court of the United States 505 U.S. 1003 (1992)

In 1986, plaintiff David Lucas paid $975,000 for two beachfront lots on the Isle of Palms along the South Carolina coast, planning to eventually build one home for himself and another for a wealthy buyer. Nineteen months later the state passed a Beachfront Management Act, which banned construction close to the shore in order to prevent flying debris and other environmental damage from Atlantic storms. Because the new regulation prevented his constructing either house, which he believed rendered his land "valueless," he sued the state, seeking "just compensation" under the Takings Clause of the Fifth Amendment. The trial court found in favor of Lucas and awarded him $1.2 million. On appeal, the state argued successfully that a landowner had no right to harm his land, which Lucas would be doing by constructing the homes, and the trial court verdict was reversed. Lucas then appealed the case to the U.S. Supreme Court.

Justice Scalia

Prior to Justice Holmes' exposition in *Pennsylvania Coal Co. v. Mahon*, it was generally thought that the Takings Clause reached only a "direct appropriation" of property, or the functional equivalent of a "practical ouster of [the owner's] possession."

Nevertheless, our decision in *Mahon* offered little insight into when, and under what circumstances, a given regulation would be seen as going "too far" for purposes of the Fifth Amendment. In 70-odd years of succeeding "regulatory takings" jurisprudence, we have generally eschewed any "set formula" for determining how far is too far. We have, however, described at least two discrete categories of regulatory action as compensable without case-specific inquiry into the public interest advanced in support of the restraint. The first encompasses regulations that compel the property owner to suffer a physical "invasion" of his property. In general (at least with regard to permanent invasions), no matter how minute the intrusion, and no matter how weighty the public purpose behind it, we have required compensation.

The second situation in which we have found categorical treatment appropriate is where regulation denies all economically beneficial or productive use of land. As we have said on numerous occasions, the Fifth Amendment is violated when land-use regulation "does not substantially advance legitimate state interests or denies an owner economically viable use of his land."

Affirmatively supporting a compensation requirement is the fact that regulations that leave the owner of land without economically beneficial or productive options for its use—typically, as here, by requiring land to be left substantially in its natural state—carry with them a heightened risk that private property is being pressed into some form of public service under the guise of mitigating serious public harm.

The trial court found Lucas's two beachfront lots to have been rendered valueless by respondent's enforcement of the coastal-zone construction ban. Under Lucas's theory of the case, which rested upon our "no economically viable use" statements, that finding entitled him to compensation. By neglecting to dispute the findings enumerated in the Act or otherwise to challenge the legislature's purposes, petitioner "concede[d] that the beach/dune area of South Carolina's shores is an extremely valuable public resource; that the erection of new construction contributes to the erosion and destruction of this public resource; and that discouraging new construction in close proximity to the beach/dune area is necessary to prevent a great public harm." In the court's view, these concessions brought petitioner's challenge within a long line of this Court's cases sustaining against Due Process and Takings Clause challenges against the State's use of its "police powers" to enjoin a property owner from activities akin to public nuisances [e.g., order to destroy diseased cedar trees to prevent infection of nearby orchards].

It is correct that many of our proper opinions have suggested that "harmful or noxious uses" of property may be proscribed by government regulation without the requirement of compensation. For a number of reasons, however, we think the South Carolina Supreme Court was too quick to conclude that that principle decides the present case. The "harmful or noxious uses" principle was the Court's early attempt to describe in theoretical terms why government may, consistent with the Takings Clause, affect property values by regulation without incurring an obligation to compensate—a reality we nowadays acknowledge explicitly with respect to the full scope of the State's police power.

The legislature's recitation of a noxious-use justification cannot be the basis for departing from our categorical rule that total regulatory takings must be compensated. If it were, departure would virtually always be allowed.

Where the State seeks to sustain regulation that deprives land of all economically beneficial use, we think it may resist compensation only if the logically antecedent inquiry into the nature of the owner's estate shows that the proscribed use interests were not part of his title to begin with.

Where "permanent physical occupation" of land is concerned, we have refused to allow the government to decree it anew (without compensation), no matter how weighty the asserted "public interests" involved, though we assuredly would permit the government to assert a permanent easement that was a preexisting limitation upon the landowner's title. We believe similar treatments must be accorded confiscatory regulations, i.e., regulations that prohibit all economically beneficial use of land.

On this analysis, the owner of a lake bed, for example, would not be entitled to compensation when he is denied the requisite permit to engage in a landfilling operation that would have the effect of flooding others' land. Such regulatory action may well have the effect of eliminating the land's only economically productive use, but it does not proscribe a productive use that was previously permissible under relevant property and nuisance principles. The use of these properties for what are now expressly prohibited purposes was always unlawful, and it was open to the State at any point to make the implication of those background principles of nuisance and property law explicit.

The "total taking" inquiry we require today will ordinarily entail analysis of, among other things, the degree of harm to public lands and resources, or adjacent private property, posed by the claimant's proposed activities, the social value of the claimant's activities and their suitability to the locality in question, and the relative ease with which the alleged harm can be avoided through measures taken by the claimant and the government (or adjacent private landowners) alike. The fact that a particular use has long been engaged in by similarly situated owners ordinarily imports a lack of any common-law prohibition (though changed circumstances or new knowledge may make what was previously permissible no longer so). So also does the fact that other landowners, similarly situated, are permitted to continue the use denied to the claimant.

It seems unlikely that common-law principles would have prevented the erection of any habitable or productive improvements on petitioner's land. We emphasize that to win its case … South Carolina must identify background principles of nuisance and property law that prohibit the uses he now intends in the circumstances in which the property is presently found. Only on this showing can the State fairly claim that, in proscribing all such beneficial uses, the Beachfront Management Act is taking nothing.

Reversed, and *remanded*, in favor of Appellant, Lucas.

One of the factors that many commentators believed was critical to the court's ruling in *Lucas* was the fact that the law that led to his inability to develop his land had been enacted after Lucas had acquired his property. However, in the 2001 case of *Palazzolo v. Rhode Island*,[35] the Supreme Court held by a 5–4 vote that someone who bought property after restrictions on development were in place could still challenge the restrictions as an unconstitutional "taking" of private property.

Many advocates of private property rights now believe that the Takings Clause has taken on a new importance because of cases such as *Lucas* and *Whitney v. United States*,[36] wherein a federal court found that the federal Surface

---

[35] 533 U.S. 606 (2001).

[36] 512 U.S. 374, 114 S.Ct. 2309 (1994).

Critical Thinking About the Law

As do other cases we have studied, Case 5-5 represents a conflict between two sets of interests. On one hand, society in the form of government has many legitimate concerns—safety, environmental protection, maintenance of a transportation network, and so on—that interfere with the interests of individual property owners. On the other hand, imagine the outrage felt by individual property owners when they see an outside body in the form of the state seizing their property.

Critical thinking about the legal reasoning used by Judge Scalia can help improve your response to this conflict of legitimate interests.

1. Justice Scalia dismisses the "noxious use" principle as an inappropriate tool for determining compensation under the Takings Clause on the grounds that this principle is ambiguous. Yet, while dismissing this principle, Scalia himself offers in its place another ambiguous basis for justifying a taking. Try to identify the ambiguity in Scalia's own principle for a legitimate state "taking."

   Clue: Locate the section in the decision in which Scalia spells out what is required for a legal "taking."

2. Environmentalists were very distressed by this decision. Yet, one thing we have stressed in our approach to critical thinking about the law is the importance of the specifics in the fact pattern. How do the facts in this case make the decision much less a threat to environmental regulation than it might appear to be at first?

   Clue: Imagine that you could create facts related to *Lucas*. Which facts would you change that would have moved Scalia in the direction of affirming the decision of the South Carolina Supreme Court?

Mining and Reclamation Act constituted a taking with respect to one mining company whose land became completely useless as a result of the act. Whether the "Property Firsters," as they call themselves, will be successful in the future remains to be seen, but they have clearly brought back attention to an argument against regulation that had been fairly dormant for the past 50 years. And they are using their arguments primarily to challenge a broad range of environmental laws involving matters from forcing cleanups of hazardous waste sites to restricting grazing and rationing water, as well as land use planning statutes.

For example, in *Dolan v. Tigard,*[37] the owner of a store in the city's business district sued when her receipt of a permit to double the size of her store and pave its gravel parking lot was made contingent on the condition that she dedicate a sixth of her land to the city. She was to make part of the land, which was in a floodplain, a public recreational greenway and part of a bike trail that could help reduce the increased congestion in the area that might result from the expansion of her store. The U.S. Supreme Court found that there was no evidence of a reasonable relationship between the floodplain easement required of Dolan and the impact of the new building. They held that the city had the right to take the easement for the greenway, but it had to provide just compensation for the regulatory taking.

Using the Fifth Amendment to bring individual challenges to land use regulations and zoning laws is a very time consuming process, so many property rights organizations have instead focused on trying to pass state laws that would make it easier for property owners to get compensation when their property values fall because of new regulations. In 2004, such groups achieved their

---

[37] 926 F.2d 1169 (1991).

greatest success with the passage of Ballot Measure 37 in the state of Oregon. The measure, which is expected to be upheld by the courts when challenged, provides that any property owner who can prove that environmental or zoning laws have hurt their investments can force the government to compensate them for their losses or get an exemption from the rules. Other states that have laws providing compensation for aggrieved property owners are Florida, Texas, Louisiana, and Mississippi, but these laws provide compensation only after a particular loss threshold has been reached, usually a 25 percent reduction in the property's value. Those laws also allow compensation only for losses caused by new land use laws. Whether the passage of the legislation in Oregon indicates the beginning of a new wave of legislation remains to be seen.

A final problem that often causes confusion among businesspersons is the question of the extent of Fifth Amendment protections for corporations. The Fifth Amendment protection against self-incrimination has not been held to apply to corporations. However, some decisions have raised questions about this long-standing interpretation. In *United States v. Doe*,[38] the U.S. Supreme Court determined that even though the contents of documents may not be protected under the Fifth Amendment, a sole proprietor should have the right to show that the act of producing the documents would entail testimonial self-incrimination as to admissions that the records existed. Therefore, the sole proprietor could not be compelled to produce the sole proprietorship's records.

In the subsequent case of *Braswell v. United States*,[39] however, the Court clearly distinguished between the role of a custodian of corporate records and a sole proprietor. In *Braswell*, the defendant operated his business as a corporation, with himself as the sole shareholder. When a grand jury issued a subpoena requiring him to produce corporate books and records, Braswell argued that to do so would violate his Fifth Amendment privilege against self-incrimination. The U.S. Supreme Court denied Braswell's claim and said that, clearly, subpoenaed business records are not privileged, and, because Braswell was a custodian for the records, his act of producing the records would be in a representative capacity, not a personal one, so the records must be produced. The Court stated that, had the business been a sole proprietorship, Braswell would have had the opportunity to show that the act of production would have been self-incriminating. Because his business was a corporation, he was acting as a representative of a corporation, and regardless of how small the corporation, he could not claim a privilege. The Court of Appeals for the Eighth Circuit recently applied the Supreme Court's decision in the *Braswell* case, as the appellate court ordered a woman to produce corporate documents, even though the corporation's charter was revoked.[40] The appellate court reasoned that the subpoena of documents from an inactive corporation does not constitute a violation of the corporate custodian's Fifth Amendment rights.

THE FOURTEENTH AMENDMENT

The **Fourteenth Amendment** is important because it applies the Due Process Clause to the state governments. It has been interpreted to apply almost the entire Bill of Rights to the states, with the exceptions of the Fifth Amendment

Fourteenth Amendment
Applies the entire Bill of Rights, excepting parts of the Fifth Amendment, to the states.

---

[38] 465 U.S. 605 (1984).

[39] 487 U.S. 99 (1988).

[40] *In re*: Grand Jury Subpoena, 75 Fed. Appx. 562 (2003).

right to indictment by a grand jury for certain types of crimes and the right to trial by jury.

The Fourteenth Amendment is also important because it contains the Equal Protection Clause, which prevents the states from denying "the equal protection of the laws" to any citizen. This clause has been a useful tool for people attempting to reduce discrimination in this country. Its significance in this area is examined in Chapter 20.

SUMMARY

The framework of our nation is embodied in the U.S. Constitution, which established a system of government based on the concept of federalism. Under this system, the power to regulate local matters is given to the states; the federal government is granted limited powers to regulate activities that substantially affect interstate commerce. All powers not specifically given to the federal government are reserved to the states.

The Commerce Clause is the primary source of the federal government's authority to regulate business. The same clause restricts states from passing regulations that would interfere with interstate commerce. The state and federal governments are limited in their regulations by the amendments to the Constitution, especially the Bill of Rights. The First Amendment, for example, protects our individual right to free expression; commercial speech is also entitled to a significant amount of protection in this area.

Other important amendments for the businessperson are the Fourth Amendment, which protects one's right to be free from unwarranted searches and seizures, and the Fifth Amendment, which establishes one's right to due process. A final amendment that has a significant impact on the legal environment is the Fourteenth Amendment, which applies most of the Bill of Rights to the states and also contains the Equal Protection Clause.

REVIEW QUESTIONS

5-1 Explain the relationship between the Supremacy Clause and the doctrine of federal preemption.

5-2 How does the Commerce Clause affect federal regulation of business activities?

5-3 What is police power?

5-4 How does the Commerce Clause affect state regulation of business?

5-5 Explain why you believe the courts have found each of the following to either constitute or not constitute a regulatory taking: (a) a city

ordinance reducing the size limit for freestanding signs within the city limits, forcing plaintiff to replace his sign; (b) a city ordinance prohibiting billboards along roads in residential areas of the city; (c) the refusal of the Army Corps of Engineers to grant Florida Rock Company a permit to allow it to mine limestone that lay beneath a track of wetlands.

5-6 How does the First Amendment protection of private speech differ from the protection of commercial speech?

5-7 Voters in the State of California decide that the tobacco industry is having too great an impact on the outcome of local referenda limiting smoking in public places. To curb the influence of that powerful lobby, so that the fate of the legislation is more clearly reflective of the will of "the people," they pass a law prohibiting firms in the tobacco industry and tobacco industry associations from (1) purchasing advertising related to smoking-related referenda and (2) making cash contributions to organizations involved in campaigns related to antismoking legislation. Several tobacco firms challenge the law. What is the constitutional basis for their challenge? Why will they be likely to succeed or fail?

5-8 Ms. Crabtree is given a one-year, nontenured contract to teach English at Haddock State University, a public institution. After her contract year ends, she is not offered a contract for the next year and is not given any explanation as to why she is not being rehired. She sues the school, arguing that her right to procedural due process has been violated. Is she correct?

5-9 The State of Ohio decides that Ohio's landfills are becoming too full at too rapid a pace, so it passes a law banning the import of waste generated out of state. Several landfill operators have contracts with out-of-state generators, so they sue the state to have the statute declared void. What arguments will each side make in this case? What is the most likely decision? Why?

5-10 Chen opens a small business. As business thrives, he decides to incorporate. He becomes the corporation's president and also its sole shareholder.

Chen comes under investigation for tax fraud and is subpoenaed to produce the corporate tax records for the prior three years. He challenges the subpoena on the grounds that it violates his Fifth Amendment right not to incriminate himself. Must he comply with the subpoena?

5-11 Congress passed the Americans with Disabilities Act requiring, among other provisions, that places of public accommodation remove architectural barriers to access where such removal is "readily achievable." If such removal is not "readily achievable," the firm must make its goods or services available through alternative methods if such methods are readily achievable. To comply with the law, Ricardo's Restaurant will have to construct a ramp at the entrance to the restaurant and two ramps within the dining area, rearrange some of the tables and chairs, and remodel the restrooms so that they will accommodate wheelchairs. Because of the expenditures Ricardo will have to make to comply with the law, he challenges the law as being a taking of private property without just compensation in violation of the Fifth Amendment. Does the law violate the Fifth Amendment?

5-12 Plaintiffs owned a piece of lakeside property. The land was subsequently rezoned to prohibit high-density apartment complexes and restrict the use of the property to single family dwellings. On what basis would the plaintiffs claim their constitutional rights had been violated by the zoning change? Would they be correct?

CASE PROBLEMS

5-13 In 1972, using the power it was given by the Commerce Clause to regulate interstate commerce, Congress passed the Clean Water Act to reduce the pollution of U.S. waters. Congress gave the Army Corps of Engineers (Corps) the power to approve or deny permits to discharge dredged or fill materials into navigable waters, and Congress gave the Environmental Protection Agency (EPA) the power to veto the Corps's permits. In 1975 a federal judge decided that this provision also applied to wetlands that were adjacent to navigable waters. Subsequent regulatory and court decisions further

expanded federal power through the adoption of the "migratory bird rule" in 1986, which gave the Corps the authority to also issue permits for the filling of isolated wetlands if those wetlands were used by migratory birds.

In 1994 a consortium of suburban Chicago municipalities selected as a solid waste disposal site an abandoned sand and gravel pit with excavation trenches that had evolved into permanent and seasonal ponds. Because the operation called for filling in some of the ponds, the consortium contacted the Corps to determine whether it needed a permit. Because the ponds were used as habitat for migratory birds, the Corps required the consortium to apply for a permit. When the Corps refused to grant the permit, the consortium challenged both the denial of the permit on its merits and the authority of Congress to regulate bodies of water that were not interstate. In other words, it argued that the migratory bird rule was beyond the scope of the federal government's authority. Explain why you believe that Congress either did or did not exceed its authority under the Commerce Clause. *Solid Waste Agency of Northern Cook County v. United States Army Corps of Engineers et al.*, 531 U.S. 159 (2001)

5-14 Del Monte Dunes wanted to develop a 37.6-acre oceanfront parcel located in the city of Monterey. The parcel itself was zoned for multifamily residential use under the city's general zoning ordinance. The planning commission rejected four applications, although the city overruled the planning commission on the last rejection, referring the application back to the commission. Each subsequent rejection made greater demands on the landowner and also decreased the number of housing units the developer could build. A fifth application was also rejected by the planning commission. The city overruled the planning commission, approving one of the site plans, and the landowner obtained a permit. After a year of planning, the landowner went back with the final plan, which the city's architecture committee recommended for approval. However, the planning commission rejected the final plan, and on appeal, the city also rejected the plan.

The city made general findings that the landowners had not provided adequate access for the development (even though the landowners had twice changed the specific access plans to comply with the city's demands and maintained they could satisfy the city's new objections if granted an extension), that the plan's layout would damage the environment (even though the location of the development on the property was necessitated by the city's demands for a public beach, view corridors, and a buffer zone next to the state park), and that the plan would disrupt the habitat of the Smith's Blue Butterfly (even though the plan would remove the encroaching ice plant and preserve or restore buckwheat habitat on almost half of the property, and even though only one larva had ever been found on the property).

After five years, five formal decisions, and 19 different site plans, respondent Del Monte Dunes decided the city would not permit development of the property under any circumstances. Del Monte Dunes filed suit against the city. Explain the constitutional basis of its lawsuit. How do you believe the Supreme Court ultimately decided this case? Why? *City of Monterey v. Del Monte Dunes*, 520 U.S. 687, 119 S.Ct. 1624 (1999)

5-15 The State of Washington established a program to provide legal services for the needy. The program was called Interest on Lawyers' Trust Accounts (IOLTA), involving the requirement that clients deposit their legal payments into trust accounts, whereby the interest earned on such accounts would be channeled to a nonprofit organization. This organization would then use the interest earned as funds for charitable legal services and educational purposes. The program was later extended to include nonlawyer limited practice officers (LPOs).

Several parties, including two individuals who frequently bought and sold real estate, brought suit against the nonprofit organization, alleging that payments they made to LPOs via IOLTA accounts resulted in an unlawful taking of interest earned on those accounts. Because they did not receive just compensation for this taking, the two individuals contended that the organization violated the individuals' Fifth Amendment rights.

The district and appellate courts both argued that there had been no taking, and even if there had been a taking, the amount of just compensation would be zero. The two individuals appealed. Explain why you believe the U.S. Supreme Court either upheld or overturned the decision of the appellate court. *Brown v. Legal Foundation of Washington*, 538 U.S. 216 (2003)

5-16 The Federal Communications Commission (FCC) prohibited radio and television broadcasters from carrying advertising about private, commercial gambling casinos. Broadcasters believed that the FCC could not constitutionally prohibit them from advertising legal casino gambling in Louisiana and Mississippi. The lower courts upheld the restrictions on advertising and the broadcasters appealed. Using the test from *Central Hudson*, explain why you believe the U.S. Supreme Court either affirmed or overturned the lower courts' ruling. *Greater New Orleans Broadcasting Association v. United States*, 119 S.Ct. 1923 (1999)

5-17 Steven Dewayne Bond was a passenger on a Greyhound bus going from California to Little Rock, Arkansas. The bus stopped, as it was required to do, at the permanent Border Patrol checkpoint in Sierra Blanca, Texas. A Border Patrol agent boarded the bus to check the immigration status of its passengers. After reaching the back of the bus, having satisfied himself that the passengers were lawfully in the United States, the agent began walking toward the front. Along the way, he squeezed the soft luggage that passengers had placed in the overhead storage space above the seats.

Bond was seated four or five rows from the back of the bus. As the agent inspected the luggage in the compartment above Bond's seat, he squeezed a green canvas bag and noticed that it contained a bricklike object. Bond admitted that the bag was his and agreed to allow the agent to open it. When he opened the bag, the agent discovered a "brick" of methamphetamine. The brick had been wrapped in duct tape until it was oval-shaped and then rolled in a pair of pants.

Bond was indicted for conspiracy to possess, and possession with intent to distribute, methamphetamine. He moved to suppress the drugs, arguing that the agent had conducted an illegal search of his bag. His motion was denied, and the district court found him guilty on both counts and sentenced him to 57 months in prison. On appeal, he conceded that other passengers had access to his bag, but contended that the agent manipulated the bag in a way that other passengers would not. The court of appeals rejected this argument, stating that the fact that Agent Cantu's manipulation of petitioner's bag was calculated to detect contraband is irrelevant for Fourth Amendment purposes. Thus, the court upheld the denial of the motion to suppress. Bond appealed the denial to the U.S. Supreme Court. What argument would you make on behalf of Bond? How do you believe the U.S.

Supreme Court ruled on this appeal? *Bond v. United States*, 529 U.S. 334, 120 S.Ct. 1462 (2000)

5-18 During an altercation in California, police officers shot Oliverio Martinez and placed him under arrest, but the police never provided Martinez with Miranda warnings. Martinez required medical treatment for his severe wounds. Patrol supervisor Chavez proceeded to question Martinez about his conduct while Martinez was receiving medical treatment at a nearby hospital. Although Martinez was not charged with a crime or tried for his actions, Martinez filed suit against the patrol supervisor, alleging that Chavez violated Martinez's Fifth Amendment privileges against self-incrimination. Martinez also argued that Chavez used coercive questioning, thereby violating Martinez's Fourteenth Amendment due process rights.

The district court granted summary judgment for Martinez, and the Court of Appeals for the Ninth Circuit also concluded that the patrol supervisor violated Martinez's Fifth Amendment and Fourteenth Amendment rights. Chavez appealed. Explain why you believe the Supreme Court either affirmed or reversed the appellate court's decision. *Chavez v. Martinez*, 538 U.S. 760 (2003)

ASSIGNMENT ON THE INTERNET

This chapter introduces you to the many constitutional principles that govern business activities. One such principle is that of free speech and the extent to which it applies to commercial speech. For example, should advertisements for pharmaceuticals be subject to Federal Drug Administration (FDA) regulations and limitations?

Read the summary from a recent Supreme Court decision about the advertising of pharmaceuticals from the pharmaceutical industry found at: www.oyez.org/oyez/resource/case/1462. Can you determine from the summary if the *Central Hudson* test was applied to the case? If so, how?

 ## ON THE INTERNET

www.aclu.org/FreeSpeech/FreeSpeechMain.cfm The ACLU is one of the largest organizations devoted to the protection of free speech and this site serves as an informative tool in understanding the various efforts to protect the First Amendment right.

www.law.umkc.edu/faculty/projects/ftrials/conlaw/home.html This site explores various issues of constitutional law, including the Commerce Clause, taxation, commercial speech, and the Takings Clause. Each issue includes brief summations of landmark court cases in that area of the law.

www.landmarkcases.org/gibbons/power.html Landmark Supreme Court cases interpreting the Commerce Clause can be found at this site. Pay close attention to how Congress has used to Commerce Clause to police and regulate businesses.

www.oyez.org/oyez/portlet/directory/400/411 The Oyez Directory, a United State Supreme Court Web site, provides salient cases in all major areas of constitutional law. This link displays recent commercial speech disputes that have been decided by the Supreme Court.

6

CYBERLAW AND BUSINESS

- **CYBERLAW AND BUSINESS: HOW LAW CHANGES AS SOCIETY CHANGES**
- **INTELLECTUAL PROPERTY ISSUES IN CYBERSPACE**
- **E-COMMERCE ISSUES**
- **EMPLOYMENT LAW ISSUES IN CYBERSPACE**
- **THE WAR AGAINST CYBERCRIME**

Laws that govern cyberspace are changing daily. Companies such as Napster start, thrive, and then change as a consequence of legal challenges that test the boundaries of cyberspace. They are replaced by new companies, such as Grokster, Ltd., which offer new business models and raise new legal questions for courts to resolve. Some companies have also tried to establish themselves as online businesses, only to discover they need bricks and mortar in addition to an online presence to survive. News stories have chronicled the dark side of the Internet, for example, the proliferation of child pornography, computer viruses, and identity theft. This area of law is dynamic and shows how traditional legal rules can adapt to meet challenges in cyberspace.

The chapter presents issues that fall under a wide range of legal topics, including a general discussion of how legal issues in cyberspace provide an opportunity for managers to see how law changes as society changes; an overview of the new slant on intellectual property issues and e-commerce; an outline of issues related to privacy and online marketing; a summary of employment issues in cyberspace, including employment-at-will in cyberspace and online harassment; and an explanation of how government regulators and law enforcement officials are working with the business community to battle the war against cybercrime.

CYBERLAW AND BUSINESS: HOW LAW CHANGES AS SOCIETY CHANGES

THE FLEXIBILITY OF LAW

In Chapter 1, the text explained the flexible nature of law. In particular, the chapter explained that as the business environment changes, the legal system adjusts to those changes. Businesspeople expect the law to provide a path that allows them to achieve their business goals. Currently, the legal system is adapting to the most important changes in the business environment that are being brought about by the Internet and e-commerce (i.e., the increasing commercial uses of the World Wide Web). Business conducted on the Internet is not constricted by territorial boundaries; consumers who make purchases with a click of a mouse expect businesses to respond quickly and efficiently. The same is true of business-to-business commerce. As Exhibit 6-1 indicates, those who interact with the Internet and e-commerce have learned new concepts to describe transactions.

In this new world without boundaries, American citizens are getting to see just how flexible our legal system is and experiencing firsthand the tensions between clashing values and ethical norms. Recent cases, such as the lawsuits between the motion picture and recording industries and those who use their products without paying for them, have raised important questions:

- Is the "wide open, no standards" format of cyberspace a strength or a weakness when it comes to e-commerce?[1]

EXHIBIT 6-1

THE LANGUAGE OF CYBERSPACE

When the United States Supreme Court first decided a case involving cyberspace in 1997 in *Reno v. ACLU*, 521 U.S. 844 (see the next section of the chapter), the Court defined cyberlaw terms.

Here are some definitions created from that case:

The Internet: "an international network of interconnected computers . . . 'a unique and wholly new medium of worldwide human communication'" (pp. 849–850).

Online services: "offer access to their own extensive proprietary networks as well as a link to the much larger resources of the Internet . . . [examples are America Online, Compuserv . . .]" (p. 850).

Cyberspace: "Tools . . . [examples are e-mail, chat rooms, the World Wide Web] . . . constitute a unique medium—known to its users as 'cyberspace'—[which is] located in no particular geographical location but available to anyone, anywhere in the world, with access to the Internet" (p. 851).

World Wide Web: "The best known category of communication over the Internet . . . [It] allows users to search for and retrieve information stored in remote computers, as well as, in some cases, to communicate back to designated sites . . . the Web consists of a vast number of documents stored in different computers all over the world. Some of these documents are simply files containing information. However, more elaborate documents, known as Web 'pages,' are also prevalent" (p. 852).

---

[1]Steven M. H. Wallman and Kathleen M. H. Wallman, "Law and Electronic Commerce: The Next Frontier," *3 Telecommunications Reports International Journal* (1999), at **www.brook.edu/views/articles/wallman/1999winter.thm**.

- Will cyberspace meet society's expectation that speech should remain free?

- Will freedom of speech clash with the concept of security and intellectual property rights?

- Will cyberspace facilitate free trade, or will citizens see darker sides to freedom?

- Who benefits in a world in which geographical, physical, and political limits do not apply? Who might suffer?

- What kind of legal system does an increasingly technologically based society need?

CHANGES IN THE WAYS COURTS FUNCTION

On a more practical level, those who administer the law are starting to see how changes brought about by the Internet are changing the way they function. Some groups are starting to resolve small claims disputes online through services such as SquareTrade.com. Actors in the traditional legal system may appreciate this trend, as many courts are unable to handle the increased caseload brought about by questions raised by e-commerce transactions.

In the meantime, however, traditional courts are grappling with important issues that arise from a borderless world. For example, before a court can reach a decision in a case, it must be sure it has the power to hear the case. Recall that jurisdiction is the power of a court to hear a case and render a binding decision. Courts must have jurisdiction over both the subject matter and a person or property.

As e-commerce has evolved, courts have had to decide whether (1) a court can establish jurisdiction over a nonresident person or business based on the presence of a Web site in a particular forum and (2) defendants who use the Internet to transact business are "purposefully availing"[2] themselves of doing business in every state in the United States and throughout the world.

Generally, courts have held that the mere presence of a Web site in a particular forum is not enough to give a court personal jurisdiction over a nonresident defendant. Specific cases have considered the extent of **interactivity** of a Web site to determine whether the site subjects the defendant to personal jurisdiction. Although the Pennsylvania case of *Zippo Manufacturing Co. v. Zippo Dot Com Inc.*[3] is not binding on other jurisdictions, many courts have used the sliding scale the court developed in that case as the basis for their decisions about personal jurisdiction (see Exhibit 6-2).

The toughest cases are the ones that fall in the middle of the scale. Businesses that want to engage in e-commerce do not want to have to defend themselves in expensive litigation if a dispute arises. Issues arising from order forms, toll-free numbers for ordering from anywhere in the world, consumer

interactivity The extent to which a Web site involves two-way communication between the site and user.

---

[2] Recall that we learned in *World-Wide Volkswagen Corporation v. Woodson*, 444 U.S. 286 (1980), that corporations that "purposefully avail" themselves of the privilege of conducting activities within the forum state have clear notice that they are subject to suit in that forum.

[3] 952 F.Supp. 1119 (W.D. Pa. 1997).

The defendant clearly transacts business over the Internet Does the defendant enter into contracts that require knowingly and repeatedly transmitting computer files over the Internet? Does the defendant sell goods over the Internet? The more accessible the Web site is in a particular forum and the more commerce is transacted, the more likely it is that the defendant is subject to personal jurisdiction in that forum.

The user exchanges information with the Web site How much does the site interact with the user? The more interactive the site, the more likely the court will find that in personam jurisdiction exists.

The Web site is passive Does the defendant merely advertise its services on a Web site? This low level of interactivity is not enough to establish in personam jurisdiction.

EXHIBIT 6-2

ZIPPO'S **SLIDING SCALE: THREE LEVELS OF INTERACTIVITY**

interaction with a salesperson, and e-mail to the Web site can all lead to disputes that end up in court. Courts are just now making decisions related to these topics.

You have already learned about four values that underlie ethical decision making. You learned about four values that influence business ethics: freedom, security, justice, and efficiency. Step into the shoes of a judge who is trying to decide where to draw the line in one of the "middle" cases related to personal jurisdiction. Would a judge who values freedom over other values draw the line at a different place than one who values security above other values? What about a judge who cherishes the value of efficiency? Why is the ethical norm of justice less relevant than the other values when deciding on questions related to jurisdiction?

CHALLENGES TO THE LIMITS AND POWERS OF GOVERNMENT

Actions Taken by the Federal Government As the legal system adjusts to the explosive growth of the Internet and World Wide Web, state and federal governments are redefining their roles. At the federal level, individuals who follow business news have watched the Justice Department use antitrust laws to protect free markets by putting a stop to Microsoft's alleged abuse of its monopoly power.[4] The government is also providing protection in the area of e-commerce. Later in this chapter, you will read about how a variety of public and private actors are working together to stop cybercrime related to e-commerce.

Citizens also count on the United States Supreme Court to provide a check on Congress. In Case 6-1, the United States Supreme Court considers a First Amendment case concerning a state law creating liability for transmitting certain material over the Internet.

---

[4] See *U.S. v. Microsoft*, 65 F.Supp. 2d 1 (D.D.C. 1999). In 1999, in a preliminary ruling, Judge Thomas Penfield Jackson did find that Microsoft holds monopoly power with its Windows operating system and that it used its power to harm both consumers and competitors. In June 2000, Judge Jackson used a final ruling, which called for Microsoft to be split into two companies, one for the Windows operating system, and one for its Internet and other businesses. In June 2001, in *U.S. v. Microsoft*, 253 F.2d 34 (2001), the Court of Appeals affirmed the decision in part, reversed it in part, and remanded it in part. In September 2001, the Department of Justice decided to stop seeking the breakup of Microsoft.

CASE 6-1

Janet RENO, Attorney General of the United States, et al., Appellants v. American Civil Liberties Union, et al., Appellee

Supreme Court of the United States 521 U.S. 844 (1997)

This case was the first case involving the limits and powers of government to regulate the Internet to be heard by the United States Supreme Court. The American Civil Liberties Union (ACLU) and the federal government asked the Court to decide whether Congress violated the free speech protections of the First Amendment of the United States Constitution when it passed the Communications Decency Act (CDA). A Pennsylvania district court had found this legislation unconstitutional under the First Amendment.

The CDA created criminal liability for the online transmission of "indecent" and "patently offensive" material to minors. In addition, it created a defense for defendants who, in good faith, took effective actions to restrict access by minors to indecent material or for those defendants who conditioned access on the provision of a credit card, debit account, adult access code, or adult personal identification number. However, because technology does not currently exist that would allow senders to block minors but not adults from accessing Internet communications, the CDA would limit adult-to-adult communications in addition to communications with minors.

In this case, the Court considered these issues: (1) Does the Internet enjoy the fullest degree of First Amendment protection? (2) Is the CDA unconstitutionally overbroad? (3) Can the CDA be considered a "cyberzone" and analyzed as a time, place, and manner regulation since it applies to all of cyberspace? (4) Did Congress demonstrate that it could not find less restrictive means of advancing its interest in protecting children from indecent speech?

After deciding that the contested provisions of the CDA were content-based blanket restrictions on speech and, thus, could not be analyzed as time, place, and manner regulations, the Court applied "strict scrutiny" to the statute.

Justice Stevens

Neither before nor after the enactment of the CDA have the vast democratic fora of the Internet been subject to the type of government supervision and regulation that have attended the broadcast industry. Moreover, the Internet is not as "invasive" as radio or television. The District Court specifically found that "[c]ommunications over the Internet do not 'invade' an individual's home or appear on one's computer screen unbidden. Users seldom encounter content 'by accident.'" It also found that "[a]lmost all sexually explicit images are preceded by warnings as to the content," and cited testimony that "'odds are slim' that a user could come across a sexually explicit site by accident."

In *Sable* [*Communications of Cal., Inc.*], a company engaged in the business of offering sexually oriented prerecorded telephone messages (popularly known as "dial-a-porn") challenged the constitutionality of an amendment to the Communications Act that imposed a blanket prohibition on indecent as well as obscene interstate commercial telephone messages. We held that the statute was constitutional insofar as it applied to obscene messages but invalid as applied to indecent messages. In attempting to justify the complete ban and criminalization of indecent commercial telephone messages, the Government ... [argued] that the ban was necessary to prevent children from gaining access to such messages. We agreed that "there is a compelling interest in protecting the physical and psychological well-being of minors" which extended to shielding them from indecent messages that are not obscene by adult standards. ... [However, we could not allow the blanket prohibition on indecent messages because] "the dial-it medium requires the listener to take affirmative steps to receive the communication. ..."

[T]he Internet ... provides a relatively unlimited, low-cost capacity for communication of all kinds. The Government estimates that "[a]s many as 40 million people use the Internet today, and that figure is expected to grow to 200 million by 1999." This dynamic, multifaceted category of communication includes not only traditional print and news services, but also audio, video, and still images, as well as interactive, real-time dialogue. Through the use of chat rooms, any person with a phone line can become a town crier with a voice that resonates farther than it could from any soapbox. Through the use of Web pages, mail exploders, and newsgroups, the same individual can become a pamphleteer. As the District Court found, "the content on the Internet is as diverse as human thought." We agree with its conclusion that our cases provide no basis for qualifying the level of First Amendment scrutiny that should be applied to this medium.

The District Court was correct to conclude that the CDA effectively resembles the ban on "dial-a-porn" invalidated in *Sable*. In *Sable*, this Court rejected the argument that we should defer to Congressional judgment that nothing less than a total ban would be effective in preventing enterprising youngsters from gaining access to indecent communications. *Sable* thus made clear that the mere fact that a statutory regulation of speech was enacted for the purpose of protecting children from exposure to sexually explicit material does not foreclose inquiry into its validity. ... [T]hat inquiry embodies an "over-arching commitment" to make sure that Congress has designed its statute to accomplish its purpose "without imposing an unnecessarily great restriction on speech."

The breadth of the CDA's coverage is wholly unprecedented. ... [T]he scope of the CDA is not limited to commercial speech or commercial entities. Its open-ended prohibitions embrace all nonprofit entities and individuals posting indecent messages or displaying them on their own computers in the presence of minors. ...

The breadth of this content-based regulation of speech imposes an especially heavy burden on the Government to explain why a less restrictive provision would not be as effective as the CDA. It has not done so. The arguments in this Court have referred to possible alternatives such as requiring that indecent material be "tagged" in a way that facilitates parental control of material coming into their homes, making exceptions for messages with artistic or educational value, providing some tolerance for parental choice, and regulating some portions of the Internet—such as commercial

web sites—differently than others, such as chat rooms ... [W]e are persuaded that the CDA is not narrowly tailored. ...

We agree with the District Court's conclusion that the CDA places an unacceptably heavy burden on protected speech, and that the defenses do not constitute the sort of "narrow tailoring" that will save an otherwise patently invalid constitutional provision. In *Sable*, we remarked that the speech restriction at issue there amounted to "burn[ing] the house to roast the pig." The CDA, casting a far darker shadow over free speech, threatens to torch a large segment of the Internet community.

[T]he growth of the Internet has been and continues to be phenomenal. As a matter of constitutional tradition, in the absence of evidence to the contrary, we presume that governmental regulation of the content of speech is more likely to interfere with the free exchange of ideas than to encourage it. The interest in encouraging freedom of expression in a democratic society outweighs any theoretical but unproven benefit of censorship.

Affirmed in favor of the Appellee,
American Civil Liberties Union.

Critical Thinking About the Law

As you know, courts often use analogies when making decisions. Often, once the Court decides which analogy it will use, it has decided who will win and lose the case. That is true in Case 6-1 in which the Court scrutinized the CDA. Please refer to Case 6-1 and consider the following questions:

1. The United States Supreme Court decided that the *Sable* case is a good analogy to the case before the Court. Once the government realized the Court saw *Sable* as a good analogy, the government knew it was likely to lose and that the CDA would be struck down. How so?

   Clue: Reread the discussion of *Sable*, paying particular attention to the level of scrutiny the Court applied to the law challenged in that case.

2. If you were a member of Congress who had a hand in drafting the CDA, how would you modify this legislation in light of the Court's opinion?

   Clue: Reread the Court's discussion of how the CDA is too broad and think of ways to make the law narrower in scope.

In 2000, the United States Supreme Court decided another First Amendment case in a way that affirms its commitment to First Amendment protection of speech. In *U.S. v. Playboy Entertainment, Inc.*,[5] Playboy Entertainment Group challenged a federal law that required cable systems to limit sexually explicit channels to late-night hours. The Court ruled that Congress overstepped its

[5] 529 U.S. 803 (2000).

bounds when it passed the Telecommunications Act of 1996.[6] This act required operators to scramble sexually explicit channels in full or limit programming on such channels to certain hours.

At issue in *Playboy* was Section 505 of this act that responded to the problem of "signal bleed" in cable television, which refers to the momentary bits of video and/or audio from some channels (i.e., Playboy channels) viewers may sometimes see or hear while watching other programs.[7] Section 505 required blocking technology to be installed in every household in every cable system that offers adult programming, including two-thirds of homes without children.[8] Alternatively, cable operators could restrict transmission of adult networks from 6:00 A.M. to 10:00 P.M.[9]

In striking down Section 505, the Court emphasized that when technology allows users of communication tools to choose what they see or hear, those users rather than the government should do the choosing. In effect, the Court ruled in favor of individual choice over government regulation. Legal experts expect this decision to place restrictions on Congress's efforts to regulate speech in cyberspace.[10]

State Actions State governments are also adjusting to changes brought about by the use of the Internet and World Wide Web. State legislatures have passed statutes that attempt to balance freedom with other ethical norms, such as security for children. In 2002, for example, Pennsylvania passed the Internet Child Pornography Act. This act forced Internet service providers to block customers' access to Web sites thought to be distributing child pornography. The Pennsylvania law was the first state attempt to impose criminal liability on Internet service providers when they had no direct relationship with the content source.[11] In September 2004, a federal district court declared the statute an unconstitutional restriction on free speech as it blocked an extensive amount of innocent speech.[12]

Another example of how states are responding to the evolving nature of cyberspace relates to Internet wine sales. Today, approximately two dozen states ban direct shipment of wine from out of state to in-state residents, even though they allow in-state wineries to pursue direct shipment to in-state residents.[13] In its 2004–2005 term, the United States Supreme Court will attempt to reconcile the Commerce Clause (which prohibits discrimination against interstate commerce) and the Twenty-First Amendment (which gives states the authority to regulate access to alcohol).[14] States that have placed restrictions on shipment of wines from out of state want to make sure they protect minors and collect taxes on the products. Consumers and winery owners want a more fluid wine market. They like the idea of goods flowing freely across state lines.

---

[6] Linda Greenhouse, "Court Overrules Law Restricting Cable Sex Shows," *New York Times*, May 23, 2000, pp. A1, A20.

[7] "Playboy Enterprises, Inc. Applauds Court Ruling", *PR Newswire*, May 22, 2000.

[8] *Id.*

[9] *Id.*

[10] *Id.*, p. A20.

[11] *Center for Democracy & Technology v. Pappert*, (E.D. Pa. 2004), available at 2004 WL 2005938.

[12] *Id.*

[13] Reuters, "Wine Laws Challenged in N.Y.," *National Law Journal*, February 21, 2000.

[14] Marcia Coyle, "New High Court Term Won't Be a Quiet One," *National Law Journal*, September 13, 2004, pp. 1, 11.

A final example focuses on challenges to states' traditional regulatory role. Traditionally, states have regulated the way consumers gain access to prescription drugs. E-commerce has changed the way consumers gain access to these drugs because the Internet does not respect state or international boundaries. Consequently, some health law lawyers believe states can no longer regulate effectively and that citizens will see ongoing debates about whether federal regulators should expand their power to regulate in this area.[15] Federal regulators promise to protect consumers from harm without dampening the pharmaceutical industry's interest in innovation.[16]

INTELLECTUAL PROPERTY ISSUES IN CYBERSPACE

PATENTS

A **patent** protects a product, process, invention, machine, or plant produced by asexual reproduction. The government grants an exclusive property right when an invention is novel and useful. Also, the invention must be genuine and not obvious. This exclusive property right lasts for 20 years.

Historically, inventors have patented physical inventions. Now, however, inventors want to apply for patents to protect Internet business methods and technologies, such as methods for streaming digital audio and video.[17] **Patent infringement** occurs when someone uses, sells, or manufactures the patented invention without the patent holder's permission. In a recent line of cases, a company called Acadia Research has filed lawsuits against distributors of adult videos, asserting that these distributors infringed on patents that cover methods for streaming digital audio and video.[18] Legal experts expect to see more lawsuits such as these, asking for protection for specific technologies rather than more tangible inventions.

TRADEMARKS

A **trademark** is a distinctive mark, word, design, picture, or arrangement used by the producer of a product that tends to cause consumers to identify the product with the producer. The goal of trademark law is to protect the right of commercial businesses to create marks consumers will identify with a particular producer. An issue that has arisen recently in cyberspace is whether "keywording" violates the spirit of fair competition that trademark law is supposed to protect.[19] **Keywording** occurs when advertisers pay to have their advertisements displayed when a computer user types in certain keywords. For example, travel site Expedia might buy the search terms "Orbitz" and "Travelocity" so that when

patent Protects a product, process, invention, machine, or plant produced by asexual reproduction.

patent infringement Occurs when someone uses, sells, or manufactures the patented invention without the patent holder's permission.

trademark A distinctive mark, word, design, picture, or arrangement used by the producer of a product that tends to cause consumers to identify the product with the producer.

keywording Occurs when advertisers pay to have their advertisements displayed when a computer user types in certain keywords.

---

[15] Kenneth Korenchuk, "21st-Century Technology Meets 20th-Century Laws: Tension Between Old Divisions of Federal and State Jurisdiction Impedes Growth of Web Rx Biz," *National Law Journal*, April 10, 2000, p. B19.

[16] *Id.*, p. B21.

[17] Robert Gerber, "Internet Litigation and the Battle to Protect Intellectual Property Rights," *Mondaq Business Briefing*, September 15, 2004, retrieved as 2004 WL 69984378.

[18] *Id.*

[19] *Id.*

Linking Law & Business

Human Resource Management

In the field of human resource management, you have learned about nondisclosure agreements and noncompete agreements. These agreements are useful in protecting intellectual property including patents. Employers can use contracts with employees to reward employees who make discoveries that add value to the firm. The firm itself owns the intellectual property the employee created.

a user enters a search using "Orbitz" or "Travelocity," an ad for Expedia will pop up nearby. Travel site competitors Orbitz and Travelocity will want to use trademark law to protect their keywords.

domain name Text names matched to particular Internet protocols or addresses.

Similar issues arise regarding the use of domain names. **Domain names** are text names matched to particular Internet protocols or addresses. They have become trademarks that allow us to identify products with producers. For instance, you probably identify the domain name "Amazon.com" with a particular product (books). It is clear that domain names are more to businesses than mere addresses.

Trademarks and Piracy As these domain names have become more valuable, they have provided an opportunity for **cybersquatters** (or **cyberpirates**) to engage in questionable acts to make a profit. Typically, cybersquatting occurs when an individual or business intentionally obtains a domain name registration for a company's trademark so it can sell the domain name back to the trademark owner; the individual "pirates" the domain name.

cybersquatters *or* **cyberpirates** Individuals or businesses that intentionally obtain a domain name registration for a company's trademark so that it can sell the domain name back to the trademark owner.

Another form of cybersquatting occurs when an individual or business registers a domain name that is the same or similar to a preexisting trademark that belongs to someone else. The intent is to confuse the consumer. For instance, a cybersquatter might register the domain name "eBuy," hoping the consumer will be confused and believe "eBuy" is "eBay," a well-known online auction site.

Still another problem occurs when two businesses have good faith desires to use the same domain name. For instance, more than one e-commerce consulting firm might want to use the domain name "e-solutions.com." Domain names are like telephone numbers; they must be unique to a single owner to work. It would not be possible for two companies to use the domain name "e-solutions.com" unless they agreed to share a Web site.

warehousing An act of bad faith that occurs when an individual or business registers domain names in the hope that the name can be sold to a business.

Additionally, the law does not respond to a problem known as **warehousing**, which occurs when an individual or business registers names with a hope of later selling the name to a business that wants a particular name. This idea of warehousing is similar to cybersquatting but without the bad faith component.

The Anticybersquatting Consumer Protection Act In November 1999, the United States became the first country to pass legislation aimed directly at these types of activities. The Anticybersquatting Consumer Protection Act responds to the first two problems just described—traditional piracy and intentional confusion. The act gives courts the power to forfeit, cancel, or transfer domain names. This was not possible under traditional intellectual property laws, which provide remedies for trademark dilution, unfair competition, false advertising, and counterfeiting. Under the new law, cybersquatters may be required to pay both actual and statutory damages that range from $1,000 to $100,000 per domain name. This new legislation does not respond to the problem of two businesses registering the same domain or the problem of warehousing. Undoubtedly, future legislation will deal with these matters.

COPYRIGHTS

Copyrights protect the *expression* of creative ideas. Copyrights protect fixed forms of expression, not ideas themselves. Copyrights protect a diverse range of creative works, such as books, periodicals, musical compositions, plays, motion pictures, sound recordings, lectures, works of art, and computer programs. For a work to be copyrightable, it must be fixed (i.e., set out in a tangible medium of expression), original, and creative. Copyrights are protected under common law. A person who wants to make sure he or she can collect damages from a copyright infringer protects his or her work by registering it with the Register of Copyrights and providing two copies of the work to the Library of Congress.

copyright The exclusive legal right to reproduce, publish, and sell the fixed form of expression of an original creative idea.

Copyrights and Piracy If a person believes someone is infringing on his or her copyright, that person may ask a court to enjoin the infringer from reproducing the copyrighted work. In response alleged infringers often assert the **fair use doctrine**, which provides that a copyrighted work may be reproduced for a range of purposes, including criticism, news reporting, and teaching. In Case 6-2, the court considers what it means for a company to engage in direct copyright infringement and what the company must assert to establish a defense based on the fair use doctrine.

fair use doctrine A legal doctrine providing that a copyrighted work may be reproduced for purposes of "criticism, comment, news reporting, teaching (including multiple copies for classroom use), scholarship, and research."

CASE 6-2

A & M Records, Inc. v. Napster, Inc.
United States Court of Appeals for the Ninth Circuit (California) 239 F. 3d 1004 (2001)

Record companies and music publishers sued Napster. Napster is a free online music trading service. The company provides software that facilitates the transmission and retention of digital audio files (called MP3 files) by users. Users download Napster's MusicShare software, which allows them to access the directory and index on a Napster server to locate MP3 files on other users' hard drives. Users download MP3 files from other users' hard drives. Although the MP3 files do not transfer through Napster's servers, users must access Napster's system to get access to file names and routing data.[20]

The plaintiffs sought an injunction against Napster, asking a trial court to prohibit Napster from facilitating the

copying, downloading, or distributing of thousands of plaintiffs' copyrighted musical compositions and sound recordings without the plaintiffs' permission. In May and July 2000, Judge Marilyn Hall Patel issued two opinions, both of which supported the injunction plaintiffs requested. She rejected several of Napster's claims, including claims that its service constituted fair use, that its service constituted valid sampling or space-shifting, and that the First Amendment protected the company's service. In the excerpt that follows, an appellate court decides whether the trial court applied the law correctly when deciding to issue the injunction. The excerpt focuses on direct copyright infringement and selected parts of the court's discussion of fair use.

---

[20] Other peer-to-peer technologies exist that do not store directories on a central server. One example is Grokster, which is discussed later in this chapter.

Circuit Judge Beezer

A. Infringement

Plaintiffs must satisfy two requirements to present a prima facie case of direct infringement: (1) they must show ownership of the allegedly infringed material and (2) they must demonstrate that the alleged infringers violate at least one exclusive right granted to copyright holders under 17 U.S.C. § 106. ... Plaintiffs have sufficiently demonstrated ownership. The record supports the district court's determination that "as much as eighty-seven percent of the files available on Napster may be copyrighted and more than seventy percent may be owned or administered by plaintiffs."

The district court further determined that plaintiffs' exclusive rights under § 106 were violated: "here the evidence establishes that a majority of Napster users use the service to download and upload copyrighted music. ... And by doing that, it constitutes—the uses constitute direct infringement of plaintiffs' musical compositions, recordings." ... The district court also noted that "it is pretty much acknowledged ... by Napster that this is infringement." We agree that plaintiffs have shown that Napster users infringe at least two of the copyright holders' exclusive rights: the rights of reproduction, § 106(1); and distribution, § 106(3). Napster users who upload file names to search the index for others to copy violate plaintiffs' distribution rights. Napster users who download files containing copyrighted music violate plaintiffs' reproduction rights. Napster asserts an affirmative defense to the charge that its users directly infringe plaintiffs' copyrighted musical compositions and sound recordings.

B. Fair Use

Napster contends that its users do not directly infringe plaintiffs' copyrights because the users are engaged in fair use of the material. ... Napster identifies three specific alleged fair uses: sampling, where users make temporary copies of a work before purchasing; space-shifting, where users access a sound recording through the Napster system that they already own in audio CD format; and permissive distribution of recordings by both new and established artists.

The district court considered factors listed in 17 U.S.C. § 107, which guide a court's fair use determination. These factors are: (1) the purpose and character of the use;

(2) the nature of the copyrighted work; (3) the "amount and substantiality of the portion used" in relation to the work as a whole; and (4) the effect of the use upon the potential market for the work or the value of the work. ... The district court concluded that Napster users are not fair users. We agree.

[The court then agreed with the district court that the first three factors weigh against a finding of fair use.]

4. Effect of Use on Market

Addressing this factor, the district court concluded that Napster harms the market in "at least" two ways: it reduces audio CD sales among college students and it "raises barriers to plaintiffs' entry into the market for the digital downloading of music." The district court relied on evidence plaintiffs submitted to show that Napster use harms the market for their copyrighted musical compositions and sound recordings. ... Notably, plaintiffs' expert, Dr. E. Deborah Jay, conducted a survey (the "Jay Report") using a random sample of college and university students to track their reasons for using Napster and the impact Napster had on their music purchases. The court recognized that the Jay Report focused on just one segment of the Napster user population and found "evidence of lost sales attributable to college use to be probative of irreparable harm for purposes of the preliminary injunction motion.".... [The court then discusses additional studies offered by the plaintiffs.]

As for defendant's experts, plaintiffs objected to the report of Dr. Peter S. Fader, in which the expert concluded that Napster is *beneficial* to the music industry because MP3 music file-sharing stimulates more audio CD sales than it displaces. The district court found problems in Dr. Fader's minimal role in overseeing the administration of the survey and the lack of objective data in his report. ... [The court then concluded that the district court demonstrated a proper exercise of discretion in using the studies to reject a fair use defense. Then, the court considered Napster's sampling and space-shifting arguments and concluded that the district court did not abuse its discretion in finding that these uses do not constitute a fair use.]

Affirmed in favor of A & M Records, Inc.

---

contributory copyright infringement The act of presenting material on a Web site that encourages site users to violate copyright laws.

Contributory Copyright Infringement In *A & M Records, Inc. v. Napster*, the court also ruled that it was likely that Napster had engaged in **contributory copyright infringement**. Contributory copyright infringement occurs when one, with knowledge of an infringing activity, induces, causes, or materially contributes to the infringing conduct of another. The court stated that liability exists if Napster engaged in conduct that encouraged or assisted infringers. The court ruled that Napster had facilitated transmission and retention of digital files by its users and had actual knowledge that specific infringing material was available on its system. Napster had failed to remove infringing material.

Critical Thinking About the Law

Courts often use ambiguous language when crafting definitions. Case 6-2 gives us an opportunity to take a look at ambiguous language. It also presents a good reminder of the importance of a particular set of facts in determining the outcome of a case.

1. Identify one ambiguous word or phrase in the court's decision in Case 6-2, and show how that ambiguity affects your willingness to accept the court's conclusion.

   Clue: Consider Napster's main defense.

2. If you could change one fact in Case 6-2 to make it less likely the judge would rule against Napster, which fact would you change?

   Clue: Look at how the district court responds to reports from experts.

In 2004, a California federal appeals court issued a ruling regarding peer-to-peer technologies that was more favorable to online music trading services. In *Metro-Goldwyn-Mayer Studios, Inc. v. Grokster Ltd.,*[21] the United States Court of Appeals for the Ninth Circuit (California) considered online music trading services that differ from Napster's original format in that they do not store directories on a central server. In particular, the court considered whether software distributors Grokster Ltd. and StreamCast Networks, Inc., were liable to songwriters, music publishers, and motion picture studios for copyright infringement based on the theory of contributory copyright infringement.

Distributors of peer-to-peer file-sharing computer networking software can be liable for contributory infringement only if they had knowledge of copyright infringement by users of their software. In *Grokster*, Grokster's and StreamCast's decentralized services meant they would not have knowledge of infringement by users. The peer-to-peer file-sharing networking software did nothing to encourage or assist infringers. Additionally, the court noted that the technology at issue in the case has many noninfringing uses. This fact makes peer-to-peer file-sharing software more like copiers, tape recorders, and video recorders. All of these products can be and are used in ways that do not violate copyright laws.[22]

The recording industry, through the Recording Industry of America (RIAA), and the motion picture industry, through the Motion Picture Association of America (MPAA), are unlikely to be discouraged by the court's decision in *Grokster*. Both organizations are pursuing several strategies to protect the rights of copyright holders. The RIAA and MPAA have filed copyright infringement lawsuits against individuals and companies throughout the world.[23] Additionally, both organizations are lobbying Congress, seeking legal reform to provide criminal penalties for copyright infringers.[24]

---

[21] 380 F.3d 1154 (2004).

[22] *Id.,* p. 1167.

[23] Gerber, *supra* note 16.

[24] *Id.*

E-COMMERCE ISSUES

This chapter has already presented several topics that fall under the general topic of e-commerce. However, the increasing importance of e-commerce raises key legal issues, many of which remain unresolved, such as whether and how states can collect taxes on sales transacted on the Internet. In this section, you will learn about three significant topics that directly affect e-commerce transactions: privacy, online marketing, and cybersignatures.

PRIVACY

When people express concerns about privacy in the context of cyberspace, they usually mean they either want to be free from external *surveillance* or to be able to control their private *information*. For example, people might be concerned that a marketing company can monitor which Web sites they visit and compile a profile that would be used for targeted marketing campaigns; someone who is considering banking online might worry that others can look into his or her account and learn facts about their finances.

The concept of privacy is especially important to e-commerce. Many people are afraid to have their personal information floating in cyberspace where hackers can get it. It does not matter that these fears may not be realistic. The more confident consumers are about how companies protect their privacy, the likelier they will be to engage in e-commerce.

Public Sector Protection The law of privacy is under increased scrutiny as cyberspace becomes more important to society. At the federal level, the United States Supreme Court has interpreted the U.S. Constitution to provide a privacy right in only limited circumstances. One federal statute, the Privacy Act of 1974, places limits on which information the federal government can collect and how the government can use that information. This act generally prohibits the government from disclosing data without an individual's consent.

At the federal level, government regulators have passed privacy guidelines for those who process information about individuals, from patient medical information to purchasing patterns. For instance, Congress passed the Electronic Communications Privacy Act of 1986 (ECPA) to respond to concerns about the impact of computer data banks on individual privacy.[25] The ECPA prohibits any person from knowingly revealing to any other person the contents on an electronic communication while that communication is in transmission or in electronic storage. This law provides a basis for individuals to sue Internet service providers and others who fail to protect e-mail and voice mail privacy.

Law in this area is especially dynamic. In *In Re DoubleClick Inc., Privacy Litigation*, for example, a federal district court decided in 2001 that a business, DoubleClick Inc., an Internet advertiser, had not violated the EPCA when it created consumer profiles by placing cookies (small text files) on users' hard drives.[26] In 2002, however, while appeals were pending, DoubleClick settled the lawsuit with plaintiffs. The plaintiffs, represented by state attorneys general, had been concerned that the advertiser was creating consumer profiles in violation

---

[25] The Privacy Act often conflicts with the Freedom of Information Act.

[26] *In Re DoubleClick, Inc., Privacy Litigation*, 154 F. Supp. 2d 497 (S.D.N.Y., 2001).

of privacy laws. DoubleClick agreed to pay damages to plaintiffs. The company also agreed to operate more transparently. It agreed, for instance, to allow individual consumers to access the profiles the company had created about them.

More recent statutes include the Children's Online Privacy Protection Act of 1998 (COPPA) and the Financial Services Modernization Act of 1999 (FSMA). COPPA requires Web sites that collect personal information from children to provide notice on the site of what information will be collected and how it will be used. Additionally, the site must obtain parental consent to collect information from children under age 13. The FSMA aims to provide Internet consumers more control over who has access to their banking information.

Private Sector Protection In the private sector, privacy laws vary by state and industry. Common law also protects privacy. Common law varies from state to state. States have typically recognized some kind of privacy tort. The torts most helpful to individuals who operate in cyberspace are those that remedy damage caused by public disclosure of private facts and damage caused when a person uses another person's information or identity inappropriately.

In addition to tort law, contract law provides some remedies. Most businesses and Web sites post privacy policies, which are contracts.[27] These privacy policies range from brief notices that let consumers know the site is secure to policies with pages of details. The goal of privacy policies is to let Internet users know how a company will collect personal data about the consumer and what the company will do with the information it collects. The policies also reassure consumers that sites are secure.

Privacy policies have been the subject of lawsuits that list a variety of theories, including the theories of unfair or deceptive trade practices and fraud. Recently, a subscriber to Yahoo! sued this Internet service provider for violating his privacy.[28] Yahoo! let AnswerThink Consulting Group Inc. know the name of an Ohio man who used the screen name Aquacool_2000 (Aquacool). Yahoo! let AnswerThink know Aquacool's name after AnswerThink subpoenaed the information. AnswerThink wanted to know which of their employees posted negative comments about his boss on a bulletin board maintained by Yahoo! After finding Aquacool's identify, AnwerThink fired him. Aquacool has filed suit against Yahoo!, claiming the Internet service provider should have at least informed him prior to disclosing the information. The lawsuit alleges breaches of constitutional and contractual rights to privacy.

ONLINE MARKETING

Increasingly, marketers are advertising products on the Internet. Marketers view the Internet as a significant opportunity to reach out to customers throughout the world. This new advertising format brings with it both opportunities and the threat of misleading or deceptive advertising strategies and fraud.

Consumer rights advocates are especially concerned about the possibility that marketers will violate consumers' privacy rights by collecting information about them without their knowledge and/or consent. This chapter considered

---

[27] It is important to note that privacy policies posted on Web sites become contracts only if the user accepts them.

[28] Lauren Gard, "User Sues Yahoo! Over Privacy Rights: Ohio Company Used Subpoena to Learn Name of Worker Who Criticized It," *National Law Journal*, May 29, 2000, p. B4.

Linking Law & Business

Marketing

In the field of marketing, you learned about the concept of direct-to-consumer (DTC) advertising. This form of marketing uses television and/or Web sites to allow marketers to reach out to consumers directly, rather than marketing to an intermediary, such as a doctor. The first DTC advertising was for a hair-loss treatment called Rogaine. A television advertisement encouraged consumers to ask their doctors for Rogaine.

privacy issues in the preceding section. As you will learn in the section on cybercrime, criminals are finding creative ways to use e-commerce to their advantage. Consumers are worried that the kinds of scams consumers experience through the telephone and mail will invade the Internet.

In Case 6-3, the court considers an online marketing issue. In particular, the court considers whether companies that advertise prescription drugs directly to consumers on television and Web sites have a duty to warn them about the dangers of the drugs. With direct-to-consumer advertising of prescription drugs on the rise, more courts will be considering these types of issues.

CASE 6-3

Saray Perez, (Plaintiff-Appellant) v. Wyeth Laboratories, Inc., (Respondent)
Supreme Court of New Jersey 734 A.2d 1245 (1999)

The following opinion considers whether a drug manufacturer that markets its product directly to consumers has a duty to warn consumers directly of foreseeable risks associated with the drug. In the past, when consumers enjoyed traditional doctor–patient relationships in which doctors "knew best" and informed patients of product dangers, legal standards required drug manufacturers to communicate with physicians rather than consumers about product dangers. Manufacturers did so through product literature or labels that listed a drug's risks. Manufacturers escaped liability by educating prescribing physicians ("learned intermediaries"), who passed information along to consumers.

This case arose when plaintiffs filed a product liability action against Wyeth Laboratories, which makes Norplant, a surgically implanted contraceptive. After plaintiffs filed their lawsuit, Wyeth filed for a summary judgment against the consumers, and a trial court granted that motion. The trial court ruled that the "learned intermediary doctrine" applies to direct marketing of prescription drugs to consumers. The trial court also ruled that Wyeth satisfied its duty to warn consumers about poten-

tially harmful side effects of its product because the company had complied with advertising, labeling, and warning requirements imposed by the Food and Drug Administration (FDA). In other words, Wyeth had met FDA requirements for educating prescribing physicians. The appellate court decides whether the "learned intermediary" doctrine is outdated in a world in which doctors in cyberspace write prescriptions for patients whom they have never seen.

Justice O'Hern

We believe that when mass marketing of prescription drugs seeks to influence a patients' choice of drug, a pharmaceutical manufacturer that makes direct claims to consumers for the efficacy of its project should not be unqualifiedly relieved of a duty to provide proper warnings of the dangers or side effects of the product.

Direct advertising of drugs to consumers alters the calculus of the learned intermediary doctrine. … First, with rare and wonderful exceptions, the " 'Norman Rockwell' image of the family doctor no longer exists." Informed consent requires a patient-based decision rather than the paternalistic approach of the 1970s. The decision to take a drug is "not exclusively a matter for medical judgment." ...Second, because managed care has reduced the time allotted per patient, physicians have considerably less time to inform patients of the risks and benefits of a drug. ... Third, having spent $1.3 billion on advertising in 1998, drug manufacturers can hardly be said to "lack effective means" to communicate directly with patients when their advertising campaigns can pay off in close to billions in dividends. Consumer-directed advertising of pharmaceuticals thus belies each of the premises on which the learned intermediary doctrine rests.

Prescription drug manufacturers that market their products directly to consumers should be subject to claims by consumers if their advertising fails to provide an adequate warning of the product's dangerous propensities. [We conclude that] the learned intermediary doctrine does not apply to the direct marketing of drugs to consumers. ... The direct marketing of drugs to consumers generates a corresponding duty requiring manufacturers to warn of defects in the product.

Reversed in favor of the Plaintiff-Appellant, Perez.

 ## Critical Thinking About the Law

When a person engages in critical thinking, it is important that he or she learns to compare arguments and recognize strengths as well as weaknesses in arguments. Another important skill for a person to apply when engaging in critical thinking is recognizing the ethical norms that underlie decision making.
Please refer to Case 6-3 and consider the following questions:

1. What is particularly good about this court's reasoning in deciding that the learned intermediary doctrine is outdated?

    Clue: Reread the part of the decision in which the court explains how individuals' relationships to their doctors have changed over time.

2. In rejecting the learned intermediary doctrine, which ethical norm is the court showing it prefers?
    Clue: Figure out who benefits from the court's decision and how this group benefits.

CYBERSIGNATURES

In 2000, Congress passed the Electronic Signatures in Global and National Commerce Act, which is commonly referred to as E-SIGN. The purpose of this legislation is to make it easier for businesses to create valid contracts over the Internet. In particular, E-SIGN outlines how businesses can create valid contracts electronically with methods that imitate the effect of written signatures on paper. E-SIGN allows a wide range of authentication possibilities. Some of these possibilities are surprisingly low tech. For instance, the law allows the use of information unique to a customer, such as a mother's maiden name.[29] On the high-tech end, E-SIGN allows individuals and businesses to create digital signatures using encryption software. This authentication procedure involves a third party who holds the identity of the two parties and can use software to make sure only the two parties involved in a contract can obtain and sign the document.

---

[29] Nancy R. Mandell, "ESIGN: Been There, Done That! Federal Electronic Signature Legislation Catches Up to Securities Industry Practices," *On Wall Street*, July 1, 2001, 2001 WL 2271745.

EMPLOYMENT LAW ISSUES IN CYBERSPACE

PRIVACY VERSUS EMPLOYMENT-AT-WILL

Not only does privacy matter in the context of business-to-consumer and business-to-business transactions, but it also is important in the context of employment. Employee monitoring is a growing issue:

- Are employers allowed to record employee keystrokes as they occur?[30]
- Can employers fire employees who type words like *union* and *strike* frequently?[31]
- Can employers keep track of which Web sites employees visit?
- Can employers ban employee access to certain sites?

Courts throughout the country are considering these questions. These issues highlight the employees' right to privacy and employers' right to control what happens in the workplace.

In Case 6-4, a Pennsylvania court makes a decision about how much privacy employees can expect from their employers. As you read the case, consider your own workplace e-mail communications. Could you end up in the same situation as Smyth?

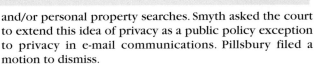

CASE 6-4

Michael A. Smyth v. The Pillsbury Company
United States District Court, E.D. Pennsylvania 914 F.Supp. 97 (1996)

This case arose when Pillsbury Company fired Michael A. Smyth for transmitting inappropriate and unprofessional comments over Pillsbury's e-mail system. In particular, Smyth made threats related to sales management (he threatened to "kill the backstabbing bastards") and referred to a holiday party the company had planned as the "Jim Jones Koolaid affair."[32] Pillsbury had repeatedly assured its employees that it would keep all e-mail communications confidential. After his employer read Smyth's comments, the company fired him.

At issue in the case is whether Smyth can maintain a wrongful discharge action under the public policy exception to the employment at will doctrine. A Pennsylvania court had previously stated that it was possible that a discharge related to an employer's tortious invasion of an employee's privacy might violate public policy. The court made this statement in the context of privacy related to an employer's drug and alcohol policy that requires urinalysis

and/or personal property searches. Smyth asked the court to extend this idea of privacy as a public policy exception to privacy in e-mail communications. Pillsbury filed a motion to dismiss.

District Judge Weiner

As a general rule, Pennsylvania does not provide a common law cause of action for the wrongful discharge of an at-will employee such as plaintiff. Pennsylvania is an employment at-will jurisdiction and an employer "may discharge an at-will employee with or without cause, at pleasure, unless restrained by some contract."

However, in the most limited of circumstances, exceptions have been recognized where discharge of an at-will employee threatens or violates a clear mandate of public policy. A "clear mandate" of public policy must be of a type that "strikes at the heart of a citizen's social right, duties

---

[30] Stephen Lesavich, "Keystroke Spies: Conflicting Rights," *National Law Journal*, May 22, 2000, p. A23.

[31] *Id.*

[32] Jim Jones is the cult leader whose followers committed mass suicide by drinking a poisoned drink in Jonestown, Guyana, in 1978.

and responsibilities." This recognized public policy exception is an especially narrow one.

Plaintiff claims that his termination was in violation of "public policy which precludes an employer from terminating an employee in violation of the employee's right to privacy as embodied in Pennsylvania common law."

[W]e find that the plaintiff has failed to state a claim upon which relief can be granted. In the first instance ... we do not find a reasonable expectation of privacy in e-mail communications voluntarily made by an employee to his supervisor over the company e-mail notwithstanding any assurances that management would not intercept such communications. Once plaintiff communicated the alleged unprofessional comments to a second person (his supervisor) over an e-mail system, which was apparently utilized by the entire company, any reasonable expectation was lost. Significantly, the defendant did not require plaintiff, as in the case of a urinalysis or personal property search, to disclose any personal information about himself. Rather, plaintiff voluntarily communicated the alleged unprofessional comments over the company e-mail system. We find no privacy rights in such communications.

In the second instance, even if we found that an employee had a reasonable expectation of privacy in the contents of his e-mail communications over the company e-mail system, we do not find that a reasonable person would consider the defendant's interception of these communications to be a substantial and highly offensive invasion of his privacy. Again, we note that by intercepting such communications, the company is not ... requiring the employee to disclose any personal information about himself or invading the employee's person or effects. Moreover, the company's interest in preventing inappropriate and unprofessional comments or even illegal activity over its e-mail system outweighs any privacy interest the employee may have in those comments.

In sum, we find that the defendant's actions did not tortiously invade the plaintiff's privacy and, therefore, did not violate public policy.

Granted motion to dismiss filed by the Defendant, Pillsbury Company.

Critical Thinking About the Law

As a critical thinker, you know there are many ways to phrase the issue. How a judge decides to describe the issue often tells the reader who is likely to win the case. Case 6-4 helps readers think about ways to word an issue. It also presents a good reminder of the importance of analogies in legal reasoning.

1. In Case 6-4, the judge chose carefully how to word the issue. Step into Smyth's shoes and write the issue as he saw it. In other words, if Smyth, through his lawyers, were allowed to state the issue, how would the issue read?

   Clue: Reread the part of the case containing Smyth's main arguments.

2. Smyth wants the court to look at what happened to him regarding privacy and view any violations as comparable to violations of privacy related to urinalysis and/or personal property searches. Why does the court reject Smyth's comparison?

   Clue: Reread the part of the decision in which the court discusses privacy rights.

ONLINE HARASSMENT

In the *Smyth* case, the employer wanted to control the employee's behavior at the expense of the employee's privacy. Employers might not react the same way to online harassment. Online harassment usually involves peer-to-peer harassment. Some employers are less likely to assert control to protect one employee from another. For example, some companies might look the other way when employees are looking at pornographic Web sites during the working day and possibly thereby are harassing other employees. Other companies might assert control and put a stop to this unproductive activity.

Later in this book, you will learn that *hostile environment* sexual harassment occurs when an employee's behavior creates an intimidating, hostile, or offensive workplace for other employees. Generally, courts have held employers responsible for employee behavior when they knew or should have known of an employee's inappropriate behavior. To escape liability, employers also need to conduct sexual harassment training and have clear workplace policies prohibiting harassing behavior.

Recent online harassment cases have raised several interesting questions, including:

- Can employers be vicariously liable for defamation?

- How do courts decide when an employer-sponsored Internet bulletin board is part of the workplace?

- Can an Internet service provider be held responsible for defamatory comments on online bulletin boards?

Recently, a New Jersey court ruled that employers have a duty to remedy online harassment when they notice that "employees are engaged in a pattern of retaliatory harassment using a work-related online forum."[33] In this case, Tammy Blakey, a Continental Airlines pilot, had already won a federal sexual harassment suit in 1997. In the 1997 federal lawsuit, Blakey succeeded in proving Continental Airlines had failed to protect her from sexual harassment, including the airline's failure to remove pornography from planes Blakey was flying. Other pilots had placed the pornography in planes specifically to make her uncomfortable. After a five-week trial, a jury awarded Blakey $875,000, which included $500,000 for emotional distress.[34]

In 1995, while the federal litigation was underway, the case took a new twist. Blakey's fellow pilots started using an electronic bulletin board to discuss the *Blakey* case. From February to July 1995, several male pilots posted comments about Blakey on the pilots' online computer bulletin board called the "Crew Members Forum." This electronic bulletin board was maintained by CompuServ and provided information to pilots and crew members about their schedules and flight assignments. Pilots posted comments on the Crew Members Forum that questioned Blakey's ability to pilot a plane. Coworkers also called her a "feminazi" and accused her of filing the federal lawsuit "to get a quick buck."[35]

The focus of the state case was on the comments employees posted on the Crew Members Forum. In this New Jersey case, Blakey sought damages for defamation, hostile environment sexual harassment under the state's antidiscrimination statute, business libel, and intentional infliction of emotional distress.[36] The court ruled that although the electronic bulletin board was located outside the workplace, it was an extension of the workplace. In remanding the case back to the trial court, the appellate court instructed the trial court to consider whether Continental derives a "substantial benefit" from the electronic bulletin board and whether this bulletin board is "sufficiently integrated in the workplace" to require the employer to put a stop to harassment.[37] The court explained that if the online

---

[33] Mary P. Gallaher, "Employee May Sue for Online Slur," *National Law Journal*, June 19, 2000, p. B1.

[34] A judge reduced the jury's award to $625,000. A significant portion of this award was for attorney fees.

[35] *Id.*

[36] *Id.*

[37] *Id.*

bulletin board is actually work related, Continental will be liable for messages that created a hostile work environment for Tammy Blakey.

As a consequence of the appellate court's ruling, it would be wise for employers throughout the country to take a serious look not only at how employees are using technology to make unprofessional comments about their employers (as in the *Smyth* case) but also at how employees are using technology to inflict damage on their coworkers. If employers find peer sexual harassment online, they should take action to stop the harassment.

THE WAR AGAINST CYBERCRIME

As technology evolves and expands opportunities, criminals are finding new ways to cause harm to the public. They are creating brand-new crimes such as denial-of-service attacks and identity theft. Additionally, criminals are adding new twists to some old crimes, such as illegal gambling and insider trading. This section explains these four crimes to illustrate some of the challenges law enforcement officials are facing in the area of cybercrime.

DENIAL-OF-SERVICE ATTACKS

In spite of developments in computer security such as firewalls and encryption, computer criminals are finding ways to threaten e-commerce. One of the most common of these tactics is a **denial-of-service attack**. A denial-of-service attack occurs when hackers clog a Web site's equipment by sending too much unsolicited commercial or "junk" e-mail at one time.[38] This form of e-mail is also called **spam**. A quick flood of spam can slow the site's performance and/or crash the site. Law enforcement officers are able to stop the attacks by getting companies, Internet service providers, and telecommunications suppliers to work together to write programs to reject requests that are clogging equipment.[39]

Federal and state law enforcement officers try to stay one step ahead of cybercriminals. Sometimes they face many challenges, including the lack of private sector cooperation from companies such as Yahoo! and eBay.[40] These companies do not want to call attention to weaknesses in their computer security systems. They also fear officers will confiscate their computers to search for evidence that may be stored in the hard drive. In addition, law enforcement officers face (1) obstacles presented by technology, such as vanishing evidence, (2) difficulty locating and identifying criminals who operate through the Internet, and (3) the lack of sufficient financial resources.

More recently, however, actors in the private sector have wanted to work with law enforcement officials to put a stop to spamming. Both the National Cyber-Forensics and Training Alliance, a nonprofit organization, and Direct Marketing Association, a trade association, have worked with the Department of Justice (DOJ) and Federal Bureau of Investigation (FBI) to protect legitimate e-mail marketing and stop spamming.[41]

denial-of-service attack A crime that occurs when hackers clog a Web site's equipment by sending it too many requests for information.

spam Unsolicited commercial or "junk" e-mail.

[38] Ira Sager, "Cybercrime: First Yahoo! Then eBay. The Net's Vulnerability Threatens E-Commerce—and You," *Business Week,* February 21, 2000, 37, 40.

[39] *Id.,* p. 39.

[40] David E. Rovella, "Preparing for a New Cyberwar: Justice Dept. Seeks Lawyers, Revised Laws to Fight Net Crimes," *National Law Journal,* May 20, 2000, pp. A1, A9.

[41] Saul Hansell, "Technology: Junk E-Mail and Fraud Are Focus of Crackdown," *New York Times,* August 25, 2004.

Linking Law & Business

Management Information Systems

In the field of management information systems, you have learned about the concept of encryption. Encryption software protects transactions and communications over the Internet. This software also adds challenges to law enforcement, since encryption software enhances the security and privacy of criminals as well.

IDENTITY THEFT

identity theft A form of fraud in which an individual assumes someone else's identity information as his or her own.

Law enforcement officials have also linked spam to the relatively new crime of identity theft. **Identity theft** is a form of fraud in which an individual assumes someone else's identity information as his or her own. Spammers with criminal intent sometimes use junk e-mailing to engage in online profiling. Spammers have been able to gather personal information about computer users, including account and/or Social Security numbers. If criminals are able to steal this kind of information, they can use it to engage in a pattern of criminal behavior. For example, criminals can use personal information to obtain false driver's licenses, which they can then use to open additional credit card and checking accounts to perpetuate additional acts of fraud.

Criminals who pursue identity theft can sometimes accumulate a significant collection of assets. For instance, husband and wife confidence artists Nalin and Meena Rawal engaged in acts of identity theft that allowed them to obtain cash and telephone service, a $20,000 Honda for their son to take to college, a $23,000 Mercedes vehicle, a $600,000 house, and even laser eye surgery for Meena Rawal.[42] Most of their swindling was made possible by use of Meena Rawal's real estate license and Nalin Rawal's notary public license. Law enforcement officials caught the Rawals, and both Meena and Nalin are serving jail sentences and are expected to pay restitution to their victims.

The Federal Trade Commission (FTC), a federal agency responsible for helping consumers who have become victims of identity theft, gives several recommendations for how individuals can prevent identity theft. For example, the FTC recommends that individuals refrain from giving out personal information over the telephone or mail unless they have initiated the contact or are sure they know the individual or business they are dealing with.[43] Another tip is to leave your Social Security card in a secure place. The agency also recommends that you guard your mail and trash. Finally, the FTC recommends that your passwords that provide access to accounts are not obvious.[44] Exhibit 6-3 presents the FTC's tips for Internet users who want to prevent identity theft.[45]

---

[42] *People v. Rawal*, Court of Appeal, Fourth District, Division 3, California, available as 2004 WL 1453525 (Cal. App. 4 Dist.), June 28, 2004.

[43] **www.consumer.gov/idtheft/protect_againstidt.html#5.**

[44] *Id*. This site gives a more exhaustive list of tips than the text has presented.

[45] *Id*.

Keep your virus protection software up-to-date.

Do not open files or click on hyperlinks sent by strangers.

If you use a high-speed Internet connection, use a firewall program to prevent hackers from taking over your computer.

Use a secure browser.

Try to refrain from storing financial information on your laptop.

Use complicated passwords, such as those that use a combination of letters, numbers, and symbols.

Delete personal information when you dispose of a computer.

Prefer Web sites with privacy policies.

EXHIBIT 6-3

IDENTITY THEFT PREVENTION FOR INTERNET USERS

INSIDER TRADING

Cybercriminals have also found creative ways to manipulate the stock market to their advantage. For instance, some criminals have discovered how easy it is to manipulate stock prices by posting false information on Internet bulletin boards.[46] Other criminals have used the Internet to engage in traditional **insider trading**. Insider trading is the use of material, nonpublic information to purchase or sell securities in violation of a duty the person owes to the company whose stock the person is trading.

For example, in one case, a part-time clerk at Goldman, Sachs & Company was charged with insider trading after he allegedly made $8.4 million on illegal tips.[47] By using an America Online chat room, he was able to draw others into his scam. He exchanged inside information for kickbacks with friends in both the real and virtual worlds. In this case, the clerk used inside information (i.e., nonpublic information he got through his job) and then engaged in manipulation (i.e., added false information to the inside information), showing he could pursue both new and traditional forms of illegal trading at the same time.

insider trading The use of material, nonpublic information to purchase or sell securities in violation of a duty the person owes to the company whose stock the person is trading.

INTERNET GAMBLING

Another challenge for law enforcement officers is how to regulate gambling on the Internet. Some states make gambling a crime and are quick to shut down gambling sites that operate through servers located in their states. However, even if a state bans companies in that state from providing access to gambling, they cannot control companies whose servers are located outside their jurisdiction.

Some people argue that attempts to limit Internet gambling are inappropriate. They ask why a person is allowed to physically travel to Las Vegas to gamble but not allowed to travel to Las Vegas via the Internet to gamble.[48] Should states be allowed to make decisions about how to protect the moral welfare of their residents? Ultimately, Congress will pass legislation that answers questions about how to regulate Internet gambling. Congress has already considered some statutes and is likely to pass legislation in the near future.

---

[46] Rovella, *supra* note 39, p. A9.

[47] Christopher Drew, "Nineteen Charged with Insider Trading Using the Internet and a Clerk," *New York Times*, March 15, 2000, p. C1.

[48] The American Bar Association's Committee on Cyberspace Law, *Cyberspace Law Developments— Annual Survey* (paper presented at the spring 1998 meeting, St. Louis, MO.), p. 32.

SUMMARY

The legal system adjusts to the changing needs of those who must obey law. The Internet and World Wide Web have raised important questions about how law should change.

As the legal system adjusts to the explosive growth of the Internet and World Wide Web, actors in state and federal governments are redefining their roles. For example, the United States Supreme Court makes sure Congress is not overstepping its bounds when passing legislation that places limits on speech on the Internet. Additionally, courts are changing the way they function. For example, new rules govern in personam jurisdiction.

Intellectual property law is also changing. For example, domain names have become valuable trademarks. These domain names have become so valuable that cyberpirates may want to take advantage of trademark owners by intentionally obtaining a domain name registration for a company's trademark and then trying to sell that domain name back to the trademark owner. Copyright law is also facing challenges. In response to challenges, courts are coming up with creative new concepts, such as contributory copyright infringement, which occurs when creators of a Web site present material on the site that encourages visitors to their site to violate copyright laws. At the same time, courts are recognizing the impact of technological change on property rights. This recognition is allowing courts to reconsider and redefine the rights of individuals who create songs, movies, and other forms of intellectual property.

Many e-commerce issues are arising in cyberspace. Individuals are increasingly concerned about their privacy rights. Online marketing is triggering some lawsuits and investigations by administrative agencies. How to establish cybersignatures is an important topic.

Employment issues in cyberspace include new reasons for employers to fire employees (e.g., when they use e-mail inappropriately) and new opportunities for employees to harass one another in the context of cyberspace.

Government regulators are waging a war against cybercrime. Government actors are responding to denial of service attacks, identity theft, insider trading, and illegal gambling. Increasingly, government actors are working through alliances in the private sector. Many individuals and groups in the private sector are starting to appreciate their interest in battling cybercrime.

REVIEW QUESTIONS

6-1 Explain two specific challenges states are facing as they try to regulate the Internet.

6-2 Explain how the concepts of domain names, trademarks, and cybersquatting are related.

6-3 Explain the concept of contributory copyright infringement and how legal interpretations of that concept have evolved from *Napster* to *Grokster*.

6-4 Explain how a person can use a cybersignature and why the subject of cybersignatures is significant.

6-5 Explain how the Internet is giving employers the opportunity to show they understand the employment-at-will doctrine.

6-6 Explain two specific kinds of crime that are on the rise as the use of the Internet has increased.

REVIEW PROBLEMS

6-7 Congress decides it wants to issue a total ban on online advertising of prescription medicines. If a pharmaceutical company challenges this total ban, is the company likely to be successful?

6-8 You are an employee who has just discovered that an e-mail message you thought you sent to your close friend at work was sent to an entire department. In this message, you disclose the fact that you believe your boss is having an extramarital affair with someone else at the company. If your boss finds out, can she fire you for sending the message? Does it matter whether your news is true?

6-9 Suppose you are the attorney general of your state. You want to file an action against a gaming corporation. You want to seek an injunction against the company, asking it to stop Internet gambling opportunities available to residents of your state via the Internet. Are you likely to be successful in getting the injunction?

6-10 Paul led a crime ring that used computers to engage in a variety of fraudulent activities, including obtaining credit card numbers and passing them along to others to use illegally. If Paul is prosecuted and found guilty of this crime, what is his likely jail sentence? What factors will help determine the sentence?

6-11 Suppose HighTech Inc., the owner of the trademark *high-tech* sued, seeking an injunction against the owner of the trademark *hitech*. Suppose HighTech wants to stop the owner of the trademark *hitech* from using that mark. How will a court decide whether to issue the injunction?

6-12 LookinGood sued Babes, Inc., for copyright violation after Babes, Inc., copied photographs from LookinGood's Web site and put them on its own Web site, babes.com. LookinGood can provide proof of its copyright. In particular, Babes, Inc., copied ten copyrighted photographs of five models. How much is Babes, Inc., likely to have to pay LookinGood? Does it matter that Babes, Inc.'s behavior was willful?

CASE PROBLEMS

6-13 Several record companies, owners of copyrights in musical recordings, sued an Internet company, MP3.Com, Inc., for copyright infringement. This company makes MP3 files of recordings available to subscribers. MP3.Com explains that its service allows customers to store, customize, and listen to recordings contained on their CDs from any place where they have a connection. The service requires subscribers to prove they already own the CD, or the subscriber must purchase the CD from one of MP3.Com's cooperating online retailers. MP3.Com claims its service amounts to "fair use." Does the court agree with this description and, consequently, find no copyright violation? *UMG Recordings, Inc. v. MP3.Com*, 92 F.Supp.2d 349 (2000)

6-14 Eileen Weber suffered injuries while she was staying at a hotel in Italy. She filed a lawsuit against Jolly Hotels in federal district court in New Jersey. Jolly Hotels is an Italian corporation that is affiliated with a Massachusetts travel agency. This agency books tour groups at Jolly and had solicited Eileen Weber's business. In addition, Jolly Hotels advertises its hotel over the Internet. Was Weber successful in asserting in personam jurisdiction over Jolly Hotels? *Weber v. Jolly Hotels*, 977 F.Supp.327 (1997)

6-15 The board of trustees of the Loudoun County Library decided to provide Internet access to its patrons. This library is a public library. Although the trustees decided to provide Internet access, they also decided to block access to child pornography, obscene material, and material that could be harmful to juveniles as defined by Virginia law. Mainstream Loudoun, an association of individuals, sued the library trustees. They asserted that the library's decision to block access to certain Web sites violates the First Amendment. What was the result? *Mainstream Loudoun v. Board of Trustees of the Loudoun County Library*, 2 F.Supp.2d 783 (1998)

6-16 Terri Welles designed a Web site featuring herself as "Terri Welles—Playmate of the Year 1981." Welles was in fact Playboy's playmate of the year in 1981. Welles uses the terms "Playboy" and "Playmate" as meta tags. Meta tags are words a Web site designer inserts into a Web site's keywords field. These tags increase the likelihood that a search will yield a particular Web site. Playboy Enterprises also has its own Web sites to promote its magazine and models. The terms "Playboy," "Playmate," and "Playmate of the Year" are trademarks of Playboy Enterprises, Inc. This corporation sued Welles over her use of the terms "Playboy" and "Playmate." Was Welles forced to change her Web site design? *Playboy Enterprises, Inc. v. Welles*, 7 F.Supp.2d 1098 (1998)

6-17 Nissan Motor Co. Ltd. sued Nissan Computer Corporation alleging Nissan Computer's use of the domain names "nissan.com" and "nissan.net" infringed on its "Nissan" trademark. What factors did the court use to determine that Nissan Motor Co. was likely to prevail on its infringement claim? *Nissan Motor Co. Ltd. v. Nissan Computer Corporation*, 89 F.Supp.2d 1154 (C.D. Cal. 2000)

6-18 In Chapter 3, you read that Kenneth Zeran brought a negligence action against America Online, Inc. (AOL), alleging that AOL unreasonably delayed removing defamatory messages posted by an unidentified third party. Zeran was a hoax victim whose business phone number appeared on an Internet electronic bulletin board, advertising items that featured slogans that glorified the Oklahoma City bombing. After Zeran sued AOL, he also sued a radio station owned by Diamond Broadcasting, Inc. He sued the radio station for defamation, false light invasion of privacy, and intentional infliction of emotional distress. He argued that the station violated Oklahoma law when it read Zeran's phone number over the air and encouraged listeners to call him. Was Zeran able to hold Diamond Broadcasting, Inc. liable for its role in the hoax? *Zeran v. Diamond Broadcasting, Inc*, 203 F.3d 714 (2000)

ASSIGNMENT ON THE INTERNET

Industry trade associations play an important role in advocating for particular changes in the law. For example, the Recording Industry Association of America (RIAA) plays an important role in advocating for changes in the law to protect its property interests. You can find the RIAA at www.riaa.org.

This assignment asks you to search the Internet to find two additional trade associations that advocate for changes in cyberlaw. In particular, you should (1) identify trade associations that represent the interests of a group this chapter has highlighted (e.g., Internet ser-

vice providers), (2) look on each trade association's Web site to discover the particular legal reforms each trade association advocates, and (3) write a short paper that describes the advocacy work of the two trade associations you discovered.

Finally, engage in an Internet search to find trade associations and/or nonprofit organizations that are in an adversarial relationship with the two associations you found. For example, the interests of the Center for Democracy and Technology are different from those of Internet service providers. See www.cdt.org.

 ## ON THE INTERNET

www.ftc.gov/bcp/conline/edcams/kidzprivacy Look at this site to see how the Federal Trade Commission educates a range of stakeholders (e.g., teachers, parents) about the Children's Online Privacy Protection Act (COPPA).

www.cybercrime.gov Look here to see how the criminal division of the U.S. Department of Justice is battling cybercrime.

www.ncfta.net Check out the National Cyber-Forensics and Training Alliance, a partnership between the public and private sectors (e.g., industry, academia, and law enforcement) that shares information and resources related by cyber incidents.

www.the-dma.org If you look at the Web site for the Direct Marketing Association, it will give you some ideas to help you complete the preceding Assignment on the Internet.

7

WHITE-COLLAR CRIME AND THE BUSINESS COMMUNITY

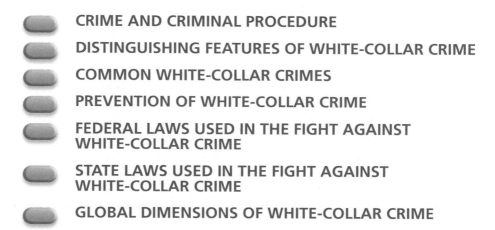

- **CRIME AND CRIMINAL PROCEDURE**
- **DISTINGUISHING FEATURES OF WHITE-COLLAR CRIME**
- **COMMON WHITE-COLLAR CRIMES**
- **PREVENTION OF WHITE-COLLAR CRIME**
- **FEDERAL LAWS USED IN THE FIGHT AGAINST WHITE-COLLAR CRIME**
- **STATE LAWS USED IN THE FIGHT AGAINST WHITE-COLLAR CRIME**
- **GLOBAL DIMENSIONS OF WHITE-COLLAR CRIME**

In 2003, Jay Jones, founder and CEO of Commercial Financial Services, was sentenced to five years in prison after pleading guilty to conspiracy. Jones artificially inflated the financial success of his debt-collection company in hopes of gaining increased investments in his company. When it was discovered that the debt-collection rate was inflated, the company went bankrupt, leaving 4,000 employees without jobs and more than $1 billion in worthless bonds. Yet, news of this white-collar crime received little attention outside of Tulsa, Oklahoma, where the company was headquartered. Unfortunately, this story has become just one of many recent large and complex white-collar crime scandals. During the previous year, telemarketing fraud resulted in losses in the United States and Canada of close to $40 billion, whereas the cost of health care fraud in the United States alone was predicted to be as high as $50 billion in 2003.[1] That year, more than $48 billion was lost

---

[1] Associated Press Report, "Insurers Predict $50 Billion in Health Care Losses," St. Petersburg Times On-Line, **www.sptimes.com/2003/11/13/Business/Insurers_predict_50_b.shtml**, November 13, 2003.

by financial institutions and businesses, whereas individuals lost an estimated $5 billion to one of the fastest-growing white-collar crimes: identity theft, a crime whereby a thief obtains credit in someone else's name and charges thousands of dollars in that person's name.

White-collar crimes—crimes committed in a commercial context—occur every day. Collectively, these crimes often result in millions of dollars of damages. In recent years, as corporate crimes such as the ones detailed in Table 7-1 and Table 7-2 become more publicized, people's attitudes toward corporations and white-collar crime are being affected.

The future manager must be prepared to respond to a growing lack of public confidence and to avoid becoming a corporate criminal. He or she must find ways to develop a corporate climate that discourages, not encourages, the commission of white-collar crime. This chapter will help the reader prepare to face the challenges posed by corporate crime. The first section defines crime and briefly explains criminal procedure. Next, the factors that distinguish corporate crime from street crime are discussed. The third section explains in detail some of the more common white-collar crimes. The fourth section introduces some ideas for how we can reduce the incidence of white-collar crime. The fifth and sixth sections discuss the federal and state responses to white-collar crime. An overview of the international dimensions of white-collar crime is then provided.

Critical Thinking About the Law

Why should we be concerned about white-collar crime? You can use the following critical thinking questions to help guide your thinking about white-collar crime as you study this chapter.

1. If a judge strongly valued justice, do you think he or she would give an easier sentence to a business manager who embezzled $50,000 than to a person who robbed a bank of $50,000? Why?

   Clue: Think about the definitions of justice offered in Chapter 1.

2. As a future business manager, you may be forced to make tough decisions regarding white-collar crime. Imagine that you discover that one of your employees planned to offer a bribe to an agent from the Environmental Protection Agency to prevent your company from being fined. Although the result of the potential bribe could greatly benefit your company, you know that the bribe is illegal. What conflicting ethical norms are involved in your decision?

   Clue: Review the list of ethical norms offered in Chapter 1.

3. White-collar crime is typically not violent crime. Therefore, many people assume that street crime is more serious and should receive harsher punishments. Can you generate some reasons why that assumption is false? Why might white-collar crime deserve a more severe sentence?

   Clue: Reread the introductory paragraphs that provide information about white-collar crime. Why might a business manager deserve a more severe sentence than a young woman committing a robbery? What are the consequences of both actions?

TABLE 7-1 RECENT WHITE-COLLAR CRIMES

Martin Bramson, Businessman. Sentence: 30 Years

Bramson, 52, directed the largest malpractice insurance scam in U.S. history. His decade-long insurance scam swindled doctors across the country out of more than $10 million and siphoned millions of dollars through a maze of phony companies and nearly 600 bank accounts worldwide. Bramson ran the scam with the help of his brother and father, setting up 53 foreign-licensed insurance companies and selling cut-rate malpractice insurance over the phone to physicians nationwide. The Bramsons collected premiums but refused to pay large claims from doctors and their patients, prosecutors said.

Bramson pleaded guilty in 1997 to conspiracy, mail fraud, and money laundering. He was sentenced to 30 years in prison and was fined in excess of $1 million. As part of his plea bargain, Bramson agreed to cooperate with efforts to locate millions in assets still believed to be hidden in banks around the world. In exchange, the government dropped seven counts and agreed not to call him to testify against another brother, Carl, still under investigation. Eight other people, including lawyers and insurance underwriters, also have pleaded guilty in the case.

John Rigas, Corporate Founder, and Timothy Rigas, Executive: Up to 30 Years Each

John, 79, and his son Timothy, 48, used Adelphia Communications Corp. (at the time, the nation's fifth largest cable company), founded by John, as their own private bank, borrowing more than $2 billion from the company. They were convicted of stealing more than $100 million from the company including taking $1 million in cash per month, using corporate jets to fly for nonbusiness purposes, and purchasing a collection of 22 cars with company money. To cover their actions they routinely reported fabricated numbers to investors and lenders and stole millions from Adelphia to prop up stock prices. Finally, in 2002 Adelphia went bankrupt, leaving thousands of people with near-worthless stock.

In 2004, John Rigas and Timothy Rigas were both convicted of one count conspiracy, 15 counts of securities fraud, and two counts of bank fraud. They could each serve up to 30 years in prison.

Jamie Olis, Vice President of Finance. Sentence: 24 Years

Jamie Olis, 38, was vice president of finance and senior director of tax planning at Dynergy, a natural gas energy company. Olis attempted to conceal more than $300 million in company debt from public investors. When the attempted concealment was discovered, millions of investor dollars were lost, including a $105 million loss suffered by 13,000 people in the California Retirement Plan.

In 2004, Olis was sentenced to 292 months in prison after being convicted of security fraud, mail fraud, and three counts of wire fraud. The 24-year sentence is one of the longest terms for fraud in U.S. history, in part because of the large financial losses to thousands of investors. In addition to the jail time, Olis was fined $25,000. However, Olis did not act alone in the concealment. Gene Foster and Helen Sharkey, both former Dynergy executives, pled guilty to conspiracy and aided in the investigation. And they entered into a plea bargain under which Foster and Sharkey were to receive sentences of up to five years in prison and $250,000 in fines.

Reed Slatkin, Investment Manager. Sentence: 14 years

For approximately 15 years, he ran a nearly $600 million Ponzi scheme that bilked hundreds of investors. His clients included people of modest means, as well as more famous people such as actor Joe Pantoliano, model Cheryl Tiegs, and attorney Greta Van Susteren. He did not treat all clients equally, paying well-known clients returns in excess of their investments from funds received from other investors.

In April 2002, he pleaded guilty to five counts of mail fraud, three counts of wire fraud, six counts of money laundering, and one count of conspiracy to obstruct justice. He was sentenced to 14 years in federal prison and ordered to pay victims $240 million in restitution.

Frank Quattrone, Wall Street Banker. Sentence: 18 Months and 2 Years Probation

Frank Quattrone, a former star technology banker, was charged with three counts of obstruction of justice related to an e-mail he forwarded to colleagues in 2000 encouraging them to "clean up" their files during a federal probe into how shares of hot initial public offerings of stock were allocated during the tech boom.

In 2004, Quattrone was found guilty of obstruction of justice. He was sentenced in September 2004 to 18 months, prison and two years, probation. He was also fined $90,000. Near the end of that year, the National Association of Securities Dealers permanently banned Quattrone from the securities industry, although he had planned to appeal the ban to the Securities and Exchange Commission.

TABLE 7-2

MAJOR WHITE-COLLAR CRIMES UNDER INVESTIGATION

Richard Scrushy, CEO of Health South

In late 2003, Richard Scrushy was indicted on 85 counts related to his efforts to defraud investors. The indictment charges Scrushy with conspiracy, mail and wire fraud, securities fraud, and money laundering. The government is seeking forfeiture of more than $278 million that Scrushy gained through the alleged illegal activities.

From 1996 through 2002, Scrushy received more than $267 million in compensation from the company, which provides outpatient surgery. Frauding investors, Scrushy added $2.7 billion in fictitious income to Health South's records, and Scrushy paid himself from the falsified records. In addition to the forfeiture, Scrushy faces possible fines of $36 million and 650 years in prison.

Walter Forbes, CEO of Cendant Coporation

In 2004, Walter Forbes went on trial for fraudulently inflating the company's revenue by $500 million to increase stock prices. Forbes is charged with wire fraud, mail fraud, conspiracy, and securities fraud. In addition, Forbes is also accused of insider trading of $11 million in Cendant stock only weeks before the accounting scandal was discovered. The former vice president is also charged with similar crimes. The CFO has testified against both the vice president and Forbes, saying that he was asked to be "creative" in reorganizing revenue.

Kenneth Lay, CEO of Enron

In 2004, Kenneth Lay went on trial, pleading not guilty to 11 felony counts, including wire fraud, bank fraud, securities fraud, and conspiracy for his part in falsifying Enron's financial reports, and denying that he profited enormously from his fraudulent acts. The extent of the fraud was discovered when the energy company went bankrupt in late 2001.

The Securities and Exchange Commission also filed a civil complaint against Lay, which could lead to more than $90 million in penalties and fines. Lay is accused of selling large amounts of stock at artificially high prices resulting in an illegal profit of $90 million.

As a result of the accounting fraud, Enron's stock plummeted, leaving thousands of people with near-worthless stock, hitting retirement funds especially hard.

Bernie Ebbers, CEO of WorldCom

In 2004, Bernie Ebbers, former CEO of the bankrupt phone company, WorldCom, pleaded not guilty to three counts of fraud and conspiracy. The accounting fraud, which involved hiding expenses and inflating revenue reports, left $11 billion in debt at the time of the bankruptcy. The former CFO of WorldCom, Scott Sullivan, pleaded guilty to fraud and has agreed to assist in the prosecution of Ebbers. Sullivan faces up to 25 years in prison for his role in the accounting scandal. (Update: Ebbers convicted of Fraud in 2005)

In addition, MCI is suing Ebbers to recover more than $400 million in loans that he took from WorldCom, now called MCI.

Dennis Kozlowski, CEO of Tyco International

Facing a second trial in early 2005 after a mistrial, Dennis Kozlowski faces charges of corruption and larceny for stealing more than $600 million from Tyco International and failing to pay more than $1 million in federal taxes. Kozlowski had Tyco pay for such over-the-top expenses as a $15,000 umbrella holder and a $2,200 garbage can. Kozlowski faces up to 30 years in prison.

CRIME AND CRIMINAL PROCEDURE

CRIME

Criminal law is designed to punish an offender for causing harm to the public health, safety, or morals. Criminal laws prohibit certain actions and specify the range of punishments for such conduct. The proscribed conduct generally includes a description of both a wrongful behavior (an act or failure to act where one has a duty to do so) and a wrongful intent or state of mind. The legal term for wrongful intent is *mens rea* (guilty mind). An extremely limited number of crimes do not require *mens rea*. These crimes are the "strict liability," or regulatory, crimes. They occur most commonly in heavily regulated industries and arise when a regulation has been violated. Regulatory crimes are created when the legislature decides that the need to protect the public outweighs the traditional requirement of *mens rea*. Because of the absence of the *mens rea* requirement for regulatory crimes, punishment for their violation is generally less severe than it is for wrongful behavior. In some states, punishment is limited to fines.

Crimes are generally classified as treason, felony, misdemeanor, or petty crime, on the basis of the seriousness of the offense. Treason is engaging in war against the United States or giving aid or comfort to its enemies. **Felonies** include serious crimes such as murder or rape, punishable by death or imprisonment in a penitentiary. Defendants charged with a felony are entitled to a jury trial. **Misdemeanors** are considered less serious crimes and are punishable by a fine or by imprisonment of less than a year in a local jail. An assault (a threat to injure someone) and disorderly conduct would be examples of misdemeanors. In most states, **petty crimes** are considered a subcategory of misdemeanors. They are usually punishable by a fine or by incarceration for six months or less. A building code violation would be an example of a petty crime. The statute defining the crime generally states whether it is a felony, misdemeanor, or petty crime. The more serious the offense, the greater the stigma that attaches to the criminal.

> **felony** A serious crime that is punishable by death or imprisonment in a penitentiary.
>
> **misdemeanor** A crime that is less serious than a felony and is punishable by fine or imprisonment in a local jail.
>
> **petty crime** A minor crime punishable, under federal statutes, by fine or incarceration of no more than six months.

CRIMINAL PROCEDURE

Criminal proceedings are initiated somewhat differently from civil proceedings. The procedures may vary slightly from state to state. In general, however, the case begins with an **arrest** of the defendant. The police must, in almost all cases, obtain an arrest warrant before arresting the defendant and taking him or her into custody. A magistrate will issue the arrest warrant when there is **probable cause** to believe that the suspect committed the crime. A magistrate is a public official who has the power to issue warrants; he or she is the lowest-ranking judicial official. Probable cause exists if it appears likely, from the available facts and circumstances, that the defendant committed the crime. An arrest may be made by a police officer without a warrant, but only if probable cause exists and there is not time to secure a warrant. An arrest without a warrant would most commonly be made when police are called to the scene of a crime and catch the suspect committing the crime or fleeing from the scene.

> **arrest** To seize and hold under the authority of the law.
>
> **probable cause** The reasonable inference from the available facts and circumstances that the suspect committed the crime.

The Miranda Warnings. At the time of the arrest, the suspect must be informed of her or his legal rights. These rights are referred to as the **Miranda rights**, and if the defendant is not informed of these rights, any statements the defendant makes at the time of the arrest will be inadmissible at the defendant's trial. These rights are listed in Table 7-3.

Despite the courts' effort to create an "objective rule to give clear guidance to the police," many arrests and interrogations create significant questions about the application of the Miranda warnings. In 2004 alone, the Supreme Court issued three separate decisions clarifying the application and use of the Miranda warnings.

> **Miranda rights** Certain legal rights—such as the right to remain silent to avoid self-incrimination and the right to an attorney—that a suspect must be immediately informed of upon arrest.

TABLE 7-3

THE MIRANDA WARNINGS

Before any questioning by authorities, the following statements must be made to the defendant:

1. "You have the right to remain silent and refuse to answer any questions."

2. "Anything you say may be used against you in a court of law."

3. "You have the right to consult an attorney before speaking to the police and have an attorney present during any questioning now or in the future."

4. "If you cannot afford an attorney, one will be appointed for you before the questioning begins."

5. "If you do not have an attorney available, you have the right to remain silent until you have had an opportunity to consult with one."

6. "Now that I have advised you of your rights, are you willing to answer any questions without an attorney present?"

The Court held in *United States v. Patane*[2] that physical evidence found through statements made without the Miranda warnings were admissible in court so long as those statements were not forced by the police; the incriminating statements, however, would not be admissible.

In *Missouri v. Seibert*,[3] the Supreme Court found that a confession made after the Miranda warnings could not be admissible if the police first ask for the confession, then give the Miranda warnings and ask for the same confession. Delivering the opinion of the Court, Justice Souter wrote, "*Miranda* addressed interrogation practices … likely … to disable [an individual] from making a free and rational choice" about speaking, and held that a suspect must be "adequately and effectively" advised of the choice the Constitution guarantees. The object of question-first is to render *Miranda* warnings ineffective by waiting for a particularly opportune time to give them, after the suspect has already confessed."

Finally, in the case of *Yarborough v. Alvarado*,[4] the Court examined the ambiguity of when a person is "in custody" and, therefore, when a person is entitled to the Miranda warnings. The "in custody" standard is whether a reasonable person would feel free to leave or end questioning. However, such a standard can be influenced by a person's age and education. Yet, the Court held that maintaining a clear and objective standard for police is more important, and considerations of age and education "could be viewed as creating a subjective inquiry." The Court found that the admission of guilt to police by Alvarado, age 17, during an interview was admissible even though he had not been read his Miranda warnings because he was never "in custody."

Hundreds of cases have sought to clarify the Miranda warnings since they were first created in 1966 in *Miranda v. Arizona*. The most recent cases, just discussed, suggest the importance the judicial system places on informing suspects of their constitutional rights and privileges.

first appearance
Appearance of the defendant before a magistrate, who determines whether there was probable cause for the arrest.

Booking and First Appearance. After the defendant has been arrested, he or she will be taken to the police station for booking, the filing of criminal charges against the defendant. The arresting officer will then file a criminal complaint against the defendant. Shortly after the complaint is filed, the defendant will make his or her **first appearance** before the magistrate. At this time, the

---

[2] 124 S. Ct. 2620 (2004).
[3] 124 S. Ct. 2601 (2004).
[4] 124 S. Ct. 2140 (2004).

magistrate will determine whether there was probable cause for the arrest. If there was not, the suspect will be set free and the case will be dismissed.

If the offense is a minor one, and the defendant pleads guilty, the magistrate may accept the guilty plea and sentence the defendant. Most defendants, however, maintain they are innocent. The magistrate will make sure the defendant has a lawyer and, if the defendant is indigent, will appoint a lawyer for him or her. The magistrate will also set bail at this time. **Bail** is an amount of money that is paid to the court to ensure that the defendant will return for trial. In some cases, especially in white-collar crimes, if the magistrate believes that the defendant has such "ties to the community" that he or she will not try to flee the area to avoid prosecution, the defendant may be released without posting bail. In such cases, the defendant is said to be released "on his [or her] own recognizance."

bail An amount of money the defendant pays to the court upon release from custody as security that he or she will return for trial.

Information or Indictment. If the crime is a misdemeanor, the next step is the prosecutor's issuance of **information**, a formal written accusation or charge. The information is usually issued only after the prosecutor has presented the facts to a magistrate who believes that the prosecution has sufficient grounds to bring the case.

information A formal written accusation in a misdemeanor case.

In felony cases, the process begins with a presentation by the prosecutor (the prosecuting officer representing the United States or the state) of the facts surrounding the crime to a **grand jury**, a group of individuals under oath who are presented with evidence of a crime. The grand jury has the power to subpoena witnesses and require them to produce documents and tangible evidence. If the grand jury is convinced by a preponderance of the evidence that there is reason to believe that the defendant may have committed the crime, an indictment (a formal, written accusation) is issued against the defendant. A grand jury does not make a finding of guilt; it simply decides whether there is enough evidence that the defendant committed the crime to justify bringing the defendant to trial. Government resources are limited, and the prosecution may not always believe it has sufficient evidence to get an indictment, let alone prove beyond a reasonable doubt that the defendant committed the crime, so not every crime is prosecuted. The prosecutor's office must make the decision in each case. Usually the decision to seek an indictment depends on whether the prosecution believes it can get a conviction and whether the interests of justice would be served by prosecuting the crime.

grand jury a group of individuals who determine whether theirs is enough evidence to try a defendant.

At the federal level, almost all criminal prosecutions are initiated by the indictment process, and the decision whether to prosecute is generally guided by the *Principles of Federal Prosecution*, published by the Justice Department in 1980. These *Principles* state that the primary consideration in the indictment decision is whether the existing admissible evidence is sufficient to obtain a conviction for a federal crime. Even if sufficient evidence does exist, the prosecutor's office might choose not to prosecute a crime if no substantial federal interest would be served by doing so, if the defendant could be efficiently prosecuted in another jurisdiction, or if an adequate noncriminal alternative to criminal prosecution exists. The factors that influence whether a substantial federal interest exists are listed in Table 7-4. The *Principles* clearly recognize that, at least when a federal crime is at issue, other noncriminal actions may offer fairer or more efficient ways to respond to the criminal conduct. Some alternatives might be to institute civil proceedings against the defendant or to refer the complaint to a licensing board or the professional organization to which the criminal belongs.

Another alternative to indictment is pretrial diversion, often referred to as PTD. Pretrial diversion attempts to divert certain criminal offenders from the

TABLE 7-4

FACTORS FOR DETERMINING A SUBSTANTIAL FEDERAL INTEREST AND THE *PRINCIPLES FOR FEDERAL PROSECUTION*

1. Federal law enforcement priorities established by the Department of Justice
2. Deterrent effect
3. The subject's culpability
4. The subject's willingness to cooperate
5. The subject's personal circumstances
6. The probable sentence
7. The possibility of prosecution in another jurisdiction
8. Noncriminal alternatives to prosecution

traditional criminal justice system into a program of supervision and services. A PTD participant signs an agreement with the government acknowledging responsibility for the act at issue but not admitting guilt. The participant agrees to be supervised by the U.S. Probation Office and to comply with the terms established for the agreed-upon period of the agreement, up to 18 months. Special conditions, which vary according to the alleged circumstances and the criminal activity, might include participating in community programs or paying restitution. If the participant complies with the agreement, the matter is closed. If not, he or she will then be prosecuted.

Once there has been an indictment, the next step is the **arraignment**. The defendant appears in court and enters a plea of guilty or not guilty. A defendant who enters a plea of not guilty is entitled to a trial before a petit jury. If the defendant declines a jury trial, the case is heard by a judge. This procedure is called a bench trial.

A defendant may also enter a plea of **nolo contendere**. This plea is one by which the defendant does not admit guilt but agrees to not contest the charges. The advantage of a nolo contendere plea over a plea of guilty is that the former cannot be used against the defendant in a civil suit.

arraignment Formal appearance of the defendant in court to answer the indictment by entering a plea of guilty or not guilty.

nolo contendere A plea of no contest that subjects the defendant to punishment but is not an admission of guilt.

plea bargaining The negotiation of an agreement between the defendant's attorney and the prosecutor whereby the defendant pleads guilty to a certain charge or charges in exchange for the prosecution reducing the charges.

Plea Bargaining. At any time during the proceedings, the parties may engage in **plea bargaining**, which is a process of negotiation between the defense attorney and the public prosecutor or district attorney. The result of this process is that the defendant pleads guilty to a lesser offense, in exchange for which the prosecutor drops or reduces some of the charges. Plea bargaining benefits the criminal by eliminating the risk of a greater penalty. It benefits the prosecutor by giving her or him a sure conviction and by reducing what is generally an overwhelming caseload. It saves both parties the time and expense of a trial.

Plea bargaining is used extensively for white-collar crimes, generally at a much earlier stage than for street crimes. In white-collar cases, plea bargaining often occurs even before the indictment. This process, as well as other modifications of criminal procedures in white-collar crime cases, helps to make the white-collar criminal seem "less a criminal" and, thus, reduces the likelihood of severe punishment.

Burden of Proof. If the case goes to trial, the burden of proof is usually on the prosecutor. The burden of proof has two aspects: the burden of production of evidence and the burden of persuasion. The burden of production of evidence of all of the elements of the crime is placed on the prosecution. Thus, the prosecution must present physical evidence and testimony that prove all elements of the crime. The burden of producing evidence of any affirmative defenses (defenses in which the defendant admits to doing the act but claims some reason for not being held responsible, such as insanity, self-defense, intoxication, or coercion) lies with the defendant.

The prosecution also bears the burden of persuasion. This means that the prosecutor must convince the jury beyond a reasonable doubt that the defendant committed the crime. In some states, a defendant who presents evidence of an affirmative defense must persuade the jury of the existence of the defense by a preponderance of the evidence. This means that the defense must prove that it is more likely than not that the defense exists. In other states, the burden of persuasion lies with the prosecutor to show beyond a reasonable doubt that the defense does not exist.

The actual trial itself is similar to a civil trial, and the role of the prosecutor or district attorney is similar to that of the plaintiff's attorney. One major difference, however, is that the defendant in a criminal case cannot be compelled to testify, and the finder of fact is not to hold the exercise of this right against the defendant. This right to not testify is guaranteed by the constitutional provision in the Fifth Amendment that no person "shall be compelled in any criminal case to be a witness against himself."

Defenses. Obviously, one of the most common defenses is that the defendant did not do the act in question. But even if the defendant did commit the act, there are a number of affirmative defenses that might be raised to preclude the defendant from being convicted of the crime. Affirmative defenses may be thought of as excuses for otherwise unlawful conduct. Four of the most common are entrapment, insanity, duress, and mistake.

Entrapment occurs when the idea for the crime was not the defendant's but was, instead, put into the defendant's mind by a police officer or other government official. An extreme example might be a case in which a government official first suggests to an employee that he or she could make good money by altering certain corporate records. Then the official shows up at the employee's home at night with a key to the office where the records are kept and reminds the employee that the record keeper is on vacation that week. The official also reminds the employee that most of the other workers rarely stay late on Friday nights, so Friday after work might be an ideal time to get the books. If prosecuted for fraud, the employee could raise the defense of entrapment.

Entrapment is not always easy to prove, however. Police are allowed to set up legitimate "sting" operations to catch persons engaged in criminal activity. The key to a legitimate sting is that the defendant was "predisposed" to commit the crime; the officer did not put the idea in the defendant's head. If an officer dresses up like a prostitute and parades around in an area where prostitution is rampant, a potential customer who solicits sex could not raise the charge of entrapment against a charge of soliciting a prostitute. Most cases, however, fall between our two examples, and it is often difficult to predict whether the entrapment defense will be successful.

Insanity is one of the best-known criminal defenses, although it is not used nearly as frequently as its notoriety might imply. Insanity is a defense when a person's mental condition prevents him or her from understanding the wrongful nature of the act he or she committed or from distinguishing wrong from right.

Duress occurs when a person is forced to commit a wrongful act by a threat of immediate bodily harm or loss of life, and the affirmative duress defense can be used by a person who claims he or she was forced to commit a crime. For example,

entrapment An affirmative defense claiming that the idea for the crime did not originate with the defendant but was put into the defendant's mind by a police officer or other government official.

insanity defense An affirmative defense claiming that the defendant's mental condition precluded understanding the wrongful nature of the act he or she committed or distinguishing wrong from right in general.

duress defense An affirmative defense claiming that the defendant was forced to commit the wrongful act by threat of immediate bodily harm or loss of life.

EXHIBIT 7-1

STEPS OF A CRIMINAL PROSECUTION

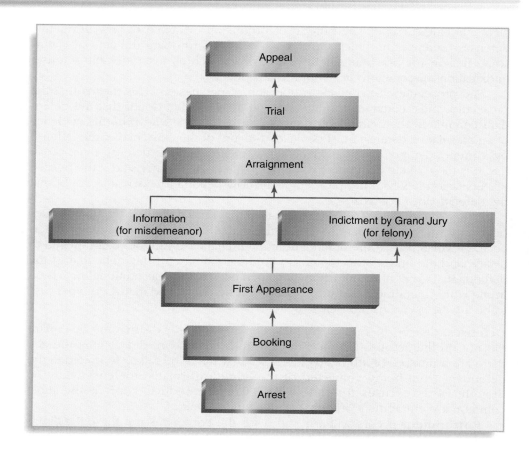

if Sam holds a gun to Jim's head and tells him to forge his employer's signature on a company check or he will be shot, Jim can raise the defense of duress to a charge of forgery. This defense is generally not available to a charge of murder.

A **mistake of fact** may sometimes be raised when that mistake vitiates the criminal intent. For example, if Mary takes Karen's umbrella from a public umbrella rack, thinking it is hers, she can raise mistake as a defense to a charge of theft.

A mistake of law, however, is generally not a defense. A person could not, for example, fail to include payment received for a small job on his or her income tax return because of a mistaken belief that income for part-time work of under $100 did not have to be reported.

Any defendant who does not prevail at the trial court can appeal the decision, just as in a civil case. The steps of a criminal action are set out in Exhibit 7-1.

mistake-of-fact defense An affirmative defense claiming that a mistake made by the defendant vitiates criminal intent.

DISTINGUISHING FEATURES OF WHITE-COLLAR CRIME

white-collar crime A crime committed in a commercial context by a member of the professional–managerial class.

An initial problem with any discussion of **white-collar crime** is its definition. The term white-collar crime does not have a precise meaning. The term was first made popular in 1939 by sociologist Edwin Sutherland, who defined white-collar crime as "crime committed by a person of respectability and high social status in the course of his occupation." Traditionally, it has been the classification of those crimes committed in a commercial context by members of the professional and managerial classes. It includes such diverse acts as bribery of corporate or government officials and violations of federal regulations such as the Occupational Safety and Health Act and the Internal Revenue Service Code. In this book, we will use the traditional definition. For illustrations of some white-collar criminals and the crimes for which they were convicted, see Table 7-1 at the beginning of this chapter. Table 7-2 features some white-collar crimes currently under investigation.

THE CORPORATION AS A CRIMINAL

One of the distinguishing features of white-collar crime is that sometimes the "criminal" may be difficult to identify. In a street crime, the identity of the criminal is fairly clear: It is the person who committed the act. If a person hires another to commit a crime, the person doing the hiring is likewise guilty of a crime. In the case of white-collar crime, the crime is often committed on behalf of a corporation, which is defined as an artificial legal entity or an artificial person. An important question, then, is whether liability can be imposed on the corporation for the criminal acts committed by employees of the corporation on behalf of the corporation.

Initially, the courts said no. Because a corporation had no mind, it could not have the mental state necessary to commit a crime. This rule was first eroded by the imposition of liability on corporations for so-called **strict liability offenses**, those for which no state of mind is required. These generally were cases in which corporate employees failed to take some action required by a regulation. For example, under most blue sky laws (state regulations of securities), it is a violation to file a false statement of a company's financial condition with a state's secretary of state. Filing a false statement is a crime, even if the corporate officer filing the statement believed it was true, as no state of mind is required to commit the crime.

strict liability offense An offense for which no state of mind is required.

The courts then began to impose liability on corporations for criminal acts of the employees by imputing the state of mind of the employee to the corporation. Today, as a general rule, the only crimes for which a corporation is not held liable are those that are punishable only by incarceration. Obviously, the rationale for this rule is that the punishment could not be carried out. Some states have even eliminated this problem by passing a statute that provides for specific fines for corporations that commit offenses otherwise punishable by incarceration only.

Many corporate executives may not realize the extent to which a corporation today can be held liable for the acts of its employees. That liability can extend down to acts of even the lowest-level employees and even to acts in violation of corporate directives, as long as two conditions are met. First, the conduct must be within the scope of the employee agent's authority. Second, the action must have been undertaken, at least in part, to benefit the corporation. Some examples of employee actions for which corporations have been held liable include employees physically harming a customer for not paying his bill,[5] supervisor or employee sexually harassing another employee,[6] and a car salesman's obtaining automobile loans for the dealership's customers by misrepresenting financial data to the lending bank.[7]

---

[5] *Crane Brothers, Inc. v. May*, 556 S.E. 2d 865 (2001).
[6] *Pennsylvania State Police v. Suders*, 124 S. Ct. 2342 (2004).
[7] *Commonwealth v. Duddie Ford, Inc.*, 551 N.E. 2d 1211 (1990).

Many states have passed statutes imposing criminal liability on partnerships under the same circumstances as those under which liability is imposed on a corporation. In the absence of such a statute, liability is not imposed on the partnership because a partnership is not a legal person.

ARGUMENTS IN SUPPORT OF CORPORATE LIABILITY

Needless to say, there is no consensus about whether, as a matter of policy, corporations should be held criminally liable. Some of the arguments in favor of such liability include the following:

1. Imposing financial sanctions against the corporation will result in lower dividends for the shareholders, which, in turn, will prompt the shareholders to take a more active role in trying to make sure that the corporation behaves legally. They will carefully select directors who will scrupulously monitor corporate behavior and will express concern when anything appears to be unethical or illegal.

2. In situations in which the crime is an omission and the responsibility for performing the omitted duty is not clearly delegated to any specific party, the duty rests with no particular individual. Therefore, there is no one to blame, and the corporation cannot be held responsible. If no one, not even the corporation, is held liable, there is no incentive to obey the laws.

3. Closely related to reason 2 is the fact that there are a tremendous number of suspects in a corporation. Most enforcement agencies do not have the resources to investigate the large number of employees involved and to build cases against each. It is much easier and less expensive for the government to investigate and bring a case against the corporation as an entity.

4. The fact that many decisions are committee decisions—or else decisions made by an initial person or group and then approved by several tiers of management—again makes it hard to point the finger at one individual. Sometimes one individual is responsible for making an initial decision, and then someone else is responsible for implementing that decision.

5. A further reason is that corporate personnel are expendable. To lose a manager because of a conviction does not really harm the enterprise that profited from the wrongdoing. In fact, it allows the firm to externalize the costs of the criminal behavior, that is, to absolve itself of guilt in the eyes of the public. The manager takes the blame, and the corporation, which profited from the manager's illegal act, continues to thrive.

6. Even if one could impose liability on one or two individuals, it is unfair to single them out for punishment when the behavior in question probably resulted from a pattern of behavior common to the entire corporation.

7. Some people assume that the beneficiaries of crime committed on behalf of the corporation are the shareholders, because they may get higher dividends if corporate crime keeps costs lower. To fail to impose sanctions on the corporation would be to allow the shareholders to benefit from the illegal activity.

8. If an action is taken against the corporation, the criminal act will be linked to the corporation in the public's mind. In a market-oriented society such as ours, disclosure of full information about businesses is essential for consumers to make informed decisions about the types of firms with which they want to transact business.

ARGUMENTS IN OPPOSITION TO CORPORATE LIABILITY

The following are arguments against imposing liability on corporations:

1. Imposing fines on corporations is a waste of time and effort because the fines are never going to be severe enough to act as a deterrent. Even if more substantial fines were imposed, the firms would simply pass on the losses to consumers in the form of increased product prices. Thus, it would really be the consumers of the corporation's products who would be punished.

2. Some people believe that the shareholders' dividends may be reduced if fines are imposed on the corporation because the cost of the fines will reduce the profits available for dividend payments. Reducing dividends, it is argued, is unfair because in most corporations, the shareholders really do not have any power to control corporate behavior.

3. Because criminal prosecutions of corporations are not well publicized, they do not harm the corporation's public image. The corporations have enough money and public relations personnel to easily overcome any negative publicity with a well-run advertising campaign designed to polish their public image. For example, the prosecution of Revco of Ohio for defrauding Medicaid of hundreds of thousand of dollars resulted in only a temporary decline of the value of Revco's stock.[8]

IMPOSITION OF LIABILITY ON CORPORATE EXECUTIVES

Another potential candidate for liability in the case of white-collar crime is the corporate executive. Top-level corporate executives, as a group, have tremendous power through their control over national corporations. When these corporations earn record-setting profits, top-level executives rush forward to take credit for their corporations' successes. However, these same executives do not rush forward to take responsibility for their corporations' criminal violations.

In fact, very few corporate officials are held liable by law enforcement for the actions of their companies.[9] This lack of liability is believed to occur because of the delegation of responsibility to lower tiers of management and reliance on unwritten orders, which allows top-level management to frequently protect itself from liability for the results of its policy decisions.

Traditionally, imposing liability on executives has been difficult because the criminal law usually requires an unlawful act to be accompanied by an unlawful intent (*mens rea*). In cases of violations of federal regulations, corporate executives often argue that they are not the ones directly responsible for filing the documents or conducting the studies. They certainly never explicitly ordered that such regulations be disregarded. In response to recent high-profile corporate scandals, Congress and the Securities and Exchange Commission have created more stringent certification requirements for CEOs, CFOs, and other corporate officials. For example, the Sarbanes-Oxley Act of 2002 holds high-ranking corporate officials responsible for the validity and accuracy of their

---

[8] D. Vaughan, *Controlling Unlawful Organizational Behavior* (Chicago: University of Chicago Press, 1983).

[9] Timothy P. Glynn, *Beyond "Unlimiting" Shareholder Liability: Vicarious Tort Liability for Corporate Officers*, 57 VAND. L. REV. 329 (2004).

financial statements. Failure to comply with the financial statement certification or certification of false information is a corporate fraud under the act, punishable with fines that range from $1 million to $5 million and prison sentences from 10 to 20 years. This act is discussed in greater detail in Chapter 22.

As the following case shows, however, the courts are recognizing that corporate executives who have the power and authority to secure compliance with the law have an affirmative duty to do so. Failure to uphold that duty can lead to criminal sanctions.

CASE 7-1

United States v. Park
United States Supreme Court 421 U.S. 658 (1975)

Defendant Park, the president of a national food-chain corporation, was charged, along with the corporation, with violating the federal Food, Drug, and Cosmetic Act by allowing food in the warehouse to be exposed to rodent contamination. Park had conceded that he was responsible for the sanitary conditions as part of his responsibility for the "entire operation" but claimed that he had turned the responsibility for sanitation over to dependable subordinates. He admitted at the trial that he had received a warning letter from the Food and Drug Administration regarding the unsanitary conditions at one of the company's warehouses.

The trial court found the defendant guilty. The court of appeals reversed. The case was appealed to the U.S. Supreme Court.

Chief Justice Burger

The question presented was whether "the manager of a corporation, as well as the corporation itself, may be prosecuted under the Federal Food, Drug, and Cosmetic Act of 1938 for the introduction of misbranded and adulterated articles into interstate commerce." In *Dotterweich*, a jury had disagreed as to the corporation, a jobber purchasing drugs from manufacturers and shipping them in interstate commerce under its own label, but had convicted Dotterweich, the corporation's president and general manager.

In reversing the judgment of the Court of Appeals and reinstating Dotterweich's conviction, this Court looked to the purposes of the Act and noted that they "touch phases of the lives and health of people which, in the circumstances of modern industrialism, are largely beyond self-protection." It observed that the Act is of "a now familiar type" which "dispenses with the conventional requirement for criminal conduct—awareness of some wrongdoing. In the interest of the larger good it puts the burden of acting at hazard upon a person otherwise innocent but standing in responsible relation to a public danger."

Central to the Court's conclusion that individuals other than proprietors are subject to the criminal provisions of the Act was the reality that "the only way in which a corporation can act is through the individuals who act on in its behalf." The Court also noted that corporate officers had been subject to criminal liability under the Federal Food and Drugs Act of 1906, and it observed that a contrary result under the 1938 legislation would be incompatible with the expressed intent of Congress to "enlarge and stiffen the penal net" and to discourage a view of the Act's criminal penalties as a "license fee for the conduct of an illegitimate business."

At the same time, however, the Court was aware of the concern which was the motivating factor in the Court of Appeals' decision, that literal enforcement "might operate too harshly by sweeping within its condemnation any person however remotely entangled in the proscribed shipment." A limiting principle, in the form of "settled doctrines of criminal law" defining those who "are responsible for the commission of a misdemeanor," was available. In this context, the Court concluded, those doctrines dictated that the offense was committed "by all who … have … a responsible share in the furtherance of the transaction which the statute outlaws."

The rule that corporate employees who have "a responsible share in the furtherance of the transaction which the statute outlaws" are subject to the criminal provisions of the Act was not formulated in a vacuum. Cases under the Federal Food and Drugs Act of 1906 reflected the view both that knowledge or intent were not required to be proved in prosecutions under its criminal provisions, and that responsible corporate agents could be subjected to the liability thereby imposed. Moreover, the principle had been recognized that a corporate agent, through whose act, default, or omission the corporation committed a crime, was himself guilty individually of that crime.

The rationale of the interpretation given the Act in *Dotterweich*, as holding criminally accountable the persons whose failure to exercise the authority and supervisory responsibility reposed in them by the business organization, resulted in the violation complained of, has been confirmed in our subsequent cases. Thus, the Court has reaffirmed the proposition that "the public interest in the purity of its food is so great as to warrant the imposition of the highest standard of care on distributors." In order to make "distributors of food the strictest censors of their merchandise," the Act punishes "neglect where the law requires care, and inaction where it imposes a duty." "The accused, if he does not will the violation, usually is in a position to prevent it with no more care than society might reasonably expect and no more exertion than it might reasonably extract from one who assumed his responsibilities."

Thus, *Dotterweich* and the cases which have followed reveal that in providing sanctions which reach and touch the individuals who execute the corporate mission—and this is by no means necessarily confined to a single corporate agent or employee—the Act imposes not only a positive duty to seek out and remedy violations when they occur but also, and primarily, a duty to implement measures that will insure that violations will not occur. The requirements of foresight and vigilance imposed on responsible corporate agents are beyond question demanding, and perhaps onerous, but they are not more stringent than the public has a right to expect of those who voluntarily assume positions of authority in business enterprises whose services and products affect the health and well-being of the public that supports them.

The Act does not, as we observed in *Dotterweich*, make criminal liability turn on "awareness of some wrongdoing" or "conscious fraud." The duty imposed by Congress on responsible corporate agents is, we emphasize, one that requires the highest standard of foresight and vigilance, but the Act, in its criminal aspect, does not require that which is objectively impossible. The theory upon which responsible corporate agents are held criminally accountable for "causing" violations of the Act permits a claim that a defendant was "powerless" to prevent or correct the violation to "be raised defensively at a trial on the merits."

... [I]t is equally clear that the Government established a prima facie case when it introduced evidence sufficient to warrant a finding by the trier of the facts that the defendant had, by reason of his position in the corporation, responsibility and authority either to prevent in the first instance, or promptly to correct, the violation complained of, and that he failed to do so. The failure thus to fulfill the duty imposed by the interaction of the corporate agent's authority and that statute furnishes a sufficient causal link. The considerations which prompted the imposition of this duty, and the scope of the duty, provide the measure of culpability.

Reversed in favor of the Government.

Critical Thinking About the Law

Although it never explicitly stated it as such, the Court in Case 7-1 was guided by a fundamental principle: To the extent that one has authority, she or he also has responsibility and can be liable for criminal action. This guiding principle played a significant role in the Court's justification (i.e., reasoning) for its decision.

Context was very important in the formulation of this principle as well as in its application to Case 7-1. Key facts, primary ethical norms, and judicial precedent were important elements of this context. Consequently, the questions that follow will focus on those aspects of Case 7-1.

1. What key fact was very important to the Court in its determination of Park's guilt?

   Clue: Think again about the Court's guiding principle in this case. You want to identify the key fact that allowed the Court to apply the principle to this particular case.

2. Precedent plays a crucial role in the Court's reasoning and, thus, in its decision. What key precedent in criminal law did the *Dotterweich* decision dispense with, thereby clearing the way for the guiding principle discussed previously to have greater significance and making conviction in the present case possible?

   Clue: Reread the section in which Justice Burger discusses the *Dotterweich* decision.

EXHIBIT 7-2 WHITE-COLLAR PRISON CAMPS

Elgin is the original "club fed." This prison's open dorms hold 50 men who sleep in two-person cubicles. The prison has an actual music department that sponsors inmate bands and has instruments prisoners can check out. Sports options include softball, basketball, soccer, flag football, weight machines, and free weights.

Morgantown is a compound in the beautiful Blue Ridge Mountains, where deer can sometimes be sighted. It holds 300 people in dorms where men sleep in two-person cubicles. Inmates can lift weights, play pool and Ping-Pong, and take courses in leather working, art, and wood carving. They can participate in apprenticeship programs in baking, commercial photography, computer technology, air-conditioning systems, landscaping, printing presses, painting, and plumbing.

Allenwood has dorms that house up to 80 men in two-person cubicles and offers inmates soccer, basketball, flag football, universal weight machines, free weights, pool, and Ping-Pong tables. The prison provides 150- and 500-hour certificate programs in horticulture, as well as a music program with inmates providing instruction.

At *Nellis,* located in North Las Vegas, inmates sleep four to a cubicle in air-conditioned dorms where they can play softball, soccer, and flag football. They can work out in a gym that offers universal weight machines, stationary bikes, stair steppers, pool tables, and Ping-Pong tables.

Although the *Park* case demonstrates that corporate executives may be found guilty of committing a corporate crime, few actually are convicted. Even when they are convicted, harsh penalties are not likely to be imposed. And even when they do go to prison, because they are not seen as security risks, they are often sent to prisons that some would argue are nicer than motels many people can afford to stay in on vacations! See Exhibit 7-2 for a glimpse of some of these prisons where white-collar criminals are likely to end up.

A primary reason for the limited number of convictions is the diffusion of responsibility. It is often difficult to establish who was responsible for the criminal act. Another problem related to corporate structure is that everyone usually has a specific job, and putting all of the pieces of the crime together is difficult. The reader should remember that the burden of proof is on the prosecution. Corporate executives also tend to have high-caliber counsel who specialize in defending white-collar criminals. These skilled attorneys, often paid for by the corporation or, when not unlawful, by an insurance carrier, usually get involved during the initial investigation of the case and perceive one of their key functions as keeping evidence out of the hands of the prosecutor. They often regard themselves as having lost the case if they do not prevent their client from being indicted or if they do not at least get the charge reduced to the lowest possible misdemeanor.[10] Another alleged reason for the limited number of convictions of corporate executives is that they are generally persons with a great deal of knowledge, including knowledge

---

[10] K. Mann, *Defending White-Collar Crime* (New Haven: Yale University Press, 1985), p. 10.

of inefficiencies and improprieties on the part of the government officials who are regulating them. It is argued that regulators are unlikely to press for prosecution when their own ineptness may be revealed in the process.

IMPOSITION OF LIABILITY ON LOWER-LEVEL CORPORATE CRIMINALS

Although much debate has been generated over the extent to which the corporation and its top executives should be held liable for crimes committed on behalf of the corporation, it is important to remember that lower-level and midlevel corporate employees can also be held liable for their individual criminal actions, and imposition of liability on the corporation does not in any way preclude the imposition of liability on the individual actor. It is likewise no excuse on the part of employees that they were committing the wrongful act only because their employer instructed them to do so.

FACTORS ENCOURAGING THE COMMISSION OF WHITE-COLLAR CRIME

White-collar crime can be distinguished from street crime by some of the factors that facilitate its commission (Table 7-5). Recognition of these factors is not meant to excuse this behavior; instead, it may be used to help devise ways to control corporate crime. As an informed corporate manager, your knowledge of these factors may help you to avoid the temptation to engage in criminal activities and to discourage others from doing so.

Initially, we must recognize that many people in our society value material success above all else. When the focus of our energies is on material success, we are much more willing to engage in illegal means to achieve our goal than we would be if our focus were on, for instance, ethical conduct. With the stress on success, the line between illegality and a shrewd business deal becomes blurred. The culture of some corporations creates an atmosphere in which corporate crime may thrive. For instance, if rewards such as salary and promotion are tied to meeting short-term goals, employees may use whatever means available to help them achieve those goals.

Once illegal behavior is initiated, it tends to become institutionalized because of a phenomenon referred to by social psychologist Irving Janis as groupthink.[11]

TABLE 7-5

FACTORS FACILITATING THE COMMISSION OF WHITE-COLLAR CRIME

1. Societal stress on material success, without equal emphasis on means of achieving success.
2. Linkage of corporate rewards of salary and promotion to accomplishing short-term goals.
3. Groupthink.
4. Ease of rationalizing illegal behavior.
5. Dispersion of decision making.
6. Retention of status by persons convicted of white-collar crime.
7. The lack of an adversarial relationship between the corporation and government regulators.
8. Poor personnel policies that leave employees feeling insecure, unappreciated, and underpaid.

[11] D. Goleman, "Following the Leader," *Science*, October 1985, p. 18.

In groupthink, there is an implicit agreement not to bring up upsetting facts. In the corporation, where junior managers' success depends to some degree on the approval of senior managers, a junior manager would be extremely reluctant to criticize a senior manager's actions. One dramatic instance of this dynamic is the *E. F. Hutton* case, in which the practice of writing illegal checks spread throughout the company. Nobody wanted to bring up the upsetting fact that perhaps the practice was illegal. Instead, managers just went along.[12]

Another factor making white-collar crime easy to commit is the fact that decision making is often distributed among various individuals. Because responsibility is diffuse, individuals may feel only very limited personal responsibility for the results of their actions. This spreading of responsibility also results in an awareness that the likelihood of getting caught is small. Another factor related to the complex organizational structure of a corporation is that once a decision has been made, many people implement it. Thus, even if a manager has second thoughts about a decision, it is often too late to stop the process. Also, once a decision has been made, when it is implemented by others the decision maker feels limited responsibility.

The businesspersons who are unlucky enough to get caught do not automatically lose their status among their peers. Some, in fact, may be admired. Violations of the law are not necessarily violations of businesspersons' ethical codes. It is important to note that, unlike street criminals, who usually recognize that they are committing crimes, white-collar criminals are frequently regarded by themselves and their peers as respectable, law-abiding citizens.

In some instances, corporate crime is facilitated because the supposed adversarial relationship between the corporation and the government agency "watchdog" does not exist. Top corporate executives and high-level government officials may share similar values and lifestyles. Business managers often make career moves directly to a government agency regulating that business, and then back to business. These factors may make some government officials reluctant to crack down on businesspersons, and businesspersons' awareness of this reluctance contributes to an environment in which white-collar crime can be tolerated.

Finally, the corporation's personnel and operating procedures often encourage the employees to commit white-collar crimes. While many of the previously discussed factors are not easily amenable to change, personnel and operating policies are under the direct control of management and, therefore, business managers concerned about white-collar crime can have an impact on the likelihood of its occurrence by carefully examining their corporate policies. For example, employees are much more likely to commit white-collar crimes when corporate policies lead to a lack of job security, inadequate pay, a lack of recognition for outstanding work, perceived inequities among salaries of employees, poor promotion opportunities, inadequate expense accounts or unreasonable budget expectations, poor training, or poor communication practices.

SENTENCING OF WHITE-COLLAR CRIMINALS

Another feature that some would say distinguishes white-collar crime is in the attitudes of the judges in handing down sentences for these crimes. A public perception that judges were not giving long enough sentences to white-collar

---

[12] *Id.*

criminals and were not imposing large enough fines led to the adoption of the 1991 Sentencing Guidelines for use by federal judges. These guidelines are said to provide "just punishment, adequate deterrence, and incentives for organizations to maintain internal mechanisms for preventing, detecting, and reporting criminal conduct in all aspects of their activity."[13] Until early 2005, these guidelines were in fact mandatory restrictions on the judge's sentencing authority. Today, these guidlines are just what their name implies: guidelines.

Under these sentencing guidelines, a fine is a product of a "base fine" and a "culpability score." The base fine is the greatest of the company's gain, the victim's loss, or a dollar amount corresponding to an offense level. The culpability score provides a multiplier that is applied to the base fine. The culpability score is determined by looking at a chart of potential mitigating and aggravating factors. An example of an aggravating factor might be that high levels of management were aware of the criminal activity but did nothing to stop it. Mitigating factors would be having a meaningful compliance program in effect at the time of the offense and upper management's taking steps to remedy the harm, discipline the offender, and prevent a recurrence. Because of the difference that these aggravating and mitigating factors can have on the amount of the fine—a crime with a base fine of $5 million, for example, could be as low as $2 million or as high as $20 million, depending on the culpability score—supporters hope that the guidelines will not only result in fairer penalties but actually have a major impact on the way firms operate.

When the sentencing guidelines were established, there was a concern about the lack of prison time served by most white-collar criminals and the general judicial leniency for white-collar crimes. Consequently, some confinement was mandated for almost all white-collar offenses. Sentences are determined similarly to the way fines are, with a base sentence and culpability factor. However, judges were given discretion, under extraordinary circumstances, to modify the sentence and depart from the guidelines and may impose alternative penalties as described later in this section. Some of the factors that allow departure include "substantial cooperation" of the defendant; extraordinary effects of a prison sentence on third parties, including the defendant's family; an overstatement of loss from the crime; and diminished capacity.

Some critics of the guidelines argue that although prison sentences are required for a broad range of white-collar crimes, the sentences for these crimes are still much less than for street crimes. For example, the base sentence for an antitrust violation is as low as two to eight months.[14] During 2001, the average sentence in the 8,328 cases of fraud was 22.9 months.

The power of the sentencing guidelines began to crumble as a result of the 2004 United States Supreme Court decision in *Blakely v. Washington*,[15] in which the high court ruled that under the Sixth Amendment, juries, not judges, should determine the facts that increase sentences beyond guideline maximums. In that case, the facts admitted into evidence supported a maximum sentence of 53 months. However, the judge imposed a sentence of 90 months after finding that the defendant had acted with deliberate cruelty, a statutorily enumerated ground for departing from the standard range. The Washington State Supreme Court had rejected the defendant's argument that the judge's acting on facts not admitted

---

[13] C. C. Dow and R. J. Muehl, "Are Policies Keyed to New Sentencing Guidelines?" 35 *Securities Management 98*, November 1992.

[14] G. N. Racz, "Exploring Collateral Consequences: *Koon v. United States*, Third Party Departures from Federal Sentencing Guidelines," *New York University Law Review 72* (1997), p. 1462.

[15] 542 U.S., 125 S.Ct 2531(2004).

into evidence denied him his constitutional right to have a jury determine, beyond a reasonable doubt, all facts legally essential to his sentence. On appeal the United States Supreme Court agreed with the defendant and overturned the state court's decision.

While this case involved a state sentencing law, the decision immediately called into question the validity of the Federal Sentencing Guidelines. Within a month of the decision in Blakely, two circuit courts of appeal had ruled that the guidelines were unconstitutional, with the judge in one case stating that, "In order to comply with Blakely and the Sixth Amendment, the mandatory system of fixed rules calibrating sentences automatically to facts found by judges must be displaced by an indeterminate system in which the Federal Sentencing Guidelines in fact become "guidelines" in the dictionary-definition sense."[16] He further said that instead of judges viewing the guidelines as mandatory, they should "view the guidelines in general as recommendations to be considered and then applied only if the judge believes they are appropriate and in the interests of justice in the particular case."[17]

A similar holding applied to the federal courts in the 2005 consolidated case of *United States v. Booker*[18] and *United States v. Fanfan*.[19] The key question in the cases was whether judges can increase criminal sentences based on arguments from prosecutors that juries never considered. The high court found that the mandatory guidelines, are unconstitutional. The mandatory sentencing scheme of the guidelines when coupled with its reliance on juidicial fact finding, is incompatible with the Sixth Amendment. District Courts now still calculate sentencing ranges under the guidelines, but these ranges are now considered merely advisory. Subsequent congressional action on the matter is anticipated.

Even before these rulings, judges had departed from the guideline under extraordinary circumstances, and sometimes also used alternative sentencing instead of imposing prison sentences or fines. One alternative to prison that judges favor for white-collar offenders is community service. Offenders have been assigned to perform such services as giving speeches about their wrongful acts to business and civic groups and working among the poor in drug rehabilitation clinics. A corporate criminal who dumped industrial waste into San Diego's sewers, claiming it was domestic sewage, received a $250 fine and three years' probation, with an unusual twist: For violating waste disposal laws, he was required to complete a hazardous materials course, perform 120 hours of volunteer work for the Veterans of Foreign Wars, and spend 40 hours at the city's pump station where waste is discharged by trucks into the city's sewage treatment system. The man was also ordered to inform the waste haulers who came into the pump station that he had falsified a report describing the type of waste he was discharging.[20]

Another popular alternative to prison is occupational disqualification. The white-collar criminal is prohibited for a specific period from engaging in an occupation in which she or he would be able to commit the same crime again. Policing such a prohibition is difficult, so if a corporation really wants the convicted employee's services, it can easily adjust the employee's job title to make it appear the job is one the employee can legally hold.

---

[16] US v. Montgomery, 03-5256 (6th Cir. July 14, 2004).

[17] *Id.*

[18] No. 03-104 (2004).

[19] No. 03-105 (2004).

[20] K. Balint, "Falsifier on Waste," *San Diego Union-Tribune*, August 21, 1993.

An alternative touted as saving money for the taxpayers is house arrest, or home confinement. The criminal is not allowed to leave home for the period of incarceration and is compelled to wear an unremovable sensor that allows government officials to detect his or her location at all times. In some cases, the defendant is allowed to serve his or her prison term on weekends.

COMMON WHITE-COLLAR CRIMES

Thus far, we have focused on the white-collar criminal, but any study of white-collar crime must include consideration of who the victims are and what some of the precise crimes are. The victims of white-collar crime are widespread, and they vary according to the precise crime committed. White-collar crimes may be committed against the public in general, as when environmental regulations are violated; against consumers, as when they are forced to pay higher prices because of violations of the antitrust laws or when they die because the products they purchased were made without undergoing the tests required by the Pure Food, Drug, and Cosmetic Act; against the taxpayers, as when income taxes are not paid; and against the corporation itself, as when employees steal from their employer. When the victims are the corporation the criminal works for, we sometimes refer to the crime as an intrabusiness crime. Estimates of the annual costs of intrabusiness crime range from $4 billion to $44 billion. In this section, we examine some of the more common white-collar crimes, noting their elements and their victims.

BRIBERY

Bribery is the offering, giving, soliciting, or receiving of money or any object of value for the purpose of influencing a person's action, especially a government official. The law against bribery is necessary to protect the integrity of the government and to ensure that the government functions fairly and efficiently. Bribery would include paying a judge to rule in favor of a party and giving a senator free use of your condominium if he or she votes for a particular piece of legislation. For example, in 2004, a Wisconsin district attorney, Joe Paulus, pleaded guilty to taking bribes in 22 cases in return for plea bargaining shorter sentences. In one case, Paulus recieved $48,000 from a defense lawyer so that his client would receive a shorter sentence. Paulus received a sentence of 33 months in prison in addition to financial penalties, which include the amount taken in bribes.

Some states broaden their definition of bribery to include certain payoffs in a commercial context. It is often considered bribery to offer to confer a benefit upon an employee or agent of another in an attempt to influence that agent's behavior on behalf of his or her employer or principle without that employer or principle's knowledge. Thus, an employee's offer to pay a contracting officer $5,000 in exchange for that officer's promise to purchase all the widgets his or her employer needs the next year would be considered a bribe in many states.

bribery The offering, giving, soliciting, or receiving of money or any object of value for the purpose of influencing the judgment or conduct of a person in a position of trust, especially a government official.

VIOLATIONS OF FEDERAL REGULATIONS

During the past few decades, regulatory agencies have been created and federal regulations enacted to control business. Analogous state regulations have also been enacted. Some are primarily regulations of economic matters; others are designed to protect the health, safety, and welfare of employees, consumers, and the public in general. You will study many of the regulations in the public law part of this book, Chapters 17 through 24.

Violation of any of these regulations constitutes a white-collar crime. The victims of these crimes vary according to the regulation that has been violated. For example, Occupational Safety and Health Act standards are established to protect the health and safety of workers. When these standards are violated, the violation is a criminal act that victimizes the employee, who is working under less safe or less healthful conditions than those required by law. When examining these different regulations in later chapters of this book, the reader should consider who would be victimized by violations of each of the regulations. The reader who has a clear understanding of who might be hurt by such violations may be careful not to violate those regulations when he or she is a manager.

Violations of these regulations are often not perceived as criminal because they are frequently remedied outside the traditional courtroom setting. These regulations are often enforced by the appropriate regulatory agency through the issuance of a warning, a recall of defective products, or a consent agreement (a contract in which the violator agrees to cease engaging in the illegal activity). A cease-and-desist order may also be issued, ordering the corporation to cease violating the law and imposing a fine on the corporation for each day it violates the order. Warning letters are often the first approach of the regulatory agency, and the prudent businessperson should heed them. In cases of substantial violations, regulatory agencies may, of course, seek to impose fines on the corporation or manager responsible for the violation or may ask the court to impose a prison sentence on an offender.

The maximum monetary penalty that can be issued for violating federal regulations enacted to control business varies according to the regulation in question. For example, the maximum corporate penalty for violating the antitrust law is $1 million, a rarely awarded sum, which is not very large compared with the billions of dollars of assets and sales of some violators. For other acts, maximums are much lower. For example, $1,000 is the maximum for a first offense under the Pure Food, Drug, and Cosmetics Act, and $10,000 is the maximum for Occupational Health and Safety Act violations.

The maximum fines for individuals vary; $10,000 under acts such as the Pure Food, Drug, and Cosmetics Act and the Securities Exchange Act is typical. Maximum prison sentences usually range from six months to one year, with a few acts allowing up to five-year sentences. The imposition of maximum sentences is rare.

CRIMINAL FRAUD

criminal fraud Intentional use of some sort of misrepresentation to gain an advantage over another party.

Criminal fraud is a generic term that embraces a wide variety of means by which an individual intentionally uses some sort of misrepresentation to gain an advantage over another person. State fraud statutes vary, but most require proof of three elements: (1) an intent to defraud, (2) the commission of a fraudulent act, and (3) the accomplished fraud. It is very difficult to prove fraud, especially the first element: the intent to defraud. Some common fraudulent acts that occur in the corporate setting are:

1. *Defalcation*, the misappropriation of trust funds or money held in a fiduciary capacity.

2. *False entries*, the making of an entry into the books of a bank or corporation that is designed to represent the existence of funds that do not exist.

3. *False token*, a false document or sign of existence used to perpetrate a fraud, such as making counterfeit money.

4. *False pretenses*, a designed misrepresentation of existing facts or conditions by which a person obtains another's money or goods, such as the writing of a worthless check.

5. *Forgery*, the material altering of anything in writing that, if genuine, might be the foundation of a legal liability.

6. *Fraudulent concealment*, the suppression of a material fact that the person is legally bound to disclose.

This list is by no means all-inclusive, but it demonstrates the broad variety of actions captured by the term *fraud*.

A person or corporation that uses the mail to execute a scheme or artifice to defraud the public out of money or property may be prosecuted under the federal law that prohibits mail fraud. Likewise, a person or corporation that uses the telephone, telegraph, television, radio, or other device to transmit a fraudulent message may be prosecuted for the federal crime of wire fraud. Mail fraud claims can be brought in a wide range of situations. Seeking greater deterrence of mail and wire fraud, Congress passed the White-Collar Crime Penalty Act of 2002, as part of the Sarbanes-Oxley Act. The act increased maximum prison sentences for mail and wire fraud from five years to a new maximum of 20 years.

As the following case indicates, the likelihood that a fraudulent scheme will succeed is inconsequential to the decision of guilt or innocence.

CASE 7-2

United States v. Gray
Eleventh Circuit Court of Appeals 367 F. 3d 1263 (2004)

The appellant, Kevin Gray, was found guilty of mail fraud. He had attempted to convince a businessman, Frank Patti, who was on trial for tax evasion and faced substantial jail time, that for $ 85,000 he would bribe the jury, thus avoiding the threat of jail for the businessman. However, the methods used by the appellant were, at times, hardly believable. As a result, the appellant seeks a judgment of acquittal on the ground that his fraudulent scheme was "so absurd" that a person of ordinary prudence would not have believed it; the scheme, therefore, fell outside the realm of conduct proscribed by the mail fraud statute.

Circuit Judge Tjoflat

On May 8, 2002, a federal grand jury in the Northern District of Florida returned an indictment charging the appellant on one count of mail fraud. He pled not guilty, and the case proceeded to trial before a jury. The jury, hav-

ing received evidence establishing the facts set forth above, found the appellant guilty, and the district court sentenced him to prison for twenty-eight months. This appeal followed.

The appellant's initial attack on his conviction is that the evidence was insufficient to make out a case of mail fraud. He argues that to prove the crime of mail fraud, the Government must establish that the defendant "intended to create a scheme 'reasonably calculated to deceive persons of ordinary prudence and comprehension.'" Additionally, it must show that the defendant took some action in furtherance of his scheme—to bring it to fruition—in the form of a material misrepresentation made to the would-be victim that "a reasonable person would have acted on." It is on this peg that the appellant hangs his hat, contending that a reasonable person would not have acted on his representations when considered as a whole. In bolstering his argument, he draws attention to his statement to Patti that $85,000 would be needed to bribe three of the jurors who would be trying his case: $35,000 for J-1, and $25,000 each for J-2 and J-3. The appellant contends that a reasonable person would know that since the pool from which these jurors would be selected would not be known until April 15—when the pool assembled at the courthouse for the trial—the representation had to be phony.

While it is true that statements like the one he cites would seem absurd or fanciful to a reasonable person, the mail fraud statute does not require that every representation a defendant utters while executing his scheme must be credible. Instead, the statute requires proof that the defendant's scheme to defraud involved the use of material, false representations or promises. The initial representations the appellant made to Patti satisfy this requirement.

In the letter to Patti, the appellant made a false promise: "we can assure you ... no imprisonment but you must pay the agreed tax settlement issued by the court." In addition, he falsely represented that an undisclosed number of sympathizers—including "our mutual friend" and "our associates in Pensacola"—would work to extricate Patti from his legal predicament if the businessman would agree to follow certain instructions. True, the letter did not identify precisely how the writer and these sympathizers would help Patti, but this omission did not render the letter devoid of any material misrepresentations that were capable of prompting a reasonable person to act as Patti did. What the appellant overlooks is that the mail fraud statute "punishes unexecuted, as well as executed, schemes. This means that the government can convict a person for mail fraud even if his targeted victim never encountered the deception—or, if he encountered it, was not deceived." All that the Government needs to show to establish the *mens rea* element of the offense is that the defendant anticipated the intended victim's reliance, and the appellant's anticipation of Patti's reliance can be inferred from, among other things, the fact that he was prepared to call Patti at the pay phone at the time and location specified in the letter.

Because the letter received by Patti contained false material representations from the appellant as part of an effort to receive cash payments from the desperate businessman, the crime of mail fraud was complete when the appellant delivered the letter via FedEx to Patti.

Affirmed in favor of the Prosecution.

Fraud can range from a single act that victimizes one individual to a long-term scheme that victimizes thousands. In the corporate setting, fraud is sometimes committed by managers to make themselves look better so that they can secure promotions at the expense of others who perhaps deserve the promotions. Fraudulent entries in corporate records may result in artificially inflating the purchase price of stock at the expense of its purchasers. Fraud may also be committed against the corporation and, thus, against the shareholders, as when an employee on a bonus system fraudulently reports sales before they have been completed to collect an early bonus or "pads" his or her expense account. The more autonomy employees have, and the fewer people overseeing their actions, the greater the likelihood of their committing fraud.

Consumers may also be victims of corporate fraud, as when businesspersons make false representations in advertising and labeling. Consumers may also be victimized by the fraudulent substitution of inferior goods for higher-quality ones.

One of the fastest-growing forms of fraud is identity theft, whereby one's credit card, Social Security number, driver's license number, and other personal information are used for fraudulent purposes. According to the Federal Trade Commission (FTC), more than 9.9 million Americans were victims of identity theft in 2002, costing over $53 billion to businesses and consumers. To combat this growing and costly form of fraud, Congress passed the Identity Theft and Assumption Deterrence Act of 1998, making identity theft a federal felony punishable by up to 25 years in prison. The act also requires the FTC to help victims restore their credit. In addition, the FTC and other federal agencies suggest methods for reducing the likelihood of identity theft, including restricting the use of your Social Security number to occasions when it is legally required, reviewing your credit report at least twice a year, and proceeding with caution before personal information is given over the Internet.

Linking Law & Business

Accounting

When people initially think about how to detect fraud, they may think that fraud detection is the auditor's responsibility. However, if you remember what you learned about the role of an auditor from your accounting class, you would quickly recognize that while an auditor may discover something that tips him or her off that fraud has occurred, fraud detection is not the auditor's responsibility. It is useful, when thinking about fraud detection, to keep in mind the differences between the role of independent auditors and the role of fraud examiners, which the following list will remind you of:

- Auditors follow a program; fraud examiners look for the unusual.
- Auditors look for errors and omissions; fraud examiners look for oddities and exceptions.
- Auditors assess internal control risk; fraud examiners "think like a criminal" and look for holes in the controls.
- Auditors use the concept of materiality with amounts higher than a fraud examiner would use.
- Auditors usually start fresh with materiality each year; fraud examiners look at cumulative materiality.
- Auditors work with financial accounting and auditing logic; fraud examiners think about motive, opportunity, and integrity.

Keeping these differences in mind, it is easy to see why, when fraud is suspected, the wise manager may wish to hire a fraud examiner, rather than simply rely on either an internal or external audit, to settle the question of whether fraud has occurred.

LARCENY

Another frequently occurring type of white-collar crime is larceny. **Larceny** is a matter of state criminal law, so the definition may vary slightly by state, but it can generally be defined as the secretive and wrongful taking and carrying away of the personal property of another with the intent to permanently deprive the rightful owner of its use or possession. The means of carrying out this crime is stealth: Larceny is not carried out by means of fear or force, which is the means of committing a robbery, and it is not carried out by means of false representation, which is one means of committing fraud. Larceny is commonly called theft by persons without legal training.

Most states distinguish petty larceny from grand larceny, with the distinction based on the value of the item. Grand larceny involves items of higher value than those involved in petty larceny. It is usually considered a felony and, thus, is punishable by either a more severe fine or a longer term of imprisonment, or both.

In the corporate context, larceny generally involves employees' taking the employer's property. Common instances of larceny include an employee's taking home stationery or supplies from the office.

larceny The secretive and wrongful taking and carrying away of the personal property of another with the intent to permanently deprive the rightful owner of its use or possession.

EMBEZZLEMENT

Another white-collar offense is **embezzlement**. This crime is commonly defined as the wrongful conversion of the property of another by one who is lawfully in possession of that property. In some states, by statute, the crime may

embezzlement The wrongful conversion of the property of another by one who is lawfully in possession of that property.

be committed only by certain classes of people, such as fiduciaries, attorneys, and public officials. As the reader might guess, larceny and embezzlement sometimes overlap. Like larceny, embezzlement is usually divided into degrees based on the value of the property embezzled. Some states also treat different kinds of embezzlers differently; that is, those embezzling from different types of institutions or those holding different types of positions may be distinguished.

COMPUTER CRIMES

As technology evolves, so do ways of committing corporate crime. With the arrival of the computer and the increasing automation of many facets of business, an area of crime has developed that society has not yet found an effective means of handling. No one knows the exact cost of computer crime each year, but estimates range from $300 million to $40 billion.

For the most part, computer crime, rather than being a new type of crime, is a means of making traditional crimes easier to commit. See Exhibit 7-3 for examples of some typical computer crime techniques. Think about how many employees have access to a computer at work. When the number of individuals with home computers is added, there are myriad opportunities available for computer crime. Computer systems must now be protected from management, lower-level employees, and outsiders, sometimes known as hackers. With all these individuals having access to computers, a continuing increase in the amount of computer crime seems highly likely. Not only do computers make crime easier, but it appears that computers also make crime more profitable. According to federal officials, the average loss in a bank robbery is $3,200, and the average loss in a nonelectronic embezzlement is $23,500. But in a computer fraud, the average loss is $500,000.

Computer crimes are also not frequently prosecuted; some analysts estimate that less than 1 percent of those who engage in computer fraud are actually prosecuted. One reason these criminals are so successful is that many computer crimes are extremely difficult to detect. Even if the crime is detected, if the victim is a business, it will often not prosecute because it does not want its competitors to know that its system was vulnerable. A final problem with convicting people of computer crimes is that the crimes sometimes do not fit precisely within the statutory definition of traditional crimes.

Partially in response to this lack of adequate statutes under which to prosecute computer crime, Congress passed the Counterfeit Access Device and Computer Fraud and Abuse Act of 1984. The act not only imposes criminal sanctions but also allows parties injured by a violation to bring a civil action to

EXHIBIT 7-3

COMMON COMPUTER CRIME TECHNIQUES

 PIGGYBACKING—A nonauthorized person gains access to a terminal when an authorized person failed to sign off or an unauthorized person discovers an authorized user's password and signs on using that password.

 IMPOSTER TERMINAL—Using a home computer with a telephone modem to gain access to a mainframe computer by cracking the password code and then using the computer free of charge.

 TROJAN HORSE—Covertly placing instructions in a computer program that will generate unauthorized functions.

 SALAMI SLICING—Stealing tiny amounts of money off large numbers of inputs (such as taking a penny off each entry) and transferring them into one's personal account.

recover compensatory damages for the losses they incurred because of the violation. This act was subsequently amended by passage of the Computer Fraud and Abuse Act of 1986 (CFAA), which expanded the coverage of the act. Congress continued to expand the scope of the law in 1989, 1990, 1994, 1996, and 2001. The most recent amendment to CFAA was passed as part of the USA Patriot Act to provide broader scope for prosecution of computer crimes. Under the latest version of the act, seven categories of activities are regulated:

1. The unauthorized use of or access to a computer to obtain classified military or foreign policy information with the intent to harm the United States or to benefit a foreign country.
2. Accessing a computer without authority or in excess of authority, protected computers (government computers, computers in financial institutions, or those used in interstate commerce).
3. The intentional, unauthorized access to a federal computer and the use, modification, destruction, or disclosure of data it contains or the prevention of authorized persons' use of such data.
4. Accessing a protected computer without or in excess of authority with the intent to obtain something of value.
5. Knowingly causing the transmission of a program, code, or command, and as a result causing damage to a protected computer.
6. The fraudulent transfer of computer passwords or other similar data that could aid unauthorized access that either (a) affects interstate commerce or (b) permits access to a government computer.
7. Transmitting in interstate or foreign commerce any threat that could cause damage to a protected computer with the intent to extort something of value.

One important issue that had to be clarified under this act was whether the act would be violated if persons knowingly accessed a computer without permission but did so not knowing what damage they would cause by their action. That issue was settled by the following case, which has become one of the classic computer crime cases.

As it may seem as if the federal statute is fairly comprehensive, there are still a number of computer crimes that do not really violate that act. Those crimes must be prosecuted, if at all, under one of the state computer crime statutes, which now exist in every state in some form, or under one of the traditional crime statutes.

As society attempts to find ways to respond to computer crimes, we have initially attempted to categorize the crimes. Following is just one way to categorize and think about these crimes.

Destruction of Data. Destruction of data is one of the biggest problems facing business today. A person with expertise in programming can create what is commonly referred to as a **virus**, a program designed to rearrange, replace, or destroy data. Once a virus is planted in a computer's instructions, it can spread to other systems or programs by rapidly copying itself. Hence, if a computer virus is not caught early, it can be extremely destructive.

A number of software programs have been developed to detect and destroy viruses. These programs, however, are reactive, not proactive. Every time a new type of virus is discovered, a new antiviral program must be developed. By 2004, there were over 80,000 known viruses, so keeping antivirus software current is no easy task, but it is essential. In 2003, it was estimated that computer viruses and **worms** cost businesses over $55 billion in damages.

virus A computer program that destroys, damages, rearranges, or replaces computer data.

worm A program that travels from one computer to another but does not attach itself to the operating system of the computer it "infects." It differs from a "virus," which is also a migrating program, but one that attaches itself to the operating system of any computer it enters and can infect any other computer that uses files from the infected computer.

CASE 7-3

United States v. Robert Tappan Morris
Second Circuit Court of Appeals 928 F.2d 504 (1991)

Defendant-appellant Morris was a first-year graduate student in Cornell University's computer science Ph.D. program in the fall of 1988. There Morris engaged in various discussions with fellow graduate students about the security of computer networks and his ability to penetrate it. In October 1988, he began work on a computer program, later known as a "worm." The goal of this program was to demonstrate the inadequacies of current security measures on computer networks by exploiting the security defects that Morris had discovered. The tactic he selected was to release a worm into network computers that could spread across a national network of computers after being inserted at one computer location connected to the network.

Morris sought to program the Internet worm to spread widely without drawing attention to itself. The worm was supposed to occupy little computer operation time and, thus, not interfere with normal use of the computers. He programmed the worm to make it difficult to detect and read, so that other programmers would not be able to "kill" the worm easily.

On November 2, 1988, Morris released the worm from a computer at the Massachusetts Institute of Technology. MIT was selected to disguise the fact that the worm came from Morris at Cornell. Morris soon discovered that the worm was replicating and reinfecting machines at a much faster rate than he had anticipated. Ultimately, many machines at locations around the country either crashed or became "catatonic." When Morris realized what was happening, he contacted a friend at Harvard to discuss a solution. Eventually, they sent an anonymous message from Harvard over the network, instructing programmers how to kill the worm and prevent reinfection. However, because the network route was clogged, this message did not get through until it was too late. Computers were affected at numerous installations, including leading universities, military sites, and medical research facilities. The estimated cost of dealing with the worm at each installation ranged from $200 to more than $53,000.

Morris was found guilty, following a jury trial, of violating 18 U.S.C. Section 1030(a)(5)(A), which makes it illegal for anyone to intentionally access without authorization a category of computers known as "[f]ederal interest computers" and to damage or prevent authorized use of information in such computers, causing loss of $1,000 or more. He was sentenced to three years of probation, 400 hours of community service, a fine of $10,050, and the costs of his supervision. He appealed to the Circuit Court of Appeals. A key issue in his appeal was whether the government must prove not only that the defendant intended to access a federal interest computer but also that the defendant intended to prevent authorized use of the computer's information and thereby cause loss.

Circuit Judge Jon O. Newman

We conclude that Section 1030(a)(5)(A) does not require the Government to demonstrate that the defendant intentionally prevented authorized use and thereby caused loss.

The intent requirement in Section 1030(a)(5)(A) covers anyone who (5) intentionally accesses a federal interest computer without authorization, and by means of one or more instances of such conduct alters, damages, or destroys information in any such federal interest computer, or prevents authorized use of any such computer or information, and thereby (A) causes loss to one or more others of a value aggregating $1,000 or more during any one year period; ...

The district court concluded that the intent requirement applied only to the accessing and not to the resulting damage. Judge Munson found recourse to legislative history unnecessary because he considered the statute clear and unambiguous. However, the Court observed that the legislative history supported its reading of Section 1030(a)(5)(A).

Morris argues that the Government had to prove not only that he intended the unauthorized access of a federal interest computer, but also that he intended to prevent others from using it, and thus cause a loss. The adverb "intentionally," he contends, modified both verb phrases of the section. The Government urges that since punctuation sets the "accesses" phrase off from the subsequent "damages" phrase, the provision unambiguously shows that "intentionally" modifies only "accesses." ... With some statutes, punctuation has been relied upon to indicate that a phrase set off by commas is independent of the language that followed. In the present case, we do not believe the comma after "authorization" renders the text so clear as to preclude review of the legislative history.

The first federal statute dealing with computer crimes was passed in 1984. ... The specific provision under which Morris was convicted was added in 1986, along with some other changes. ... First, the 1986 amendments changed the scienter requirement in Section 1030(a)(2) from "knowingly" to "intentionally." The subsection now covers anyone who (2) intentionally accesses a computer without authorization or exceeds authorized access. ...

According to the Senate Judiciary Committee, Congress changed the mental state requirement in Section 1030(a)(2) for two reasons. Congress sought only to proscribe intentional acts of unauthorized access, not "mistaken, inadvertent, or careless" acts of unauthorized access. ... Also, Congress expressed concern that the "knowingly" standard "might be inappropriate for cases involving computer technology." The concern was that a scienter requirement of "knowingly" might encompass the acts of an individual "who inadvertently 'stumble[d] into' someone else's computer file or computer data," especially where such an individual was authorized to use a particular computer. ... The Senate Report concluded that "[t]he substitution of an 'intentional' standard is designed to focus Federal criminal prosecution on those whose conduct evinces a clear intent to enter, without proper authorization, computer files or data belonging to another." This use of a mens rea standard to make sure that inadvertent accessing was not covered is also emphasized in the Senate Report's discussion of Section 1030(a)(3) and Section 1030(a)(5), under which Morris was convicted. ... The rationale for the mens rea requirement suggests that it modifies only the "accesses" phrase, which was the focus of Congress's concern in strengthening the scienter requirement.

Affirmed in favor of the United States.

Destruction of data may also be more limited. For example, a disgruntled employee who is fired might program his computer to destroy a section of data every time a file is saved. Before anyone realizes what has occurred, valuable data may be lost.

Technology and the Legal Environment

Are We Prepared to Fight Cybercrime?

After the worldwide attack by the Philippine "love bug" virus, and the difficult time that nation had in prosecuting the perpetrator of the cybercrime, McConnell International LLC, a global technology policy and management consulting firm, undertook a study to determine the readiness of most countries to successfully prosecute those who committed cybercrimes. Their conclusion was that in most countries around the world, existing laws are likely to be unenforceable against such crimes, meaning that businesses and governments must rely solely on technical measures to protect themselves from those who would steal, deny access to, or destroy valuable information. This unfortunate state of the law is very important because the number of cybercrimes seems to be continually escalating. For example, according to the Computer Emergency Response Team Coordination Center (CERT/CC), the number of reported incidences of security breaches in the first three quarters of 2000 rose by 54 percent over the total number of reported incidences in 1999 (see www.cert.org.). What makes these figures all the more frightening, however, is that some corporations and governments would not want to admit being victims of cybercrimes, so the figures must be an understatement of the scope of the problem.

McConnell International's report analyzes the state of the law in 52 countries. It finds that only ten of these nations have amended their laws to cover more than half of the kinds of crimes that need to be addressed. Although many of the others have initiatives under way, most countries do not have laws that cover cybercrimes. For example, in many countries, laws that prohibit physical acts of trespass or breaking and entering do not cover their "virtual" counterparts.

To prepare the report, McConnell International asked global technology policy officials in the 52 countries to provide copies of their laws that would be used to prosecute criminal acts involving both private and public sector computers. Countries that provided legislation were evaluated to determine whether their criminal statutes had been extended into cyberspace to cover ten different types of cybercrime in four categories: data-related crimes, including interception, modification, and theft; network-related crimes, including interference and sabotage; crimes of access, including hacking and virus distribution; and associated computer-related crimes, including aiding and abetting cybercriminals, computer fraud, and computer forgery.

Thirty-three of the countries surveyed had not yet updated their laws to address any type of cybercrime. Of the remaining countries, nine have enacted legislation to address five or fewer types of cybercrime, and ten have updated their laws to prosecute against six or more of the ten types of cybercrime. Among those nations that had substantially or fully updated their laws were the United States, Canada, Japan, and the Philippines. To see the full report, go to www.mcconnellinternational.com/services/cybercrime.htm.

Unlawful Appropriation of Data or Services. Employees at work are often provided expensive computer systems and software. They have access to vast amounts of data. When employees use their work computers or data accessed through these computers in a manner not authorized by their employer, they have engaged in theft of computer services or data.

Entering of Fraudulent Records or Data into a Computer System. Entering fraudulent records includes altering a person's credit rating electronically and breaking into a university's computer system and changing someone's course grades.

Financial Crimes. Fraud, embezzlement, and larceny are now easier to accomplish by computer. An employee could electronically transfer ownership of funds from a corporate account to a personal account. Any object subject to lawful transfer electronically can also be stolen electronically.

PREVENTION OF WHITE-COLLAR CRIME

We should all be interested in the prevention of white-collar crime because we are all its victims in more than one aspect of our lives. We are victims as consumers, shareholders, responsible employees, taxpayers, and citizens in general. The suggested ways for reducing white-collar crime are numerous and varied. Some ideas are utopian, but others can be put into practice immediately.

First, we will examine some of the ways in which corporate crime committed on behalf of the corporation may be prevented. One suggestion is to replace state chartering of corporations with federal chartering. Proponents argue that such chartering would prevent competition among states, which may lead to bribery and state officials' routinely overlooking corporate violations of the laws. As a part of federal chartering (or until then, by state law), corporations could be required to have outside directors (directors who are not also officers or managers). A counterargument to that suggestion is that outside directors do not have a significant impact on the behavior of management. They have neither the knowledge nor the interest to provide effective supervision.

An even more innovative suggestion, put forward by Christopher Stone,[21] is that each corporation doing over a certain amount of business be required to have a general public director (GPD). The GPD would have an office at the corporation with a small staff, would be given access to corporate books and records, and would represent the public interest in the ongoing functions of the corporation. General public directors would sit on corporate committees and advise corporate officials about the legality of their activities. These public-interest watchdogs would be full-time workers paid from tax money. Stone further suggested that special public directors (SPDs), who would function like GPDs except that they would work in a special area such as workplace safety or antitrust, be assigned to corporations that have committed a series of violations in any specific area. Special public directors would attempt to prevent further violations of a similar nature.

Two other proposals are to link the amounts of fines to the benefits obtained by the violations and to increase the amount of both corporate and individual fines. Over 90 percent of the fines paid by corporations between 1975 and 1976

---

[21] C. Stone, *Where Law Ends: The Social Control of Corporations* (New York: Harper and Row, 1976), pp. 122–183.

were less than $5,000. When imposed on a relatively small corporation, one with annual sales of $300 million, such fines are analogous to giving a person who earns $15,000 a year a two-and-a-half-cent fine.[22] Hence, fines as they currently exist do not really serve any deterrent function. Likewise, requiring greater and mandatory prison sentences for corporate executives found to have violated federal and state regulations might cause them to take these laws more seriously. Some also suggest elimination of the nolo contendere plea.

Because it is believed that the courts are unlikely to impose stiff fines on either corporations or convicted executives, the imposition of equity fines has been proposed. If a company is convicted of a white-collar crime, it would be forced to turn over a substantial block of its stock to a victims' compensation fund. This relinquishing of the company's stock would make its executives' holdings worth less. It would also provoke the ire of shareholders, whose holdings would be diluted, and might prompt them to call for the ouster of the responsible executives. Finally, it might put pressure on managers, who realize that the existence of a block of stock in one place would make a takeover attempt easier.

It is also believed that regulations are often broken because of ineffective monitoring by agencies. One remedy, it is argued, would be to increase the operating budgets of the regulatory agencies to allow them to hire more people to monitor corporations and to improve the training of regulatory agency employees. A related argument is that the regulations themselves are often vague and complex. Simplification of these laws would make them more understandable and easier to follow. It would also make violations of these laws easier to recognize and prosecute.

Linking Law & Business

Management

Responsibility is defined as the obligation to complete specific activities. Typically, managers will assign individuals to a particular position in which they are entrusted with the responsibility of carrying out a task. Job activities are often divided by the functional similarity method, which is a basic method for separating duties in the organization. There are four interconnected steps in this method: (1) Examine organizational objectives; (2) delegate appropriate activities to meet established objectives; (3) design specific jobs for each activity; and (4) place individuals with responsibility for each specific job.

Another guide to the functional similarity method suggests that overlapping responsibility should be avoided. Overlapping responsibility refers to situations in which more than one person has responsibility for a specific task. When more than one employee is assigned to a certain task, there is a greater likelihood for employee conflicts and poorer working relationships.

However, there is a disadvantage to avoiding overlapping responsibility. When individuals are given greater responsibility and autonomy, there is also a greater possibility for fraudulent activities. When there are fewer people working along with an individual, there may be a greater temptation to engage in fraud. Thus, managers should weigh the costs and risks associated with the level of responsibility given to employees before dividing responsibility for various activities.

---

[22] G. Stricharchuk and A. Pasztor, "New Muscle in False Claims Act May Help in Combating Fraud Against the Government," *Wall Street Journal*, December 19, 1986, p. 19.

Of course, these suggestions are all ideas that are beyond the direct control of most corporate managers. There are, however, some very practical things that managers can do to reduce the likelihood of white-collar crimes being committed by their employees. First, have a well-defined company code of ethics that the employees read and sign. Make sure that the employees understand that dishonest and unethical behavior is not acceptable. Second, provide a hot line for anonymous tips. Employees should be encouraged to use the hot line to report any instances of fraud on the part of other employees. Third, provide an employee assistance program. Often employees commit fraud and other white-collar crimes because they are having problems with substance abuse, gambling, or money management. If they can get assistance with these problems, it may prevent their trying to solve them by committing crimes against the company. Finally, conduct proactive fraud auditing.

FEDERAL LAWS USED IN THE FIGHT AGAINST WHITE-COLLAR CRIME

THE RACKETEER INFLUENCED CORRUPT ORGANIZATIONS ACT (RICO)

Racketeer Influenced Corrupt Organizations Act (RICO) Prohibits persons employed by or associated with an enterprise from engaging in a pattern of racketeering activity, which is broadly defined to include almost all white-collar crimes as well as acts of violence.

In the eyes of many plaintiffs' attorneys and prosecutors, a major weapon in the fight against white-collar crime can be found in Title IX of the Organized Crime Control Act of 1970,[23] the **Racketeer Influenced Corrupt Organizations Act**, or **RICO**, as it is commonly called. This statute was originally enacted to help fight organized crime, but its application in the commercial context soon became apparent. In fact, a study by the Task Force on Civil RICO of the American Bar Association revealed that only about 9 percent of the RICO cases involved what is commonly considered organized crime; 37 percent were cases involving common-law fraud in a commercial setting, and 40 percent involved securities fraud allegations.[24]

RICO is such a powerful statute because it allows any person whose business or property is injured by a violation of the statute to recover treble damages plus attorney's fees in a civil action. So this is a case in which a civil lawsuit may help prevent criminal action.

How does one violate RICO? RICO prohibits persons employed by or associated with an enterprise from engaging in a pattern of racketeering activity. Judicial interpretations have interpreted *pattern* to mean more than one act. Thus, RICO cannot be used against the one-time violator. What constitutes racketeering activity, however, has been very broadly defined to include almost all criminal actions, including acts of violence, the provision of illegal goods and services, bribery, antitrust violations, securities violations, and fraud.

RICO has been used so successfully in many of these areas that many corporate and brokerage firm attorneys are making appeals to the legislature through the press to limit the application of RICO. They argue that the statute is unfair because it does not require that a defendant be convicted of the alleged criminal activity before a civil RICO suit can be brought. They argue that this lack of a requirement of a prior conviction leads to spurious lawsuits and encourages out-of-court settlements by intimidated legitimate businesspersons. Opponents also argue that the courts are or will be "flooded" with such lawsuits

---

[23] 18 U.S.C.A., Sections 1961 et seq. (West Publishing Co., 1998).
[24] Stricharchuk and Pasztor, *supra* note 13.

and, thus, valuable resources will be wasted. They also argue that the law was designed to attack "organized crime," not employees of "legitimate businesses," against whom it is now being successfully used.

Proponents of RICO argue that the law should continue in force as it is. They point out that fraud is a national problem, costing the nation more than $200 billion each year.[25] Proponents further believe that given our lack of success in prosecuting criminal fraud cases in the past, we should retain this tool, which may allow us to punish persons who have been able to escape criminal prosecution. Criminal activity in "legitimate" businesses is a major problem facing the country today, and curing it can only enhance the reputations of those in the business world. If a corporation and its officers are not engaging in illegal or quasi-legal activities, they have nothing to fear from RICO.

FALSE CLAIMS ACT

A largely ignored 141-year-old federal law has come back to life since 1986 and is now being used vigorously in the fight against white-collar crime. Under the False Claims Act, private citizens may sue employers on behalf of the government for fraud against the government. A successful party may receive 25 percent of the amount recovered if the government chooses to intervene in the action or 30 percent if the government does not participate in the suit. Between the law's amendment in 1986 to encourage private whistle-blowers and September 2003, the government has recovered over $15 billion through a total of 4,294 cases under this act.[26] Recoveries for the fiscal year ending September 30, 2003, alone tallied a record $2.1 billion, a 75 percent increase over the prior year's recoveries of $1.1 billion.[27]

The act also offers protection to persons using the law to sue their employer. An employer may be held liable to the employee for twice the amount of back pay plus special damages if found guilty of retaliation. Between the law's amendment in 1986 to encourage private whistle-blowers and July 2001, the government paid whistle-blowers a total of $722 million.[28]

The recently enacted Sarbanes-Oxley Act contains a provision that provides safeguards to protect whistle-blowers, as does the Homeland Security Act of 2002. The new provisions were encouraged after whistle-blowers received much attention with the rise in corporate fraud scandals. Perhaps no whistle-bower is more notable in the business world than Sherron Watkins. As the vice president for corporate development at Enron, Watkins wrote several letters to chairman Kenneth Lay exposing corporate officials Andrew Fastow and Jeffery Skilling for committing the fraud. While the Enron matter remains for the courts to decide the facts of the case and assign blame, Watkins has played a significant role in exposing the company's failures. Because of the important role whistle-blowers can play in revealing fraud or other illegal behavior, Congress is currently considering passage of the federal Whistle-Blower Protection Act, which would expand safeguards for whistle-blowers who are fearful of future employment discrimination.

---

[25] Mann, *supra* note 6, p. 86.

[26] The False Claims Act Legal Center, **www.taf.org/statistics.htm**, accessed August 15, 2004.

[27] Dept. of Justice Press Release, "Justice Dept. Civil Fraud Recoveries Total $2.1 Billion For Fiscal Year 2003 False Claims Act Recoveries Exceed $12 Billion Since 1986," **www.usdoj.gov/opa/pr/2003/November/03_civ_613.htm**, November 10, 2003.

[28] Alice Demoner, "Lawmakers, Justice Department Officials Question Whistleblower Payoffs," Knight-Ridder Tribune News Service, July 29, 2001, 2001 WL 25947333.

The False Claims Act has also been used in a wide variety of circumstances. It has been used by an employee claiming that his employer, a school, helped its students fraudulently obtain millions of dollars in federal financial aid; by an employee who claimed that his employer, a defense contractor, knowingly manufactured defective parts for use in a guided missile system; and more recently by employees of hospitals, doctors, and nursing homes that are over-billing Medicare claims. Claims related to health care fraud make up the biggest share of the claims, whereas the second greatest percentage of claims comes from fraud in defense procurement contracts.

Because of Justice Department estimates that fraud costs the taxpayers as much as $100 billion a year,[29] there are many proponents of the use of this act. Its use is encouraged because it motivates persons in the best positions to be aware of fraud to report its occurrence. Employers who know that their employees may bring an action if asked to engage in fraud may be deterred from engaging in such acts.

Opponents of the use of the False Claims Act cite a variety of reasons. Some fear that frivolous or politically motivated lawsuits may be brought. Others say that the 60-day time period during which the Justice Department has to decide whether to join in the action is too brief and places an undue burden on the department. During that limited time period, the government must decide whether to join in a complex suit that may take years to resolve.

For now, at least, use of the False Claims Act is increasing. But as the rising number of large judgments to whistle-blowers keeps making headlines—at least a dozen whistle-blowers thus far have collected over $15 million each—more people are starting to question whether the whistle-blower "rewards" are a wise use of taxpayers' money. Some have proposed capping the amount a whistle-blower can collect at $10 or $15 million. Those who have collected some of the awards above those amounts, however, have said that such a cap probably would have kept them from reporting the fraud. Since the majority of the awards are below $10 million, with the median award from 1986–mid-2001 being around $150,000, it seems unlikely that amending the law to provide a cap will be a major item on the congressional agenda in the near future.

SARBANES-OXLEY ACT

The large number of high-profile companies engaged in fraudulent acts in recent years led to the passage of the Sarbanes-Oxley Act of 2002. This act, fully discussed in Chapter 22, establishes new rules regarding corporate accounting, government oversight, and financial regulations. Although the act applies only to publicly held companies, many of the act's rules will influence the behavior of private and nonprofit organizations. Specifically, the act seeks to eliminate the conflicts of interests that can lead to fraudulent activity. For example, the act establishes the Public Company Accounting Oversight Board, which seeks to ensure proper accounting practices, mandates the separation of audit and nonaudit services, and requires corporate officials to certify their financial statements, which makes those officials responsible and liable for fraudulent statements.

---

[29] H. Berleman, "A Few Big Penalties Make for a Record Year," *National Law Journal*, October 24, 1994.

STATE LAWS USED IN THE FIGHT AGAINST WHITE-COLLAR CRIME

Some states have whistle-blower statutes that protect employees who testify against their employers. Some state acts also allow government whistle-blowers to bring actions against the state government, and a few—namely Texas, California, and Alaska—even allow government-employee whistle-blowers to seek punitive damages.

Although a whistle-blower statute with unlimited potential for recovery may sound like a good idea, not everyone supports such laws. Sometimes cases under these statutes have surprising outcomes. The following case demonstrates the application of Texas's Whistleblower Act.

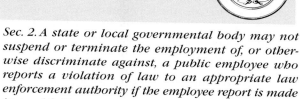

CASE 7-4

Texas Department of Human Services v. George Green
Court of Appeals of Texas 855 S.W.2d 136 (1993)

Plaintiff-appellant George Green brought an action for retaliatory discharge against his former employer, the Texas Department of Human Services (DHS), alleging that he had been fired because he kept informing his supervisors of what he believed was a pattern of fraud and corruption among DHS procurement officers. He had reported a series of corrupt activities to his superiors, and, when they failed to take corrective actions, he had threatened to go outside the agency. He was then thoroughly investigated and ultimately terminated for a 13-cent unauthorized phone call and a missed physical therapy session while on sick leave. The trial court, in a jury trial, awarded him $3,459,831.87 in compensatory damages, $10 million in punitive damages, and $160,000 in attorney fees, plus interest. DHS appealed, and the court of appeals affirmed. DHS then filed a motion for rehearing with the court of appeals.

Justice Smith

In its first point of error, DHS argues that the trial court erred in rendering judgment on the verdict because governmental immunity bars both the suit and the liability for an award of damages against DHS, a state agency.

DHS argues that the legislature must not have intended to waive governmental immunity because the Whistleblower Act permits a public employee to recover actual and unlimited exemplary damages, "as the surreal verdict in this suit demonstrates." DHS maintains that the Act only creates a cause of action against individual state or local officials and not against the governmental entity itself as employer.

The relevant portions of the Act prohibiting retaliation and creating certain remedies for public employees state:

Sec. 2. A state or local governmental body may not suspend or terminate the employment of, or otherwise discriminate against, a public employee who reports a violation of law to an appropriate law enforcement authority if the employee report is made in good faith.

Sec. 3. (a) A public employee whose employment is suspended or terminated in violation of this Act is entitled to:

(1) reinstatement in his former position; (2) compensation for wages lost during the period of suspension or termination; and (3) reinstatement of any fringe benefits or seniority rights lost because of the suspension or termination.

In determining whether the legislature unambiguously waived the State's governmental immunity with these words, we are guided by this Court's previous examination of the Act's text. ... [W]e determined that the statute as a whole evidences two legislative purposes: (1) to protect public employees from retaliation by their employer when, in good faith, employees report a violation of law, and (2) in consequence, to secure lawful conduct on the part of those who direct and conduct the affairs of public bodies.

In effecting the first goal, the legislature directed its proscription of retaliatory firing against a "state or local governmental body," and not against the individual supervisors through whom that body might act. From the legislature's focus on the governmental body as the fountainhead of the prohibited conduct, we perceive an unambiguous intent to direct the Act's penalties at the same entity. This understanding is wholly consistent with the Act's second goal, securing lawful conduct from those who manage the affairs of the governmental body. In its wisdom, the legislature obviously determined that subjecting the governmental body, and not the individual agent, to the Act's highest penalties would enhance the Act's deterrent effect. Because it thus bears the primary risk for violations of the Act, the governmental body has the principal incentive to oversee the conduct of its agents to the greater protection of public employees.

In light of the legislature's purposes, we decline to read the Act as limiting a public employee's cause of action for retaliation to a suit against an individual supervisor. Indeed, such an interpretation cannot be reconciled with section 5(a) of the Act, which provides for a civil penalty not to exceed $1,000 to be imposed against individual supervisors for violations of the Act. The attorney general or appropriate prosecuting attorney sues to collect this penalty, and because any funds collected must be deposited in the state treasury's general revenue fund, an injured public employee derives no benefit from a penalty levied under section 5.

Nowhere else does the Act expressly refer to individual supervisors, much less target them for liability. Thus, the express mention of individual supervisors in section 5(a) and nowhere else constrains us to interpret the Act's other sections as excluding additional liability of individual supervisors. Because governmental bodies (including state agencies) are, therefore, the manifest object of the Act's other liability provisions, we must decline DHS's invitation to extend the liability of individual supervisors when the legislature itself has not done so.

Suit against a governmental body that retaliates for whistle-blowing activities plainly falls within the terms, as well as the spirit and purpose, of the Whistleblower Act.

The Texas Supreme Court has noted the importance of the legislative safeguards afforded by a whistle-blower cause of action:

In a democratic, free enterprise system, a commitment to whistle-blowing represents a fundamental confidence in the ability of individuals to make a difference. Society can never eradicate wrongdoing, but it can shield from retaliation those citizens who, urged on by their integrity and social responsibility, speak out to protect its well-being.

We conclude that the Act unambiguously waives the governmental immunity from suit. Complaints about "surreal verdicts" resulting from the Act's failure to limit liability for actual or exemplary damages should be addressed to the legislature, not the judiciary.

The jury's finding must be upheld unless it is so against the great weight and preponderance of the evidence as to be manifestly unjust or erroneous. We are not free to substitute our judgment for the jury's simply because we may disagree with the verdict.

We conclude that this is more than the scintilla of evidence required to defeat the no-evidence challenge to the jury's finding that Green's whistle-blowing activities resulted in DHS's retaliatory firing; we also hold that the finding is factually sufficient.

Affirmed in favor of Plaintiff, Green.

GLOBAL DIMENSIONS OF WHITE-COLLAR CRIME

White-collar crime is not a problem just in the United States. It is a worldwide problem. Ironically, improvements in technology have increased the amount of white-collar crime on a worldwide scale by creating more opportunities for skilled employees to commit such crimes. For example, the availability of credit cards that can be used worldwide has increased the opportunities for credit card fraud.

When companies operate multinationally, they may be able to avoid regulation and escape the jurisdiction of any nation by not really basing their operations in any country. One example of a company that was able to successfully engage in criminal behavior for years without detection was Investor's Overseas Services (IOS). This company was much admired until its collapse in 1970. Using sales representatives recruited worldwide, IOS was able to persuade clients to invest $2.5 billion in a variety of mutual fund companies. Sales kept growing until the company finally went broke and the investors lost their money.

To some extent, IOS had been able to operate in a fraudulent manner because the company was not domiciled in any country or group of countries, and, thus, it was subject to no particular country's regulation. Managers registered and domiciled their funds wherever they could in order to avoid taxation and regulation.

Critical Thinking About the Law

The primary objective of the court in Case 7-4 was to examine whether a governmental body is subject to suit and liability for damages under the Whistleblower Act. In determining that governmental bodies indeed are subject to such legal remedies, the court offered rather elaborate reasoning, some of it based on precedent.

The purpose of these critical questions is to improve your skills in identifying a court's reasoning, for only after that has been done can you begin to evaluate.

1. One type of justification for its decision is the court's explanation of why a governmental body may be subject to suit and liability under the Whistleblower Act. Reproduce the court's support for this justification.

   Clue: The bulk of the support can be found within the court's discussion of the act's first goal.

2. Implicit beliefs (assumptions) often slip into legal reasoning. Their presence is normal and necessary. However, the accuracy of these beliefs needs to be questioned when they are both debatable and extremely important for the court's reasoning. Otherwise, unquestioned assumptions end up moving us toward a conclusion that a critical thinker might reject.

   For example, in Case 7-4 the court claims that placing maximum penalties on the governmental body itself results in maximizing the deterrent effect intended by the act. Can you think of any reason why the result of this logic might not create the heightened supervision assumed by the court?

   Clue: Would you be more attentive to your behavior if a penalty could fall on you directly or if the penalty could fall only on the organization to which you belong?

Consequently, they were able to do things that no company domiciled in one country could do. The prudent manager should make sure that any multinational firm with which he or she does business is domiciled in some country.

Another factor leading to the commission of white-collar crime on an international scale is the unfortunate lack of cooperation among the police of different countries. This situation may be changing, however. In April 2001, the United States and 12 other countries agreed to start sharing confidential data about the complaints they receive from consumers in a bid to crack down on cross-border Internet fraud.

The FTC voted unanimously to begin pooling its U.S. complaints with those from other countries to create a single database, something an FTC spokesperson said would "greatly improve international law enforcement agencies' ability to address cross-border Internet fraud and deception."[30]

The countries participating in the project, in addition to the United States, are Australia, Canada, Denmark, Finland, Hungary, Mexico, New Zealand, Norway, South Korea, Sweden, Switzerland, and the United Kingdom. Under the agreement, law enforcement agencies in each country will have access to the database through a single, password-protected Web site, the agency said. FTC officials said the information will tip them off to Internet scam artists.

Another important global initiative, the Convention on Cybercrime, is being undertaken by the United States, Canada, Japan, and the 43 members of the

---

[30] U.S., 12 Other Countries to Hit Internet Fraud," April 25, 2001, **news.findlaw.com/legalnews/s/20010424/techinternetfraud.html.**

Council of Europe (COE). Initiated in 1997, at the end of June 2001, after 27 drafts, a final version was agreed upon, paving the way for international rules governing copyright infringement, online fraud, child pornography, and hacking. The three main topics covered by the convention are harmonization of the national laws that define offenses, definition of investigation and prosecution procedures to cope with global networks, and establishment of a rapid and effective system of international cooperation. The Draft Convention on Cybercrime can be found at www.privacyinternational.org/issues/cybercrime/coe/cybercrime-final.html.

The Convention will come into effect on July 1, 2005. At this time it is impossible to foresee whether the Convention, upon going into effect, will render significant results or if additional countries will choose to sign.

SUMMARY

Criminal law is that body of laws designed to punish persons who engage in activities that are harmful to the public health, safety, or welfare. A crime generally requires a wrongful act and a criminal intent.

Criminal procedure is similar to civil procedure, but there are some significant differences. A criminal prosecution begins with the issuance of an information by a magistrate or an indictment by a grand jury. The next step is the arraignment, which is followed by the trial, and then, in some cases, an appeal.

White-collar crimes—crimes committed in a commercial context—may be as costly to society as street crimes, but they are more difficult to prosecute and often carry relatively light sentences. Some of the more common white-collar crimes are larceny, the secretive and wrongful taking of another's property; embezzlement, the wrongful conversion of property that one has lawful possession of; and violations of federal regulations. Increasingly, computers are being used to commit white-collar crime, making the detection of these crimes even more difficult.

Attempts are being made to fight white-collar crime on the federal level through such statutes as RICO and the False Claims Act. Some states have now passed whistle-blower statutes to help fight white-collar crime.

When thinking about white-collar crime, it is important to remember that one of the drawbacks of increasing globalization is that it has led to increasing amounts of white-collar crime carried out across borders. Criminals have taken advantage of the lack of international cooperation among law enforcement officials.

REVIEW QUESTIONS

7-1 What is the purpose of criminal law?

7-2 Explain how crimes are classified.

7-3 Explain the basic procedural stages in a criminal prosecution.

7-4 State two alternative definitions of white-collar crime and give an example of one crime that

fits under both definitions and another crime that would fit only one of the definitions.

7-5 Explain the rationale for imposing criminal liability on corporations.

7-6 Explain two sentencing alternatives to prison for white-collar criminals.

REVIEW PROBLEMS

7-7 Rawlsworth is an employee of General Sam Corporation. One of Rawlsworth's jobs is to monitor the amount of particular pollutants and to record the results on a form that is submitted to the Environmental Protection Agency. This self-monitoring is required by law to ensure that firms limit the amount of particular pollutants they discharge. One day the firm's equipment is malfunctioning, and so Rawlsworth records that the firm's discharge is in excess of the lawful amount. When Matheson, Rawlsworth's supervisor, sees what he has done, Matheson tells him to change the records to state that the firm is in compliance and, in the future, never to record such violations. When Rawlsworth calls the vice president to report this violation, he is told that the vice president does not take care of such matters and does not want to know about them. Rawlsworth then falsifies the records as instructed. When the falsification is discovered, who can be held criminally liable? Why?

7-8 Several corporations were convicted of violating the Sherman Act as a result of an unlawful agreement among their agents that the suppliers who supported an association to attract tourists would be given preferential treatment over those who did not contribute financially to the association. The corporations appealed on the grounds that the corporate agents involved were acting contrary to general corporate policy. Was the defense valid?

7-9 Defendant Laffal was the president of a corporation that operated a restaurant. It was alleged that prostitutes frequented the restaurant, picking up men there and returning them after a short time, thus making the restaurant an illegal "bawdy house" in violation of the state criminal law. Laffal argued that he could not be charged with operating a bawdy house because he was never present when any of the illegal acts took place and he did not even know they were going on. Was Laffal correct?

7-10 Evans was a loan officer for a bank and in this capacity had approved several loans to Docherty, all of which were legitimate and were repaid on time. Evans asked Docherty to apply for a loan from the bank for $2,000 and then to give the money to Evans, who would repay the loan. Evans explained that he could not obtain the loan himself because bank policy did not allow borrowing from the bank. Docherty agreed. Was Evans's or Docherty's behavior illegal?

7-11 Defendant managed a corporation charted for the purpose of "introducing people." He obtained a loan from a Mrs. Russ by telling her that he wanted the loan to build a theater on company property and that the loan would be secured by a mortgage on the property. The loan was not repaid; the mortgage was not given to the lender because the corporation owned no property. The defendant, in fact, simply deposited the money in the corporate account and used it to pay corporate debts. What crime, if any, had the defendant committed?

7-12 Jones worked for a small community college teaching business students how to set up inventories on various computer programs. The college had purchased the software and was licensed to use several copies of it for educational purposes. Jones started his own small business on the side and used the software for his own firm's inventory control. He saw his own use as "testing" the product to make sure he was teaching students to use a process that really worked. Is his behavior lawful or unlawful? Why?

CASE PROBLEMS

7-13 The charitable nonprofit orgaization, VietNow, hired a for-profit telemarketing corporation to solicit donations to aid Vietnam veterans. The contract held between VietNow and the telemarketers provided that the telemarketers would retain 85 percent of the gross receipts from Illinois donors. The Illinois attorney general filed a complaint against the telemarketers, asserting fraud by falsely representing that a significant amount of each dollar would aid the Vietnam veterans, while in fact, less than 15 cents on each dollar went to the charitable organization.

The telemarketers moved to dismiss the fraud claims under the First Amendment. The circuit court affirmed and the claims were dismissed. Upon appeal, the appellate court agreed with the lower court as did the Supreme Court of Illinois. The appeals court reasoned that the telemarketers' statements were alleged to be false because they failed to disclose the percentage information to donors, and the attorney general's complaint was an attempt to limit telemarketing activity on the basis of a percentage-rate limitation.

The case was finally appealed to the United States Supreme Court. Did the Court agree with the Supreme Court of Illinois and all the lower courts? Should the First Amendment defense be allowed in this case of alleged fraud? List the reasons you would give in support of your position. *Madigan v. Telemarketing Associates, Inc.*, 123 S. Ct. 1829 (2003).

7-14 Thomas Rybicki, Fredric Grae, and the law firm of Grae, Rybicki & Partners were convicted by a jury trial of mail fraud, wire fraud, and conspiracy to commit mail fraud. Rybicki and Grae made payments or kickbacks to middlemen who would in return approach insurance company adjusters to arrange more favorable settlements in personal injury lawsuits. It was understood that both the middleman and the adjuster would share a percentage of the settlement. Rybicki and Gae took considerable measures to conceal the payments made to the middlemen and adjusters.

The government did not seek to prove that the amount of the settlements had been inflated above what would have been a reasonable range for the particular cases. Instead, the government argued that the settlements were necessarily inflated above the amount that Rybicki's clients would have been willing to accept by at least the amount paid to the middlemen and insurance adjusters. The government was able to prove that these transactions took place over wires through phone calls and the mail.

Upon conviction, Rybicki and Grae appealed, arguing that because the government failed to prove that the appellants intended to cause, or actually caused, economic harm to the insurance companies, there was insufficient evidence to establish that their actions actually constituted fraud. Do Rybicki and Grae have reason to have their convictions overturned? Does the appeals court accept their argument? How would you decide the case? Why? *United States v. Rybicki*, 287 F. 3d 257 (2003).

7-15 Cedric Kushner Promotions, Ltd., a corporation that promotes boxing events, sued Don King, the president and sole shareholder of Don King Productions, a corporation that also promotes boxing events. The lawsuit against King claimed that King conducted boxing-related events in violation of the Racketeer

Influenced Corrupt Organizations Act (RICO). The district court dismissed the case and the appeals court affirmed the reasoning that Don King was not acting as a separate "person" from the corporation, Don King Productions. If no separation exists between the corporation and the person, then RICO does not hold. The case was appealed to the Supreme Court. How should the Court resolve this dispute? Why? How does the Court determine if a separation exists between the corporation and the person? *Cedric Kushner Promotions, Ltd. v. Don King*, 121 S. Ct. 2087 (2001).

7-16 Reginald Fortner was a detention officer at a Georgia County Detention Center where he was accused of taking bribes from inmates on four different occasions in exchange for delivering contraband, such as tobacco products. The bribes, however, were only $30 on two occasions and $20 on two other occasions. Consequently, the trial court dismissed the charges after finding that the small amounts of cash taken by Fortner did not constitute bribery. The state appealed the trial court's decision. Did the trial court err in its dismissal of the bribery charges? Does the amount gained by the defendant matter in determining bribery? *The State v. Fortner*, 264 Ga. App. 783 (2003).

7-17 The FBI questioned Dickerson about his knowledge of a recent bank robbery. During the interrogation Dickerson confessed to robbing the bank; however, at the time of the confession Dickerson was not a suspect, was not under arrest, and was free to leave. At issue is that Dickerson's confession was not preceded by his Miranda warning. Consequently, Dickerson's lawyer sought to exclude the confession from his trial because it was obtained without the proper Miranda warning. The district court agreed and suppressed the confession. Upon appeal, the decision to suppress was reversed because the confession was voluntarily given. Dickerson appealed to the Supreme Court. How does the issue of custody affect the Court's decision? How do you think the Court should rule? Does the Court agree with you? *Dickerson v. United States*, 120 S. Ct. 2326 (2000).

7-18 Defendant Middleton had been a personal computer administrator for an Internet service provider. Dissatisfied with his job, he quit but retained an e-mail account as a customer. Using a company program he was familiar with, he logged on, switched his account to that of a particular receptionist, and thereby obtained the ability to create new accounts and to add features to and delete existing accounts.

His activity was discovered, and his e-mail account was terminated. But he later logged on to a test account and used it to gain access to the company's main computers. He then accessed the account of a sales representative and created two new accounts, through which he gained access to another company computer used for administrative functions. He then changed all the administrative passwords, altered the computer's registry, and deleted the entire billing system and two internal databases.

He was discovered, arrested and convicted, and sentenced. What law did he violate? Explain how that law would apply to his case. *United States v. Middleton*, 231 F.3d 1207 (9th Cir. 2000).

ASSIGNMENT ON THE INTERNET

You have now learned several approaches to deter white-collar crime in this chapter, including federal laws such as the RICO and False Claims Act, individual state laws, and the proposed GPD. However, there are many other independent steps a business can take to ensure that employees do not engage in illegal behavior. Use the Internet to find what other businesses are doing to prevent white-collar crime. You can begin by visiting this **www.theiia.org/iia/index.cfm?doc_id=1330**.

As a business manager, what additional deterrents to white-collar crime would you create or adopt? How does *United States v. Park*, discussed earlier in this chapter, affect your attitude toward the responsibility of a manager to prevent white-collar crime?

 ## ON THE INTERNET

www.nw3c.org This site is the location of the National White-Collar Crime Center, which provides investigative support services to fight against white-collar crimes.

www.ffhsj.com/firmpubs.php?topic=White-Collar+Crime A bibliography of articles on white-collar crime.

www.ussc.gov At this Web site, you can find the text of the U.S. Sentencing Guidelines Manual.

www.usdoj.gov/criminal/fraud.html This is the Web site of the division of the Department of Justice that prosecutes fraud and white-collar crime.

www.wccfighter.com White-Collar Crime Fighter is a Web site and monthly publication designed to detect and prevent white-collar crime. This site provides current articles and news reports that you might find helpful in applying the information learned in this chapter.

corporate.findlaw.com/industry/white If you wish to find laws particular to your state about white-collar crime, visit this site. Also provided are articles and recent cases involving white-collar crime from your state.

www.corporatecrimereporter.com The Corporate Crime Reporter provides articles, links, and reports on current white-collar crime cases and investigations.

8

ETHICS, SOCIAL RESPONSIBILITY, AND THE BUSINESS MANAGER

- **DEFINITION OF BUSINESS ETHICS AND SOCIAL RESPONSIBILITY**
- **THEORIES OF ETHICAL THOUGHT**
- **CODES OF ETHICS**
- **SCHOOLS OF SOCIAL RESPONSIBILITY**
- **GLOBAL DIMENSIONS OF ETHICS AND SOCIAL RESPONSIBILITY**

On December 2, 1984, in Bhopal, India, lethal methylisocyanate gas (MIC) leaked from a chemical plant owned by Union Carbide India Ltd., killing approximately 2,000 people and injuring thousands more, many of whom are still receiving treatment. Union Carbide's chairman, Warren Anderson, a lawyer, flew to India with a pledge of interim assistance totaling $7 million and medical support. He was arrested and deported from the country. Lawsuits on behalf of the deceased and injured were brought by U.S. law firms as well as by the government of India.

The price of Union Carbide stock dropped from $48 to $33. In August 1984, GAF Corporation attempted to take over Union Carbide. Union Carbide successfully fought off the takeover attempt in 1985. On May 13, 1986, a federal court judge dismissed the personal injury and wrongful death actions, stating that the complaints should be more properly heard in a court in India. The judge attached certain conditions to the dismissal, one of which was that Union Carbide would have to agree to pay any damages rendered by an Indian court. The trail began in August 1988 in a New Delhi court amidst rumors that a former disgruntled employee had sabotaged Union Carbide's Bhopal plant, causing the gas leakage. In January 1988, Union Carbide shares traded on the New York Stock Exchange for $49, and the much leaner company was one of the 30 companies making up the composite Dow Jones Industrial Average. It might be helpful to read this case set out in edited form in Chapter 9. For additional and update facts though 2004. (See *Comment* after case).

In an unrelated, but similarly disturbing situation, the death toll for accidents involving Ford Explorers equipped with Firestone tires rose to at least 174 by June 2001, and the number of reported injuries topped 700. Ford recalled most of the Firestone tires on Explorers, and eventually it switched to other brands. Meanwhile, the tire manufacturer maintained that the problem was not the tires but the design of the Explorer. As the two companies continued to try to place responsibility primarily on each other, consumers continued to purchase Ford Explorers, although not quite at the same rate as before all the negative publicity.

The Bhopal incident in 1984, along with a stream of insider trading cases beginning in 1986 and continuing into the 1990s, as well as a number of white-collar crime cases in the early 2000s (highlighted in Chapter 7) have brought a heightened awareness of the need for debate as to whether the business community has a responsibility solely to shareholders or to other stakeholders as well.

Such cases force us to ask ourselves: What should be the legal rules that businesses must obey in their daily operations? Additionally, there are ethical questions that force us to consider how we should behave if we are to live in a better world. Business ethics is the study of the moral practices of the firms that play such an important role in shaping that better world.

Whenever you wonder whether a business decision requires us to think about ethics, simply ask yourself: will this decision affect the quality of life of other people? If the answer is yes, the decision involves ethics. We think you will agree that business ethics is an extremely important aspect of our environment because almost all business decisions influence the quality of our lives.

This chapter presents material on business ethics in a neutral way. Readers are left to make their own choices about what part ethics should play in business decision making and about whether the business community, the trade groups that represent it, and individual managers should act in a "socially responsible" manner. The chapter includes (1) a broad definition of ethics and social responsibility; (2) some recognized theories of ethical thought and their application to business problems; (3) a discussion of individual, corporate, trade association, and professional ethical codes; and (4) schools of social responsibility as applied to business problems. The chapter ends with a brief discussion of some current trends in the area of ethics and social responsibility as well as some proposals now being debated, which, if implemented, would change the structure of corporate governance.

Critical Thinking About the Law

Business ethics is perhaps one of the most personal and emotional areas in business decision making. Business ethics can be confusing and complex because a right or wrong answer often does not exist. Because this area is so emotional and controversial, it is extremely important to use your critical thinking skills when thinking about business ethics. It would be very easy to make arguments based on your gut reaction to cases such as the Bhopal gas incident. However, you should carefully use your critical thinking skills to draw an informed conclusion. The following questions can help you begin to understand the complexity surrounding business ethics.

1. As critical thinkers, you have learned that ambiguous words—words that have multiple possible meanings—can cause confusion in the legal environment. Perhaps the best example of ambiguity in the legal environment is the phrase *social responsibility*. What definitions of responsibility can you generate?

   Clue: Consider the Bhopal incident. Do you think Union Carbide would have the same definition of social responsibility as the families of the victims of the accident in India?

2. It is quite common for individuals, businesses, judges, and juries to each have different meanings of the phrase *social responsibility*. Preferences for certain ethical norms might account for these different meanings. If executives of a company thought that security was extremely important, how might their definition of social responsibility be affected?

   Clue: Remember the definitions of security in Chapter 1. If Union Carbide valued security, how might the company treat the victims of the Bhopal incident?

3. Your friend discovers that you are taking a Legal Environment of Business class. He says, "I'm extremely angry at the cigarette companies. They knew that cigarettes cause cancer. Don't those companies have a responsibility to protect us?" Because you are trained in critical thinking, you know that his question does not have a simple answer. Keeping your critical thinking skills in mind, how would you intelligently respond to his question?

   Clue: Consider the critical thinking questions about ambiguity, ethical norms, and missing information.

DEFINITION OF BUSINESS ETHICS AND SOCIAL RESPONSIBILITY

BUSINESS ETHICS

ethics The study of what makes up good and bad conduct inclusive of related actions and values.

business ethics The study of what makes up good and bad conduct as related to business activities and values.

Ethics is the study of good and bad behavior. **Business ethics** is a subset of the study of ethics and is defined as the study of what makes up good and bad business conduct. This conduct occurs when the firm acts as an organization, as well as when individual managers make decisions inside the organization. For example, there may be differences between the way Warren Anderson personally looked at the Bhopal tragedy (a failure of the plant to implement company operating standards) and the way the corporation's board of directors and the chemical industry did (the Indian government allowed people to live too close to the plant). It is important to look at "business" ethics not as a single monolithic system but from the perspective of individual managers, corporations, and industry-wide ethical concerns. Each may judge a particular happening in a different way.

How these groups think depends on their ethical norms and on their philosophy or theory of ethics. To help you understand their thinking, we include a discussion of three schools of ethical thought. Individual managers, corporations,

Linking Law & Business

Business Ethics

Managers often attempt to encourage ethical practices in the workplace. A significant reason for managers' concern with ethics is to portray their organizations in a favorable light to consumers, investors, and employees. As a means of creating an ethical workplace, there are several methods that managers should implement that you may recall from your management class: (1) Create a code of ethics, which is a formal statement that acts as a guide for making decisions and actions within an organization. Distribution and continual improvement of the code of ethics are also important steps. (2) Establish a workplace or office for the sole purpose of overseeing organizational practices to determine if actions are ethical. (3) Conduct training programs to encourage ethical practices in the organization. (4) Minimize situations in which unethical behavior is common and create conditions in which people are likely to behave ethically. Two practices that often result in unethical behavior are to give unusually high rewards for good performance and uncommonly harsh punishments for poor performance. By eliminating these two causal factors of unethical behavior, managers are more likely to create conditions in which employees choose to behave ethically within the organization. Therefore, a manager's hope to represent the organization in a respectable manner may be achieved through the execution of these methods.

Source: S. Certo, *Modern Management* (Upper Saddle River, N.J.: Prentice Hall, 2000), pp. 66–69.

or industries may belong to any one of the schools, as each school has its advocates and refinements. In addition, each school attempts to explain why an action is right or wrong and how one knows it to be right or wrong.

THE SOCIAL RESPONSIBILITY OF BUSINESS

The **social responsibility** of business is defined as a concern by business about both its profit-seeking and its non-profit-seeking activities and their intended and unintended impact on groups and individuals other than management or the owners of a corporation (e.g., consumers, environmentalists, and political groups). Since the late 1960s, an outcry has arisen for business to be more socially responsible. This outcry of public concern has resulted in part from three factors:

social responsibility
Concern of business entities about profit and nonprofit activities and their unintended impact on others directly or indirectly involved.

1. *The complexity and interdependence of a postindustrial society.* No individual or business is an island unto itself. If a company builds a chemical plant in Bhopal, India, and its primary purpose is to make profits for its shareholders, can it be held responsible to the public that lives around the plant when there is a gas leak? The public is dependent on the firm's good conduct, and the firm is dependent on the public and its political representatives to supply labor, an adequate water supply, tax forgiveness, roads, and so on.

2. *Political influence that has translated public outcry for socially responsible conduct into government regulation.* Whether a malfunction occurs at a nuclear plant at Three Mile Island or a human disaster is caused by a gas leak in Bhopal, India, the political arm of government at all levels sees the solution in the form of more regulation. This attitude pleases the government's constituents and makes its official more electable.

3. *Philosophical differences about what should be the obligations of business.* Neoclassical economic theory would argue that the sole purpose of business is to make a profit for its investing shareholders, who, in turn, reinvest, creating expanded or new businesses that employ more people, thus creating a higher standard of living.

Others hold different theories of social responsibility. Some would argue for a managerial or coping approach; that is, "throw money" at the problem when it occurs, such as the Bhopal disaster, and it will go away. Others would argue a more encompassing theory of social responsibility that purports that business, like any other institution in our society (e.g., unions, churches), has a social responsibility not only to shareholders (or members or congregations) but also to diverse groups, such as consumers and political, ethnic, racial group, and gender-oriented organizations. These and other schools of social responsibility are discussed later in this chapter.

THEORIES OF ETHICAL THOUGHT

CONSEQUENTIAL THEORIES

Ethicists, businesspeople, and workers who adhere to a consequential theory of ethics judge acts as ethically good or bad based on whether the acts have achieved their desired results. The actions of a business or any other societal unit are looked at as right or wrong only in terms of whether the results can be rationalized.

This theory is best exemplified by the utilitarian school of thought, which is divided into two subschools: act utilitarianism and rule utilitarianism. In general, adherents of this school judge all conduct of individuals or businesses on whether it brings net happiness or pleasure to a society. They judge an act ethically correct after adding up the risks (unhappiness) and the benefits (happiness) to society and obtaining a net outcome. For example, if it is necessary for a company to pay a bribe to a foreign official in order to get several billion dollars in airplane contracts, utilitarians would argue, in general, that the payment is ethically correct because it will provide net happiness to society; that is, it will bring jobs and spending to the community where the airplane company is located. If the bribe is not paid, the contracts, jobs, and spending will go to a company somewhere else.

Act utilitarians determine if an action is right or wrong on the basis of whether that individual act (the payment of a bribe) alone brings net happiness to the society

TABLE 8-1

THEORIES OF ETHICAL THOUGHT

Consequential Theories	Acts are judged good or bad based on whether the acts have achieved their desired results. Acts of the business community or any other social unit (e.g., government, school, fraternity, and sorority). Act and rule utilitarianisms are two subschools.
Deontological Theories	Actions can be judged good or bad based on rules and principles that are applied universally.
Humanist Theories	Actions are evaluated as good or bad depending on whether they contribute to improving inherent human capacities such as intelligence, wisdom, and self-restraint.

as opposed to whether other alternatives (e.g., not paying the bribe or allowing others to pay the bribe) would bring more or less net happiness. Rule utilitarians argue that an act (the payment of the bribe) is ethically right if the performance of similar acts by all similar agents (other contractors) would produce the best results in society or has done so in the past. Rule utilitarians hold the position that whatever applicable rule has been established by political representatives must be followed and should serve as a standard in the evaluation of similar acts. If payment of bribes has been determined by the society to bring net happiness, and a rule allowing bribes exists, then rule utilitarians would allow the bribe. On the other hand, the Foreign Corrupt Practices Act of 1977, as amended in 1988, which forbids paying bribes to foreign government officials to get business that would not have been obtained without such a payment, is an example of a standard that rule utilitarians would argue must be followed but that would lead to a different result. So the act utilitarians might get the airplane plant, but the rule utilitarians, if they were following the Foreign Corrupt Practices Act, would not.

We must note that both act and rule utilitarians focus on the consequences of an act and not on the question of verifying whether an act is ethically good or bad.[1] Either one of these theories can be used by individuals or businesses to justify their actions.[2] Act utilitarians use the principle of utility (adding up the costs and benefits of an act to arrive at net happiness) to focus on an individual action at one point in time. Rule utilitarians believe that one should not consider the consequences of a single act in determining net happiness but, instead, should focus on a general rule that exemplifies net happiness for the whole society. Case 8-1 illustrates a rule-utilitarian view of jurisprudence.

DEONTOLOGICAL THEORIES

Deontology is derived from a Greek word meaning "duty." For advocates of deontology, rules and principles determine whether actions are ethically good or bad. The consequences of individual actions are not considered. The golden rule, "do unto others as you would have them do unto you," is the hallmark of the theory.

Absolute deontology claims that actions can be judged ethically good or bad on the basis of absolute moral principles arrived at by human reason regardless of the consequences of an action, that is, regardless of whether there is net happiness.[3] Immanuel Kant (1724–1804) provided an example of an absolute moral principle in his widely studied "categorical imperative." He stated that a person ought to engage only in acts that he or she could see becoming a universal standard. For example, if a U.S. company bribes a foreign official in order to obtain a contract to build airplanes, then U.S. society and business should be willing to accept the principle that foreign multinationals will be free morally to bribe U.S. government officials in order to obtain defense contracts. Of course, the reverse will be true if nonbribery statutes are adopted worldwide. Kant, as part of his statement of the categorical imperative, assumed that everyone is a rational being having free will, and he warned that one ought to "treat others as having

---

[1] W. LaCroix, *Principles for Ethics in Business*, rev. ed. (Washington, D.C.: University Press, 1979), p. 12.

[2] See B. Brennan, "Amending the Foreign Corrupt Practices Act of 1977: Clarifying or Gutting a Law," *Journal of Legislation* 2 (1984), pp. 78–81, for an examination of the rule and act utilitarian schools of thought within the context of the proposed amending process of the 1977 Foreign Corrupt Practices Act.

[3] La Croix, *supra* note 2, p. 13.

intrinsic values in themselves, and not merely as a means to achieve one's end."[4] For deontologists such as Kant, ethical reasoning means adopting universal principles that are applied to all equally. Segregation of one ethnic or racial group is unethical because it denies the intrinsic value of each human being and, thus, violates a general universal principal. See the case that follows in which the court appears to leave the decision making to a trial jury.

HUMANIST THEORIES

A third school of thought, the humanist school, evaluates actions as ethically good or bad depending on what they contribute to improving inherent human capacities such as intelligence, wisdom, and self-restraint. Many natural law theorists (examined in Chapter 2) believe that humans would arrive by reason alone at standards of conduct that ultimately derive from a divine being or another ultimate source such as nature. For example, if a U.S. business participates in bribing a foreign official, it is not doing an act that improves inherent human capacities such as intelligence and wisdom; thus, the act is not ethical. In a situation that demanded choice, as well as the use of the intelligence and restraint that would prevent a violation of law (the Foreign Corrupt Practices Act of 1977), the particular business would have failed ethically as well as legally.

Case 8-1 illustrates a consequential theory of ethics, but if read carefully, the other two schools of thought outlined here could be argued as well.

CASE 8-1

Pavlik v. Lane
U.S. Court of Appeals 3r Cir.,
135 F.3d 876 (1998)

Pavlik (plaintiff) filed a suit, on behalf of his son, against Lane (defendant) and others. Butane, a fuel used in lighters, had a warning on each distributed can "DO NOT BREATHE SPRAY." Zeus was the brand name under which butane was distributed in small aerosol cans. Pavlik's son died after intentionally inhaling the contents of one of the cans. The plaintiff argued that the warning on the can did not warn users adequately of the hazards of butane. The defendants argued for a summary judgment claiming the warning was adequate and a 20-year-old young man must have been aware of the dangers of butane. The federal district court granted a summary judgment. The plaintiff appealed.

Justice Backer
[A]n otherwise properly designed product may still be unreasonably dangerous (and therefore "defective") for

strict liability purposes if the product is distributed without sufficient warnings to apprise the ultimate user of the latent dangers in the product.

[W]e have serious doubts that the Zeus warning (on the can) sufficiently warns users of the potentially fatal consequences of butane inhalation, and we are not convinced of its adequacy. More specifically, the "DO NOT BREATHE SPRAY" warning appears to give the user no notice of the serious nature of the danger posed by inhalation, intentional or otherwise, and no other language on the Zeus can does so. Yet, we similarly cannot find that such a directive is inadequate as a matter of law, and so we must leave the question for the jury.

Reversed for plaintiff,
and *remanded* to the trial court for new trial.

---

[4] R. Wolff, ed., *Foundations of the Metaphysics of Moral Thought and Critical Essays* (New York: Bobbs-Merrill, 1964), p. 44.

CODES OF ETHICS

INDIVIDUAL CODES OF ETHICS

When examining business ethics, one must recognize that the corporations, partnerships, and other entities that make up the business community are a composite of individuals. If the readers of this book are asked where they obtained their ethical values, they might respond their values come from parents, church, peers, teachers, brothers and sisters, or the environment. In any event, corporations and the culture of a corporation are greatly influenced by what ethical values individuals bring to them. Often business managers are faced with a conflict between their individual ethical values and those of the corporation. For example, a father of three young children, who is divorced and their sole support, is asked by his supervisor to "slightly change" figures that will make the tests on rats of a new drug look more favorable when reported to the Food and Drug Administration. His supervisor hints that if he fails to do so, he may be looking for another job. The individual is faced with a conflict in ethical values: individual values of honesty and humaneness toward potential users of the drug versus business values of profits, efficiency, loyalty to the corporation, and the need for a job. Which values should he adopt?

Individual Ethical Codes versus Groupthink

On January 28, 1986, just 74 seconds into its space shuttle launch, *Challenger* exploded, killing the first schoolteacher in space, Christa McAuliffe, and six other astronauts on board. A presidential commission was set up and found that faulty O-rings in the booster rockets were to blame. Two engineers testified before the commission that they opposed the launch but were overruled by their immediate supervisor and other officials of the Thikol Corporation that manufactured the booster rockets. Warnings by the two engineers of problems with the O-rings continued to take place until the day before the launch. After the launch one engineer was assigned to "special projects" for the firm. Another took leave and founded a consulting firm.

On September 11, 2001, two planes flew into ("Twin Towers") of the World Trade Center in New York City; one plane flew into the Pentagon in Washington, D.C., and another flew into a field near Pittsburgh, Pennsylvania. Approximately 3,000 people were killed by terrorists flying the planes. Again, a presidential commission was set up. In 2004 the commission reported that the failure of intermediate-level employees to be heard within intelligence agencies, as well as the inability of agencies such as the CIA (Central Intelligence Agency), DIA, (Defense Intelligence Agency), and NSA (National Security Agencies) to bring early warning information forward to the decision makers (in the White House), were in part responsible for the events that took place. The CIA director resigned and other officials at some agencies retired. A new structure was set up for intelligence gathering in 2004 which allows a single individual to be responsible for intelligence provided to the President of the United States.

These factual situations are very different, but when reading the presidential commissions' testimonies it appears, in both cases, there were conflicts between individual ethical values and groupthink. *Groupthink* here will be defined as a form of thinking that people engage in when they are involved in a cohesive in-group,

continued on the next page

striving for unanimity, which overrules a realistic appraisal of alternative courses of action. Groupthink refers "to a deterioration of mental efficiency, reality testing, and moral efficiency that results from in-group pressures."[1] For the engineers in the *Challenger* case and the middle-level managers of intelligence agencies, the question always will remain—were they part of a groupthink process that altered the outcome? Are there important factual differences in these cases: private sector employment (Thikol) as opposed to public sector intelligence agencies?

Groupthink, on the other hand, may be necessary in our society. Without it, how would we organize our corporations, the military, and government agencies? If we allowed everyone to think independently, would anyone follow orders in the military or build rocket boosters in industry? Also, people often do not think like whistle-blowers (see discussion of the Sarbanes-Oxley Act later in this chapter and in Chapter 22) for fear of losing their status and their jobs, which are often necessary to support egos and families.

Before answering any of the questions posed here, return to Chapter 1 and review the eight steps in critical thinking outlined there.

---

[1] Irving L., Janis, *Victims of Groupthink* (Boston: Houghton-Mifflin, 1972).

CORPORATE CODES OF ETHICS

The sum total of individual employees' ethical values influences corporate conduct, especially in a corporation's early years. The activities during these years, in turn, form the basis of what constitutes a corporate culture or an environment for doing business. In a free-market society, values of productivity, efficiency, and profits become part of the culture of all companies. Some companies seek to generate productivity by cooperation between workers and management; others motivate through intense production goals that may bring about high labor turnover. Some companies have marketed their product through emphasis on quality and service; others emphasize beating the competition through lower prices.[5] Over time, these production and marketing emphases have evolved into what is called a corporate culture, often set forth in corporate codes.

Approximately 90 percent of all major corporations have adopted codes of conduct since the mid-1960s. In general, the codes apply to upper- and middle-level managers. They are usually implemented by a chief executive officer or a designated agent. They tend to provide sanctions ranging from personal reprimands that are placed in the employee's file to dismissal. Some formal codes allow for due process hearings within the corporation, in which an employee accused of a violation is given a chance to defend himself or herself. With many employees bringing wrongful dismissal actions in courts of law, more formal internal procedures are developing to implement due process requirements. A study of corporate codes reveals that the actions most typically forbidden are:[6]

- Paying bribes to foreign government officials
- Fixing prices

---

[5] C. Power and D. Vogel, *Ethics in the Education of Business Managers* (Hastings-on-Hudson, N.Y.: Hastings Center, 1980), p. 6.

[6] See K. Chatov, "What Corporate Ethics Statements Say," *California Management Review 22* (1980), p. 20.

- Giving gifts to customers or accepting gifts from suppliers

- Using insider information

- Revealing trade secrets

Corporate Ethics: Internal Housecleaning

Following several financial scandals involving companies such as Enron, Martha Stewart Living, Inc., Imclone Systems, WorldCom, Inc. (now MCI), and Tyco International (see Chapter 7 for analysis of some of these), Congress passed the Sarbanes-Oxley Act in 2002. This act required publicly traded companies to set up confidential internal systems by April 2003 so that employees and others could have a method of reporting possible illegal or unethical auditing and accounting practices as well as other areas including sexual harassment.

Web reporting systems such as Ethicspoint allow employees of companies to click on an icon on their computers and anonymously be linked to the reporting services. Employees may report alleged unethical or illegal activity. The reporting system then alerts a management person or the audit committee of the board of directors to any possible problem. Other systems include a special phone number (800 or 900). None are perfect but the key factor is that Sarbanes-Oxley has given impetus to "cleaning house" internally.

Whistle-blowing protection under Section 806 of Sarbanes-Oxley[1] prohibits any publicly traded company from "discharging, demoting, suspending, threatening or otherwise discriminating against an employee who provides information to the government or assists in a government investigation regarding conduct that an employee believes may be a violation of the securities laws." Penalties as noted in Chapter 22 are both civil and criminal in nature.

---

[1] H.R. 3782 signed into law by President George W. Bush on July 30, 2002, effective on August 29, 2002. Pub. L. 109–204; 15 U.S.C. Section 78d (I)–(3) codified in Exchange Act, Section 4. See Chapter 22 for a full discussion.

INDUSTRY CODES OF ETHICS

In addition to corporate ethical codes, industry codes exist, such as those of the National Association of Broadcasters or the National Association of Used Car Dealers. In most cases, these codes are rather general and contain either affirmative inspirational guidelines or a list of "shall-nots." A "hybrid model" including "dos and don'ts" generally addresses itself to subjects such as:[7]

- Honest and fair dealings with customers

- Acceptable levels of safety, efficacy, and cleanliness

- Nondeceptive advertising

- Maintenance of experienced and trained personnel, competent performance of services, and furnishing of quality products

---

[7] See R. Jacobs, "Vehicles for Self-Regulation: Codes of Conduct, Credentialing and Standards," in *Self-Regulation*, conference proceedings (Washington, D.C.: Ethics Resource Center, 1982), p. 83.

Most trade associations were formed for the purpose of lobbying Congress, the executive branch, and the regulatory agencies, in addition to influencing elections through their political action committees (PACs). They have not generally been effective in monitoring violations of their own ethical codes. In light of the reasons for their existence and the fact that membership dues support their work, it is not likely that they will be very effective disciplinarians.

However, some effective *self-regulating mechanisms* do exist in industries. In Chapter 23, the reader will see that self-regulating organizations (SROs) such as the National Association of Securities Dealers and the New York Stock Exchange have carried out authority delegated to them by the Securities and Exchange Commission in an extremely efficient manner. In addition, the Council of Better Business Bureaus, through its National Advertising Division (NAD), has provided empirical evidence that self-regulation can be effective. The NAD seeks to monitor and expose false advertising through its local bureaus and has done an effective job, receiving commendations from a leading consumer advocate, Ralph Nader.[8]

PROFESSIONAL CODES OF ETHICS

Within a corporation, managers often interact with individual employees who have "professional" codes of conduct that may supersede corporate or industry-wide codes in terms of what activities they can participate in and still remain licensed professionals. For example, under the Model Code of Professional Responsibility, a lawyer must reveal the intention of his or her client to commit a crime and the information necessary to prevent the crime.[9] When a lawyer, a member of the law department of Airplane Corporation X, learns that his company deliberately intends to bribe a high-level foreign official in order to obtain an airplane contract, he may be forced, under the Model Code, to disclose this intention because the planned bribe is a violation of the Foreign Corrupt Practices Act of 1977, as amended, an act that has criminal penalties. Failure to disclose could lead to suspension or disbarment by the lawyer's state bar. Management must be sensitive to this and to the several professional codes that are to be discussed.

Professionals is an often-overused term, referring to everything from masons to hair stylists to engineers, lawyers, and doctors. When discussing professions or professionals here, we mean a group that has the following characteristics:

- Prelicensing mandatory university educational training, as well as continuing education requirements.

- Licensing-exam requirements.

- A set of written ethical standards that is recognized and continually enforced by the group.

- A formal association or group that meets regularly.

- An independent commitment to the public interest.

- Formal recognition by the public as a professional group.

---

[8] See R. Tankersley, "Advertising: Regulation, Deregulation and Self-Regulation," in *Self-Regulation*, conference proceedings, *supra* note 7, at 45.

[9] See Model Code of Professional Responsibility DR 4-401(C) and Formal Op. 314 (1965).

Management must often interact with the professions outlined in the following paragraphs. Each of them has a separate code of conduct. An awareness of this factor may lead to a greater understanding of why each group acts as it does.

Accounting. The American Institute of Certified Public Accountants (AICPA) has promulgated a Code of Professional Ethics and Interpretive Rules. The Institute of Internal Auditors has set out a Code of Ethics, as well as a Statement of Responsibilities of Internal Auditors. In addition, the Association of Government Accountants has promulgated a Code of Ethics.

Disciplinary procedures are set forth for individuals as well as for firms in the Code of Professional Ethics for Certified Public Accountants (CPAs). Membership in the AICPA is suspended without a hearing if a judgment of conviction is filed with the secretary of the institute as related to the following:[10]

- A felony as defined under any state law.
- The willful failure to file an income tax return, which the CPA as an individual is required to file.
- The filing of a fraudulent return on the part of the CPA for his or her own return or that of a client.
- The aiding in the preparation of a fraudulent income tax return of a client.

The AICPA Division for CPA Firms is responsible for disciplining firms as opposed to individuals. Through its SEC Practice and its Private Company sections, this division requires member firms to (1) adhere to quality-control standards, (2) submit to peer review of their accounting and audit practices every three years, (3) ensure that all professionals participate in continuing education programs, and (4) maintain minimum amounts of liability insurance.

Accountants' ethical responsibility is reinforced by the Sarbanes-Oxley Act of 2002, which was passed by Congress following a series of financial scandals (see Chapters 7 and 22).[11] A Public Company Accounting Oversight Board was created and provisions that require auditor independence were included in this statute. Under Section 802 of the act, accountants are required to maintain working papers on file relating to an audit or review for five years. A willful violation will be subject to a fine or imprisonment for up to ten years or both.

Other statutory provisions affecting accountants include Sections 11 and 12 (2) of the 1933 Securities Act, as well as Section 10(b) and (18) of the 1934 Exchange. The 1933 act deals with accountant liability for false statements or omission of a material fact in auditing financial statements required for registration of securities. A defense is due diligence and a reasonable belief that the work is complete.

Under the 1934 act Sections 10(b), accountants are liable for false and misleading reports required by the act (see Chapter 22). Willful violations bring criminal penalties. Additionally, provisions of the Internal Revenue Code provide criminal penalties (felony) for tax preparers who willfully prepare or assist in preparing a false return.[12] Additionally, tax preparers who negligently or willfully understate tax liability are subject to criminal penalties. Failure to provide a taxpayer with a copy of his or her return may subject a tax preparer to criminal penalties.[13]

---

[10] See AICPA Professional Standards, vol. 2, Disciplinary Suspension and Termination of Membership Hearing, GL 730.01.

[11] H.R. 3762 signed into law by President George W. Bush on July 30, 2002, effective August 30, 2002.

[12] 26 U.S.C. Section 7208 (2).

[13] 26 U.S.C. Section 7101 (a) (36).

Insurance and Finance. The American Society of Chartered Life Underwriters (ASCLU) had adopted a Code of Ethics consisting of eight Guides to Professional Conduct and six Rules of Professional Conduct. The Guides are broad in nature, whereas the Rules are specific. Enforcement of the Code of Ethics is left primarily to local chapters. Discipline includes reprimand, censure, and dismissal. A local chapter can additionally recommend suspension or revocation to a national board. Very few disciplinary actions have been forthcoming.[14]

In addition, the Society of Chartered Property and Casualty Underwriters (CPCC) has a Code of Ethics consisting of seven Specified Unethical Practices, as well as three Unspecified Unethical Practices of a more general nature. On receipt of a written and signed complaint, the president of the society appoints a three-member conference panel to hear the case. If a panel finds a member guilty of an "unspecified unethical practice," the president directs the member to cease such action. If a member is found guilty of a "specified unethical practice," the society's board of directors may reprimand or censure the violator or suspend or expel her or him from membership in the society.

Law. The American Bar Association's Model Rules of Professional Responsibility were submitted to the highest state courts and the District of Columbia for adoption, after the association's House of Delegates approved them in August 1983 (before then, the states had adopted the Model Code of Professional Responsibility). There are nine canons of professional responsibility. From these are derived Ethical Considerations and Disciplinary Rules. The Model Rules set out a minimal level of conduct that is expected of an attorney. Violation of any of these rules may lead to warnings, reprimands, public censure, suspension, or disbarment by the enforcement agency of the highest state court in which the attorney is admitted to practice. Most state bar disciplinary actions are published in state bar journals and local newspapers, so lawyers and the public in general are aware of attorneys who have been subject to disciplinary action.

The case excerpted here illustrates some legal problems surrounding professional ethical codes when they result in price-fixing.

CASE 8-2

Bates v. State Bar of Arizona
United States Supreme Court
433 U.S. 350 (1977)

Plaintiff-appellants Bates and O'Steen, licensed to practice law in the state of Arizona, opened a "legal clinic" in 1974. The clinic provided legal services to people with modest incomes for approximately two years, after which the clinic placed an advertisement in the *Arizona Republic*, a daily newspaper circulated in the Phoenix area, stating prices charged for legal services. The plaintiffs conceded that this advertisement was a violation of Disciplinary Rule 2-101(B) incorporated in Rule 29(a) of the Arizona Supreme Court rules, which stated in part:

A lawyer shall not publicize himself or his partner or associate, or any other lawyer affiliated with him or his firm, as a lawyer through newspapers, or magazine advertisements, radio, television announcements, display advertisements in the city telephone directories or other means of commercial publicity, nor shall he authorize others to do so in his behalf.

A complaint was initiated by the president of the State Bar of Arizona, and a hearing was held before a three-member

---

[14] See R. Horn, *On Professions, Professionals, and Professional Ethics* (Malvern, Penn.: American Institute for Property and Liability Underwriters, 1978), p. 74.

special local administrative committee. The committee recommended to the Arizona Supreme Court that each of the plaintiffs be suspended from practice for not less than six months. The court agreed and ordered the plaintiffs suspended. The plaintiffs appealed to the U.S. Supreme Court.

Justice Blackmun

The heart of the dispute before us today is whether lawyers may constitutionally advertise the prices at which certain routine services will be performed. Numerous justifications are proffered for the restriction of such price advertising. We consider each in turn:

1. *The Adverse Effect on Professionalism.* Appellee places particular emphasis on the adverse effects that it feels price advertising will have on the legal profession. The key to professionalism, it is argued, is the sense of pride that involvement in the discipline generates. It is claimed that price advertising will bring about commercialization, which will undermine the attorney's sense of dignity and self-worth. The hustle of the marketplace will adversely affect the profession's service orientation, and irreparably damage the delicate balance between the lawyer's need to earn and his obligation selflessly to serve. Advertising is also said to erode the client's trust in his attorney. Once the client perceives that the lawyer is motivated by profit, his confidence that the attorney is acting out of a commitment to the client's welfare is jeopardized. And advertising is said to tarnish the dignified public image of the profession.

We recognize, of course, and commend the spirit of public service with which the profession of law is practiced and to which it is dedicated. The present Members of this Court, licensed attorneys all, could not feel otherwise. And we would have reason to pause if we felt that our decision today would undercut that spirit. But we find the postulated connection between advertising and the erosion of true professionalism to be severely strained. At its core, the argument presumes that attorneys must conceal from themselves and from their clients the real-life fact that lawyers earn their livelihood at the bar. We suspect that few attorneys engage in such self-deception. And rare is the client, moreover, even one of modest means, who enlists the aid of an attorney with the expectation that his services will be rendered free of charge.

Moreover, the assertion that advertising will diminish the attorney's reputation in the community is open to question. Bankers and engineers advertise, and yet these professionals are not regarded as undignified. In fact, it has been suggested that the failure of lawyers to advertise creates public disillusionment with the profession. The absence of advertising may be seen to reflect the profession's failure to reach out and serve the community.

Studies reveal that many persons do not obtain counsel even when they perceive a need because of the feared price of services or because of an inability to locate a competent attorney. Indeed, cynicism with regard to the profession may be created by the fact that it long has publicly eschewed advertising, while condoning the actions of the attorney who structures his social or civic associations so as to provide contacts with potential clients.

2. *Inherently Misleading Nature of Attorney Advertising.* It is argued that advertising of legal services inevitably will be misleading. The argument that legal services are so unique that fixed rates cannot meaningfully be established is refuted by the record in this case. The appellee State Bar itself sponsors a Legal Services Program in which the participating attorneys agree to perform services like those advertised by the appellants at standardized rates.

3. *The Adverse Effect on the Administration of Justice.* Advertising is said to have the undesirable effect of stirring up litigation. But advertising by attorneys is not an unmitigated source of harm to the administration of justice. It may offer great benefits. Although advertising might increase the use of the judicial machinery, we cannot accept the notion that it is always better for a person to suffer a wrong silently than to redress it by legal action.

4. *The Undesirable Economic Effects of Advertising.* It is claimed that advertising will increase the overhead costs of the profession, and that these costs then will be passed along to consumers in the form of increased fees. Moreover, it is claimed that the additional cost of practice will create a substantial entry barrier, deterring or preventing young attorneys from penetrating the market and entrenching the position of the bar's established members.

These two arguments seem dubious at best. Neither distinguishes lawyers from others and neither appears relevant to the First Amendment. The ban on advertising serves to increase the difficulty of discovering the lowest cost seller of acceptable ability. As a result, to this extent attorneys are isolated from competition, and the inventive to price competitively is reduced. Although it is true that the effect of advertising on the price of services has not been demonstrated, there is revealing evidence with regard to products: where consumers have the benefit of price advertising, retail prices often are dramatically lower than they would be without advertising. It is entirely possible that advertising will serve to reduce, not advance, the cost of legal services to the consumer.

The entry-barrier argument is equally unpersuasive. In the absence of advertising, an attorney must rely on his contacts with the community to generate a flow of business. In view of the time necessary to develop such contacts, the ban in fact serves to perpetuate the market position of established attorneys. Consideration of entry-barrier problems would urge that advertising be allowed so as to aid the new competitor in penetrating the market.

5. *The Adverse Effect of Advertising on the Quality of Service.* It is argued that the attorney may advertise a given "package" of service at a set price, and will be inclined to provide, by indiscriminate use, the standard package regardless of whether it fits the client's needs … Even if advertising leads to the creation of "legal clinics" like that of appellants—clients that emphasize standardized procedures for routine problems—it is possible that such clinics will improve service by reducing the likelihood of error.

6. *The Difficulties of Enforcement.* Finally, it is argued that the wholesale restriction is justified by the problems of enforcement if any other course is taken. Because the public lacks sophistication in legal matters, it may be particularly susceptible to misleading or deceptive advertising by lawyers.

It is at least somewhat incongruous for the opponents of advertising to extol the virtues and altruism of the legal profession at one point, and, at another, to assert that its members will seize the opportunity to mislead and distort. We suspect that, with advertising, most lawyers will behave as they always have: They will abide by their solemn oaths to uphold the integrity and honor of their profession and of the legal system.

In sum, we are not persuaded that any of the proffered justifications rise to the level of an acceptable reason for the suppression of all advertising by attorneys. As with other varieties of speech, it follows as well that there may be reasonable restrictions on the time, place, and manner of advertising.

The constitutional issue in this case is only whether the State may prevent the publication in a newspaper of appellants' truthful advertisement concerning the availability and terms of routine legal services. We rule simply that the flow of such information may not be restrained, and we therefore hold the present application of the disciplinary rule against appellants to be violative of the First Amendment.

Reversed in favor of Plaintiff, Bates.

Critical Thinking About the Law

As you know, a judge's reasoning is not always clear. In the course of writing an opinion, a judge may discuss an assortment of topics. Your task, as a reader, is to organize those topics into a meaningful pattern and then locate the reasoning in the decision. Only then are you ready to think critically about the case. The following questions should help you better understand the reasoning in Case 8-2.

1. The Court clearly listed the reasons the State Bar of Arizona offered for restricting price advertising. Justice Blackmun evaluated those reasons. As critical thinkers, you realize that identifying the link between the conclusion and reasons is imperative. What reasons did the Court offer for allowing attorneys to advertise their prices?

   Clue: Remember that the Court concluded that, under the First Amendment, the state may not suppress advertising by attorneys. What reasons did Justice Blackmun use to reach this conclusion?

2. What primary ethical norm dominated the Court's consideration of the advertisement of prices for attorney services?

   Clue: Go back to the Court's examination of the reasons offered by the State Bar of Arizona. Look closely at Justice Blackmun's response to reason 3. Furthermore, consider the last two paragraphs of the opinion.

3. Suppose the State Bar of Arizona had introduced evidence that advertising causes the price of attorney's services to increase. Do you think Justice Blackmun would have come to a different conclusion? Why or why not?

   Clue: Look at the discussion of undesirable economic effects on advertising. Consider the primary ethical norm you identified in question 2. Do you think Justice Blackmun would consider this piece of evidence to be extremely persuasive?

SCHOOLS OF SOCIAL RESPONSIBILITY

Early in this chapter, the social responsibility of business was defined as concern by business about both its profit and its nonprofit activities and their intended and unintended impact on others. As you will see, theories of ethics and schools of social responsibility are not necessarily mutually exclusive. For example, the primary purpose of a steel company is to make a profit for its individual and institutional shareholders. The unintended effects of this company's actions might be that the surrounding community has polluted waters and homes are affected by ash that falls from the company's smokestack. Similarly, in the Union Carbide incident set out at the beginning of this chapter, the purpose of Union Carbide India Ltd. was to make a profit for its shareholders. By doing so, it was able to employ people. The unintended effect of this activity was a gas leak that killed approximately 2,000 people and injured many more. The question in both of these cases is, What responsibility, if any, do firms have for the unintended effects of their profit-seeking activity? This section of the chapter discusses five views of social responsibility that seek to answer that question: profit oriented, managerial, institutional, professional obligation, and regulation. Each of these schools reflects, or is an implementation of, the ethical values or culture of a corporation. The reader should analyze each, realizing, as in the case of ethical theories, that each has its strong advocates but that the "answer" may not lie in any one.

PROFIT-ORIENTED SCHOOL

The profit-oriented school of social responsibility begins with a market-oriented concept of the firm that most readers were exposed to in their first or second course in economics. Holders of this theory argue that business entities are distinct organizations in our society and their sole purpose is to increase profits for shareholders. Businesses are to be judged solely on criteria of economic efficiency and

TABLE 8-2

SCHOOLS OF SOCIAL RESPONSIBILITY

Profit-Oriented School	Business entities are distinct organizations in our society whose sole purpose is to increase profits for shareholders.
Managerial School	Advocates of this theory argue that business entities (particularly large ones) have a number of groups that they must deal with. They include not only stockholders but also employees, customers, activist groups, and government regulators, all of whom may make claims on the entities' resources.
Institutional School	Business entities have a responsibility to act in a manner that benefits all society.
Professional Obligation School	Business managers and members of boards of directors must be certified as "professionals" before they assume managerial responsibilities. They must have a responsibility to the public interest beyond making profits. The Sarbanes-Oxley Act (see Chapters 7 and 22) may be leading in that direction.
Regulation School	All business units are accountable to elected officials. See the Sarbanes-Oxley Act, as to dealing with independent financial audits (see Chapter 22).

how well they contribute to growth in productivity and technology. Corporate social responsibility is shown by managers who maximize profits for their shareholders, who, in turn, are able to reinvest such profits, providing for increased productivity, new employment opportunities, and increased consumption of goods. Classical economists, who advocate this position, recognize that there will be unintended effects of such profit-seeking activities (externalities) that affect society and cannot be incorporated into or passed on in the price of output. They would argue that this is the "social cost" of doing business. Such social costs are a collective responsibility of the government. Individual businesses should not be expected to voluntarily incorporate in their product's price the cost of cleaning up water or air, because this incorporation will distort the market mechanism and the efficient use of resources. Profit-seeking advocates argue that, when government needs to act in a collective manner, it should act in a way that involves the least interference with the efficiency of the market system, preferably through direct taxation.

In summary, efforts at pollution control, upgrading minority workers, and bringing equality of payment to the workforce are all tasks of government, not of the private sector, which is incapable of making such choices and is not elected in a democratic society to do so. Its sole responsibility is to seek profits for its shareholders. The accompanying box represents an important set of issues.

"Old Joe Camel" was adopted by R. J. Reynolds (RJR) in 1913 as the symbol for the brand Camel. In late 1990, RJR revived Old Joe with a new look in the form of a cartoon that appealed to young smokers.

In December 1991, the *Journal of the American Medical Association (JAMA)* published three surveys that found the cartoon character Joe Camel reached children very effectively.[15] Of children between ages 3 and 6 who were surveyed, 51.1 percent of them recognized Old Joe Camel as being associated with Camel cigarettes. The 6-year-olds were as familiar with Joe Camel as they were with the Mickey Mouse logo for the Disney Channel.

An RJR spokeswoman claimed that "just because children can identify our logo doesn't mean they will use our product." Since the introduction of Joe Camel, however, Camel's share of the under-18 market has climbed to 33 percent from 5 percent. Among 18–24-year-olds, Camel's market share has climbed to 7.9 percent from 4.4 percent.

The Centers for Disease Control reported in March 1992 that smokers between ages 12 and 18 preferred Marlboro, Newport, or Camel cigarettes, the three brands with the most extensive advertising.[16]

Teenagers throughout the country were wearing Joe Camel T-shirts. Brown & Williamson, the producer of Kool cigarettes, began testing a cartoon character for its ads, a penguin wearing sunglasses and Day-Glo sneakers. Company spokesman Joseph Helewicz stated that the ads were geared to smokers between 21 and 35 years old. Helewicz added that cartoon advertisements for adults were not new and cited the Pillsbury Doughboy and the Pink Panther as effective advertising images.

In mid-1992, then–Surgeon General Novella, along with the American Medical Association, began a campaign called "Dump the Hump" to pressure the tobacco industry to stop ad campaigns that teach kids to smoke. In 1993, the FTC staff recommended a ban on the Joe Camel ads. In 1994, then–Surgeon General Joycelyn

---

[15] K. Deveny, "Joe Camel Ads Reach Children," *Wall Street Journal*, December 11, 1991, p. B-1.
[16] *Id.*

Elders blamed the tobacco industry's $4 billion in ads for increased smoking rates among teens. RJR's tobacco division chief, James W. Johnston, responded, "I'll be damned if I'll pull the ads." RJR put together a team of lawyers and others it referred to as in-house censors to control Joe's influence. A campaign to have Joe wear a bandana was nixed, as was one for a punker Joe with pink hair.

In 1994, RJR CEO James Johnston testified before a congressional panel on the Joe Camel controversy and stated, "We do not market to children and will not," and added, "We do not survey anyone under the age of 18."

Internal documents about targeting young people were damaging. A 1981 RJR internal memo on marketing surveys cautioned research personnel to tally underage smokers as "age 18." A 1981 Philip Morris internal document indicated information about smoking habits in children as young as 15 was important because "today's teenager is tomorrow's potential regular customer." Other Philip Morris documents from the 1980s expressed concerns that Marlboro sales would soon decline because teenage smoking rates were falling.

A 1987 marketing survey in France and Canada by RJR before it launched the Joe Camel campaign showed that the cartoon image with its fun and humor attracted attention. One 1987 internal document used the phrase "young adult smokers" and noted a campaign targeted at the competition's "male Marlboro smokers ages 13–24."

A 1997 survey of 534 teens by *USA Today* revealed the following:

Ad	Have Seen Ad	Liked Ad
Joe Camel	95%	65%
Marlboro Man	94%	44%
Budweiser Frogs	99%	92%

Marlboro was the brand smoked by most teens in the survey. The survey found 28 percent of teens between ages 13 and 18 smoked—an increase of 4 percent since 1991. In 1987, Camels were the cigarette of choice for 3 percent of teenagers when Joe Camel debuted. By 1993, the figure had climbed to 16 percent.

In early 1990, the Federal Trade Commission (FTC) began an investigation of RJR and its Joe Camel ads to determine whether underage smokers were illegally targeted by the ten-year Joe Camel Campaign. The FTC had dismissed a complaint in 1994 but did not have the benefits of the newly discovered internal memos.

In late 1997, RJR began phasing out Joe Camel. New Camel ads featured healthy-looking men and women in their twenties, in clubs and swimming pools, with just a dromedary logo somewhere in the ad. RJR also vowed not to feature the Joe Camel character on nontobacco items such as T-shirts. The cost of the abandonment was estimated at $250 million.

Philip Morris proposed its own plan to halt youth smoking in 1996, which included no vending machine ads, no billboard ads, no tobacco ads in magazines with 25 percent or more youth subscribers, and limits on sponsorships to events (rodeos, motor sports) where 75 percent or more of attendees were adults.

In 1998, combined pressure from Congress, the state attorneys general, and ongoing class action suits produced what came to be known as "the tobacco settlement." In addition to payment of $206 billion, the tobacco settlement in all of its various forms bars outdoor advertising, the use of human images (Marlboro man) and cartoon characters (Joe Camel), and vending-machine sales. This portion of the settlement was advocated by those who were concerned about teenagers and their attraction to cigarettes via these ads and their availability in machines.

MANAGERIAL SCHOOL

Advocates of the managerial school of social responsibility argue that businesses, particularly large institutions, have a number of interest groups or constituents both internally and externally that they must deal with regularly, not just stockholders and a board of directors. A business has employees, customers, suppliers, consumers, activist groups, government regulators, and others that influence decision making and the ability of the entity to make profits. In effect, modern managers must balance conflicting claims on their time and the company's resources. Employees want better wages, working conditions, and pensions; suppliers want prompt payment for their goods; and consumers want higher-quality goods at lower prices. These often conflicting demands lead advocates of a managerial theory of social responsibility to argue that the firm must have the trust of all groups, both internal and external. Thus, it must have clear ethical standards and a sense of social responsibility for its unintended acts in order to maximize profits and to survive in the short and long run. A firm that seeks to maximize short-run profits and ignores the claims of groups, whether they be unions, consumer activists, or government regulators, will not be able to survive in the complex environment that business operates in.

If one reviews the Union Carbide India Ltd. incident described earlier, it is clear that the explosion in Bhopal, India, had at least three consequences: (1) It precipitated an attempt by GAF to take over the company. (2) Union Carbide made a successful but costly attempt to fight off this takeover. (3) The value of the stock decreased and, thus, the investors suffered large losses. Advocates of managerial theory would point to the investors' trust in management's ability to deal with this disaster as being important to how the market evaluated Union Carbide's stock. They also would argue that the management of Johnson & Johnson took decisive action in dealing with the poison in its Tylenol product and was, thus, perceived by investors and customers as being trustworthy.[17] As a result its stock value recovered relatively quickly.

In this case, see the conflicting claims of stakeholders.

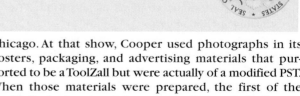

CASE 8-3

Cooper Industries v. Leatherman Tool Group, Inc.
United States Supreme Court
121 S.Ct. 1678 (2001)

Leatherman (plaintiff) sued Cooper (defendant) in federal district court for unfair competition. Leatherman Tool Group, Inc., manufactured and sold a multifunctional tool called the PST that improved on the classic Swiss army knife. Leatherman dominated the market for multifunctional pocket tools. In 1995, Cooper Industries, Inc., decided to design and sell a competing multifunctional tool under the name "ToolZall." Cooper introduced the ToolZall in August 1996 at the National Hardware Show in Chicago. At that show, Cooper used photographs in its posters, packaging, and advertising materials that purported to be a ToolZall but were actually of a modified PST. When those materials were prepared, the first of the ToolZalls had not yet been manufactured. A Cooper employee created a ToolZall "mock-up" by grinding the Leatherman trademark from a PST and substituting the unique fastenings that were to be used on the ToolZall. At least one of the photographs was retouched to remove a

---

[17] See M. Krikorian, "Ethical Conduct: An Aid to Management," Address at Albion College, Albion, Mich., April 16, 1985.

curved indention, where the Leatherman trademark had been. The photographs were used, not only at the trade show, but also in marketing materials and catalogs used by Cooper's sales force throughout the United States.

The lower court found for Leatherman in the amount of $50,000 in compensatory damages and $4.5 million in punitive damages.

Cooper appealed to the court of appeals, which affirmed the lower court seeing no "abuse of discretion" by the lower court as to punitive damages. Cooper appealed to the U.S. Supreme Court petitioning for a de novo review of the facts as to the size of the punitive damages.

Justice Stevens

Although compensatory damages and punitive damages are typically awarded at the same time by the same decision maker, they serve distinct purposes. The former are intended to redress the concrete loss that the plaintiff has suffered by reason of the defendant's wrongful conduct. The latter, which have been described as "quasi-criminal," operate as private fines intended to punish the defendant and to deter future wrongdoing. A jury's assessment of the extent of a plaintiff's injury is essentially a factual determination, whereas its imposition of punitive damages is an expression of its moral condemnation. The question whether a fine is constitutionally excessive calls for the application of a constitutional standard to the facts of a particular case, and in this context de novo review of that question is appropriate.

Reversed and *remanded* based on a de no standard in favor of Cooper, to determining whether the punitive damage award is excessive.

INSTITUTIONAL SCHOOL

Advocates of an institutional school of social responsibility for business argue that business entities have a responsibility to act in a manner that benefits all of society just as churches, unions, courts, universities, and governments have. Whether a single proprietorship, a partnership, or a corporation, a business is a legal entity in our society that must be held responsible for its activities. Proponents of this theory argue that the same civil and criminal sanctions should be applied to business activities that injure the social fabric of a society (e.g., the pollution of water and air) as are applied to acts of individuals and of other institutions. When managers fail to deal adequately with "externalities," they should be held accountable not only to their board of directors but also to government enforcement authorities and individual citizens as well.

PROFESSIONAL OBLIGATION SCHOOL

Advocates of a professional obligation school of social responsibility state that business managers and members of boards of directors should be certified as "professionals" before they can assume managerial responsibility. In our discussion of professional ethical codes, we defined professionals as persons having (1) educational entrance requirements and continuing-education standards, (2) licensing-exam requirements, (3) codes of conduct that are enforced, (4) a formal association that meets regularly, and (5) an independent commitment to the public interest. Advocates of a professional obligation theory argue that business directors and managers, like doctors and lawyers, have a responsibility to the public beyond merely making profits and that the public must be able to be sure that they are qualified to hold their positions. They should be licensed by meeting university requirements and passing a state or national test. They should be subject to a disciplinary code that could involve revocation or suspension of their license to "practice the management of a business" if they are found by state or national boards to have failed to meet their codified responsibilities. Such responsibilities would include accountability for the unintended effects of their profit-making activities (externalities).

REGULATION SCHOOL

A regulation school of social responsibility sees all business units as accountable to elected public officials. Proponents of this theory argue that, because business managers are responsible only to a board of directors that represents shareholders, the corporation cannot be trusted to act in a socially responsible manner. If society is to be protected from the unintended effects of profit-making business activities (e.g., pollution, sex discrimination in the workplace, and injuries to workers), it is necessary for government to be involved. The degree of government involvement is much debated by advocates of this theory. Some would argue in the extreme for a socialist state. Others argue for government representatives on boards of directors, and still others argue that government should set up standards of socially responsible conduct for each industry. The last group advocates an annual process of reporting conduct, both socially responsible and otherwise, similar to the independent financial audits required now by the SEC of all publicly registered firms. The growth of ethics offices within corporations has played a role in dealing with ethical and legal problems. Sometimes these offices are mandated by courts when sentencing takes place in white-collar criminal cases. Often corporations set up such offices as preventive measures.

GLOBAL DIMENSIONS OF ETHICS AND SOCIAL RESPONSIBILITY

Code of Conduct for Transnational Corporations. A United Nations effort to prevent misconduct by transnational corporations has been promulgated. Four objectives include:

1. *Respect for national sovereignty in countries where such companies operate.* Often transnational companies operate in developing nations where governments are less stable and more corrupt, making this goal very difficult to carry out.

2. *Adherence to sociocultural values.* The code seeks to prevent transnational companies from imposing value systems that are detrimental to those of the host country.

3. *Respect for human rights.* Companies should not discriminate on the basis of race, color, sex, religion, language, political, or other opinion. In developing nations this sometimes is very difficult when the host country does discriminate based on some of these factors.

4. *Abstention from corrupt practices.* Transnational corporations shall refrain from the offering, promising, or giving of any payment, gift, or other advantage to a public official, or refraining from performing a duty in accordance with a business transaction.

Corruption is endemic to many developing countries and a way of doing business. The United States has set forth one approach and the Organization for Economic and Cultural Development another. See Chapter 22 for a discussion of the Foreign Corrupt Practices Act of 1977 as amended in 1988 and the International Securities Enforcement Cooperation Act of 1990 (OECD).

SUMMARY

We have sought to define ethics and social responsibility within the context of business associations. We examined consequential theories of ethics based on the consequences of the company's actions. In contrast, deontology schools of ethics are based on duties. Humanist theories of ethics evaluate actions as good or bad based on how the actions improved inherent human capacities. Codes of ethics emanating from businesses and professions were also examined. Five schools of social responsibility based on the unintended effects of corporate and human conduct were examined. Finally, global dimensions of ethical and socially responsible conduct are highlighted with an examination of the United Nations' Code of Conduct for Transnational Corporations.

REVIEW QUESTIONS

8-1 Define the humanist theory of ethics. On the basis of this theory and a reading of the *Union Carbide* case synopsis, do you think that Union Carbide acted ethically after the Bhopal, India, incident? Explain.

8-2 List the differing views on whether corporations should act in a socially responsible manner. Explain each one.

8-3 How are professional codes of ethics different from individual codes? Explain.

8-4 What actions are typically forbidden by corporate codes? Explain.

8-5 Why are industry ethical codes not generally effective? Explain.

REVIEW PROBLEMS

8-6 A, a middle-level manager of Drug Company X, has been told by her boss, B, to change some figures on the percentage of rats that died as a result of injections of a new drug that will need Food and Drug Administration approval. The percentage of animals that died in the testing will need to be reported as lower, she is told. A is the single mother of two children and makes $65,000 a year. Choose one ethical theory outlined in the chapter and, on the basis of that theory, advise A what to do.

8-7 B knows that 200 percent cost overruns exist because of the negligence of the management of Company Y in carrying out a federal government contract to build an airplane. He works in the comptroller's office and has been told by his boss to "keep his mouth shut" when the auditors from the General Accounting Office (a government agency) come. He is told that there will be "severe consequences" if he does not keep quiet. He earns $65,000 annually and is the father of three children attending private colleges. His wife works at home but is not compensated. Select a single ethical theory and advise B what he should do.

8-8 C, a student at University Z, learns a method of bypassing the telephone system to make free telephone calls. C tells his roommate, D. How would you advise D to act on the basis of one of the ethical theories discussed in this chapter?

8-9 You are hiring a new manager for your department. You have several good applicants. Assume that the one who is best suited for the job in training and experience has also been found to have done one of the things listed below. How would knowing what the person has done affect your decision? Would your answer be the same regardless of which theory of ethical thought you applied? Examine each factual situation below and explain how your answer is affected.

    (a) The individual listed on his résumé that he had an M.B.A. from Rutgers. He does not have an M.B.A.

    (b) The individual listed that his prior salary was $40,000. The prior salary was actually $43,000.

8-10 You are a purchasing manager for Alphs Corporation. You are responsible for buying two $1 million generators. Your company has a written policy prohibiting any company buyer from receiving a gratuity in excess of $50 and requiring that all gratuities be reported. The company has no policy regarding whistle-blowing. A salesperson for a generator manufacturer offers to arrange it so that you can buy a $20,000 car for $7,000. The car would be bought from a third party. You decline the offer. Do you now report it to your superior? To the salesperson's superior? How would the various schools of social responsibility influence your decision? Pick one school to justify your decision. Explain.

8-11 You are a lab technician for the Standard Ethical Drug Company. You run tests on animals and prepare a summary that is then doctored by your superior to make a drug appear safe when in fact it is not. Your supervisor determines your salary and has significant influence on whether you retain the job. You are the sole source of support of your two children, have no close relative to help you, and are just making it financially. Jobs equivalent to yours are difficult to find. You are convinced that if the company markets the drug, the risk of cancer to the drug users will increase significantly. The drug provides significant relief for hemorrhoids. What will you do? Which school of social responsibility would be the basis for your decision. Explain.

CASE PROBLEMS

8-12 Combs worked for AT&T for ten years, from 1979 through 1989, in the Phoenix area. Combs hurt her back while lifting a heavy mail sack. Thereafter, the AT&T doctors restricted her to lifting no more than 10 to 15 pounds. Despite this restriction, her supervisor insisted that she do the same work as all other employees in the mailroom. Combs refused to lift more than 15 pounds, and her supervisor treated this refusal as a resignation by Combs. Combs was denied unemployment benefits because she had "resigned" her job "voluntarily." Should Combs be entitled to unemployment benefits? Did she resign or was she fired? If she was fired, was the firing proper or improper? *Combs v. Board of Review*, 636 A. 2d 122 (1994).

8-13 Richard and Suzanne Weinstein owned Elm City Cheese Company. Elm City sold its products to three major customers that used the cheese as a "filler" to blend into their cheeses. In 1982, Mark Federico, a certified public accountant, became Elm City's accountant and the Weinsteins' personal accountant. Federico's duties went beyond typical accounting work, and when the Weinsteins were absent, Federico was put in charge of operations. In 1992, Federico was made a vice president of the company, and a year later he was placed in charge of day-to-day operations. He also continued to serve as Elm City's accountant. He resigned as Elm City's employee and as its accountant in 1995. Less than two years later, Federico opened Lomar Foods, Inc., to make the same products as Elm City by the same process and to sell the products to the same customers. Federico located Lomar closer to Elm City's suppliers. Elm City filed a suit in a Connecticut state court against Federico and Lomar, alleging, among other things, misappropriation of trade secrets. Elm City argued that it was entitled to punitive damages because Federico's conduct was "willful and malicious." Federico responded in part that he did not act willfully and maliciously because he did not know that Elm City's business details were trade secrets. Were Federico's actions "willful and malicious"? Were they ethical? Explain. *Elm City Cheese Company v. Federico*, 251 Conn. 59 (1999).

8-14 The Johns-Manville Corporation made a variety of building and other products. It was a major producer of asbestos, which was used for insulation in buildings. It has been medically proven that excessive exposure to asbestos causes asbestosis, a fatal lung disease. Thousands of employees of the company and consumers who were exposed to asbestos and contracted this fatal disease sued the company for damages.

As a response, the company filed for reorganization bankruptcy. It argued that if it did not, an otherwise viable company that provided thousands of jobs and served a useful purpose in this country would be destroyed, and that without the declaration of bankruptcy a few of the plaintiffs who first filed their lawsuits would win awards of millions of dollars, leaving nothing for the remainder of the plaintiffs. Under the bankruptcy court's protection, the company was restructured to survive. As part of the release from bankruptcy, the company contributed money to a fund to pay current and future claimants. The fund is not large enough to pay all injured persons the full amount of their claims.

Was is ethical for Johns-Manville to declare bankruptcy? [*In re Johns-Manville Corporation*, 36 B.R. 727 (B.C.S.D.N.Y. 1984)] Select a school of social responsibility that the board of directors may use to rationalize its conduct in declaring bankruptcy. Explain.

8-15 Richard Fraser was an "exclusive career insurance agent" under a contract with Nationwide Mutual Insurance Co. Fraser leased computer hardware and software from Nationwide for his business. During a dispute between Nationwide and the Nationwide Insurance Independent Contractors Association, an organization representing Fraser and other exclusive career agents, Fraser prepared a letter to Nationwide competitors asking whether they were interested in acquiring the represented agents' policyholders. Nationwide obtained a copy of the letter and searched its electronic file server for e-mail indicating that the letter had been sent. It found a stored e-mail that Fraser had sent to a coworker indicating that the letter had been sent to at least one competitor. The e-mail was retrieved from the coworker's file of already received and discarded messages stored on the receiver. When Nationwide canceled its contract with Fraser, he filed a suit in a federal district court against the firm, alleging, among other things, violations of various federal laws that prohibit the interception of electronic communications during transmission. Had Nationwide acted ethically in retrieving the e-mail? Which school of socially responsible conduct did Richard Fraser represent in his conduct? Explain. Which school did Nationwide represent? Explain. *Fraser v.*

Nationwide Mutual Insurance Co., 135 F.Supp.3d 623 (E.D.Pa 2001).

8-16 Charles Zandford was a securities broker for Prudential Securities, Inc., in Annapolis, Maryland. In 1987, he persuaded William Wood, an elderly man in poor health, to open a joint investment account for himself and his mentally retarded daughter. The stated investment objectives for the account were "safety of principal and income." The Woods gave Zandford discretion to manage their account and to engage in transactions for their benefit without prior approval. Relying on Zandford's promise to "conservatively invest" their money, the Woods entrusted him with $419,255. Zandford immediately began writing checks to himself on the account. Paying the checks required selling securities in the account. Before William's death in 1991, all of the money was gone. Zandford was convicted of wire fraud and sentenced to more than four years in prison. The Securities and Exchange Commission (SEC) filed a suit in a federal district court against Zandford, alleging in part misappropriation of $343,000 of the Woods' securities and seeking disgorgement of that amount. Which theory of ethics did Zanford represent? Explain. Which theory of ethics did the SEC represent? Explain. *SEC v. Zandford*, 535 U.S. 813 (2002).

ASSIGNMENT ON THE INTERNET

This chapter introduces you to three theories of ethical thought and five schools of social responsibility. Explore how the three theories of ethical thought are put into practice. Using the Internet, find the code of ethics for a business or corporation that does business in your city or town. This site provides links to codes of ethics for hundreds of corporations: **www.business-ethics.com**.

Applying your critical thinking skills, determine if the code of ethics chosen relies more heavily on one theory of ethical thought than the others. Are there aspects of that business's code of ethics that you would like to see changed? Why?

 ## ON THE INTERNET

www.business-ethics.com This site provides codes of ethics from hundreds of corporations and articles detailing current trends or methods of bringing ethics into the business environment.
ethics.acusd.edu/index.html Ethics Updates is designed primarily to be used by ethics instructors and their students. It is intended to provide updates on current literature.
www.legalethics.com This comprehensive ethics page provides numerous hotlinks to other valuable Web sites.
www.ethicsweb.ca/resources/business/institutions.html This site contains links to numerous business ethics centers and institutions, as well as business ethics consultants.
www.mapnp.org/library/ethics/ethics.htm#anchor1419177 This site provides information on managing ethics in the workplace. A number of links also address the social responsibility of a business.
www.globalethics.org The Web site for the Global Ethics Institute provides information about business ethics from countries around the world.

9

THE INTERNATIONAL LEGAL ENVIRONMENT OF BUSINESS

 **DIMENSIONS OF THE INTERNATIONAL ENVIRONMENT OF BUSINESS**

METHODS OF ENGAGING IN INTERNATIONAL BUSINESS

RISKS OF ENGAGING IN INTERNATIONAL BUSINESS

LEGAL AND ECONOMIC INTEGRATION AS A MEANS OF ENCOURAGING INTERNATIONAL BUSINESS ACTIVITY

GLOBAL DISPUTE RESOLUTION

At the outset of Chapter 2, we noted that U.S. managers can no longer afford to view their firms as doing business on a huge island between the Pacific and Atlantic oceans. Existing and pending multilateral trade agreements open vast opportunities to do business in Europe and Asia, throughout the Americas, and indeed throughout the world. If present and future U.S. managers do not become aware of these opportunities, as well as the attendant risks, they and their firms will be at a competitive disadvantage vis-à-vis foreign competitors from all over the world.

This chapter (1) introduces the international environment of business; (2) sets forth the methods by which companies may engage in international business; (3) indicates the risks involved in such engagement; (4) describes organizations that work to bring down tariff barriers and, thus, encourage companies of all nations to engage in international business; and (5) indicates the means by which disputes between companies doing business in the international arena are settled. Please note carefully that when we use the word *companies* in an international context, we are referring not only to private sector firms but also to nation-state subsidized entities and government agencies that act like private sector companies.

═ Critical Thinking About the Law ═

Because of the widespread international opportunities and advances in communication, business managers must be aware of the global legal environment of business. As you will soon learn, the political, economic, cultural, and legal dimensions are all important international business considerations. The following questions will help sharpen your critical thinking about the international legal environment of business.

1. Consider the number of countries that might participate in an international business agreement. Why might ambiguity be a particularly important concern in international business?

   Clue: Consider the variety of cultures as well as the differences in languages. How might these factors affect business agreements?

2. Why might the critical thinking questions about ethical norms and missing information be important for international businesses?

   Clue: Again, consider the variety of cultures involved in international business. Why might identifying the primary ethical norms of a culture be helpful?

3. What ethical norm might influence the willingness to enter into agreements with foreign companies?

   Clue: How might international agreements differ from agreements between two U.S. companies?

DIMENSIONS OF THE INTERNATIONAL ENVIRONMENT OF BUSINESS

Doing international business has political, economic, cultural, and legal dimensions. Although this chapter emphasizes the legal dimensions of international business transactions, business managers need to be aware of those other important dimensions as well. (Ethical dimensions were examined in Chapter 8.)

POLITICAL DIMENSIONS

Managers of firms doing international business must deal with different types of governments, ranging from democracies to totalitarian states. They are concerned with the stability of these governments and with whether economic decisions are centralized or decentralized. In the Marxist form of government, such as existed in the former Soviet Union and in Eastern Europe until recent years, economic decisions were centralized and there was political stability. This would seem to be an ideal environment in which to do business from a multinational business manager's perspective. But it was not ideal, because a centralized economy limits the supply of goods coming from outside a country, the price that can be charged for goods inside the country, and the amount of currency that can be taken out of the country by multinational businesses.

In 1998, 88 of the world's 191 countries were categorized as "free" in the sense that they were perceived as having high political and civil liberties (e.g., Australia, Belgium, Luxembourg, Finland, and the United States, to name a few). Fifty-three countries were classified as "partly free" because they enjoyed limited political rights and civil liberties (e.g., Egypt, China, Ethiopia, and North Korea).[1] A trend toward democratization seems to be under way. The percentages of the total population living in free, partly free, and not free conditions in recent years are as follows:[2]

	1990	*1998*	*2003*
Free	38.9	21.7	41.4
Partly Free	21.8	39.1	23.2
Not Free	19.0	39.2	35.4

Despite the collapse of communism and the development of new political systems professing support of free enterprise in Eastern Europe and throughout the former Soviet Union, companies in the industrialized nations have delayed investing in most of these areas because they are uncertain of their political stability and willingness to adhere to economic agreements. The situation is similar in China, where an early rush to invest has been slowed by foreign companies' experiences with a seemingly capricious government. For example, McDonald's leased a prime location in Beijing from the centralized government but found itself ousted a few years later when the government revoked the lease in order to allow a department store to be built on that site. Moreover, doubts about the Chinese government's intention to honor its agreement with the British government that Hong Kong will retain its separate political and economic status for 50 years after the 99-year British lease expired in 1997 has led one longtime Hong Kong trading company, Jardine, to move its headquarters to the Bahamas.

ECONOMIC DIMENSIONS

Every business manager should do a country analysis before doing business in another nation-state. Such an analysis not only examines political variables but also dissects a nation's economic performance as demonstrated in its rate of economic growth, inflation, budget, and trade balance. There are four economic factors that especially affect business investment:

1. *Differences in size and economic growth rate of various nation-states.* For example, when McDonald's decided to engage in international business, the company initially located its restaurants only in countries that already had high growth rates. As more and more developing nations moved toward a market economy, McDonald's expanded into Russia, China, Brazil, Mexico, and other countries deemed to have potentially high growth rates.

2. *The impact of central planning versus a market economy on the availability of supplies.* When McDonald's went into Russia, it had to build its own food-processing center to be certain it would get the quality of beef it needed. Furthermore, because of distribution problems, it used its own trucks to move supplies.

3. *The availability of disposable income.* This is a tricky issue. Despite the fact that the price of a Big Mac, french fries, and a soft drink equals the average Russian worker's pay for four hours of work, McDonald's is serving thousands of customers a day at its Moscow restaurant.

4. *The existence of an appropriate transportation infrastructure.* Decent roads, railroads, and ports are needed to bring in supplies and then to transport

---

[1] Adrian Karatnycky, "Freedom Gains," *San Diego Union Tribune*, December 27, 1998, p. 61.

[2] Adrian Karatnycky, *Freedom in the World* (New York: Freedom House, 2002), p. 6.

them within the host country. McDonald's experience in Russia is common-place. Multinational businesses face transportation problems in many developing countries.

The World Bank classifies economies into one of the following categories according to per capita GNP:[3]

Low Income	755 or less
Middle Income	756–9,265
High Income	9,266 or more

CULTURAL DIMENSIONS

Culture may be defined as learned norms of a society that are based on values, beliefs, and attitudes. For example, if people of the same area speak the same language (e.g., Spanish in most of Latin America, with the exception of Brazil and a few small nations), the area is often said to be culturally homogeneous. Religion is a strong builder of common values. In 1995, the Iranian government outlawed the selling and use of satellite communications in Iran on the grounds that they presented "decadent" Western values that were undermining Muslim religious values.

A failure to understand that some cultures are based on ascribed group membership (gender, family, age, or ethnic affiliation) rather than on acquired group membership (religious, political, professional, or other associations), as in the West, can lead to business mistakes. For example, gender- and family-based affiliations are very important in Saudi Arabia, where a strict interpretation of Islam prevents women from playing a major role in business. Most Saudi women who work hold jobs that demand little or no contact with men, such as teaching or acting as doctors only for women.

culture The learned norms of a society that are based on values, beliefs, and attitudes.

Linking Law & Business

Global Business

Your management class may have discussed the growing trend of globalization. One level of an organization's involvement in the international arena is the multinational corporation. There are three basic types of employees in multinational corporations: (1) expatriates—employees living and working in a country where they are not citizens; (2) host-country nationals—employees who live and work in a country where the international organization is headquartered; (3) third-country nationals—employees who are expatriates in a country (working in one country and having citizenship in another), while the international organization is located in another country. Typically, organizations with a global focus employ workers from all three categories. However, the use of host-country nationals is increasing, considering the cost of training and relocating expatriates and third-country nationals. By hiring more host-country nationals, managers may spend less time and money training employees to adapt to new cultures, languages, and laws in foreign countries. In addition, managers may avoid potential problems related to sending employees to work in countries where they do not have citizenship or understand the culture; thus, managers may still obtain organizational objectives through cheaper and respectable means by hiring a greater number of host-country nationals.

Source: S. Certo, *Modern Management* (Upper Saddle River, N.J.: Prentice Hall, 2000), pp. 78, 84–85.

---

[3] *The World Bank Atlas, 2003,* (Washington, D.C.: The World Bank, 2002).

Another important cultural factor is the attitude toward work. Mediterranean and Latin American cultures base their group affiliation on family and place more emphasis on leisure than on work. We often say that the Protestant ethic, stressing the virtues of hard work and thrift, is prevalent in Western and other industrialized nations. Yet the Germans refuse to work more than 35 hours a week and take 28 days of paid vacation every year. The average hourly wage is higher in Germany than in the United States, and German workers' benefits far outpace those of U.S. workers.

Business managers must carefully consider language, religion, attitudes toward work and leisure, family versus individual reliance, and numerous other cultural values when planning to do business in another nation-state. They also need to find a method of reconciling cultural differences between people and companies from their own nation-state and those from the country in which they intend to do business.

LEGAL DIMENSIONS

Business managers have to be guided both by the national legal system of their own country and the host country and by international law when they venture into foreign territory.

National Legal Systems. When deciding whether to do business in a certain country, business managers are advised to learn about the legal system of that country and its potential impact in such areas as contracts, investment, and corporate law. The five major families of law are (1) common law, (2) Romano-Germanic civil law, (3) Islamic law, (4) socialist law, and (5) Hindu law (Table 9-1).

The common-law family is most familiar to companies doing business in the United States, England, and 26 former British colonies. The source of law is primarily case law, and decisions rely heavily on case precedents. As statutory law has become more prominent in common-law countries, the courts' interpretation

TABLE 9-1

FAMILIES OF NATIONAL LAW AND HOW THEY AFFECT INTERNATIONAL BUSINESS

Family	Characteristics
Common law	Primary reliance is on case law and precedent instead of statutory law. Courts can declare statutory law unconstitutional.
Romano-Germanic civil law	Primary reliance is on codes and statutory law rather than case law. In general, the high court cannot declare laws of parliament unconstitutional (an exception is the German Constitutional Court).
Islamic law	Derived from the *Shari'a*, a code of rules designed to govern the daily lives of all Muslims.
Socialist law	Based on the teachings of Karl Marx. No private property is recognized. Law encourages the collectivization of property and the means of production and seeks to guarantee national security. According to classical Marxist theory, both the law and the state will fade away as people are better educated to socialism and advance toward the ultimate stage of pure communism.
Hindu law	Derived from the *Sastras*. Hindu law governs the behavior of people in each caste (hereditary categories that restrict members' occupations and social associations). Primarily concerned with family matters and succession. Has been codified into India's national legal system.

of laws made by legislative bodies and of regulations set forth by administrative agencies has substantially increased the body of common law.

Countries that follow the Romano-Germanic civil law (e.g., France, Germany, and Sweden) organize their legal systems around legal codes rather than around cases, regulations, and precedents, as do common-law countries. Thus, judges in civil-law countries of Europe, Latin America, and Asia resolve disputes primarily by reference to general provisions of codes and secondarily by reference to statutes passed by legislative bodies. However, as the body of written opinions in civil-law countries grows, and as they adopt computer-based case and statutory systems such as Westlaw and Lexis, the highest courts in these countries are taking greater note of case law in their decisions. Civil-law systems tend to put great emphasis on private law, that is, law that governs relationships between individuals and corporations or between individuals. Examples are the law of obligations, which includes common-law contracts, torts, and creditor–debtor relationships. In contrast to common-law systems, civil-law systems have an inferior public law: This is law that governs the relationships between individuals and the state. In fact, their jurists are not extensively trained in such areas as criminal, administrative, and labor law.[4]

More than 600 million Muslims in approximately 30 countries that are predominantly Muslim, as well as many more Muslims living in countries where Islam is a minority religion, are governed by Islamic law.[5] In many countries, Islamic law, as encoded in the *Shari'a*, exists alongside the secular law. In nations that have adopted Islamic law as their dominant legal system (e.g., Saudi Arabia), citizens must obey the *Shari'a*, and anyone who transgresses its rules is punished by a court. International business transactions are affected in many ways by Islamic law. For example, earning interest on money is forbidden, though a way around this stricture can be found be setting up Islamic banks that, in lieu of paying interest on accounts, pay each depositor a share of the profits made by the bank.

Socialist-law systems are based on the teachings of Karl Marx and Vladimir Lenin (who was, incidentally, a lawyer). Right after the Bolshevik Revolution of 1917 in Russia, the Czarist legal system, which was based on the Romano-Germanic civil law, was replaced by a legal system consisting of People's Courts staffed by members of the Communist Party and peasant workers. By the early 1930s, this system had been replaced by a formal legal system with civil and criminal codes that has lasted to this day. The major goals of the Soviet legal system, were: (1) to encourage collectivization of the economy; (2) to educate the masses as to the wisdom of socialist law; and (3) to maintain national security.[6] Most property belonged to the state, particularly industrial and agricultural property. Personal (not private) property existed, but it could be used only for the satisfaction and needs of the individual, not for profit—which was referred to as "speculation" and was in violation of socialist law. Personal ownership ended either with the death of the individual or with revocation of the legal use and enjoyment of the property. Socialist law is designed to preserve the authority of the state over agricultural land and all means of production. It is still enforced in North Korea, Cuba, and to some degree, Libya, but the countries that made up the old Soviet Union and the East European bloc have been moving toward Romano-Germanic civil-law systems and private-market economies in the last decade.

---

[4] Id. at 437–438.

[5] Id. at 437–438.

[6] Id. at 176–179.

Hindu law, called *Sharmasastra*, is linked to the revelations of the Vedas, a collection of Indian religious songs and prayers believed to have been written between 100 B.C. and A.D. 300 or 400.[7] It is both personal and religious. Hindus are divided into social categories called castes, and the rules governing their behavior are set out in texts known as *Sastras*. The primary concerns of Hindu law are family matters and property succession. Four-fifths of all Hindus live in India; most of the remaining Hindus are spread throughout Southeast Asia and Africa, with smaller numbers living in Europe and the Americas. After gaining independence from England in 1950, India codified Hindu law. Today it plays a prominent role in Indian law alongside secular statutory law, which, especially in the areas of business and trade, uses legal terminology and concepts derived from common law. Both the Indian criminal and civil codes strongly reflect the British common-law tradition.[8] The Civil code is important when outsourcing, and intellectual property law are discussed.

public international law
Law that governs the relationships between nation-states.

private international law
Law that governs the relationships between private parties involved in international transactions. Includes international business law.

International Law. The law that governs the relationships between nation-states is known as **public international law**. **Private international law** governs the relationships between private parties involved in transactions across national borders. In most cases, the parties negotiate between themselves and set out their agreements in a written document. In some cases, however, nation-states subsidize the private parties or are signators to the agreements negotiated by those parties. In such instances, the distinction between private and public international law is blurred.

The sources of international law can be found in (1) custom; (2) treaties between nations, particularly treaties of friendship and commerce; (3) judicial decisions of international courts such as the International Court of Justice; (4) decision of national and regional courts such as the U.S. Supreme Court, the London Commercial Court, and the European Court of Justice; (5) scholarly writings; and (6) international organizations. These sources will be discussed throughout this text.

International business law includes laws governing (1) exit visas and work permits; (2) tax and antitrust matters and contracts; (3) patents, trademarks, and copyrights; (4) bilateral treaties of commerce and friendship between nations and multilateral treaties of commerce such as the North American Free Trade Agreement (NAFTA), the European Union (EU), and the World Trade Organization (WTO). All will be explored later in this chapter.

METHODS OF ENGAGING IN INTERNATIONAL BUSINESS

For purposes of this chapter, methods of engaging in international business are classified as (1) trade, (2) international licensing and franchising, and (3) foreign direct investment.

TRADE

international trade The export of goods and services from a country and the import of goods and services into a country.

We define **international trade** generally as exporting goods and services from a country and importing the same into a country. There are two traditional theories of trade relationships. The theory of absolute advantage, which is the older theory, states that an individual nation should concentrate on exporting the goods

---

[7] Id. at 449.
[8] Id. at 468–471.

that it can produce most efficiently. For example, Sir Lanka (formerly Ceylon) produces tea more efficiently than most countries can and, thus, any surplus in Sri Lanka's tea production should be exported to countries that produce tea less efficiently. The theory of comparative advantage arose out of the realization that a country did not have to have an absolute advantage in producing a good in order to export it efficiently; rather, it would contribute to global efficiency if it produced specialized products simply more efficiently than others did. To illustrate this concept, let's assume that the best attorney in a small town is also the best legal secretary. Because this person can make more money as an attorney, it would be more efficient for her to devote her energy to working as a lawyer and to hire a legal secretary. Similarly, let's assume that the United States can produce both wheat and tea more efficiently than Sri Lanka can. Thus, the United States has an absolute advantage in its trade with Sri Lanka. Let us further assume that U.S. wheat production is comparatively greater than U.S. tea production vis-á-vis Sri Lanka. That is, by using the same amount of resources, the United States can produce two and a half times as much wheat but only twice as much tea as Sri Lanka. The United States then has a comparative advantage in wheat over tea.[9]

In this simplified example, we made several assumptions: that there were only two countries and two commodities involved; that transport costs in the two countries were about the same; that efficiency was the sole objective; and that political factors were not significant. In international trade, things are far more complex. There are many nations and innumerable products involved, and political factors are often more potent than economic considerations.

Trade is generally considered to be the least risky means of doing international business, because it demands little involvement with a foreign buyer or seller. For small and middle-sized firms, the first step toward involvement in international business is generally to hire an export management company, which is a company licensed to operate as the representative of many manufacturers with exportable products. These management companies are privately owned by citizens of various nation-states and have long-standing links to importers in many countries. They provide exporting firms with market research, identify potential buyers, and assist the firms in negotiating contracts.

Export trading companies, which are governed by the Export Trading Act in the United States, comprise those manufacturers and banks that either buy the products of a small business and resell them in another country or sell products of several companies on a commission basis. Small and medium-sized exporting companies may also choose to retain foreign distributors, which purchase imported goods at a discount and resell them in the foreign or host country. Once a company has had some experience selling in other countries, it may decide to retain a foreign sales representative. Sales representatives differ from foreign distributors in that they do not take title to the goods being exported. Rather, they usually maintain a principal–agency relationship with the exporter.

INTERNATIONAL LICENSING AND FRANCHISING

International licensing is a contractual agreement by which a company (licensor) makes its trade secrets, trademarks, patents, or copyrights (intellectual property) available to a foreign individual or company (licensee) in return

international licensing A contractual agreement by which a company (licensor) makes its intellectual property available to a foreign individual or company (licensee) for payment.

[9] J. Daniels, L. Radebaugh, and D. Sullivan, *International Business*, 10th ed. (Upper Saddle River, N.J.: Pearson Prentice Hall, 2004), pp. 148, 49.

either for royalties or for other compensation based on the volume of goods sold or a lump sum. All licensing agreements are subject to restrictions of the host country, which may include demands that its nationals be trained for management positions in the licensee company, that the host government receive a percentage of the gross profits, and that licensor technology be made available to all host-country nationals. Licensing agreements can differ vastly from country to country.

international franchising
A contractual agreement whereby a company (licensor) permits another company (licensee) to market its trademarked goods or services in a particular nation.

International franchising permits a licensee of a trademark to market the licensor's goods or services in a particular nation (e.g., Kentucky Fried Chicken franchises in China). Often companies franchise their trademark to avoid a nation-state's restrictions on foreign direct investment. Also, political instability is less likely to be a threat to investment when a local franchisee is running the business. Companies considering entering into an international franchise agreement should investigate bilateral treaties of friendship and commerce between the franchisor's nation and the franchisee's nation, as well as the business laws of the franchisee country.

In some instances, licensing and franchising negotiations are tense and drawn out because businesses in many industrialized nations are intent on protecting their intellectual property against "piracy" or are adamant about getting assurances that franchising agreements will be honored. These are major legitimate concerns. For example, between 1994 and 1999, the United States threatened to impose sanctions against China because of that nation's sale of pirated U.S. goods as well as its failure to comply with international franchising requirements. A series of last-minute agreements encouraged by Chinese and U.S. businesses averted the sanctions, which would have proved expensive for private and public parties in both countries. By the year 2000, the Congress and the president of the United States granted normal trade relations with China and left open the opportunity for the latter to join the World Trade Organization (WTO).[10] In June 2001, with a China–U.S. agreement on agriculture, a major barrier to entrance was overcome.

In November 2001, China and Taiwan entered the WTO, after considerable negotiations between the western nations over many issues. For example, at China's insistence, all membership documents refer to it as the People's Republic of China, while Taiwan will be referred to as the Separate Customs Territory of Taiwan, Penghu, Kinmen, and Matsu. The latter three islands are under the control of Taiwan. Taiwan is not recognized as an independent nation but as a territory belonging to the mainland. (See Chapter 24 for a discussion of franchising.)

FOREIGN DIRECT INVESTMENT

Direct investment in foreign nations is usually undertaken only by established multinational corporations. Foreign direct investment may take one of two forms: The multinational either creates a wholly or partially owned and controlled foreign subsidiary in the host country or enters into a joint venture with an individual, corporation, or government agency of the host country. In both cases, the risk for the investing company is greater than is the risk in international trade and international franchising and licensing because serious amounts of capital are flowing to the host country that are subject to its government's restrictions and its domestic law.

---

[10] See "Backers Hope China Pact Will Promote Reform," *USA Today*, September 20, 2000, p. 10.

Large multinationals choose to create **foreign subsidiaries** for several reasons: (1) to expand their foreign markets, (2) to acquire foreign resources, including raw materials, (3) to improve their production efficiency, (4) to acquire knowledge, and (5) to be closer to their customers and competitors. Rarely do all these reasons pertain in a single instance. For example, U.S. companies have set up foreign subsidiaries in Mexico, Western Europe, Brazil, and India for quite different reasons. Mexico provided cheap labor and a location close to customers and suppliers for U.S. automobile manufacturers. In the case of Western Europe, the impetus was both a threat and an opportunity. The member nations of the European Union (EU) have been moving to eliminate all trade barriers among themselves, while at the same time imposing stiffer tariffs on goods and services imported from non-EU countries. U.S. companies have been rushing to establish foreign subsidiaries in EU countries, not only to avoid being shut out of this huge lucrative market but also to expand sales among its approximately 380 million people. Brazil is not only the largest potential market in Latin America, but it also offers low labor and transportation costs, making it ideal for U.S. automakers desiring to export to neighboring Latin American countries. Union Carbide, Inc., a producer of chemicals and plastics, decided to establish a subsidiary in India, where cheap labor (including highly skilled chemists and engineers) and low-cost transportation enabled the parent company to produce various materials cheaply and, thus, boost its bottom line. The Indian subsidiary turned out to be a very expensive investment for Union Carbide after the Bhopal disaster. The civil suit that resulted illustrates an issue that is often overlooked by managers of multinationals when setting up subsidiaries in foreign nation-states: Should a parent corporation be held liable for the activities of its foreign subsidiary? Although the case presented here is framed in a jurisdictional context (whether a U.S. court or an Indian court should hear the suit), you should bear in mind the issue of corporate parent liability as you read it.

foreign subsidiary A company that is wholly or partially owned and controlled by a company based in another country.

CASE 9-1

In Re Union Carbide Corporation Gas Plant Disaster at Bhopal, India, in December, 1984 v. Union Carbide Corporation
United States Court of Appeals
809 F.2d 195 (2d Cir. 1987)

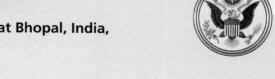

The government of India (UOI) and several private class action plaintiffs (Indian citizens) sued Union Carbide India Limited (UCIL) and the parent corporation, Union Carbide Corporation (UCC), for over $1 billion after a disaster at a chemical plant operated by UCIL in 1984. There was a leak of the lethal gas methylisocyanate from the plant on the night of December 2, 1984. The deadly chemicals were blown by wind over the adjacent city of Bhopal, resulting in the deaths of more than 2,000 persons and the injury of more than another 200,000 persons. UCIL is incorporated under the laws of India; 50.9 percent of the stock is owned by UCC, 22 percent is owned or controlled by the government of India, and the balance is owned by

23,500 Indian citizens. The federal district court (Judge Keenan) granted UCC's motion to dismiss the plaintiffs' action on the grounds that Indian courts, not U.S. courts, were the appropriate forum for the suit. The plaintiffs appealed this decision.

Judge Mansfield

As the district court found, the record shows that the private interests of the respective parties weigh heavily in favor of dismissal on grounds of *forum non conveniens*. The many witnesses and sources of proof are almost entirely located in India, where the accident occurred, and could not be compelled to appear for trial in the United States. The Bhopal plant at the time of the accident was operated by some 193 Indian nationals, including the managers of seven operating units employed by the Agricultural Products Division of UCIL, who reported to Indian Works Managers in Bhopal. The plant was maintained by seven functional departments employing over 200 more Indian nationals. UCIL kept daily, weekly, and monthly records of plant operations and records of maintenance, as well as records of the plant's Quality Control, Purchasing, and Stores branches, all operated by Indian employees. The great majority of documents bearing on the design, safety, start-up and operation of the plant, as well as the safety training of the plant's employees, is located in India. Proof to be offered at trial would be derived from interviews of these witnesses in India and study of the records located there to determine whether the accident was caused by negligence on the part of the management or employees in the operation of the plant, by fault in its design, or by sabotage. In short, India has greater ease of access to the proof than does the United States.

The plaintiffs seek to prove that the accident was caused by negligence on the part of UCC in originally contributing to the design of the plant and its provision for storage of excessive amounts of the gas at the plant. As Judge Keenan found, however, UCC's participation was limited and its involvement in plant operations terminated long before the accident. Under 1973 agreements negotiated at arm's length with UCIL, UCC did provide a summary "process design package" for construction of the plant and the services of some of its technicians to monitor the progress of UCIL in detailing the design and erecting the plant. However, the UOI controlled the terms of the agreements and precluded UCC from exercising any authority to "detail design, erect and commission the plant," which was done independently over the period from 1972 to 1980 by UCIL process design engineers who supervised, among many others, some 55 to 60 Indian engineers employed by the Bombay engineering firm of Humphreys and Glasgow. The preliminary process design information furnished by UCC could not have been used to construct the plant. Construction required the detailed process design and engineering data prepared by hundreds of Indian engineers, process designers, and subcontractors. During the ten years spent constructing the plant, the design and configuration underwent many changes.

In short, the plant has been constructed and managed by Indians in India. No Americans were employed at the plant at the time of the accident. In the five years from 1980 to 1984, although more than 1,000 Indians were employed at the plant, only one American was employed there and he left in 1982. No Americans visited the plant for more than one year prior to the accident, and during the five-year period before the accident the communications between the plant and the United States were almost nonexistent.

The vast majority of material witnesses and documentary proof bearing on causation of and liability for the accident is located in India, not the United States, and would be more accessible to an Indian court than to a United States court. The records are almost entirely in Hindi or other Indian languages, understandable to an Indian court without translation. The witnesses for the most part do not speak English but Indian languages understood by an Indian court but not by an American court. These witnesses could be required to appear in an Indian court but not in a court of the United States. India's interest is increased by the fact that it has for years treated UCIL as an Indian national, subjecting it to intensive regulations and governmental supervision of the construction, development, and operation of the Bhopal plant, its emissions, water and air pollution, and safety precautions. Numerous Indian government officials have regularly conducted on-site inspections of the plant and approved its machinery and equipment, including its facilities for storage of the lethal methylisocyanate gas that escaped and caused the disaster giving rise to the claims. Thus India has considered the plant to be an Indian one and the disaster to be an Indian problem. It therefore has a deep interest in ensuring compliance with its safety standards.

Affirmed in favor of Defendant, Union Carbide.

COMMENT: The Bhopal victims filed their claims in U.S. courts against UCC because the parent company had more money than the subsidiary (UCIL). Also, suing the parent made it more likely that the case would be heard in U.S. courts, which are considered to be far better forums for winning damages in personal injury actions than Indian courts are. After the lawsuits were removed to an Indian court, UCC agreed to pay $470 million to the Bhopal disaster victims. Union Carbide's stock substantially decreased in value, and UCC was threatened by a takeover (the attempt was thwarted in 1985). More than half of UCC was subsequently sold or spun off, including the Indian subsidiary (UCIL). In 1989, the Indian Supreme Court ordered UCC to pay $470 million to compensate Bhopal victims. Criminal charges against the company and its officials were dropped. About 12,000 people worked for UCC in 1995, in contrast to the 110,000 employed by the company a decade earlier. In 1998 Dow chemical acquired Union Carbide. On December 2nd, 2004 (the 20th Anniversary of the plant explosion) there has been no clean up.

Joint ventures, which involve a relationship between two or more corporations or between a foreign multinational and an agency of a host-country government or a host-country national, are usually set up for a specific under-

Critical Thinking About the Law

Please refer to Case 9-1 and consider the following questions:

1. Highlight the importance of facts in shaping a judicial opinion by writing an imaginary letter that, had it been introduced as evidence, would have greatly distressed Union Carbide Corporation.

   Clue: Review the first part of the decision, in which Judge Mansfield discussed the extent of UCC's involvement in the plant where the accident occurred. What facts would counter his statement that the parent company had only "limited" involvement?

2. Suppose a U.S. plant exploded, resulting in extensive deaths in the United States. Further suppose that all the engineers who built the plant wrote and spoke German only. Could Judge Mansfield's decision be used as an analogy to seek dismissal of a negligence suite against the owners of the plant?

   Clue: Review the discussion of the use of legal analogies in Chapter 1 and apply what you read to this question.

3. What additional information, were it to surface, would strengthen Union Carbide's request for a dismissal of the case described?

   Clue: Notice the wide assortment of facts that Judge Mansfield organized to support his decision.

---

taking over a limited period of time. Many developing countries (such as China) allow foreign investment only in the form of a joint venture between host-country nationals and the multinationals. Recently, there have been three-way joint ventures among United States–based multinationals (e.g., automobile companies such as Chrysler and General Motors), Japanese multinationals (e.g., Mitsubishi and Honda), and Chinese government agencies and Chinese nationals. Joint ventures are also used in host countries with fewer restrictions on foreign investment, often to spread the risk or to amass required investment sums that are too large for one corporation to raise by itself. Some of these joint ventures are private associations, with no host government involvement.

joint venture Relationship between two or more persons or corporations, or an association between a foreign multinational and an agency of the host government or a host country national, set up for a specific business undertaking or a limited time period.

RISKS OF ENGAGING IN INTERNATIONAL BUSINESS

Unlike doing business in one's own country, the "rules of the game" are not always clear when engaging in business in a foreign country, particularly in what we have classified as middle- and low-income economies. Here we set out the four primary risks that managers engaged in international business may face: (1) expropriation of private property by the host foreign nation, (2) the application of the sovereign immunity doctrine and the act-of-state doctrine to disputes between foreign states and U.S. firms, (3) export and import controls, and (4) currency controls and fluctuations in currency values.

EXPROPRIATION OF PRIVATE PROPERTY

Expropriation—the taking of private property by a host-country government either for political or for economic reasons—is one of the greatest risks companies take when they engage in international business. Thus, it is essential for business

expropriation The taking of private property by a host country government for political or economic reasons.

managers to investigate the recent behavior of host-country government officials, particularly in countries that are moving from a centrally planned economy toward one that is market oriented (e.g., Russia and Eastern European nations). One method of limiting risk in politically unstable countries is to concentrate on exports and imports (trade) and licensing and franchising. Another is to take advantage of the low-cost insurance against expropriation offered by the Overseas Private Investment Corporation (OPIC). If a U.S. plant or other project is insured by OPIC and is expropriated, the U.S. firm receives compensation in return for assigning to OPIC the firm's claim against the host country government.

bilateral investment treaty Treaty between two parties to outline conditions for investment in either country.

Bilateral investment treaties (BITs), which are negotiated between two governments, obligate the host government to show fair and nondiscriminatory treatment to investors from the other country. The BIT also includes a promise of prompt, adequate, and effective compensation in the event of expropriation or nationalization.

SOVEREIGN IMMUNITY DOCTRINE

sovereign immunity doctrine States that a government expropriating foreign-owned private property is immune from the jurisdiction of courts in the owner's country.

Another risk for companies engaged in international business is the **sovereign immunity doctrine**, which allows a government expropriating foreign-owned private property to claim that it is immune from the jurisdiction of courts in the owner's country because it is a government, rather than a private sector entity. In these cases, the company whose property was expropriated often receives nothing because it cannot press its claims in its own country's courts, and courts in the host country are seldom amenable to such claims.

The sovereign immunity doctrine has been a highly controversial issue between the United Sates and certain foreign governments in developing nations. To give some protection to foreign businesses without impinging on the legitimate rights of other governments, the U.S. Congress in 1976 enacted the Foreign Sovereign Immunities Act (FSIA), which shields foreign governments from U.S. judicial review of their public, but not their private, acts. The FSIA grants foreign nations immunity from judicial review by U.S. courts unless they meet one of the FSIA's private exceptions. One such exception is the foreign government's involvement in commercial activity. Case 9-2 clarifies the U.S. Supreme Court's definition of commercial activity under the FSIA. Note how the Court emphasizes the nature of the Nigerian government's action by asking whether it is the type of action a private party would engage in.

CASE 9-2

Keller v. Central Bank of Nigeria
United States Court of Appeals
277 F. 3d. 811 (6th Cir. 2002)

Prince Arthur Ossai, a government official in Nigeria, entered into a contract with Henry Keller (plaintiff), a sales representative for H.K. Enterprises, Inc., a Michigan-based manufacturer of medical equipment. They agreed that among other things, Ossai would have exclusive distribution right to sell H.K. products in Nigeria, which would buy $4.1 million of H.K. equipment for $6.63 mil-

lion, plus a $7.65 million "licensing fee." Ossai said that, first, $25.5 million on deposit in the Central Bank of Nigeria (CBN) had to be transferred into an account set up by Keller. CBN employees charged Keller $28,950 in fees for the transaction, but the funds were never transferred. Keller and H.K. filed a suit in a federal district court against the CBN and others, asserting in part a claim under the Racketeer Influenced and Corrupt Organizations Act (RICO). The defendants filed a motion to dismiss under the Foreign Sovereign Immunities Act (FSIA). The court denied the motion, concluding that the claim fell within the FSIA's "commercial activity" exception. The defendants appealed to the U.S. Court of Appeals for the Sixth Circuit.

Justice Norris

[The defendants] claim that the illegality of the deal alleged precludes a finding that it is a commercial activity. The FSIA defines "commercial activity" as "either a regular course of commercial conduct or a particular commercial transaction or act." The commercial character of an activity shall be determined by reference to the nature of the course of conduct or particular transaction or act, rather than by reference to its purpose. [W]hen a foreign government acts, not as regulator of a market, but in the manner of a private player within it, the foreign sovereign's actions are commercial within the meaning of the FSIA.

In the instant case, the conduct was a deal to license and sell medical equipment, a type of activity done by private parties and not a "market regulator" function. The district court correctly concluded that this was a commercial activity, and that any fraud and bribery involved did not render the plan non-commercial.

Defendants claim that plaintiffs cannot establish another element of the commercial activity exception, namely, that there was a direct effect in the United States. [A]n effect is "direct" if it follows as an immediate consequence of the defendant's activity.

In this case, defendants agreed to pay but failed to transmit the promised funds to an account in a Cleveland bank. Other courts have found a direct effect when a defendant agrees to pay funds to an account in the United States and then fails to do so. The district court in the instant case correctly concluded, in accord with the other [courts], that defendant's failure to pay promised funds to a Cleveland account constituted a direct effect in the United States.

Affirmed for Plaintiff.

Critical Thinking About the Law

Context plays a vital role in any legal decision. The existence or nonexistence of certain events directly affects the court's verdict. In Case 9-2, the court applies the regulations of FSIA to the specific facts of the case. If certain facts exist, the federal statute protects the plaintiff, and the court should appropriately reject the defendant's motion to dismiss. Otherwise, the CBN is immune, and the statute does not protect the plaintiff.

Understanding the facts is the starting point for legal analysis. The following questions encourage you to consider the significance of the facts in Case 9-2.

1. What are the facts that are critical in the court's ruling in favor of the plaintiff?
    Clue: Reread the introductory paragraph.

2. Look at the facts you found. To illustrate the importance of context, which fact, if it had not been included in the case, might have resulted in the court's granting the defendant's motion to dismiss?
    Clue: Find the elements of the federal statute that the judge discusses and use these elements as a guide to highlight the most significant facts.

ACT-OF-STATE DOCTRINE

The **act-of-state doctrine** holds that each sovereign nation is bound to respect the independence of every other sovereign state and that the courts of one nation will not sit in judgment on the acts of the courts of another nation done within that nation's own sovereign territory. This doctrine, together with the sovereign immunity doctrine, substantially increases the risk of doing business in a foreign

act-of-state doctrine States that each sovereign nation is bound to respect the independence of every other sovereign national and that the courts of one nation will not sit in judgment on the acts of the courts of another nation.

country. Like the sovereign immunity doctrine, the act-of-state doctrine includes some court-ordered exceptions, such as when the foreign government is acting in a commercial capacity or when it seeks to repudiate a commercial obligation.

Congress made it clear in 1964 that the act-of-state doctrine shall not be applied in cases in which property is confiscated in violation of international law, unless the president of the United States decides that the federal courts should apply it. As Case 9-3 demonstrates, the plaintiff has the burden of proving that the doctrine should not apply—that is, that the courts should sit in judgment of public acts of a foreign government, in this case, a former government.

CASE 9-3

Republic of the Philippines v. Ferdinand E. Marcos
United States Circuit Court of Appeals
862 F.2d 1355 (9th Cir. 1988)

The Republic of the Philippines (plaintiff) brought a civil suit against its former president, Ferdinand Marcos, and his wife, Imelda (defendants), asserting claims under the Racketeer Influenced Corrupt Organizations Act (RICO) and other applicable U.S. law. The Republic alleges that the Marcoses (and other defendants) arranged for investments in real estate in Beverly Hills, California, of $4 million fraudulently obtained by the Marcoses; that the Marcoses arranged for the creation of two bank accounts in the name of Imelda Marcos at Lloyds Bank of California totaling over $800,000, also fraudulently obtained by the Marcoses; and that the Marcoses transported into Hawaii money, jewels, and other property worth over $7 million, also fraudulently obtained by them. The key to the Republic's entire case is the allegation that the Marcoses stole public money. The federal district court entered a preliminary injunction enjoining the Marcoses from disposing of any of their assets except to pay attorneys and their living expenses. The Marcoses appealed.

Justice Noonan
Before determining whether issuance of an injunction was appropriate we must consider two defenses which, if accepted, would block trial of the case the Marcoses maintain. First, that their acts are insulated because they were acts of state not reviewable by our courts, and second, that any adjudication of these acts would involve the investigation of political questions beyond our court's competence. The classification of certain acts as "acts of state," with the consequence that their validity will be treated as beyond judicial review, is a pragmatic device, not required by the nature of sovereign authority and inconsistently applied in international law. The purpose of the device is to keep the judiciary from embroiling the courts and the country in the affairs of the foreign nation whose acts are challenged. Minimally viewed, the classification keeps a court from making pro-

nouncements on matters over which it has no power, maximally interpreted, the classification prevents the embarrassment of a court defending a foreign government that is "extant at the time of suit." The "continuing vitality" of the doctrine depends on its capacity to reflect the proper distribution of functions between the judicial and political branches of the government on matters bearing upon foreign relations.

As a practical tool for keeping the judicial branch out of the conduct of foreign affairs, the classification of "act of state" is not a promise to the ruler of any foreign country that his conduct, if challenged by his own country after his fall, may not become the subject of scrutiny in our courts. No estoppel exists insulating a deposed dictator from accounting. No guarantee has been granted that immunity may be acquired by an ex-chief magistrate invoking the magic words "act of state" to cover his or her past performance.

In the instant case the Marcoses offered no evidence whatsoever to support the classification of their acts as acts of state. The burden of proving acts of state rested upon them. They did not undertake the proof.

Bribetaking, theft, embezzlement, extortion, fraud, and conspiracy to do these things are all acts susceptible of concrete proof that need not involve political questions. The court, it is true, may have to determine questions of Philippine law in determining whether a given act was legal or illegal. But questions of foreign law are not beyond the capacity of our courts. The court will be examining the acts of the president of a country whose immediate political heritage is from our own. Although sometimes criticized as a ruler and at times invested with extraordinary power, Ferdinand Marcos does not appear to have had the authority of an absolute autocrat. He was not the state, but the head of the state, bound by the laws that applied to him. Our courts have had no difficulty in distinguishing the legal acts of a deposed ruler from his acts for personal profit that lack a basis in law.

Affirmed for Plaintiff, Republic of the Philippines.

Critical Thinking About the Law

1. At the outset of Case 9-3, Justice Noonan acknowledges a key ambiguity in this case that will require clarification before announcing his decision. How does that ambiguity affect the reasoning?

   Clue: Notice the key concept in the first of the two defenses used by the Marcoses.

2. What behavior of the Marcoses made it highly unlikely that the first defense would be effective?

   Clue: Review Justice Noonan's rationale for not honoring the defense.

3. What ethical norm is implicit in the Marcoses' struggle against the preliminary injunction?

   Clue: Look back at the discussion of the ethical norms and eliminate those that seem inconsistent with the Marcoses' behavior and interests.

EXPORT AND IMPORT CONTROLS

Export Controls. Export controls are usually applied by governments to militarily sensitive goods (e.g., computer hardware and software) to prevent unfriendly nations from obtaining these goods. In the United States, the Department of State, the Department of Commerce, and the Defense Department bear responsibility, under the Export Administration Act and the Arms Export Control Act, for authorizing the export of sensitive technology. Both criminal and administrative sanctions may be imposed on corporations and individuals who violate these laws.

Export controls often prevent U.S. companies from living up to negotiated contracts. Thus, they can damage the ability of U.S. firms to do business abroad.

Import Controls. Nations often set up import barriers to prevent foreign companies from destroying home industries. Two such controls are tariffs and quotas. For example, the United States has sought historically to protect its domestic automobile and textile industries, agriculture, and intellectual property (copyrights, patents, trademarks, and trade secrets). Intellectual property has become an extremely important U.S. export in recent years, and Washington has grown more determined than ever to prevent its being pirated. After several years of frustrating negotiations with the People's Republic of China, the U.S. government decided to threaten imposition of 100 percent tariffs on approximately $1 billion of Chinese imports in 1995, and again in 1996 and 1997. In retaliation, the Chinese government has threatened several times to impose import controls on many U.S. goods. Washington took action only after documenting that hundreds of millions of dollars' worth of "pirated" computerized software (including videodiscs, law books, and movies) was being produced for sale within China and for export to Southeast Asian nations in violation of the intellectual property laws of both China and the United States, as well as international law. The documentation showed that 29 factories owned by the state of Communist Party officials were producing pirated goods. A last-minute settlement in which the Chinese government pledged to honor intellectual property rights prevented a trade war that would have had bad implications for workers in import-export industries in both countries. American consumers also would have suffered because Chinese imports would have been twice as expensive had the 100 percent tariff taken effect—though the effect on consumers would have been offset by an increase in imports of the affected goods from other foreign countries (e.g., English and Japanese bikes would have replaced Chinese bikes in demand).

Another form of import control is the imposition of antidumping duties by two U.S. agencies, the International Trade Commission (ITC) and the International Trade Administration (ITA). The duties are levied against foreign entities that sell the same goods at lower prices in U.S. markets than in their own to obtain a larger share of the U.S. market (i.e., entities that practice "dumping"). An illustration of this conflict is set out in Case 9-4.

CURRENCY CONTROLS AND FLUCTUATIONS IN CURRENCY VALUES

Currency Controls. Currency controls are usually found in lower-income and lower-middle-income countries where regulations may restrict the conversion of domestic currency into foreign currency (e.g., the U.S. dollar) and the repatriation of foreign currency (e.g., taking U.S. dollars out of India). The latter type of restriction limits foreign multinationals from repatriating more than a certain percentage of the funds they have invested in the host country. Some countries impose an income (withholding) tax on repatriated earnings. Businesspeople

---

CASE 9-4

United States v. Haggar Apparel Company
United States Supreme Court
526 U.S. 380 (1999)

Haggar Apparel Company (Haggar) ships a fabric to Mexico with threads and zippers to make pants. A subsidiary has the trousers sewn and permapressed, and then shipped back to the United States. Under federal agency regulations, this process of shipping out goods and reshipping back to the United States is exempt from a duty that is charged against other imports. However, the U.S. Custom Service levied a duty on Haggar pants, under a regulation that makes all permapressing operations to be an additional step in manufacturing, not incidental to the assembly process. Haggar filed a suit against the United States in the U.S. Court of International Trade, seeking a refund of the duty. The court ruled in Haggar's favor, and the U.S. Court of Appeals for the Federal Circuit affirmed. The federal government appealed.

Justice Kennedy

The [Haggar Company] claims the regulation binds the Custom Service when they classify imported merchandise but does not bind the importers. The statutory scheme does not support this limited view of the force and effect of regulation.

Respondent [Haggar] relies on the specific direction to the Secretary to make rules of classification for "the various

ports of entry" to argue that the statute authorizes promulgation of regulations that do nothing more than ensure that customs officers in field offices around the country classify goods according to a similar and consistent scheme. The regulations issued under the statute have no bearing, says respondent, on the right of the importer. We disagree. The phrase in question is explained by the simple fact that *classification decisions must be made at the port where goods enter.* We shall not assume Congress was concerned only to ensure that customs officials at the various ports of entry make uniform decisions but that it had no concern for uniformity once the goods entered the country and judicial proceedings commenced. *The tariffs do not mean one thing for customs officers and another for importers.* [Emphasis added.] Particularly in light of the fact that the agency utilized the notice-and-comment rulemaking process before issuing the regulations, the argument that they were not intended to be entitled to judicial deference implies a sufficient departure from conventional contemporary administrative practice that we ought not to adopt it absent a different statutory structure and more express language to this effect in the regulations themselves.

Reversed the lower court's decisions
in favor of the United States.

need to be aware that currency controls are common both in developing and developed nations and that doing business in countries that impose them requires investment for the long term.

Currency Fluctuations. Doing international business involves the exchange of foreign currencies in the buying and selling of goods and services. Significant fluctuations in currency values, especially if they are unanticipated and, therefore, unprepared for, can present painful problems for businesses. For example, in July through September 1997 the world saw currencies of some Asian countries, vis-à-vis the U.S. dollar, fall dramatically. For many years, these countries had linked their currencies to the dollar. When their currencies were delinked, high growth rates, inflation, and easy bank loans led to financial crises. Some Asian political leaders blamed the crises on monetary speculators, who in turn placed the blame on more fundamental economic indicators. With the resulting devaluation of currencies, such countries as Malaysia, Thailand, Indonesia, the Philippines, and South Korea saw their exports to developed nations plunge and investors flee. If it took many more ringgits (Malaysia), bahts (Thai), rupiahs (Indonesia), pesos (Philippines), and wons (Korea) per U.S. dollar to recover their return on investments, investors moved their money to other locations (e.g., the United States, Europe, Latin America). In economies that were highly dependent on foreign investment, this strategy led to cutbacks on major projects that would have provided local growth and employment. Most important, in October and November 1997, stock markets fell worldwide for several days, showing the interdependency of national and international institutions. The International Monetary Fund, the U.S. government, and private U.S. commercial banks "pumped" more than $100 million into the five nations mentioned here in January 1998. The opposite effect took place in 2002–2004 when the U.S. dollar fell vis-à-vis other currencies. Japan sought to temporarily hold the dollar value stable. See Exhibit 9-1.

International Commerce and Currency Markets

As shown in Exhibit 9-1, exchange rates and currency fluctuations manipulated by the Japanese government cost it nearly 15 trillion yen ($142 billion) in order to prop up the U.S. dollar during the period from January to March 29, 2004. Without the Japanese action the dollar would have slid lower and Japanese exporters would have had difficulty in selling abroad. Note in the exhibit that near the end of March Japan decided not to prop up the currency as it had in previous months and the dollar dropped 1.2 percent to a four year-low of $104.35 and 0.9 percent against the euro, the latter rising to $1.23. Japan's withdrawal has important implications: (1) Its huge intervention up until the end of March translated into losses for big U.S. banks and hedge funds and lessened performance for Americans' overseas investments, and (2) the market manipulation by Japan ran counter to the traditional supply and demand mechanism that Japan and the United States had long agreed to when dealing with the foreign exchange market. By intervening in the market, Japan created an artificial volatility in these markets.

In such a financial crisis, U.S. and other exporters hedge against exchange risks by contracting with a bank. In return for a fee (based on risk), the bank assumes the risk of currency fluctuation by guaranteeing the exporter a fixed number of dollars in exchange for the foreign currency it receives. **Hedging** is

hedging Exporting companies contract with a bank that guarantees the exporter a fixed number of U.S. dollars in exchange for payment of the goods it receives in a foreign currency. The exporting company pays a fee to the bank. The fee is based on the risk the bank is taking that the foreign currency will fluctuate.

EXHIBIT 9-1

MANIPULATING EXCHANGE RATES

Source: Bloomberg Financial Markets, Ministry of Finance

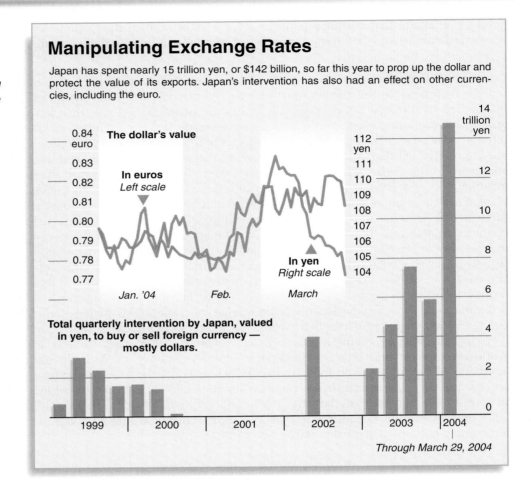

Manipulating Exchange Rates

Japan has spent nearly 15 trillion yen, or $142 billion, so far this year to prop up the dollar and protect the value of its exports. Japan's intervention has also had an effect on other currencies, including the euro.

The dollar's value

In euros
Left scale

In yen
Right scale

Jan. '04   Feb.   March

Total quarterly intervention by Japan, valued in yen, to buy or sell foreign currency — mostly dollars.

1999   2000   2001   2002   2003   2004

Through March 29, 2004

a practice managers involved in international business should be thoroughly knowledgeable about, especially if they are dealing with developing nations where currency fluctuations can be quite erratic.

LEGAL AND ECONOMIC INTEGRATION AS A MEANS OF ENCOURAGING INTERNATIONAL BUSINESS ACTIVITY

Table 9-2 summarizes a number of groups that have been formed to assist businesspeople in carrying out international transactions. These groups range from the World Trade Organization (formerly the General Agreement on Tariffs and Trade),which is attempting to reduce tariff barriers worldwide, to the proposed South American Common Market, which would form a duty-free zone for all the nations of South America. The most ambitious organization is the European Union (EU), which is in the process of forming a Western European political and economic community with a single currency and a common external tariff barrier toward nonmembers.

Multinational corporations are learning that doing international business is much easier when they are aware of the worldwide and regional groups listed in the table. We will describe three of these groups: the WTO, the EU, and NAFTA. We chose to examine these three because they represent three different philosophies and structures of legal and economic integration, not because we do not appreciate the major effects of other integrative groups outlined in Table 9-2.

TABLE 9-2

LEGALLY AND ECONOMICALLY INTEGRATED INSTITUTIONS

Name	*Members and Purpose*
World Trade Organization (WTO)	Replaced General Agreement on Tariffs and Trade (GATT) in 1995 and the most favored nation clause, with the normal trade relations principle. 144 member nations. Goal is to get the nations of the world to commit to the trade principles of nondiscrimination and reciprocity so that, when a trade treaty is negotiated between two members, the provisions of that bilateral treaty will be extended to all WTO members. All members are obligated to harmonize their trade laws or face sanctions. The WTO, through its arbitration tribunals, is to mediate disputes and recommend sanctions.
European Union (EU)	Composed of 25 European member states. Established as the European Economic Community (later called the European Community) by the Treaty of Rome in 1957. Goal is to establish an economic "common market" by eliminating custom duties and other quantitative restrictions on the import and export of goods and services between member states. In 1986 the treaty was amended by the Single European Act (SEA), providing for the abolition of all customs and technical barriers between nations by December 31, 1992. In 1991, the Maastricht Summit Treaty proposed monetary union, political union, and a "social dimension" (harmonizing labor and Social Security regulations) among EU members. All aspects have not been approved by all members.
North American Free Trade Agreement (NAFTA)	The United States, Canada, and Mexico are members at present; Chile has been invited to join. NAFTA seeks to eliminate barriers to the flow of goods, services, and investments among member nations over a 15-year period, starting in 1994, the year of its ratification. Unlike the European Union, NAFTA is not intended to create a common market. Whereas European Union states have a common tariff barrier against non-EU states, members of NAFTA maintain their own individual tariff rates for goods and services coming from non-NAFTA countries.
Organization for Economic Cooperation and Development (OECD)	Established in 1951. Western European nations with Australia, New Zealand, United States, Canada, Japan, Russia, and some Eastern European nations as associate members. The OECD's original purpose was to promote economic growth after World War II. Today it recommends and evaluates options on environmental issues for its members and establishes guidelines for multinational corporations when operating in developed and developing countries.

TABLE 9-2
(continued)

European Free Trade Association (EFTA)	Founded in 1960 and originally composed of Finland, Sweden, Norway, Iceland, Lichtenstein, Switzerland, and Austria. EFTA has an intergovernmental council that negotiates treaties with the EU. Finland, Sweden, and Austria left the EFTA in 1995 and joined the EU. EFTA in the future will have only minor significance.
Andean Common Market (ANCOM)	Composed of Bolivia, Venezuela, Colombia, Ecuador, and Peru. ANCOM seeks to integrate these nations politically and economically through a commission, the Juanta Andean Development Bank, and a Reserve Fund and a Court of Justice. Founded in 1969, its goals have been set back by national interests.
Mercado Commun del Ser Mercosul (Mercosul)	Composed of Argentina, Brazil, Paraguay, and Uruguay. Mercosul's purposes are to reduce tariffs and eliminate nontariff barriers among members and to establish a common external tariff. The organization was founded in 1991, and these goals were to be met by December 31, 1994. For political reasons they have not been fully met.
South American Common Market	A duty-free common market comprised of countries in the ANCOM and Mercosul groups came about on January 1, 1995. On that date, tariffs were ended on 95 percent of goods traded among Brazil, Argentina, Paraguay, and Uruguay. All three nations adopted common external tariffs.
Asia-Pacific Economic Corporations (APEC)	Formed in 1989. A loosely organized group of 15 developed and developing Pacific Group (APEC) nations, including Japan, China, United States, Canada, and New Zealand. APEC is not a trading bloc and has no structure except for a secretariat.
Association of Southeast Asian Nations (ASEAN)	Formed in 1967. Composed of Indonesia, Malaysia, Vietnam, Philippines, Singapore, Thailand, and Brunei. ASEAN's purpose is to encourage economic growth of member nations by promoting trade and industry. There have been tariff reductions between members and ASEAN's secretariat has represented nations vis-à-vis other regional groups such as the EU.
Gulf Cooperation Council (GCC)	Founded in 1982. Composed of Saudi Arabia, Kuwait, Bahrain, Qatar, the United Arab Emirates, and Oman. The GCC's purposes are to standardize industrial subsidies, eliminate trade barriers among members, and negotiate with other regional groups to obtain favor able treatment for GCC goods, services, and investments.

THE WORLD TRADE ORGANIZATION

Purpose and Terms. On January 1, 1995, the 47-year-old General Agreement on Tariffs and Trade (GATT) organization was replaced by a new umbrella group, the World Trade Organization (WTO). The WTO has the power to enforce the new trade accord that evolved out of seven rounds of GATT negotiations, with more than 140 nations participating. All 144 signators to this accord have agreed to reduce their tariffs and subsidies by an average of one-third on most goods over the next decade, agricultural tariffs and subsidies included. Economists estimate that this trade pact will result in tariff reductions totaling $744 billion over the next ten years.

Moreover, the accord, which the WTO will supervise, prohibits member countries from placing limits on the quantity of imports (quotas). For example, Japan will have to end its ban on rice imports, and the United States will have to end its import quotas on peanuts, dairy products, and textiles. Furthermore, the agreement bans the practice of requiring high local content of materials for manufactured products such as cars. It also requires all signatory countries to protect patents, trademarks, copyrights, and trade secrets. (See Chapter 14 for discussion of these topics, which fall under the umbrella of intellectual property.)

General Impact. The accord created the World Trade Organization, which consists of all nations whose governments approved and met the GATT–Uruguay Round Accord.[11] Each member state has one vote in the Ministerial Conference, with no single nation having a veto. The Conference meets at least biannually, and a General Council meets as needed. The Conference may amend the charter created by the pact—in some cases, by a two-thirds vote; in others, by a three-fourths vote. Changes will apply to all members, even those that voted no.

The WTO has been given the power to set up a powerful dispute-resolution system with three-person arbitration panels. Each panel follows a strict schedule for dispute-resolution decisions, and WTO members may veto its findings. This is a matter of great concern to the United States, and it figured prominently in the House and the Senate debates preceding approval of the WTO. U.S. farmers (and other groups), who had previously won decisions before GATT panels, saw these decisions vetoed by the European Union countries that subsidize the production of soybeans and other agricultural products; they enthusiastically supported the new WTO process. Environmentalists and consumer groups, on the other hand, feared that the WTO would overrule U.S. environmental laws and in other ways infringe on the sovereignty of the nation. To assuage these fears, the framers of the accord added a provision that allows any nation to withdraw upon six months' notice. Congress also attached a condition to its approval that calls for the setting up of a panel of U.S. federal judges to review the WTO panels' decisions.

Impact on Corporate Investment Decision Making. The WTO pact makes it less risky for multinationals to source parts—that is, to have them built in cheap-labor countries and then brought back to the multinational's home country for use in making a product (e.g., brakes for automobiles). Industries that are expected to shift quickly to buying parts from all over the world for their products include computers, telecommunications, and other high-tech manufacturing. It is anticipated that with a freer flow of goods across borders, businesses will gain increased economies of scale by building parts-manufacturing plants at a location that serves a wide market area.

Because the tariff cuts are to be introduced gradually over a six-year period and are to be finalized only after ten years, the impact on trade will not be immediate. However, once the major nations ratify the WTO pact, companies will begin to make investment and employment decisions predicated on dramatic reductions in tariffs, subsidies, and other government-established deterrents to free trade.

---

[11] Uruguay Round Amendments Act, Pub. L. 103-465, was approved by Congress on December 8, 1994. One hundred eight states signed the final act embodying the results of the Uruguay round of multilateral trade negotiations. Bureau of National Affairs, *International Reporter*, Vol. 11, p. 11 (April 20, 1994). Sixteen more states have joined since 1994.

Technology and the Legal Environment

WTO Says U.S. Ban on Online Gambling Violates International Law

The island nation of Antigua and Barbuda (plaintiff) brought a case against the United States to a WTO panel. The nation licenses companies (19) that offer (sports) betting and casino games (e.g., blackjack) over the Internet. It argued that the United States is in violation of international law by prohibiting cross-border gambling operations via the Internet. The plaintiff argues that the U.S. trade policy does not prohibit cross-border gambling operations.

The WTO panel ruled in favor of Antigua and Barbuda. In its decision in 2004, the panel stated that U.S. policy prohibiting online gambling operations emanating from the plaintiff nation violates international law. WTO panels do not have to give reasons for their decisions. The United States has a right to appeal the decision to a separate court of appeals and is expected to do so.

Some important legal, political, and cultural considerations:

1. WTO panel decisions only apply to the set of facts and case before it. Internet gambling using credit cards takes place in the Caribbean, Costa Rica, Great Britain, and Canada. Although this case is not precedent, the United States should expect more legal action as several million customers are at stake, and revenues from offshore casinos are important to nation states that operate Internet casinos.

2. Present federal law in the United States makes it illegal to bet over the Internet if not allowed by individual states. Although untested as legal theory, the Justice Department is seeking to crack down on broadcasters and print media that accept advertising from offshore Internet casinos claiming they are aiding and abetting an illegal enterprise. The airwaves are controlled by the Federal Communications Commission. Some questions are being raised: (a) Is the lobbying of American gambling companies against Internet betting (emanating from abroad) the real reason for the U.S. government stand? American companies have a lock on U.S. gambling and do not want to lose it to worldwide Internet casino interests; (b) Based on international trade law, countries allowing online casino gambling may seek to raise tariffs on services or goods of U.S. companies doing business (e.g., AT&T) within their jurisdiction as a way of retaliating against U.S. Policy. Will this bring an expression of concern from U.S. companies to members of Congress? Does AT&T contribute to the reelection of members of Congress? Do gambling interests provide funds for reelection bids? Will there be a clash of interests?

THE EUROPEAN UNION

Purpose. Today's 25-member European Union (EU) grew out of the European Economic Community (later called the European Community) established by six Western European nations through the Rome Treaty of 1957. Its goals are to create a "customs union" that would do away with internal tariffs among the member states and to create a uniform external tariff to be applied to all nonmembers. The EU is thoroughly committed to achieving the free movement of goods, services, capital, and people across borders (Exhibit 9-2).

The EU's ambitious plan to create an immense "common market" of 380 million people and $4 trillion worth of goods was greatly strengthened by the 1986 signing of the Single European Act (SEA), which set a deadline for economic integration of December 31, 1992, and instituted new voting requirements to make passage of EU legislation easier. A treaty that was proposed at the Maastricht Summit in 1991 was ratified in 1993. It provided for (1) monetary union through the creation of a single currency for the entire EU, (2) political union, and (3) a "social dimension" through the establishment of

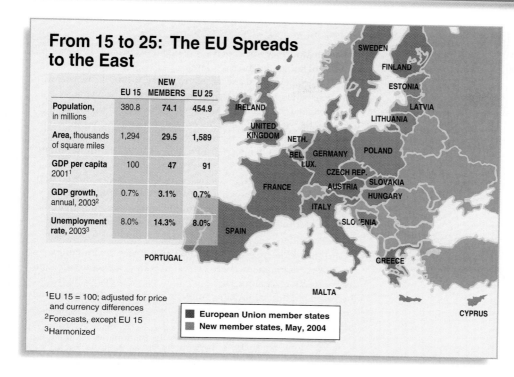

From 15 to 25: The EU Spreads to the East

	EU 15	NEW MEMBERS	EU 25
Population, in millions	380.8	74.1	454.9
Area, thousands of square miles	1,294	29.5	1,589
GDP per capita 2001[1]	100	47	91
GDP growth, annual, 2003[2]	0.7%	3.1%	0.7%
Unemployment rate, 2003[3]	8.0%	14.3%	8.0%

[1]EU 15 = 100; adjusted for price and currency differences
[2]Forecasts, except EU 15
[3]Harmonized

■ European Union member states
■ New member states, May, 2004

EXHIBIT 9-2

FROM 15 TO 25: THE EU SPREADS TO THE EAST

Source: Eurostat, The United Nations Population Reference Bureau; (Gapminder. org).

uniform labor and Social Security regulations. The leaders of the 12 nations at the time agreed to the creation of a European Monetary Institute by 1994, a European Central Bank by 1998, and a uniform European currency unit (ECU) by 1999 (Table 9-3). Three new members (Finland, Austria, and Sweden) joined the EU in 1994, bringing the total to 15 nations.

In May 2004, ten nations joined the EU: Cyprus, Czech Republic, Estonia, Hungary, Latvia, Lithuania, Malta, Poland, Slovakia, and Slovenia. Bulgaria, Romania, and Turkey's applications may be accepted later.

Structure. The European Union consists of a Council of Ministers, a Commission, a parliament (Assembly), and the European Court of Justice (with the addition of the Court of First Instance).

Council of Ministers. The Council of Ministers is composed of one representative from each of the member nations. Its purposes are to coordinate the economic policies of member states and, more recently, to negotiate with nonmember states. In the past, the Council generally rubber-stamped legislation proposed by the Commission, but this docility is less assured as the Council begins to flex some of the authority granted it by the SEA and the Maastricht Treaty.

Commission. The Commission consists of 20 members who represent the EU, not national concerns. It is responsible for the EU's relations with international organizations such as the United Nations and the World Trade Organization. Member states are apportioned voting power in the Commission on the basis of their population and economic power. The Commission elects a president from among its members. Each Commission member supervises a functional area (e.g., agriculture or competition) that may be affected by several

TABLE 9-3

KEY ELEMENTS OF THE TREATY OF MAASTRICHT

Agreement	Goals and Stumbling Blocks
Monetary Union	• European Monetary Institute was created on January 1, 1994, and started operating on January 1, 1999. • A single currency issued any day after January 1, 1999, is the goal of 25 nations who meet three standards: (1) Annual budget deficit cannot exceed the ceiling of 3 percent of gross domestic product; (2) the public debt limit for each country must not exceed 60 percent of gross domestic product; and (3) a country's inflation rate must be lower than 2.9 percent, based on a complex formula set out in 1997. • Great Britain was allowed to opt out of the EC currency union until an unspecified date. It opposes monetary union for ideological reasons. • Denmark was also allowed to opt out pending a referendum on the issue, a constitutional requirement. The Danish government backs monetary union.
Political Union	• EC jurisdiction in areas including industrial affairs, health, education, trade, environment, energy, culture, tourism, and consumer and civil protection. Member states vote to implement decisions. • Increased political cooperation under a new name—European Union. Permanent diplomatic network of senior political officials created in the EC capitals. • Great Britain rejected EC-imposed labor legislation, forcing the removal of the so-called social chapter from the treaty. It will be implemented separately by the other 14 members, officials said.
Federalism	• EC leaders dropped reference to an EC "with a federal goal." Instead, the political Union accord describes the community as "an ever-closer union in which political decisions have to be taken as near to the people as possible." • Great Britain rejected the "federalism" as the embodiment of what it feels would be an encroaching EC superstate.
Foreign Affairs	• EC states move toward a joint foreign policy, with most decisions requiring unanimity. • Great Britain wanted the ability to opt out of any joint decision. How this provision will be interpreted by the various sides is yet to be seen.
Defense	• The Western European Union, a long-dormant group of nine EC states, will be revived to act as the EC's defense body but linked to the NATO alliance. • Although France and Germany supported a greater military role for the Union, Great Britain, Italy, and others did not want to see NATO's influence diluted.
European Parliament	• The 518-member EC assembly gets a modest say in shaping some EC legislation. Its new powers fall short of what the assembly had sought (i.e., an equitable sharing of the right to make EC laws with the EC governments). • Great Britain and Denmark refused to grant the assembly broader powers.

directorates. There are 22 directorates (Exhibit 9-3), which are actually run by "supranational" civil servants called director generals. In theory, the directorates serve the Commission, but, in fact, the director generals often heavily influence legislation as it moves through the Commission.

- External Relations
- Economic and Financial Affairs
- Internal Market and Industrial Affairs
- Competition
- Employment, Social Affairs, and Education
- Agriculture
- Transportation
- Development
- Personnel and Administration
- Information, Communication, and Culture
- Environment, Nuclear Safety, and Civil Protection; Science; Research and Development
- Telecommunication, Information Industry, and Innovation
- Fisheries
- Financial Institutions and Company Law
- Regional Policy
- Energy
- Credit and Investment
- Budgets
- Financial Control
- Customs Union and Indirect Taxation
- Coordination of Structural Instruments
- Enterprise Policy, Distributive Trades, Tourism, and Cooperatives

EXHIBIT 9-3

DIRECTORATES OF THE EUROPEAN UNION

Parliament. The Parliament (Assembly) is made up of representatives elected from each nation-state for a term set by the nation-state. The representatives come from most of the major European political factions (Socialists, Christian Democrats, Communists, Liberals, and so on), and each of the parties in the Parliament also exists in the member states. The Parliament elects a president to preside over its deliberations. The Parliament's general powers are to (1) serve as a consultative body to the council, (2) refer matters affecting EU interests to the Commission or Council, (3) censure the Commission when necessary, (4) assent to trade agreements with countries outside the EU, (5) amend the EU budget, and (6) participate with the Commission in the legislative procedure.

European Court of Justice. The European Court of Justice performs the functions of arbiter and final decision maker in conflicts between EU law and individual member states. The national courts of member states are obligated to follow EU law and Court of Justice decisions. The Court of First Instance was established in 1989 to reduce the workload of the Court of Justice. It has jurisdiction over appeals of the Commission's decisions on mergers and acquisitions. It also sets the penalties for price fixing when non-EU companies are involved.

Impact. *Unity of Law.* Agricultural, environmental, and labor legislation is being made uniform throughout the 25 member nations, with allowances and subsidies for the poorer members. The national courts of member states are now following decisions of the European Court of Justice.

Economic Integration. The SEA and the Maastricht Treaty have pushed the EU members to eliminate tariff and nontariff barriers among themselves. British and French differences over the creation of a single currency have forced the suspension of this goal.

Political Union. The political union envisioned by the Maastricht Treaty has been an elusive goal for the EU because member states (and their citizens) have proved more reluctant to make the necessary compromises on national sovereignty than the treaty's architects anticipated. Nonetheless, the EU is the only regional organization that has in place the sophisticated structure required to make political union a realistic possibility. A draft of the new charter for the EU was under consideration in 2004.

A Constitution for 450 Million People

The 105 delegates making up the Convention of the Future of Europe codified a draft constitution for the 25 members of the European Union (Union or EU) in June 2003. The Union comprises 450 million people (larger than all but China and India) with an economy of $9 trillion (about the same as the United States). One year later in June 2004, the Constitution was adopted (but not ratified) by the heads of state. The Constitution will have primacy over any nation-state law. It sets out voting rules and trade policy for the Union. In 400 articles, the Constitution outlines in detail areas such as transportation, justice, and social policy that must be harmonized with the member states. It also sets out a new organizational structure with a powerful council, a president, one foreign minister, a strong public prosecutor arm, and a Parliament with the power to pass legislation if approved by at least 15 member countries (or 65 percent of the population). The Constitution fails to set out a common foreign and security policy; thus, the sovereignty of nation-states is upheld in part. Each nation-state's Parliament must ratify the Constitution before it can come into force. Denmark, Ireland, Great Britain, and four other countries must have a national referendum by virtue of their constitutions, whereas others may choose to do so for political reasons. There are still many issues to be resolved, for example, how to share power between small nation-states (Spain) and large countries (Germany), or how to share the budget of the Union in order to help poorer nation-states.

NORTH AMERICAN FREE TRADE AGREEMENT

Purpose. The North American Free Trade Agreement (NAFTA), ratified in 1994, seeks to eliminate barriers to the flow of goods, services, and investments among Canada, the United States, and Mexico over a 15-year period. NAFTA envisions a gradual phasing out of these barriers, with the length of the phaseout varying from industry to industry. The ultimate goal is a totally free trade zone among the three member states, with eventual inclusion of Central and Latin American countries. So far, the only country invited to join the founding members is Chile.

Structure. NAFTA is administered by a three-member Trade Commission, which oversees a Secretariat and arbitral panels.

Trade Commission. Staffed by trade ministers from each of the three nations, the Trade Commission meets once a year and makes its decisions by consensus. It supervises the implementation of the treaty and resolves disputes over interpretation. The daily operations of NAFTA are conducted by ad hoc working groups appointed by the three governments.

Secretariat. The permanent Secretariat is composed of national sections (departments) representing each member country. Its purposes are to provide technical support for the Trade Commission and to put together arbitral panels to resolve disputes between members.

Arbitral Panels. The treaty has detailed arbitration provisions for settling disputes, particularly those involving dumping of goods (selling a good in a member country at a lower price than at home) and interpretations of the treaty. Though the arbitration proceedings are designed especially to resolve disputes between member nations, the treaty encourages private parties to use them as well. If they do, they must agree to abide by the arbitral panel's decision.

Each arbitral panel has five members, chosen from a roster of 30 legal experts from NAFTA and non-NAFTA countries. Within 90 days, the panel will give the disputant countries a confidential report. Over the next 14 days, the disputants may present their comments on the report to the panel. Within 30 days of the issuance of the initial report, the arbitral panel must present its final report to the parties and to the Trade Commission, which publishes it. The countries then have 30 days to resolve their dispute, or if the panel has found one party wrong, the other may legally retaliate.

Impact. NAFTA has not only brought together three North American neighbors of different historical and cultural background, but it has also provided a model of economic integration for other countries in Central and Latin America.

It has had an impact on each country's exports and imports. It has served as an institution to arbitrate disputes. For example, the U.S. government has filed a complaint on behalf of United Parcel Service (UPS), and one of the first arbitral panels was set up. UPS believed it was being hampered by NAFTA government regulations in Mexico, which limit the size of delivery trucks to be used in delivering packages. The arbitral panel ruled in favor of UPS.

GLOBAL DISPUTE RESOLUTION

Many times, when private or public parties enter into an international business agreement, they incorporate means for resolving future disputes (e.g., arbitration clauses) into the agreement. Another form of protection for firms doing business internationally is the insurance some nation-states offer domestic companies to encourage them to export (e.g., United States Overseas Private Investment Corporation). Still, the two methods used most frequently to resolve irreconcilable differences between parties involved in international transactions are arbitration and litigation.

ARBITRATION

Arbitration is a dispute-resolution process whereby parties submit their disagreements to a private individual decision maker they agree on or to a panel of decision makers whose selection has been provided for in the contract the parties signed. Arbitration clauses in contracts involving international business transactions should meticulously stipulate what law will govern the arbitration, where

arbitration A dispute-resolution method whereby the disputant parties submit their disagreement to a mutually agreed upon neutral decision maker or one provided for by statute.

and when the arbitration will take place, what language will be used, and how the expenses of arbitration will be shared. They also stipulate a waiver of judicial (court) review by both parties to the dispute. All these matters should be carefully negotiated when the contract is being drafted. Arbitration of disputes may also come about through treaties. For instance, the United Nations Convention on the Recognition of Foreign Arbitral Awards encourages use of arbitration agreements and awards. The World Bank's International Center for the Settlement of Investment Disputes (ICSID), created in 1965 by treaty (the Washington Convention), provides to disputants arbitration rules as well as experienced arbitrators, and the International Chamber of Commerce offers a permanent arbitration tribunal. Finally, individual countries have arbitration associations that provide experienced arbitrators to parties desiring assistance in settling their disputes.

We presented a detailed explanation of the arbitration process in Chapter 4. Here we provide a case that demonstrates how important it is for businesses to understand the nature of international arbitration and the meaning of any documents they sign.

CASE 9-5

Republic of Nicaragua v. Standard Fruit Company and Steamship Company
United States Court of Appeals
937 F.2d 469 (9th Cir. 1991)

Plaintiff-appellant Nicaragua sued Standard Fruit and its parent companies, the defendants. Standard Fruit, a wholly owned subsidiary of Standard Fruit Company (SFC) and Steamship Company (Steamship), was involved in the production and purchase of bananas in Nicaragua. Steamship purchased the bananas from SFC. In 1979, a Nicaraguan rebel group known as the Sandinistas overthrew the government of Nicaragua and attempted to negotiate with Standard Fruit for more control over the banana industry in their country. When the negotiations proved unsuccessful, the Sandinistas took over the industry by decree and nullified all leases of plantations and purchase contracts. Standard Fruit stopped doing business in Nicaragua. After three days of negotiations, Steamship signed a memorandum, termed "an agreement in principal," that provided for the renegotiation of existing contracts and included an arbitration clause that stated:

> *Any and all disputes arising under the arrangements contemplated hereunder ... will be referred to mutually agreed mechanisms or procedures of international arbitration, such as the rules of the London Arbitration Association.*

The implementing contracts provided for in the memorandum were never renegotiated, but Standard Fruit resumed business in Nicaragua for two years and then left the country for good in 1982. Nicaragua then sued in a United States District Court, requesting the court to compel Steamship to arbitrate Nicaragua's breach-of-contract suit.

Steamship argued that the arbitration clause in the memorandum was too vague and broad to be enforceable and that it merely referred to the creation of a formal clause that would be included in the renegotiated contracts. The district court agreed and ruled in favor of the defendants, granting their request for a summary judgment. Nicaragua appealed.

Judge Ferguson

We hold that although it was the court's responsibility to determine the threshold question of arbitrability, the district court improperly looked to the validity of the contract as a whole and erroneously determined that the parties had not agreed to arbitrate this dispute. Instead, it should have considered only the validity and scope of the arbitration clause itself. In addition, the district court ignored strong evidence in the record that both parties intended to be bound by the arbitration clause. As all doubts over the scope of an arbitration clause must be resolved in favor of arbitration, and in light of the strong federal policy favoring arbitration in international commercial disputes, Nicaragua's motion to compel arbitration should have been granted. Whether the Memorandum was binding, whether it covered banana purchases, and whether Standard Fruit Company was bound by it are all questions properly left to the arbitrators. Finally, genuine disputes of fact exist as to the intent of the parties and the validity and scope of the Memorandum.

Reversed, in favor of Plaintiff-Appellant, Nicaragua.

LITIGATION

When contracts do not contain arbitration clauses and there is no other alternative (such as mediation or conciliation) available, **litigation** may be the only way to resolve a dispute between parties. In some private international business contracts, a choice-of-forum clause is included so that the parties know which family of law is to be applied in case of a dispute and what nation's courts will be used. When negotiating contracts in the international arena, managers should make sure that choice-of-forum clauses are specific on both these questions, for what family of law governs and which nation's courts are used can make a major difference in the outcome. Because there is no single international court or legal system capable of resolving all commercial disputes between private parties, a choice-of-forum clause should be negotiated in all agreements involving major transactions. London's Commercial Court, established in 1895, is the most popular neutral forum for resolving commercial litigation, owing to its 100 years of experience.

Most of the international and regional organizations discussed in this chapter emphatically encourage the arbitration of private contractual disputes because the arbitration process is a quicker and less public means of resolving disputes than litigation. In certain areas of the world (particularly the Far East), companies and governments seek to avoid litigation.

litigation A dispute-resolution process that involves going through the judicial system; a lawsuit.

Globalization Or Not?

In most all of the chapters in this text we have examined the globalization aspect of several areas of business ethics and law. We have attempted to present some factual bases in setting out the discussion. Below you will find a debate that is taking place all over the world. We invite you to participate in this sometime vigorous discussion of whether globalization of business helps or hurts societies all over the world. It is skillfully summarized by Professor Murray Wiedenbaum in his text *Business and Government in the Global Marketplace*.

Pros	*Cons*
"Accelerates economic growth, increasing living standards"	"Generates widespread poverty in the pursuance of corporate greed"
"Offers consumers greater variety of products and at lower prices"	"Results in greater income inequality"
"Increases jobs and wages and improves working conditions"	"Moves jobs to low-wage factories that abuse workers' rights"
"Encourages a greater exchange of information and use of technology"	"Provides opportunity for criminal and terrorist groups to operate on a global scale"
"Provides wealth for environmental cleanup"	"Pollutes local environments that lack ecological standards"
"Helps developing nations and lifts millions out of poverty"	"Traps developing countries in high debt loads"
"Extends economic and political freedoms"	"Threatens national sovereignty"
"Raises life expectancy, health standards, and literacy rates"	"Worsens public health and harms social fabrics of agricultural-based societies"

Source: M. Wiedenbaum, *Business and Government in the Global Marketplace*, 7th ed. (Upper Saddle River, N.J.: Prentice Hall, 2004), p. 190.

SUMMARY

The political, economic, cultural, and legal dimensions of the international environment of business need to be considered by managers undertaking international business ventures, although the emphasis in this book is on legal and ethical issues. The major families of law are common law, which relies primarily on case law and precedent; civil law, which relies primarily on codes and statutory law; Islamic law, which relies on the *Shari'a*, a religious code of rules; socialist law, which is based on Marxism-Leninism and does not recognize private property; and Hindu law, which relies primarily on the *Sastras*, a religious code.

International law is divided into public international law, governing the relationships between nation-states, and private international law, governing the relationships between private parties involved in international transactions.

The major methods of engaging in international business are trade, international licensing and franchising, and foreign direct investment. The principal risk of engaging in international business are expropriation, the sovereign immunity doctrine and the act-of-state doctrine, export and import controls, and currency controls and fluctuations (particularly in developing nations).

World and regional integrative organizations, especially the World Trade Organization, the European Union, and NAFTA, are making a strong impact on international business. Arbitration and litigation are the major methods of international dispute resolution.

REVIEW QUESTIONS

9-1 Contrast the common-law family with the socialist-law family.

9-2 Which of the methods of engaging in international business discussed in this chapter is least risky for a foreign multinational company? Explain.

9-3 Define the following:
   a. expropriation
   b. doctrine of sovereign immunity
   c. act-of-state doctrine
   d. arbitration clause
   e. choice-of-forum clause

9-4 Explain how currency fluctuations affect companies doing international business.

9-5 Why was the GATT Pact, creating the World Trade Organization, so important to doing international business? Explain.

9-6 Why is arbitration preferred to litigation as a means of resolving international business disputes? Explain.

REVIEW PROBLEMS

9-7 Royal Bed and Spring Company, a U.S. distributor of furniture products, entered into an exclusive distributorship agreement with a Brazilian manufacturer of furniture products. Under the terms of the contract, Royal Bed was to distribute in Puerto Rico the furniture products manufactured by Famossul in Brazil. The contract contained forum-selection and choice-of-law clauses, which designated the juridical district of Curitiba, State of Parana, Brazil, as the judicial forum and the Brazilian Civil Code as the law to be applied in the event of any dispute. Famossul terminated the exclusive distributorship and suspended the shipment of goods without just cause. Puerto Rican law refuses to enforce forum-selection clauses providing for foreign venues as a matter of public policy. In what jurisdiction should Royal Bed bring suit? Explain.

9-8 A, a U.S. company, entered into a contract with C, a Swiss subsidiary of General Motors, to sell Chevrolet automobiles in Aruba. An arbitration clause in the parties' agreement provided that all disputes would be settled by arbitration in accordance with Aruban law. Aruba follows Dutch civil law. A argues that only U.S. law can apply because the contract was made in the United States. Is A correct? Explain.

9-9 Zapata entered into a contract with a German corporation to use one of Zapata's oil-drilling rigs off the coast of Italy. The contract stated, "Any dispute arising must be treated before the London Court of Justice." A severe storm damaged the oil rig as it was being towed through the Gulf of Mexico. Zapata filed suit in federal district court. Does the U.S. court have jurisdiction to decide the dispute? What is the purpose behind a choice-of-forum clause, and should the clause be enforced?

9-10 The members of the International Association of Machinists (IAM) were disturbed by the high price of oil and petroleum-derived products in the United States. They believed that the actions of the Organization of Petroleum Exporting Countries (OPEC) were the cause of the high prices. Therefore, the IAM sued OPEC's member countries in a federal district court, alleging that these countries' price-setting

activities violated U.S. antitrust law. OPEC argued the act-of-state doctrine as a defense. Who do you think won? Explain why.

9-11 Dr. Will Pirkey, a U.S. otolaryngologist, signed an employment contract in which he agreed to work for two years at the King Faisal Hospital in Saudi Arabia. Before his departure, Pirkey received his employment contract, which contained a clause providing that his agreement with the hospital would be construed in accordance with Saudi Arabian law. Because of the assassination of King Faisal and for other reasons, Pirkey did not go to Saudi Arabia as agreed and is now contesting the choice-of-law provision of his employment contract as unconscionable. He asks that his home state's laws (New York) should apply. Who will win this case? Explain why.

9-12 U.S. Company owned a subsidiary in France that had a contract to deliver compressors for use in the Soviet natural gas pipeline then under construction. The U.S. government banned the export of goods to the Soviet Union by U.S. companies or U.S.-controlled foreign companies, and U.S. company complied with the ban by ordering its French subsidiary to stop delivery of the compressors. The French government, however, ordered delivery. U.S. Company delivered the compressors. The U.S. government thereupon instituted a criminal action against U.S. Company. What is U.S. Company's defense? Explain.

CASE PROBLEMS

9-13 Tonoga, Ltd. (Taconic) is a manufacturer incorporated in Ireland with its principal place of business in New York. In 1997, Taconic entered into a contract with a German construction company to supply special material for a tent project designed to shelter religious pilgrims visiting holy sites in Saudi Arabia. Most of the material was made in and shipped from New York. The company did not pay Taconic and eventually filed for bankruptcy. Another German firm, Werner Voss Architects and Engineers, acting as an agent for the government of Saudi Arabia, guaranteed the payments due Taconic to induce it to complete the project. When Taconic received all but the final payment, the firm filed a suit in a federal district court against the government of Saudi Arabia, claiming breach of the guaranty and seeking to collect, in part, about $3 million. The defendant filed a motion to dismiss based, in part, on the doctrine of sovereign immunity.

Under what circumstances does this doctrine apply? Should this suit be dismissed under the "commercial activity" exception? Explain. *Tonoga, Ltd. v. Ministry of Public Works and Housing of Kingdom of Saudi Arabia*, 135 F.Supp. 2d 350 (N.D.N.Y. 2001).

9-14 George Janini and other employees of Kuwait University (the plaintiffs) were terminated from their positions following Iraq's invasion of Kuwait in August 1990. Following the invasion, the government of Kuwait issued a decree stating, among other things, that contracts concluded between the government and those non-Kuwaiti workers were automatically abrogated because of the impossibility of enforcement due to the Iraqi invasion. The plaintiffs sued Kuwait University in a U.S. court, alleging that their termination breached their employment contracts, which required nine months' notice before termination. The plaintiffs sought back pay and other benefits to which they were entitled under their contracts. The university claimed that, as a government-operated institution, it was immune from the jurisdiction of U.S. courts under the doctrine of sovereign immunity. Will an exception apply to the university's activities with respect to the plaintiffs? *Janini v. Kuwait University*, 43 F.3d 1534 (D.C. Cir. 1995)

9-15 In 1996, the International Trade Administration (ITA) of the U.S. Department of Commerce assessed antidumping duties against Koyo Seiko Co., NTN Corp., on certain tapered roller bearings and their components imported from Japan. In assessing these duties, the ITA requested information from the makers about their home market sales. NTN responded in part that its figures should not include many sample and small-quantity sales, which were made to enable customers to decide whether to buy the products. NTN provided no evidence to support this assertion, however. In calculating the fair market value of the bearings in Japan, the ITA determined, among other things, that sample and small-quantity sales were within the makers' ordinary course of trade. Koyo and others appealed these assessments to the U.S. Court of International Trade. NTN objected in part to the ITA's inclusion of sample and small quantity sales. Should the court order the ITA to recalculate its assessment on the basis of NTN's objection? Explain. *Koyo Seiko Co. v. United States*, 186 F.Supp.2d 1332 (CIT [Court of International Trade] 2002).

ASSIGNMENT ON THE INTERNET

As this chapter demonstrates, there are many important issues to consider before engaging in international business. Pick a country that you know little about and using the following Web site (**www.lib.uchicago.edu/~llou/forintlaw.html**), research the issues you think most important to consider before doing business in that country. What are its cultural, economic, political, and legal dimensions?

What are its trade laws? Does it belong to any international treaties or organizations?

If you cannot find all the information you need, make a list of detailed questions you would want answered. Finally, for each of the questions you researched, explain why that question was significant in your thinking.

 ## ON THE INTERNET

www.asil.org/resource/ergintr1.htm#Researching Use this site, maintained by the American Society of International Law, to guide you in researching international law issues on the internet.

www.washlaw.edu/forint/forintmain.html This page provides links to primary foreign and international legal resources, research aids, and sites useful for international business.

www.loc.gov/law/guide/nations.html This link to the Law Library of Congress's Nations of the World contains legal information for each country around the world.

www.icj-cij.org This page contains information about and ruling of the International Court of Justice.

www.un.org/law The website of the United Nations International Law provides useful information, including treaties governing business transactions and trade law.

www.nafta-sec-alena.org/DefaultSite/index.html The homepage of the North American Free Trade Agreement (NAFTA) contains many legal texts as well as methods for dispute settlement.

Part Two

PRIVATE LAW AND THE LEGAL

ENVIRONMENT OF BUSINESS

art Two explores areas of private law that impact on the legal environment
of business. It opens with a discussion of contract law, then proceeds to
examine the law of torts, product liability law, property law, agency law,
and finally, the law of business associations.

10

THE LAW OF CONTRACTS
AND SALES—I

- DEFINITION, SOURCES, AND CLASSIFICATIONS
  OF CONTRACT LAW
- ELEMENTS OF A LEGAL CONTRACT
- CONTRACTS THAT MUST BE IN WRITING
- PAROL EVIDENCE RULE
- THIRD-PARTY BENEFICIARY CONTRACTS
  AND ASSIGNMENT OF RIGHTS

It is a fundamental requirement of a free enterprise economy that entities in the private sector and at all levels of government be able to enter into agreements that are enforceable by courts of law. Without the assurance that business agreements are legally enforceable, everyday commercial dealings would be difficult to carry out. Contract law has evolved to provide enterprises with the sense of predictability and security they need to flourish and to produce quality products.

Contract law affects several other areas of law discussed in this book. When we take up the law of torts and product liability (Chapters 12 and 13), for instance, much of our discussion will concern breaches of warranty of merchantability, fitness, or usefulness. In our review of the law of business associations (Chapter 16), we will examine contracts between principal and agents, employer and employees, and partners in partnership agreements. You will see when we analyze antitrust law (Chapter 23) that contracts that unreasonably restrain trade are prohibited. The basis for our discussion of labor law (Chapter 19) is collective bargaining agreements and what practices incorporated into those agreements government regulation will tolerate. Finally, when we discuss the relationship between management and consumers (Chapter 24), the law of contracts will be our starting point. So contract law is immensely significant in the legal environment of business.

This chapter begins with a definition and classification of contract law. It analyzes the six elements of a contract; then explains which contracts must be in writing in order to be enforceable, the parol evidence rule, and the nature of third-party beneficiary contracts and assignment of rights.

DEFINITION, SOURCES, AND CLASSIFICATIONS OF CONTRACT LAW

DEFINITION

A **contract** is generally defined as a legally enforceable exchange of promises or an exchange of a promise for an act that assures parties to an agreement that their promises will be enforceable. Contract law brings predictability to the exchange. For example, if a corporation manufacturing video recorders enters

contract A legally enforceable exchange of promises or an exchange of a promise for an act.

═══ Critical Thinking About the Law ═══

Contract law promotes predictability in exchange. In other words, as a future business manager, you might enter into a contractual agreement in which you agree to pay a certain amount of money in exchange for another business's goods or services. Because contracts are legally enforceable, you are much more likely to receive these goods at the price on which you both agreed when there is an existing contract. Hence, there is greater predictability, and less risk, when a contract exists, because the possibility of a lawsuit deters businesses from deviating from the terms of a contract. Therefore, contracts keep businesses and individuals accountable to the agreements they make.

Predictability and accountability are only two reasons for the importance of contract law. But underlying these reasons, certain primary ethical norms have greater priority than others. As you consider the benefits of contract law, this critical thinking exercise will urge you to think about the *primary ethical norms* that influence the law of contracts (see Chapter 1).

1. Which primary ethical norm would be most important to someone who viewed contract law as a crucial method of promoting predictability in exchange?

   Clue: This person might want to ensure that his business runs smoothly, even though some of his operations depend on another business or individual to honor the terms of the contract.

2. If someone were mostly concerned with contract law's keeping businesses and individuals accountable to their agreements, which primary ethical norm would this person value the most?

   Clue: This person might be fearful that other businesses or individuals might not perform as they agreed, thereby harming those depending on their performance.

3. Even though a contract exists between two businesses, courts may decide not to honor the existing contract because the contract would threaten fair competition in a particular industry. This principle underlies the reasoning for Congress's creating antitrust legislation, which you will read more about in Chapter 23. In these kinds of situations in which a court declares a contract to be unfair, which ethical norms would the court hold in highest priority?

   Clue: One of the reasons that a court would strike down a contractual agreement is that the court wants to maximize consumer welfare, while derogating the interests of large corporations.

into an agreement with a retailer to provide a fixed number of video recorders each month, the retailer knows that it can rely on the corporation's promise and advertise the availability of those video recorders to its customers, because if the manufacturer reneges on the agreement, it is enforceable in a court of law. Contracts are essential to the workings of a private enterprise economy. They assist parties in the buying and selling of goods, and they make it possible to shift risks to parties more willing to bear them.

SOURCES OF CONTRACT LAW

Contract law is grounded in the case law of the state and federal courts, as well as state and federal statutory law. Case law, or what is often known as the common law because it originates with the law of English courts, governs contracts dealing with real property, personal property, services, and employment contracts. Statutory law, particularly the Uniform Commercial Code (UCC), generally governs contracts for the sale of goods. The UCC has been adopted in whole or in part by all 50 states and the District of Columbia. This chapter integrates case law with the UCC.

Case Law. The law of contracts originated in judicial decisions in England and the United States. Later, states and the federal courts modified their case law through the use of statutory law. Nonetheless, the formation of contract law and its understanding are based on fundamental principles set out by the courts and, more recently, in the *Restatement of the Law of Contracts*. The restatement summarizes contract principles as set out by legal scholars. Case law (or common law) applies to contracts that cover real property (land and anything attached permanently therein), personal property, services, and employment contracts.

Uniform Commercial Code. In order to obtain uniformity among state laws, particularly as applicable to sales contracts, the National Conference of Commissioners on Uniform State Laws and the American Law Institute drafted a set of commercial laws applicable to all states. This effort was called the *Uniform Commercial Code (UCC)*. Gradually, the states adopted the document in whole or in part. Businesses now had uniform requirements that expedite interstate contracts. In general, Article II of the UCC allows more liberal requirements to form and perform contracts than are allowed in contracts based on common-law principles. Particular differences are noted in sections of this and the next chapter. Article II is being revised to provide coverage of contracts dealing with electronic data processing, licenses, leases, and matters dealing with computer software.

CLASSIFICATIONS OF CONTRACTS

express contract An exchange of oral or written promises between parties that are enforceable in a court of law.

implied contract One that is established by the conduct of a party rather than by the party's written or spoken words.

Terms that refer to types of contracts are sprinkled throughout this text. So that you will clearly understand what we are talking about, we define several classifications of contracts here.

Express and Implied Contracts. An **express contract** is an exchange of oral or written promises between parties that are enforceable in a court of law. Note that oral and written promises are equally enforceable. An **implied contract** is one that is established by the conduct of a party rather than by the party's written or spoken words. For example, if you go to the dentist in an emergency and have a tooth extracted, you and the dentist have an implied agreement contract: She will extract your throbbing tooth in a professional manner and you will pay her for her service. The existence and content of an implied contract are determined by the reasonable-person test: Would a reasonable person expect the conduct of the parties to constitute an enforceable contract?

Unilateral and Bilateral Contracts. A **unilateral contract** is defined as an exchange of a promise for an act. For example, if City A promises to pay a reward of $5,000 to anyone who provides information leading to the arrest and conviction of the individual who robbed a local bank, the promise is accepted by the act of the person who provides the information. A **bilateral contract** involves the exchange of one promise for another promise. For example, Jones promises to pay Smith $5,000 for a piece of land in exchange for Smith's promise to deliver clear title and a deed at a later date.

unilateral contract An exchange of a promise for an act.

bilateral contract The exchange of one promise for another promise.

Void, Voidable, and Valid Contracts. A contract is **void** if at its formation its object is illegal or it has serious defects in its formation (e.g., fraud). If Jones promises to pay Smith $5,000 to kill Clark, the contract is void at its formation because killing another person without court sanction is illegal. A contract is **voidable** if one of the parties has the option of either withdrawing from the contract or enforcing it. If Jones, a 17-year-old in a state where the legal age for entering an enforceable contract is 18, executes an agreement with Smith, an adult, to buy a car, Jones can rescind (cancel) the contract before he is 18 or shortly thereafter. A **valid contract** is one that is not void, is enforceable, and meets the six requirements discussed later in this chapter.

void contract One that at its formation has an illegal object of serious defects.

voidable contract One that gives one of the parties the option of withdrawing.

valid contract One that meets all legal requirements for a fully enforceable contract.

Executed and Executory Contracts. An **executed contract** is one for which all the terms have been performed. In our earlier example, if Jones agrees to buy Smith's land for $5,000, and Smith delivers clear title and a deed and Jones gives Smith $5,000, the necessary terms (assuming no fraud) have been carried out or performed. In contrast, an executory contract is one for which all the terms have not been completed or performed. If Jones agrees to paint Smith's house for $2,500 and Smith promises to pay the $2,500 upon completion of the paint job, the contract remains executory until the house is completely painted. The importance of complete performance will be shown when discharge and remedies for a breach of contract are examined in Chapter 11.

executed contract One for which all the terms have been performed.

Quasi-Contract. A **quasi-contract** is a court-imposed agreement to prevent unjust enrichment of one party when the parties had not really agreed to an enforceable contract. For example, while visiting his neighbor, Johnson, Jones sees a truck pull up at his own residence. Two people emerge and begin cutting his lawn and doing other landscaping work. Jones knows that neither he nor his wife contracted to have this work performed; nevertheless, he likes the job that's being done, so he says nothing. When the landscapers finish, they put a bill in Jones's mailbox and drive off. It turns out that the landscapers made an honest mistake: They landscaped Jones's property when they were supposed to landscape Smith's. Jones refuses to pay the bill, arguing that he did not contract for this work. He even calls the landscapers unflattering names. The court orders Jones to pay, finding that he was unjustly enriched. (Jones would not have had to pay if he had not been in a position to correct the mistake before it took place. That is, Jones would not have had to pay had this mistaken landscaping occurred while he and his wife were vacationing in Paris.) Quasi-contracts are rare.

quasi-contract A court-imposed agreement to prevent the unjust enrichment of one party when the parties had not really agreed to an enforceable contract.

"No, Mr. Foster, I'm afraid that keeping your fingers crossed during the signing of the contract did not render it unenforceable."

COPYRIGHT © ARNOLD R. GLICK 1994.

ELEMENTS OF A LEGAL CONTRACT

A valid contract has six elements: (1) legal offer, (2) legal acceptance, (3) consideration, (4) genuine assent, (5) competent parties, and (6) a legal object. When these six elements are present, a legally enforceable contract usually exists.

LEGAL OFFER

legal offer An offer that shows objective intent to enter into the contract, is definite, and is communicated to the offeree.

The contractual process begins with a **legal offer**. "I will pay you $2,000 for your 1978 Cutlass," Smith says to Jones. Smith has initiated a possible contract and is known as the *offeror*. Jones is the *offeree*. In order for Smith's offer to be valid, by common-law principles, it must meet three requirements:

1. The offer must show *objective intent* to enter into the contract. The court will look at the words, conduct, writing, and, in some cases, deliberate omissions of the offer. The court will not concern itself with subjective measurements, such as what was in the person's mind at the time of entering the contract. It will simply ask whether a reasonable person who listened to Smith's statements would conclude that there was a serious intent to make an offer.

2. The offer must be *definite*; that is, there must be some reference to subject matter, quantity of items being offered, and price of the items. In Smith's offer, all three references are present. Article II of the UCC, because it is intended to govern daily transactions in goods, is less stringent. It allows the price and other terms—but not subject matter or quantity—to remain open or to be based on an industry standard of "reasonableness." X offers to sell "20 widgets that are needed" to Y at a "reasonable price with specific terms

to be negotiated" is an example of the more open-ended approach to legal offers taken by the UCC (Section 2-204). Also, the courts weigh industry custom and prior dealings to determine whether the terms are definite.

3. The offer must be *communicated* to the party (offeree) intended by the offeror. Smith's offer was communicated directly to Jones, but what of an offer by Bank X to pay for information leading to the arrest and conviction of Y, a robber? Z does not know of the reward, but several days after it is offered, she sees Y running out of a store with something in his hand. Z apprehends Y. Should she get the reward from Bank X? The bank's offer of a reward was not communicated to her, so the technical requirements of contract law have not been met. Most state courts, however, and many state statutes, provide that Z will be able to collect, for it is public policy to encourage citizens to assist in apprehending criminals.

In the following case, the court examined an advertisement's intent, its definiteness, and to whom it was communicated in determining whether a legal offer existed.

CASE 10-1

Satellite Entertainment Center v. Keaton
Superior Court of New Jersey Appellate Division,
789 A. 21.662 (2002)

In 1993, John Keaton decided to open a barbecue restaurant in Jersey City, New Jersey, and entered into a six-year lease with George Williams to occupy a portion of Williams's building. After Williams died, Morris Winograd, the owner of Satellite Entertainment Center, Inc., bought the building. Winograd planned to renovate the entire premises to open a new restaurant and bar. In September 1995, Winograd asked Keaton how much it would cost to buy his business. Keaton named a price of $175,000. Keaton later claimed, as corroborated by witnesses, that Winograd said he would pay that amount. He wanted Keaton out by the end of the year, and he wanted Keaton to manage the new enterprise. Keaton vacated the premises by December. In January, Winograd began paying Keaton a salary but did not pay him the $175,000, despite repeated requests. In April 1997, Winograd terminated Keaton. In a subsequent claim in a New Jersey state court against Satellite and Winograd, Keaton (plaintiff) sought the $175,000. Winograd denied agreeing to pay Keaton anything. The court ruled in Keaton's favor. Winograd appealed to a state intermediate appellate court, claiming in part that the alleged agreement should not be enforced because it did not include the essential terms of an enforceable contract.

Justice Lesfmann

We reject the claim that Winograd's contractual undertaking to pay $175,000 to Keaton should be invalidated for lack of specificity concerning the terms of the contract. The basic terms of this very simple agreement were clear.

First, the price was firm: it was $175,000. So too was the description of what Winograd was purchasing. He was buy-

ing all of Keaton's business, including whatever tangible assets, inventory of "good will" might be involved. However, none of those assets were particularly significant to Winograd. Thus, it is not surprising that the parties did not, for example, itemize with specificity the inventory or the furniture of Keaton's business which was to be turned over to Winograd. To Winograd, those details were unimportant. The critical point, and the real reason for Winograd's payment of $175,000, was Keaton's agreement to vacate the property by the end of 1995, which he did.

Winograd also argues that the contract was too vague for enforcement because there was no description of the interest rate or the due date of the payment for the right to interest. He claims further that without a specified due date, the [payment] should be regarded as due on demand.

It is a settled principle that when the essential parts of a contract are spelled out, a court will not refuse to enforce that contract because some of its less critical terms have not been articulated. In such a case, the court will imply a reasonable missing term or, if necessary, will receive evidence to provide a basis for such an implication. And that is particularly true when there has been part performance of the contract, or—as here—where one of the parties (Keaton) has fully performed his part of the bargain.

Here the heart of the contract is the dollar amount to be paid to Keaton and Keaton's obligation to vacate the premises for Winograd's use. The incidental terms do not bar enforcement of the essential agreement between the parties.

Affirmed for the Plaintiff.

Methods of Termination of an Offer. There are generally five methods of termination of an offer under the common law.

1. *Lapse of time.* The failure of the offeree to respond within a reasonable time (e.g., 30 days) will cause an offer to lapse.

2. *Death of either party.* However, the death of the agent of a corporation will not terminate the contract because the company will continue in most cases.

3. *Destruction of the subject matter.* If the item contracted for cannot be replaced because of an accident not the fault of the offeror, the offer may be terminated.

4. *Rejection by the offeree.* If the offeree does not accept the offer, it is terminated.

5. *Revocation by the offeror.* If the offeror withdraws the offer before the offeree accepts it, the offer is terminated. The *UCC* differs somewhat from the common law in methods of termination of an offer. Here are some examples.

Rejection by the Offeree. At *common law* a counteroffer by the offeree constitutes rejection (method 4 above) and brings about a termination of the offer. For example, suppose Jones offers to sell his house for $200,000 and no more or less. If Smith offers Jones $185,000, Smith has terminated the original offer and now has set forth a counteroffer ($185,000), which Jones can either accept or reject.

The *Uniform Commercial Code, 2-207,* allows for modification by offerees when dealing with the sale of goods. For example, in the case of nonmerchants, such as Smith and Jones above, a counteroffer by the offeree (Smith) does not constitute a rejection because there is still a clear intent to contract, but the additional term added by the offeree will not become part of the contract. For example, suppose Smith offers to sell his bicycle to Jones for $300. If Jones tells Smith that he will buy his bicycle for the amount of $300 if he (Smith) paints it black, a contract exists even if the painting of the bicycle was not part of the original offer by Smith.

If both parties to a contract for goods are *merchants,* under *Section 2-207,* added terms to a contract by an offeree will become additional terms and part of an enforceable contract unless one of the following conditions exists: (1) The added terms are material to the contract; or (2) the offeror limited the term of the original offer to the offeree by placing it in writing; or (3) one of the parties objects to any added term within a reasonable period of time.

Revocation by the Offeror. At *common law* the offer is terminated if the offeror notifies the offeree that the offer is no longer good before the offeree accepts it (revocation; method 5 above). An offeree can forestall that type of termination by paying an offeror an amount of money to keep the offer open for a time. This tactic is called an *option,* and usually it will exist for 30 days. During this time the offeror can neither sell the property to another nor revoke the offer. Under the *UCC, Section 2-205,* a firm offer made by a merchant in writing, and signed by the merchant with another, must be held open for a definite period (three months). The firm offer cannot be revoked, and no consideration is required (the offeree need not buy an option).

LEGAL ACCEPTANCE

legal acceptance An acceptance that shows objective intent to enter into the contract, that is communicated by proper means to the offeror, and that mirrors the terms of the offer.

Legal acceptance involves three requirements that must be met. In order for an acceptance to be valid:

1. An intent to accept must be shown by the offeree.

2. The intent must be communicated by proper means.

3. The intent must satisfy, or "mirror," the terms of the offer.

Intent to Accept. There must be objective intent (words, conduct, writing) similar to that required of a legal offer. If Jones offers to sell Smith his 1978 Cutlass for $2,000 and Smith responds by stating, "I'll think it over," there is no objective intent to accept because there exists no present commitment on the part of Smith. In general, silence does not constitute acceptance unless prior conduct of the parties indicates that they assume that it does.

Communication of Acceptance. In general, any "reasonable means of communication" may be used in accepting an offer, and acceptances are generally binding upon the offeror when dispatched. Both industry custom and the subject matter will determine "reasonableness" in the eyes of a court. However, if the offeror requires that acceptance be communicated only in a certain form (e.g., letter), any other form that is used by the offeree (e.g., telegram) will delay the effectiveness of the acceptance until it reaches the offeror. If the offer states that "acceptance must be by mail" and the mails are used, the acceptance is effective upon deposit at the post office. If a telegram is used instead of mail, the acceptance will not be effective until it reaches the offeror. The strictest interpretation of this rule (known as the "mailbox rule") states that any acceptance of variance with the terms of the offer cannot form a contract even when received by the offeror.

Knowing whether there has been a valid acceptance is not always easy, as the following case involving Pamela Lee Anderson, of *Baywatch* fame, illustrates.

CASE 10-2

The Private Movie Company, Inc. v. Pamela Lee Anderson et al.
Superior Court of California, County of Los Angeles (1997)

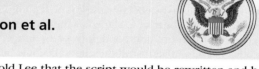

The plaintiff, Private Movie Company (Efraim), sued the defendant, Pamela Lee Anderson (Lee), for $4.6 million, alleging that she breached both an oral and a written contract so that she could work on a different project. The plaintiff claimed that an oral contract existed on November 18, 1994, when the parties agreed on all of the principal terms of a "deal," at the conclusion of a "business meeting" at the offices of defendant's personal manager. The plaintiff claimed that a written contract was entered into on December 21, 1994, when the plaintiff's lawyer sent the defendant copies of a "long-form" contract (Exhibit 10-1). The plaintiff claimed that Exhibit 10-1 was a written embodiment of the oral agreement reached on November 18, 1994.

The somewhat confusing facts that were testified to, and disputed, at trial made it difficult for the judge to determine whether a contract existed. The events began in October 1994, when plaintiff's attorney, Blaha, sent plaintiff's script to defendant's agent. After several conversations, an offer was sent to her agent. At trial, Efraim testified that Lee had said she loved the script and the character, but she testified that she was concerned about the nudity and sexual content of the script. Efraim said

that he told Lee that the script would be rewritten and he would do whatever she wished regarding the nudity.

On November 18, a business meeting was held by Efraim, his attorney, the defendant's agents (Joel and Stevens) and manager (Brody), and the director, to negotiate a contract. Those present at the meeting testified that agreement was reached on a specific makeup person, security, trailer to be provided for Lee, start date, and expenses, and per diem. The issue of limiting the amount of nudity used in the trailer or any of the advertising material was raised. The issue of nudity in the film was apparently resolved by an understanding that Brody (defendant's manager) would provide a list of dos and don'ts and that Private Movie would abide by them. The structure of the agreement was also discussed with an understanding that there would be two contracts—i.e., an acting contract and a consulting contract—thereby allowing Private Movie to save money relating to payment of benefits. The issue of the sexual content or simulated sex in the movie script was not raised at the meeting. Nor was the issue of the rewrite of the script raised at the meeting. At the end of the meeting, Efraim asked defendant's agent whether the deal was closed if Anderson's compensation was increased to $200,000. He said yes.

A few days later Efraim had his attorney draft the agreement with the increased compensation. Several drafts were exchanged between the attorney and defendant's agent, all containing the following nudity clause:

> NUDITY. The parties hereto acknowledge that the Picture will include "nude and/or simulated sex scenes." Player has read the screenplay of the Picture prior to receipt of the Agreement and hereby consents to being photographed in such scenes, provided that such "nude and simulated sex scenes" will not be banged nor photographed in a manner different from what has been agreed to unless mutually approved by Artist and producer.

The rewritten script was sent to defendant on December 27, 1994. Plaintiff's attorney testified that he called defendant on December 29, 1994, and she said the script was great, but she wanted a different makeup artist and would split the difference in cost. Defendant testified that she recalled no such phone call. She said that she reviewed the script on January 1, 1995, saw that the simulated sex scenes remained, and called her manager to tell him she would not do the film.

Plaintiff found a less well known actress to make the film and brought his action against the defendant.

Justice Horowitz

When the parties orally or in writing agree that the terms of a proposed contract are to be reduced to writing and signed by them before it is to be effective, there is no binding agreement until a written contract is signed. If the parties have orally agreed on the terms and conditions of a contract with the mutual intention that it shall thereupon become binding, but also agree that a formal written agreement to the same effect shall be prepared and signed, the oral agreement is binding regardless of whether it is subsequently reduced to writing.

Whether it is the intention of the parties that the agreement should be binding at once, or when later reduced to writing, or to a more formal writing, is an issue to be determined by reference to the words the parties used, as well as [based on] all of the surrounding facts and circumstances.

One of the essential elements to the existence of a contract is the consent of the parties. This consent must be freely given, mutual, and communicated by each party to the other.

Consent is not mutual unless the parties all agree upon the same thing in the same sense. Ordinarily, it is the outward expression of consent that is controlling. Mutual consent arises out of the reasonable meaning of the words and acts of the parties, and not from any secret or unexpressed intention or understanding. In determining if there was mutual consent, the Court considers not only the words and conduct of the parties, but also the circumstances under which the words are used and the conduct occurs.

Parties may engage in preliminary negotiations, oral or written, before reaching an agreement. These negotiations only result in a binding contract when all of the essential terms are definitely understood and agreed upon even though the parties intend that formal writing including all of these terms shall be signed later.

An acceptance of an offer must be absolute and unconditional. All of the terms of the offer must be accepted without change or condition. A change in the terms set forth in the offer, or a conditional acceptance, is a rejection of the offer.

Plaintiff has presented no testimony that Lee, on 11/18/94, the date which Plaintiff alleged that an oral contract was created, personally agreed to perform in the movie *Hello, She Lied*; Plaintiff, therefore, has the burden of proving that Joel and/or Stevens, her "agent" and "manager," had the authority to bind her to an oral written contract.

The parties do not and did not agree on the definition of "simulated sex." Clearly the performance of simulated sexual scenes in the film was important and material to both Lee and Efraim. Efraim stated that he would abide by whatever Lee wanted in this regard.

Nudity and sexual content are material deal points that must be resolved before there can be a binding contract. An agreement concerning sexual content or simulated sex was not reached in this instance. Lee did not agree to the terms relating to simulated sex or to the script offered by the Plaintiff.

Plaintiff's letter of 1/13/95 to Lee claims she "agreed to perform simulated sex scenes, and the exact type of nudity had been agreed upon in detail." Efraim claimed in deposition that Lee agreed to perform simulated sex scenes and agreed to the draft contract to confirm that fact. Blaha testified that Paragraph 9 was a correct statement of the agreement. In deposition he stated it was a mistake. The rewritten script has three or four scenes that depict simulated sex. It is obvious that the "offer" made by Plaintiff concerning this issue was not complete and unqualified, nor was there any acceptance of this issue that was complete and unqualified.

Brody and Joel testified to their opinion that they thought they had "closed the deal" on 11/18/94 or shortly thereafter. Such perceptions have very little legal relevance. Brody testified that he had authority to negotiate this contract. Joel never spoke with Lee concerning the transaction and did not negotiate points such as script rewrite or sexual content.

Plaintiff has failed to prove by a preponderance of the evidence that Lee entered into an oral or written contract to perform in the movie *Hello, She Lied*.

Judgment in favor of Defendant, Lee.

Satisfying, or "Mirroring," the Terms of the Offer. Under the common law, to be valid, the acceptance must satisfy, or "mirror," the terms of the offer. For example, if Jones offers to sell Smith his Cutlass for $2,000, and Smith responds

Critical Thinking About the Law

We know that language is not usually clear. Words convey information but not always the information that the speaker or writer intends. Ambiguity refers to these words and phrases that do not have a clear meaning. These ambiguous terms might result in another person's misinterpreting what the writer or speaker actually meant. In contract law, ambiguity could create problems between an offeror and offeree, as the two parties might not be in agreement on the same terms of the contract if the contract contains ambiguous language. In Case 10-2, the parties thought they understood each other. However, key ambiguous phrases created confusion in the contract negotiations and, consequently, raised concerns about whether there was actual consent by both parties.

As business managers, it is imperative that you demand clear definitions in the contracts that you offer and accept. The following questions pertaining to Case 10-2 urge you to consider the importance of ambiguity in contract law.

1. **What key ambiguous phrases did the court discuss?**

    Clue: Find the legal term in dispute that the judge defined. Also, look for ambiguity in the specific elements of the contractual negotiations between the plaintiff and the defendant.

2. **How has the ambiguity in the alleged contract affected the court's reasoning?**

    Clue: Do you think the court would have ruled differently had the ambiguity not existed in Case 10-2?

by saying, "I'll give you $1,800," this is not a legal acceptance but a counteroffer by Jones, which then must be accepted by Smith in order for the terms of the counteroffer to be satisfied and a contract to take place. Under the *UCC, Section 2-207*, acceptance does not have to be a mirror image of the offer. Terms can be added to the contract without constituting a counteroffer if they meet one of the three conditions listed in the section on methods of termination of an offer.

CONSIDERATION

Consideration is defined as a bargained-for exchange of promises in which a legal detriment is suffered by the promisee. For example, Smith promises Jones that if she gives up her job with Stone Corporation, he will employ her at Brick Corporation. The two requirements of consideration are met: (1) Smith (promisor) has bargained for a return promise from Jones (promisee) that she will give up her job; (2) when Jones gives up her job, she has lost a legal right, the contractual right to her present job with Stone Corporation. The reader should note that *legal* detriment (giving up a *legal* right or refraining from exercising a legal right) must take place. *Economic* detriment is not necessary. For example, a student agrees to not go to any bars during fall semester in exchange for his mother's promise to give him $500. The student's giving up his right to go to the bars is a legal detriment because he now cannot do something he previously could legally do.

consideration A bargained-for exchange of promises in which a legal detriment is suffered by the promisee.

Adequacy of Consideration. In general the courts have not been concerned with the amount of consideration involved in a contract, especially in a business context. If one party makes a bad deal with another party—that is, if the consideration is inadequate—the courts will usually refuse to interfere. Unless a party can show fraud, duress, undue influence, or mistake, the court will not intervene on behalf of a plaintiff. Sufficiency of consideration as opposed to adequacy will be examined by the court. Sufficiency of consideration requires both a bargained-for exchange of promises and legal detriment to the promisee.

Preexisting Duty Rule. In defining consideration, we said that a legal detriment to a promisee requires the giving up of a legal right or the refraining from exercising a right. Logically, the courts have then declared that if a party merely agrees to do what he or she is required to do, there exists no detriment to the promisee. For example, Smith contracted with Jones for Jones to build him a house by April 1, 1988, for $150,000. On February 1, 1988, Jones came to Smith and said that, because of the number of jobs he had, he wouldn't be able to finish by April unless Smith agreed to a bonus of $10,000. Smith agreed to the bonus, and the house was completed by April 1. Smith refused to pay, claiming that there was a *preexisting duty* on the part of Jones because he had a contractual duty to finish by April 1. Jones took him to court but lost the suit because no consideration existed for the bonus agreement. There is an important exception to the preexisting duty rule: The *UCC*, which applies to the sale of goods, states that an agreement modifying the original contract needs no consideration to be binding.

Promises Enforceable Without Consideration. The courts have enforced certain contracts when the requirements of consideration were not met, using the doctrine of *promissory estoppel* to do so. This doctrine requires (1) a promise justifiably relied on by the promisee, (2) substantial economic detriment to the promisee, and (3) an injustice that cannot be avoided except by enforcing the contract. Consider this hypothetical example. An elderly couple pledged in writing to leave $1 million to their family church for a building fund if the church raised another $1 million. The church accepted the offer, raised the matching funds, and contracted with an architect and builder. The couple died and, in their will, left the money to another church. When the family church sued the deceased's estate on the basis of the promissory estoppel doctrine, the court awarded it the full amount pledged, even though a *bargained-for exchange of promises* did not exist. There was a justifiable reliance by the family church upon the couple's promise, causing substantial economic injury to the church, and injustice could not be avoided in any other way.

Liquidated and Unliquidated Debts. A *liquidated debt* exists when there is no dispute about the amount or other terms of the debt. If A owes B and C $500,000, and B and C agree to accept $100,000 as settlement for the debt, they are not precluded from suing A later on for the balance. The courts reason that the first agreement by A to pay a particular amount ($500,000) to B and C was supported by consideration. The second agreement to pay $100,000 was not because A had a preexisting duty to pay $500,000, and there was, therefore, no legal detriment on A's part to support B and C's promise to accept the lesser amount.

An *unliquidated debt* exists when there is a dispute between the parties as to the amount owed by the debtor. If there is an agreement similar to the preceding one, except that the amount A originally owed B and C is in dispute, the general rule is that there exists consideration for the second agreement, and the creditors cannot come back and sue for the balance of what they thought they were owed. B and C would have no claim for the full $500,000, but would be limited to $100,000. The rationale is that new consideration was given for the second agreement. There exists a legal detriment because B and C are giving up a legal right to sue for an *unspecified debt*. The debtor is also giving up a legal right because there is *uncertainty* as to what he or she owes in an unliquidated debt situation.

GENUINE ASSENT

When two parties enter into a legally enforceable contract, it is presumed that they have entered of their own free will and that the two parties understand the content of the contract in the same way. If *fraud, duress, undue influence,* or *mutual mistake* exists, **genuine assent**, or a "meeting of the minds," has not taken place, and grounds for rescission (cancellation) of the contract exist. Table 10–1 lists the factors that prevent genuine assent.

Fraud. Fraud consists of (1) a misrepresentation of a *material* (significant) fact, (2) made with *intent to deceive* the other party, (3) who reasonably *relies* upon the misrepresentation, (4) and as a result is *injured.* For example, Smith enters into a contract to sell a house to Jones. The house is 12 years old, and Smith notices that the basement is sinking. She fails to tell Jones. After Jones moves in, she finds that the house is sinking about two feet a year. In this case, there existed a misrepresentation of a material fact because there existed a duty on the part of Smith to disclose the fact that the house was sinking. Furthermore, there existed knowledge of the fact with intent to deceive. The law does not require that an evil motive exist, but only that the selling party (Smith) knew and recklessly disregarded the fact that the house was sinking. Reliance existed on the part of Jones, who thought the house was habitable, and of course injury to Jones took place because the house was not worth what she paid for it. The cost of preventing further sinking of the house would be part of the damages involved. The case here illustrates fraud based on a unique set of facts.

TABLE 10-1

FACTORS PREVENTING GENUINE ASSENT

- Fraud
- Duress
- Undue influence
- Bilateral mistake
- Unilateral mistake

genuine assent Assent to a contract that is free of fraud, duress, undue influence, and mutual mistake.

fraud Misrepresentation of a material fact made with intent to deceive the other party to a contract, who reasonably relied on the misrepresentation and was injured as a result. See also *criminal fraud.*

CASE 10-3

Stambovsky v. Ackley and Ellis Realty
Supreme Court, Appellate Division, State of New York
169 A.D.2d 254 (1991)

Plaintiff Stambovsky purchased a home from Ackley, who was represented by Ellis Realty. After entering the contract but before closing, Stambovsky learned that the house was said to be possessed by poltergeists, reportedly seen by Ackley and her family on numerous occasions over the previous nine years. As a resident of New York City, Stambovsky was unaware that apparitions seen by the Ackleys were reported in the *Reader's Digest* and the local press of Nyack, New York. The house was also included in 1989 on a five-home walking tour, in which the house was described as "a riverfront Victorian (with ghost)." Stambovsky brought an action for rescission of the contract, arguing that the reputation of the house impaired the present value of the property and its resale value. He argued that the failure of the Ackleys and Ellis Realty Company to disclose the nature of the house as

haunted was fraudulent in nature. The defendants argued that the principle of caveat emptor (buyer beware) applied in the state of New York and they had no affirmative duty to disclose nonmaterial matters. They moved for dismissal. The lower court granted the dismissal. The plaintiff appealed.

Judge Rubin

While I agree with [the] Supreme Court [New York's trial court] that the real estate broker, as agent for the seller, is under no duty to disclose to a potential buyer the phantasmal reputation of the premises and that, in his pursuit of a legal remedy for fraudulent misrepresentation against the seller, plaintiff hasn't a ghost of a chance, I am nevertheless moved by the spirit of equity to allow the buyer to seek rescission of the contract of sale and recovery of his down payment. New York law fails to recognize any remedy for damages incurred as a result of the seller's mere silence, applying instead the strict rule of caveat emptor. Therefore, the theoretical basis for granting relief, even under the extraordinary facts of this case, is elusive if not ephemeral.

"Pity me not, but lend thy serious hearing to what I shall unfold."

(William Shakespeare, *Hamlet*, Act I, Scene V [Ghost]).

From the perspective of a person in the position of plaintiff herein, a very practical problem arises with respect to the discovery of a paranormal phenomenon: "Who you gonna' call?" as the title song to the movie *Ghostbusters* asks. Applying the strict rule of caveat emptor to a contract involving a house possessed by poltergeists conjures up visions of a psychic or medium routinely accompanying the structural engineer and Terminix man on an inspection of every home subject to a contract of sale. It portends that the prudent attorney will establish an escrow account lest the subject of the transaction come back to haunt him and his client—or pray that his malpractice insurance coverage extends to supernatural disasters. In the interest of avoiding such untenable consequences, the notion that a haunting is a condition which can and should be ascertained upon reasonable inspection of the premises is a hobgoblin that should be exorcised from the body of legal precedent and laid quietly to rest.

The doctrine of caveat emptor requires that a buyer act prudently to assess the fitness and value of his purchase and operates to bar the purchaser who fails to exercise due care from seeking the equitable remedy of rescission. For the purposes of the instant motion to dismiss the action, the plaintiff is entitled to every favorable inference that may reasonably be drawn from the pleadings; specifically, in this instance, that he met his obligation to conduct an inspection of the premises and a search of available public records with most meticulous inspection and the search would not reveal the presence of poltergeists at the premises or unearth the property's ghoulish reputation in the community. Therefore, there is no sound policy reason to deny plaintiff relief for failing to discover a state of affairs that the most prudent purchaser would not be expected to even contemplate.

The case law in this jurisdiction dealing with the duty of a vendor of real property to disclose information to the buyer is distinguishable from the matter under review. The most salient distinction is that existing cases invariably deal with the physical condition of the premises and other factors affecting its operation. No case has been brought to this court's attention in which the property value was impaired as the result of the reputation created by information disseminated to the public by the seller (or, for that matter, as a result of possession by poltergeists). Where a condition that has been created by the seller materially impairs the value of the contract and is peculiarly within the knowledge of the seller or unlikely to be discovered by a prudent purchaser exercising due care with respect to the subject transaction, nondisclosure constitutes a basis for rescission as a matter of equity. Any other outcome places upon the buyer not merely the obligation to exercise care in his purchase but rather to be omniscient with respect to any fact that may affect the bargain. No practical purpose is served by imposing such a burden upon a purchaser. To the contrary, it encourages predatory business practice and offends the principle that equity will suffer no wrong to be without a remedy.

In the case at bar, defendant seller deliberately fostered the public belief that her home was possessed. Having undertaken to inform the public at large, to whom she has no legal relationship, about the supernatural occurrences on her property, she may be said to owe no less a duty to her contract vendee. It has been remarked that the occasional modern cases that permit a seller to take unfair advantage of a buyer's ignorance but has created and perpetuated a condition about which he is unlikely to even inquire, enforcement of the contract (in whole or in part) is offensive to the court's sense of equity. Application of the remedy of rescission, within the bounds of the narrow exception to the doctrine of caveat emptor set forth herein, is entirely appropriate to relieve the unwitting purchaser from the consequences of a most unnatural bargain.

Reversed in favor of Plaintiff, Stambovsky.

Dissenting Opinion

The parties herein were represented by counsel and dealt at arm's length. This is evidenced by the contract of sale, which contained various riders and a specific provision that all prior understandings and agreements between the parties were merged into the contract, that the contract completely expressed their full agreement and that neither had relied upon any statement by anyone else not set forth in the contract. There is no allegation that defendants, by some specific act, other than the failure to speak, deceived the plaintiff. Nevertheless, a cause of action may be sufficiently stated where there is a confidential or fiduciary relationship creating a duty to disclose and there was a failure to disclose a material fact, calculated to induce a false belief. However, plaintiff herein has not alleged and there is no basis for concluding that a confidential or fiduciary relationship existed between these parties to an arm's length transaction such as to give rise to a duty to disclose. In addition, there is no allegation that defendants thwarted plaintiff's efforts to fulfill his responsibilities fixed by the doctrine of caveat emptor.

Critical Thinking About the Law

Although judges frequently rely on legal precedent, there is no fixed standard by which judges must give a certain weight to precedent. In other words, judges differ in the degree to which they show deference to legal precedent and legislative acts. Consequently, several judges viewing the same case and same set of facts could reach conflicting decisions. As you learned in the chapter about the American legal system, there are different philosophies of judges: those who believe in judicial restraint and those who believe in judicial activism. Underlying these two philosophies are varying degrees of importance that judges give to the four primary ethical norms. (See Chapter 1.) The degree of importance that a judge attaches to each of these ethical norms plays a significant role in the shaping of a judge's reasoning and the court's conclusion. The following questions pertaining to Case 10-3 encourage you to consider the importance of primary ethical norms in a judge's reasoning.

1. Which primary ethical norm was guiding the judge's reasoning in the majority opinion?

   Clue: Consider the factors the judge discussed in favoring the plaintiff's interests over the defendant's interests.

2. To further illustrate the significance of ethical norms, to which ethical norm did the dissenting judge give highest priority?

   Clue: Similar to the first question, why do you think the judge held the defendant's interests over the plaintiff's interests?

3. What missing information would help you better evaluate the court's reasoning?

   Clue: Find the reasons the plaintiff provides for a rescission of the contract. What omitted evidence could have made the plaintiff's case more convincing?

Duress. Another factor that prevents **genuine assent** of the parties is **duress**, defined as any wrongful act or threat that prevents a party from exercising free will when executing a contract. The state of mind of the party at the time of entering into the contract is important. If Smith, when executing a contract with Jones to sell a house, holds a gun on Jones and threatens to shoot Jones if he refuses to sign the contract, grounds exist for rescission of the contract. Duress is not limited to physical threats, however. Threats of economic ruin or public embarrassment also constitute duress.

duress Any wrongful act or threat that prevents a party from exercising free will when executing a contract.

Undue Influence. If one party exerts mental coercion over the other party, there is **undue influence** and, therefore, no genuine assent. There are two court-established requirements for undue influence: (1) There must be a dominant–subservient relationship between the contrasting parties (e.g., a doctor–patient, lawyer–client, or any trusting relationship); (2) this dominant-subservient relationship must allow one party to influence the other in a mentally coercive way. An example of coercion that meets these requirements is a dying patient's contracting with a family doctor to sell his family land at an unreasonably low price in order to pay his doctor bills.

undue influence Mental coercion exerted by one party over the other party to the contract.

Mistake. A **mistake** also prevents a meeting of the minds, or genuine assent. If both parties made an error as to a material fact, a *mutual*, or *bilateral*, mistake has occurred, and as a general rule the courts will rescind such contracts. But if an error is made by only one party to the contract, a *unilateral* mistake has occurred, and the courts will generally not grant the mistaken party a rescission of the contract. An exception to this rule is made if the nonmistaken party knew

mistake Error as to material fact. A bilateral mistake is one made by both parties; a unilateral mistake is one made by only one party to the contract.

or should have known of the mistake. For example, if five contractors bid on a $10 million hospital project and Smith's bid is $2 million below all other bids because of an accountant's error, the hospital should have known of the error before accepting the bid, especially if Smith had immediately notified the hospital of the mathematical error and the contract was executory in nature.

COMPETENT PARTIES

competency A person's ability to understand the nature of the transaction and the consequences of entering into it at the time the contract was entered into.

The fifth essential element of a legally enforceable contract is **competency** of the parties. A person is presumed to be competent at the time of entering into a contract, so most people who raise the defense of a lack of capacity must prove that at the time the contract was entered into the individual did not have the ability to understand the nature of the transaction and the consequences of entering into it. This defense often arises when contracts involve minors or insane or intoxicated persons.

Minors. A minor is a person under the legal age of majority. The states differ as to age of majority for entering into enforceable contracts. The age of majority for contractual capacity should not be confused with the age at which one can drink or can vote in state and federal elections. Contracts made by minors are voidable and can be *disaffirmed* by the minor at any time before the minor becomes of a majority age or shortly thereafter. If the minor fails to disaffirm a contract, he or she will be considered to have *ratified* (approved) it and is, thus, legally bound. For example, Smith, at age 17 years, three months, entered into a contract with Jones to buy the latter's automobile for $2,000. The state in which the contract was executed had a majority age of 18. After using the automobile for two years and a month, Smith returned the auto and asked for his $2,000 back, minus depreciation on the car, because he was only 17 when he entered the contract and he claimed that, therefore, the contract was voidable. Smith was not allowed to disaffirm his contract because he had ratified the agreement by failing to disaffirm it before age 18 or shortly thereafter.

A minor is generally liable for the reasonable value (not the contract or the market value) of *necessaries* (food, clothing, shelter), which enable the minor to live in a manner he or she is accustomed to. To avoid the issues of what constitutes a necessary, prudent businesspeople check purchasers' ages very carefully and require a parent or guardian to cosign a loan when the borrower is a minor. For example, a student who is a minor for contractual purposes is not able to obtain a loan at a bank without a parent's signature, and merchants generally will check to see if a charge card in the possession of a minor is issued in a parent's name.

The following case illustrates the principle of disaffirmance and ratification by a minor.

CASE 10-4

Mitchell v. Mitchell
Court of Appeals of Kentucky,
963 S.W.2d 222 (Ky.App. 1998)

Sherri R. Mitchell was injured while she was a passenger in an automobile owned by her father, Donnie Fee, and operated by her husband, Michael J. Mitchell. Sherri, who was 17, executed a release settling her bodily injury claim for $2,500. No conservator was appointed at the time of the execution of the release. Sometime later, Sherri filed a lawsuit seeking a determination that the settlement she had signed was null and void owing to her capacity as a minor at the time she signed the release. The lower court found for the defendant.

Justice Williams

Kentucky statutes define a minor as anyone under the age of eighteen. Ordinarily, contracts executed by minors are enforceable by the minors; but the minors may avoid the contract if it is not affirmed after they reach adulthood. Put differently, although minors have the legal capacity to contract, they have the privilege of avoiding the contract. Although certain exceptions to this general rule exist (e.g., the minor's liability for necessaries), none applied to this case. The privilege bestowed on a minor to avoid contracts made during infancy is given for policy reasons. The law presumes that infants, like the other classes of disabilities, lack sufficient maturity or experience to bargain effectively with those who have attained legal age. Accordingly, courts must scrutinize closely any transaction that may result in a financial loss to infants or in a depletion of their estates. Granted, the marriage of an infant emancipates the minor. But as Kentucky precedents

hold, parental emancipation, while it may free the infant from parental control, does not remove all the disabilities of infancy. Emancipation does not, for example, enlarge or affect the minor's capacity or incapacity to contract. To some, it may seem ironic that a minor can drive a car yet not be bound by the contract to purchase that car or be responsible for his or her torts and crimes yet unable to settle a dispute against a tortfeasor. The distinction hinges on the fact that all too frequently a contract involves negotiation and thought beyond the maturity of most people under the age of eighteen. Hence, Kentucky courts should not adopt a rule that marriage by the minor somehow classifies him or her as more mature and intelligent than his or her unmarried counterpart. Logic and common sense would not encourage such a result, since marriage by a minor often in itself might indicate a lack of wisdom and maturity. Kentucky statutes provide a means by which a court can appoint a conservator so as to protect the financial interests of a married minor. Although the lack of such appointment will not render the contract void, a minor such as Sherri remains free to avoid her obligations under the contract.

Reversed in favor of Plaintiff.

Insanity. If a person is adjudicated by a court of law to be insane, or is *de facto* (in fact) insane at the time of entering into a contract, the individual will be allowed to disaffirm a contract. Court-appointed guardians may also disaffirm such agreements.

Intoxication. A person who is intoxicated to the degree that understanding the nature of the contract and its consequences is impossible will be able to disaffirm a contract in all cases but those involving necessaries. It is the degree of intoxication that the court will look at. In order to disaffirm, the intoxicated individual will have to return the item bought. In the case of necessaries, the intoxicated individual is not allowed to disaffirm but is held liable for the reasonable value of such items.

LEGAL OBJECT

The sixth necessary element of a contract is a **legal object**. This means that the subject matter of the agreement must be lawful. If it is not, the contract is void at its inception. Contracts that are in violation of state or federal statutes, as well as those in violation of case law, are void as a matter of public policy.

legal object Contract subject matter that is lawful under statutory and case law.

Statutory Law. State statutes that forbid wagering agreements (betting) and usurious (defined as exorbitant) finance charges or interest rates on loans, as well as those aimed at licensing and regulation, have been the source of much adjudication. If Smith practices law in a state without being admitted to practice before its highest state court, the courts will generally not enforce any contracts Smith made with clients for services rendered. Smith may also be subject to criminal charges. State statutes require licensing of nurses, doctors, accountants, real estate agents, electricians, and many other groups (the list varies from state to state) in order to protect the public from incompetents. Some opponents of these statutes argue that they were enacted at the behest of interest groups to decrease the supply of individuals in a particular profession or trade and, hence, prevent competition. Whatever their origin, however, courts will not enforce contracts made by unlicensed providers of these services.

Case Law. Often, when there is a question as to whether a contract has a lawful object, statutory law does not indicate clearly whether the contract is void or unenforceable. For example, agreements not to compete are found to be contrary to the public policy of fostering competition, and there are federal and state antitrust laws (statutes) making price-fixing between competitors illegal and void. However, when an otherwise lawful contract of employment contains a no-competition clause whereby an employee agrees not to be employed by a competitor of his or her employer, the courts will look at whether the restriction on the employee is for a *reasonable* time and area. In addition, it will look at the relative bargaining power of the employer and employee and the hardship on the employee contractually forbidden to work for another employer in the same industry. As the following case shows, each factual situation is carefully examined, and the standard of reasonableness is used to determine whether the contract is enforceable.

CASE 10-5

Moore v. Midwest Distribution, Inc.
Arkansas Court of Appeals,
65 S. W3d 490 (2002)

Moore began working in the product display business in 1997 for Hubb Group (HG). In 1999, HG terminated his contract. Moore went to work for Midwest Distribution, Inc., which also set up product displays as a contractor for HG. Midwest asked Moore to sign a "Service Work for Hire Agreement" under which Moore agreed that, for one year after the termination of his employment, he would not "provide, or solicit or offer to provide to any present or former Customer of Contractor, or become directly or indirectly interested in any person or entity which provides, or solicits or offers to provide, any services to such Customers." The agreement applied "to those geographical areas in which the Contractee acts as independent contractor including, but not limited to, the State of Arkansas, Illinois, Iowa, Kansas, Missouri, Nebraska, New Mexico, Oklahoma, Texas, and any other state that contractor has granted a contract or agreement within." Moore then quit this job to work for Jay Godwin, who also contracted with HG. Midwest Distribution filed a suit in an Arkansas state court against Moore, seeking to enjoin him from providing services to Godwin. The court issued a temporary injunction. Moore appealed to the state court of appeals.

Justice Crabtree

The test of reasonableness of contracts in restraint of trade is that the restraint imposed upon one party must not be greater than is reasonably necessary for the protection of the other and not so great as to injure a public interest. Where a covenant not to compete grows out of an employment

relationship, the courts have found an interest sufficient to warrant enforcement of the covenant only in those cases where the covenantee provided special training, or made available trade secrets, confidential business information or customer lists, and then only if it is found that the covenantee was able to use information so obtained to gain an unfair competitive advantage.

In the present case, appellee's [Midwest] president, Kevin Barrett, testified that appellant [Moore] had been provided with no special training. In addition, he stated that appellant had not been provided with any trade secrets, confidential business information, or customer lists. Further, Mr. Barrett testified that appellant was not using information he obtained from appellee to gain an unfair advantage over appellee, except how to install "fixtures and stuff." We hold that appellant did not use any information to gain an unfair competitive advantage over appellee. As such, we hold that appellee did not have a legitimate interest to be protected by the agreement.

We are also persuaded that the geographical area included in the agreement is too broad. The geographical area in a convenant not to compete must be limited in order to be enforceable. The restraint imposed upon one party must not be greater than is reasonably necessary for protecting the other party. In determining whether the geographic restriction is reasonable, the trade area of the former employer is viewed. Where a geographic restriction is greater than the trade area, the restriction is too broad and the covenant not to compete is void.

In the case at bar [before the court], the agreement precluded appellant from working in the trade of setting up displays in any of the nine states listed. The agreement included the state of Oklahoma. However, appellee did not conduct any business in Oklahoma. We find that it is not reasonable to restrict appellant from working in a state he never worked in before. By including in the scope of the non-compete agreement's geographic restriction a state that appellant has never worked in, appellee more broadly limited appellant's working than is reasonably necessary to protect appellee's trade area.

Reversed for Moore.

CONTRACTS THAT MUST BE IN WRITING

Most contracts need not be in writing. They are enforceable as long as the six elements of a contract exist. However, the Statute of Frauds, which originated in England in 1677, requires certain business contracts to be in writing. Originally, those contracts listed in this section, and some other nonbusiness contracts, were required to be in writing because they were thought to be the most likely situations in which perjury would occur. Today, each state requires by statute that various contracts be written in order to be enforceable.

In most states, the requirements for a written contract include some evidence of writing and the signature of the party being sued. The writing should reasonably outline the terms and state who are the parties to the agreement. Contracts governed by the *UCC, Section 2-201*, do not have these requirements. The party suing may have the only evidence of writing with his or her signature on it. Often, between merchants, confirmation memoranda summarize oral agreements and are satisfied by only one party. The nonsigning party must simply review the memorandum. The Statute of Frauds is satisfied if the nonsigning party agrees to its content.

The business-related contracts in this section are those that most frequently fall *within* the Statute of Frauds. They, therefore, must be in writing to be enforceable.

CONTRACTS FOR THE SALE OF AN INTEREST IN LAND

An "interest in land" includes mortgages, easements (an easement is a contract that allows a party to cross your land, for example, with electrical wires), and, of course, the land itself and the buildings on it. Leases for longer than one year usually have to be in writing.

A notable exception to the requirement that contracts for sale of an interest in land must be written is part performance. For example, if substantial improvements have been made on a piece of property by a lessee in reliance on an oral commitment by the lessor to sell, the oral contract will be enforced.

CONTRACTS TO PAY THE DEBTS OF ANOTHER

If Smith promises to pay Jones's debt to the bank should Jones be unable to pay it, this contract must be in writing under the Statute of Frauds. In this case, Smith has *secondary liability to the bank*. If, however, Smith tells the bank that she will act as a surety for Jones's debt, Smith has a *primary liability to the bank*. This agreement is not within the Statute of Frauds and, therefore, may be enforced even if oral.

In the first situation, Smith's promise was *conditional* in nature. That is, on condition that Jones does not pay, the bank may look to Smith, but first it must look to Jones. In the second situation, the bank may first look to Smith. It does not have to go to Jones at all because it has a guarantor or surety agreement with Smith.

Linking Law & Business

Accounting

Land is treated specially not just in the law but in other disciplines as well. As you may recall from your accounting class, land is classified as a long-term operational asset. One distinguishing characteristic of land is that land is not subject to depreciation or depletion. In other words, land is considered to have an infinite life because it is not destroyed by use. If an organization makes a basket purchase, or acquires several assets in a single transaction, then the amount paid should be carefully divided between the land and the other assets on the organizational financial statements. Therefore, the balance sheet will reflect the nondepreciable nature of the land, while allowing noticeable depreciation or depletion of the other assets purchases.

Source: T. Edmonds, F. McNair, E. Milam, and P. Olds, *Fundamental Financial Accounting Concepts* (New York: McGraw-Hill, 2000), pp. 408–410.

CONTRACTS NOT PERFORMABLE IN ONE YEAR

A contract must be in writing if it specifies that it will last longer than one year. For example, in most states, a baseball player who agrees to play for a team for three years at $2 million a year must sign a written contract in order for it to be enforceable. If, however, no date is set in the contract for the completion of performance, the contract need not be in writing. For example, an agreement to provide help for a person until that person dies does not fall within the Statute of Frauds and, thus, does not have to be in writing to be enforceable.

SALE OF GOODS OF $500 OR MORE

Under the *Uniform Commercial Code, Section 2-201*, contracts for the sale of goods of $500 or more fall within the Statute of Frauds and must be in writing to be enforced. There are three exceptions to this rule: (1) One of the parties to a suit admits in writing or in court to the existence of an oral contract; (2) a buyer accepts and uses the goods; (3) the contract is between merchants, and the merchant who is sued received a written confirmation of the oral agreement and did not object within ten days. In all of these instances, the oral contract will be enforced even if for goods worth $500 or more.

NONBUSINESS CONTRACTS

Non-business-related contracts that must be in writing to be enforceable are (1) contracts in consideration of marriage and (2) contracts of an executor or administrator to answer for the debts of a deceased person.

PAROL EVIDENCE RULE

The **parol** (oral) **evidence rule** states that when parties have executed a *written* agreement, which is complete on its face, *oral* agreements made *prior to* or at the *same time* as the written agreement that *vary*, *alter*, or *contradict* it are invalid. Such

TABLE 10-2

EXCEPTIONS TO THE PAROL EVIDENCE RULE

1. Oral agreements used to prove a subsequent modification of the written agreements are admissible.

2. Oral agreements to clear up ambiguity in the written agreement are admissible.

3. Oral agreements to prove fraud, mistake, illegality, duress, undue influence, or lack of capacity are admissible.

4. Oral agreements concerning collateral matters not germane to the written agreement are admissible.

oral agreements will not be allowed to be introduced in evidence by most state courts. For example, suppose that Smith enters into a written contract with Jones to sell him a two-year-old Chevy Citation for $5,000 and "all warranties are excluded" under the terms of the contract. At the time of signing, Smith orally tells Jones, "Don't worry, we'll warranty all parts and labor." This oral agreement made at the time of execution will not be allowed into evidence because it varies from the written agreement. Exceptions to the parol evidence rule are set out in Table 10-2.

Under the *UCC, Section 2-202*, written memoranda that are intended to be a final expression of the parties' agreement cannot be contradicted by prior or contemporaneous oral agreement but may be explained or supplemented orally by course of dealing or usage of trade, by course of performance, or by evidence of consistent additional terms. This *UCC* rule allows the courts to admit into evidence oral testimony with regard to written agreements that would ordinarily be inadmissible under case law.

parol evidence rule When parties have executed a written agreement that is complete on its face, oral agreements made prior to, or at the same time as, the written agreement that vary, alter, or contradict it are invalid.

THIRD-PARTY BENEFICIARY CONTRACTS AND ASSIGNMENT OF RIGHTS

TYPES OF THIRD-PARTY BENEFICIARY CONTRACTS

So far, our discussion has focused on contracts between two parties (usually Smith and Jones). However, two parties may enter into a contract with the clear intent to benefit a third party; in these cases, there is a *third-party beneficiary contract*. There are two kinds of third-person beneficiary contracts: donee and creditor.

A **donee-beneficiary contract** exists when the purpose of the promisee in obtaining a promise from the promisor is to make a gift to a third person. For example, Liberty Insurance Company (promisor) promises to pay Smith (third party) a sum of $100,000 upon the death of Jones (promisee) in exchange for Jones's payment of a yearly premium. Under this third-party donee-beneficiary contract, Smith may sue Liberty Insurance Company if it fails to pay the $100,000 upon the death of Jones.

A third-party **creditor-beneficiary contract** exists when the purpose of the promisee in requiring a promisor's performance to be made to a third person is to fulfill a legal obligation of the promisee to the third person. For example, Smith (promisee) works for Jones (promisor) in exchange for Jones's promise to pay Taylor $6,000 that Smith owes. Under this third-party creditor-beneficiary contract, if Smith does the work and Jones refuses to pay, Taylor may sue both Jones and Smith.

donee-beneficiary contract One in which the promisee obtains a promise from the promisor to make a gift to a third party.

creditor-beneficiary contract One in which the promisee obtains a promise from the promisor to fulfill a legal obligation of the promisee to a third party.

EXHIBIT 10-1

ASSIGNMENT OF
CONTRACT RIGHTS

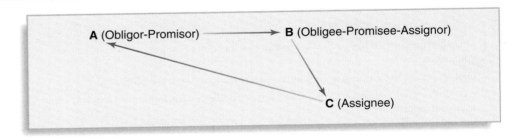

Note that insurance contracts and all forms of creditor collection agreements are third-party beneficiary contracts. These types of agreements are obviously very important in our economy.

ASSIGNMENT OF RIGHTS

assignment The present transfer of an existing right.

An **assignment** is the *present* transfer of an existing right. Contracts between two parties may be assigned to a third party under certain conditions. Suppose that B, a manufacturing company, sells A, a retail company, 600 bicycles at $100 apiece on credit. A, known as the obligor-promisor, agrees to pay B, the obligee-promisee-assignor, $60,000. A does not pay and, therefore, B has the right to sue A. But B has another choice: to assign this right to C, a collection agency, and receive immediate cash from C. In effect, B is assigning to C, known as the assignee, A's promise to pay in the future in exchange for receiving cash from C now (Exhibit 10-1). C has the right to sue both A and B. That is, if the collection agency is unable to collect the money from the retailer, it may sue not only the retailer but also the manufacturer to recover the cash it advanced in anticipation of collecting the debt.

The conditions attached to most assignments are that unless the obligor (A) receives notice of assignment by the obligee-assignor (B), the obligor has no duty to the assignee (C). Once that notice is received, however, the assignee "stands in the shoes" of the obligee.

Certain classes of assignments are not recognized by law:

1. Assignments that materially change the duty of the obligor.
2. Assignments forbidden by state statute.
3. Any assignment forbidden by the original contract between the obligor-promisor and the obligee-promisee.

SUMMARY

A contract is defined as a legally enforceable exchange of promises. The sources of contract law are case law from state and federal courts and statutory law from the federal and state legislatures, particularly from the *Uniform Commercial Code*. Contracts may be classified as express or implied, unilateral or bilateral, void or voidable or valid; executed or executory; and quasi.

The six necessary elements of a legal contract are (1) a legal offer, (2) a legal acceptance, (3) a consideration, (4) genuine assent, (5) competent parties, and (6) a legal object. The *Uniform Commercial Code* differs somewhat from the common law in its requirements for contracts. Table 10-3 outlines some of the differences.

Area of Comparison	Common Law	UCC
Contract application	Real property, services, and employment contracts	Sale of goods contracts
Requirements for offer	Includes subject matter, price, and quantity	Includes subject matter and quantity while leaving price and other terms open
Option agreements	Needs consideration for all option agreements	No consideration needed
Requirements for acceptance	Terms of acceptance are mirror image of offer	Mirror image not necessary; additional terms allowed if one of three requirements is met
Requirements for consideration	Consideration required for contract to be enforceable except under doctrine of promissory estoppel	Consideration not needed for modifications
Statute of Frauds (contracts that must be in writing)	Real estate contracts, contracts not performable in one year; paying the debt of another	Sales of goods of $500 or more with three exceptions

TABLE 10-3

COMPARISON BETWEEN COMMON LAW AND THE *UNIFORM COMMERCIAL CODE (UCC)*

Some types of contracts fall within the Statute of Frauds and, therefore, must be in writing to be enforceable. The parol evidence rule invalidates most oral agreements made before or at the same time as a written contract that alter or contradict the terms of the contract.

Third-party beneficiary contracts may be of either the donor-beneficiary or the creditor-beneficiary type. A contract made between two parties may be assigned to a third party under certain conditions.

REVIEW QUESTIONS

10-1 How is a contract generally defined?

10-2 Explain the distinction between a void and a voidable contract; between an executed and an executory contract; between a unilateral and a bilateral contract.

10-3 Describe the three requirements for a valid acceptance.

10-4 Describe the three requirements for a valid offer.

10-5 Explain how an offer can be terminated.

10-6 Explain the difference between liquidated and unliquidated debts.

REVIEW PROBLEMS

10-7 Fisher, an employment agency, sued Catani, a minor, for breach of contract for the balance due the agency of $101.25 as a commission for finding Catani employment. The defendant disaffirmed his contract with the agency while still a minor two months after obtaining the job and one month after he quit. Can he disaffirm? Explain.

10-8 Robinson was employed as an assistant manager in Gallagher Drug Company Store. He was accused of theft and embezzlement, which he admitted to, and was fired. The following day, at company headquarters, he signed a contract promising to repay the company $2,000. Robinson made payments totaling $741, and then stopped. Gallagher sued for the balance. Robinson's defense was that he had signed the agreement under duress. What logical problem would there be in Robinson's arguing that he became aware of the duress after he attended a support group for unemployed managers?

10-9 Osborne, a former chairman of the board of Locke Steel Company, entered into an agreement with Locke that, on retirement, he would hold himself available for consultation and would not work for any direct or indirect competitors of the company. In exchange for these promises, the company agreed to pay Osborne $15,000 a year for the rest of his life. After paying for two years, the company stopped payments when Osborne refused to consent to a modification of the agreement. The defendant argued that there was no consideration because the contract was based on past services and, thus, there was no detriment to the promisee (Osborne). Who won? Explain.

10-10 Fisher, an inexperienced businessman, bought equipment and chinchillas from Division West Chinchilla in order to start a chinchilla ranch. Fisher got into the business because Division West had told him that chinchilla ranching was an "easy undertaking … and no special skills were required." Fisher lost money operating the ranch. He sued, claiming that he had relied on Division West's fraudulent representations. Who won? Explain.

10-11 William Story promised his nephew that he would pay him $5,000 if he gave up "using tobacco, swearing, and playing cards and billiards until he was 21." The nephew did so and asked his uncle for the money. His uncle agreed to pay, but died before he did so. The uncle's estate refused to pay, arguing that there was no consideration for the uncle's promise. Should the court uphold the agreement in this case? Why or why not?

CASE PROBLEMS

10-12 In 1987, United Parcel Service Company and United Parcel Service of America, Inc. (together known as "UPS") decided to change its parcel delivery business from relying on contract carriers to establishing its own airline. During the transition, which took 16 months, UPS hired 811 pilots. At the time, UPS expressed a desire to hire pilots who remained throughout that period with its contract carriers, which included Orion Air. A UPS representative met with more than 50 Orion pilots and made promises of future employment. John Rickert, a captain with Orion, was one of the pilots. Orion ceased operation after the UPS transition, and UPS did not hire Rickert, who obtained employment about six months later as a second officer with American Airlines but at a lower salary. Rickert filed a suit in a Kentucky state court against UPS, claiming, in part, fraud based on the promises made by the UPS representative. UPS filed a motion for a directed verdict. What are the elements for a cause of action based on fraudulent misrepresentation? In whose favor should the court rule in this case? *United Parcel Service, Inc. v. Rickert*, 996 S.W.2d 464 (Ky. 1999)

10-13 Peoples Group (D.L.) placed an ad in a Missouri newspaper to recruit admissions representatives, who were hired to recruit Missouri residents to attend D. L.'s college in Florida. Donald Hawley responded to the ad. He signed, in Missouri, an "Admissions Representative Agreement." The agreement was mailed to D. L.'s president, who signed it in his office in Florida. The agreement

provided in part that D. L. would pay Hawley a commission if he successfully recruited students for the school in Missouri. While attempting to make one of his first calls on his new job, Hawley was accidentally shot and killed. On the basis of his death, a claim was filed in Florida for workers' compensation. (Under Florida law, when an accident occurs outside Florida, workers' compensation benefits are payable only if the employment contract was made in Florida.) Is this admissions representative agreement a bilateral or a unilateral contract? Explain. *D.L. Peoples Group, Inc. v. Hawley*, 804 So.2d 561 (Fla. App. 1 Dist. 2002)

10-14 Southwick Homes, Ltd. develops and markets residential subdivisions. William McLinden and Ronald Coco are the primary owners of Southwick Homes. Coco is also the president of Mutual Development Co. Whiteco Industries, Inc., wanted to develop lots and sell homes in Schulien Woods, a subdivision in Crown Point, Indiana. In September 1996, Whiteco sent McLinden a letter enlisting Southwick Homes to be the project manager for developing and marketing the finished lots (lots where roads had been built and on which utility installation and connections to water and sewer lines were complete); the letter set out the roles and expectations of each of the parties, including the terms of payment. In October 1997, Whiteco sent Coco a letter naming Mutual Development the developer and general contractor for the houses to be built on the finished lots. A few months later, Coco told McLinden that he would not share the profits from the construction of the houses. McLinden and others filed a suit in an Indiana state court against Coco and others, claiming, in part, a breach of fiduciary duty. The defendants responded that the letter to McLinden lacked such essential terms as to render it unenforceable. Did the McLinden letter include these terms of an enforceable contract? In whose favor should the court rule? Explain. *McLinden v. Coco,* 765 N.E.2d 606 (Ind.App. 2002)

10-15 Time Warner and Fox, two powerful, experienced, and skilled electronic-media giants, negotiated for, but failed to reach agreement on, the carriage of the Fox News Channel by Time Warner. Fox filed an action against Time Warner for fraud and promissory estoppel, relying on Time Warner's oral assurances during the negotiations to the effect of "We are in agreement," "We will certainly reach agreement," "Signing an agreement with you is our top priority after we arrange an important merger," and "All the details are set," when in fact, the gritty details had not been agreed upon. Simultaneously, Time Warner was considering alternate arrangements with others, which it ultimately embraced—to Fox's disappointment—partly, it can be assumed, because some of Time Warner's management was hostile to, and never wanted an agreement with, Fox.

The parties did participate in intensive and complex negotiations, but they never reached—or even approached— agreement on the essentials to a contractual relationship. Time Warner filed a motion for summary judgment. Why do you believe the court did or did not grant Time Warner's motion? *Fox News Network, L.L.C. v. Time Warner, Inc.,* 1997 WL 271720 (E.D.N.Y., May 16, 1997)

10-16 Castle and Harlan, an investment firm, entered into an agreement with the federal government to buy Western Empire Federal Savings and Loan. Under the agreement, Castle Harlan was to invest a nominal amount in the bank and arrange for others to invest much more, in exchange for, among other things, a promise that for two years Western Empire would not be subject to certain restrictions in federal regulations. Castle, Harlan, and the other investors filed a suit in the U.S. court of federal claims against the government, alleging breach of contract. The government filed a motion to dismiss all of the plaintiffs except Castle and Harlan, on the ground that the others did not sign the contract between the government and Castle and Harlan. Is the government correct? Should the court dismiss the claims brought by the other investors? *Castle v. United States,* 42 Fed. Cl. 859 (1999)

ASSIGNMENT ON THE INTERNET

This chapter provides information on the numerous requirements of traditional contract law. However, new ways of deciding contract disputes may be needed as the Internet allows more people to enter into contracts through cyberspace. Using the links that follow or by visiting www.jurisdiction.com/ecom3.htm, discover three

new issues of contract law that arise out of electronic contracts that are not addressed in this chapter.

Then use your critical thinking skills to apply the existing law to these new issues. Will the existing law resolve the new issues? What direction do you predict courts will take on the questions you have discovered? (See Chapter 11 for additional information)

 ## ON THE INTERNET

www.loc.gov From this site you can find links to a wealth of information about contracts.
www.law.cornell.edu/topics/contracts.html This site will provide more links to information about contract law.
www.lectlaw.com/formb.htm Multiple contract examples and forms are provided on this Web site.
www.legaldocs.com This site provides information about how to prepare contracts and contains legal forms to use as a template for you own contract.
www.findlaw.com/01topics/07contracts/gov_agencies.html This site contains links to government agencies that regulate contracts.
www.biercekenerson.com/Articles/E-Contracts.htm Court cases involving electronic contracts are increasing, and this Web site contains a number of the more important cases that are setting precedent.

11

THE LAW OF CONTRACTS AND SALES—II

- **METHODS OF DISCHARGING A CONTRACT**
- **REMEDIES FOR A BREACH OF CONTRACT**
- **E-CONTRACTS**
- **GLOBAL DIMENSIONS OF CONTRACT AND SALES LAW**

In our discussion of the law of contracts in Chapter 10, we were concerned that agreements be enforceable. We noted that without enforceability of contract law by a court, there would be no predictability for enterprises that produce and sell goods. Without this there would be no security and financial stability for a firm. We would see the risk of loss increase and entrepreneurship decline if contracts were not enforceable at all levels of the manufacturing, marketing, and distribution of services and goods.

In this chapter we will carefully examine the methods by which a contract can be discharged (particularly through performance), as well as the remedies that are possible for firms and individuals who are injured by a breach of contract for the sale of goods (Articles 2 and 2A of the UCC). E-contracts are highlighted and distinguished from traditional contract principles. This chapter also addresses the international dimensions of contracts and sales agreements.

Critical Thinking About the Law

In the previous chapter, we emphasized the importance of predictability and stability for those who enter into contracts. Yet, we do not want parties to jump immediately to the belief that they have a contract every time they talk about an exchange. Instead, we want to make it possible for people to talk about an exchange without having actually made a commitment to the exchange. Why?

To aid your critical thinking about issues surrounding contract formation and performance, let's look at a fact pattern involving concert tickets.

Jennifer and Juan were recently involved in a breach-of-contract case. Juan had two extra tickets to a Garth Brooks concert, and he agreed to sell these tickets to Jennifer. After they had agreed about the price, Juan promised to give the tickets to Jennifer the next day. But the next day, Jennifer did not want the tickets. Jennifer had discovered that it was an outdoor, afternoon concert. Jennifer argued that she should not have to buy the tickets because she is allergic to sunlight and unable to spend any extended period of time outside. The judge ruled in favor of Jennifer.

1. What ethical norms seem to dominate the judge's thinking? (See Chapter 1)

    Clue: We have said that security is one reason for enforcing contracts. Review your list of ethical norms. Which norms seem to conflict with security in this case?

2. What missing information might be helpful in this case?

    Clue: To help you think about missing information, ask yourself the following question. Would the fact that Juan knew that Jennifer was allergic to sunlight affect your thinking about this case?

3. What ambiguous words might be troublesome in this case?

    Clue: Examine the reasoning that Jennifer uses to argue that she should be released from the contract.

METHODS OF DISCHARGING A CONTRACT

When a contract is terminated, it is said to be *discharged*. A contract may be discharged by performance (complete or substantial), mutual agreement, conditions precedent and subsequent, impossibility of performance, or commercial impracticality.

DISCHARGE BY PERFORMANCE

In most cases, parties to an agreement discharge their contractual obligation by doing what was required by the terms of the agreement. Many times, however, performance is substantial rather than complete. Traditional common law allowed suits for breach of contract if there was not **complete performance** of every detail of the contract. Today, however, the standard is **substantial performance**. This standard requires (1) completion of nearly all the terms of the agreement, (2) an honest effort to complete all the terms, and (3) no *willful* departure from the terms of the agreement. Courts usually find substantial performance when there is only a *minor* breach of contract. For example, A, a contractor, agreed to build a house with five bedrooms for B. By the terms of the agreement, each of the rooms was to be painted blue. By mistake, one was painted pink, and B refused to pay A the $10,000 balance due on the house. The court awarded A

complete performance
Completion of all the terms of the contract.

substantial performance
Completion of nearly all the terms of the contract plus an honest effort to complete the rest of the terms coupled with no willful departure from any of the terms.

$10,000 minus the cost of painting the wrongly painted room, finding that the departure from the contract terms was slight and unintentional and, therefore, insufficient for B to refuse to perform (pay) as agreed to in the contract.

If the breach is *material*, the injured party may terminate the contract and sue to recover damages. A material breach is one that is substantial and, usually, intentional. Today, courts allow a party to "cure" a material breach if the time period within which a contract is supposed to be performed has not lapsed. The following classic case concerns a dispute over whether there was a minor or a material breach of contract by a home builder and which of two rules the court should use to measure damages.

CASE 11-1

Plante v. Jacobs
Supreme Court of Wisconsin
103 N.W.2d 296 (1960)

Plaintiff-appellee Plante sued defendants-appellants the Jacobs to obtain a lien on their property to recover $26,765 owed Plante by the Jacobs. Plante had agreed to build a house on a lot owned by the Jacobs according to specifications. A dispute arose when the misplacement of a wall caused the living room to be smaller than specified. The amount unpaid was approximately 25 percent of the contracting price. The wall would cost $4,000 to tear down and rebuild. Real estate experts claimed that the value of the house was not affected by the smaller width of the living room. The plaintiff conceded that he had failed to provide gutters and downspouts, a sidewalk, closet clothes poles, and other small items amounting to $1,601.95. However, he claimed that he had substantially performed the contract. Defendants argued that Plante had not substantially performed and, therefore, there was a material breach of the contract. The lower court ruled in favor of Plante for $4,152.90. The Jacobs appealed.

Justice Hallows

Substantial performance as applied to construction of a house does not mean that every detail must be in strict compliance with the specifications and the plans. Something less than perfection is the test of specific performance unless all details are made the essence of the contract. This was not done here. There may be situations in which features or details of construction of special or of great personal importance, which if not performed, would prevent a finding of substantial performance of the contract. In this case the plan was a stock floor plan. No detailed construction of the house was shown on the plan. There were no blueprints. The specifications were standard printed forms with some modifications and additions written in by the parties. Many of the problems that arose during the construction had to be solved on the basis of practical experience. No mathematical rule relat-

ing to the percentage of the price, of cost of completion, or of completeness can be laid down to determine substantial performance of a building contract. Although the defendants received a house with which they are dissatisfied in many respects, the trial court was not in error in finding the contract was substantially performed.

The next question is what is the amount of recovery when the plaintiff has substantially, but incompletely, performed. For substantial performance the plaintiff should recover the contract price less the damages caused the defendant by the incomplete performance. Both parties agree the correct rule for damages due to faulty construction amounting to such incomplete performance is the difference between the value of the house if it had been constructed in strict accordance with the plans and specifications. This is the diminished-value rule. The cost of replacement or repair is not the measure of such damage, but is an element to take into consideration in arriving at value under some circumstances. The cost of replacement or the cost to make whole the omissions may equal or be less than the difference in value in some cases and, likewise, the cost to rectify a defect may greatly exceed the added value to the structure as corrected. The defendants argue that under this rule their damages are $10,000. The plaintiff on review argues the defendants' damages are only $650. Both parties agree the trial court applied the wrong rule to the facts.

The trial court applied the cost-of-repair or replacement rule as to several items, stating when there are a number of small items of defect or omission, which can be remedied without the reconstruction of a substantial part of the building or a great sacrifice of work or material already wrought in the building, the reasonable cost of correcting the defect should be allowed.

The trial court disallowed certain claimed defects because they were not proven. This finding was not against the great weight and clear preponderance of the evidence and will not be disturbed on appeal. Of the remaining defects claimed by the defendants, the court allowed the cost of replacement or repair except as to the misplacement of the living-room wall. Whether a defect should fall under the cost-of-replacement rule or be considered under the diminished-value rule depends upon the nature and magnitude of the defect. This court has not allowed items of such magnitude under the cost-of-repair rule as the trial court did. Viewing the construction of the house as a whole and its cost we cannot say, however, that the trial court was in error in allowing the cost of repairing the plaster cracks in the ceilings, the cost of mud jacking and repairing the patio floor, and the cost of reconstructing the non-weight-bearing and nonstructural patio wall. Such reconstruction did not involve an unreasonable economic waste.

The item of misplacing the living-room wall under the facts of this case was clearly under the diminished-value rule. There is no evidence that defendants requested or demanded the replacement of the wall in the place called for by the specifications during the course of construction. To tear down the wall now and rebuild it in its proper place would involve a substantial destruction of the work, if not all of it, which was put into the wall and would cause additional damage to other parts of the house and require replastering and redecorating the walls and ceilings of at least two rooms. Such economic waste is unreasonable and unjustified. The rule of diminished value contemplates the wall is not going to be moved. Expert witnesses for both parties, testifying as to the value of the house, agreed that the misplacement of the wall had no effect on the market price. The trial court properly found that the defendants suffered no legal damage, although the defendants' particular desire for specified room size was not satisfied.

It would unduly prolong this opinion to detail and discuss all the disputed items of defects of workmanship or omissions. We have reviewed the entire record and considered the points of law raised and believe the findings are supported by the great weight and clear preponderance of the evidence and the law properly applied to the facts.

Affirmed in favor of Plaintiff, Plante.

Critical Thinking About the Law

Although rules of law provide guidance in courts' reasoning in subsequent cases, judges are not tightly bound by these rules. As you already read, common law previously required complete performance to discharge a contract. However, common law evolved to require only substantial performance. But the shift to a less strict requirement for contract performance does not occur arbitrarily. Judges who lessened the requirements for discharge by performance provided reasons for applying a different standard. These judges were also influenced by ethical norms that differed from ethical norms of judges in previous cases. Hence, the standard for discharge by performance changed. Similarly, the previous case illustrates how judges weigh the reasons for and against certain rules of law. In this case, the judge evaluated the reasons for applying either the diminished-value rule or the cost-of-replacement rule. In addition, the judge's reasoning is influenced by primary ethical norms, as the judge places greater priority on certain ethical norms relative to others. The following questions encourage you to consider the impact that reasons and ethical norms (Chapter 1) have on a judge's reasoning. Please refer to Case 11-1 and consider the following questions:

1. What reasons did the court provide to prefer the diminished-value rule instead of the cost-of-replacement rule, specifically in relation to the dispute about the living-room wall?

    Clue: Reread the two paragraphs in which the court discusses the "magnitude of the defect" and economic waste.

2. Consider the court's reasoning in applying the diminished-value rule. What primary ethical norms underlie the court's preference?

    Clue: Look at the list of primary ethical norms and compare the two rules the court discussed. Consider the ethical norms that would be most conducive to the diminished-value rule, which places a less stringent burden on builders to make homes in accordance with strict standards.

Uniform Commercial Code and Performance. The substantial performance doctrine does not apply to the sale of goods. The performance of a sale or lease contract requires the seller or lessor to transfer and deliver what is known as *conforming goods* (perfect tender rule). The buyer or lessee must accept and pay for the conforming goods. The UCC states an exception to the perfect tender rule. If the goods or tender of delivery fail to conform to the contract in any respect, the buyer has the following options: (1) to reject all the goods, (2) to accept all that are tendered, or (3) to accept any number of units the buyer chooses to and reject the rest. The buyer must generally give notice to the seller of any defect in the goods or tender of delivery and then allow the seller a reasonable time to "cure" the defect.

DISCHARGE BY MUTUAL AGREEMENT

Subsequent to the making of a contract, the parties may agree that they should rescind (cancel) the contract because some unforeseen event took place that makes its fulfillment financially impracticable. For example, if A agrees to build B a house for $150,000, and then, when building the basement, runs into an unforeseen and incorrectable erosion factor, both parties may want to cancel the agreement, with restitution to A for expenditures on the basement construction. The contract is then said to be discharged by mutual agreement.

Sometimes the parties wish to rescind an original agreement and substitute a new one for it. This type of discharge by mutual agreement is called *accord and satisfaction*. If the parties wish to substitute new parties for the original parties to the agreement, this is called *novation*. Note that novation does not change contractual duties; it merely changes the parties that will perform those duties. Suppose a rock star (original party) is unable to perform at a concert because of illness, and a star of the same stature (substitute party) agrees to appear instead. If all parties, including the concert impresario, agree to the substitution, there is discharge by mutual agreement.

Linking Law & Business

Management and Production

Quality is defined as the extent to which a product functions as intended. The measure of excellence for a product is ranked primarily by the purchaser based on certain characteristics and features, but the managers must oversee production processes to ensure that quality standards are being met. Managers are continuing to realize that an improvement in the quality of products leads toward greater productivity for the organization. By emphasizing greater quality, a firm will probably spend less time and money on repairing defective products. Also, manufacturing quality products reduces the chance of production mistakes and inefficient use of materials. One method of providing a greater assurance that an organization is producing quality products is with statistical quality control. This is a process by which a certain percentage of products for inspection is determined to ensure that organizational standards for quality are met. Organizations that place a strong emphasis on quality, possibly by implementing an effective statistical quality control strategy, are less likely to be faced with having their goods rejected under the perfect tender rule or facing litigation for a breach of contract over defective products. Thus, a serious and consistent emphasis on quality reaps many benefits for an organization.

Source: S. Certo, *Modern Management* (Upper Saddle River, N.J.: Prentice Hall, 2000), pp. 445, 447.

CASE 11-2

Architectural Systems, Inc. v. Gilbane Building Company
U.S. District Court, Maryland,
760 F. Supp 79 (1991)

Carley Capital Group (Carley) was the owner of a project in the city of Baltimore known as "Henderson's Wharf." The project was designed to convert warehouses into residential condominiums. On September 4, 1987, Carley hired Gilbane Building Company (Gilbane) to be the general contractor and construction manager for the project. Gilbane hired Architectural Systems, Inc. (ASI), as the subcontractor to perform drywall and acoustical tile work on the project. The subcontract included the following clause: "It is specifically understood and agreed that the payment to the trade contractor is dependent, as a condition precedent, upon the construction manager receiving contract payments from the owner."

Gilbane received periodic payments from Carley and paid ASI as work progressed. By late 1988, ASI had satisfactorily performed all of its obligations under the subcontract and submitted a final bill of $348,155 to Gilbane. Gilbane did not pay this bill because it had not received payment from Carley. On March 10, 1989, Carley filed for bankruptcy. ASI sued Gilbane, seeking payment.

Justice Young

ASI argues that it did not assume the credit risk simply by the inclusion of the statement "as a condition precedent" in the subcontract. It may not be sound business practice to accept such a business proposal but that is what occurred. The provision unambiguously declares that Gilbane is not obligated to pay ASI until it first received payment by the owner. The cause for the owner's nonpayment is not specifically addressed and could be due to a number of causes, including insolvency.

A provision that makes a receipt of payment by the general contractor a condition precedent to its obligation to pay the subcontractor transfers from the general contractor to the subcontractor the credit risk of non-payment by the owner for any reason (at least for any reason other than the general owner's own fault), including insolvency of the owner.

Decision in favor of Gilbane.

DISCHARGE BY CONDITIONS PRECEDENT AND SUBSEQUENT

Condition Precedent. A **condition precedent** is a particular event that must take place in order to give rise to a duty of performance. If the event does not take place, the contract may be discharged. For example, when Smith enters into a contract with Jones to sell a piece of real estate, a clause in the agreement requires that title must be approved by Jones's attorney before closing and execution of the contract for sale. If Jones's attorney does not give this approval before the closing, then Jones is discharged from the contract. The following case illustrates discharge of a contract by a condition precedent.

condition precedent A particular event that must take place to give rise to a duty of performance of a contract.

Condition Subsequent. A **condition subsequent** is a particular future event that, when following the execution of a contract, terminates the contract. For example, a homeowner's insurance contract may discharge the insurer from responsibility for coverage in the event of an "act of war" (condition subsequent).

condition subsequent A particular event that, when following the execution of a contract, terminates it.

DISCHARGE BY IMPOSSIBILITY OF PERFORMANCE

In early common law, when disruptive unanticipated events (e.g., war) occurred after parties entered into a contract, the contract was considered enforceable anyway. Thus, if a shipping line could not transport goods it had agreed to transport because of a wartime blockade, or if it could transport the goods but had to take a more expensive route to do so, it (or its insurance carrier) was required to pay damages or absorb the costs of a longer route. Courts today take the view that if an unforeseeable event makes a promisor's performance objectively impossible, the contract is discharged by **impossibility of performance**.

impossibility of performance Situation in which the party cannot legally or physically perform the contract.

"Objectively impossible" is defined as meaning that no person or company could legally or physically perform the contract.

This defense for nonperformance is used most frequently in three circumstances. First is the death or illness of a promisor whose personal performance is required to fulfill the contract when no substitute is possible. Say a world-renowned artist is commissioned to paint an individual's portrait. If the artist dies, the contract is discharged because there is no substitute for the artist. Second is a change of law making the promised performance illegal. For example, if A enters into a contract with B to sell B her home to be used for residential purposes, and subsequent to their agreement the property is zoned commercial, the contract will be discharged. The final circumstance is the destruction of the subject matter. If A enters into a contract with B to buy all the hay in B's barn and the barn burns down with the hay in it before shipment takes place, the contract is discharged because performance is impossible.

Discharge by Commercial Impracticability. The courts have sought to enlarge the grounds for discharge of a contract by adding the concept of **commercial impracticability**, defined as a situation in which performance is impracticable because of unreasonable expense, injury, or loss to one party. In effect, a situation that was not foreseeable, or whose nonoccurrence was assumed at the time the contract was executed, occurs, making performance of the contract unreasonably expensive or injurious to a party. For example, a plastics manufacturer becomes extremely short of raw materials because of a war and an embargo on oil coming from the Middle East. The manufacturer's contracts with retailers for plastic goods will be discharged in most cases if the court finds that the manufacturer could not have anticipated the war and had no alternative source of materials costing about the same price.

In the following case the New York Court of Appeals (New York's highest court) decided this precedent-setting case as to whether one party can seek adequate assurance of future performance of another if there is reason to be concerned that there may be a breach of contract.

commercial impracticability Situation that makes performance of a contract unreasonably expensive, injurious, or costly to a party.

CASE 11-3

Norcon Power v. Niagara Mohawk Power Corp.
Court of Appeals of New York
705 N.E. 2d 656 (N.Y. 1998)

In 1989, Norcon Power Partners, L. P., an independent power producer, entered into a contract with Niagara Mohawk Power Corporation, a public utility provider, whereby Niagara Mohawk agreed to purchase electricity generated at Norcon's Pennsylvania facility for a period of 25 years. There were three pricing periods under the contract. In the first period, Niagara Mohawk paid six cents per kilowatt-hour for electricity. In the second and third periods, the price paid by Niagara Mohawk was based on "avoided cost," which was calculated using the cost that Niagara Mohawk would incur to generate electricity itself or to purchase it from other sources. In the second period, Niagara Mohawk's payments were capped by a ceiling price. In the third period, the price paid by Niagara

Mohawk was not subject to a cap or a floor. Payments made by Niagara Mohawk in the third period were adjusted to account for any balance existing in the adjustment account that operated in the second period.

In February 1994, Niagara Mohawk wrote to Norcon stating that, based on revised avoided cost estimates, substantial credits in Niagara Mohawk's favor would occur in the adjustment account during the second pricing period. As a result, the company's analysis indicated that the cumulative avoided cost account would exceed $610 million by the end of the second period. Concerned that Norcon would be unable to satisfy the escalating credits in the third period, Niagara Mohawk demanded that Norcon provide adequate assurance that it would duly perform all of its future repayment obligations. Norcon sued Niagara Mohawk, seeking a declaration that Niagara Mohawk had no contractual right to demand adequate assurance.

The district court found that New York common law ruled in favor of the plaintiff. The decision was appealed to the U.S. Court of Appeals for the Second Circuit, which certified the question to the New York Court of Appeals for assistance in the correct application of New York law.

Justice Belladosa

The Court is persuaded that the policies underlying the UCC 2-609 counterpart should apply with similar cogency for the resolution of this kind of controversy. [Section 2-609 of the UCC provides that a party to a contract for the sale of goods has the right to demand assurances of future performance from the other party when grounds for insecurity exist. If no such assurances are provided, the party may assume that a repudiation has occurred.] A useful analogy can be drawn between the contract at issue and a contract for the sale of goods. If the contract here was in all respects the same, except that it was for the sale of oil or some other tangible commodity instead of the sale of electricity, the parties would unquestionably be governed by the demand for adequate assurance of performance factors in UCC 2-609. We are convinced to take this prudent step because it puts commercial parties in these kinds of disputes at relatively arm's-length equilibrium in terms of reliability and uniformity of governing legal rubrics. The availability of the doctrine may even provide an incentive and tool for parties to resolve their own differences, perhaps without the necessity of judicial intervention. Open, serious renegotiation of dramatic developments and changes in unusual contractual expectations and qualifying circumstances would occur because of and with an eye to the doctrine's application.

The various authorities, factors and concerns, in sum, prompt the prudence and awareness of the usefulness of recognizing the extension of the doctrine of demand for adequate assurance, as a common law analogue. It should apply to the type of long-term commercial contract between corporate entities entered into by Norcon and Niagara Mohawk here, which is complex and not reasonably susceptible of all security features being anticipated, bargained for and incorporated in the original contract. Norcon's performance, in terms of reimbursing Niagara Mohawk for credits, is still years away. In the meantime, potential quantifiable damages are accumulating and Niagara Mohawk must weigh the hard choices and serious consequences that the doctrine of demand for adequate assurance is designed to mitigate.

Reversed for Defendant.

Critical Thinking About the Law

Legal analogies permeate legal reasoning. However, simply because a court introduces an analogy in a judicial decision does not necessarily mean the analogy is persuasive. Analogies become more convincing only when they reflect significant similarities in terms of the facts between two situations. Alternatively, analogies become less convincing when they contain significant differences. The two questions below urge you to evaluate the court's reliance on legal analogies. Please refer to Case 11-3 and consider the following questions:

1. On what analogy did the court base its decision in this case?
   Clue: The court explicitly mentions the analogy in the first paragraph of the opinion.

2. Why did the court believe this analogy was convincing? Do you agree? Why or why not?
   Clue: Recall that an analogy is more convincing when there is a lack of significant differences.

REMEDIES FOR A BREACH OF CONTRACT

The fact that a court will enforce a contract does not mean that one party will automatically sue if the other breaches. Businesspeople need to consider several factors before they rush to file a lawsuit: (1) the likelihood of the suit's succeeding, (2) whether they wish to maintain a business relationship with the breaching party, (3) the possibility of arbitrating the dispute through a third party, thus avoiding litigation, and (4) the cost of arbitration or litigation as opposed to the revenues to be gained from enforcing the contract.

Remedies for a breach of contract are generally classified according to whether the plaintiff requests monetary damages ("legal" remedies) or nonmonetary damages (equitable remedies).

MONETARY DAMAGES ("LEGAL" REMEDIES)

monetary damages Dollar sums awarded for a breach of contract; "legal" remedies.

Monetary damages (often referred to as "exemplary") include compensatory, punitive, nominal, and liquidated damages.

compensatory damages Monetary damages awarded for a breach of contract that results in higher costs or lost profits for the injured party.

Compensatory Damages. The purpose of **compensatory damages** is to place the injured (nonbreaching) party to a contract in the position that that party would have been in had the terms of the contract been performed. For example, if a firm contracted to buy 8,000 widgets at $10 apiece to be delivered by August 15, the buyer has a right to go out and buy the widgets from another source if they are not delivered by the contract date. Suppose the widgets bought from the other source cost $10.50 apiece. In that case, the buyer can sue for the 50-cent difference in price per unit plus court costs. If the buyer cannot obtain widgets anywhere else, it can sue for lost profits.

The courts have set out three standards that the plaintiff-buyer must meet in order to recoup lost profits:

1. The plaintiff-buyer must show that it was reasonably foreseen by the defendant-seller that if he or she did not deliver the promised goods, the buyer would have no alternative source and, thus, would lose profits.

2. The plaintiff-buyer must show the amount of the damages with reasonable certainty; the buyer cannot just speculate about what this amount is.

3. The plaintiff-buyer must show that he or she did everything possible to mitigate damage—that is, that he or she looked for other possible sources of the goods.

In the landmark case that follows, a famous actress and dancer is involved in the litigation of a contract that involves the mitigation of damages.

punitive damages Monetary damages awarded in excess of compensatory damages for the sole purpose of deferring similar conduct in the future.

Punitive Damages. Damages in excess of compensatory damages that the court awards for the sole purpose of deterring the defendant and others from doing the same act again are known as **punitive damages**. They are infrequently awarded in contract cases.

nominal damages Monetary damages of a very small amount (e.g., $1) awarded to a party that is injured by a breach of contract but cannot show real damages.

Nominal Damages. Sometimes the court awards a very small sum (usually $1) in **nominal damages** to a party that is injured by a breach of contract but cannot show real damages. Generally in these cases, the court also enables the injured party to recover court costs, though not attorney's fees.

CASE 11-4

Shirley Parker v. Twentieth Century Fox Film Corporation
Supreme Court of California
474 P.2d 689 (1970)

Shirley Parker is the legal name of well-known actress Shirley MacLaine, who contracted with Twentieth Century Fox Film Corporation to play the female lead in a picture entitled *Bloomer Girl*, a musical. The film corpora-

tion decided against making the film, and so notified Parker, but offered to employ her in another film, *Big Country*. The compensation was the same but the picture was a western to be shot in Australia as opposed to a musical. Parker was given one week to accept. She didn't and sued Twentieth Century Fox, seeking recovery of $750,000 plus interest. The defendants argued against the awarding of damages to Parker because, they claimed, she failed to mitigate damages by accepting the part in *Big Country*. The trial court awarded summary judgment to Parker. Twentieth Century Fox appealed.

Justice Burke

The complaint sets forth two causes of action. The first is for money due under the contract; the second, based upon the same allegations as the first, is for damages resulting from defendant's breach of contract. Defendant, in its answer, admits the existence and validity of the contract, that plaintiff complied with all the conditions, covenants and promises and stood ready to complete the performance, and that defendant breached and "anticipatorily repudiated" the contract. It denies, however, that any money is due to plaintiff either under the contract or as a result of its breach, and pleads as an affirmative defense to both causes of action plaintiff's allegedly deliberate failure to mitigate damages, asserting that she unreasonably refused to accept its offer of the leading role in *Big Country*.

Plaintiff moved for summary judgment under Code of Civil Procedure Section 437c, the motion was granted, and summary judgment for $750,000 plus interest was entered in plaintiff's favor. This appeal by defendant followed.

As stated, defendant's sole defense to this action, which resulted from its deliberate breach of contract, is that in rejecting defendant's substitute offer of employment, plaintiff unreasonably refused to mitigate damages.

The general rule is that the measure of recovery by a wrongfully discharged employee is the amount of salary agreed upon for the period of service, less the amount the employer affirmatively proves the employee has earned or with reasonable effort might have earned from other employment. However, before projected earnings from other employment opportunities not sought or accepted by the discharged employee can be applied in mitigation, the employer must show that the other employment was comparable, or substantially similar, to that of which the employee has been deprived; the employee's rejection of or failure to seek other available employment of a different or inferior kind may not be resorted to in order to mitigate damages.

In the present case defendant has raised no issue of reasonableness of efforts by plaintiff to obtain other employment; the sole issue is whether plaintiff's refusal of defendant's substitute offer of *Big Country* may be used in mitigation. Nor, if the *Big Country* offer was of employment different or inferior when compared with the original *Bloomer Girl* employment, is there an issue as to whether or not plaintiff acted reasonably in refusing the substitute offer. Despite defendant's arguments to the contrary, no case cited or that our research has discovered holds or suggests that reasonableness is an element of a wrongfully discharged employee's option to reject, or fail to seek, different or inferior employment lest the possible earnings therefrom be charged against him in mitigation of damages.

Applying the foregoing rules to the record in the present case, with all intendment in favor of the party opposing the summary judgment motion—here, defendant—it is clear that the trial court correctly ruled that plaintiff's failure to accept defendant's tendered substitute employment could not be applied in mitigation of damages because the offer of the *Big Country* lead was of employment both different and inferior, and that no factual dispute was presented on that issue. The mere circumstances that *Bloomer Girl* was to be a musical review calling upon plaintiff's talents as a dancer as well as an actress, and was to be produced in the City of Los Angeles, whereas *Big Country* was a straight dramatic role in a "Western Type" story taking place in an opal mine in Australia, demonstrates the difference in kind between the two employments; the female lead as a dramatic actress in a western-style motion picture can by no stretch of imagination be considered the equivalent of or substantially similar to the lead in a song-and-dance production.

Additionally, the substitute *Big Country* offer proposed to eliminate or impair the director and screenplay approvals accorded to plaintiff under the original *Bloomer Girl* contract, and thus constituted an offer of inferior employment. No expertise or judicial notice is required in order to hold that the deprivation or infringement of an employee's rights held under an original employment contract converts the available "other employment" relied upon by the employer to mitigate damages, into inferior employment, which the employee need not seek or accept.

In view of the determination that defendant failed to present any facts showing the existence of a factual issue with respect to its sole defense—plaintiff's rejection of its substitute employment offer in mitigation of damages— we need not consider plaintiff's further contention that for various reasons, plaintiff was excused from attempting to mitigate damages.

Affirmed in favor of Plaintiff, Parker.

Liquidated Damages. Liquidated damages are usually set in a separate clause in the contract. The clause generally stipulates that the parties agree to pay so much a day for every day beyond a certain date that the contract is not completely performed. Liquidated damage clauses are frequently found in general contractors' agreements with individuals, corporations, and state or local

liquidated damages
Monetary damages for nonperformance that are stipulated in a clause in the contract.

Critical Thinking About the Law

Remedies are among the more visible actions by which judges express their views about ethical norms. Notice that in Case 11-4 the California Supreme Court could conceivably have affirmed the trial court's judgment for Parker and then decided to reduce the damages. However, the court was disturbed enough by the harm caused by Twentieth Century Fox that it affirmed what was at the time a substantial damage award.

Please refer to Case 11-4 and consider the following questions:

1. Decide what damage award each of the four primary ethical norms outlined in Chapter 1 compels in Case 11-4 and present a rationale for why that norm compels that particular damage award. You are not looking so much for a specific number here. Instead, you are asking the question, "Which of these norms propel the damage award higher and which argue for minimal damages?"

   Clue: Remember that one form of ethical reasoning focuses on the consequences of following an ethical norm in a particular situation. For instance, what would be the impact on efficiency if the damage award were even higher than that affirmed by the court?

2. If you were the judge in Case 11-4, what argument would you make in defending the size of the damages awarded by the trial court?

   Clue: Use ethical reasoning to support your desired remedy.

---

equitable remedies
Nonmonetary damages awarded for breach of contract when monetary damages would be inadequate or impracticable.

agencies in situations in which it is essential that a building project be completed on time. Such clauses help the contracting parties avoid going to court and seeking a judicial determination of damages—with all the attendant delays and expenses. The concept of liquidated damages is illustrated in Case 11-5.

EQUITABLE REMEDIES

When dollar damages are inadequate or impracticable as a remedy, the injured party may turn to nondollar or **equitable remedies**. Equitable remedies include rescission, reformation, specific performance, and injunction.

CASE 11-5

California and Hawaiian Sugar Company v. Sun Ship, Inc.
U.S. Court of Appeals
(9th Cir.) 794 F.2d 1433 (1986)

The California and Hawaiian Sugar Company (C&H), a California corporation, is an agricultural cooperative owned by 14 sugar plantations in Hawaii. It transports raw sugar to its refinery in Crockett, California. Sugar is a seasonal crop, with about 70 percent of the harvest occurring between April and October. C&H requires reliable seasonal shipping of the raw sugar from Hawaii to California. Sugar stored on the ground or left unharvested suffers a loss of sucrose and goes to waste.

After C&H was notified by its normal shipper that it would be withdrawing its services as of January 1981, C&H commissioned the design of a large hybrid vessel consisting of a barge attached to a tug. After substantial negotiations, C&H contracted with Sun Ship, Inc. (Sun Ship), a Pennsylvania corporation, to build the vessel for $25,405,000. The contract, which was signed in the fall of 1979, provided a delivery date of June 30, 1981. The contract also contained a liquidated damage clause calling for a payment of $17,000 per day for each day that the vessel was not delivered to C&H after June 30, 1981. Sun Ship did not complete the vessel until March 16, 1982. The vessel was commissioned in mid-July 1982 and christened the *Moku Pahu*.

During the 1981 season, C&H was able to find other means of shipping the crop from Hawaii to its California refinery. Evidence established that actual damages suffered by C&H because of the nonavailability of the vessel from Sun Ship were $368,000. When Sun Ship refused to pay the liquidated damages, C&H filed suit to require payment of $4,413,000 in liquidated damages under the contract. The district court entered judgment in favor of C&H and awarded the corporation $4,413,000 plus interest. Sun Ship appealed.

Justice Noonan

Contracts are contracts because they contain enforceable promises, and absent some overriding public policy, those promises are to be enforced. Where each of the parties is content to take the risk of its turning out in a particular way, why should one be released from the contract, if there were no misrepresentation or other want of fair dealing? Promising to pay damages of a fixed amount, the parties normally have a much better sense of what damages can occur. Courts must be reluctant to override their judgment. Where damages are real but difficult to prove, injustice will be done the injured party if the court substitutes the requirements of judicial proof for the parties' own informed agreement as to what is a reasonable measure of damages. The liquidated damage clause here functions in lieu of a court's determination of the consequential damages suffered by C&H.

Proof of this loss is difficult. Whatever the loss, the parties had promised each other that $17,000 per day was a reasonable measure. The court must decline to substitute the requirements of judicial proof for the parties' own conclusion. The *Moku Pahu*, if available on June 30, 1981, was a great prize, capable of multiple employments and enlarging the uses of the entire C&H fleet. When sophisticated parties with bargaining parity have agreed what lack of this prize would mean, and it is now difficult to measure what the lack did mean, the court will uphold the parties' bargain.

Affirmed in favor of Plaintiff, C&H.

Rescission. Rescission is defined as the canceling of a contract. Plaintiffs who wish to be put back in the position they were in before entering into the contract often seek rescission. In cases of fraud, duress, mistake, or undue influence (discussed in Chapter 10), the courts will generally award rescission.

rescission Cancellation of a contract.

Reformation. The correction of terms in an agreement so that they reflect the true understanding of the parties is known as **reformation**. For example, if A enters into an agreement to sell B 10,000 widgets at $.50 a unit when the figure should have been $5.50 a unit, A will petition the court for reformation of the contract.

reformation Correction of terms in an agreement so that they reflect the true understanding of the parties.

Specific Performance. A court order compelling a party to perform in such a way as to meet the terms of the contract is called **specific performance**. Courts are reluctant to order specific performance unless (1) a unique object is the subject matter of the contract (e.g., an antique or artwork) or (2) real estate is involved. To obtain a specific performance order, the plaintiff must generally show that dollar damages (damages "at law") are inadequate to compensate for the defendant's breach of contract. Even then, a court will often refuse to grant the order if it is incapable of or unwilling to supervise it. For these reasons, specific performance in contract cases is infrequently granted.

specific performance A court order compelling a party to perform in such a way as to meet the terms of the contract.

Injunctions. Injunctions are temporary (e.g., 30 days) or permanent orders of the court preventing a party to a contract from doing something. The plaintiff must show the court that dollar damages are inadequate and that irreparable harm will be done if the injunction is not granted. For instance, if an opera singer contracts with an opera company to sing exclusively for the company and then later decides to sing for other opera companies, the court may grant an injunction to prevent her from singing for the other companies. Injunctions, like specific performance, are seldom granted in contract law cases.

injunction Temporary or permanent court order preventing a party to a contract from doing something.

CASE 11-6

Potter v. Oster
Supreme Court of Iowa
426 N.W.2d 148 (1988)

The parties, though sharing a common interest in agribusiness, present a study in contrasts. Plaintiff Charles Potter is a farm laborer, and his wife, Sue, is a homemaker and substitute teacher. They have lived all their lives within a few miles of the real estate in question. Defendant Merrill Oster is an agricultural journalist and recognized specialist in land investment strategies. He owns Oster Communications, a multimillion-dollar publishing concern devoted to furnishing farmers the latest in commodity market analysis and advice on an array of farm issues.

In May 1978, Oster contracted with Florence Stark to purchase her 160-acre farm in Howard County, Iowa, for $260,000 on a 10-year contract at 7 percent interest. Oster then sold the homestead and nine acres to Charles and Sue Potter for $70,000. The Potters paid $18,850 down and executed a ten-year installment contract for the balance at 8.5 percent interest. Oster then executed a contract with Robert Bishop for the sale of the remaining 151 acres as part of a package deal that included the sale of 17 farms for a sum exceeding $5.9 million.

These back-to-back contracts collapsed like dominoes in March 1985 when Bishop failed to pay Oster and Oster failed to pay Stark the installments due on their respective contracts. Stark commenced forfeiture proceedings (proceedings to retake the property because Oster failed to perform a legal obligation—payment under the contract—and, thus, forfeited his right to the land). The Potters had paid every installment when due under their contract with Oster and had included Stark as a joint payee with Oster on their March 1, 1985, payment. But they were financially unable to exercise their right to advance the sums due on the entire 160 acres in order to preserve their interest in the nine acres and homestead. As a result, their interest in the real estate was forfeited along with Oster's and Bishop's and they were forced to move from their home in August 1985.

The Potters then sued Oster to rescind their contract with him, claiming restitution damages for all consideration paid. Trial testimony revealed that the market value of the property had decreased markedly since its purchase. Expert appraisers valued the homestead and nine acres between $27,500 and $35,000. Oster himself placed a $28,000 value on the property; Potter, $39,000. Evidence was also received placing the reasonable rental value of the property at $150 per month, or a total of $10,800 for the six-year Potter occupancy.

The district court concluded that the Potters were entitled to rescission of the contract and return of the consideration paid including principal and interest, cost of improvements, closing expenses, and taxes for a total of $65,169.37. From this amount the court deducted $10,800 for six years' rental, bringing the final judgment to $54,369.37.

On appeal, Oster challenged the judgment. He claimed that Potter had an adequate remedy at law for damages, which should have been measured by the actual economic loss sustained.

Judge Neuman

This is a suit in equity brought by the plaintiffs to rescind an installment land contract based on the seller's inability to convey title. The question on appeal is whether, in an era of declining land values, returning the parties to the status quo works an inequitable result. We think not. Accordingly, we affirm the district court judgment for rescission and restitution.

The facts are largely undisputed. Because the case was tried in equity, our review is *de novo*. We give weight to the findings of the trial court, particularly where the credibility of witnesses is concerned, but we are not bound thereby.

Rescission is a restitutionary remedy, which attempts to restore the parties to their positions at the time the contract was executed. The remedy calls for a return of the land to the seller, with the buyer given judgment for payments made under the contract plus the value of improvements, less reasonable rental value for the period during which the buyer was in possession. The remedy has long been available in Iowa to buyers under land contracts when the seller has no title to convey.

Rescission is considered an extraordinary remedy, however, and is ordinarily not available to a litigant as a matter of right but only when, in the discretion of the court, it is necessary to obtain equity. Our cases have established three requirements that must be met before rescission will be granted. First, the injured party must not be in default. Second, the breach must be substantial and go to the heart of the contract. Third, remedies at law must be inadequate.

The first two tests are easily met in the present case. The Potters are entirely without fault in this transaction. They tendered their 1985 installment payment to Oster before the forfeiture, and no additional payments were due until 1986. On the question of materiality, Oster's loss of equitable title [ownership rights protected in equity] to the homestead by forfeiture caused not only substantial, but total breach of his obligation to ensure peaceful possession [an implied promise made by a landowner, when selling or renting land, that the buyer or tenant will not be evicted or disturbed by the landowner or a person having a lien or superior title] and convey marketable title under the Oster–Potter contract. Only the third test—the inadequacy of damages at law—is contested by Oster on appeal. ... Restoring the status quo is the goal of the restitutionary remedy of rescission. Here, the district court accomplished the goal by awarding the Potters a sum representing all they had paid under the contract rendered worthless by Oster's default. Oster contends that in an era of declining land values, such a remedy goes beyond achieving the status quo and results in a windfall to the Potters. Unwilling to disgorge the benefits he has received under the unfulfilled contract, Oster would have the court shift the "entrepreneurial risk" [the risk assumed by one who initiates, and provides or controls the management of, a business enterprise] of market loss to the Potters by limiting their recovery to the difference between the property's market value at breach ($35,000) and the contract balance ($27,900). In other words, Oster claims the court should have awarded ... damages. ...

... [L]egal remedies are considered inadequate when the damages cannot be measured with sufficient certainty. Contrary to Oster's assertion that the Potters' compensation should be limited to the difference between the property's fair market value and contract balance at time of breach, ... damages are correctly calculated as the difference between contract price and market value at the time of performance. Since the time of performance in this case would have been March 1990, the market value of the homestead and acreage cannot be predicted with any certainty, thus rendering such a formulation inadequate.

Most importantly, the fair market value of the homestead at the time of forfeiture is an incorrect measure of the benefit the Potters lost. It fails to account for the special value the Potters placed on the property's location and residential features that uniquely suited their family. For precisely this reason, remedies at law are presumed inadequate for breach of a real estate contract. Oster has failed to overcome that presumption here. His characterization of the transaction as a mere market loss for the Potters, compensable by a sum that would enable them to make a nominal down payment on an equivalent homestead, has no legal or factual support in this record. ...

... In summary, we find no error in the trial court's conclusion that the Potters were entitled to rescission of the contract and return of all benefits allowed thereunder, less the value of reasonable rental for the period of occupancy. ...

Affirmed in favor of Plaintiff, Potter.

REMEDIES FOR BREACH OF A SALES CONTRACT (GOODS)

Remedies for the Seller. Under the UCC, remedies for the seller resulting from the buyer's breach include the following:

- *The right to recover the purchase price* if the seller is unable to sell or dispose of goods (*Section 2-709[1]*)

- *The right to recover damages* if the buyer repudiates a contract or refuses to accept the goods (*Section 2-708[1]*).

Remedies for the Buyer. If a seller breaches a sales contract by failing to deliver conforming goods or repudiating the contract prior to delivery, the buyer has a choice of remedies under the UCC:

- *The right to obtain specific performance* when the goods are unique or remedy at law is inadequate (*Section 2-716[1]*).

- *The right to recover damages after cancellation* of the contract.

- *The right to reject the goods* if the goods or tender fail to conform to the contract, or the right to keep some goods and reject the others.

- *The right to recover damages* for accepted goods *if the seller is notified of the breach* within a reasonable time (*Section 2-714[11]*).

In the following case, the court determined who is considered a "buyer" under the UCC provision noted previously.

CASE 11-7

Yates v. Pitman Manufacturing, Inc.
Supreme Court of Virginia
514 S.E.2d 605 (1999)

Pitman Manufacturing, Inc. (Pitman), when selling a construction crane in 1980 to Shelton Wilton Equipment, certified that the outrigger on the crane could be seen from its "activating location." In 1991, Carbon Corporation owned the crane. Ira Stiltner, an employee of Carbon Corporation, was delivering equipment to Baldwin Coal (Baldwin), but could not see Ed Yates, an employee of Baldwin, who was releasing the chains from the crane truck's bed. The outrigger dropped on Yates's foot. In the lower court, Yates (plaintiff) argued that a breach of warrant on the part of Pitman existed. Pitman argued that under UCC Section 2-607(3), reasonable notice was not given. Yates argued that he was not the buyer of the crane and, thus, did not have to give notice. The lower court ruled in favor of Pitman. Yates appealed.

Justice Stephenson

First, we consider whether the trial court erred in holding that Yates was required to provide Pitman with notice of breach of warranty as a prerequisite to recovery therefore. The issue is one of first impression for this Court.

To resolve the issue, we look to [Virginia] Code [Section] 8.2-607(3), the only provision of the Sales title of the Uniform Commercial Code (the UCC) that requires notice to be given to a seller of goods. The section provides, in pertinent part, the following:

> Where a tender has been accepted the buyer must within a reasonable time after he discovers or should have discovered any breach notify the seller of breach or be barred from any remedy.

It is firmly established that, when a statute is clear and unambiguous, a court must accept its plain meaning and not resort to extrinsic evidence or rules of construction. The pertinent language in the Code is unambiguous and clearly states that "the buyer must notify the seller of [the] breach." Thus, accepting the statute's plain meaning, it is apparent that the notice of breach is required from the "*buyer*" of the goods. [Emphasis added.]

In the present case, Yates was not the buyer of the crane unit. Therefore, the notice requirement of the Code does not preclude Yates from maintaining a breach of warranty action.

We hold, therefore, that only buyers, i.e., those who buy or contract to buy goods from a seller, must give notice of breach of warranty to the seller as a prerequisite to recovery. Consequently, the trial court erred in ruling that Yates was required to have given Pitman such notice.

Reversed in favor of Yates, Plaintiff.

E-CONTRACTS

In Chapter 10, and this chapter, we have examined the traditional principles governing contracts for the sale of real and personal property, as well as the sale and lease of goods as defined by the UCC. E-contracts (contracts entered into electronically via computers or satellite) are now an everyday part of a cyberspace era. While using many of the traditional principles when entering into online contracts, minimum provisions should include:

- remedies that are available to the buyer if any of the goods contracted for are defective
- a statement of the referral policy of the seller
- a statement of how goods are to be paid for
- a forum selection clause, which indicates the location and/or forum where a dispute will be settled should one arise
- a disclaimer of liability provision by the seller for certain uses of a good sold
- the manner in which an offer can be accepted (e.g., by "click on"). Similarly, an acceptance may be used by traditional principles or by Section 2-2204 of UCC (previously studied in Chapter 10)

- click-on terms that indicate an agreement of the terms outlined in an offer
- browse-wrap terms that are enforceable (or binding) without offeree's active consent as with "click-on terms"

E-SIGNATURES

In the year 2000, Congress enacted a law entitled Electronic Signatures in Global and National Commerce Act (E-SIGN),[1] allowing consumers and businesses to sign contracts online and making e-signatures just as binding as ones in ink. Such contracts as those for bank loans and brokerage accounts may be entered into over the Internet 24 hours a day. This prevents delays that arise from paper contracts that need to be written, mailed, signed, and then returned. The cost of drawing up paperwork, mailing it, and storing agreements will be eliminated in favor of electronic retention.

The law went into effect on October 1, 2000, but questions were raised as to whether people would be able to forge electronic signatures on everything from online purchases to credit card applications. The law does not specify what constitutes a digital signature. Possible requirements include (1) a password that must be entered into a form on a Web page, with the Web site having to confirm that it belongs to a certain person, or (2) the use of hardware such as thumbprint scanning devices that plug into personal computers and transmit the thumbprint over the Internet to a business, which would keep it on file for authenticity purposes.

State laws governing e-signatures differ from state to state. Some states prohibit documents from being signed with e-signatures (e.g., California) whereas others do not. In 1999 the National Conference on Commissions on Uniform State Law and the American Law Institute set out the Uniform Electronic Transcription Act (UETA),[2] which sought to bring uniformity to this area of the law. The law indicates that a signature may not be denied legal enforceability solely because of its electronic form. The UETA has been adopted in whole or in part by more than 40 states.

THE UNIFORM COMPUTER INFORMATION TRANSACTION ACT (UCITA)[3]

Prior to World War II, the common law of contracts was sufficient to handle most of the transactions in an agricultural society. As the distribution and manufacturing of goods tended to dominate commerce, the Uniform Commercial Code (UCC) was drafted by the National Conference of Commissioners on Uniform State Law, a consortium of lawyers, judges, businesspeople, and legal scholars. Individual states gradually adopted all or part of it. For purposes of the law of contracts, Article 2 (Sales) and 2A (Leases) have been of significance, as shown in this and the preceding chapter.

As the world of computers and electronic commerce developed in the 1980s and 1990s, the common law of contracts and the UCC did not provide adequate guidelines, because the cyberspace economy is largely based on electronic contracts and the licensing of information. Questions developed as to how to enforce e-contracts, as well as what consumer protection should be provided. In July 1999, the National Conference of Commissioners issued the UCITA. It has been adopted by two states as of 2004.

[1] 15 U.S.C. Section 700 et seq.
[2] UETA 102 (8) and (25).
[3] UCITA Section 102.

SCOPE OF THE UCITA

It should be emphasized that the UCITA deals only with information that is electronically disseminated. Under this act, a computer information transaction is an agreement to create, transfer, or license computer information. Not covered are licenses of information for traditional copyrighted materials such as books or magazines.

Many of the provisions of the UCITA are similar to Article 2 of the UCC. For example, a licensing agreement may be interpreted by the courts using express terms of the agreement, as well as course of performance and usage. However, there are several differences with licensing agreements under the UCITA.

- The party who sells the right to use a piece of software (licensor) can control the right of use by the buyer (licensee). In a mass market this is extremely important. An exclusive license means that for its duration, the licensor will not grant to any other person rights to the same information. This is a matter of serious negotiation both nationally and internationally, with firms as well as with governments.

- If a contract requires a fee of more than $5,000, it is enforceable only if it is authenticated. To authenticate means to sign a contract or execute an electronic symbol, sound, or message attached to or linked with the record. Authentication may be attributed to his or her agent. Authentication may be proven if a party uses information or if he or she engages in operations that authenticate the record.

THE BUSINESS COMMUNITY: CRITICISMS OF THE UCITA

The UCITA would favor software makers because clickwrap agreements are favored by the act, and there would be uniformity to such agreements. This still leaves the question of enforcement of such agreements when working with other business entities or governments.

Debate exists among those who want uniformity and critics who believe software makers would use uniformity to argue that they are not responsible for defective software sold. For example, who is going to be responsible for a software virus? Will consumers read the fine-print disclaimers? Some would argue that problems associated with e-contracts are similar in dealing with contracts for real property, goods, and personal property.

GLOBAL DIMENSIONS OF CONTRACT AND SALES LAW

As more nations in Europe, Latin America, and Asia have shifted toward market-oriented economies, international trade has increased, and, along with it, contracts implementing transactions between foreign entities (either governments or private companies) and U.S. companies have increased. International and regional treaties lowering or eliminating tariffs have hastened the trend to free trade. (See Chapter 9 for a detailed description of recent trade pacts.)

Given this accelerating trend toward free trade, the United Nations Commission on International Trade Law drafted the Convention on Contracts for the International Sale of Goods (CISG)[4] to provide uniformity to international transactions. The CISG covers all contracts for the sale of goods in coun-

---

[4] 15 U.S.C. app. (1997).

tries that have ratified it. Parties to a contract can choose to adhere to all or part of the CISG, or they may select other laws to govern their transactions.

On January 1, 1988, CISG was approved as a treaty and incorporated into U.S. federal law. As a treaty, it overrides conflicting state laws dealing with contracts. Each of the 50 states is now examining conflicts between the Uniform Commercial Code (as adopted in the state) and the CISG, which supersedes it.

Some of these differences between the CISG and the UCC are highly significant. For example, under the CISG, a contract is formed when the seller (offeror) receives the acceptance from the offeree, whereas under the UCC, a contract is formed when the acceptance is mailed or otherwise transmitted. To take another example, under the CISG, a sales contract of any amount is enforceable if it is oral, whereas the UCC requires a written contract for a sale of goods of $500 or more.

Present and future business managers must become knowledgeable about these and other differences between the UCC and the CISG to avoid costly and time-consuming litigation as international transactions in goods increase. You might want to review Chapter 9 at this point to refresh your memory of the methods and details of international transactions.

Technology and the Legal Environment

International E-Commerce

A group of leading companies involved in the Internet online and e-commerce industries (AOL Time Warner, Microsoft, and AT&T) sought to establish "Guidelines for Merchant-to-Consumer Transactions" in June 2000 with the purpose of becoming less reliant on many countries' laws.[5] The guidelines covered marketing practice, cancellation, return and refund policies, privacy, and warranty information, among many aspects of customer transactions.

Additionally, this e-commerce group also set forth a "Statement on Global Jurisdiction" that deals with global transactions conducted over the Internet. It also addresses the question of merchants' ability to use online dispute-resolution mechanisms to resolve disputes[6].

[5] "E-Commerce Group Proposes Guidelines for Consumer Protection Group," PR News Wire, June 6, 2000.
[6] Electronic Commerce and Protection Group, **www.ecommercegroup.org**.

SUMMARY

Contracts are discharged by performance, mutual agreement, conditions precedent and subsequent, and sometimes through impossibility of performance. Remedies for breach of contract include dollar remedies such as lost profits, punitive, nominal, and liquidated damages. Often, when dollar damages are insufficient, the court will rely on equitable remedies (nondollar damages) such as rescission, restitution, specific performance, and reformation.

Contract laws became more uniform with the ratification by many nations of the Convention on Contracts for the International Sale of Goods. This has wide implications for the conduct of international transactions.

E-contracts require some minimum provisions that may be slightly different than common-law principles. With the help of statutory and case law, e-contracts are now becoming part of everyday business transactions.

REVIEW QUESTIONS

11-1 Describe the criteria used by the courts in determining lost profits.

11-2 What is the CISG? Why is it important to present and future businesspeople?

11-3 What is meant by "impossibility of performance"?

11-4 What is the standard a court uses to award dollar damages when lost profits are involved?

11-5 Why should a party who has not breached a contract be required to mitigate the damages of the breaching party?

11-6 What are some provisions that should be included in e-contracts?

REVIEW PROBLEMS

11-7 Silver was a journeyman electrician who was occasionally employed by A.O.C. Corporation, an apartment management company. He did some electrical work for A.O.C. over a four-month period and submitted a bill for $893. The defendant refused to pay, claiming the contract lacked a legal object because the plaintiff was not licensed as an electrical contractor in Detroit or the state of Michigan. The state licensing statute exempted "minor work," and the plaintiff claimed that his work rewiring a hallway in an apartment building managed by A.O.C. was "minor." What critical thinking skills would you use to speculate on who might win this case?

11-8 Ace contracted with Jones to do certain remodeling work on the building owned by Jones. Jones supplied the specifications for the work. The contract price was $70,000. After the work was completed, Jones was dissatisfied and had Clay, an expert, compare the work done with the specifications provided. Clay testified that the work had been done improperly by Ace and that it would cost about $6,000 to correct the mistakes of Ace. If Jones refuses to pay any amount to Ace, what recourse, if any, does Ace have against Jones? Explain.

11-9 On January 4, General Contractors, Inc., entered into a contract with Julius and Penelope Jones to construct a house fit for occupancy by June 1. What is the legal consequence if General Contractors fails to complete the house by June 1 but does finish it by June 20? What would be the consequence if the contract stated that with regard to the June 1 deadline, "time is of the essence"? Suppose further that by May 10 no work had yet been started by General Contractors. When contacted by Julius, General Contractors' president states that due to other projects still pending, he is unable to build the house until late November. What legal recourse, if any, do Julius and Penelope have against General Contractors?

11-10 A contractor agreed to build a skating rink for the plaintiff at a price of $180,000. The rink was to be completed by December 1 and was designed to replace a similar but older rink that the plaintiff rented for $800 a month. A clause in the contract awarded the plaintiff "$100 per day in liquidated damages" for each day after December 1 that the rink was not completed. Was this a valid liquidated damages clause? Explain.

11-11 On April 15, Don Construction contracted to build a house for Jessup. The contract price was $55,000. The agreement contained a provision stating that the builder would deduct $1,000 a day from the contract price for each day the house was not completed after August 15. It was not completed until September 15. Don Construction refused to deduct $30,000 from the contract price. Jessup refused to sue. Don Construction sued, claiming the $1,000 a day was a penalty clause, not a liquidated damages clause. What was the result? Explain.

11-12 Julius W. Erving ("Dr. J") entered into a four-year contract to play exclusively for the Virginia Squires of the American Basketball Association. After one year, he left the Squires to play for the Atlanta Hawks of the National Basketball Association. The contract signed with the Squires provided that the team have his contract set aside for fraud. The Squires counterclaimed and asked for arbitration. Who won? Explain.

11-13 TWA had a sale/leaseback agreement with Connecticut National Bank. Because of the Gulf War, air travel was decreased and it was having trouble making its payments. Discuss the extent to which TWA could use commercial impracticability or impossibility as a defense for nonpayment.

CASE PROBLEMS

11-14 In May 1996, O'Brien-Shiepe Funeral Home, Inc., in Hempstead, New York, hired Teramo & Co. to build an addition to O'Brien's funeral home. The parties' contract did not specify a date for the completion of the work. The city of Hempstead issued a building permit for the project on June 14, and Teramo began work about two weeks later. There was some delay in construction because O'Brien asked that no work be done during funeral services, but by the end of March 1997, the work was substantially complete. The city of Hempstead issued a "Certificate of Completion" on April 15. During the construction, O'Brien made periodic payments to Teramo, but there was a balance due of $17,950, which O'Brien did not pay. To recover this amount, Teramo filed a suit in a New York state court against O'Brien. O'Brien filed a counterclaim to recover lost profits for business allegedly lost due to the time Teramo took to build the addition and for $6,180 spent to correct problems caused by poor work. Who won? Explain. *Teramo & Co., v. O'Brien-Shiepe Funeral Home, Inc.*, 725 N.Y.S. 2d 87 (2001)

11-15 Mr. and Mrs. Evanoski filed a suit against All-Around Travel agency for money paid for their trip. They signed an insurance contract that required 72 hours' notice for cancellation. Mrs. Evanoski came down with a sudden illness on the day they were to leave. Could they invoke the doctrine of impossibility of performance? Who won? Explain. *Evanoski v. All-Around Travel*, 684 N.Y. 5.2d 342 (Sup. 1998)

11-16 Katherine Lane enrolled her 18-month-old daughter in day care with Kindercare Learning Centers, Inc. (Kindercare). Lane's daughter had been prescribed medication, and Lane filled out an authorization form granting Kindercare's employees permission to administer the medication to her daughter that day. Just after 5:00 P.M., one of the employees placed the child, who had fallen asleep, in a crib in the infant room. At approximately 6:00 P.M., the employees, apparently unaware that Lane's daughter was still sleeping in the crib, locked the doors of the facility and went home for the day. Shortly thereafter, Lane returned to the facility to pick up her daughter and found the facility locked and unlit. An officer then broke a window and retrieved the child from the building. The child was upset after the incident but not physically harmed. When Lane went into the facility to retrieve her daughter's belongings, she apparently found the medication authorization form and observed that it had not been initialed to indicate that an employee had given the med-

ication to the child. As a result of the incident, Lane alleged that she had suffered emotional distress. Michigan law allowed the recovery of emotional damages for breach of contracts of a personal nature but not for breaches involving commercial, or pecuniary, contracts. Should Lane prevail on her claim in this case? *Lane v. Kindercare Learning Centers*, Inc., 588 N.W.2d 715 (Mich. App. 1998)

11-17 Adolf and Ida Krueger contracted with Pisani Construction, Inc., to erect a metal building as an addition to an existing structure. The two structures were to share a common wall, and the frames and panel heights of the new building were to match those of the existing structure. Shortly before completion of the project, however, it was apparent that the roofline of the new building was approximately three inches higher than that of the existing structure. Pisani modified the ridge caps of the buildings to blend the rooflines. The discrepancy had other consequences, however, including misalignment of the gutters and windows of the two buildings, which resulted in an icing problem in the winter. The Kruegers occupied the new structure but refused to make the last payment under the contract. Pisani filed a suit in a Connecticut state court to collect. Did Pisani substantially perform its obligations? *Pisani Construction, Inc. v. Krueger*, 791 A.2d 634 (2002)

11-18 William West, an engineer, worked for Bechtel Corporation, an organization of about 160 engineering and construction companies, which is headquartered in San Francisco, California, and operates worldwide. Except for a two-month period in 1985, Bechtel employed West on long-term assignments or short-term projects for 30 years. In October 1997, West was offered a position on a project with Saudi Arabian Bechtel Co. (SABCO), which West understood would be for two years. In November, however, West was terminated for what he believed was his "age and lack of display of energy." After his return to California, West received numerous offers from Bechtel for work that suited his abilities and met his salary expectations, but he did not accept any of them and did not look for other work. Three months later, he filed a suit in a California state court against Bechtel, alleging in part breach of contract and seeking the salary he would have earned during two years with SABCO. Bechtel responded in part that, even if there had been a breach, West had failed to mitigate his damages. Is Bechtel correct? *West v. Bechtel, Corp.*, 117 Cal. Rptr. 2d 647 (2002)

ASSIGNMENT ON THE INTERNET

This chapter briefly introduces the Uniform Computer Information Transaction Act (UCITA) as a means of regulating the increasing volume of e-commerce and electronic contracts. However, not everyone is in favor of the UCITA. Using the Internet, search for articles and opinions that present multiple perspectives about how the UCITA influences business operations.

You can begin by visiting the Americans for Fair Electronic Commerce Transactions (AFECT) site (www.ucita.com). What arguments does it present against UCITA? Then visit the Virginia Technology Council (leg.vptc.org/UCITA/consumer.html) to read positions in favor of UCITA.

Now draft a brief response to what you have read. Would you support or oppose wider enactment of UCITA? Why? Would you recommend any changes be made if your state was considering adopting parts of UCITA? What would those changes be?

 ## ON THE INTERNET

cisgw3.law.pace.edu/cisg/text/database.html The CISG can be found at this page, set up by the Institute of Commercial Law.

www.law.cornell.edu/ucc/2/overview.html This site contains the relevant part of the Uniform Commercial Code to contracts and sales.

www.lectlaw.com/files/bul08.htm This site provides more information on nonperformance and breach of contract.

www.cisg.law.pace.edu/cisg/text/treaty.html Here you can find the United Nations Convention of Contracts for the International Sale of Goods.

www.law.cornell.edu/topics/contracts.html Use this site to access recent contract-law cases.

www.law-counsel.com/Legal_information/contract_law This site address some common questions about international contract law.

THE LAW OF TORTS

- THE GOALS OF TORT LAW
- DAMAGES AVAILABLE IN TORT CASES
- CLASSIFICATIONS OF TORTS
- GLOBAL DIMENSIONS OF TORT LAW

We said in Chapter 2 that the law is divided into criminal law and civil law. The division, however, is not airtight. Although a given set of actions may constitute a crime or a wrong against the state and, thus, may give rise to a criminal prosecution, the same set of actions may also constitute a tort, a civil wrong that gives the injured party the right to bring a lawsuit against the wrongdoer to recover compensation for the injuries. We define a **tort** as an injury to another's person or property.

This chapter discusses torts as if they were the same across the country—and, in general, they are—but you should keep in mind that tort law is state law and so may vary somewhat from state to state. The total amount of tort litigation has been declining since 1996.[1] Even so, tort law is and will continue to be an important area of law and an essential subject for the student of the legal environment of business, because managers who fail to have a basic understanding of tort law are placing themselves and the company's stakeholders at risk.

---

[1] Ted Rohrlich, "America's Litigation Explosion Has Fizzled," *Los Angeles Times*, February 1, 2001.

≡ Critical Thinking About the Law ≡

Tort law allows compensation for individuals whose person or property has been injured. Applying some critical thinking questions to tort law can help you better understand this chapter.

1. As discussed in Chapter 1, courts have preferences for certain ethical norms. Using critical thinking skills will help us understand how those norms have shaped legal reasoning about tort law. It is quite possible for two judges hearing a tort case to disagree on a verdict. One reason for the different verdicts is their disagreement over which ethical norms are most important. What conflicting ethical norms are inherent in tort law?

   Clue: Think of the definitions of the primary ethical norms in Chapter 1. If a judge strongly values freedom, what ethical norm might conflict with the judge's loyalty to freedom? Why?

2. Loyalty to certain ethical norms will influence your attitude toward compensating injured individuals. Remember that the majority of civil jury trials involve torts. If you value efficiency, how might the large number of tort cases in the court system affect your thinking about tort law?

   Clue: Why would this large number of tort cases not trouble a person who values justice over efficiency?

3. One of the critical thinking skills you have learned to use is identifying ambiguous words. Words with multiple possible meanings can result in different interpretations of a law. In tort law, this issue is especially important. Look at the definition of a tort. How does the definition of the word *injury* influence thinking about tort cases?

   Clue: Again, consider the number of tort cases in the courts. How would the number of court cases change if we loosely defined the word *injury*? What ethical norms would influence our definition of injury?

THE GOALS OF TORT LAW

tort An injury to another's person or property; a civil wrong.

Tort cases are commonly referred to as *personal injury cases*, although a tort case may involve harm solely to property. The primary goal of tort law is to compensate innocent persons who are injured or whose property is injured as a result of another's conduct, but tort law also fulfills other important societal goals. It discourages private retaliation by injured persons and their friends. It also promotes citizens' sense of a just society by forcing responsible parties to pay for the injuries they have caused. Finally, it deters future wrongs because potential wrongdoers are aware that they will have to pay for the consequences of their harmful acts.

For example, if Sam takes Judy's car without her permission and wrecks it, he has committed a tort. If there were no tort law, she would get no compensation from Sam and would have to use her own money to have the car repaired or to buy a new one. She would feel that she lived in an unjust world. She might even be tempted to seek revenge against Sam by breaking his car window. Others, seeing what Sam has gotten away with, would be less likely to be careful with other people's property in the future. However, because we have tort law, Judy can sue Sam and receive compensation from him for the damage he did to her car. She will then feel that she has received justice and will not be inclined to take any private retaliatory actions against Sam. Others, knowing that Sam had to pay for the harm he caused, may be deterred from committing torts themselves.

DAMAGES AVAILABLE IN TORT CASES

The victim of a tort may sue the wrongdoer, or *tortfeasor*, and has the potential to recover from among three types of damages: *compensatory*, *nominal*, and *punitive* (Table 12-1). All three types of damages were defined and discussed in Chapter 11 in relation to breaches of contract. Here we describe their specific application to tort cases.

COMPENSATORY DAMAGES

The most common type of damages sought in tort cases are compensatory damages. Compensatory damages are designed to make the victim whole again, that is, to put the victim in the position he or she would have been in had the tort never taken place. They include compensation for all of the injuries to the victim and his or her property that were caused by the tortfeasor. Typical items covered by this class of damages are medical bills, lost wages, property repair bills, and compensation for pain and suffering. Note that attorneys' fees are not considered an item of compensatory damages, even though it would be virtually impossible for a victim to bring suit without the services of an attorney. Because the plaintiffs in personal injury cases must usually pay their attorneys by giving them a portion of the compensatory damages they are awarded, some people argue that compensatory damages do not fully compensate tort victims.

NOMINAL DAMAGES

Sometimes the plaintiff is unable to prove damages that would necessitate compensation. In such a case, the court may award the victim nominal damages (damages in name only). The sum of such awards is minuscule, usually $1, but recovery of nominal damages may be important because it allows the plaintiff to seek punitive damages. Punitive damages cannot be awarded alone but must accompany an award of compensatory or nominal damages. An illustration of a case in which nominal damages were of utmost importance is the case of the death-row inmate in South Carolina who received nominal damages of only 10 cents from his case against prison guards.[2] This sum allowed the plaintiff—in this case, the inmate—to seek punitive damages. However, this award was also

Type	Purpose	Amount	
Compensatory	To put the plaintiff in the position he or she would have been in had the tort never occurred	Sufficient to cover all losses caused by the tort, including compensation for pain and suffering	**TABLE 12-1** **TYPES OF TORT DAMAGES**
Nominal	To recognize that the plaintiff has been wronged.	A nominal amount—usually $1 to $5.	
Punitive	To punish the defendant.	Determined by the severity of the wrongful conduct and the wealth of the defendant.	

---

[2] "Lawyer Gets $30,000 Fee Award for 10-cent Win," 95 LWUSA 1037 (1995).

Linking Law & Business

Marketing

The establishment of torts for the purpose of deterring future crimes relates to a familiar concept in the field of marketing. This idea, advertising, is defined as the "presentation and promotion of ideas, goods, or services by an identified sponsor." Advertisers hope that what they are promoting will gain acceptance by the general public. Similarly, the law of torts is created to promote fair and just behavior among civilians. One intent of torts is that potential wrongdoers will refrain from injuring other persons or their property because of the consequences entailed in tort laws.

Source: P. Kotler and G. Armstrong, *Principles of Marketing* (Upper Saddle River, N.J.: Prentice Hall, 2001), p. 543.

important for other reasons. For example, it may change the prison guards' behavior in the future. Or, because the inmate won, even though the damages were only nominal, perhaps the public will see the case as involving an important legal issue.

PUNITIVE DAMAGES

When the act of the tortfeasor is flagrant, unconscionable, or egregious, the court may award the victim punitive damages. These damages are designed to not only punish the tortfeasor for willfully engaging in extremely harmful conduct but also to deter others from engaging in similar conduct. Punitive damages are considered by some legal scholars to be especially useful in deterring manufacturers from making unsafe products. If there were no possibility of incurring punitive damages, manufacturers might calculate how much money they would have to spend fighting and settling lawsuits resulting from the sale of a defective product and then calculate the cost of making a safer product. If it turned out to be cheaper to produce the defective product and compensate injured victims than to make a safer product, rational manufacturers would be likely to produce the defective product. The risk of incurring punitive damages, however, is often sufficient to convince manufacturers to produce the safe product.

Some people disagree with this reasoning. They claim that the costs of compensatory damages alone are a sufficient incentive to produce only safe products. They further argue that the almost unrestricted ability to award punitive damages gives juries too much power.

In recent years, there have been many attempts by insurance companies and tort reform groups to limit the amount of punitive damages that can be assessed. These advocates of tort reform have tried repeatedly to get the courts to strike down punitive damages as unconstitutional on the grounds that such damages violate defendants' due process rights. This argument was unsuccessful until 1994. That year, in the case of *Honda Motor Company v. Oberg*,[3] the Supreme Court handed business firms their first victory in their campaign

---

[3] 114 S.Ct. 2331 (1994).

against punitive damages. This case, in which the high court struck down a punitive damages award as being a violation of due process, was unusual in two respects. First, the punitive damages were over five times the amount of the compensatory damages. Second, the state law had no provision for judicial review of the amount of the punitive damage award, whereas every other state allows such a review. It was Oregon's denial of judicial review of the amount of punitive damages that the U.S. Supreme Court said violated the Due Process Clause. Because of its unusual facts, *Honda v. Oberg* was not very instructive as to when punitive damages would be so excessive as to violate due process. In the following case, the Supreme Court finally set forth a workable test.

CASE 12-1

BMW of North America, Inc. v. Ira Gore, Jr.
United States Supreme Court
116 S.Ct. 1589 (1995)

Plaintiff Ira Gore, Jr., brought an action against BMW's American distributor and the dealer who had sold him a car, alleging that the dealer's failure to disclose that the car had been repainted after being damaged before delivery constituted suppression of a material fact. The failure to notify the plaintiff was consistent with the company policy not to advise its dealers, and hence their customers, of predelivery damage to new cars when the cost of repair amounted to less than 3 percent of the car's suggested retail price. The jury returned a verdict finding BMW liable for compensatory damages of $4,000. In addition, the jury assessed $4 million in punitive damages, based on a determination that the nondisclosure policy constituted "gross, oppressive or malicious" fraud. The Alabama Circuit Court affirmed. The distributor and manufacturer appealed. The Alabama Supreme Court conditionally affirmed the punitive damage award after reducing the award to $2 million.

Justice Stevens

The Due Process Clause of the Fourteenth Amendment prohibits a State from imposing a "grossly excessive" punishment on a tortfeasor. The question presented is whether a $2 million punitive damages award ... exceeds the constitutional limit.

Punitive damages may properly be imposed to further a State's legitimate interests in punishing unlawful conduct and deterring its repetition. In our federal system, States necessarily have considerable flexibility in determining the level of punitive damages that they will allow in different classes of cases and in any particular case. Most States that authorize exemplary damages afford the jury similar latitude, requiring only that the damages awarded be reasonably necessary to vindicate the State's legitimate interests in punishment and deterrence. Only when an award can fairly be categorized as "grossly excessive" in relation to these interests does it enter the zone of arbitrariness that violates the Due Process Clause of the Fourteenth Amendment.

For that reason, the federal excessiveness inquiry appropriately begins with an identification of the state interests that a punitive award is designed to serve. We therefore focus our attention first on the scope of Alabama's legitimate interests in punishing BMW and deterring it from future misconduct.

No one doubts that a State may protect its citizens by prohibiting deceptive trade practices and by requiring automobile distributors to disclose presale repairs that affect the value of a new car. But the States need not, and in fact do not, provide such protection in a uniform manner. That diversity demonstrates that reasonable people may disagree about the value of a full disclosure requirement.

We may assume, arguendo, that it would be wise for every State to adopt Dr. Gore's preferred rule, requiring full disclosure of every presale repair to a car, no matter how trivial and regardless of its actual impact on the value of the car. But while we do not doubt that Congress has ample authority to enact such a policy for the entire Nation, it is clear that no single State could do so, or even impose its own policy choice on neighboring States. Similarly, one State's power to impose burdens on the interstate market for automobiles is not only subordinate to the federal power over interstate commerce, but is also constrained by the need to respect the interests of other States. We think it follows from these principles of state sovereignty and comity that a State may not impose economic sanctions on violators of its laws with the intent of changing the tortfeasors' lawful conduct in other States.

The award must be analyzed in the light of the same conduct, with consideration given only to the interests of

Alabama consumers, rather than those of the entire Nation. When the scope of the interest in punishment and deterrence that an Alabama court may appropriately consider is properly limited, it is apparent for reasons that we shall now address that this award is grossly excessive. Elementary notions of fairness enshrined in our constitutional jurisprudence dictate that a person receive fair notice not only of the conduct that will subject him to punishment but also of the severity of the penalty that a State may impose. Three guideposts, each of which indicates that BMW did not receive adequate notice of the magnitude of the sanction that Alabama might impose for adhering to the nondisclosure policy, lead us to the conclusion that the $2 million award against BMW is grossly excessive: the degree of reprehensibility of the nondisclosure; the disparity between the harm or potential harm suffered by Dr. Gore and his punitive damages award; and the difference between this remedy and the civil penalties authorized or imposed in comparable cases.

Perhaps the most important indicium of the reasonableness of a punitive damages award is the degree of reprehensibility of the defendant's conduct. As the Court stated nearly 150 years ago, exemplary damages imposed on a defendant should reflect "the enormity of his offense." Thus, we have said that "nonviolent crimes are less serious than crimes marked by violence or the threat of violence." Similarly, "trickery and deceit" are more reprehensible than negligence.

In this case, none of the aggravating factors associated with particularly reprehensible conduct is present. The harm BMW inflicted on Dr. Gore was purely economic in nature. The presale refinishing of the car had no effect on its performance or safety features, or even its appearance for at least nine months after his purchase. BMW's conduct evinced no indifference to or reckless disregard for the health and safety of others. To be sure, infliction of economic injury, especially when done intentionally through affirmative acts of misconduct, or when the target is financially vulnerable, can warrant a substantial penalty. But this observation does not convert all acts that cause economic harm into torts that are sufficiently reprehensible to justify a significant sanction in addition to compensatory damages. Dr. Gore contends that BMW's conduct was particularly reprehensible because nondisclosure of the repairs to his car formed part of a nationwide pattern of tortious conduct. Certainly, evidence that a defendant has repeatedly engaged in prohibited conduct while knowing or suspecting that it was unlawful would provide relevant support for an argument that strong medicine is required to cure the defendant's disrespect for the law.

Dr. Gore's second argument for treating BMW as a recidivist is that the company should have anticipated that its actions would be considered fraudulent in some, if not all, jurisdictions. This contention overlooks the fact that actionable fraud requires a material misrepresentation or omission. This qualifier invites line drawing of just the sort engaged in by States with disclosure statutes and by BMW. We do not think it can be disputed that there may exist minor imperfections in the finish of a new car that can be repaired (or indeed, left unrepaired) without materially affecting the car's value. There is no evidence that BMW acted in bad faith when it sought to establish the appropriate line between presumptively minor damage and damage requiring disclosure to purchasers. For this purpose, BMW could reasonably rely on state disclosure statutes for guidance. In this regard, it is also significant that there is no evidence that BMW persisted in a course of conduct after it had been adjudged unlawful on even one occasion, let alone repeated occasions.

Finally, the record in this case discloses no deliberate false statements, acts of affirmative misconduct, or concealment of evidence of improper motive.

We accept, of course, the jury's finding that BMW suppressed a material fact which Alabama law obligated it to communicate to prospective purchasers of repainted cars in that State. But the omission of a material fact may be less reprehensible than a deliberate false statement, particularly when there is a good faith basis for believing that no duty to disclose exists. That conduct is sufficiently reprehensible to give rise to tort liability, and even a modest award of exemplary damages, does not establish the high degree of culpability that warrants a substantial punitive damages award. Because this case exhibits none of the circumstances ordinarily associated with egregiously improper conduct, we are persuaded that BMW's conduct was not sufficiently reprehensible to warrant imposition of a $2 million exemplary damages award.

The second and perhaps most commonly cited indicium of an unreasonable or excessive punitive damages award is its ratio to the actual harm inflicted on the plaintiff. The principle that exemplary damages must bear a reasonable relationship to compensatory damages has a long pedigree. Our decisions in both *Haslip* and *TXO* endorsed the proposition that a comparison between the compensatory award and the punitive award is significant.

In *Haslip* we concluded that even though a punitive damages award of "more than four times the amount of compensatory damages" might be "close to the line," it did not cross the line into the area of constitutional impropriety. *TXO* refined this analysis by confirming that the proper inquiry is, "whether there is a reasonable relationship between the punitive damages award and the harm likely to result from the defendant's conduct as well as the harm that actually has occurred." Thus, in upholding the $10 million award in TXO, we relied on the difference between that figure and the harm to the victim that would have ensued if the tortious plan had succeeded. That difference suggested that the relevant ratio was not more than 10 to 1.

The $2 million in punitive damages awarded to Dr. Gore by the Alabama Supreme Court is 500 times the amount of his actual harm as determined by the jury. Moreover, there is no suggestion that Dr. Gore or any other BMW purchaser was threatened with any additional potential harm by BMW's nondisclosure policy. The disparity in this case is thus dramatically greater than those considered in *Haslip* and *TXO*.

Of course, we have consistently rejected the notion that the constitutional line is marked by a simple mathematical formula, even one that compares actual and potential damages to the punitive award. Indeed, low awards of compensatory damages may properly support a higher ratio than high compensatory awards, if, for example, a particularly egregious act has resulted in only a small amount of economic damages. A higher ratio may also be justified in cases in which the injury is hard to detect or the monetary value of noneconomic harm might have been difficult to determine.

Comparing the punitive damages award and the civil or criminal penalties that could be imposed for comparable misconduct provides a third indicium of excessiveness. [A] reviewing court should "accord 'substantial deference' to legislative judgments concerning appropriate sanctions for the conduct at issue." In this case the $2 million economic sanction imposed on BMW is substantially greater than the statutory fines available in Alabama and elsewhere for similar malfeasance.

We cannot accept the conclusion of the Alabama Supreme Court that BMW's conduct was sufficiently egregious to justify a punitive sanction that is tantamount to a severe criminal penalty.

The fact that BMW is a large corporation rather than an impecunious individual does not diminish its entitlement to fair notice of the demands that the several States impose on the conduct of its business. Indeed, its status as an active participant in the national economy implicates the federal interest in preventing individual States from imposing undue burdens on interstate commerce. While each State has ample power to protect its own consumers, none may use the punitive damages deterrent as a means of imposing its regulatory policies on the entire Nation.

As in *Haslip*, we are not prepared to draw a bright line marking the limits of a constitutionally acceptable punitive damages award. Unlike that case, however, we are fully convinced that the grossly excessive award imposed in this case transcends the constitutional limit.

Reversed and *remanded* in favor of Appellant, BMW.

The impact of the *BMW* case has spread beyond tort cases. For example, the *BMW* test handed down for determining whether a punitive award is excessive—by looking at (1) the reprehensibility of the conduct, (2) the ratio of punitive damages to compensatory damages, and (3) comparable civil and criminal penalties for the same crime—has been used to hold as unreasonable a punitive damages award in a discrimination case.

In 2003, the United States Supreme Court reaffirmed and attempted to clarify the *BMW* rule when holding in *State Farm v. Campbell*[4] that a punitive damage award was grossly excessive and violated the Due Process Clause. In *Campbell*, plaintiffs sued their auto insurance carriers alleging bad-faith failure to settle a claim against them within policy limits. The jury found in favor of plaintiffs, awarding $2.6 million in compensatory damages. The jury further awarded $145 million in punitive damages, primarily because of evidence that State Farm's conduct was part of a long-standing pattern and practice of dishonest and fraudulent acts against policyholders.

The trial court reduced the punitive award to $25 million, but the Utah Supreme Court, in an extensive opinion evaluating the evidence, reinstated the jury's verdict. The U.S. Supreme Court granted review of whether the punitive damages award violated the standards of *BMW v. Gore* by a constitutionally excessive ratio to compensatory damages and by punishing the defendant in part for out-of-state conduct not directly affecting the plaintiffs.

The Supreme Court reiterated from *Gore v. BMW* that the most important indicium of the reasonableness of a punitive damages award is the degree of reprehensibility of the defendant's conduct and noted that the reprehensibility of a defendant is determined by considering whether "the harm caused was physical as opposed to economic; the tortious conduct evinced an indifference to or a reckless disregard of the health or safety of others; the target of the conduct had

---

[4] 123 S. Ct. 1513 (2003).

financial vulnerability; the conduct involved repeated actions or was an isolated incident; and the harm was the result of intentional malice, trickery, or deceit, or mere accident."[5] The Court also noted that punitive damages should be awarded only if the defendant's culpability, after having paid compensatory damages, is so reprehensible as to warrant the imposition of further sanctions to achieve punishment or deterrence.

In applying the first prong of the *BMW* case, the high court found that while the defendant's direct conduct against the plaintiff was reprehensible enough to warrant some modest punitive damages, the trial court erred in allowing the jury to consider the defendant's out-of-court conduct toward other policyholders, and without this improperly considered evidence of out-of-state conduct, the defendant's conduct in failing to settle the claim within its policy limits was not sufficiently reprehensible to warrant such a large punitive damages award.

While the Court once again refused to draw a line as to what ratio of compensatory to punitive damages was acceptable, it did give some additional guidance by saying that "[o]ur jurisprudence and the principles it has now established demonstrate... that, in practice, few awards exceeding a single-digit ratio between punitive and compensatory damages, to a significant degree, will satisfy due process."[6]

Although this significant Supreme Court decision involving punitive damages appears to have led to even more damage awards being overturned, most people fail to recognize that even before *BMW* and *Campbell*, most multimillion-dollar damages awards by juries making headlines and fueling the debate over limiting punitive damages were rarely paid and certainly not promptly paid. In September 1995, for example, a federal jury in Alaska slapped Exxon Corporation with the largest punitive damage award ever imposed on a corporation—$5 billion awarded to 14,000 people who were injured by the Exxon *Valdez* oil spill in March 1989. Before the time for filing post-trial material had closed, Exxon had filed a total of 22 motions. Eventually, the appellate court ordered the trial judge to reduce the "excessive" award, so District Court Judge Holland reduced the punitive damages award to $4 billion. In January 2004, Judge Holland ordered Exxon Mobil to pay not only the $4.5 billion award for compensatory and punitive damages but also an additional $2 billion in interest. As of July 2004, Exxon Mobil still had not paid the award. See Table 12-2 for some examples of appeals courts' reductions of extravagant punitive damages awarded by juries.

State courts tend to take a more active role in limiting punitive damages. For example, on February 2, 1994, the Texas Supreme Court handed down a decision in the case of *Transportation v. Moriel*[7] that is expected to make it more difficult for plaintiffs in that state to recover punitive damages, and many commentators believe that the ruling will influence decision makers in other states. Moriel suffered a broken pelvis and became impotent as a result of having a stack of countertops fall on him while he was working. He sued the insurance company when it delayed payment on some of his medical bills. The jury awarded Moriel $101,000 in compensatory damages, with $100,000 of that total being for mental anguish, and $1 million in punitive damages. The state court of appeals affirmed the verdict. The Texas Supreme Court struck down the puni-

---

[5] Id., p. 1516.

[6] Id., p. 1524.

[7] 879 S. W. 2d 10 (1994).

TABLE 12-2 SOME MAJOR PUNITIVE DAMAGE AWARDS IN RECENT YEARS

Case	Jury Award	Ultimate Resolution
Frankson v. Browne & Williamson	A jury awarded the widow Gladys Frankson $350,000 in compensatory damages and $20 million in punitive damages following the death of her husband, who died from lung cancer caused by his using the defendant's cigarettes.	In June 2004, the Supreme Court of New York did not strictly follow the 4–1 ratio in *State Farm v. Campbell*, but they held that the punitive damages were still excessive and reduced the punitive damage award to $5 million if the plaintiff agreed to the new amounts. Otherwise, the judge directed a new trial upon punitive damages.
Diamond Woodworks, Inc. v. Argonaut Insurance Company	A jury awarded compensatory damages and $14 million in punitive damages to an employee who was denied insurance benefits after being injured at his place of employment.	The trial court reduced the punitive damages to $5.5 million, but the appellate court granted defendant's motion for a new trial only if defendant agreed to a remittitur of $1 million in punitive damages, in accordance with the 4–1 ratio established in *State Farm v. Campbell*.
Conroy v. Owens-Corning Fiberglass	A jury awarded $3.37 million in compensatory damages and $54 million in punitive damages to the families of three men who contracted mesothelioma from long-term workplace exposure to asbestos.	On appeal, punitive damages were reduced from $18.2 million per plaintiff to $1 million and one cent per plaintiff. Plaintiffs then settled for an undisclosed amount.
Liebeck v. McDonald's	A jury awarded Stella Liebeck $2.9 million in damages, including $2.7 million in punitive damages for extensive burns she received when she spilled hot coffee (170° F) on her legs. Jurors were influenced by McDonald's having known that prior customers had received severe burns from the coffee.	The trial court reduced the award by 77 percent to $640,000. The parties subsequently settled the case for an undisclosed amount.
Proctor v. Davis	In 1991, a jury ordered the defendant to pay plaintiff Proctor and his wife $127.78 million in damages, including $124.57 million in punitive In damages. Mr. Proctor's left eye had shriveled when an ophthalmologist accidentally injected an Upjohn product called Depo-Medrol into the plaintiff's eye.	In 1992, the trial judge cut nearly $90 million from the punitive award, reducing the judgment to $38.2 million. In 1994, the appellate judge reduced the punitive damages to the amount of the compensatory damages, leaving a judgment of $6.2 million.

tive damages award, holding that an insurance company's refusal to pay a claim does not justify punitive damages unless the failure to pay was in bad faith and the insurer knew that its action would probably bring about extraordinary harm such as "death, grievous physical injury or genuine likelihood of financial catastrophe." Another example of a state's attempt to limit punitive damages is California Governor Arnold Schwarzenegger's proposal to place a 75 percent tax on punitive damages. Schwarzenegger argues that a tax would still achieve the desired ends of punishing defendants and deterring future bad acts, while also promoting the public good more directly with more tax money.[8]

Many pieces of legislation designed to reform tort law have been proposed at both the federal and state levels during the past several years. The majority of

---

[8] Adam Liptak, "Schwarzenegger Sees Money for State in Punitive Damages," *New York Times*, May 30, 2004, p. A16.

these proposals contained provisions limiting punitive damages. For example, in 1995, the proposed federal Common Sense Legal Reform Act contained a provision limiting punitive damages in certain types of tort cases—namely, torts involving defective products (so-called product liability cases, which are discussed in Chapter 13). This legislation would allow punitive damages in such cases only when the plaintiff could prove by clear and convincing evidence that the harm suffered was caused by "actual malice." Such damages would also be limited to $250,000 or three times the actual economic harm incurred by the plaintiff, whichever was greater. Part of this legislation, including the cap on punitive damages, was passed in 1996, but was vetoed by President Clinton. Until 2005, reformers at the federal level have had very little success. In response to arguments that state tort laws lack uniformity, the Class Action Fairness Act, was proposed, which would transfer jurisdiction in large, multi-state class action tort suits from state courts to federal courts. Because state courts commonly give multimillion-dollar awards in class action suits, the new legislation would most likely result in less lucrative awards in federal courts. This act finally passed and was signed into law in February of 2005.

Tort reform advocates at the state level have been more successful thus far. Almost every state has passed some sort of tort reform legislation. Since 1986, thirty-four of these state tort reform laws limited punitive damages awards in some fashion.[9] However, many of these reform efforts have been struck down by the courts.

> **intentional tort** A civil wrong that involves taking some purposeful action that the defendant knew, or should have known, would harm the person, property, or economic interests of the plaintiff.

> **negligent tort** A civil wrong that involves a failure to meet the standard of care a reasonable person would meet and, because of that failure, harm to another resulted.

CLASSIFICATIONS OF TORTS

> **strict liability tort** A civil wrong that involves taking action that is so inherently dangerous under the circumstances of its performance that no amount of due care can make it safe.

There are three classifications of torts: intentional, negligent, and strict liability. The primary distinguishing feature among them is the degree of willfulness of the wrongful conduct. **Intentional torts** are those wherein the defendant took some purposeful action that he or she knew, or should have known, would harm the plaintiff. **Negligent torts** involve carelessness on the part of the defendant. Finally, **strict liability torts** involve inherently dangerous actions and impose liability on the defendant regardless of how careful he or she was. Defenses for the various categories of torts differ, as do the types of damages generally awarded (Table 12-3).

INTENTIONAL TORTS

Intentional torts, the most "willful" torts, include a substantial number of carefully defined wrongful acts. What each of these acts has in common is the element of intent. *Intent* here does not mean a specific determination to cause harm to the plaintiff; rather, it means the determination to do a specific physical act that may lead to harming the plaintiff's person, property, or economic interests.

---

[9] Congressional Budget Office, The Effects of Tort Reform: Evidence from the States (June 2004).

TABLE 12-3 CATEGORIES OF TORTS

Type	Description and Examples	Common Defenses	Type of Damages Usually Awarded
Intentional Torts	Purposeful action that results in harm	Specific to subtype	
Against Persons	Assault and battery	• Self-defense • Defense of another • Defense of property	Compensatory damages for medical bills, lost wages, and pain and suffering

	Defamation	• Truth
		• Privilege
		  Absolute (congressional and courtroom speech)
		  Conditional (speech concerning public figures or in employment context)
			Compensatory damages for measurable financial losses

	Invasion of privacy	• Waiver by plaintiff of right to privacy	Compensatory damages for any resultant economic loss and pain and suffering
	False imprisonment	• Posted warnings of observation	Compensatory damages for treatment of physical injuries and lost time at work
	Intentional infliction of emotional distress	• Shopkeepers' privilege	Compensatory damages for treatment of physical illness resulting from the emotional distress
Against property	Trespass to realty		Compensatory damages for harm caused to property and losses suffered by rightful owner
	Trespass to personalty		Compensatory damages for harm to the property
	Conversion		Compensatory damages for full value of converted item
Against economic interests	Disparagement	• Truth	Compensatory damages for actual economic loss
	Intentional interference with a contract	• No knowledge of contract	Compensatory damages for loss of expected benefits from the contract
	Unfair competition		Compensatory damages for lost profits
	Misappropriation	• Independent origination • Denial of discussion of idea	Compensatory damages for economic losses
Negligent Torts	Careless action that results in harm	• No duty • No breach of duty • No causation (actual or proximate) • No damages suffered by the plaintiff • Contributory negligence by plaintiff • Pure comparative negligence • Modified comparative negligence	Compensatory damages for injuries, including medical bills, lost time from work, harm to property, and pain and suffering
Strict Liability Torts	Action that is so inherently dangerous that no amount of due care can make it safe	• Assumption of risk	Compensatory damages for personal injury and harm to property

Intentional torts can be divided into three categories based on the interest being harmed: torts against persons, torts against property, and torts against economic interests. The following sections discuss a number of specific torts that fall into each category, along with the defenses to each.

Intentional Torts Against Persons. There are a number of torts against persons. We will discuss five of the most common ones: assault and battery, defamation, privacy torts, false imprisonment, and intentional infliction of emotional distress.

Assault and Battery. Torts against persons consist of harm to another's physical or mental integrity. One of the most common torts against the person is assault. An **assault** is the intentional placing of another in fear or apprehension of an immediate, offensive bodily contact. All of those elements must be present for an assault to exist. Thus, if the defendant pointed a gun at the plaintiff and threatened to shoot, and the plaintiff believed the defendant would shoot, an assault would have taken place. However, if the plaintiff thought the defendant was joking when making the threat, there was no assault because there was no apprehension on the part of the plaintiff. Likewise, a threat to commit harm in a week is not an assault because there is no question of immediate bodily harm. But a threat made with an unloaded gun, as long as the plaintiff does not know the defendant is incapable of carrying out the threat, is an assault.

> **assault** Intentional placing of a person in fear or apprehension of an immediate, offensive bodily contact.

An assault is frequently, but not always, followed by a **battery**, which is an intentional, unwanted, offensive bodily contact. Punching someone in the nose is a battery. However, accidentally bumping into someone on a crowded street is not. The term *bodily contact* has been broadly interpreted to include such diverse situations as the defendant's using a projectile, such as a gun, to make physical contact with the plaintiff, and a defendant's pulling a chair out from under the plaintiff. A number of well-known figures, such as Mike Tyson, have been sued for battery.

> **battery** Intentional unwanted and offensive bodily contact.

Defenses to Assault and Battery. The most common defense to a battery is *self-defense*. If one is attacked, one may repel the attacker—but with only that degree of force reasonably necessary to protect oneself. In most states, if a third person is in trouble, one may defend that person with the same degree of force that one would reasonably use to defend oneself, so long as the third party is unable to act in his or her own defense and there is a socially recognized duty to defend that person. This defense is often referred to as *defense of another.*

A third defense that may be raised against a charge of battery is *defense of property*. A person can use reasonable force to defend home and property from an intruder. However, deadly force in defense of property is rarely, if ever, considered justified.

Defamation. Another tort that most people have heard of is defamation. **Defamation** is the intentional publication (communication to a third party) of a false statement that is harmful to the plaintiff's reputation. If the defamation is published in a permanent form—for example, in a piece of writing or on television—the tort is called **libel**; if it is spoken, it is called **slander**.

> **defamation** Intentional publication (communication to a third party) of a false statement that is harmful to the plaintiff's reputation.

> **libel** Publication of a defamatory statement in permanent form.

Once a plaintiff proves the elements of a case of libel, "general" damages are presumed as a matter of law. These damages provide the plaintiff com-

> **slander** Spoken defamatory statement.

pensation for harms that are hard to quantify but which would almost certainly arise from libel, such as feeling of humiliation and the loss of standing in the community. In the case of slander, however, the plaintiff must prove "special damages," which means that in order to recover damages, the plaintiff must demonstrate an actual monetary loss flowing from the slanderous statement.

There is an exception to this limitation on damages, however, and the exception is for statements that constitute *slander per se*. These are statements that are considered by their very nature to be so obviously harmful to a person that no proof of special damages is needed. Traditionally, statements are considered slander per se if they are statements that (1) one has a loathsome communicable disease; (2) one has committed improprieties in the performance of his or her profession; (3) one has committed or been imprisoned for a serious crime; and (4) an unmarried female is not chaste.

One example of a libel case is the Warnaco claim against Calvin Klein. On the *Larry King Live* television show, Calvin Klein accused Warnaco, the company that manufactures Calvin Klein jeans and underwear, of making and selling substandard Calvin Klein products. In response, Warnaco brought a libel claim against Calvin Klein personally.[10] Another example of a libel case is Lance Armstrong's suit against a British coauthor, who accused Armstrong in a new book of taking performance-enhancing drugs during his journey in winning a world-record six Tour de France titles.[11]

There are limits as to what is considered defamation. For instance, someone can say something that is potentially harmful to one's reputation but not suffer any consequences for saying it if the statement is merely one of *opinion* and not a statement of a *fact*. For example, in a 1997 case, Randolph Cook claimed to have had a past relationship with Oprah Winfrey. During that relationship, he claimed, Winfrey used cocaine regularly. Cook had contacted several media outlets with his claim. After Winfrey heard about this, she called Cook a liar, both privately and publicly. Cook sued Winfrey for defamation, among other things. However, since calling someone a liar is only an opinion, and one cannot be sued for stating one's opinion, the case was dismissed.[12] Likewise, it was not defamatory for employees of Apple Computer Company to refer to the famous astronomer Carl Sagan as "butthead astronomer."[13]

Defamation has become a little more confusing since people began communicating over the Internet. This medium of communication has generated two questions. First, when does a false statement made over this information network constitute defamation? Second, who can be held liable if defamation does exist? Both the legislature and the courts have been grappling with these issues. The following case illustrates one court's approach.

---

[10] *National Law Journal*, February 16, 1998, p. B9.

[11] Samuel Abt, "Armstrong Hotter Off Bike Than On as Pyrenees Loom," *New York Times*, July 16, 2004.

[12] *Cook v. Winfrey*, 975 F.Supp. 1045 (N.D. Ill, 1977).

[13] *Carl Sagan v. Apple Computer Co.*, 874 F. Supp. 1972 (1994).

CASE 12-2

Optinrealbig.com v. Ironport Systems (SpamCop.net)
United States District Court for the Northern District of California
323 F. Supp ad 1037 (2004)

Plaintiff Optin, a company that sends bulk commercial e-mails, motioned for a preliminary injunction against a wholly owned subsidiary of Ironport Systems called SpamCop, an interactive Internet-based service that tries to reduce spam. Optin argued that it is not a sender of spam ("spammer") but a sender of legitimate commercial e-mails. SpamCop collects complaints from recipients of spam and sends recipients' complaints and the spam messages in reports to Internet service providers (ISPs). Optin contended that these complaints were inflated in number because SpamCop allegedly sent numerous copies of the same complaint to several ISPs, thereby causing ISPs to reduce the bandwidth they permitted Optin. Moreover, Optin argued that SpamCop's policy of removing the recipients' e-mail addresses in its reports to ISPs inhibited Optin's removal of such recipients from their bulk e-mail lists. Plaintiff Optin sought a preliminary injunction against SpamCop for allegedly making slanderous and libelous statements, sending reports to ISPs other than Optin's primary ISP, and removing recipients' e-mail addresses in SpamCop's reports.

Judge Armstrong

From the facts in the record, at the very least, SpamCop's reports can strongly influence or play an important role in an ISP's decision to sanction senders, such as Optin.

[Communications Decency Act] CDA § 230 provides, "No provider or user of an interactive computer service shall be treated as the publisher or speaker of any information provided by another information content provider." The purpose of this section is "to maintain the robust nature of Internet communication and accordingly, to keep government interference in the medium to a minimum." "Congress recognized the threat that tort-based lawsuits pose to freedom of speech in the new and burgeoning Internet medium. The imposition of tort liability on service providers for the communications of others represented, for Congress, simply another form of intrusive government regulation of speech." Through § 230, Congress "sought to prevent lawsuits from shutting down websites and other services on the Internet." Thus, under § 230, interactive service providers and users cannot be held liable for the republication or redistribution of statements "provided by any other content provider."

The Court's review of the case law, supra, focuses on publication. In the case at hand, the parties agree that in addition to publishing the reports of registered users, SpamCop distributes them by forwarding copies of the reports to third parties who are not subscribers to SpamCop's services. Although the Ninth Circuit has not directly addressed the issue of distributors, it has observed that courts have consis-

tently found that the CDA does not distinguish between publishers and distributors. "Congress made no distinction between publishers and distributors in providing immunity from liability." "If computer service providers were subject to distributor liability, they would face potential liability each time they receive notice of a potentially defamatory statement—from any party, concerning any message."

The focus is not on the distribution list, it is on the content of the e-mail and the distributor's complicity in shaping that content. Moreover, the Court is not persuaded that sending reports to non-subscribers somehow affects the immunity of a distributor. Nor is it persuaded that Congress intended such distribution to affect immunity. Rather, Congress has chosen to provide "immunity even where the interactive service provider has an active, even aggressive role in making available content prepared by others." Distributing content to non-subscribers may be perceived as aggressive activity, but it does not destroy the distributor's immunity.

Reviewing the case law and the statute, it appears that the focus on distributor liability is and should be conterminous with the focus on publisher liability: content. Just like a publisher, if a distributor alters the content, then the distributor may be liable. Thus, to determine whether or not SpamCop is immune, the Court must determine whether SpamCop has contributed to the content. Optin argues that SpamCop has contributed to the content of the reports in two ways. First, it has included information in the reports. Second, by sending out numerous reports, it affects the impact of the reports.

[W]hen SpamCop sends out the reports, it removes the registered user's name and includes the following statement: "This message is brief for your comfort. Please follow links for details." The links lead a recipient back to SpamCop's website, where SpamCop explains its business, provides an opt-out, and cautions that it cannot guarantee the veracity of the report. These activities cannot be considered a contribution to the content. They do not alter, shape, or even edit the content.

With respect to the impact, it may be true that SpamCop is aggressive in mailing the reports to any and all ISPs that it can identify in the mailing header of the purported spam. Optin has failed to show, however, that SpamCop sends multiple copies of the same report to the same recipient in order to inflate its impact. Even if Optin had, the Court is not persuaded that multiple mailings would amount to an alteration in the content found within each report. The content of each republished report remains the same and a recipient may identify them as multiple copies of the same report. In addition, in terms of the traditional role of a distributor, the Court perceives no substantive difference between distributing one copy of an item once, and distributing the same item numerous times.

Setting aside these questions, though, Optin still faces a fundamental hurdle in its claim for trade libel—malice. It has not submitted any evidence that SpamCop has particular malice towards it. Without even a hint of malice, it is difficult to say that Optin has a likelihood of prevailing on the merits of its trade libel claim. At the hearing, Optin also argued that the multiple mailings have harmed Optin's reputation because third party ISPs are now less likely to contract with Optin to provide bandwidth. This, however, must be countered by the numerous news articles that clearly establish that Optin's reputation as a spammer precedes it. It is being sued by the state of New York and Microsoft Corporation. It has been described as a spammer in numerous press articles and it has been found by one Internet analysis group to be the third largest spammer in the world.

Moreover, to the degree that SpamCop's practice does inflate the number of actual reports or otherwise harms Optin's reputation, it is the ISPs themselves who allow SpamCop's reports to impact their perception of Optin and affect their decision making. Whether they choose to rely entirely on SpamCop's reports, or ignore them, or to conduct some investigation on their own, it is the ISPs who ultimately make the decision whether or not to terminate Optin's bandwidth. In addition, because SpamCop reproduces the purported Spam in full, the ISPs can actually determine for themselves whether or not Optin has complied with CAN-SPAM by providing a valid and functioning opt-out link.

Damage to a business's goodwill is typically an irreparable injury because it is difficult to calculate. It is true that when SpamCop sends out reports to ISPs, these reports affect Optin's reputation and goodwill. This does not mean, however, that SpamCop is fully responsible for any damage these reports make to Optin's goodwill. First, there is the fact that Optin's reputation precedes it. Second, SpamCop cannot be held entirely responsible for the decisions these ISPs make. These ISPs may be more likely to assume that Optin is a spammer because they are already aware of Optin's reputation. Thus, it would take fewer reports to persuade these ISPs to terminate Optin's bandwidth.

[T]he Court is quite wary that requiring SpamCop to provide the e-mail addresses of the registered users would have a chilling effect. Registered users concerned about retaliatory actions or loss of privacy would be less likely to post reports. The Court must balance this chilling effect and the public interest in free speech on the one hand, with Optin's obligations under CAN-SPAM and the public's interest in its compliance with that Act. Although Optin has not demonstrated that SpamCop is under a legal duty to provide Optin these e-mail addresses, Optin alleges that if it does not have them, then it is at risk of violating CAN-SPAM. Then again, it is Optin's responsibility to ensure that its own opt-out procedures work, no one else's. Quite simply, the public's interest in protecting privacy and free speech outweigh whatever risks Optin faces from its own faulty programming.

It is hereby ordered that Optin's motion for a preliminary injunction is denied. Pursuant to § 230 of the Communications Decency Act, SpamCop is immune from liability for publishing or distributing the reports of registered users. Even if SpamCop were not immune, Optin has failed to demonstrate that it is likely to prevail on the merits or that the balance of hardships tips in its favor.

Judgment in favor of Defendant, SpamCop.

Critical Thinking About the Law

In every legal case, there are at least two separate conclusions. The plaintiff believes the court should rule one way, whereas the defendant thinks the court should rule another. In Case 12-2, Plaintiff OptIn provided one conclusion, but the court supported a conclusion more similar to SpamCop's conclusion. The court's reasoning provides the answer for why the court reached its particular conclusion. The following questions address the court's reasoning.

1. Identify the court's conclusion in Case 12-2.

   Clue: Reread the final paragraph of the court's decision.

2. What are the reasons the court provides to support this conclusion?

   Clue: Look at the court's application of the Communications Decency Act as well as the court's response to OptIn's argument.

3. To demonstrate the significance of primary ethical norms in court decisions such as this one, identify the ethical norm that would have reversed the OptIn decision.

   Clue: This norm is related to prioritizing the plaintiff's rights over those of the defendant in cases such as Case 12-2.

Defenses to Defamation. There are two primary types of defenses to a defamation action: truth and privilege. It is often stated that truth is an absolute defense. In other words, if I make an honest statement that harms the reputation of the defendant, there has been no defamation. However, for the ordinary plaintiff, a defendant cannot use the excuse that he or she thought the statement was true. It is only when a possible privilege exists that the defendant's incorrect belief about the truth of the statement is important.

Privilege is the second type of defense in a defamation action. Most privileges arise under certain circumstances in which our society has decided that encouraging people to speak is more important than protecting people's reputations.

absolute privilege The right to make any statement, true or false, about someone and not be held liable for defamation.

There are two types of privilege: absolute and qualified, or conditional. When an **absolute privilege** exists, one can make any statement, true or false, and cannot be sued for defamation. There are very few situations in which such a privilege exists. The Speech and Debate Clause of the U.S. Constitution gives an absolute privilege to individuals speaking on the House and Senate floors during congressional debate. This privilege will encourage the most robust debate possible over potential legislation. Another absolute privilege arises in the courtroom during a trial.

conditional privilege The right to make a false statement about someone and not be held liable for defamation provided the statement was made without malice.

The other type of privilege is a qualified or **conditional privilege**. A conditional privilege provides that one will not be held liable for defamation unless the false statement was made with malice. Malice has a special meaning in a defamation case. *Malice* means knowledge of the falsity of the statement or reckless disregard for the truth. In other words, the defendant either knew the statement was false or could have easily discovered whether it was false.

The most often used conditional privilege is the *public figure privilege*. People in the public eye, such as politicians, often find themselves the victims of false rumors. When a defendant has made a false statement about a public figure—a person who has thrust herself or himself into the public eye and who generally has access to the media—the defendant will raise the public figure

Technology and the Legal Environment

CAN-SPAM: Putting Spam on the Stand

Spam, or unsolicited commercial e-mail, occupies over one half of all electronic mail traffic. The flooding of these unwanted messages prompted Congress to impose regulations on such messages. For instance, Congress passed the Controlling the Assault of Non-Solicited Pornography and Marketing Act of 2003 (i.e., "CAN-SPAM Act"), which took effect in January 2004. The act states, "Most of these messages are fraudulent or deceptive in one or more respects." Consequently, Congress created three provisions for "spammers." First, spammers must clearly label their messages as advertisements, avoiding misleading or untruthful subject lines that function simply to entice readers to view such messages. Second, spammers must provide a clear and convenient opt-out option in their messages, whereby recipients may reject future e-mails from these spammers. Third, spammers must send messages from legitimate return addresses, while also including the sender's postal address. However, these three restrictions on spammers do not apply in situations in which a recipient has given prior affirmative consent to receive spam messages. Congress created this federal act to preempt most state laws against spammers, while making exceptions for state laws related to deceptive information in commercial electronic mail. The Federal Trade Commission, along with other federal and state agencies and attorney generals, can bring suit against spammers. Violations of the CAN-SPAM Act could result in civil and criminal penalties, including heavy fines and possible imprisonment.

privilege as a defense for defamation. If the defendant proves that the plaintiff is a public figure, the plaintiff will have to additionally prove that the defamation was made with malice (defined as knowledge of the falsity or reckless disregard for the truth) in order to recover for defamation.

The reason for this privilege to comment freely about public figures as long as statements are made without malice is to encourage open discussion about persons who have a significant impact on our lives. Also, because these people generally have access to the media, they are in a position to defend themselves and, therefore, need less protection than an ordinary private citizen.

A libel or slander case brought by a public figure sometimes appears quite complex. First, the public figure plaintiff proves that the defendant made a false statement that harmed the plaintiff's reputation. Then the defendant must prove that the plaintiff is in fact a public figure. Then the burden of proof shifts back to the plaintiff, who must prove that the statements were made with malice (Exhibit 12-1).

There are two kinds of public figures: public figures for all purposes and public figures for a limited purpose. The *public figure for all purposes* was defined in the foregoing paragraph. Movie stars, musicians, and politicians fall into that category. The *public figure for a limited purpose* is a private figure who achieves substantial media attention for a specific activity. That person is then considered a public figure for matters related to that activity. For example, the leader of an antiabortion group would be considered a public figure for matters related to abortion. Thus, if the activist brought a defamation suit against a defendant who falsely stated that the activist had undergone three abortions as a teenager, the activist would have to prove that the defendant knew the statement was false, or acted recklessly, without even trying to check the veracity of the claim. On the other hand, had the defendant claimed that the activist had stolen money from at least three former employers, no public figure privilege would arise and it would not be necessary for the activist to prove that the claim had been made with malice.

Some people are trying to argue that the public figure privilege should apply in another context: when the defamatory statement is published over the Internet. The rationale for this privilege is twofold. First, remember that part of the reason for the public figure privilege is that the public figure who has been

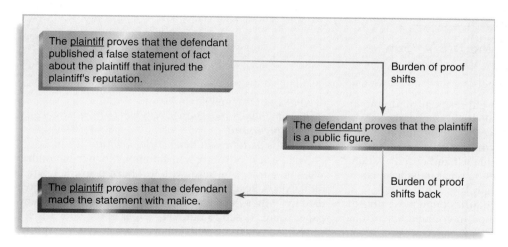

EXHIBIT 12-1

THE SHIFTING BURDEN OF PROOF IN A DEFAMATION CASE

The plaintiff proves that the defendant published a false statement of fact about the plaintiff that injured the plaintiff's reputation.

Burden of proof shifts

The defendant proves that the plaintiff is a public figure.

Burden of proof shifts back

The plaintiff proves that the defendant made the statement with malice.

defamed has access to the media and, therefore, has the ability to defend himself or herself. Likewise, when a person is defamed over the Internet, with a few keystrokes, the defamed party can respond. Thus, there is less need for the stronger legal protection we ordinarily give to the private party. A second reason is that we want to encourage free expression and the exchange of ideas on the Internet. Requiring a plaintiff to prove malice would encourage such free discussion because people would not have to be worried about making errors when they speak about others.

Another use of the conditional privilege arises with respect to job recommendations. To encourage employers to give honest assessments of their former employees, an employer who makes a false statement about a former worker can be held liable only if the statement is made with malice.

Privacy Torts. Although truth may be an absolute defense to defamation, one is not necessarily allowed to reveal everything one knows about another person. The recently developed tort of *invasion of privacy* is used to allow a person to keep private matters confidential. Just as defamation has two forms, libel and slander, the tort of invasion of privacy is really four distinct torts: (1) public disclosure of private facts, (2) false light, (3) appropriation, and (4) invasion of privacy.

public disclosure of private facts A privacy tort that consists of unwarranted disclosure of a private fact about a person.

Public disclosure of private facts occurs when the defendant makes public a fact about the plaintiff that the plaintiff is entitled to keep private. The disclosure must be unwarranted and the plaintiff must have not waived his or her right to privacy. For example, if the defendant worked in a clinic and revealed the names of women who had obtained abortions at the clinic, the defendant would be liable for public disclosure of private facts.

false light A privacy tort that consists of intentionally taking actions that would lead observers to make false assumptions about the person.

False light occurs when you do not actually make a defamatory statement about someone, but by your actions you place the person in a false light. For example, a neighborhood newsletter publishes a story captioned "Gang Warfare Growing in Our Community," and between the caption and the article is an untitled photo of four girls sitting on the hood of a car. The photo is clear enough that the girls' identities are obvious. If these girls are not gang members, they have been placed in a false light and may sue the publisher.

Often illustrations in tabloids may lead to false-light claims. The following case provides an illustration of this tort.

CASE 12-3

Nellie Mitchell v. Globe Inc. D/B/A "Sun"
United States District Court, W.D. Arkansas,
786 F. Supp. 791 (1992)

Plaintiff Mitchell was a 96-year-old resident of Mountain Home, Arkansas, who since 1963 had operated a newsstand on the town square as well as delivering newspapers. Known to almost everyone in this small Ozark Mountain town, she supported herself and raised a family as a single parent for many years on what must have been the meager earnings of a "papergirl."

The October 2 edition of the *Sun* contained a photograph of the plaintiff, Mrs. Mitchell, in conjunction with a story entitled:

SPECIAL DELIVERY
World's oldest newspaper carrier, 101, quits because she's pregnant!
"I guess walking all those miles kept me young."

The "story" purported to be about "paper gal Audrey Wiles" in Stirling, Australia, who had been delivering papers for 94 years. Readers were told that Ms. Wiles became pregnant by "Will," a "reclusive millionaire" she met on her newspaper route. "I used to put Will's paper in the door when it rained, and one thing just kind of led to another."

In words that could certainly have described Nellie Mitchell, the article, which was in the form and style of a factual newspaper account, said: "[S]he's become like a city landmark because nearly everyone at one time or another has seen her trudging down the road with a large stack of papers under her arm."

A photograph of Nellie, apparently "trudging down the road with a large stack of papers under her arm" was used in conjunction with the story. The picture used in the October 2 edition of the *Sun* had been used by the defendant in a reasonably factual and accurate article about Mrs. Mitchell published in another of the defendant's publications, the *Examiner*, in 1980.

The case was tried by a jury that found that the defendant's conduct had invaded Mrs. Mitchell's privacy by placing her in a false light and had amounted to an intentional infliction of emotional distress. The jury awarded the plaintiff $650,000 in compensatory damages and $850,000 in punitive damages.

Defendant filed a motion for judgment as a matter of law or, alternatively, for remittitur of the jury award or, alternatively, for new trial.

Chief Judge Waters

Testimony at trial indicated that most of the defendant's articles are created "TOH" or "top of the head," in the words of John Vadar, editor of the *Sun*. That is, the authors, none of whom use their real name, are given a headline and a picture and then "make up" the accompanying stories. In fact, according to the evidence, the editor and perhaps others "make up" a series of headlines for stories to appear in each issue, and they are placed on a table. The "reporters" or perhaps, according to defendant's contentions at the trial, their "authors of fiction" select from this list the stories they wish to write....

In order to prevail on this claim [of false light], the plaintiff has the burden of proving by clear and convincing evidence the following:

One, that the false light in which she was placed by the publicity would be highly offensive to a reasonable person, and

Two, that the defendant acted with actual malice in publishing the statements at issue in this case.

Actual malice means that Globe International intended, or recklessly failed to anticipate, that readers would construe the publicized matter as conveying actual facts or events concerning Mrs. Mitchell. ...

Defendant argues that there was no evidence of intentional conduct on the part of Globe. It is further argued that no one understood the story to state actual facts about Mrs. Mitchell. ...

The court cannot say as a matter of law that the article is incapable of being interpreted as portraying actual events or facts regarding the plaintiff. The "facts" conveyed are not so inherently impossible or fantastic that they could not be understood to convey actual facts. Nor can we say that no person could take them seriously. Moreover, even if the headline and certain facts contained in the article could not be reasonably believed, other facts, e.g., the implication of sexual promiscuity, could reasonably be believed. ...

In making this determination we "consider the surrounding circumstances in which the statements were made, the medium by which they were published and the audience for which they were intended." ... No distinction is made between those articles that are wholly fictional and the articles that are intended to be factual. Fictional articles are not denoted as such. The *Sun* apparently intends for the readers to determine which articles are fact and which are fiction or what percentage of a given article is fact or fiction. ...

[T]he court believes the jury could have, and apparently did, find that the defendant intended their readers to construe the article in question as conveying actual facts or events concerning Mrs. Mitchell or at the very least that the defendant recklessly failed to anticipate that the article would be so construed. The court believes the publication methods utilized by the defendant make it reasonable for the jury to draw such a conclusion.

Motion denied.

Appropriation of a person's name for commercial gain occurs when a defendant uses another's name or likeness without that person's permission for commercial gain. This tort, for example, prohibits a cereal company from putting an athlete's picture on its cereal box without obtaining the athlete's permission.

The final privacy tort is **invasion of privacy**, which occurs when someone invades another's solitude, seclusion, or personal affairs when that person has the right to expect privacy. Some examples of invasion of privacy would include wiretapping and using someone's password to gain access to the person's electronic mail messages. Or an owner of an ice skating rink who installed two-way mirrors in the women's dressing room would have committed an invasion of privacy because the skaters should be able to expect a certain degree of privacy in a dressing room. Of course, the degree of privacy one should reasonably expect varies greatly. For example, if one is trying on clothes in a

appropriation A privacy tort that consists of using a person's name or likeness for commercial gain without the person's permission.

invasion of privacy A privacy tort that consists of encroaching on the solitude, seclusion, or personal affairs of someone who has the right to expect privacy.

department store fitting room where signs are posted saying that the "area is under observation to deter shoplifting," it would not be unreasonable for the store to have authorized security guards of the same sex as the dressing room occupants observing the dressing rooms.

false imprisonment The intentional restraint or confinement, by force or threat of force, of a person against that person's will and without justification.

False Imprisonment. **False imprisonment** is the intentional restraint or confinement of a person against that person's will and without justification. The tort protects our freedom of movement. The confinement cannot be by moral force alone. There must be either physical restraint, such as locking a door; physical force, such as holding someone down; or threats of physical force.

Most cases of false imprisonment are brought against security guards and retailers. In fact, this tort is brought so frequently against retailers who have detained a person suspected of shoplifting that it has become known as the "shopkeepers' tort." In most states, retailers who detain suspected shoplifters for questioning are entitled to raise "the shopkeepers' privilege." Under this privilege a merchant who has reason to believe a person has shoplifted may detain the person for questioning about the incident. The detention must be conducted in a reasonable manner, and the suspect can be held for only a reasonable time. Following is a case that illustrates reasonable detention.

CASE 12-4

Shirley Gordon v. May Department Store Company
New York Supreme Court, Appellate Division,
1998 N.Y. Slip Op. 08712

On March 21, 1994, Plaintiff Shirley Gordon, a part-time employee at a Lord & Taylor Department Store, was stopped as she was leaving the store and store security personnel searched her bag. She did not object to the search. No stolen merchandise was found, and she left within a few minutes of being detained. She then sued the retail store for false imprisonment. The trial court denied the store's motion for summary judgment and appeal was taken.

Judges Ritter, Santucci, Altman, and Krausman
In order to sustain a claim for false imprisonment, the plaintiff must prove that (1) the defendant intended to confine, (2) the plaintiff was conscious of the alleged confinement, (3) the plaintiff did not consent to the confinement, and (4) the confinement was not otherwise privileged.

The plaintiff admitted at her examination before trial that she was not under the impression that she was not free to leave the store at any point during the day in question. The affidavit that she submitted in opposition to the motion for summary judgment did not raise any genuine issue of fact in this regard. We find no merit to the plaintiff's contention that the brief search of her bag resulted in an unreasonable detention.

Reversed in favor of defendant.

intentional infliction of emotional distress Intentionally engaging in outrageous conduct that is likely to cause extreme emotional pain to the person toward whom the conduct is directed.

Even if one is successful in bringing an action for false imprisonment, damages are often not easy to prove. Obviously, a person who is physically restrained might have medical bills for treatment of physical injuries, but most cases do not involve physical harm. Usually plaintiffs ask for a monetary award to compensate them for lost time off work, pain and suffering from the mental distress, and humiliation.

Intentional Infliction of Emotional Distress. One of the newest torts against the person is **intentional infliction of emotional distress**. This tort arises when the defendant engages in outrageous, intentional conduct that is likely to cause extreme emotional distress to the party toward whom such conduct is directed. For example, if a debt collector called a debtor and told him that he was a police officer and he was sorry to inform him that his wife had just been killed in an auto accident, and her last words to the medic at the scene of the crash had been, "God must be punishing me for our not paying our debts," such conduct would most likely be interpreted as the intentional infliction of emotional distress.

In most states, to recover damages for intentional infliction of emotional distress, the plaintiff must demonstrate some physical symptoms caused by his or her emotional distress. For example, in the preceding example, if the plaintiff had high blood pressure, and after hearing the message he had a heart attack, the heart attack would provide the basis for his injury. Other physical symptoms commonly arising from emotional distress include headaches, a sudden onset of high blood pressure, hives, chills, inability to sleep, or inability to get out of bed.

While some people may argue that the requirement of physical harm puts an undue burden on the plaintiff, others fear that without the physical symptoms of harm, it would be too easy to successfully recover damages in a situation in which there is not any real harm. For example, some would argue that a 1998 suit filed against Dennis Rodman of the Chicago Bulls for intentional infliction of emotional distress provides an illustration of abuse of the tort. Rodman and a friend were playing craps at the Mirage Hotel in Las Vegas. While playing, Rodman allegedly rubbed the dealer's bald head for good luck. The dealer claimed that this act caused him "embarrassment, indignity, degradation, and anger." Because of the severe results of Rodman's head rubbing, the dealer sought damages in excess of $10,000.[14]

Intentional Torts Against Property. The foregoing torts arise when persons are harmed. The second category of intentional torts involves damage to property. **Trespass to realty**, also called **trespass to real property**, occurs when a person intentionally enters the land of another or causes an object to be placed on the land of another without the landowner's permission. Trespass to realty also occurs when one originally enters another's land with permission, is told to leave, and yet remains on the land. It is no defense to argue that one did not know that the land belonged to another; the intent refers to intentionally being on that particular piece of land.

Trespass to personalty occurs when one intentionally interferes with another's use and enjoyment of his or her personal property. It is usually of short duration, and the trespasser is liable for any harm caused to the property or any loss suffered by the true owner as a result of the trespasser's having used the property.

Conversion is a more extreme wrong. It occurs when the defendant deprives the owner of his or her use and enjoyment of personal property. Traditionally, the tort required the defendant's permanent removal of the property from the owner's possession and control, such that the item could not be recovered or restored to its original condition. Today, however, a serious deprivation, even if not permanent, may constitute conversion. The plaintiff usually recovers damages for the full value of the converted item.

If I take my neighbor's car for a drive without permission, but I return it unharmed before the owner knows I have it, I have committed trespass to personalty, but the true owner has no damages. If I take the car and hit a tree, damaging the bumper before I return the car, I have again committed trespass to personalty and will be liable for the cost of repairing the car. If I take the car

trespass to realty (trespass to real property) Intentionally entering the land of another or causing an object to be placed on the land of another without the landowner's permission.

trespass to personalty Intentionally exercising dominion and control over another's personal property.

conversion Intentional permanent removal of property from the rightful owner's possession and control.

---

[14] Across the USA: Nevada, **www.lawyersweekly.com** [accessed June 29, 1998].

and sell it to a salvage firm that tears the car apart and sells its parts, I have committed conversion and will be liable for replacing the car.

Intentional Torts Against Economic Interests. Torts against economic interests are the torts that most commonly arise within the business context. One such tort is **disparagement**.

disparagement
Intentionally defaming a business product or service.

To win a disparagement case, a plaintiff must prove four elements. First, the defendant made a false statement of a material fact about the plaintiff's business, product or service. In general, the types of statements that are actionable are statements about the quality, honesty, or reputation of the business, as well as statements about the ownership of the business property. The second element is publication. Remember, publication in the context of any kind of defamation action means communication to a third party. So if the defendant makes disparaging comments about the plaintiff's business in a public address to a consumer group or in an advertisement, the defendant has published the statement.

Third, there must be harm to the reputation of the business, product, or service. Finally, there must be actual economic loss as a result of the false statements. Proving the economic loss that provides a basis for compensatory damages is not always easy. Usually damages will be based on a decrease in profits that can be linked to the publication of the false statement. An alternative, although a less common way to prove damages, would be to demonstrate that the plaintiff had been negotiating a contract with a third party, but the third party lost interest shortly after the publication of the false statement. The profits the plaintiff would have made on the contract would be the damages. Table 12-4 lists the elements of disparagement.

In 13 states, a closely related tort has been created: *food disparagement*. Dubbed "veggie libel" and "banana bills" by their critics, these laws provide ranchers and farmers a cause of action when someone spreads false information about the safety of a food product. The first major test of one of these laws came in a $6.7 million case filed by a rancher in a federal district court against talk show host Oprah Winfrey and one of her guests. They were discussing the potential for U.S. cattle to contract mad cow disease, and, at one point, Oprah said that was it—the conversation had stopped her from ever eating a burger again. After the broadcast, which the show's producers said tried to show both sides of the issue, the price of cattle futures fell.

The Texas law at issue provides that anyone who says that a perishable food product is unsafe, knowing the statement is false, may be required to pay damages to the producer of the product. The defendants originally asked that the case be dismissed on the grounds that the law unconstitutionally interferes with free speech. The judge dismissed the food disparagement claims on the grounds that the cattlemen did not prove that "knowingly false" statements were made and that a perishable food was not involved. The jury then decided there was no case under traditional business disparagement law, as well.

TABLE 12-4

ELEMENTS OF DISPARAGEMENT

1. A false statement of a material fact about the plaintiff's product or service
2. Publication
3. Damage to the reputation of the product or service
4. Economic loss

Another tort against economic interests is the tort of **intentional interference with a contract**, a complex and difficult tort to prove. In order to prove the tort of intentional interference with a contract, the plaintiff must demonstrate that:

1. The plaintiff had a valid contract with a third party.
2. The defendant knew of the contract and its terms.
3. The defendant took action knowing that it was highly likely to cause the third party to breach the contract with the plaintiff.
4. The defendant undertook the action for the purpose of causing the third party to breach the contract.
5. The third party did in fact breach the contract.
6. As a result of the breach, the plaintiff was injured.

> **intentional interference with a contract** Knowingly and successfully taking action for the purpose of enticing a third party to breach a valid contract with the plaintiff.

Some of the most common cases concerning intentional interference with contracts in the business setting involve employers taking employees from another firm when they know the employee has a contract for a set period of time. Luring an employee from a successful competitor is often a delicate situation. There is no problem if the employee does not have a contract for a fixed period of time, but if the employee is indeed bound by a contract of employment for a fixed term or by a contractual agreement to not work for a competitor for a set period of time, then pursuit of the employee makes a second employer with knowledge of the contract open to liability.

A third tort against economic interest is **unfair competition**. Our legal system assumes that individuals go into business for the purpose of making a profit. Competition is supposed to drive inefficient firms out of business because the more efficient firms will be able to provide less expensive goods and services. For this system to work, however, firms must be in business to make a profit. Therefore, it is unlawful for a person to go into business for the purpose of causing a loss of business to another without regard for his or her own profit.

> **unfair competition** Entering into business for the sole purpose of causing a loss of business to another firm.

For example, assume that Mark wants to open a painting business, but his father wants him to go to college. When Mark opens his business, his father starts a competing firm and is able to underbid every job his son bids because he, the father, is willing to lose money. He just wants to force his son out of business. The father, in this case, is engaging in unfair competition.

Misappropriation is another tort against economic interest that is difficult to prove. **Misappropriation** occurs when a person presents an unsolicited idea for a product, service, or even method of marketing to a business with the expectation of compensation if the idea is used by the firm and the firm subsequently uses the idea without compensating the individual. The individual may have the basis for an action for misappropriation.

> **misappropriation** Use of an unsolicited idea for a product, service, or marketing method without compensating the originator of the idea.

The firm may always defend on the grounds that it had already independently come up with the idea that the plaintiff had proposed. The firm may also deny that the idea was even discussed. It is, therefore, extremely important that anyone offering an unsolicited idea to a firm have that idea and the offer to the firm documented.

NEGLIGENT TORTS

Elements of Negligence. The second classification of torts is negligent torts. **Negligence** results not from the willful wrongdoing of a party but from carelessness. A person is said to be negligent when her or his behavior falls below the standard of care necessary to protect others from an unreasonable risk of harm. To prove negligence, a plaintiff must establish four elements:

> **negligence** Failure to live up to the standard of care that a reasonable person would meet to protect others from an unreasonable risk of harm.

(1) duty, (2) breach of duty, (3) causation, and (4) damages. Failure to establish any one of those elements precludes recovery by the plaintiff.

The first element to be proved is *duty*. The duty is the standard of care that the defendant owes the plaintiff. Under certain circumstances, a law establishes the duty of care for a particular party, but the courts generally use a "reasonable person" standard. Under this standard, the defendant must have exercised the degree of care and skill that a reasonable person would have exercised in similar circumstances to protect the plaintiff from an unreasonable risk of injury.

The reasonable-person standard is an objective standard; it is an illustration of how members of society would expect an individual to act in a certain situation. Thus, the reasonable person is careful and wise. In negligence cases, a judge or jury must determine what the reasonable person would do in a situation and compare this standard to the actions of the individual in the case before it.

One of the reasons that a future business manager should be knowledgeable about duty of care is that courts generally expect businesses to meet a reasonable duty of care for customers who enter onto the businesses' property. Thus, businesses must warn customers about potential risks they might encounter while on the property, or even better, make sure that the property is safe for customers. However, if a business attempts to warn its customers about potential hazards, the business might still be considered negligent. For example, in a case decided in Los Angeles,[15] a woman sued the House of Blues restaurant because she tripped over lumber that was being stored on the front porch of the restaurant. Although the lumber was marked with yellow construction tape, the woman received $91,366 in damages.

The next element to be proved is a *breach of duty*. Once the plaintiff establishes the duty required of the defendant under the circumstances, the plaintiff must show that the defendant's conduct was not consistent with that duty. For example, a reasonable person does not leave a campfire burning unattended in the woods. A defendant who builds a campfire and then goes home without putting out the campfire has breached her or his duty of care to the owner of the campground and to other campers whose safety is endangered by the unguarded campfire.

The third element is *causation*. Causation is really two elements: actual cause and proximate cause. *Actual cause* is a factual matter of whether the defendant's conduct resulted in the plaintiff's injury. The breach of the duty must have resulted directly in the plaintiff's harm. To ascertain whether the breach of duty was the actual cause of the plaintiff's harm, one must ask, "If the defendant had obeyed his or her duty, would the plaintiff still have been injured?" If the answer is no, then the defendant's breach was the actual cause of the plaintiff's harm.

Proximate cause is a question of how far society wishes to extend liability. In the majority of states, proximate cause is defined as foreseeability. Proximate cause exists if both the plaintiff and the type of injury incurred by the plaintiff are foreseeable. For example, it is foreseeable that if a tire falls off a car, the car may run off the road and hit a pedestrian. It is not foreseeable that the pedestrian will be carrying dynamite, which he will throw when he sees the car moving toward him, causing the dynamite to explode, causing vibrations that shatter a window six blocks away, and causing glass to fly and cut a secretary. Neither the secretary nor the secretary's injury would be foreseeable, so the secretary would not succeed in a suit for negligence against the manufacturer of the car in most states because of the lack of proximate cause. Proximate cause,

---

[15] *Haywood v. Baseline Construction Company*, No. SC004942, Los Angeles County Superior Court (1999).

however, would not prevent the pedestrian from suing in this example, because a pedestrian is a foreseeable victim when a car goes out of control.

In a minority of states, the courts do not differentiate between actual and proximate cause; once actual cause is proved, proximate cause is said to exist. Thus, in the minority of states, both the pedestrian and the secretary would be able to recover in the foregoing example.

Damages, or compensable injury, are the final element. The defendant's action must have resulted in some harm to the plaintiff for which the plaintiff can be compensated. A party cannot bring an action in negligence seeking only nominal damages. A recent example of negligence involved the tragic death of R&B vocalist Aaliyah Dana Haughton, who died August 25, 2001, in an airplane accident, following the completion of her music video titled "Rock the Boat."[16] Blackground Records, who entered into a recording agreement with Aaliyah, brought suit against Instinct Productions, a company that produced Aaliyah's music video and made transportation arrangements for the filming. Blackground sued Instinct for negligence, claiming that Blackground and Instinct shared a long, trusting relationship, from which Instinct owed a duty to Blackground to provide safe transportation for Aaliyah. Blackground argued that Instinct breached this duty, causing foreseeable economic harm to Blackground, whose financial success depended primarily on Aaliyah. When this book went to press, the case was still before the New York Supreme Court.

In any negligence case, the plaintiff must show that the defendant owed a duty of care to the plaintiff and breached that duty, causing foreseeable harm to the plaintiff for which the plaintiff is seeking compensation. Place yourself in the plaintiff's position to see that proving negligence would often be difficult. Frequently, direct proof of the defendant's negligent conduct does not exist because it was destroyed and there were no witnesses to the negligent act. To make it easier for plaintiffs to recover in negligence cases, most courts have adopted two doctrines: *res ipsa loquitur* and *negligence per se*.

Res ipsa loquitur literally means "the thing speaks for itself." The plaintiff uses this doctrine to allow the judge or jury to infer that the defendant's negligence was the cause of the plaintiff's harm when there is no direct evidence of the defendant's lack of due care. To establish *res ipsa loquitur* in most states, the plaintiff must demonstrate that:

> **res ipsa loquitur** Legal doctrine that allows a judge or a jury to infer negligence on the basis of the fact that accidents of the type that happened to the plaintiff generally do not occur in the absence of negligence on the part of the someone in the defendant's position.

1. The event was of a kind that ordinarily does not occur in the absence of negligence.

2. Other responsible causes, including the conduct of third parties and the plaintiff, have been sufficiently eliminated.

3. The indicated negligence is within the scope of the defendant's duty to the plaintiff.

Proof of these elements does not require a finding of negligence; it merely permits it.

One of the earliest uses of *res ipsa loquitur* was the case of *Escola v. Coca-Cola*.[17] In that case, the plaintiff, a waitress, was injured when a bottle of Coca-Cola that she was removing from a case exploded in her hand. From the facts that (1) bottled soft drinks ordinarily do not spontaneously explode, and (2) the bottles had been sitting in a case, undisturbed, in the restaurant for approximately 36 hours

---

[16] Negligence Action Brought Against Video Producer Over Air Crash Death of Popular Singer Advances, 2 New York Law Journal, June 3, 2004.

[17] 150 P.2d 436 (1944).

before the plaintiff simply removed the bottle from the case, the jury reasonably inferred that the defendant's negligence in the filling of the bottle resulted in its explosion. The plaintiff, therefore, could recover without direct proof of the defendant's negligence. The doctrine has subsequently been used in numerous accident cases in which there has been no direct evidence of negligence. Note that the jury does not have to infer negligence, but it may. The defendant's best response to the use of this doctrine is to try to demonstrate other possible causes of the accident.

negligence per se Legal doctrine that says when a statute has been enacted to prevent a certain type of harm and the defendant violates that statute, causing that type of harm to befall the plaintiff, the plaintiff may use proof of the violation as proof of negligence.

Another doctrine that may aid the plaintiff is **negligence per se**. If a statute is enacted to prevent a certain type of harm and a defendant violates that statute, causing that type of harm to befall the plaintiff, the plaintiff may use proof of the violation of the statute as proof of negligence. For example, it is unlawful to sell certain types of glue to minors because they may inhale it to obtain a euphoric feeling. Such a use of the glue may lead to severe health problems or death. If a retailer sold such glue to a minor who died from sniffing the glue, proof of the sale in violation of the statute establishes negligence per se by the retailer.

Defenses to Negligence. Although the courts have created the two foregoing doctrines to help the plaintiff establish his or her case, the courts also accept certain defenses that will relieve a defendant from liability, even if the plaintiff has successfully established the elements of negligence.

contributory negligence A defense to negligence that consists of proving the plaintiff did not exercise the ordinary degree of care to protect against an unreasonable risk of harm and that this failure contributed to causing the plaintiff's harm.

Initially, all states made available a strong defense to negligence: **contributory negligence**. Under this defense, the defendant must prove that (1) the plaintiff did not exercise the degree of care that one would ordinarily exercise to protect oneself from an unreasonable risk of harm, and (2) this failure contributed to causing the plaintiff's own harm. Proof of such contributory negligence is an absolute bar to recovery. In other words, once the defendant proves that the plaintiff was contributorily negligent, the defendant wins the lawsuit and will not have to pay any damages to the plaintiff. Because of the harshness of this defense, many states adopted the *last-clear-chance doctrine* (Exhibit 12-2). Under this doctrine, once the defendant establishes contributory negligence on the part of the plaintiff, the plaintiff may still recover by showing that the defendant had the last clear opportunity to avoid the accident that resulted in the plaintiff's loss.

comparative negligence A defense that allocates recovery based on percentage of fault allocated to plaintiff and defendant; available in either pure or modified form.

assumption of the risk A defense to negligence based on showing that the plaintiff voluntarily and unreasonably encountered a known risk and that the harm that the plaintiff suffered was the harm that was risked.

The adoption of this doctrine, however, still left a lot of situations in which an extremely careless defendant caused a great deal of harm to a plaintiff who was barred from recovery because of minimal contributory negligence. Thus, today, most states have replaced the contributory negligence defense with either pure or modified **comparative negligence**. Under a pure comparative negligence defense, the court determines the percentage of fault of the defendant, and that is the percentage of damages for which the defendant is liable. Damages under modified comparative negligence are calculated in the same manner, except that the defendant must be more than 50 percent at fault before the plaintiff can recover. Twenty-eight states have modified comparative negligence, 13 have pure comparative negligence, and 9 have contributory negligence. Remember, every state adopts one of these three defenses. The parties do not get to pick from among them. However, if a party resides in a state that uses a defense that is not favorable to that party, he or she can always argue that the state should change its law to accept a different defense. For example, a plaintiff residing in a state that still allows the contributory negligence defense might try to argue that the state should follow the trend and modernize its law by moving to modified comparative negligence and abolishing the contributory negligence defense.

Another defense that may be used in a negligence case is **assumption of the risk**. The defendant must show that the plaintiff voluntarily and unreasonably

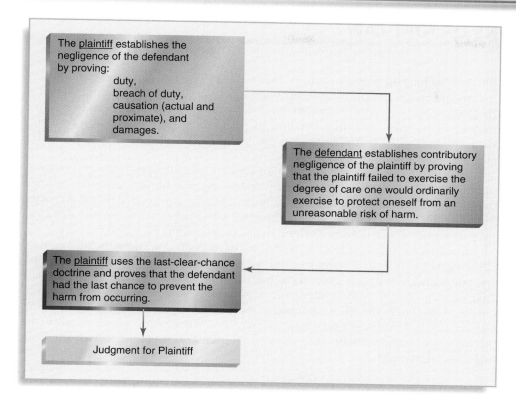

EXHIBIT 12-2

APPLICATION OF THE LAST-CLEAR-CHANCE DOCTRINE

The plaintiff establishes the negligence of the defendant by proving:

    duty,
    breach of duty,
    causation (actual and proximate), and
    damages.

The defendant establishes contributory negligence of the plaintiff by proving that the plaintiff failed to exercise the degree of care one would ordinarily exercise to protect oneself from an unreasonable risk of harm.

The plaintiff uses the last-clear-chance doctrine and proves that the defendant had the last chance to prevent the harm from occurring.

Judgment for Plaintiff

encountered a known risk. To successfully use this defense, the defendant must establish that the harm suffered was indeed the risk assumed. For example, in one case, a plaintiff was using a grinding wheel while wearing only his eyeglasses and not the safety goggles provided by his employer to keep the pieces of stone chips and dust from flying into his eyes. The defective grinding wheel exploded into three pieces, and one piece flew into the plaintiff's eye, blinding him. When the plaintiff sued the defendant manufacturer, the defendant raised the defense of assumption of the risk. The court struck down that attempted use of the defense, noting that the wearing of safety goggles was not intended to prevent harm from exploding grinding wheels, and that if any risks were assumed by the plaintiff, it was the risk of getting a small stone chip in his eye. As the plaintiff could not have known that the wheel would explode, he could not have assumed the risk.

STRICT LIABILITY TORTS

A third type of tort is a strict liability tort. Under this theory, the defendant is engaged in an activity that is so inherently dangerous under the circumstances of its performance that no amount of due care can make it safe. The activity does have some social utility, however, so we do not want to prohibit it entirely. Consequently, we allow people to engage in such activities but hold them strictly liable for any damages caused by engaging in these activities. Inherently dangerous activities include blasting in a populated area and keeping nondomesticated animals. As the reader will see in the next chapter, in today's society, strict liability has had perhaps its greatest impact on cases involving products that are considered unreasonably dangerous.

GLOBAL DIMENSIONS OF TORT LAW

With the increasing globalization of business, it is becoming more common for citizens of foreign countries to temporarily reside in the United States, as well as for U.S. citizens to reside abroad for long periods of time. There are also a number of people with dual citizenship. It is, therefore, a realistic possibility that one might get a tort judgment in the United States and need to enforce that judgment in a foreign nation.

Although many European nations are signatories to treaties regarding enforcement of foreign judgments, the United States has not signed any such treaties. Therefore, the extent to which a U.S. judgment will be enforced in a foreign nation depends on that nation's laws. For example, some nations will review the judgment to ensure that it does not offend their country's notion of due process.

One area in which at least two nations have been unwilling to fully enforce U.S. judgments is with respect to punitive damage awards. Both a German federal court and an English court have ruled that punitive damage awards violate their nation's public policy interest in maintaining a purely compensatory tort system. They have, therefore, refused to enforce U.S. punitive damages awards. As international business and, thus, international litigation continue to grow, the U.S. business manager will have to become increasingly familiar with the policies of foreign courts.

SUMMARY

Tort law provides a means for an injured party to obtain compensation from the party whose actions caused the injury. Tort law provides three types of damages. Compensatory damages, which are the most common, are designed to put the plaintiff in the position he or she would have been in had the tort not occurred. Nominal damages, available only in intentional tort cases, are a minimal amount, such as $1, and signify that the defendant's behavior was wrongful but caused no harm. Punitive damages are assessed in addition to compensatory damages when the defendant's conduct is egregious. Punitive damages are designed primarily to punish the defendant and deter such conduct in the future.

Torts are classified as intentional, negligent, or strict liability, depending on the degree of willfulness required for the tort. The most willful are the intentional torts, which are further categorized by the interest that is injured. Intentional torts against the person include assault, battery, defamation, intentional infliction of emotional distress, false imprisonment, and the privacy torts. Intentional torts against property include trespass to realty, trespass to personalty, and conversion. Intentional torts against economic interests include disparagement, intentional interference with contractual relations, misappropriation, and unfair competition.

Negligence can be thought of as the tort of carelessness. To prove negligence, one must prove four elements: (1) duty of care, (2) breach of duty, (3) causation, and (4) damages. Negligence per se and *res ipsa loquitur* are two doctrines that may help the plaintiff prove negligence. Defenses to negligence include contributory negligence, modified and pure comparative negligence, and assumption of the risk.

Strict liability occurs when one causes injury to another by engaging in an unreasonably dangerous activity.

As more citizens of foreign nations reside in the United States, and more citizens of the United States reside in foreign nations, it becomes increasingly likely that one might get a tort judgment in the United States and need to enforce it in a foreign country. The enforceability of such a judgment depends on that foreign nation's laws. And if one is attempting to enforce that judgment in either Germany or England, any punitive damages award will not be enforced.

REVIEW QUESTIONS

12-1 Evaluate the arguments for and against restricting the availability of punitive damages. Explain why you would tend to agree more with one position than the other.

12-2 Distinguish intentional torts from negligent torts.

12-3 Define an assault and a battery and explain how the two are related.

12-4 Explain why it is harder to win a defamation action if you are a public figure.

12-5 Explain the relationship between trespass and personalty and conversion.

12-6 Your state is proposing to pass a food disparagement law. Construct the strongest arguments in support of and in opposition to such a law. Explain how emphasizing the importance of different ethical norms could lead to a different attitude toward the proposed law.

REVIEW PROBLEMS

12-7 Karen writes Bob a long letter in which she falsely accuses him of stealing her bike. Bob is outraged because no one has ever questioned his character in that way before. He is so incensed that he shows the letter to several colleagues, as well as to his boss. A few weeks later, he applies for a promotion and is turned down. When he asks his boss why he lost the promotion, his boss, very reluctantly, says he believed that a number of people were concerned about his integrity in light of the recent accusations about his involvement in a bicycle theft. Bob sues Karen for defamation and intentional infliction of emotional distress. Why will he probably succeed or fail on each claim?

12-8 Madeline enters into a contract with Canyon Canoes to go on a weeklong canoe trip down a river. The contract states that, although the firm provides experienced guides and high-quality equipment, they are not insurers of the adventurers' safety. The firm cannot be responsible for harm resulting from ordinary dangers of outdoor activities. Madeline is injured when the Coleman stove she was provided with explodes. The explosion was caused by an inadequate repair that had been made by Canyon Canoes. The company raises the defense of assumption of the risk when she sues it for negligence. Why is or is this not a valid defense?

12-9 Action Advertising hired Alice Jones as an account executive. She signed an employment contract under which she agreed to work for the agency for a one-year term for an annual salary of $45,000. After the manager of Creative Ads had seen an exceptional set of ads Jones had created, he called Jones, asking her whether she would be interested in changing jobs. When Jones explained that she was bound by contract for six more months, the manager said that the contract was unenforceable and further offered to double her salary if she came to work for him, because he did not believe she was being paid what she was worth. If Jones quits and goes to work for Creative, is there a tort? If so, what would the remedy be? If not, why not?

12-10 Sam was driving in excess of the speed limit and ran a red light at 11 P.M. He hit Suzanne's car, which was crossing the intersection when he ran the red light. Sam had not seen Suzanne's car because of his excess speed and also because she was driving a black car and had not turned on her headlights. Suzanne suffered extensive injuries and sued Sam for negligence. Detail the manner in which she tried to prove her case and describe how Sam attempted to defend himself. How do you think the court would resolve this dispute? How would the state in which the case arose affect the outcome?

12-11 Bill is having marital difficulties and has an affair with Sara, from whom he contracts herpes. Hoping to work out his marital problems, he does not inform his wife of his infection. Four years later, Bill and his wife, Eva, divorce. A month later, before she has had any relationships with other men, Eva discovers she has herpes. Knowing she could have contracted the disease from only one person, she sues her husband for negligence, battery, and intentional infliction of emotional distress. What arguments would she make to support each of these causes of action? Explain how you believe the court would respond to each argument.

12-12 Devo Dynamite is imploding a building. Despite taking every known safety precaution and imploding the building at a time when the least traffic is likely to be in the area, the implosion is not perfect, and Ron, a passerby, is injured by a piece of flying debris. What tort may Devo be accused of committing? Explain why Ron is either likely or unlikely to be successful in his legal action.

CASE PROBLEMS

12-13 Briney owned an unoccupied farmhouse. Frustrated by vandals entering the house, he set up a spring gun to discharge in the event that anyone entered a bedroom of the old building. Katko and his companion had broken into the house to find and steal old bottles and dated fruit jars. When they opened the bedroom door, the gun automatically discharged, shooting Katko in the leg. He sued Briney for battery. The jury entered an award for Katko for $20,000 in actual damages and $10,000 in punitive damages.

Briney filed a motion for a new trial, which the trial court judge denied. He appealed the denial of the motion to the state supreme court. How do you think the court ruled? Why? *Katko v. Briney*, 183 N.W.3d 657 (1971)

12-14 Dominique Gantt informed her employer, a private security company, that she had obtained a protective order barring her ex-boyfriend from abusing, threatening, or contacting her anywhere, including her home and "place of employment." Upon notification, Gantt's employer informed all of its supervisors that Gantt was to be assigned only to secure interior posts so that her ex-boyfriend could not gain access to her. But Gantt's supervisor, who personally knew Gantt's ex-boyfriend, appparently believing that the estranged couple "should talk," permitted her ex-boyfriend access to Gantt. Gantt's supervisor allowed her ex-boyfriend to have phone contact with Gantt on several occasions. Then, on December 7, 1996, Gantt's supervisor stationed her outside the building at an unsecured post, where she was promptly contacted via phone by her ex-boyfriend. After the phone call, Gantt asked to be moved to an interior post. Her supervisor refused her request. Shortly after Gantt's request was denied, her ex-boyfriend showed up at Gantt's position outside the building. Her ex-boyfriend then, at gunpoint, kidnapped Gantt from her workplace and held her captive for six hours, assaulting and raping her.

Gantt sued her employer seeking damages for her resulting severe emotional distress, claiming that after the attack she has suffered recurrent nightmares, anxiety attacks, and mild agoraphobia. In light of the evidence presented, should the case have been decided in the defendant's favor on a motion for summary judgment? How do the plaintiff's allegations support her claim for intentional infliction of emotional distress? *Gantt v. Security, USA, Inc.*, 356 F.3d 547 (2004)

12-15 Christopher Zaffer was driving a tractor-trailer westbound on Interstate 40 in Tennessee when his rig became disabled due to mechanical problems. Zaffer moved the tractor-trailer completely into the emergency breakdown lane (the shoulder) where the tractor was clearly visible at least 1,000 feet away by oncoming traffic. He then placed the orange-triangle warning devices required by Tennessee statute and federal regulation behind the tractor-trailer to signal to approaching traffic that his rig was disabled.

Approximately five hours later, Diane Rupe and her two grandsons struck the back end of Zaffer's truck, killing Zaffer, Rupe, and one of her grandsons. Rupe's next of kin brought suit against Zaffer's employer and Zaffer's estate claiming Zaffer negligently left his disabled rig on the highway for five hours, causing the accident. What would Rupe's next of kin have to prove to win the case? Who ultimately won the case? *Kellner v. Budget Car and Truck Rental, Inc.*, 2004 FED App. 0059P (6th Cir. 2004)

12-16 An advertisement for Killian's Irish Red Beer that appeared in the February 1994 swimsuit issue of *Sports Illustrated* featured a drawing of a pitcher in the windup position. Don Newcombe, ex-Dodger pitcher, and his friends immediately recognized the drawing as a picture of him. Coors Brewing Company, which makes Killian's, argued that although the drawing was copied from a photograph of Newcombe, the drawing did not contain his name or his facial features. Furthermore, the drawing did not depict specific uniforms or team names. However, Newcombe argued that because his stance was so unique, he could be identified in the drawing. Therefore, he brought a suit against Coors Brewing Company. On what grounds was his suit based? Does he have a case? Why or why not? *Newcombe v. Coors*, 98 S.O.S 7327 (9th Cir. 1998)

12-17 A week after O.J. Simpson was acquitted for the double murders of Nicole Brown Simpson and Ronald Goldman, the *National Examiner* ran the following front-page headline: "Cops Think Kato Did It! … he fears they want him for perjury, say pals." The cops did not believe that Kaelin committed the murders, and the publisher of the *National Examiner* did not believe that the cops suspected Kaelin. When questioned, the news editor stated that "It" referred to perjury. Furthermore, the editor stated that he was concerned that the headline did not accurately reflect the article inside the publication. Kaelin demanded a retraction. When the *National Examiner* refused, he filed suit. On what grounds did Kaelin file suit? Was

his suit successful? Why or why not? *Brian Kato Kaelin v. Globe Communications Corp.*, 162 F.3d 1036 (9th Cir. 1998)

12-18 Karin Gray worked at AT&T for approximately one month when she missed more than a week's worth of work due to a non-work-related injury. Gray submitted the proper injury forms to AT&T; however, due to inconsistencies in the forms AT&T did not certify Gray's forms. Upon contacting the doctor listed on the forms, AT&T was informed that the doctor did not have any records of Gray's visit. AT&T began to investigate Gray's claims, leading to its termination of Gray for falsifying corporate documents. Gray's supervisor (Garrett) told Gray, the investigation team, Garrett's supervisor, and the human resources manager about the reasons Gray was fired. When Gray filed for unemployment benefits, AT&T forwarded Gray's termination information to the company processing the unemployment claim. Gray filed a defamation suit against AT&T, contending AT&T defamed her by publishing statements that she committed disability fraud. Was Gray successful in her suit? Why or why not? *Gray v. AT&T Corp.*, 357 F.3d 763 (2004)

ASSIGNMENT ON THE INTERNET

Now that you have a basic understanding of tort law, use the Internet and your critical thinking skills to evaluate arguments for tort reform. Find at least two Web sites, other than those that follow, with opposing views on the issue of tort reform. What is the primary argument of each one? What ethical norms support each argument?

After evaluating the arguments of others, formulate your own position about one aspect or area of tort reform. What ethical norms have you used in formulating your position?

The following links may be helpful in searching for other sites with positions on tort reform.

 ## ON THE INTERNET

www.atra.org This site, home of the American Tort Reform Association, provides a broad range of information on issues related to tort reform.

www.atrafoundation.org The American Tort Reform Foundation also provides useful information and facts related to tort reform. Compare this site with that of ATRA (www.atra.org.).

cspinet.org/foodspeak If you were bothered by the ideas of veggie libel laws, you will want to check out this site maintained by the Foodspeak Coalition.

www.mds.rmit.edu.au/law/defame.html This site examines the issue of defamation on the Internet. Use your knowledge from the previous chapter on cyberlaw when discussing torts in cyberspace.

www.law.cornell.edu/topics/torts.html Use the links at this Web site to explore recent court cases involving torts.

www.findlaw.com/01topics/22tort Provided at this site are several links to tort law resources, such as state and local laws, cases, and several databases.

13

PRODUCT AND SERVICE LIABILITY LAW

 **THEORIES OF RECOVERY IN PRODUCT LIABILITY CASES**

MARKET SHARE LIABILITY

SERVICE LIABILITY

GLOBAL DIMENSIONS OF PRODUCT LIABILITY LAW

When consumers enter a store to purchase a product, they assume that the product will do the job the manufacturer claims it will do without injuring the consumer or anyone else. The consumer may not be aware that each year over 33.4 million injuries and an average of 24,400 deaths result from the use of products purchased in the U.S. marketplace. Deaths, injuries, and property damage from consumer products incidents cost the nation more than $700 billion annually.[1] Such injuries have resulted in the filing of numerous lawsuits, with estimates of the number of product liability cases ranging as high as 1 million a year. Given the substantial number of product-related injuries and the amount of ensuing litigation, the businessperson in today's society will probably become involved in some aspect of product liability litigation, either as a plaintiff or as an employee of a defendant. This chapter discusses the most significant aspects of this area of law, known as product liability, in order to help the student function as a prudent consumer and businessperson.

Product liability law developed out of *tort law*, discussed in the previous chapter. This chapter begins by introducing the three primary theories of recovery in product liability cases and the defenses raised in such cases.

---

[1] U.S. Consumer Product Safety Commission, **www.cpsc.gov/about/about.html** accessed June 28, 2004.

When examining these theories, the reader should recognize how they rely on the traditional tort theories discussed in Chapter 12. These sections are followed by an introduction to the concept of enterprise liability, a concept that has slightly broadened the potential reach of product liability cases. Closely related to the concept of product liability is service liability, which is discussed in the next section. Although they are not obvious at first, product liability law does have global implications, and these are discussed in the final section of this chapter.

Critical Thinking About the Law

Manufacturers owe a certain responsibility to consumers. Consumers should be able to reasonably use a product without its causing harm to them or others. After you read the following case, answer the critical thinking questions that will enhance your thinking about product liability law.

Katherine purchased a can of hair spray from her local drugstore. When she removed the cap from the hair spray can, the can exploded in her hands. She suffered third-degree burns on her hands and face and was unable to work for three months.

Katherine sued the hair spray manufacturer after she discovered that another woman had suffered an identical accident when using the same brand of hair spray. The jury awarded Katherine $750,000 in compensatory damages.

1. Katherine's lawyer described a previous case in which an individual was injured because a product exploded. Two years earlier, a woman walking down a row of hair care products in a supermarket had been injured when three cans of hair spray spontaneously exploded. She lost her sight because of the explosion, and a jury awarded her $2.2 million in damages. Katherine's lawyer argued that because the previous woman had been compensated, Katherine should be awarded $2 million in damages for her injuries. Do you think the earlier case is similar enough to Katherine's case for Katherine to recover damages? Why?

   Clue: How are the cases similar and different? How does the fact that Katherine purchased the product affect your thinking about the earlier case?

2. The manufacturer argued that, because it places a warning on the hair spray cans, it is free from responsibility for injury. The can states, "Warning: Flammable. Contents under pressure." However, the jury ruled in favor of Katherine. What ethical norm seems to have shaped the jury's thought?

   Clue: Study the list of ethical norms in Chapter 1. The manufacturer argued that it should not have to assume responsibility because the can has a warning. What ethical norm is consistent with offering greater protection for the consumer?

3. What additional information about this case would make you more willing to state your own opinion about the situation?

   Clue: What information about the product would change your thinking about the responsibility of the manufacturer? For example, suppose that Katherine discovered that an identical accident occurred with the same brand of hair spray. How might knowing the date that the similar accident occurred influence your thinking about Katherine's case?

THEORIES OF RECOVERY IN PRODUCT LIABILITY CASES

Product liability law developed out of tort law. A glance at the three primary theories of recovery in product liability cases reveals a relationship between product liability and tort law. The three theories of recovery used in product liability cases are *negligence*, *breach of warranty*, and *strict product liability*. A plaintiff usually brings an action alleging as many of these three grounds as possible, although often a suit based on strict product liability is the easiest to prove.

NEGLIGENCE

Negligence has been one of the theories traditionally used by plaintiffs in product liability cases. To successfully recover using a negligence theory, the plaintiff must prove the elements of negligence explained in Chapter 12. The plaintiff must establish that the defendant manufacturer owed a duty of care to the plaintiff, that the defendant breached that duty of care, that this breach of duty caused the plaintiff's injury, and that the plaintiff suffered actual, compensable injury.

The Privity Limitation. An early problem using negligence as a theory of recovery for an injury caused by a defective product was the problem of establishing duty. Originally, the courts said that a plaintiff who was not the purchaser of the defective product could not establish a duty of care and, thus, could not recover. This limitation was based on the concept of *privity*. Privity means that one is a party to a contract. In the earliest known product liability case, *Winterbottom v. Wright*,[2] the British court in 1842 laid the basis for the long-standing rule that to recover for an injury caused by a defective product, the plaintiff must establish privity. In other words, before a manufacturer or seller of a defective good could owe a duty to the plaintiff, the plaintiff must have purchased that good directly from the defendant who manufactured it. Because plaintiffs rarely purchase goods from the manufacturer, few such suits were initially brought.

The years of the privity limitation tended to be a grim period for injured consumers. Gradually, especially in cases of defective food, the courts began to do away with the requirement of privity, and it was essentially abolished in the landmark 1916 case of *MacPherson v. Buick Motor Company*.[3]

In *MacPherson v. Buick*, the court held the remote manufacturer of an automobile with a defective wheel liable to the plaintiff when the wheel broke and the plaintiff was injured. In that case, Judge Cardozo stated that the presence of a sale does not control the duty; if the elements of a product are such that it is harmful to individuals if negligently made, and if the manufacturer knows that the product will be used by other than the purchaser without new tests, then "irrespective of contract, the manufacturer of this thing is under a duty to make it carefully." By the holding in this New York case, which was quickly followed by similar holdings in other states, the court did away with the requirement of privity, thereby allowing a negligent manufacturer to be held responsible for a defective product's causing injuries to someone with whom the defendant manufacturer had no contract.

---

[2] 152 Eng. Rep. 402 (1842).
[3] 11 N.E. 1050 (1916).

Eradication of the privity requirement and the subsequent increase in the liability of producers and sellers reflected a shift in social policy toward placing responsibility for injuries on those who market a product that could foreseeably cause harm if proper care were not taken in its design, manufacture, and labeling. Increasingly, the courts indicated that defendants should be responsible for their affirmative acts when they knew that such actions could cause harm to others. Also, because the manufacturer and seller derive economic benefits from the sale and use of the product, it seemed fair to impose liability on them if they earned profits from a defectively made product.

Thus, the abolition of the privity limitation opened the door for negligence as a theory of liability to be used in cases in which people were injured because of the lack of care of a product manufacturer or seller. There are now a number of negligent acts or omissions that typically give rise to negligence-based product liability actions, which are listed in Table 13-1. We will now discuss the most common of these negligence-based product liability actions: negligent failure to warn and negligent design.

Negligent Failure to Warn. Most of the product liability actions grounded in negligence involve allegations of failure to warn or inadequate warning. To bring a successful negligence case for failure to warn, the plaintiff must demonstrate that the defendant knew or should have known that, without a warning, the product would be dangerous in its ordinary use or in any *reasonably foreseeable use*. In determining whether a reasonable manufacturer would have given a warning in a particular situation, the courts frequently consider the likelihood of the injury, the seriousness of the injury, and the ease of warning.

There is generally no duty to warn of dangers arising from unforeseeable misuses of a product or from obvious dangers. A producer, for example, need not give a warning that a sharp knife could cut someone. Similarly, some plaintiffs have argued that fast-food restaurants, like McDonald's, are liable to consumers for their obesity-related health problems because the restaurants failed to warn customers of the unhealthy attributes of fast food. In *Pelman v. McDonald's*, the plaintiff alleged that McDonald's failed to warn customers of the "ingredients, quantity, qualities and levels of cholesterol, fat, salt and sugar content and other ingredients in those products, and that a diet high in fat, salt, sugar and cholesterol could lead to obesity and health problems."[4] In his decision dismissing the plaintiff's claims against McDonald's, Judge Sweet specifically stated that "this opinion is guided by the principle that legal consequences should not attach to the consumption of hamburgers and other fast food fare unless consumers are unaware of the dangers of eating such food."

TABLE 13-1

COMMON NEGLIGENT ACTIONS LEADING TO PRODUCT LIABILITY CASES

- Negligent failure to warn
- Negligent provision of an inadequate warning
- Negligent design
- Negligent manufacture
- Negligent testing or failure to test
- Negligent advertising

---

[4] 237 F. Supp.2d. 512, (S.D.N.Y 2003).

Because consumers know, or should reasonably know, the potential negative health effects associated with eating fast food, the plaintiff's claim was dismissed. However, if the plaintiffs can allege that McDonald's food is dangerous in a manner not known to consumers, their claims may survive in the future. Plaintiffs' hopes of recovering from McDonald's may be thwarted by a bill called "Personal Responsibility in Food Consumption." This bill, currently being considered in Congress, would bar plaintiffs from bringing "frivolous" claims against fast food restaurants in an attempt to recover for consumers' obesity and diabetes.

Often a defendant gives a warning but does so in a manner not clearly calculated to reach those whom the defendant should expect to use the product. If the product is to be used by someone other than the original purchaser, the manufacturer is generally required to put some sort of warning on the product itself, not just in a manual that comes with the product. If children or those who are illiterate are likely to come into contact with the product and risk harm from its use, picture warnings may be required.

Products designed for intimate bodily use, especially drugs and cosmetics, often give rise to actions based on negligent failure to warn because the use of these products frequently causes adverse reactions. When a toxic or allergic reaction causes harm to the user of a cosmetic or an over-the-counter drug, many courts find that there is no duty to warn unless the plaintiff proves (1) that the product contained an ingredient to which an appreciable number of people would have an adverse reaction, (2) that the defendant knew or should have known, in the exercise of ordinary care, that this was so, and (3) that the plaintiff's reaction was due to his or her membership in this abnormal group.[5]

Other courts, however, determine negligence by looking at the particular circumstances of the case and weighing the amount of danger to be avoided with the ease of warning. For example, in a 1995 case against McNeil Consumer Products Company, a jury awarded over $8.8 million to a man who suffered permanent liver damage as a result of drinking a glass of wine with a Tylenol capsule. Although the corporation had known for years that combining a normal dose of Tylenol with a small amount of wine could cause massive liver damage in some people, the company failed to put a warning to that effect on the label. The jury did not accept the company's argument that the reaction was so rare that no warning was necessary.[6]

The marketing of prescription drugs is unique because the manufacturer almost never has any communication with the user, only with the physician who prescribes the drug for the user. In these cases, the courts have generally held that drug manufacturers have a duty to provide adequate warnings to physicians to enable them to decide whether to prescribe the drug or to disclose the risk to the patient. The manufacturer must warn the physician of any chance of a serious adverse reaction, no matter how small the risk may be. Prescription drugs are frequently the subject of product liability cases, as described in Table 13-2.

Initially, almost all successful product liability actions based on negligence were for breach of the duty to warn. The range of successful actions was so limited because a number of influential people believed the idea that competition and the open marketplace provided the best means for ensuring that products

---

[5] W. Page et al., *Prosser and Keeton on Torts*, 5th ed. (St. Paul, Minn.: West 1984), p. 687.

[6] *Benedict v. McNeil Consumer Products Co.*, 1992 WL 729052 (L.R.P. Jury).

TABLE 13-2 PRESCRIPTION DRUGS THAT HAVE LED TO PRODUCT LIABILITY CLAIMS

Product	*Case Status and Legal Claims*
Accutane (prescription drug to treat cystic acne)	Accutane is known to cause birth defects in children. Despite the fact that the manufacturer included several warnings and a drawing of a deformed baby on the packaging, a small number of women were still getting pregnant while taking Accutane. As of April 2002, the manufacturer required women seeking a prescription for the drug to commit to using two forms of birth control and test negatively on two pregnancy tests. Additionally, some people taking Accutane reported experiencing severe despression; some have committed suicide. Parents of a 14-year-old boy who committed suicide while taking Accutane have sued the manufacturer for negligence. In April 2002, a teenage boy taking Accutane was killed after he flew a small plane into a Florida offic building; his mother is suing the manufacturer for wrongful death.
Baycol (prescription drug to lower cholesterol)	Plaintiffs reportedly experienced rhabdomyolysis, a kidney disorder in which toxic muscle cells are released into the bloodstream. Patients can then develop fatal organ failure. Plaintiffs frequently bring claims of failure to warn or defectively designed drug. The manufacturer voluntarily removed Baycol from market because of the legal claims against the manufacturer. As of January 2004, the manufacturer, Bayer, estimated that it had settled approximately 2,000 Baycol cases but still faced approximately 10,000.
Fen-Phen (Redux) (drug to treat obesity)	Some patients experienced heart valve disease after using Fen-Phen to lose weight. In January 2004, a $3.75 billion trust was created as a settlement between patients and drug manufacturer, American Home Products, to compensate patients injured from Fen-Phen use. Under the settlement agreement, eligible patients may be entitled to compensation, diet drug prescription refunds, and echocardiography screenings.
Prempro (prescription drug to relieve menopausal symptoms)	Researchers determined that women taking Prempro were more likely to suffer breast cancer, stroke, heart disease, blood clots, and dementia. After this research, the FDA approved new labels emphasizing these increased risks. Approximately 6 million women had been taking Prempro before the researchers announced the increased health risks associated with Prempro use.
Paxil (antidepressant) Similar claim has been brought from use of Zoloft, another antidepressant.	Patients taking Paxil reportedly had withdrawal reactions and problems: anxiety, agitation, confusion, dizziness, fatigue, headache, insomnia, irritability, nausea, palpitations, sweating, sleep disturbances, sensory disturbances, tremor, and vision distortion. As of April 2004, there were about 1,500 Paxil withdrawal plaintiffs in over 30 states. These cases were consolidated into Multi-District Litigation. Plaintiffs frequently bring the following claims: intentional misrepresentation, fraud, negligence, strict liability, and warranty claims.
Serzone (antidepressant)	Some patients taking Serzone experienced liver damage or liver failure, as well as some deaths. As a result, in November 2003, the manufacturer, Bristol-Myers Squibb, announced it would voluntarily remove Serzone from the market. Several class actions have been filed against the manufacturer.
Zicam (over-the-counter nasal gel to remedy the common cold)	Plaintiffs contend that after using Zicam, they lost their sense of smell and taste. As of April 2004, there were about 70 plaintiffs who had been injured through Zicam use. Plaintiffs argue that the Zicam manufacturer knew or should have known about the potential dangers associated with the use of nasal medications containing zinc. Use of zinc can cause nerve damage. Furthermore, plaintiffs argue that the manufacturer failed to provide sufficient warnings to the users of the products even though the side effects of using zinc compounds have been documented.

will have optimal safety features. Those who believe in the sanctity of the market feel that the manufacturer's job is to see that the purchaser is an *informed* purchaser and is not deceived about the safety of a product.[7]

Negligent Design. The foregoing attitude generally prevailed until approximately 1960, when the courts began, in a limited number of cases, to impose liability based on negligence in the sale of *defectively designed products*. Such liability is imposed only when a reasonable person would conclude that despite any warnings given

---

[7] See R. Coase, "The Problem of Social Cost," *Law and Economics* 3 (1960), p. 1.

with the product, the risk of harm outweighed the utility of the product as designed. Courts have found a wide variety of products to be negligently designed, including weed killers, gas stations, BB guns, airplanes, and traffic signs. One example of negligent design can be found in a 1998 case against Scepter Weed Killer Company. The firm was sued because it did not warn that corn crops could be damaged if the weed killer had been used on soybean crops the previous year. Many farmers suffered crop damage because they were unaware of this problem. The company was found guilty of negligent design because it did not adequately test the product prior to putting it on the market. Therefore, the design of the product was considered faulty, but its inadequacy could have been prevented.[8]

In bringing an action for negligence in design, a plaintiff must generally prove that the product design (1) is inherently dangerous, (2) contains insufficient safety devices, or (3) consists of materials that do not satisfy standards acceptable in the trade.

In general, an action for product liability based on negligence is accompanied by a claim grounded in strict liability (discussed later). The strict liability claims are usually easier to prove. With the growing acceptance of strict liability, negligence has become less important as a theory of liability. Another reason for the lack of favor for negligence as a theory of recovery is the broad range of defenses available for such actions.

Negligence Per Se. In the previous chapter, the concept of negligence per se was introduced. As you know from that discussion, violation of a statutory duty is considered negligence per se. That concept is also used in negligence-based product liability cases.

When a statute establishes product standards, the manufacturer has a duty to meet those standards imposed by the statute. If a manufacturer does not meet those standards, the manufacturer has breached its duty of reasonable care and as long as the plaintiff can establish that the breach of the statutory duty caused injury, the plaintiff can recover under negligence per se.

Statutes that might be violated and lead to negligence per se actions include the Flammable Fabrics Act of 1953, the Food, Drug, and Cosmetics Act of 1938, and the Hazardous Substances Labeling Act of 1960.

Defenses to a Negligence-Based Product Liability Action. All of the defenses to negligence discussed in the negligence section of the torts chapter are available in product liability cases based on negligence. Remember that the plaintiff's own failure to act reasonably can provide a defense. Depending on the state in which the action is brought, the plaintiff's negligence will allow the defendant to raise the defense of *contributory, modified comparative,* or *pure comparative negligence.* If contributory negligence is proved, the plaintiff is barred from recovery. In a state where the defense of pure comparative negligence is allowed, the plaintiff can recover for only that portion of the harm attributable to the defendant's negligence. In a modified contributory negligence state, the plaintiff can recover the percentage of harm caused by the defendant as long as the jury finds the plaintiff's negligence responsible for less than 50 percent of the harm. So, if a jury finds the defendant to be responsible for 60 percent of the plaintiff's harm, the plaintiff could recover nothing in a contributory negligence state and recover damages for 60 percent of his or her injuries in a modified or pure comparative negligence

---

8 "Farmer Can Sue Weed Killer Manufacturer—No Federal Preemption," *Lawyer's Weekly USA,* **www.lawyersweekly.com.**

state. If the defendant were only 40 percent responsible, however, the plaintiff would be able to recover 40 percent of his or her injuries only in the pure comparative negligence state and nothing in the other two.

Another defense available in product liability cases based on negligence is *assumption of the risk.* A plaintiff is said to assume the risk when he or she voluntarily and unreasonably encounters a known danger. If the consumer knows that a defect exists but still proceeds unreasonably to make use of the product, he or she is said to have voluntarily assumed the risk of injury from the defect and cannot recover.

In deciding whether the plaintiff did indeed assume the risk, the trier of fact may consider such factors as the plaintiff's age, experience, knowledge, and understanding. The obviousness of the defect and the danger it poses are also relevant factors. If a plaintiff knows of a danger but does not fully appreciate the magnitude of the risk, the applicability of the defense is a question for the jury to determine. In most cases, when an employee uses an unsafe machine at work, she or he is not presumed to assume the risk because most courts recognize that the concept of voluntariness is an illusion in the workplace. Earlier, however, employees attempting to sue manufacturers of defective machines for injuries at work were defeated by this defense.

In many states, *misuse* of the product is raised as a defense in negligence-based product liability cases. It is generally accepted that such a misuse must be unreasonable or unforeseeable to constitute a defense. When a defendant raises the defense of product misuse, what he or she is really arguing is that the harm was caused not by the defendant's negligence but by the plaintiff's failure to use the product in the manner in which it was designed to be used.

Statutory defenses are also available to defendants. To ensure that there will be sufficient evidence from which a trier of fact can make a decision, states have **statutes of limitations** that limit the time within which all types of civil actions may be brought. The statute of limitations for tort actions and, thus, for negligence-based product liability cases is from one to six years from the date of injury. Maine and North Dakota are the only states with six-year statutes of limitations, and Kentucky, Louisiana, and Tennessee are the only states with one-year statutes of limitation. Most states' statutes are from two to four years. Moreover, if the injured party is a minor, the statute of limitations does not start running until the injured party reaches age 18.

statute of limitations A statute that bars actions arising more than a specified number of years after the cause of the action arises.

States also have **statutes of repose**, which provide an additional limitation in product liability cases by barring actions arising more than a specified number of years after the product was purchased. Statutes of repose are usually much longer than statutes of limitations; they are often at least 10 years, and frequently are 25 or 50 years. Statutes of repose may seem unduly harsh on consumers who may be injured as a result of a latent defect in a product. On the other hand, to make the manufacturer liable in perpetuity is felt by some to be unduly harsh on manufacturers and sellers because of the resulting uncertainty about possible liability. Those who worry about the seller's liability, however, should remember that the older the product is, the more difficult it will be for the plaintiff to prove negligence on the part of the defendant.

statute of repose A statute that bars actions arising more than a specified number of years after the product was purchased.

The **state-of-the-art defense** is used by the defendant to demonstrate that his or her alleged negligent behavior was reasonable, given the available scientific knowledge existing at the time the product was sold or produced. If a case is based on the defendant's negligent defective design of a product, the state-of-the-art defense refers to the technological feasibility of producing a safer product

state-of-the-art defense A product liability defense based on adherence to existing technologically feasible standards at the time the product was manufactured.

at the time the product was manufactured. In cases of negligent failure to warn, the state-of-the-art defense refers to the scientific knowability of a risk associated with a product at the time of its production. This is a valid defense in a negligence case because the focus is on the reasonableness of the defendant's conduct. Demonstrating that, given the state of scientific knowledge, there was no feasible way to make a safer product does not always preclude liability. The court may find that the defendant's conduct was still unreasonable because even in the product's technologically safest form, the risks posed by the defect in the design so outweighed the benefits of the product that the reasonable person would not have produced a product of that design.

An earlier section revealed that failure to comply with a safety standard may lead to the imposition of liability. An interesting question is whether the converse is true. Does *compliance with safety regulations* constitute a defense? There is no clear answer to that question. Sometimes, however, compliance with federal laws may lead to the defense that use of state tort law is preempted by a federal statute designed to ensure the safety of a particular class of products. The following case illustrates one situation in which the court accepted the preemption argument and found that compliance with a federal statute designed to regulate medical devices relieved a manufacturer from potential tort liability.

CASE 13-1

Irene M. Green and Martin Green, Appellants v. Richard L. Dolsky, M.D., and Collagen Corporation
Superior Court of Pennsylvania,
641 A.2d 600 (1994)

Plaintiff Irene Green developed an autoimmune disease after she was treated with Zyderm collagen implant. Zyderm is injected under the skin to fill in wrinkles and is regulated as a Class III medical device under the Medical Device Amendments Act of 1976 (MDA). When the plaintiff sued defendants Collagen Corporation and the doctor who treated her, on the basis of theories of negligence, strict liability, and breach of warranty, the defendants filed a motion for summary judgment on the grounds that the MDA preempted the Greens' state tort claims. The trial court agreed and granted the motion. Plaintiffs appealed to the Pennsylvania Superior Court.

Judge Johnson

Under the supremacy clause of the United States Constitution, federal law is "the supreme Law of the Land; and the Judges in every State shall be bound thereby, any Thing in the Constitution or Laws of any State to the Contrary notwithstanding." As a result, all conflicts between federal and state laws must be resolved in favor of federal law. In determining whether a conflict between state and federal law exists, a court looks to congressional intent.

Generally, preemption may be express or implied, and it is compelled whether Congress' command is explicitly stated in the statute's language or implicitly contained in its structure and purpose. When Congress is silent on the matter, state law will be preempted by federal law "when (a) compliance with both state and federal law is impossible or (b) when state law stands as an impediment to a federal purpose."

Pursuant to the MDA, the FDA classifies all medical devices into one of three categories. Class III devices, such as Zyderm, are subject to the most extensive controls "to provide reasonable assurance of … safety and effectiveness." Class III devices must obtain pre-market approval from the FDA because they "present a potential unreasonable risk of illness or injury."

Thus, the extensive pre-market approval process requires a manufacturer to submit a detailed application to the FDA, including information pertaining to product specifications, intended use, manufacturing methods, and proposed labeling. An appointed panel of experts conducts a comprehensive review of the application and prepares a report and recommendation. Within six months of receipt of the application, the FDA must either approve the device for sale, or reject it for additional information or testing. The MDA also imposes extensive post-approval regulations to keep the FDA apprised of any new information or safety findings relating to Class III devices. The FDA may withdraw approval of the product permanently, or suspend its approval temporarily if it determines that the device has become unsafe or its labeling inadequate.

In enacting the MDA, Congress was not only interested in protecting the individual use, but it was also interested in encouraging research and development and allowing new and improved medical devices to be marketed without delay. In the MDA, Congress included an express preemption provision. State requirements which, in effect, establish new substantive requirements for a medical device in a regulated area, such as labeling, are preempted. Since Congress has provided an express preemption provision in the MDA, we must determine whether the Green's state law tort claims fall within the scope of that provision by imposing requirements in addition to or different from those mandated by the FDA.

In *King v. Collagen Corp.* [a similar case], the plaintiff, Jane King, contracted an auto-immune disease after receiving a test dose of Zyderm. King filed suit against Collagen, the manufacturer, alleging strict liability, breach of warranty of merchantability, negligence. ... Collagen filed a motion for summary judgment on the basis that the MDA preempted King's claims. The United States District Court for the District of Massachusetts agreed.

The First Circuit Court of Appeals affirmed after finding that (1) the extensive pre-market approval process and the similarly extensive post-approval regulations were indications that the FDA had established specific "requirements" within the meaning of Section 360k of the MDA and (2) King's state law tort claims would impose additional or different requirements than those mandated by the FDA, in contravention of Section 360k.

In *Stamps v. Collagen Corp.* [another similar case], guided by the express language of Section 360k(a), the Fifth Circuit Court of Appeals determined that Stamps' claims were preempted by federal law because first, the state tort law claims would constitute requirements in addition to or different from the MDA, and, second, these requirements would relate to either the safety or effectiveness of Zyderm and Zyplast. "State tort causes of action— to the extent they relate to safety, effectiveness, or other MDA requirements—constitute requirements 'different from, or in addition to' the Class III process; they are, therefore, preempted."

In the present case, the Greens claim that the district court erred in granting summary judgment on the basis that the MDA preempted their state tort law claims. Here, we are constrained to agree with the rationale in *King* and *Stamps*, and we conclude that a finding in favor of the Greens on any of their alleged state tort law claims would impose additional or different requirements on Collagen, whose product, Zyderm, has already received FDA approval. Such requirements are in conflict with the MDA and, thus, the Greens' state law claims are therefore preempted.

Affirmed in favor of Defendants,
Dolsky and Collagen Corp.

The court's decision in the *Green* case turned to a great extent on the intent of Congress in passing the legislation that set the standards. Each preemption case requires careful scrutiny of the purpose of the statute, and the opposite result often occurs. For example, in *Tebbetts v. Ford Motor Company*,[9] the plaintiff alleged that the 1988 Ford Escort was defectively designed because it did not have a driver's-side air bag. Ford raised the preemption defense, arguing that it had complied with federal safety regulations under the National Traffic and Motor Vehicle Safety Act (NTMVS), and that such compliance preempted recovery under state product liability laws. The court analyzed the legislative history of the act, as well as the language of the law itself. Finding a clause in the law that stated that "[c]ompliance with any Federal motor vehicle safety standard issued under this act does not exempt any person from any liability under common law," the court found that the Tebbetts were not preempted from bringing their product liability action.

Oil companies have had mixed results in cases in which they have argued that the Clean Air Act preempts their liability for MTBE water contamination. In an attempt to reduce air pollution in certain areas, Congress mandated that gasoline contain an oxygenate, which allows gasoline to burn more cleanly. However, Congress did not require that a particular oxygenate be used. Most oil companies added the oxygenate MTBE (Methyl Tertiary Butyl Ether) to gasoline. Unfortunately, very small amounts of MTBE can contaminate drinking water. It affects the smell and taste of water and may cause health problems. Public water utilities and private individuals, faced with millions of dollars of

---

[9] 665 A2d 345 (N.H. 1995).

cleanup costs, began suing oil companies for damages to resolve the water contamination. In response, oil companies, raising the preemption defense, argue that because the government required them to add an oxygenate to gasoline, oil companies should not be responsible for the water contamination. Plaintiffs argue that oil companies chose to use MTBE; other oxygenates, like ethanol, were available. Several courts have concluded that the Clean Air Act preempts oil companies' liability, but other courts have reached the opposite conclusion, emphasizing the fact that oil companies had a choice. Furthermore, these courts argue that the purpose of the Clean Air Act was to address air pollution, and the MTBE water contamination is a problem too far removed from the purposes of the Clean Air Act to preempt product liability claims associated with MTBE.

From the foregoing discussion of negligence, it is apparent that negligence is a valid theory on which to base a product liability case. However, from a plaintiff's perspective, it offers too many defenses to the manufacturer and the seller. An alternative theory of liability is breach of warranty.

STRICT LIABILITY IN CONTRACT FOR BREACH OF WARRANTY

warranty A guarantee or binding promise that goods (products) meet certain standards of performance.

express warranty A warranty that is clearly stated by the seller or manufacturer.

implied warranty A warranty that automatically arises out of a transaction.

implied warranty of merchantability A warranty that a good is reasonably fit for ordinary use.

The Uniform Commercial Code (UCC) provides the basis for recovery against a manufacturer or seller on the basis of breach of warranty. A **warranty** is a guarantee or a binding promise. Warranties may be either **express** (clearly stated by the seller or manufacturer) or **implied** (automatically arising out of a transaction). Either type may give rise to liability (see Table 13-3). Two types of implied warranties may provide the basis for a product liability action: warranty of merchantability and warranty of fitness for a particular purpose.

Implied Warranty of Merchantability. The **implied warranty of merchantability** is a warranty or guarantee that the goods are reasonably fit for ordinary use. This warranty arises out of every sale, unless it is expressly and clearly excluded. According to the UCC, to meet the standard of merchantability, the goods:

1. Must pass without objection in the trade under the contract description.
2. Must be of fair or average quality within the description.
3. Must be fit for the ordinary purpose for which the goods are used.
4. Must run, with variations permitted by agreement, of even kind, quality, and quantity within each unit and among all units involved.
5. Must be adequately contained, packaged, and labeled as the agreement may require.
6. Must conform to any affirmations or promises made on the label or the container.[10]

TABLE 13-3

WARRANTIES THAT MAY GIVE RISE TO LIABILITY

Express Warranties	*Implied Warranties*
• Written or oral description of good	• Of merchantability
• Promise or affirmation of fact about the good	• Of fitness for a particular purpose
• Sample or model of the good	

---

[10] *UCC, Section 2-314.*

If the product does not conform to those standards and, as a result of this non-conformity, the purchaser or his or her property is injured, the purchaser may recover for breach of implied warranty of merchantability. For example, some health care workers are using this theory to try to recover damages because they have developed latex protein toxic syndrome. When HIV rates began climbing, health workers uniformly used latex gloves to prevent transmission of the disease. However, some health workers started to develop an allergy to the proteins in the rubber latex. For some people, the allergy became so severe that they could not tolerate being in a room with a single latex balloon; consequently, they could no longer work in a profession that required them to wear latex gloves. These plaintiffs argue that glove manufacturers knew of the dangers of latex allergies but did not attempt to minimize the amount of protein in the gloves.

The UCC expressly provides that an injury to a person or property proximately caused by a breach of warranty is a recoverable type of consequential damage. The use of this warranty is limited, however, in two respects: (1) It is made only by one regularly engaged in the sale of that type of good, and (2) the seller may sometimes avoid liability by expressly disclaiming liability, or by limiting liability to replacement of the defective goods. The UCC, however, has restricted the applicability of the latter limitation by a provision declaring that a limitation of consequential damages for injury to a person in the case of consumer goods is prima facie "unconscionable." *Unconscionability* is a concept meaning gross unfairness. Under the UCC, unconscionable contract clauses are unenforceable. Thus, if a disclaimer is unconscionable, it will not be enforced.

Privity is not a problem in an action based on breach of warranty because of *UCC Section 2-318.* This section allows states to adopt one of three alternatives to allow nonpurchasers to recover for breach of warranty. The most liberal alternative allows any person injured by the defective product to sue. One issue that frequently arises in product liability cases involving breach of the warranty of merchantability is whether there is a breach of this warranty when the alleged breach arises from a naturally occurring characteristic of the product. This problem typically arises in cases involving food. Is it a breach of the warranty of merchantability when there is a bone in a fish fillet or a pit in an olive jar labeled "pitted olives"? The following case sets forth the two tests that are used in various jurisdictions.

CASE 13-2

Williams v. Braum Ice Cream Stores, Incorporated
Oklahoma Court of Appeals,
534 P.2d 700 (1974)

Plaintiff Williams purchased a cherry-pecan ice cream cone from the defendant's shop. While eating the ice cream, she broke her tooth on a cherry pit that was in the ice cream. She sued defendant Braum Ice Cream Stores, Inc., for breach of implied warranty of merchantability. The trial court ruled in favor of the defendant, and the plaintiff appealed.

Judge Reynolds

There is a division of authority as to the test to be applied where injury is suffered from an object in food or drink sold to be consumed on or off the premises. Some courts hold there is no breach of implied warranty on the part of a restaurant if the object in the food was "natural" to the food served. These jurisdictions recognize that the vendor is held to impliedly warrant the fitness of food, or that he may be liable in negligence in failing to use ordinary care in its preparation, but deny recovery as a matter of law when the substance found in the food is natural to the ingredients of the type of food served. This rule, labeled the "foreign-natural test" by many jurists, is predicated on the view that the practical difficulties of separation of ingredients in the course of food preparation (bones from meat or fish, seeds from fruit, and nutshell from the nut meat) is a matter of common knowledge. Under this natural theory, there may be a recovery only if the object is "foreign" to the food served. How far can the "foreign-natural test" be expanded? How many bones from meat or fish, seeds from fruit, nutshells from the nut meat or other natural indigestible substances are unacceptable under the "foreign-natural test"?

The other line of authorities hold that the test to be applied is what should "reasonably be expected" by a customer in the food sold to him.

[State law] provides in pertinent part as follows:

(1) … a warranty that the goods shall be merchantable is implied in a contract for their sale if the seller is a merchant with respect to goods of that kind. Under this section the serving for value of food or drink to be consumed either on the premises or elsewhere is a sale.
(2) Goods to be merchantable must be at least such as … (c) are fit for the ordinary purposes for which such goods are used;…

In *Zabner v. Howard Johnson's Inc.* … the Court held:

The "Foreign-natural" test as applied as a matter of law by the trial court does not recommend itself to us as being logical or desirable. The reasoning applied in this test is fallacious because it assumes that all substances which are natural to the food in one stage or another of preparation are, in fact, anticipated by the average consumer in the final product served. …

Categorizing a substance as foreign or natural may have some importance in determining the degree of negligence of the processor of food, but it is not determinative of what is unfit or harmful in fact for human consumption. A nutshell natural to nut meat can cause as much harm as a foreign substance, such as a pebble, piece of wire, or glass. All are indigestible and likely to cause injury. Naturalness of the substance to any ingredients in the food served is important only in determining whether the consumer may reasonably expect to find such substance in the particular type of dish or style of food served.

The "reasonable expectation" test as applied to an action for breach of implied warranty is keyed to what is "reasonably" fit. If it is found that the pit of a cherry should be anticipated in cherry-pecan ice cream and guarded against by the consumer, then the ice cream was reasonably fit under the implied warranty.

In some instances, objects which are "natural" to the type of food but which are generally not found in the style of the food as prepared, are held to be the equivalent of a foreign substance.

We hold that the better legal theory to be applied in such cases is the "reasonable expectation" theory, rather than the "naturalness" theory as applied by the trial court. What should be reasonably expected by the consumer is a jury question, and the question of whether plaintiff acted in a reasonable manner in eating the ice cream cone is also a fact question to be decided by the jury.

Reversed and remanded in favor of Plaintiff, Williams.

Implied Warranty of Fitness for a Particular Purpose. A second implied warranty that may be the basis for a product liability case is the **implied warranty of fitness for a particular purpose**. This warranty arises when a seller knows that the purchaser wants to purchase a good for a particular use. The seller tells the consumer that the good can be used for that purpose, and the buyer reasonably relies on the seller's expertise and purchases the product. If the good cannot be used for that purpose, and, as a result of the purchaser's attempt to use the good for that purpose, the consumer is injured, a product liability action for breach of warranty of fitness for a particular purpose is justified. For example, if a farmer needed oil for his irrigation engine, and he went to a store and told the seller exactly what model irrigation engine he needed oil for, the seller would be creating an implied warranty of fitness for a particular purpose by picking up a can of oil, handing it to the farmer, and saying, "This is the product you need." If the farmer purchases the recommended oil, uses it in the engine, and the engine explodes because the oil was not heavy enough, the seller would have breached the warranty of fitness for a particular purpose. If the farmer were injured by the explosion, he would be able to recover on the basis of breach of warranty.

implied warranty of fitness for a particular purpose A warranty that arises when the seller tells the consumer a good is fit for a specific use.

Express Warranties. The seller or the manufacturer may also be held liable for breach of an express warranty. An express warranty is created by a seller in one of three ways: by describing the goods, by making a promise or affirmation of fact about the goods, or by providing a model or sample of the good. If the goods fail

Critical Thinking About the Law

The criteria selected are important in determining the outcome of a case. Simply put, depending on the court's selection from many possible criteria, it can reach multiple conclusions. Judging a case according to criteria X, Y, and Z can yield a vastly different decision than if the same case were judged according to criteria A, B, and C.

Case 13-2 illustrates the foregoing assertion. The trial court had made a legal decision based on criterion X, namely the "foreign-natural" test. However, the appeals court held that the trial court must redecide the case, this time on the basis of criterion Y, or the "reasonable expectation" test.

The critical thinking questions enable you to examine carefully the key differences between the two tests, including the possible implications. The larger project of the questions is to increase your awareness of the extent to which a legal decision is dependent upon the criteria chosen to reach that decision.

1. What is the fundamental difference between the nature of the two tests discussed by the court in Case 13-2?

   Clue: Reread the discussion of the two tests to formulate your answer.

2. Which of the two tests is more likely to yield ambiguous reasoning when applied?

   Clue: Refer to your answer to Question 1.

---

to meet the description, fail to do what the seller claimed they would do, or fail to be the same as the model or sample, the seller has breached an express warranty. For example, if a 200-pound man asks a seller whether a ladder will hold a 200-pound man without breaking, the seller who says that it will is affirming a fact and is, thus, expressly warranting that the ladder will hold a 200-pound man without breaking. If the purchaser takes the ladder home and climbs up on it, and if it breaks under his weight, causing him to fall to the ground, he may bring a product liability action against the seller on the basis of breach of an express warranty.

A fairly recent example of an express warranty is the claim that many companies made that their software was "Y2K compliant." When the nation was in fear of a possible chaotic result of the year 2000, many computer companies came out with "Year 2000–compliant" software. However, this claim was usually written outside of the contract and, therefore, was an express warranty. Because businesses had the potential to lose a lot of money after Y2K, they felt that they needed someone to help reimburse what they might lose. Many decided that the easiest targets would be these "Y2K-safe" software companies because the businesses could sue on the basis of breaking an express warranty.[11]

Defenses to Breach-of-Warranty Actions. Two common defenses used in cases based on breach of warranty arise from the UCC and make sense in a commercial setting when a transaction is between two businesspeople, but they make little sense in the context of a consumer injury. Therefore, the courts have found ways to limit the use of these defenses in product liability cases in most states.

The first such defense is that the purchaser failed to give the seller notice within a reasonable time after he or she knew or should have known of the breach of warranty, as required by the UCC. Obviously, most consumers would not be aware of this rule, and as a result, many early breach-of-warranty cases

---

[11] J.L. Dam, "Can Business Sue for Cots of Fixing the 'Year 2000' Problem?" *Lawyers Weekly USA,* **www.lawyersweekly.com.**

were lost. Most courts today avoid this requirement by holding (1) that a long delay is reasonable under the particular circumstances, (2) that the section imposing the notice requirement was not intended to apply to personal injury situations, or (3) that the requirement is inapplicable between parties who have not dealt with each other, as when a consumer is suing a manufacturer.

The second defense is the existence of a **disclaimer**. A seller or manufacturer may relieve himself or herself of liability for breach of warranty in advance through the use of disclaimers. The disclaimer may say (1) that no warranties are made ("as is"), (2) that the manufacturer or seller warrants only against certain consequences or defects, or (3) that liability is limited to repair, replacement, or return of the product price.

disclaimer Disavowal of the liability for breach of warranty by the manufacturer or seller of a good in advance of the sale of the good.

Again, these disclaimers make sense in a commercial context but seem somewhat harsh in the case of consumer transactions. Thus, the courts do not look with favor on disclaimers. First, the disclaimer must be clear; in many cases, courts have rejected the defendant's use of a disclaimer as a defense on the grounds that the retail purchaser either did not see the disclaimer or did not understand it. Thus, any businessperson using disclaimers to limit liability must be sure that the disclaimers are very plainly stated on an integral part of the product or package that will not be removed before retail purchase by the consumer. In some cases, however, despite clear disclaimers, courts have held disclaimers to consumers invalid, stating either that these disclaimers are unenforceable *adhesion contracts* resulting from gross inequities of bargaining power and are, therefore, unenforceable, or that they are *unconscionable* and contrary to the policy of the law. The UCC, in fact, now contains a provision stating that a limitation of consequential damages for injury to a person in the case of consumer goods is prima facie unconscionable.

The *statute of limitations* may also be used defensively in a case based on strict liability for breach of warranty. Under the UCC, the statute of limitations runs four years from the date on which the cause of action arises. In an action based on breach of warranty, the cause of action, according to the UCC, arises at the time of the sale. This rule would severely limit actions for breach of warranty, as defects often do not cause harm immediately. Section 2-725(2) of the UCC, however, changes the time that the cause of action arises to the date when the breach of warranty is or should have been discovered when a warranty "explicitly extends to the future performance of the goods, and the discovery of the breach must await the time of performance." This section, when applicable, makes the statute of limitations less of a potential problem for the plaintiff. In a few states, courts have simply decided to apply the tort statute of limitations as running from the date of injury or the date when the defect was or should have been discovered to all product liability cases grounded in breach of warranty.

STRICT LIABILITY IN TORT

The third and most prevalent theory of product liability used during the past three decades is strict liability in tort, established in the 1963 case of *Greenman v. Yuba Power Products Company*[12] and incorporated in Section 402A of the *Restatement (Second) of Torts*. This section reads as follows:

1. One who sells any product in a defective condition, unreasonably dangerous to the user or consumer or his family is subject to liability for physical harm thereby caused to the ultimate user or consumer, or to his property, if

---

[12] 59 Cal. 2d 57 (1962).

a. the seller is engaged in the business of selling such a product, and

b. it is expected to and does reach the consumer or user without substantial change in the condition in which it was sold.

2. The rule stated in Subsection (1) applies although

a. the seller has exercised all possible care in the preparation and sale of his product, and

b. the user or consumer has not bought the product from or entered into any contractual relation with the seller.

Under this theory, the manufacturer, distributor, or retailer may be held liable to any reasonably foreseeable injured party. Unlike causes of action based on negligence or, to a lesser degree, breach of warranty, product liability actions based on strict liability in tort focus on the *product*, not on the producer or seller. The degree of care exercised by the defendant is not an issue in these cases. The issue in such cases is whether the product was in a "defective condition, unreasonably dangerous" when sold. To succeed in a strict liability action, the plaintiff must prove that:

1. The product was defective when sold,

2. The defective condition rendered the product unreasonably dangerous, and

3. The product was the cause of the plaintiff's injury.

The defect is usually the most difficult part of the case for the plaintiff to establish. A product may be defective because of (1) some flaw or abnormality in its construction or marketing that led to its being more dangerous than it otherwise would have been, (2) a failure by the manufacturer or seller to adequately warn of a risk or hazard associated with the product, or (3) a design that is defective. For example, in 1966, Mr. Dolinski purchased a bottle of Squirt from a vending machine and drank most of the contents. He soon felt ill and discovered a decomposed mouse and mouse feces at the bottom of the bottle. He suffered physical and mental distress and avoided soft drinks after this experience. Under strict liability in tort, he sued that bottle manufacturer and distributor, Shoshone Coca-Cola bottling company, and a jury awarded him $2,500. Moreover, this case was the first case in which the Nevada state courts recognized the doctrine of strict liability.

A defect in manufacture or marketing generally involves a specific product's not meeting the manufacturer's specifications. Proof of such a defect is generally provided in one or both of two ways: (1) Experts testify as to the type of flaw that could have caused the accident that led to the plaintiff's injury; (2) evidence of the circumstances surrounding the accident lead the jury to infer that the accident must have been caused by a defect in the product. Notice how in the following case the court makes an analogy to *res ipsa loquitur* when finding the existence of a defect caused by the defendant.

CASE 13-3

Welge v. Planters Lifesavers Company
Court of Appeals for the Seventh Circuit
17 F.3d 209 (1994)

Richard Welge loved to sprinkle peanuts on his ice cream sundaes. Karen Godfrey, with whom Welge boarded, bought a 24-ounce vacuum-sealed plastic-capped jar of Planters peanuts for him at a Kmart. To obtain a $2 rebate from the maker of Alka-Seltzer, Godfrey needed proof of her purchase of the jar of peanuts. So, using an Exacto knife, she removed the part of the label that contained the bar code. She then placed the jar on top of the refrigerator for Welge. About a week later, Welge removed the plastic seal from the jar, uncapped it, took some peanuts, replaced the cap, and returned the jar to the top of the refrigerator. A week after that, he took down the jar, removed the plastic cap, spilled some peanuts into his left hand to put on his sundae, and replaced the cap with his right hand—but as he pushed the cap down on the open jar, the jar shattered. His hand, continuing in its downward motion, was severely cut and, he claimed, became permanently impaired.

Welge filed products liability actions against Kmart, which sold the jar of peanuts to Godfrey; Planters, which manufactured the product (filled the glass jar with peanuts and sealed and capped it); and Brockway, which manufactured the glass jar and sold it to Planters. After pretrial discovery, the defendants moved for summary judgment. The district judge granted the motion on the ground that the plaintiff had failed to exclude possible causes of the accident other than a defect introduced during the manufacturing process. The plaintiff appealed.

Justice Posner

No doubt there are men strong enough to shatter a thick glass jar with one blow. But Welge's testimony stands uncontradicted that he used no more than the normal force that one exerts in snapping a plastic lid onto a jar. So the jar must have been defective. No expert testimony and no fancy doctrine are required for such a conclusion. A nondefective jar does not shatter when normal force is used to clamp its plastic lid on. The question is when the defect was introduced. It could have been at any time from the manufacture of the glass jar by Brockway (for no one suggests that the defect might have been caused by something in the raw materials out of which the jar was made) to moments before the accident. But testimony by Welge and Godfrey … excludes all reasonable possibility that the defect was introduced into the jar after Godfrey plucked it from a shelf in the KMart store. From the shelf she put it in her shopping cart. The checker at the check-out counter scanned the bar code without banging the jar. She then placed the jar in a plastic bag. Godfrey carried the bag to her car and put it on the floor. She drove directly home, without incident. After the bar-code portion of the label was removed, the jar sat on top of the refrigerator except for the two times Welge removed it to take peanuts out of it. Throughout this process it was not, so far as anyone knows, jostled, dropped, bumped, or otherwise subjected to stress beyond what is to be expected in the ordinary use of the product. Chicago is not Los Angeles; there were no earthquakes. Chicago is not Amityville either; no supernatural interventions are alleged. So the defect must have been introduced earlier, when the jar was in the hands of the defendants.

But, they argue, this overlooks two things. One is that Karen Godfrey took a knife to the jar. And no doubt one can weaken a glass jar with a knife. But nothing is more common or, we should have thought, more harmless than to use a knife or a razor blade to remove a label from a jar or bottle. People do this all the time with the price labels on bottles of wine. Even though mishandling or misuse, by the consumer or by anyone else (other than the defendant itself), is a defense … to a products liability suit … and even if, as we greatly doubt, such normal mutilation as occurred in this case could be thought a species of mishandling or misuse, a defendant cannot defend against a products liability suit on the basis of a misuse that he invited. The Alka-Seltzer promotion to which Karen Godfrey was responding when she removed a portion of the label of the jar of Planters peanuts was in the KMart store. It was there, obviously, with KMart's permission. By the promotion KMart invited its peanut customers to remove a part of the label on each peanut jar bought, in order to be able to furnish the maker of Alka-Seltzer with proof of purchase. If one just wants to efface a label one can usually do that by scraping it off with a fingernail, but to remove the label intact requires the use of a knife or a razor blade. Invited misuse is no defense to a products liability claim. Invited misuse is not misuse. …

Even so, the defendants point out, it is always possible that the jar was damaged while it was sitting unattended on the top of the refrigerator, in which event they are not responsible. Only if it had been securely under lock and key when not being used could the plaintiff and Karen Godfrey be certain that nothing happened to damage it after she brought it home. That is true—there are no metaphysical certainties—but it leads nowhere. Elves may have played ninepins with the jar of peanuts while Welge and Godfrey were sleeping; but elves could remove a jar of peanuts from a locked cupboard. The plaintiff in a products liability suit is not required to exclude every possibility, however fantastic or remote, that the defect which led to the accident was caused by someone other than one of the defendants. The doctrine of *res ipsa loquitur* teaches that an accident that is unlikely to occur unless the defendant was negligent is itself circumstantial evidence that the defendant was negligent. The doctrine is not strictly applicable to a products liability case because unlike an ordinary accident case the defendant in a products case has parted with possession and control of the harmful object before the accident occurs. … But the doctrine merely instantiates the broader principle, which is as applicable to a products case as to any other tort case, that an accident can itself be evidence of liability. … If it is the kind of accident that would not have occurred but for a defect in the product, and if it is reasonably plain that the defect was not introduced after the product was sold, the accident is evidence that the product was defective when sold. The second condition (as well as the first) has been established here, at least to a probability sufficient to defeat a motion for summary judgment. Normal people do not lock up their jars and cans lest something happen to damage these containers while no one is looking. The probability of such damage is too remote. It is not only too remote to make a rational person take measures to prevent it; it is too remote to defeat a products liability suit should a container prove dangerously defective.

Of course, unlikely as it may seem that the defect was introduced into the jar after Karen Godfrey bought it if the plaintiffs' testimony is believed, other evidence might make their testimony unworthy of belief—might even show, contrary to all the probabilities, that the knife or some mysterious night visitor caused the defect after all. The fragments of glass into which the jar shattered were preserved and were examined by experts for both sides. The experts agreed that the jar must have contained a defect but they could not find the fracture that had precipitated the shattering of the jar and they could not figure out when the defect that caused the fracture that caused the collapse of the jar had come into being. The defendants' experts could neither rule out, nor rule in, the possibility that the defect had been introduced at some stage of the manufacturing process. The plaintiff's expert noticed what he thought was a preexisting crack in one of the fragments, and he speculated that a similar crack might have caused the fracture that shattered the jar. This, the district judge ruled, was not enough.

But if the probability that the defect that caused the accident arose after Karen Godfrey bought the jar of Planters peanuts is very small—and on the present state of the record we are required to assume that it is—then the probability that the defect was introduced by one of the defendants is very high.

… The strict-liability element in modern products liability law comes precisely from the fact that a seller subject to that law is liable for defects in his product even if those defects were introduced, without the slightest fault of his own for failing to discover them, at some anterior stage of production. … So the fact that KMart sold a defective jar of peanuts to Karen Godfrey would be conclusive of KMart's liability, and since it is a large and solvent firm there would be no need for the plaintiff to look further for a tortfeasor. This point seems to have been more or less conceded by the defendants in the district court—the thrust of their defense was that the plaintiff had failed to show that the defect had been caused by any of them—though this leaves us mystified as to why the plaintiff bothered to name additional defendants.

… Evidence of KMart's care in handling peanut jars would be relevant only to whether the defect was introduced after sale; if it was introduced at any time before sale—if the jar was defective when KMart sold it—the source of the defect would be irrelevant to KMart's liability. In exactly the same way, Planters' liability would be unaffected by the fact, if it is a fact, that the defect was due to Brockway rather than to itself. To repeat an earlier and fundamental point, a seller who is subject to strict products liability is responsible for the consequences of selling a defective product even if the defect was introduced without any fault on his part by his supplier or by his supplier's supplier.

… Here we know to a virtual certainty (always assuming that the plaintiff's evidence is believed, which is a matter for the jury) that the accident was not due to mishandling after purchase but to a defect that had been introduced earlier.

Reversed and remanded in favor of Plaintiff, Welge.

When a plaintiff is seeking recovery based on a design defect, he or she is not impugning just one item, but an entire product line. If a product is held to be defectively designed in one case, a manufacturer or seller may recognize that this particular case may stimulate a huge number of additional lawsuits. Thus, defendants are very concerned about the outcome of these cases. Therefore, the availability of this type of action has a greater impact on encouraging manufacturers to produce safe products than does the availability of any other type of product liability action.

For example, hundreds of claims, ranging from property damage to personal injury and wrongful death, have been brought in federal and state courts against Firestone and Ford for Firestone's ATX, ATX II, and Wilderness AT tires. Plaintiffs argue that the tires have a design defect that causes the treads to prematurely separate, leading to tire blowouts. Firestone issued a recall for these tires in August 2000, but plaintiffs argue that the recall was not sufficient to warn customers about the tire defects. Furthermore, plaintiffs allege that Firestone had knowledge of the defects earlier but failed to disclose this knowledge. In an attempt to encourage efficiency, the federal cases have been consolidated to the Southern District Court in Indiana at least for the purposes of discovery.

Although all the states agree that manufacturers may not market defectively designed products, there is no uniform definition of a defective design. Two tests have evolved to determine whether a product is so defective as to be unreasonably dangerous. The first test, set out in the *Restatement (Second) of Torts*, is the consumer expectations test. This test asks the question: Did the product meet the standards that would be expected by a reasonable consumer? Such a test relies on the experiences and expectations of the ordinary consumer and, thus, is not answered by the use of expert testimony about the merits of the design.

The second is the feasible alternatives test, sometimes referred to as the risk-utility test. In applying this test, the court generally looks at seven factors:

1. The usefulness and desirability of the product—its utility to the user and to the public as a whole.

2. The safety aspects of the product—the likelihood that it will cause injury, and the probable seriousness of the injury.

3. The availability of a substitute product that would meet the same need and not be as unsafe.

4. The manufacturer's ability to eliminate the unsafe character of the product without impairing its usefulness or making it too expensive to maintain its utility.

5. The user's ability to avoid danger by the exercise of care in the use of the product.

6. The user's anticipated awareness of the dangers inherent in the product and their avoidability, because of general public knowledge of the obvious condition of the product or of the existence of suitable warnings or instructions.

7. The feasibility, on the part of the manufacturer, of spreading the loss by adjusting the price of the product or carrying liability insurance.[13]

The following case illustrates the difference between these two tests.

CASE 13-4

Sperry–New Holland, a Division of Sperry Corporation v. John Paul Prestage and Pam Prestage
Supreme Court of Mississippi
617 So.2d 248 (1993)

Plaintiff-appellees John and Pam Prestage sued defendant for damages arising out of an accident in which Mr. Prestage's foot and lower leg were caught in a combine manufactured by defendant-appellant Sperry–New Holland. Plaintiffs' first cause of action was based on the theory of strict product liability. A jury awarded John $1,425,000 for his injuries and Pam $218,750 for loss of consortium (the ability to engage in sexual relations with one's spouse). Defendant appealed.

Judge Prather
Sperry raises several issues. ...

Issue A: The court erred in applying a "risk-utility" analysis instead of a "consumer expectation" analysis.

This case requires a re-examination of Mississippi products liability law. Two competing theories of strict liability in tort can be extrapolated from our case law. While our older decisions applied a "consumer expectations" analysis in products cases, recent decisions have turned on an analysis under "risk-utility." In this case, Sperry claims that the trial court erred in applying a "risk-utility" theory of recovery, and not a "consumer expectations" theory. Prestage argues that while "consumer expectations" was the law at one time, recent cases have embraced "risk-utility." We today apply a "risk-utility" analysis and write to clarify our reasons for the adoption for that test.

The purpose of [strict] liability is to ensure that the costs of injuries resulting from defective products are

---

[13] J. Wade, "On the Nature of Strict Tort Liability for Products," *Mississippi Law Journal* 44 (1994).

borne by the manufacturers that put such products on the market rather than by the injured persons who are powerless to protect themselves.

State Stove explicitly holds that the extent of strict liability of a manufacturer for harm caused by its product is not that of an ensurer. However, strict liability does relieve the plaintiff of the onerous burden of proving negligence (i.e., fault). Fault is supplied as a matter of law.

Section 402A is still the law in Mississippi. How this Court defines the phrases "defective conditions" and "unreasonably dangerous" used in 402A dictates whether a "consumer expectations" analysis or a "risk-utility" analysis will prevail. Problems have arisen because our past decisions have been unclear and have been misinterpreted in some instances.

"Consumer Expectations" Analysis

The term "consumer expectations" comes from comment i to Section 402A. It states:

> The rule stated in this section applies only where the defective condition of the product makes it unreasonably dangerous to the user or consumer. … The article sold must be dangerous to an extent beyond that which would be contemplated by the ordinary consumer who purchases it, with the ordinary knowledge common to the community as to its characteristics.

In a "consumer expectations" analysis, "ordinarily the phrase 'defective condition' means that the article has something wrong with it, that it did not function as expected." Comment g of Section 402A defines "defective condition" as "a condition not contemplated by the ultimate consumer, which will be unreasonably dangerous to him." Thus, in a "consumer expectations" analysis, for a plaintiff to recover, the defect in a product which causes his injuries must not be one which the plaintiff, as an ordinary consumer, would know to be unreasonably dangerous to him. In other words, if the plaintiff, applying the knowledge of an ordinary consumer, sees a danger and can appreciate that danger, then he cannot recover for any injury resulting from that appreciated danger.

"Risk-Utility" Analysis

In a "risk-utility" analysis, a product is "unreasonably dangerous" if a reasonable person would conclude that the danger-in-fact, whether foreseeable or not, outweighs the utility of the product. Thus, even if a plaintiff appreciates the danger of a product, he can still recover for any injury resulting from the danger provided that the utility of the product is outweighed by the danger that the product creates. Under the "risk-utility" test, either the judge or the jury can balance the utility and danger-in-fact, or risk, of the product.

Around the country, the test generally employed to determine liability for products defects is the "risk-utility" test. In recent years, the "risk-utility" test has replaced the "consumer expectations" test in defective design cases. "Risk-utility" has become the trend in most federal and state jurisdictions. This Court has clearly moved away from a "consumer expectations" analysis and has moved towards "risk-utility." Consistent with the national trend, the two most recent decisions of this Court applied a "risk-utility" analysis to strict products liability.

A "risk-utility" analysis best protects both the manufacturer and the consumer. It does not create a duty on the manufacturer to create a completely safe product. Creating such a product is often impossible or prohibitively expensive. Instead, a manufacturer is charged with the duty to make its product reasonably safe, regardless of whether the plaintiff is aware of the product's dangerousness. This is not to say that a plaintiff is not responsible for his own actions. In balancing the utility of the product against the risk it creates, an ordinary person's ability to avoid the danger by exercising care is also weighed.

Having here reiterated this Court's adoption of a "risk-utility" analysis for product liability cases, we hold, necessarily, that the "patent danger" bar is no longer applicable in Mississippi. Under a "risk-utility" analysis, the "patent danger" rule does not apply. In "risk-utility," the openness and obviousness of a product's design is simply a factor to consider in determining whether a product is unreasonably dangerous.

There is sufficient evidence to show that Prestage tried his case under a "risk-utility" analysis. It is also clear from the record that the trial court understood "risk-utility" to be the law in Mississippi and applied that test correctly.

Affirmed in favor of Plaintiff, Prestage.

Impact of the Restatement (Third) of Torts. Even though elements of Section 402A of the *Restatement (Second) of Torts* have come to be adopted in all states, and it is generally considered to be the foundation of modern product liability law, there has been a lot of dissatisfaction over the law. That dissatisfaction resulted in what may be the biggest change in product liability law since the passage of Section 402A: the adoption on May 20, 1997 of the American Law Institute's *Restatement (Third) of Torts: Product Liability*, which is intended to replace Section 402A.

Critical Thinking About the Law

Case 13-4 provides another illustration of the importance of criteria selection in determining the outcome of a case. When Sperry–New Holland appealed the case, it did not focus on the facts or on the court's conclusion. Instead, the appeal focused on the test used by the court to decide the case. There was the presumption in the defendant's appeal that if the "consumer expectations" test had been used instead of the "risk-utility" analysis, the decision likely would have been different.

The questions that follow will help you to think more critically about the court's decision to use risk-utility analysis in Case 13-4.

1. To demonstrate your awareness of the guiding power of ethical norms, identify the primary ethical norm that would lead to the use of risk-utility analysis.

    Clue: To answer this question, you want to reread the court's discussion of each test.

2. In Case 13-4, the court selects risk-utility analysis as the test to apply in making its decision. What are its reasons for making this selection?

    Clue: You know the court's holding. Every group of sentences that answers the question "*Why* is that the holding?" provides a reason.

Under the *Restatement (Third)*, "one engaged in the business of selling or otherwise distributing products who sells or distributes a defective product is subject to liability for harm to persons or property caused by the defect." The seller's liability, however, is determined by a different standard, depending on which type of defect is involved: (1) a manufacturing defect, (2) a design defect, or (3) a defective warning.

When the defect is one in the manufacture, liability is strict. A manufacturing defect is said to exist when "the product departs from its intended design." The new rule imposes liability in such a case regardless of the care taken by the manufacturer.

The *Restatement (Third)* adopts a reasonableness standard for design defects. It states that "a product is defective in design when the foreseeable risks of the harm posed by the product could have been reduced or avoided by the adoption of a reasonable alternative design by the seller … and the omission of the alternative design renders the product not reasonably safe." In the comments, the *Restatement* lists a number of factors the court can use to determine whether a reasonable alternative design renders the product not reasonably safe. These factors include "the magnitude and probability of the foreseeable risks of harm, the instructions and warnings accompanying the product, and the nature and strength of consumer expectations regarding the product, including expectations arising from product portrayal and marketing … the relative advantages and disadvantages of the product as designed and as it alternatively could have been designed … the likely effects of the alternative design on product longevity maintenance, repair and esthetics, and the range of consumer choice among products." Thus, the *Restatement (Third)* has in effect shifted to a risk-utility test.

Regarding the third category, warning defects, the *Restatement (Third)* has likewise adopted a reasonableness standard. "A product is defective because of inadequate instructions or warnings when the foreseeable risks of harm posed by the product could have been reduced or avoided by the provision of reasonable instructions or warnings by the seller … and the omission of the warnings renders the product not reasonably safe."

Many lawyers think that the changes brought about by the newest *Restatement* will have a deep impact on product liability law well into the twenty-first century.

Defenses to a Strict Product Liability Action. *Product misuse*, discussed as a defense to a negligence-based action, is also available in a strict product liability case. *Assumption of the risk* is likewise raised as a defense in a strict liability action. However, controversy has arisen over whether the state-of-the-art defense should be allowed in cases in which the cause of action is based on strict liability. In most strict liability cases, courts have rejected the use of this defense, stating that the issue is not what the producers knew at the time the product was produced, but whether the product was defectively dangerous. In the 1984 case of *Elmore v. Owens Illinois, Inc.* a claim arose from the plaintiff's contracting asbestosis. The plaintiff's job required him to handle a product manufactured by the defendant that contained 15 percent asbestos. The Supreme Court of Missouri ruled that the state of the art of a product has no bearing on the outcome of a strict liability claim because the issue is the defective condition of the product, not the manufacturer's knowledge, negligence, or fault.

The refusal of most courts to allow the state-of-the-art defense in strict liability cases makes sense if we consider the social policy reasons for imposing strict liability. One of the reasons for imposing strict liability is that the manufacturers or producers are best able to spread the cost of the risk; this risk-spreading function does not change with the availability of scientific knowledge.

The argument against this position, however, is equally compelling to some. If the manufacturer has indeed done everything as safely and carefully as available technology allows, it seems unfair to impose liability on the defendant. After all, how else could he or she have manufactured the product?

LIABILITY TO BYSTANDERS

Sometimes the person injured by the defective product is not a purchaser, nor even an owner of the product. The question arises as to whether strict product liability can be used by someone other than the owner or user of the product. The following case provides the rationale of one court that chose to allow recovery by a bystander.

Linking Law & Business

Management

In your management class, you learned about total quality management (TQM), a process by which all members within an organization function to achieve goals associated with product quality. TQM places a strong emphasis on the importance of high-quality products for three reasons: (1) to promote a positive image for the organization; (2) to lower costs and increase market share; and (3) to decrease liability costs associated with defective products. By improving quality, an organization is less likely to manufacture potentially dangerous products. Thus, it is probable that the organization will be faced with fewer strict liability charges.

Source: S. Certo, *Modern Management* (Upper Saddle River, N.J.: Prentice Hall, 2000), pp. 504–505.

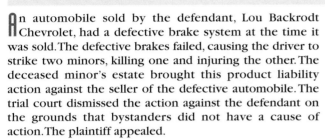

CASE 13-5

James A. Peterson, Administrator of the Estate of Maradean Peterson, et al. v. Lou Backrodt Chevrolet Company
Appellate Court of Illinois,
307 N.E. 2d 729 (1974)

An automobile sold by the defendant, Lou Backrodt Chevrolet, had a defective brake system at the time it was sold. The defective brakes failed, causing the driver to strike two minors, killing one and injuring the other. The deceased minor's estate brought this product liability action against the seller of the defective automobile. The trial court dismissed the action against the defendant on the grounds that bystanders did not have a cause of action. The plaintiff appealed.

Justice Guild

The question of whether a bystander can employ the doctrine of strict liability in a lawsuit has been thoroughly considered by reviewing courts and legal commentators. These authorities indicate that permitting the bystander to maintain an action based on strict tort liability is the more enlightened approach. This has been the result when this issue has been considered in light of Illinois law. The rationale behind this result is best expressed by this statement of the California Supreme Court in *Elmore v. American Motors Corp.*

If anything, bystanders should be entitled to greater protection than the consumer or user where injury to bystanders from the defect is reasonably foreseeable. Consumers and users, at least, have the opportunity to inspect for defects and to limit their purchases to articles manufactured by reputable manufacturers and sold by reputable retailers, whereas the bystander ordinarily has no such opportunities. In short, the bystander is in greater need of protection from defective products which are dangerous, and if any distinction should be made between bystanders and users, it should be made ... to extend greater liability in favor of the bystanders.

... the doctrine of strict liability in tort is available in an action for personal injuries by a bystander against the manufacturer and the retailer.

We agree with the California Supreme Court's cogent reasoning and hold that it is equally applicable when directed to those in the business of selling used cars.

Reversed and remanded in favor of Plaintiff, Peterson.

Critical Thinking About the Law

Some of the most important decisions made by the courts concern the scope of a given law. With their decisions, courts determine what classes, groups, and so on will or will not be protected by certain laws. Inevitably, courts must grapple with questions related to the four primary ethical norms in making these decisions.

Case 13-5, the court supported the applicability of strict tort liability to third parties, or "bystanders." The primary objective of the questions that follow is to enable you to recognize the role ethical norms played in the court's liberal interpretation of strict tort liability.

1. **What primary ethical norm dominates the court's reasoning in Case 13-5?**

   Clue: To answer this question, you want to reread the excerpted paragraph from the California Supreme Court decision.

2. **To demonstrate your ability to recognize the importance of judicial decisions in shaping law, identify the term used by the court that is potentially ambiguous and most likely will require further interpretation in future cases.**

   Clue: This ambiguous term is not an adjective as is the general rule. Its interpretation will decide who will or will not be protected.

MARKET SHARE LIABILITY

Throughout the chapter, the focus has been on product liability cases in which the plaintiff knows who produced the defective product. Sometimes, however, injuries resulting from defects in a products begin showing up 10 or 20 years after exposure to the product. By this time, even though injury can be traced to the defective product, the plaintiffs cannot trace the product to any particular manufacturer. Often a number of manufacturers produced the same product, and the plaintiff would have no idea whose product had been used. A plaintiff may have even used more than one manufacturer's product.

In this type of situation, the courts have had to balance the interests of the plaintiffs in recovering for injuries caused by defective products with the manufacturers' interests in not being held liable for injuries caused by a product they did not produce. The primary means used to resolve this dilemma today is the **market share theory**, created in 1980 by the California Supreme Court in the case of *Sindell v. Abbott Laboratories*.[14]

market share theory
A theory of recovery in liability cases according to which damages are apportioned among all the manufacturers of a product based on their market share at the time the plaintiff's cause of action arose.

In the *Sindell* case, the plaintiffs' mothers had all taken a drug known as diethylstilbestrol (DES) during pregnancies that had occurred before the drug was banned in 1971. Because the drug had been produced 20 years before the plaintiffs suffered any effects from the drug their mothers had taken, it was impossible to trace the defective drug back to each manufacturer who had produced the drug that had caused each individual's problems. In order to balance the competing interests of the victims, who had suffered injury from the drug, and the defendants, who did not want to be held liable for a drug they did not produce, the court allowed the plaintiffs to sue all of the manufacturers who had produced the drug at the time that the plaintiffs' mothers had used the drug. Then the judge apportioned liability among the defendant-manufacturers on the basis of the share of the market they had held at the time that the drug had been produced.

Since *Sindell*, a number of other courts have applied and refined the market share theory, primarily in drug cases. One trial court judge in a Pennsylvania DES case laid out the four factors that are generally necessary for applying market share liability: (1) All defendants are tortfeasors; (2) the allegedly harmful products are identical and share the same defective qualities; (3) plaintiff is unable through no fault of his or her own to identify which defendant caused his or her injury; and (4) the manufacturers of substantially all of the defective products in the relevant area and during the relevant time are named as defendants.[15]

Other courts have modified the market share approach of *Sindell*. For example, in *Collins v. Eli Lilly Company*,[16] a 1984 DES case, the court rejected the market share theory applied in *Sindell* and instead held that the plaintiff need sue only one maker of the allegedly defective drug. If the plaintiff can prove that the defendant manufactured a drug of the type taken by the plaintiff's mother at the time of the mother's pregnancy, that defendant can be held liable for all damages. However, the defendant may join other defendants and the jury may apportion liability among all defendants. The court stated that this approach could also be applied to cases that were factually similar to the DES cases.

---

[14] 607 P2d 924 (1980).

[15] *Erlich v. Abott Lab*, 5 Phila.249 (1981).

[16] 342 N.W. 2d 37 (Sic.1984).

Not all states have adopted the enterprise liability or market share theory. At least one case has questioned whether the theory could be applied to cases based on fraud or breach of warranty. In *Brown v. Abbott Laboratories*,[17] the court refused to extend the theories to such cases because they focused not on the product, but on the behavior of the manufacturer. Likewise, at least one California court has refused to allow the market share theory to be used to award punitive damages.[18]

And attempts to extend the theory to products other than drugs have not met with much success. For example, in 2003, the court refused to allow the city of Gary to rely on market share theory to prove damages in negligence action against handgun manufacturers, wholesalers, and dealers because of the wide mix of lawful and unlawful conditions as well as many potentially intervening acts by nonparties.[19]

SERVICE LIABILITY

Along with the growth in lawsuits for defective products, there has also been an increase in the number of lawsuits brought for defective services. These actions are generally brought when someone or someone's property is harmed as a result of an inadequately performed service.

Unlike in the product liability area, strict liability has rarely been applied to services. The few cases in which a strict liability standard has been applied involved cases in which the defendant provided both a good and a service, such as a restaurant owner's serving spoiled food.

malpractice suits Service liability suits brought against professionals, usually based on a theory of negligence, breach of contract or fraud.

Most service liability cases involve services provided by professionals, such as doctors, lawyers, engineers, real estate appraisers, and accountants. Actions against these professionals are generally referred to as **malpractice suits** and are usually based on a theory of negligence, breach of contract, or fraud. Malpractice actions against professionals are rising at an extremely rapid rate. For example, by the early 1970s, there had been only about 700 legal malpractice decisions reported; today that many legal malpractice cases occur each year.

The businessperson, however, is most likely to become involved in a malpractice action involving accountant malpractice. The next section, therefore, explores the liability of accountants.

ACCOUNTANTS' LIABILITY

One group that has seen increasing liability is accountants. Much of their potential liability has come from the securities laws. Accountants' liability under these laws is discussed in Chapter 22.

Accountants' liability for malpractice generally arises under actions for negligence, fraud, or breach of contract. Under a malpractice action based on negligence, the plaintiff must prove the same elements discussed in previous sections on negligence: duty, breach of duty, causation, and damages.

The accountant's duty is said to be that of using the degree of care, skill, judgment, and knowledge that can reasonably be expected of a member of the accounting profession. Two sets of standards have been developed by the

---

[17] 751 P.2d 470 (1995).

[18] *Magallanes v. E.R. Squibb & Sons*, 167 Cal. App. 878 (1985).

[19] *City of Gary ex rel. King v. Smith & Wesson Corp.*, 801 N.E.2d 1222, Prod.Liab.Rep. (CCH) P 16,862 (Ind. 2003).

American Institute of Certified Public Accountants, the professional accountants' association, that help determine reasonable care. A reasonable accountant should, at minimum, follow the Generally Accepted Accounting Principles (GAAPs) and the Generally Accepted Auditing Standards (GAASs). These two codes provide standards against which to measure an accountant's practices.

A major issue in accounting malpractice is the question of to whom the accountant's duty is owed. States are not in agreement about to whom an accountant can be held liable. Of course, the accountant is always liable to his or her clients. Third parties who have relied on the accountant's work present a problem, however.

There are three alternative rules used by states to define the parameters of the accountant's liability to third parties. The first, and oldest, rule is often referred to as the **Ultramares Doctrine**. Under this rule, the accountant is liable to only those in a privity-of-contract relationship. In other words, only the party who contracted for the accountant's work may sue. For example, if a client contacted an accountant to prepare a statement that the accountant knew was going to be used to secure a loan from the First Founding Bank, First Founding could not sue the accountant for malpractice in a state that followed the Ultramares Doctrine, because there was no contractual relationship between First Founding and the accountant.

Ultamares Doctrine Rule making accountants liable only to those in a privity-of-contract relationship with the accountant.

A somewhat more liberal rule is found in Section 552 of the *Restatement (Second) of Torts*. This rule holds that accountants will be liable to a limited class of intended users of the information. Thus, the accountant owes a duty to the client and any class of persons the accountant knows is going to be receiving a copy of his or her work. Under this rule, First Founding *could* recover in the preceding example.

The broadest rule applies in an extremely limited number of states. The smallest minority of states holds the accountant liable to any reasonably foreseeable user of the statement the accountant prepares. Exhibit 13-1 illustrates the states that adhere to each rule.

In the following case, the Supreme Court of Florida in 1990 decided to increase the extent of liability of accountants. In explaining its rationale for the extension, the court provided a good discussion of the alternative rules of liability.

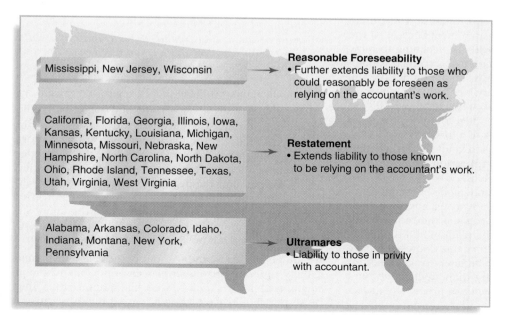

EXHIBIT 13-1

LIABILITY OF ACCOUNTANTS TO THIRD PARTIES

CASE 13-6

First Florida Bank v. Max Mitchell and Company
Supreme Court of Florida
558 So.2d 9 (1990)

Plaintiff First Florida Bank sued defendant accounting firm Max Mitchell for preparing inaccurate financial statements that plaintiff had relied on when it decided to make a loan to Max Mitchell's client. The statements were prepared by Max Mitchell and Company with knowledge that they were to be used by the plaintiff in its loan decision and were in fact delivered to the plaintiff bank by the defendant. The trial court decided in favor of the plaintiff bank, and the defendant accounting firm appealed.

Justice Grimes

When an accountant fails to exercise reasonable and ordinary care in preparing the financial statements of his clients and where that accountant personally delivers and presents the statements to a third party to induce that third party to loan to or invest in the clients, knowing that the statements will be relied upon by the third party in loaning to or investing in the client, is the accountant liable to the third party in negligence for the damages the third party suffers as a result of the accountant's failure to use reasonable and ordinary care in preparing the financial statements, despite a lack of privity between the accountant and the third party?

The seminal case on this subject is *Ultramares Corp. v. Touche*. In that case the court held that a lender which had relied upon inaccurate financial statements to its detriment had no cause of action against the public accounting firm which had prepared them because of the lack of privity between the parties. In declining to relax the requirement of privity, the court observed: "If liability for negligence exists, a thoughtless slip or blunder, the failure to detect a theft or forgery beneath the cover of deceptive entries, may expose accountants to a liability in an indeterminate amount for an indeterminate time to an indeterminate class. The hazards of a business conducted on these terms are so extreme as to kindle doubt whether a flaw may not exist in the implication of a duty that exposes one to these consequences."

The doctrine of privity has undergone substantial erosion in Florida. Indeed, in cases involving injuries caused by negligently manufactured products the requirement that there be privity between the plaintiff and the manufacturer has been abolished. Further, this Court held that a general contractor could sue an architect or engineer for damages proximately caused by their negligence on a building project despite the absence of privity of contract between the parties.

In the more than fifty years which have elapsed since *Ultramares*, the question of an accountant's liability for negligence where no privity exists has been addressed by many courts. There are now essentially four lines of authority with respect to this issue.

1. Except in cases of fraud, an accountant is only liable to one with whom he is in privity or near privity.

2. An accountant is liable to third parties in the absence of privity under the circumstances described in section 552, *Restatement (Second) of Torts* (1976), which reads in pertinent part:

   "§552. Information Negligently Supplied for the Guidance of Others (1) One who, in the course of his business, profession or employment, or in any other transaction in which he has a pecuniary interest, supplies false information for the guidance of others in their business transactions, is subject to liability for pecuniary loss caused to them by their justifiable reliance on the information, if he fails to exercise reasonable care or competence in obtaining or communicating the information. (2) Except as stated in Subsection (3), the liability stated in Subsection (1) is limited to loss suffered (a) by the person or one of a limited group of persons for whose benefit and guidance he intends to supply the information or know that the recipient intends to supply it: and (b) through reliance upon it in a transaction that he intends the information to influence or knows that the recipient so intends or in a substantially similar transaction."

3. An accountant is liable to all persons who might reasonably be foreseen as relying upon his work product.

4. An accountant's liability to third persons shall be determined by the balancing of various factors, among which are the extent to which the transaction was intended to affect the plaintiff, the foreseeability of harm to him, the degree of certainty that the plaintiff suffered injury, the closeness of the connection between the defendant's conduct and the injury suffered, the moral blame attached to the defendant's conduct, and the policy of preventing future harm.

We are persuaded by the wisdom of the rule which limits liability to those persons or classes of persons whom an accountant "knows" will rely on his opinion rather than those he "should have known" would do so because it takes into account the fact that an accountant controls neither his client's accounting records nor the distribution of his reports.

We conclude that the standard set forth in the *Restatement (Second) of Torts* Section 552 (1976) represents the soundest approach to accountants' liability for negligent misrepresentation. It constitutes a middle ground between the restrictive *Ultramares* approach advocated by defendants and the expansive "reasonably foreseeable" approach advanced by plaintiffs. It recognizes that liability should extend not only to those with whom the accountant is in privity or near privity, but also to those persons, or classes of persons, whom he knows and intends will rely on this opinion, or whom he knows his client intends will so rely. On the other hand, as the commentary makes clear, it prevents extension of liability in situations where the accountant "merely knows of the ever-present possibility of repetition to anyone, and the possibility of action in reliance upon (the audited financial statements), on the part of anyone to whom it may be repeated." As such it balances, more so than the other standards, the need to hold accountants to a standard that

accounts for their contemporary role in the financial world with the need to protect them from liability that unreasonably exceeds the bounds of their real undertaking.

There remains the need to apply this rule to the facts at hand. At the time Mitchell prepared the audits for C. M. Systems, it was unknown that they would be used to induce the reliance of First Florida Bank to approve a line of credit for C. M. Systems. Therefore, except for the unusual facts of this case, Mitchell could not be held liable to the bank for any negligence in preparing the audit. However, Mitchell actually negotiated the loan on behalf of his client. He personally delivered the financial statements to the bank with the knowledge that it would rely upon them in considering whether or not to make the loan. Under this unique set of facts, we believe that Mitchell vouched for the integrity of the audits and that his conduct in dealing with the bank sufficed to meet the requirements of the rule which we have adopted in this opinion.

Reversed and remanded in favor of Plaintiff, First Florida Bank.

Critical Thinking About the Law

Case 13-6 provides another illustration of the extent to which the criteria selected by the court shapes their judgment about the case. Because of our esteem for the court and the judicial system in general, we tend to believe that any set of criteria used to judge the facts and circumstances of a case are the criteria for judging that case. We presume that judging the case by those criteria yields the "right" judgment. Justice Grimes himself explicitly stated that there existed four different sets of criteria that have been used to judge such cases. He chose one.

Consequently, one project of the questions that follow is to prod you to think more deeply about the extent to which the standards (i.e., criteria) we use to judge the world influence that judgment, with the courtroom being no exception.

1. Understanding the issue at hand is a necessary condition for critically thinking about legal reasoning. What key fact makes the issue of Case 13-6 an issue at all?

   Clue: Under certain circumstances there would have been no question of the accountant's liability. Why is there a question of his liability in Case 13-6?

2. To ensure that you understand the importance of criteria selection for legal decisions, explain the likely outcome of Case 13-6 had the court adopted the criteria used in the *Ultramares* case.

   Clue: Read again the court's review of *Ultramares*.

The rule in this case has been used to extend liability to third parties adversely affected by the performance of other professionals. For example, in 1991, the case was cited to justify allowing a condominium association to sue an engineer who had been retained to inspect buildings and to make structural reports before an apartment building was converted into a condominium.[20] The

---

[20] *Bay Garden Manor Condominium Association v. James Marks*, 576 So. 2d 744 (1991).

case was also cited to allow a real estate appraiser to be sued by a bank that relied on an inaccurate appraisal of property.[21]

The potential of accountants being sued is not only being expanded by the slow demise of the Ultramares Doctrine, which extends the number of persons who can sue the accountant, but the activities for which they can be held liable is also expanding. In 1994, a jury in California handed down the first massive verdict against an accounting firm for its work as a litigation consultant in *Mattco Forge, Inc. v. Arthur Young.*[22] In 1986, Mattco filed suit against General Electric Company (G.E.) and hired Ernst & Young as litigation consultants to provide a damage analysis. The firm made numerous errors, including re-creating documents that existed before the lawsuit. When the re-creations were discovered, the case against G.E. was dismissed. Mattco then sued Ernst & Young for malpractice and fraud. The case was initially dismissed, but on appeal the Supreme Court of California held that accountants were "not immune for malpractice arising out of litigation support services." The case was then tried and resulted in the award of $14.2 million compensatory damages and $27.8 million in punitive damages. On appeal, the plaintiff's damages were reduced to out-of-pocket expenses because the plaintiffs had failed to prove an essential element of a malpractice claim: that had it not been for the malpractice of the defendants, the plaintiff would have won the case. It is only by proving this "case within a case" that the plaintiff in such a malpractice case can show damages. Thus, the appellate court clarified the standard for malpractice cases arising out of litigation support services.

GLOBAL DIMENSIONS OF PRODUCT LIABILITY LAW

Businesspersons are concerned with the transnational aspects of products liability law primarily in two situations: (1) when they sell an imported product that causes injury to a consumer in the United States and (2) when they manufacture and export a product that causes harm to a consumer in a foreign country. In both instances, the U.S. corporation may be subject to liability for the injury.

Liability for a defective product that injures a consumer may be imposed on everyone in the chain of distribution of the product from the retailer to the manufacturer. In about 80 percent of the cases, it is the manufacturer on whom plaintiffs tend to concentrate, because the manufacturer is usually responsible for the defect and has the greatest assets. If the manufacturer of a defective product is a company located in another country, a U.S. importer, wholesaler, distributor, or retailer may find herself or himself liable for the injuries caused by a defective imported product. When a manufacturer is located in a foreign country, the plaintiff often simply sues only the retailer and the wholesaler. Because they do business in the state where the consumer lives, the court can easily assert personal jurisdiction over them. The foreign corporation may sometimes argue successfully that the corporation does not have enough minimum contracts with the state to allow the assertion of jurisdiction over the foreign manufacturer under the state's long-arm statute.

---

[21] *First State Bank v. Albright and Associates of Ocala, Inc.*, 561 So. 2d 1326 (1990).
[22] 5 Cal. App 4th 39 (1992).

Even if the long-arm statute is satisfied, a potential problem arises in conjunction with service. Although the means of service acceptable in the United States are acceptable for serving corporations in most countries, the Hague Convention on the Service of Judicial and Extrajudicial Documents in Civil and Commercial Matters (adhered to by 28 countries, including most of the major trading partners of the United States) requires that the foreign defendant receive actual notice of the suit. This requirement is sometimes difficult to satisfy.

Still another consideration for the plaintiff is the collectability of the judgment. If the foreign defendant has no assets in the United States and refuses to pay, the plaintiff will be forced to ask the courts in the country where the manufacturer is located to execute a judgment against the defendant's assets there. With all of these potential problems resulting from an action against a foreign manufacturer, a plaintiff is very likely to simply sue those U.S. businesses in the chain of distribution. The prudent businessperson who sells foreign goods should be aware of this potential liability problem.

In the case of U.S. products sold abroad, U.S. manufacturers may be brought before the foreign courts. Since the late 1970s, European and other foreign countries have been adopting increasingly strict product liability rules, holding manufacturers, distributors, and retailers liable for injuries caused by defective products on theories similar to those used in the United States, such as breach of warranty, negligence, and strict liability.

Each country has its own set of rules, so the prudent businessperson will become familiar with the rules of the country to which he or she is exporting a product. New Zealand, for example, took a unique approach in its 1972 Accident Compensation Act. This law provides for almost automatic payment of compensation for pecuniary damages, such as medical expenses and lost wages, while excluding most claims for pain and suffering.[23] Another example of how foreign laws may vary is found in France, where the courts systematically refuse to enforce contract clauses that attempt to limit a manufacturer's liability to repairing or replacing defective products in cases of both personal and commercial loss.

Foreign importers, retailers, and wholesalers of goods manufactured in the United States are not at all reluctant to join U.S. manufacturers in lawsuits in order to distribute the cost of the judgment. Obtaining jurisdiction over U.S. manufacturers presents some difficulties for some foreign courts, but most countries are more permissive than the U.S. courts in their grounds for jurisdiction, so it is much easier for a foreign court to obtain jurisdiction over a U.S. manufacturer than it is for a U.S. court to obtain jurisdiction over a foreign manufacturer. U.S. courts generally enforce judgments rendered by foreign courts as long as the principles used to obtain jurisdiction over the person are reasonably similar to those accepted in the United States and the substantive law reasonably conforms to our sense of justice. Thus, it is extremely important that businesspersons remember that selling a product overseas does not mean freedom from product liability considerations. Product standards for goods sold overseas should be just as high as for goods sold domestically. In fact, extra precautions may need to be taken. For example, warning labels and instructions should always be printed in the languages spoken in the countries where the goods will be sold.

---

[23] G. Palmer, "Compensation for Personal Injury: A Requiem for the Common Law in New Zealand," *Journal of Compensation Law* 21 (1972), p. 1.

SUMMARY

Product liability law grew out of tort law and relies on basic tort theories. A product liability action can be based on negligence, breach of warranty, or strict product liability. The easiest of these to prove is strict product liability.

A product liability action may be brought by any party who is injured by a defective product, even if he or she did not purchase the product. An action based on strict product liability may even be brought by a bystander.

The defendant may be a retailer, distributor, or manufacturer. Sometimes, when the producer of the product cannot be clearly identified, as in the case of a drug, the theory of enterprise liability (market share theory) may be used to bring an action against all manufacturers of a product.

Service liability is analogous to product liability but is for defective services. Another difference between the two is that negligence is generally the only theory of liability available in a service liability case. Most service liability cases involve professional malpractice, such as accountant or medical malpractice.

Just because a U.S. corporation manufactures goods for sale overseas, the goods should not be less safe than those produced for American consumption. The manufacturer of a shoddy exported product may find himself or herself defending an action brought in a foreign court. Conversely, an importer in the United States should be especially careful inspecting the imported goods because a U.S. plaintiff may not want to sue the foreign producer, leaving the U.S. importer as the primary defendant.

REVIEW QUESTIONS

13-1 Explain what privity is and what impact it had on the development of product liability law.

13-2 Explain the elements one would have to prove to bring a successful product liability case based on negligence.

13-3 Explain the defenses one can raise in a product liability case based on negligence.

13-4 Explain the various types of warranties that provide the basis for product liability cases based on breach of warranty.

13-5 Explain the difference between the "foreign-natural" and consumer expectations tests.

13-6 Explain the defenses available in a breach-of-warranty case.

REVIEW PROBLEMS

13-7 Jack Clark was eating a chicken enchilada at Mexacoli Rose restaurant when he swallowed a chicken bone. The bone lodged in his throat and had to be removed in the emergency room of a local hospital. What is the primary factor that will determine whether Mr. Clark's product liability lawsuit is successful?

13-8 Five people died of carbon monoxide poisoning from a gas heater that had been improperly installed in a cabin by the owner, who had not extended the vent pipe far enough above the roofline. The instruction manual had stated that the pipe needed to be vented outside but did not specify how far outside the vent pipe needed to extend, other than having a drawing that showed it extending beyond the roofline. The manual also said, "Warning: to ensure compliance with local codes, have installed by a gas or utility inspector." Do the decedents' estates have a product liability action for failure to warn? Why or why not?

13-9 The plaintiff was injured when a fire extinguisher failed to work when it was needed to put out a fire. Could the defendant manufacturer of the fire extinguisher raise the defense of contributory negligence against the plaintiff if the plaintiff's negligence started the fire? Why or why not?

13-10 Mattie was injured when she lost control of the car she was driving because of a tire blowout. The tire was guaranteed by the manufacturer "against failure from blowouts." The guarantee also limited the manufacturer's liability to repair or replacement of any defective tire. Can Mattie sue under strict liability breach of warranty and recover damages for her injury? Why or why not?

13-11 Bob was waiting at the crosswalk for the light to turn green. As he stood there, a car that was stopped in the road next to him suddenly exploded. There had been a defect in the engine that had caused the explosion. Will Bob be able to bring a strict product liability action against the manufacturer of the engine?

13-12 National Bank was deciding whether to loan money to Pateo Corporation. It asked Pateo to provide a copy of the company's most recent audit. When doing the audit, the auditors, Hamble & Humphries, failed to follow up on evidence indicating that one of the firm's managing partners might be siphoning money out of the corporation's funds. Relying on the audit, the bank made the loan. Six months later Pateo went into bankruptcy, primarily because one partner had stolen funds from the corporation and then had fled the country. Can the bank bring an action against Hamble & Humphries? Why is your answer dependent on the state in which the case arose?

CASE PROBLEMS

13-13 Yong Cha Hong bought some take-out fried chicken from Roy Rogers Restaurant, owned by the Marriott Corporation. When she was eating one of the chicken wings she had purchased, she bit into something that she thought was a worm. The experience caused her extreme physical and emotional distress, and she sued the Marriott Corporation for breach of implied warranty of merchantability, seeking damages of $500,000. Marriott provided evidence of expert analysis that showed that the object at issue was not a worm or other parasite, but was probably either a chicken aorta or trachea, and argued for summary judgment on the grounds that there could be no recovery as a matter of law because the offending item was a part of the chicken and, therefore, not a foreign object. Discuss the outcome of Marriott's motion for summary judgment. *Yong Cha Hong v. Marriott Corp.,* 3 UCC Rep. Serv. 2d 83 (1987)

13-14 Faberge USA manufactured Aqua Net hair spray, which is sold in an aerosol can. The propellant contained in the hair spray, along with the alcohol, makes the liquid highly flammable. The can contains a warning label that reads, "Do not puncture" and "Do not use near fire or flame."

Fourteen-year-old Alison Nowak tried to use a newly purchased can of Aqua Net, but the spray valve would not work. She decided to open the can and empty its contents into another spray container. She decided to use a can opener to open the bottle. She was standing in the kitchen near a gas stove when she punctured the can. When liquid from the can rushed out, it was ignited by the pilot light of the stove, causing a flame that burned the girl over 20 percent of her body, causing her to be permanently disfigured.

She sued under a theory of strict liability, arguing that Faberge had failed to warn of the dangers of the flammability of the product. The jury found in favor of the plaintiff and awarded her $1.5 million, and Faberge appealed. How do you believe the appellate court would rule in this case? Why? *Nowak v. Faberge USA, Inc.,* 32 F.3d 755 (1994)

13-15 In 1994, Don Walter Kitchen Distributors installed new cabinets in the home of David and Corrine Bako. Mrs. Bako soon thereafter contacted an employee of Don Walter to provide a stain for the wood trim on the first floor to match the cabinets. The stain was provided to the Bakos by Don Walter, which ordered the stain through Crystal Cabinet Works. The stain came in unmarked cans. When Mrs. Bako subsequently contacted Don Walter for a slightly different color of stain for the floor, she was put directly in contact with a Crystal employee. Mrs. Bako ordered stain for the floor, which was again received without a label or any instructions.

After applying the stain the Bakos bought a polyurethane topcoat for the stain. After application of the topcoat, severe and permanent damage to their woodwork occurred. It turned out that the stain was lacquer-based and, therefore, incompatible with a polyurethane topcoat.

The Bakos sued Crystal and Don Walker for breach of express warranties, breach of implied warranty of fitness for a particular purpose, breach of implied warranty of merchantability, products liability, and negligence. The Bakos sought $100,000 in damages. The trial court ruled in favor of the Bakos but awarded them only $24,683.02. The Bakos appealed and Crystal cross-appealed. The court of appeals found in favor of the defendants on the breach of warranty claims. Can you explain what the court's reasoning might have been? *David Bako et al. v. Crystal Cabinet Works, Inc., et al.*, 2001 Ohio App. LEXIS 2120 (2001)

13-16 Douglas Martin had been drinking when he went to see his friend Marcel Nadeau. As the two were leaving to get more beer, Martin saw Nadeau's .38 Colt Mustang pistol. Nadeau removed the magazine and handed the gun to Martin. Nadeau turned away briefly, and when he turned back around, Martin had the gun in his hand, pointed toward his head. Nadeau heard the gun discharge; Martin died not long after. Valerie-Ann Bolduc, acting as administrator of Martin's estate, sued Colt's Manufacturing Company, Inc., for negligent design.

In Massachusetts, for a plaintiff to prevail in a negligent design case, he or she must show both that the defendant failed to exercise reasonable care to eliminate avoidable or foreseeable dangers to the user and that there is a functional alternative design that would reduce the product's risk. Bolduc alleged that neither Martin nor Nadeau knew that the gun would fire with the magazine removed. She also alleged that there is an alternative design that includes a feature to stop the gun from firing when the magazine is disconnected. Thus, it appears that Bolduc satisfied both prongs of the Massachusetts test. Yet the district court ruled that Bolduc could not prevail on the claim and dismissed the case. What are possible reasons the district court used to find that Colt had not negligently designed the product? *Valerie-Ann Bolduc v. Colt's Manufacturing Company, Inc.*, 968 F. Supp. 16 (1997)

13-17 Christopher Nadel was in the car with his father, Paul, and his grandmother, Evelyn, when they pulled into Burger King for breakfast. Christopher was seated in the center of the front seat, between Paul and Evelyn; two of Christopher's classmates were in the back seat. The group ordered several breakfast sandwiches at the drive-thru as well as two cups of coffee. Evelyn was burned on her right leg by the coffee when she tasted it to see how hot it was. As she was placing the coffee back in the carrier, Paul pulled out onto the street and Christopher began to scream that he was being burned. Either one or both cups of coffee had spilled onto Christopher's foot and Christopher was subsequently treated for second-degree burns to his right foot.

The Nadels, on behalf of Christopher, sued the owner of the particular Burger King franchise that they stopped at and Burger King Corporation itself, alleging, among other claims, product liability for a defectively designed product and for failure to warn of the dangers of handling a liquid served as hot as their coffee.

Both the owner of the Burger King and Burger King Corporation moved for summary judgment and the trial court granted both motions. Burger King Corporation argued that it was immune to the product liability claims because it was not a manufacturer, seller, or supplier of the coffee. The Nadels appealed. Do you think the court of appeals agreed that Burger King Corporation was immune to the product liability claims? Why or why not? *Christopher Nadel et al. v. Burger King Corporation and Emil, Inc.*, 119 Ohio App. 3d 578, 695 N.E.2d 1185 (1997)

13-18 June Sutowksi is the daughter of a woman who took diethylstilbestrol (DES) while pregnant. Sutowski sued Eli Lilly and several other manufacturers of DES for her in utero exposure to DES that caused harm to her reproductive system. Sutowski sued in federal court under market share theory but the case was removed to the Supreme Court of Ohio because it was unclear what Ohio's position was with regard to the market share liability theory. In one previous case, the Sixth Circuit Court stated that Ohio would not adopt the market share theory of liability in DES cases. In a case decided just before the Sixth Circuit case, the Ohio Supreme Court held that suits could survive the enactment of the Ohio Products Liability Act if the statute did not specifically forbid the suits. The Ohio Products Liability Act stated that manufacturers would not be held liable under enterprise liability in any case or held liable under alternative liability unless all tortfeasors were named. The majority noted that market share theory had not gained wide acceptance outside of California and that this case would enter Ohio under the many states that refused to recognize market share liability. Two lively dissents were written. The dissenters found for the plaintiff using the exact cases the majority used to find for the defendant. What critical thinking questions might the dissenters have applied to the majority's decision to find in favor of the plaintiff? *Sutowski v. Eli Lilly & Company et al.*, 82 Ohio St. 3d 347, 696 N.E.2d 187 (1998)

ASSIGNMENT ON THE INTERNET

At the Legacy Tobacco Documents Library, legacy.library.ucsf.edu, you can find internal tobacco documents from the files of top tobacco companies. Within this site, at www.library.ucsf.edu/tobacco/litigation/summary.html, you can find a summary chart of tobacco lawsuits by state. Select one of the states to view the complaints filed in the case. Read the complaint to find out what claims (i.e., negligence, strict liability, breach of warranty) the plaintiff is bringing.

Find out what type of relief the plaintiff is seeking (i.e., damages, injunction, etc).

Earlier in this chapter, we discussed the failure to warn claims against the fast-food industry, and we noted that Congress is considering banning all obesity-related claims against fast-food restaurants. Write a paper in which you compare the fast-food litigation to the tobacco litigation.

 ## ON THE INTERNET

www.cpsc.gov This site is the home of the U.S. Consumer Product Safety Commission.
www.productslaw.com This site provides links to a wide variety of sites containing product liability information.
www.law.cornell.edu/topics/products_liability.html This site contains a brief overview of product liability and provides several links to liability law as well as recent product liability court cases.
news.findlaw.com/legalnews/us/pl Visit this site for the latest product liability news stories.
hcch.e-vision.nl/index_en.php This site contains information from the Hague Conference on Private International Law. Here you will also find links to additional sources on international product liability law.
www.briefreporter.com/productsliability.htm This site contains summaries of recent product liability cases.
europa.eu.int/comm/consumers/cons_safe/prod_safe/defect_prod/index_en.htm The Web site of the European Union's Consumer Affairs contains information about product liability within the European Union.

14

LAW OF PROPERTY: REAL, PERSONAL, AND INTELLECTUAL

- REAL PROPERTY
- INTERESTS IN REAL PROPERTY
- VOLUNTARY TRANSFER OF REAL PROPERTY
- INVOLUNTARY TRANSFER OF REAL PROPERTY
- RESTRICTIONS ON LAND USE
- PERSONAL PROPERTY
- INTELLECTUAL PROPERTY
- GLOBAL DIMENSIONS OF PROPERTY LAW

When people hear the word *property*, they generally think of physical objects: land, houses, cars. However, this pattern of thought reflects an incomplete understanding of the concept of property. **Property** is a bundle of rights and interests in relation to other persons with reference to a tangible or intangible object (Exhibit 14-1). The essence of the concept of property is that the state provides the mechanism to allow the owner to exclude other people.

By virtue of this right, persons with great amounts of property have an especially significant amount of power. Because possessing property facilitates the acquisition of even more property, the identification of those who possess a disproportionate amount of property rights provides insight into the dynamics of influence and authority in our society.

property A bundle of rights, in relation to others, to possess, use, and dispose of a tangible or intangible object.

Critical Thinking About the Law

Property is directly related to the power that one has in society. Some individuals argue that the government should offer more protection for property owners. Others argue that in a fair country, citizens would have similar amounts of property because property provides a basis for so many other decisions. Property rights actually exist as a matter of degree. A property owner has some rights, but he or she must tolerate some restrictions on those rights. The following questions will help you think critically about the link between property rights and power.

1. If a group of politicians passed a law to increase protection of property rights, what ethical norm probably led to this legislation?

   Clue: Review the list of ethical norms in Chapter 1. Which ethical norm seems most likely to cause increased protection of property?

2. If a group of radical politicians proposed a law that reduced personal property protection and redistributed some property rights to the poor, what ethical norm was probably behind this action?

   Clue: Again, review the list of ethical norms.

3. According to Bill Gates's Web site, Bill Gates has a net worth that makes him richer than all but 48 countries. His development of intellectual property has created his considerable wealth. How do you think he would react to Questions 1 and 2?

   Clue: Which law do you think he would be most willing to support? Why?

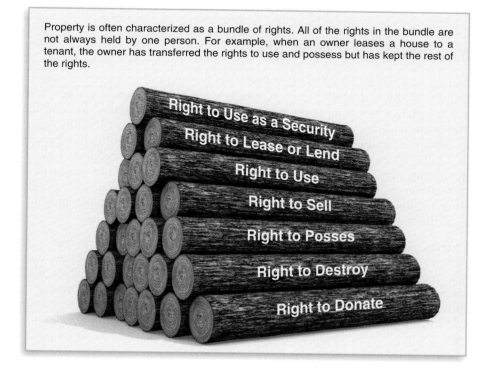

Property is often characterized as a bundle of rights. All of the rights in the bundle are not always held by one person. For example, when an owner leases a house to a tenant, the owner has transferred the rights to use and possess but has kept the rest of the rights.

Right to Use as a Security
Right to Lease or Lend
Right to Use
Right to Sell
Right to Posses
Right to Destroy
Right to Donate

EXHIBIT 14-1

PROPERTY AS A BUNDLE OF RIGHTS

Property rights are not the same in every society, nor are they static. In reading this chapter, think about how property rights could be different and what impact that difference would have both on the legal environment of business and on society as a whole.

Because different types of property give their owners different rights, and because different bodies of law govern different types of property, we will discuss the three primary types of property in separate sections. Initially, this chapter focuses on *real property*, that is, land and anything permanently attached to it. The next section discusses *personal property*, both tangible (capable of being detected by the senses) and intangible (incapable of being detected by the senses). The third section shifts to *intellectual property*, that is, things created primarily by mental rather than physical processes.

REAL PROPERTY

real property Land and everything permanently attached to it.

Real property is land and everything permanently attached to it. One's rights to a property depend on the type of interest that one has in that property. These types of interests are described in detail in the next section. Once one has an interest, the law provides the means to convey or transfer that interest.

Although most conveyances are voluntary, the government may require involuntary conveyances to benefit the public and may place restrictions on the use of property to protect the public health, safety, and welfare.

DEFINITION OF REAL PROPERTY

Although the definition of *real property* in the previous paragraph may have sounded straightforward, many disputes have arisen over whether certain items are real or personal property. The law says that an item that is *attached* to the land is a part of the realty. What does *attached* mean? Usually, an item is considered attached if its removal would cause damage to the property. Thus, built-in appliances are generally a part of the real property, whereas freestanding ones are not. Sometimes, however, an item is not really permanently affixed to the land, but its functioning is said to be essential to the functioning of the structure. In such cases, the courts usually find the item to be part of the real property.

fixture An item that is initially a piece of personal property but is later attached permanently to the realty and is treated as part of the realty.

Fixtures. An item that is initially a piece of personal property, but is later attached permanently to the realty, is known as a **fixture** and is treated as part of the realty. Thus, if a person rents another's property and installs a built-in microwave oven, the oven is a fixture and becomes part of the realty. The tenant may not remove the oven when he or she leaves. There are two exceptions to this rule.

First, the parties may agree that specific fixtures will be treated as personal property. To be enforceable, such an agreement must be in writing.

The second exception is for *trade fixtures*. A trade fixture is a piece of personal property that is affixed to realty in conjunction with the lease of a property for a business. When an entrepreneur opens an ice cream parlor in a leased building, the freezers he or she installs are trade fixtures. These are treated as personal property because of a presumption that neither party intends such fixtures to become a permanent part of the realty. The businessperson will need the freezers at any new location, and new business tenants will have different needs.

However, in Arizona, a state appellate court found that improvements made by companies to land leased from the city were the property of the city. In this instance, two air service businesses, Air Commerce Center, LLP, and Airport Properties, held interest in public land at Scottsdale Municipal Airport. Although the air-service-related improvements that Airport Properties built would appear to be trade fixtures, the court found that the companies held only a possessory interest in the improvements, which were determined to be the property of the city.[1]

EXTENT OF OWNERSHIP

Any concept of land obviously includes the surface of the land, but legally, more is included. The landowner is entitled to the airspace above the land, extending to the atmosphere. Ownership of land also includes **water rights**, the legal ability to use water flowing across or underneath one's property.

Water rights, however, are somewhat restricted, in that one cannot divert water flowing across the property in such a manner as to deprive landowners downstream of the use of water from the stream.

Ownership of land usually also encompasses the land below the surface, including **mineral rights**, the legal ability to dig or mine the minerals from the earth. However, these mineral rights may be sold or given to someone other than the person who owns the surface of the land.

> **water rights** The legal ability to use water flowing across or underneath one's property.

> **mineral rights** The legal ability to dig or mine the minerals from the earth below the surface of one's land.

INTERESTS IN REAL PROPERTY

Not all interests in land are permanent. The duration of one's ownership depends on the type of estate one is said to hold. The estate that one has also determines what powers one has in regard to using the land. Exhibit 14-2 briefly summarizes these interests, which are described in detail in the following sections.

FEE SIMPLE ABSOLUTE

The most complete estate is the **fee simple absolute**. When most people talk about owning property, they usually have in mind a fee simple absolute. If one has a fee simple absolute, one has all rights to own and possess that land. When the owner of a fee simple absolute interest dies, the interest passes to the owner's heirs.

> **fee simple absolute** The right to own and possess the land against all others, without conditions.

---

[1] *Airport Properties v. Maricopa County, Arizona*, 195 Ariz. 89; 985 P.2d 574 (1999).

EXHIBIT 14-2

ESTATES IN LAND. NOTICE THAT THE RIGHTS OF THE HOLDER DECREASE AS YOU MOVE UP THE PYRAMID.

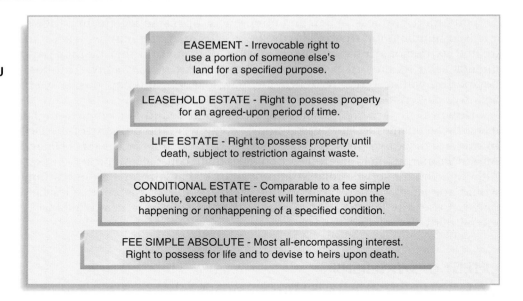

EASEMENT - Irrevocable right to use a portion of someone else's land for a specified purpose.

LEASEHOLD ESTATE - Right to possess property for an agreed-upon period of time.

LIFE ESTATE - Right to possess property until death, subject to restriction against waste.

CONDITIONAL ESTATE - Comparable to a fee simple absolute, except that interest will terminate upon the happening or nonhappening of a specified condition.

FEE SIMPLE ABSOLUTE - Most all-encompassing interest. Right to possess for life and to devise to heirs upon death.

CONDITIONAL ESTATE

conditional estate The right to own and possess the land, subject to a condition whose happening (or nonhappening) will terminate the estate.

The interest of a **conditional estate** is the same as that of a fee simple absolute, except that it is subject to a condition, the happening or nonhappening of which will terminate the interest. For example, Rose may own a farm subject to the condition that Rose never grow cotton. Once Rose grows cotton, the condition has occurred, and the land either reverts to the former owner or is transferred in accordance with the terms of the deed (the instrument that is used to convey real property). Conversely, a conditional estate could be set up so that the holder would own the farm as long as the primary crop planted every year was corn. Failure to meet the condition would terminate the estate.

LIFE ESTATE

life estate The right to own and possess the land until one dies.

A **life estate** is the right to own and possess property until one dies. The use of a life estate may be more restricted than that of a fee simple absolute. The party who will take possession of the property upon the death of the holder of the life estate has an interest in making sure that the value of the property does not substantially decline as a result of neglect or abuse by the holder of the life estate. Thus, the holder is not allowed to waste the property. The holder cannot use the property in such a way as to destroy its value to future holders. Nor can the life tenant neglect to make necessary repairs to the property to prevent its destruction.

The following case provides an illustration of the type of behavior that the courts have found to constitute waste.

CASE 14-1

Sauls v. Crosby
District Court of Appeals of Florida,
258 So. 2d 326 (1972)

Appellant and defendant Annie Sauls conveyed a future interest in certain property to plaintiff-appellees Dan and Bertha Crosby, reserving for herself a life estate in the property. When she attempted to cut timber on the property to sell, the holders of the future interest sought to enjoin her from doing so. The district court held that defendant Sauls was not entitled to cut timber and keep the proceeds for herself. Defendant Sauls appealed.

Judge Rawls

On the 9th day of October 1968, appellant conveyed to appellees certain lands situated in Hamilton County, Florida, with the following reservation set forth in said conveyance: "The Grantor herein, reserves a life estate in said property." By this appeal appellant now contends that the trial court erred in denying her, as a life tenant, the right to cut merchantable timber and enjoy the proceeds.

The English common law, which was transplanted on this continent, holds that it is waste for an ordinary life tenant to cut timber upon his estate when the sole purpose is to clear the woodlands. American courts today as a general rule recognize that an ordinary life tenant may cut timber and not be liable for waste if he uses the timber for fuel; for repairing fences and buildings on the estate; for fitting the land for cultivation; or for use as pasture if the inheritance is not damaged and the acts are conformable to good husbandry; and for thinning or other purposes which are necessary for the enjoyment of the estate and are in conformity with good husbandry.

In this jurisdiction a tenant for life or a person vested with an ordinary life estate is entitled to the use and enjoyment of his estate during its existence. The only restriction on the life tenant's use and enjoyment is that he not permanently diminish or change the value of the future estate of the remainderman. This limitation places on the "ordinary life tenant" the responsibility for all waste of whatever character.

An instrument creating a life tenancy may absolve the tenant of responsibility for waste by stating that the life tenant has the power to consume or that the life tenant is without impeachment for waste. Thus, there is a sharp distinction in the rights of an ordinary life tenant or life tenant without impeachment for waste or life tenant who has the power to consume. An ordinary life tenant has no right to cut the timber from an estate for purely commercial reasons and to do so is tortious conduct for which the remainderman may sue immediately.

In the case before us, the trial court was concerned with the rights of an ordinary life tenant and correctly concluded that appellant "does not have the right to cut merchantable timber from the land involved in this suit unless the proceeds of such cutting and sale are held in trust for the use and benefit of the remaindermen. ..."

Affirmed in favor of Plaintiff, Crosby.

Critical Thinking About the Law

A judge's reasoning explains the conditions under which certain actions are either legal or illegal. These conditions reveal the extent to which a court's decision depends on not only the existence of a certain set of facts but also the court's earlier determinations about the appropriate structure of those conditions.

Though brief, the court's decision in Case 14-1 is loaded with contingencies or limits to the boundaries of the decision. The following questions will help you both to identify and to evaluate those contingencies.

1. To ensure that you are aware of the contingent nature of the court's decision, identify all of the conditions listed by the court in Case 14-1 that would have made the defendant's actions legally acceptable.

   Clue: Go back through the court's reasoning and pinpoint when it is acceptable for an ordinary life tenant to cut timber.

2. As you now know from performing the task assigned in Question 1, the court provides a condition under which Sauls could have cut timber for commercial purposes. What ethical norm is implicit in this condition?

   Clue: Think about what a person who objects to the plaintiff's being allowed to keep the money would say. Would such a person say that this allowance is unjust, inefficient, a detriment to security, or a violation of liberty?

future interest The present right to possess and own the land in the future.

Future Interest. A person's present right to possession and ownership of land in the future is a **future interest** and usually exists in conjunction with a life estate or a conditional estate. For example, Sam owns a life estate in Blueberry Farm, and, on Sam's death, fee simple absolute ownership of the land will pass to Jane. Jane has a future interest in Blueberry Farm. As a result of her interest, she may sue Sam to enjoin him from engaging in waste of the property.

LEASEHOLD ESTATES

leasehold The right to possess property for an agreed-upon period of time stated in a lease.

lease The contract that transfers possessory interest in a property from the owner (lessor) to the tenant (lessee).

A **leasehold** is not an ownership interest. It is a *possessory* interest. One who has a leasehold is entitled to exclude all others, including the property owner under most circumstances, for the period of the lease and is entitled to use the property for any legal purpose that is not destructive of other occupiers' rights or prohibited by the terms of the lease. The **lease** is the contract that transfers the possessory interest. It generally specifies the property to be leased, the amount of the rent payments and when they are due, the duration of the leasehold, and any special duties or rights of either party. It is signed by both parties. The owner of the property is the lessor, or landlord. The holder of the lease is the lessee, or tenant.

Although the rights and obligations of the landlord and the tenant may be altered by the lease, some states have statutes requiring landlords to keep the premises in good repair and allowing tenants to withhold their rent if the landlord fails to do so. The landlord may enter the property only in an emergency, with permission of the tenant to make repairs, or with notice to the tenant near the end of the leasehold to show the property to a potential tenant. If the tenant fails to make the agreed-upon rental payments, the landlord may bring an action to evict the tenant.

Unless prohibited by the lease, a tenant may move out of the property and sublease it to another party. The initial tenant, however, still remains liable to the landlord for payment of rent due for the entire term of the lease.

EASEMENTS

easement An irrevocable right to use some portion of another's land for a specific purpose.

An **easement** is an irrevocable right to use some portion of another's land for a specific purpose. The party holding the easement does not own the land in question but has only the right to use it. Easements generally arise in one of three ways: express agreement, prescription, or necessity.

An *easement by express agreement* arises when the landowner expressly agrees to allow the holder of the easement to use the land in question for the agreed-upon purpose. For example, a utility company may have an easement to run power lines across one's property. The easement should be described on the deed to the property or recorded in the county office that keeps property records to protect the holder of the easement when the property is sold.

An *easement by prescription* arises under state law. When one openly uses a portion of another's property for a statutory period of time, an easement arises. In many states, the time period is 25 years.

An *easement by necessity* arises when a piece of property is divided and, as a result, one portion is landlocked. The owner of the landlocked portion has an easement to cross the other parcel for purposes of entrance to and exit from the land.

LICENSE

A **license** is a temporary, revocable right to be on someone else's property. When one opens a business, the public is given a license to enter the property to purchase the good or services provided by the business.

CO-OWNERSHIP

We have been referring to the holders of interest in land in the singular. Ownership of land may also be held by multiple persons, as well as by business organizations. Whenever there is ownership by multiple parties, it is important to know what type of ownership exists because different forms give different rights to the owners.

The three types of **co-ownership** are tenancy in common, joint tenancy, and tenancy by the entirety. Regardless of which type of tenancy exists, all tenants have the equal right to occupy all the property. Their other interests are described here and are summarized in Table 14-1.

Tenancy in common occurs most frequently. Owners may own unequal shares of the property, may sell their interest without consent of the other owners, and may have their interest attached by a creditor. Upon the death of the tenant in common, his or her heirs receive the property interest.

Under **joint tenancy**, all are co-owners of equal shares and may sell their shares without the consent of other owners. Their interest can be attached by creditors. Upon the death of a joint tenant, his or her interest is divided equally among the remaining joint owners.

Tenancy by the entirety exists only when co-owners are a married couple. One cannot sell his or her interest without the consent of the other, and creditors of only one cannot attach the property. Upon the death of one, full ownership of the property passes to the other. Upon divorce, tenancy by the entirety automatically becomes tenancy in common.

CONDOMINIUMS AND COOPERATIVES

Two forms of co-ownership that have become increasingly popular over the past 20 years are condominiums and cooperatives.

Condominiums. In a condominium ownership interest, the owner acquires title to a "unit" within a building, along with an undivided interest in the land, buildings, and improvements of the "common areas" of the development. When

license A temporary, revocable right to be on someone else's property.

co-ownership Ownership of land by multiple persons or business organizations; all tenants have an equal right to occupy all of the property.

tenancy in common Form of co-ownership of real property in which owners may have equal or unequal shares of the property, may sell their shares without the consent of the other owners, and may have their interest attached by creditors.

joint tenancy Form of co-ownership of real property in which all owners have equal shares in the property, may sell their shares without the consent of the other owners, and may have their interest attached by creditors.

tenancy by the entirety Form of co-ownership of real property, allowed only to married couples, in which one owner cannot sell without the consent of the other and the creditors of only one owner cannot attach the property.

TABLE 14-1

JOINT OWNERSHIP

Type	Division of Ownership	Rights of Owners' Creditors	Ownership of Property upon Death
Tenancy in common	Equal or unequal shares	Can attach interest	Transferred to heirs
Joint tenancy	Equal shares	Can attach interest	Divided among other joint tenants
Tenancy by the entirety	Equal shares	Cannot attach interest	Goes to surviving spouse

the condominium is developed, a Declaration of Covenants and Restrictions (called CC&Rs) is filed. This document contains the architectural and use restrictions for the condominium development, assessments, and instructions for forming the condominium association that will manage the condominium. The association has the power, as provided in the CC&Rs, to levy assessments against the unit owners in order to manage, maintain, insure, repair, and replace the common areas. The association likewise has the authority to fine unit owners who do not comply with the CC&Rs. The following case illustrates the type of conflict that often arises out of this form of ownership.

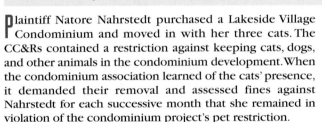

CASE 14-2

Natore A. Nahrstedt v. Lakeside Village Condominium Association, Inc. et al., and Respondents
Supreme Court of California,
8 Cal 4th 361, 878 P.2d 1275 (1994)

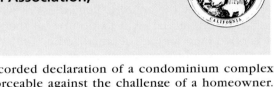

Plaintiff Natore Nahrstedt purchased a Lakeside Village Condominium and moved in with her three cats. The CC&Rs contained a restriction against keeping cats, dogs, and other animals in the condominium development. When the condominium association learned of the cats' presence, it demanded their removal and assessed fines against Nahrstedt for each successive month that she remained in violation of the condominium project's pet restriction.

Nahrstedt then brought a lawsuit against the association, its officers, and two of its employees, asking the trial court to invalidate the assessments, to enjoin future assessments, to award damages for violation of her privacy when the association "peered" into her condominium unit, and to declare the pet restriction "unreasonable" as applied to indoor cats (such as hers) that are not allowed free run of the project's common areas. She asserted that the restriction was "unreasonable" as applied to her because she kept her three cats indoors and because her cats were "noiseless" and "created no nuisance." She also claimed that she was unaware of the restriction when she moved in.

The association counterclaimed for enforcement of fines that it had imposed. Agreeing with the premise underlying the owner's complaint, the court of appeals concluded that the association could enforce the restriction only upon proof that plaintiff's cats would be likely to interfere with the right of other homeowners "to the peaceful and quiet enjoyment of their property" and enjoined the enforcement of the restriction. However, the court denied her other causes of action. The plaintiff then appealed to the state supreme court.

Justice Kennard

[T]he issue before us is not whether in the abstract pets can have a beneficial effect on humans. Rather, the narrow issue here is whether a pet restriction that is contained in the recorded declaration of a condominium complex is enforceable against the challenge of a homeowner. The Legislature has required that courts enforce the covenants, conditions, and restrictions contained in the recorded declaration of a common interest development "unless unreasonable."

Because a stable and predictable living environment is crucial to the success of condominiums and other common interest residential developments, and because recorded use restrictions are a primary means of ensuring this stability and predictability, the Legislature has afforded such restrictions a presumption of validity and has required of challengers that they demonstrate the restriction's "unreasonableness" by the deferential standard applicable to equitable servitudes.

Under this standard established by the Legislature, enforcement of a restriction does not depend upon the conduct of a particular condominium owner. Rather, the restriction must be uniformly enforced in the condominium development to which it was intended to apply unless the plaintiff owner can show that the burdens it imposes on affected properties so substantially outweigh the benefits of the restriction that it should not be enforced against any owner.

Restrictions on property use are not the only characteristic of common interest ownership. Ordinarily, such ownership also entails mandatory membership in an owners' association, which, through an elected board of directors, is empowered to enforce any use restrictions contained in the project's declaration or master deed and to enact new rules governing the use and occupancy of property within the project.

… [O]wners' associations "can be a powerful force for good or for ill" in their members' lives. Therefore, anyone who buys a unit in a common interest development with knowledge of its owners' associations' discretionary power accepts "the risk that the power may be used in a way that benefits the commonality but harms the individual." Generally, courts will uphold decisions made by the governing board of an owners' association so long as they represent good faith efforts to further the purposes of the common interest development, are consistent with the development's governing documents, and comply with public policy. Thus, subordination of individual property rights to the collective judgment of the owners' association together with restrictions on the use of real property comprise the chief attributes of owning property in a common interest development.

Of course, when an association determines that a unit owner has violated a use restriction, the association must do so in good faith, not in an arbitrary or capricious manner, and its enforcement procedures must be fair and applied uniformly, in reliance on the CC&R's.

As we have explained, when, as here, a restriction is contained in the declaration of the common interest development and is recorded with the county recorder, the restriction is presumed to be reasonable and will be enforced uniformly against all residents of the common interest development unless the restriction is arbitrary, imposes burdens on the use of lands it affects that substantially outweigh the restriction's benefits to the development's residents, or violates a fundamental public policy.

We conclude, as a matter of law, that the recorded pet restriction of the Lakeside Village condominium development prohibiting cats or dogs but allowing some other pets is not arbitrary, but is rationally related to health, sanitation, and noise concerns legitimately held by residents of a high-density condominium project such as Lakeside Village, which includes 530 units in 12 separate 3-story buildings. Nahrstedt's complaint alleges no facts that could possibly support a finding that the burden of the restriction on the affected property is so disproportionate to its benefit that the restriction is unreasonable and should not be enforced. Also, the complaint's allegations center on Nahrstedt and her cats (that she keeps them inside her condominium unit and that they do not bother her neighbors), without any reference to the effect on the condominium development as a whole, thus rendering the allegations legally insufficient to overcome section 1354's presumption of the restriction's validity.

[As to the privacy claim, there is no case law that provides] any support for the position that the recognized scope of autonomy privacy encompasses the right to keep pets: courts that have considered condominium pet restrictions have uniformly upheld them.

Judgment in favor of the Defendant, Lakeside Village Condominium Homeowners' Association, Inc.

Cooperatives. Whereas condominiums often involve developments consisting of multiple buildings, each of which contains two or more units, cooperatives are more commonly used for ownership interests in apartment buildings. In a cooperative, the investor resident acquires stock in the corporation that owns the facility and receives a permanent lease on one unit of the facility. A board of directors is generally elected from among the unit owners to manage the facility. All unit owners are bound by rules established by the cooperative's board of directors. Commonly, the cooperative will provide that a member may be evicted for violation of the rules, and upon eviction, the cooperative will repurchase the evicted member's unit.

VOLUNTARY TRANSFER OF REAL PROPERTY

The value of property is heightened by the owner's ability to transfer that property. In general, the owner may transfer the property to anyone for any amount of consideration or for no consideration. He or she may transfer all or any portion of the property.

In order to transfer property, however, the owner must follow the proper procedures. These are *execution*, *delivery*, *acceptance*, and, to protect the recipient of the property, *recording* (Exhibit 14-3). Unless something to the contrary is stated, it is presumed that a conveyance of ownership is the conveyance of a fee simple absolute.

EXHIBIT 14-3

STEPS IN A CONVEYANCE

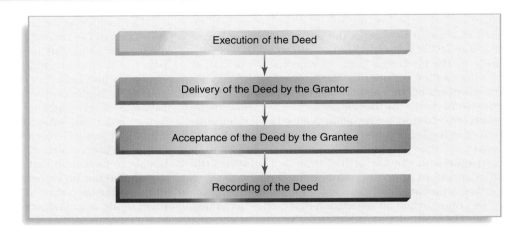

Execution of the Deed

Delivery of the Deed by the Grantor

Acceptance of the Deed by the Grantee

Recording of the Deed

EXECUTION

deed Instrument of conveyance of property.

The first step in a voluntary transfer is the execution of the deed. The **deed**, as shown in Exhibit 14-4, is the instrument of conveyance. A properly drafted deed:

1. Identifies the grantor (the person conveying the property) and the grantee (the person receiving the property).
2. Contains words that express the grantor's intent to convey the property.
3. Identifies the type and percentage of ownership.
4. States the price paid for the property, if any.
5. Contains a legal description of the physical boundaries of the property (not the street address).
6. Specifies any easements or restrictions on use of the land.
7. Identifies any warranties or promises made by the grantor in conjunction with the conveyance.

general warranty deed A deed that promises that the grantor owns the land and has the right to convey it and that the land has no encumbrances other than those stated in the deed.

General Warranty Deed. Two basic types of deeds are generally used to transfer ownership of property. The first, a **general warranty deed**, is preferred by grantees because it contains certain warranties or promises by the grantor. Although such covenants may vary slightly from state to state, they generally include the following.

1. The covenant of *seisen*—a promise that the grantor owns the interest that he or she is conveying.
2. The covenant of the *right to convey*—a promise that the grantor has the right to convey the property.
3. The covenant against *encumbrances*—a promise that there are no mortgages or liens against the property that are not stated in the deed.
4. The covenant for *quiet enjoyment*—a promise that the grantee will not be disturbed by anyone who has a better claim to title of the property and a promise to defend the grantee's title against such claims or to reimburse the grantee for any money spent in the defense or settlement of such claims.
5. The covenant of *further assurances*—the promise that the grantor will provide the grantee with any additional documents that the grantee needs to perfect his or her title to the property.

Form 1-A 8 Legal News, Toledo, Ohio

WARRANTY DEED

Received and Recorded at _____ M.	TRANSFERRED _____
RECORDER	AUDITOR
	PER _____

Know All Men By These Presents:

That Sam Seller

in consideration of $88,000 *the grantor* ,

to be *paid by* Betty Buyer

whose present mail address is 2028 North Main, Bowling Green, Ohio *the grantee*

the receipt whereof is hereby acknowledged, do es *hereby BARGAIN, SELL and CONVEY to said Grantee*

and her *heirs, successors and assigns forever, the following described real estate, situate in the County of* Wood *, State of Ohio: viz:*

Lot 57, plat 32 in
Green Hills Subdivision

and all the estate, right, title and interest said grantor has *or ought to have in and to said described premises, together with the privileges and appurtenances to the same belonging, but subject to zoning ordinances, restrictions of record and public utility or other easements of record.*

Grantor acquired title to the above described premises by instrument recorded in Vol. **LXVI** , Page **12**

To Have and To Hold the same to the said Grantee , and to his *heirs, successors and assigns forever;* Grantor is *hereby covenanting that* he is *the true and lawful owner* of said premises and is *well seized of the same in fee simple, and ha* s *good right and full power to bargain, sell and convey the same in the manner aforesaid, and that the premises so conveyed are clear, free and unencumbered and that* he will *warrant and defend the same against all claims whatsoever, except taxes and assessments due and payable* .

IN WITNESS WHEREOF, The said Sam Seller has

hereunto set his *hand this* 17 *day of* May *in the year of our Lord* One Thousand Nine Hundred and eighty-eight

Signed, acknowledged and Delivered in the presence of

The State of Ohio, **Wood** County, ss.

BE IT REMEMBERED, That on the 17th *day of* May *in the year of our Lord* One Thousand Nine Hundred and eighty eight *, before me, the subscriber, a Notary Public within and for* said county, personally came Sam Seller

the grantor in the above conveyance, and acknowledged the signing thereof to be his *voluntary act and deed, for the purpose therein mentioned.*

IN WITNESS WHEREOF, I have hereunto subscribed my name and affixed my official seal on the day and year aforesaid.

Notary Public, Lucas County, Ohio.
My Commission Expires 9-26-95

This Instrument Prepared By: **Andrea Attorney**

EXHIBIT 14-4

A GENERAL WARRANTY DEED

quitclaim deed A deed that simply transfers to the grantee the interest that the grantor owns in the property.

Quitclaim Deed. The other type of deed, which is more desirable from the grantor's perspective, is the **quitclaim deed**. With such a deed, the grantor simply transfers to the grantee the interest that the grantor owns in the property being conveyed. The grantor makes no additional covenants. Obviously, most grantees would be very reluctant to accept a quitclaim deed.

Once the properly drafted deed has been signed by the grantor and the grantee, it is said to have been *executed*. Many states require the signing of the deed to be witnessed or notarized (witnessed by an official of the state who certifies that she or he saw the parties sign the deed and was provided evidence that the signatories were who they purported to be).

DELIVERY

Once executed, the deed must be *delivered*, or transferred, to the grantee with the intent of transferring ownership to the grantee. The delivery may be made directly to the grantee or to a third party who has been instructed to transfer the deed to the grantee.

ACCEPTANCE

The final essential step is *acceptance* by the grantee. This is the grantee's expression of intent to possess the property. Acceptance is presumed when the grantee retains possession of the deed.

RECORDING

Recording is not essential for the transfer of ownership, but it is so important to securing the grantee's rights to the property that it should always be a part of the process of conveyance. Recording is the filing of the deed (as well as any other documents related to realty, such as mortgages) with the appropriate county office. This office varies by state and may be the county clerk's office or the county recorder's office. Recording gives the world notice of the transfer. It is significant because in many states, if there are two deeds allegedly conveying the same piece of property, the owner of the property is the one whose deed was recorded first.

INVOLUNTARY TRANSFER OF REAL PROPERTY

Transfer of ownership interests in property may also occur without the owner's knowledge, or even against his or her will, by either adverse possession or condemnation.

adverse possession Acquiring ownership of realty by openly treating it as one's own, with neither protest nor permission from the real owner, for a statutorily established period of time.

ADVERSE POSSESSION

Most states provide that when a person openly treats realty as his or her own, without protest or permission from the real owner, for a statutorily established period of time, ownership is automatically vested in that person. Each state has its own exact requirements for **adverse possession**, but the necessary possession is often described as having to be actual (the party resides on or uses the land as would an owner), open (not secretive), and notorious (without the owner's permission). Some state laws require specific acts such as the payment of real estate taxes. Others require that the adverse possessor took possession of the land "under color of title," that is, thinking that he or she was the lawful possessor of the land.

CONDEMNATION

Condemnation is a process by which the government acquires the ownership of private property for a public use over the protest of the owner of the property. The property owner may have been contesting either the taking itself or the price that the government was willing to pay for the taking. Condemnation proceedings occur as a result of the government's exercise of its right of **eminent domain**, which was briefly discussed in Chapter 5. Remember from the discussion of the Takings Clause that the right of eminent domain is the constitutional right of the government to take private property, on payment of just compensation, for a purpose that will benefit the general welfare. This taking may be by any level of government or, in limited cases, by private companies fulfilling a public or governmental function.

In a case arising in Atlantic City, New Jersey, a private company, Trump Plaza, wanted to take private property belonging to Vera Coking. Trump Plaza argued that because casino gambling was integral to Atlantic City's prosperity, turning Vera Coking's property into a parking lot was a governmental function, even though Trump Plaza was a private business. Trump Plaza argued further that the expansion of the private business would provide jobs, thereby benefiting the city. The mayor of Atlantic City agreed, stating, "We are rebuilding Atlantic City. The future of this city is not Vera Coking's boarding house."[2] What do you think about this reasoning?

Under the right of eminent domain, the government first approaches the property, owner with an offer of payment. If the owner objects to the transfer or the parties cannot agree on a price, the government institutes condemnation proceedings. The court then determines whether the governmental purpose is legitimate. If it determines that it is, the court then determines the fair market value of the property. Once this price has been paid, ownership is transferred to the governmental body that brought the action.

Sometimes the government wishes to use its eminent domain power to take property, and the owner questions whether the taking is really for a public purpose. That question may be especially difficult when the property to be acquired will be subsequently conveyed to another private individual, as in the previously described scenario involving Trump Plaza. In the early 1980's, we started seeing an increasing number of cases where city and state economic redevelopment agencies were using the power of eminent domain to take private property and transfer it to another private business for the ostensible public use of economic development, or job creation.

The case that seemed to stimulate the increase in takings for economic redevelopment was the now famous Michigan State Supreme Court case of

condemnation The process whereby the government acquires the ownership of private property for a public use over the protest of the owner.

eminent domain The constitutional right of the government to take privately owned real property for a public purpose in exchange for a just compensation to the owner.

---

[2] D. Timmons and L. Womack, "Eminent Domain or Domination?" *Real Estate Issues,* Winter 1999/2000, p. 44.

Poletown Neighborhood Council v. City of Detroit and the Detroit Economic Development Corporation.[3] In that case, the *Detroit Economic Development Corporation* sought to acquire a large parcel of land on which members of the plaintiff organization, Poletown Neighborhood Council, resided and had small businesses. Once the development agency had acquired the land through the use of the city's eminent domain power, that property would be conveyed to General Motors to expand their plant. Plaintiffs, who did not want their community destroyed, sued the city and the development council on the grounds that they were attempting to abuse their power of eminent domain to unconstitutionally take private property for a private use.

In decisions that surprised many legal scholars, the lower and appellate courts upheld the taking. When the case was appealed to the state supreme court, the high court likewise held that the use of eminent domain was constitutional. The court said that the heart of this dispute was whether the proposed condemnation is for the primary benefit of the public or the private user, and they went on to say that once a legislature declared that a particular government action met a public need and serves a public purpose, that finding is entitled to deference from the court.

After this case, most courts appeared to give state agencies very broad latitude in cases involving takings for private development, finding public use when there is any plausible argument that the public will benefit from the new use. And this broad latitude was not just given in cases where individuals' property was being taken. Increasingly, governments began using eminent domain to transfer property from one business to another. For instance, in June of 2000, Costco, a large retail chain, wanted to expand its warehouse in Lancaster, California. Afraid of losing the large store, which threatened to move if it could not expand, the city considered using its eminent domain powers to acquire an adjacent 99 Cents Only store so Costco could obtain the property. This example demonstrates that even business may be at risk of losing their property to larger, more powerful businesses.

As the number of these private property transfers continued to rise, however, a slowly increasing number of cases started backing off from giving so much deference to states in economic development situations. For example, in a 2002 case involving the condemnation of property located next to a racetrack for the construction of additional parking, the Illinois supreme court sided with the property owner, stating that it was "a violation of the constitutional public use limitation for a government agency to take unoffending property in order to convey it for the expansion of parking of another private business."[4] The court said that the power of eminent domain is to be "exercised with restraint and not abandon."[5]

Finally, in the late summer of 2004, in the following case, the Michigan Supreme Court overturned the Poletown decision that had been the stimulus for the use of eminent domain in so many of these economic redevelopment situations.

---

[3] 304 N.W. 2d 455 (1981).

[4] Southwestern Illinois Development Authority bv. National City Environmental, L.L.C., 199 Ill. 2d 225, 768 N.E. 1 (2002).

[5] *Id.*

CASE 14-3

County of Wayne, Plaintiff-Appellee v. Edward Hathcock, et al., Defendant-Appellant
Supreme Court of Michigan
471 Mich. 445, 684 N. W. 2d. 765 (2004)

The Pinnacle Project called for the construction of a state-of-the-art business and technology park, with a conference center, hotel accommodations, and a recreational facility in a 1,300-acre area adjacent to Metropolitan Airport. The county believed that the Project would create thirty thousand jobs and add $350 million in tax revenue, while broadening the County's tax base from predominantly industrial to a mixture of industrial, service, and technology; and enhance the image of the County in the development community.

Having acquired over one thousand acres, the county determined that an additional forty-six parcels distributed in a checkerboard fashion throughout the project area were needed for the business and technology park. The county apparently determined that further efforts to negotiate additional voluntary sales would be futile and decided instead to invoke the power of eminent domain. The County brought an action to condemn the remaining parcels of land for the project. The property owners contested the takings, arguing, among other claims, that the taking was unconstitutional because the Pinnacle Project did not constitute a public use. Relying heavily on the Poletown case, the Circuit Court, Wayne ruled in favor of county. The property owners appealed. The Court of Appeals affirmed the lower court's decision, and the property owners appealed to the Michigan State Supreme Court.

Justice J. Young

We are presented again with a clash of two bedrock principles of our legal tradition: the sacrosanct right of individuals to dominion over their private property, on the one hand and, on the other, the state's authority to condemn private property for the commonwealth. ...

The question presented here is a fairly discrete one: are the condemnation of defendants' properties and the subsequent transfer of those properties to private entities pursuant to the Pinnacle Project consistent with the common understanding of "public use" at ratification? For the reasons stated below, we answer that question in the negative.

2. "Public Use" and Private Ownership

When our Constitution was ratified in 1963, it was well-established in this Court's eminent domain jurisprudence that the constitutional "public use" requirement was not an absolute bar against the transfer of condemned property to private entities. It was equally clear, however, that the constitutional "public use" requirement worked to prohibit the state from transferring condemned property to private entities for a private use. Thus, this Court's eminent domain jurisprudence—at least that portion concerning the reasons for which the state may condemn private property—has focused largely on the area between these poles.

Justice Ryan's Poletown dissent accurately describes the factors that distinguish takings in the former category from those in the latter. ... Accordingly, we conclude that the transfer of condemned property is a "public use" when it possess one of the three characteristics in our pre-1963 case law identified by Justice Ryan.

First, condemnations in which private land was constitutionally transferred by the condemning authority to a private entity involved "public necessity of the extreme sort otherwise impracticable. ..."

Second, this Court has found that the transfer of condemned property to a private entity is consistent with the constitution's "public use" requirement when the private entity remains accountable to the public in its use of that property ...

Finally, condemned land may be transferred to a private entity when the selection of the land to be condemned is itself based on public concern. In Justice Ryan's words, the property must be selected on the basis of "facts of independent public significance," meaning that the underlying purposes for resorting to condemnation, rather than the subsequent use of condemned land, must satisfy the Constitution's public use requirement.

The primary example of a condemnation in this vein is found in In re Slum Clearance. ... In that case, we considered the constitutionality of Detroit's condemnation of blighted housing and its subsequent resale of those properties to private persons. The city's controlling purpose in condemning the properties was to remove unfit housing and thereby advance public health and safety; subsequent resale of the land cleared of blight was "incidental" to this goal. We concluded, therefore, that the condemnation was indeed a "public use," despite the fact that the condemned properties would inevitably be put to private use. In re Slum Clearance turned on the fact that the act of condemnation itself, rather than the use to which the condemned land eventually would be put, was a public use. Thus ... the condemnation was a "public use" because the land was selected on the basis of "facts of independent public significance" namely, the need to remedy urban blight for the sake of public health and safety.

3. Poletown, the Pinnacle Project, and Public Use

The exercise of eminent domain at issue here—the condemnation of defendants' properties for the Pinnacle Project and the subsequent transfer of those properties to private entities—implicates none of the saving elements noted by our pre-1963 eminent domain jurisprudence.

The Pinnacle Project's business and technology park is certainly not an enterprise "whose very existence depends on the use of land that can be assembled only by the coordination central government alone is capable of achieving."

Second, the Pinnacle Project is not subject to public oversight to ensure that the property continues to be used for the commonwealth after being sold to private entities. Rather, plaintiff intends for the private entities purchasing defendants' properties to pursue their own financial welfare with the single-mindedness expected of any profit-making enterprise. ... No formal mechanisms exist to ensure that the businesses that would occupy what are now defendants' properties will continue to contribute to the health of the local economy.

Finally, there is nothing about the act of condemning defendants' properties that serves the public good in this case. The only public benefits cited by plaintiff arise after the lands are acquired by the government and put to private use. Thus, the present case is quite unlike Slum Clearance because there are no facts of independent public significance (such as the need to promote health and safety) that might justify the condemnation of defendants' lands.

We can only conclude, therefore, that no one sophisticated in the law at the 1963 Constitution's ratification would have understood "public use" to permit the condemnation of defendants' properties for the construction of a business and technology park owned by private entities. ...

Indeed, the only support for plaintiff's position in our eminent domain jurisprudence is the majority opinion in Poletown. In that opinion ..., a majority of this Court concluded that our Constitution permitted the Detroit Economic Development Corporation to condemn private residential properties in order to convey those properties to a private corporation for the construction of an assembly plant.

... [T]he majority [in Poletown]conflated the broad construction of "public purpose" in our taxation jurisprudence with the more limited construction of "public purpose" in the eminent domain context.

This inconsistency aside, the majority opinion in Poletown is most notable for its radical and unabashed departure from the entirety of this Court's pre-1963 eminent domain jurisprudence. The opinion departs from the "common understanding" of "public use" at the time of ratification in two fundamental ways. First, the majority concluded that its power to review the proposed condemnations is limited because "[t]he determination of what constitutes a public purpose is primarily a legislative function, subject to review by the courts when abused, and the determination of the legislative body of that matter should not be reversed except in instances where such determination is palpable and manifestly arbitrary and incorrect."

The majority derived this principle from a plurality opinion of this Court and supported the application of the principle with a citation of an opinion of the United States Supreme Court concerning judicial review of congressional acts under the Fifth Amendment of the federal constitution. Neither case ... is persuasive authority for the use to which they were put by the Poletown majority.

As Justice Ryan's dissent noted: "In point of fact, this Court has never employed the minimal standard of review in an eminent domain case which is adopted by the [Poletown] majority. ... Notwithstanding explicit legislative findings, this Court has always made an independent determination of what constitutes a public use for which the power of eminent domain may be utilized."

Second, the Poletown majority concluded, for the first time in the history of our eminent domain jurisprudence, that a generalized economic benefit was sufficient ... to justify the transfer of condemned property to a private entity. Before Poletown, we had never held that a private entity's pursuit of profit was a "public use" for constitutional takings purposes simply because one entity's profit maximization contributed to the health of the general economy. ...

Every business, every productive unit in society, does, ... contribute in some way to the commonwealth. To justify the exercise of eminent domain solely on the basis of the fact that the use of that property by a private entity seeking its own profit might contribute to the economy's health is to render impotent our constitutional limitations on the government's power of eminent domain. Poletown's "economic benefit" rationale would validate practically any exercise of the power of eminent domain on behalf of a private entity. ... Indeed, it is for precisely this reason that this Court has approved the transfer of condemned property to private entities only when certain other conditions—those identified in our pre-1963 eminent domain jurisprudence in Justice RYANS Poletown dissent—are present.

Because Poletown's conception of a public use—that of "alleviating unemployment and revitalizing the economic base of the community" has no support in the Court's eminent domain jurisprudence before the Constitution's ratification, its interpretation of "public use" ... cannot reflect the common understanding of that phrase among those sophisticated in the law at ratification. Consequently, the Poletown analysis provides no legitimate support for the condemnations proposed in this case and, for the reasons stated above, is overruled.

We conclude that the condemnations proposed in this case do not pass constitutional muster because they do not advance a public use.

Reversed and remanded in favor of the Defendant.

While the *Hathcock* case is an interpretation of public use under Michigan's state constitution, the reasoning can be persuasive in any case involving the interpretation of public use, just as the reasoning in Poletown was persuasive in so many cases involving the same question with respect to other similar state constitutions and the United States constitution.

The influence of *Hathcock* may end up being limited, however, because at the time this book went to press, the United States Supreme Court was poised to render a decision in the appeal of *Susette Kello v. City of New London,*[6] another recent case in which the definition of public use is called into question. In Kello, the city of New London was faced with economic hard times and high unemployment, and the city's development corporation had come up with a plan that would allegedly generate between 1,736 and 3,169 new jobs and generate a minimum of $680,544 in property tax revenues for the city.[7] Relying heavily on the reasoning in Poletown, the high court in Connecticut ruled that the city could use its power of eminent domain to take the private property of a number of residents for the purpose of constructing a state park, new residences, research and development facilities, office space, and retail space.[8] Many are predicting that the United States Supreme Court will follow the reasoning in *Hathcock* and overturn the decision in *Kello,* thereby restoring the earlier, more restrictive interpretation of public use and giving property owners a greater degree of security.

RESTRICTIONS ON LAND USE

No one is allowed to use the land in a completely unrestricted manner. As previously indicated, the doctrine of waste prohibits some uses and abuses of land. There are other such restrictions, both voluntary and involuntary.

RESTRICTIVE COVENANTS

Parties may voluntarily enter into **restrictive covenants**, that is, promises to use or not to use their land in particular ways. These covenants are generally included in the deeds and are binding on the owners as long as the covenants are for lawful acts. For example, a restrictive covenant not to construct buildings higher than three stories would be lawful and enforceable, whereas a covenant never to convey property to minorities would be unlawful and, thus, unenforceable.

restrictive covenants Promises by the owner, generally included in the deed, to use or not to use the land in particular ways.

ZONING

Zoning is the restriction of the use of property to allow for the orderly growth and development of a community and to protect the health, safety, and welfare of its citizens. Zoning may restrict the type of use to which land may be put, such as residential, commercial, industrial, or agricultural. Zoning laws may also regulate land use in geographic areas on the basis of such factors as the intensity (single or multifamily dwellings), the size, or the placement of buildings.

zoning Government restrictions on the use of private property in order to ensure the orderly growth and development of a community and to protect the health, safety, and welfare of citizens.

[6] 268 Conn. 1, 843 A.2d 500 (2004).
[7] *Id.,* p.10.
[8] *Id.*

When new zoning ordinances are enacted by a community, there is generally a public hearing on the proposed change in zoning. Often the community allows a nonconforming use of a particular property when the zoning of an area changes. This exception to the zoning law occurs when the property in question was being used for a purpose not allowed under the new zoning statutes, but because of the prior use, the owner is allowed to continue using the property in the nonconforming manner.

A landowner who wished to use her or his land in a manner prohibited by zoning laws may seek a variance from the appropriate governmental unit, usually a zoning board or a planning commission. A **variance** is permission to use a piece of land in a manner prohibited by the zoning laws. Variances are generally granted to prevent undue hardship.

Sometimes persons negatively affected by a zoning law challenge that ordinance. Zoning is allowed under the police power, the power of the state to regulate to protect the health, safety, and welfare of the public. To be a valid exercise of such power, the zoning ordinance must not be arbitrary or unreasonable. An ordinance is unreasonable if (1) it encroaches on the private property rights of landowners without a substantial relationship to a legitimate government purpose, or (2) there is no reasonable relationship between the ends sought to be obtained and the means used to attain those ends.

Zoning is also unreasonable if it is totally destructive of the economic value of a property holder's land. In such cases, the zoning is really a constructive taking of the property, and the party whose land is so affected is entitled to just compensation. This type of challenge is frequently made, but it is rarely successful.

variance Permission given to a landowner to use a piece of his or her land in a manner prohibited by the zoning laws; generally granted to prevent undue hardship.

OTHER STATUTORY RESTRICTIONS ON LAND USE

In addition to zoning ordinances, states often use their police power to pass laws affecting individuals' use of their property. For example, some states have passed historic preservation statutes whereby certain buildings with historical importance are subject to certain restrictions. Owners of such structures may be required to keep the buildings in good repair or might be required to have any alterations to the buildings' facade approved prior to modification.

Like zoning laws, any laws restricting people's use of their property may be subject to constitutional challenge. The following case illustrates the type of land use regulations that are increasingly being challenged. In this case, the Court clarified and toughened its requirement that government planners produce specific justifications when they condition building permits on a party's rendering a portion of the property for public use.

CASE 14-4

Dolan v. City of Tigard
United States Supreme Court
114 S.Ct. 2309 (1994)

Plaintiff Dolan sought a permit from defendant City of Tigard to expand her store and pave her parking lot. The city conditioned granting her permit on her dedication of a portion of her property for (1) a public greenway to minimize flooding that would otherwise be likely to result from her construction and (2) a pedestrian/bicycle pathway to decrease congestion in the business district.

Plaintiff Dolan appealed the decision of the planning commission to the Land Use Board of Appeals, which found that the land dedication requirements were reasonably related to her proposed construction and, therefore, did not constitute a taking. The state court of appeals and state supreme court both affirmed the decision in favor of the city. Plaintiff Dolan appealed to the U.S. Supreme Court.

Justice Rehnquist

One of the principal purposes of the Takings Clause is "to bar Government from forcing some people alone to bear public burdens which, in all fairness and justice, should be borne by the public as a whole." Without question, had the city simply required petitioner to dedicate a strip of land along Fanno Creek for public use, rather than conditioning the grant of her permit to redevelop her property on such a dedication, a taking would have occurred. Such public access would deprive petitioner of the right to exclude others, "one of the most essential sticks in the bundle of rights that are commonly characterized as property."

On the other side of the ledger, the authority of state and local governments to engage in land use planning has been sustained against constitutional challenge. ... A land use regulation does not effect a taking if it "substantially advance[s] legitimate state interests" and does not "den[y] an owner economically viable use of his land."

Petitioner contends that the city has forced her to choose between the building permit and her right under the Fifth Amendment to just compensation for the public easements. Petitioner does not quarrel with the city's authority to exact some forms of dedication as a condition for the grant of a building permit, but challenges the showing made by the city to justify these exactions. She argues that the city has identified "no special benefits" conferred on her, and has not identified any "special quantifiable burdens" created by her new store that would justify the particular dedications required from her which are not required from the public at large.

In evaluating petitioner's claim, we must first determine whether the "essential nexus" exists between the "legitimate state interest" and the permit condition exacted by the city. If we find that a nexus exists, we must then decide the required degree of connection between the exactions and the projected impact of the proposed development.

Undoubtedly, the prevention of flooding along Fanno Creek and the reduction of traffic congestion in the Central Business District qualify as the type of legitimate public purposes we have upheld. It seems equally obvious that a nexus exists between preventing flooding along Fanno Creek and limiting development within the creek's 100-year floodplain. Petitioner proposes to double the size of her retail store and to pave her now-gravel parking lot, thereby expanding the impervious surface on the property and increasing the amount of stormwater run-off into Fanno Creek.

The same may be said for the city's attempt to reduce traffic congestion by providing for alternative means of transportation. In theory, a pedestrian/bicycle pathway provides a useful alternative means of transportation for workers and shoppers: "Pedestrians and bicyclists occupying dedicated spaces for walking and/or bicycling … remove potential vehicles from streets, resulting in an overall improvement in total transportation system flow."

The second part of our analysis requires us to determine whether the degree of the exactions demanded by the city's permit conditions bear the required relationship to the projected impact of petitioner's proposed development.

"The distinction, therefore, which must be made between an appropriate exercise of the police power and an improper exercise of eminent domain is whether the requirement has some reasonable relationship or nexus to the use to which the property is being made or is merely being used as an excuse for taking property simply because at that particular moment the landowner is asking the city for some license or permit."

We think a term such as "rough proportionality" best encapsulates what we hold to be the requirement of the Fifth Amendment. No precise mathematical calculation is required, but the city must make some sort of individualized determination that the required dedication is related both in nature and extent to the impact of the proposed development.

We turn now to analysis of whether the findings relied upon by the city here, first with respect to the floodplain easement and second with respect to the pedestrian/bicycle path, satisfied these requirements.

It is axiomatic that increasing the amount of impervious surface will increase the quantity and rate of stormwater flow from petitioner's property. The city has never said why a public greenway, as opposed to a private one, was required in the interest of flood control. We conclude that the findings upon which the city relies do not show the required reasonable relationship between the floodplain easement and the petitioner's proposed new building.

With respect to the pedestrian/bicycle pathway, we have no doubt that the city was correct in finding that the larger retail sales facility proposed by petitioner will increase traffic on the streets of the Central Business District. Dedications for streets, sidewalks, and other public ways are generally reasonable exactions to avoid excessive congestion from a proposed property use. But on the records before us, the city has not met its burden of demonstrating that the additional number of vehicle and bicycle trips generated by the petitioner's development reasonably relate to the city's requirement for a dedication of the pedestrian/bicycle pathway easement.

As Justice Peterson of the Supreme Court of Oregon explained in his dissenting opinion, however, "[t]he findings of fact that the bicycle pathway system 'could offset some of the traffic demand' is a far cry from a finding that the bicycle pathway system *will*, or is *likely* to, offset some of the traffic demand." No precise mathematical calculation is required, but the city must make some effort to quantify its findings in support of the dedication for the pedestrian/bicycle pathway beyond the conclusory statement that it could offset some of the traffic demand generated.

Cities have long engaged in the commendable task of land use planning, made necessary by increasing urbanization particularly in metropolitan areas such as Portland. The city's goals of reducing flooding hazards and traffic congestion, and providing for public greenways, are laudable, but there are outer limits to how this may be done. "A strong public desire to improve the public condition [will not] warrant achieving the desire by a shorter cut than the constitutional way of paying for the change."

Reversed and remanded in favor of Plaintiff, Dolan.

This case is frequently relied on by courts in cases that arise when a city attempts to impose burdens on property owners wishing to develop their property.[9] For example, when the town of Flower Mound wished to condition the building of a residential development on the developer's replacing of an adjacent asphalt street with a concrete one, the court struck down the requirement, finding that the required nexus between the safety and durability of the road and a rebuilding of the road did not exist. The court found that the interests of the city were legitimate, but the requirement of completely reconstructing the road was not roughly proportionate to the impact of the additional traffic that would result from the new development.[10] In other words, there was no reasonable relationship between the burden resulting from the development and the required method of alleviating that burden.

PERSONAL PROPERTY

personal property All property that is not real property; may be tangible or intangible.

tangible property Personal property that is material and movable (e.g., furniture).

intangible property Personal property that does not have a physical form and is usually evidenced in writings (e.g., an insurance policy).

title Ownership of property.

All property that is not real property is **personal property**. As previously explained, personal property may be either tangible or intangible. **Tangible property** includes movable items, such as furniture, cars, and other goods. **Intangibles** include such items as bank accounts, stocks, and insurance policies.

Because most intangibles (with the exception of some of those classified as intellectual property and discussed later) are evidenced by writings, most of the following discussion applies to both tangible and intangible property. The primary concerns that arise in conjunction with personal property involve (1) the means of acquiring ownership of the property and (2) the rights and duties arising out of a bailment. Both are discussed here in detail.

VOLUNTARY TRANSFER OF PERSONAL PROPERTY

The most common means by which personal property is acquired is by its voluntary transfer, as a result of either a purchase or a gift. Ownership of property is referred to as **title**, and title to property passes when the parties so intend. When there is a purchase, the acquiring party gives some consideration to the seller in exchange for title to the property. In most cases, this transfer of ownership requires no formalities, but in a few cases, changes of ownership must

---

[9] *Town of Flower Mound v. Stafford Estates Ltd. Partnership*, 2004 WL 1048331 (Tex.).
[10] *Id.*

- Delivery
- Donative Intent
- Acceptance

EXHIBIT 14-5

ELEMENTS OF A GIFT

be registered with a government agency. The primary transfers requiring such formalities include sales of motor vehicles, watercraft, and airplanes. Transfer of such property requires that a certificate of title be signed by the seller, taken to the appropriate governmental agency, and then reissued in the name of the new owner.

Gifts are distinguished from purchases in that there is no consideration given for a gift. As the reader knows, a promise to make a gift is, therefore, unenforceable. Once properly made, however, a gift is an irrevocable transfer.

For a valid gift to occur, three elements must be present (Exhibit 14-5). First, there must be a delivery of the gift. This delivery may be actual, that is, the physical presentation of the gift itself. Or it may be constructive, that is, the delivery of an item that gives access to the gift or represents it, such as the handing over of the keys to a car. Second, the delivery must be made with **donative intent** to make a present, as opposed to future, gift. The donor makes the delivery with the purpose of turning over ownership at the time of delivery. The final element is acceptance, a willingness of the donee to take the gift from the donor. Usually, acceptance is not a problem, although a donee may not want to accept a gift because he or she does not want to feel obligated to the donor or because he or she believes that ownership of the gift may impose some unwanted legal liability.

donative intent Intent to transfer ownership to another at the time the donor makes actual or constructive delivery of the gift to the donee.

INVOLUNTARY TRANSFERS OF PERSONAL PROPERTY

Involuntary transfers involve the transfer of ownership of property that has been abandoned, lost, or mislaid. The finder of such property may acquire ownership rights to such property through possession.

Abandoned property is property that the original owner has discarded. Anyone who finds that property becomes its owner by possessing it.

Lost property is property that the true owner has unknowingly or accidentally dropped or left somewhere. He or she has no way of knowing how to retrieve it. In most states, the finder of lost property has title to the lost good against all except the true owner.

Mislaid property differs from lost property in that the owner has intentionally placed the property somewhere but has forgotten its location. The person who owns the realty on which the mislaid property was placed has the right to hold the mislaid property. The reason is that it is likely that the true owner will return to the realty looking for the mislaid property.

In some states, the law requires that before becoming the owner of lost or mislaid property, a finder must place an ad in the paper that will give the true owner notice that the property has been found or must leave the property with the police for a statutorily established reasonable period of time. Some state laws require both.

BAILMENTS

bailment A relationship in which one person (the bailor) transfers possession of personal property to another (the bailee) to be used in an agreed-on manner for an agreed-on period of time.

A **bailment** of personal property is a special relationship in which one party, the *bailor*, transfers possession of personal property to another, the *bailee*, to be used by the bailee in an agreed-on manner for an agreed-on time period.

One example of a bailment is when a person leaves his or her coat in a coat-check room. The person hands his or her coat to the clerk and is given a ticket identifying the object of the bailment so that it can be reclaimed. The bailment may be gratuitous or for consideration. It may be to benefit the bailor, the bailee, or both. If the bailment is intended to benefit only the bailor, the bailee is liable for damage to the property caused by the bailee's gross negligence. If the bailment is solely for the bailee's benefit, then the bailee is responsible for harm to the property caused by even the slightest lack of due care on the part of the bailee. If the bailment is for the mutual benefit of both bailee and bailor, the bailee is liable for harm to the bailed property arising out of the bailee's ordinary or gross negligence. If the property is harmed by an unpreventable "act of God," there is no liability on the part of the bailee under any circumstances. These general rules notwithstanding, the parties to a bailment contract can limit or expand the liability of the bailee by contract. In general, conspicuous signs (e.g., "We are not responsible for lost items") have been held sufficient to limit liability.

If the bailee is to receive compensation for the bailment, the bailee may retain possession of the bailed property until payment is made. In most states, when the bailor refuses to provide the agreed-on compensation to the bailee, the property may ultimately be sold by the bailee after proper notice and a hearing. The proceeds are first used to pay the bailee and to cover the costs of the sale. The remaining proceeds then go to the bailor.

In addition to their duty to pay bailees their agreed-on compensation, a bailor must also warn the bailee of any hidden defects in the bailed goods. If such a warning is not given and the defect injures the bailee, the bailor is liable to the bailee for the injuries.

INTELLECTUAL PROPERTY

Intellectual property consists of the fruits of one's mind. The laws of intellectual property protect property that is primarily the result of mental creativity rather than physical effort. This category includes trademarks, trade secrets, patents, and copyrights, all of which are discussed in the following paragraphs.

TRADEMARKS

trademark A distinctive mark, word, design, picture, or arrangement used by the producer of a product that tends to cause consumers to identify the product with the producer.

A **trademark** is a distinctive mark, word, design, picture, or arrangement used by a seller in conjunction with a product and tending to cause the consumer to identify the product with the producer. Even the shape of a product or package may be a trademark if it is nonfunctional.

Even though the description of a trademark is very broad, there has still been substantial litigation over precisely what features can and cannot serve as a trademark. In the following case, the U.S. Supreme Court grappled with the issue of whether a color can be a trademark.

CASE 14-5

Qualitex Company v. Jacobson Products Company
United States Supreme Court,
514 U.S. 159 (1995)

For years, the plaintiff, Qualitex Company, colored the dry-cleaning press pads it manufactured a special shade of green-gold. When Jacobson Products, a competitor, started coloring its pads the same shade of green-gold, Qualitex sued Jacobson Products for trademark infringement. The defendant challenged the legitimacy of the trademark, arguing that color alone should not qualify for registration as a trademark.

The district court found in favor of the plaintiff, but the Ninth Circuit reversed, holding that color alone could not be registered as a trademark. The plaintiff appealed to the U.S. Supreme Court.

Justice Breyer

The Lanham Act gives a seller or producer the exclusive right to "register" a trademark, to prevent his or her competitors from using that trademark. Both the language of the Act and the basic underlying principles of trademark law would seem to include color within the universe of things that can qualify as a trademark. The language of the Lanham Act describes that universe in the broadest of terms. It says that trademarks "includ[e] any word, name, symbol, or device, or any combination thereof." Since human beings might use as a "symbol" or "device" almost anything at all that is capable of carrying meaning, this language, read literally, is not restrictive. The courts and the Patent and Trademark Office has [*sic*] authorized for use as a mark a particular shape (of a Coca-Cola bottle), a particular sound (of NBC's three chimes) and even a particular scent (of plumeria blossoms or sewing thread). If a shape, a sound, and a fragrance can act as symbols why, one might ask, can a color not do the same?

A color is also capable of satisfying the more important part of the statutory definition of a trademark, which requires that a person "us[e]" or "inten[d] to use" the mark

> *To identify and distinguish his or her goods, including a unique product, from those manufactured or sold by others and to indicate the source of the goods, even if that source is unknown.*

True, a product's color is unlike "fanciful," "arbitrary," or "suggestive" words or designs, which almost automatically tell a customer that they refer to a brand. The imaginary word "Suntost," or the words "Suntost Marmalade," on a jar of orange jam immediately would signal a brand or a product "source"; the jam's orange color does not do so. But, over time, customers may come to treat a particu-

lar color on a product or its packaging (say, a color that in context seems unusual such as pink on a firm's insulating material or red on the head of a large industrial bolt) as signifying a brand. And, if so, that color would have come to identify and distinguish the goods—i.e., "to indicate" their "source"—much in the way that descriptive words on a product (say, "Trim" on nail clippers or "Car-Freshener" on deodorizer) can come to indicate a product's origin. In this circumstance, trademark law says that the word (e.g., "Trim"), although not inherently distinctive, has developed "secondary meaning." ("Secondary meaning" is acquired when "in the minds of the public, the primary significance of a product feature ... is to identify the source of the product rather than the product itself"). Again, one might ask, if trademark law permits a descriptive word with secondary meaning to act as a mark, why would it not permit a color, under similar circumstances, to do the same?

It would seem, then, that color alone, at least sometimes, can meet the basic legal requirements for use as a trademark. It can act as a symbol that distinguishes a firm's goods and identifies their source, without serving any other significant function. The green-gold color acts as a symbol. Having developed secondary meaning (for customers identified the green-gold color as Qualitex's), it identifies the press pads' source. And, the green-gold color serves no other function. Accordingly, unless there is some special reason that convincingly militates against the use of color alone as a trademark, trademark law would protect Qualitex's use of the green-gold color on its press pads.

Respondent Jacobson Products says that there are four special reasons why the law should forbid the use of color alone as a trademark. We shall explain why we find them unpersuasive.

Jacobson says that, if the law permits the use of color as a trademark, it will produce uncertainty and unresolvable court disputes about what shades of a color a competitor may lawfully use. Because lighting will affect perceptions of protected color, competitors and courts will suffer from "shade confusion" as they try to decide whether use of a similar color on a similar product does, or does not, confuse customers and thereby infringe on a trademark.

We do not believe that color, in this respect, is special. Courts traditionally decide quite difficult questions about whether two words or phrases or symbols are sufficiently similar, in context, to confuse buyers. They have had to compare, for example, such words as "Bonamine" and "Dramamine" (motion-sickness remedies); "Huggies" and

"Dougies" (diapers); "Cheracol" and "Syrocol" (cough syrup); "Cyclone" and "Tornado" (wire fences): and "mattres" and "1-800-Mattres" (mattress franchisor telephone numbers). Legal standards exist to guide courts in making such comparisons. We do not see why courts could not apply those standards to a color, replicating, if necessary, lighting conditions under which a colored product is normally sold. Indeed, courts already have done so in cases where a trademark consists of a color plus a design, i.e., a colored symbol such as a gold stripe (around a sewer pipe), a yellow strand of wire rope, or a "brilliant yellow" band (on ampules).

Jacobson argues that colors are in limited supply. If one of many competitors can appropriate a particular color for use as a trademark, and each competitor then tries to do the same, the supply of colors will soon be depleted.

This argument is unpersuasive, however, largely because it relies on an occasional problem to justify a blanket prohibition. When a color serves as a mark, normally alternative colors will likely be available for similar use by others. Moreover, if that is not so—if a "color depletion" or "color scarcity" problem does arise—the trademark doctrine of "functionality" normally would seem available to prevent the anticompetitive consequences that Jacobson's argument posits.

The functionality doctrine forbids the use of a product's feature as a trademark where doing so will put a competitor at a significant disadvantage because the feature is "essential to the use or purpose of the article" or "affects [its] cost or quality." For example, this Court has written that competitors might be free to copy the color of a medical pill where that color serves to identify the kind of medication (e.g., a type of blood medicine) in addition to its source. And, the federal courts have demonstrated that they can apply this doctrine in a careful and reasoned manner, with sensitivity to the effect on competition. Lower courts have permitted competitors to copy the green color of farm machinery (because customers wanted their farm equipment to match) and have barred the use of black as a trademark on outboard boat motors (because black has the special functional attributes of decreasing the apparent size of

the motor and ensuring compatibility with many different boat colors).

Where a color serves a significant nontrademark function, courts will examine whether its use as a mark would permit one competitor (or a group) to interfere with legitimate (nontrademark-related) competition through actual or potential exclusive use of an important product ingredient. That examination should not discourage firms from creating aesthetically pleasing mark designs, for it is open to their competitors to do the same. But, ordinarily, it should prevent the anticompetitive consequences of Jacobson's hypothetical "color depletion" argument, when, and if, the circumstances of a particular case threaten "color depletion."

Jacobson points to many older cases—including Supreme Court cases—in support of its position. These Supreme Court cases, however, interpreted trademark law as it existed before 1946, when Congress enacted the Lanham Act. The Lanham Act significantly changed and liberalized the common law to "dispense with more technical prohibitions," most notably, by permitting trademark registration of descriptive words (say, "U-Build-It" model airplanes) where they had acquired "secondary meaning." The Lanham Act extended protection to descriptive marks by making clear that (with certain explicit exceptions not relevant here), "Nothing ... shall prevent the registration of a mark used by the applicant which has become distinctive of the applicant's goods in commerce." This language permits an ordinary word, normally used for a nontrademark purpose (e.g., description), to act as a trademark where it has gained "secondary meaning." Its logic would appear to apply to color as well.

Jacobson argues that there is no need to permit color alone to function as a trademark because a firm already may use color as part of a trademark, say, as a colored circle or colored letter or colored word. This argument begs the question. One can understand why a firm might find it difficult to place a usable symbol or word on a product and, in such instances, a firm might want to use color, pure and simple, instead of color as part of a design.

Reversed in favor of Plaintiff, Qualitex Company.

A trademark used *intrastate* is protected under state common law. To be protected in *interstate* use, the trademark must be registered with the U.S. Patent Office under the Lanham Act of 1947. Several types of marks, listed in Table 14-2, are protected under this act.

If a mark is registered, the holder of the mark may recover damages from an infringer who uses it to pass off goods as those of the mark owner. The owner may also obtain an injunction prohibiting the infringer from using the mark. Only the latter remedy is available for an unregistered mark.

TABLE 14-2

TYPES OF MARKS PROTECTED UNDER THE LANHAM ACT

1. *Product trademarks:* Marks affixed to a good, its packaging, or its labeling.

2. *Service marks:* Marks used in conjunction with a service.

3. *Collective marks:* Marks identifying the producers as belonging to a larger group, such as a trade union.

4. *Certification marks:* Marks licensed by a group that has established certain criteria for use of the mark, such as "U.L. Tested" or "Good Housekeeping Seal of Approval."

To register a mark with the Patent Office, one must submit a drawing of the mark and indicate when it was first used in interstate commerce and how it is used. The Patent Office conducts an investigation to verify those facts and will register a trademark as long as it is not generic, descriptive, immoral, deceptive, the name of a person whose permission has not been obtained, or substantially similar to another's trademark.

It is sometimes difficult to determine whether a trademark will be protected. And once the trademark is issued, it is not always easy to predict when a similar mark will be found to infringe upon the registered trademark. The following case demonstrates a typical analysis used in a trademark infringement suit.

CASE 14-6

Toys Я Us, Inc. v. Canarsie Kiddie Shop, Inc.
District Court of the Eastern District of New York,
559 F. Supp. 1189 (1983)

Beginning in 1960, plaintiff Toys "Я" Us, Inc., sold children's clothes in stores across the country. The firm obtained a registered trademark and service mark for Toys "Я" Us in 1961 and aggressively advertised and promoted its products using these marks. In the late 1970s, defendant Canarsie Kiddie Shop, Inc., opened two children's clothing stores within two miles of a Toys "Я" Us shop, and contemplated opening a third. The owner of Canarsie Kiddie Shop, Inc., called the stores Kids "r" Us. He never attempted to register the name. Toys "Я" Us sued for trademark infringement in the federal district court.

Judge Glasser
In assessing the likelihood of confusion and in balancing the equities, this Court must consider the now classic factors. …

1. Strength of the Senior User's Mark
… "[T]he term 'strength' as applied to trademarks refers to the distinctiveness of the mark, or more precisely, its tendency to identify goods sold under the mark as emanating from the particular, although possibly anonymous, source." A mark can fall into one of four general categories, which, in order of ascending strength, are: (1) generic; (2) descriptive; (3) suggestive; and (4) arbitrary or fanciful. The strength of a mark is generally dependent both on its place upon the scale and on whether it has acquired secondary meaning.

A generic term "refers, or has come to be understood as referring to the genus of which the particular product is a species." A generic term is entitled to no trademark protection whatsoever, since any manufacturer or seller has the right to call a product by its name.

A descriptive mark identifies a significant characteristic of the product, but is not the common name of the product. A mark is descriptive if it "informs the purchasing public of the characteristics, quality, functions, uses, ingredients, components, or other properties of a product, or conveys comparable information about a service." To achieve trademark protection a descriptive term must have attained secondary meaning, that is, it must have "become distinctive of the applicant's goods in commerce."

A suggestive mark is one that "requires imagination, thought, and perception to reach a conclusion as to the nature of the goods." These marks fall short of directly describing the qualities or functions of a particular product or service, but merely suggest such qualities. If a term is suggestive, it is entitled to protection without proof of secondary meaning.

Arbitrary or fanciful marks require no extended definition. They are marks which in no way describe or suggest the qualities of the product.

The Toys "Я" Us mark is difficult to categorize.

The strength of the plaintiff's mark must be evaluated by examining the mark in its entirety. … I agree that the Toys "Я" Us mark serves to describe the business of the plaintiff, and in this sense is merely descriptive. This descriptive quality, however, does require some "imagination, thought, and perception" on the part of the consumer since the plaintiff's mark, read quite literally, conveys the message, "we are toys," rather than "we sell toys."

Whether the "leap of imagination" required here is sufficient to render the mark suggestive rather than descriptive is a question with no clear-cut answer. Such an absolute categorization is not essential, however, since the defendants concede that through the plaintiff's marketing and advertising efforts the Toys "Я" Us mark has acquired secondary meaning in the minds of the public, at least in relation to its sale of toys. Such secondary meaning assures that the plaintiff's mark is entitled to protection even if it is viewed as merely descriptive. Because I find that through the plaintiff's advertising and marketing efforts the plaintiff's mark has developed strong secondary meaning as a source of children's products, it is sufficient for purposes of this decision to note merely that the plaintiff's mark is one of medium strength, clearly entitled to protection, but falling short of the protection afforded an arbitrary or fanciful mark.

2. Degree of Similarity Between the Two Marks

… [T]he key inquiry is … whether a similarity exists which is likely to cause confusion. This test must be applied from the perspective of prospective purchasers. Thus, it must be determined whether "the impression which the infringing [mark] makes upon the consumer is such that he is likely to believe the product is from the same source as the one he knows under the trademark." In making this determination, it is the overall impression of the mark as a whole that must be considered.

Turning to the two marks involved here, various similarities and differences are readily apparent. The patent similarity between the marks is that they both employ the phrase, "Я" Us. Further, both marks employ the letter "R" in place of the word "are," although the plaintiff's mark uses an inverted capitalized "R," while the defendants generally use a non-inverted lower case "r" for their mark.

The most glaring difference between the marks is that in one the phrase "Я" Us is preceded by the word "Toys," while in the other it is preceded by the word "Kids." Other differences include the following: plaintiff's mark ends with an exclamation point, plaintiff frequently utilizes the image of a giraffe alongside its mark, plaintiff's mark is set forth in stylized lettering, usually multi-colored, and plaintiff frequently utilizes the words, "a children's bargain basement" under the logo in its advertising.

I attach no great significance to the minor lettering differences between the marks, or to the images or slogans usually accompanying the plaintiff's mark. … While the marks are clearly distinguishable when placed side by side, there are sufficiently strong similarities to create the possibility that some consumers might believe that the two marks emanated from the same source. The similarities in sound and association also create the possibility that some consumers might mistake one mark for the other when seeing or hearing the mark alone. The extent to which these possibilities are "likely" must be determined in the context of all the factors present here.

3. Proximity of the Products

Where the products in question are competitive, the likelihood of consumer confusion increases. … [B]oth plaintiff and defendants sell children's clothing; … the plaintiff and defendants currently are direct product competitors.

4. The Likelihood That Plaintiff Will "Bridge the Gap"

… "[B]ridging the gap" refers to two distinct possibilities; first, that the senior user presently intends to expand his sales efforts to compete directly with the junior user, thus creating the likelihood that the two products will be directly competitive; second, that while there is no present intention to bridge the gap, consumers will assume otherwise and conclude, in this era of corporate diversification, that the parties are related companies. … I find both possibilities present here.

5. Evidence of Actual Confusion

Evidence of actual confusion is a strong indication that there is a likelihood of confusion. It is not, however, a prerequisite for the plaintiff to recover.

6. Junior User's Good Faith

The state of mind of the junior user is an important factor in striking the balance of the equities. In the instant case, Mr. Pomeranc asserted at trial that he did not recall whether he was aware of the plaintiff's mark when he chose to name his store Kids "r" Us in 1977.

I do not find this testimony to be credible. In view of the proximity of the stores, the overlapping of their products, and the strong advertising and marketing effort conducted by the plaintiff for a considerable amount of time prior to the defendants' adoption of the name Kids "r" Us, it is difficult to believe that the defendants were unaware of the plaintiff's use of the Toys "Я" Us mark.

The defendants adopted the Kids "Я" Us mark with knowledge of plaintiff's mark. A lack of good faith is relevant not only in balancing the equities, but also is a factor supporting a finding of a likelihood of confusion.

7. Quality of the Junior User's Product

If the junior user's product is of a low quality, the senior user's interest in avoiding any confusion is heightened. In the instant case, there is no suggestion that the defendants' products are inferior, and this factor therefore is not relevant.

8. Sophistication of the Purchasers

The level of sophistication of the average purchaser also bears on the likelihood of confusion. Every product, because of the type of buyer that it attracts, has its own distinct threshold for confusion of the source or origin.

The goods sold by both plaintiff and defendants are moderately priced clothing articles, which are not major expenditures for most purchasers. Consumers of such goods, therefore, do not exercise the same degree of care in buying as when purchasing more expensive items. Further, it may be that the consumers purchasing from the plaintiff and defendants are influenced in part by the desires of their children, for whom the products offered by plaintiff and defendants are meant.

9. Junior User's Goodwill

[A] powerful equitable argument against finding infringement is created when the junior user, through concurrent use of an identical trademark, develops goodwill in their mark. Defendants have not expended large sums advertising their store or promoting its name. Further, it appears that most of the defendants' customers are local "repeat shoppers," who come to the Kids "r" Us store primarily because of their own past experiences with it. In light of this lack of development of goodwill, I find that the defendants do not have a strong equitable interest in retaining the Kids "r" Us mark.

Conclusion on Likelihood of Confusion

[T]he defendants' use of the Kids "r" Us mark does create a likelihood of confusion for an appreciable number of consumers.

In reaching this determination, I place primary importance on the strong secondary meaning that the plaintiff has developed in its mark, the directly competitive nature of the products offered by the plaintiff and defendants, the plaintiff's substantially developed plans to open stores similar in format to those of the defendants', the lack of sophistication of the purchasers, the similarities between the marks, the defendants' lack of good faith in adopting the mark, and the limited goodwill the defendants have developed in their mark.

Judgment for the Plaintiff, Toys "Я" Us.

Critical Thinking About the Law

Legal reasoning and decision making almost always entail a reliance on tradition. Yet, in Case 14-6, the court's deference to tradition is especially strong. In applying the "classic factors" to the case, the court judges the present case on the basis of the way in which an allegedly similar earlier case was judged.

The implications of relying on tradition in legal reasoning are quite significant. The questions that follow will help you to consider this significance more deeply.

1. To demonstrate your ability to recognize analogous reasoning, identify the implicit analogy that pervades the court's reasoning in Case 14-6.

   Clue: Consider the source of the "classic factors."

2. What important piece of missing information hinders your ability to make a sound critical judgment about the appropriateness of the court's reasoning?

   Clue: Refer to your answer to Question 1; it is directly related to this question.

The potential for consumer confusion seems to be a very important consideration in a trademark infringement case. In the "Dentyne Ice" chewing gum case, the court ruled that there was little possibility for consumer confusion between "Dentyne Ice" and "Icebreakers" because Dentyne was a common household name; thus, Dentyne did not infringe on Nabisco's trademark.

TRADE DRESS

trade dress The overall appearance and image of a product that has acquired secondary meaning.

The term **trade dress** refers to the overall appearance and image of a product. Trade dress is entitled to the same protection as a trademark. To succeed on a claim of trade dress infringement, a party must prove three elements: (1) The trade dress is primarily nonfunctional; (2) the trade dress is inherently distinctive or has acquired a secondary meaning; and (3) the alleged infringement creates a likelihood of confusion.

The main focus of a case of trade dress infringement is usually on whether or not there is likely to be consumer confusion. For example, in a recent case, Tour 18, Limited, a golf course, copied golf holes from famous golf courses without permission of the course owners.[11] In copying a hole from one the most famous courses in the country, Harbour Town Hole 19, it even copied the Harbour Town Lighthouse, which is the distinctive feature of that hole. In its advertising, Tour 18 prominently featured pictures of this hole, including the lighthouse. The operator of the Harbour Town course sued Tour 18 for trade dress infringement. The court found that there was infringement and made Tour 18 remove the lighthouse and disclaim in its advertising any affiliation with the owner of the Harbour Town course.

Trade dress violations occur over a wide range of products. Two very different examples of trade dress infringement include *Bubba's Bar-B-Q Oven v. The Holland Company*,[12] and *Two Pesos v. Taco Cabana*.[13] In the first case, Bubba had almost exactly copied the physical appearance of Holland Company's very successful gas-fired barbecue grill, which the court found to be trade dress infringement. In the second case, the court found that Taco Cabana's trade dress consisted of "a festive eating atmosphere having interior dining and patio areas decorated with artifacts, bright colors, paintings and murals"; "a patio that has interior and exterior areas with the interior patio capable of being sealed off from the outside patio by overhead garage doors"; a stepped exterior of the building that has "a festive and vivid color scheme using top border paint and neon stripes"; and "bright awnings and umbrellas." When Two Pesos opened a series of competing Mexican restaurants that mimicked those features almost perfectly, the court found them to be guilty of trade dress infringement.

FEDERAL TRADEMARK DILUTION ACT OF 1995

Under the Lanham Act, trademark owners were protected from the unauthorized use of their marks on only competing goods or related goods where the use might lead to consumer confusion. Consequently, a mark might be used without permission on completely unrelated goods, thereby potentially diminishing the

---

[11] *Pebble Beach Co. v. Tour 18, Ltd.* 942 F. Supp. 1513.

[12] 175 F.3d 1013 (1999).

[13] 112 S.Ct. 2753 (1994).

Technology and the Legal Environment

Trademarks and Domain Names

If a business has a very strong trademark, what better domain name to have than that trademark? Unfortunately, the same trademark may be owned by two companies selling noncompeting goods, yet there can be only one user of any single domain name. For example, apple is a trademark owned by both a computer company and the company that produces the Beatles' records. Both cannot establish a site identified as apple.com.

Domain names are important because they are the way people and business are located on the Web. A domain name is made up of a series of domains separated by periods. Most Web sites have two domains. The first-level domain, the one that the address ends with, generally identifies the type of site. For example, if it is a government site, it will end in gov. An educational site will end in edu, a network site in net, an organization in org, and a business in com. These top-level domain names are the same worldwide.

The second-level domain is usually the name of whoever maintains the site. For a college, for example, it would be an abbreviation of the college, as in bgsu. Businesses will generally want to use their firm name or some other trademark associated with their product, because that name will obviously make it easiest for their customers to find them.

So how does a firm go about securing a domain name that reflects its trademark? Network Solutions, Inc. (NSI), which is funded by the National Science Foundation, is responsible for registering domain names. This entity acts on behalf of the Internet Network Information Center, which handles the daily administration of the domain name system in the United States.

Initially, you applied to the NSI to use your desired domain name, and as long as no one else held that name, registration was granted. Since 1995, however, the NSI has been a little more careful in handing out names. Anyone seeking to register a domain name must now state in their application that the name will not infringe on anyone else's intellectual property rights and that the registrant intends to use the name on a regular basis on the Internet.

A party may lose registration of a name by not using it for more than 90 days. Or the domain name may be canceled if the registrant lied on the registration application. If a firm has a registered trademark and finds that someone is using its trademark as a domain name, and that party does not also have ownership of that mark, the firm may give written notice to the NSI, and under its Domain Dispute Policy, they will most likely put the name "on hold," meaning that no one can use the name. Of course, if that party had registered its domain name before the firm had obtained the trademark, then there is probably nothing it can do. The party will be entitled to retain its domain name.

Some firms have tried to get the domain name they desire by going to another country. That alternative is certainly a possibility. However, many countries require that a firm be incorporated within their borders before it can gain the right to the domain name there. And an additional problem is that trademark law relating to domain names is even more unclear abroad.

For the new entrepreneur, the best advice is to try to simultaneously apply for federal trademark protection and register the domain name. And for those not yet on the Web, the sooner you get your domain name, the more likely you are to get the name you want. And if you feel that your mark is being violated by another's domain name, you may want to sue them for infringement, because the unauthorized use of another's trademark in a domain name has been found to be illegal. But you may be in for quite a fight because this is a new area of the law.

value of the mark. In response to this problem, a number of states passed trademark dilution laws, which prohibited the use of "distinctive" or "famous" trademarks, such as McDonald's, even without a showing of consumer confusion.

In 1995, Congress made similar protection available at the federal level by passing the Federal Trademark Dilution Act of 1995. In one of the first cases decided under this law, the court said that the protection available under this act extended not just to identical marks but also to similar marks. In that case, Ringling Brothers–Barum & Bailey challenged Utah's use of the slogan "The Greatest Snow on Earth" as diluting its famous slogan, "The Greatest Show on Earth." In denying Utah's motion to dismiss because the slogans were not identical, the court said that the marks need not be identical.

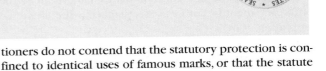

CASE 14-7

Victor Moseley and Kathy Moseley et al., dba Victor's Little Secret v. V Secret Catalogue, Inc. et al.
Supreme Court of the United States
537 U.S. 418, 123 S.Ct.1115 (2003)

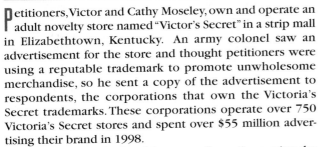

Petitioners, Victor and Cathy Moseley, own and operate an adult novelty store named "Victor's Secret" in a strip mall in Elizabethtown, Kentucky. An army colonel saw an advertisement for the store and thought petitioners were using a reputable trademark to promote unwholesome merchandise, so he sent a copy of the advertisement to respondents, the corporations that own the Victoria's Secret trademarks. These corporations operate over 750 Victoria's Secret stores and spent over $55 million advertising their brand in 1998.

Respondents asked petitioners to discontinue using the name, and they responded by changing the store's name to "Victor's Little Secret." Respondents then filed a lawsuit containing four separate claims for (1) trademark infringement, alleging that petitioners' use of their trade name was "likely to cause confusion and/or mistake"; (2) unfair competition, alleging misrepresentation; (3) "federal dilution" in violation of the Federal Trademark Dilution Act (FTDA); and (4) trademark infringement and unfair competition in violation of the common law of Kentucky. The dilution count was premised on the claim that petitioners' conduct was "likely to blur and erode the distinctiveness" and "tarnish the reputation" of the Victoria's Secret trademark.

Finding that the record contained no evidence of actual confusion between the parties' marks, the district court concluded that "no likelihood of confusion exists as a matter of law" and entered summary judgment for the Moseleys on the infringement and unfair competition claims. With respect to the FTDA claim, however, the court ruled for V Secret Catalogue, and the Moseleys appealed. The Sixth Circuit affirmed, finding that respondents' mark was "distinctive" and that the evidence established "dilution" even though no actual harm had been proved.

Justice Stevens

… The Victoria's Secret mark is unquestionably valuable and petitioners have not challenged the conclusion that it qualifies as a "famous mark" within the meaning of the statute. Moreover, as we understand their submission, peti-

tioners do not contend that the statutory protection is confined to identical uses of famous marks, or that the statute should be construed more narrowly in a case such as this.

The District Court's decision in this case rested on the conclusion that the name of petitioners' store "tarnished" the reputation of respondents' mark, and the Court of Appeals relied on both "tarnishment" and "blurring" to support its affirmance. Petitioners have not disputed the relevance of tarnishment, presumably because that concept was prominent in litigation brought under state antidilution statutes and because it was mentioned in the legislative history. … Indeed, the contrast between the state statutes, which expressly refer to both "injury to business reputation" and to "dilution of the distinctive quality of a trade name or trademark," and the federal statute which refers only to the latter, arguably supports a narrower reading of the FTDA.

… The relevant text of the FTDA provides that "the owner of a famous mark" is entitled to injunctive relief against another person's commercial use of a mark or trade name if that use "causes dilution of the distinctive quality" of the famous mark. This text unambiguously requires a showing of actual dilution, rather than a likelihood of dilution.

This conclusion is fortified by the definition of the term "dilution" itself. That definition provides:

"The term 'dilution' means the lessening of the capacity of a famous mark to identify and distinguish goods or services, regardless of the presence or absence of—

"(1) competition between the owner of the famous mark and other parties, or

"(2) likelihood of confusion, mistake, or deception."

The contrast between the initial reference to an actual "lessening of the capacity" of the mark, and the later reference to a "likelihood of confusion, mistake, or deception" in the second caveat confirms the conclusion that actual dilution must be established.

Of course, that does not mean that the consequences of dilution, such as an actual loss of sales or profits, must also be proved. … We do agree, however, with that court's conclusion that, at least where the marks at issue are not identical, the mere fact that consumers mentally associate the junior user's mark with a famous mark is not sufficient to establish actionable dilution. As the facts of that case demonstrate, such mental association will not necessarily reduce the capacity of the famous mark to identify the goods of its owner, the statutory requirement for dilution under the FTDA. For even though Utah drivers may be reminded of the circus when they see a license plate referring to the "greatest snow on earth," it by no means follows that they will associate "the greatest show on earth" with skiing or snow sports, or associate it less strongly or exclusively with the circus. "Blurring" is not a necessary consequence of mental association. (Nor, for that matter, is "tarnishing.")

The record in this case establishes that an army officer who saw the advertisement of the opening of a store named "Victor's Secret" did make the mental association with "Victoria's Secret," but it also shows that he did not therefore form any different impression of the store that his wife and daughter had patronized. There is a complete absence of evidence of any lessening of the capacity of the Victoria's Secret mark to identify and distinguish goods or services sold in Victoria's Secret stores or advertised in its catalogs. The officer was offended by the ad, but it did not change his conception of Victoria's Secret. His offense was directed entirely at petitioners, not at respondents. Moreover, the expert retained by respondents had nothing to say about the impact of petitioners' name on the strength of respondents' mark.

Noting that consumer surveys and other means of demonstrating actual dilution are expensive and often unreliable, respondents and their amici argue that evidence of an actual "lessening of the capacity of a famous mark to identify and distinguish goods or services," may be difficult to obtain. It may well be, however, that direct evidence of dilution such as consumer surveys will not be necessary if actual dilution can reliably be proved through circumstantial evidence—the obvious case is one where the junior and senior marks are identical. Whatever difficulties of proof may be entailed, they are not an acceptable reason for dispensing with proof of an essential element of a statutory violation. The evidence in the present record is not sufficient to support the summary judgment on the dilution count, and the judgment is therefore reversed.

Judgment for Petitioners.

TRADE SECRETS

A **trade secret** is a process, product, method of operation, or compilation of information that gives a businessperson an advantage over his or her competitors. Inventions and designs may also be considered trade secrets. A trade secret is protected by the common law from unlawful appropriation by competitors as long as it is kept secret and comprises elements not generally known in the trade.

Competitors may discover the "secret" by any lawful means, such as reverse engineering or by going on public tours of plants and observing the use of trade secrets. Discovery of the secret means there is no longer a trade secret to be protected.

In order to enjoin a competitor from continuing the use of a trade secret or to recover damages caused by the use of the secret, a plaintiff must prove that:

1. A trade secret actually existed.

2. The defendant acquired it through unlawful means such as breaking into the plaintiff's business and stealing it or securing it through misuse of a confidential relationship with the plaintiff or one of the plaintiff's present or former employees.

3. The defendant used the trade secret without the plaintiff's permission.

> **trade secret** A process, product, method of operation, or compilation of information used in a business that is not known to the public and that may bestow a competitive advantage on the business.

PATENTS

A **patent** protects a product, process, invention, machine, or plant produced by asexual reproduction. For this protection to be granted, certain criteria must be satisfied (Exhibit 14-6). First, the object of the patent must be *novel*, or new. No one else must have previously made or published the plans for this object. The second criterion is that it be *useful*, unless it is a design patent. It must provide

> **patent** Grants the holder the exclusive right to produce, sell, and use a product, process, invention, machine, or asexually reproduced plant for 20 years.

EXHIBIT 14-6

CRITERIA FOR A PATENT

- Novel
- Useful
- Nonobvious

some utility to society. The final criterion is that it be *nonobvious*. The invention must not be one that the person of ordinary skill in the trade could have easily discovered. When a patent is issued for an object, it gives its holder the exclusive right to produce, sell, and use the object of the patent for 20 years. The holder of the patent may license, or allow others to manufacture and sell, the patented object. In most cases, patents are licensed in exchange for the payment of royalties, a sum of money paid for each use of the patented process.

The only restriction on the patent holder is that he or she may not use the patent for an illegal purpose. The two most common illegal purposes would be tying arrangements and cross-licensing. A **tying arrangement** occurs when the patent holder issues a license to use the patented object only if the licensee agrees also to buy some nonpatented product from the holder. **Cross-licensing** occurs when two patent holders license each other to use their patents only on the condition that neither licenses anyone else to use his or her patent without the other's consent. Both of these activities are unlawful because they tend to reduce competition.

To obtain a patent, one generally contacts an attorney licensed to practice before the U.S. Patent Office. The attorney does a *patent search* to make sure that no other similar patent exists. If it does not, the attorney fills out a patent application and files it with the Patent Office. The Patent Office evaluates the application, and, if the object meets the criteria already described, a patent is issued.

Once the patent is issued, the holder may bring a patent infringement suit in a federal court against anyone who uses, sells, or manufactures the patented invention without the permission of the patent holder. A successful action may result in an injunction prohibiting further use of the patented item by the infringer and also an award of damages. Sometimes, however, the result of the case is that the holder loses the patent. This loss would occur when the infringer is able to prove that the Patent Office should not have issued the patent in the first place.

A common dilemma facing an inventor is whether to protect an invention through patent or trade secret law. If the inventor successfully patents and defends the patent, the patent holder has a guarantee of an exclusive monopoly on the use of the invention for 20 years, a substantial period of time. The problem is that, once this period is over, the patented good goes into the public domain and everyone has access to it. There is also the risk that the patent may be successfully challenged and the protection lost prematurely.

Trade secret law, on the other hand, could protect the invention in perpetuity. The problem is that once someone discovers the secret lawfully, the protection is lost.

tying arrangement A restraint of trade wherein the seller permits a buyer to purchase one product or service only if the buyer agrees to purchase a second product or service. For example, a patent holder issues a license to use a patented object on condition that the licensee agree to also buy nonpatented products from the patent holder.

cross-licensing An illegal practice in which two patent holders license each other to use their patented objects only on condition that neither will license anyone else to use those patented objects without the other's consent.

copyright The exclusive legal right to reproduce, publish, and sell the fixed form of an expression of an original creative idea.

COPYRIGHTS

Copyrights protect the *expression* of creative ideas. They do not protect the ideas themselves but only their fixed form of expression. Copyrights protect a diverse range of creative works, such as books, periodicals, musical compositions, plays, motion pictures, sound recordings, lectures, works of art, and computer programs. Titles and short phrases may not be copyrighted.

There are three criteria for a work to be copyrightable (Exhibit 14-7). First, it must be *fixed*, which means set out in a tangible medium of expression. Next, it must also be *original*. Finally, it must be *creative*.

A copyright automatically arises under common law when the idea is expressed in tangible form and carries appropriate notice. However, if the work is freely distributed without notice of copyright, the work falls into the public domain. A copyrighted work that is reproduced with the appropriate notice affixed is protected for the life of its creator plus 70 years, or if the owner is a publisher, for 95 years after the date of publication or 120 years after creation.

Under the common law of copyright, any infringer may be enjoined from reproducing a copyrighted work. For the creator to be able to sue the infringer to recover damages arising from the infringement, however, the copyrighted work must be registered. One may register a work by filing a form with the Register of Copyright and providing two copies of the copyrighted materials to the Library of Congress. Whenever the work is reproduced, it must be accompanied by the appropriate notice of copyright. Printed works, for example, must be published with the word *copyright* and the symbol © or the abbreviation *copr.*, followed by the first date of publication and the name of the copyright owner. Once the work is registered, as long as it is always accompanied by the notice of copyright when reproduced, the holder of the copyright has the additional right to sue any infringer for damages caused by the infringer's use of the copyrighted materials and to recover any profits made by the infringer on the copyrighted material.

A source of controversy involving copyrighted works is the application of the **fair use doctrine**. This doctrine provides that a portion of a copyrighted work may be reproduced for purposes of "criticism, comment, news reporting, teaching (including multiple copies for classroom use), scholarships, and research." When deciding whether the use is fair, the court not only looks at the purpose of the use but also looks at the amount of the work that is used and whether the use has any impact on the commercial value of the copyrighted work.

Under this broad conception of fair use, parody is also protected. But it is difficult to know when the author has taken so much of the original that the court will find infringement and not fair use. For example, in 2001, the estate of the author of *Gone with the Wind* sought an injunction to block the publication of *The Wind Done Gone*. The author of the second text said it was a parody of the former book and a portrayal of life in the Old South from a black point of view. However, the estate of the author of *Gone with the Wind* claimed that the second book was an illegal sequel that infringed on the older work, citing the book's direct taking of characters, character traits, scenes, settings, physical

fair use doctrine A legal doctrine providing that a portion of a copyrighted work may be reproduced for purposes of "criticism, comment, news reporting, teaching (including multiple copies for classroom use), scholarships, and research."

- Fixed Form
- Original
- Creative

EXHIBIT 14-7

CRITERIA FOR A COPYRIGHT

descriptions, and plot from the copyrighted novel, as well as its appropriation of direct quotes from the novel.[14]

The district court initially granted the injunction, finding that (1) the works were substantially similar; (2) the overriding purpose of *The Wind Done Gone* was to create a sequel, not a parody, although the book was partially transformative; (3) the book used more of the original work than necessary to obtain a parodic effect; (4) the effect of the allegedly infringing use on the market value of the original novel weighed in favor of the copyright owners; (5) the owners showed substantial likelihood of success on the merits; (6) the defendant publisher did not rebut the presumption of irreparable injury; (7) the balance of harms weighed in favor of the owners; and (8) competing public interests weighed in favor of preserving the owners' copyright interests.[15]

However, on appeal, the higher court overturned the district court's decision, claiming the injunction was an unlawful prior restraint of speech under the First Amendment. The court looked at the record and did not believe that the plaintiffs had made a strong enough case that (1) there was a substantial likelihood that the plaintiffs would prevail on the merits, (2) that the plaintiffs would suffer irreparable harm if the injunction were not granted, (3) that the threatened injury to the defendant outweighed that to the defendant, and (4) that the granting of the injunction would be in the public interest, which are the necessary prerequisites for the granting of a preliminary injunction.[16]

The Wind Done Gone went on sale June 28, 2001, with the following words encircled on its cover: "An Unauthorized Parody." The appellate court accurately predicted that plaintiffs would not find success on the merits. Had the plaintiffs succeed however, they would have been entitled to a permanent injunction and most likely damages in the amount of the profits made from the infringing work.

GLOBAL DIMENSIONS OF PROPERTY LAW

The primary international protection for intellectual property is offered through multilateral conventions. These treaties are generally administered by the World Intellectual Property Organization, a specialized agency of the United Nations.

THE BERNE CONVENTION OF 1886

The Berne Convention of 1886, to which 81 countries are now signatories, is the oldest treaty designed to protect artistic rights. Four basic principles underlie obligations of signatories to the treaty:

1. The national treatment principle requires each member nation to protect artists of all signatory nations equally.

---

[14] *Mitchell and Joseph Reynolds Mitchell V. Houghton Mifflin Co.*, 58 U.S.P.Q.2d 1652 (2001).

[15] *Id.*

[16] *Mitchell and Joseph Reynolds Mitchell v. Houghton Mifflin Co.*, 252 F.3d 265 (2001).

2. The nonconditional protection principle requires that protection not be conditioned on the use of formalities although the country of origin may require registration or a similar formality.

3. The protection independent of protection in the country of origin principle allows nationals of nonsignatory countries to protect works if they are created in a member country.

4. The common rules principle establishes minimum standards for granting copyrights that all nations must meet.

UNIVERSAL COPYRIGHT CONVENTION

Although the United States, China, and Russia are now signatories to the Berne Convention, they and other nations had not signed the treaty in the 1950s because they disagreed with some of its provisions. Consequently, they decided to enter into another convention that would not contravene the rights of anyone under the Berne Convention and would be loose enough for all nations to sign. This new document was the Universal Copyright Convention. The document went into effect in 1950 and was revised, along with the Berne Convention, in 1971. Today, 93 nations have signed either the 1952 or the 1971 version.

The Universal Copyright Convention differs from the Berne Convention primarily by allowing members to establish formalities for protection and making exceptions to common rules as long as the exceptions are not inconsistent with the essence of the treaty. It also does not require signatory countries to protect authors' rights.

THE PARIS CONVENTION OF 1883

The Paris Convention now has 101 members who have agreed to protect so-called industrial rights, such as inventions and trademarks. Unfair competition is also restricted under the Paris Convention.

The treaty has been revised several times, and not all members have signed all versions. Although the treaty is highly complex, it has three basic principles: (1) *national treatment*, as defined under the Berne Convention; (2) *the right of priority*, which allows a national of a member state 12 months after filing in his or her home nation to file an application in any other member state and have the date of application be considered the date of the filing in the home nation; and (3) *common rules*, which set out minimum standards of protection in all states. These common rules include such items as outlawing false labeling and protecting trade names of companies from member states even without registration.

PATENT COOPERATION TREATY

The Patent Cooperation Treaty contains a provision for making application for a patent in any member state an international application that would be as effective as filing individually in all member states. When the application is filed in any member state, the application is then forwarded to an international search authority.

Despite the existence of such agreements, enforcement in foreign countries is often very lax. In 1994, problems with blatant trademark infringement in China were so severe that President Clinton threatened to impose trade sanctions if enforcement was not improved.

SUMMARY

Property is a bundle of rights in relation to a tangible object, the most significant of which is probably the right to exclude others. Property can be divided into three categories: real property, land and anything permanently attached to it; personal property, tangible movable objects and intangible objects; and intellectual property, property that is primarily the result of one's mental rather than physical efforts. Real property can be transferred voluntarily or involuntarily. Voluntary transfers include transfer by gift or sale. Adverse possession and condemnation are the two involuntary means. Personal property likewise can be transferred voluntarily through a gift or sale. It may also be transferred involuntarily if it is lost or mislaid.

The primary forms of intellectual property we protect are trademarks, copyrights, patents, and trade secrets. Unlike most property, which is protected by state law, the first three forms of intellectual property are protected by federal statutes. Intellectual property is protected internationally primarily by the use of treaties. Such treaties include the Universal Copyright Convention, the Berne Convention, and the Paris Convention of 1883.

REVIEW QUESTIONS

14-1 Explain why each of the following is or is not real property.

   a. A fence   d. A built-in oven

   b. A tree   e. A refrigerator

   c. A house trailer

14-2 Define the primary estates in land.

14-3 Explain the circumstances under which each of the following types of ownership would be most desirable. Give reasons for your responses.

   a. Joint tenancy

   b. Tenancy in common

   c. Tenancy by the entirety

14-4 Explain how the ownership of land may be transferred.

14-5 Explain how a general warranty deed differs from a quitclaim deed.

14-6 What are the similarities and differences between condemnation and adverse possession?

REVIEW PROBLEMS

14-7 The plaintiff owned land in an area zoned for buildable private parks. The city rezoned the land to allow only parks open to the public. This rezoning effectively prohibited the plaintiff from generating any sort of income from the land. Was the plaintiff correct in his contention that this constituted a deprivation of property without due process of law?

14-8 Judy worked the morning shift at Wild Oats. She bought a Pepsi but got too busy to drink it, so she left it on a shelf behind the counter to drink the next day. Cindy was working that afternoon. She got thirsty and asked her coworkers if the Pepsi belonged to any of

them. When no one claimed it, she opened the bottle, saw some fine print on the underside of the cap, and read, "You have won a million dollars." When Judy found out what happened, she confronted Cindy and claimed the prize as hers. Explain who should receive the prize money and why.

14-9 Hallman spent the night at the New Colonial Hotel. On inquiry, he was told that the bellboy would take care of his car. The bellboy took the car to a nearby parking lot and left the car and keys with the lot attendant. He gave Hallman a claim check bearing the name of the lot and stamped "New Colonial." When Hallman went to pick up his car, the side window was broken and over $500 worth of personal property was missing. Who was liable for the missing personalty and the damage to the car? Why?

14-10 Thrifty Inn decides to open a motel along an interstate that will provide cheap lodging. It calls the motel Sleep McCheap. McDonald's seeks to enjoin Thrifty Inns from using the name, claiming that it violates the McDonald's trademark as well as the McStop trademark that the firm has for its one-stop business that provides cheap food, cheap lodging, and cheap gas. Will the injunction be granted? Why or why not?

14-11 Amerec Corporation had developed a secret, unpatented process for producing methanol and had

built a special plant where it was going to use this process. The Christophers were hired by a competitor of Amerec to take aerial photographs of the construction. Amerec sued the photographers for misappropriation of trade secrets. What defenses might the Christophers raise? Would these be successful?

14-12 Professor Kendall wants students to read three articles from a recently published journal. The professor, who is concerned about the students' expenditures for books, photocopies the articles and places them on reserve. The publisher of the journal sues the professor for copyright infringement. What defense will the professor raise? Would this defense be successful?

CASE PROBLEMS

14-13 The Casino Reinvestment Development Authority (CRDA) sought to take the property of several private property owners under the power of eminent domain. The property taken would be given to a local casino for the purposes of expansion and the construction of additional parking. As a result of the expansion, the CRDA stated that the public would benefit by increased employment, increased tourism, and alleviation of traffic congestion. The landowners challenged the constitutionality of the taking. Do you think the proposed condemnation was constitutional? How do you think the court decided? *CRDA v. Banin*, 727 A.2d 102 (1998)

14-14 A church owns and occupies several lots within a subdivision in the Country Club District in Kansas City. When the church proposed the building of a new parking lot, the nonprofit association overseeing the Country Club District filed suit to enforce a restrictive covenant that precluded the building on any lots for anything other than "private residence purposes." The trial court ruled in favor of the association and the church appealed claiming circumstances have changed, making the restrictive convenant unenforcable. Was the church successful with its argument? Why or why not? *Country Club Dist. Homes Assn. v. Country Club Christian Church*, 118 SW3d 185 (Ct. App., Mo., 2003)

14-15 Origins Natural Resources owns the trademark "Origins." It primarily used the mark on a highly successful line of cosmetics that are sold nationally, and had used the mark on a few clothing items. Kotler, the defendant, wanted to use the trademark "Natural Origins" on a line of upscale women's clothing. The trademark "Natural Origins" looked nothing like the "Origins" mark used on the cosmetics.

Origins Natural Resources filed for an injunction against the defendant, arguing that the use of "Natural Origins" constituted infringement and diluted the value of the "Origins" trademark. Why do you think the court either granted or denied the injunction? *Origins Natural Resources, Inc. v. Kotler*, 2001 WL 492429 (S.D. N.Y., 2001)

14-16 Marketing Displays, Inc. (MDI), held now-expired utility patents for a "dual-spring design" mechanism that keeps temporary road and other outdoor signs upright in adverse wind conditions. After the patents expired, TrafFix Devices, Inc., a competitor, began marketing sign stands with a dual-spring mechanism copied from MDI's design. MDI claimed that its sign stands were recognizable to buyers and users because the patented design was visible near the sign stand's base, so the company brought suit under the Trademark Act of 1964 for, among other claims, trade dress infringement.

TrafFix filed a motion for summary judgment, arguing that no reasonable trier of fact could determine that MDI had established secondary meaning in its alleged trade dress; that is, consumers did not associate the dual-spring design's look with MDI. TrafFix also argued that there could be no trade dress protection for the motion. The Sixth Circuit disagreed. How do you believe the U.S. Supreme Court ruled in this case, and why? *TrafFix Devices, Inc. v. Marketing Displays, Inc.*, 121 S.Ct. 1255 to 121 S.Ct. 1255 (2001)

14-17 Dippin' Dots Inc. markets and sells a brightly colored, flash-frozen ice cream it calls "dippin' dots," consisting of free-flowing small beads (or dots) of ice cream. Dippin' Dots owns the patent to the flash-freezing process it uses to make its ice cream. Frosty Bites Distribution is a competitor to Dippin' Dots that sells brightly colored flash-frozen ice cream, called Frosty Bites, that are mostly popcorn-shaped, as well as small and spherical in shape. Dippin' Dots brought suit against Frosty Bites alleging trade dress infringement. Dippin' Dots claims that Frosty Bites are substantially similar in appearance to Dippin' Dots. What elements must Dippin' Dots prove to win its case? Why do you believe Dippin' Dots was or was not successful? *Dippin' Dots, Inc. v. Frosty Bites Dist.*, LLC, 2004 U.S. App. LEXIS 9217 (11th Cir, 2004)

14-18 Plaintiff Columbia Pictures Industries, Inc., brought a copyright infringement action against Miramax Films Corporation. The successful motion picture *Men in Black*, produced by Columbia Pictures, grossed over $250 million at the box office in 1997. In advertising the film, Columbia produced a copyrighted "MIB Poster" and two copyrighted "MIB trailers" shown in theaters. The poster shows Will Smith and Tommy Lee Jones standing in front of the New York City skyline. They hold oversized weapons, and the copy reads: "Protecting the Earth from the Scum of the Universe." The movie trailers use the same slogan and show a shadow of Smith and Jones superimposed over the letters *MIB*.

In 1998, Miramax Films Corporation produced the film *The Big One*. This was a documentary concerning corporate America's quest for profits at the expense of jobs and plant closings. Prior to the release, Miramax also produced posters and movie trailers. The posters featured Michael Moore, the writer and director of the film, standing in front of the New York City skyline with an oversized microphone. The copy reads: "Protecting the Earth from the Scum of Corporate America." The slogan is used again in the movie trailer, and the trailer ends with a picture of Moore superimposed over the letters *TBO*.

The promotions for *The Big One* were pulled after Miramax received complaints from Columbia Pictures. Columbia argued that Miramax used copyrighted material to generate profits for the film. Miramax contended that it was protected under the fair use doctrine and argued that the films were not similar in nature. Whom do you think the court decided in favor of? Why? *Columbia Pictures Industries, Inc. v. Miramax Films Corp.*, 11 F. Supp 1179 (1998)

ASSIGNMENT ON THE INTERNET

This chapter introduced you to government regulation and protection of various forms of property. One such regulation and protection used by the government is zoning. Using the Web site links that follow (www.megalaw.com/top/zoning.php would be most useful), find a recent court case in which a zoning law was challenged, or where the plaintiff argued that a zoning law resulted in a taking of property.

Once you have found such a case, identify the court's reasoning and the ethical norms used in such reasoning. Was the particular zoning law found to be unreasonable? Now, compare the reasoning of your case to that of *Dolan v. City of Tigard*. Are the ethical norms different or the same?

 ## ON THE INTERNET

www.benedict.com Find out more about copyrights from "The Copyright Website."

www.uspto.gov This is the Web site of the United States Patent and Trademark Office.

www.wipo.int This is the home page of the World Intellectual Property Organization.

www.intelproplaw.com The Intellectual Property Law Server provides useful information on patent, trademark, and copyright intellectual property. The many links at this site contain laws, articles, and cases of interest.

sunsite.berkeley.edu/Copyright This site contains ample links to articles, journals, and research tools regarding property rights, especially intellectual property rights.

www.lucs.org The Land Use Controls site provides information about institutional controls in such areas such as brownefields and superfund sites.

www.megalaw.com/top/zoning.php Visit this site for recent court cases on zoning issues and links to local governments' zoning laws and regulations.

15

AGENCY LAW

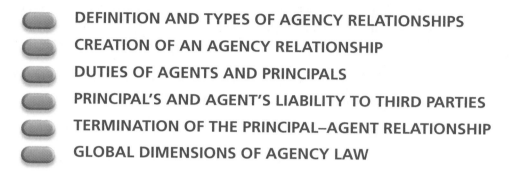

- DEFINITION AND TYPES OF AGENCY RELATIONSHIPS
- CREATION OF AN AGENCY RELATIONSHIP
- DUTIES OF AGENTS AND PRINCIPALS
- PRINCIPAL'S AND AGENT'S LIABILITY TO THIRD PARTIES
- TERMINATION OF THE PRINCIPAL–AGENT RELATIONSHIP
- GLOBAL DIMENSIONS OF AGENCY LAW

Agency law has become more prominent in our complex postindustrial society. In an earlier period, when business owners (principals) did most or all of their business on a one-to-one basis with their customers (third parties), agents played a very small role in the business environment. As business entities became larger and conducted far-flung transactions within the United States and worldwide, businesspeople felt a need to hire domestic and foreign agents to represent their interests to potential customers.

This chapter examines the following matters: (1) the definition and creation of an agency relationship, as well as employment relationships; (2) the rights and duties of agents and principals toward each other and toward third parties; (3) the law of contracts and torts as they affect agency relationships; and (4) the global dimensions of agency law.

Critical Thinking About the Law

Agency law is based on a trusting relationship between two parties or individuals. Critical thinking skills, such as identifying ethical norms and missing information, are especially important when thinking about agency relationships.

1. Agency relationships are frequently used in modern society. Businesses increasingly rely on agents to conduct their business with customers. What ethical norms would businesses expect their agents to hold in carrying out their responsibilities?

   Clue: Look at the list of ethical norms and ask yourself: Which would be most important to a business?

2. As you will soon learn, agency relationships can be formed by informal oral agreements or by formal written contracts. Judges are often faced with the task of determining whether an agency relationship exists in informal oral agreements or formal written contracts or whether an agency relationship exists after an agent has performed a task. What kinds of information would be especially important to a judge in deciding whether an agency relationship had been established?

   Clue: What would tend to happen if a business formed a relationship with an employee to carry out a task?

3. Consider the definitions of justice in Chapter 1. How might the fact that the agent has already performed the task affect the judge's decision?

   Clue: Do any of the definitions of justice give special guidance here?

DEFINITION AND TYPES OF AGENCY RELATIONSHIPS

DEFINITION OF AGENCY

agency A fiduciary relationship between two persons in which one (the agent) acts on behalf of, and is subject to the control of, the other (the principal).

Agency is defined as a fiduciary relationship (one of trust and confidence) between two persons in which they mutually agree that one person (the agent) will act on behalf of the other (the principal) and be subject to the latter's control and consent. For example, a corporate officer who enters into contracts that legally bind the corporation is representing the corporation as an agent.

Provided they are able to understand the instructions of a principal, most people have the capacity to act as agents. For example, a minor can be employed by a principal to act as an agent in making an offer of employment to a third person. The minor's lack of capacity to enter a contract is immaterial here because the contract is between the principal and the third party. (However, the minor's lack of contractual capacity means that any agreement between the minor and the principal may be voided by the minor before he or she reaches majority age or shortly thereafter.)

TYPES OF AGENCY RELATIONSHIPS

principal–agent relationship One in which the principal gives the agent expressed or actual authority to act on the former's behalf.

Agency law is concerned with three types of relationships: principal–agent, employer–employee, and employer–independent contractor. These relationships are summarized in Table 15-1.

Principal–Agent. The **principal–agent relationship** (Exhibit 15-1) is one in which the principal (usually an employer) hires an agent (employee) and gives the agent either expressed or actual authority to act on the principal's behalf.

Principal–agent	Agent is hired by principal to act on his or her behalf subject to the latter's control and consent.
Employer–employee	Employer controls the physical conduct and determines the details of performance of employee.
Employer–independent contractor	Employer does not control the details of performance and conduct of independent contractor.

TABLE 15-1

TYPES OF AGENCY RELATIONSHIPS

Expressed authority arises from specific statements made by the principal to the agent. **Actual authority** includes expressed authority and implied authority—that authority customarily given to an agent in an industry, trade, or profession. The principal–agent relationship is the most basic type of agency relationship. It is, in fact, the foundation of the next two types of agency relationships we discuss: that between employer and employee and that between principal and independent contractor.

Employer–Employee. The employer–employee relationship evolved out of the traditional master–servant relationship, in which a master employed a servant to perform services and the servant's conduct was subject to the master's physical control. Under the doctrine of **respondeat superior**, the master was responsible for the acts of servants that were within the scope of their employment. In the postindustrialized version of this arrangement, the **employer–employee relationship**, the employee is subject to the control of the employer and, in accordance with expressed or implied authority, may enter into contractual relationships on behalf of the employer. In general, any agent who works for pay is considered an employee, and any employee, unless specifically limited, who deals with a third party is given agent's status. The employer–employee relationship is the only agency relationship that encompasses workers' compensation, Social Security, and unemployment compensation laws (as well as numerous other state and federal laws), thus its importance. It is also important to distinguish the employer–employee relationship from an **employer–independent contractor relationship**, which normally does not fall under these statutes, and that is an important distinction in the legal environment of business.

expressed authority
Authority that arises from specific statements made by the principal (employer) to the agent (employee).

actual authority Includes expressed authority as well as implied authority, or that authority customarily given to an agent in an industry, trade, or profession.

respondeat superior Legal doctrine imposing liability on a principal for torts committed by an agent who is employed by the principal and subject to the principal's control.

employer–employee relationship One in which an agent (employee) who works for pay and is subject to the control of the principal (employer) may enter into contractual relationships on the latter's behalf.

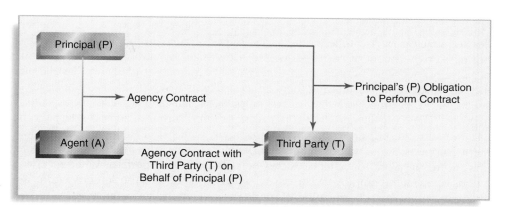

EXHIBIT 15-1

PRINCIPAL–AGENCY RELATIONSHIP

Linking Law & Business

Finance

In finance you have examined agency relationships and particularly costs associated with such. For example, if both parties to a relationship are utility maximizers, there is reason to believe the agent will not act in the best interest of the principal. The principal can limit divergencies from his or hes interest by establishing appropriate incentives for the agent by monitoring costs of agents. In addition, in some situations it pays the agent to expend resources (bonding costs) to make sure the principal is not harmed.

The sum of agency costs include:

1. Monitoring expenditures by the principal
2. Bonding expenditures by the agent
3. Residual loss

Source: M. Jensen, and W. H. Mecking, "Agency Costs and the Theory of the Firm," *Journal of Financial Economics*, 3 (1976), pp. 79, 81.

---

employer–independent contractor relationship
One in which the agent (independent contractor) is hired by the principal (employer) to do a specific job but is not controlled with respect to physical conduct or details of work performance.

Employer–Independent Contractor. Independent contractors are hired by the employer to do a specific job but are not controlled with respect to their physical conduct or the details of their work performance. In this type of agency relationship, the employer is normally not subject to payments into workers' compensation pools and Social Security or to liability for the torts of the independent contractor. (Torts, you will recall, are wrongful acts, other than breaches of contract, for which damages may be obtained.) For example, the employer of a taxi driver who is an independent contractor and owns his or her own cab is not liable in most cases for damages when the driver injures another person in an accident.

When called on to distinguish between an employee and an independent contractor, it is the degree of control the employer has over the agent that courts scrutinize. Courts also consider such factors as (1) whether the hired persons had a distinct occupation or profession, (2) whether they supplied their own tools and equipment, (3) whether they were employed only for a specific time period, (4) whether they were paid hourly or on completion of a job, and (5) what degree of skill was required to do the job.

In order to escape paying unemployment insurance taxes, as well as medical benefits, many employers in recent years have classified their workers as independent contractors or part-time workers. A common strategy in the highly competitive business environment of the 1990s was to "downsize" by cutting back on the number of employees in a corporation through early retirement plans and layoffs and then to "restructure" by rehiring them as "consultants" (independent contractors) to accomplish the same work they did as employees. This is essentially a cost-cutting measure. The "consultants" draw a per diem or lump sum instead of a salary for the job they are hired to perform, and the company saves on health care, unemployment compensation, and Social Security benefits. In turn, the independent contractors are free to work for others besides their old employer, perhaps while receiving a pension from the employer. The case that follows indicates the scrutiny courts are giving to employers' classification of workers as independent contractors.

CASE 15-1

Daws Critical Care Registry, Inc. v. Department of Labor, Employment Security Division
Connecticut Superior Court,
622 A.2d 222 (1992)

Daws Critical Care Registry (plaintiff), a professional nurse agency, is appealing a decision by the administrator of the Connecticut Unemployment Compensation Act of the Connecticut Department of Labor (defendant) that Daws should pay unemployment taxes to the department. Daws argues that the nurses it supplies to medical facilities are independent contractors and, therefore, it is not liable for this tax. Daws supplies nurses to medical facilities on request from a list of nurses it maintains, then bills the medical facilities and pays the nurses a set wage depending on their qualifications. Nurses may work for other agencies as well as Daws.

Justice Healy

Under the Unemployment Compensation Act the term "employment" means: "Service performed by an individual shall be deemed to be employment subject to this chapter irrespective of whether the common law relationship of master and servant exists, unless and until it is shown to the satisfaction of the administrator that (A) such individual has been and will continue to be free from control and direction in connection with the performance of such service; and (B) such service is performed either outside the usual course of the business for which the service is performed or is performed outside of all the places of business of the enterprise for which the service is performed; and (C) such individual is customarily engaged in an independently established trade, occupation, profession or business of the same nature as that involved in the service performed. ..." This is the act's ABC test.

This statute not only codifies common law rules used to determine the existence of an employe–employee relationship, but also incorporates what is known "in Connecticut and throughout the country in similar legislation as the 'ABC test' [which is used] to ascertain whether an employer–employee relationship exists under the act." For the plaintiff to prove that it is not an employer and, thus, has no liability under the act for unemployment taxes, it must show that it has satisfied all three prongs of the ABC test.

In taking up the ABC test in the present case, part A will be examined first. Under that part Daws bore the burden of proving under the statute that its nurses have "been and will continue to be free from any control or direction" in connection with the performance of such service, "both under [their] contract [for the performance of service] and in fact." Part A of the test invokes essen-

tially the same criteria as the independent contractor test at common law: The fundamental distinction between an employee and an independent contractor depends upon the existence or nonexistence of the right to control the means and methods of work. The test of the relationship is the right to control. It is not the fact of actual interference with the control, but the right to interfere, that makes the difference between an independent contractor and a servant or agent.

The court is aware that the test of the relationship does not depend upon the actual exercise of the right to control by Daws but that the existence of the right to control is sufficient. But it is submitted that Daws did not have the general right to control their nurses. It had no such control or even the right to control over the means and methods of the nurses' services rendered at the medical facilities where their assignments took them. Daws's function, after satisfying itself that a nurse was "competent," was fairly limited to arranging times mutually convenient for the nurse and the particular medical facility where the nurse's services were to be rendered and examining a nurse's pay invoices when submitted to it for payment and in making payment. It did not have "the right to general control of the activities." Once the assignment to a particular medical facility was offered by Daws and undertaken by a Daws nurse, the nurse went there and, subject to the protocol of that facility, rendered her professional services under that facility's direction. The lack of a right to control is further indicated by the proof that no representative of Daws ever visited a medical facility to check on the performance of any of their nurses. The court also notes that Daws did not conduct any orientations for its nurses nor did it have any manual of instructions that it issued to them. ... There is no question but that Daws processed the invoices submitted to it by its nurses for payment for their nursing services at whatever medical facility they might work. These invoices were on forms provided by Daws and the times indicated thereon as having been worked had to be certified to by a supervisor at that particular facility before being processed by Daws. Payment was at an hourly rate. The defendant, in arguing that the Daws nurses are employees, maintains that "the hourly rate of pay criterion is not merely satisfied; instead a comprehensive pay scheme on an hourly and continuing basis during a nurse's performance of service is established. This apparently is to suggest that the "hourly rate criterion" he contends for is to be distinguished, as the defendant claims, from payment of an independent contractor at the end of an entire project without taking account of the number of hours worked on the project. This court believes otherwise. "The manner of remuneration, whether in wages, salary commission, by piece or job, is not decisive or controlling in determining whether one is an employee or an independent contractor exercising control over the manner of his own work." In other words, the methods used to determine the payment to be made for the work done is not of controlling significance. The reality is that the payor (Daws), in effect, served in the nature of conduit for payment.

Under all the evidence, the court concludes that the facts demonstrate ... that Daws did satisfy part A of the ABC test.

Part B of the ABC test in our statute says: "such service is performed either outside the usual course of the business for which the service is performed or is performed outside of all the places of business of the enterprise for which the service is performed."

Daws argues that it, in effect, brokers nursing personnel. A "broker" has been said generally to be one whose business it is to bring buyer and seller together. A "broker" has also been said to be a "middleman or negotiator between parties." There can be little question but that Daws is in the business of providing, indeed brokering, nurses to its clients: medical facilities. There also can be little question but that the nurses so provided furnished their professional services at the particular medical facility. Once, however, they went on an assignment, Daws had no control over them, certainly, as to how they performed their services. Daws was not in the business of providing health care at any client's medical facility. The simple and overriding fact is that Daws does not perform patient care but it brokers nurses. In so doing it is Daws' nurses who perform nursing services when at medical facilities, which is a function beyond the usual course of Daws' business and beyond what, in fact, it holds itself out to do. Part B has been satisfied by the plaintiff and the defendant's conclusion to the contrary cannot stand.

Part C of the ABC test provides that "such individual is customarily engaged in an independently established trade, occupation, profession or business of the same nature as that involved in the service performed." Here the court notes that part C in our statute refers to "an independently established trade, occupation, profession or business. ..." The Daws nurses were in a "profession." The term "profession" implies "knowledge of an advanced type in a given field of science or learning gained by a prolonged course of specialized instruction and study." The Daws nurses were in an independently established profession as the result of having been licensed by the state after completing a long course of instruction and study. They were also "customarily" so engaged in that profession as defined. This is called "independently established." [W]ell over a majority of Daws nurses worked for other agencies at other medical facilities performing similar services while also working on assignments through Daws. The performance of such "like services" was independent of "whatever connection" they had with Daws and the continued performance of such "like services" was "not subject to their relationship with the principal (Daws)." The independently established nature of their nursing profession permits them to continue therein even after their relationship with Daws terminates.

Reversed in favor of Plaintiff, Daws.

Critical Thinking About the Law

When courts establish legal tests, they describe conditions that must be met for the test to be passed. In Case 15-1, the plaintiff hoped it could meet the standards of the ABC test for avoiding the legal responsibilities attached to an agency relationship.

To meet this test, a large range of facts had to be present. If the facts all fell into place in a particular way, the plaintiff would prevail.

1. **Identify specific facts from Case 15-1 that permitted the plaintiff to prevail.**

    Clue: Go to the location in the decision where the court is going step-by-step through the test, and pick out a few instances in which one part of the test was met because of a particular set of circumstances.

2. **What "facts," had they existed, would have caused the plaintiff to lose this case?**

    Clue: Read the court's statement of the necessary conditions for establishing agency. Then create some "facts" that would satisfy those conditions.

"TEMPS": Employees or Independent Contractors?

In 1990, Microsoft Corporation was found by the IRS to have hundreds of workers who were employees of the company as opposed to independent contractors, based on the control that Microsoft exercised over such workers. Instead of contesting the IRS ruling, which required the company to pay back payroll taxes, Microsoft required most of its former independent contractors to become associated with employment agencies and work for Microsoft as "temps." If they didn't, they were laid off. Those workers who didn't sign up with an agency sued Microsoft, claiming that they were employees of the company and were entitled to participate in the stock option plan. Microsoft argued that each of the workers had signed an independent contractor agreement and, thus, they were not eligible for benefits. At the Ninth Circuit Court of Appeals level, the court held that the "temps" were "common-law employees" under agency law. Furthermore, the court stated that being an employee of a temporary employment agency did not prevent the workers from being a common-law employee of Microsoft at the same time. *Vizcaino v. Microsoft*, 173 F.3d 713 (9th Cir. 1999).

CREATION OF AN AGENCY RELATIONSHIP

Agency relationships can be informal oral agreements or formal written contracts. Under the Statute of Frauds (see Chapter 10), some states require that all agency contracts be in writing.

Most such relationships grow out of the consent of two parties, the principal indicating in some way that the agent should act on its behalf and the agent agreeing to do so. An agency relationship may be formed through (1) expressed agency, (2) implied authority, (3) ratification of the agent's previous acts by the principal, or (4) apparent agency (Table 15-2).

EXPRESSED AGENCY OR AGENCY BY AGREEMENT

An agency relationship formed through oral or written agreement between the principal and agent is known as an **expressed agency**, or **agency by agreement**. Under the Statute of Frauds, agency agreements that will last longer than one year must be in writing. An exclusive agency

expressed agency (agency by agreement) Agency relationship formed through oral or written agreement.

Agency Relationships	Method of Creation
Expressed agency, or agency by agreement	Formed by detailed written or oral agreement. A power-of-attorney document is often used to establish this relationship.
Agency by implied authority	Formed in situations in which custom and circumstances determine the agent's authority to do business for the principal.
Agency through ratification	Formed when an unauthorized act of an agent is accepted by the principal.
Agency by estoppel, or apparent authority	Formed when a principal leads a third party to believe that a certain person is acting as agent for the principal. The principal is estopped from denying the agency relationship.

TABLE 15-2

HOW AGENCY RELATIONSHIPS ARE CREATED

contract is a type of agreement whereby the principal agrees that it will not employ any other agent for a period of time or until a particular job is completed. If the principal fails to live up to this agreement, the agent may file a breach-of-contract suit to recover monetary damages plus court costs and attorney's fees.

power of attorney
An agency agreement used to give an agent authority to sign legal documents on behalf of the principal.

A legal document used to establish an agency relationship is called a **power of attorney**. It gives the agent the authority to sign legal documents on behalf of the principal. Many states allow powers of attorney for both business and health care purposes. In the latter kind of power of attorney, the principal designates in writing an individual (agent) who will act for the principal in the event of a serious illness that renders the principal mentally incompetent to make decisions concerning his or her own medical care. The agent is usually given the authority to make such decisions in consultation with physicians. The power of attorney for business purposes may be a general document that gives the agent broad powers to act on the principal's behalf (Exhibit 15-2), or it may be a more limited document that authorizes the agent to act only in matters enumerated in the agreement. Many people now incorporate by reference powers of attorney for both health and business purposes into their wills or trusts.

AGENCY BY IMPLIED AUTHORITY

agency by implied authority Agency relationship in which customs and circumstances, rather than a detailed formal agreement, determine the agent's authority.

When a principal and agent create an agency, they often do not set out every detail of the agent's authority in the written or oral agreement. In **agency by implied authority**, customs, circumstances, and the facts of a situation determine the authority of the agent to do business on behalf of the principal.

Unless the agency contract says otherwise, courts have generally allowed agents to:

1. Receive payments of money due principal.
2. Enter into contracts for incidentals.
3. Employ or discharge employees.
4. Buy equipment and supplies.

In the following case, the court indicates the extent to which implied authority will be granted to an agent.

CASE 15-2

Penthouse International v. Barnes
United States Court of Appeals,
792 F.2d 943 (9th Cir. 1986)

Priscilla Barnes was a hostess at a club in Hollywood, California, when she was approached by a freelance photographer (Dunas) who sold nude photographs to *Penthouse* magazine. Dunas was an independent contractor. He asked Barnes to pose nude. She agreed but did not want her actual name used. Dunas agreed to her terms, and

Barnes signed a "Release, Authorization and Agreement Form" that gave *Penthouse* the right to "republish photographic pictures or portraits." Dunas added the term "AKA" ("also known as") on the contract to indicate that the photographs would not be published under her actual name but under a pseudonym. *Penthouse* did so in 1976. Later

Barnes became a well-known television broadcaster for a station in Los Angeles. When *Penthouse* informed her, in 1983, that it wished to republish her nude photograph, she threatened to sue, claiming Dunas had implied agency to write the term "AKA" and, thus, *Penthouse* was bound. *Penthouse* requested a declaratory judgment from the federal district court allowing it to republish a nude photo of the defendant. The district court found for Barnes and issued an injunction against *Penthouse*. *Penthouse* appealed.

Judge Boochever

Under California law, questions regarding the existence of agency are questions of fact that we review for clear error. California Civil Code Section 2316 defines actual authority as "such as a principal intentionally confers upon the agent, or intentionally, or by want of ordinary care, allows the agent to believe himself to possess." At issue is whether Dunas contracted to act on behalf of *Penthouse*.

Penthouse instructed photographers "to get a signed model release and not to alter the release in any way, without our permission." However, *Penthouse* carried Dunas's name on its masthead, gave him blank *Penthouse* contracts, may have given him business cards, and had him present contracts to models. Thus, although the record conflicts as to whether Dunas was an actual agent of *Penthouse*, on review, we cannot find that the district court clearly erred in finding Dunas to be a *Penthouse* agent.

Having found that the district court did not err in characterizing Dunas as an agent, we next turn to whether Dunas was acting within the scope of his authority by modifying the contract. Barnes does not contend nor is there evidence that Dunas possessed express actual authority to modify the contract. Dunas, however, had implied actual authority. Implied actual authority requires that (1) Dunas believe he was authorized to modify the contract based on *Penthouse* conduct known to him or (2) such a belief was reasonable.

Circumstantial evidence exists that Dunas placed "AKA" on other contracts with no objection from *Penthouse*. In June 1974, a year and a half before Barnes posed, contracts prepared by Dunas had "AKA" on them. Further, *Penthouse* internal memoranda reflect an understanding among *Penthouse* employees that "AKA" added to a contract meant that *Penthouse* was to associate a fictitious name with a woman's photograph. The evidence thus indicates that Dunas reasonably believed he was authorized to add "AKA" and modify the contract to require that only a fictitious name be used.

Affirmed in favor of Defendant, Barnes.

Critical Thinking About the Law

One of the primary purposes of a judge's opinion is to explain the court's reasoning in a particular case. A judge's opinion is not arbitrary, in the sense that a judge must give due consideration to relevant facts and rules of law for any legal issue. From a judge's opinion, we are, therefore, able to know not only a judge's conclusion but also why the judge ruled for one party over another. These opinions provide the court's rationale in a particular case, which may be later used as precedent for subsequent cases that contain similar fact patterns. In Case 15-2, the judge provided several reasons to support the court's conclusion. The next two questions relate to the judge's reasoning in Case 15-2.

1. What reasons did the judge provide for ruling in favor of the defendant?

   Clue: To ensure that you have found a reason, ask yourself whether what you have listed answers to the question: "Why did the court rule for the defendant?"

2. What aspects of the court's reasoning were particularly strong or weak? Remember that simply because reasons are given does not mean that these reasons are necessarily strong.

   Clue: Reverse roles in this case and assume you were the plaintiff's lawyer. With which parts of the judge's opinion would you still disagree based on the court's reasoning? Would there be parts of the judge's reasoning with which, even though you were the opposing party, you would agree?

EXHIBIT 15-2

POWER OF ATTORNEY

Power of Attorney

Know All Men by These Presents: That _____

_____

the undersigned (jointly and severally, if more than one) hereby make, constitute and
appoint _____

_____

My true and lawful Attorney for me and in my name, place and stead and for my use and benefit:

(a) To ask, demand, sue for, recover, collect and receive each and every sum of money, debt, account, legacy, bequest, interest, dividend, annuity and demand (which now is or hereafter shall become due, owing or payable) belonging to or claimed by me, and to use and take any lawful means for the recovery thereof by legal process or otherwise, and to execute and deliver a satisfaction or release therefor, together with the right and power to compromise or compound any claim, or demand;

(b) To exercise any or all of the following powers as to real property, any interest therein and/or any building thereon; To contract for, purchase, receive and take possession thereof and of evidence of title thereto; to lease the same for any term or purpose, including leases for business residence, and oil and/or mineral development; to sell exchange, grant or convey the same with or without warranty; and to mortgage, transfer in trust, or otherwise encumber or hypothecate the same to secure payment of a negotiable or non-negotiable note or performance of any obligation or agreement;

(c) To exercise any or all of the following powers as to all kinds of personal property and goods, wares and merchandise, chosen in action and other property in possession or in action; To contract for, buy sell, exchange, transfer and in any legal manner deal in and with the same and to mortgage, transfer in trust, or otherwise encumber of hypothecate the same to secure payment of a negotiable or non-negotiable note or performance of any obligation or agreement.

(d) To borrow money and to execute and deliver negotiable or non-negotiable notes therefore with or without security; and to loan money and receive negotiable or non-negotiable notes therefor with such security as said Attorney shall deem proper;

(e) To create, amend, supplement and terminate any trust and to instruct and advise the trustee of any trust wherein I am or may be trustor or beneficiary, to present and vote stock, exercise stock rights, accept and deal with any dividend, distribution or bonus, join in any corporate financing, reorganization, merger, liquidation, consolidation or other action and the extension, compromise, conversion, adjustment, enforcement or foreclosure, singly or in conjunction with others of any corporate stock, bond, note, debenture or other security; to compound, compromise, adjust, settle and satisfy any obligation secured or unsecured, owing by or to me and to give or accept any property and/or money whether or not equal to or less in value than the amount owing in payment settlement or satisfaction thereof;

(f) To transact business of any kind or class and as my act and deed to sign, execute, acknowledge and deliver any deed, lease, assignment or lease, covenant, indenture indemnity, agreement, mortgage, deed of trust, assignment of mortgage or of the beneficial interest under deed of trust, extension or renewal of any obligation, subordination or waiver or priority, hypothecation, bottomry, charter-party, bill of lading, bill of sale, bill, bond, note, whether negotiable, receipt, evidence of debt, full or partial release or satisfaction of mortgage judgment and other debt, request for partial or full reconveyance of deed or trust and such other instruments in writing of any kind or class as may be necessary or proper in the premises.

Giving and Granting unto my said Attorney full power and authority to do and perform all and every act and thing whatsoever, requisite, necessary or appropriate to be done in and about the premises as fully to all intents and purposes as I might or could do if personally present, hereby ratifying all that my said Attorney shall lawfully do or cause to be done by virtue of these presents. The powers and authority hereby conferred upon my said Attorney shall be applicable to all real and personal property or interests therein now owned or hereafter required by me and wherever situate.

My said Attorney is empowered hereby to determine in said Attorney's sale discretion the time when, purpose for and manner in which any power herein conferred upon said Attorney shall be exercised, and the conditions, provisions and covenants of any instrument or document which may be executed by said Attorney pursuant hereto and in the acquisition or disposition of real or personal property, my said Attorney shall have exclusive power to fix the terms thereof for cash, credit, and/or property, and if on credit with or without security.

The undersigned, if a married person, hereby further authorizes and empowers my said Attorney, as my duly authorized agent, to join in my behalf, in the execution of any instrument by which any community real property or any interest therein, now owned or hereafter acquired by my spouse and myself, or either of us, is sold, leased, encumbered, or conveyed.

When the contest to requires, the masculine gender includes the feminine and/or neuter, and the singular number includes the plural.

Witness my hand this _____ **day of** _____ **, 19** _____.
STATE OF OHIO
COUNT OF WOOD   } SS

On _____ before me, the undersigned,
a Notary Public in and for said State personally
appeared _____

_____

_____

_____ personally known
to me (or proved to me on the basis of satisfactory
evidence) to be the person _____ whose name
_____ subscribed to the within instrument and
acknowledged that _____ executed the same.
WITNESS my hand and official seal.
Signature _____

_____
        Name (Typed or Printed)   (This area for official seal)

agency by ratification
Agency relationship in which an unauthorized agent commits the principal to an agreement and the principal later accepts the unauthorized agreement, thus ratifying the agency relationship.

AGENCY THROUGH RATIFICATION BY PRINCIPAL

Agency by ratification occurs when a person misrepresents himself or herself as an agent and the principal accepts (ratifies) the unauthorized act. If the principal accepts the results of the agent's act, then the principal is bound, just as if he or she had authorized the individual to act as an agent. Two conditions are necessary for the ratification to be effective: (1) The principal must have full knowledge of the agent's action, and (2) the existence of the principal must be clear to the third party at the time of the agent's unauthorized act. For example, Max Black tells his friend Mary Ann Jones, a realtor, that if she ever finds anyone who is ready, willing, and able to sell a certain kind of computer franchised store, he will buy it. Jones finds such a store, cannot reach Black, and has never been his agent, but she enters into the agreement with the franchisor anyway and signs the contract "Mary Ann Jones, agent for Max Black." Jones is not Black's agent. However, if Black decides to honor the contract, he will have ratified an agency relationship, and Jones will most likely get a commission.

AGENCY BY ESTOPPEL, OR APPARENT AUTHORITY

If a third person is led by a principal to believe that a certain individual is the principal's agent, then there appears to be authority for the agent to act and the principal is estopped from denying that the individual is an agent. It is the writing, words, or acts, or some combination thereof, of the principal that creates the **agency by estoppel**, or **apparent authority** for the agent to act; the third party relies on the principal's conduct. In reading the case that follows, note carefully the court's focus on the principal's actions in the negative application of the legal doctrine of **estoppel**.

> **agency by estoppel (apparent authority)** An agency relationship in which the principal is estopped from denying that someone is the principal's agent after leading a third party to believe the person is an agent.
>
> **estoppel** A legal bar to either alleging or denying a fact because of one's own previous words or actions to the contrary.

CASE 15-3

Miller v. McDonald's Corporation
Court of Appeals of Oregon,
945 P.2d 1107 (1997)

Plaintiff, Joni Miller (Miller) sued defendant McDonald's Coroporation (McDonald's) for damages resulting from injuries suffered when she bit into a sapphire stone when eating a Big Mac Sandwich that she purchased at McDonald's restaurant in Tigard, Oregon owned and operated by a company 3K.

In this case, there is an issue of fact about whether defendant held 3K out as its agent. Everything about the appearance and operation of the Tigard McDonald's identified it with defendant and with the common image for all McDonald's restaurants that defendant has worked to create through national advertising, common signs and uniforms, common menus, common appearance, and common standards. The possible existence of a sign identifying 3K as the operator does not alter the conclusion that there is an issue of apparent agency for the jury. There are issues of fact of whether that sign was sufficiently visible to the public, in light of plaintiff's apparent failure to see it, and of whether one sign by itself is sufficient to remove the impression that defendant created through all of the other indicia of its control.

Defendant does not seriously dispute that a jury could find that it held 3K out as its agent. Rather, it argues that there is insufficient evidence that plaintiff justifiably relied on that holding out. It argues that it is not sufficient for her to prove that she went to the Tigard McDonald's because it was a McDonald's restaurant. Rather, she also had to prove that she went to it because she believed that McDonald's Corporation operated both it and the other McDonald's restaurants that she had previously patronized.

[I]n this case plaintiff testified that she relied on the general reputation of McDonald's in patronizing the Tigard restaurant and in her expectation of the quality of the food and service that she would receive. Especially in light of defendant's efforts to create a public perception of a common McDonald's system at all McDonald's restaurants, whoever operated them, a jury could find that plaintiff's reliance was objectively reasonable. The trial court erred in granting summary judgment on the apparent agency theory. Miller appealed.

Justice Warren

The issue on summary judgment is whether there is evidence that would permit a jury to find defendant vicariously liable for injuries. McDonald's claims it is not liable because the 3K Corporation owns the restaurant. 3K owned and operated the restaurant under a License Agreement with McDonald's that required 3K to operate in a manner consistent with the "McDonald's System." The Agreement provided that 3K was not an independent contractor and was responsible for all obligations and liabilities, including claims based on injury, illness, or death directly or indirectly resulting from the operation of the restaurant.

Miller thought that McDonald's owned, controlled, and managed the restaurant because its appearance and menu were similar to that of other McDonald's restaurants. Miller testified, she went to the Tigard McDonald's because she relied on defendant's reputation and because she wanted to obtain the same quality of service, standard of care in food preparation, and general attention to detail that she had previously enjoyed at other McDonald's restaurants.

Reversed and remanded for Plaintiff, Miller.

DUTIES OF AGENTS AND PRINCIPALS

PRINCIPAL'S DUTIES TO AGENT

Through an evolution of case law and scholarly writing, it is now generally recognized that a principal (employer) owes four duties to an agent (employee): (1) a duty of compensation, (2) a duty of reimbursement and indemnification, (3) a duty of cooperation, and (4) a duty to provide safe working conditions. These duties are either part of a written contract or implied by law.

Duty of Compensation. In the absence of a written agreement, it is implied that a principal will compensate the agent for services rendered, either when services are contracted for or when they are completed. If the parties cannot agree on the amount, courts will usually indicate that the compensation should be calculated on the basis of what is reasonable or customary. For example, lawyers and real estate brokers are sometimes paid on a **contingency fee** (commission) basis.

contingency fee Agent's compensation that consists of a percentage of the amount the agent secured for the principal in a business transaction.

indemnity Obligation of the principal to reimburse the agent for any losses the agent incurs while acting on the principal's behalf.

Duty of Reimbursement and Indemnification. An **indemnity** is an obligation on the part of an individual (principal) to make good (or reimburse) another person (agent) against any losses incurred when the latter is acting on the former's behalf. All necessary expenses can be recouped by the agent, but the agent is not entitled to expenses arising out of tortious conduct (e.g., negligence) or unlawful activities (e.g., bribes paid to suppliers).

Duty of Cooperation. The principal must do nothing to interfere with the reasonable conduct of an agent as agreed upon in an express or implied contract. For example, if a franchisor (principal) agrees with a franchisee (agent) that the latter has an exclusive right to sell a specific item within a geographic territory, the franchisor cannot legally compete with the franchisee by setting up another franchisee within that territory. If the franchisor does establish a competitive franchisee, the first franchisee can sue for breach of contract, asking either for lost profit, court costs, and attorney's fees or for specific performance.

Duty to Provide Safe Working Conditions. The principal has a duty to its agent to provide safe working conditions. Federal legislation such as the Occupational Safety and Health Act (discussed in Chapter 18) set standards designed to create a safe working environment for employees. Employers who repeatedly violate those standards may be fined or imprisoned or both.

AGENT'S DUTIES TO PRINCIPAL

Just as a principal has legal duties to an agent, the agent has legal obligations toward the principal. They are loyalty, obedience, accounting, and performance.

Duty of Loyalty. Courts have often indicated that the agent's most important obligation is fiduciary. The fiduciary obligation includes loyalty to the principal—that is, acting on behalf of one principal only to avoid conflicts of interest, communicating all material information to the principal, and refraining from acting in a manner that is adverse to the principal's interest.

Duty of Obedience. The agent has the duty to follow all reasonable and lawful instructions of the principal. If the manufacturer of a drug to alleviate the symptoms of the common cold tells its advertising department, salespeople, and distributors to tout the product as a cure for the common cold, these agents have no duty to follow the instructions because they are in violation of Section 5 of the Federal Trade Commission Act (see Chapter 24).

Duty of Accounting. Whenever the principal requests an accounting of money or property, it is the duty of the agent to hand over the requested material. When courts have been asked to determine how the duty of accounting is met, their answers have varied from case to case, but the keeping of accurate books that can be viewed by the principal is the minimum activity expected.

Duty of Performance. In all agency relationships, courts have indicated that agents must use reasonable care and skill in performing their work. This is generally taken to mean that agents must live up to the standards of performance expected of people in their occupation. Note in the following case the court's concern about whether an insurance company (agent) failed to meet the duty of performance to the deceased (principal) because it did not buy a life insurance contract.

CASE 15-4

Bias v. Advantage International, Inc.
United States Court of Appeals,
905 F.2d 1558 (D.C. Cir. 1990)

Leonard Bias's estate (plaintiff) sued Advantage International, Inc. (defendant), claiming that Advantage had failed to obtain a $1 million insurance policy on Leonard Bias as directed. Bias was an outstanding basketball player at the University of Maryland. On June 17, 1986, he was drafted in the first round by the Boston Celtics of the National Basketball Association. On June 19, 1986, he died in his dormitory room of an overdose of cocaine. Advantage obtained a summary judgment from the trial court, in which the court noted that even if Advantage had attempted to obtain an insurance policy, it would have been denied because of Bias's cocaine use. The estate appealed to the U.S. Court of Appeals, arguing that there was a genuine issue of fact as to

whether Bias was a cocaine user and that that fact should have been presented to the jury.

Justice Sentelle

The testimony of Long and Gregg (former teammates of Bias) clearly tends to show that Bias was a cocaine user. The testimony of Bias's parents to the effect that they knew Bias well and did not know him to be a drug user does not rebut the Long and Gregg testimony about Bias's drug use on particular occasions. The drug test results offered by the Estate may show that Bias had no cocaine in his system on the dates when the tests were administered, but, as the District Court correctly notes, these tests speak only to Bias's abstention during the periods preceding the tests. The tests do not rebut the Long and Gregg testimony that on a number of occasions Bias ingested cocaine in their presence.

The Estate could have deposed Long and Gregg, or otherwise attempted to impeach their testimony. The Estate also could have offered the testimony of other friends or teammates of Bias who were present at some of the gatherings described by Long and Gregg, who went out with Bias frequently, or who were otherwise familiar with his social habits. The Estate did none of these things. The Estate is not entitled to reach the jury merely on the supposition that the jury might not believe the defendants' witnesses. We thus agree with the District Court that there was no genuine issue of fact concerning Bias's status as a cocaine user.

The defendants offered evidence that every insurance company inquires about the prior drug use of an applicant for a jumbo policy at some point in the application process. The Estate failed to name a single particular company or provide other evidence that a single company existed which would have issued a jumbo policy in 1986 without inquiring about the applicant's drug use. Because the Estate has failed to do more than show that there is "some metaphysical doubt as to the material facts," the District Court properly concluded that there was no genuine issue of material fact as to the insurability of a drug user.

Affirmed in favor of Defendant, Advantage.

Critical Thinking About the Law

You should be alert to the human element that figures into all legal reasoning. Because a human being and not a computer is weighing the evidence in a case and rendering decisions, there is always the possibility that reasonable people will disagree about legal judgments. Judges, as humans, are not infallible.

Therefore, we need to focus on how a decision is reached as opposed to blindly accepting the decision itself. Indeed, as we emphasized in Chapter 1, the process of legal decision making is central to critical thinking about the law. The questions that follow will aid you in the process-centered task of thinking critically about the judge's treatment of the evidence presented in Case 15-4.

1. What evidence concerning Bias's alleged drug use is in conflict?

   Clue: Examine the judge's discussion of whether Bias was a regular cocaine user.

2. The judge resolves this conflicting evidence by ruling that the testimony affirming Bias's drug use is not disproved by evidence to the contrary. You might have reached a different conclusion. Even if you did not, how and why might someone else have made a different judgment?

   Clue: You want to think about not only the quality of the evidence that suggests that Bias was not a drug user but also the quality of the evidence that suggests that he was.

PRINCIPAL'S AND AGENT'S LIABILITY TO THIRD PARTIES

Principals are normally responsible for the acts of their agents if those acts come within the scope of the agents' employment. Principals, then, can be held liable when agents enter contracts, commit torts within the scope of their employment, and commit crimes while acting on behalf of the principal (Table 15-3).

CONTRACTUAL LIABILITY

The purpose of a principal–agency relationship is to enable the principal to expand business through the use of agents who can negotiate agreements with third parties that the principal would find it difficult or impossible to contact. To

TABLE 15-3

DUTIES OF PRINCIPALS AND AGENTS

Principal's Duties to Agency

Duty of Cooperation	Must cooperate with and assist the agent in the performance of the agent's duties and the accomplishment of the agency.
Duty to Provide Safe Working	Must provide safe working conditions, warn agents of dangerous conditions, and repair and conditions remedy unsafe conditions.
Duties of Reimbursement and Indemnification	Must reimburse an agent for all expenses paid that were authorized by the principal, within the scope of the agency, and necessary to discharge the agent's duties. Must indemnify the agent for any losses suffered because of the principal's acts.
Duty of Compensation	Must pay the agent agreed-upon compensation. If there is no agreement, the principal must pay what is customary in the industry, or, if there is no custom, then the reasonable value of the services.

Agent's Duties to Principal

Duty of Performance	Performance of the lawful duties expressed in the agency contract with reasonable care, skill, and diligence.
Duty of Notification	Duty to notify principal of any information he or she learns that is important to the agency. Information learned by the agent in the course of the agency is imputed to the principal.
Duty of Loyalty	Duty not to act adversely to the interests of the principal. The most common breaches of loyalty are: **1.** *Self-dealing.* Agent cannot deal with the principal unless his or her position is disclosed and the principal agrees to deal with the agent. **2.** *Usurping an opportunity.* Agent cannot unsurp (take) an opportunity belonging to the principal as his or her own. **3.** *Competing with the principal.* Agents are prohibited from competing with the principal during the course of an agency unless the principal agrees.
Duty of Obedience	Must obey the lawful instructions of the principal during the performance of the agency.
Duty of Accountability	Must maintain an accurate accounting of all transactions undertaken on the principal's behalf. A principal may demand an accounting from the agent at any time.

do their job, therefore, agents must be authorized to enter into contracts. A principal's liability for an agent's contracts depends in large part on whether the principal is disclosed or undisclosed to the third party at the time of the execution of the agreement.

E-Commerce: Intelligent Agents

When discussing agency law in this chapter and contract law in Chapters 11 and 12, we have discussed relationships between human beings and entities represented by individual corporations, partnerships, or franchisors. Usually, the agent acted within the scope of her or his expressed or implied authority. Today, electronic agents (e-agents) such as computer programs are used in e-commerce to perform such tasks as searching the Web for the best price on a service or good.

As discussed in Chapter 11, "click-on agreements" often are part of e-commerce. The terms of such an agreement must be recognized by an intelligent agent. Failing to observe such terms by the agent (A) may bind a principal (P), especially in a lengthy franchise agreement. Also, it may be important that certain click-on agreements exempt third parties (T) from liability. In order to avoid such problems, click-on agreements are now being developed for online stores that are more easily understood by e-agents.

The Uniform Electronic Transaction Act (UETA) (previously discussed in Chapter 11) allows e-agents to bind principals. When an individual or business entity places an order over the Internet, the principal or company that takes the order from an e-agent cannot disclaim the order.

LIABILITY OF DISCLOSED, PARTIALLY DISCLOSED PRINCIPALS, AND UNDISCLOSED PRINCIPALS

disclosed principal One whose identity is known by the third party when the latter enters into an agreement negotiated by the agent.

partially disclosed principal One whose identity is not known to the third party at the time of the agreement, though the third party does know the agent represents a principal.

undisclosed principal One whose identity and existence are both unknown to the third party.

A **disclosed principal** is one whose identity is known by the third party at the time he or she enters into the agreement; the third party is aware that the agent is acting on behalf of this principal. A **partially disclosed principal** is one whose identity is not known to the third party at the time of the agreement; the third party does know, however, that the agent represents a principal. In both these cases, the agent has actual authority and, therefore, the principal is liable. For example, if Jones (agent) enters into an agreement with Thomas (third party) to buy a new car on behalf of Smith, Inc. (principal), Smith will be liable for the contract. Disclosure of a principal is usually shown in the agent's signature on the contract (e.g., "Smith, Inc., by Jones, Agent").

LIABILITY OF UNDISCLOSED PRINCIPAL

When the third party is aware of neither the identity of the principal nor the agency relationship, the agent may be liable to the third party if the principal does not perform the terms of the contract. **Undisclosed principal**–agent relationships are lawful and are often used by wealthy people to conceal their involvement in a negotiation. For example, Jones, a famous tycoon, hires Smith to go to an auction to bid on a castle. Jones wishes to remain undisclosed because he fears the other bidders will "bid up" the price if they know he is bidding. In this case, both Jones and Smith are liable to the seller whose castle is being auctioned.

TORT LIABILITY

Under the doctrine of respondeat superior, a principal (employer) may be liable for the intentional or negligent torts of his or her agent (employee) if such acts are committed within the scope of the agent's employment. If the unauthorized acts are committed outside the scope of employment, liability shifts to the agent. So the crucial issue for the courts is whether the employee was acting within the scope of employment when the tort took place.

Two criteria used by the courts to decide this issue are: (1) Was the agent or employee acting in the principal's interest? (2) Was the agent or employee authorized to be in the particular place that he or she was in at the time of the commission of the tort? For example, Smith, an employee of Brennan Pizza Company, is authorized to deliver pizza in a vehicle owned by the company but not to make any stops in between delivering the pizza and returning the company vehicle to Brennan Pizza. Smith stops off at a local tavern after delivering the last pizza. Shith comes out of the tavern and hits a third party, Jones, who is walking across the street in a legal manner. If Jones sues the company and Smith, the court must decide these questions: Should the company be held liable? Should the agent, Smith, be held liable? Or should they be held liable jointly and severally? In most states, the agent would be liable given this factual situation because she was not authorized to be where she was at the time of the accident. Where company rules against the tortious activity are in place, courts generally rule against the agent. Were the company and Smith found to be **jointly/severally liable**, the agent would have had to indemnify the principal for what the company has to pay. Practically speaking, though, an agent like Smith usually does not have the money to pay either damages or indemnities. Under the "deep pocket" concept, Brennan Pizza Company alone would pay damages because it has the money to do so. Whether an employee was acting within the scope of his or her employment at the time of an accident is often not clear-cut, as the following case illustrates.

> **joint/several liability** The legal principle that makes two or more people liable for a judgment, either as individuals or in any proportional combination. Under this principle, a person who is partially responsible for a tort can end up being completely liable for damages.

CASE 15-5

Sussman v. Florida East Coast Properties, Inc.
District Court of Appeals of Florida,
557 So.2d 74 (1995)

Elizabeth Paraiso was a fitness instructor at a health spa owned by Florida East Coast Properties (Florida Properties). She was asked by a fellow employee to pick up a birthday cake for another employee. Paraiso deviated five blocks from her route to work to pick up the cake. She picked up the cake, and while driving to work she reached over to prevent the cake from falling off the seat. As a result her car struck Sussman, who was sitting on a bench waiting for a bus. Sussman sued Florida Properties for damages resulting from injury. Trial court ruled in favor of Florida Properties. Sussman appealed.

Justice Ferguson
The conduct of an employee is within the scope of his employment, for the purpose of determining the employer's vicarious liability to third persons injured by

the employee, only if (1) the conduct is of the kind the employee is hired to perform, (2) the conduct occurs substantially within the time and space limits authorized or required by the work to be performed, and (3) the conduct is activated at least in part by a purpose to serve the master.

The employee detoured on her way to work to stop at a supermarket, where she purchased a cake for a fellow employee's birthday celebration. Although she was enroute to her place of employment when she struck and injured a pedestrian with her personal vehicle, she was outside the scope of the employer's business as a matter of law. The employee's deposition testimony supports the finding that the purchase of the cake was outside the scope of duties the employee was employed to perform.

Affirmed for Defendant, Florida East Properties, Inc.

CRIMINAL LIABILITY

Principals are generally not liable for criminal acts (e.g., murder, rape, price-fixing, extortion) of their agents because it is difficult to show the intent of the principal that is required for liability for such crimes. However, this general rule has two major exceptions: (1) when a principal participates directly in the agent's crime and (2) when the principal has reason to know there is a violation of law taking place by employees or agents (see *United States v. Park* in Chapter 7). For an example of the first exception, assume that a refinery threatens to terminate Jones (employee) unless he agrees to set the prices of gasoline in a certain location and communicate those prices to all company-owned and independent dealers using the refinery's gasoline. If Jones does what he is told and is caught, both the refinery and Jones will be prosecuted under the Sherman Act for price-fixing (see Chapter 24). The defense of Jones that he was just an employee following his employer's orders when he fixed prices will not be acceptable. On the other hand, if Jones refuses to do what his employer is demanding and is discharged, he can sue the refinery on the basis of the tort of wrongful discharge (see Chapter 20).

TERMINATION OF THE PRINCIPAL–AGENT RELATIONSHIP

The principal–agent relationship may be terminated by agreement or by operation of law.

TERMINATION BY AGREEMENT

Either of the parties may decide to terminate the principal–agent relationship. When such a relationship is terminated, all third parties who dealt with the agent should be given actual notice by the principal. Constructive notice may be given to others through advertisement in newspapers published in areas where the agent operated on behalf of the principal.

Some agency relationships are terminated by a lapse of time. For example, Jones agrees with Smith that Smith will serve as his agent for business purposes until May 20, 1996. On that day, Smith's actual or apparent authority lapses. Once again, the principal should notify all relevant third parties at the termination.

TERMINATION BY LAW

When the principal–agent relationship is terminated by law, there is no requirement to give notification to relevant third parties. The five most common methods of termination by operation of law are: (1) death of one of the parties, even if the other party is unaware of that death, (2) insanity of one of the parties, (3) bankruptcy of the principal, (4) impossibility of performance, which may come about through the destruction or loss of subject matter or a change in the law, and (5) an outbreak of war, particularly when the agent's country is at war with the principal's country.

GLOBAL DIMENSIONS OF AGENCY LAW

As global business by multinational, midsize, and even small corporations has expanded, many U.S. businesses have hired foreign agents to represent them abroad. With the lowering of tariff barriers through such treaties as the North American Free Trade Agreement and the World Trade Organization, foreign agents will become ever more essential to the movement of goods and services across national boundaries. So it behooves managers in businesses of all sizes to become knowledgeable about the exporting companies, distributors, and sales agents they contract with and the rules that govern those agents in their own countries. We covered the general aspects of these treaties and the international legal environment of business in Chapter 9. Here we encapsulate some of the major differences between agency law and practice in the United States and in two importing trading partners of U.S. business: Japan and the European Union.

JAPAN

In Japan, agents must disclose whom they are representing, and third parties often require proof that agents are acting on behalf of a particular principal. Unlike in the United States, an agent in Japan must have expressed authority to act, and principals are held liable for acts of agents within their limited range.

EUROPEAN UNION (EU)

European Union principals are bound to act in good faith toward their agents. If there is no written contract, compensation is based on customary practice in the location where the agent is acting. Agents are also expected to act in good faith. All items in negotiations must be communicated to the principal, and the agent is bound to follow the principal's instructions quite literally. Most agency agreements are assumed to be for an indefinite time; thus, notice of one, two, and three months, respectively, is required to terminate a relationship of one, two, and three years' duration.

U.S. AGENTS ABROAD

From just these two examples you can see how agency law elsewhere can differ significantly from agency law in the United States. Managers should carefully review a host country's laws on agency before carrying on business in that country.

There are special complications for managers when the law of the host country conflicts with the Foreign Corrupt Practices Act (FCPA) of 1977, as amended in 1988. Although that act allows remuneration to lower-level foreign agents and officials to expedite the handling of goods that U.S. businesses are seeking to sell in another country, it strictly forbids payments to political officials of a certain level. Because companies are liable for both civil and criminal sanctions for violating the FCPA, managers must keep a close watch over the actions of hired foreign agents as well as over the actions of their own employees abroad.

SUMMARY

An agency relationship is a fiduciary relationship in which the agent acts on behalf of, and is subject to the control of, the principal. There are three types: principal–agent, employer–employee, and employer–independent contractor. The four methods of creating an agency relationship are (1) through expressed agency (agency by agreement), (2) by implied authority, (3) through ratification by the principal, and (4) by estoppel, or apparent authority. The duties of the principal to the agent are compensation for services rendered, reimbursement for expenses and indemnification for losses, cooperation, and provision of safe working conditions. Those of the agent toward the principal are loyalty, obedience to reasonable and lawful instructions, an accurate accounting, and skillful and careful performance.

Principals are liable to third parties for contracts made by their agents on their behalf, torts committed by the agent within the scope of the agent's employment, and crimes committed by the agent at the principal's direction.

Agency relationships may be terminated by mutual consent or by operation of law.

Managers doing international business need to be aware of the sometimes significant differences between agency law in the United States and agency law in other countries.

REVIEW QUESTIONS

15-1 Explain the doctrine of respondeat superior.

15-2 Define apparent and actual authority.

15-3 Describe the agent's duties to the principal.

15-4 Distinguish an agent from an independent contractor.

15-5 Is a principal responsible for all contracts entered into by an agent? Explain.

15-6 Why must a principal notify a third party of the termination of an agency relationship? Explain.

REVIEW PROBLEMS

15-7 Profit Corporation authorized Anderson, an employee, to find a buyer for used equipment that Profit intended to sell. Anderson believed that he had authority to contract for the sale of the equipment, but in fact he did not. Anderson found a prospective buyer, Caveat Corporation, and contracted with Caveat on behalf of Profit for the sale of the equipment to Caveat. In this contract, Anderson warranted that the equipment was fit for Caveat's particular needs. A responsible officer of Profit read the contract and directed that the equipment be shipped to Caveat. The equipment did not meet the special needs of Caveat, and Caveat refused to pay for it. Profit sued Caveat for the contract price. Who will win this case and why?

15-8 Mrs. Terry sees a cashmere sweater she likes in Peters Department Store but notices that it is slightly soiled. Alice, the sales clerk, agrees to mark it down from $55 to $40, which she has no authority to do. Mrs. Terry consents, asks that the sweater be delivered, and promises to pay COD. The manager of Peters sees the item being wrapped, corrects the bill, and sends it out to Mrs. Terry. On seeing her sweater accompanied by a bill for $55, Mrs. Terry calls and is told by Peters that Alice had no authority to knock down the price and that she should either pay the bill or return the sweater. Is Mrs. Terry entitled to the bargain? Why or why not?

15-9 Owner orally authorized Agent to sell his house. Agent completed a sale of the house to Buyer. When Buyer attempted to enforce the contract against Owner, Buyer was told that the contract was not enforceable because Owner's agency relation with Agent was not in writing. Must Owner have given Agent written authorization?

15-10 Owner listed his house with Penelope, a real estate broker, granting Penelope an exclusive right to sell Owner's house. Penelope entered negotiations with Buyer, who seemed interested in purchasing the property. Buyer found the price agreeable but he insisted on including in the sales contract a clause giving him the right to cancel the contract if he could not get a loan to finance his purchase. At the closing, Buyer exercised his right to cancel, giving as his reason inability to procure a loan. Penelope turned to Owner and claimed that she was entitled to her commission even though the sale did not go through. Must Owner pay Penelope a commission?

15-11 Julius and Olga Sylvester owned an unimproved piece of land near King of Prussia, Pennsylvania. They were approached by Beck, a real estate broker, who asked if they were willing to sell their land, stating that an oil company was interested in buying, renting, or leasing the property. The Sylvesters said that they were only interested in selling, and they authorized Beck to sell the property for $15,000. Several weeks later, Beck phoned the Sylvesters and offered to buy the property for himself for $14,000. Olga asked, "What happened to the oil company?" and Beck responded, "They are not interested. You want too much money for it." The Sylvesters sold the property to Beck. A month later, Beck sold the property to Epstein for $25,000. When the Sylvesters learned that Beck had realized a huge profit in a quick resale of the property, they sued Beck, claiming that he owed them the $9,000 profit. Does Beck owe the Sylvesters the money?

15-12 Peter authorized Arnon, a grain broker, to buy at the market 20,000 bushels of wheat for Peter. At the time, Arnon had in storage 5,000 bushels belonging to Johnson, who had authorized Arnon to sell for him. Arnon also had 15,000 bushels that she owned. Arnon transferred these 20,000 bushels to Peter's name and charged Peter the current market price. Shortly thereafter, and before Peters had used or sold the wheat, the market price declined sharply. Peters refused to pay for the wheat and tried to cancel the contract. Can he cancel? Explain.

CASE PROBLEMS

15-13 Greif Brothers Corp., a steel drum manufacturer, owned and operated a manufacturing plant in Youngstown, Ohio. In 1987, Lowell Wilson, the plant superintendent, hired Youngstown Security Patrol, Inc. (YSP), a security company, to guard Greif property and "deter thieves and vandals." Some YSP security guards, as Wilson knew, carried firearms. Eric Bator, a YSP security guard, was not certified as an armed guard but nevertheless took his gun in a briefcase to work. While working at the Greif plant on August 12, 1991, Bator fired his gun at Derrell Pusey, in the belief that Pusey was an intruder. The bullet struck and killed Pusey. Pusey's mother filed a suit in an Ohio state court against Greif and others, alleging in part that her son's death was the result of YSP's negligence, for which Greif was responsible. Greif filed a motion for directed verdict. Who wins? Explain. *Pusey v. Bator*, 94 Ohio St. 3d 275, 762 N.E. 2d 968 (2002)

15-14 Ford Motor Credit Co. is a subsidiary of Ford Motor Co. with its own offices, officers, and directors. Ford Credit buys contracts and leases of automobiles entered into by dealers and consumers. Ford Credit also provides inventory financing for dealers' purchases of Ford and non-Ford vehicles and makes loans to Ford and non-Ford dealers. Ford Credit is not subject to any agreement with Ford Motor "restricting or conditioning" its ability to finance the dealers' inventories or the consumers' purchases or leases of vehicles. A number of plaintiffs filed a product liability suit in a Missouri state court against Ford Motor. The plaintiffs asserted that Ford Credit, which had an office in the jurisdiction, acted as Ford's "agent for the transaction of its usual and customary business" there. Is Ford Credit an agent of Ford Motor? Explain. *State ex rel. Ford Motor Co. v. Bacon*, 63 S.W.3d 641 (Mo. 2002)

15-15 John Dunning was the sole officer of the R.B. Dunning Company and was responsible for the management and operation of the business. When the company rented a warehouse from Samuel and Ruth Saliba, Dunning did not say that he was acting for the firm. The parties did not have a written lease. Business faltered and the firm stopped paying rent. Eventually, it went bankrupt and vacated the property. The Salibas filed a suit in a Maine state court against Dunning personally, seeking to recover the unpaid rent. Dunning claimed the debt belonged to the company because he had only been acting as its agent. Who is liable for the rent and why? *Estate of Saliba v. Dunning*, 682 A.2d 224 (Me. 1996)

15-16 Federated Financial Reserve Corporation leases consumer and business equipment. As part of its credit-approval and debt-collection practices, Federated hires credit collectors, whom it authorizes to obtain credit reports on its customers. Janice Caylor, a Federated collector, used this authority to obtain a report on Karen Jones, who was not a Federated customer but who was the former wife of Caylor's roommate, Randy Lind. When Jones discovered that Lind had her address and how he had obtained it, she filed a suit in a federal district court against Federated and the others. Jones claimed in part that they had violated the Fair Credit

Reporting Act, the goal of which is to protect consumers from the improper use of credit reports. Under what theory might an employer be held liable for an employee's violation of a statute? Does that theory apply in this case? Explain. *Jones v. Federated Financial Reserve Corp.*, 144 F.3d 961 (6th Cir. 1998)

15-17 Juanita Miller filed a complaint in an Indiana state court against Red Arrow Ventures, Ltd., Thomas Hayes, and Claudia Langman, alleging that they had breached their promise to make payments on a promissory note issued to Miller. The defendants denied this allegation and asserted a counterclaim against Miller. After a trial, the judge announced that, although he would be ruling against the defendants, he had not yet determined what amount of damages would be awarded to Miller. Over the next three days, the parties' attorneys talked and agreed that the defendants would pay Miller $21,000. The attorneys exchanged correspondence acknowledging this settlement. When the defendants balked at paying this amount, the trial judge issued an order to enforce the settlement agreement. The defendants appealed to a state intermediate appellate court, arguing that they had not consented to the settlement agreement. What is the rule regarding the authority of an agent to agree to a settlement? How should the court apply the rule in this case? Why? *Red Arrow Ventures, Ltd. v. Miller*, 692 N.E.2d 939 (Ind. App. 1998)

ASSIGNMENT ON THE INTERNET

Using one of the two Web sites that follow, or another Web site of your choosing, find a recent case involving the principal–agency law. Read the case and determine the issue being decided, the court's holding or conclusion, and the reasons cited for the holding. Next, identify the ideas discussed in this chapter that were used in the court's reasoning. Do you agree with the court's reasoning? Why?

 ## ON THE INTERNET

www2.chass.ncsu.edu/garson/pa765/agent.htm This site provides a brief discussion on the principal–agent theory in business management. The site also contains suggested readings for further research.

www.law.cornell.edu/topics/agency.html The Legal Information Institute's site on agency contains a brief overview and links to recent court cases involving agency law.

16

LAW AND BUSINESS ASSOCIATIONS

- **THE MOST COMMON FORMS OF BUSINESS ORGANIZATION IN THE UNITED STATES**
- **LIMITED LIABILITY COMPANIES**
- **FACTORS INFLUENCING A BUSINESS MANAGER'S CHOICE OF ORGANIZATIONAL FORM**
- **SPECIALIZED FORMS OF BUSINESS ASSOCIATIONS**
- **GLOBAL DIMENSIONS OF BUSINESS ASSOCIATIONS**

The world of business is much more complex than is ordinarily supposed. Businesses vary greatly in size, of course, but they also differ dramatically in form, and organizational form has a tremendous impact on the amount of regulation to which a business is subject, as well as on the rights and responsibilities of its owners.

The first section of this chapter introduces the three most common types of business associations found in this country—the sole proprietorship, the partnership, and the corporation. It describes how these organizational forms are created and terminated and identifies some of the important players in each. The second part of this chapter discusses a relatively new business form— limited liability companies. The third section presents a detailed look at the factors that cause businesspeople to choose one of these organizational forms initially and the reasons they sometimes change from one form to another.

There are other types of business associations that are less well known than the principal three, and the fourth section discusses several of those specialized forms of business. The final section raises some of the questions business managers need to ask before they decide on the form their involvement in international markets will take.

Critical Thinking About the Law

We point out in this chapter that the organizational form of a business will determine the amount of regulation that a firm experiences. Furthermore, owners will have different rights and responsibilities according to the organizational form. Although you will learn about the major organizational forms later in this chapter, you can prepare to use your critical thinking skills while you consider business associations by asking yourself the following questions.

1. This question is not a formal critical thinking question, but it lays the groundwork for critical thinking about forms of business organization. Think about the businesses that you interact with every day. For example, where do you buy groceries? Who cuts your hair? Where did you buy this book? Why should the community even care whether these businesses are owned by a single person or by hundreds of shareholders?

    Clue: Ask yourself what the community expects from businesses and how these different forms of ownership would affect the extent to which those expectations are fulfilled.

2. Joan wants to open a business that specializes in selling fine wines. She believes that, as long as she follows the law of selling alcohol only to individuals 21 years of age or older, the government should not impose any other regulation on her business activity. What ethical norm seems to dominate Joan's thinking?

    Clue: Think about the list of ethical norms in Chapter 1. Which norm seems most consistent with little or no governmental regulation? Which ethical norm seems to conflict with the idea of little governmental regulation?

3. One of the factors that might influence business owners to choose one organizational form over another is the liability associated with that organizational form. For example, in a sole proprietorship, the owner is liable for all losses, whereas owners in a corporation have limited liability. Vanessa has a chance to be either a sole proprietor or a shareholder in a corporation. She chooses to become a sole proprietor, even though she considers this option to be riskier. Which ethical norms might be guiding her decision to become a sole proprietor?

    Clue: Look closely at the list of ethical norms. Which norms seem consistent with Vanessa's choice? Can you generate any other ethical norms that seem to influence her decision?

THE MOST COMMON FORMS OF BUSINESS ORGANIZATION IN THE UNITED STATES

The most common forms of business organization in the United States are the sole proprietorship, the partnership, and the corporation (Table 16-1). We examine each of these organizational forms in turn, beginning with the oldest and simplest: the sole proprietorship.

sole proprietorship A business owned by one person, who has sole control over management and profits.

THE SOLE PROPRIETORSHIP

Someone who decides to go into business alone is creating a **sole proprietorship**. Forming a sole proprietorship requires few legal formalities, and the enterprise is subject to minimal governmental regulation. The proprietor has

TABLE 16-1

ALTERNATIVE FORMS OF BUSINESS ORGANIZATION

Sole proprietorship	Person going into business on his or her own, responsible for all profits and losses.
Partnership (general)	Voluntary association of two or more persons to carry on a business as co-owners for profit. A limited liability partnership is a voluntary association, as is a general partnership, but one or more partners contribute capital only, and those partners play no role in management. Their liability is limited to the amount of capital they contribute.
Corporation	A legal entity created by state law that raises capital by issuing stocks and bonds to investors, who become shareholders and owners of the corporation. Corporations can be classified as public or private and are further distinguished as multinational, professional, closely held, or Subchapter S.

total control of management and retains all profits of the business, which are taxed as personal income to the proprietor. The proprietor is also personally liable for all losses incurred by the proprietorship.

THE PARTNERSHIP

Types of Partnership. When two or more people wish to be involved in the ownership of a business, either a limited or a general partnership may be formed. Under the Uniform Partnership Act (UPA), the law that governs partnerships in most states, a **partnership** is defined as a voluntary association of two or more persons formed to carry on a business as co-owners for profit. As in a sole proprietorship, the profits of a partnership are taxed only as income to the partners. More recently the Revised Uniform Partnership Act (RUPA) has been adopted in more than 30 states. Others continue with the UPA. The RUPA states that a partnership is no longer dissolved just because a partner leaves, clarifies the fiduciary duties of partners, and establishes a formula for valuing a partnership interest during a buyout. It also provides greater protection for the limited liability partner (to be discussed later in this chapter).

In a **general partnership**, all profits are divided among the partners, and all partners are personally liable for partnership debts. For example, if James and Carol decide to operate a florist shop as co-owners in a general partnership, each of them makes an initial contribution in the form of cash, realty, business supplies, or services. They take an equal role in the management of the business, with each expected to contribute services. They split the profits equally (assuming that no other proportion has been specified in a written partnership agreement). At the end of the first year, they file a partnership return with the Internal Revenue Service that shows the partnership's profit or loss. If the partnership makes a profit, James and Carol each pay income tax on half the profits; if the partnership incurs a loss, each deducts one-half of that loss from his or her ordinary income. The partnership itself pays no taxes. If the business fails, both James and Carol can be sued by creditors and forced to pay the partnership's debts out of their personal resources. The following case illustrates the elements of a general partnership.

partnership A voluntary association of two or more persons formed to carry on a business as co-owners for profit.

general partnership A partnership in which management responsibilities and profits are divided (usually equally) among the partners, and all partners have unlimited personal liability for the partnership's debts.

CASE 16-1

Tarnausky v. Tarnausky
U.S. Court of Appeals
147 F 2d 674 (8th Cir. 1998)

In the late 1960s, Morris and T. R. Tarnausky bought a cattle ranch (Christ Place) with their mother, Mary. Morris and T. R. opened a bank account used to deposit proceeds from the ranch as well as to pay taxes, make mortgage payments, and buy supplies and animals. All activities were done jointly by the brothers, including the purchase of machinery and cattle, as well as filing state and federal income tax returns. By 1980, Mary gave up her interest in the ranch. Some years later, T. R. gave up the bookkeeping chores. Morris sent a notice of dissolution to T. R. Subsequently, T. R. (plaintiff) filed suit against Morris for his share of the assets of the partnership. The federal district court ordered payment of $250,000 by Morris to T. R. Morris appealed to the U.S. Court of Appeals.

Justice Gibson

Elements are critical to the existence of a partnership. These elements are: (1) an intention to be partners; (2) co-ownership of the business; and (3) profit motive.

First, T. R. and Morris reported their farming activities on state and federal partnership income tax returns. Morris and T. R. opened a joint bank account. From this account, they made the Christ Place property payments,

purchased cattle, seed, and related supplies. These actions by Morris and T. R. evidence their intent to be partners.

The second element necessary for a partnership includes the sharing of profits and losses as well as the power of control in the management of the business.

[A]fter completing a sale of cattle or grain, the brothers would deposit their share of the income in their joint account. From this account, the brothers jointly paid expenses. Morris and T. R. would allocate the year's profits on the partnership income tax return equally between themselves. This sharing of profits is evidence that Morris and T. R. were partners.

Morris was "in charge" of livestock production and "administered" equipment purchases, and T. R. was "in charge" of paperwork and finances. This is evidence that T. R. and Morris both had the power of control over management of the business. Control, when combined with profit sharing, strongly suggests the existence of a partnership.

The final critical element of a partnership is profit motive, and there is no dispute that the farming business was operated with such motive.

Affirmed in favor of Plaintiff, T. R. Tarnausky.

limited partnership A partnership that has one general partner, who is responsible for managing the business, and one or more limited partners, who invest in the partnership but do not participate in its management and whose liability is limited to the amount of capital they contribute.

Now suppose that Shelly wishes to invest in James and Carol's partnership but has no desire to take part in its management because she does not want to incur unlimited liability. In most states, she could join the business as a limited partner, and the partnership would then become a limited partnership. **Limited partnerships** have at least one general partner and one limited partner and are easily identifiable because they must include the word *limited* (or an abbreviation of it) in their names. Except for the special status accorded to limited partners and the necessity of strictly following the statutory scheme for the formation of a limited partnership (described later in this section), general and limited partnerships function similarly. The primary law governing limited partnerships is the Revised Uniform Limited Partnership Act (RULPA), which has been adopted by 48 states. The question of how much management activity a limited partner can engage in before losing the special status granted by statute is still unsettled.

> **Who Has Limited Liability in a Partnership?**
> *Limited Liability Limited Partnership (LLLP).* The liability of a general partner is the same as that of the limited partners. The liability is to the amount of investment made in the firm by each partner.
> *Limited Liability Partnership (LLP).* This form is for professionals who do business as partners. The major advantage allows a partnership to continue even if there

exists liability for one of the partners for tort liability. If a client sues one of the partners for malpractice and wins a large judgment, and the firm's insurance does not cover it all, all the partners are not jointly and separately liable.

Creating a Partnership. Initially in many partnerships, there is no written partnership agreement; the partners informally split the capital contribution and work between them. In the absence of a written agreement, the Uniform Partnership Act (UPA) controls. For example, the UPA requires partners to share profits equally. Now James and Carol may not have intended an equal distribution of profits when they went into business, and such a distribution may be unfair because Carol does 90 percent of the work and the less energetic James does a mere 10 percent. But if they have no written agreement, James can legally claim 50 percent of the profits. To avoid conflicts over management responsibilities, borrowing power, profit sharing, and other common bones of contention in a partnership, the partners should set out the rights and responsibilities of each partner in a written partnership agreement at the outset. Exhibit 16-1 lists some of the items that should be included in such an agreement.

Under the RUPA, which is described earlier in this chapter, most of the act consists of rules that will apply unless the partnership agreement states differently. This will force all partnerships to be carefully created. All parties engaged in an existing partnership or creating a new one should be careful to see if the RUPA has been adopted in the state where the partnership agreement is formed.

Relationship Between Partners. The Uniform Partnership Act requires that each partner have a fiduciary relationship to the partnership and act in good faith for the benefit of the partnership. In most general partnerships, each partner has one vote in decisions pertaining to the management of the business, though in some instances—such as a decision to merge with another partnership—a unanimous vote may be required.

Read Exhibit 16-1 carefully, for it will give you a good idea of the issues that should be resolved before people enter into a business partnership. The relationship between partners will go much more smoothly if the parties agree

---

- Name and address of partnership
- Name and address of partners
- Purpose of partnership
- Duration of partnership
- Amount and type of investment of each partner (e.g., cash, realty, services)
- Loans to partnership
- How profits and losses are to be shared
- Management and voting power of each partner
- Method of settling disputes that should arise
- Cross-insurance of partners
- Duties of each partner
- How books are to be set up and maintained
- Banking arrangements—who has authority to deposit and withdraw
- Who has authority to borrow money in the name of the partnership
- Who does the hiring and firing of employees

EXHIBIT 16-1

ITEMS INCLUDED IN PARTNERSHIP AGREEMENTS

beforehand on how much each will invest, the management duties each will undertake, methods of dispute resolution, banking arrangements and borrowing policies for the business, and how the books will be kept. Then look at Exhibit 16-2, which is a model form for a general partnership agreement. It does not contain variables it might be wise to include for specific kinds of partnerships, but it is a useful starting point for drafting such an agreement.

Terminating a Partnership. A partnership, unlike a corporation, does not have perpetual existence. It can "die" when partners leave the partnership, the partnership is merged with another business or goes bankrupt, or the partnership agreement expires.

On its "deathbed," a partnership goes through a process called "dissolution and winding-up." Dissolution prevents any new business from taking place, whereas **winding-up** involves completing all unfinished transactions, paying off debts, dividing any remaining profits, and distributing assets.

THE CORPORATION

The partnership is the most common form of business organization in the United States. However, the dominant business organizational form is the **corporation**, a legal entity created by state law that raises capital by issuing stock to investors, who own the corporation. Although the corporation may have many owners, it is legally treated as a single person. Before we go into the laws governing the creation, financing, and operation of corporations, we need to explain how corporations are classified. (See Table 16-2.)

Classification of Corporations. All corporations are broadly classified as either public or private. They are further differentiated as closely held, publicly held, multinational, Subchapter S, professional, or limited liability corporations. Not-for-profit corporations also exist under state laws, and quality under federal and state tax laws.

Closely Held Corporation. The greatest number of corporations in this country are private, or **closely held corporations**. The stock of these corporations is not traded on any of the national securities exchanges. Instead, it is usually held by a small group of people, often members of the same family or close friends, who serve as directors as well as officers and active managers of the corporation. When the corporation is formed, these original owners frequently enter into an agreement to restrict the sale of stock to the initial shareholders. By limiting ownership in this way, they retain control of the corporation.

Publicly Held Corporation. Those corporations whose stock is traded on the national exchanges are known as **publicly held corporations**. Although technically governed by the same rules as closely held corporations (except for securities law, which is discussed in Chapter 22), their operations are much different from those of closely held corporations. Publicly held corporations have numerous shareholders who are simply investors. Real control rests in the hands of the officers and managers, who may own some stock, though generally not a majority or controlling amount.

When the term *corporation* is used in this book, a publicly held corporation is meant unless otherwise specified. Although some regulations apply only to publicly held corporations, in most instances the same laws apply to both public and private corporations. The impact of such laws differs, though, depending on

winding-up The process of completing all unfinished transactions, paying off outstanding debts, distributing assets, and dividing remaining profits after a partnership has been terminated or dissolved.

corporation An entity formed and authorized by state law to act as a single person and to raise capital by issuing stock to investors who are the owners of the corporation.

closely held corporation A corporation whose stock is not traded on the national securities exchanges but is privately held by a small group of people.

publicly held corporation A corporation whose stock is traded on at least one national securities exchange.

EXHIBIT 16-2

MODEL GENERAL PARTNERSHIP AGREEMENT FORM

Kubasek-Brennan-Browne
PARTNERSHIP AGREEMENT

This agreement, made and entered into as of the [Date], by and among Kubasek-Brennan-Browne (referred to as "Partners").

WITNESSETH:

Whereas, the Parties hereto desire to form a General Partnership (hereinafter referred to as the "Partnership"), for the term and upon the conditions hereinafter set forth;

Now, therefore, in consideration of the mutual covenants hereinafter contained, it is agreed by and among the Parties hereto as follows:

Article I
BASIC STRUCTURE

Form. The Parties hereby form a General Partnership pursuant to the Laws of the State of Newgarth.

Name. The business of the Partnership shall be conducted under the name of Kubasek-Brennan-Browne.

Place of Business. The principal office and place of business of the Partnership shall be located at 2130 Foot Street, Justin, Newgarth, or such other place as the Partners may from time to time designate.

Term. The Partnership shall commence on [Date], and shall continue for [Number] years, unless earlier terminated in the following manner:

(a) By the completion of the purpose intended, or

(b) Pursuant to this Agreement, or

(c) By applicable Newgarth law, or

(d) By death, insanity, bankruptcy, retirement, withdrawal, resignation, expulsion, or disability of all of the then Partners.

Article II
MANAGEMENT

Managing Partners. The Managing Partner(s) shall be all partners.

Voting. All Managing Partner(s) shall have the right to vote as to the management and conduct of the business of the Partnership according to their then Percentage Share of [Capital/Income]. Except otherwise herein set forth a majority of such [Capital/Income] shall control.

Percentage Share of Profits. Distribution to the Partners of net operating profits of the Partnership shall be made quarterly in the percentage agreed upon (40%, 40%, 20%).

whether the affected corporation is public or private. The reason for our focus on public rather than private corporations is the same as our reason for emphasizing corporations rather than partnerships: impact on society. Public corporations are wealthier than any other form of business organization and, therefore, the impact of regulation on these corporations has the greatest effect on society.

EXHIBIT 16-2
(continued)

Article III
DISSOLUTION

Dissolutions. In the event that the Partnership shall hereafter be dissolved for any reason whatsoever, a full and general account of its assets, liabilities and transactions shall at once be taken. Such assets may be sold and turned into cash as soon as possible and all debts and other amounts due the Partnership collected. The proceeds thereof shall thereupon be applied as follows:

(a) To discharge the debts and liabilities of the Partnership and the expenses of liquidation.

(b) To pay each Partner or his legal representative any unpaid salary, drawing account, interest or profits to which he shall then be entitled and in addition, to repay to any Partner his capital contributions in excess of his original capital contribution.

(c) To divide the surplus, if any, among the Partners or their representatives as follows: (1) First (to the extent of each Partner's then capital account) in proportion to their then capital accounts; (2) Then according to each Partner's then Percentage Share of Capital/Income.

Right to Demand Property. Each partner shall have the right to demand and receive property in kind for his distribution.

Article IV
MISCELLANEOUS

Accounting Year, Books, Statements. The Partnership's fiscal year shall commence on January 1st of each year and shall end on December 31st of each year. Full and accurate books of account shall be kept at such place as the Managing Partner(s) may from time to time designate, showing the condition of the business and finances of the Partnership; and each Partner shall have access to such books of account and shall be entitled to examine them at any time during ordinary business hours.

Arbitration. Any controversy or claim arising out of or relating to this Agreement shall only be settled by arbitration in accordance with the rules of the American Arbitration Association's chosen Arbitrator, and shall be enforceable in any court having competent jurisdiction.

Witness	**Partners**
J. Foster	Kubasek-Brennan-Browne
_____	_____

multinational (transnational) corporation
A corporation whose production, distribution, ownership, and management span several nations.

Multinational or Transnational Corporation. This relatively new type of publicly held corporation now dominates the world economy. It is called a **multinational**, or **transnational**, **corporation** because it does not restrict its production to a single nation and generally maintains worldwide distribution sites. Its stock is usually traded on the securities exchanges of several nations,

TABLE 16-2

TYPES OF CORPORATIONS

Closely Held	Corporations held by a small group of people whose stock is not traded on national securities exchanges.
Publicly Held	Corporations whose stock is traded on the national exchange (discussed in Chapter 22) and is held by numerous shareholders. This form will be emphasized in this text.
Domestic, Foreign, Alien	A corporation is held to be *domestic* in the state in which it incorporates. If a corporation is formed in one state but does business in another, it is referred to in the other state as a *foreign corporation*. A corporation formed in one country but doing business in the United States is referred to in the United States as an *alien* corporation.
Multinational	A corporation that maintains worldwide distribution and manufacturing, trades on exchanges of many nation-states, and that has officers and managers who are citizens of many states.
Subchapter S	A corporation that organizes and operates as a domestic business corporation but for tax purposes is treated like a partnership.
Professional	A corporation that allows physicians, lawyers, dentists, accountants, and other professionals to incorporate to take advantage of health and pension plan tax deductions.
Nonprofit	Corporation not formed for purposes of making a profit (e.g., charitable, religious, educational, and health care organizations).

and its managers are often citizens of different countries. Through their tremendous wealth, power, and reach, multinationals have a strong impact on societies all over the world.

Subchapter S Corporation. This type of closely held corporation is best described as a hybrid of the corporation and the partnership. The **Subchapter S corporation** is organized and operates as a regular business corporation but for tax purposes is treated like a partnership. To qualify for Subchapter S treatment under the Internal Revenue Code, a domestic corporation must (1) have no more than 35 shareholders, all of whom are individuals, estates, or certain types of trusts, and none of whom is a nonresident alien; (2) have only one class of stock outstanding; and (3) not be a member of an affiliated group of corporations. All shareholders must consent to the election of Subchapter S status.

Professional Corporation. The **professional corporation** is a fairly new form of business organization intended for doctors, lawyers, dentists, accountants, and other professionals who were once unable to incorporate legally. Most states now have passed statutes permitting specified professionals to incorporate so that they can take the tax advantages of deductions for health and pension plans that are allowable under the corporate form. In most states, the professional corporation differs from other corporations in that the owners are not accorded limited liability for professional acts. (It is generally considered contrary to public policy to grant professionals limited liability for their negligence.)

Nonprofit Corporation. Type of corporation that is formed for purposes other than making a profit. Some examples include: hospitals, educational institution, charities and religious groups. Most are private in nature but not necessarily so. Nonprofit corporations are used by groups as a way to carry out transactions and own property without individuals (who belong to a group) being

Subchapter S corporation A business that is organized like a corporation but, under Internal Revenue Code Subchapter S, is treated like a partnership for tax purposes so long as it abides by certain restrictions pertaining to stock, shareholders, and affiliations.

professional corporation A corporation organized by doctors, dentists, lawyers, accountants, or other professionals specified in state statutes.

held liable. Often in legal papers they are referred to as *eleemosynary* institutions (private corporations created for charitable and benevolent purposes).

Creating a Corporation. Corporations are creatures of state, not federal, law. Each of the 50 states, as well as the District of Columbia, Puerto Rico, and Guam, has a general incorporation statute that stipulates the articles of incorporation to be used in that state. These articles, generally standardized forms, identify the name of the corporation, its registered address and resident agent, the general purpose of the business, the classes of stock to be issued by the corporation and their face value, and the names and mailing addresses of the incorporators (Exhibit 16-3). The articles, accompanied by the required fees, are filed with the secretary of state of the state of incorporation, who then issues a certificate of incorporation. Upon issuance of the certificate, the corporation holds its first board meeting, at which a board of directors is elected, bylaws are enacted, and corporate stock is issued. The bylaws are the governing regulations of the corporation and often are the basis for litigation when directors act on behalf of the shareholders of the corporation. The Delaware Supreme Court is considered the most influential of all courts in the nation with regard to corporate governance and the chief arbiter of conflicts between corporations and between shareholders and a single corporation. More than 50 percent of *Fortune* 100 companies are registered in Delaware. Anyone who merges, sues, or manages a Delaware corporation is subject to Delaware law as interpreted by its courts. More recently there has been significant controversy surrounding the appointment and reappointment of state supreme court justices and the politicizing of appointments made by the commission that recommends candidates to the governor.

Two primary concerns of state corporate laws are the financing of the corporation and its operation. These two areas are necessarily entwined, but they are separated here for discussion purposes. Laws governing these two areas of corporate activity are primarily state regulations, though most states are guided by a modified version of the Revised Model Business Corporations Act (RMBCA).

Financing a Corporation. Financing is the acquiring of funds or capital for the operation or expansion of a corporation. Corporations generally engage in two types of financing: debt and equity. Debt financing may be described as the taking out of loans; equity financing is accomplished by the sale of ownership interest in the corporation.

Debt Financing. A corporation can issue three primary types of debt instruments: notes, bonds, and debentures. **Notes** are short-term loans. **Bonds** are usually long-term loans secured by a lien or mortgage on corporate assets. **Debentures** are usually unsecured long-term corporate loans.

In all forms of debt financing, corporations incur a liability to the holder of the debt security. Periodic interest payments are generally required. Interest payments on debt securities are tax deductible, whereas dividend payments made to owners under equity financing are not. This difference in the tax treatment of the two types of financing is one reason for the heavy reliance on debt financing by corporations. Even though debt financing offers distinct tax advantages to both the corporation and investors, there is always the risk that a corporation that relies too much on debt financing will be deemed too thinly capitalized by the Internal Revenue Service (IRS), which will then treat any loans made by shareholders as capital contributions.

Equity Financing. All business corporations must raise operating capital through the sale of **stock**, or equity securities. Exhibit 16-4 reproduces a stock certificate, which evidences one's ownership of stock. Shareholders—persons

notes Short-term loans.

bonds Long-term loans secured by a lien or mortgage on corporate assets.

debentures Unsecured long-term corporate loans.

stock The capital that a corporation raises through the sale of shares that entitle their holders to certain rights of ownership.

EXHIBIT 16-3

ARTICLES OF
INCORPORATION OF
BRENNAN-KUBASEK
CORPORATION

Article I
NAME

The name of this corporation is Brennan-Kubasek Corporation.

Article II
REGISTERED OFFICE AND RESIDENT AGENT

The registered office of the corporation is 15650 Id Rd., Newgarth, Ohio.

The resident agent at that address is M. Neil Browne.

Article III
NATURE OF BUSINESS

The nature and purpose of the business to be conducted or promoted are:
To engage in any lawful conduct or activity for which corporations may be
organized in the State of Ohio.

Article IV
CAPITAL STOCK

This corporation is authorized to issue forty thousand (40,000) shares of common
stock without par value.

Article V
INCORPORATORS

The names and mailing addresses of the incorporators are as follows:
B. A. Brennan—600 Jelly Street, Newgarth, Ohio
N. Kubasek—800 Minor Street, Newgarth, Ohio

Article VI
INITIAL DIRECTORS

The powers of the incorporators are to terminate upon the filing of these Articles of
Incorporation, and the names and mailing address of the persons who are to serve
as directors until the first annual meeting of stockholders or until their successors
are elected and qualified are:
B. A. Brennan—600 Jelly Street, Newgarth, Ohio
N. Kubasek—800 Minor Street, Newgarth, Ohio

Article VII
BYLAWS

The power to adopt, repeal, and amend the bylaws of this corporation shall reside
in the Board of Directors of this corporation.
IN TESTIMONY WHEREOF, we have hereunto set our names this

_____ day of _____.

who purchase shares of stock—generally acquire rights to control the corporation through voting, to receive income through dividends, and, upon dissolution of the corporation, to share in the net assets in direct proportion to the
number of shares they own.

EXHIBIT 16-4

STOCK CERTIFICATE

Authorized use by Viacom
International, Inc.

The number of shares of stock must be authorized in the corporation's articles of incorporation. All shares authorized by the articles need not be issued or sold to shareholders immediately, but no shares may be issued that are not authorized. Under the Revised Model Business Corporations Act, the articles of incorporation must authorize (1) one or more classes of stock that entitle their owners to unlimited voting rights and (2) one or more classes of stock (these may be the same classes as those with voting rights) that entitle their owners to receive the net assets of the corporation upon dissolution. This provision of the RMBCA ensures that there will be a class of shareholders with the power to elect directors and make other important decisions and a class of shareholders who will share in the residuary (remaining assets) of the corporation on its termination.

Classes of Stock. Most states allow corporations to authorize and issue different classes of stock, with different rights attaching to the different classes. The limitations and preferences of each class must be stated in the articles of incorporation. The two primary classes of stock are common and preferred.

Traditionally, **common stock** has carried with it the right to vote, the right to participate in income through dividends, and the right to participate in the net assets on liquidation. Common stock has no preferential rights (described in the next paragraphs) and, therefore, common stockholders bear the greatest risk of loss. If a corporation has only one class of stock, it is ordinarily assumed to be common stock.

Preferred stock is given special preferences relating to either the payment of dividends or the distribution of assets. Most preferred stock is preferred as to dividends, meaning that in every year in which the corporation pays a dividend,

common stock A class of stock that entitles its owner to vote for the corporation's board of directors, to receive dividends, and to participate in the net assets upon liquidation of the corporation.

preferred stock A class of stock that entitles its owner to special preferences relating to either dividends or the distribution of assets.

Linking Law & Business

Financial Accounting

As a consequence of the disadvantages involved with debt financing, users of financial statements use ratios to assess the risk. However, using one ratio or even several ratios is not the basis for effectively analyzing financial statements. It is imperative that ratios be used concurrently with one another and with other information, including historical facts, because the usefulness of ratios depends on the likelihood that history will repeat itself. One example of a ratio that evaluates the risk involved in debt financing is the times-interest-earned ratio. This ratio is computed by dividing a firm's earnings before interest and taxes (EBIT) by the interest expense. The times-interest-earned ratio is used for the purpose of determining how many times an organization can pay interest expenses using available earnings for interest payments. The higher the ratio, the more likely it is that the firm will be able to make its interest payments. A firm's inability to make interest payments can lead to bankruptcy; therefore, a higher ratio indicates that there is less risk for the firm.

Source: T. Edmonds, F. McNair, E. Milam, and P. Olds, *Fundamental Financial Accounting Concepts* (New York: McGraw-Hill, 2000), pp. 480–482.

---

the preferred shareholders are paid before the common shareholders at a rate stipulated in the articles of incorporation.

If the stock is *cumulative preferred*, the preferred shareholders do not lose their rights to a dividend during a year in which no dividends are paid. Rather, their rights to each year's unpaid dividends accumulate. Thus, during the next year in which dividends are paid, the preferred shareholders receive all past dividends that have accumulated plus the present year's dividend before any dividends are paid to the common shareholders.

If the stock is *participating preferred*, the preferred shareholders first receive their dividends at the preferred rate. The common shareholders receive dividends at the same rate. The remaining income is shared, on a pro rata basis, by the common and preferred stockholders.

If the stock is *liquidation preferred*, upon liquidation of the corporation, preferred shareholders receive either the par value of their stock or a specified monetary amount before the common shareholders share pro rata in the remainder of the assets. Liquidation preferences may also be participating.

Finally, preferred stock may be *convertible*. At the holder's request, such stock may be exchanged for common stock at a stated ratio.

Preferred stock frequently has limited voting rights. It is also generally redeemable, meaning that the corporation has the right to exchange each preferred share for a prespecified monetary amount.

All these distinctions may become irrelevant as more states adopt the Revised Model Business Corporations Act. The RMBCA stipulates that the various classes of stock and the number of shares in each class that may be issued must be stated in the articles of incorporation, but it omits references to such classes of stock as "preferred" and "common." If only one class of stock is designated in the articles of incorporation, it is presumed that the shares carry both the right to vote and the right to participate in corporate assets. If more than one class of stock is authorized, either the distinguishing designation and preferences, limitations, and rights of those classes must be listed or the board of directors must be authorized to designate such features at a later date.

capital structure The percentage of each type of capital—debt, preferred stock, and common equity—used by the corporation.

This broad flexibility given to the directors to affect the **capital structure** of the corporation may be desirable from management's perspective. However, it does not benefit the shareholders, because it may dilute their interests. It is also contrary to present trends in securities regulations (discussed in Chapter 22).

Under the RMBCA, corporations can also issue rights to purchase a stated number of shares at a stated price, usually for a stated period of time. Legal documents, called **stock warrants**, that certify these rights may be freely traded. Employees may receive such rights as compensation in the form of **stock options**. However, when employees are granted the rights to purchase shares at a stated price, these rights cannot be traded. A major issue is whether a stock option will become an expense item under a Financial Accounting Board proposal scheduled to take effect in 2005. Strong opposition from technology and accounting firms exists.[1] A major issue is whether director, officer and employee stock options will become expense items under a Financial Accounting Board (FASB) proposal. In December 2004 the FASB unanimously adopted the expense item rule, which is scheduled to take affect in July of 2005. Further, the FASB has told companies that if they expect to buy back shares of their own company stock in connection with a stock option plan, they must declare an estimate of how many shares they will buy back. Often, buy back programs are used to prevent options and new shares that result from diluting stock prices and earnings per share. This decision of the FASB will be appealed to the SEC, and may be overturned by Congress.

stock warrant A document authorizing its holder to purchase a stated number of shares of stock at a stated price, usually for a stated period of time; may be freely traded.

stock option A stock warrant issued to employees; cannot be traded.

Consideration. Stocks and warrants are issued in return for consideration—that is, something of value. That consideration cannot be less than the stated value of the shares. If a corporation issues shares for less than the stated value, the shareholder remains liable to the corporation for the difference between the stated value and the amount of consideration actually paid.

par value The nominal or face value of a stock or bond.

Traditionally, the minimum amount for which a share could be issued was called the **par value**. In general, this amount was so low (often $1) that the likelihood of a buyer not paying at least that much for the stock was slim. The total par value of all stock initially issued by a corporation was known as stated capital. Some states allowed the issuance of no-par stock, which is stock that does not have a stated par value, but when a corporation issued no-par stock, the board of directors still had to designate a stated value for the stock. The sum of the stated values was the stated capital of the corporation.

The RMBCA has done away with the terms *par*, *no par*, and *stated capital*. Now, before issuing any shares, the board of directors must determine that the amount of consideration received or about to be received is adequate. When the corporation receives the consideration for which the board of directors authorized the issuance of the shares, the shares are deemed fully paid.

Under the RMBCA and most current state laws, the consideration paid for the stock may be in the form of money, property, or past services. The RMBCA also allows for payment by promissory notes and agreements to provide future services.

In some states, problems can arise over the valuation of a nonmonetary consideration. Most states use the good faith rule, which presumes that the valuation of the property or services given as consideration for the stock was

---

[1] See "Expensive Habit: Employees Stock Options Are No Free Lunch for Shareholders," *Barron's*, July 5, 2004, p. 12.

fair as long as it was honestly made—in other words, there was no fraud or bad faith on the part of the directors in making their valuation, and they exercised the degree of care that ordinarily prudent persons in their position would exercise.

Operation of the Corporation. The question of how the corporation is financed can be answered relatively easily. As the previous section explained, the corporation is financed by debt and equity security holders. The answer to the question of who manages the corporation is not quite so simple. Even legal experts disagree to some extent over who actually manages the corporation, as well as over who should manage it.

Three groups theoretically have a voice in the management of the corporation: the shareholders, the board of directors, and the corporate officers and managers. Formal responsibility for management of the corporation is vested in its board of directors, who are elected by the shareholders. These directors determine policy matters and appoint the officers who carry out those policies and manage the everyday affairs of the corporation. Exhibit 16-5 illustrates the division of responsibility in this corporate hierarchy of shareholders, board of directors, and officers and managers.

The Role of the Shareholders. The shareholders are the owners of the corporation, yet they have no direct control over its operation. They are not agents of the corporation and cannot act on its behalf. Their control of the corporation is limited to exercising their right to vote at shareholders' meetings and, through that voting, to select the board of directors who will set corporate policy.

Most corporations are obliged to hold an annual shareholders' meeting at a time specified in the corporate bylaws. In addition, special shareholders' meetings may be called by the board of directors, the holders of more than 5 percent of the shares entitled to cast a vote at such meetings, or anyone else authorized to do so under the corporate bylaws.

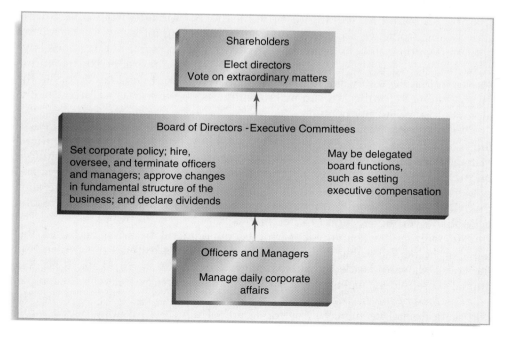

EXHIBIT 16-5

THE CORPORATE HIERARCHY

proxy A document by which shareholders or a publicly held company can transfer their rights to vote at a shareholders' meeting to a second party.

Shareholders vote at the shareholders' meetings either in person or by a **proxy**, which is a written delegation of authority to cast one's votes. Most shareholders vote by proxy, and it is this process of proxy election that has led many people to question whether shareholders really have any say in operating the corporation.

The proxy election is usually run by a proxy committee of corporate executives, who, under the Security and Exchange Commission's Proxy Rules, must use a ballot form to solicit proxies. The form must state that the shares held by the shareholder will be voted in accordance with the way the shareholder marks the ballot. The shareholder has the option to indicate on the ballot that he or she wishes to allow the proxy committee to vote the shares in any way it sees fit. The proxy committee also sends all shareholders a statement of resolutions on which the shareholders are to vote, as well as a biographical sketch of each of the candidates for the board of directors.

This process sounds efficient, even benign. However, because shareholders of major corporations are scattered across the country and could not realistically attend a shareholders' meeting, the proxy process gives management effective control over the election. By placing on the ballot only the names of those candidates management wishes to see elected to the board of directors, management, in essence, selects the board. Although a shareholder can write in the name of another candidate, the cost of communicating with other shareholders makes the prospects for a write-in candidate quite slim.

Any shareholder may also engage in proxy solicitation. However, the costs of doing so are almost prohibitive. In a fight between a shareholder and the corporate proxy committee for proxies, the corporate committee has access to corporate funds, corporate office materials such as paper and duplicating machinery, corporate clerical personnel, and also the corporate legal staff. The shareholders have only their personal funds.

In recent years, the proxy forms sent out by proxy committees of major corporations have sometimes contained resolutions submitted by politically active shareholders who understand how the corporate machinery operates. Most of these resolutions have sought to change the corporation's social policies; for example, resolutions seeking to prohibit the corporation from investing in countries that practice apartheid and from withholding information from shareholders regarding the environmental impact of the corporation's activities have been popular in the last decade or so. The public-interest proxy resolution shown in Exhibit 16-6 was proposed by a shareholder of General Motors in the proxy statement for the 1985 annual meeting. Its objective was to force General Motors to be politically neutral.

When these types of resolutions appear on proxy forms, the management of the corporation usually suggests that shareholders vote against them. Management also generally includes a strong argument against such resolutions on the proxy statement on which the proposal appears. Thus, even if a shareholder does get a resolution on the ballot, the chances of its passing are slim, though there are more frequent and more vigorous fights over policy resolutions than over the election of directors.

Recognizing that shareholder voting occurs primarily by proxy and, thus, that the shareholders' meeting really serves no purpose but to fulfill the demands of the law, Delaware decided to abolish the requirement that corporations hold an annual shareholders' meeting. Other states may soon follow Delaware's example.

The Role of the Board of Directors. Most incorporation laws state that the corporation shall be managed by the board of directors. Although such a rule

Resolved: That the stockholders of General Motors, assembled in annual meeting in person and by proxy, hereby recommended that the Corporation affirm the political nonpartisanship of the Corporation. To this end the following practices are to be avoided.

(a) The handing of contribution cards of a single political party to an employee by a supervisor.

(b) Requesting an employee to send a political contribution to an individual in the corporation for subsequent delivery as part of a group of contributions to a political party or fund-raising committee.

(c) Requesting an employee to issue personal checks blank as to payee for subsequent forwarding to a political party, committee, or candidate.

(d) Using supervisory meetings to announce that contribution cards of one party are available and that anyone desiring cards of a different party will be supplied one on request to his supervisor.

(e) Placing a preponderance of contribution cards of one party at mail station locations.

EXHIBIT 16-6

SHAREHOLDER RESOLUTION

may reflect the behavior of the directors of a closely held corporation who are also its officers, it does not describe the behavior of the directors of publicly held corporations. Nor does it describe the behavior that most people expect from directors of publicly held corporations.

Recognizing that most directors are not going to become involved in daily corporate affairs, the RMBCA in its statement on the role of the board of directors says merely that the corporation shall be managed "under the direction of" the board. This provision does seem to make it clear, however, that the directors are expected to function at least as overseers and policymakers. In this role, the board of directors generally must authorize or approve (1) the payment of dividends, changes in financing, and other capital changes; (2) the selection, supervision, and removal of officers and other executive personnel; (3) the determination of executive compensation and pension plans; (4) the adoption, amendment, or repeal of the corporate bylaws; and (5) the establishment of policy regarding products, services, and labor relations. Unfortunately, most corporate boards abdicate their policymaking function and merely rubber-stamp decisions already made by the officers and managers of the corporation. Rarely does a board challenge an action taken by its corporate officers.

The board, like the shareholders, must function as a group. Unlike shareholders, however, directors are not allowed to vote by proxy. Instead, they are supposed to vote in person at a formal directors' meeting. The rationale for this traditional restriction is that corporations derive benefits from the consultation, discussion, and collective judgment of their boards. Today, however, the laws in most states have been relaxed enough so that board members may act informally, without a meeting, when all the directors consent to such action in writing.

The Role of the Officers and Managers. The officers and managers are responsible for the actual management of corporate affairs. Unlike directors and shareholders, officers are agents of the corporation. Technically, they are appointed and supervised by the board of directors, but because the officers of the company control the proxy election, it is usually the directors who serve at the pleasure of the corporate officers.

Traditional statutes provided that a corporation must have certain officers, such as a president, a vice president, and a treasurer. The RMBCA, however, makes no such stipulations.

EXHIBIT 16-7

CEO PAY: THE BENEFITS AND COSTS TO SHAREHOLDER AND EMPLOYEES

Following the exposure of high salaries, and other financial problems, involving companies and individuals inclusive of ENRON, WorldCom, Adelphia, and Richard Grasso, (formerly of the New York Stock Exchange,)[1] the compensation of officers of corporations has been spotlighted. The decisions for compensation to be paid to a CEO and other officers of a publicly held corporation, are made by the compensation committee of the board of directors. The board of directors is often made up of present and past CEOs, of corporations, nominated informally by the CEO of the company itself and voted on by the full board. Reforms on how compensation, committees are formed, and what members of the board are eligible, have taken place.

Boards representing shareholders pay large sums to CEOs and other officers of a corporation for several reasons:

- *Big pay packages pay off.* CEOs should be paid based on stock market performance of the company. There are up and down years in the market, but generally qualified CEOs are needed for direction.
- If CEOs own stock, they have the same interest as shareholders. Better performance means better profits and better dividends for all.

Some doubt this analysis, arguing that compensation of CEOs should be awarded based on the following reasons:

- Compensation committees of board of directors seek to keep compensation packages similar to those in other corporations in the same sector.
- Compensation committees seek to raise compensation packages in order to keep CEOs from going to other companies; and often tie such packages to stock performance.
- One study indicates talented CEOs will exercise his/her power wisely as officers of the corporation independent of their compensation package.[2]

---

[1] WSJ/Mercer, "CEO Compensation Survey," April 12, 2003 *Wall Street Journal* pp. R-6–10; and "Grasso Lawsuit Fallout Hits Other Executives," *Wall Street Journal*, May 25, 2003, pp. C1, C6.

[2] J. Collins, "Good to Great: Why Some Companies Make the Leap And Others Don't," *USA Today*, June 10, 2003 p. 13A.

Fiduciary Obligations of Directors, Officers, and Managers. As previously noted, the shareholders do not have any direct control over the corporation's operations. Whenever the property of one party is placed in the control of another, however, a fiduciary relationship exists between the two. Thus, certain obligations, called fiduciary duties, are placed on property holders to ensure that they will treat the property as carefully as if it were their own. Because the shareholders own the corporation (property) but its care is entrusted to the directors, officers, and managers, a fiduciary relationship exists between the shareholders and the officers, managers, and directors. The standards of conduct—and, thus, the fiduciary duties—imposed by the RMBCA on officers and directors of corporations are almost identical. Both are required to exercise their duties:

> *(1) in good faith; (2) with the care an ordinarily prudent person in a like position would exercise under similar circumstances; and (3) in a manner he reasonably believes to be in the best interests of the corporation. (Sections 8.30 and 8.42 of the RMBCA)*

There is a potential breach of this duty to act in the best interests of the corporation when a corporate officer or director takes personal advantage of an opportunity that, in all fairness, should have belonged to the corporation. The following classic case illustrates the **corporate opportunity doctrine**.

corporate opportunity doctrine A doctrine, established by case law, that says corporate officers, directors, and agents cannot take personal advantage of an opportunity that in all fairness should have belonged to the corporation.

CASE 16-2

Irving Trust Company v. Deutsch
United States Court of Appeals
73 F.2d 121 (2d Cir. 1934)

The plaintiff, Irving Trust, was the trustee in bankruptcy proceedings for Sonora Products Corporation of America (formerly Acoustic Products Company). The defendants were directors of Acoustic Products. Before it went bankrupt, Acoustic had tried to secure certain patent rights held by De Forest Radio Company. An agent of Acoustic, named Bell, made an offer on the company's behalf for a third of the stock in De Forest, which would have increased Acoustic's chances of getting the patent rights. Acoustic's president, Deutsch, was authorized to obtain financing for the stock purchase but was unable to do so. He and two other directors and Bell then purchased the stock themselves and later sold it for a substantial profit. When Irving Trust sought to hold the defendants liable to the corporation for the amount of the profits, the district court dismissed the trustee's petition for relief. Irving Trust appealed.

Justice Swan

The theory of the suit is that a fiduciary may make no profit for himself out of a violation of duty to his cestui [the beneficiary or person for whom the trust was established] even though he risks his own funds in the venture, and that anyone who assists in the fiduciary's dereliction is likewise liable to account for the profit so made. Concretely, the argument is that members of the Biddle syndicate, three of whom, Messrs. Biddle, Deutsch, and Hammond, were directors and one, Mr. Bell, its agent in procuring the contract, appropriated to themselves Acoustic's rights under its contract with Reynolds & Co., for 200,000 shares of De Forest stock, when as fiduciaries they were obligated to preserve those rights for Acoustic and were forbidden to take a position where personal interest would conflict with the interest of their principal. The other defendants are claimed to have assisted in their dereliction. In answer to this argument, the defendants do not deny the principle, but dispute its applicability to the facts.

The main defense asserted is that Acoustic by reason of its financial straits had neither the funds nor the credit to make the purchase and that the directors honestly believed that by buying the stock for themselves they could give Acoustic the advantage of access to the De Forest patents, while at the same time taking a stock speculation for their own benefit. In support of the proposition that the prohibition against corporate officers acting on their own behalf is removed if the corporation is itself financially unable to enter into the transaction, the appellees cite *Hannerty v. Standard Theater Co.*, 109 Mo. 297, 19 S.W. 82. While these facts raise some question whether Acoustic actually lacked the funds or credit necessary for carrying out its contract, we do not feel justified in reversing the District Court's finding that it did. Nevertheless, they tend to show the wisdom of a rigid rule forbidding directors of a solvent corporation to take over for their own profit a corporate contract on the plea of the corporation's financial inability to perform. If the directors are uncertain whether the corporation can make the necessary outlays, they need not embark upon the venture; if they do, they may not substitute themselves for the corporation any place along the line and divert possible benefits into their own pockets. "Uncompromising rigidity has been the attitude of courts of equity when petitioned to undermine the rule of undivided loyalty by the 'disintegrating erosion' of particular exceptions."

The defendant Bell was Acoustic's agent in the original negotiations with Reynolds, and it is urged by the plaintiff that as such agent he was a fiduciary precluded from making profits out of the subject-matter of his agency. On his behalf it is contended that his agency was ended when he delivered to Acoustic the written offer of Reynolds & Co. and that his participation in the Biddle syndicate was not by virtue of his former agency relationship nor because of any information he had obtained as Acoustic's agent; that he stands like any stranger to whom the syndicate might have offered a participation. But, even if the fact of his agency be disregarded, we think there is an applicable principle which requires him to account, namely, that one who knowingly joins a fiduciary in an enterprise where the personal interest of the latter is or may be antagonistic to his trust becomes jointly and severally liable with him for the profits of the enterprise. Although Bell testified that "My knowledge of what Acoustic did or intended to do with respect to Reynolds' offer of March 31st was limited to what Deutsch told me around the 9th of April," and although precisely what he was told does not appear, nevertheless Bell says that on April 7th or 9th he agreed with Mr. Deutsch that, if the latter was not successful in raising the purchase money for the stock from his own associates, he would join him to the extent of $25,000. This agreement, made at a time when the offer was still open for acceptance by the corporation, brings Bell within the principle above enunciated.

Reversed as against Bell, Biddle, Deutsch, and Hammond.

Affirmed as to the other defendants.

Although a corporate opportunity must be offered to the corporation, it will not necessarily be accepted by the corporation. Once an opportunity is rejected by a vote of the disinterested members of the board of directors, that opportunity no longer belongs to the corporation.

When the corporation cannot take advantage of an opportunity because of financial constraints, a director or officer must do his or her best to secure financing of the opportunity by the corporation, although neither need go so far as to lend the corporation money. In general, taking personal advantage of the opportunity when financing is clearly unavailable is allowed. However, as *Irving Trust v. Deutsch* demonstrates, some courts have strictly applied the duty of undivided loyalty and held that such action usurps a corporate opportunity.

conflict of interest
A conflict that occurs when a corporate officer or director enters into a transaction with the corporation in which he or she has a personal interest.

Another potentially troublesome situation occurs when an officer or a director, or a corporation in which the officer or director has an interest, enters into a transaction with the corporation. This problem, known as a **conflict of interest**, is specifically addressed by the RMBCA. The act provides that a transaction will not be voided because of a conflict of interest when any one of the following is true: (1) The material facts of the transaction and the director's interest were disclosed or known to the board of directors or a committee thereof, and it authorized, approved, or ratified the transaction; (2) the material facts of the transaction and the director's interest were known or disclosed to the shareholders entitled to vote, and they approved, authorized, or ratified the transaction; or (3) the transaction was fair to the corporation. Use of the broad language, "the transaction was fair," seems to give the utmost flexibility to directors. In many states that have not adopted the RMBCA, directors can protect themselves from conflict-of-interest charges through full disclosure and ratification by the board of directors.

business judgment rule
A rule that says corporate officers and directors are not liable for honest mistakes of business judgment.

We have said that officers and directors are required to exercise their duties in a manner they reasonably believe to be in the best interests of the corporation. Under the **business judgment rule**, the courts generally avoid second-guessing corporate executives and let stand any business decisions made in good faith that are uninfluenced by personal considerations.

In determining whether a director's conduct fulfills the duty of care, the courts are aided by RMBCA, which states that a director is entitled to rely on information and reports provided or prepared by (1) officers or employees of the corporation whom the director reasonably believes are reliable and competent, (2) legal counsel or accountants in regard to matters that the director believes are within that professional's competence, or (3) a committee of directors of which the director is not a part, if he or she reasonably believes they merit confidence. The use courts make of the business judgment rule is illustrated in the following case. Note carefully the court's emphasis on the financial expertise required when discussing the question of a valuation study.

CASE 16-3

Smith v. Van Gorkom
Delaware Supreme Court
488 A.2d 858 (1985)

In order to take advantage of a favorable tax situation, defendant Van Gorkom, chief executive of Trans Union Corporation ("Trans Union" or "the Company"), solicited a merger offer from Pritzker, an outside investor. Van Gorkom acted on his own and arbitrarily arrived at a buyout price of $55 per share. Without any investigation, the full Trans

Union board accepted the offer informally. The offer was proposed two more times before its formal acceptance by the board. Plaintiff Smith and other shareholders brought suit, claiming that the board had failed to give due consideration to the offer. The trial court held that the shareholder vote approving the merger should not be set aside because the stockholders had been "fairly informed" by the board of directors before they voted on it.

It also found that, because the board had considered the offer three times before formally accepting it, it had acted in an informed manner and was, therefore, entitled to the protection of the business judgment rule. Plaintiffs appealed.

Justice Horsey

On Friday, September 19, Van Gorkom called a special meeting of the Trans Union Board for noon the following day. . . .

Van Gorkom began the Special Meeting of the Board with a twenty-minute oral presentation. Copies of the proposed Merger Agreement were delivered too late for study before or during the meeting. He reviewed the Company's ITC and depreciation problems and the efforts theretofore made to solve them. He discussed his initial meeting with Pritzker and his motivation in arranging that meeting. Van Gorkom did not disclose to the Board, however, the methodology by which he alone had arrived at the $55 figure, or the fact that he first proposed the $55 price in his negotiations with Pritzker.

Van Gorkom outlined the terms of the Pritzker offer as follows: Pritzker would pay $55 in cash for all outstanding share, of Trans Union stock upon completion of which Trans Union would be merged into new T Company, a subsidiary wholly-owned by Pritzker and formed to implement the merger; for a period of 90 days, Trans Union could receive, but could not actively solicit, competing offers; the offer had to be acted on by the next evening, Sunday, September 21; Trans Union could only furnish to competing bidders published information, and not proprietary information; the offer was subject to Pritzker obtaining the necessary financing by October 10, 1980; if the financing contingency were met or waived by Pritzker, Trans Union was required to sell to Pritzker one million newly-issued shares of Trans Union at $38 per share.

The Board meeting of September 20 lasted about two hours. . . . The directors approved the proposed Merger Agreement. . . .

On February 10, the stockholders of Trans Union approved the Pritzker merger proposal. Of the outstanding shares, 69.9% were voted in favor of the merger, 7.25% were voted against the merger, and 22.85% were not voted.

The determination of whether a business judgment is an informed one turns on whether the directors have informed themselves "prior to making a business decision of all material information reasonably available to them."

In the specific context of a proposed merger of domestic corporations, a director has a duty under 8 Del. C 251(b), along with his fellow directors, to act in an informed and deliberate manner in determining whether to approve an agreement of merger before submitting the proposal to the stockholders. Certainly in the merger context, a director may not abdicate that duty by leaving to the shareholders alone the decision to approve or disapprove the agreement.

On the record before us, we must conclude that the Board of Directors did not reach an informed business judgment on September 20, 1980 in voting to "sell" the company for $55 per share pursuant to the Pritzker cash-out merger proposal. Our reasons, in summary, are as follows:

The directors (1) did not adequately inform themselves as to Van Gorkom's role in forcing the "sale" of the Company and in establishing the per share purchase price; (2) were uninformed as to the intrinsic value of the Company; and (3) given these circumstances, at a minimum, were grossly negligent in approving the "sale" of the Company upon two hours' consideration, without prior notice, and without the exigency of a crisis or emergency.

Without any documents before them concerning the proposed transaction, the members of the Board were required to rely entirely upon Van Gorkom's 20-minute oral presentation of the proposal. No written summary of the terms of the merger was presented; the directors were given no documentation to support the adequacy of $55 price per share for sale of the Company; and the Board had before it nothing more than Van Gorkom's statement of his understanding of the substance of an agreement, which he admittedly had never read, nor which any member of the Board had ever seen.

There was no call by the Board, either on September 20 or thereafter, for any valuation study or documentation of the $55 price per share as a measure of the fair value of the Company in a cash-out context. It is undisputed that the major asset of Trans Union was its cash flow. Yet, at no time did the Board call for a valuation study taking into account that highly significant element of the Company's assets.

The record also establishes that the Board accepted without scrutiny Van Gorkom's representation as to the fairness of the $55 price per share for sale of the Company—a subject that the Board had never previously considered. The Board thereby failed to discover that Van Gorkom had suggested the $55 price to Pritzker and, most crucially, that Van Gorkom had arrived at the $55 figure based on calculations designed solely to determine the feasibility of a leveraged buy-out. No questions were raised either as to the tax implications of a cash-out merger or how the price for the one million share option granted Pritzker was calculated.

We do not say that the Board of Directors was not entitled to give some credence to Van Gorkom's representation that $55 was an adequate or fair price. . . . The issue is whether the directors informed themselves as to all information that was reasonably available to them. Had they done so, they would have learned of the source and derivation of the $55 price and could not reasonably have relied thereupon in good faith.

The defendants ultimately relied on the stockholder vote of February 10 for exoneration. The defendants contend that the stockholders' "overwhelming" vote approving the Pritzker Merger Agreement had the legal effect of curing any failure of the Board to reach an informed business judgment in its approval of the merger.

The burden must fall on defendants who claim ratification based on shareholder vote to establish that the shareholder approval resulted from a fully informed electorate. On the record before us, it is clear that the Board failed to meet that burden.

To summarize: we hold that the directors of Trans Union breached their fiduciary duty to their stockholders (1) by their failure to inform themselves of all information

reasonably available to them and relevant to their decision to recommend the Pritzker merger; and (2) by their failure to disclose all material information such as a reasonable stockholder would consider important in deciding whether to approve the Pritzker offer.

We hold, therefore, that the Trial Court committed reversible error in applying the business judgment rule in favor of the director defendants in this case.

Reversed in favor of Plaintiff, Smith.

Critical Thinking About the Law

The standards we use to make judgments are often ambiguous. For example, in judging someone's character we might consider whether that person is fair, honest, and reasonable. To the extent that standards such as "fair" and "honest" and "reasonable" do not have universal meanings, they are ambiguous.

As you are well aware by this time, courts are not exempt from this tendency to use ambiguous standards in judging. The facts of a case are important in determining how ambiguous standards will be applied.

An important critical thinking skill is the ability to recognize ambiguous language in a court's opinion, for without this recognition, you are not prepared to make an informed decision about whether the court's application of standards was merited by the facts of the case. The questions that follow are intended to help you improve this critical thinking skill.

1. To demonstrate your ability to recognize ambiguous language, identify at least two examples, from Case 16-3, of such language in the court's opinion.

   Clue: Remember that adjectives are often ambiguous.

2. The court applies this ambiguous language in a manner unfavorable to the defendant. What reasons does the court provide for doing so?

   Clue: If the defendant had met the standards by which he was being judged, the decision would have been favorable to him. Another way of phrasing this question is: Why didn't the court find that he met these standards?

COMMENT: *In Cinerama Inc. v. Technicolor Inc.*, 663 A.2d 1156 (1995) the Supreme Court of Delaware distinguished the *Van Gorkom* case and held that the defendant (Technicolor) board of directors did not violate its duty of loyalty when as interested directors they participated in a unanimous vote to repeal the company's supermajority provisions. The court stated that an "entire fairness analysis is required" when considering how a board of directors discharges its fiduciary duties. The Delaware Supreme Court affirmed the chancery court's decision in favor of the defendants despite the fact that the interested directors had played a major part in negotiating the merger of their company without disclosing their material conflicts of interest to shareholders such as the plaintiff, Cinerama. In *Brehm v. Eisner*, Supreme Court of Delaware, 746 A.2d 244 (2000), the issue was whether stockholders may impose personal liability on the directors of a Delaware corporation for lack of due care and for waste of corporate assets. The legal questions referring to corporate governance and compliance with statutory and case were found not to have been violated. The appeals court affirmed the dismissal of the action of the lower court (chancery court). The appeals court stated that the lucrative buyout of the former president of Disney (Ovitz) did not constitute waste by the board. In the absence of fraud, disagreements were not grounds for imposing personal liability based on breach of fiduciary duty with regard to the board.

In January 2003, E. Norman Veasey, chief justice of the Delaware Supreme Court, indicated in a roundtable discussion on executive compensation at the University of Delaware[2] that corporate directors could be held personally liable if they fail to act in good faith and thus breach their fiduciary duty to shareholders.

Experts in the area of corporate governance seemed to interpret such comments as meaning that the independence of a board's compensation committee from the CEO will be looked at by the court carefully in terms of good faith as outlined in this chapter. The large number of companies incorporated in Delaware make such comments particularly important.

On March 2, 2004, the chairman and chief executive of Walt Disney Company (Michael Eisner) lost his position as chairman after an estimated 43 percent of voting shareholders declined to support his reelection. Other nominees to the board received fewer dissenting votes. Roy Disney, nephew of the founder, led the dissenting shareholders. Despite the no-confidence vote, Mr. Eisner still had the directors' support as CEO. In October of 2004, Mr. Eisner announced his resignation effective in 2005.

LIMITED LIABILITY COMPANIES

BACKGROUND

The **limited liability company (LLC)** is a hybrid form of business organization. It allows entrepreneurs and small business owners to enjoy the same limited personal liability that shareholders in a corporation have while retaining the status of partners in a partnership. The LLC is federally taxed, not as a corporation, but as a partnership, so taxes are paid personally by members of the LLC. Limited liability corporation members share in the profits from the business and exercise management control without these actions affecting their profit share or limited liability status. The LLC differs from the Subchapter S corporation in that other corporations, partnerships, and foreign investors can be LLC members, and there is no limit on the number of members.

limited liability company (LLC) A hybrid corporation-partnership, such as the Subchapter S corporation, but with far fewer restrictions.

THE UNIFORM LIMITED LIABILITY ACT

The National Conference on Uniform State Law (comprised of lawyers, academics, and judges) issued the Uniform Limited Liability Company Act (ULLCA). This act covers the formation, operation, and termination of LLCs. Each state through its legislature must determine whether the ULLCA will become state law. Forty-eight states have adopted all or part of the Uniform Act as its state statute.

LLC CHARACTERISTICS

The LLC is a separate legal person (or entity) under state law. It can sue or be sued, enforce contracts, and be found civilly and criminally liable for violations of law (ULLCA, Section 201).

---

[2] J. Becker, "Delaware Justice Warns Boards of Liability for Executive Pay," *Wall Street Journal,* January 6, 2003, p. A-14.

The owners of the LLC are called members. They are not personally liable to third parties for the debts, obligations, and liabilities of an LLC beyond an individual's capital contribution—that is, they are under a limited liability (ULLCA, Section 303[9]). A member is personally liable for the debts of an LLC only if he or she agrees to it in writing or if it is so stated in the articles of incorporation. An example of personal liability is set out in the case that follows.

CASE 16-4

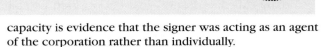

Creative Resource Management Inc. v. Soskin
Court of Appeals of Tennessee, WL
813420 (1998)

Nashville Pro Hockey, LLC, was a limited liability company organized under the laws of Tennessee. The LLC owned and operated the Nashville Nighthawks, a minor league professional hockey team. On September 4, 1996, Nashville Pro Hockey, LLC, contracted with Creative Resource Management, Inc. (CRM), plaintiff, whereby CRM, for fees and other consideration, would provide employee leasing services to Nashville Pro Hockey, LLC. The contract was signed by Barry Soskin, the president of Nashville Pro Hockey, LLC. A paragraph in the contract provided: "By affixing my hand and seal to this agreement, I personally guarantee any and all payments payable as represented and outlined in this agreement."

Nashville Pro Hockey, LLC, failed, owing CRM $29,626. CRM sued Nashville Pro Hockey, LLC, and Barry Soskin to recover the unpaid compensation. Soskin defended, alleging that his signature on the contract was in his representative capacity only and not in his individual capacity as a guarantor. The trial court agreed and granted summary judgment to Soskin. CRM appealed.

Justice Cain

The well-settled precedent in Tennessee suggests that a corporate officer's signature preceded by a corporation's capacity is evidence that the signer was acting as an agent of the corporation rather than individually.

This rule, however, must yield where the language of the contract compels a different conclusion. The language of the contract involved in the case at bar distinguishes this case from the general rule. This case concerns a contract, which contains personal guarantee language in the body of the contract.

The words "I personally guarantee any and all payments payable as represented and outlined in this agreement" reflect indisputably a guarantee by someone. Soskin insists that he signed only as a representative of the limited liability company. CRM insists that his signature imposes personal liability upon him. The stark fact is that the words "I personally guarantee" are meaningless if applied to Nashville Pro Hockey, LLC and not to Barry Soskin individually. Since the words "I personally guarantee" cannot refer to Nashville Pro Hockey, LLC, and retain any meaning at all in the text of this agreement, they must of necessity reflect the personal guarantee of Barry Soskin.

Reversed in favor of Plaintiff, CRM.

CREATING A LIMITED LIABILITY COMPANY

The following steps are important in creating an LLC:

- Choose a state where the LLC will be doing most of its business.
- Select a name. It is important to make sure the state's statute governing the LLC is met and the name is not already used. The words *limited liability company* or the abbreviation *LLC* should be used or other language approved by Section 105(a), as adopted by the state statute. Reserve the name by filing the application with the secretary of state, following a determination as to whether the proposed company name is federally trademarked by another company.

Critical Thinking About the Law

Ethical norms act as the lenses through which we view particular situations. Individuals who give greater weight to one ethical norm could easily view the same set of facts as another person but view those facts in a different light. These differing lenses do not necessarily suggest that one person has the correct view and the other does not. Instead, these lenses simply influence an individual's perception of certain events, which could lead to disagreement between individuals who are wearing ethical lenses of varying colors. Disagreements on the basis of contrasting ethical lenses are easily seen in the relationship between plaintiffs and defendants. These opposing sides often disagree about what should be the outcome of a case, even when they agree about most of the facts. In Case 16-4, Soskin and CRM viewed the same set of facts; they agreed that there was a contract, signed by Barry Soskin, and the clause in dispute stated "I personally guarantee." But Soskin and CRM vehemently disagreed about who should be liable—the individual or the limited liability company. The next two questions ask you to view the facts of Case 16-4 while trying on a couple different ethical lenses.

1. Make a list of the facts in Case 16-4.

   Clue: Reread the introductory section. Be sure to consider the relevant rules of law in this case.

2. Assume you are Defendant Soskin in Case 16-4. What ethical norm would be most important to you when viewing the fact of the case as you make your argument? To enhance your understanding of the ways in which ethical norms influence your perception of given facts, now pretend you are a business manager for CRM. With which primary ethical norm are you most likely to view this case?

   Clue: Focus on the way in which each party would interpret the defendant's capacity in signing the agreement.

- Under the ULLCA, an LLC may be formed by one or more persons by delivering articles of organization to the secretary of state. The LLC comes into existence at the time of filing by the secretary (ULLCA, Section 202).

DURATION OF THE LLC

Unless an LLC has specified otherwise in its articles of organization, its duration is unlimited or at will, meaning that it has no specific term.

FINANCING OF THE LLC

Members' contributions to the LLC may be in the form of money; real, personal, tangible, and intangible property (e.g., often a patent); or contracts for services, promissory notes, or other agreements to contribute (ULCC, Section 401).

CONTROL CONSIDERATIONS

Members of an LLC should have an operating agreement that will outline responsibilities, voting rights, and how the LLC is to be managed, at minimum. Often outside management companies are hired. Experienced counsel and accountants should be involved in the drafting of such an agreement.

TAX RAMIFICATIONS

As noted previously, the LLC does not pay taxes. Income and losses are passed through to members to be reported on individual tax returns. Accountants and tax lawyers should be hired to set up this "flow-through" treatment on tax returns.

FACTORS INFLUENCING A BUSINESS MANAGER'S CHOICE OF ORGANIZATIONAL FORM

There is no ideal form for a business venture. Each of the forms we discussed in this chapter has advantages and disadvantages. The entrepreneur, with the counsel of an attorney and an accountant or tax expert, should carefully weigh the advantages and disadvantages of different organizational forms for the type of business the entrepreneur wishes to open. The principal factors influencing the choice of organizational form are (1) tax ramifications, (2) control considerations, (3) potential liability of the owners, (4) ease and expense of formation and operation, (5) transferability of ownership

TABLE 16-3 COMPARISON OF ALTERNATIVE FORMS OF BUSINESS ORGANIZATION

Organizational Form	Tax Ramifications	Control Considerations
Sole proprietorship	Profits taxed directly to proprietor as ordinary income and losses deducted by proprietor.	Sole proprietor has total control.
General partnership	A federal income tax return must be filed for information only. Profits taxed to partners as ordinary income and losses deducted by partners. Profits and losses shared equally unless changed by partnership agreement.	Each partner is entitled to equal control. Can be changed by partnership agreement.
Limited partnership (limited liability partnership)	Same as general partnership.	Same as for general partners. Limited partners cannot take part in management.
Public corporation	Profits taxed as income to corporation and again as income to owners when distributed as dividends.	Separation of ownership and control. No control over daily management decisions.
Subchapter S corporation	Taxed as a partnership.	Separation of ownership and control. No control over daily management decisions.
Limited liability company	Taxed as a partnership.	Control over daily management decisions.

interests, and (6) the projected life of the organization. Table 16-3 gives an overview of how these six factors differ for each organizational form.

SPECIALIZED FORMS OF BUSINESS ASSOCIATIONS

In addition to the three major forms of business associations emphasized in this chapter, there are several specialized forms of doing business. These forms, summarized in Table 16-4, have become increasingly significant for raising capital, producing goods and services, and marketing them—in many cases, across national borders. You will note in our discussion of these specialized forms that they arise out of private contractual relationships and often are not regulated by state or federal governments.

Liability	Ease and Expense of Formation	Transferability of Ownership Interests	Lifetime
Sole proprietor has unlimited personal liability.	No formalities or expenses required other than those specific to the business to be operated.	Nontransferable.	Limited to life of proprietor.
Each partner has unlimited personal liability for debts of the partnership.	No formalities or expenses required other than those specific to the business to be operated. Written agreement advisable.	Nontransferable.	Limited to life of partners.
Same as for general partners. Liability of limited partner is limited to his or her capital contribution.	Added expense and time required to draw up and file written partnership agreement. Failure to comply with formalities will result in loss of limited partnership.	Nontransferable.	Limited to life of general partners.
Liability limited to loss of capital contribution.	Expense and time required to comply with statutory formality. Must receive charter from state; usually required to register and pay fees to operate in states other than state of incorporation.	Generally unlimited, except by shareholder agreements.	Unlimited.
Liability limited to loss of capital contribution.	Same as for public corporation; must follow IRS rules carefully or lose Subchapter S status.	Ownership interests limited to no more than 35 shareholders; all must be individuals, estates, or certain types of trusts, and no shareholder may be a nonresident alien. Shares may not be issued or transferred to more than 35 shareholders.	Unlimited.
Liability limited to loss of capital contribution.	Same as for public corporation; must follow IRS rules carefully or lose limited liability status.	No limitation on number of members.	Unlimited.

TABLE 16-4 SPECIALIZED FORMS OF BUSINESS ASSOCIATIONS

Form	Description
Cooperative	A not-for-profit business created by individuals to market products.
Joint-stock company	A partnership agreement in which individuals agree to take stock ownership while retaining partnership liability.
Syndicate	An investment group created primarily for the purpose of financing a purchase, usually a single transaction.
Joint venture	A partnership, individual, or corporation that pools labor and capital for a limited period of time.
Franchising	A method of marketing goods through a private agreement whereby the franchisor allows use of its trade name, trademark, or copyright in exchange for a percentage of the gross profits made by the franchisee. Federal and state laws govern franchising.

COOPERATIVE

cooperative A not-for-profit organization formed by individuals to market products.

A **cooperative** is a not-for-profit organization formed by individuals to market products. For example, farmers often agree to pool their crops in order to sell them in larger quantities so they can get the best price from distributors. Any profits made by the cooperative are shared by members. The dividends of a cooperative are paid to members in direct proportion to the amount of business they conduct with the organization yearly.

JOINT STOCK COMPANY

joint stock company A partnership agreement in which members of the company own shares that are transferable, but all goods are held in the name of the members, who assume partnership liability.

A **joint stock company** is a partnership agreement in which members agree to stock ownership in exchange for partnership liability. Although members own shares that are transferable (as in a corporation), the joint stock company is treated as a partnership because all goods are held in the name of the partners, who are held personally liable when sued successfully by a third party.

SYNDICATE

syndicate An investment group that privately agrees to come together for the purpose of financing a large commercial project that none of the syndicate members could finance alone.

A **syndicate** is an investment group that makes a private agreement to come together for the purpose of financing a large commercial project (e.g., a hotel or a sports team) that the individual members (partnerships or corporations) could not finance alone. The advantage of a syndicate is that it can raise large amounts of capital quickly. The disadvantage is, if the project fails, the syndicate members may be held liable for a breach of the agreement by a third party.

JOINT VENTURE

joint venture Relationship between two or more persons or corporations, or an association between a foreign multinational and an agency of the host government or a host country national; set up for a specific business undertaking or a limited time period.

When individuals, partnerships, or corporations make a private agreement to finance, produce, and sell goods, securities, or commodities for a limited purpose and/or a limited time, they have formed a **joint venture**. Joint ventures are a popular way for developing nations (e.g., China) to attract foreign capital. Typically, two companies (say, Chrysler and Bank of America) join with foreign companies (say, Chinese state auto companies) to finance, produce, and market goods. In the United States, General Motors and Toyota Corporation entered into a joint venture to produce the highly successful Saturn line of cars.

FRANCHISING

A **franchising** relationship is based on a private commercial agreement between the franchisor, who owns a trade name or trademark, and the franchisee, who sells or distributes goods using the trade name or trademark. It is a method of marketing goods or services.

The franchisee usually pays a percentage of the gross sales to the franchisor in exchange for use of the trademark name, construction of the building, and numerous other services. Usually the franchisee is a local entrepreneur whom the franchisor supplies with goods to be sold under conditions set out under the agreement. Failure to meet such conditions (e.g., not keeping a fast-food restaurant clean) may lead to termination of the franchise agreement.

franchising A commercial agreement between a party that owns a trade name or trademark (the franchisor) and a party that sells or distributes goods or services using that trade name or trademark (the franchisee).

LAWS GOVERNING FRANCHISING

When franchising exists based on contractual relationship, traditional common law applies for nongoods. Article 2 of the UCC applies when the franchisor–franchisee is involved in sales agreements.

Terms of a Franchise Agreement

Generally, the agreement is a standard form contract prepared by the franchisor. Franchise agreements cover the following topics:

1. *Quality control standards.* The franchisor's most important assets are its name and reputation. The quality control standards set out in the franchise agreement—such as the franchisor's right to make periodic inspections of the franchisee's premises and operations—are intended to protect these assets. Failure to meet the proper standards can result in loss of the franchise.

2. *Training requirements.* Franchisees and their personnel usually are required to attend training programs either on site or at the franchisor's training facilities.

3. *Covenant not to compete.* Covenants not to compete prohibit franchisees from competing with the franchisor during a specific time and in a specified area after the termination of the franchise. Unreasonable (overextensive) covenants not to compete are void.

4. *Arbitration clause.* Most franchise agreements contain an arbitration clause providing that any claim or controversy arising from the franchise agreement or an alleged breach thereof is subject to arbitration. The U.S. Supreme Court has held such clauses to be enforceable.

5. *Other terms.* Capital requirements include: restrictions on the use of the franchisor's trade name, trademarks, and logo; standards of operation; duration of the franchise; recordkeeping requirements; sign requirements; hours of operation; prohibition as to the sale of assignment of the franchise; conditions for the termination of the franchise; and other specific terms pertinent to the operation of the franchise and the protection of the parties' rights.

Franchise Fees

Franchise fees payable by the franchisee are usually stipulated in the franchise agreement. The franchisor may require the franchisee to pay any or all of the following fees:

1. *Initial license fee.* A lump-sum payment for the privilege of being granted a franchise.

2. *Royalty fee.* A fee for the continued use of the franchisor's trade name, property, and assistance that is often computed as a percentage of the franchisee's gross sales.

> 3. *Assessment fee.* A fee for such things as advertising and promotional campaigns and administrative costs, billed either as a flat monthly or annual fee or as percentage of gross sales.
>
> 4. *Lease fees.* Payment for any land or equipment leased from the franchisor, billed either as a flat monthly or annual fee or as a percentage of gross sales or other agreed-upon amount.
>
> 5. *Cost of supplies.* Payment for supplies purchased from the franchisor.

In addition there are federal and state laws that are designed to protect franchisees from terminating the agreement without good cause.

FEDERAL AND STATE LAWS

Federal Laws. The Franchise Rule promulgated by the Federal Trade Commission requires a franchisor to disclose all material facts to a franchisee before entering into a franchise agreement. (See Chapter 24 for a discussion of this rule.)

State Laws. State deceptive trade practices acts and the Uniform Franchise Law set out by the National Conference of Commissioners on Uniform State Laws seek to make all states' franchise laws similar. This law must be adopted by each state legislature before it is applicable in a state.

GLOBAL DIMENSIONS OF BUSINESS ASSOCIATIONS

It is inevitable that the worldwide trend to market-oriented economies will raise the demand for the investment capital and manufactured goods and services of the industrialized world. This certainty, together with the forging of international and regional agreements to lower or eliminate tariffs and other barriers to trade in recent years (see Chapter 9), is spurring many corporations, partnerships, and proprietorships that were once strictly domestic businesses to become transnational, multinational, or international buyers and sellers of goods and services.

In deciding whether to take the plunge into international waters, managers of small, midsize, and large businesses need to ask the following questions:

- Is there a demand for the product in the targeted country or countries?
- Are there legal obstacles in the targeted country that need to be carefully considered?
- Is managing an international business at a distance a realistic possibility for the firm?
- Will management be able to deal successfully with currency fluctuations?
- Is the risk of political interference by the target country's government too great to make doing business in that country worthwhile?
- Is there a serious risk of nonperformance, nonpayment, or loss of property or freight in the country or region the firm is considering entering?

If the responses to those questions indicate that the firm should go ahead, managers need to determine the optimal level of global involvement by answering these questions:

- Should the firm directly export to another firm in the target country, or should it hire an export trading company to market its products?

- Should the firm license the use of its products under an international licensing agreement? For example, international franchising is a form of licensing in which franchisees in the targeted countries are allowed to use the franchisor's name in exchange for a percentage of the gross profits. This specialized business form is the preferred way to go international among fast-food retailers such as McDonald's, Wendy's, and Pizza Hut. If the firm holds a patent, trademark, or copyright on its product, however, it must always be concerned about possible efforts by businesses or individuals in the target country to circumvent multilateral and bilateral international agreements.

- Should the firm go international by joint ventures, mergers, or acquisitions? These alternatives, which involve investment of large sums of capital, seem most appropriate for large multinational companies.

Outsourcing

The increase in outsourcing of manufacturing and service sector jobs despite political opposition (e.g., Democrats, unions, prisoners, and others) brought into focus a dilemma for private and public sector companies in developed nations worldwide. Cost savings on goods and services and increased exports to fast-growing developing countries versus loss of jobs and "heat" from politicians presents problems for many private sector companies. Candidates in the 2004 presidential elections offered contrasting views on this subject. Also, doing a cost–benefit analysis with regard to outsourcing does not produce many hard numbers. For example, if there is an outsourcing of some jobs to India, how is that balanced against Indians buying more U.S. services, and U.S. citizens being able to buy cheaper goods manufactured in India?[1] Legal questions also exist at the federal and state levels.

There were six different tax bills introduced into congress in 2004 that had amendments aimed at curbing outsourcing. They were lobbied against, warning that taxpayers' costs would go up if outsourcing were curbed. The U.S. Chamber of Commerce and other lobbying groups were successful in bottling up legislation in Congress. The Chamber represents multinationals and others that are proponents of outsourcing.[2] An amendment to a federal omnibus appropriations act was passed in 2004. It prohibited some government jobs from being outsourced.

At the state level some 35 states have introduced anti-outsourcing bills. None of the bills have passed in a form that would curtail outsourcing. Indiana and Maryland passed a nonbinding preference act for hiring in-state companies for state contracts as opposed to one performed by a contractor from a site located outside the United States. Both the Chamber and unions lobbied in opposition to each other at the state legislative level. The business lobby indicated that anti-outsourcing legislation would interfere with work done on everything from roads to state employee pension plans, where in the latter case Indiana subcontractors had produced the software running the system. Another example was in Maryland, where foreign nationals were employed in its overseas study program at the University of Maryland. Compromises were made in the two state legislatures (Indiana and Maryland). No other bills have passed.[3]

---

[1] Jon E. Hilsenrath, "Behind Outsourcing Debate: Surprisingly Few Hard Numbers," *Wall Street Journal*, April 12, 2004, pp. A-1, A-7.
[2] M. Schroeder, "States Efforts' to Curb Outsourcing Stymied," *Wall Street Journal*, April 16, 1984, p. A-4.
[3] *Id.*

SUMMARY

The sole proprietorship, the partnership, and the corporation are the three major forms of business organizations in the United States.

Factors influencing the choice of one of these three types of business associations include tax ramifications, control considerations, liability of owners, and, less significantly, ease and expense of ownership, transferability of properties, and the projected life of the business. The sole proprietorship allows the owner to have total control of management, assets, and profits; the owner also has unlimited personal liability. General partners usually exercise equal control over management and profits; they, too, incur unlimited personal liability. Limited partners forgo management control in return for limited liability. In both sole proprietorships and partnerships, profits are taxed as personal income to the owners. All corporations offer limited liability to owners. Owners of private corporations often exercise managerial control. In Subchapter S and limited liability companies, profits are taxed as in a partnership. Owners (shareholders) of public corporations exert no managerial control; profits of these corporations are subject to double taxation.

Specialized forms of business associations are the cooperative, joint stock company, syndicate, joint venture, and franchising.

Business organizations should ask some basic questions before they enter global markets. Once they have decided to go ahead, they need to decide the optimal level of involvement and marketing methods.

REVIEW QUESTIONS

16-1 Identify the primary differences between a limited partnership and a general partnership.

16-2 Describe the various types of corporations discussed in this chapter.

16-3 Identify the factors that an entrepreneur should consider in selecting an organizational form for a business.

16-4 Describe the circumstances under which a partnership would offer greater tax advantages than a corporation.

16-5 Explain why it is somewhat misleading to assert that the corporate form provides limited liability for its owners, whereas the partnership form saddles its owners with unlimited liability.

16-6 What is a single tax advantage of a limited liability company?

REVIEW PROBLEMS

16-7 A truck owned by Thoni Trucking Company was involved in an accident that caused severe injuries to the Fosters (plaintiffs). After learning of the accident, the owner (defendant) of all but two shares of the stock in Thoni Trucking and the rest of the board of directors, which consisted of the majority owner's wife and his father, transferred substantial corporate assets to themselves as salary and dividends. The remaining assets and business operations were transferred to another company that the defendant owned. In the midst of these activities, the defendant kept sending misleading information to the plaintiffs, first telling them to seek recovery from the defendant corporation, then advising them that the corporation had no assets. Would the defendant's actions allow him to reduce his liability?

16-8 Jumping Jills, Inc., was a corporation that provided trampolines for the use of the public. Defendant

Jones owned 80 percent of the stock of Jumping Jills, Inc.; his wife owned 10 percent; and his stepson owned the remaining 10 percent. Jones also owned a drive-in theater located next to the trampoline business. The finances of the two businesses were kept completely separate; the family finances were kept separate from both businesses. The public had no notice that the ownership of the two businesses was similar. Jumping Jills employed two persons. It had been in business for only three months when young Banks was injured on one of its trampolines. Jumping Jills' insurance company went bankrupt and, thus, could not compensate Banks for his injuries. The corporation itself had no assets, so Banks sought to recover from the major shareholder, Jones. Would Banks be successful?

16-9 Alder, Svingos, and Shaw owned an equal number of shares in a corporation that was organized to run a restaurant. They entered into a shareholders' agreement that provided, among other things, that all corporate changes, including changes in the corporate structure, would have to be approved by a unanimous vote of the shareholders. When Alder and Shaw tried to sell the business, Svingos alleged that this sale would violate the shareholders' agreement. Shaw and Alder argued that the pertinent provision was void because it should have been contained in the articles of incorporation, not in the shareholders' agreement. Was the shareholders' agreement enforceable in this case?

16-10 Dunn and Welch both appeared to operate Ruidoso Downs Feed Concession. Dunn sought to obtain credit for Ruidoso Downs from Anderson Hay and Grain Company. Relying on Dunn's financial position, Anderson extended the credit. Dunn was the person who was responsible for making sure that the payments were made. When Ruidoso Downs could not pay Anderson, Anderson brought an action against Dunn, alleging that, as a partner, Dunn was personally liable for the debts the partnership could not repay. Dunn defended on the grounds that he was not a partner because there was no formal partnership agreement between him and Welch. Was Dunn liable?

16-11 Kline was both president and one of two directors of Fayes, Inc. The business, the ladies' ready-to-wear department of a department store, was supervised by a general manager and operated under a five-year written lease. In March, the renewal lease was sent to Kline, as president. He held the lease for eight months and then had it redrawn as a personal lease in his name. The new lease became effective July 1, but the corporation continued to operate until July 31, when Kline seized all of the assets, including the inventory and fixtures. Did the corporation have any legal recourse?

16-12 Hugo and Charles were brothers who did business as partners for several years. When Hugo died, Charles was appointed administrator of his estate. Tax returns disclosed that the partnership business continued to operate just as it had before Hugo's death and that Hugo's estate received the profits and was charged with the losses of the business. Did Charles have the authority to continue the partnership business after the dissolution of the partnership brought about by Hugo's death, and are the assets of Hugo's estate chargeable with the liabilities of the partnership incurred after Hugo's death?

CASE PROBLEMS

16-13 C. B. Management Company operated McDonald's restaurants in Cleveland, Ohio, under a franchise agreement with McDonald's Corporation. The agreement required C. B. to make monthly payments of certain percentages of the gross sales to McDonald's. If any payment was more than 30 days late, McDonald's had the right to terminate the franchise. When C. B. defaulted on the payments in July 1997, McDonald's gave notice of 30 days to comply or surrender possession of the restaurants. McDonald's demanded that C. B. vacate the restaurants. C. B. refused. McDonald's filed a suit in a federal district

court against C. B., alleging violations of the franchise agreement. C. B. counterclaimed in part that McDonald's had breached the implied covenant of good faith and fair dealing. McDonald's filed a motion to dismiss C. B.'s counterclaim. Will the court agree? Explain. *McDonald's Corp. v. C. B. Management Co.*, 13 F. Supp 2d 705 (N.D. Ill. 1998)

16-14 Charles Pace and Maria Fuentez were shareholders of Houston Industries Inc., (HII), and employees of Houston Lighting & Power, a subsidiary of HII, when they lost their jobs because of a company-wide reduction in its workforce. Pace, as a shareholder, three times wrote to HII, demanding that the board of directors terminate certain HII directors and officers and file a suit to recover damages for breach of fiduciary duty. Three times, the directors referred the charges to board committees and an outside law firm, which found that the facts did not support the charges. The board also received input from federal regulatory authorities about the facts behind some of the charges. The board notified Pace that it would refuse his demands. In response, Pace and Fuentez filed a shareholders' derivative suit in a Texas state court against Don Jordan and the other HII directors, contending that the board's investigation was inadequate. The defendants filed a motion for summary judgment, arguing that the suit was barred by the business judgment rule. How should the court rule? Why? *Pace v. Jordan*, 999 S.W.2d 615 1 (1999)

16-15 In 1957, Ott Chemical Company manufactured chemicals at its plant near Muskegon, Michigan, and both intentionally and unintentionally dumped hazardous substances in the soil and groundwater near the plant. In 1965, CPC International, Inc., incorporated a wholly owned subsidiary (Ott II) to buy Ott's assets. Ott II then continued both the chemical production and dumping. Ott II's officers and directors had positions and duties at both CPC and Ott.

In 1972, CPC sold Ott II to Story Chemical, which operated the plant until its bankruptcy in 1977. Aerojet General Corporation bought the plant from the bankruptcy trustee and manufactured chemicals there until 1986.

In 1969, the EPA filed suit to recover the costs of cleanup on the plant site and named CPC, Aerojet, and the officers of the now defunct Ott and Ott II. Can the corporation and Ott officers be held liable? What theories would the EPA advance? Explain. *United States v. Best Foods*, 118 S.Ct. 1876 (1998)

16-16 Macinac Cellular Corporation offered to sell Robert Broz a license to operate a cellular phone system in Michigan. Broz was a director of Cellular Information Systems, Inc. (CIS). CIS, as a result of bankruptcy proceedings, was in the process of selling its cellular holdings. Broz did not formally present the opportunity to the CIS board, but he told some of the firm's officers and directors, who replied that CIS was not interested. At the time, PriCellular, Inc., a firm that wanted the Michigan license, was attempting to buy CIS. Without telling PriCellular, Broz bought the license himself. After PriCellular took over CIS, the company sued Broz, alleging that he had usurped a corporate opportunity. Has Broz done anything wrong? Discuss. *Broz v. Cellular Information Systems, Inc.*, 673 A2d 148 (Del. 1996)

16-17 A group of shareholders of Mercury Finance Company filed suit against certain Mercury corporate directors, alleging that the directors had intentionally overstated the company's earnings and financial performance in documents filed with the Securities and Exchange Commission and in communications to shareholders. In subsequent years, as these misrepresentations came to light, the company and its shareholders lost essentially all of its former $2 billion value. After they were sued for negligence, lack of care, and breach of fiduciary duty, the directors argued that a cause of action for disclosure violations only exists when the directors are requesting action by the shareholders. What should be the result? Explain. *Malone v. Brincat*, 722 A.2d 5 (Del. 1998)

16-18 The board of directors of a California banking corporation made a variety of decisions regarding loans, expenses, and other financial issues, shortly before the bank became insolvent. The directors obtained advice from a number of outside consultants before making their decisions and acted in good faith to do what they believed was in the best interest of the corporation. The directors were later sued for negligence by the federal agency that took over the bank. What will their defense be? Explain. *FDIC v. Castetter*, 184 F.3d 1040 (9th Cir. 1999)

ASSIGNMENT ON THE INTERNET

This chapter introduces the common forms of business organization in the United States. However, business structures outside the United States are often very different. Use the Internet to determine some of the major differences in business organization between the United States and the European Union. You can begin your search by visiting the Eurolegal Services Web site at www.eurolegal.org/webresources/eustartup.htm.

If you were looking to start a business in the European Union, what would you do differently than if you were to start the business in the United States? The following Web sites may also assist you in your search.

 ## ON THE INTERNET

www.irs.gov/faqs/faq-kw127.html The Internal Revenue Service (IRS) provides information about limited liability corporations at this site.

www.mycorporation.com/index.htm This is the site of a private firm that assists small companies and businesses as to become incorporated.

www.llc-reporter.com/28.htm This site provides an analysis of the Uniform Limited Liability Company Act.

www.eurolegal.org/webresources/eustartup.htm This site contains information about starting a corporation in the European Union.

www.hg.org/corp.html This site provides links to useful information on corporate law and recent court cases that decide issues of corporate law.

www.lexfori.net/france/incorp_france.html This site provides information about starting a corporation in France and the various structures corporations can take in that country.

Part Three

PUBLIC LAW AND THE LEGAL
ENVIRONMENT OF BUSINESS

Part Three focuses on the public laws that regulate the legal environment of business. Because most public laws governing the legal environment are administered and created by administrative agencies, this part opens with a chapter introducing administrative agencies. After this foundational chapter, we examine laws affecting employees in the workplace, laws governing employee benefits, labor–management relationships, and employment discrimination. The focus then shifts to laws governing the physical environment, followed by those governing securities, antitrust, and consumer protection.

17

THE LAW OF ADMINISTRATIVE AGENCIES

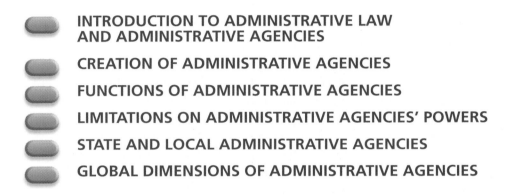

- **INTRODUCTION TO ADMINISTRATIVE LAW AND ADMINISTRATIVE AGENCIES**
- **CREATION OF ADMINISTRATIVE AGENCIES**
- **FUNCTIONS OF ADMINISTRATIVE AGENCIES**
- **LIMITATIONS ON ADMINISTRATIVE AGENCIES' POWERS**
- **STATE AND LOCAL ADMINISTRATIVE AGENCIES**
- **GLOBAL DIMENSIONS OF ADMINISTRATIVE AGENCIES**

The first two federal administrative agencies—the Interstate Commerce Commission (ICC) (no longer in existence) and the Federal Trade Commission (FTC)—were created by Congress in the late nineteenth century and early twentieth century during an era of reform. Congress felt that the anticompetitive conduct of railroads and other corporations could best be controlled by separate administrative agencies with defined statutory mandates. In another era of reform following the stock market crash of 1929 and the beginning of the Great Depression, Congress saw a need for additional agencies to assist a free market economy and to act in the public interest— hence, the creation of such agencies as the Securities and Exchange Commission (SEC), the National Labor Relations Board (NLRB), and the Federal Communications Commission (FCC). From time to time since then, new administrative agencies have been established, until today there are some 76 federal administrative agencies affecting nearly every aspect of life in the United States.[1] For example, the clothes we wear are subject to regula-

---

[1] Office of the Register, *General Index: Code of Federal Regulations*, rev. ed. (Washington, D.C.: National Archives, General Services Administration, January 1, 1999).

tion by the Consumer Product Safety Commission (CPSC); the cars we drive are subject to regulation by the National Highway Safety Transportation Board (NHSTB) and the Environmental Protection Agency (EPA); and the television we watch and the out-of-state telephone calls we make are subject to regulation by the Federal Communications Commission (FCC).

Because government agencies have such a powerful effect on business, businesspeople need to understand the laws (regulations) these agencies are empowered to create and the rules of procedure they use to make such laws. The impact of administrative agency regulations on business and society is a primary focus of this text. Although we emphasize the role of federal administrative agencies, each of the 50 states, the District of Columbia, and Puerto Rico, as well as counties, cities, and some towns, have administrative agencies that also regulate business and societal conduct. In this chapter, we define administrative law and administrative agencies and discuss the reasons for their growth, how they were created, and their functions. We also explore the federal administrative agencies' relationship to the executive, legislative, and judicial branches of government, as well as the institutions and laws that limit the power of administrative agencies. We end the chapter with a brief consideration of the global dimensions of administrative agencies.

Critical Thinking About the Law

As a future business leader, you will certainly encounter many governmental regulations. Congress created administrative agencies, in part, because it could not hope to address the enormous variety and number of concerns that are now covered by administrative agencies. Although you will not learn about every administrative agency in this chapter, you can jump-start your thinking about administrative agencies by answering these critical thinking questions.

1. Your roommate states that people do not have to follow the regulations passed by administrative agencies because these regulations are not laws. She argues that only Congress can make laws. Which critical thinking question needs to be applied to settle this disagreement?

   Clue: Do you and your roommate agree on the meaning of the words she is using?

2. Some individuals may argue that the creation of regulations by administrative agencies promotes unfair restrictions on business. What ethical norm seems to be behind this thought?

   Clue: If you want fewer restrictions from the government, what ethical norm is influencing your thought? What ethical norm seems to conflict with the wish for fewer governmental regulations?

3. Congress assumes that the administrative agencies will effectively address problems in their respective areas. For example, the EPA ensures compliance with environmental laws. If Matt makes the assumption that environmental problems are so complex and widespread that the EPA could not hope to make a difference, what conclusion do you think Matt would draw regarding administrative agencies?

   Clue: Think about a contrary assumption. If Matt assumed that the administrative agencies were effective, would he be more likely to support the regulations passed by the various agencies?

INTRODUCTION TO ADMINISTRATIVE LAW AND ADMINISTRATIVE AGENCIES

ADMINISTRATIVE LAW

administrative law Any rule (statute or regulation) that directly or indirectly affects an administrative agency.

For the purposes of this text, **administrative law** is defined broadly as any rule (statute or regulation) that affects, directly or indirectly, an administrative agency. These rules may be procedural or substantive, and they may come from the legislative, executive, or judicial branch of government or from the agencies themselves. A **procedural rule** generally has an impact on the internal processes by which the agencies function or prescribes methods of enforcing rights. For example, under the Administrative Procedure Act (APA), an administrative agency must give adequate notice to all parties involved in an agency hearing. A **substantive rule** defines rights of parties. An example is an act of Congress that forbids the Federal Trade Commission (FTC) from applying the antitrust laws to all the Coca-Cola bottlers in the United States. In this instance, the rights and regulations of both the FTC and the Coca-Cola bottlers were defined by Congress.

procedural rule A rule that governs the internal processes of an administrative agency.

substantive rule A rule that creates, defines, or regulates the legal rights of administrative agencies and the parties they regulate.

ADMINISTRATIVE AGENCIES

administrative agency Any body that is created by the legislative branch to carry out specific duties.

An **administrative agency** is any body that is created by the legislative branch (e.g., Congress, a state legislature, or a city council) to carry out specific duties. Some agencies are not situated wholly in the legislative, executive, or judicial branch of government. Instead, they may have legislative power to make rules for an entire industry, judicial power to adjudicate (decide) individual cases, and executive power to investigate corporate misconduct. Examples of such independent federal administrative agencies are the Environmental Protection Agency, the Federal Communications Commission, and the Interstate Commerce Commission; at the state level, examples are public utilities commissions and building authorities; at the city level, examples are city planning commissions and tax appeals boards.

independent administrative agency An agency whose appointed heads and members serve for fixed terms and cannot be removed by the president except for reasons defined by Congress.

Types. Administrative agencies are generally classified as independent or executive. **Independent administrative agencies**, such as the FTC and the SEC, are usually headed by a board of commissioners, who are appointed for a specific term of years by the president with the advice and consent of the Senate. A commissioner can be removed before serving out a full term only for causes defined by Congress, not at the whim of the president—which is why these agencies are called independent.

executive administrative agency An agency located within a department of the executive branch of government; heads and appointed members serve at the pleasure of the president.

 Executive administrative agencies are generally located within departments of the executive branch of government. For example, the Occupational Safety and Health Administration (OSHA) is located in the Department of Labor and the National Transportation Safety Board (NTSB) in the Department of Transportation. Heads and members of these boards have no fixed term of office. They serve at the pleasure of the president, meaning they can be removed from their positions by the chief executive at any time.

 Table 17-1 lists the major independent and executive agencies of the federal government.

Independent Agencies	Executive Agencies	TABLE 17-1
Commodity Futures Trading Commission (CFTC)	Federal Deposit Insurance Corporation (FDIC)	**SELECTED ADMINISTRATIVE AGENCIES**
Consumer Product Safety Commission (CPSC)	General Services Administration (GSA)	
Equal Employment Opportunity Commission (EEOC)	International Development Corporation Agency (IDCA)	
Federal Communications Commission (FCC)	National Aeronautics and Space Administration (NASA)	
Federal Trade Commission (FTC)	National Science Foundation (NSF)	
Interstate Commerce Commission (ICC)	Occupational Safety and Health Administration (OSHA)	
National Labor Relations Board (NLRB)		
National Transportation Safety Board (NTSB)	Office of Personnel Management (OPM)	
Nuclear Regulatory Commission (NRC)	Small Business Administration (SBA)	
Securities and Exchange Commission (SEC)	Veterans Administration (VA)	

Reasons for Growth. Administrative agencies have proliferated rapidly since the late 1890s for the following reasons:

1. *Flexibility.* Unlike the court proceedings studied in Chapter 3, administrative agency hearings are not governed by strict rules of evidence. For example, hearsay rules are waived in most cases.

2. *Need for expertise.* The staff of each of the agencies has technical expertise in a relatively narrow area, gained from concentrating on that area over the years. It would be impossible, for example, for 435 members of the House of Representatives and 100 senators to regulate the television, radio, and satellite communication systems of the United States on a daily basis. Only the FCC staff has that expertise.

3. *Prevention of overcrowding in courts.* If administrative agencies did not exist, our highly complex, often litigious, society would have to seek redress of grievances through the federal and state court systems. As explained in Chapter 4, both corporations and individuals are already seeking alternatives to the overburdened court system.

Linking Law & Business

Management

The word *administrative* or *administration* is often used in other disciplines such as management and international business. Often individuals are hired to "administer" (direct or lead) a company or a specific project within a company in the private sector. The use of such language has a far different meaning when used in the public sector as set out in this chapter. Thus, often administrative law is taken to mean a set of rules directly applicable to the administrator or officer of a private sector entity. Also, does administrative law under the Administrative Procedure Act apply to the president or the dean of the College of Business at a private university? Are they administrators or are they instructors, lecturers, or professors? Does this make a difference? Does language as used by different disciplines become important?

4. *Expeditious solutions to national problems.* After the 1929 stock market crash and the ensuing Depression, Congress sought to give investors confidence in the securities markets by creating the Securities and Exchange Commission in 1934. The SEC was intended to be a "watchdog" agency that would ensure full disclosure of material information to the investing public and prevent a repetition of the fraudulent practices that marked the freewheeling 1920s. When the public became concerned about the deterioration of the nation's water, land, and air, Congress created the Environmental Protection Agency to implement clean air, water, and waste regulations.

All those reasons for the existence of administrative agencies are now being challenged by proponents of deregulation—or no regulation—of industry. The debate between advocates of returning to a period in our history when market forces were the sole regulators of business conduct and champions of administrative agency regulation is highlighted throughout the public law section of this text.

CREATION OF ADMINISTRATIVE AGENCIES

Exhibit 17-1 gives an idea of the proliferation of administrative agencies at the federal level from 1900 to 1999. Because all these agencies affect individuals, the business community, and society as a whole, it is important for you to know how and why they were created.

Congress creates these agencies through statutes called **enabling legislation**. In general, an enabling statute delegates to the agency congressional **legislative power** for the purpose of serving the "public interest, convenience, and necessity." Armed with this mandate, the administrative agency can issue rules that control individual and business behavior. In many instances, such rules carry criminal as well as civil penalties. In Chapter 22, you will see how the SEC, using its mandate under the 1933 and 1934 Securities Acts, can both fine and criminally prosecute individuals involved in insider trading. The enabling statute also delegates **executive power** to the agency to investigate potential violations of rules or statutes. Chapter 23 sets out the wide-ranging investigative powers of the SEC staff. Finally, the enabling statutes delegate **judicial power** to the agency to settle or adjudicate any disputes it may have with businesses or individuals. For example, the SEC, using its congressional mandate under the 1933 and 1934 Securities Acts, has prescribed rules governing the issuance of, and trading in, securities by businesses as well as by brokers and underwriters. Administrative law judges assigned to the SEC adjudicate cases in which individuals or corporations may have violated the rules.

Because the framers of the U.S. Constitution carefully separated the legislative (Article I), executive (Article 2), and judicial powers of government into three distinct branches, some people complain that allowing administrative agencies (Article III) to exercise all three powers violates the spirit of the Constitution. Critics go so far as to state that these agencies constitute a "fourth branch of government." In 1995 the House of Representatives and the Senate

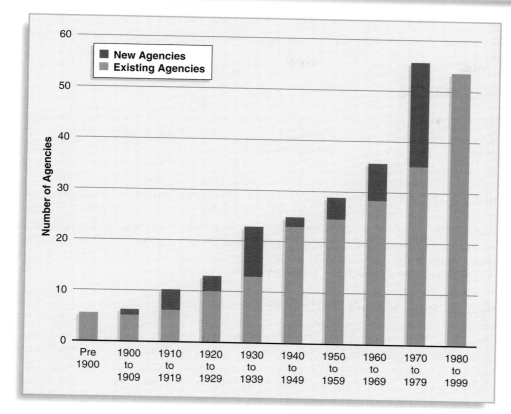

EXHIBIT 17-1

GROWTH OF FEDERAL REGULATORY AGENCIES

Source: From M. L. Weidenbaum, *Business and Government in the Global Marketplace*, 7th ed. © 2004, p. 30. Reprinted by permission of Prentice Hall, Inc., Upper Saddle River, N.J., and the Center for the Study of American Business.

overwhelmingly passed a bill that would require all administrative agencies (both executive and independent) to do a cost–benefit analysis of any proposed regulation that would cost the economy more than $25 million. All agencies would also have to identify possible alternatives to the proposed regulation that would require no government action, as well as varying actions customized for different regions of the country, and "the use of market-based mechanisms." The Office of Management and Budget (OMB) reviews all proposed rules judged to be "major." Since OMB (located in the executive branch) recommends annual budgets to Congress for each administrative agency, it has influence over all rule making.

FUNCTIONS OF ADMINISTRATIVE AGENCIES

Administrative agencies perform the following functions: (1) rule making; (2) adjudication of individual cases brought before administrative law judges by agency staff; and (3) administrative activities, which include (a) informal advising of individual businesses and consumers, (b) preparing reports and doing studies of industries and of consumer activities, and (c) issuing guidelines for the business community and others as to what activities are legal in the eyes of the agency staff.

RULE MAKING

We said that administrative agencies are authorized to perform the legislative function of making rules or regulations by virtue of the enabling statutes. For example, the enabling statute of the Occupational Safety and Health Administration (OSHA) gave the secretary of labor authority to set "mandatory safety and health standards applicable to businesses affecting interstate commerce." The secretary was also given the power to "prescribe such rules and regulations that he may deem necessary to carry out the responsibilities under this act." In some cases, the procedures for implementing the rule-making function are spelled out in the enabling act. If they are not, agencies follow the three major rule-making models—formal, informal, and hybrid—outlined in the **Administrative Procedure Act (APA)** of 1946.

Administrative Procedure Act (APA) Establishes the standards and procedures federal administrative agencies must follow in their rule-making and adjudicative functions.

Formal Rule Making. Section 553(c) of the APA requires formal rule making when an enabling statute or other legislation states that all regulations or rules must be enacted by an agency as part of a formal hearing process that includes a complete transcript. This procedure provides for (1) an agency notice of proposed rule making to the public in the *Federal Register*; (2) a public hearing at which witnesses give testimony on the pros and cons of the proposed rule, each witness is cross-examined, and the rules of evidence are applied; and (3) the making and publication of formal findings by the agency. On the basis of these findings, an agency may or may not promulgate a regulation. Because of the expense and time involved in creating a formal transcript and record, most enabling statutes do not require agencies to go through a formal rule-making procedure when promulgating regulations.

Informal Rule Making. As provided by Section 553 of the APA, informal rule making applies in all situations in which the agency's enabling legislation or other congressional directives do not require another form. The APA requires that the agency (1) give prior notice of the proposed rule by publishing it in the *Federal Register*; (2) provide an opportunity for all interested parties to submit written comments; and (3) publish the final rule, with a statement of its basis and purpose, in the *Federal Register*. Exhibit 17-2 lays out the five-step process for promulgating a rule according to the informal rule-making model. Executive and independent agencies are required to set out a cost–benefit analysis in Step 1 of the process.

Informal rule making is the model most often used by administrative agencies because it is efficient in terms of time and cost. No formal public hearing is required, and no formal record need be established, as in formal rule making. However, parties opposed to a particular rule arrived at through informal rule making often seek to persuade the appellate courts that the agency in question did not take important factors into account when the rule was being made.

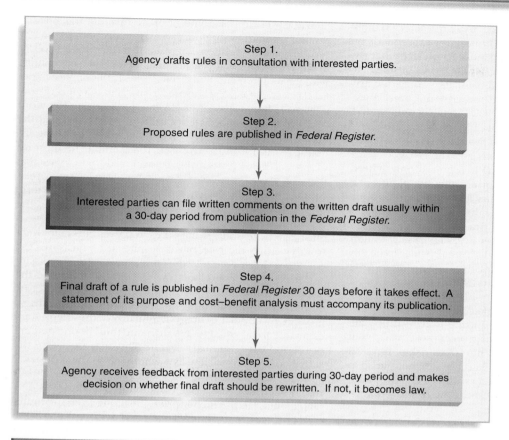

EXHIBIT 17-2

STEPS IN THE INFORMAL RULE-MAKING PROCESS

Step 1.
Agency drafts rules in consultation with interested parties.

Step 2.
Proposed rules are published in *Federal Register*.

Step 3.
Interested parties can file written comments on the written draft usually within a 30-day period from publication in the *Federal Register*.

Step 4.
Final draft of a rule is published in *Federal Register* 30 days before it takes effect. A statement of its purpose and cost–benefit analysis must accompany its publication.

Step 5.
Agency receives feedback from interested parties during 30-day period and makes decision on whether final draft should be rewritten. If not, it becomes law.

CASE 17-1

American Dental Association v. Martin
United States Court of Appeals
984 F.2d 823 (7th Cir. 1993)

In 1991, the Occupational Safety and Health Administration (OSHA) promulgated a rule to protect health care workers from viruses that can be transmitted in the blood of patients. The rule requires employers in the health care industry to take certain precautions relating to the handling of contaminated instruments (such as needles), the disposal of contaminated waste, and the use of protective clothing (such as gloves, masks, and gowns). The rule also requires employers to provide vaccinations for hepatitis B for their employees and confidential blood testing of workers following accidental exposures (such as being stuck with a contaminated needle). The American Dental Association (ADA) and two other groups asked a federal court to review the rule. The ADA argued, among other things, that OSHA had failed to establish that dental workers were sufficiently at risk to benefit from the rule. Furthermore, the rule would

unnecessarily burden consumers with increased medical costs and, hence, diminished care.

Justice Posner
In deciding to impose this extensive array of restrictions on the practice of medicine, nursing, and dentistry, OSHA did not (indeed is not authorized to) compare the benefits with the costs and impose the restrictions on finding that the former exceeded the latter. Instead it asked whether the restrictions would materially reduce a significant workplace risk to human health without imperiling the existence of, or threatening massive dislocation to, the health care industry.

OSHA cannot impose onerous requirements on an industry that does not pose substantial hazards to the safety or health of its workers. But neither is the agency required to proceed workplace by workplace, which would require it to promulgate hundreds of thousands of separate rules. It is not our business to pick the happy medium between these extremes. It is OSHA's business. If it provides a rational explanation for its choice, we are bound. It explained that while the cost of compliance with the precautions that the CDC has recommended (and OSHA has required) against bloodborne pathogens varies in a readily determinable fashion from industry to industry, the risk of infection does not. The risk goes with practices (so protective clothing is required only where being splashed with blood or other infective liquid can reasonably be anticipated, whether it is a dentist's office or a hospital operating room) rather than with industries, and the rule is therefore based on practices rather than on industries. The HIV or HBV carrier bears menace with him as he makes the rounds from health care provider to health care provider. The risk of blood splatters and needlesticks is greater in some medical procedures than in others, but a dental hygienist is as likely to be splattered by blood contained in saliva as is many a worker in a hospital or a doctor's office. The idea behind requiring universal precautions for health care workers is to protect those workers in any situation in which there is a nontrivial risk of physical contact with a patient's blood, and these situations arise in dentists' offices as well as in doctors' offices and hospitals. OSHA was required neither to quantify the risk to workers' health nor to establish the existence of significant risk to a scientific certainty. It is true that because fewer people have dental than medical insurance, and therefore more people pay for dental care out of their own pockets, the higher price of dentistry that is a likely consequence of the rule will have a greater impact on demand; and inadequate dental care is a source of pain and suffering. But again the dental association made no effort to quantify this impact, though techniques for doing so exist in economics.

The dental association complains that the rule goes too far in requiring dentists to "ensure" that their employees comply with the requirements of the rule. They say this imposes strict liability, which OSHA acknowledges it cannot do. It is reasonably plain, however, that OSHA did not by using the word "ensure" seek to impose strict liability. It explained that the employer's responsibility doesn't end with furnishing his employees with protective gear, for example; he must do everything he can reasonably be expected to do to see that they use it. Like an employer made liable for his employee's conduct not by the principle of respondeat superior (a form of strict liability) but by the negligence principle, the employer subject to OSHA's rule on bloodborne pathogens must take all reasonable measures to prevent his employees from violating the rule, but if despite these measures the employee violates the rule, the employer is off the hook.

The costs of compliance with OSHA's rule, once the issue of strict liability for unforeseeable misconduct by employees is laid to one side, can hardly be thought so great as to imperil dentistry. Annualized, these costs are estimated to be equal to less than one-third of one percent of the industry's annual revenue. This may overstate the actual cost, not to society as a whole but to the industry.

[T]he dental association's argument [is] that OSHA's rule is likely to cause a deterioration in dental care as dental patients flee the higher prices resulting from the industry's efforts to shift some of the costs of compliance with the rule to its customers. There are some omitted costs, as we have noted, but not enough to make a decisive difference; nor does the association emphasize them.

Plaintiff ADA's petition to review the rule *denied*.

Hybrid Rule Making. Interested parties often complained that informal rule making gave them little opportunity to be heard other than in writing. Both Congress and the executive branch wanted administrative agencies to do a cost–benefit analysis of proposed regulations. Out of this input from the public and two branches of government came hybrid rule making, which combines some of the aspects of formal and informal rule making. This model requires the agency to give notice of a proposed regulation, set a period for public comments, hold a public hearing, and have a cost–benefit analysis done by an independent executive agency.

Exempted Rule Making. Section 553 of the APA allows the agencies to decide whether there will be public participation in rule-making proceedings relating to "military or foreign affairs" and "agency management or personnel," as well as in proceedings relating to "public property, loans, grants, benefits or contracts" of an agency. Public notice and comment are also not required when the agency is making interpretive rules or general statements of policy.

It is generally conceded that proceedings dealing with military and foreign affairs often require speed and secrecy, both of which are incompatible with public notice and hearings.

Critical Thinking About the Law

You are now aware that facts are the building blocks for any legal case. Judges are presented with the facts of the case and make decisions on the basis of how those facts relate to relevant case law and statutory law. However, judges never receive all the facts, just some of the facts, as the court's acquiring all the relevant facts would take too much time and energy to unveil. Hence, judges make decisions to the best of their ability on the information they have received, but this does not imply that judges have not heard or considered other important pieces of information. When we evaluate the quality of a judge's reasons, we are often confronted with unanswered questions related to significant omitted information. Therefore, our analysis of a judge's decision would benefit from the revelation of additional information.

In Case 17-1 involving a dispute between the ADA and OSHA, fails to include certain facts that would aid a reader in his or her evaluation of the court's reasoning. The following questions prompt you to consider missing information that would help you better evaluate the quality of the judge's reasoning in Case 17-1.

1. If you were Justice Posner in Case 17-1, what missing information would you want to consider before making your decision?

   Clue: Consider the arguments that both sides make in relation to the positive and negative aspects of OSHA's placing more stringent rules on dentists. In other words, what additional evidence would help you evaluate the efficacy of OSHA's regulatory measures?

2. There is an intimate nexus between the critical thinking skills of ambiguity and missing information. Ambiguity refers to a lack of clarification about the meaning of certain words. We could consider this lack of definitional clarity as being one form of missing information. What are several examples of relevant ambiguity in the court's reasoning?

   Clue: Avoid the temptation of thinking that you and Justice Posner share the same definition of certain phrases. Try to think of multiple interpretations of ambiguous phrases that make sense within the context of the argument but could easily lead to different conclusions based on which interpretation you choose.

Judicial Review of Rule Making. After a regulation is promulgated by an administrative agency and is published in the *Federal Register*, it generally becomes law. Appellate courts have accepted agency-promulgated regulations as law unless a business or other affected groups or individuals can show that:

1. The congressional delegation of legislative authority in the enabling act was unconstitutional because it was too vague and not limited.
2. An agency action violated a constitutional standard, such as the right to be free from unreasonable searches and seizures under the Fourth Amendment. For example, if an agency such as OSHA promulgated a rule that allowed its inspectors to search a business property at any time without its owners' permission and without an administrative search warrant, that rule would be in violation of the Fourth Amendment.
3. The act of an agency was beyond the scope of power granted to it by Congress in its enabling legislation.

Judicial review of administrative agency action provides a check against agency excesses that can prove very costly to the business community. Excerpted here is a case that exemplifies that kind of judicial review when constitutional standards are important.

CASE 17-2

Food and Drug Administration v. Brown & Williamson Tobacco Corporation
United States Supreme Court
529 U.S. 120 (2000)

The Food and Drug Administration (FDA) is a federal administrative agency empowered to administer the Food, Drug, and Cosmetic Act (FDC Act). The FDA can regulate "drugs" and medical "devices." Based on its perceived power under the FDA Act, the FDA enacted a rule regulating tobacco products. The rule:

1. Prohibits the sale of cigarettes and smokeless tobacco to persons younger than 18.

2. Requires retailers to verify through photo identification the age of all purchasers younger than 27.

3. Prohibits the sale of cigarettes in quantities smaller than 20.

4. Prohibits the distribution of free samples.

5. Prohibits sales through self-service displays and vending machines except in adult-only locations.

6. Requires print advertising appear in black-and-white, text-only format.

7. Prohibits outdoor advertising within 1,000 feet of any public school or playground.

8. Prohibits the distribution of any promotional items, such as T-shirts or hats, bearing the manufacturer's brand.

9. Prohibits a manufacturer from sponsoring any athletic, musical, artistic, or other social or cultural event using its brand name.

10. Requires that the statement "A Nicotine-Delivery Device for Persons 18 or Older" appear on all tobacco products.

A group of tobacco manufacturers and advertisers filed a lawsuit in district court, asserting that the FDA did not have authority to regulate tobacco as a "drug" or "device" that delivered nicotine to the body. The district court certified the issue to the court of appeals, which held that the FDC Act did not grant the FDA power to regulate tobacco products. The FDA appealed.

Justice O'Connor

Regardless of how serious the problem an administrative agency seeks to address, it may not exercise its authority in a manner that is inconsistent with the administrative structure that Congress enacted into law. Congress has foreclosed the removal of tobacco products from the market. A provision of the United States Code currently in force states that "the marketing of tobacco constitutes one of the greatest basic industries of the United States with ramifying activities which directly affect interstate and foreign commerce at every point, and stable conditions therein are necessary to the general welfare." More importantly, Congress has directly addressed the problem of tobacco and health through legislation on six occasions since 1965. See Federal Cigarette Labeling and Advertising Act (FCLAA), Public Health Cigarette Smoking Act of 1969, Alcohol and Drug Abuse Amendments of 1983, Comprehensive Smoking Education Act, Comprehensive Smokeless Tobacco Health Education Act of 1986, and Alcohol, Drug Abuse, and Mental Health Administration Reorganization Act. When Congress enacted these statutes, the adverse health consequences of tobacco use were well known, as were nicotine's pharmacological effects. Nonetheless, Congress stopped well short of ordering a ban. Instead, it has generally regulated the labeling and advertisement of tobacco products.

Considering the FDC Act as a whole, it is clear that Congress intended to exclude tobacco products from the FDA's jurisdiction. A fundamental precept of the FDC Act is that any product regulated by the FDA—but not banned—must be safe for its intended use. Consequently, if tobacco products were within the FDA's jurisdiction, the FDC Act would require the FDA to remove them from the market entirely. But a ban would contradict Congress's clear intent as expressed in its more recent, tobacco-specific legislation. The inescapable conclusion is that there is no room for tobacco products within the FDC Act's regulatory scheme.

By no means do we question the seriousness of the problem that the FDA has sought to address. The agency has amply demonstrated that tobacco use, particularly among children and adolescents, poses perhaps the single most significant threat to public health in the United States. Nonetheless, no matter how important, conspicuous, and controversial the issue, an administrative agency's power to regulate in the public interest must always be grounded in a valid grant of authority from Congress. And, in our anxiety to effectuate the congressional purpose of protecting the public, we must take care not to extend the scope of the statute beyond the point where Congress indicated it would stop. Reading the FDC Act as a whole, as well as in conjunction with Congress's subsequent tobacco-specific legislation, it is plain that Congress has not given the FDA the authority that it seeks to exercise here.

Affirmed for defendants Brown & Williamson.

ADJUDICATION

In carrying out its adjudicative function in individual cases as opposed to rule making for whole industries, the administrative agency usually pursues a four-step process. After receiving a complaint alleging violation of an administrative law, the agency notifies the party against whom the complaint is made and conducts an investigation into the merits of the complaint. If the agency staff finds the complaint has merit, it next negotiates with the party to see if it can get the party to voluntarily stop the violation. If negotiation is unsuccessful, the third step is to file a complaint with an administrative law judge (ALJ). Step 4 consists of a hearing and decision by the ALJ. The party may appeal the ALJ's decision to the full commission or agency head and ultimately to a federal court of appeals and the U.S. Supreme Court.

All these steps are guided by the APA, which sets out minimum procedural standards for administrative agency adjudication. Enabling statutes that create agencies often add other procedural requirements. Finally, case law arising out of appeals of agency decisions to the U.S. circuit courts of appeal and the U.S. Supreme Court provides further guidelines for agencies in carrying out their adjudicative function. In the following detailed description of the four-step adjudicative process for federal administrative agencies, we use the Federal Trade Commission (FTC) as a representative agency. You will find it easier to follow our discussion if you look first at the organizational outline of the FTC provided in Exhibit 17-3 and the summary of adjudication and judicial review of agency decision making given in Exhibit 17-4.

Investigation and Complaint. The Federal Trade Commission (FTC), which includes the Bureau of Competition and the Bureau of Consumer Protection, is obliged to conduct an investigation whenever it receives a complaint from other government agencies, competitors, or consumers. For example, upon receiving a complaint about a mouthwash product that is advertised as killing germs and protecting people from sore throat, the commission examines the product to see if the statement has any scientific validity. Should the commission's staff find that the advertising is "deceptive" or "unfair" within the meaning of Section 5 of the Federal Trade Commission Act, it will seek to stop the advertising campaign in one of two ways:

1. *Voluntary compliance.* The staff will ask the corporation to voluntarily stop the advertising campaign. Usually, no penalty is assessed if the company agrees to do this.

2. *Consent order.* If voluntary compliance is not obtained, the staff notifies the mouthwash company that it has 10 days to enter into a consent order, or the staff will issue a formal complaint.

Most cases are closed at this stage because, under a **consent order**, the company does not have to admit that it was deceptive or unfair in its advertising; it only has to promise that it will not do such unlawful advertising again and agree to the remedy that the commission imposes. The latter may be some form of corrective advertising that tells the public that the mouthwash does not kill germs. A consent order helps the commission staff to obtain a binding cease-and-desist order with limited effort and time. It also benefits the company, because by agreeing to a consent order, the company avoids both an admission of guilt and the

consent order An agreement by a business to stop an activity an administrative agency alleges to be unlawful and to accept the remedy the agency imposes; no admission of guilt is necessary.

EXHIBIT 17-3 FEDERAL TRADE COMMISSION

Source: U.S. Government Manual 2002–03 (Washington, D.C.: Office of the Federal Register), 2003, p. 722.

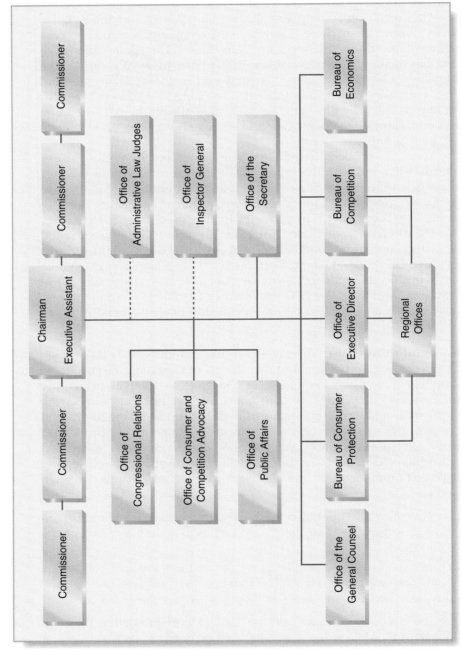

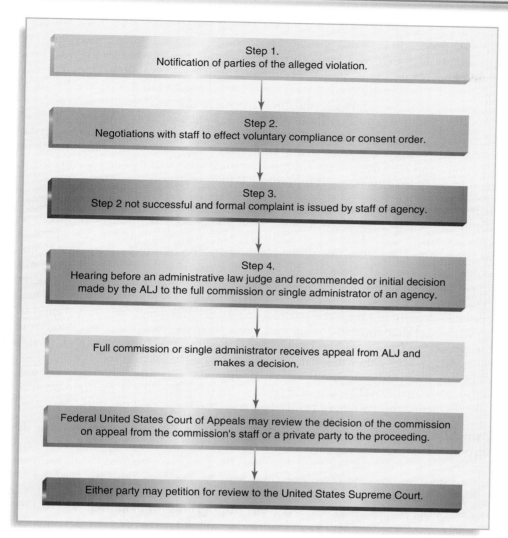

EXHIBIT 17-4

ADJUDICATION AND JUDICIAL REVIEW OF AGENCY DECISION MAKING

Step 1.
Notification of parties of the alleged violation.

Step 2.
Negotiations with staff to effect voluntary compliance or consent order.

Step 3.
Step 2 not successful and formal complaint is issued by staff of agency.

Step 4.
Hearing before an administrative law judge and recommended or initial decision made by the ALJ to the full commission or single administrator of an agency.

Full commission or single administrator receives appeal from ALJ and makes a decision.

Federal United States Court of Appeals may review the decision of the commission on appeal from the commission's staff or a private party to the proceeding.

Either party may petition for review to the United States Supreme Court.

cost of litigation and shareholder and consumer lawsuits that might ensue if the next steps in the adjudication process—a formal complaint and a hearing by an administrative law judge—resulted in an adverse decision for the company.

Formal Complaint and Hearing. If the case is not settled by voluntary compliance or a consent order, the commission's staff, usually through the FCC's Office of the General Counsel (see Exhibit 17-3), will issue a formal complaint listing the charges against the mouthwash company and will request that certain penalties be assessed by the **administrative law judge (ALJ)**. Administrative law judges, who number approximately 1,150, are selected on the basis of a merit exam and are assigned to specific administrative agencies. They usually come from within the federal administrative bureaucracy and are given life tenure. Administrative law judges are noted for their independence, even though they may be assigned to a particular independent or executive agency for a number of years.[2]

administrative law judge (ALJ) A judge, selected on the basis of a merit exam, who is assigned to a specific administrative agency.

----

[2] See "Administrative Law Judges Are Washington's Potent Hybrids," *New York Times*, December 3, 1980; and "Symposium: Administrative Law Judges," *Western New England Law Review* 6 (1984), p. 1.

A hearing before an ALJ may take several months or years. It resembles a judicial proceeding in that it includes notice to the parties, discovery, and the presentation of evidence by both the staff of the commission and the accused party (the respondent), direct examination and cross-examination of the witnesses, and presentation of motions and arguments to the ALJ. However, there is no jury at these hearings, and they are more informal than court proceedings. For instance, an ALJ will often intervene to ask questions and to take note of evidence that neither of the parties has introduced. At times, in fact, the ALJ becomes a severe questioner of both parties, especially in hearings involving disability and welfare claims. Thus, adjudicative proceedings are less adversarial and more investigative, or inquisitorial, than court proceedings.

Initial or Recommended Decision. After the hearing is completed, both the commission staff and the respondent submit proposed findings of facts and conclusions of law. Under the APA, the ALJ must then prepare an initial or recommended decision. An initial decision becomes the final agency action unless an appeal is taken to the full commission by either the staff or the respondent. In contrast, a recommended decision is not final; it has to be acted on by the full commission or by the head of the agency. Agency heads and commissions are not required to defer to the ALJ's factual findings. It should be remembered that commissioners and agency heads are political appointees of the president and may have political or policy reasons for overruling an ALJ's decision. Should either the staff or the respondent appeal a full commission's decision to a federal circuit court of appeals, the court is likely to give deference to the ALJ's factual findings because the ALJ is the person who actually heard the witnesses testify and read the submitted exhibits.

preponderance of evidence A legal standard whereby a bare majority (51 percent) of the evidence is sufficient to justify a ruling.

Appeal to the Full Commission. If the losing party (the agency staff or the respondent) does not agree with the ALJ's decision, it may appeal to the full commission, in the case of the FTC, or to the head of an executive department (or agency), in the case of an executive agency. In the mouthwash case we are using as an example, a majority of the commission members must rule in favor of one of the parties on the basis of a **preponderance of evidence** standard (51 percent or more). The APA requires that the commission state factual, legal, and policy bases for its decision. This requirement makes the agency responsible for its decision both to the public and to the courts that may later review it.

Judicial Review of Adjudicative Proceedings. If the party that loses at the full-commission or agency-head level in an adjudicative proceeding wishes to appeal, it must file a motion for appeal with the federal circuit court of appeals that has jurisdiction in the case. Briefs are filed by both parties, and the court hears oral argument. The court also reviews the whole record, including the ALJ's findings, in the case. It does not review the commission's factual findings as long as they are supported by substantial evidence in the record. (The substantial evidence rule requires that the court find that a reasonable person, after reviewing the record, would make the same findings the agency did.) Rather, it reviews the commission's legal findings to ensure that (1) it acted in a constitutionally approved way; (2) it acted within the scope of its jurisdiction as outlined by the enabling statute; and (3) it followed proper statutory procedures and did not act in an arbitrary or capricious manner. In the following case, you will note the court's application of some of these standards.

CASE 17-3

Warner Lambert v. Federal Trade Commission
United States Court of Appeals
562 F.2d 49 (D.C. Cir. 1977)

The product Listerine was advertised by the Warner Lambert Company (petitioner) as a preventive or cure for the common cold. Listerine had been on the market since 1879 and had been advertised as described since 1921. The FTC ordered Warner Lambert to cease and desist its advertising and to allocate $10 million to corrective advertising that included a statement "Contrary to prior advertising." The ALJ ruled in favor of the FTC staff. The petitioner appealed to the full commission, which affirmed most of the ALJ's findings. Warner Lambert appealed to the court of appeals.

Justice Wright

The first issue on appeal is whether the Commission's conclusion that Listerine is not beneficial for colds or sore throats is supported by the evidence. The Commission's findings must be sustained if they are supported by substantial evidence on the record viewed as a whole. We conclude that they are. Both the ALJ and the Commission carefully analyzed the evidence. They gave full consideration to the studies submitted by petitioner. The ultimate conclusion that Listerine is not an effective cold remedy was based on six specific findings of fact.

First, the Commission found that the ingredients of Listerine are not present in sufficient quantities to have any therapeutic effect. This was the testimony of two leading pharmacologists called by Commission counsel. The Commission was justified in concluding that the testimony of Listerine's experts was not sufficiently persuasive to counter this testimony.

Second, the Commission found that in the process of gargling it is impossible for Listerine to reach the critical areas of the body in medically significant concentration. The liquid is confined to the mouth chamber. Such vapors as might reach the nasal passage would not be in therapeutic concentration. Petitioner did not offer any evidence that vapors reached the affected areas in significant concentration.

Third, the Commission found that even if significant quantities of the active ingredients of Listerine were to reach the critical sites where cold viruses enter and infect the body, they could not interfere with the activities of the virus because they could not penetrate the tissue cells.

Fourth, the Commission discounted the results of a clinical study conducted by petitioner that contends that in a four-year study schoolchildren who gargled with Listerine had fewer colds and cold symptoms than those who did not gargle with Listerine. The Commission found that the design

and execution of the "St. Barnabas Study" made its results unreliable. For the first two years of the four-year test no placebo was given to the control group. For the last two years the placebo was inadequate: the control group was given colored water which did not resemble Listerine in smell or taste. There was also evidence that the physician who examined the test subjects was not blinded from knowing which children were using Listerine and which were not, that his evaluation of the cold symptoms of each child each day may have been imprecise, and that he necessarily relied on the non-blinded child's subjective reporting. Both the ALJ and the Commission analyzed the St. Barnabas Study and the expert testimony about it in depth and were justified in concluding that its results are unreliable.

Fifth, the Commission found that the ability of Listerine to kill germs by millions on contact is of no medical significance in the treatment of colds or sore throats. Expert testimony showed that bacteria in the oral cavity, the "germs" which Listerine purports to kill, do not cause colds and play no role in cold symptoms. Colds are caused by viruses. Further, "while Listerine kills millions of bacteria in the mouth, it also leaves millions. It is impossible to sterilize any area of the mouth, let alone the entire mouth."

Sixth, the Commission found that Listerine has no significant beneficial effect on the symptoms of sore throat. The Commission recognized that gargling with Listerine could provide temporary relief from a sore throat by removing accumulated debris irritating the throat. But this type of relief can also be obtained by gargling with salt water or even warm water. The Commission found that this is not the significant relief promised by petitioner's advertisements. It was reasonable to conclude that "such temporary relief does not 'lessen the severity' of a sore throat any more than expectorating or blowing one's nose 'lessens the severity' of a cold."

Petitioner contends that even if its advertising claims in the past were false, the portion of the Commission's order requiring "corrective advertising" exceeds the Commission's statutory power. The argument is based upon a literal reading of Section 5 of the Federal Trade Commission Act, which authorizes the Commission to issue "cease and desist" orders against violators and does not expressly mention any other remedies. The Commission's position, on the other hand, is that the affirmative disclosure that Listerine will not prevent colds or lessen their severity is absolutely necessary to give effect to the prospective cease and desist order; a hundred years of false claims could have built up a large reservoir of erroneous consumer belief, which would persist, unless corrected, long after petitioner ceased making the claims.

The need for the corrective advertising remedy and its appropriateness in this case are important issues. But the threshold question is whether the Commission has the authority to issue such an order. We hold that it does based on the legislative history of the Federal Trade Commission Act of 1914, the Wheeler-Lea Act Amendments of 1938, and the 1975 amendments, along with case precedents interpreting the act.

Having established that the Commission does have the power to order corrective advertising in appropriate cases, it remains to consider whether use of the remedy against Listerine is warranted and equitable. We have concluded that part 3 of the order should be modified to delete the phrase "Contrary to prior advertising." With that modification, we approve the order.

Our role in reviewing the remedy is limited. The Supreme Court has set forth the standard:

> The Commission is the expert body to determine what remedy is necessary to eliminate the unfair or deceptive trade practices which have been disclosed. It has wide latitude for judgment and the courts will not interfere except where the remedy selected has no reasonable relation to the unlawful practices found to exist.

The Commission has adopted the following standard for the imposition of corrective advertising:

> If a deceptive advertisement has played a substantial role in creating or reinforcing in the public's mind a false and material belief which lives on after the false advertising ceases, there is clear and continuing injury to competition and to the consuming public as consumers continue to make purchasing decisions based on the false belief. Since this injury cannot be averted by merely requiring respondent to cease disseminating the advertisement, we may appropriately order respondent to take affirmative action designed to terminate the otherwise continuing ill effects of the advertisement.

We think this standard is entirely reasonable. It dictates two factual inquiries: (1) Did Listerine's advertisements play a substantial role in creating or reinforcing in the public's mind a false belief about the product? and (2) Would this belief linger on after the false advertising ceases? It strikes us that if the answer to both questions is not yes, then Listerine may be wasting their massive advertising budgets. Indeed, it is more than a little peculiar to hear petitioner assert that its commercials really have no effect on consumer belief.

Affirmed with modifications in favor of Respondent, Commission.

Critical Thinking About the Law

As a future business manager you likely will have consultants who will attempt to persuade you of the quality and appropriateness of their proposals. Important to you will be not only what the proposal is but also why you should accept it. Whenever we ask the question "Why?" we are looking for reasons.

Learning to ask "why" is a relatively simple but crucial skill to develop. Unless you ask a consultant why you should accept a proposal, you might approve a bad proposal or reject a good one for no good reason.

Case 17-3 presents you with an opportunity to develop the skill of asking why.

1. The court gives a rationale for its finding that the FTC has the authority to order corrective advertising. What missing information do you need before you can evaluate the quality of this rationale?

   Clue: Find the paragraph in which the court provides its rationale. Ask yourself why the court believes the rationale is sound. Next ask yourself what more you would like to know before being confident about the quality of the court's rationale.

2. The court ordered that "contrary to prior advertising" be deleted from the corrective advertising. What reasons did the court give for this deletion?

   Clue: Imagine that the court is asked to explain why the deletion is desirable.

3. When trying to stop false advertising and seeking a remedy for it, the FTC is faced with a clash between two primary ethical norms. Identify those norms.

   Clue: Tackle this question one part at a time. What primary ethical norm is promoted by eliminating false advertising? What primary ethical norm is promoted by permitting the advertising?

AGENCY ADMINISTRATIVE ACTIVITIES

In addition to rule making and adjudication, executive and independent agencies perform a variety of tasks that are less well known but equally important to the average individual or business. The most significant of these are:

1. *Advising businesses and individuals concerning what an agency considers legal or not legal.* The antitrust merger guidelines we discuss in Chapter 23 are an example of an attempt by the Justice Department and the FTC to advise all interested parties about what conduct will be considered violations of Section 7 of the Clayton Act. More generally, lawyers representing interested parties meet daily with agency officials to receive informal comments or advice.

2. *Conducting studies of industry and markets.* Agencies such as the FTC, OSHA, and the FDA carry out studies to determine the level of economic concentration in an industry, dangerous products in the workplace, and the harmful effects of legal drugs.

3. *Providing information to the general public* on myriad matters through answering phone calls, distributing pamphlets, and holding seminars.

4. *Licensing of businesses in certain areas,* such as radio and television stations (FCC).

5. *Managing property.* The General Services Administration (GSA) is the largest landlord in the country. It buys, sells, and leases all property used by the U.S. government.

LIMITATIONS ON ADMINISTRATIVE AGENCIES' POWERS

STATUTORY LIMITATIONS

Certain federal statutes, summarized in Table 17-2, limit the power of administrative agencies and their officials. We have already discussed the Administrative Procedure Act. You should carefully review the brief descriptions of the other statutes listed in the table. It is important that you know, both as a future business manager and as an individual citizen, their major provisions. For instance, under the Federal Register Act of 1933, the Federal Privacy Act of 1974, and the Freedom of Information Act of 1966 as amended in 1974 and 1976, the decision-making processes of administrative agencies are open to the public. This legislation prevents secret, arbitrary, or capricious activity by the "fourth branch of government." And, as you have seen, judicial review of administrative agencies' rule-making and adjudication functions serves a similar purpose. Note also that private citizens have a means of relief against improper acts by employees of federal administrative agencies through the Federal Tort Claims Act of 1946, which forces agencies to waive sovereign immunity for their tortious actions and those of their employees. Tortious actions under this act include assault, battery, abuse of prosecution, false arrest, and trespass. For example, if an inspector from the EPA illegally enters a business property after being told to leave, the inspector, as well as the agency, may be held liable.

We said earlier that agencies were exempted from holding open hearings in certain circumstances, chiefly when proceedings concern military matters or foreign affairs. Some agencies have tried to stretch the exemption to cover proceedings in other "sensitive" matters.

TABLE 17-2 FEDERAL STATUTES LIMITING ADMINISTRATIVE AGENCIES' AUTHORITY

Statute	Summary of Provisions
Federal Register Act of 1933	Created the Federal Register system, which mandates the publication of all notices of federal agency meetings, proposed regulations, and final regulations in the *Federal Register*. The Federal Register system includes the *Government Manual*, which lists information, updated yearly, about each administrative agency, and the *Code of Federal Regulations* (CFR), which codifies regulations promulgated by agencies of the federal government.
Freedom of Information Act of 1966 (FOIA)	Requires each agency to publish in the *Federal Register* places where the public can get information from the agency, procedural and substantive rules and regulations, and policy statements. Also, the FOIA requires each agency to make available for copying on request such items as staff manuals, staff instruction orders, and adjudicated opinions, as well as interpretations of policy statements. Nine exceptions exist that enable an agency to deny an FOIA request by the public, a business, or other groups.
Government in Sunshine Act of 1976 (Sunshine Act)	Requires each agency headed by a collegiate body to hold every portion of a business meeting open to public attendance. A collegiate body exists if the agency is headed by two or more individuals, the majority of whom are appointed by the president and confirmed by the Senate.
Federal Privacy Act of 1974 (FPA)	Prevents an agency from disclosing any record in a system of records, by any means of communication, to any person or agency without the written authority of the individual. Eleven exceptions to the statute allow information to be released by the agency without the consent of individuals. Some exceptions are (1) to meet an FOIA request; (2) for use by the Selective Service System; (3) for use by another federal agency in civil or criminal law enforcement; (4) for use by a committee of the Congress; or (5) to meet a court order. Also, under the FPA, an individual may obtain information and correct errors in his or her record.
Administrative Procedure Act (APA)	The APA requires that certain uniform procedures be followed by all federal administrative agencies when performing their rule-making and adjudicative functions.
Federal Tort Claims Act of 1946 (FTCA)	Requires the federal government to waive sovereign immunity and to assume liability for the tortious act of its employees if nondiscretionary functions are being carried out by the employee.
Regulatory Flexibility Act of 1980	Requires analysis, which measures the cost that a proposed rule would impose on a business (particularly a small business).
Small Business Regulatory Enforcement Fairness Act of 1996 (SBREFA)	Congress may review a proposed regulation for sixty days. The SBREFA helps enforce the Regulatory Flexibility Act to make sure federal agencies seek to reduce the impact of new regulations on small businesses.
Congressional Review Act of 1996	This law, in effect, gives Congress a "veto power" over every single regulation agencies pass. Under this statute, a regulation cannot take effect until at least 60 working days have passed since the regulation was promulgated. If, during the 60-day period, a majority of the members of Congress pass a resolution of disapproval of the rule, and either the president signs it or Congress overrules his veto of it, the regulation is nullified.

INSTITUTIONAL LIMITATIONS

Executive Branch. The power of administrative agencies is limited by the executive branch through (1) the power of the president to appoint the heads of the agencies, (2) the power of the Office of Management and Budget (OMB) to recommend a fiscal year budget for each agency, and (3) presidential executive orders.

The president not only appoints the head of each administrative agency but also designates some lower-level heads of departments and divisions that do not come under the federal civil service system. Naturally, presidential appointees tend to have the same philosophical bent as the chief executive and are often of the same party. In this way, the president gains some influence over both independent and executive agencies.

Presidents exercise even greater influence over executive agencies through the budget process and executive orders. In 1981, for instance, President Reagan signed Executive Order 12291, which requires executive agencies to perform a cost–benefit analysis before promulgating a major federal regulation. A major federal regulation is one that will cost businesses $100 million or more to comply with. To take another example, this one concerning the budget process, Executive Order 12498, signed in 1985 (also by President Reagan), extended the OMB's powers so that it now has authority over "pre-rule-making action" by executive agencies. This executive order requires civilian government agencies to submit a Draft Regulatory Program listing all pre-rule-making and other significant actions they intend to take in a fiscal year. These Draft Regulatory Programs become part of the Administration's Regulatory Program. Once that program is published by the OMB, no agency may deviate from the plan without approval from the OMB unless forced to do so by the courts. Note that these executive orders affect executive administrative agencies. Independent administrative agencies have been requested to comply voluntarily with these orders, and some have done so. A bill passed by the House of Representatives and the Senate in 1995, and discussed in this chapter under "Creation of Administrative Agencies," applies to both executive and independent administrative agencies.

Legislative Branch. Congress limits the authority of administrative agencies through its (1) oversight power, (2) investigative power, (3) power to terminate an agency, and (4) power to advise and consent on presidential nominations for heads of administrative agencies.

When Congress creates an agency, it delegates to that agency its own legislative power over a narrow area of commerce, say, human rights. Each year, through one of its oversight committees, it determines whether the agency has been carrying out its mandated function. Suppose, for example, that the House Energy and Commerce Committee's Subcommittee on Consumer, Finance, and Telecommunications finds that the SEC is not enforcing laws against insider trading and fraud. The full committee will investigate and, if it finds dereliction, will order the SEC to enforce the laws as it is charged to do.

The greatest legislative limitation on agency power, however, lies in Congress's right to approve or disapprove an agency budget submitted by the executive branch (the OMB). If Congress disagrees with the agency's actions, it can slash the budget or refuse to budget the agency at all. The latter action, of course, will shut down the agency. On the other hand, if Congress believes that the executive branch is shortchanging an agency for some reason, it can raise that agency's budget above the amount proposed by the OMB.

Judicial Branch. The courts can curb administrative agencies' rule-making and adjudicative excesses by reversing or modifying such actions, as we explained earlier in this chapter. You might want to go back to that portion of the chapter at this point and reread the standards used by the courts in reviewing these agency functions.

STATE AND LOCAL ADMINISTRATIVE AGENCIES

Each of the 50 states, the District of Columbia, and territories such as Puerto Rico and Guam have created state and local administrative agencies to carry out tasks assigned to them by their legislative bodies. Most have utilities commissions (or the equivalent) that regulate local and in-state telephone rates, and are similar to the Federal Communications Commission, which regulates telephone rates for calls between states (or interstate). Agencies that regulate state-chartered banks, workers' compensation, state universities, and state taxes are common at the state level and are assigned duties by the state legislature. At the city and county level, real estate planning boards, zoning commissions, and supervisory boards are just a few of the administrative agencies that have a profound effect on the life of all citizens and should not be overlooked by future business leaders when determining where their companies will be located.

GLOBAL DIMENSIONS OF ADMINISTRATIVE AGENCIES

Like the United States, other nations have created administrative agencies to carry out important government functions. In some cases, they have more unfettered authority than their U.S. counterparts. Japan's Ministry of International Trade and Industry, Ministry of Finance, and Ministry of Foreign Affairs, for example, are often thought to be more powerful than elected Japanese politicians. Educated Japanese compete to work for these powerful agencies, which deeply influence trade, foreign affairs, and domestic issues.

The U.S. Trade Representative's Office, the Commerce Department's International Division, and the State Department share power over trade matters and regularly meet with and influence their administrative agency counterparts in Japan and Europe, particularly in the European Union. Recently, the Securities and Exchange Commission (SEC) entered into memoranda of agreement with Switzerland and other European countries, as well as with several Caribbean nations, to obtain disclosure of numbered bank accounts suspected of being used to harbor illegal profits from insider trading and other fraudulent activities in the United States (these topics are discussed in Chapter 22).

SUMMARY

Administrative law is defined broadly as any rule (statute or regulation) that directly or indirectly affects an administrative agency. The Administrative Procedure Act (APA) provides procedural guidelines for federal agencies; these guidelines are often copied, in whole or in part, by state and local administrative agencies.

The major functions of administrative agencies are rule making, adjudication, and the carrying out of numerous administrative activities. The executive, judicial, and legislative branches of government limit the power of federal agencies in numerous ways. In addition, several federal statutes limit the authority of administrative agencies.

Federal administrative agencies meet with their counterparts in other nations and enter into international agreements that aid the enforcement powers of U.S. agencies.

REVIEW QUESTIONS

17-1 Why did Congress create administrative agencies?

17-2 What are the two major functions of administrative agencies?

17-3 Explain the distinction between executive administrative agencies and independent administrative agencies.

17-4 Describe how the courts check the power of administrative agencies.

17-5 Describe how the executive branch of government checks the power of administrative agencies.

17-6 Describe how the legislative branch of government checks the power of administrative agencies.

REVIEW PROBLEMS

17-7 The Occupational Safety and Health Administration (OSHA) promulgated a rule limiting employees' exposure to cotton dust during the manufacture of cotton products because serious diseases were traced to exposure to such dust. The cotton industry argued that the standard was beyond the scope of OSHA's authority in that it failed to reflect a reasonable relationship between the costs of compliance for the industry and the benefits to people working in the cotton industry. OSHA and the secretary of labor argued that they did not need to perform a cost–benefit analysis to justify the standard but needed only to show that the standard reduced the risk of illness to an extent that was technologically and economically feasible. Who won this case, and why?

17-8 Under the Clean Air Act, the EPA can regulate gasoline additions if they "endanger the public welfare." Scientific evidence showed that lead emissions from gasoline constituted 90 percent of all the lead in the air and that this lead could be absorbed into the body. The EPA promulgated regulations requiring a step-by-step reduction of the lead content of gasoline. Gasoline manufacturers challenged EPA's rule-making procedure, claiming that it was arbitrary and capricious because the evidence supporting the agency's decision was unsound. They claimed that air was only one of several sources of the lead absorbed by the body. The EPA argued that the evidence it had marshaled was sufficient to justify the regulations. Who won this case, and why?

17-9 The Federal Communications Commission (FCC) promulgated rules prohibiting cable television from broadcasting feature films more than three years old but less than ten years old in addition to certain other programs. Home Box Office (HBO) argued that these rules were arbitrary and capricious and that they discriminated against cable companies. The FCC countered that the regulations were necessary to prevent siphoning off of movies by cable companies from (free) network television. Who won this case, and why?

17-10 In 1969, the secretary of transportation approved a plan to extend an interstate highway through Overton Park in Memphis, Tennessee. A group of environmentalists petitioned the courts, seeking to enjoin the Department of Transportation (DOT) from financing the project. They argued that under the Federal Aid Highway Act, federal funds could not be used for highway construction through a public park if a "feasible and prudent alternative" existed. DOT personnel produced affidavits indicating that the secretary had considered other alternatives and argued that, unless there was substantial evidence to the contrary, the secretary's decision should be upheld by the reviewing court. Who won this case, and why?

17-11 The Federal Trade Commission (FTC) instituted proceedings against the Soft Drink Bottling Company, alleging violations of laws prohibiting unfair methods of competition. The complaint against Soft Drink Bottling challenged the validity of exclusive bottling agreements between the company and franchised bottlers, who had to agree not to sell the company's products outside a designated territory. Soft Drink Bottling asked the FTC to include the 513 bottlers in the case. The FTC refused to do so on the ground that inclusion of so many bottlers would make the case unmanageable—although it said that any bottlers who wished to could intervene in the case. Soft Drink Bottling decided to appeal the decision to a federal court. Did the court entertain the action?

17-12 One of the hottest business issues today is the outrageously lavish pay of many chief executive officers (CEOs) vis-à-vis corporate profits. In 1990, for example, United Airlines' CEO got $18.3 million—1,200 times what a new flight attendant makes—even though United's profits had fallen by 71 percent that year! The Interstate Commerce Commission would like to regulate CEO pay. Does it have the authority to do so? Explain.

CASE PROBLEMS

17-13 The U.S. Patent and Trademark Office (PTO) denied an application for a patent on a method for increasing computer security, finding that it was not original. On appeal, the federal circuit court of appeals reversed, holding that the PTO fact-finding was "clearly erroneous." The appellate court did not find the process "arbitrary and capricious" and did not discuss the "substantial evidence" rule. The patent applicant then appealed to the U.S. Supreme Court. Did the appellate court use the appropriate standard for reviewing the agency's action? Why or why not? *Dickinson v. Zurko*, 119 S.Ct. 1816 (1999)

17-14 OSHA issued what it called a "directive" in which it announced a new program. Under the program, called the Cooperative Compliance Program, certain employers with low rates of workplace injuries would be allowed to participate in a special arrangement, in which OSHA would work with the employer to improve illness and injury rates and the employer would face a reduced chance of a random OSHA inspection. The issuance of the "directive" was challenged by industry groups, because it had been issued by OSHA without any rule-making procedures—formal or informal—and no opportunity for "notice and comment." OSHA defended the process, arguing that the directive was a type of policy or procedural rule (and, therefore, not subject to the APA rule-making procedures) rather than a substantive rule. What should the result be and why? *Chamber of Commerce of the United States v. OSHA*, 174 F.3d 206 (D.C. Cir. 1999)

17-15 American Message Centers (AMC) provides answering services to retailers. Calls to a retailer are automatically forwarded to AMC, which pays for the calls. AMC obtains telephone service at a discount from major carriers, including Sprint. Sprint's tariff (a public document setting out rates and rules relating to Sprint's services) states that the "subscriber shall be responsible for the payment of all charges for service." When AMC learned that computer hackers had obtained the access code for AMC's lines and had made nearly $160,000 in long-distance calls, it asked Sprint to absorb the cost. Sprint refused. AMC filed a complaint with the Federal Communications Commission (FCC), claiming in part that Sprint's tariff was vague and ambiguous, in violation of the Communications Act of 1934 and FCC rules. These laws require that a carrier's tariff "clearly and definitely" specify any "exceptions or conditions which in any way affect the rates named in the tariff." The FCC rejected AMC's complaint. AMC appealed the FCC's decision to a federal appellate court, claiming that the FCC's decision to reject AMC's complaint was arbitrary and capricious. What should the court decide? *American Message Centers v. Federal Communications Commission*, 50 F.3d 35 (D.C. Cir. 1995)

17-16 OSHA is part of the U.S. Department of Labor. OSHA issued a "directive" under which each employer in selected industries was to be inspected unless it adopted a "Comprehensive Compliance Program"—a safety and health program designed to meet standards that in some respects exceeded those otherwise required by law. The Chamber of Commerce of the United States objected to the directive and filed a petition for review with the U.S. Court of Appeals for the District of Columbia Circuit. The chamber claimed, in part, that OSHA did not use proper rule-making procedures in issuing the directive. OSHA argued that it was not required to follow those procedures because the directive itself was a "rule of procedure." OSHA claimed that the rule did not alter the rights or interests of parties, "although it may alter the manner in which the parties present themselves or their viewpoints to the agency." What are the steps of the most commonly used rule-making procedure? Which steps are missing in this case? *Chamber of Commerce of the United States v. U.S. Department of Labor*, 74 F.3d 206 (D.C. Cir. 1999)

17-17 Lion Raisins, Inc., is a family-owned business that grows and markets raisins to private enterprises. In May 1999, a USDA investigation reported that Lion appeared to have falsified inspectors' signatures, given false moisture content, and changed the grade of raisins on three USDA raisin certificates issued between 1996 and 1998. Lion was subsequently awarded five more USDA contracts. In January 2001, however, the USDA awarded these contracts to other bidders and, on the basis of the May 1999 report, suspended Lion from participating in government contracts for one year. Lion filed a suit in the U.S. Court of Federal Claims against the USDA, seeking, in part, lost profits on the school lunch contracts on the ground that the USDA's suspension was arbitrary and capricious. Who won? Explain. *Lion Raisins, Inc. v. United States*, 51 Fed Cl. 238 (2001)

ASSIGNMENT ON THE INTERNET

This chapter introduces administrative law and several administrative agencies. However, there are many agencies not discussed that play a significant role in creating regulations. Use the Internet to discover three federal administrative agencies not discussed in this chapter. Explain the purpose of each agency and state at least two recent rules or regulations it has issued. The Web sites listed in the following section may be of use in discovering the many federal administrative agencies.

 ## ON THE INTERNET

www.whitehouse.gov/government/independent-agencies.html This site, maintained by the White House, contains links to federal agencies and commissions.

www.gsa.gov/Portal/gsa/ep/home.do?tabId=0 This site provides information about most administrative agencies.

www.abanet.org/adminlaw/process.html Here is the site to go to if you have ideas about how to improve the way administrative agencies cooperate.

www.law.cornell.edu/topics/administrative.html The Legal Information Institute's site on administrative agencies, including recent administrative law judicial decisions.

www.constitution.org/ad_state/y5063e03.htm This site contains a discussion of the constitutional issues related to administrative activities.

www.oalj.dol.gov This is the site of the Office of Administrative Law Judges.

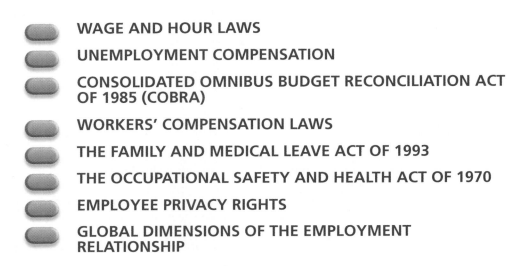

18

THE EMPLOYMENT RELATIONSHIP

- **WAGE AND HOUR LAWS**
- **UNEMPLOYMENT COMPENSATION**
- **CONSOLIDATED OMNIBUS BUDGET RECONCILIATION ACT OF 1985 (COBRA)**
- **WORKERS' COMPENSATION LAWS**
- **THE FAMILY AND MEDICAL LEAVE ACT OF 1993**
- **THE OCCUPATIONAL SAFETY AND HEALTH ACT OF 1970**
- **EMPLOYEE PRIVACY RIGHTS**
- **GLOBAL DIMENSIONS OF THE EMPLOYMENT RELATIONSHIP**

One way to think about the employment relationship is that it is a contractual relationship between the employer and employee: The employer agrees to pay the employee a certain amount of money in exchange for the employee's agreement to render specific services. Early in our history, the employer and employee were free to determine all the conditions of their employment relationship. Today, however, both the federal and state governments specify many of the conditions under which that relationship exists.

This chapter will explain many of the conditions that the government imposes. The first five sections will focus on the laws that affect employee wages and benefits: wage and hour laws; unemployment compensation legislation; the Consolidated Omnibus Budget Reconciliation Act of 1985 (COBRA); state workers' compensation laws; and the Family and Medical Leave Act. The sixth and seventh sections shift to protecting worker safety and health and privacy rights. The final section focuses on the international dimensions of the employment relationship.

494

Critical Thinking About the Law

Employers are required by law to provide specific employment conditions for their employees. For example, minimum wage and hours laws help to ensure that the worker will not be required to work an extraordinary number of hours for little pay.

Why do we have laws to protect workers? One reason for these laws is the belief that employees cannot protect themselves in the workplace. Because they have very little power over the employer, we have traditionally offered protection for employees to prevent their exploitation.

After you read the following case, answer the critical thinking questions that will sharpen your thinking about employee benefits.

Mike works full time at a large factory. As he is preparing to go home after his shift, he sees his boss yelling angrily at the television in his office. The news station had just reported a new law passed by Congress that requires employers to provide paid leave for the birth of a child. Both mothers and fathers will receive the paid leave. Mike's boss thinks the new law is an outrageous restriction on employers. Mike, however, is happy about the new law because his wife is pregnant. He will be happy to stay home with his wife when she has the baby.

1. Mike's opinion and his employer's opinion about the new law obviously conflict. Their respective ethical preferences are one important cause of their disagreement. What ethical norm seems to be dominating the employer's thought?

   Clue: Why is the employer upset? Review your list of ethical norms; try to match one of the norms to the reason why the employer is angry.

2. Mike's boss makes the following argument: "It is ridiculous that the government would make me pay my employees to sit at home! They are my employees. I should get to decide if employees should be allowed to leave for the birth of a child." Do you see any problems with this argument?

   Clue: How does the employer's argument conflict with the reason for offering employee benefits?

3. Before you make a judgment about the worth of the new law, is there any additional information that would help your thinking?

   Clue: What information seems to be missing? Several crucial pieces of information about the paid leave are not offered in the news report.

WAGE AND HOUR LAWS

Employers do not have complete freedom anymore to pay workers any wages they choose or to require them to work any number of hours. Several federal laws impose minimum wage and hour requirements. For example, the Davis–Bacon Act[1] requires that contractors and subcontractors working on government projects pay the "prevailing wage." The most pervasive law regulating wages and hours, however, is the Fair Labor Standards Act[2] (FLSA), which covers all employers engaged in interstate commerce or the production of goods for interstate commerce.

One of the most significant aspects of the FLSA is its requirement that a minimum wage of a specified amount be paid to all employees in covered industries. This specified amount is periodically raised by Congress to compensate for

---

[1] 40 U.S.C., Section 276a–276a-5 (1998).
[2] U.S.C., Sections 201–260 (1998).

increases in the cost of living caused by inflation. The most recent increase took effect on September 1, 1997, when the minimum wage rose to $5.15 per hour.

The FLSA also requires that employees who work more than 40 hours in a week be paid no less than one and one-half times their regular wage for all the hours beyond the standard 40-hour workweek. Four categories of employees, however, are excluded from this provision of the law: executives, administrative employees, professional employees, and outside salespersons. To prevent employers from taking advantage of these exemptions, however, the act generally requires that these employees earn at least a minimum amount of income and spend a certain amount of time engaged in specified activities before they can fall into each of those exempted categories. Recently, several groups of Taco Bell employees brought class action suits against Taco Bell because the company allegedly shaved hours off the employee time cards to avoid paying employees overtime. Taco Bell settled one of the suits for $13 million. In the other case, the jury found Taco Bell guilty and awarded damages of $1.5 million.[3]

Taco Bell is not alone, however. A seemingly unending list of well-known companies appear to have attempted to avoid paying overtime, often by miscategorizing nonmanagerial employees as managers. For example, in 2002, Starbucks and UPS collectively agreed to pay $36 million in damages to settle claims by groups of workers who had been misclassified as "managers." In July of that same year, Radio Shack settled an overtime class action suit for just under $30 million.[4] CVS agreed to pay an undisclosed sum to settle claims of pharmacists that they were not salaried, exempt employees, and Petco agreed to pay its managers and assistant managers in California up to $25 million to settle their claims that they were not exempt from being paid overtime pay.[5]

In 2001, a California court of appeals upheld all but $1.2 million of the largest class action overtime award thus far, a $90 million award to claims adjusters at Farmer's Insurance Exchange who had been incorrectly classified as "exempt" employees and not paid the overtime to which they were entitled.[6]

According to the Department of Labor (DOL), the number of wage and hour class action suits now exceeds the number of employment discrimination cases under all federal discrimination statutes combined.[7] During 2002, the DOL alone collected $212 million in back wages and overtime for employees, which is 60 percent more than the amount collected during 2000.

Perhaps in an attempt to quell some of this litigation, the Bush administration made substantial changes to the DOL overtime regulations. In August 2004, the new DOL rules went into effect, redefining eligibility requirements for overtime protection. Under these new rules, workers earning less than $23,660 a year are guaranteed overtime protection, which is estimated to affect 1.3 million workers. However, other changes to the rules remove overtime protection from an estimated 4–6 million workers. One such change redefines "executive" to include those workers whose job is primarily manual or routine labor but who

---

[3] "Taco Bell Loses Second Big Back-Pay Case As Ore. Jury Affirms Time-Card Tampering Charge," *Nation's Restaurant News*, March 26, 2001, p. 3.

[4] "Costco Sued for Unpaid Overtime Wages," M2 Presswire, 2003 WL 133014792299 (2/21/03).

[5] Connie Robbins Gentry, "Off the Clock," *Chain Store Age*, 79, no. 2, 2003 WL 13301250 (2/01/03).

[6] David Haase and Ross Friedman, "Overtime Requirements," *National Law Journal*, 26, no. 3, p. 13 (3/29/04).

[7] *Id.*

also perform supervision. The new definition of "executive" removes overtime protection from 1.4 million supervisors. Other key definitions, such as "professional" or "administrative," were changed, resulting in a net loss of workers with overtime protection. As fewer employees are guaranteed overtime protection, the number of overtime-related lawsuits may drop.[8]

To ensure that employers comply with the FLSA, the law imposes record-keeping requirements on employers. For each nonexempt employee, the employer must maintain the following records: (1) employee's full name and Social Security number; (2) address, including zip code; (3) birth date, if under 18; (4) sex and occupation; (5) time and day of week when employee's work-week begins; (6) hours worked each day; (7) total hours worked each work-week; (8) basis on which employee's wages are paid (e.g., "$6 an hour," "$220 a week," "piece work"); (9) regular hourly pay rate; (10) total daily or weekly straight time earnings; (11) total overtime earning for the workweek; (12) all additions to or deductions from the employees wages; (13) total wages paid each pay period; (14) date of payment and the pay period covered by each payment.[9]

Finally, to ensure that employees become aware of their rights, the employer must post in a conspicuous place a poster similar to the one in Exhibit 18-1.

UNEMPLOYMENT COMPENSATION

Having a minimum wage provides a great deal of security for employees when they are working, but what happens to those who lose their jobs? In 1935, Congress passed the Federal Unemployment Tax Act,[10] which created a state system that provides unemployment compensation to qualified employees who lose their jobs. Under this act, employers pay taxes to the states. These tax dollars are deposited into the federal government's Unemployment Insurance Fund.

Each state then has an account from which it has access to the money in the fund. States then set up their own system of allocating these funds, determining such matters as how the amount of compensation is determined and how long it can be collected. Eligibility requirements must also be set, with most states requiring, at minimum, that an applicant was not fired for just cause or did not voluntarily quit. Some states are more generous than others in setting up their eligibility requirements. For example, although states generally require that employees did not voluntarily quit, some will allow an employee to still receive unemployment if he or she quit because of a compelling reason, as in the 2000 case of *Beachem v. Unemployment Compensation Board of Review*.[11] In that case, Mr. Beachem, a welder living in Pennsylvania, was a single parent of a son who began having emotional and behavioral problems. The son was living with Beachem's mother in Alabama at the time, and Beachem quit his job to move to Alabama to care for the boy after exhausting all possible child care options. He found a job in Alabama but was laid off after a month, too soon to collect unemployment compensation in that state, so he filed for benefits in Pennsylvania. The court found

---

[8] Economic Policy Institute, "Longer Hours, Less Pay," **www.epinet.org/content.cfm/briefingpapers_bp152** (accessed 9/15/04).

[9] www.dol.gov/esa/regs/compliance/whd/whdfs21.htm (accessed 9/15/04).

[10] 426 U.S.C., Sections 3301–3310.

[11] *Beachem v. Unemployment Compensation Board of Review*, 2000 WL 1357484 (Cmwlth. Ct., Pa. 2000).

EXHIBIT 18-1 YOUR RIGHTS UNDER THE FAIR LABOR STANDARDS ACT POSTER

Your Rights Under the Fair Labor Standards Act

Federal Minimum Wage

$4.75 per hour
beginning October 1, 1996

$5.15 per hour
beginning September 1, 1997

Employees under 20 years of age may be paid $4.25 per hour during their first 90 consecutive calendar days of employment with an employer.

Certain full-time students, student learners, apprentices, and workers with disabilities may be paid less than the minimum wage under special certificates issued by the Department of Labor.

Tip Credit – Employers of "tipped employees" must pay a cash wage of at least $2.13 per hour if they claim a tip credit against their minimum wage obligation. If an employee's tips combined with the employer's cash wage of at least $2.13 per hour do not equal the minimum hourly wage, the employer must make up the difference. Certain other conditions must also be met.

Overtime Pay

At least $1\frac{1}{2}$ times your regular rate of pay for all hours worked over 40 in a workweek.

Child Labor

An employee must be at least **16** years old to work in most non-farm jobs and at least **18** to work in non-farm jobs declared hazardous by the Secretary of Labor. Youths **14** and **15** years old may work outside school hours in various non-manufacturing, non-mining, non-hazardous jobs under the following conditions:

No more than –
  • **3** hours on a school day or **18** hours in a school week;
  • **8** hours on a non-school day or **40** hours in a non-school week.

Also, work may not begin before **7 a.m.** or end after **7 p.m.**, except from **June 1** through **Labor Day**, when evening hours are extended to **9 p.m.** Different rules apply in agricultural employment.

Enforcement

The Department of Labor may recover back wages either administratively or through court action, for the employees that have been underpaid in violation of the law. Violations may result in civil or criminal action.

Fines of up to $10,000 per violation may be assessed against employers who violate the child labor provisions of the law and up to $1,000 per violation against employers who willfully or repeatedly violate the minimum wage or overtime pay provisions. This law prohibits discriminating against or discharging workers who file a complaint or participate in any proceedings under the Act.

Note: • Certain occupations and establishments are exempt from the minimum wage and/or overtime pay provisions.
  • Special provisions apply to workers in American Samoa.
  • Where state law requires a higher minimum wage, the higher standard applies.

For Additional Information, Contact the Wage and Hour Division office nearest you – listed in your telephone directory under United States Government, Labor Department.

This poster may be viewed on the Internet at this address: http://www.dol.gov/esa/regs/compliance/posters/flsa.htm

The law requires employers to display this poster where employees can readily see it.

U.S. Department of Labor
Employment Standards Administration
Wage and Hour Division
Washington, D.C. 20210

WH Publication 1088
Revised October 1996

that "a cause of necessitous and compelling nature exists where there are circumstances that force one to terminate his employment that are real and substantial and would compel a reasonable person under those circumstances to act in the same manner,"[12] and allowed him to receive benefits.

CONSOLIDATED OMNIBUS BUDGET RECONCILIATION ACT OF 1985 (COBRA)

COBRA ensures that employees who lose their jobs or have their hours reduced to a level at which they are no longer eligible to receive medical, dental, or optical benefits can continue receiving benefits for themselves and their dependents under the employer's policy. By paying the premiums for the policy, plus up to a 2 percent administration fee, employees can maintain the coverage for up to 18 months or 29 months for a disabled worker. Employees have 60 days after coverage would ordinarily terminate to decide whether to maintain the coverage.

This obligation does not arise if the employee was fired for gross misconduct or if the employer decides to eliminate the benefit for all current employees. Employers who refuse to comply with the law may be required to pay up to 10 percent of the annual cost of the group plan or $500,000, whichever is less.

WORKERS' COMPENSATION LAWS

Unlike many other laws affecting the employment relationship, workers' compensation legislation is purely state law. Our coverage of this topic must, therefore, be rather generalized. Prudent businesspeople will familiarize themselves with the workers' compensation statutes of the states within which their companies operate.

COVERAGE

Workers' compensation laws provide financial compensation to employees or their dependents when the covered employee of a covered employer is injured on the job. For administrative convenience, most states exclude certain types of businesses and small firms from coverage. A few states also allow employers to "opt out" of the system. These states may likewise give the employee the opportunity to reject coverage.

Workers' compensation is said to be "no fault" because recovery does not depend on showing that the injury was caused by an error of the employer. Think of workers' compensation as analogous to insurance: The employer pays premiums based on the frequency of accidents in the employer's business, and the employees receive insurance-like benefits if injured.

To recover workers' compensation benefits, the injured party must demonstrate that she or he is an employee as opposed to being an independent contractor. This distinction, which was discussed in Chapter 15, is based on the degree of control the employer can exert over the worker: The greater the degree

workers' compensation laws State laws that provide financial compensation to covered employees or their dependents when employees are injured on the job.

---

[12] *Id.*

of control, the more likely the party will be considered an employee. Factors showing employer control include the employer's dictating how the job is to be done, providing the tools to do the job, and setting the worker's schedule. In contrast, in employer–independent contractor relationships, the employer generally specifies the task to be accomplished but has no control over how the task is done. A broker hired by a firm to sell a piece of property is an example of an independent contractor.

The employee must also establish that the injury occurred on the job. This means it must have taken place during the time and within the scope of the claimant's employment. Once an employee is on company property, the courts generally find that the employee was on the job. This finding is based on the application of what is commonly called the premises rule.

More difficult, however, is the situation of the employee who is injured on the way to or from work. If the employee works fixed hours at a fixed location, injuries on the way to or from work are generally noncompensable. But some states provide for exceptions to this rule. One exception, known as the special-hazards exception, applies when a necessary means of access to the employer's premises presents a special risk, even if the hazardous area is beyond the control of the employer. For example, if an employee must make a left-hand turn across a busy thoroughfare to enter the company parking lot, this situation has been held to be a risk of employment; therefore, employees involved in accidents while making a left-hand turn into their employers' parking lots have been allowed compensation under this exception.

Another exception occurs when an employee is requested to run an errand for the employer on the way to or from work. In general, compensation is allowed for injuries sustained during the course of running the errand.

Sometimes, as a consequence of the job, an employee is forced to temporarily stay away from home. What if the employee is injured while away from home? In some states, reasonable injuries suffered while away from work are covered. In a New York case, a typist was required to travel to Canada to transcribe depositions. While showering in her hotel, she fell and injured herself. She filed a successful workers' compensation claim.

The elements necessary for recovery under workers' compensation laws are summarized in Exhibit 18-2.

RECOVERABLE BENEFITS

The amounts and types of benefits recoverable under workers' compensation are specified by each state's relevant statute. Most statutes cover medical, hospital, and rehabilitation expenses. In some cases, expenses for unusual items have been allowed as necessary. For example, a New York court ruled that a claimant who had become a quadriplegic as a result of a work-related accident was entitled to recover the cost of building a self-contained apartment attached to his

EXHIBIT 18-2

ELEMENTS REQUIRED FOR A SUCCESSFUL WORKERS' COMPENSATION CLAIM

1. Claimant is an employee, as opposed to an independent contractor.

2. Both claimant and employer are covered by the state workers' compensation statute.

3. The injury occurred while the claimant was on the job and acting within the scope of the claimant's employment.

parents' home. The claimant, who had formerly been highly independent, had been placed in a nursing home after the accident, but the depression caused by his injury was so compounded by being surrounded by infirm, elderly people that he had tried to commit suicide three times. Thus, the court felt that, in this case, the apartment qualified under the statute as "other treatment" or "appliances" necessary to treat the worker for his work-connected injury.

Compensation under state statutes also generally includes payment for lost wages. When employees become disabled as a result of their injury, most states have a schedule that determines the amount of compensation for the disability, as well as compensation schedules for loss of body parts. Thus, an employee who lost a toe in an industrial accident, even though not disabled as a result, would be entitled to some compensation for the loss.

THE CLAIMS PROCESS

Most workers' compensation claims are handled by a state agency responsible for administering the compensation fund and adjudicating claims. In general, an employee who is injured fills out a claim form and files it with the responsible administrative agency. A representative of the agency then verifies the claim with the employer. If the employer does not contest the claim—and most do not—an employee of the bureau (usually called a "claims examiner") investigates the claim and determines the proper payment.

If either the amount or the validity of the claim is contested, there is an informal hearing before a regional office of the agency. Most states provide for an appeals process within the agency. A dissatisfied party who has exhausted the administrative appeals process may appeal to the state trial court of general jurisdiction.

BENEFITS OF THE WORKERS' COMPENSATION SYSTEM

Workers' compensation systems are often touted as benefiting workers. In many ways, they do. Before we had workers' compensation statutes, an employee who was injured on the job could successfully gain compensation from his or her employer only if able to prove that the injury was caused by the employer's negligence. Such proof was often difficult to produce.

Recovery was further restricted by the availability of powerful defenses. If the employee's own negligence contributed to the injury, the employee could not recover because of the defense of contributory negligence. Under the fellow servant rule, an employee could not recover if the act of another employee caused or contributed to the injury. And in some cases, the courts would say that if the claimant employee engaged in work knowing that it presented a particular safety risk, that employee had assumed the risk of injury and, therefore, the employer was not liable.

Overall, then, workers' compensation helps employees because it has removed from them the burden of having to prove employer negligence and has made all the defenses just mentioned irrelevant to compensation claims. Today, employees can obtain compensation in situations in which formerly they could not have recovered. The system also helps employees because they do not need to hire an attorney to recover. Many injured workers have never used attorneys and would not know how to seek legal help. They might also fear retaliation from their employers for bringing suit.

Certain aspects of workers' compensation, however, work to the detriment of employees and to the benefit of employers. In most states, employees who are covered by workers' compensation statutes do not have the right to bring personal injury lawsuits against their employers. Because the payment schedule adopted under any state law is a political compromise heavily influenced by business lobbies, the amount of compensation given is minimal—generally far less than the amount a party could recover through a successful lawsuit brought against the employer.

Some people argue that claimants are not completely compensated under most payment schedules and that workers' compensation laws compel employees to give up the chance of a large (or full) recovery in exchange for certain, but minimal, recovery. Because employers simply make regular payments to the workers' compensation fund, the costs of occupational injuries are a routine part of their operating expenses. Companies do not have to worry about incurring substantial unanticipated losses; at most, they may find their premiums increased if the number of claims filed against them goes up. For instance, a Texas state judge threw out a $12.7 million jury award against Exxon in a wrongful death suit because the victim's family had accepted $15,000 from a workers' compensation claim 22 years prior. With interest, the jury award would have forced Exxon to pay $107 million. This example demonstrates one way in which workers' compensation laws can be seen as "insurance" against large jury awards for companies.

Some people argue further that, by reducing potential costs for workplace injuries in this manner, workers' compensation has made employers more careless about employee safety than they would be if they had to fear huge damage awards.

THE FAMILY AND MEDICAL LEAVE ACT OF 1993

Family and Medical Leave Act (FMLA) A law designed to guarantee that workers facing a medical catastrophe or certain specified family responsibilities will be able to take needed time off from work without pay but without losing medical benefits or their job.

On August 5, 1993, the **Family and Medical Leave Act (FMLA)** went into effect. This law was designed to guarantee that workers facing an unexpected medical catastrophe or the birth or adoption of a child would be able to take needed time off from work. The act was hailed by its supporters as a "breakthrough" in U.S. law, and it was feared by its opponents as an unwieldy encumbrance upon business. So far, the jury is still out on the act's effectiveness.

MAJOR PROVISIONS

The Family and Medical Leave Act is a highly complex piece of legislation, containing six titles divided into 26 sections. The regulations, designed to guide the implementation of the act, are eight times longer than the statute itself! No wonder many employers were still not in full compliance with the act a year after it became effective.

The act covers all public employers and private employers of 50 or more employees. Covered employers must formulate a family leave policy and revise employee handbooks accordingly. The policy must provide all eligible employees with up to 12 weeks of leave during any 12-month period for any of the following family-related occurrences:

- The birth of a child
- The adoption of a child

- The placement of a foster child in the employee's care

- The care of a seriously ill spouse, parent, or child

- A serious health condition that renders the employee unable to perform any of the essential functions of his or her job

To exercise one's rights under the FMLA, an employee whose need for a leave is foreseeable must advise the employer of that need at least 30 days prior to the anticipated date on which the leave needs to begin, or as soon as practicable. A typical foreseeable leave would be one for the birth of a child.

If the leave is unforeseeable, notice must be given as soon as practicable. "As soon as practicable" is defined as within one or two business days from when the need for the leave becomes known.

The act does not provide a clear definition of exactly what type of notice is necessary. At minimum, the employee must inform the employer of why the employee needs the leave, and, if possible, the length of time needed. The FMLA does not have to be specifically mentioned in the request.

Courts look at the facts of each case individually to determine whether notice was sufficient. The following case illustrates how confusing the issue of adequacy of notice can be.

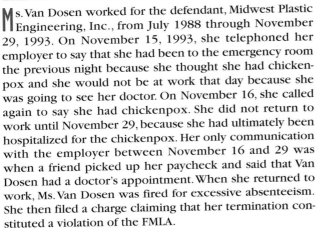

CASE 18-1

Reich, Secretary of Labor v. Midwest Plastic Engineering
United States District Court
934 F. Supp. 266 (W.D. Mich 1995)

Ms. Van Dosen worked for the defendant, Midwest Plastic Engineering, Inc., from July 1988 through November 29, 1993. On November 15, 1993, she telephoned her employer to say that she had been to the emergency room the previous night because she thought she had chickenpox and she would not be at work that day because she was going to see her doctor. On November 16, she called again to say she had chickenpox. She did not return to work until November 29, because she had ultimately been hospitalized for the chickenpox. Her only communication with the employer between November 16 and 29 was when a friend picked up her paycheck and said that Van Dosen had a doctor's appointment. When she returned to work, Ms. Van Dosen was fired for excessive absenteeism. She then filed a charge claiming that her termination constituted a violation of the FMLA.

District Judge Holmes Bell

The Act is silent regarding the notice that an employee must provide to her employer when the need for leave is not foreseeable. The regulations, however, provide: … "An employee shall provide at least verbal notice sufficient to make the employer aware that the employee needs FMLA-qualifying leave, and the anticipated timing and duration of the leave. The employee need not expressly assert rights under the FMLA, but may only state that leave is needed for [a covered reason]. The employer should inquire further of the employee if it is necessary to have more information about whether FMLA leave is being sought by the employee, and obtain the necessary details of the leave to be taken. In the case of medical conditions, the employer may find it necessary to inquire further to determine if the leave is because of a serious health condition and may request medical certification to support the need for such leave.

[T]he Court must now determine whether Ms. Van Dosen informed Midwest of her condition with sufficient detail to make it evident that the requested leave was protected as FMLA-qualifying leave. The Court can illustrate … with a hypothetical involving two eligible employees.

Both employees were involved in separate car accidents on Sunday. The first employee incurred substantial injuries as a result of his accident, which necessitated his being hospitalized for several weeks. The second employee sustained no injuries in his accident.

Neither employee came to work on Monday, the first because he was in the hospital and the second because he decided to go fishing. Each employee called the employer on Monday morning and reported that he would not be at work that day and that he had been involved in a car accident on Sunday. Under the Act and the regulations, the first employee clearly had a "serious health condition," and the second clearly did not. But neither employee provided the employer with adequate notice of his need for FMLA leave. While each employee told the employer that he had been involved in a car accident on Sunday, neither employee informed the employer of his condition with sufficient detail to make it evident to the employer that the absence was protected as FMLA-qualifying leave—a person who is involved in a car accident does not necessarily incur a serious health condition.

To provide adequate notice to the employer of his need for FMLA leave, the first employee should have stated that he had been hospitalized as the result of the accident. Such a statement by the employee would have informed his employer of his condition with sufficient detail to make it evident that the requested leave was protected as FMLA-qualifying leave. An employer should not have to speculate as to the nature of an employee's condition.

Turning to the present case, Ms. Van Dosen communicated with Midwest regarding her condition and need for leave on only three occasions prior to the termination of her employment on November 29—her November 15 telephone message, her November 16 conversation with Mr. Adams, and [her friend's] conversation with Mr. Long on November 19. In the course of these communications, Ms. Van Dosen failed to communicate sufficient information to inform Midwest of her condition with sufficient detail to make it evident to Midwest that her leave was the result of a "serious health condition" and was, therefore, protected as FMLA-qualifying leave. Specifically, the Court finds that she did not communicate that she was under the continuing treatment of a health care provider for her condition of chickenpox, nor did she communicate that she had received inpatient care at Vencor Hospital as the result of her having chickenpox.

Furthermore, even if Midwest had not already terminated Ms. Van Dosen's employment prior to her November 29 conversation with Mr. Long, and even if she had communicated these facts to Mr. Long during that conversation, the Court nevertheless concludes that the defendant still did not violate the Act. As previously indicated, [the act] required that Ms. Van Dosen provide notice to Midwest "as soon as practicable." Surely, if Ms. Van Dosen was able to go to the bank on the afternoon of November 19, she was "practically" able to notify Midwest of her condition at least by that date.

Finally, Midwest was permitted to require Ms. Van Dosen to report periodically on her status and intent to return to work. Mr. Long specifically told [her friend] to have Ms. Van Dosen bring in a doctor's slip verifying her condition on Monday, November 22. Ms. Van Dosen failed to do this. Moreover, she failed even to call in on that day to explain either her absence or her failure to bring in the slip and did not call in on November 23, 24, or 29.

Thus, even if she had adequately notified Midwest of her need for FMLA leave—which she did not do—she failed to update Midwest as to her status and intent to return to work as Mr. Long had demanded and Midwest's policies required. This alone gave Midwest a ground to terminate Ms. Van Dosen's employment.

Judgment in favor of Defendant, Midwest Plastic Engineering.

Upon termination of their leaves, employees must be restored to the same position or one that involves substantially equivalent skills, effort, responsibility, and authority. And, although the leave can be unpaid, the employer must continue health insurance benefits during the leave period. The employer may also require an employee to substitute paid time off for unpaid leave. For example, an employee who has four weeks of accrued sick leave and two weeks of vacation and wishes to take a 12-week leave for the birth of a new baby may be required to take the paid vacation and sick leave plus six weeks of unpaid leave.

SERIOUS MEDICAL CONDITION

One of the most contentious issues under the FMLA is what constitutes a medical condition that is serious enough to invoke the protections of the act. That issue is discussed in the following case.

CASE 18-2

Kimberly Miller v. AT&T Corporation
United States Court of Appeals Fourth Circuit
250 F.3d 820 (2000)

Kimberly Miller, plaintiff-appellee, was employed by defendant AT&T, and had missed a number of days of work for various reasons. Under the company's attendance policy, she would be terminated if she had any more unexcused absences. Absences covered by FMLA were not unexcused absences. On December 26, 1996, Miller began feeling ill while at work. She completed her shift that day but was too ill to work on the 27th. The following day, she called in sick and sought treatment at an urgent care center. The doctor diagnosed her as suffering from the flu and determined that

she was severely dehydrated. He also conducted a blood test, which revealed that Miller's white blood cell and platelet counts were significantly lower than normal.

After administering intravenous fluids, the doctor directed Miller to take over-the-counter medications to alleviate her symptoms and to return on December 30 for reevaluation. On December 30, Dr. Sommerville examined her and conducted another blood test, which revealed that Miller's white blood cell and platelet counts were still low, although the platelet level had improved and Miller felt better.

At the conclusion of her initial visit on December 28, Miller was given a work-excuse slip for December 28 through 31. On December 31, Miller telephoned the urgent care center and requested a work-excuse slip for January 1, explaining that she was feeling better but needed an additional day off work. The urgent care center granted this request.

Miller filed for FMLA leave for the days she missed. The company denied her request because it did not consider the flu to be a serious health condition. This denial made her absence unexcused, and she was consequently terminated.

She sued her employer for unlawful denial of benefits under FMLA. The district court granted her motion for partial summary judgment as to liability, and thereafter awarded back pay and attorneys' fees. The employer appealed.

Circuit Judge Wilkins

… AT&T contends that it did not violate the FMLA because the illness for which Miller sought FMLA leave—an episode of the flu—was not a serious health condition as defined by the Act and implementing regulations; that if Miller's flu was a serious health condition under the applicable regulations, those regulations are contrary to congressional intent and are therefore invalid. …

The FMLA entitles an eligible employee to as many as 12 weeks of unpaid leave per year for "a serious health condition that makes the employee unable to perform the functions of the position of such employee." The Act defines "serious health condition" as an illness, injury, impairment, or physical or mental condition that involves

(A) inpatient care in a hospital, hospice, or residential medical care facility; or
(B) continuing treatment by a health care provider.

Thus, as is relevant here, an eligible employee is entitled to FMLA leave for an illness that incapacitates the employee from working and for which the employee receives "continuing treatment," a term the FMLA does not define.

The FMLA grants the Secretary of Labor authority to promulgate regulations implementing the Act. Pursuant to this authority, the Secretary promulgated the following regulation:

A serious health condition involving continuing treatment by a health care provider includes …:
(i) A period of incapacity (i.e., inability to work) of more than three consecutive calendar days … that also involves:
(A) Treatment two or more times by a health care provider …; or

(B) Treatment by a health care provider on at least one occasion which results in a regimen of continuing treatment under the supervision of the health care provider.

The regulations further provide that "treatment" "includes (but is not limited to) examinations to determine if a serious health condition exists and evaluations of the condition."

The FMLA allows an employer to require that a request for leave for an employee's serious health condition be supported by a certification from the employee's health care provider. Among other things, the employer may require that the certification include "appropriate medical facts" regarding the condition. If the employer doubts the validity of a certification, it may require the employee to obtain a second opinion at the employer's expense. In the event of a conflict between the two opinions, the employer may require the employee to obtain a third opinion, again at the employer's expense. The opinion of the third health care provider is binding on both parties. …

We turn first to AT&T's contention that Miller's flu was not a "serious health condition" under the Act and regulations. First, AT&T contends that Miller cannot satisfy the regulatory criteria for a serious health condition because she did not receive "treatment" on two or more occasions. Failing this, AT&T argues that even if Miller qualified for FMLA leave under the regulatory criteria for "continuing treatment," the regulations specifically exclude the flu from FMLA coverage.

We begin with AT&T's contention that Miller did not receive treatment from Dr. Sommerville on two or more occasions. AT&T asserts that Miller's second visit to Dr. Sommerville—during which he conducted a physical examination and drew blood—did not constitute "treatment" because Dr. Sommerville simply evaluated Miller's condition. However, this assertion is contradicted by the regulations, which define "treatment" to include "examinations to determine if a serious health condition exists and evaluations of the condition." Under this definition, Miller's second visit to Dr. Sommerville clearly constituted "treatment."

AT&T next argues that even if Miller satisfies the regulatory criteria for a "serious health condition," the regulations nevertheless specifically exclude the flu and other minor illnesses from coverage under the FMLA. AT&T points to the following regulatory language:

Ordinarily, unless complications arise, the common cold, the flu, ear aches, upset stomach, minor ulcers, headaches other than migraine, routine dental or orthodontia problems, periodontal disease, etc., are examples of conditions that do not meet the definition of a serious health condition and do not qualify for FMLA leave.

According to AT&T, this regulation establishes that absent complications, the flu is never a serious health condition even if the regulatory test is satisfied. We disagree.

In light of our conclusion that Section 825.114(c) does not preclude FMLA coverage of an episode of the flu when the regulatory definition of a serious health condition is satisfied, we need not decide whether Miller suffered from any complications.

There is unquestionably some tension between subsection (a), setting forth objective criteria for determining whether a serious health condition exists, and subsection (c), which states that certain enumerated conditions "ordinarily" are not serious health conditions. Indeed, that tension is evidenced by Miller's illness. Miller was incapacitated for more than three consecutive calendar days and received treatment two or more times; thus, she satisfied the regulatory definition of a serious health condition under subsection (a). But, the condition from which Miller suffered—the flu—is one of those listed as being "ordinarily" not subject to coverage under the FMLA. AT&T urges us to resolve this tension by holding that subsection (c) essentially excepts the enumerated ailments from FMLA coverage even when an individual suffering from one of those ailments satisfies the regulatory criteria of subsection (a).

… Complications, per se, need not be present to qualify as a serious health condition if the regulatory … tests are otherwise met. The regulations reflect the view that, ordinarily, conditions like the common cold and flu (etc.) would not be expected to meet the regulatory tests, not that such conditions could not routinely qualify under FMLA where the tests are, in fact, met in particular cases.

[W]e nevertheless conclude that Section 825.114(c) is properly interpreted as indicating merely that common ailments such as the flu normally will not qualify for FMLA leave because they generally will not satisfy the regulatory criteria for a serious health condition.

Whenever possible, this court must reconcile apparently conflicting provisions. That is not difficult to do here. 29 C.F.R. Section 825.114(c) provides that "ordinarily" the flu will not qualify as a serious health condition. Presumably, this is because the flu (and the other conditions listed in the regulation) ordinarily will not meet the objective criteria for a serious health condition, inasmuch as such an illness normally does not result in an inability to work for three or more consecutive calendar days or does not require continuing treatment by a health care provider. Section 825.114(c) simply does not automatically exclude the flu from coverage under the FMLA. Rather, the provision is best read as clarifying that some common illnesses will not ordinarily meet the regulatory criteria and thus will not be covered under the FMLA.

Affirmed, in favor of Plaintiff, Miller.

Critical Thinking About the Law

Courts and legislatures are very aware of the dangers of ambiguity; they are alert to the same critical thinking problems that you are learning to watch for. So they will intentionally design decisions and legislation to clarify concepts that would otherwise interfere with the predictability that is one of the criteria for any legal system.

The following questions, pertaining to Case 18-2, will enable you to think once more about ambiguity and its effects, as you are urged to identify instances where others have clarified potential ambiguity.

1. Locate instances in the FMLA where those who drafted the legislation tried explicitly to avoid ambiguity.

   Clue: Go to each place in the decision where language from the FMLA is reported and look for instances in the act where terms are being clarified or defined.

2. Is the court being asked to see the FMLA as ambiguous regarding the flu?

   Clue: Does the flu come in different forms, such that sometimes it would be covered under FMLA and sometimes it would not?

REMEDIES FOR VIOLATIONS OF FMLA

If an employer fails to comply with the FMLA, the penalties can be substantial. The plaintiff may recover damages for unpaid wages or salary, lost benefits, denied compensation, and actual monetary losses up to an amount equivalent to the employee's wages for 12 weeks, as well as attorney fees and court costs. If the plaintiff can prove bad faith on the part of the employer, double damages may be awarded. An employee may also be entitled to reinstatement or promotion.

Although most awards under FMLA have not been extremely large, the size of the awards is beginning to grow. One of the larger awards was made in 1996. A California worker who was demoted, and then fired, for taking time off from work for surgery for a brain tumor was awarded $313,000.[13] In 1999 a state trooper was denied time off to care for his pregnant wife and then, subsequently, his daughter when his wife became ill during and after the pregnancy. He was subsequently awarded $375,000.[14] Many employment law specialists are now seeing the FMLA as an act that employers must carefully follow.

THE OCCUPATIONAL SAFETY AND HEALTH ACT OF 1970

Employees worry about more than compensation. They also want to work in a safe environment. Although working can be hazardous to one's health and safety, not all jobs are equally hazardous. The most dangerous industry is mining, followed by construction, agriculture, and transportation. The safest industries are the service industries. Fortunately workplaces are getting safer. Exhibit 18-3 illustrates the declining rates of occupational injuries in the U.S. workplace.

Occupational Safety and Health Act (OSH Act) A regulatory act designed to provide a workplace free from recognized hazards that are likely to cause death or serious harm to employees.

The primary regulatory measure designed to provide a safer workplace is the **Occupational Safety and Health Act** of 1970 (**OSH Act**). The OSH Act requires every employer to "furnish to each of his employees … employment … free from recognized hazards that are likely to cause death or serious physical harm! …" To ensure that this objective will be met, Congress, under the OSH Act, authorized the creation of three agencies: the Occupational Safety and Health Administration (OSHA), the National Institute for Occupational Safety and Health (NIOSH), and the Occupational Safety and Health Review Commission (OSHRC).

OCCUPATIONAL SAFETY AND HEALTH ADMINISTRATION (OSHA)

Occupational Safety and Health Administration (OSHA) The agency responsible, under the OSH Act, for setting and enforcing standards for occupational health and safety.

The most important of these agencies is the **Occupational Safety and Health Administration (OSHA)**. It has both a standard-setting and an enforcement role. In addition, it undertakes educational programs among employers and employees. In the 30 years since OSHA's establishment in 1971, workplace fatalities have been cut by 60 percent and occupational injury and illness rates by 40 percent, despite a near doubling of the American workforce during that time.

Standard Setting. OSHA sets the standards for occupational health and safety in the United States. These standards are frequently opposed by labor and management but for different reasons. In general, labor organizations criticize them for insufficiently protecting employees' health and safety, whereas employer groups claim they are unnecessarily stringent and too costly.

In establishing health standards, OSHA has used the following four-step process since 1981:

1. The agency asks whether the hazard presents a "significant risk" that warrants intervention.

2. If it does, OSHA decides whether regulatory action can reduce the risk.

---

[13] *Kline v. Walmart Stores, Inc.*, No. CA-95-0056 (post-trial motions denied October 1996).
[14] *Knussman v. State of Maryland et al.*, 65 F. Supp. 353 (1999).

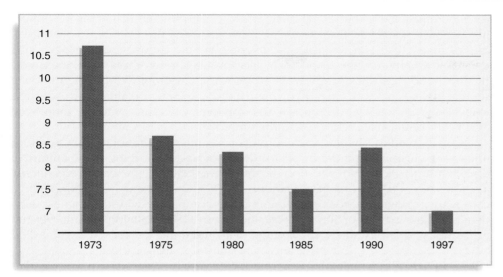

EXHIBIT 18-3

OCCUPATIONAL INJURY AND ILLNESS INCIDENCE RATES (PER 100 FULL-TIME WORKERS, SELECTED YEARS, INCLUDING CASES WITH AND WITHOUT LOST WORKDAYS)

Source: Adapted from Safety and Health Statistics, stats.bls.gov/news.release/osh.t06.htm.

3. If it can, the agency establishes a standard to reduce the risk "to the extent feasible," taking into account both technological and economic feasibility.

4. OSHA then analyzes the cost-effectiveness of various implementation options to determine which will achieve its goals most efficiently.[15]

Enforcement. OSHA is charged with enforcing the OSH Act through unannounced inspections and the levying of fines against violators. The goals of OSHA inspections are to find and correct existing hazards and to encourage employers to eliminate hazards before inspection.

OSHA conducts several different types of inspections. In order of priority, these are imminent danger inspections, when OSHA learns of a hazard that can be expected to cause physical harm or death; catastrophe and fatality investigations, whenever an accident hospitalizes five or more workers or causes a death; employee complaints, when an employee alleges a violation and requests an inspection; special inspection programs, including those aimed at certain hazards or industries; and, finally, programmed or random inspections. Follow-up inspections may also be conducted at any time.

OSHA's budget strongly affects the number of inspectors the agency has and, hence, the number of inspections. The agency's budget obviously fluctuates annually. For fiscal year 2001, its budget was $426 million. The agency had a staff of 2,370 workers, including 1,170 inspectors. The states running their own OSHA state programs had 2,948 state employees, including 1,275 inspectors. During fiscal year 2000, OSHA inspected 36,350 workplaces. The states running their own OSHA programs conducted an additional 54,510 inspections.

Inspection Procedure. The safety and health compliance officer conducting the inspection arrives at the plant, usually unannounced, presents his or her credentials, and asks to meet with the person in charge and a union representative to explain the purpose of the visit. The inspector then asks to see any relevant

---

[15] *Preventing Illness and Injury in the Workplace* (Washington, D.C.: Office of Technology Assessment, 1985), p. 16.

records. Since 1981, the policy of OSHA has been for the inspector in a safety inspection to calculate from these employer records the average lost-workday rate of injury. If it is lower than the average for the industry, the inspection is ended. If it is higher, the inspector walks through the workplace, taking notes, pictures, and exposure samples when relevant. An employer or an employee representative, or both, may accompany the inspector on this tour. After the inspection, the inspector discusses any apparent violations with the employer. Any citations are usually mailed to the employer at a later date.

As we noted in Chapter 5, an employer has the constitutional right to refuse to allow an inspection if the inspector does not have a warrant. If the employer does refuse to allow an inspection, however, the OSHA representative generally just goes to court and obtains a warrant. In 1997, OSHA launched a cooperative compliance program under which about 500 companies with the highest accident and illness rates or the greatest number of OSHA citations would get full inspections, whereas about 12,250 firms with more modest records were asked to create health and safety programs to avoid tough inspections.

Penalties. When violations are found, compliance inspectors may issue citations for violations. These violations fall into three categories: willful or repeat, serious, and nonserious. The maximum fines for serious or nonserious violations is $7,000 per day of noncompliance, whereas the maximum for a willful or repeat violation is up to $70,000 per violation. If a willful violation results in the death of a worker, criminal penalties may be imposed. For a first conviction, a fine of up to $10,000 and six months in jail are possible. For subsequent convictions, the penalty may be up to $20,000 and one year in jail.

Penalties can mount when firms have multiple violations. For example, during 1999, OSHA cited Ford Motor Company with 25 safety violations in its Buffalo Stamping Plant and fined the automaker $175,000. All but about $15,000 arose from 16 repeat violations—more than OSHA found in all of 1996! Moreover, in 2001, one company, Rocky Mountain Steel Mills (a subsidiary of Oregon Steel Mills), was fined $487,000 for 1,078 violations of 107 workplace safety standards. Although 22 of the violations were "repeat," none were designated "willful." Just two years earlier, Rocky Mountain Steel Mills had been fined $400,000.[16]

In addition to citing companies for safety violations, OSHA, through its voluntary participation program (VPP), recognizes companies that have created a particularly safe workplace by designating them as "Star" work sites. These sites, which have put into practice outstanding safety and health programs, are not targeted by OSHA for regularly scheduled programmed inspections. However, these sites tend to have fewer employee illnesses and injuries.

The program began in 1982 and is highly selective. Approximately 1,000 workplaces now participate in the program, and fewer than 150 businesses have logged nine years or more in this prestigious program.[17] An illustration of a company receiving recognition as a "Star" site is an Eaton manufacturing plant whose 714 worker facility had an exemplary safety and health program, and its lost workday injury and illness rate was 86% below the industry average.[18]

---

[16] "USWA Welcomes Comprehensive OSHA Inspection of Rocky Mountain Steel," **www.uswa.org/press/c.f. 030100.html**, March 1, 2000.

[17] "Eaton Corporation Earns Another 'Star' from OSHA," OSHA Press Release 03-955-Kan/KC-OSHA-33, December 19 2003 **www.osha.gov/pls/oshaweb/owadisp.show document?p table=NEWS RELEASES&p id=10593**.

[18] *Id.*

Public Education. Since 1975, OSHA has provided free, confidential, on-site consultations with employers seeking to bring their businesses up to OSHA standards. Any unsafe or unhealthful working conditions discovered during consultations are not reported to the OSHA inspection staff, as long as the firm commits itself to correcting any serious job safety and health hazards found during the consultation. The steps of a typical consultation are found in Exhibit 18-4 below. OSHA also sponsors a Targeted Training Program, which provides short-term grants to employers, employees, and nonprofit organizations to address health and safety issues about which OSHA has particular concerns.

State Plans. Under the present OSH Act, a state may regulate its own workplaces if it establishes a program providing for the establishment and enforcement of standards that will be at least as effective as the federal standards. As of August 2004, 25 states plus Puerto Rico and the Virgin Islands had established such programs.

OCCUPATIONAL SAFETY AND HEALTH REVIEW COMMISSION (OSHRC)

The **Occupational Safety and Health Review Commission (OSHRC)** is an independent review body before which an employer can contest the issuance of a citation by OSHA, the amount of the penalty, or the time within which abatement is expected. A hearing is conducted before an administrative law judge, whose ruling becomes OSHRC's final order 30 days after it is issued, provided it is not contested. Within the 30-day period, any party may request a review of the decision by OSHRC, which is automatically granted. A final order is issued after the review is completed. The final order may be appealed to a circuit court of appeals.

Occupational Safety and Health Review Commission (OSHRC) An independent body that reviews OSHA citations, penalties, and abatement periods that are contested by an employer.

NATIONAL INSTITUTE FOR OCCUPATIONAL SAFETY AND HEALTH (NIOSH)

The **National Institute for Occupational Safety and Health (NIOSH)** was established under the OSH Act to identify occupational health and safety problems, to develop controls to prevent occupational accidents and diseases, and to disseminate its findings. This body functions primarily as a research facility that attempts to make its findings on hazards available to those who can use them. Although independent of OSHA, NIOSH provides OSHA with information on which the agency bases many of its "criteria documents," recommendations for health and safety standards that contain supporting evidence and bibliographical references.

OSHA, NIOSH, and OSHRC work together to implement the OSH Act. By taking advantage of the assistance offered by these agencies and by meeting the standards that OSHA has established, businesspeople can make their workplaces safer and more healthful. It may even be in their interests to do so, for often the increased costs of providing a safer workplace are more than offset by the benefits employers derive from reduced absenteeism, fewer workers' compensation claims, and less work time lost because of accident investigations.

National Institute for Occupational Safety and Health (NIOSH) A research facility established by the OSH Act to identify occupational health and safety problems, develop controls to prevent occupational accidents and diseases, and disseminate its findings, particularly to OSHA.

EXHIBIT 18-4

STEPS OF A CONSULTATION ADAPTED FROM CONSULTATION PROGRAM FOR SMALL BUSINESSES, DECEMBER 9, 2004

www.osha.gov/dcsp/smallbus iness/consult.html.

Walk through

Together, the employer and consultant will examine conditions in the workplace. OSHA strongly encourages maximum employee participation in the walk-through. Talking with employees during the walk-through helps the consultant identify and judge the nature and extent of specific hazards.

The consultant studies the entire workplace or the specific operations designated by the employer and discusses the applicable OSHA standards. Consultants also will point out other safety or health risks that might not be cited under OSHA standards, but still pose safety or health risks to employees. They may suggest other measures to prevent future hazardous situations.

A comprehensive consultation also includes (1) appraisal of all mechanical and environmental hazards and physical work practices, (2) appraisal of the present job safety and health program or establishment of one, (3) a conference with management on findings, (4) a written report of recommendations and agreements, and (5) training and assistance with implementing recommendations.

Opening Conference

Upon arrival at the site, the consultant will first meet with the employer in an opening conference to briefly review the consultant's role and the obligations of the employer.

Initiation

The consulting process is initiated by a confidential phone call or letter to OSHA. A consultant will discuss the employer's specific needs and set up a visit date.

Abatement and Follow-through

Following the closing conference, the consultant sends the employer a detailed written report explaining the findings and confirming any abatement periods agreed upon. Consultants may also contact the employer from time to time to check the firm's progress. Ultimately, OSHA requires hazard abatement so that each consultation visit achieves its objective—effective employee protection. If you fail to eliminate or control identified serious hazards (or an imminent danger) according to the plan and within the limits agreed upon or an agreed-upon extension, the situation must be referred from consultation to an OSHA enforcement office for appropriate action, although these situations almost never arise.

Closing Conference

The consultant then reviews detailed findings with the employer in a closing conference. Problems, possible solutions, and abatement periods to eliminate or control any serious hazards identified during the walk-through are discussed. In rare instances, the consultant may find an "imminent danger" situation during the walk-through. If so, immediate action must be taken to protect all employees. In certain other situations that would be judged a "serious violation" under OSHA criteria, the employer and the consultant are required to develop and agree to a reasonable plan and schedule to eliminate or control that hazard. The consultants will offer general approaches and options to to the employer, and may also suggest other sources for technical help.

EMPLOYEE PRIVACY RIGHTS

Not only is safety an important concern of employees, but also they are increasingly concerned about privacy on the job. Privacy issues arise in a broad array of contexts, including the hiring process, monitoring of employee performance on the job, and the use of new technology.

ELECTRONIC MONITORING AND COMMUNICATION

Increasing use of technology in the workplace has raised a number of new privacy issues. When, for example, can employers monitor employees' telephone conversations, read their e-mail, or listen to their voice mail? The legal issues related to workplace privacy involve the common-law tort of invasion of privacy (discussed in Chapter 12) and the Omnibus Crime Control and Safe Streets Act of 1968,[19] as amended by the Electronic Communications Privacy Act (ECPA) of 1986.[20]

The Omnibus Crime Control Act prohibits employers from listening to the private telephone conversations of employees or disclosing the contents of those conversations. Employers are allowed to ban personal calls and monitor calls for compliance, but once they determine that a call is personal, they are not allowed to continue listening to the conversation. Violators may be subject to fines of up to $10,000.

The Electronic Communications Act extended employee's privacy rights to electronic forms of communication including e-mail and cellular phones. The act prohibits the intentional interception of electronic communications or the intentional disclosure or use of the information obtained through such interception.

Linking Law & Business

Management

In your management class, you may have learned about several theories of motivation related to human needs. The most widely known and accepted theory is Maslow's hierarchy of needs. This concept, developed by Abraham Maslow, includes five fundamental human needs: physiological; security, or safety; social; esteem; and self-actualization. As previously mentioned, the OSH Act of 1970 has promoted safer working environments via the aid of the three agencies established by Congress. Therefore, one of the five needs in Maslow's hierarchy, specifically safety needs, has been endorsed by congressional legislation. Because the statutes under the OSH Act encourage employers to create a safer workplace and better satisfy safety needs, managers have a more probable means of motivating employees to perform to the degree that they are able to accomplish a particular task. Thus, advocating safer workplaces could potentially result in motivated employees, which is an essential element in attaining organizational goals.

Source: S. Certo, *Modern Management* (Upper Saddle River, N.J.: Prentice Hall, 2000), pp. 354, 358–359.

---

[19] U.S.C., Section 2210 et seq.

[20] U.S.C., Sections 2510–2521.

The act, however, includes a "business-extension exemption" that allows employers to monitor employee telephone conversations in the ordinary course of their employment, as long as the employer does not continue to listen to conversations once he or she recognizes that they are of a personal nature. Such monitoring is often needed by employers to improve job performance and to offer some protection to employees from harassing calls from the public. A second exception arises when the employees consent to the monitoring of their conversations. The following case illustrates the application of this law.

CASE 18-3

Fraser v. Nationwide Mutual Insurance Company
United States Court of Appeals for the Third Circuit
352 F.3d 107 (2003)

Plaintiff Fraser's employment at Nationwide was terminated after e-mails revealed that he had divulged company trade secrets. Nationwide believed Fraser had become disloyal to the company and, consequently, the company searched its own main file server for e-mails showing disloyal conduct. Fraser then filed a lawsuit against Nationwide, claiming wrongful termination and a violation of the ECPA. The district court found in favor of defendant, Nationwide, on summary judgment. Plaintiff appealed.

Circuit Judge Ambro

Nationwide argues … that it terminated Fraser because he was disloyal. It points out that Fraser drafted a letter to two competitors expressing … dissatisfaction with Nationwide and seeking to determine whether [the competitors] would be interested in acquiring the policyholders of the agents. Fraser claims that the letters only were drafted to get Nationwide's attention and were not sent.

When Nationwide learned about these letters, it claims that it became concerned that Fraser might also be revealing company secrets to its competitors. It therefore searched its main file server—on which all of Fraser's e-mail was lodged—for any e-mail to or from Fraser that showed similar improper behavior. Nationwide's general counsel testified that the e-mail search confirmed Fraser's disloyalty. Therefore, on the basis of the two letters and the e-mail search, Nationwide terminated Fraser's agreement. It is this search of his e-mail that gives rise to Fraser's claim for damages under the Electronic Communications Privacy Act of 1986 (ECPA).

Fraser argues that, by accessing his e-mail on its central file server without his express permission, Nationwide violated Title I of the ECPA, which prohibits "intercepts" of electronic communications such as e-mail. The statute defines an "intercept" as "the aural or other acquisition of the contents of any wire, electronic, or oral communication through the use of any electronic, mechanical, or other device." Nationwide argues that it did not "intercept" Fraser's e-mail within the meaning of Title I because an "intercept" can only occur contemporaneously with transmission and it did not access Fraser's e-mail at the initial time of transmission.

Every circuit court to have considered the matter has held that an "intercept" under the ECPA must occur contemporaneously with transmission.

[W]hen Congress amended the Wiretap Act in 1986 (to create what is now known as the ECPA) to extend protection to electronic communications, it "did not intend to change the definition of 'intercept.' [T]he differences in definition between "wire communication" and "electronic communication" in the ECPA supported its conclusion that stored e-mail could not be intercepted within the meaning of Title I. A "wire communication" under the ECPA was (until recent amendment by the USA Patriot Act) "any aural transfer made in whole or in part through the use of facilities for the transmission of communications by the aid of wire, cable, or other like connection between the point of origin and the point of reception … *and such term includes any electronic storage of such communication*." By contrast, an "electronic communication" is defined as "any transfer of signs, signals, writing, images, sounds, data, or intelligence of any nature transmitted in whole or in part by a wire, radio, electromagnetic, photoelectronic or photooptical system … but does *not include … any wire or oral communication*." Thus, because "wire communication" explicitly included electronic storage but "electronic communication" did not, there can be no "intercept" of an e-mail in storage, as an e-mail in storage is by definition not an "electronic communication."

We … hold that there has been no "intercept" within the meaning of Title I of ECPA.

We *affirm* the District Court's grant of summary judgment in favor of Nationwide.

The key question in cases involving employer monitoring and interception of employee communications via e-mail, telephone, or voice mail is whether the employee had a reasonable expectation of privacy with respect to the communication in question. Therefore, many employment law specialists recommend that, to minimize the likelihood of being sued by employees for invasion of privacy and to keep good morale in the workplace, employers should have written employee privacy policies that are explained to employees and printed in employee handbooks. The Society of Human Resource Management, in a 1997 survey, found that nearly 80 percent of participants had e-mail, yet only 36 percent had policies defining proper e-mail use and only 34 percent had written privacy policies.

Privacy policies should cover matters from employer surveillance policies to control of and access to medical and personnel records, to drug testing, and to all issues unique to the electronic workplace. Exhibit 18-5 provides a sample of a good electronic mail policy.

A related privacy concern in the workplace is the use of surveillance cameras. Again, the courts fall back on the reasonable expectation of privacy. Closed-circuit cameras are increasingly being used to combat employee theft, to monitor employee performance, and to safeguard employees. Clearly visible cameras are generally not challenged. As one arbitrator said, "Since one of the supervisor's jobs is to observe employees at work, such supervision cannot be said to interfere with an employee's right to privacy, even if it is done by a camera." However, this logic did not hold in a recent case involving a very well-known employer. During the night shift at Wal-Mart, a visible surveillance camera recorded four employees eating candy and nuts from damaged incoming boxes (which was against store policy). When Wal-Mart fired them for theft, the four employees sued the corporation, and won $5 million each. The employees received the money in part because of "slander" and "emotional distress," but more relevantly, because of Wal-Mart's eavesdropping. So sometimes employers can get into trouble for taking action based on what is seen on a surveillance camera—even if it is in plain sight.[21]

Hidden cameras may generally be placed in areas where employees do not have reasonable expectation of privacy, such as hallways. Installation of video cameras in bathrooms, however, may prompt claims of invasion of privacy. In cases in which a plant is unionized, the courts may consider the installation of a closed-circuit television monitoring system to be an issue that the firm must bargain over with the union because it changes working conditions.

DRUG TESTING

In the interests of safety, and also to have a more productive workforce, employers have been increasingly interested in using drug testing for employees. Employer interest in drug testing was also encouraged by Congress in 1988, when it passed the Drug-Free Workplace Act, which required employers that receive federal aid or do business of $25,000 or more with the federal government to develop an antidrug policy for employees, provide drug-free awareness programs for them, make them aware of assistance programs for those with drug problems, and warn them of penalties for violating the company's drug-free policies.

Employers, however, must be careful when establishing drug-testing policies, because employees may challenge such policies on grounds that they violate their state or federal constitutional rights, their common-law privacy rights, or state or

---

[21] "Wal-Mart Employees Win $20 Million After Being Fired for Eating Company Candy," **www.lawyersweekly.com.**

EXHIBIT 18-5

**ELECTRONIC MAIL POLICY
AND EMPLOYEE
ACKNOWLEDGMENT**

Source: Copyright 1997,
Robert B. Fitzpatrick,
Fitzpatrick & Associates,
reprinted from "Technology
Advances in the Information
Age: Effects on Workplace
Privacy Issues," SB ALI-ABA
261 (1997).

ELECTRONIC MAIL POLICY

* E-mail is the property of the company and should be used solely for work-related purposes.

* Employees are prohibited from sending messages that are harassing, intimidating, offensive, or discriminatory.

* Each employee will be given a password to access e-mail. Your password is personal and should not be shared with anyone else. However, the company retains a copy of all passwords and has a right to access e-mail at any time for any reason without notice to the employee. The employee has NO expectation of privacy or confidentiality in the e-mail system.

* The employee must sign and return an Acknowledgment and Consent form indicating receipt and acceptance of our company's policy.

ACKNOWLEDGMENT

I understand that the company's electronic mail and voice mail systems (herein together referred to as "the company's systems") are company property and are to be used for company business. I understand that [excessive] use of the company's systems for the conduct of personal business is strictly prohibited.

I understand that the company reserves the right to access, review, and disclose information obtained through the company's systems at any time, with or without advance notice to me and with or without my consent. I also understand that I am required to notify my supervisor and the company's Security Department if I become aware of any misuse of the company's systems.

I confirm that I have read this employee acknowledgment and have had an opportunity to ask questions about it. I also agree to abide by the terms of the company's policy in this regard a copy of which has been provided to me.

AGREED TO THIS _____ DAY OF _____ , 19_____ .

_____

Witness _____   Employee Signature _____

local drug-testing laws. Because of the variation among states regarding drug testing, employers must examine both the statutory and case law in their state very closely before implementing a drug-testing policy. With that caution in mind, however, some broad generalizations can be made.

Drug testing generally arises in four different contexts, and standards may be different for each. The most commonly occurring drug testing is preemployment testing. Most states allow preemployment drug testing. Sometimes a prospective employee will try to sue the employer for requiring preemployment drug testing, but as long as the drug tests do not violate discrimination laws, the tests are usually accepted. In one case, a man failed his preemployment drug test and sued the physicians because he thought that they must have made a mistake: The drug test came up positive, and he claimed that he had never taken any drugs. He did not win his case, however, because the physicians were hired by the employer, and not by the plaintiff; hence, they owed no duty to the plaintiff. Interestingly, however, in a case the following year in a different state, the state supreme court imposed liability on a drug-testing firm whose negligent testing as part of an employer's substance abuse testing program led to the plaintiff's termination.[22] The employer could not be sued because he or she is allowed to reject a prospective employee on any grounds, as long as he or she is not violating discrimination laws.[23]

Most states also recognize the legitimacy of drug testing as a part of a periodic physical, assuming that proper standards for drug testing are followed. The third context in which drug testing may be used is one in which the employer has a reasonable suspicion that an employee may be under the influence of drugs in the workplace. "Reasonable suspicion" generally requires the employer to have some evidence, such as an unexplainable drop in performance, to justify the tests. If the employer does have such sound evidence, the test is generally upheld. The most controversial area is that of random drug testing, on which the courts are split. Random drug testing is most likely to be upheld when an employee may pose a safety risk to others by doing a job while under the influence of drugs and when employees have been informed in advance in writing of the random drug-testing policy.

Private sector employers have much greater freedom to require drug testing than do employers in the public sector. Whereas private employers may be restricted only by state constitutions and state and local laws, federal entities are also restricted by the Constitution. The following case provides the Supreme Court's most recent response to a challenge to drug testing as a violation of individuals' Fourth Amendment right to be free from unreasonable searches.

CASE 18-4

Chandler v. Miller et al.
United States Supreme Court
117 SCt. 1295 (1997)

A Georgia statute requires candidates for designated state offices to certify that they have taken a urinalysis drug test within 30 days prior to qualifying for nomination or election and that the test result was negative. Plaintiff, Chandler, along with other Libertarian Party nominees for state offices, filed an action one month before the deadline for submission of the certificates, naming the governor (Miller) and state administrative officials as defendants. They asserted that the drug tests required by the law violated their rights under the First, Fourth, and Fourteenth Amendments to the United States Constitution.

---

[22] *Ney v. Axelrod*, 723 A 2d 719 (Sup. Ct. Pa 1999).

[23] *Duncan v. Afton, Inc.* (1999 WL 1073434, sup. C t. Wyo.)

Justice Ginsburg

The Fourth Amendment requires the government to respect "[t]he right of the people to be secure in their persons ... against unreasonable searches and seizures." This restraint on government conduct generally bars officials from undertaking a search or seizure absent individualized suspicion. Searches conducted without grounds for suspicion of particular individuals have been upheld, however, in "certain limited circumstances."

We confront in this case the question of whether [Georgia's] requirement ranks among the limited circumstances in which suspicionless searches are warranted. Relying on this Court's precedents sustaining drug-testing programs for student athletes, customs employees, and railway employees, the United States Court of Appeals for the Eleventh Circuit judged Georgia's law constitutional.

Georgia was the first, and apparently remains the only, state to condition candidacy for state office on a drug test.

It is settled law, the court accepted, that the drug tests required by the statute rank as searches. But, as was true of the drug-testing programs at issue in *Skinner* and *Von Raab*, the [circuit] court reasoned, Section 21-2-140 serves "special needs," interests other than the ordinary needs of law enforcement. The court therefore endeavored to "balance the individual's privacy expectations against the Government's interests to determine whether it [was] impractical to require a warrant or some level of individualized suspicion in the particular context." Examining the state interests involved, the court acknowledged the absence of any record of drug abuse by elected officials in Georgia. Nonetheless, the court observed, "[t]he people of Georgia place in the trust of their elected officials ... their liberty, their safety, their economic well-being, [and] ultimate responsibility for law enforcement." Consequently, "those vested with the highest executive authority to make public policy in general and frequently to supervise Georgia's drug interdiction efforts in particular must be persons appreciative of the perils of drug use." The court further noted that "[t]he nature of high public office in itself demands the highest levels of honesty, clear-sightedness, and clear-thinking."

Turning to petitioners' privacy interests, the Eleventh Circuit emphasized that the tests could be conducted in the office of the candidate's private physician, making the "intrusion here ... even less than that approved in *Von Raab*." Furthermore, the candidate would control release of the test results: Should the candidate test positive, he or she could forfeit the opportunity to run for office, and in that event, nothing would be divulged to law enforcement officials.

Another consideration, the court said, is the reality that "candidates for high office must expect the voters to demand some disclosures about their physical, emotional, and mental fitness for the position." Concluding that the State's interests outweighed the privacy intrusion caused by the required certification, the court held the statute, as applied to petitioners, not inconsistent with the Fourth and Fourteenth Amendments.

[W]e note, first, that the testing method the Georgia statute describes is relatively noninvasive; therefore, if the "special need" showing had been made, the State could not be faulted for excessive intrusion. The State permits a candidate to provide the urine specimen in the office of his or her private physician; and the results of the test are given first to the candidate, who controls further dissemination of the report.

Because the State has effectively limited the invasiveness of the testing procedure, we concentrate on the core issue: Is the certification requirement warranted by a special need? Our precedents establish that the proffered special need for drug testing must be substantial—important enough to override the individual's acknowledged privacy interest, sufficiently vital to suppress the Fourth Amendment's normal requirement of individualized suspicion. Georgia has failed to show a special need of that kind. Respondents' defense of the statute rests primarily on the incompatibility of unlawful drug use with holding high state office. The statute is justified, respondents contend, because the use of illegal drugs draws into question an official's judgment and integrity; jeopardizes the discharge of public functions, including antidrug law enforcement efforts; and undermines public confidence and trust in elected officials. The statute, according to respondents, serves to deter unlawful drug users from becoming candidates and thus stops them from attaining high state office. Notably lacking in respondents' presentation is any indication of a concrete danger demanding departure from the Fourth Amendment's main rule. Nothing in the record hints that the hazards respondents broadly describe are real and not simply hypothetical for Georgia's polity.

In contrast to the effective testing regimes upheld in [precedents, omitted] Georgia's certification requirement is not well designed to identify candidates who violate antidrug laws. Nor is the scheme a credible means to deter illicit drug users from seeking election to state office. The test date—to be scheduled by the candidate any time within 30 days prior to qualifying for a place on the ballot—is no secret. As counsel for respondents acknowledged at oral argument, users of illegal drugs, save for those prohibitively addicted, could abstain for a pretest period sufficient to avoid detection. Moreover, respondents have offered no reason why ordinary law enforcement methods would not suffice to apprehend such addicted individuals, should they appear in the limelight of a public stage.

What is left, after close review of Georgia's scheme, is the image the State seeks to project. By requiring candidates for public office to submit to drug testing, Georgia displays its commitment to the struggle against drug abuse. The suspicionless tests, according to respondents, signify that candidates, if elected, will be fit to serve their constituents free from the influence of illegal drugs. But Georgia asserts no evidence of a drug problem among the State's elected officials, those officials typically do not perform high-risk, safety-sensitive tasks, and the required certification immediately aids no interdiction effort. The need revealed, in short, is symbolic, not "special," as that term draws meaning from our case law.

The greatest dangers to liberty lurk in insidious encroachment by men of zeal, well-meaning but without understand-ing. However well-meant, the candidate drug test Georgia has devised diminishes personal privacy for a symbol's sake. The Fourth Amendment shields society against that state action.

Reversed in favor of Plaintiff, Chandler.

Critical Thinking About the Law

The primary objective in Case 18-4 was to determine whether the State of Georgia could require candidates for state offices to be tested for drugs before qualifying for election. However, a more abstract version of the same issue is the following: When may a public employer impinge on the privacy rights of a potential employee? The court provides an answer to the question, and your task as a critical thinker is to find the answer and evaluate its worth. The following critical thinking questions will help you complete that task.

1. If the State of Georgia could have demonstrated one element, it would have won its case. What is that element, and why would Georgia have won?

   Clue: This question requires you to identify the conclusion and reasons. If one element had been demonstrated by the state, the court would have come to a different conclusion.

2. The court uses a certain definition of *special need*. Do you think this definition is adequate?

   Clue: Go back to the definition of *special need* in the reasoning. Then reread the ambiguity section in the first chapter of this book. On the basis of what you know about ambiguity, make a judgment about the clarity of the definition.

OTHER TESTING

In recent years, the number of companies that use some form of preemployment testing has significantly increased. The time and costs of preemployment testing are offset in the long run because businesses are able to reduce turnover rates and low productivity by carefully screening applicants before they are offered a job. In addition, preemployment testing often saves businesses money by paring down the applicant pool efficiently and with some assurance that applicants are treated consistently.

Businesses, however, must be careful to ensure that their tests do not violate discrimination laws or the Americans with Disabilities Act. Tests should only measure what is necessary for the performance of a job. For example, a typing test that screens out those applicants who cannot use their hands is acceptable if the position is for a typist. However, tests should seek to accommodate those with disabilities if their disability does not impair the performance of a job.

Of the many forms of preemployment testing, polygraph testing has received the greatest amount of legal action. In 1988, Congress passed the Employee Polygraph Protection Act. This law prevents employers from using lie detector tests while screening job applicants. It also prohibits administering lie detector tests randomly, but it does allow their use in specific instances in which there has been an economic injury to the employer's business. The act also provides an exception to allow private security companies and those selling controlled substances to use lie detector testing of applicants and current employees. The Labor Department may seek fines of up to $10,000 against firms that violate the act.

Skills testing, such as a typing test or a professional exam, are widely used and generally legal so long as the tests examine necessary skills for the job. Much less used are aptitude tests that seek to evaluate the general abilities of an applicant. Aptitude tests often leave the employer open to discrimination lawsuits if the tests are not carefully written for specific information necessary to job performance.

Another type of test is a medical test. These are used when the applicant must be in good health to assure safety and good job performance. For example, airline pilots must undergo regular medical examinations to assure their health and the safety of their passengers.

Public sector employoees are granted an additional level of protection from discriminatory testing. Federal employees are protected under the Uniform Guidelines on Employee Selection Procedures of 1978. These procedures are evaluated and enforced by the the federal Equal Employment Opportunity Commission.

GLOBAL DIMENSIONS OF THE EMPLOYMENT RELATIONSHIP

Although some of the benefits described in this chapter may seem significant, laws in some other nations ensure much greater benefits for workers. One area in which other nations provide significantly greater benefits is parental leave. Workers in this country are guaranteed up to 12 weeks of unpaid leave; most European countries require a guaranteed paid leave. For example, in France, Austria, and Finland, paid parental leave begins six weeks before childbirth; it extends to ten weeks after birth in France, eight weeks in Austria, and almost one year in Finland. French working mothers are then entitled to an additional unpaid job-protected leave until their children reach age 3. Altogether, over 120 nations require paid maternity leave, with the Czech Republic providing 24 weeks of paid leave. One of the reasons why such extensive benefits can be offered in those nations, however, is that the tax-funded social insurance/social security systems provide most of the money for these benefits.

Another area in which employees have fewer rights in the United States is that of vacation time. The United States, unlike most European nations, does not mandate any minimum amount of annual vacation time for employees. But in Ireland, for example, the Holiday Act of 1973 guarantees every worker, regardless of how long he or she has been with a company, three weeks of paid vacation time and nine additional days off for public holidays. Luxembourg also has tremendous holiday benefits. Irrespective of the employee's age, he or she is given 25 days of holiday, 12 of which must be taken in succession. Additionally, Luxembourg workers are given time off for 10 public holidays.

Swedish law requires employees be given five weeks of vacation time. After five years of employment, the time is increased to ten weeks. Denmark also mandates no less than five weeks of paid vacation a year. Spanish law requires employers to grant no less than 30 days of holiday in addition to the country's 14 paid public ones. In contrast to these European countries, the United Kingdom, like the United States, has no laws requiring employers to give paid or even unpaid holidays.

To try to ensure that workers around the world receive the rights and benefits described in this chapter, the United Nations Commission on Human Rights developed the International Covenant on Economic, Social, and Cultural Rights. This covenant does not really bind any employers, but it gathers its strength by documenting and publicizing where its terms are not followed.

SUMMARY

The employment relationship today is still a contract between the employer and employee, but the national and state governments specify certain parameters of this relationship. Laws that affect wages and hours include the Davis–Bacon Act, the Fair Labor Standards Act, and the Federal Unemployment Tax Act.

The Family and Medical Leave Act ensures that workers will be able to take necessary time off from work when they or members of their family suffer from a serious medical condition. COBRA ensures that if an employee loses his or her job, he or she will be able to purchase health insurance for up to 18 months. The Occupational Safety and Health Act tries to secure safe working conditions for employees, but if they are injured on the job, workers' compensation laws provide benefits to compensate them for the injury or disability they received.

A final concern of workers and employers is the extent of worker privacy rights. Federal employees have more rights in this area than private employees, because the public employer has to comply with the Fourth Amendment, but private employers must still be sure they do not violate state and federal laws designed to protect worker privacy. The prudent employer today will have a written privacy policy that clearly sets out when employees should have a reasonable expectation of privacy and when they should not. When comparing other countries' employee benefits with those in the United States, one area where the United States offers less protection to employees is with respect to family leave benefits.

REVIEW QUESTIONS

18-1 What benefits do employees receive under the Fair Labor Standards Act?

18-2 Explain how workers' compensation laws benefit both employers and employees but in different ways.

18-3 What requirements are imposed on an employer by the Family and Medical Leave Act?

18-4 What remedies can an employee seek if an employer violates the Family and Medical Leave Act?

18-5 Explain the relationship between OSHA and NIOSH.

18-6 Explain the principles you would want to keep in mind when drafting an employee privacy policy for a firm.

REVIEW PROBLEMS

18-7 In early December, Decco Manufacturing Corporation underwent a major downsizing and laid off 40 percent of its employees. Robert Banks was not laid off, but he thought that he probably would be laid off in the near future unless business got dramatically better. In fact, his supervisor told him that he would probably be laid off in early January. Robert decided that if he was going to get laid off anyway, he would rather have the time between jobs over the holidays, so he quit and filed for unemployment compensation. Should he be able to collect workers' compensation?

18-8 Karen Jenner was a teacher at Northwood Junior High. Every year, to raise money for charity, the school sponsored a faculty–student basketball game. Teachers were required to participate in the event in some manner, either by playing on the team, selling tickets, or working at the concession stand. Karen chose to play on the team and was injured when she collided with another player during the game. She filed a claim for workers' compensation, which her employer contested. Explain why you believe her claim is either valid or invalid.

18-9 Nellie Mandle worked as a machine operator. She had been told on numerous occasions that if her press ever jammed up, she was not to stick her hand in to unjam it, but rather, she was to use a special safety fork with a long handle that would allow her to unjam the machine without inserting any part of her hand into the press. Her machine jammed, and she looked around for the safety fork. Realizing that the worker on the previous shift must have removed the fork, she reached her hand inside the machine to unjam it. Before she could remove her hand, the machine cycled, catching her hand and injuring it severely. She filed a workers' compensation claim, which her employer contested because she caused the injury by her disobedience of the safety rules. Evaluate the employer's argument.

18-10 Caroline Williams works for a firm that has a written policy that prohibits the use of company telephones for personal use. Employees have been told that the company randomly monitors telephone conversations to enforce this policy. Caroline uses a company telephone to call her doctor to find out the results of a blood test she had taken to determine whether she had contracted a sexually transmitted disease. Her employer intercepted the phone call and, once he heard her question, he stayed on the line to find out the results of her test. Discuss why you believe the employer's behavior is lawful or unlawful. If unlawful, what penalty should he receive?

18-11 Michael Meuter was an employee in a hospital emergency room. He used an extension phone to call one of the workers in the pharmacy to order some drugs for the emergency room. After placing his request, he started to complain to the pharmacy worker about his supervisor, calling him a number of offensive names. Unknown to Michael, his supervisor was listening to the conversation. Was the supervisor's listening to the conversation lawful?

18-12 Ginny Morris applied for a job as an executive assistant to the president of a software firm. She received high evaluations from those on the hiring committee and was told that she looked like an excellent candidate for the job, but before a final decision could be made, she would have to take a drug test so that the firm could be confident that she did not use any illegal drugs and a lie detector test to ensure that she would be someone who could be entrusted with trade secrets. Discuss whether you believe there are any problems with the firm's requests.

CASE PROBLEMS

18-13 Mary Guess worked for Sharp Manufacturing Company of America ("Sharp") as an assembly-line worker. On November 6, 1998, one of Guess's coworkers lacerated his hand, which resulted in some of the coworker's blood getting on Guess's hand. Although there was no penetrating injury to Guess, she testified that she had open cuts on her hands as well as a fresh manicure.

Guess testified that as a result of getting this blood on her hands, she was "out of control," "nervous," "screaming for help," "upset," "shaking," and "hysterical." She explained that she believed the blood that she got on her hands to be HIV positive. Her subjective conclusion that her coworker had AIDS was based on the following: The coworker was sick all the time; he had been isolated in the work environment; he had friends at work who had died of AIDS; he appeared very frail; he was on the mailing list of a gay rights organization; and he "looked and acted gay."

Guess was diagnosed with Post-Traumatic Stress Disorder (PTSD) caused by the "work related injury of November 1998." Guess's doctors testified that her psy-chological condition was caused by her fear of being exposed to HIV-positive blood.

Dr. Michael Gelfand, an infectious disease specialist, testified that Guess had been tested five times for HIV and all five tests were negative. Dr. Gelfand testified that Guess's chance of becoming infected was infinitely small by virtue of the unknown status of the source and the mechanism of claimed contact.

Guess filed a workers' compensation claim seeking relief based on a chronic mental disorder that arose after she came into contact with the blood of a coworker, whom she believed to be HIV positive. The chancery court for Shelby County found that Guess had suffered a vocational disability as a result of the psychological consequences of the event and awarded benefits. Sharp appealed claiming the evidence did not prove that Guess had suffered a compensable injury under workers' compensation. How did the appellate court rule? Why? *Guess v. Sharp Manufacturing Co. of America*, 114 S.W.3d 480 (2003)

18-14 Leah Meadows worked at Dollar General as an assistant manager. On May 29, 2001, she was operating the cash register when Bill Bewley, a customer with whom Meadows had been briefly acquainted, approached her to ring up a sale of motor and transmission oil. Bewley questioned Meadows about a third party and then verbally assaulted her. After Meadows had rung up the sale, Bewley threw the bag containing the oil at her, striking her in the right eye. Meadows did not immediately notice any problems with her vision but gradually began to realize that she could not see out of her right eye. She was diagnosed with a detached retina and underwent surgery on June 12, 2001.

Prior to the assault, Meadows's uncorrected vision in her right eye was 20/200 and she wore contact lenses in both eyes. After the surgery, her uncorrected vision remained 20/200. Meadows's physician, John W. Ellis, M.D., opined that, as a result of the accident, Meadows suffered 36 percent permanent partial disability to the right eye, over and above any prior impairment. Meadows filed for workers' compensation. Dollar General challenged

Meadows's claim for workers' compensation. The trial court found in Meadows's favor and Dollar General appealed, claiming the injuries Meadows suffered were not related to work. How do you believe the appellate court ruled? What reasons do you think the court used to justify its decision? *Dollar General Corp. v. Meadows*, 2003 OK CIV APP 13 (2002)

18-15 Margaret Russell worked at a hospital as a patient accounts adjustment representative. By mid-January 2000, Russell had been disciplined three times for unscheduled absences. Under the hospital's progressive disciplinary system, Russell was suspended for three days without pay after her third transgression and risked termination if her absenteeism continued.

On May 31, 2000, Russell slipped and fell at work. She was diagnosed with a fractured right elbow and a sprained ankle, which she later learned was actually fractured. When Russell fell, she also aggravated an existing wrist condition for which she had been receiving treatment before she fell. The physician told Russell that she could return to work but restricted the use of her right arm.

Throughout the course of the next 10 days, Russell worked a number of partial days, complaining of pain related to the injuries she suffered when she slipped and fell. Due to her pain, she left work early or did not show up at all for a number of days. Russell received treatment during this time from several different doctors.

On Monday, June 13, Russell was fired for her excessive absenteeism. Thereafter, Russell filed a lawsuit claiming that the hospital had retaliated against her for exercising a protected FMLA right. The protected right she claims is the right to be absent from work during the period between May 31 and June 9, 2000, for a seri-ous health condition. Was Russell successful in her FMLA claim? Why or why not? *Russell v. North Broward Hospital*, 346 F.3d 1335 (2003)

18-16 Mr. and Mrs. Lewis worked for Holsum. Holsum's company rule D-1 states that written reprimands will be issued for "[f]ailure to notify authorized company personnel not less than one (1) hour before scheduled reporting time when unable to report for duty." After the third offense, company rule D-1 calls for the discharge of the employee. Holsum's attendance policy provides: "If given a return-to-work date by the doctor, report this date when you call in. If you actually return on this date, no other phone call is required. If no date is given, or the date is changed by the doctor, you must call in advance every day you are scheduled."

On December 17, Mrs. Lewis suffered an asthma attack at work. She checked into a hospital and remained there for four days, through the evening of December 21. Her treating physician wrote Lewis an off-work slip dated December 18. The off-work slip stated that Lewis "is currently hospitalized" at St. Joseph Medical Center. It did not indicate when Mrs. Lewis could return to work. Mr. Lewis delivered the off-work slip to Holsum. Although Mrs. Lewis was scheduled to work on December 19, she did not appear and Holsum designated the day as time off for FMLA leave.

From December 21 through December 28, Mrs. Lewis and her husband both had scheduled to take time off from work using their vacation time. Holsum scheduled Mrs. Lewis to return to work on December 29; she was also scheduled to work on December 31 and January 2 of that same week. Mrs. Lewis, however, did not return to work on December 29, nor did she show up for work on December 31 or January 2. Furthermore, Mrs. Lewis did not call into work on any of these days to inform Holsum of her need to be absent. Mrs. Lewis admitted that throughout the relevant time period, she had access to a telephone. Nor did her husband, who worked on those days, give notice to anyone that Mrs. Lewis would not be in.

Because Mrs. Lewis failed to call in or show up for work on three consecutive days that she was scheduled to work, she was terminated on January 2, 1998, consistent with Holsum's company rules, its attendance policy, and a Holsum–Union Labor Agreement. Mrs. Lewis had a follow-up appointment with her doctor that same day. The doctor gave her an off-work slip dated December 17 through January 8, indicating that she could return to work on January 8. Her husband delivered the slip to Holsum on January 2, but her manager did not receive the slip until the next day.

Mrs. Lewis sued, claiming that her termination violated the FMLA. The lower court granted summary judgment in favor of Holsum, which Mrs Lewis appealed. What do you think the outcome of the appeal was? Why? *Rebecca Lewis v. Holsum of Fort Wayne, Inc.*, 278 F3d 706 (7th Cir. 2002)

18-17 Pillsbury Company provided an e-mail system for its employees so they could communicate with one another. Employees were told that their e-mail was confidential and would not be used against them. Smyth, a Pillsbury employee, wrote an e-mail message to his supervisor in which he criticized sales management at the firm and threatened to "kill the backstabbing bastards." When other members of the management team intercepted his e-mail message, Smyth was fired for transmitting inappropriate and unprofessional comments. Smyth believed that his termination violated his

privacy rights. Do you think the court agreed with Smyth? Why or why not? *Smyth v. Pillsbury Co.*, 914 F. Supp. 97 (1996)

18-18 The Customs Service instituted a drug-testing program that analyzed urine specimens of employees who applied for promotion to positions involving interdiction of illegal drugs, requiring them to carry firearms or handle classified materials. The employee union challenged the program as unconstitutional because there was no history of drug abuse problems among Customs Service employees. The U.S. district court upheld the drug-testing program. Explain how you believe the U.S. Supreme Court ruled on appeal and why it reached that conclusion. *Service Employees, National Treasury Employees Union, et al., Petitioners v. William Von Raab, Commissioner, United States Customs Service*, 489 U.S. 660 (1989)

ASSIGNMENT ON THE INTERNET

Laws that govern employment relationships indicate the ethical norms a particular country or state wishes to advance. This can be seen no more clearly than in cases of family or medical leave. Visit the Web site for the Clearing House in International Development in Child, Youth, and Family Policies (www.childpolicyintl.org) and compare the family and medical leave policies of the United States

with other industrialized countries around the world. Write a paper in which you address the following questions: How does the United States compare on a world scale when it comes to employee benefits for family leave? What does this comparison say about the ethical norms of the United States in areas of employment relationships?

 ## ON THE INTERNET

www.benefitslink.com/index.html BenefitsLink is a site that provides information about employee benefits, including articles about employee benefits, the full texts of new regulations, and links to other related sites.
www.dol.gov At this site, the home page of the Department of Labor, you can find all the information you would need as an employer to make sure that you are in compliance with the Fair Labor Standards Act.
www.osha-slc.gov The Web page of the Occupational Safety and Health Administration provides information about worker health and safety, including how to file a complaint. It also provides the text of the Occupational Safety and Health Act of 1970, as well as OSHA standards, regulations, and directives.
www.hr.ucdavis.edu/Pubs/All/Fmla_booklet This site contains a document entitled "Family and Medical Leave … What Every Supervisor Should Know," which provides a good overview of the FMLA and illustrates its implementation by a public employer.
www.unhchr.ch/html/menu3/b/a_cescr.htm At this page, you can find the International Covenant on Economic, Social, and Cultural Rights.
www.privacyfoundation.org To learn more about privacy issues related to employment, go to this site.
www.opm.gov/oca/leave/HTML/fmlafac2.asp This is the Web site of the federal government's Office of Personnel Management. Here you can find information about the Family and Medical Leave Act.
www.privacyrights.org The Privacy Rights Clearinghouse is an organization dedicated to protecting privacy in areas that include places of employment. Visit this site to read about workplace privacy.

19

LAWS GOVERNING LABOR–MANAGEMENT RELATIONS

- **STRUCTURE OF THE PRIMARY U.S. LABOR LEGISLATION AND THE MECHANISMS FOR ITS ENFORCEMENT**
- **LABOR ORGANIZING**
- **THE COLLECTIVE BARGAINING PROCESS**
- **STRIKES, PICKETING, AND BOYCOTTS**
- **GLOBAL DIMENSIONS OF LABOR–MANAGEMENT RELATIONS**

I n the early 1800s, labor unions were very rare. Despite the mistreatment of workers by management during the Industrial Revolution, most attempts to organize employees throughout the nineteenth and early twentieth centuries were treated by the courts as criminal conspiracies. Finally, in the midst of the economic chaos of the Great Depression, Congress enacted laws giving employees the right to organize and to bargain collectively over wages and terms and conditions of employment.

Union strength has fluctuated in the years since unions were legalized. Over a third of U.S. workers were organized in the post–World War II period. By 1983, however, only 20.1 percent of workers were unionized, and, by 2003, the percentage had fallen to 12.9 percent, or 15.8 million workers. Moreover, in 2003, the median weekly earnings of workers who were union members were $760, compared with $599 per week for nonunion workers.[1] Not all occupations are equally organized. Exhibit 19-1 shows the percentages of workers organized by occupational group in 2000.

---

[1] www.bls.gov/news.release/union2.nr0.htm.

EXHIBIT 19-1

HERE PERCENTAGE OF EMPLOYED UNION–REPRESENTED WAGE AND SALARY WORKERS, BY OCCUPATION, 2000

Source: Adapted from www.bls.gov/news.release/union2.nr0.htm.

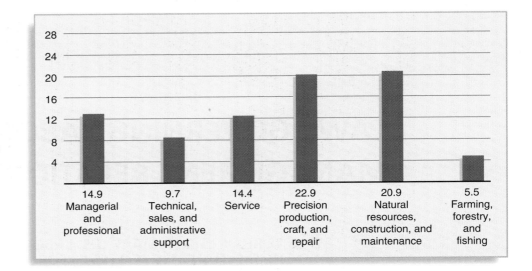

| 14.9 Managerial and professional | 9.7 Technical, sales, and administrative support | 14.4 Service | 22.9 Precision production, craft, and repair | 20.9 Natural resources, construction, and maintenance | 5.5 Farming, forestry, and fishing |

Although organized workers are still not in as powerful a position as their employers, they are distinctly better off than they were during most of our nation's existence. The primary basis for their improved status is the National Labor Relations Act (NLRA), which was passed in 1935. The NLRA is the focus of this chapter.

The first section briefly outlines the structure and enforcement of the NLRA and the Landrum-Griffin Act, the primary pieces of operative labor

Critical Thinking About the Law

Many people hold strong feelings about unions. Workers who belong to unions often view unions as positive forces that work to their benefit. On the other hand, employers are often suspicious of the activity of unions. As you consider the aspects of labor law in this chapter, be aware of the role of biases in complex legal issues. The following critical thinking questions will help you consider the role of biases and ethical norms in labor legislation.

1. In the language of ethical norms, what function do unions serve for workers?

    Clue: Remember the list of ethical norms and reread the beginning paragraphs of this chapter. How do labor unions help workers? Can you match this answer to an ethical norm?

2. What role do you think personal ethical norms should play in thinking about labor legislation?

    Clue: Could paying attention to these ethical norms benefit the workers or employers in any manner?

3. Your coworkers have been excitedly talking for days about plans to unionize. You are unsure if you will join the union. One of your coworkers argues that joining the union will help you get a raise. What questions do you have for your coworker about missing information?

    Clue: Think about any possible costs associated with getting a raise.

TABLE 19-1 THE TWO FACES OF UNIONS

Collective Face	Monopoly Face
Unions primarily provide a collective voice through which workers can express their job-related concerns.	Unions are institutions that primarily serve to raise wages above competitive levels.
Unions increase efficiency because unionized firms have lower employee turnover rates so the employer spends less money and time training new employees.	Unions decrease efficiency by securing unmerited wage increases for their workers, thereby causing a misallocation of resources.
Because unions usually negotiate contracts that base wage increases primarily on seniority, older workers are more likely to help newer ones and a more cooperative workplace will exist, thereby increasing efficiency.	Unions decrease efficiency by causing strikes that result in lost production and obtaining special contract provisions that reduce productivity.
Unions decrease inequality of wage distribution within the firm because they will try to raise the wages of the below-average workers up to those of the average; for solidarity purposes, they have to try to make the wages of those in the bargaining unit more equal.	Unions increase the existing inequality of wage distribution by providing higher wages for unionized workers at the expense of nonunionized workers.
Unions are democratic institutions, representing the interests of workers in general in the political process.	Unions gain their power through coercion and the threat of physical violence and use that power to lobby for legislation to restrict competition in their respective industries.

Source: Adapted from R. B. Freeman and J. L. Medoff, *What Do Unions Do?* (New York: Basic Books, 1994).

legislation. The next three sections discuss specific areas of labor–management relations governed by the NLRA: organizing, collective bargaining, and the collective activities of striking, picketing, and boycotting. The chapter concludes with a consideration of the international dimensions of labor law.

Before you start to read about our system of labor laws, take a few minutes to examine Table 19-1, which summarizes the two conflicting views of the role of unions in economics and society. Whether one thinks labor laws should strengthen or restrain labor organizations depends largely on which of the two "faces" of unions one thinks is "prettier."

STRUCTURE OF THE PRIMARY U.S. LABOR LEGISLATION AND THE MECHANISMS FOR ITS ENFORCEMENT

Three major pieces of legislation govern labor–management relations in the United States today: the Wagner Act of 1935, the Taft–Hartley Act of 1947, and the Landrum–Griffith Act of 1959 (the last is cited also as the Labor–Management Reporting and Disclosure Act, or LMRDA). The Taft–Hartley Act amended the Wagner Act, so they are jointly referred to as the National Labor Relations Act (NLRA). In this section, we briefly describe the primary features of each of these acts and discuss those situations in which the business manager is most likely to need an understanding of these laws.

THE WAGNER ACT OF 1935

The **Wagner Act** (cited also as the **NLRA**) was the first major piece of federal legislation adopted explicitly to encourage the formation of labor unions. Many supporters of this act recognized that a number of labor problems were caused by gross inequality of bargaining power between employers and employees. They hoped that the Wagner Act would bring about industrial peace and raise the standard of living of U.S. workers. The act was to accomplish those goals by facilitating the formation of labor unions as a powerful collective voice for employees and by providing for **collective bargaining** between employers and unions as a means of obtaining the peaceful settlement of labor disputes. The key section of the Wagner Act is Section 7. This section provides:

> *Employees shall have the right to self-organization, to join, form or assist labor organizations, to bargain collectively through representatives of their own choosing, and to engage in concerted activities for the purpose of collective bargaining or other mutual aid and protection.*

Employees' Section 7 rights are protected through Section 8(a) of the act, which prohibits specific "employer unfair labor practices." These practices are delineated in Table 19-2. Section 9 of the act sets forth the procedures, including the secret ballot election, by which the exclusive employee-bargaining-unit representative (union) is to be chosen.

The final important provision of the Wagner Act authorized an administrative agency, the **National Labor Relations Board (NLRB)**, to interpret and enforce the act. It also provided for judicial review in designated federal courts of appeal.

THE TAFT–HARTLEY ACT OF 1947

The passage of the Wagner Act led to a growth in unionization and an increase in workers' power. Given that they had almost no power before, any power workers obtained was bound to look like a dramatic increase. Thus, the public's perception of union power may have been greater than the actual power of unions. At any rate, this perception led to the passage of the **Taft–Hartley Act**, which was designed to curtail the powers the unions had apparently acquired under the Wagner Act.

Section 8(b) of the Taft–Hartley Act, titled Union Unfair Labor Practices, bars unions from engaging in certain specified activities (see Table 19-3). The act also (1) amended Section 7 of the Wagner Act to include the right of employees

TABLE 19-2

**EMPLOYER UNFAIR LABOR
PRACTICES**

Section	Prohibited Practice
8(a)1	Interference with employees' Section 7 rights.
8(a)2	Employer-dominated unions.
8(a)3	Discrimination by employers in hiring, firing, and other employment matters because of union activity.
8(a)4	Retaliation against an employee who testifies or makes charges before the National Labor Relations Board.
8(a)5	Failure to engage in good-faith collective bargaining with duly certified unions.

Section	Prohibited Practice
8(b)1	Restraining or coercing employees' exercise of their Section 7 rights.
8(b)2	Forcing the employer to discriminate against employees on the basis of union or antiunion activity.
8(b)3	Failing to engage in good-faith collective bargaining with the employer.
8(b)4	Striking, picketing, and engaging in secondary boycotts for illegal purposes.
8(b)5	Charging excessive union dues or initiation fees in a union shop.
8(b)6	Featherbedding (charging employers for services not performed).
8(b)7	Picketing for recognition or to force collective bargaining under certain circumstances.

TABLE 19-3

UNION UNFAIR LABOR PRACTICES

to refrain from engaging in collective activity, (2) made collective bargaining agreements enforceable in federal district courts, and (3) provided a civil damages remedy for parties injured by certain prohibited union activities.

THE LANDRUM–GRIFFITH ACT OF 1959

The final major piece of labor legislation is the **Landrum–Griffith Act**, which primarily governs the internal operations of labor unions. This act's passage was prompted by congressional hearings that uncovered evidence of looting of union treasuries by some powerful union officials and of corrupt, undemocratic practices in some labor unions. The act requires certain financial disclosures by unions and establishes civil and criminal penalties for financial abuses by union officials. It also includes a section, known as "labor's bill of rights," that gives employees protection against their own unions. The rights established by the Landrum–Griffith Act are summarized in Table 19-4.

Landrum–Griffith Act
Governs the internal operation of labor unions.

Section	Right
101(A)1	*Equal Rights.* Every union member has an equal right to nominate candidates, to vote in elections, and to attend and fully participate in membership meetings, subject to the organization's reasonable constitution and bylaws.
101(A)2	*Freedom of Speech and Assembly.* Members have the right to meet freely with one another at any time and to express any views about the labor organization, candidates for office, or business affairs at organization meetings, subject to reasonable rules pertinent to conduct of meetings.
101(A)3	*Dues, Initiation Fees, and Assessments.* Increases in local union dues, initiation fees, or assessments must be voted on by a majority of the members through secret ballot.
101(A)4	*Protection of Right to Sue.* Labor organizations cannot prohibit members from bringing any legal actions, including those against the organization. Organizations may require that members first exhaust reasonable hearing procedures established by the organization.
101(A)5	*Safeguards Against Improper Discipline.* No member may be fined or otherwise disciplined except for nonpayment of dues without being (1) served with written notice of specific charges, (2) given a reasonable time to prepare a defense, and (3) afforded a full and fair hearing.

TABLE 19-4

EMPLOYEE RIGHTS UNDER THE LANDRUM–GRIFFITH ACT

THE NATIONAL LABOR RELATIONS BOARD (NLRB)

Structure. The National Labor Relations Board (NLRB), as we stated earlier, is the administrative agency responsible for the interpretation and enforcement of the National Labor Relations Act. Its structure is diagrammed in Exhibit 19-2. The NLRB's three primary functions are:

1. Monitoring the conduct of the employer and the union during an election to determine whether workers want to be represented by a union.

2. Preventing and remedying unfair labor practices by employers or unions.

3. Establishing rules and regulations interpreting the act.

The NLRB is composed of five members, each appointed by the president with the advice and consent of the Senate. Members serve staggered five-year terms. The board meets in Washington, D.C. Three-member panels decide routine cases involving disputes between employees, union, and employer, but the entire board may hear significant cases.

The general counsel of the NLRB, also appointed by the president with the advice and consent of the Senate, fulfills the role of a prosecutor in unfair labor practice cases by overseeing the investigation and prosecution of unfair practice charges before the board. If a board decision is subsequently challenged in court, it is the general counsel who represents the board before the appellate court.

Obviously, there are far too many cases for the board and general counsel to handle each one personally. Instead, most cases are handled by 34 regional offices, located in major cities across the country. These regional offices are headed by a regional director, appointed and overseen by the general counsel.

EXHIBIT 19-2

THE NATIONAL LABOR RELATIONS BOARD

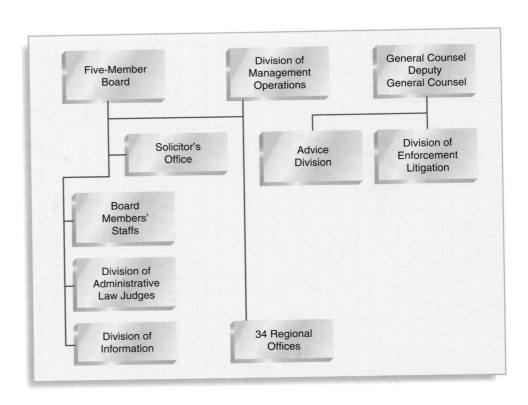

The regional director and his or her staff are directly responsible for investigating charges of unfair labor practices, which they prosecute before administrative law judges (ALJs). They are also responsible for conducting representation elections, in which employees of a firm decide whether they wish to be represented by a union.

Jurisdiction. Just as a civil court must have jurisdiction over the parties before it, the NLRB must have jurisdiction over the parties before it in both representation and unfair labor practice cases. The basis for NLRB jurisdiction is found in the NLRA, under which Congress granted jurisdiction to the NLRB over any business "affecting commerce," with certain specific exceptions. Any employer or employee not covered by the NLRA need not abide by its provisions. (Noncovered employees and employers, however, may be covered by state labor laws.) Employees specifically omitted from NLRA coverage are those who work in federal, state, and local government; employees in the transportation industry and those covered by the Railway Labor Act; independent contractors; agricultural workers; household domestics; and persons employed by a spouse or parent.

Also excluded from NLRB jurisdiction are supervisors and managerial employees and confidential employees. Much litigation has arisen over disputed definitions of *managerial employee* and *supervisor*. One of the employee groups that is facing the greatest difficulty today over the issue of whether or not they are supervisors is nurses. Thus far, the NLRB and the courts have been carefully examining the duties of the nurses in each individual case, with the nurse's eligibility depending on the circumstances. It was thought for a while that the NLRB had finally come up with a workable test for what constituted "independent judgment," which characterizes an employee as a supervisor. The board had said that employees do not exercise "independent judgment" when they exercise "ordinary professional or technical judgment in directing less skilled employees to deliver services in accordance with employer-specified standards." However, the United States Supreme Court rejected that test in the following case.

Even though the Court does not suggest what the test to determine "independent judgment" should be, many commentators believe this decision may make it harder for health care personnel to organize. Others feel that it will also affect organizing of computer programmers, pharmacists, lawyers, and other professionals.

CASE 19-1

National Labor Relations Board v. Kentucky River Community Care, Inc. et al.
Supreme Court of the United States ,
121 S.Ct. 1861 (2001)

Defendant-respondent Kentucky River Community Care, Inc., operated a residential care facility named Caney Creek for people with mental retardation and mental illness. The facility employed approximately 110 professional and nonprofessional employees, in addition to roughly a dozen concededly managerial or supervisory employees. In 1997, the Kentucky State District Council of Carpenters petitioned the National Labor Relations Board to represent a single unit of all 110 potentially eligible employees at Caney Creek.

At the ensuing representation hearing, the defendant-respondent objected to the inclusion of the facility's six registered nurses in the bargaining unit, arguing that they were "supervisors" and, therefore, excluded from the class of "employees" subject to the act's protection and includable in the bargaining unit.

At the representation hearing, the board's regional director included the nurses in the unit. When the defendant-respondent refused to bargain with the union, the board's general counsel filed an unfair labor practice complaint. The board granted the general counsel summary judgment on the basis of the representation determination, but the Sixth Circuit refused to enforce the board's order. It rejected the board's interpretation of "independent judgment," explaining that the board had erred by classifying "the practice of a nurse supervising a nurse's aide in administering patient care" as "'routine' [simply] because the nurses have the ability to direct patient care by virtue of their training and expertise, not because of their connection with 'management'."

Justice Scalia

The Act expressly defines the term "supervisor" in Section 2(11), which provides:

> The term "supervisor" means any individual having authority, in the interest of the employer, to hire, transfer, suspend, lay off, recall, promote, discharge, assign, reward, or discipline other employees, or responsibly to direct them, or to adjust their grievances, or effectively to recommend such action, if in connection with the foregoing the exercise of such authority is not of a merely routine or clerical nature, but requires the use of independent judgment.

The text of Section 2(11) of the Act that we quoted above, sets forth a three-part test for determining supervisory status. Employees are statutory supervisors if (1) they hold the authority to engage in any 1 of the 12 listed supervisory functions, (2) their "exercise of such authority is not of a merely routine or clerical nature, but requires the use of independent judgment," and (3) their authority is held "in the interest of the employer." The only basis asserted by the Board, before the Court of Appeals and here, for rejecting respondent's proof of supervisory status with respect to directing patient care was the Board's interpretation of the second part of the test—to wit, that employees do not use "independent judgment" when they exercise "ordinary professional or technical judgment in directing less-skilled employees to deliver services in accordance with employer-specified standards." The Court of Appeals rejected that interpretation, and so do we.

Two aspects of the Board's interpretation are reasonable, and hence controlling on this Court. First, it is certainly true that the statutory term "independent judgment" is ambiguous with respect to the degree of discretion required for supervisory status. Many nominally supervi-

sory functions may be performed without the "exercis[e of] such a degree of … judgment or discretion … as would warrant a finding" of supervisory status under the Act. It falls clearly within the Board's discretion to determine, within reason, what scope of discretion qualifies.

Second, as reflected in the Board's phrase "in accordance with employer-specified standards," it is also undoubtedly true that the degree of judgment that might ordinarily be required to conduct a particular task may be reduced below the statutory threshold by detailed orders and regulations issued by the employer. So, for example, in *Chevron Shipping Co.* … the Board concluded that "although the contested licensed officers are imbued with a great deal of responsibility, their use of independent judgment and discretion is circumscribed by the master's standing orders, and the Operating Regulations, which require the watch officer to contact a superior officer when anything unusual occurs or when problems occur."

The Board, however, argues further that the judgment even of employees who are permitted by their employer to exercise a sufficient degree of discretion is not "independent judgment" if it is a particular kind of judgment, namely, "ordinary professional or technical judgment in directing less-skilled employees to deliver services." The first five words of this interpretation insert a startling categorical exclusion into statutory text that does not suggest its existence. The text, by focusing on the "clerical" or "routine" (as opposed to "independent") nature of the judgment, introduces the question of degree of judgment that we have agreed falls within the reasonable discretion of the Board to resolve. But the Board's categorical exclusion turns on factors that have nothing to do with the degree of discretion an employee exercises. … Let the judgment be significant and only loosely constrained by the employer; if it is "professional or technical" it will nonetheless not be independent. The breadth of this exclusion is made all the more startling by virtue of the Board's extension of it to judgment based on greater "experience" as well as formal training? … What supervisory judgment worth exercising, one must wonder, does not rest on "professional or technical skill or experience"? If the Board applied this aspect of its test to every exercise of a supervisory function, it would virtually eliminate "supervisors" from the Act.

As it happens, though, only one class of supervisors would be eliminated in practice, because the Board limits its categorical exclusion with a qualifier: Only professional judgment that is applied "in directing less-skilled employees to deliver services" is excluded from the statutory category of "independent judgment." This second rule is no less striking than the first, and is directly contrary to the text of the statute. Every supervisory function listed by the Act is accompanied by the statutory requirement that its exercise "requir[e] the use of independent judgment" before supervisory status will obtain, but the Board would apply its restriction upon "independent judgment" to just 1 of the 12 listed functions: "responsibly to direct." There is no apparent textual justification for this asymmetrical limitation, and the Board has offered none. Surely no conceptual justification can be found in the proposition that supervisors exercise professional, technical, or experienced judgment only when they direct other employees. Decisions "to hire, ... suspend, lay off, recall, promote, discharge, ... or discipline" other employees, ibid., must often depend upon that same judgment, which enables assessment of the employee's proficiency in performing his job. ... Yet in no opinion that we were able to discover has the Board held that a supervisor's judgment in hiring, disciplining, or promoting another employee ceased to be "independent judgment" because it depended upon the supervisor's professional or technical training or experience. When an employee exercises one of these functions with judgment that possesses a sufficient degree of independence, the Board invariably finds supervisory status.

The Board's refusal to apply its limiting interpretation of "independent judgment" to any supervisory function other than responsibly directing other employees is particularly troubling because just seven years ago we rejected the Board's interpretation of part three of the supervisory test that similarly was applied only to the same supervisory function. ... In *Health Care*, the Board argued that nurses did not exercise their author-

ity "in the interest of the employer," as Section 152(11) requires, when their "independent judgment [was] exercised incidental to professional or technical judgment" instead of for "disciplinary or other matters, i.e., in addition to treatment of patients." It did not escape our notice that the target of this analysis was the supervisory function of responsible direction.

"Under Section 2(11)," we noted, "an employee who in the course of employment uses independent judgment to engage in 1 of the 12 listed activities, including responsible direction of other employees, is a supervisor. Under the Board's test, however, a nurse who in the course of employment uses independent judgment to engage in responsible direction of other employees is not a supervisor. We therefore rejected the Board's analysis as "inconsistent with ... the statutory language," because it "rea[d] the responsible direction portion of Section 2(11) out of the statute in nurse cases." ... It is impossible to avoid the conclusion that the Board's interpretation of "independent judgment," applied to nurses for the first time after our decision in *Health Care*, has precisely the same object. This interpretation of "independent judgment" is no less strained than the interpretation of "in the interest of the employer" that it has succeeded.

Affirmed in favor of Defendant, Kentucky River Community Care.

Critical Thinking About the Law

The rules of law provide a starting point from which judges try to make the appropriate ruling in a particular case. The Court's first step, therefore, in making a ruling is often to decide which laws and case precedents are applicable to the issue in dispute. Then judges must decide how to apply the relevant laws and previous Court decisions to the facts of the case. In Case 19-1, the Court examined the relevant portion of a section in the NLRA. Most of the Court's opinion addressed the way that the act should apply to the facts of the case. Specifically, the Court questioned whether nurses were covered by the NLRB or whether nurses were considered supervisors who were outside the NLRB's jurisdiction. The following questions urge you to pay close attention to the Court's reasoning for favoring one interpretation of the act over another.

1. The primary point of contention in Case 19-1 involved ambiguity in several phrases of the act. Identify these ambiguous phrases.

   Clue: Look at the Court's discussion of the board's three-part test for determining supervisory status.

2. Why did the Court prefer its interpretation of the ambiguous phrases over the NLRB's interpretation?

   Clue: Consider the reasons the Court provides for interpreting the ambiguous phrases less broadly, unlike the board's interpretation that consequently excluded more employees from supervisory status.

Just because Congress has granted the NLRB the authority to act in a given case does not mean that the board will act. The board does not have unlimited funds. Consequently, the NLRB has established its own set of guidelines, which it uses to determine whether it will exercise jurisdiction over an employer. These guidelines are basically designed to determine whether a firm does a significant amount of business and, thus, has enough employees to justify the expenditure of NLRB resources; they are established industry by industry (e.g., a transit system must have a total annual business volume of at least $250,000). The employer must supply the figures the board needs to determine whether it should assert jurisdiction.

Procedures in Representation Cases. An important function of the NLRB and the general counsel is to ensure that employees will be uncoerced in their choice of a bargaining representative or in choosing not to be represented by a union. Under NLRB procedures, set out in Exhibit 19-3, a petition for a representation election is initially filed with the regional director (1) by the

EXHIBIT 19-3

STEPS IN A REPRESENTATION PROCEEDING

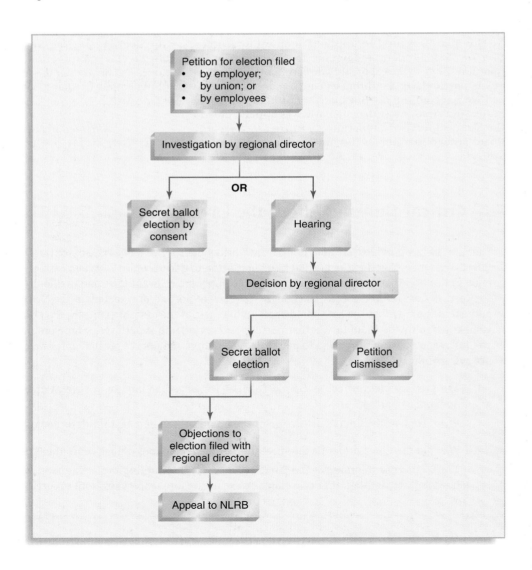

union, when it can demonstrate it has the support of over 30 percent of the employees it seeks to represent (known as "majority support"); (2) by the employer, when two or more unions are claiming to be the exclusive representative of the employees or when one union claims to have majority support; or (3) by the employees themselves. The union demonstrates its support by submitting authorization cards. Each card is signed by an employee and states that the employee gives the union the authority to act as the employee's exclusive bargaining representative.

Once the petition is filed, the regional director conducts an investigation to determine whether the employer is under the jurisdiction of the NLRB, whether the group of employees the union is seeking to represent is covered by the NLRA, whether the group of employees seeking representation is an appropriate bargaining unit (discussed in more detail later), and whether there is sufficient support (30 percent) for the union. If these findings are affirmative, the director will see whether all parties will consent to an election. If they will not, the regional office holds a hearing to receive evidence on whether an election should be held and, if so, which employees are entitled to vote. The transcript of the hearing is given to the regional director, who decides whether a question of representation exists and an election should be held. An affirmative decision results in an election by secret ballot, conducted by a representative of the regional office. In fiscal year 2003, the NLRB conducted 2937 representation elections, and workers chose union representation in 53.8 percent of the elections.[2]

After the election, the losing party may file objections to the outcome of the election with the regional director, who either orders a new election or certifies the results. The decision may be appealed to the board.

Procedures in Unfair Labor Practice Cases. A second important function of the NLRB is to prevent and remedy unfair labor practices by both employers and employees. An unfair labor practice charge is initiated when an aggrieved employee, union, or employer files an unfair labor practice charge with the appropriate regional office. (A sample charge is pictured in Exhibit 19-4.) In fiscal year 2003, 28,781 unfair labor charges were filed with the NLRB.[3] After regional office employees, called field examiners, investigate the charge, the regional director decides whether to issue a complaint. If a complaint is issued, an attorney from the regional office tries to resolve the complaint informally.

If informal negotiations are unsuccessful, the regional office attorney prosecutes the case before an administrative law judge. In fiscal year 2003, NLRB administrative law judges issued 399 decisions.[4] The ALJ issues an order recommending a remedy or suggesting a dismissal, in either case stating the rationale and evidence for the decision. If no party objects to the decision within 20 days, it automatically becomes a final order of the NLRB. If an order is issued and any party fails to abide by it, the board must petition a U.S. court of appeals for an enforcement order. The procedure in unfair labor practice cases is diagrammed in Exhibit 19-5.

Given the cumbersome nature of this procedure, it is easy to see how an unfair labor practice can continue for a substantial period of time. During the

---

[2] NLRB, Sixty-Eighth Annual Report of the NLRB for Fiscal Year Ended September 30, 2003, p. 1, available at **www.nlrb.gov/nlrb/shared_files/brochures**.

[3] NLRB, Sixty-Eighth Annual Report of the NLRB for Fiscal Year Ended September 30, 2003, p. 1, available at **www.nlrb.gov/nlrb/shared_files/brochures**.

[4] *Id.*, p. 2.

EXHIBIT 19-4

**FORM FOR FILING AN
UNFAIR LABOR PRACTICE
CHARGE**

	UNITED STATES OF AMERICA	DO NOT WRITE IN THIS SPACE	
	NATIONAL LABOR RELATIONS BOARD	Case	Date Filed
	CHARGE AGAINST EMPLOYER		

INSTRUCTIONS

File an original and 4 copies of this charge with NLRB Regional Director for the region in which the alleged unfair labor practice occurred or is occurring.

I EMPLOYER AGAINST WHOM CHARGE IS BROUGHT

a Name of Employer	b Number of workers employed

c Address, street, city, state, zip code	d Employer Representative	e Telephone No.

f Type of Establishment: factory, mine, wholesaler, etc.	g Identify principal product or service

h The above-named employer has engaged in and is engaging in unfair labor practices within the meaning of section 8 (a) subsections
———————————————————————————— (1) and first subsections of the National Labor
Relations Act and these unfair labor practices are unfair practices affecting commerce within the meaning of the Act

2 Basis of the Charge (set forth a clear and concise statement of the facts constituting the alleged unfair labor practices)

By the above and other acts, the above-named employer has interfered with, restrained, and coerced employees in the exercise of the rights guaranteed in Section 7 of the Act

3 Full name of the party filing charge (labor organization: give full name including local name and number)

4a Address (street and number, city, state and ZIP code)	4b Telephone No.

5 Full name of national or international labor organization which is an affiliate or constituent unit (to be filled in when charge is filed by a labor organization)

6 DECLARATION

I declare that I have read the above charge and that the statements are true to the best of my knowledge and belief.

B ————————————————————— ——————————————
Signature of representative making charge (title if any)

Address ————————————————————— ——————————— —————————
Telephone No. (date)

WILLFUL FALSE STATEMENTS ON THIS CHARGE CAN BE PUNISHED BY FINE AND IMPRISONMENT (U.S. CODE, TITLE 18, SECTION 1001)

mid-1980s, it took, on average, 48 days to complete an investigation, 94 days to hand down a decision after the close of an unfair labor practice hearing, and an additional 116 days before the board issued an order.

There are a couple of instances in which appeal to the board is available. First, if the regional director refuses to issue a complaint, the charging party may appeal to the general counsel in Washington, D.C. Such appeals are almost always denied. Second, a party dissatisfied with the administrative law judge's decision may file an appeal, called an exception to the recommended order,

EXHIBIT 19-5

PROCEDURES FOR AN UNFAIR LABOR PRACTICE CASE

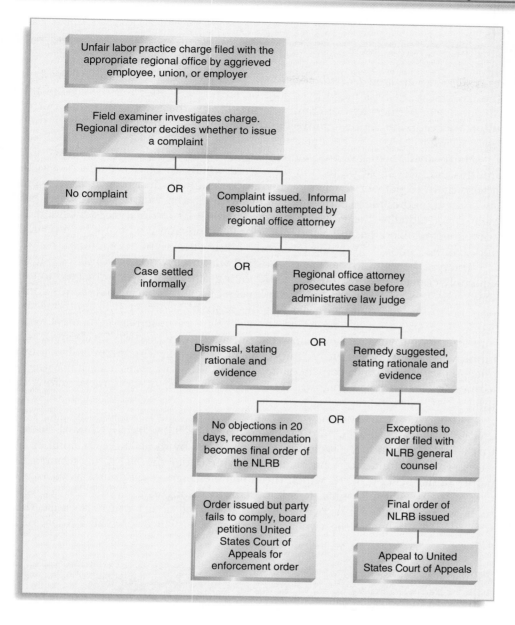

with the board in Washington. Briefs are then filed with the board, and, in extremely rare instances, oral arguments are heard. The board then issues its final order. In fiscal year 2003, the board issued 865 decisions.[5]

It should be noted that no one is actually required to honor an NLRB order, because the board has no contempt-of-court powers. Instead, when its order is not followed, the NLRB brings an enforcement proceeding in a circuit court of appeals asking the court to order the parties to abide by its order. A party who is dissatisfied with the board's order may also appeal to a circuit court of appeals.

---

[5] *Id.*, p. 16.

LABOR ORGANIZING

In a 1936 novel titled *In Dubious Battle,* John Steinbeck graphically described the extreme hardships faced by union organizers just after the passage of the Wagner Act. Derided as Communist sympathizers, they were often run out of town by company representatives and sometimes even by the workers they were trying to help.

Many small-town law enforcement officers were indebted to business during this era. The most protection they were willing to offer organizers was to advise them to get out of town. Many labor organizers lost their lives or were severely injured in these early unionization battles, and victories were often not clear-cut. Gradually, the violence directed against labor organizers subsided as companies realized that the National Labor Relations Act would not be repealed and that the courts were going to enforce employees' right to organize.

Today, when employees are dissatisfied with their working conditions, they generally contact a national union representing other employees engaged in the same type of work. For example, employees of a shop that manufactures components for automobile engines would probably contact the United Auto Workers (UAW) Union. The union then sends a representative to meet with interested employees and explain what unionization would do for them. If the employees want to pursue a unionization effort, the organizer helps them engage in a campaign to convince a majority of the workers to accept the union as their exclusive representative. Table 19-5 lists some of the largest unions in the United States today.

During the course of this organizing campaign, certain activities of both employers and employees are prohibited by the NLRA and by "board rules," that is, rules of conduct developed over the years by the NLRB in a number of cases. The constraints on employers' behavior under the NLRA are found primarily under Section 8(a)1, which prohibits interference with employees' exercise of their Section 7 rights. It is important to distinguish conduct that constitutes an unfair labor practice from violations of board rules, because the remedies available for the two are different. A violation of board rules may

TABLE 19-5

SOME OF THE LARGEST UNIONS IN THE UNITED STATES AS OF 2000

Union Name	Number of Members
National Education Association (NEA)	2,530,000
International Brotherhood of Teamsters (IBT)	1,402,000
Service Employees International Union (SEIU)	1,374,000
United Food and Commercial Workers International Union (UFCW)	1,308,722
American Federation of State, County, and Municipal Employees (AFSCME)	1,300,000
Laborers' International Union of North America (LIUNA)	818,412
International Association of Machinists and Aerospace Workers (IAM)	730,673
International Brotherhood of Electrical Workers (IBEW)	727,837
American Federation of Teachers (AFT)	706,973
International Union, United Automobile, Aerospace and Agricultural Implement Workers of America (UAW)	671,853

Source: Adapted from "Unions in U.S. with More Than 100,000 Members," www.lraonline.org/charts.php?id=25.

result in the NLRB's setting aside the results of an election and ordering a new one. In contrast, the commission of an unfair labor practice by the employer may cause the board to ignore the election results altogether and order the employer to bargain with the union without a new election. The latter remedy occurs only in cases in which the employer's conduct was so egregious as to make it impossible to hold a fair election and the union had previously collected authorization cards signed by a majority of the employees.

BOARD RULES

Board rules are designed to guarantee a fair election. One very important rule, the **24-hour rule**, prohibits both union representatives and employers from making speeches to "captive audiences" of employees within 24 hours of a representation election. A captive audience exists when the employees have no choice but to listen to the speech.

> **24-hour rule** Prohibits both union representatives and employers from making speeches to "captive audiences" of employees within 24 hours of a representative election.

Another important board rule requires employers to file with the regional director a list of the names and addresses of all employees eligible to vote within seven days after an election order is issued. This list, known as the *Excelsior list* (after the case that created it), is then made available to the union or union organizers by the regional director.

It is essential that employers be aware of these and other board rules, because their violation may result in the setting aside of an election, even when the behavior does not constitute an unfair labor practice. All unfair labor practices, whether by employers or employees, are also considered violations of the board's election rules.

UNFAIR LABOR PRACTICES BY EMPLOYERS

In fiscal year 2003, the majority of claims of unfair labor practices by employers (10,132 claims) alleged that the employer illegally discharged workers or engaged in other illegal discrimination against employees.[6] The second largest category of unfair labor practices alleged that employers refused to bargain (10,081 charges).

Interference with Organizing. Section 8(a)1 of the National Labor Relations Act prohibits employer interference, restraint, or coercion of employees in the exercise of their Section 7 rights. It is sometimes difficult for a businessperson to know when her or his speech or conduct rises to the level of coercion, restraint, or interference. To make the issue even more complicated, Section 8(c) expressly provides that the expression of a view, argument, or opinion is not evidence of an unfair labor practice as long as it does not contain any threats of reprisals or promises of benefits.

As these sections have been interpreted since 1969, employers are allowed to communicate to employees their general views on unions or their specific views on a particular union, even to the point of predicting the impact that unionization would have on the company, so long as these statements do not amount to threats of reprisals or promises of benefits. To keep within these bounds, an employer must carefully phrase any predictions and be sure they are based on objective facts; in essence, the consequences that the employer

---

[6] NLRB, Sixty-Eighth Annual Report of the NLRB for Fiscal Year Ended September 30, 2003, p. 6, available at **www.nlrb.gov/nlrb/shared_files/brochures**.

predicts must be outside the control of the employer. Examples of threats of reprisals that constitute unfair labor practices are threats to close a plant if the employees organize, threats to discharge union sympathizers, and threats to discontinue present employee benefits, such as coffee breaks or employee discounts. An example of a promise of benefits that constitutes an unfair labor practice is the announcement of a new employee profit-sharing plan a few days before the election.

No-solicitation rules of employers may also constitute an employer unfair labor practice because they interfere with communications among employees. In order for employees to exercise their Section 7 rights, they must be able to communicate with one another.

Businesspeople must understand what types of organizing behavior can lawfully be prohibited and what prohibitions would constitute unfair labor practices. Understandably, employers do not want employees to use work time or company property to organize, and, in general, they may prohibit union solicitation and the distribution of literature during work time. During nonwork time, such as lunch and coffee breaks, employers may prohibit organizing activity on company property only if there are legitimate safety or efficiency reasons for doing so and the restraint is not manifestly intended to thwart organizing efforts. The burden of proof is on the employer to demonstrate these safety or efficiency concerns. The following case provides an illustration of an employer's engaging in unfair labor practices during an organizing campaign.

CASE 19-2

Frazier Industrial Company, Inc. v. National Labor Relations Board
United States Court of Appeals, District of Columbia Circuit,
213 F.3d 750, 164 L.R.R.M. (BNA) 2516 (2000)

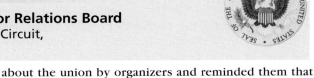

During the start-up phase of defendant Frazier Industrial Company's Idaho plant, the plant manager hired nine welders and nine other employees to perform fabrication, maintenance, painting, and other duties. One of the welders, John Ramirez, started working for the company on March 7. Beginning in April, he solicited employees to attend organizational meetings and to sign union authorization cards. He spoke with more than half of the plant's workforce about the union and spoke with at least one person about unionization daily or every other day before his discharge. He spoke with them before and after work and while on break. He repeatedly spoke to those who were noncommittal, but once someone said they opposed the union, he quit trying to recruit them.

During the next several months, supervisors asked workers why certain employees wanted a union, and upon hearing that perhaps employees wanted better pay or better benefits, one supervisor said that "before the company went union they would either hire nonunion or shut the plant down." They continually asked employees whether they were being harassed about the union by organizers and reminded them that the company had a policy prohibiting the discussion of unions on the job, although other personal matters could be discussed.

In June 1996, Ramirez was discharged because other employees were complaining that he was bothering them all the time and his behavior was affecting productivity.

He sought relief from the NLRB, alleging that his termination was an unfair labor practice. At his hearing, the administrative law judge (ALJ) found that the company had violated Section 8(a)(1) by threatening to discharge employees who engaged in union activities, coercively interrogating employees about their union activities and sympathies, threatening employees that it would close the plant if employees chose union representation, and maintaining and enforcing a rule prohibiting union talk while permitting other nonwork discussions. The board also adopted the judge's findings that the company had violated Section 8(a)(1) and (a)(3) by discharging Ramirez because of his union activity and ordered reinstatement and back pay. The NLRB adopted the ALJ's findings. The company appealed.

Circuit Judge Rogers

Section 8(a)(1) and (3) of the Act makes it an unfair labor practice for an employer "to interfere with, restrain or coerce employees in the exercise of the rights guaranteed" by the Act, and "by discrimination in regard to hire or tenure of employment or any term or condition of employment to encourage or discourage membership in any labor organization." To establish a causal nexus between adverse employment decisions and an employee's union affiliation, the complaining party must first show that protected activity "was a 'motivating factor'" in the adverse employment decision, and then the employer may show that it would have made the adverse decision even had the employee not engaged in the protected activity.

To establish an employer's discriminatory motive, the Board may "consider such factors as the employer's knowledge of the employee's union activities, the employer's hostility toward the union, and the timing of the employer's action." In addition, evidence that an employer has violated Section 8(a)(1) of the Act can support an inference of anti-union animus. The court will affirm the findings of the Board unless they are "unsupported by substantial evidence in the record considered as a whole," or unless the Board "acted arbitrarily or otherwise erred in applying established law to the facts."

The company maintains that, even if Ramirez's actions constituted protected activities, its termination of Ramirez's employment was lawful because it would have discharged him in the absence of protected conduct for his insubordination and dishonesty. We hold that there is substantial evidence in the record to support the Board's conclusions that Ramirez's conduct was protected union activity under the Act, that the company violated the Act by discharging Ramirez for engaging in such protected union activity, and that the company's other proffered reasons for termination of Ramirez's employment—insubordination and dishonesty—are insufficient to meet its burden.

In support of its contention that Ramirez's conduct was not protected by the Act because he was engaged in repeated harassment of fellow employees during work time resulting in frequent interruptions of work, the company relies on [a case], which held that "an employee who disrupts other employees during working hours is not engaged in a protected activity even though he is discussing union business." Similarly, Board precedent states that "activity that would otherwise be protected may lose that protection if the means by which that activity is conducted are sufficiently abusive or threatening." Under such precedent, the company contends, the fact that Ramirez was attempting to organize the company's work force is immaterial because he had no legitimate protected interest in repeatedly approaching and harassing his co-workers while they were trying to work. Although this interpretation of evidence may be reasonable, the Board's finding to the contrary was supported by substantial evidence in the record.

The Board found that Ramirez's activities were protected because "it is clear that ... all of Ramirez's worktime solicitations were brief and did not involve any obvious disruption in production." Adding that "there is no evidence that employees whom Ramirez solicited more than once ever even told him that he was interfering with their work or that further solicitations would have that effect," the Board found that although Ramirez tenaciously solicited employees to sign cards, attend the union's meetings, or meet individually with a union organizer, he did not pursue such matters with employees over their expressed objections. On the contrary, the Board found that "his persistence, in the main, resulted in those instances where he received tepid or inconclusive responses from the employees with whom he spoke." The Board thus concluded that Ramirez's conduct, while persistent, did not rise "to the level of unprotected harassment."

*Judgment of NLRB **affirmed**.*

It is not always easy to predict when employer conduct is going to be found unlawful, as in many cases the court is trying to strike a balance between the employer's private property rights and the employees' rights to communicate with one another during an organizing campaign. For example, in *Guardian Industries Corporation v. National Labor Relations Board*,[7] Guardian had maintained a bulletin board upon which it would post, on its employees' behalf, "for sale" cards. When asked to post notices of upcoming union organizing meetings on this board, the employer refused. The union filed an unfair labor practice charge, arguing that once employees were given access to the bulletin board for one purpose, they should have access to it for all purposes, including organizing.

The court found that there was nothing unlawful about Guardian's behavior. The company had never allowed announcements of any meetings to be posted, so it was not unlawfully discriminating against the organizing employees in this instance. It is only in instances in which an employer has opened up bulletin boards

---

[7] 49 F.3d 317 (1995).

for all employee postings and then disallowed postings related to organizing that courts have found an employer in violation of the National Labor Relations Act.

Thus far, we have been concerned with employee solicitations and distributions. Nonemployee organizers have fewer rights than employee organizers. As long as they have some way to communicate with employees (and they do in almost all cases now because they are entitled to the *Excelsior* list of names and addresses of employees), nonemployee organizers may be prohibited from entering the employer's property, including private parking lots. The courts have held that in the case of nonemployee organizers, the employer's private property rights will be protected, as the following case illustrates.

CASE 19-3

Lechmere, Inc. v. NLRB
United States Supreme Court,
112 S.Ct. 841 (1992)

Lechmere, Inc., owns and operates a retail store in a shopping plaza. The company also owns part of the plaza parking lot, which is separated from the highway by a 46-foot-wide strip of grass-covered public property. During a union organizing campaign, nonemployee organizers placed handbills on cars in the employee section of the parking lot. Lechmere then denied organizers access to the lot. The organizers responded by distributing handbills and picketing on the grassy strip. They also contacted about 20 percent of Lechmere's employees directly.

The organizers filed a charge with the NLRB, alleging that Lechmere's denial of access to the parking lot to the organizers constituted an unfair labor practice. An ALJ ruled in the organizers' favor, recommending that Lechmere be ordered to cease and desist from barring the organizers from the lot. The NLRB affirmed and issued the order. Lechmere appealed, and the U.S. Court of Appeals affirmed, enforcing the order. Lechmere appealed to the U.S. Supreme Court.

Justice Thomas

By its plain terms, the NLRA confers rights only on employees, not on unions or their nonemployee organizers. [H]owever, we recognized that insofar as the employees' "right of self-organization depends in some measure on [their] ability … to learn the advantages of self-organization from others," Section 7 of the NLRA may, in certain limited circumstances, restrict an employer's right to exclude nonemployee union organizers from his property.

As a rule an employer cannot be compelled to allow distribution of union literature by nonemployee organizers on his property. As with many other rules, however, we recognized an exception. Where "the location of a plant and the living quarters of the employees place the employees beyond the reach of reasonable union efforts to communicate with them," employers' property rights may be "required to yield to the extent needed to permit communication of information on the right to organize."

"While an employer may not always bar nonemployee union organizers from his property, his right to do so remains the general rule. To gain access, *the union has the burden of showing that no other reasonable means of communicating its organizational message to the employees exists* or that the employer's access rules discriminate against union solicitation. That the burden imposed on the union is a heavy one is evidenced by the fact that the balance struck by the Board and the courts under the *Babcock* accommodation principle has rarely been in favor of trespassory organizational activity."

In *Babcock*, we held that the Act drew a distinction "of substance," between the union activities of employees and nonemployees. In cases involving *employee* activities, we noted with approval, the Board "balanced the conflicting interests of employees to receive information on self-organization on the company's property from fellow employees during nonworking time, with the employer's right to control the use of his property." In cases involving *nonemployee* activities, however, the Board was not permitted to engage in that same balancing. *Babcock*'s teaching is straightforward: Section 7 simply does not protect nonemployee union organizers *except* in the rare case where "the inaccessibility of employees makes ineffective the reasonable attempts by nonemployees to communicate with them through the usual channels." Our reference to "reasonable" attempts was nothing more than a common sense recognition that unions need not engage in extraordinary feats to communicate with inaccessible employees—not an endorsement of the view that the Act protects "reasonable" trespasses. Where reasonable alternative means of access exist, Section 7's guarantees do not authorize trespasses by nonemployee organizers, even "under … reasonable regulations" established by the Board.

The threshold inquiry in this case, then, is whether the facts here justify application of *Babcock*'s inaccessibility exception.

As we have explained, the exception to *Babcock*'s rule is a narrow one. It does not apply wherever nontrespassory access to employees may be cumbersome or less-than-ideally effective, but only where "*the location of a plant and the living quarters of the employees* place the employees beyond the reach of reasonable union efforts to communicate with them." Classic examples include logging camps, mining camps, and mountain resort hotels. *Babcock*'s exception was crafted precisely to protect the Section 7 rights of those employees who, by virtue of their employment, are isolated from the ordinary flow of information that characterizes our society. The union's burden of establishing such isolation is, as we have explained, "a heavy one," and one not satisfied by mere conjecture or the expression of doubts concerning the effectiveness of nontrespassory means of communication.

The Board's conclusion in this case that the union had no reasonable means short of trespass to make Lechmere's employees aware of its organizational efforts is based on a misunderstanding of the limited scope of this exception. Because the employees do not reside on Lechmere's property, they are presumptively not "beyond the reach," of the union's message. Although the employees live in a large met-ropolitan area (Greater Hartford), that fact does not in itself render them "inaccessible" in the sense contemplated by *Babcock*. Their accessibility is suggested by the union's success in contacting a substantial percentage of them directly, via mailings, phone calls, and home visits. Such direct contact, of course, is not a necessary element of "reasonably effective" communication; signs or advertising also may suffice. In this case, the union tried advertising in local newspapers; the Board said that this was not reasonably effective because it was expensive and might not reach the employees. Whatever the merits of that conclusion, other alternative means of communication were readily available.

Thus, signs displayed, for example, from the public grassy strip adjoining Lechmere's parking lot would have informed the employees about the union's organizational efforts. (Indeed, union organizers picketed the shopping center's main entrance for months as employees came and went every day.) Access to employees, not success in winning them over, is the critical issue—although success, or lack thereof, may be relevant in determining whether reasonable access exists. Because the union in this case failed to establish the existence of any "unique obstacles," that frustrated access to Lechmere's employees, the Board erred in concluding that Lechmere committed an unfair labor practice by barring the nonemployee organizers from its property.

Reversed in favor of Appellee, Lechmere.

Critical Thinking About the Law

Suppose that you are a midlevel manager in a firm who notices that one of the employees for whom you are responsible is not working very hard. After warning the employee several times, you finally go to your supervisor to report the situation. At this point, your supervisor must decide where she places the burden of proof with respect to your grievance. Basically, she can request either that you prove that the employee is slacking in his duties or that the employee prove that he is not slacking off. If she places the burden of proof on you, in essence she is saying, "I assume that the employee is working hard. That is the solid position from which you must move me to convince me of the validity of your grievance." In this case, the employee is innocent until proven guilty. On the other hand, if she places the burden of proof on the employee, a quite different situation arises. With that placement, she is conveying her assumption that the employee is less than diligent in his work and that he must prove otherwise. In this scenario, the employee is guilty until proven innocent.

As you can see, where the burden of proof is placed in a court of law is very important to the outcome of the case. In a very crude sense, by not placing the burden of proof on one party, those interpreting a law are saying that they tend to accept that party's argument. The other party has the burden of proof; it must disprove the first party's argument to the court's satisfaction.

Because the burden of proof is such a crucial factor in any dispute, it is important to be sensitive to who must bear that burden in particular conflicts.

1. Who had the burden of proof in Case 19-3

   Clue: The Court explicitly answered this question.

2. What ethical norm guided the placement and nature of the burden of proof in Case 19-3?

   Clue: Focus on the crucial role of private property rights in Justice Thomas's reasoning.

Domination or Support of Labor Organizing. In addition to the NLRA's all-encompassing Section 8(a)1, there are other subsections of 8(a) that set forth specific behaviors that constitute unfair labor practices; a violation of any of these sections is simultaneously a violation of Section 8(a)1. For example, under Section 8(a)2, an employer cannot dominate, support, or interfere with a labor organization. Thus, in response to an organizing campaign by one union, the employer cannot aid some of its employees in contacting a different union to compete for the right to represent the workers at that plant. Nor can the employer play any role in establishing or operating any committee or other organization designed to represent or aid employees in their dealings with the employer over wages, rates of pay, or other terms and conditions of employment.

The employer must also be careful about voluntarily recognizing a union claiming to represent a majority of the employees. If the employer recognizes a union that does not represent the majority of employees, that is a violation of Section 8(a)2, even if the employer was acting in good faith.

A union dominated by an employer will be disestablished; that is, it may never again represent those employees. A union unlawfully supported by an employer will be decertified; that is, it will not be able to represent the employees until it has been certified as a result of a new representation election monitored by the NLRB.

One of the major concerns facing labor relations specialists at present is the impact of Section 8 on some of the more cooperative labor–management programs that employers are trying to put in place today. Many commentators from both business and academia have cited the traditional adversarial relationship between labor and management as being at least partially responsible for productivity problems in many industries.[8] Consequently, U.S. management has been experimenting with programs to increase cooperation between labor and management. There is strong evidence that these programs do boost productivity.[9] However, many of them have been found to constitute unfair labor practices.

We will discuss three of the most common of these new programs: quality circles, autonomous and semiautonomous work groups, and labor–management committees. All bring labor and management together in an attempt to solve mutual problems; yet, in instituting these programs, management may be violating the NLRA.

A **quality circle** is a small group of workers that meets regularly on a voluntary basis to analyze work problems and recommend solutions to management. Discussions are typically led by a supervisor from the area in which the employees work. Although the focus is typically on such production problems as reducing scrap, solutions may involve matters traditionally classified as "working conditions," such as plant layout and scheduling. Quality circles may also be used to educate workers in such areas as group dynamics, problem solving, and statistical quality control.

One of the best-known uses of quality circles is Ford's Employee Involvement program, a voluntary program developed in cooperation with the UAW. Workers meet voluntarily in small groups with their supervisors to provide suggestions for improving production. Participants also receive training in group problem-solving techniques. The recommendations and results of the

quality circle A small group of workers that voluntarily meets on a regular basis, under the leadership of a supervisor, to discuss work problems and recommend solutions to management.

---

[8] C. Farrell and M. J. Mandell, "Industrial Policy," *Business Week*, April 6, 1992, pp. 70–75; and B. Childs, "United Motors: An American Success Story," *Labor Law Journal* 40 (1989), p. 453.

[9] Childs, *supra* note 2.

groups are published. Since the implementation of this program, the number of grievances at Ford plants has fallen, and employee job satisfaction ratings have increased. So far, Ford's plan has not been challenged in the courts.

Autonomous work group programs organize workers into teams. Some teams are led by a supervisor appointed by management; others are led by a worker elected from among the team members. The group is given a task to perform, and it determines how it will accomplish the task. Depending on the industry, the "task" may be anything from building refrigerators to processing an insurance claim. The group's authority may range from deciding how and when subtasks are to be performed to disciplining group members, scheduling overtime, and interviewing job applicants for the team. Teams that have less authority are known as semiautonomous work groups.

The essence of the autonomous work team is that with increased responsibility will come increased motivation. A program using semiautonomous work groups has been successfully implemented at the General Motors–Toyota plant in Fremont, California, for example. This plant had a history of contentious labor–management relations, but after the semiautonomous work groups were set up, management noticed substantial improvements in the quality of the plant's products and a reduction in the number of grievances filed by workers.

Labor–management committees provide a forum in which workers can communicate directly with upper management. Worker participants on these committees are either elected by their fellow workers or appointed by management. They usually serve for a limited time, such as six months, to ensure maximum participation.

Under a literal interpretation of the NLRA, most participatory committees would appear to constitute labor organizations. In fact, in the leading U.S. Supreme Court case on this issue, *NLRB v. Cabot Carbon Co.*,[10] the Court found that "employee committees" established by the employer to allow employees to discuss with managers such issues as safety, increased efficiency, and grievances at nonunion plants and departments are labor organizations. Numerous decisions since *Cabot* have followed this strict interpretation. The dilemma for management is that these committees are rather useless unless they are allowed to discuss issues that have an impact on working conditions, but having such discussions makes them illegal employer-dominated labor organizations under the NLRA.

Recently, the NLRB and a few appellate courts have created two narrow exceptions to the strict interpretation the Supreme Court set forth in *Cabot*. The first exception arises when all of the workers in a bargaining unit or plant participate in the program. In that situation, the committee does not "represent" the employees because it comprises all the employees; if it does not represent employees, it cannot be a labor organization and, hence, cannot be construed as an employer-dominated union. In other words, participation in an employee group is legal, but representation of other employees is not.

The second exception involves a situation in which employees carry out a traditional management function. In such cases, the employee group no longer "deals with" management because it is performing the delegated function itself.

You can see from these examples that the National Labor Relations Board and some of the courts are trying very hard to find a way to allow cooperative labor–management programs to exist. Remember, even if a labor–management committee is found to constitute a labor organization, to be unlawful, the committee must be dominated or supported by the employer.

autonomous/semiautonomous work group A team of workers, led by either a supervisor appointed by management or a worker elected by the team, that determines for itself how it will accomplish the work task it is given to perform. Those groups with full authority over all subtasks, scheduling of overtime, and hiring of new team members are autonomous; those with less authority are semiautonomous.

labor–management committee A forum in which workers communicate directly with upper management. May be illegal under the NLRA if the committee has an impact on working conditions, unless all workers in a bargaining unit or a plant participate or the employees on the committee are carrying out a traditional management function.

---

[10] 360 U.S. 203 (1959).

Linking Law & Business

Management

Your management class may have discussed several different approaches to management. One type is the behavioral approach, which emphasizes an increase in productivity based on a better understanding of people. Proponents of this approach believe that a better understanding of human behavior by the management, while adapting an organization to its workers, will lead to greater organizational success. The behavioral approach to management highlights the human relations movement, which places a strong emphasis on the people-oriented aspect of a firm. The human relations movement involves the observation of relations among people in organizations to determine the relational impact on a firm's success. By developing a better understanding of human behavior, managers are equipped for engaging in healthier relations with their employees. Therefore, the overall efficiency of the organization may increase. As already mentioned in this section, adversarial relations, on the other hand, between a company's management and employees may lead to productivity problems. The programs that we have been discussing—quality circles, autonomous and semiautonomous work groups, and labor–management committees—are several means of enhancing organizational productivity by improving employer-employee relations. Thus, a lawful use of these programs may result in better relational interactions with employers and employees, which could boost organizational productivity.

Source: S. Certo, *Modern Management* (Upper Saddle River, N.J.: Prentice Hall, 2000), pp. 32–33.

The traditional test[11] asks whether the committee is structurally independent of management. Most participatory committees have some minimal association with management that would render them unfair under this strict test. Again, however, some circuit courts are using two factors to minimize the impact of this holding on participatory programs. First, the court asks whether the employers had good motives in establishing the plan. Second, the court asks whether the employees are satisfied with it.

Applying this two-part analysis, the court may then distinguish illegal domination and support from legal cooperation.[12] In the case in which this two-part test was initially set forth, the court focused on the NLRA's goal, which is to protect employee free choice, and said that employees should be free to enter into cooperative arrangements with their employers as long as the employer does not try to use the plan to interfere with free choice.

So the courts are bending over backward to find these cooperative arrangements between labor and management legal. Yet, until there is a change in the NLRA to specifically allow such cooperative programs, or until the Supreme Court clearly upholds their validity, employers adopting such programs should be fully aware of the potential problems.

One final issue of concern with respect to employee-involvement plans is whether participation on some of the more powerful committees places workers in the category of managerial or supervisory employees, thereby putting them at risk of losing their right to bargain collectively under the NLRA. For example, after

---

[11] This test was established in *NLRB v. Newport News Shipbuilding and Drydock Co.*, 308 U.S. 241 (1939).

[12] *Chicago Rawhide v. NLRB*, 221 F.2d 165 (1955).

a union at the College of Osteopathy and Medicine won an increased managerial voice for its members, the employees lost their right to bargain collectively.[13]

Discrimination Based on Union Activity. An employer who discriminates against employees because of their union activity is in violation of Section 8(a)3. An ambiguous situation arises when a marginal employee who is also an organizer for a union is fired. The NLRB will have to determine whether the firing was motivated by the employee's poor performance or by the employee's union activity. Discharge of even the most strident union activist is legal as long as the primary motivation for the firing was poor performance rather than union activity. In such cases, courts look at such factors as how others who engage in similar misconduct have been treated by the employer.

Firing is the ultimate form of discrimination, but other forms of discrimination, such as reducing break time and unfavorable treatment in job and overtime assignments, also constitute violations of Section 8(a)3.

UNFAIR LABOR PRACTICES BY EMPLOYEES

Unfair labor practices by employees are less common in organizing campaigns than unfair labor practices by employers, perhaps because when a union is trying to gain representational status, it generally does not have enough power to engage in such practices. The sections of the NLRA most applicable to unions during the organizing period are 8(b)1, which prohibits restraint or coercion of employees in the exercise of their Section 7 rights; 8(b)2, which prohibits forcing the employer to discriminate to encourage or discourage union activity; and 8(b)7, which prohibits picketing for recognition when another union has been certified or when the picketing union has lost an election within the past year.

ORGANIZING THE APPROPRIATE UNIT

The purpose of all organizing activity is for the union to gain the right to be the exclusive representative of employees in negotiations with the employer over wages, hours, and terms and conditions of employment. Because the potential power of the union clashes with the employer's desire to maintain control over the workplace, organizational campaigns can become very heated. In any organizing campaign, the first step for the union is to gain the support of a substantial number of the members (generally 30 percent) of an appropriate bargaining unit so that a board-run election may be ordered.

As mentioned previously, an important question in this initial stage is: What is the **appropriate bargaining unit**? The appropriate unit, as defined by the NLRA, is one that can "ensure the employees the fullest freedom in exercising the rights guaranteed by the Act." In making such a determination, the regional director of the NLRB examines a number of alternatives. An entire plant may be an appropriate unit; so may a single department of highly skilled employees; and so may all the employees of a single employer located at more than one facility (e.g., all employees of a group of retail stores located in a metropolitan area).

In determining whether a proposed bargaining unit is appropriate, the NLRB considers primarily whether there is a mutuality of interest among the proposed members of the unit. All proposed members should have similar skills, wages,

appropriate bargaining unit May be an entire plant, a single department, or all employees of a single employer, as long as there is a mutuality of interest among the proposed members of the unit.

---

[13] 265 N.L.R.B. 295 (1982).

hours, and working conditions, for only then is it possible for a union to look out for the interests of all members. Other factors considered include the desires of the employees, the extent of organization, and the history of collective bargaining of the employer and of the industry in which the employer operates. In the following case decision in 2004, the NLRB considered whether graduate students are an appropriate bargaining unit. Note that unlike the other cases in this chapter, the text of this case is the NLRB decision rather than a court decision.

CASE 19-4

Brown University *and* International Union, United Automobile, Aerospace and Agricultural Implement Workers of America, UAW AFL–CIO, Petitioner.
National Labor Relations Board Case 1–RC–21368 July 13, 2004

On November 16, 2001, a regional director issued a decision determining that 450 teaching assistants, research assistants, and proctors at Brown University were employees within the meaning of Section 2(3) of the NLRA and constitute an appropriate unit for collective bargaining. Brown University filed a request for review with the NLRB. In an earlier case involving New York University (NYU), the board concluded that graduate student assistants are employees under Section 2(3) of the act and, therefore, are to be extended the right to engage in collective bargaining. Here, the board revisits the issue.

Decision on Review and Order by Chairman Battista and Members Liebman, Schaumber, Walsh, and Meisburg

In *Adelphi University*, 195 NLRB 639 (1972), the Board held that graduate student assistants are primarily students and should be excluded from a unit of regular faculty. In *Leland Stanford*, 214 NLRB 621 (1974), the Board went further. It held that graduate student assistants "are not employees within the meaning of Section 2(3) of the Act." The common thread in both opinions is that these individuals are students, not employees. The Board found that the research assistants were not statutory employees because, like the graduate students in *Adelphi*, supra, they were "primarily students." In support of this conclusion, the Board cited to the following: (1) the research assistants were graduate students enrolled in the Stanford physics department as Ph.D. candidates; (2) they were required to perform research to obtain their degree; (3) they received academic credit for their research work; and (4) while they received a stipend from Stanford, the amount was not dependent on the nature or intrinsic value of the services performed or the skill or function of the recipient, but instead was determined by the goal of providing the graduate students with financial support. For over 25 years, the Board adhered to the *Leland Stanford* principle.

The Supreme Court has recognized that principles developed for use in the industrial setting cannot be "imposed blindly on the academic world." *NLRB v. Yeshiva University*, 444 U.S. 672, 680–681 (1980), citing *Syracuse University*, 204 NLRB 641, 643 (1973). While graduate programs may differ somewhat in their details, the concerns raised … here forcefully illustrate the problem of attempting to force the student–university relationship into the traditional employer–employee framework. It is clear to us that graduate student assistants, including those at Brown, are primarily students and have a primarily educational, not economic, relationship with their university. Accordingly, we overrule *NYU* and return to the pre-*NYU* Board precedent.

The [NLRA] was premised on the view that there is a fundamental conflict between the interests of the employers and employees engaged in collective bargaining under its auspices and that "'[t]he parties … proceed from contrary and to an extent antagonistic viewpoints and concepts of self-interest.'"

> *[T]he damage caused to the nation's commerce by the inequality of bargaining power between employees and employers was one of the central problems addressed by the Act. A central policy of the Act is that the protection of the right of employees to organize and bargain collectively restores equality of bargaining power between employers and employees and safeguards commerce from the harm caused by labor disputes. The vision of a fundamentally economic relationship between employers and employees is inescapable.*

The Board's long-standing rule that it will not assert jurisdiction over relationships that are "primarily educational" is consistent with these principles. We emphasize the simple, undisputed fact that all the petitioned-for individuals are students and must first be enrolled at Brown to be awarded a TA, RA, or proctorship. Even students who have finished their coursework and are writing their dissertation must be enrolled to receive these awards. Further, students serving as graduate student assistants spend only a limited number of hours performing their duties, and it is beyond dispute that their principal time commitment at Brown is focused on obtaining a degree and, thus, being a student. Also, as shown below, their service as a graduate student assistant is part and parcel of the core elements of the Ph.D. degree. Because they are first and foremost students, and their status as a graduate student assistant is contingent on their continued enrollment as students, we find that they are primarily students.

We also emphasize that the money received by the TAs, RAs, and proctors is the same as that received by fellows. Thus, the money is not "consideration for work." It is financial aid to a student.

Besides the purely academic dimension to this relationship is the financial support provided to graduate student assistants because they are students. Attendance at Brown is quite expensive. Brown recognizes the need for financial support to meet the costs of a graduate education. This assistance, however, is provided only to students and only for the period during which they are enrolled as students. Further, the vast majority of students receive funding.

Thus, in light of the status of graduate student assistants as students, the role of graduate student assistantships in graduate education, the graduate student assistants' relationship with the faculty, and the financial support they receive to attend Brown, we conclude that the overall relationship between the graduate student assistants and Brown is primarily an educational one, rather than an economic one.

Consistent with long-standing Board precedent, and for the reasons set forth in this decision, we declare the federal law to be that graduate student assistants are not employees within the meaning of Section 2(3) of the Act.

Order

The Regional Director's Decision and Direction of Election is *reversed*, and the petition is *dismissed*.

The appropriateness of the proposed bargaining unit is the first issue that the staff of the regional office determines when it receives a petition for a representation election. Once that issue has been resolved, employer and union representatives try to reach an agreement on such matters as the time and place of the election, standards for eligibility to vote, rules of conduct during the election, and the means for handling challenges to the outcome of the election. If the parties cannot reach agreement, the NLRB regional director determines these matters and orders an election.

If the union obtains signed authorization cards from over 50 percent of the appropriate employee unit, it may ask the employer to recognize the union on the basis of this showing of majority support alone. Realizing it is futile to try to prevent the union from representing its employees, the employer may decide that it would ultimately be beneficial to recognize the union and begin the bargaining process on an amicable note. Such behavior is risky, however, because it may constitute a violation of Section 8(a)1, which prohibits employers from interfering with employees' Section 7 right of free choice. In other cases, the employer may wish to avoid the risk of violating Section 8(a)2, which prohibits employer-dominated unions and may, therefore, request that the union file a petition for certification. Having a board-run election to ensure that there indeed is majority support protects the employer.

If a union receives a majority of the votes and the election results are not challenged, the board will certify the union as the exclusive bargaining representative of the employees of that unit. If two or more unions are seeking to represent employees, and neither one of the unions nor "no union" receives a majority of the votes, there will be a runoff election between the choices that got the first and second greatest number of votes. Once a valid representation election has been held and there has been either a certification of a representative union or a majority vote for no union, there cannot be another election for one year. Nor can there be an election during the term of a collective bargaining agreement, unless either the union is defunct or there is such a division in the ranks of the union that it is unable or unwilling to represent the employees.

THE COLLECTIVE BARGAINING PROCESS

good-faith bargaining
Following procedural standards laid out in Section 8 of the NLRA; failure to bargain in good faith, by either the employer or the union, is an unfair labor practice.

Shortly after a union has been certified, or recognized, the collective bargaining process begins. Both the employer and the bargaining unit representative are required by the NLRA to bargain collectively in good faith with respect to wages, hours, and other terms and conditions of employment. Note that the requirement is only to bargain in good faith, not to reach an agreement. The board has no power to order the parties to accept any contract provision; it can only order them to bargain.

To a great extent, **good-faith bargaining** is defined procedurally. Under Section 8(d), the parties must (1) meet at reasonable times and confer in good faith; (2) sign a written agreement if one is reached; (3) when intent on terminating or modifying an existing contract, give 60 days' notice to the other party with an offer to confer over proposals, and give 30 days' notice to the federal or state mediation services in the event of a pending dispute over the new agreement; and (4) neither strike nor engage in a lockout during the 60-day notice period.

Failure of the employer to bargain in good faith is an unfair labor practice under Section 8(a)5. Employers violate this section not only by disregarding proper procedural standards but also by assuming a take-it-or-leave-it attitude. So if the employer takes a position and says it will alter it only if new information shows its proposal to contain incorrect assumptions, this is not good-faith bargaining. Employers who refuse to provide the union with relevant information that it requests and needs in order to responsibly represent the employees in the bargaining process are also engaging in an unfair labor practice. Relevant information includes job descriptions, time-study data, financial data supporting a company claim that it is unable to meet union demands, and competitive wage data to support a company claim that the union is demanding noncompetitive wage rates.

Taking unilateral action on a matter subject to bargaining is also an unfair employer labor practice under Section 8(a)5. One example is giving employees a raise or additional benefits during the term of a collective bargaining agreement without first consulting the union. This behavior would have the effect of undermining the union as a bargaining representative and, thus, would be unlawful.

Because bargaining is meant to secure benefits for employees, there are fewer cases of union refusals to bargain, but failure of a union to bargain in good faith is a violation of Section 8(b)3. Thus, unions may not violate any of the procedural requirements already delineated, nor may they refuse to sign a contract after an agreement has been reached or insist on bargaining for clauses that fall outside the scope of mandatory bargaining.

mandatory subjects of collective bargaining
Subjects over which the parties must bargain, including rates of pay, wages, hours of employment, and other terms and conditions of employment.

permissive subjects of collective bargaining
Subjects that are not primarily about conditions of emploment and, therefore, need not be bargained over.

SUBJECTS OF BARGAINING

All subjects of bargaining are either mandatory or permissive. Many people mistakenly assume that wages are the only real issue that unions bargain over. As Table 19-6 illustrates, unions have been successful in negotiating higher wages for workers in most progressions. However, the scope of bargaining items is much more expansive than merely wages. **Mandatory subjects of collective bargaining** are those over which the parties must bargain: rates of pay, wages, hours of employment, and other terms and conditions of employment. Failure to bargain over these subjects constitutes an unfair labor practice. All other bargaining subjects are **permissive** and need not be bargained over. Management decisions concerning the

Occupation	Union Earnings	Nonunion Earnings	
Management, professional, and related occupations	$896	$886	**TABLE 19-6**
Professional and related occupations	$885	$883	**UNION AND NONUNION EARNINGS BY OCCUPATION, 2003**
Service occupations	$606	$382	
Sales and office occupations	$629	$530	
Natural resources, construction, and maintenance occupations	$851	$558	
Production, transportation, and material moving occupations	$688	$493	

Note: These numbers are median weekly earnings for full-time wage and salary workers.

Source: Adapted from **www.aflcio.org/aboutunions/joinunions/whyjoin/uniondifference/uniondiff5.cfm**.

commitment of capital and the basic scope of the enterprise, for instance, are not primarily about conditions of employment and, thus, are not mandatory. Inclusion of a permissive subject in the bargaining process in one year, even if that results in its inclusion in a collective bargaining agreement, does not make that subject an issue of mandatory bargaining in any future contract. The only subjects that cannot be included in the bargaining process are illegal terms, such as a contract clause that would require unlawful discrimination by the employer.

Unions have traditionally tried to expand the scope of mandatory items. Mandatory items concerning wages include piece rates, shift differentials, incentives, severance pay, holiday pay, vacation pay, profit sharing, stock option plans, and hours (including overtime provisions). Mandatory items concerning conditions of employment include layoff and recall provision, seniority systems, promotion policies, no-strike and no-lockout clauses, grievance procedures, and work rules. In the following case, the U.S. Supreme Court examined the issue of whether changes in prices offered in a company cafeteria were subject to mandatory bargaining.

CASE 19-5

Ford Motor Company v. NLRB
United States Supreme Court,
441 U.S. 488 (1979)

Ford Motor Company provided its employees with in-plant cafeteria and vending services. Although Ford contracted out these services to an independent caterer, the company retained the right to review and approve the quality and price of the food. Ford notified the union of pending price increases, and the union sought to bargain over these increases. When Ford refused to bargain over the issue, the union filed an unfair labor practice charge with the NLRB, alleging a violation of Section 8(a)5.

The NLRB decided in favor of the union, finding the prices of food available in the plant cafeteria to be within the scope of "other terms and conditions of employment,"

which the employer must bargain over. The U.S. Court of Appeals enforced the order to bargain. Ford then appealed to the U.S. Supreme Court.

Justice White

The Board has consistently held that in-plant food prices are among those terms and conditions of employment defined in Section 8(d) and about which the employer and union must bargain under Sections 8(a)5 and 8(b)3. Because it is evident that Congress assigned to the Board the primary task of construing these provisions in the course of adjudicating charges of unfair refusals to bargain and because the "classification of bargaining subjects as 'terms or conditions of employment' is a matter concerning which the Board has special expertise," its judgment as to what is a mandatory bargaining subject is entitled to considerable deference.

Of course, the judgment of the Board is subject to judicial review; but if its construction of the statute is reasonably defensible, it should not be rejected merely because the courts might prefer another view of the statute. [W]e have refused enforcement of Board orders where they had "no reasonable basis in law," either because the proper legal standard was not applied or because the Board applied the correct standard but failed to give the plain language of the standard its ordinary meaning. We have also parted company with the Board's interpretation where it was "fundamentally inconsistent with the structure of the Act" and an attempt to usurp "major policy decisions properly made by Congress." [W]e could not accept the Board's application of the Act where we were convinced that the Board was moving "into a new area of regulation which Congress had not committed to it."

The Board is vulnerable on none of these grounds in this case. Construing and applying the duty to bargain and the language of Section 8(d), "other terms and conditions of employment," are tasks lying at the heart of the Board's function. ... [W]e conclude that the Board's consistent view that in-plant food prices and services are mandatory bargaining subjects is not an unreasonable or unprincipled construction of the statute and that it should be accepted and enforced.

The terms and conditions under which food is available on the job are plainly germane to the "working environment." Furthermore the company is not in the business of selling food to its employees, and the establishment of in-plant food prices is not among those "managerial decisions, which lie at the core of entrepreneurial control." The Board is in no sense attempting to permit the Union to usurp managerial decisionmaking; nor is it seeking to regulate an area from which Congress intended to exclude it.

Including within Section 8(d) the prices of in-plant-supplied food and beverages would also serve the ends of the National Labor Relations Act. "The object of this Act was not to allow governmental regulation of the terms and conditions of employment, but rather to ensure that employers and their employees could work together to establish mutually satisfactory conditions. As illustrated by the facts of this case, substantial disputes can arise over the pricing of in-plant-supplied food and beverages. National labor policy contemplates that areas of common dispute between employers and employees be funneled into collective bargaining. The assumption is that this is preferable to allowing recurring disputes to fester outside the negotiation process until strikes or other forms of economic warfare occur.

The trend of industrial practice supports this conclusion. In response to increasing employee concern over the issue, many contracts are now being negotiated that contain provisions concerning in-plant food services. In this case, as already noted, local agreements between Ford and the Union have contained detailed provisions about nonprice aspects of in-plant food services for several years. Although not conclusive, current industrial practice is highly relevant in construing the phrase "terms and conditions of employment."

Ford nevertheless argues against classifying food prices and services as mandatory bargaining subjects because they do not "vitally affect" the terms and conditions of employment and because they are trivial matters over which neither party should be required to bargain.

There is no merit to either of these arguments. Here, the matter of in-plant food prices and services is an aspect of the relationship between Ford and its own employees.

As for the argument that in-plant food prices and services are too trivial to qualify as mandatory subjects, the Board has a contrary view, and we have no basis for rejecting it. It is also clear that the bargaining-unit employees in this case considered the matter far from trivial since they pressed an unsuccessful boycott to secure a voice in setting food prices. They evidently felt, and common sense also tells us, that even minor increases in the cost of meals can amount to a substantial sum of money over time.

Ford also argues that the Board's position will result in unnecessary disruption because any small change in price or service will trigger the obligation to bargain. The problem, it is said, will be particularly acute in situations where several unions are involved, possibly requiring endless rounds of negotiations over issues as minor as the price of a cup of coffee or a soft drink.

These concerns have been thought exaggerated by the Board. Its position in this case, as in all past cases involving the same issue, is that it is sufficient compliance with the statutory mandate if management honors a specific union request for bargaining about changes that have been made or are to be made. The Board apparently assumes that, as a practical matter, requests to bargain will not be lightly made. Moreover, problems created by constantly shifting food prices can be anticipated and provided for in the collective bargaining agreement. Furthermore, if it is true that disputes over food prices are likely to be frequent and intense, it follows that more, not less, collective bargaining is the remedy. This is the assumption of national labor policy, and it is soundly supported by both reason and experience.

Finally, Ford asserts that to require it to engage in bargaining over in-plant food service prices would be futile because those prices are set by a third-party supplier, ARA. It is true that ARA sets vending machine and cafeteria prices, but under Ford's contract with ARA, Ford retains the right to review and control food services and prices. In any event, an employer can always affect prices by initiating or altering a subsidy to the third-party supplier such as that provided by Ford in this case, and will typically have the right to change suppliers at some point in the future. To this extent the employer holds future, if not present, leverage over in-plant food services and prices.

Affirmed in favor of Appellee, NLRB.

STRIKES, PICKETING, AND BOYCOTTS

In 2003, fourteen major work stoppages occurred.[14] Major work stoppages may occur through worker-initiated strikes or employer-initiated lockouts. These 14 major work stoppages idled 129,2000 workers and led to 4.1 million idle work-days.[15] The prudent businessperson needs to understand the National Labor Relations Act not only as it applies to labor organizing and collective bargaining but also as it applies to three other common occurrences in labor–management relations: strikes, picketing, and boycotts.

STRIKES

A **strike**, simply defined, is a temporary, concerted withdrawal of labor. It is the ultimate weapon used by employees to secure recognition or to gain favorable terms in the collective bargaining process because it can be so costly to employers. For example, in 2001, pilots employed by the Delta Airlines' Comair unit went on an eight-week strike in an attempt to receive pay raises. The pilot strike caused Delta to lose approximately $1.5 million to $2 million in revenue per day.[16]

> **strike** A temporary concerted withdrawal of labor.

However, not all strikes are legal, and employees engaging in certain types of legal strikes may still lose their jobs as a consequence of striking. The type of strike that one is engaged in is determined both by the purpose of the strike and by the methods used by the strikers.

Lawful Strikes. A lawful **economic strike** is a nonviolent work stoppage for the purpose of obtaining better terms and conditions of employment under a collective bargaining agreement. Because this type of strike is a protected activity, strikers are entitled to return to their jobs once the strike is over. However, employers are allowed to fill economic strikers' jobs while the strike is taking place, and if permanent replacements are hired, strikers are not entitled to return to their jobs. This ability of the employer to replace economic strikers permanently tends to make the strike a less potent weapon than it at first appears.

> **economic strike** A nonviolent work stoppage for the purpose of obtaining better terms and conditions of employment under a collective bargaining agreement.

Because of the ability of the employer to permanently replace workers engaged in an economic strike if they first hire permanent replacement workers, unions have fought to try to get Congress to pass legislation prohibiting the use of permanent replacement workers. Workers did achieve a minor victory in 1995, when President Clinton issued an executive order prohibiting federal contractors with government contracts worth over $100,000 from hiring permanent replacements for strikers. If any such firm does hire replacement workers, the labor secretary is to notify the head of any agencies that have contracts with such firms, and the contracts are to be terminated and no contracts are to be made with said firms in the future.

Even if replaced, however, economic strikers still are entitled to vote in representational elections at their former place of employment within one year of their replacement or until they find "regular and substantially similar employment" elsewhere, whichever comes first. Any permanently replaced economic

---

[14] Major Work Stoppages in 2003, **www.bls.gov/news.release/wkstp.nr0.htm**.

[15] *Id.*

[16] N. Fonti, "Comair Permanently Cuts 200 Pilot Jobs," *Atlanta Journal and Constitution*, May 17, 2001.

striker is also entitled to be rehired when any job vacancies arise at the former place of employment.

Employees may also lawfully engage in a strike over employer unfair labor practices. An **unfair labor practice strike** is a nonviolent work stoppage in protest against an employer's committing an unfair labor practice. Employees engaged in such a strike are entitled to return to their jobs at the end of the strike. If the employer fires such strikers, they will be able to sue for reinstatement and back pay for the time during which they were unlawfully prohibited from working.

unfair labor practice strike
A nonviolent work stoppage for the purpose of protesting an employer's commission of an unfair labor practice.

Unlawful Strikes. Strikes are unlawful when either their means or their purpose is unlawful. Strikes with unlawful means include (1) *sit-down strikes*, wherein employees remain on the job but cease working; (2) *partial strikes*, wherein only some of the workers leave their jobs; and (3) *wildcat strikes*, which are strikes that are not authorized by the parent union and that are frequently in violation of the collective bargaining agreement. Strikes that include acts of violence or blockading of exits or entrances of a plant are also strikes with unlawful means.

Strikes with an unlawful purpose include *jurisdictional strikes*, which are work stoppages for the purpose of forcing an employer to resolve a dispute between two unions. Jurisdictional strikes are most common in the construction industry, where two unions often disagree over which trade (and, thus, which union's members) is entitled to do a particular type of work on a given project.

Also unlawful are a number of strikes that fall into the category of secondary strikes. A *secondary strike* occurs when the unionized workers of one employer go on strike to force their employer to bring pressure on another employer with whom the union has a dispute.

When employees engage in a strike with unlawful means or an unlawful purpose, they are not legally protected and, therefore, may be discharged by their employer. For example, in 2003, the NLRB decided that a strike by an employer's security guards was not protected because the union failed to take reasonable precautions to protect the employer's operations from foreseeable dangers resulting from security guards' work stoppage. Because the strike was not protected, the employer's termination of the security guards was lawful.[17]

BOYCOTTS

boycott A refusal to deal with, purchase goods from, or work for a business.

A **boycott** is a refusal to deal with, purchase goods from, or work for a business. Like a strike, it is a means used to prohibit a company from carrying on its business so that it will accede to union demands. Primary boycotts are legal; that is, a union may boycott an employer with whom the union is directly engaged in a labor dispute.

Secondary boycotts, like secondary strikes, are illegal. A secondary boycott occurs when unionized employees who have a labor dispute with their employer boycott another employer to force it to cease doing business with their employer.

secondary boycott A boycott against one employer to force it to cease doing business with another employer with whom the union has a dispute.

One type of secondary boycott is legal under the NLRA in the construction and garment industries. That is the "hot cargo agreement," an agreement between the union and the employer that union members need not handle nonunion goods and that the employer will not deal with nonunion employers. This type of secondary boycott is considered an unfair labor practice under Section 8(b) in all other industries, however.

---

[17] NLRB, Sixty-Eighth Annual Report of the NLRB for Fiscal Year Ended September 30, 2003, p. 23, available at **www.nlrb.gov/nlrb/shared_files/brochures**.

PICKETING

Picketing is the stationing of individuals outside an employer's place of business for the purpose of informing passersby of the facts of a labor dispute. Picketing usually accompanies a strike, but it may occur alone, especially when employees want to continue to work in order to draw a paycheck.

Just as there are numerous types of strikes and boycotts, there are multiple types of picketing with different degrees of protection. **Informational picketing**, designed to truthfully inform the public of a labor dispute between an employer and employees, is protected. This protection may be lost, however, if the picketing has the effect of stopping deliveries and services to the employer. Picketing designed to secure a stoppage of service to the employer is called signal picketing and is not protected.

Jurisdictional picketing, like jurisdictional strikes, occurs when two unions are in dispute over which union's workers are entitled to do a particular job. If one union pickets because work was assigned to the other union's members, this action is unlawful; jurisdictional disputes are resolved by the NLRB under an expedited procedure, so there is no need to take coercive action against the employer. The other union or the employer may secure an injunction to preserve the status quo until the board resolves the dispute.

Organizational, or **recognitional**, **picketing**, which is designed to force the employer to recognize and bargain with an uncertified union, is illegal when (1) another union has already been recognized as the exclusive representative of the employees, and the employer and employees are operating under a valid collective bargaining agreement negotiated by that union; (2) there has been a valid representation election within the past year; or (3) the union has been picketing for longer than 30 days without filing a petition for a representation election.

When (1) and (2) are not applicable, a union may picket for up to 30 days while attempting to secure signed authorization cards from over 30 percent of the employees. Once the appropriate signatures have been obtained, the union may then file its petition for recognition and continue picketing to inform the public of the company's refusal to recognize the union.

Picketing, like striking, may be illegal because of its means. Violent picketing is, of course, unlawful. So is massed picketing, though this type of unlawful activity is somewhat more difficult to define. It is said to exist when the pickets are so massed as to be coercive or to block entrances and exits. In cases interpreting this term, the courts have tended to find unlawful massed picketing when there have been so many picketers before a gateway to a plant that free entry or exit is made difficult or almost impossible.

picketing The stationing of individuals outside an employer's place of business to inform passersby of the fact of a labor dispute.

informational picketing Picketing designed to truthfully inform the public of a labor dispute.

jurisdictional picketing Picketing by one union to protest an assignment of jobs to another union's members.

organizational (recognitional) picketing Picketing designed to force the employer to recognize and bargain with an uncertified union.

GLOBAL DIMENSIONS OF LABOR–MANAGEMENT RELATIONS

Many U.S. corporations have moved their operations overseas to obtain cheaper labor costs. Our laws permit this. But whereas a corporation's foreign operations are not subject to U.S. labor laws, most countries have labor laws of their own to which U.S. companies are subject. Likewise, foreign companies with plants in the United States must comply with our labor laws.

Many scholars argue that it would be desirable to have uniform labor laws across the world, or at least among all the industrialized nations. Their reasons differ. Some believe that there are certain inherent rights of workers that should be protected regardless of where they live and work. Others believe that uniformity would make it easier for multinationals that have a presence in many countries because then their labor practices could be uniform throughout all their operations.

The likelihood of a worldwide uniform labor law is almost nonexistent, if only because different countries' leaders have very different philosophies about the purpose of labor law. There are a few similarities, however, among most countries' labor laws. For example, in almost all countries a worker has the right to refuse to perform unsafe work.[18]

The International Labor Organization (ILO), to which 174 nations now send government, management, and labor delegates, has attempted to create some uniformity among the labor laws of member nations. The ILO formulates conventions and recommendations for labor legislation that can be adopted by all countries. These include minimum specifications and often provisions for national or traditional variations on those basics. Enforcement procedures are generally left to the individual nations.[19] The ILO has promulgated 182 conventions and 190 recommendations; there have been over 6,600 ratifications of these.[20] Although there are still more differences than similarities in labor laws from country to country, the ILO has generated some harmonizing of laws.

SUMMARY

The National Labor Relations Act is the primary legislation governing labor–management relations. Section 7 of the NLRA sets forth the rights of employees, and Section 8(a) identifies specific employer behaviors, called unfair labor practices, that are prohibited. Employee unfair labor practices are set out in Section 8(b). The Landrum–Griffith Act was passed to ensure proper internal governance of labor organizations.

The administrative agency responsible for oversight and enforcement of the NLRA is the National Labor Relations Board. The board is primarily responsible for ensuring that organizing campaigns are conducted fairly and that neither employers nor employees commit unfair labor practices. Prospects for a worldwide uniform labor law are negligible, but the International Labor Organization is attempting to create some harmony among the labor laws of member nations.

REVIEW QUESTIONS

19-1 Explain why some people support unions whereas others oppose them.

19-2 Explain the relationship between Section 7 and Section 8 of the NLRA.

19-3 Explain why someone would argue that the existence of Section 8(a)1 really makes Sections 8(a)2–5 unnecessary.

19-4 Describe the roles of the National Labor Relations Board and its general counsel.

19-5 What is the difference between violating a board rule and committing an unfair labor practice?

19-6 What advice would you give to an employer who wants to adopt some form of employee participation program but is concerned about the legality of such programs?

---

[18] M. Lennard, "The Right to Refuse Unsafe Work," *Comparative Labor Law Journal* 4 (1981), p. 217.
[19] International Labor Organization (ILO), *The ILO: What It Is, What It Does*, February 10, 2000.
[20] *Id.*

REVIEW PROBLEMS

19-7 A national union wanted to organize the employees of Dexter Thread Mills. The company parking lot was adjacent to a public highway, separated from the highway by a 10-foot-wide grassy public easement. The union sought to distribute handbills in the parking lot; the company sought to exclude the union from the lot. Was the union allowed to distribute the handbills on the company lot?

19-8 Keystone, a producer of pretzels, employed about 40 people. Six months after the plant was sold, Local 6 obtained authorization cards from 17 employees out of a perceived potential bargaining unit of 29 employees. Keystone authorized one employee who had antiunion sentiments to conduct surveillance of union activities and report back to management. Keystone officials also interrogated two prounion employees and gave a raise to a union foe while denying one to a union adherent. They solicited and promised to resolve employee grievances and to grant benefits. They conducted an employee meeting on a holiday: Employees who attended were paid and responded to an employee poll. Through its president, the company expressed satisfaction about the negative response to unionization reflected by the poll. Could the union file a successful unfair-labor-practice charge?

19-9 Otis Elevator was acquired by United Technologies (UT) in 1975. A review of Otis's operations showed its technology to be outdated. The company's products were poorly engineered and were losing money. Its production and research facilities were scattered across the United States with many duplications of work. Research, in particular, was done at two separate New Jersey facilities, one of which was extremely outdated. UT did all of its research at a major research and development center in Connecticut; some research for Otis was also done there. UT decided to transfer Otis research from the two New Jersey locations to an expanded facility in Connecticut in order to strengthen the overall research effort and to allow Otis to redesign its product. The union representing Otis employees alleged that UT had engaged in an unfair labor practice by refusing to bargain with the union over its decision to relocate the work. Was UT's refusal to bargain over this decision a violation of Section 8(a)5?

19-10 The clerks at Raley's were represented by the Independent Drug Clerks Association (IDCA). When the Retail Clerks Union (Retail Clerks) began a campaign to oust IDCA, Raley's maintained a neutral posture. Retail Clerks picketed the store in July. Could Raley's obtain an injunction prohibiting the picketing?

19-11 The workers at the Big R Restaurant were trying unsuccessfully to negotiate a new contract. On Monday, all of the busboys called in sick. On Tuesday, all the cooks called in sick. On Wednesday, the waitresses all called in sick. Was there anything unlawful about the employees' behavior? If so, what recourse does the employer have?

19-12 Ajax manufacturing company was unionized in 1998 and had been operating under a contract negotiated at the beginning of that year. Several new workers were hired near the end of the year, and they thought a stronger union was needed. They began picketing the employer to recognize a different union as the representative of the workers, or at minimum to have a decertification election. Is their picketing legal? Why or why not?

CASE PROBLEMS

19-13 Employees in the entertainment department of the Taj Mahal Casino were attempting to organize themselves into a union. The employees included stage technicians, convention lounge technicians, and entertainment event technicians. The employer also maintained a list of 40 "on-call" employees who performed the same functions as the regular technicians on an intermittent basis, whenever more technicians were needed. Whenever the casino needed to hire new full-time employees, it hired the casu- als with the greatest number of hours already worked at the casino. In 1990, casuals averaged 7 hours per week; in early 1991, 17 hours per week. The employees sought to have their bargaining unit include both full-time and casual employees. Apply the facts of this case to the criteria used in determining the appropriate bargaining unit and explain how the case should be decided. *Trump Taj Mahal Associates Ltd. v. International Alliance of Theatrical Stage Employees*, 306 NLRB 57 (1992)

19-14 GranCare, Inc., operates a 282-bed nursing home in Bayside, Wisconsin, a suburb of Milwaukee. The home is divided into several units, the largest being a nursing department consisting of a director of nursing, an assistant director of nursing, 19 registered nurses (RNs), 38 LPNs, 90 certified nursing assistants (CNAs), and a handful of clerical employees. At any nursing home, someone has to perform basic tasks such as helping groom, feed, and toilet the residents and changing their bed linens. Here those tasks primarily fall to CNAs, the largest employee group, and everyone in this case agrees that they are not supervisors under the NLRA.

Above the CNAs are Audubon's LPNs, and above the LPNs are the RNs. Everyone agrees that the RNs, 19 of them at Audubon, are supervisors under the NLRA. The LPNs lie between the two.

The differences between Audubon's three levels of nursing department personnel are largely based on education and training: RNs have more of both, are paid more money, and have higher licenses. By virtue of their licenses, RNs can perform advanced tasks, such as initiating IVs, which LPNs cannot do. RNs regularly attend meetings regarding Medicare staffing and rehabilitation, and they often interact with physicians. If nursing employees are absent, RNs are responsible for scheduling replacements. RNs, unlike LPNs, often work from supervisory offices for which they are given keys. RNs also perform evaluations of the CNAs and attend weekly management meetings with GranCare's director of nursing. Also, RNs are salaried and do not punch a time clock.

CNAs and LPNs, on the other hand, are paid by the hour and punch time clocks to signal their arrival at and departure from work. During the evening hours, when few workers are on hand, a single "house supervisor RN" is in charge of the facility. This is compatible with Wisconsin law, which the parties tell us requires that an RN be present at the home at all times.

LPNs act as "charge nurses," meaning they are expected to "take charge" by directing the CNAs, using discipline when necessary, and handling complaints. LPNs, according to GranCare, are told that "the role of the Charge Nurse is more than passing meds and doing treatments. The Charge Nurse is a 'management' role in assisting the RN, supervision and direction of CNAs, communicating with MDs, team work with the CNAs (i.e., feeding, answering lights, etc.)."

The union organized the CNAs and LPNs over GranCare's contention that LPNs were supervisors and, thus, should not have been included in the bargaining unit. GranCare refused to recognize and bargain with the union, and the NLRB issued an order requiring the employer to bargain with the union. Why do you believe that the court of appeals ultimately either granted or rejected the petitioner's request for enforcement? *NLRB v. GranCare, Inc.*, 170 F.3d 662 (1998)

19-15 ATC operates the city bus system in Santa Clarita, California. ATC's bus drivers were represented by the Teamsters, which had a collective bargaining agreement with ATC that was in effect from November 1996 to August 2001. Pursuant to a provision contained in the collective bargaining agreement, ATC provided space for a bulletin board for the union to use.

In mid-2000, the United Transportation Union ("the UTU") sought to become the employees' collective bargaining representatives. The board scheduled an election between the Teamsters and the UTU for January 3, 2001.

On December 7 or 8, a notice was posted on the bulletin board announcing a special meeting for all drivers/operators to be held at a local hotel. After seeing the notice, ATC operations manager, Sheri Camuso, removed it from the bulletin board. The following week, on December 14 or 15, a similar notice was posted. Again, Camuso removed the notice within hours. Camuso claimed that ATC's corporate headquarters had told her that the company must remain neutral in the upcoming election and ATC would no longer allow the Teamsters to post notices concerning the election. On December 26, ATC distributed a memorandum concerning the posting of union materials. It stated in part that to preserve " 'employer neutrality' … there shall be no literature posted of any kind by either the UTU or the Teamsters on the bulletin boards."

The election was held as scheduled on January 3, 2001, and the UTU defeated the Teamsters. Following the election, the Teamsters filed objections to the election as well as an unfair labor practices claim. Given your understanding of the NLRA, did ATC commit an unfair labor practice? Why or why not? *ATC Vancom, CA v. NLRB*, 370 F.3d 692 (2004)

19-16 In June 2000, two agents of the American Postal Workers Union entered the Postal Service's Bulk Mail Center to solicit drivers employed by Mail Contractors of America (MCOA), a company that hauls mail by truck for the Postal Service. The two agents, neither of which was employed by the Postal Service, went to a lounge to solicit membership from drivers. Johnson, a Postal Service employee, joined the two agents in the lounge. Upon finding the three men talking, a supervisor, after consulting with a manager, instructed them to leave the Bulk Mail Center, which they did. The supervisor and the manager acted pursuant to the Postal Service's Southeast Area Office Policy. The office policy was to remain neutral, neither hindering nor helping union organization, as well as to prohibit all solicitations. The union filed an unfair labor practice charge. Did the Postal Service commit an unfair labor practice? What reasons did the NLRB give for its conclusion? *American Postal Worker's Union v. NLRB*, 370 F.3d 25 (2004)

19-17 In June 2002, Lynch Construction was building a maintenance facility on the Greenbrier's property. The union determined that Lynch Construction violated its agreement with the union by hiring employees represented by a different labor union to work on the Greenbrier project. To protest this alleged breach of agreement, the union set up a picketing stand a few feet from the Greenbrier's property line near the Greenbrier's employee entrance on the public right-of-way along U.S. Highway 60, a major thoroughfare of the county with heavy traffic and a speed limit of 55 mph. The union was not protesting the Greenbrier, but rather Lynch Construction, and thus the picketers were not employees of the Greenbrier.

On June 20, the Greenbrier notified local police about the picketing. When the police arrived, they notified the picketers that they were required to have a permit for assembly. After filing for a permit and finding out the granting of said permit would be delayed, the picketers returned.

On June 24, after the picketers had returned, the Greenbrier again notified the police about the picketers. Greenbrier cited public safety and the 55 mph speed limit on the highway as the main reasons for its concern.

Ultimately, the city attorney decided to let the picketers continue without a permit. The union subsequently filed suit with the NLRB against Greenbrier alleging that Greenbrier unlawfully interfered with the union's right to lawfully picket by contacting the police to have the picketers removed from the premise or arrested. Did Greenbrier's actions constitute an unfair labor practice by interfering with the union's right to picket? Why or why not? *CSX Hotels, Inc. v. NLRB*, 2004 U.S.App. LEXIS 15391 (2004)

19-18 Electromation, Inc., a manufacturer of electrical components, reduced wages, bonuses, and benefits for employees, while tightening attendance and leave policies. In response to employees' complaints, Electromation set up five "action committees," each made up of six employees and two management representatives. The purpose of the committees was to make suggestions to management about such policies as the treatment of absentee employees and employee remuneration. The Teamsters Union, which had been trying to organize Electromation's workers, filed an unfair labor practice charge against the company, arguing that the committees were comparable to a union dominated by management. The NLRB agreed. On appeal, did the Seventh Circuit Court of Appeals uphold the decision of the NLRB? Why or why not? *Electromation v. NLRB*, 35 F.3d 1148 (1994)

ASSIGNMENT ON THE INTERNET

You have learned many laws and regulations that govern labor–management relations. Many of those laws and regulations are used in each of the National Labor Relations Board's decisions. Visit the NLRB's Web site that contains recent decisions (www.nlrb.gov/nlrb/legal/decisions/default.asp) and read at least two decisions.

What information from this chapter helps you better understand the decisions? What were the reasons given for the decisions? When reading, pay careful attention to how the board interpreted or resolved ambiguity in the law. Finally, what ethical norms support the decisions?

ON THE INTERNET

www.nlrb.gov/nlrb/home/default.asp This site is the home page of the National Labor Relations Board.
www.aflcio.org Find out about the AFL-CIO at this site.
www.iisg.nl/~w3vl/index.html This site, Labor History and Business, is a virtual library site that would be a good place to begin research on any labor topic.
www.opm.gov/lmr Links are provided at the Office of Personnel Management that are useful to better understanding labor–management relations.
www.dol.gov The home page for the Department of Labor provides a wealth of useful information and links. This is a good place to begin research in areas of employment law, especially the Bureau of Labor Statistics.
www.flra.gov/index.html At this site you will find the Federal Labor Relations Authority, which administers labor management for the entire federal workforce.

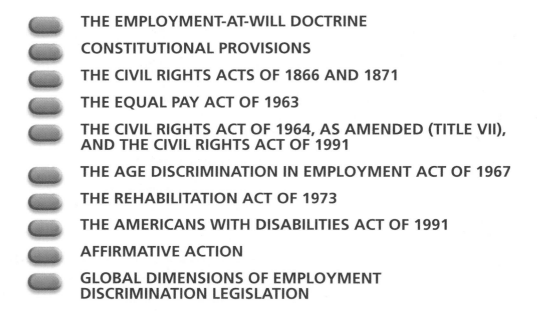

20

EMPLOYMENT DISCRIMINATION

Being an employer was so much easier one hundred years ago. Managers could use almost any criteria for hiring, promoting, and firing employees. Today, employers' decision-making powers are restricted by both federal and state legislation. This chapter focuses on the laws that limit employers' abilities to use any criteria they wish in hiring, firing, and promoting employees.

The right of the employer to terminate an employment relationship was originally governed almost exclusively by the employment-at-will doctrine, which is discussed in the first section of this chapter. The second section discusses the constitutional provisions that affect an employer's ability to hire and fire workers. The following six sections discuss each of the major pieces of federal legislation designed to prohibit discrimination in employment relations. These acts are discussed in the order in which they were enacted. The ninth section discusses the increasingly controversial subject of affirmative action. Global dimensions of employment discrimination are discussed in the final section.

Critical Thinking About the Law

You will soon be a businessperson, and you may be responsible for hiring, promoting, and firing people. When you do hold this position, you will need to be aware of federal and state laws that prohibit discrimination in employment. Why do you think the government has prohibited discrimination in employment? What ethical norm does the government emphasize by prohibiting discrimination in employment? The government seems to emphasize justice, in the sense that it wants all human beings to be treated equally, regardless of class, race, gender, age, and so on. Reading the following case and answering the critical thinking questions will sharpen your thinking about laws prohibiting employment discrimination.

Tom, Jonathan, and Bob were hired to work as executive secretaries at a major corporation. The other secretaries for the corporation were surprised that three men were hired as secretaries when no man had ever before been hired as a secretary at this corporation. All secretaries were required to type 20 five-page reports each day in addition to completing work for their respective departments. After the male secretaries had been working at the corporation for approximately one month, they received pay raises. None of the female secretaries received raises. When the women asked the manager why the male secretaries had received raises, the manager claimed that the men were performing extra duties and consequently received raises.

1. The manager claimed that the men received raises because they were performing extra duties. Can you identify any potential problems in the manager's response?

   Clue: What words or phrases are ambiguous in the manager's response?

2. The female secretaries decided to bring a suit against the corporation. They claimed that they did not receive raises because of their gender. Pretend that you are a lawyer, and the female secretaries have come to you with their complaint. After talking with the secretaries, you realize that you need to find out some additional information. What additional information might be helpful in this case?

   Clue: The female secretaries claimed that the male secretaries received raises because they are male. Can you think of any alternative reasons why the men might have received raises?

3. You discover only one case regarding equal pay that was decided in your district. In this case, both men and women performed hard labor in a factory, but only men received offers to work during the third shift. Those workers who worked the third shift received an additional $30 per hour. The women in this factory claimed that they were not asked to work the third shift because of their gender. The factory argued that the women who worked at the factory were not physically strong enough to endure the work of the third shift. The court ruled in favor of the women. Do you think that you should use this case as an analogy? Why or why not?

   Clue: How are the two cases similar? How are they different?

THE EMPLOYMENT-AT-WILL DOCTRINE

In all industrial democracies except the United States, workers are protected by law from unjust termination. The traditional "American rule" of employment has been that a contract of employment for an indeterminate term is terminable at will by either party. Thus, an employee who did not have a contract for a specific length of time could be terminated at any time, for any reason.

This **employment-at-will doctrine** has been justified by the right of the employer to control his or her property. It has also been justified on the grounds that it is fair because both employer and employee have the equal right to terminate the relationship. Some may question the latter justification

employment-at-will doctrine A contract of employment for an indeterminate term is terminable at will by either the employer or the employee; the traditional "American rule" governing employer–employee relations.

because the employer can almost always replace a terminated employee, whereas it is not equally easy for the employee to find new employment. Thus, the employment-at-will doctrine places the employer in a position to treat employees arbitrarily.

Partially because of the abuse that can occur under this doctrine, it has been slowly restricted by state and federal legislation, as well as by changes in the common law. One of the first pieces of legislation to restrict the employer's right to freely terminate employees was the National Labor Relations Act (discussed in the previous chapter), which has reduced the number of employees covered by the employment-at-will doctrine. This reduction has occurred because the act gives employees the right to enter into collective bargaining agreements, which usually restrict the employer's ability to terminate employees except for "just cause." The employees covered by these agreements are, thus, no longer "at-will" employees.

The effect of the doctrine has also been restricted by a growing number of common law and state statutory exceptions. Such exceptions usually fall into three categories: implied contract, violations of public policy, and implied covenant of good faith and fair dealing. In some states, the courts find that an implied contract may arise from statements made by the employer in advertising the position or in an employment manual. For example, sometimes a company provides an employment manual delineating the grounds for termination but not containing any provision for termination "at will." Under such circumstances, if the court finds that the employee reasonably relied on the manual, the court will not apply the employment-at-will doctrine and will allow termination only for reasons stated in the manual. Or, if certain procedures, such as notice and a hearing, are stated as being used to terminate an employee, such procedures must be followed or the termination is unlawful. Thirty-two states and the District of Columbia recognize this exception.

public policy exception
An exception to the employment-at-will doctrine that makes it unlawful to dismiss an employee for taking certain actions in the public interest.

The **public policy exception** prohibits terminations that contravene established public policy. "Public policy" varies from state to state, but some of the more common terminations deemed unlawful include dismissals based on actions "in the public interest," such as participation in environmental or consumer protection activities, and dismissals resulting from "whistle-blowing." Many states have also cut away at the employment-at-will doctrine with laws that specifically prohibit the termination of employees in retaliation for such diverse activities as serving jury duty, doing military service, filing for or testifying at hearings for workers' compensation claims, whistle-blowing, and refusing to take lie detector tests. A total of 33 states accept the public policy exception.

implied covenant of good faith and fair dealing
An exception to the employment-at-will doctrine that is based on the theory that every employment contract, even an unwritten one, contains the implicit understanding that the parties will deal fairly with each other.

Seven states recognize the **implied covenant of good faith and fair dealing** exception. This theory holds that every employment contract, even an unwritten one, contains an implicit understanding that the parties will deal fairly with one another. Because there is no clear agreement on what constitutes "fair treatment" of an employee, this theory is not often used.

Many federal laws also restrict the employment-at-will doctrine. Employees cannot be fired for filing a complaint, testifying, or causing a hearing to be instituted regarding the payment of the minimum wage, equal pay, or overtime. Pursuit of a discrimination claim is likewise statutorily protected.

The doctrine of employment-at-will, however, still exists and is strongly adhered to in many states. So, although the doctrine is being cut back and, therefore, business managers of the future cannot rely on the continued availability of

TABLE 20-1 EXCEPTIONS TO EMPLOYMENT-AT-WILL DOCTRINE

Public Policy Exception	*Implied Contract Exception*	*Good Faith and Fair Dealing Exception*
Alaska, Arizona, California, Connecticut, Florida, Georgia, Hawaii, Illinois, Indiana, Kansas, Kentucky, Louisiana, Maryland, Michigan, Minnesota, Missouri, Nevada, New Hampshire, New Jersey, New Mexico, New York, North Carolina, Ohio, Oklahoma, Oregon, South Carolina, Tennessee, Texas, Virginia, Washington, West Virginia, Wisconsin	Alabama, Arizona, California, Colorado, Connecticut, Georgia, Idaho, Illinois, Indiana, Kansas, Kentucky, Maine, Maryland, Michigan, Minnesota, Missouri, Nebraska, Nevada, New Jersey, New Mexico, New York, North Carolina, Ohio, Oregon, South Dakota, Tennessee, Texas, Vermont, Washington, West Virginia, Wisconsin, Wyoming, District of Columbia	Alaska, Arizona, California, Colorado, Connecticut, Massachusetts, Minnesota, Montana

this doctrine, it may be a long time before the doctrine is no longer applicable. However, as its applicability varies from state to state, familiarity with the doctrine's parameters in one's own state is extremely important. Table 20-1 lists a breakdown of which states accept each of the three major exceptions.

CONSTITUTIONAL PROVISIONS

The beginnings of antidiscrimination law can be traced back to three constitutional provisions: the Fifth Amendment, which states that no person may be deprived of life, liberty, or property without due process of law; the Thirteenth Amendment, which abolished slavery; and the Fourteenth Amendment, which granted former slaves all the rights and privileges of citizenship and guaranteed the equal protection of the law to all persons. These provisions alone, however, were not sufficient to prohibit the unequal treatment of citizens on the basis of their race, sex, age, religion, and national origin. Congress needed to enact major legislation to bring about a reduction in discrimination. These laws are referred to as civil rights laws and antidiscrimination laws. They are summarized in Table 20-2 and discussed in detail in the following sections.

Civil Rights Act of 1866
Guarantees that all persons in the United States have the same right to make and enforce contracts and have the full and equal benefit of the law.

THE CIVIL RIGHTS ACTS OF 1866 AND 1871

The first major civil rights act was passed immediately after the Civil War: the **Civil Rights Act of 1866** (42 U.S.C.A. Section 1981). This act was designed to effectuate the Thirteenth Amendment and guarantees that all persons in the United States have the same right to make and enforce contracts and have full and equal benefit of the law. The **Civil Rights Act of 1871** (42 U.S.C.A. Section 1982) prohibited discrimination by state and local governments. Initially used only when there was state action, today these acts are also used against purely private discrimination, especially in employment.

Civil Rights Act of 1871
Prohibits discrimination by state and local governments.

TABLE 20-2 FEDERAL STATUTES PROHIBITING DISCRIMINATION IN EMPLOYMENT

Law	*Prohibited Conduct*	*Remedies*
Civil Rights Acts of 1866 and 1871, codified as 42 U.S.C. Sections 1981 and 1982	Discrimination based on *race* and *ethnicity*.	Compensatory damages, including several years of back pay, punitive damages, attorneys' fees, court costs, and court orders.
Equal Pay Act of 1963	Wage discrimination based on *sex*.	Back pay, liquidated damages equivalent to back pay (if defendant was not acting in good faith), attorneys' fees, and court costs.
Civil Rights Acts of 1964 (Title VII) of 1991	Discrimination in terms and conditions of employment based on *race, color, religion, sex*, or *national origin*.	Back pay for up to two years, remedial seniority, compensatory damages, punitive damages (may be limited due to class), attorneys' fees, court costs, and court orders for whatever actions are appropriate, including reinstatement and affirmative action.
Age Discrimination in Employment Act of 1969	Discrimination in terms and conditions of employment on the basis of *age* when the affected individual is age 40 or older.	Back pay, liquidated damages equal to back pay (if defendant acted willfully), attorneys' fees, court costs, and appropriate court orders including reinstatement.
Rehabilitation Act of 1973	Discrimination by government or governmental contractor based on a *handicap*.	Back pay, attorney's fees, court costs, and court orders for appropriate affirmative action.
Americans with Disabilities Act of 1991	Discrimination in employment based on a *disability*.	Hiring, promotion, reinstatement, back pay, reasonable accommodation, compensatory damages, and punitive damages.

APPLICABILITY OF THE ACTS

Initially, these acts were interpreted very narrowly to prohibit discrimination based only on race. For several years, circuit courts of appeals were split as to how race is defined. In June 1986, the U.S. Supreme Court resolved that issue by holding that both an Arabic and a Jewish individual were protected by the Civil Rights Act of 1866. Justice White, writing the majority opinion in *Saint Francis College et al. v. Majid Ghaidan Al-Khazraji*,[1] said that it was clear from the legislative history that the act was intended to protect from discrimination "identifiable classes of persons who are subjected to intentional discrimination solely because of their ancestry or ethnic characteristics," even if those individuals would be considered part of the Caucasian race today. Thus, today these laws have a broader application.

Remedies The acts themselves do not have specific provisions for remedies. A wide variety of both legal remedies (money damages) and equitable remedies (court orders) have been awarded under these statutes. The courts are free under

---

[1] 483 U.S. 1011 (1987). The accompanying case filed by a Jewish plaintiff was *Chaare Tefila Congregation et al. v. John William Cobb et al.*, 481 U.S. 615 (1987).

these acts to award compensatory damages, damages designed to make the plaintiff "whole" again, which may amount to several years of back pay. The courts may also award punitive damages, an amount intended to penalize the defendant for wrongful conduct. Finally, the courts may require the defendant to pay the plaintiff's attorney's fees.

Procedural Limitations Unlike most antidiscrimination laws, the Civil Rights Acts of 1866 and 1871 do not require the plaintiff to first attempt to resolve the discrimination problem through any administrative procedures. The plaintiff simply files the action in federal district court within the time limit prescribed by the state statute of limitations, requesting a jury trial if one is desired. Often a claim under the 1866 or 1871 Civil Rights Act will be added to a claim under another antidiscrimination statute.

THE EQUAL PAY ACT OF 1963

The next major piece of federal legislation to address the problem of discrimination was the **Equal Pay Act of 1963**, an amendment to the Fair Labor Standards Act. Enacted at a time when the average wages of women were less than 60 percent of those of men, the act was designed with a very narrow focus: to prevent wage discrimination based on sex within a business establishment. It was primarily designed to remedy the situations in which women, working alongside men or replacing men, were being paid lower wages for doing substantially the same job.

Equal Pay Act of 1963
Prohibits wage discrimination based on sex.

The act, as stated in 29 U.S.C.A. Section 206(d)1, prohibits any employer from discriminating within any "establishment"

> between employees on the basis of sex by paying wages to employees in such establishment at a rate less than the rate at which he pays wages to employees of the opposite sex … for equal work on jobs the performance of which requires equal skill, effort, and responsibility, and which are performed under similar working conditions, except where payment is made pursuant to (i) a seniority system; (ii) a merit system; (iii) a system which measures earnings by quantity or quality of production; or (iv) differential based on any factor other than sex.

In the typical Equal Pay Act case, the burden of proof is initially on the plaintiff to show that the defendant-employer pays unequal wages to men and women for doing equal work at the same establishment. Two questions result: What is equal work, and what is an establishment?

EQUAL WORK

The courts have interpreted *equal* to mean substantially the same in terms of all four factors listed in the act: skill, effort, responsibility, and working conditions. If the employer varies the actual job duties affecting any one of those factors, there is no violation of the act. For example, if jobs are equal in skill and working conditions, but one requires greater effort, whereas the other requires greater responsibility, the jobs are not equal. Obviously, a sophisticated employer could easily vary at least one duty and then pay men and women different wages or salaries.

Skill is defined as experience, education, training, and ability required to do the job. Effort refers to physical or mental exertion needed for performance of the job. Responsibility is measured by the economic and social consequences that would result from a failure of the employee to perform the job duties in question. Similar working conditions refers to the safety hazards, physical surroundings, and hours of employment. However, an employer is entitled to pay a shift premium to employees working different shifts, as long as he or she does not use sex as a basis for determining who is entitled to work the higher-paying shifts.

Extra Duties. Sometimes employers try to justify pay inequities on the grounds that employees of one sex are given extra duties that justify their extra pay. The courts scrutinize these duties very closely. The duties are sufficient to preclude a finding of equal work only if:

1. The duties are actually performed by those receiving the extra pay.

2. The duties regularly constitute a significant portion of the employee's job.

3. The duties are substantial, as opposed to inconsequential.

4. Additional duties of a comparable nature are not imposed on workers of the opposite sex.

5. The extra duties are commensurate with the pay differential.

6. In some jurisdictions, the additional duties must be available on a nondiscriminatory basis.

Establishments. One business location is obviously an establishment, but if an employer has several locations, they may all be considered part of the same establishment on the basis of an analysis of the company's labor relations policy. The greater the degree of centralized authority for hiring, firing, wage setting, and other human resource matters, the more likely the courts are to find multiple locations to be a single establishment. The more freedom each facility has to determine its own human resource policies, the more likely a court will find it to be independent of other facilities.

DEFENSES

Once an employee establishes that an employer is paying different wages to employees of different sexes doing substantially equal work, there are certain defenses that the employer can raise. These are, in essence, legal justifications for paying unequal wages to men and women.

The first defense that an employer may use is that the pay differential is based on one of the four statutory exceptions found in the Bennet Amendment to the Equal Pay Act. If the wage differential is based on one of these four factors, the differential is justified and the employer is not in violation of the act. The four factors are:

1. A bona fide seniority system.

2. A bona fide merit system.

3. A pay system based on quality or quantity of output.

4. Factors other than sex.

The first three are fairly straightforward. Seniority-, merit-, and productivity-based wage systems must be enacted in good faith and must be applied to both men and women. As minimal evidence of good faith, any such system should be written down.

The fourth factor presents greater problems. Such factors as greater availability of females and their willingness to work for lower wages do not constitute factors other than sex. One factor that is frequently litigated is training programs. A training program that requires trainees to rotate through jobs that are normally paid lower wages will be upheld as long as it is a bona fide training program and not a sham for paying members of one sex higher wages for doing the same job. The court will look at each case individually, but factors that would lead to a training program's being found bona fide include a written description of the training program that is available to employees, nondiscriminatory access to the program for members of both sexes, and demonstrated awareness of the availability of the program by employees of both sexes.

REMEDIES

An employer found to have violated the act cannot remedy the violation by reducing the higher-paid workers' wages or by transferring those of one sex to another job so that they are no longer doing equal work.

A person who has been subject to an Equal Pay Act violation may bring a private action under Section 16(b) of the act and recover back pay in the amount of the differential paid to members of the opposite sex. If the employer had not been acting in good faith in paying the discriminatory wage rates, the court will also award the plaintiff damages in an additional amount equal to the back pay. A successful plaintiff is also entitled to attorney's fees.

THE CIVIL RIGHTS ACT OF 1964, AS AMENDED (TITLE VII), AND THE CIVIL RIGHTS ACT OF 1991

The year after it passed the Equal Pay Act, Congress passed the Civil Rights Act of 1964. **Title VII** of this act is the most common basis for lawsuits premised on discrimination, because it covers a broader area of potential claimants than does either of the previously discussed statutes. Title VII prohibits employers from (1) hiring, firing, or otherwise discriminating in terms and conditions of employment and (2) segregating employees in a manner that would affect their employment opportunities on the basis of their race, color, religion, sex, or national origin. These five categories are known as protected classes.

> **Title VII** The statute that prohibits discrimination in hiring, firing, or other terms and conditions of employment on the basis of race, color, religion, sex, or national origin.

APPLICABILITY OF THE ACT

Employers covered by the act include only those who have 15 or more employees, this year or last, for 20 consecutive weeks, and are engaged in a business that affects interstate commerce. In 1994, the term *employer* was broadened to include the U.S. government, corporations owned by the government, and agencies of the District of Columbia. The act also covers Indian tribes, private clubs, unions, and employment agencies.

In addition to prohibiting discrimination by covered employers, unions, and employment agencies, the act also imposes recordkeeping and reporting requirements on these parties. Covered parties must maintain all records regarding employment opportunities for at least six months. Such records include job applications, notices for job openings, and records of layoffs. If an employment discrimination charge is filed against the employer, such records must be kept until the case is concluded. Annual reports (known as EEO-1 forms) that contain information concerning the number of minorities in various job classifications must be filed annually with the Equal Employment Opportunity Commission (EEOC) by employers of more than 100 workers. A copy of this form is provided in Exhibit 20-1. Finally, each covered employer must display a summary of the relevant portions of Title VII where the employees can see it. The notice must be printed in a language that the employees can read.

PROOF IN EMPLOYMENT DISCRIMINATION CASES

The burden of proof in a discrimination case is initially on the plaintiff. The plaintiff attempts to establish discrimination in one of three ways: (1) disparate treatment, (2) disparate impact, or (3) harassment.

disparate treatment cases
Discrimination cases in which the employer treats one employee less favorably than another because of that employee's color, race, religion, sex, or national origin.

Disparate Treatment. Disparate treatment occurs when one individual is treated less favorably than another because of color, race, religion, sex, or national origin. The key in such cases is proving the employer's unlawful discriminatory motive. This process is referred to as building a prima facie case.

The plaintiff must establish the following set of facts: (1) The plaintiff is within one of the protected classes; (2) he or she applied for a job for which the employer was seeking applicants for hire or promotion; (3) the plaintiff possessed the minimum qualifications to perform that job; (4) the plaintiff was denied the job or promotion; and (5) the employer continued to look for someone to fill the position.

Once the plaintiff has established those facts, the burden shifts to the defendant to articulate legitimate and nondiscriminatory business reasons for rejecting the plaintiff. Such reasons for a failure to promote, for instance, might include a poor work record or excessive absenteeism. If the employer meets this burden, the plaintiff must then demonstrate that the reasons the defendant offered were just a pretext for a real discriminatory motive. In other words, the alleged reason was not the real reason; it was just put forth because it sounded good. One way in which the plaintiff can demonstrate pretext is by showing that the criteria used to reject the plaintiff were not applied to others in the same position. Introduction of past discriminatory policies would also be relevant, as would statistics indicating a general practice of discrimination by the defendant. At the pretext stage, the issue of proving an employer's intent to discriminate first appears and is usually the key to the plaintiff's winning or losing the case. Exhibit 20-2 shows how the burden of proof shifts in a disparate treatment case.

disparate impact cases
Discrimination cases in which the employer's facially neutral policy or practice has a discriminatory effect on employees that belong to a protected class.

Disparate Impact. As complex as disparate treatment cases are, disparate impact cases are even more difficult to establish. **Disparate impact cases** arise when a plaintiff attempts to establish that an employer's facially neutral employment policy or practice has a discriminatory impact on a protected class. In other words, a requirement of the policy or practice applies to everyone equally, but, in application, it disproportionately limits employment opportunities for a particular protected class.

EXHIBIT 20-1 EEO-1 FORM

Joint Reporting Committee
- Equal Employment Opportunity Commission
- Office of Federal Contract Compliance Programs (Labor)

I OF I

EQUAL EMPLOYMENT OPPORTUNITY

EMPLOYER INFORMATION REPORT EEO-1
1994

RETURN COMPLETED REPORT TO:
THE JOINT REPORTING COMMITTEE
P.O. BOX 779
NORFOLK, VA 23501

PHONE: (804) 461-1213

Section A—TYPE OF REPORT
Refer to instructions for number and types of reports to be filed.

I. Indicate by marking in the appropriate box the type of reporting unit for which this copy of the form is submitted (MARK ONLY ONE BOX).

(1) ☐ Single-establishment Employer Report

Multi-establishment Employer:
(2) ☐ Consolidated Report (Required)
(3) ☐ Headquarters Unit Report (Required)
(4) ☐ Individual Establishment Report (Submit one for each establishment with 50 or more employees)
(5) ☐ Special Report

2. Total number of reports being filed by this Company (Answers on Consolidated Report only) _____

Section B—COMPANY IDENTIFICATION (To be answered by all employers)

	OFFICE USE ONLY
I. Parent Company	
a. Name of parent company (owns or controls establishment in item 2) omit if same as label	a.
Address (Number and street)	
City or town / State / ZIP code	b.
	c.
2. Establishment for which this report is filed. (Omit if same as label)	
a. Name of establishment	
Address (Number and street) / City or town / County / State / ZIP code	d.
	e.
b. Employer identification No. (IRS 9-DIGIT TAX NUMBER)	f.

c. Was an EEO-1 report filed for this establishment last year?   Yes ☐ No ☐

Section C—EMPLOYERS WHO ARE REQUIRED TO FILE (To be answered by all employers)

☐ Yes ☐ No   I. Does the entire company have at least 100 employees in the payroll period for which you are reporting?

☐ Yes ☐ No   2. Is your company affiliated through common ownership and/or centralized management with other entities in an enterprise with a total employment of 100 or more?

☐ Yes ☐ No   3. Does the company or any of its establishments (a) have 50 or more employees AND (b) is not exempt as provided by 41 CFR 60-1.5. AND either (1) is a prime government contractor or first-tier subcontractor, and has a contract, subcontract, or purchase order amounting to $50,000 or more, or (2) serves as a depository of Government funds in any amount or is a financial institution which is an issuing and paying agent for U.S. Savings Bonds and Savings Notes?

→ If the response to question C-3 is yes, please enter your Dun and Bradstreet identification number (if you have one): ☐☐☐☐☐☐☐☐

NOTE: If the answer is yes to questions I, 2, or 3, complete the entire form, otherwise skip to Section G.

NSN 7540-00-180-6384

EXHIBIT 20-1 *(Continued)*

Section D—EMPLOYMENT DATA

Employment at this establishment—Report all permanent full-time and part-time employees including apprentices and on-the-job trainees unless specifically excluded as set forth in the instructions. Enter the appropriate figures on all lines and in all columns. Blank spaces will be considered as zeros.

JOB CATEGORIES		OVERALL TOTALS (SUM OF COL. B THRU K) A	MALE					FEMALE				
			WHITE (NOT OF HISPANIC ORIGIN) B	BLACK (NOT OF HISPANIC ORIGIN) C	HISPANIC D	ASIAN OR PACIFIC ISLANDER E	AMERICAN INDIAN OR ALASKAN NATIVE F	WHITE (NOT OF HISPANIC ORIGIN) G	BLACK (NOT OF HISPANIC ORIGIN) H	HISPANIC I	ASIAN OR PACIFIC ISLANDER J	AMERICAN INDIAN OR ALASKAN NATIVE K
Officials and Managers	1											
Professionals	2											
Technicians	3											
Sales Workers	4											
Office and Clerical	5											
Craft Workers (Skilled)	6											
Operatives (Semi-Skilled)	7											
Laborers (Unskilled)	8											
Service Workers	9											
TOTAL	10											
Total employment reported in previous EEO—1 report	11											

NOTE: Omit questions 1 and 2 on the Consolidated Report.

1. Date(s) of payroll period used: 2. Does this establishment employ apprentices:

                    1 ☐ Yes   2 ☐ No

Section E—ESTABLISHMENT INFORMATION *(Omit on the Consolidated Report)*

1. What is the major activity of this establishment? (Be specific, i.e., manufacturing steel castings, retail grocer, wholesale plumbing supplies, title insurance, etc.) Include the specific type of product or type of service provided, as well as the principal business or industrial activity.

OFFICE USE ONLY

Section F—REMARKS

Use this item to give any identification data appearing on last report which differs from that given above, explain major changes in composition or reporting units and other pertinent information.

Section G—CERTIFICATION *(See instructions G)*

Check One

1 ☐ All reports are accurate and were prepared in accordance with the instructions (check on consolidated only).

2 ☐ This report is accurate and was prepared in accordance with the instructions.

Name of Certifying Official	Title	Signature	Date
Name of person to contact regarding this report (Type or print)	Address (Number and Street)		
Title	City and State	ZIP Code	Telephone Number (Including Area Code.)	Extension

All reports and information obtained from individual reports will be kept confidential as required by Section 709(e) of Title VII.
WILLFULLY FALSE STATEMENTS ON THIS REPORT ARE PUNISHABLE BY LAW, U.S. CODE, TITLE 18, SECTION 1001.

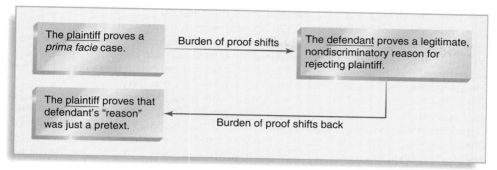

EXHIBIT 20-2

THE SHIFTING BURDEN OF PROOF IN A DISPARATE TREATMENT CASE

To establish a case of discrimination based on disparate impact, the plaintiff must first establish statistically that the rule disproportionately restricts employment opportunities for a protected class. Then the burden of proof shifts to the defendant to demonstrate that the practice or policy is a business necessity. The plaintiff, at this point, can still recover by proving that the "necessity" was promulgated as a pretext for discrimination.

The first two steps for proving a prima facie case of disparate impact were laid out in *Griggs v. Duke Power Company.*[2] In that case, the employer-defendant required all applicants to have a high school diploma and a successful score on a professionally recognized intelligence test for all jobs except that of laborer. By establishing these criteria, he proposed to upgrade the quality of his workforce.

The plaintiff demonstrated the discriminatory impact by showing that 34 percent of the white males in the state had high school diplomas, whereas only 12 percent of the black males did, and by introducing evidence from an EEOC study showing that 58 percent of the whites, compared with 6 percent of the blacks, had passed tests similar to the one given by the defendant. The defendant could show no business-related justification for either employment policy, so the plaintiff was successful. Not all employees of Duke Power needed to be smart or possess high school diplomas. After all, when does a student in high school learn how to install power lines or repair company vehicles? Requiring a high IQ or high school or college diploma may be necessary for some jobs but not for all jobs at Duke Power.

The following case illustrates the application of the disparate treatment theory.

CASE 20-1

Fickling et al. v. New York State Department of Civil Service
United States District Court, Southern District of New York,
909 F. Supp. 185 (1995)

Juliette Fickling and other plaintiffs were employed as temporary Social Welfare Eligibility Examiners by Westchester County. In 1989 and 1990, each plaintiff took and failed, more than once, the civil service examination for the position of Eligibility Examiner with Westchester County.

On March 15, 1991, each plaintiff was terminated because her failing test score precluded her placement on the "eligible list" for the position of Eligibility Examiner. Each plaintiff, except one, had received satisfactory to excellent performance evaluations from at least one of her supervisors prior to her termination.

---

[2] 401 U.S. 424 (1971).

Initially, access to the position of Eligibility Examiner is controlled by competitive examination; the applicants must attain a score of 70 on the examination to be placed on an Eligibility Examiner "eligible list." Plaintiffs had been employed as temporary Eligibility Examiners because Westchester County did not have an "eligible list" at the time. Temporary Eligibility Examiners may become permanent, however, only by passing the examination.

Plaintiffs sued, claiming their termination due to failing the competitive exam was unlawful because the exam had a racially disparate impact on minorities and failed to serve defendants' employment goal of fair competition.

District Judge Parker

The examinations had a disparate impact on African-Americans and Hispanics in Westchester County and statewide. In Westchester County, the impact ratios (% minority passing/%white passing) at the cutoff score on the 1989 examination ranged from 52.8% to 66.2% for African-Americans and between 43.1% and 56.6% for Hispanics. For the 1990 examination, the pass rate for African-Americans was between 40.4% and 50.8% of the white pass rate while Hispanics passed at between 25.5% and 34.9% of the white rate. Statewide, the impact ratio at the cutoff score on the 1989 examination ranged from 41.8% to 53.7% for African-Americans and between 36.6% and 44.6% for Hispanics and on the 1990 examination was between 38.2% and 43.1% for African-Americans and between 25.0% and 40.3% for Hispanics. ...

The New York State DCS created the examinations based upon a job analysis conducted in 1975. The job analysis identified the knowledge, skills, and abilities ("KSAs") required for successful performance in the Eligibility Examiner position. ...

Defendants concede that the examinations at issue tested only 13 of the 49 KSAs (approximately 27%) identified by the summary report of the job analysis. ...

The New York State DCS has never done a predictive validity study on the examinations at issue. ...

It is clear from these lists that the examinations tested mainly reading comprehension. In addition, 38% of the questions required arithmetic. The ability to do arithmetic however was found to be unimportant to successful job performance in the 1989–91 job analysis. The examinations did not test written expression or oral expression, except the ability to describe eligibility requirements in a comprehensible manner, despite the fact that these abilities were found to be very important to successful job performance in the 1989–91 job analysis.

... Only 13 of the 49 KSAs identified by the 1975 job analysis as necessary to the successful performance of the job were tested by the examinations at issue here. Dr. Daido testified that the other 36 KSAs could not be tested by a written instrument. She testified that 24 of the untested KSAs were full performance KSAs; that is, they could only be learned on the job. The EEOC Guidelines make it clear that testing for material that can only be learned on the job is inappropriate.

... [T]he Court concludes that the examinations were needlessly unrepresentative. Excluding those KSAs that could only be learned on the job, the examinations at issue tested only 50% of the remaining KSAs identified in the 1975 job analysis study. The test seized upon relatively minor aspects of the Eligibility Examiner job, such as reading comprehension and arithmetic, and ignored others.

Under the Guidelines, "where cutoff scores are used, they should normally be set so as to be reasonable and consistent with normal expectations of acceptable proficiency within the work force." ... "[A] criterion-related study is not necessarily required" in order to establish a basis for the cutoff score; the employer may rely on "a professional estimate of the requisite ability levels, or, at the very least, by analyzing the test results to locate a logical 'break-point' in the distribution of scores." ...

Defendants, however, have offered no such basis. They rely merely upon the New York State Civil Service Commission President's Regulations which set 70% of the total possible score as the passpoint, and set the passpoint two standard errors of measurement below 70% to guard against false negatives. ...

Because I find that the examinations had a significant disparate impact and defendants have failed to offer credible evidence that the examinations served the legitimate business goal of fair competition in civil service employment, I find for the plaintiffs.

Order in favor of Plaintiffs, Fickling et al.

Harassment. The third way to prove discrimination is to demonstrate harassment. Harassment is a relatively new basis for a discrimination claim; it first developed in the context of discrimination based on sex and then evolved to become applicable to other protected classes.

The definition of **sexual harassment** stated in the EEOC Guidelines and accepted by the U.S. Supreme Court is "unwelcome sexual advances, requests for sexual favors, and other verbal or physical conduct of a sexual nature" that implicitly or explicitly makes submission a term or condition of employment;

makes employment decisions related to the individual dependent on submission to or rejection of such conduct, or has the purpose or effect of creating an intimidating, hostile, or offensive environment.

The courts have recognized two distinct forms of sexual harassment. The first is often referred to as quid pro quo. This type of unlawful behavior occurs when a supervisor makes sexual demands on someone of the opposite sex and this demand is reasonably perceived as a term or condition of employment. The basis for this rule is that similar demands would not be made by the supervisor on someone of the same sex.

The second form of sexual harassment involves the creation of a hostile environment. The following case demonstrates the standards used by the U.S. Supreme Court to determine whether an employer's conduct has indeed created a hostile work environment.

sexual harassment
Unwelcome sexual advances, requests for sexual favors, and other verbal or physical conduct of a sexual nature that explicitly or implicitly makes submission a term or condition of employment or that creates an intimidating, hostile, or offensive environment.

CASE 20-2

Teresa Harris v. Forklift Systems, Inc.
United States Supreme Court,
510 U.S. 17 (1994)

Plaintiff Harris was a manager for defendant Forklift Systems, Inc. During her tenure at Forklift Systems, plaintiff Harris was repeatedly insulted by defendant's president and, because of her gender, subjected to sexual innuendos. Numerous times, in front of other employees, the president told Harris, "You're just a woman, what do you know?" He sometimes asked Harris and other female employees to remove coins from his pockets and made suggestive comments about their clothes. He suggested to Harris in front of others that they negotiate her salary at the Holiday Inn. When Harris complained, he said he would stop. He did not stop, however, so she quit and filed an action against the defendant for creating an abusive work environment based on her gender.

The district court found in favor of the defendant, holding that some of the comments were offensive to the reasonable woman but were not so serious as to severely affect Harris's psychological well-being or to interfere with her work performance. The court of appeals affirmed. Plaintiff Harris appealed to the U.S. Supreme Court.

Justice O'Connor

In this case we consider the definition of a discriminatorily "abusive work environment" (also known as a "hostile work environment") under Title VII.

Title VII of the Civil Rights Act of 1964 makes it "an unlawful employment practice for an employer ... to discriminate against any individual with respect to his compensation, terms, conditions, or privileges of employment, because of such individual's race, color, religion, sex, or national origin." As we made clear in *Meritor Savings Bank v. Vinson*, this language "is not limited to 'economic' or 'tangible' discrimination. The phrase 'terms, conditions, or privileges of employment' evinces a congressional intent 'to strike at the entire spectrum of disparate treatment of men and women' in employment," which includes requiring people to work in a discriminatorily hostile or abusive environment. When the workplace is permeated with "discriminatory intimidation, ridicule, and insult," that is "sufficiently severe or pervasive to alter the conditions of the victim's employment and create an abusive working environment."

This standard, which we reaffirm today, takes a middle path between making actionable any conduct that is merely offensive and requiring the conduct to cause a tangible psychological injury. As we pointed out in *Meritor*, "mere utterance of an ... epithet which engenders offensive feelings in a employee," does not sufficiently affect conditions of employment to implicate Title VII. Conduct that is not severe or pervasive enough to create an objectively hostile or abusive work environment—an environment that a reasonable person would find hostile or abusive—is beyond Title VII's purview. Likewise, if the victim does not subjectively perceive the environment to be abusive, the conduct has not actually altered the conditions of the victim's employment, and there is no Title VII violation.

But Title VII comes into play before the harassing conduct leads to a nervous breakdown. A discriminatorily abusive work environment, even one that does not seriously affect employees' psychological well-being, can and often will detract from employees' job performance, discourage employees from remaining on the job, or keep them from advancing in their careers. Moreover, even without regard to these tangible effects, the very fact that the discriminatory conduct was so severe or pervasive that it created a work environment abusive to employees because of their race, gender, religion, or national origin offends Title VII's broad rule of workplace equality. The appalling conduct alleged in *Meritor*, and the reference in that case to environments "so heavily polluted with discrimination as to destroy completely the emotional and psychological stability of minority group workers," merely present some especially egregious examples of harassment. They do not mark the boundary of what is actionable.

We therefore believe the District Court erred in relying on whether the conduct "seriously affected plaintiff's psychological well-being" or led her to "suffer injury." Such an inquiry may needlessly focus the fact-finder's attention on concrete psychological harm, an element Title VII does not require. Certainly Title VII bars conduct that would seriously affect a reasonable person's psychological well-being, but the statute is not limited to such conduct. So long as the environment would reasonably be perceived, and is perceived, as hostile or abusive, there is no need for it also to be psychologically injurious.

This is not, and by its nature cannot be, a mathematically precise test. But we can say that whether an environment is "hostile" or "abusive" can be determined only by looking at all the circumstances. These may include the frequency of the discriminatory conduct; its severity; whether it is physically threatening or humiliating, or a mere offensive utterance; and whether it unreasonably interferes with an employee's work performance. The effect on the employee's psychological well-being is, of course, relevant to determining whether the plaintiff actually found the environment abusive. But while psychological harm, like any other relevant factor, may be taken into account, no single factor is required.

Reversed and remanded in favor of Plaintiff, Harris.

Since *Meritor*, conflicting lower court decisions have created confusion in the area of sexual harassment. It appeared that in a quid pro quo case, a company was liable regardless of its knowledge, but in a hostile environment case, a company could not be held liable without direct knowledge of the situation. Another question was whether there could be recovery when only empty threats were made.

For example, in *Jones v. Clinton*,[3] the district court judge threw out Jones's sexual harassment case against the president because Jones had no clear and tangible job detriment necessary for a quid pro quo case, and she was not subject to a hostile environment when the totality of the circumstances was viewed. Even if the allegations were true, the contacts did not constitute "the kind of pervasive, intimidating, abusive conduct"[4] necessary for a hostile environment.

The U.S. Supreme Court attempted to clarify these issues in *Ellerth v. Burlington*.[5] Ellerth was subjected to a litany of dirty jokes and sexual innuendos from her boss. He propositioned her and threatened to make her life miserable if she refused him. She refused him without reprisals and was even promoted. She did not complain about harassment but quit after a year because she could not stand the threats and innuendos.

In a decision that offered something to both plaintiffs and defendants, the high court ruled that "an employer is subject to vicarious liability to a victimized employee for an actionable hostile environment created by a supervisor with immediate (or successively higher) authority over the employee. When no tangible employment action is taken, a defending employer may raise an affirmative defense to liability ... [by showing that] (a) the employer exercised reasonable care to prevent and correct promptly any sexually harassing behavior, and (b) the plaintiff employee unreasonably failed to take advantage of any preventive or corrective opportunities provided by the employer or to avoid harm oth-

---

[3] No. LR-C-94-290 (E.D. Ark. 1998).

[4] *Id.*

[5] 118 S. Ct. 2275 (1998).

Critical Thinking About the Law

As has previously been touched upon, the judiciary most often operates in relationship to shades of gray and not to the black and white between which those shades lie. The Court's decision in Case 20-2, in large part dependent on its determination of a definition, illustrates this point.

The Court's primary test was to decide what constitutes an "abusive work environment," the second type of sexual harassment actionable under Title VII. Deciding on such a definition is not as easy as going to a legal dictionary and looking up "abusive work environment." The Court had to interpret the meaning of such an environment, and important to this interpretation were legal precedent, ambiguity, and primary ethical norms.

Hence, the questions that follow will aid in thinking critically about these factors influential to the Court's interpretation.

1. What ambiguous language did the Court leave undefined in Case 20-2?

    Clue: To find this answer, look at the Court's definition of an "objectively hostile work environment." As always, remember that ambiguities most often are adjectives.

2. In her discussion of the *Meritor Savings Bank* precedent, Justice O'Connor made it clear that the district court misinterpreted the *Meritor* decision in rendering its decision. Contrary to the district court's decision, the existence of which key fact was not necessary for the Court to find the defendant guilty of sexual harassment?

    Clue: Revisit the paragraph discussing the district court's dismissal of Ms. Harris's claim. On what basis was this dismissal made? This is the key fact whose existence the Supreme Court found not to be necessary for judgment in favor of the plaintiff.

erwise. ... No affirmative defense is available, however, when the supervisor's harassment culminates in a tangible employment action."[6] The Court then remanded the case to the lower court for a new trial.

Under limited circumstances, employers may be held liable for harassment of their employees by nonemployees. For example, if an employer knows a customer is harassing an employee but does nothing to remedy the situation, the employer may be liable. That situation arose in *Lockhard v. Pizza Hut Inc.*[7] The franchise was held liable because the company failed to take any steps to stop the harassment of a waitress by two male customers.

Same-Sex Harassment. Initially, same-sex harassment did not constitute sexual harassment. In the first appellate case on this issue, a Fifth Circuit Court of Appeals case decided in July 1994, a male employee sued his employer for sexual harassment, alleging that on several occasions his male supervisor had approached him from behind and grabbed his crotch.[8] The court of appeals affirmed the trial court's dismissal of the claim on the grounds that no prima facie case had been established. The court said that Title VII addressed gender discrimination, and harassment by a male supervisor of a male employee did not constitute sexual harassment, regardless of the sexual overtones of the harassment.

By 1997, however, the circuits were clearly split on whether one could be sexually harassed by a person of the same sex. The U.S. Supreme Court finally rendered a definitive answer to that issue in the following case.

---

[6] *Id.*

[7] 162 F.3d 1062 (10th Cir. 1998).

[8] *Garcia v. Elk Atochem*, 28 F.3d 466 (1994).

CASE 20-3

Joseph Oncale v. Sundowner Offshore Services
United States Supreme Court,
118 S.Ct. 998 (1998)

Oncale was working for respondent Sundowner Offshore Services on a Chevron U.S.A., Inc., oil platform in the Gulf of Mexico. He was employed as a roustabout on an eight-man crew. Lyons, the crane operator, and Pippen, the driller, had supervisory authority. On several occasions, Oncale was forcibly subjected to sex-related, humiliating actions against him by Lyons, Pippen, and Johnson in the presence of the rest of the crew. Pippen and Lyons also physically assaulted Oncale in a sexual manner, and Lyons threatened him with rape. Oncale's complaints to supervisory personnel produced no remedial action; he eventually quit—asking that his pink slip reflect that he "voluntarily left due to sexual harassment and verbal abuse." Oncale stated, "I felt that if I didn't leave my job that I would be raped or forced to have sex."

Plaintiff Oncale brought a Title VII action against his former employer and against male supervisors and coworkers, alleging sexual harassment. The U.S. District Court granted summary judgment for defendants, and plaintiff appealed. The U.S. Court of Appeals affirmed. Plaintiff Oncale appealed to the U.S. Supreme Court.

Justice Scalia

[I]n the related context of racial discrimination in the workplace we have rejected any conclusive presumption that an employer will not discriminate against members of his own race. "Because of the many facets of human motivation, it would be unwise to presume as a matter of law that human beings of one definable group will not discriminate against other members of that group."

If our precedents leave any doubt on the question, we hold today that nothing in Title VII necessarily bars a claim of discrimination "because of ... sex" merely because the plaintiff and the defendant are of the same sex. [W]hen the issue arises in the context of a "hostile environment" sexual harassment claim, the state and federal courts have taken a bewildering variety of stances. Some, like the Fifth Circuit in this case, have held that same-sex sexual harassment claims are never cognizable under Title VII. Other decisions say that such claims are actionable only if the plaintiff can prove that the harasser is homosexual (and thus presumably motivated by sexual desire). Still others suggest that workplace harassment that is sexual in content is always actionable, regardless of the harasser's sex, sexual orientation, or motivations.

We see no justification in the statutory language or our precedents for a categorical rule excluding same-sex harassment claims from the coverage of Title VII. [M]ale-on-male sexual harassment in the workplace was assuredly not the principal evil Congress was concerned with when it enacted Title VII. But statutory prohibitions often go beyond the principal evil to cover reasonably comparable evils, and it is ultimately the provisions of our laws rather than the principal concerns of our legislators by which we are governed. Title VII prohibits "discriminat[ion] ... because of ... sex" in the "terms" or "conditions" of employment. Our holding that this includes sexual harassment must extend to sexual harassment of any kind that meets the statutory requirements.

Respondents and their amici contend that recognizing liability for same-sex harassment will transform Title VII into a general civility code for the American workplace. But that risk is no greater for same-sex than for opposite-sex harassment, and is adequately met by careful attention to the requirements of the statute. Title VII does not prohibit all verbal or physical harassment in the workplace; it is directed only at "discriminat[ion] ... because of ... sex." We have never held that workplace harassment, even harassment between men and women, is automatically discrimination because of sex merely because the words used have sexual content or connotations. "The critical issue, Title VII's text indicates, is whether members of one sex are exposed to disadvantageous terms or conditions of employment to which members of the other sex are not exposed."

Courts and juries have found the inference of discrimination easy to draw in most male–female sexual harassment situations, because the challenged conduct typically involves explicit or implicit proposals of sexual activity; it is reasonable to assume those proposals would not have been made to someone of the same sex. The same chain of inference would be available to a plaintiff alleging same-sex harassment, if there were credible evidence that the harasser was homosexual. But harassing conduct need not be motivated by sexual desire to support an inference of discrimination on the basis of sex. A trier of fact might reasonably find such discrimination, for example, if a female victim is harassed in such sex-specific and derogatory terms by another woman as to make it clear that the harasser is motivated by general hostility to the presence of women in the workplace. A same-sex harassment plaintiff may also, of course, offer direct comparative evidence about how the alleged harasser treated members of both sexes in a mixed-sex workplace. Whatever evidentiary route the plaintiff chooses to follow, he or she must always prove that the conduct at issue was not merely tinged with offensive sexual connotations, but actually constituted "discrimina[tion] … because of … sex."

And there is another requirement that prevents Title VII from expanding into a general civility code: the statute does not reach genuine but innocuous differences in the ways men and women routinely interact with members of the same sex and of the opposite sex. The prohibition of harassment on the basis of sex requires neither asexuality nor androgyny in the workplace; it forbids only behavior so objectively offensive as to alter the "conditions" of the victim's employment. "Conduct that is not severe or pervasive enough to create an objectively hostile or abusive work environment—an environment that a reasonable person would find hostile or abusive—is beyond Title VII's purview." We have always regarded that requirement as crucial, and as sufficient to ensure that courts and juries do not mistake ordinary socializing in the workplace—such as male-on-male horseplay or intersexual flirtation—for discriminatory "conditions of employment."

[T]he objective severity of harassment should be judged from the perspective of a reasonable person in the plaintiff's position, considering "all the circumstances." In same-sex (as in all) harassment cases, that inquiry requires careful consideration of the social context in which particular behavior occurs and is experienced by its target. A professional football player's working environment is not severely or pervasively abusive, for example, if the coach smacks him on the buttocks as he heads onto the field—even if the same behavior would reasonably be experienced as abusive by the coach's secretary (male or female) back at the office. The real social impact of workplace behavior often depends on a constellation of surrounding circumstances, expectations, and relationships which are not fully captured by a simple recitation of the words used or the physical acts performed. Common sense, and an appropriate sensitivity to social context, will enable courts and juries to distinguish between simple teasing or rough housing among members of the same sex, and conduct which a reasonable person in the plaintiff's position would find severely hostile or abusive.

Judgment reversed in favor of Plaintiff, Oncale.

Hostile Environment Extended. Hostile environment cases have also been used in cases of discrimination based on religion, race and even age.[9] For example, in a 1994 case,[10] Hispanic and black corrections workers demonstrated that a hostile work environment existed by proving that they had been subjected to continuing verbal abuse and racial harassment by coworkers and that the county sheriff's department had done nothing to prevent the abuse. The white employees had continually used racial epithets and posted racially offensive materials on bulletin boards, such as a picture of a black man with a noose around his neck, cartoons favorably portraying the Ku Klux Klan, and a "black officers' study guide," consisting of children's puzzles. White officers once dressed a Hispanic inmate in a straw hat, sheet, and sign that said "spic." Such activities were found by the court to constitute a hostile work environment.

STATUTORY DEFENSES

The three most important defenses available to defendants in Title VII cases are the bona fide occupational qualification (BFOQ) defense, merit, and seniority. These defenses are raised by the defendant after the plaintiff has established a prima facie case of discrimination based on disparate treatment, disparate impact, or a pattern or practice of discrimination.

Bona Fide Occupational Qualification. The BFOQ defense allows an employer to discriminate in hiring on the basis of sex, religion, or national origin when such a characteristic is necessary for the performance of the job. Note that race or color cannot be a BFOQ. Such necessity must be based on actual qualifications, not on stereotypes about one group's abilities. Being a male cannot be a BFOQ for a job

---

[9] *Crawford v. Medina General Hospital*, 96 F.3d (1997).
[10] *Snell v. Suffolk County*, 782 F.2d 1094 (1994).

because it is a dirty job or a "strenuous" job, although there may be a valid requirement that an applicant be able to lift a certain amount of weight if such lifting is a part of the job. A BFOQ does not arise because an employer's customers would prefer to be served by someone of a particular gender or national origin. Nor does inconvenience to the employer, such as having to provide two sets of restroom facilities, make a classification a BFOQ.

Merit. Most claims of merit involve the use of tests to hire or promote. The use of a professionally developed ability test that is not designed, intended, or used to discriminate, is legal. Such tests may have an adverse impact on a class, but they do not violate the act as long as they are manifestly related to job performance. The "Uniform Guidelines on Employee Selection Procedures" (UGESP) have, since 1978, contained the policy of all governmental agencies charged with enforcing civil rights, and they provide guidance to employers and other interested persons about when ability tests are valid and job related. Under these guidelines, tests must be validated in accordance with standards established by the American Psychological Association.

Three types of validation are acceptable: (1) criterion-related validity, which is the statistical relationship between test scores and objective criteria of job performance; (2) content validity, which isolates some skill used on the job and directly tests that skill; and (3) construct validity, wherein a psychological trait needed to perform the job is measured. A test that required a secretary to type and take shorthand would be content valid. A test of patience for a teacher would be construct valid.

Seniority Systems. A final statutory defense, available under Section 703(h), is a bona fide seniority system. A seniority system, in which employees are given preferential treatment based on their length of service, may perpetuate discrimination that occurred in the past. Nonetheless, such systems are considered bona fide and are, thus, not unlawful if (1) the system applies equally to all persons; (2) the seniority units follow industry practices; (3) the seniority system did not have its genesis in discrimination; and (4) the system is maintained free of any illegal discriminatory purpose.

PROTECTED CLASSES

As you know, five classes are protected under Title VII. Unique problems have arisen with regard to each of these protected classes, of which the astute business manager should be aware.

Race and Color. A primary goal of Title VII was to remedy the discrimination in employment to which blacks had been subjected since the founding of this nation. However, the act also contains a proviso stating that nothing in the act requires that preferential treatment based on an imbalance between their representation in the employer's workplace and their representation in the population at large be given to any protected class. This proviso, thus, paved the way for questions about "reverse discrimination," or discrimination against whites, as a result of employers' attempts to create a racially balanced workforce. This issue will be discussed in the section on affirmative action.

National Origin. The act prohibits discrimination based on national origin, not on alienage (citizenship of a country other than the United States). Thus, an employer can refuse to hire non–United States citizens. This prohibition applies even to owners of foreign corporations who have established firms in the United States. In the absence of a treaty between the United States and the foreign state authorizing such conduct, a corporation cannot discriminate in favor of those born in a foreign state.

Since the bombing of the Twin Towers on September 11, 2001, there has been a significant increase in charges based on national origin by individuals who are, or are perceived as being, Arab or South Asian. Many of these claims are combined with claims of discrimination based on religion. Many are based on harassment. For example, in 2004, two California auto dealers agreed to pay seven Afgnan workers $550,000 to settle their complaint of harassment based on national origin and religion. The workers alleged that they were called everything from "camel jockeys" to "bin Laden's gang." One of the women with an Arabic name was asked to call herself by an American name like Sara.[11]

During fiscal year 2003, the EEOC received 8,450 charges of national origin discrimination, and, including some charges from 2002, settled 9,172. the agency collected $21.3 million for the charging parties.[12]

Religion. Under Title VII, employers cannot discriminate against employees on the basis of religion, although an exception has been made allowing religious corporations, associations, and societies to discriminate in their employment practices on the basis of religion, but they may not discriminate on the basis of any other protected class. In Fiscal Year 2003, EEOC received 2,532 charges of religious discrimination, and resolved 2,690 such charges, recovering $6.6 million.[13]

Employers are required to make reasonable accommodation to their employees' religious needs, as long as such accommodation does not result in an undue hardship on the employer or other employees. For example, an employer has a dress code that prohibits clerical workers visible to the public from wearing hats or scarves. A Muslim worker requests that she be granted an exemption from the dress code so that she may wear the hijab (head scarf) in conformance with her Muslim beliefs. Her exemption would be a reasonable accommodation. Flexible scheduling, voluntary substitutions or swaps, job reassignments and lateral transfers are other examples of reasonable accommodations to an employee's religious beliefs. Courts will examine the requested accommodation very carefully to ensure that it does not place an undue burden on the workplace. For example, the reasonableness of accommodating an employee's request to not work on Saturday would depend on the availability of other workers who would willingly work on Saturdays.

As mentioned above, since September 11, 2001, the number of charges of religious discrimination by individuals who are or are perceived to be Muslim or Sikh has increased. From September 11, 2000 to September 11, 2001, 323 charges based on "religion-Muslim" were filed with the EEOC. The following year, 706 similar charges were filed. In 2003, the EEOC settled one of the largest workplace discrimination suits against Muslims. In that case, four Muslim Pakistani machine operators alleged that their employer, Stockton Steel, routinely gave them the worst jobs, ridiculed their daily prayers, and called them "camel jockey" and "raghead." The four workers shared a $1.1 million settlement.[14]At the time of the settlement, then EEOC Commissioner

---

[11] Bob Egelko, "Two Auto Dealers Agree to Settle Suit with Afghan Workers", *San Francisco Chronicle*, B 7, April 7, 2004.

[12] EEOC, "National Origin Discrimination," **eeoc.gov/origin/index.html** Accessed December 14, 2004.

[13] EEOC, "Religious Discrimination," **eeoc.gov/types/religion.html** Accessed December 14, 2004.

[14] Marjorie Valbrun, "U.S. Battles Bias Against Arabs and Muslims in the Workplace," *The Asian Wall Street Journal*, A6, April 14, 2003.

Steven Miller expressed hope that such cases would sensitize employers to issues of religious and ethnic discrimination.[15] Since the attacks, the EEOC has been attempting to reach out to Arab and Muslim groups to explain what illegal discrimination is and what actions they can take to enforce their rights.

Sex. Under Title VII, sex is interpreted as referring only to gender and not to preferences. Hence, homosexuals and transsexuals are not protected under the act. However, it would be sex discrimination to fire male homosexuals while retaining female homosexuals.

As noted earlier, sexual harassment is prohibited by Title VII's prohibition against discrimination based on sex. Although sexual harassment cases were not filed in large numbers immediately after Title VII's passage, there has been a tremendous increase in the number of such cases filed since law professor Anita Hill captivated the nation in late 1991 by testifying before Congress about the harassment to which she was subjected by U.S. Supreme Court nominee Clarence Thomas. According to the EEOC, there were 9,953 sexual harassment complaints filed in the year ending on October 1, 1992, an increase of 2,546 over the previous year. The number has continued to increase. In fiscal year 2003, EEOC received 13,566 charges of sexual harassment. Almost 15% of those charges were filed by males.[16]

Linking Law & Business

Management

Perhaps you learned in your organizational behavior or management class about *biculturalism*. This term refers to instances in which individuals of a particular racial or ethnic minority class have been socialized in two cultures— the dominant culture and the individual's ethnic or racial culture. Living in two cultures often increases stress, which is referred to as *bicultural stress*. Two general characteristics of bicultural stress are the following: (1) role conflict—the conflict that exists when an individual fills two competing roles due to her or his dual cultural membership; and (2) role overload—the excess expectations that result from living in two cultures. The intensity of these problems tends to increase for women of color due to the negative dynamics directed toward both women and minorities. Hiring minorities into the workplace can pose adaptation problems for some managers. Accustomed to the cultural norms of the majority, some managers may be insensitive to the bicultural stress that minorities are often burdened with. Additionally, managers may not realize that employees usually do not set aside their values and lifestyle preferences while at work. Therefore, it is important for managers to recognize differences and respond in ways that increase productivity without discriminating. This shift in management philosophy may include diversity training for managers and other employees in order to help them to raise behavioral awareness, recognize biases and stereotypes, avoid assumptions, and modify policies. Therefore, an acute sensitivity to differences in the workplace may result in a friendlier environment where productivity is increased.

Source: S. Certo, *Modern Management* (Upper Saddle River, N.J.: Prentice Hall, 2000), pp. 534–535, 544; and S. Robbins, *Organizational Behavior* (Upper Saddle River, N.J.: Prentice Hall, 2001), pp. 13–14.

---

[15] *Id.*

[16] EEOC, "Sexual Harassment," **eeoc.gov/types/sexual harassment.html** Accessed December 14, 2004.

1. Senior management must make clear its position that sexual harassment in any form will not be tolerated.

2. Have an explicit written policy on sexual harassment that is widely disseminated in the workplace and given to every new employee.

3. Make sure employees know what is, and is not, sexual harassment.

4. Provide a gender-neutral training program on sexual harassment for all employees.

5. Establish an efficient system for investigating charges of sexual harassment and punishing violators.

6. Make sure that complaints are to be filed with a neutral party, not with the employee's supervisor.

7. Thoroughly investigate and resolve every complaint, punishing every violation appropriately. If no violation is found, explain to the complainant why there was no violation.

EXHIBIT 20-3

TIPS FOR AVOIDING SEXUAL HARASSMENT CHARGES

Source: Adapted from K. Swisher, "Corporations Are Seeing the Light on Harassment," *Washington Post National Weekly Edition,* February 14–20, 1994, p. 21.

These sex discrimination cases can be quite costly. For example, in late 2000, it cost CBS $8 million to settle a sex discrimination case brought by 200 female technicians at six CBS stations.[17] The women had alleged workplace discrimination in promotions, assignments, and compensation, along with a hostile work environment. Although management admitted no guilt, it also agreed to set up mechanisms to prevent sex discrimination. Thus, it is increasingly important that businesspersons be able to recognize sexual harassment and to prevent its occurrence in the workplace. Exhibit 20-3 provides some suggestions for how managers can avoid liability for sexual harassment.

Pregnancy Discrimination Act. Shortly after Title VII's enactment, the U.S. Supreme Court ruled that discrimination on the basis of pregnancy was not discrimination on the basis of sex under Title VII.[18] In response to that decision, Congress amended Title VII by passing the Pregnancy Discrimination Act (PDA), which specifies that discrimination based on pregnancy is sex discrimination; pregnancy must be treated the same as any other disability, except that abortions for any purpose other than saving the mother's life may be excluded from the company's medical benefits. In a 1986 case interpreting the PDA, the U.S. Supreme Court concluded that Congress intended the PDA to be "a floor beneath which pregnancy disability benefits may not drop—not a ceiling above which they may not rise."[19] Consequently, the high court held that a California statute requiring unpaid maternity leave for pregnant women and reinstatement after the birth of the child was constitutional because the intent of the law was to make women in the workplace equal, not to give them favored treatment.[20]

In the summer of 2001, the PDA became the basis for the first ruling on the employment discrimination issue of gender equity in drug coverage. In a class action lawsuit against Bartell Drug Company, a Seattle judge ruled that the

---

[17] "CBS Agrees to Settle Discrimination Suit," *New York Times,* October 26, 2000, p. C16.

[18] *General Electric Co. v. Gilbert,* 429 U.S. 125 (1976).

[19] *California Federal Savings and Loan Association et al. v. Department of Fair Employment and Housing et al.,* 479 U.S. 272 (1987).

[20] *Id.*

drugstore chain discriminated against women when it excluded prescription contraceptives from its employee health plan.[21] Granting summary judgment to the plaintiff, the judge said, "Male and female employees have different sex-based disability and health care needs, and the law is no longer blind to the fact that only women can get pregnant, bear children, or use prescription contraception."[22]

ENFORCEMENT PROCEDURES

Enforcement of Title VII is a very complicated procedure and is full of pitfalls. Failure to follow the proper procedures within the appropriate time framework may result in the plaintiff's losing her or his right to file a lawsuit under Title VII. An overview of these procedures is provided in Exhibit 20-4.

The Charge. The first step in initiation of an action under Title VII is the aggrieved party's filing of a charge with the state agency responsible for enforcing fair

EXHIBIT 20-4

ANATOMY OF A TITLE VII CASE

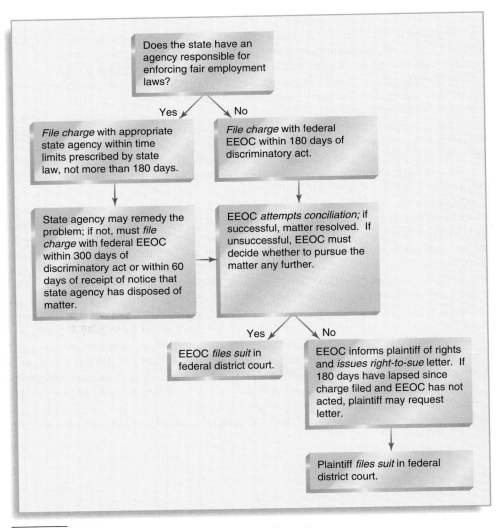

---

[21] *Erickson v. Bartell Drug Company*, 141 F.Supp. 1266 (2001).

[22] *Id*.

employment laws (a state EEOC) or, if no such agency exists, with the federal EEOC. A charge is a sworn statement that states the name of the charging party, the name(s) of the defendant(s), and the nature of the discriminatory act. In states that do not have state EEOCs, the aggrieved party must file the charge with the federal EEOC within 180 days of the alleged discriminatory act. In states that do have such agencies, the charge must be filed either with the federal EEOC within 180 days of the discriminatory act or with the appropriate state agency within the time limits prescribed by local law, which cannot be more than 180 days. If initially filed with the local agency, the charge must be filed with the federal EEOC within 300 days of the discriminatory act or within 60 days of receipt of notice that the state agency has disposed of the matter, whichever comes first. Exhibit 20-5 is a typical charge.

Conciliation and Filing Suit. Once the EEOC receives the charge, it must notify the alleged violator of the charge within ten days. After such notification, the EEOC investigates the matter in an attempt to ascertain whether there is "reasonable cause" to believe that a violation has occurred. If the EEOC does find such reasonable cause, it attempts to eliminate the discriminatory practice through conciliation. If unsuccessful, the EEOC may file suit against the alleged discriminator in federal district court.

If the EEOC decides not to sue, it notifies the plaintiff of his or her right to file an action and issues the plaintiff a right-to-sue letter. The plaintiff must have this letter in order to file a private action. The letter may be requested at any time after 180 days have elapsed since the filing of the charge. As long as the requisite time period has passed, the EEOC will issue the right-to-sue letter regardless of whether or not the EEOC members find a reasonable basis to believe that the defendant engaged in discriminatory behavior.

REMEDIES

The plaintiff bringing a Title VII action can seek both equitable and legal remedies. The courts have broad discretion to order "such affirmative action as may be appropriate."[23] Under this broad guideline, courts have ordered parties to engage in diverse activities ranging from publicizing their commitment to minority hiring to establishing special training programs for minorities.

In general, a successful plaintiff is able to recover back pay for up to two years from the time of the discriminatory act. Back pay is the difference between the amount of pay received after the discriminatory act and the amount of pay that would have been received had there been no discrimination. For example, if two years before the case came to trial the defendant refused a promotion to a plaintiff on the basis of her sex, and the job for which she was rejected paid $100 more per week than her current job, she would be entitled to recover back pay in the amount of $100 multiplied by 104. (If the salary rose at regular increments, these are also included.) The same basic calculations are used when plaintiffs were not hired because of discrimination. Such plaintiffs are entitled to the back wages that they would have received minus any actual earnings during that time. Defendants may also exclude wages for any period during which the plaintiff would have been unable to work.

---

[23] Section 706(a).

EXHIBIT 20-5 A TYPICAL CHARGE OF DISCRIMINATION FILED WITH THE EEOC

CHARGE OF DISCRIMINATION	AGENCY	CHARGE NUMBER
This form is affected by the Privacy Act of 1974; See Privacy Act Statement before completing this form.	☒ FEPA ☒ EEOC	

OHIO CIVIL RIGHTS COMMISSION _____ and EEOC
State or local Agency, if any

Name *(Indicate Mr., Ms., Mrs.)* Ms. Nellie Baldwin	Home Telephone *(Include Area Code)* (419) 863-4125	
STREET ADDRESS 826 Potter Road	CITY, STATE AND ZIP CODE Toledo, Ohio 43602	DATE OF BIRTH 11/10/56

NAMED IS THE EMPLOYER, LABOR ORGANIZATION, EMPLOYMENT AGENCY APPRENTICESHIP COMMITTEE, STATE OR LOCAL GOVERN-MENT AGENCY WHO DISCRIMINATED AGAINST ME *(If more than one list below.)*

Name Mancum Manufacturers	NUMBER OF EMPLOYEES, MEMBERS +15	TELEPHONE *(Include Area Code)* (419) 693-8296
STREET ADDRESS 896 Lewis Ave .	CITY, STATE AND ZIP CODE Toledo, Ohio 43605	COUNTY Lucas
Name	TELEPHONE NUMBER *(Include Area Code)*	
STREET ADDRESS	CITY, STATE AND ZIP CODE	COUNTY

CAUSE OF DISCRIMINATION BASED ON *(Check appropriate basis)* ☐ RACE ☐ COLOR ☒ SEX Female ☐ RELIGION ☐ NATIONAL ORIGIN ☐ RETALIATION ☐ AGE ☐ DISABILITY ☐ OTHER *(Specify)*	DATE DISCRIMINATION TOOK PLACE / / 02/ 05/ 93 ☐ CONTINUING ACTION

THE PARTICULARS ARE *(If additional space is needed, attach extra sheet(s))*:

1. I was employed by Canfield for 2 years as a machine operator general.
2. An opening for machine operator special, a higher position, was posted.
3. I applied for the position along with 4 other males and 2 females.
4. All applicants took a dexterity test.
5. I received the highest score on the test, but a male who scored second highest was promoted.
6. I was told that the posted job was "better suited for a male", but that with my test score I would be first in line when a more appropriate opening arose.

CXM/IFL:bd

☒ I also want this charge filed with the EEOC. I will advise the agencies if I change my address or telephone number and I will cooperate fully with them in the processing of my charge in accordance with their procedures.	Notary - *(When necessary for State and Local Requirements)*
	I swear or affirm that I have read the above charge and that it is true to the best of my knowledge, information and belief.
I declare under penalty of perjury that the foregoing is true and correct.	SIGNATURE OF COMPLAINANT *Ms. Nellie Baldwin*
Date	SUBSCRIBED AND SWORN TO BEFORE ME THIS DATE *(Day, month, and year)*
Charging Party *(Signature)*	

EEOC TEST FORM 5 (09/01/91)

If a plaintiff was not hired for a job because of a Title VII violation, the plaintiff may receive, in addition to back pay, remedial seniority dating back to the time when the plaintiff was discriminated against.

Perhaps the most significant change made by the 1991 Civil Rights Act was its impact on the availability of compensatory and punitive damages. Under the new act, not only plaintiffs discriminated against because of race but also those discriminated against on the basis of sex, disability, religion, or national origin may recover both compensatory damages, including those for pain and suffering, and punitive damages. In cases based on discrimination other than race, however, punitive damages are capped at $300,000 for employers of more than 500 employees; $100,000 for firms with 101 to 200 employees; and $50,000 for firms with 100 or fewer employees.

Since the passage of the Civil Rights Act of 1991, there has been a definite increase in the damages awarded under Title VII and in the amounts for which employers are willing to settle. In 1998, Astra USA agreed to the largest settlement in a sexual harassment case to date when it agreed to pay $10 million to end a lawsuit claiming widespread debauchery and sexual abuse by its management.[24]

Attorneys' fees are ordinarily awarded to a successful plaintiff in Title VII cases. They are denied only when special circumstances would render the award unjust. In those rare instances in which the courts determine that the plaintiff's action was frivolous, unreasonable, or without foundation, the courts may use their discretion to award attorneys' fees to the prevailing defendant.

THE AGE DISCRIMINATION IN EMPLOYMENT ACT OF 1967

Our society does not revere age. Many aspects of the culture reward and cater to youth. Older employees detract from a firm's "youthful" image. They are also expensive. They have accumulated raises over the years and, thus, earn more than younger employees. They have pension benefits, which the employer will have to pay when employees retire from the firm. They are sometimes viewed as rigid and unwilling to learn new technology. Thus, it is understandable that firms may attempt to discriminate against older employees. The **Age Discrimination in Employment Act of 1967 (ADEA)** was enacted to prohibit employers from refusing to hire, discharging, or discriminating in terms and conditions of employment on the basis of age. The language describing the prohibited conduct is virtually the same as that of Title VII, except that a person's being age 40 or older is the prohibited basis for discrimination.

Although the motivation for the ADEA was to prevent the unfair, negative treatment of older people in the workplace, after the legislation had been in place for several years, some began to question whether the law also prohibited giving older workers more favorable treatment. In 2004, the United States Supreme Court decided that issue in the following case.

Age Discrimination in Employment Act of 1967 (ADEA) Prohibits employers from refusing to hire, discharging, or discriminating against people in terms of conditions of employment on the basis of age.

---

[24] M. Jackson, "Better Safe … Sexual Harassment Insurance Is a Paton Company's Bottom Line," *Chicago Tribune*, April 26, 1998, p. 2.

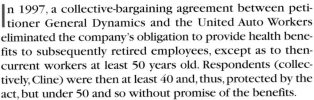

CASE 20-4

General Dynamics Land Systems, Inc. v. Dennis Cline et al.
United States Supreme Court,
540 U.S. 581 (2004)

In 1997, a collective-bargaining agreement between petitioner General Dynamics and the United Auto Workers eliminated the company's obligation to provide health benefits to subsequently retired employees, except as to then-current workers at least 50 years old. Respondents (collectively, Cline) were then at least 40 and, thus, protected by the act, but under 50 and so without promise of the benefits.

Before the Equal Employment Opportunity Commission (EEOC or Commission) Cline claimed that the agreement violated the ADEA. The EEOC agreed and invited General Dynamics and the union to settle informally with Cline. When they failed, Cline brought this action against General Dynamics under the ADEA. The district court dismissed in reliance on the Seventh Circuit's opinion in *Hamilton v. Caterpillar Inc.*, 966 F.2d 1226 (1992), that "the ADEA 'does not protect … the younger against the older'." A divided panel of the Sixth Circuit reversed. We granted certiorari to resolve the conflict among the circuits.

Justice Souter

The Age Discrimination in Employment Act of 1967 (ADEA or Act) forbids discriminatory preference for the young over the old. The question in this case is whether it also prohibits favoring the old over the young. We hold it does not.

The common ground in this case is the generalization that the ADEA's prohibition covers "discriminat[ion] … because of [an] individual's age," that helps the younger by hurting the older. In the abstract, the phrase is open to an argument for a broader construction, since reference to "age" carries no express modifier and the word could be read to look two ways. This more expansive possible understanding does not, however, square with the natural reading of the whole provision prohibiting discrimination, and in fact Congress's interpretive clues speak almost unanimously to an understanding of discrimination as directed against workers who are older than the ones getting treated better.

Congress chose not to include age within discrimination forbidden by Title VII of the Civil Rights Act of 1964, being aware that there were legitimate reasons as well as invidious ones for making employment decisions on age. Instead it called for a study of the issue by the Secretary of Labor, who concluded that age discrimination was a serious problem. When the Secretary ultimately took the position that arbitrary discrimination against older workers was widespread and persistent enough to call for a federal legislative remedy, he placed his recommendation against the background of common experience that the potential cost of employing someone rises with age, so that the older an employee is, the greater the inducement to prefer a younger substitute. The report contains no suggestion that reactions to age level off at some point, and it was devoid of any indication that the Secretary had noticed unfair advantages accruing to older employees at the expense of their juniors.

Congress then asked for a specific proposal, which the Secretary provided in January 1967. Extensive House and Senate hearings ensued. The testimony dwelled on unjustified assumptions about the effect of age on ability to work. The record thus reflects the common facts that an individual's chances to find and keep a job get worse over time; as between any two people, the younger is in the stronger position, the older more apt to be tagged with demeaning stereotype. Not surprisingly, from the voluminous records of the hearings, we have found nothing suggesting that any workers were registering complaints about discrimination in favor of their seniors.

The statutory objects were "to promote employment of older persons based on their ability rather than age; to prohibit arbitrary age discrimination in employment; [and] to help employers and workers find ways of meeting problems arising from the impact of age on employment."

In sum, except on one point, all the findings and statements of objectives are either cast in terms of the effects of age as intensifying over time, or are couched in terms that refer to "older" workers, explicitly or implicitly relative to "younger" ones. The single subject on which the statute speaks less specifically is that of "arbitrary limits" or "arbitrary age discrimination." But these are unmistakable references to the Wirtz Report's finding that "[a]lmost three out of every five employers covered by [a] 1965 survey have in effect age limitations (most frequently between 45 and 55) on new hires which they apply without consideration of an applicant's other qualifications." The ADEA's ban on "arbitrary limits" thus applies to age caps that exclude older applicants, necessarily to the advantage of younger ones.

Such is the setting of the ADEA's core substantive provision prohibiting employers and certain others from "discriminat[ion] … because of [an] individual's age," whenever (as originally enacted) the individual is "at least forty years of age but less than sixty-five years of age." The prefatory provisions and their legislative history make a case that we think is beyond reasonable doubt, that the ADEA was concerned to protect a relatively old worker from discrimination that works to the advantage of the relatively young.

Nor is it remarkable that the record is devoid of any evidence that younger workers were suffering at the expense of their elders, let alone that a social problem required a federal statute to place a younger worker in parity with an older one. Common experience is to the contrary, and the testimony, reports, and congressional findings simply confirm that Congress used the phrase "discriminat[ion] … because of [an] individual's age" the same way that ordinary people in common usage might speak of age discrimination any day of the week. This same, idiomatic sense of the statutory phrase is confirmed by the statute's restriction of the protected class to those 40 and above. If Congress had been worrying about protecting the younger against the older, it would not likely have ignored everyone under 40. The youthful deficiencies of inexperience and unsteadiness invite stereotypical and discriminatory thinking about those a lot younger than 40, and prejudice suffered by a 40-year-old is not typically owing to youth, as 40-year-olds sadly tend to find out. The enemy of 40 is 30, not 50. Even so, the 40-year threshold was adopted over the objection that some discrimination against older people begins at an even younger age; female flight attendants were not fired at 32 because they were too young. Thus, the 40-year threshold makes sense as identifying a class requiring protection against preference for their juniors, not as defining a class that might be threatened by favoritism toward seniors.

The federal reports are as replete with cases taking this position as they are nearly devoid of decisions like the one reviewed here. While none of these cases directly addresses the question presented here, all of them show our consistent understanding that the text, structure, and history point to the ADEA as a remedy for unfair preference based on relative youth, leaving complaints of the relatively young outside the statutory concern.

The Courts of Appeals and the District Courts have read the law the same way, and prior to this case have enjoyed virtually unanimous accord in understanding the ADEA to forbid only discrimination preferring young to old. The very strength of this consensus is enough to rule out any serious claim of ambiguity, and Congressional silence after years of judicial interpretation supports adherence to the traditional view.

We see the text, structure, purpose, and history of the ADEA, along with its relationship to other federal statutes, as showing that the statute does not mean to stop an employer from favoring an older employee over a younger one. The judgment of the Court of Appeals is:

Reversed in favor of General Dynamics.

As the U.S. economy started a downward turn in late 2000 and continued through 2001, an increase in age discrimination claims occurred. Charges of age discrimination filed with the EEOC rose from roughly 14,000 filed in fiscal year 1999 to 16,000 in 2000. And that pace continued through the first half of 2001, with age discrimination charges making up approximately 22.5 percent of the total charges filed with the EEOC during that period. In fiscal year 2003, the agency received 19,124 charges of age discrimination. They collected $48.9 million in benefits for aggrieved individuals.[25]

APPLICABILITY OF THE STATUTE

The ADEA applies to employers having 20 or more employees in an industry that affects interstate commerce. It also applies to employment agencies and to unions that have at least 25 members or operate a hiring hall. However, as a result of a Supreme Court ruling in *Kimel v. Florida Board of Regents*,[26] the act does not apply to state employers.

PROVING AGE DISCRIMINATION

Discrimination under the ADEA may be proved in the same ways that discrimination is proved under Title VII: by the plaintiff's showing disparate treatment or disparate impact. Most of the ADEA cases today involve termination. In order to prove a prima facie case of age discrimination involving a termination, the plaintiff must establish facts sufficient to create a reasonable inference that age was a determining factor in the termination. The plaintiff raises this inference by showing that he or she (1) belongs to the statutorily protected age group (age

---

[25] EEOC, "Age Discrimination," **eeoc.gov/types/age.html** Accessed Dec. 14, 2004.
[26] 120 S.Ct. 631 (2001).

40 or older); (2) was qualified for the position held; and (3) was terminated under circumstances giving rise to an inference of discrimination.

Until 1996, the plaintiff also had to demonstrate that he or she was replaced by someone outside the protected class. But in *O'Conner v. Consolidated Caterers Corporation*,[27] the United States Supreme Court held that replacement by someone outside the protected class was not a necessity as long as there was evidence that the termination was based on age.

If the plaintiff establishes these three facts, the burden of proof then shifts to the defendant to prove that there was a legitimate, nondiscriminatory reason for the discharge. If the employer meets this standard, the plaintiff may recover only if he or she can show by a preponderance of the evidence that the employer's alleged legitimate reason is really a pretext for a discriminatory reason.

Circuit courts have generally been split on the evidentiary standard to which a plaintiff must be held. Some courts have relied only on a pretext standard, as described earlier, while others have required a plaintiff to show direct, not just inferential, proof of discrimination, known as "pretext plus."[28] To resolve this circuit court confusion, the Supreme Court agreed to hear the following case.

CASE 20-5

Reeves v. Sanderson Plumbing Products, Inc.
United States Supreme Court,
120 S.Ct. 2097 (2000)

Roger Reeves, 57, had been an employee of Sanderson Plumbing Products, Inc., for 40 years. As the "hinge room" supervisor, Reeves, along with Joe Oswalt, mid-30s, logged employee hours, reviewed daily and weekly time sheets, and prepared monthly reports for their supervisor, Russell Caldwell, 45. When, because of absenteeism and tardiness, poor production in the area Reeves worked in became a problem, Caldwell reported it to Powe Chesnut, the director of manufacturing. A review of the time sheets did not indicate a problem, so an audit was ordered that, according to Chesnut, showed numerous errors committed by Caldwell, Oswalt, and Reeves. Chesnut recommended that Reeves and Caldwell be fired, and the company president, Sandra Sanderson, also Chesnut's wife, followed the recommendation. Reeves sued the company, claiming that his termination was wrongful discrimination under the ADEA.

A jury trial was held and the jury found the company guilty of age discrimination, awarding Reeves $35,000 in compensatory damages and $35,000 in liquidated damages. Reeves was also given $28,490.80 in front pay by the district court. Sanderson Plumbing appealed the ruling to the Fifth Circuit Court. The circuit court overturned the lower court's ruling, saying that Reeves had not introduced enough information for the jury to conclude that he had been discriminated against because of his age. Reeves appealed to the Supreme Court.

Justice O'Connor

[*McDonnell Douglas Corp. v. Green*] and subsequent decisions have "established an allocation of the burden of production and an order for the presentation of proof in … discriminatory-treatment cases." … It is undisputed that the petitioner satisfied this burden here: (i) at the time he was fired, he was a member of the class protected by the ADEA …, (ii) he was otherwise qualified for the position of Hinge Room supervisor, (iii) he was discharged by respondent, and (iv) respondent successively hired three persons in their thirties to fill petitioner's position. The burden is therefore shifted to respondent to "produc[e] evidence that the plaintiff was rejected, or someone else was preferred, for a legitimate, nondiscriminatory reason." … Respondent met this burden by offering admissible evidence sufficient for the trier of fact to conclude that petitioner was fired because of his failure to maintain accurate attendance records.

… [T]he plaintiff—once the employer produces sufficient evidence to support a nondiscriminatory explanation for its decision—must be afforded the "opportunity to prove by a preponderance of the evidence that the legitimate reasons offered by the defendant were not its true reasons, but were a pretext for discrimination." …

Petitioner … made a substantial showing that respondent's explanation was false. …

---

[27] 529 U.S. 62 (2000).

[28] M. Coyle, "How to Judge Age Bias," *National Law Journal*, March 20, 2000, p. A10.

Based on this evidence, the Court of Appeals concluded that petitioner "very well may be correct" that "a reasonable jury could have found that [respondent's] explanation for its employment decision was pretextual." ... Nonetheless, the court held that this showing, standing alone, was insufficient to sustain the jury's finding of liability. ... And in making this determination, the Court of Appeals ignored the evidence supporting petitioner's prima facie case and challenging respondent's explanation for its decision. The court confined its review of evidence favoring petitioner to that evidence showing that Chesnut had directed derogatory, age-based comments at petitioner, and that Chesnut had singled out petitioner for harsher treatment than younger employees. ... It is therefore apparent that the court believed that only this additional evidence of discrimination was relevant to whether the jury's verdict should stand. That is, the Court of Appeals proceeded from the assumption that a prima facie case of discrimination, combined with sufficient evidence for the trier of fact to disbelieve the defendant's legitimate, nondiscriminatory reason for its decision, is insufficient as a matter of law to sustain a jury's finding of intentional discrimination.

In so reasoning, the Court of Appeals misconceived the evidentiary burden borne by plaintiffs who attempt to prove intentional discrimination through indirect evidence. This much is evident from our decision in [*St. Mary's Honor Center v. Hicks*]. There we held that the factfinder's rejection of the employer's legitimate, nondiscriminatory reason for its action does not *compel* judgment for the plaintiff. ... The ultimate question is whether the employer intentionally discriminated, and proof that "the employer's proffered reason is unpersuasive, or even obviously contrived, does not necessarily establish that the plaintiff's proffered reason ... is correct." ... In other words, "[i]t is not enough ... to disbelieve the employer; the factfinder must *believe* the plaintiff's explanation of intentional discrimination." ...

In reaching this conclusion, however, we reasoned that it is permissible for the trier of fact to infer the ultimate fact of discrimination from the falsity of the employer's explanation. Specifically, we stated:

> *The factfinder's disbelief of the reason put forward by the defendant (particularly if disbelief is accompanied by a suspicion of mendacity) may, together with the elements of a prima facie case, suffice to show intentional discrimination. Thus, rejection of the defendant's proffered reasons will permit the trier of fact to infer the ultimate fact of discrimination.*

Thus, a plaintiff's prima facie case, combined with sufficient evidence to find that the employer's asserted justification is false, may permit the trier of fact to conclude that the employer unlawfully discriminated. ...

The ultimate question in every employment discrimination case involving a claim of disparate treatment is whether the plaintiff was the victim of intentional discrimination. Given the evidence in the record supporting petitioner, we see no reason to subject the parties to an additional round of litigation before the Court of Appeals rather than to resolve the matter here. The District Court plainly informed the jury that petitioner was required to show "by a preponderance of the evidence that his age was a determining and motivating factor in the decision of [respondent] to terminate him." ... The court instructed the jury that, to show that respondent's explanation was a pretext for discrimination, petitioner had to demonstrate "1, that the stated reasons were not the real reasons for [petitioner's] discharge; *and* 2, that age discrimination was the real reason for [petitioner's] discharge." (emphasis added). Given that petitioner established a prima facie case of discrimination, introduced enough evidence for the jury to reject respondent's explanation, and produced additional evidence of age-based animus, there was sufficient evidence for the jury to find that respondent had intentionally discriminated. The District Court was therefore correct to submit the case to the jury, and the Court of Appeals erred in overturning its verdict.

Reversed in favor of Plaintiff, Reeves.

Critical Thinking About the Law

So much about legal reasoning depends on taking a close look at analogies. No set of facts is ever exactly like another. But when citing precedents, each party hopes the facts in certain cases are similar enough in significant ways to cause the courts to select their cited cases as the more relevant ones in each case.

The questions here focus on the quality of the precedent cited by the defendant in Case 20-5.

1. What about *St. Mary's Honor Center v. Hicks* led to its being cited as authority by the defendant?
   Clue: Who won in *St. Mary's* and why?

2. What caused Justice O'Connor to reject the analogy of *St. Mary's* as binding in Case 20-5?
   Clue: Check her discussion of *St. Mary's* to find how she distinguished *St. Mary's* from the Reeves case.

STATUTORY DEFENSES

Bona Fide Occupational Qualification. As under Title VII, there are a number of statutory defenses available to an employer in an age discrimination case. The first is the bona fide occupational qualification. To succeed with this defense, the defendant must establish that he or she must hire employees of only a certain age to safely and efficiently operate the business in question. The courts generally scrutinize very carefully any attempt to demonstrate that age is a BFOQ.

One example of an employer's successful use of this defense is provided by *Hodgson v. Greyhound Lines, Inc.,*[29] a case in which the employer refused to hire applicants aged 35 or older. Greyhound demonstrated that its safest drivers were those between the ages of 50 and 55, with 16 to 20 years of experience driving for Greyhound. Greyhound argued that this combination of age and experience could never be reached by those who were hired at age 35 or older. Therefore, in order to ensure the safest drivers, it should be allowed to hire only applicants younger than 35. In that case, the court accepted the employer's rationale. Although safety considerations are important, to use them in establishing age as a BFOQ, the employer must indeed prove, as did the defendant in the *Greyhound* case, that safety is related to age.

Other Defenses. As under Title VII, decisions premised on the operation of a bona fide seniority system are not unlawfully discriminatory despite any discriminatory impact. Likewise, employment decisions may also be based on "reasonable factors other than age."

Executive Exemption. Even if none of the foregoing defenses are available to the employer, termination of an older employee may be legal because of the **executive exemption**. Under this exemption, an individual may be mandatorily retired after age 65 if (1) he or she has been employed as a bona fide executive for at least two years immediately before retirement, and (2) on retirement, he or she is entitled to nonforfeitable annual retirement benefits of at least $44,000.

executive exemption
Exemption to the ADEA that allows mandatory retirement of executives at age 65.

After-Acquired Evidence of Employee Misconduct. An important issue, not just for the ADEA but also for other employment discrimination claims, is whether an employer can use evidence of an employee's misconduct discovered after a charge has been found to defeat that charge. In the 1995 case of *McKennon v. Nashville Banner,*[30] a unanimous Supreme Court decided that issue in a manner that pleased lawyers that represented both businesses and plaintiffs.

In *Nashville Banner,* the plaintiff had feared being fired by the company because of age, so she copied confidential documents to use (if needed) in her subsequent lawsuit. She was, in fact, fired, and she filed a discrimination claim. The employer subsequently discovered that the plaintiff had copied the documents and argued that her ADEA action should be dismissed because she would have been fired anyway had the firm known that she had copied the

---

[29] 499 F.2d 859 (7th Cir. 1974).
[30] 63 U.S.L.W. 4105 (1995).

documents. The circuit court held that she deserved to be fired because of her misconduct and, therefore, she could not sue for discrimination.

The Supreme Court, however, overruled the appellate court and held that after-acquired knowledge of misconduct will not bar a discrimination action. However, the Supreme Court did not believe such conduct should be totally irrelevant. If the defendant can prove that the misconduct was actually substantial enough to have warranted termination of the employee, then reinstatement will not be required. The amount of back pay required will also be reduced. The employee's back pay will be calculated from the date of the unlawful discharge until the date that the evidence of misconduct was discovered. Thus, the after-acquired evidence may be used to reduce the plaintiff's relief but not to completely bar the action.

ENFORCEMENT PROCEDURES

Enforcement of ADEA is similar to the enforcement of Title VII. Under ADEA, the victim of age discrimination may file a charge with the appropriate state agency or with the EEOC within 180 days of the act. If a charge has been filed with the state agency, an EEOC charge must be filed within 300 days of the discrimination or within 30 days of receiving notice of the termination of state proceedings, whichever comes first. The charge must identify the defendant and specify the nature of the discriminatory act. On receipt of a charge, the EEOC must notify the accused and attempt to conciliate the matter. If conciliation fails, the EEOC may then bring a civil action against the violator.

A party who does not plan to file a private action may choose to file a charge with the EEOC only; if a party wishes to file a private civil action, complaints must be filed with both the appropriate state agency and the EEOC. If these complaints are filed within the appropriate time limits, a party then has three years from the date of the discriminatory act within which to file a private action under ADEA, assuming the alleged discriminatory act was willful. If the alleged discrimination is purportedly unwillful, the party has two years within which he or she must file the private action. The party, however, must wait 60 days from the date of the filing of the complaints with both the EEOC and the state agency before filing the lawsuit. If the EEOC or the state agency files an action on the matter during that time, the plaintiff is precluded from filing suit.

REMEDIES UNDER ADEA

A successful plaintiff is entitled to back pay for up to two years. In addition, in a private action by a plaintiff, he or she may be able to recover liquidated damages in an amount equal to the back pay recovered if the plaintiff can prove that the employer acted willfully. *Willfully* means that the employer was substantially aware of the possibility that he or she was in violation of the ADEA but did not attempt to ascertain the legality of his or her actions. If liquidated damages are not granted, the plaintiff is generally entitled to interest on the back pay; interest is not awarded when liquidated damages have been granted. Compensatory damages for items such as mental distress from the discrimination are occasionally, but rarely, awarded by a few courts. Likewise, punitive damages are rarely awarded.

THE REHABILITATION ACT OF 1973

Rehabilitation Act of 1973 Prohibits discrimination in employment against otherwise qualified persons who have a handicap. Applies only to the federal government, employers who have contracts with the federal government, and parties who administer programs receiving federal financial assistance.

In 1973, Congress broadened the class of individuals protected against discrimination to include the handicapped by passing the **Rehabilitation Act of 1973**. This act is designed to protect the handicapped from discrimination in employment and also to help them secure rehabilitation, training, access to public buildings, and all benefits of covered programs that might otherwise be denied them because of their handicap. It also requires that covered employers have a qualified affirmative action program for hiring and promoting the handicapped. A handicapped individual, for purposes of the act, is defined as one who has a "physical or mental impairment, which substantially limits one or more of such person's major life activities,"[31] or who has a record of such impairment. Even people who are falsely regarded as having such impairment are protected. The major provisions of this act are outlined in Table 20-3.

This act applies only to the federal government and employers who have contracts with the federal government, so its impact is relatively limited. In 1991, the Americans with Disabilities Act (ADA) was passed, which extends similar prohibitions against discrimination to private-sector employers who do not have federal contracts. Because of its broader impact, the ADA will be discussed in greater detail in the next section, but the principles discussed with respect to that act apply to the Rehabilitation Act as well.

It is important to remember neither the Rehabilitation Act nor the Americans with Disabilities Act (ADA) requires any employer to hire an unqualified individual. The acts require only the hiring of an individual with a disability who, with reasonable accommodation for his or her disability, can perform the job at the minimum level of productivity that would be expected of an individual with no disability.

Nor does this act or the ADA prohibit an employer from terminating an employee whose disability does in fact prevent him or her from doing the job. For example, in a 1994 case, a disabled employee was terminated because her disability caused her to frequently miss work without calling in sick. She had an inner ear disorder that caused nausea and vomiting when she traveled, frequently making her so

TABLE 20-3 SUMMARY OF MAJOR PROVISIONS OF REHABILITATION ACT

Section	Potential Defendant	Prohibited Conduct	Required Conduct
501	Federal departments and agencies	Cannot discriminate against otherwise qualified workers because of a handicap	Prepare and implement an affirmative action plan for hiring and promoting the handicapped
502	Federal agencies entering into contracts with private employers for property or services and the private employers entering into these contracts	Private party with government contract cannot discriminate against otherwise qualified workers because of a handicap	Contracts must contain clause requiring private employer to take affirmative action in hiring and promoting the handicapped and to not discriminate against them
504	Parties who administer programs receiving federal assistance	Discrimination by those administering programs prohibited	

[31] U.S.C. Section 706(b).

ill on the way to work that she could not continue or even call in. The plaintiff in that case had sued under the Rehabilitation Act, arguing that the Justice Department, her employer, should have reasonably accommodated her disability by allowing her to come in any time between 8 A.M. and noon and restructuring her job to allow others to do her time-sensitive tasks when she was absent. The Supreme Court disagreed, saying that such accommodation would place undue hardship on the department. The Court felt that an essential component of the job was being able to report to work and complete tasks within a reasonable period of time.[32]

THE AMERICANS WITH DISABILITIES ACT OF 1991

Like the Rehabilitation Act, the **Americans with Disabilities Act (ADA)** is intended to prevent employers from discriminating against employees and applicants with disabilities by requiring employers to make reasonable accommodations to the known physical or mental disabilities of an otherwise qualified person with a disability unless the necessary accommodation would impose an undue burden on the employer's business.

> **Americans with Disabilities Act of 1991 (ADA)** Requires that employers make reasonable accommodations to the known disabilities of an otherwise qualified job applicant or employee with a disability, unless the necessary accommodation would impose an undue burden on the employer's business.

The ADA now covers all employers of 15 persons or more, which includes approximately 660,000 businesses, so its impact has the potential to be significant. In fiscal year 2003, the EEOC received 15,377 complaints related to the act. The agency resolved 16,915 disability related charges that year, and recovered $45.3 million in monetary benefits for charging parties and other aggrieved individuals.[33]

COVERED INDIVIDUALS

The definition of an individual with a disability, for purposes of the act, is essentially the same as the definition of a handicapped individual in the Rehabilitation Act. A disability is defined as "(1) a physical or mental impairment which substantially limits one or more of the major life activities of such individual, (2) a record of such impairment, or (3) being regarded as having such an impairment."[34] A wide variety of impairments are captured under such a definition. Individuals suffering from diseases such as cancer, epilepsy, and heart disease are included, as are those who are blind or deaf. In 1998 the U.S. Supreme Court held that those who are infected with the human immunodeficiency virus (HIV), but who are not yet symptomatic, are covered.[35] Those whose past records may harm them are also protected. For example, persons who suffer from alcoholism but are not currently drinking or who are former drug addicts are protected. However, an employee who is currently a substance abuser and whose abuse would affect job performance is not protected.

Employers often find it difficult to know how the Americans with Disabilities Act applies to those who have mental disabilities. From 1992 to 1998, emotional/psychiatric impairment claims were 12 percent of all claims, second only to claims for back impairment, at 15.5 percent.[36]

---

[32] *Carr v. Reno*, 23 F.3d 525 (D.C. Cir. 1994).

[33] "Disability Discrimination" **eeoc.gov/types.ada.html**, accessed 12/14/04.

[34] 42 U.S.C. 12102 (2).

[35] 1998 WL 332958.

[36] National Council on Disability, Equal Employment Opportunity Commission, "Promises to Keep: A Decade of Federal Enforcement of the Americans with Disabilities Act," June 27, 2000, **www.ncd.gov/newsroom/publications/promises_3.htm/#6.**.

Under the ADA, employers are not only forbidden from discriminating against persons with mental disabilities but also must make reasonable accommodations for them unless such accommodations could cause undue hardship. Typical accommodations include providing a private office, flexible work schedule, restructured job, or time off for treatment.

The major problems associated with responding to a mental disability are twofold. First, many employers are not sure how to accommodate a mentally disabled person. Second, many people are afraid of mentally disabled people because some of them can be dangerous, especially people with mood disorders, who at times have violent tempers. And a firm that employs a worker who deals with the public could be liable in tort to a customer who is injured by a mentally disabled worker. How firms will respond to problems associated with mental disabilities remains to be seen.

Another type of disability that employers must be aware of is an intellectual disability. According to the EEOC, roughly 1% of Americans have an intellectual disability, and only around 31% of these individuals are employed, even though a much greater percentage would like to work.

An individual is considered to have an intellectual disability when: (1) the person's intellectual functioning level (IQ) is below 70-75; (2) the person has significant limitations in adaptive skill areas as expressed in conceptual, social, and practical adaptive skills; and (3) the disability originated before the age of 18. "Adaptive skill areas" refers to basic skills needed for everyday life, and include communication, self-care, home living, social skills, leisure, health and safety, self-direction, functional academics (reading, writing, basic math), and work.

Another major difficulty employers face under the ADA is ensuring that they do not violate the law during the interview process. The EEOC issued guidelines to help employers comply with the law. The guidelines emphasize that employers' questions must be designed to focus on whether a potential employee can do the job, not on the disability, but it is often difficult to know when a question violates the act. Exhibit 20-6 provides examples from the EEOC guidelines of acceptable and unacceptable questions.

EXHIBIT 20-6

INTERVIEWING POTENTIAL EMPLOYEES WITHOUT VIOLATING ADA

Source: Adapted from EEOC's "Enforcement Guidance on Pre-Employment Disability—Related Inquiries and Medical Examinations Under the Americans with Disabilities Act." (EEOC, 1998).

You May Ask	Do Not Ask
• Can you perform the functions of this job (essential and/or marginal), with or without reasonable accommodations?	• Do you have a disability that would interfere with your ability to perform the job?
• Can you meet the attendance requirements of this job?	• How many days were you sick last year?
• Do you illegally use drugs? Have you used illegal drugs in the past two years?	• What prescription drugs are you currently taking?
• Do you have a cold? How did you break your leg?	• Do you have AIDS? Do you have asthma?
• How much do you weigh? Do you regularly eat three meals a day?	• How much alcohol do you drink each week? Have you ever been treated for alcohol problems?

Technology and the Legal Environment

The Internet as a Public Accommodation?

As e-commerce and the use of the Internet become more common, the courts are likely to begin to treat the Internet as a public accommodation, meaning that it would be subject to the ADA, which states that "no individual shall be discriminated against on the basis of disability in the full and equal enjoyment of the goods, services, facilities, privileges, advantages, or accommodations of any place of public accommodation by any person who owns, leases to, or operates a place of public accommodation."

No one yet knows the full implications that treating the Internet as a public accommodation would have, but a lawsuit filed by the National Federation of the Blind (NFB) against America Online (AOL) may help give us an idea of what some disabled individuals would expect.

In November 1999, the NFB sued AOL, alleging that the company's software does not work with other software required to translate computer signals into braille or synthesized speech. By failing to remove communication barriers presented by its designs, thus denying the blind independent access to this service, AOL is alleged to be violating the ADA.

In July 2000, AOL and the NFB reached an agreement. NFB suspended the lawsuit against AOL and AOL promised to have appropriate software by April 2001. The lawsuit was subsequently dropped. Regulations tacked on to Section 508 of the Rehabilitation Act, which went into effect in December 2000, also assisted the blind. Under these regulations, federal agencies must construct and design their Web sites using applications and technologies making site information available to all users.

It is well worth the prudent employer's time to study these guidelines because the liability for violating the "rules for job interviews" can be substantial. In 1995 a job applicant who was asked about his disability during an interview was awarded $15,000 in compensatory damages and $30,000 in punitive damages.[37] The plaintiff was partially disfigured, partially deaf, and partially blind as a result of two brain tumor operations. The plaintiff brought up the disability himself to explain a gap in his work record, but the interviewers told him they felt uncomfortable with his disability and asked him to make them feel more comfortable by describing the condition and its treatment. They also asked whether managers or customers had a problem with him because of his disability.

ENFORCEMENT PROCEDURES

The ADA is enforced by the EEOC in the same way that Title VII is enforced. To bring a successful claim under the ADA, the plaintiff must show that he or she (1) had a disability, (2) was otherwise qualified for the job, and (3) was excluded from the job solely because of that disability.

REMEDIES

Remedies are likewise similar to those available under Title VII. A successful plaintiff may recover reinstatement, back pay, and injunctive relief. In cases of intentional discrimination, limited compensatory and punitive damages are also available. An employer who has repeatedly violated the act may be subject to fines of up to $100,000.

---

[37] *EEOC v. Community Coffee Co.*, No. H-94-1061 (S.D. Texas 1995).

AFFIRMATIVE ACTION

affirmative action plans
Programs adopted by employers to increase the representation of women and minorities in their workforces.

reverse discrimination
Discrimination in favor of members of groups that have been previously discriminated against; claim usually raised by white males.

One of the most controversial workplace issues of the past two decades has been the legitimacy of **affirmative action plans**. Ever since employers began to try to create balanced workforces by focusing on increasing their employment of minorities, there have been cries that such actions constitute **reverse discrimination**, which is a violation of the equal protection clause of the Fourteenth Amendment.

Many of the significant cases challenging affirmative action plans have arisen in contexts other than private employment. Other areas in which these programs have been challenged include school admissions policies and government policies to set aside contracts for minority businesses. Table 20-4 summarizes the major affirmative action cases. A close reading of the cases reveals the increasing scrutiny that the courts have come to apply to affirmative action policies, and it now appears that any affirmative action plan that can withstand constitutional muster must (1) attempt to remedy past discrimination, (2) not use quotas or preferences, and (3) end or change once it has met its goal of remedying past discrimination. This standard was set forth by the Supreme Court in *Adarand Constructors, Inc. v. Pena*, a case challenging a federal affirmative action program (see Table 20-4).

Many interested observers were hopeful that in 1997 the U.S. Supreme Court would hand down a definitive decision regarding affirmative action cases in the employment setting, as the high court had agreed to hear the case of *Taxman v. Board of Education* described in Table 20-4. However, the parties settled the case before it went to trial.

The next, and most recent major affirmative action case arose in the area of university admissions and is described in Case 20-6.

TABLE 20-4 MAJOR REVERSE DISCRIMINATION CASES

Case	Alleged Discriminatory Action	Outcome
Regents of the University of California. Bakke, 438 U.S. 265 (1978)	The school's special admissions policy reserved 16 out of the 100 available seats for minority applicants. Bakke was denied admission while minorities with lower test scores were admitted.	Although race could be one of a number of factors considered by a school in passing on applications, this special admission policy was illegal because a classification that benefits victims of a victimized group at the expense of innocent individuals is constitutional only where proof of past discrimination exists.
United Steelworkers v. Weber, 443 U.S. 193 (1979)	The employer and union entered into a voluntary agreement that half the openings in a skilled craft training program will go to blacks until the rough proportion of blacks in the program is equal to that of blacks in the labor force. A white male who would have been admitted to the training program absent the plan challenged the plan.	Court said it was clear that Congress did not intend to wholly prohibit private and voluntary affirmative action. To be valid, such plans must not unnecessarily trammel the rights of whites, should be temporary in nature, and should be customized to solve the past proven pattern of discrimination.
Johnson v. Santa Clara County Transportation Agency, 480 U.S. 616 (1987)	County affirmative action plan authorized agency to consider applicant's sex as a relevant factor when making promotion decisions for job classifications in which women have traditionally been underrepresented.	Court held that the plan represented a moderate, flexible case-by-case approach to gradually effecting an improvement of the representation of women and minorities in traditionally underrepresented positions. Court emphasized that the agency had identified a conspicuous imbalance in representation; that no slots were set aside for women or minorities; and no quotas were established. Race or sex could just be one of several factors considered.

Adarand Constructors, Inc. v. Pena, 515 U.S. 200 (1995)	Plaintiff submitted the lowest bid for a government contract, but the contract was awarded to a Hispanic firm submitting a higher bid. The job sent to the Hispanic firm in accordance with a government program giving 5 percent of all highway construction projects to disadvantaged construction firms.	In a landmark decision, the U.S. Supreme Court held that any federal, state, or local affirmative action program that uses racial or ethnic classifications as a basis for making decisions is subject to strict scrutiny by the courts. This level of scrutiny can be met only when (1) the program attempts to remedy past discrimination, (2) does not use quotas or preferences, and (3) will be ended or changed once it has met its goal of remedying past discrimination.
Hopwood v. State of Texas, 84 U.S. 720 (3d Cir. 1996)	Two white law school applicants were denied admission to the University of Texas Law School because of the school's affirmative action program. That program allowed admissions officials to take racial and other factors into account when admitting students.	The Court of Appeals for the Fifth Circuit held that the program violated the equal protection clause because it discriminated in favor of minorities. The U.S. Supreme Court refused to hear the case.
Taxman v. Board of Education of the Township of Piscataway, 91 F.3d 1547 (3d Cir. 1996)	The Board of Education wanted to eliminate one teaching position at Piscataway High School. A black female and white female had the same seniority and qualifications. Because minority teachers were underrepresented in the school, the board chose to lay off the white teacher to promote racial diversity.	Taxman challenged the policy as violative of Title VII. The trial court granted summary judgment in her favor. The circuit court of appeals affirmed, awarding her complete back pay. The defendants appealed to the U.S. Supreme Court, but the case was settled prior to the hearing before the high court.
Jennifer Johnson v. Board of Regents of the University of Georgia, 2001 WL 967756 (2001)	The University of Georgia had an admissions policy that awarded a fixed numerical bonus to nonwhite and male applicants that it did not give to white and female applicants. The three plaintiffs, white females who were denied admission to the University of Georgia, filed an action arguing that the use of race violated the Equal Protection Clause, among other claims.	The District Court fund in favor of the plaintiffs and entered summary judgment in their favor. Defendants appealed on the issue of preferential treatment based on race. The Circuit Court said it did not need to address the issue of whether student body diversity is a compelling interest sufficient to withstand the strict scrutiny that the court must apply to government decision making based on race. Even if it were a compelling interest, a policy that mechanically awards an arbitrary diversity bonus to every nonwhite applicant at a decisive stage in admissions, and severely limits the range of other factors relevant to diversity that may be considered at the stage, is not narrowly tailored to achieve that interest. The policy, therefore, violates the Equal Protection Clause of the Fourteenth Amendment.

Grutter v. Bollinger, 288 F.3D 732 (2003)	A white female was denied admission to the University of Michigan Law School despite a 3.8 GPA and a 161 LSAT score. She argued that the school's admissions policy, which focused on applicants' academic ability coupled with a flexible assessment of their talents, experience, and potential to contribute to the learning environment as well as the life and diversity of the law school, resulted in her being discriminated against on the basis of race.	After a 15 day bench trial, the Federal District Court found that Michigan's use of race as a factor in admissions decisions was unlawful.
		    The Sixth Circuit Court of Appeals reversed, finding the use of race to be narrowly tailored because it was used only as a potential plus factor.
		    The United States Supreme Court affirmed, agreeing that the Equal Protection Clause does not prohibit the narrowly tailored use of race in admissions decisions to further a compelling interest in obtaining the educational benefits that flow from a diverse student body.

CASE 20-6

Grutter v. Bollinger
United States Supreme Court
288 F.3d 732 (2003)

The University of Michigan Law School (Law School), one of the Nation's top law schools, follows an official admissions policy that seeks to achieve student body diversity through compliance with *University of California v. Bakke.* Focusing on students' academic abilities, coupled with a flexible assessment of their talents, experiences, and potential, the policy requires admissions officials to evaluate each applicant based on all the information available in the file, including a personal statement, letters of recommendation, an essay describing how the applicant will contribute to Law School life and diversity, and the applicant's undergraduate grade point average (GPA) and Law School Admissions Test (LSAT) score. Additionally, officials must look beyond grades and scores to so-called "soft variables," such as recommenders' enthusiasm, the quality of the undergraduate institution and the applicant's essay, and the areas and difficulty of undergraduate course selection. The policy does not define diversity solely in terms of racial and ethnic status and does not restrict the types of diversity contributions eligible for "substantial weight," but it does reaffirm the Law School's commitment to diversity with special reference to the inclusion of African-American, Hispanic, and Native-American students, who otherwise might not be represented in the student body in meaningful numbers. By enrolling a "critical mass" of underrepresented minority students, the policy seeks to ensure their ability to contribute to the Law School's character and to the legal profession.

When the Law School denied admission to petitioner Grutter, a white Michigan resident with a 3.8 GPA and 161 LSAT score, she filed this suit, alleging that respondents had discriminated against her on the basis of race in violation of the Fourteenth Amendment, Title VI of the Civil Rights Act of 1964, and 42 U.S.C. § 1981; that she was rejected because the Law School uses race as a "predominant" factor, giving applicants belonging to certain minority groups a significantly greater chance of admission than students with similar credentials from disfavored racial groups; and that respondents had no compelling interest to justify that use of race. The District Court found the Law School's use of race as an admissions factor unlawful. On appeal, the Sixth Circuit reversed, holding that Justice Powell's opinion in *Bakke* was binding precedent establishing diversity as a compelling state interest, and that the Law School's use of race was narrowly tailored because race was merely a "potential 'plus' factor" and because the Law School's program was virtually identical to the Harvard admissions program described approvingly by Justice Powell and appended to his *Bakke* opinion. Plaintiff appealed to the United States Supreme Court.

Justice O'Connor

In the landmark *Bakke* case, this Court reviewed a medical school's racial set-aside program that reserved 16 out of 100 seats for members of certain minority groups. The decision produced six separate opinions, none of which commanded a majority. Justice Powell, announcing the Court's judgment, provided a fifth vote not only for invalidating the program, but also for reversing the state court's injunction against any use of race whatsoever. In a part of his opinion that was joined by no other Justice, Justice Powell expressed his view that attaining a diverse student body was the only interest asserted by the university that survived scrutiny. Grounding his analysis in the academic freedom that "long has been viewed as a special concern of the First Amendment," Justice Powell emphasized that the " 'nation's future depends upon leaders trained through wide exposure' to the ideas and mores of students as diverse as this Nation." However, he also emphasized that "[i]t is not an interest in simple ethnic diversity, in which a specified percentage of the student body is in effect guaranteed to be members of selected ethnic groups," that can justify using race. Rather, "[t]he diversity that furthers a compelling state interest encompasses a far broader array of qualifications and characteristics of which racial or ethnic origin is but a single though important element."

Since *Bakke,* Justice Powell's opinion has been the touchstone for constitutional analysis of race-conscious admissions policies. Public and private universities across the Nation have modeled their own admissions programs on Justice Powell's views.

All government racial classifications must be analyzed by a reviewing court under strict scrutiny. But not all such uses are invalidated by strict scrutiny. Race-based action necessary to further a compelling governmental interest does not violate the Equal Protection Clause so long as it is narrowly tailored to further that interest. Context matters when reviewing such action. The Court endorses Justice Powell's view that student body diversity is a compelling state interest that can justify using race in university admissions. The Court defers to the Law School's educational judgment that diversity is essential to its educational mission. The Court's scrutiny of that interest is no less strict for taking into account complex educational judgments in an area that lies primarily within the university's expertise.

Attaining a diverse student body is at the heart of the Law School's proper institutional mission, and its "good faith" is "presumed" absent "a showing to the contrary." Enrolling a "critical mass" of minority students simply to assure some specified percentage of a particular group merely because of its race or ethnic origin would be patently unconstitutional. But the Law School defines its critical mass concept by reference to the substantial, important, and laudable educational benefits that diversity is designed to produce, including cross-racial understanding and the breaking down of racial stereotypes.

The Law School's claim is further bolstered by numerous expert studies and reports showing that such diversity promotes learning outcomes and better prepares students for an increasingly diverse workforce, for society, and for the legal profession. Major American businesses have made clear that the skills needed in today's increasingly global marketplace can only be developed through exposure to widely diverse people, cultures, ideas, and viewpoints. High-ranking retired officers and civilian military leaders assert that a highly qualified, racially diverse officer corps is essential to national security. Moreover, because universities, and in particular, law schools, represent the training ground for a large number of the Nation's leaders, the path to leadership must be visibly open to talented and qualified individuals of every race and ethnicity. Thus, the Law School has a compelling interest in attaining a diverse student body.

The Law School's admissions program bears the hallmarks of a narrowly tailored plan. To be narrowly tailored, according to Justice Powell, a race-conscious admissions program cannot "insulat[e] each category of applicants with certain desired qualifications from competition with all other applicants." Instead, it may consider race or ethnicity only as a "'plus' in a particular applicant's file"; i.e., it must be "flexible enough to consider all pertinent elements of diversity in light of the particular qualifications of each applicant, and to place them on the same footing for consideration, although not necessarily according them the same weight." The Law School's admissions program, like the Harvard plan approved by Justice Powell, satisfies these requirements. Moreover, the program is flexible enough to ensure that each applicant is evaluated as an individual and not in a way that makes race or ethnicity the defining feature of the application.

The Law School engages in a highly individualized, holistic review of each applicant's file, giving serious consideration to all the ways an applicant might contribute to a diverse educational environment. There is no policy, either *de jure* or *de facto*, of automatic acceptance or rejection based on any single "soft" variable. Also, the program adequately ensures that all factors that may contribute to diversity are meaningfully considered alongside race. Moreover, the Law School frequently accepts nonminority applicants with grades and test scores lower than underrepresented minority applicants (and other nonminority applicants) who are rejected.

The Court rejects the argument that the Law School should have used other race-neutral means to obtain the educational benefits of student body diversity, *e.g.*, a lottery system or decreasing the emphasis on GPA and LSAT scores. Narrow tailoring does not require exhaustion of every conceivable race-neutral alternative or mandate that a university choose between maintaining a reputation for excellence or fulfilling a commitment to provide educational opportunities to members of all racial groups.

The Court is also satisfied that, in the context of individualized consideration of the possible diversity contributions of each applicant, the Law School's race-conscious admissions program does not unduly harm nonminority applicants.

Finally, race-conscious admissions policies must be limited in time. The Court takes the Law School at its word that it would like nothing better than to find a race-neutral admissions formula and will terminate its use of racial preferences as soon as practicable. The Court expects that 25 years from now, the use of racial preferences will no longer be necessary to further the interest approved today.

In favor of Defendant Bollinger. Affirmed.

While this case has provided some additional guidance to those in higher education, most employers will get more help from looking to the EEOC.

The EEOC has issued guidelines in an attempt to help employers set up valid affirmative action plans. According to these guidelines, Title VII is not violated if (1) the employer determines that there is a reasonable basis for determining that an affirmative action plan is appropriate, and (2) the affirmative action plan is reasonable. Quotas are specifically outlawed by the 1991 Civil Rights Act amendments.

GLOBAL DIMENSIONS OF EMPLOYMENT DISCRIMINATION LEGISLATION

With many U.S. firms having operations overseas, the question of the extent to which U.S. laws prohibiting discrimination apply to foreign countries naturally arises. The Civil Rights Act of 1991 extended the protections of Title VII and the ADA to U.S. citizens working abroad for U.S. employers. Amendments to the ADEA

Linking Law & Business

Management

Affirmative action plans promote greater diversity in workplaces. Despite the controversial issues related to these programs, diversity itself can be advantageous to organizations. In your management class, you probably discussed some of the advantages of diversity. First, group decisions that include the contributions from diverse employees provide an advantage because there may be a greater assortment of ideas for dealing with work issues. Second, diversity may also enhance a firm's credibility with its customers in the sense that the firm is portrayed as more able to identify with customers of various backgrounds. Third, diversity can encourage greater creativity and innovation in organizations. Fourth, diversity also tends to promote a more flexible organizational structure that is beneficial when a firm is faced with a need to change. Therefore, diversity, if properly managed, could be beneficial to a firm.

Source: S. Certo, *Modern Management* (Upper Saddle River, N.J.: Prentice Hall, 2000), pp. 529–530; and S. Robbins, *Organizational Behavior* (Upper Saddle River, N.J.: Prentice Hall, 2001), p. 14.

in 1984 had already extended that act's protection in a similar manner. The provisions of these acts also apply to foreign corporations controlled by a U.S. employer.

It is not always easy to determine whether a multinational corporation will be considered "American" enough to be covered by the acts. According to guidelines issued by the EEOC in October 1993, the EEOC will initially look at where the company is incorporated but will often have to look to other factors. These other factors must also be considered when the employer is not incorporated as, for example, in the case of an accounting partnership. Some of these additional factors include the company's principal place of business, the nationality of the controlling shareholders, and the nationality and location of management. No one factor is considered determinative, and the greater the number of factors linking the employer to the United States, the more likely the employer is to be considered "American" for purposes of being covered by Title VII and the ADEA.

In determining whether a foreign corporation is controlled by a U.S. employer, the EEOC will again look at a broad range of factors. Some such factors include the interrelation of operations, common management, centralized labor relations, and common ownership or financial control over the two entities. However, a corporation that is clearly a foreign corporation and is not controlled by a U.S. entity is not subject to U.S. equal employment laws. An employer may also violate ADA and Title VII if compliance with either law would constitute an illegal action in the foreign country in which the corporation is operating.

Thus, it is important for corporate managers to be familiar with Title VII and the ADA, even when they are going to be working outside the United States.

SUMMARY

During the early years of our nation's history, the employment-at-will doctrine governed the employment relationship. Under this doctrine, an employee without a contract for a set period of time could be fired at any time, for any reason. The doctrine has been gradually eroded, and most states today employ at least one of three exceptions to the employment-at-will doctrine: the public policy exception, the implied contract exception, and implied covenant of good faith and fair dealing exception.

Civil rights laws have also eroded the employer's ability to hire and fire at will. This chapter examined those laws in the order in which they were enacted. The Civil Rights Act of 1866 prohibits employers from discriminating against individuals because of their race.

The Equal Pay Act of 1963 prohibits employers from paying male and female employees doing the same job different wages because of their sex.

Title VII prohibits employers from discriminating in terms and conditions of employment on the basis of race, color, national origin, religion, and sex. This act was amended by the Pregnancy Discrimination Act, which essentially requires employers to not discriminate against pregnancy and to treat pregnancy like any other temporary disability. Title VII was also amended by the Civil Rights Act of 1991, which expanded the remedies available under Title VII.

The Age Discrimination in Employment Act prohibits discrimination based on age against persons age 40 or over. The act is enforced similarly to the way in which Title VII is enforced.

The Rehabilitation Act requires federal agencies, those who have contracts with the federal government, and those receiving any type of federal funds to not discriminate against persons with handicaps. The Americans with Disabilities Act extended the basic protections of the Rehabilitation Act to private employers, requiring them to reasonably accommodate persons with disabilities.

Employers locating overseas must remember that they can no longer avoid Title VII and the ADEA simply by leaving the country. U.S. corporations operating in foreign nations, as well as foreign companies controlled by U.S. corporations, must follow Title VII requirements.

REVIEW QUESTIONS

20-1 Explain the employment-at-will doctrine and why some people would prefer the abolition of this doctrine whereas others feel saddened by its gradual demise.

20-2 Explain why each of the following sets of jobs would or would not be considered equal under the Equal Pay Act:

  a. Male stewards and female stewardesses on continental air flights.

  b. Male checkers of narcotics and female checkers of nonnarcotic drugs at a pharmacy.

  c. Male tailors and female seamstresses.

20-3 Explain the following aspects of the Equal Pay Act:

  a. Its purpose.

  b. The remedies available under the act.

  c. The defenses available to employers.

20-4 Explain the following aspects of Title VII:

  a. Its purpose.

  b. The remedies available under the act.

  c. The defenses available to employers.

20-5 Explain two significant ways that the Civil Rights Act of 1991 has changed the application of Title VII.

20-6 What constitutes "reasonable accommodation" under the Rehabilitation Act and the Americans with Disabilities Act?

REVIEW PROBLEMS

20-7 The City of Los Angeles provided equal monthly retirement benefits for men and women of the same age, seniority, and salary. The benefits were partially paid for by employee contributions and partially by employer contributions. Because women, on the average, live longer than men, the city required women to make contributions to the retirement fund that were 14.84 percent higher than those made by men. Was this a violation of the Civil Rights Act?

20-8 JoAnn, Ann, and Bryon were all laboratory analysts, performing standardized chemical tests on various materials. JoAnn was hired first, with no previous experience, and was trained on the job by the supervisor. She later trained Ann. When Bryon was hired, he was trained by the supervisor with the assistance of the two women. All initially worked the same shift and received the same pay. Then Bryon received a five-cent-per-hour raise and was to work a swing shift every other two weeks. Was his higher wage a violation of the Equal Pay Act?

20-9 Administrators of an Ohio Christian school refused to renew a teacher's contract after she had become pregnant on the basis of its belief that "a mother's place is in the home." When she filed sex discrimination charges under the state civil rights statute, she was fired. Was the termination unlawful?

20-10 Ellen's immediate supervisor repeatedly required her to have "closed door" meetings with him, in violation of company policy. As a consequence, rumors began to spread that the two were having an office romance, although the meetings in fact involved her boss's trying to convince her to loan him money, again in violation of company policy. When Ellen asked her immediate supervisor to try to stop the rumors, he said he found them

somewhat amusing and refused to do anything to stop them. As a consequence of the rumors, she began to be treated as an "outcast" by her coworkers and received low evaluations from other supervisors in the areas of "integrity" and "interpersonal relations." She was passed over for two promotions for which she had applied. She filed an action against her employer on the grounds that her supervisor had created a hostile environment by his refusal to stop the rumors. Do you believe she has a valid claim under Title VII? Why or why not? Are there any other causes of action she might raise?

20-11 A U.S. citizen was working at a multinational company's Zaire facility. The employer was incorporated in the state of Louisiana. When the employee was terminated, allegedly because of his age, he sought recovery under the federal ADEA and also under the Louisiana Age Discrimination in Employment Law. The employer argued that its overseas operations were not subject to the federal ADEA. Was the employer correct?

20-12 Davis, D'Elea, and Sims were former heroin or narcotics addicts. Davis and Sims were told by the city director that they could not be hired by the city because of their former habit. D'Elea was rejected from a city CETA program because of his former habit. The three sued the city, alleging that drug addiction was a handicap under the Rehabilitation Act of 1973 and that, therefore, the city's refusal to hire them was unlawful under this act. Were they correct in their contention?

CASE PROBLEMS

20-13 In 1980, at 14 years of age, Mike Tyson was placed under the supervision of Cus D'Amato, a renowned boxing figure and manager. When Tyson's mother died in 1983, D'Amato also became his legal guardian. At the beginning of Tyson's boxing career, Rooney and D'Amato agreed that Rooney would train Tyson without compensation until the fighter became a professional athlete, and when Tyson advanced to professional ranks, Rooney would be Tyson's trainer "for as long as [Tyson] fought professionally." Rooney trained Tyson for 28 months without compensation. In March 1985, Tyson turned professional and began enjoying meteoric success. D'Amato died that same year.

James Jacobs became Tyson's manager in 1986. When rumors started in some sports media that Rooney would be replaced as Tyson's trainer, Rooney queried Jacobs. To quell the speculation, Tyson allegedly authorized Jacobs

to state publicly that "Kevin Rooney will be Mike Tyson's trainer as long as Mike Tyson is a professional fighter." Jacobs allegedly sent Rooney a copy of a press release to that effect. Thereafter, Rooney continued to train Tyson and was compensated for each of Tyson's professional fights until 1988. In 1988, apparently in connection with Rooney's alleged comments regarding Tyson's divorce and other business-related litigation, Rooney read a newspaper article stating that Tyson would no longer train with Rooney. Tyson formally terminated his boxer–trainer relationship with Rooney later that year.

A federal lawsuit claiming breach of the oral agreement was filed, and the jury returned its verdict in favor of Rooney. Tyson countered after the trial that the agreement was for an indefinite duration and was terminable at will under New York law and, therefore, unenforceable as a matter of law, regardless of the jury's verdict. The district trial court agreed with Tyson's legal position and granted him the posttrial victory. The trial judge concluded that "the alleged term of the employment contract, 'for as long as Tyson boxes professionally,' does not state a term of definite duration as a matter of law" and, therefore, "the nature of the proof offered at trial cannot sustain a finding that the employment relationship was anything other than one at will." Rooney appealed.

Why do you believe the appellate court either reversed or affirmed the district court judge's ruling? *Rooney v. Tyson*, 91 NY 2d 685 (NY 1998)

20-14 Sysco operates a food wholesale distribution business. Sergio E. Fonseca alleges that he was subjected to discrimination based on his race and ethnicity beginning in 1999, soon after Don Peterson was hired as the manager of the Sysco warehouse where Fonseca is employed. Although Fonseca is the only Guatemalan working at the warehouse, there are other Hispanic employees, mostly Mexicans. Fonseca alleges that white workers consistently have received better treatment than Hispanics in similar circumstances. Fonseca alleges he was discriminated against by being harshly punished for accidents that were not his fault, when worse accidents committed by white employees went unpunished.

In addition, Fonseca was frequently passed up for overtime opportunities he should have been offered due to his seniority, according to the collective bargaining agreement. These overtime opportunities were offered to white employees with less seniority. Fonseca filed successful grievances on five of these occasions and eventually received lost overtime pay. For each of his successful grievances, Fonseca alleges that he repeatedly had to request payments, and sometimes was not paid for weeks, whereas white employees were always paid in their next paychecks.

Fonseca filed a complaint with the EEOC. He received a right-to-sue letter and timely filed a Title VII action. Sysco claims that the overtime errors were not adverse employment actions because Fonseca successfully resolved them through the grievance process and, thus, was not put out by the lost overtime. Was Sysco able to raise a successful defense to Fonseca's Title VII claim? Why or why not? *Fonseca v. Sysco Food Services, Inc.*, 2004 U.S. App. LEXIS 13814 (2004)

20-15 IBM hired Thomas Larimer in August 2000, and in May of the following year his wife, who was also an employee of IBM, gave birth to twin daughters after only 29 weeks of pregnancy. At birth the two girls suffered from a variety of serious medical conditions owing to

their prematurity. The girls were hospitalized for almost two months at a total expense of almost $200,000, all of which IBM's employee health plan paid for. The two children seemed to be healthy and normal, but there is some probability that they will develop serious physical or mental handicaps as they grow older.

Larimer was fired in August 2001, shortly after the children came home from the hospital. His principal claim is that IBM violated the Americans with Disabilities Act by firing him because his daughters are disabled. Was Larimer successful in his suit against IBM? Why or why not? *Larimer v. IBM Corp.*, 370 F.3d 698 (2004)

20-16 Brenda Healey worked as a child care specialist at Southwood Psychiatric Home. Her responsibilities included maintaining a therapeutic environment for the children and adolescents treated at the hospital. After a staff reorganization, Healey was assigned to the night shift. This shift was particularly undesirable because it entailed more housekeeping chores and less interaction with the patients. Healey was assigned to the night shift because Southwood needed a female child care specialist for that shift. Because Southwood treated both male and female patients, it contended that it was necessary to maintain a gender-based policy to meet the privacy concerns of the patients. Healey argued that the shift change was made solely on the basis of gender and, therefore, it constituted sex discrimination in violation of Title VII. Do you agree? Why or why not? *Healy v. Southwood Psychiatric Hospital*, 78 F.3d 128 (1996)

20-17 Plaintiff James Corvell was employed by Bank One Trust Company from 1992 until his termination in 2001. The plaintiff, who was 49 at the time of his termination, was replaced by someone 42. The plaintiff filed suit for wrongful termination, arguing that he had been wrongfully terminated on the basis of his age. The trial court granted the defendant's motion for a judgment on the pleadings, accepting the defendant's argument that a prima facie case for age discrimination can be established only by demonstrating replacement by someone outside the protected class. The plaintiff appealed, but the Court of Appeals affirmed the trial court's decision, and the plaintiff once again appealed. How do you think the Ohio Supreme Court, relying on precedent established by the United States Supreme Court, decided the appeal? *Coryell v. Bank One Trust Company, N.A.*, 803 N.E.2d 781, 101 Ohio St.3d 175 (2004)

20-18 Rohan, an actress and singer, suffers from post-traumatic stress disorder ("PTSD") and severe depression stemming from childhood incest and sexual abuse. Despite her mental condition, Rohan was hired by

Networkes Presentations for the role of "Lady Beaconsfield" and as a member of the "Ensemble" in the traveling musical *Jekyll & Hyde*. During rehearsals, Rohan suffered from a number of episodes, which disrupted her ability to rehearse. However, these episodes abated during the first six weeks of performances. Despite Rohan's upbeat attitude at the beginning of the tour, as her divorce was finalized and the holidays approached, she began to have episodes with increasing frequency. Rohan even had to miss one-half performance due to an episode, although she was finished with her role as Lady Beaconsfield at that point. As these episodes increased in frequency, Rohan began to talk about suicide.

After a suicide attempt, two of the play's managers met with Rohan regarding her ability to continue the tour. The management had decided to release Rohan at the beginning of the holiday break. The decision came from wanting to help her, and because she had threatened not to come back after the layoff, this would help her get more assistance for her condition and get her off the sporadic traveling schedule. This would also resolve the disruptions that the company has been dealing with over the past sev-

eral months and relieve them from the stress involved with the long bus rides that caused Rohan's episodes.

When Rohan received a message from the managers stating that they needed to talk, she demanded that if she was to be fired that she be flown home immediately. Upon returning home, Rohan filed a complaint with the Equal Employment Opportunity Commission ("EEOC"), which issued her a right-to-sue letter. Rohan filed this civil action asserting claims for wrongful discharge and hostile work environment under the ADA. After discovery, Networks moved for summary judgment, which the district court granted. As to the ADA claims, the district court held that Rohan was not a "qualified individual with a disability" and, therefore, could not bring a claim under the ADA, because she was unable to perform an essential function of her job. The district court identified that essential job function as the ability to interact with others. Rohan appealed the grant of summary judgment. What rationale did the appellate court give for its decision to affirm or reject the grant of summary judgment? *Rohan v. Networks Presentations LLC*, 2004 U.S. App. LEXIS 14103 (2004)

ASSIGNMENT ON THE INTERNET

Affirmative action remains a contentious issue in areas of employment, school admissions, and government policies. Yet, many companies use a form of affirmative action to create a diverse workforce. Using the Internet, find a company with an affirmative action policy and review the policy.

Using the test set forth in *Adarand Constructors, Inc. v. Pena* and EEOC guidelines, determine whether

the affirmative action policy would withstand a legal challenge. Why or why not? Also make a list of information not available to you on the company's Web site that would assist you in better determining the legality of its affirmative action policy.

 ## ON THE INTERNET

public.findlaw.com/employment_employee/faq.html This site provides answers to questions an employer or employee might have about the kinds of questions employers may ask during the hiring process.

www.legalshark.com Created by an attorney who practices discrimination law, this site provides much useful legal information.

www.eeoc.gov The home page of the U.S. Equal Employment Opportunity Commission provides numerous links to helpful information, including statistics, laws, regulations, and how to file a charge.

www.lawguru.com/faq/5.html Frequently asked questions about the ADA are addressed at this site.

aad.english.ucsb.edu This site is a useful resource for research on affirmative action.

www.law.cornell.edu/topics/employment_discrimination.html Here is a page that will give you information about discrimination law as well as allow you to search for statutes and cases related to employment discrimination.

www.dol.gov/asp/programs/guide.htm This Department of Labor Web site provides labor policy information and an employment law guide.

21

ENVIRONMENTAL LAW

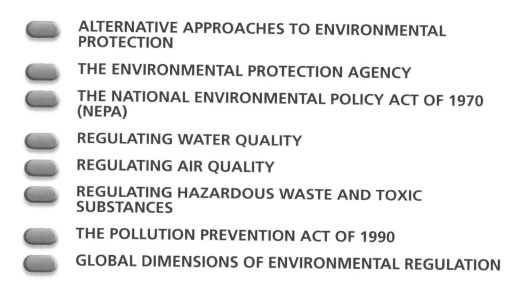

ALTERNATIVE APPROACHES TO ENVIRONMENTAL PROTECTION

THE ENVIRONMENTAL PROTECTION AGENCY

THE NATIONAL ENVIRONMENTAL POLICY ACT OF 1970 (NEPA)

REGULATING WATER QUALITY

REGULATING AIR QUALITY

REGULATING HAZARDOUS WASTE AND TOXIC SUBSTANCES

THE POLLUTION PREVENTION ACT OF 1990

GLOBAL DIMENSIONS OF ENVIRONMENTAL REGULATION

As previous chapters have demonstrated, this country has often turned to the government to solve problems created by business enterprises. Early in the history of our nation, people recognized that certain problems, such as monopolization and labor strife, were national in scope and required a national solution.

Unfortunately, we did not exercise the same degree of foresight in thinking about protecting our physical environment. We looked at our smokestack industries with pride and saw them as symbols of our great productivity and technological advances. People did not fully appreciate that the billowing smoke was making the air less healthful to breathe and that the industrial sewage dumped into rivers was killing or contaminating many forms of aquatic life. The demands placed on nature to serve as a garbage disposal grew ever greater.

Some people eventually started to realize that pollution was a negative externality. It was a cost of the product not paid for by the manufacturers in their costs of production or by consumers in the purchase price. Rather, its costs were being imposed on the community as its members were forced to breathe dirty air and to fish in impure water. People who had the misfortune of living in industrialized areas were paying even higher costs than were people in rural areas through pollution-related diseases and discomfort. Not only were these costs being borne by those who did not use or manufacture the products whose production had led to the pollution, but also, in many cases, these costs were higher than the cost of preventing the pollution in the first place.

During the late 1960s, environmental problems became a major national concern. This concern resulted in the enactment of numerous pieces of legislation designed to protect the environment and to clean up previously created problems. Before introducing contemporary environmental legislation, this chapter briefly examines a few alternatives to the regulatory approach for solving pollution problems and examines the primary agency responsible for enforcing environmental laws, the Environmental Protection Agency. These alternative approaches are becoming increasingly important to understand because the current administration believes that there has been

Critical Thinking About the Law

Why should you, as a future business manager, be concerned about environmental problems? First, you will need to be aware of environmental legislation that could affect your business. Second, as a citizen, you should be concerned about the quality of the environment for both you and future generations. Therefore, you should familiarize yourself with both environmental problems and legislation proposed as a solution to those problems. Asking the following questions about environmental law can help develop your critical thinking skills.

1. Companies are sometimes hesitant to support environmental regulation because the regulation may lead to higher costs for the business. Although a company might be required by law to comply with environmental regulation, devotion to which ethical norms might influence companies to voluntarily comply with environmental legislation?

   Clue: Examine the list of ethical norms. Although compliance might add to a company's costs, what considerations may overrule monetary concerns?

2. You work for a major automobile maker, and you are responsible for monitoring the level of pollutants in the waste produced. If the level of pollutants rises above 75, you are required to contact the Environmental Protection Agency (EPA). One day, the pollutant level is 85; however, your supervisor advises you to correct the problem yourself and to not contact the EPA. You decide to notify the EPA. What ethical norms did you consider in making your decision? How did these norms conflict?

   Clue: Consider the list of ethical norms. What ethical norm seems most successful in convincing you to obey the EPA's regulation?

3. People hold beliefs, or assumptions, about the way the world is. For example, some people do not support environmental laws. They do not support those laws because they believe that it is wasteful to spend money and time on creating laws to protect the environment. Although they will not state so, they believe that there is no environmental problem. Therefore, they do not support environmental regulation. What is ambiguous in such an analysis?

   Clue: Is it clear whether a particular event is wasteful or beneficial?

excessive regulation of the environment, and is looking for ways to cut back on many areas of environmental protection. After discussing the primary direct regulations designed to protect the environment, this chapter examines the Pollution Prevention Act of 1990, an act that has the potential to shift the focus of environmental regulation. Finally, the chapter examines the global dimensions of environmental protection.

ALTERNATIVE APPROACHES TO ENVIRONMENTAL PROTECTION

TORT LAW

Torts, as explained in Chapter 12, are injuries to one's person or property. Pollution injures citizens and their property. Our first attempts to regulate pollution were through the use of tort law, in particular, through the use of the tort of nuisance. A **nuisance** is an unreasonable interference with someone else's use and enjoyment of his or her land. If a factory was emitting black particles that settled on a person's property every day, depositing a layer of dirt on everything in the vicinity, that person might bring an action based on nuisance. He or she would be asking the court to enjoin the emission of the particulates. Before the tort of nuisance was used in attempts to stop pollution, an injunction was always granted when a nuisance was found. Nuisance, therefore, would appear to be the perfect solution to the problem of pollution. The following case, however, demonstrates why the tort of nuisance is ineffective as a means of controlling pollution.

nuisance An unreasonable interference with someone else's use and enjoyment of his or her land.

CASE 21-1

Boomer et al. v. Atlantic Cement Company
New York State Court of Appeals,
257 N.E.2d 870 (1970)

Defendant Atlantic Cement Company operated a large cement plant that emitted considerable amounts of dirt and smoke into the air. These emissions, combined with vibrations from the plant, caused damage to the plaintiffs, Boomer and other owners of property located close to the plant. The plaintiffs brought a nuisance action against the defendant, seeking an injunction. The trial court ruled in favor of the defendants; it found a nuisance but denied plaintiffs the injunction they sought. The plaintiffs appealed to the intermediate appellate court, and the judgment of the trial court was affirmed in favor of the defendant. Plaintiffs then appealed to the state's highest appellate court.

Judge Bergan

[T]here is now before the court private litigation in which individual property owners have sought specific relief from a single plant operation. The threshold question raised on this appeal is whether the court should resolve the litigation between the parties now before it as equitably as seems possible, or whether, seeking promotion of the general public welfare, it should channel private litigation into broad public objectives.

A court performs its essential function when it decides the rights of parties before it. Its decision of private controversies may sometimes greatly affect public issues. Large questions of law are often resolved by the manner in which private litigation is decided. It is a rare exercise of judicial power to use a decision in private litigation as a purposeful mechanism to achieve direct public objectives greatly beyond the rights and interests before the court.

Effective control of air pollution is a problem presently far from solution even with the full public and financial powers of government. In large measure adequate technical procedures are yet to be developed and some that appear possible may be economically impracticable.

It seems apparent that the amelioration of air pollution will depend on technical research in great depth, on a carefully balanced consideration of the economic impact of close regulation, and on the actual effect on public health. It is likely to require massive public expenditure and to demand more than any local community can accomplish and to depend on regional and interstate controls.

A court should not try to do this on its own as a byproduct of private litigation and it seems manifest that the judicial establishment is neither equipped in the limited nature of any judgment it can pronounce nor prepared to lay down and implement an effective policy for the elimination of air pollution. This is an area beyond the circumference of one private lawsuit. It is a direct responsibility for government and should not thus be undertaken as an incident to solving a dispute between property owners and a single cement plant—one of many—in the Hudson River Valley.

The cement-making operations of defendant have been found by the Court at Special Term to have damaged the nearby properties of plaintiffs in these two actions. That court accordingly found defendant maintained a nuisance and this has been affirmed at the Appellate Division. The total damage to plaintiffs' properties is, however, relatively small in comparison with the value of defendant's operation and with the consequences of the injunction which plaintiffs seek.

The ground for the denial of injunction, notwithstanding the finding both that there is a nuisance and that plaintiffs have been damaged substantially, is the large disparity in economic consequences of the nuisance and of the injunction....

[T]o grant the injunction unless defendant pays plaintiffs such permanent damages as may be fixed by the court seems to do justice between the contending parties. All of the attributions of economic loss to the properties on which plaintiffs' complaints are based will have been redressed.

The nuisance complained of by these plaintiffs may have other public or private consequences, but these particular parties are the only ones who have sought remedies and the judgment proposed will fully redress them. The limitation of relief granted is a limitation only within the four corners of these actions and does not foreclose public health or other public agencies from seeking proper relief in a proper court.

It seems reasonable to think that the risk of being required to pay permanent damages to injured property owners by cement plant owners would itself be a reasonably effective spur to research for improved techniques to minimize nuisance.

The damage base here suggested is consistent with the general rule in those nuisance cases where damages are allowed. "Where a nuisance is of such a permanent and unabatable character that a single recovery can be had, including the whole damage past and future resulting therefrom, there can be but one recovery." It has been said that permanent damages are allowed where the loss recoverable would obviously be small compared with the cost of removal of the nuisance.

Thus, it seems fair to both sides to grant permanent damages to plaintiffs which will terminate this private litigation.

Reversed in favor of Plaintiff, Boomer.

Critical Thinking About the Law

In Case 21-1, the New York Court of Appeals became the third court to find the Atlantic Cement Company guilty of committing a nuisance against the plaintiff Boomer. At the same time, the state's highest court also became the third court not to grant an injunction to halt the cement company's pollution.

At first glance, the finding of the court and its subsequent decision seem to contradict one another. However, a closer look at the case reveals that Judge Bergan, in delivering the decision, qualified when a nuisance warrants an injunction. The questions that follow will help you identify this qualification and determine the primary ethical norm to which such a qualification is tied.

1. To demonstrate your ability to follow legal reasoning, in your own words, run down the court's reasoning for its decision.

   Clue: Do not be too narrow here. You want to identify (1) why the court granted damages to the plaintiff and (2) why the court did not order an injunction.

2. The court argued that granting the plaintiff monetary damages should promote more environmentally friendly practices on the part of businesses, because they would develop technologies to prevent having to pay damages. What assumption was made by the court in this reasoning?

   Clue: Reread the court's reasoning. This assumption is related to the quantitative relationship between the damages imposed on businesses for polluting and the economic benefits of polluting for businesses.

In *Boomer*, the plaintiffs technically "won" the case because they were granted a greater remedy than the lower courts had granted; they were granted an injunction in the event that the defendant failed to pay permanent damages within a set period of time. However, they did not achieve their objective, which was to eliminate the nuisance through receipt of an injunction, the traditional remedy in a nuisance action. Thus, in *Boomer v. Atlantic Cement Company*, the court decided that before it would apply the traditional nuisance remedy to stop the pollution, it would weigh the harms that would result from the injunction against the benefits. Because of a lack of scientific knowledge, judges at the time did not see the true costs that the polluting behavior was imposing on the community. Thus, a major problem with using nuisance laws to stop pollution is that the courts will not necessarily use their authority to issue an injunction to stop the polluting behavior even when they find that a nuisance exists.

Another problem with using the tort of nuisance as a remedy is **standing**: the legal status necessary to file an action. Under common law, there are two types of nuisances: public and private. A public nuisance is one that affects a substantial number of people. A private nuisance is one that affects only a limited number of persons, or one that generally affects a large group of persons but causes some special harm to one or a few.

standing The legal status necessary to file a lawsuit.

The only person who has standing to bring an action for a public nuisance is a public official, such as the local prosecutor or the state attorney general. Such officials are often reluctant to sue polluting companies because a lawsuit might result in the closing down of that business and, consequently, a reduction in employment and tax revenues in the area.

In most states, only when the nuisance is a private nuisance does an individual plaintiff have standing to sue. Because most nuisances affect a large number of persons, there are many situations in which individuals cannot file an action and the prosecutor will not file one. In this situation, pollution continues unabated. A few states have resolved this problem by passing statutes giving private citizens standing to seek injunctive relief from public nuisances. In most states, however, this problem with tort solutions to environmental problems still exists.

The foregoing reasons amply demonstrate why nuisance actions alone are not sufficient to control pollution. Nuisance actions can be and are used, but they are primarily used as a way for plaintiffs injured by pollution to recover.

Negligence, an Alternative Tort Solution. The tort of negligence is also used sometimes in the fight against pollution. Plaintiffs must establish the elements of negligence as described in Chapter 12: duty, breach of duty, causation, and damage. Negligence would most often be used in a case in which a defendant's polluting behavior harmed a plaintiff. For example, if a defendant buried hazardous waste in the ground and the waste seeped down into the water table, contaminating the plaintiff's well water and injuring the plaintiff, the plaintiff might bring a negligence action.

Negligence actions involving hazardous materials are often difficult to bring successfully, primarily because many of the pollutants do not cause immediate harm. By the time the harm occurs, it is often difficult to link the damage to the defendant's release of the material, making the element of causation extremely difficult to prove. The availability of defenses such as contributory or comparative negligence, as well as assumption of the risk, help weaken the effectiveness of this tort. It also shares with nuisance the attribute of being reactive rather than preventing pollution in the first place.

The primary method of controlling pollution today is through direct regulation, but before we discuss the regulatory approach, some additional alternatives to regulation should be considered. These approaches were proposed before much of the pollution control legislation was enacted, and they are being discussed again as the country attempts to find more efficient ways to protect the environment.

GOVERNMENT SUBSIDIES APPROACH

One such approach is the use of government subsidies. Under a subsidy system, the government pays polluters to reduce their emissions. Some subsidies that could be used are tax breaks, low-interest loans, and grants for the purchase and installation of pollution control devices. The primary problem with this approach is that when a subsidy is for less than 100 percent of the cost, the firm that limits its pollutants must still bear substantial expenses not borne by its competitors.

EMISSION CHARGES APPROACH

Another approach is simply to charge the polluter a flat fee on every unit of pollutant discharged. Each rational polluter would theoretically reduce pollution to the point at which the cost of reducing one more unit of pollutant is greater than the emission fee. The larger the fee for each unit, the greater the motivation of firms to reduce their emissions. Difficulties in monitoring every discharge of the pollutant and in calculating the amount that should be assessed for each unit of the various pollutants are major problems with this approach. A final problem with this approach is that it may amount to licensing a continuing wrong. Some firms might simply pay the charges and continue to emit pollutants that would be difficult to clean up even with the fees collected.

MARKETABLE DISCHARGE PERMITS APPROACH

Discharge permits provide a similar approach to pollution control. The government would sell permits for the discharge of various pollutants. These pollutants could be discharged only if the polluter had the appropriate permit. Polluters would be encouraged to reduce their emissions because this reduction would enable them to sell their permits. This approach is currently being attempted on a limited scale to reduce emissions of one air pollutant, sulfur dioxide (see the discussion of acid rain control later in this chapter).

From the perspective of people wishing to reduce the total amount of pollution emitted into the environment, the primary advantage that this system offers over a system of charges is that the government actually limits the total amount of pollution through the permits; no permits will be issued once a certain amount of emissions has been authorized. To reduce pollution, the government can simply reduce the number of permits that it issues. Again, however, there is the problem of monitoring the pollution sources.

DIRECT REGULATION APPROACH

Direct regulation is the primary device currently used for protecting the environment. During the late 1970s, a comprehensive set of regulations designed to protect the environment and specifically to improve air and water quality was adopted. These regulations set specific limits on the amount of pollutants that could be discharged. One issue that must be determined when direct regulations are going to be used is whether the standards set by the regulations are "technology forcing" or "technology driven." So-called **technology forcing standards** are set primarily on the basis of health considerations, with the assumption that once standards have been established, the industries will be forced to develop the technology to meet the standards.

Technology driven standards, on the other hand, try to achieve the greatest improvements possible with existing levels of technology. Most of the early environmental regulations in this country were technology forcing. In some cases, this approach was highly successful, and impressive technological gains were made. In other cases, sufficient technology had not yet been developed, and we were unable to meet some rather lofty goals.

Environmental regulations are enforced primarily by administrative agencies. The judiciary is available as a last resort to ensure that these agencies will fulfill their obligations under the law. Because the administrative agencies are staffed by presidential appointment, the attitude of the chief executive has a substantial impact on an agency's behavior. Under different administrations, federal environmental regulations have been enforced with varying degrees of vigor.

For example, the Bush administration significantly decreased federal environmental protection, leaving the states to create and establish their own environmental laws in many areas. In 2004, a rule preventing logging and mining in over 60 million acres of the national forests was removed in favor of allowing governors to determine whether roads can be built through national forests in their states. During the same year, California, frustrated by the lack of federal action preventing greenhouse gas emissions, instituted its own emission standards for automobiles. Because 12 percent of all car sales occur in California, the state has significant power in forcing automakers to cut auto emissions. Whether the federal government's role in protecting the environment will continue to diminish remains to be seen.

The remainder of this chapter focuses primarily on direct regulation as a means of protecting the environment because, despite some minor changes in some of the environmental laws, direct regulation is still the primary means of protecting the environment. We will first examine the Environmental Protection Agency, which has primary responsibility for enforcing the direct regulations.

technology forcing standards Standards of pollution control set primarily on the basis of health considerations, with the assumption that once regulators have set the standards, industry will be forced to develop the technology to meet them.

technology driven standards Standards that take account of existing levels of technology and require the best control system possible given the limits of that technology.

THE ENVIRONMENTAL PROTECTION AGENCY

Like other areas of administrative law, environmental law is primarily made up of regulations passed by a federal agency operating under the guidance of congressional mandates. The primary agency responsible for passage and enforcement of these regulations is the **Environmental Protection Agency (EPA)**.

The EPA is the largest federal agency, having over 18,000 employees in the year 2004. The agency was created by executive order in 1972 to mount an integrated, coordinated attack on pollution in the areas of air, water, solid waste, pesticides, radiation, and toxic substances—a rather substantial mandate for any agency! The reason for placing control of all types of environmental problems within one agency was to ensure that the attack on pollution would be

Environmental Protection Agency (EPA) The federal agency charged with responsibility for conducting an integrated, coordinated attack on all forms of pollution of the environment.

integrated. In other words, Congress wanted to be certain that we would not have a regulation reducing air pollution that simply led to increased water pollution. Unfortunately, such integration did not occur. Within the agency, as Exhibit 21-1 reveals, separate offices were established for each of the areas of pollution, and there was very little interaction among them.

Recognizing the inefficiency of the EPA's organizational structure, in July 1993, EPA administrator Carol Browner took one of the first major steps toward trying to make the agency one with a truly integrated focus. She announced her decision to move all enforcement actions from the various program offices into one main enforcement office. Environmentalists applauded this change because it would make multipronged enforcement routine rather than extraordinary.

In October 1993, she carried out her plan by establishing an Office of Compliance, which has as its primary focus "providing industry with coherent information about compliance requirements." The office is divided into groups of regulators that will focus on separate sectors of the economy: energy and transportation, agriculture, and manufacturing. Browner also created a new

EXHIBIT 21-1

U.S. ENVIRONMENTAL PROTECTION AGENCY

Source:
www.epa.gov/epahome/organization.htm.

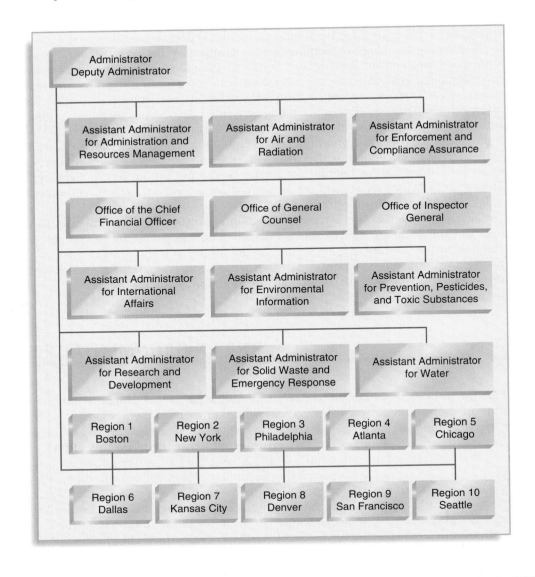

Office of Regulatory Enforcement to take on the tough responsibility of deciding which polluters would be taken to court.[1]

Exhibit 21-1 shows the organizational structure of the EPA. Office of Compliance and Enforcement is located within the authority of the Assistant Administrator for Enforcement and Compliance Assurance.

One area of special concern to business managers, especially since 1990, has been the EPA's use of criminal sanctions, including incarceration, to enforce environmental laws. These cases are not actually tried by the EPA but are passed on by the EPA to the Justice Department with a recommendation for prosecution.

Criminal enforcement continues to be a component of the EPA's enforcement program, although some environmentalists complain that this powerful tool is not being used as often as in the past. For example, in 2003, the EPA referred 228 criminal cases to the Department of Justice, as compared to an all-time high of 278 cases referred during 1997. During 2003, defendants were sentenced to a total of 1,752 months of jail; 1999 was a record year, with a high of 2,500 months sentenced. More than $71 million in criminal fines and restitution was handed down in 2003, a considerable decrease from the record of $169 million in criminal fines assessed in 1997. In terms of civil fines, 1999 was a record year for the EPA; it imposed $141 million in civil fines and a lower $25.5 million in administrative penalties.[2] But even with less emphasis on criminal enforcement, compliance with environmental standards is still an area of importance to the business manager.

Since 1994, the agency has been operating under a policy statement issued to guide its special agents in their enforcement activities. Under this policy, the agents are to look for "significant environmental harm" and "culpable conduct." The first criterion is fairly straightforward, meaning that there has been actual environmental harm or a threat of significant harm. To satisfy the second criteria, the EPA will look for a "history of repeated violations," "concealment of misconduct," or "falsification of required records," "tampering with monitoring or control equipment," and "failing to obtain required licenses or permits."[3]

By issuing this policy, the EPA is trying to put firms on notice as to when their conduct is clearly unacceptable and may subject them to criminal liability. The policy also reflects the intent of the EPA to target the worst violators and make examples of them, hoping that such prosecutions will have a deterrent effect.

A complementary policy issued in 1995, the Final Policy on Penalty Reductions,[4] encourages firms to engage in environmental self-auditing. If a firm can demonstrate that it discovered a violation and moved to correct it, the EPA will seek to reduce the penalty for the violation. Thus, the policy offers a significant benefit to firms that are trying to comply with the laws. Of course, the firm that engages in a self-audit, discovers a violation, and chooses not to change the harmful practice is setting itself up to be a candidate for a criminal prosecution. See Exhibit 21-2 for the elements of a successful environmental auditing program.

---

[1] P. Wallach and D. Levin, "Using Government's Guidance to Structure Compliance Plan," *National Law Journal*, August 30, 1993, p. S. 10.

[2] Office of Enforcement and Compliance Assurance, **es.epa.gov/oeca**.

[3] E. Devaney, *The Exercise of Investigative Discretion* (Washington, D.C.: American Law Institute, 1995).

[4] *Federal Register 60*, no. 246 (December 22, 1995).

EXHIBIT 21-2

ELEMENTS OF A SUCCESSFUL ENVIRONMENTAL SELF-AUDITING PROGRAM

- Explicit senior management support for environmental auditing and the willingness to follow up on the findings.
- An environmental auditing function independent of audited activities.
- Adequate auditor training and staffing.
- An explicit audit program, objectives, scope, resources, and frequency.
- A process that collects, analyzes, interprets, and documents information sufficient to achieve audit objectives.
- A process that includes specific procedures to promptly prepare candid, clear, and appropriate written reports on audit findings, corrective actions, and schedules for implementation.
- A process that includes quality assurance procedures to verify the accuracy and thoroughness of such audits.

THE NATIONAL ENVIRONMENTAL POLICY ACT OF 1970 (NEPA)

One of the first major environmental laws passed in this nation set forth our country's policy for protecting the environment. This act, the National Environmental Policy Act of 1970 (NEPA), has been regarded by many as the country's most influential piece of environmental legislation.

IMPLEMENTING THE NATIONAL ENVIRONMENTAL POLICY ACT

Environmental Impact Statement (EIS) A statement that must be prepared for every major federal activity that would significantly affect the quality of the human environment.

The National Environmental Policy Act is viewed as an extremely powerful piece of legislation because its primary purpose and effect have been to reform the process by which regulatory agencies make decisions. Title II of the act requires the preparation of an **Environmental Impact Statement (EIS)** for every major legislative proposal or agency action that would have a significant impact on the quality of the human environment. A substantial number of these statements are filed every year, over which a significant amount of litigation results.

Threshold Considerations. As the preceding paragraph indicates, an EIS is required when three elements are present. First, the action in question must be federal, such as the grant of a license, the making of a loan, or the lease of property by a federal agency. Second, the proposed activity must be major, that is, requiring a substantial commitment of resources. Finally, the proposed activity must have a significant impact on the human environment.

Content of the EIS. Once an agency has determined that an EIS is necessary, it must gather the information necessary to prepare the document. The NEPA requires that the EIS include a detailed statement of:

1. The environmental impact of the proposed action.

2. Any adverse environmental effects that cannot be avoided should the proposal be implemented.

3. Alternatives to the proposed action.

4. The relationship between local short-term uses of the human environment and the maintenance and enhancement of long-term productivity.

5. Any irreversible and irretrievable commitments of resources that would be involved in the proposed activity should it be implemented.

A continuing problem under the act, however, is interpreting what is meant by environmental impacts. Clearly, they extend beyond the effects on the natural environment and in some cases have been held to include noise, increased traffic and congestion, the overburdening of public facilities such as sewage and mass transportation systems, increased crime, increased availability of illegal drugs, and in a small number of cases, damage to the psychological health of those affected by the agency action. Other cases, however, have not allowed all such damages. The loss of business profits resulting from a proposed agency action has not been considered an environmental impact.

The following case illustrates how difficult it sometimes is for the court to determine what is considered a significant environmental impact that requires the filing of an EIS.

CASE 21-2

Department of Transportation v. Public Citizen
United States Supreme Court,
124 S. Ct. 2204 (2004)

The Federal Motor Carrier Safety Administration (FMCSA) prepared new regulations to allow Mexican trucking companies into the United States. To examine the effects of the new regulations on the environment, FMCSA performed an Environmental Assessment (EA) instead of an Environmental Impact Study (EIS). The latter is required only if the new regulations are likely to have a significant impact on the environmental. Public Citizen, a watchdog group, challenged the decision not to perform an EIS, asserting that FMCSA should have considered the significant environmental impact of the increased number of trucks that would be admitted into the United States. The district court sided with FMCSA because it had control only over the passage of regulations and not over the trucks admitted.

Justice Thomas

In this case, we confront the question whether the National Environmental Policy Act of 1969 (NEPA), and the Clean Air Act (CAA) require the Federal Motor Carrier Safety Administration (FMCSA) to evaluate the environmental effects of cross-border operations of Mexican-domiciled motor carriers, where FMCSA's promulgation of certain regulations would allow such cross-border operations to occur. Because FMCSA lacks discretion to prevent these cross-border operations, we conclude that these statutes impose no such requirement on FMCSA.

FMCSA's decision not to prepare an Environmental Impact Statement (EIS) can be set aside only upon a showing that it was "arbitrary, capricious, an abuse of discretion,

or otherwise not in accordance with law." Respondents criticize the EA's failure to take into account the various environmental effects caused by the increase in cross-border operations of Mexican motor carriers.

Under NEPA, an agency is required to provide an EIS only if it will be undertaking a "major Federal action," which "significantly affects the quality of the human environment." Thus, the relevant question is whether the increase in cross-border operations of Mexican motor carriers, with the correlative release of emissions by Mexican trucks, is an "effect" of FMCSA's issuance of the Application and Safety Monitoring Rules; if not, FMCSA's failure to address these effects in its EA did not violate NEPA, and so FMCSA's issuance of a finding of no significant impact cannot be arbitrary and capricious.

Respondents have only one complaint with respect to the EA: It did not take into account the environmental effects of increased cross-border operations of Mexican motor carriers. Respondents' argument that FMCSA was required to consider these effects is simple. FMCSA is barred from expending any funds to process or review any applications by Mexican motor carriers until FMCSA implemented a variety of specific application and safety-monitoring requirements for Mexican carriers. This expenditure bar makes it impossible for any Mexican motor carrier to receive authorization to operate within the United States until FMCSA issued the regulations challenged here. The promulgation of the regulations, the argument goes, would "cause" the entry of Mexican trucks (and hence also cause any emissions such trucks would produce), and the entry of the trucks is "reasonably foreseeable." Thus, the argument concludes, FMCSA must take these emissions into account in its EA when evaluating whether to produce an EIS.

Respondents' argument, however, overlooks a critical feature of this case: FMCSA has no ability to countermand the President's lifting of the moratorium or otherwise categorically to exclude Mexican motor carriers from operating within the United States. Under FMCSA's entirely reasonable reading of this provision, it must certify *any* motor carrier that can show that it is willing and able to comply with the various substantive requirements for safety and financial responsibility contained in DOT regulations; only the moratorium prevented it from doing so for Mexican motor carriers before 2001. Thus, upon the lifting of the moratorium, if FMCSA refused to authorize a Mexican motor carrier for cross-border services, where the Mexican motor carrier was willing and able to comply with the various substantive safety and financial responsibilities rules, it would violate the law.

We hold that where an agency has no ability to prevent a certain effect due to its limited statutory authority over the relevant actions, the agency cannot be considered a legally relevant "cause" of the effect. Hence, under NEPA regulations, the agency need not consider these effects in its EA when determining whether its action is a "major Federal action." Because the President, not FMCSA, could authorize (or not authorize) cross-border operations from Mexican motor carriers, and because FMCSA has no discretion to prevent the entry of Mexican trucks, its EA did not need to consider the environmental effects arising from the entry.

FMCSA did not violate NEPA regulations when it did not consider the environmental effect of the increase in cross-border operations of Mexican motor carriers in its EA. Nor did FMCSA act improperly by not performing, pursuant to the CAA and relevant regulations, a full conformity review analysis for its proposed regulations. We therefore reject respondents' challenge to the procedures used in promulgating these regulations. Accordingly, the judgment of the Court of Appeals is reversed, and the case is remanded for further proceedings consistent with this opinion.

Reversed and remanded in favor of the Dept. of transportation.

Critical Thinking About the Law

When judges encounter significant ambiguity in statutory language, their subsequent interpretation is an important element of their reasoning. As we have discussed previously, such interpretation is influenced by primary ethical norms.

Case 21-2 provides a good illustration of significant ambiguity whose interpretation has a significant, if not determinative, bearing on the Court's decision. Consequently, the questions that follow will focus on this part of the Court's reasoning with an emphasis on the impact of primary ethical norms.

1. **What significant ambiguity did the Court confront in Case 21-2?**

   Clue: Reread the section in which the Court discussed the statutory language relevant to the case.

2. **How did the Court's interpretation of this ambiguity affect the respondent's claim?**

   Clue: What did the Court find were the "effects" of FMCSA's regulations?

Another problem regarding the scope of the EIS pertains to the requirement of a detailed statement of alternatives to the proposed actions. What alternatives must be discussed, and how detailed must the discussion be? In general, any reasonable alternatives, including taking no action, must be discussed. The more likely the alternative is to be implemented, the more detailed the statement must be.

Effectiveness of the EIS Process. The EIS requirement has clearly changed the process of agency decision making, but many wonder whether the requirement has improved the quality of the decision making.

Now that the reader is familiar with this umbrella environmental act, we will examine some of the specific laws designed to protect various aspects of the environment. The focus will initially be on protecting the quality of the water.

REGULATING WATER QUALITY

Water pollution is controlled today primarily by two pieces of legislation: the Federal Water Pollution Control Act (FWPCA; also called the Clean Water Act) and the Safe Drinking Water Act. The first concentrates on the quality of water in our waterways; the second ensures that the water we drink is not harmful to our health. (Some people say that the former law protects the environment from humans, while the latter protects humans from the environment!)

THE FEDERAL WATER POLLUTION CONTROL ACT

When Congress passed the 1972 amendments to the FWPCA, it established two goals: (1) "fishable" and "swimmable" waters by 1983 and (2) the total elimination of pollutant discharges into navigable waters by 1985. These goals were to be achieved through a system of permits and effluent discharge limitations. Obviously, these goals were not attained. Many argue that no one really expected their attainment. However, they set a high goal toward which we could aspire.

Point-Source Effluent Limitations. One of the primary tools for meeting the goals of the 1972 FWPCA amendments was the establishment and enforcement of point-source effluent limitations. **Point sources** are distinct places from which pollutants can be discharged into water. Factories, refineries, and sewage treatment facilities are a few examples of point sources. Effluents are the outflows from a specific source. **Effluent limitations**, therefore, are the maximum allowable amounts of pollutants that can be discharged from a source within a given time period. Different limitations were established for different pollutants.

Under the National Pollutant Discharge Elimination System (NPDES), every point source that discharges pollutants must obtain a discharge permit from the EPA or from the state if the state has an EPA-approved plan at least as strict as the federal standards. The permits specify the types and amounts of effluent discharges allowed. The discharger is required to continually monitor its discharges and report any excess discharges to either the state or federal EPA. Discharges without a permit or in amounts in excess of those allowed by the permit may result in the imposition of criminal penalties. Enforcement of the act is left primarily to the states where there is an approved program for regulation. However, the act provides for federal monitoring, inspection, and enforcement. Citizens may also bring suit to enforce the effluent limits.

Permissible discharge limits under the discharge system are based on technological standards. Most sources today must use the Best Available Control Technology, or BACT. All new sources must meet this standard, but some existing facilities are allowed to meet a slightly lower standard, Best Practicable Control Technology (BPCT). The EPA issues regulations explaining which equipment meets these standards. These standards remain in effect.

point sources Distinct places from which pollutants are discharged into water, such as paper mills, electric utility plants, sewage treatment facilities, and factories.

effluent limitations Maximum allowable amounts of pollutants that can be discharged from a point source within a given time period.

THE SAFE DRINKING WATER ACT

The FWPCA ensures that the waterways are clean, but "clean" does not necessarily mean "fit to drink." The Safe Drinking Water Act (SDWA), therefore, sets standards for drinking water supplied by a public water supply system. A public water supply system is defined by the SDWA as a water supply system that has at least 15 service connections or serves 25 or more persons.

The SDWA requires the EPA to establish two levels of drinking water standards for potential drinking water contaminants. Primary standards are to protect human health, and secondary standards are to protect the aesthetic quality of drinking water.

Primary standards are based on maximum contaminant level goals (MCLGs) and maximum contaminant levels (MCLs) for all contaminants that had the potential to have an adverse effect on human health. MCLGs are the levels at which there are no potential adverse health effects. These are unenforceable, health-based goals. They are the high standards to which we aspire. The MCLs are the enforceable standards. They are developed from the MCLGs but also take into account the feasibility and cost of meeting the standard. By 1991, the EPA was to have set MCLs for 108 of the hundreds of contaminants found in our drinking water, and MCLs for 25 more contaminants every three years thereafter. These goals were not met, and the 1996 amendments to the SDWA gave the EPA more flexibility in setting standards so that the agency could focus on first setting standards for the contaminants that posed the greatest potential health hazards. As the reader might guess, keeping up with the ever-increasing MCLs is a difficult task for public drinking water suppliers. Monitoring these systems is also a chore. Most states do monthly monitoring. Violations may be punished by administrative fines or orders. The 1996 amendments also imposed a "right to know" provision, requiring drinking water suppliers to provide every household with annual reports on water contaminants and the health problems they may cause.

REGULATING AIR QUALITY

A second major environmental concern is protecting the quality of the air. To that end, Congress enacted the Clean Air Act in 1970. Although air quality continues to improve, the EPA estimated that in 2002 over 146 million Americans lived in areas that did not meet the ambient air quality standards for at least one of six major conventional air pollutants: carbon monoxide, lead, nitrogen oxides, suspended particulates, ozone, and sulfur dioxide.[5]

Table 21-1 illustrates some of the most common health problems caused by these pollutants. In addition to these enumerated health problems, nitrogen oxides and sulfur dioxide contribute to the formation of acid rain, which defaces buildings and causes the pH levels of lakes to reach such low levels that most plants and animals can no longer survive in them. These pollutants, frequently referred to as criteria pollutants, have been regulated primarily through national air quality standards.

THE NATIONAL AMBIENT AIR QUALITY STANDARDS (NAAQSs)

national ambient air quality standards (NAAQSs) A two-tiered set of standards developed for the chief conventional air pollutants: primary standards, designed to protect public health; and secondary standards, designed to protect public welfare.

The **national ambient air quality standards (NAAQSs)** provide the focal point for air pollution control. The administrator of the EPA establishes primary and secondary NAAQSs for criteria pollutants. Primary standards are those that the administrator determines are necessary to protect the public health, including an ade-

---

[5] EPA, "Air Trends: Six Principle Pollutants," **www.epa.gov/airtrends/sixpoll.html**, June 25, 2004.

Pollutant	Associated Problems
Carbon monoxide	Angina, impaired vision, poor coordination, lack of alertness
Lead	Neurological system and kidney damage
Nitrogen oxides	Lung and respiratory tract damage
Ozone	Eye irritation, increased nasal congestion, reduction of lung function, reduced resistance to infection
Sulfur dioxide	Lung and respiratory tract damage

TABLE 21-1

AIR POLLUTANTS AND ASSOCIATED HEALTH PROBLEMS

quate margin of safety. Secondary standards are more stringent, as they are the standards that would protect the public welfare (crops, buildings, and animals) from any known or anticipated adverse effect associated with the air pollutant for which the standard is being established. Currently, the primary and secondary standards are the same for all criteria pollutants except sulfur dioxide. The administrator of the EPA retains the authority to establish new primary and secondary standards if scientific evidence indicates that the present standards are inadequate or that such standards must be set for currently unregulated pollutants.

Once each NAAQS is established, each state has nine months to establish a **state implementation plan (SIP)** that explains how the state is going to ensure that the pollutants in the air within a state's boundaries will be kept from exceeding the NAAQSs. Under the SIPs, primary NAAQSs must be achieved within three years of their creation, and secondary standards are to be met within a reasonable time. The administrator of the EPA has to approve all SIPs. When a SIP is found inadequate, the administrator has the power to amend it or send it back to the state for revision.

In the 1990 Clean Air Act Amendments, Congress specifically addressed those areas of the country that had not yet met the NAAQSs, the so-called *nonattainment areas*. Such areas are classified in five categories ranging from "marginal" to "extreme," depending on how far out of compliance they are. New deadlines for meeting the primary standard for ozone were set, ranging from 5 to 20 years. Nonattainment areas also must establish or upgrade vehicle inspection and maintenance programs.

In addition to establishing the NAAQSs, the EPA administration is also required to determine national, uniform emission standards for new motor vehicles, as well as for new and major expansions of existing stationary sources of pollutants. The standards, established by the New Source Review program, for the new stationary sources are to reflect the best available control technology, taking into account the costs of compliance. The initial emission standards for automobiles and new stationary sources, like the NAAQSs, were not all met within the original timetables. Many of the deadlines were simply extended. In the 1990 amendments to the Clean Air Act, Congress imposed additional requirements on the automakers, mandating the use of tailpipe emissions-reduction equipment on newly manufactured vehicles, for example. In nonattainment areas, reformulated, cleaner gasolines were required beginning in 1995.

state implementation plan (SIP) A plan, required of every state, that explains how the state will meet federal air pollution standards.

NEW SOURCE REVIEW

As part of the 1977 Clean Air Act Amendments, Congress established the New Source Review (NSR) program, which regulates criteria pollutants and ensures acceptable levels of NAAQSs through mandating the installation of new pollution control technology in new or modified stationary sources. In 2002, it was estimated that the NSR regulated over 17,000 stationary sources, such as power plants, oil refineries, and chemical factors. Consequently, many view the NSR as a key provision in the Clean Air Act, as it removes millions of tons of sulfur dioxide, nitrogen oxide, and mercury from the air each year.[6]

However, the NSR may be undergoing significant changes, changes which some see as further rollbacks of longstanding environmental protections by the Bush administration. One proposed change to the NSR would allow significant maintenance, upgrades, and expansions to occur without requiring new pollution controls as long as the costs of the modifications do not exceed 20 percent of the cost of the entire "process unit." Under this new rule, major utility plant changes that cost millions of dollars and increase pollution by thousands of tons could be defined as "routine maintenance" and, thus, be exempt from Clean Air Act protections. Environmental groups have expressed strong anger toward this new rule, arguing that it will substantially harm the quality of the air, increase respiratory aliments such as asthma, and cause thousands of premature deaths. In 2004, the EPA reported that over 100 million people in the United States breathe unhealthy levels of particulates emitted from stationary sources. Citing the widespread health effects of increased particulate matter in the air, environmentalist groups have sued to stop the implementation of the changes. As of late 2004 the issue remains in federal court.

HAZARDOUS AIR POLLUTANTS

The conventional air pollutants discussed previously can be emitted into the air in somewhat substantial quantities without posing a significant risk to human health or the environment. Other air pollutants, however, may pose a significant risk to human health when even very tiny amounts are emitted. These pollutants, which are likely to cause an increase in mortality or in serious, irreversible illness, are referred to as hazardous or toxic air pollutants.

Under the 1990 Amendments to the Clean Air Act, Congress identified 189 of these hazardous air pollutants (HAP), including asbestos, benzene, mercury, and vinyl chloride, and mandated that their emissions be reduced by 90 percent by the year 2000. However, the EPA fell well short of this goal, achieving 39 percent overall HAP reduction by 2000.[7] The EPA continues to reduce HAP by requiring industries to use pollution control equipment that meets the maximum achievable control technology, or MACT, standard. In 2004, MACT standards were criticized by environmentalist for their numerous loopholes, preventing significant HAP reductions mandated by the Clean Air Act. The EPA publishes guidelines as to what equipment meets this standard.

INDOOR AIR POLLUTION

The Clean Air Act addressed primarily the outdoor air quality problems. In recent years, however, we have come to realize that the quality of the air inside the structures where people live and work has a significant impact on their

---

[6] EPA, New Source Review, Report to the President, June 2002. Can be viewed at **www.epa.gov/nsr/documents/nsr_report_to_president.pdf**.

[7] U.S. House of Representatives, Committee on Energy and Commerce, May 1, 2002, **www.law.syr.edu/faculty/driesen/cong_test.pdf**.

health. Because Americans spend roughly 90 percent of their time indoors, indoor air quality is an important issue.

The major indoor air quality issue that has recently arisen is the **sick building syndrome**. During the 1970s, buildings were made as airtight as possible for purposes of saving energy; substantial insulation was used, and windows were sealed. Consequently, building occupants became completely dependent upon artificial heating and cooling systems for airflow and circulation. If filters are not properly cleaned and maintained, fungi, bacteria, and viruses can thrive, accumulate, and circulate in the building, having a detrimental impact on the health of the occupants.

A related problem is that many building materials, office furnishings, and carpets emit harmful substances, including pesticides, upon installation. In a well-sealed building, these substances may be concentrated for up to a year. The EPA estimates that 90 percent of people's time is spent indoors and, thus, greater exposure to pesticides may be through indoor exposure.[8]

Despite the costs to human health, the Clean Air Act does not address indoor air quality. The OSHA does have some air quality regulations for workplaces; however, no agency seriously addresses the residential threat, except that the EPA tries to publicize the potential problem (see Exhibit 21-3).

sick building syndrome
Indoor air pollution caused by the absence of fresh air in overly insulated new buildings and by the emission of harmful substances found in many building materials and office furnishings.

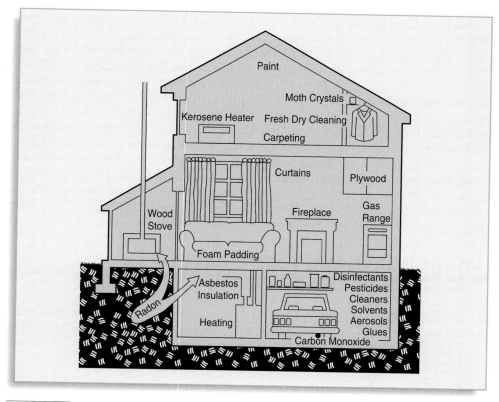

EXHIBIT 21-3

AIR POLLUTION SOURCES IN THE HOME

Source: U.S. Environmental Protection Agency, *Environmental Progress and Challenges: EPA's Update* (Washington, D.C.: U.S. Government Printing Office, 1988), p. 32.

---

[8] EPA, "The Inside Story: A Guide to Indoor Air Quality," July 9, 2004.

THE ACID RAIN CONTROL PROGRAM

acid rain Precipitation with a high acidic content (pH level of less than 5) caused by atmospheric pollutants.

One of the major air quality problems facing the United States, as well as other countries, is **acid rain**. Roughly 75 percent of acid rain is caused by emissions of sulfur dioxide and nitrogen oxide from the burning of fossil fuels by electric utilities. The 1990 Clean Air Act Amendments included an innovative approach to controlling the sulfur dioxide emissions.

Under the 1990 Clean Air Act Amendments, Congress required the EPA to establish an emissions trading program that would significantly cut the emissions of sulfur dioxide. As a result of the Acid Rain Program, sulfur dioxide emissions between 1993 and 2002 were cut by 31 percent creating a 39 percent reduction in air quality concentrations.[9]

Under the program, the EPA auctions a given number of sulfur dioxide allowances each year. A holder can emit 1 ton of sulfur dioxide for each allowance. Firms holding the allowances would be able to use the allowance to emit pollutants, "bank" their allowances for the next year, or sell their allowances to other firms. The purpose of the program is to reduce total emissions in the most efficient way possible. Those firms for which emission reduction is the cheapest will reduce their emissions extensively, whereas those for which emission reduction is extremely expensive will find it more efficient to buy allowances. Total emissions will fall because every succeeding year the number of allowances issued will be reduced, but the firms actually reducing their emissions will be the ones whose emissions can be reduced at the lowest cost.

On March 29, 1993, the first auction of EPA pollution allowances was held. More than 150,000 allowances were sold, with each allowance permitting the emission of 1 ton of sulfur dioxide. Prices for each allowance ranged from $122 to $450. Utilities were given a fixed amount of allowances and could bid for others at the auction. Some environmental groups also participated in the auction, buying allowances that they would retire unused to help clean the air.

By 1995, after three years of the program's operation, many were surprised that the price of the allowances had fallen to less than $140 per ton. Given the low price of allowances, it would have been cheaper for many firms to buy allowances, but many chose instead to install costly pollution control equipment or switch to less-polluting fuel. In 1998, a total of 150,000 allowances were offered for use that year at a price ranging from $115.01 to $228.92. In 2004, only 125,000 allowances were auctioned at an average price of $272.82. This program is often cited as a model for achieving cost-effective pollution reduction and, consequently, many people are looking at emissions trading as a possible way to meet the worldwide problem of too many harmful greenhouse gases.[10]

REGULATING HAZARDOUS WASTE AND TOXIC SUBSTANCES

When people think about pollution, they often think of air and water pollution, yet the land can be polluted too, often with tragic results. Perhaps the most dramatic of such instances was the Love Canal incident.

---

[9] EPA, Acid Rain Program, 2002 Progress Report, **www.epa.gov/airmarkets/cmprpt/arp02/2002report.pdf**, June 30, 2004.
[10] Scott Olsen, "The New Green Game: Tradable Allowances for Greenhouse Gases May One Day Become the World's Biggest Commodities Market," *Newsweek*, August 27, 2001, 000.

In 1978, state officials ordered the emergency evacuation of 240 families from the Love Canal area of Niagara Falls, New York. This residential area had been built over the site of a Hooker Chemical Company dump that contained more than 300 million tons of industrial waste. The extremely high incidences of asthma, urinary tract disease, miscarriages, and birth defects among the residents were attributed to exposure to the waste.

Most of us want to enjoy the products that technology has developed. But what price are we willing to pay for these amenities? Most of us do not wish to pay the price paid by the former residents of Love Canal. Nor would any of us want to be the businessperson whose decisions were partially responsible for such a tragedy.

Until the mid-1970s, most people were content to take advantage of newly available products without giving much thought to the by-products resulting from their manufacture. Most businesspersons were primarily concerned about creating new products and using new technology to increase production and profits. Then came a growing awareness of the potential health and environmental risks posed by the waste created in the production process. In addition to the problems created by the waste, some of the new products themselves, and their newly created chemical components, were proving to be harmful.

The potential health risks from these chemicals and wastes include a plethora of cancers, respiratory ailments, skin diseases, and birth defects. Environmental risks include not only pollution of the air and water but also unexpected explosions and soil contamination. Species of plants and animals may be threatened with extinction.

During the mid-1970s, Congress began to take a closer look at regulating waste and toxic materials. One of the problems regulators face in this area, however, is a lack of scientific knowledge concerning the impact of many chemicals on human health. We know that exposure to many chemicals causes cancer in laboratory animals. We are unable, however, to ascertain the impact of each increment of exposure. For example, we know that saccharin in some quantity can cause cancer in humans, but we do not know what quantity or whether especially sensitive persons may be affected by substantially smaller amounts. Congress has responded to these and related problems in a variety of ways.

Four primary acts are designed to control hazardous waste and toxic substances: (1) the Resource Conservation and Recovery Act of 1976 (RCRA); (2) the Comprehensive Environmental Response, Compensation, and Liability Act of 1980 (CERCLA); (3) the Toxic Substances Control Act of 1979 (TSCA); and (4) the Federal Insecticide, Fungicide, and Rodenticide Act of 1972 (FIFRA).

THE RESOURCE CONSERVATION AND RECOVERY ACT OF 1976 (RCRA)

The Resource Conservation and Recovery Act regulates both hazardous and nonhazardous waste, with the primary emphasis on controlling hazardous waste. The focus of the act is on the treatment, storage, and disposal of **hazardous waste**. (See Exhibit 21-4.) The reason for this focus was the belief that it was not necessarily the creation of waste that was the problem but rather the improper disposal of such waste. Also, it was hoped that making firms pay the true costs of safe disposal would provide the financial incentive for them to generate less waste.

The Manifest Program. The best-known component of the RCRA is its **manifest program**, which is designed to provide "cradle-to-grave" regulation of hazardous waste. A waste may be considered hazardous and, thus, fall under

hazardous waste Any waste material that is ignitable, corrosive, reactive, or toxic when ingested or absorbed.

manifest program A program that attempts to see that hazardous wastes are properly transported to disposal facilities licensed by the EPA so that the agency will have an accurate record (manifest) of the location and amount of all hazardous wastes.

EXHIBIT 21-4

WHAT IS A HAZARDOUS WASTE?

Source: Council on Environmental Quality, *Environmental Quality,* January 1993, p. 126.

According to the Resource Conservation and Recovery Act of 1976 (RCRA) and the Hazardous and Solid Waste Amendments of 1984 (RCRA amendments), a hazardous waste may be "garbage, refuse, or sludge or any other waste material" that exhibits one or more of the following characteristics:

Ignitability

Corrosivity

Reactivity (unstable under normal conditions and capable of posing dangers)

Toxicity (harmful or fatal when ingested or absorbed)

Improperly handled, hazardous wastes can contaminate surface waters and groundwater, release toxic vapors into the air, or cause other dangerous situations, such as explosions.

the manifest program in one of three ways. First, it may be listed by the EPA as a hazardous waste. Second, the generator may choose to designate the waste as hazardous. Finally, according to the RCRA, a hazardous waste may be "garbage, refuse, or sludge or any other waste material that has any one of the four defining characteristics: ignitability, corrosivity, reactivity, or toxicity."

Once a waste is designated as hazardous, it falls under RCRA's manifest program. Under this program, generators of hazardous waste must maintain records called *manifests.* These manifests list the amount and type of waste produced, how it is to be transported, and how it will ultimately be disposed of. Some wastes cannot be disposed of in landfills at all. Others must receive chemical or biological treatment to reduce toxicity or to stabilize them before they can be landfilled. If the waste is transported to a landfill, both the transporter and the owner of the disposal site must certify their respective sections of the manifest and return it to the creator of the waste. The purpose of these manifests is to provide a record of the location and amount of all hazardous wastes and to ensure that such waste will be properly transported and disposed of. Exhibit 21-5 shows the hazardous waste manifest trail. An electronic hazardous waste manifest trail is currently being developed to increase the safety of hazardous waste disposal.

All firms involved in the transportation and disposal of hazardous waste must be certified by the EPA in accordance with standards established under RCRA. Every year, approximately 12 million tons of hazardous waste are transported for treatment, storage, or disposal.

RCRA Amendments of 1984 and 1986. Congress amended RCRA in 1984 and 1986. The primary effect of the amendments was to make landfills, or hazardous waste dumps, a last resort for the disposal of many types of waste. Advanced treatment, recycling, incineration, and other forms of hazardous waste treatment are all assumed to be preferable to land disposal. Some wastes were banned from landfill disposal after 1988.

The 1986 amendment requires that companies report the amount of hazardous chemical they release into the environment each year. From 1997–2001 RCRA reported a decrease in overall chemical emissions each year. Toxic chemical emissions increased 5 percent over the previous year, which included a 3.4 percent increase in lead emissions and a 10 percent increase in mercury emissions. Environmental groups blame the lax standards of the Bush administration for the increase in toxic chemicals released into the environment.[11]

---

[11] Juliet Eilperin, "Toxic Emissions Rising, EPA Says," *Washington Post,* June 23, 2004, p. A02.

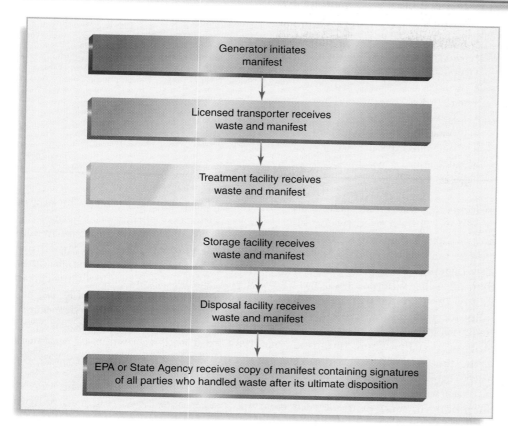

EXHIBIT 21-5

**THE HAZARDOUS WASTE
MANIFEST TRAIL**

*Source: Environmental
Programs and Challenges: EPA
Updates* (EPA, August 1988),
p. 88.

Enforcement of RCRA. RCRA is enforced by the EPA. However, states may set up their own programs as long as these programs are at least as stringent as the federal program. The EPA gives any state that has taken the responsibility for regulating its hazardous wastes the first opportunity to prosecute violators. This procedure is consistent with the EPA's enforcement of other environmental laws.

If the state fails to act within 30 days, the EPA takes action to enforce the state's requirements. The EPA may issue informal warnings; seek temporary or permanent injunctions with criminal penalties of up to $50,000 per day of violation, or civil penalties of up to $25,000 per violation, or both; or announce other penalties that the EPA administrator finds appropriate.

THE COMPREHENSIVE ENVIRONMENTAL RESPONSE, COMPENSATION, AND LIABILITY ACT OF 1980 (CERCLA), AS AMENDED BY THE SUPERFUND AMENDMENT AND REAUTHORIZATION ACT OF 1986 (SARA)

If the manifest program is followed, waste will be disposed of properly and there will be no more incidents like Love Canal. But before RCRA was enacted, there was extensive unregulated dumping. Something needed to be done to take care of cleaning up the sites created by improper disposal. Exhibit 21-6 shows some of the risks posed by these sites.

To alleviate the problems created by improper waste disposal, CERCLA authorized the creation of the **Superfund**, primarily from taxes on corporations

Superfund A fund authorized by CERCLA to cover the costs of cleaning up hazardous waste disposal sites whose owners cannot be found or are unwilling or unable to pay for the cleanup.

EXHIBIT 21-6

ENVIRONMENTAL OR PUBLIC HEALTH THREATS REQUIRING SUPERFUND EMERGENCY ACTIONS

Source: Office of Emergency and Remedial Response (Superfund), U.S. EPA, reprinted in *Environmental Programs and Challenges: EPA Updates* (EPA, August 1988), p. 96.

- Contaminated Air
- Direct Contact with Hazardous Waste
- Contaminated Drinking Water
- Ecological Damage
- Fire or Explosion Hazard
- Exposure Through Food Web
- Contaminated Ground Water
- Contaminated Soil
- Contaminated Surface Water

in industries that create significant amounts of hazardous waste. The money in Superfund is then used by the EPA or state and local governments to cover the cost of cleaning up leaks from hazardous waste disposal sites when their owners cannot be located or are unable or unwilling to pay for a cleanup. Superfund also provides money for emergency responses to hazardous waste spills other than oil spills. When an owner is found after a cleanup, or was initially unwilling to pay, the EPA may sue to recover the costs of the cleanup. Under CERCLA, liability for cleanup extends beyond the immediate owner. So-called potentially responsible parties, who may be held liable, include (1) present owners or operators of a facility where hazardous materials are stored, (2) owners or operators at the time the waste was deposited there, (3) the hazardous waste generators, and (4) those who transported hazardous waste to the site.

The following case illustrates the typical situation in which the EPA is attempting to recover money for cleanup costs. Notice how long it took from the time the hazardous condition was discovered until the cleanup and ultimate recovery of funds from the responsible party.

CASE 21-3

United States v. Harold B. Chapman, Jr.
United States Court of Appeals, Ninth Circuit,
146 F.3d 1166 (1998)

Harold B. Chapman, Jr., manufactured small metal collars and stored and resold military and commercial surplus chemicals on his five-acre parcel of land in Washoe County, Nevada. In 1989, at the request of Washoe County officials, the EPA investigated the facility and found approximately two thousand 5-gallon containers of paint, insulating oil, sulfuric acid, chloroform, alcohols, and other military surplus chemicals at the site. In addition there were one hundred 55-gallon drums of unknown substances. The majority of the drums were stored outside in an unprotected storage yard. Many of the containers were deteriorated and several drums were leaking into the soil. The soil was visibly stained in various areas.

After a preliminary assessment, Washoe County ordered Chapman to bring his property into compliance. In April 1990, Washoe County issued a misdemeanor citation to

Chapman for his failure to comply, and in May 1990 the county commissioner revoked Chapman's business license. The county then requested assistance from the EPA.

On May 24, 1990, the EPA issued an order stating that the site posed an "imminent and substantial endangerment to the public health or welfare or the environment because of the release or threatened release of hazardous substances" and ordered an immediate cleanup. Two months later Chapman submitted a plan for cleanup that the EPA deemed inadequate. A subsequent inspection in January 1991 revealed that conditions had not changed.

Because Chapman had failed to take the necessary steps to comply with the EPA's order, the EPA decided to initiate a response action and sent its contractor to visit the site. In February 1991, when the EPA was prepared to begin its response action, Chapman finally began to comply with the order. Under the supervision of the EPA, Chapman removed the containers from the site and conducted soil samples.

In April 1992, the EPA sent demand letters to Chapman requesting $33,946 for the response costs it had incurred. Chapman refused to pay the EPA's costs and the United States brought this civil action against Chapman to collect them. The district court granted summary judgment in favor of the government, and Chapman appealed.

Judge Thompson

To establish a prima facie case to recover its response costs under CERCLA Section 107, the government has to prove: (1) the site is a "facility"; (2) a "release" or "threatened release" of a hazardous substance occurred; (3) the government incurred costs in responding to the release or threatened release; and (4) the defendant is the liable party. ... Once the government presents a prima facie case for response costs, the burden shifts to the defendant to prove the government's response action was inconsistent with the National Contingency Plan. ...

Chapman argues the government failed to establish a prima facie case ... because there is a genuine issue of material fact as to whether Chapman caused a release or a threatened release of a hazardous substance on his property.

... As the district court stated, the administrative record reflected that there were consultant reports. And the facts established that two thousand drums were stored on the property. They were reported to have been rusted and corroded, and without tops, and in poor condition. And there was some evidence of visible soil stains, and soil—and actual soil sample contamination.

... Three samples were flammable, one was a corrosive basic liquid, and four others were combustible. These are hazardous substances under CERCLA. ...

The only evidence Chapman presented in opposition to the foregoing evidence were his own declarations. The district court concluded those declarations were not based upon Chapman's own observation, but were hearsay and therefore they failed to create a genuine issue of material fact. ... The assertions are secondhand hearsay and were inadequate to rebut the evidence in the administrative record presented by the EPA. That evidence established the EPA's prima facie case under CERCLA Section 107(a).

... The government having established its prima facie case under CERCLA Section 107(a), the burden then shifted to Chapman to create a genuine issue of material fact on the question of whether the EPA's response action was inconsistent with the National Contingency Plan ("NCP"). Chapman failed to do so.

... The NCP is a national plan the EPA was required to promulgate to guide federal and state response actions. ... "The NCP is designed to make the party seeking response costs choose a cost-effective course of action to protect the public health and the environment." ...

... "To prove that a response action of the EPA was inconsistent with the NCP, a defendant must prove that the EPA's response action was arbitrary and capricious."

... Chapman argues the EPA's response action was inconsistent with the NCP because the EPA's removal order was arbitrary and capricious in that it ordered removal of material from Chapman's property without first determining whether that material was hazardous. We disagree. Before issuing its Order, the EPA inventoried and sampled the containers at the site as part of its preliminary assessment. EPA Order 90-10 details the EPA's actions as well as the nature and extent of the threat at the Chapman site. ...

The EPA did not act arbitrarily or capriciously in ordering removal of the material. Prior to issuing its Order 90-10, the EPA concluded, after careful investigation and evaluation, that the site posed a threat, and removal or remedial action was necessary.

Affirmed in favor of Plaintiff, United States.

Successful actions under the CERCLA to recover costs have been less frequent than originally hoped. The fund was originally intended to be self-replenishing but was not successful in that regard. The CERCLA was amended in late 1986 by the Superfund Amendment and Reauthorization Act of 1986 (SARA). These amendments provided more stringent cleanup requirements and increased Superfund's funding to $8.5 billion, to be generated primarily by taxes on petroleum, chemical feedstocks, imported chemical derivatives, and a new "environmental tax" on corporations. Additional money was to come from general revenues, recoveries, and interest.

The future of Superfund, however, remains in question. The taxes on chemical and petroleum companies used to support Superfund cleanups expired in 1995 and require reauthorization from Congress. Consequently, in 2003, the fund was depleted of any money from the chemical or petroleum industries, shifting the cleanup burden directly to the taxpayers.[12] As of 2004, 33 of the most toxic Superfund sites no longer receive funding; the Bush administration advocates using the government's general fund, financed by taxpayers, to complete the cleanups. Because Superfund is no longer funded by polluter and industry dollars, the completion of Superfund cleanups has decreased 50 percent between the periods 1997–2000 and 2001–2003. Environmentalist warn that without a renewal of the tax on chemical and petroleum industries, Superfund will not be able to treat many of the nation's most polluted sites.

A decision by the U.S. Supreme Court in December of 2004 may further slow the cleanup of many of the nation's most toxic waste sites. In *Cooper Industries v. Aviall*,[13] the high court held that a private party *who had not been sued* in a CERCLA administrative or cost recovery action could not obtain contribution from other liable parties.

On 1981, Cooper sold Aviall four aircraft-engine maintenance shops. In the mid-nineties, Aviall admitted that several hazardous chemicals had been dumped on one site. The company subsequently sold that operation, but voluntarily paid to clean up the site to state specifications. Aviall then sued the former owner, Cooper, for $5 million to help pay for the clean-up. CERCLA provides that firms "may" seek contribution from others who might be held liable for the pollution "during or following a civil action." Cooper argued that the "may" meant, "may only," and, therefore, Aviall could not sue because the cleanup was not the result of a government action forcing them to clean the site. (In other words, because the site had been voluntarily cleaned up, the other contributors to the pollution could not have been held liable in a civil suit because there would not have been a civil suit after a clean-up.) The district court judge agreed and dismissed the case, but the court of appeals reversed their decision. The U.S. Supreme Court reinstated the district courts' dismissal.

While the ruling was a narrow one, interpreting only the contribution provision and therefore leaving open the possibility of suing under a different provision of CERCLA, environmentalists still worry that the case will have a chilling effect on voluntary cleanups of hazardous sites. Firms may now feel they have to wait until the government sues them if there is a possibility of spreading liability for the cleanup.

THE TOXIC SUBSTANCES CONTROL ACT OF 1979 (TSCA)

Toxic substances are found not only as by-products in hazardous waste but also as integral parts of some products that we use every day. Neither RCRA nor CERCLA regulates these substances. The Toxic Substances Control Act (TSCA) attempts to fill this regulatory gap. It attempts to ensure that the least amount of damage will be done to human health and the environment while allowing the greatest possible use of these substances.

toxic substance Any chemical or mixture whose manufacture, processing, distribution, use, or disposal presents an unreasonable risk of harm to human health or the environment.

The term **toxic substances** has not been clearly defined by Congress. However, by reviewing the types of substances regulated under TSCA, one would probably conclude that a toxic substance is any chemical or mixture whose manufacture, processing, distribution, use, or disposal may present an unreasonable risk of harm to human health or the environment. That is a broad definition and encompasses a large number of substances. Thus, control of these substances is a major undertaking.

---

[12] General Accounting Office, Superfund Program: Current Status and Future Fiscal Challenges, GAO/RECD-03-850, July 2003.

[13] 2004 WL 2847713 (U.S.), S. Ct. (2004).

The primary impact of TSCA comes from its procedure for evaluating the environmental impact of all chemicals, except those regulated under other acts such as the Food, Drug, and Cosmetics Act. Under TSCA, every manufacturer of a new chemical must give the EPA a premanufacturing notice (PMN) at least 90 days before the first use of the substance in commerce. The PMN contains data and test results showing the risk posed by the chemical. The EPA then determines whether the substance presents an unreasonable risk to health or whether further testing is required to establish the substance's safety. The manufacture of the product is banned when the risk of harm is unacceptable. If more testing is required, a manufacturer of the product must wait until the tests have been satisfactorily completed. Otherwise, manufacturing may begin as scheduled.

THE FEDERAL INSECTICIDE, FUNGICIDE, AND RODENTICIDE ACT OF 1972 (FIFRA)

One category of toxic substances that has been singled out for special regulatory treatment is pesticides. **Pesticides** are defined as substances designed to prevent, destroy, repel, or mitigate any pest or to be used as a plant regulator or a defoliant. Insecticides, fungicides, and rodenticides are all forms of pesticides. Pesticides are obviously highly important to us. Their use results in increased crop yields. Some pesticides kill disease-carrying insects. Others eradicate pests, such as mosquitoes, that simply cause us discomfort. Yet many pesticides have harmful side effects. Pesticides may cause damage to all species of life. When a pesticide does not degrade quickly, it may be consumed along with the crops on which it was used, potentially resulting in damage to the consumer's health. The pesticide may get washed into a stream to contaminate aquatic life and animals that drink from the stream. Once the pesticide gets into the food chain, it may do inestimable harm.

> **pesticides** Any substance designed to prevent, destroy, repel, or mitigate any pest or to be used as a plant regulator or defoliant.

In 1972, FIFRA created the registration system that is used to control pesticide use. In order for a pesticide to be sold in the United States, it must be registered and properly labeled. A pesticide will be registered when (1) its composition warrants the claims made for it; (2) its label complies with the act; and (3) the manufacturer provides data to demonstrate that the pesticide can perform its intended function, when in accordance with commonly accepted practice, without presenting unreasonable risks to human health or the environment.

A pesticide will receive general use registration if it can be sold without any restrictions. A restricted use registration will be granted if the pesticide will not cause an unreasonable risk only if its use is restricted in some manner. Typical restrictions would include allowing the pesticide to be used only by certified applicators or allowing it to be sold only during certain times of the year or only in certain regions of the country or only in certain quantities.

Registration is good for five years, at which time the manufacturer must apply for a new registration. If, at any time prior to the end of the registration period, the EPA obtains evidence that a pesticide poses a risk to human health or the environment, the agency may institute proceedings to cancel or suspend the registration.

The EPA believes that progress under FIFRA has been significant, although there are critics of the act. In 2002 alone, 186 product registrations were canceled as a result of FIFRA.[14] The following case illustrates the controversy that can arise when a pesticide's registration is canceled.

---

[14] N. Kubasek and G. Silverman, *Environmental Law* (Upper Saddle River, N.J.: Prentice Hall, 2004).

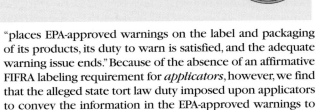

CASE 21-4

The Dow Chemical Company and Affordable Pest Control v. Ebling
Supreme Court of Indiana,
753 N.E.2d 633 (2001)

Todd and Cynthia Ebling, the plaintiffs, sued Dow Chemical and Affordable Pest Control (Affordable), the defendants, for injuries to their children alleging the defendants' failure to warn of the dangers of exposure to chemicals applied in the Eblings' home. Affordable Pest Control was responsible for applying the chemical to the Eblings' home. The trial court denied Affordable's motion for summary judgment and Affordable appealed. The appeals court found that Affordable had an obligation to warn plaintiffs them of the potential adverse effects of the chemical application. The case was appealled to the Indiana Supreme Court.

Justice Dickson

In this appeal, defendants Dow Chemical Company, Louisville Chemical Company, Inc., and Affordable Pest Control, Inc. challenged the denial of their motions for summary judgment in a damage action brought by plaintiffs Todd and Cynthia Ebling alleging that their children were injured as a result of exposure to pesticides manufactured and applied by the defendants.

The plaintiffs contend that their two young children experienced respiratory disorders, developmental delays, brain damage, and seizure disorders as a result of being repeatedly exposed to Dursban 2E and Creal-O when their apartment was regularly sprayed over an eleven-month period without their being warned of the dangers surrounding the exposure to these pesticides.

As to its appellate claim of FIFRA preemption, Affordable argues that the principles of preemption for failure to warn claims apply to pest control applicators "just as they do to manufacturers."

In regard to labeling, FIFRA, in an attempt to ensure some uniformity, contains an explicit preemption provision that prevents a state from "imposing or continuing in effect any requirements for labeling or packaging in addition to or different from those required under this Act." As an initial matter, we note agreement among a majority of jurisdictions that the phrase "any requirements" in this provision is sufficiently expansive to include both positive enactments of state law-making bodies and common law duties enforced in actions for damages.

While FIFRA requires pesticide manufacturers to affix an approved label to their product in order to sell it, applicators, either commercial or private, are not required to label anything but, as with members of the general public, applicators are prohibited from detaching, altering, defacing or destroying the label affixed to the pesticide by the manufacturer. The law is fairly settled that when a pesticide *manufacturer*

"places EPA-approved warnings on the label and packaging of its products, its duty to warn is satisfied, and the adequate warning issue ends." Because of the absence of an affirmative FIFRA labeling requirement for *applicators*, however, we find that the alleged state tort law duty imposed upon applicators to convey the information in the EPA-approved warnings to persons placed at risk does not constitute a requirement additional to or different from those imposed by FIFRA.

FIFRA specifically provides for regulation of pesticides by states, and the United States Supreme Court held in [a prior case] that FIFRA "leaves ample room for States and localities to supplement federal efforts. ..." As noted above, in [the prior case] the United States Supreme Court declined to extend FIFRA preemption to preclude local regulations requiring a pesticide applicator to give notice of pesticide use and of any label information prescribing a safe reentry time and imposing fines in the event of violations. After finding that preemption was not required by either the language of FIFRA or its legislative history, the Court also determined that there is no implied field preemption and no actual conflict between FIFRA and the local ordinance. The Court concluded by holding that FIFRA did not preempt the local governmental regulation of pesticide use.

We finally consider whether permitting a state tort claim based on Affordable's alleged failure to communicate label information to persons placed at risk frustrates the purpose of FIFRA or renders compliance with both state and federal law impossible, thereby favoring preemption under the principles of [prior court decisions]. Rather than conflicting with or frustrating the purposes of FIFRA, the opposite is true. The plaintiffs' claim that Affordable should have communicated the label information is entirely consistent with the objectives of FIFRA. The use of state tort law to further the dissemination of label information to persons at risk clearly facilitates rather than frustrates the objectives of FIFRA and does not burden Affordable's compliance with FIFRA.

We hold that FIFRA preemption does not apply to preclude the plaintiffs' action against Affordable for its failure to warn the plaintiffs by providing them with the FDA-approved label warning information. The trial court is affirmed in its denial of summary judgment to Affordable on preemption. In all other respects, the opinion of the Court of Appeals is summarily affirmed, and this cause is remanded to the trial court for further proceedings accordingly.

Affirmed in favor of plaintiff Eblings and remanded.

Pesticide Tolerances in Food. Under the Federal Food, Drug, and Cosmetic Act (FFDCA), the EPA establishes legally permissible maximum amounts of pesticide residues in processed food or in animal products such as meat or milk, as well as on food crops such as apples or tomatoes. Before a pesticide can be registered, an applicant must obtain a tolerance for that pesticide. To obtain the tolerance, the applicant must provide evidence of the level of residue likely to result and data to establish safe residue levels. Under the 1996 Food Quality Protection Act, a safe residue level is one at which there is a "reasonable certainty of no harm" from exposure to the pesticide. The law also requires distribution of a brochure on the health effects of pesticides.

THE POLLUTION PREVENTION ACT OF 1990

By now the reader is familiar with the basic provisions of our primary laws designed to reduce the harmful effects of pollution. Tremendous gains have been made under these laws. However, after 20 years of implementing these controls, it has become more costly to get increasingly smaller reductions of pollutants. Whereas initially a $1 million expenditure on end-pipe controls might have reduced emissions by 80 percent, today that same investment is likely to result in only a 5 percent reduction.

Recognition of this decline in the effectiveness of direct regulation and the consequent need to look for alternative approaches to pollution problems led to passage of the Pollution Prevention Act of 1990, in which Congress set forth the following policy:

> Pollution should be prevented or reduced at the source whenever feasible; pollution that cannot be prevented should be recycled in an environmentally safe manner, whenever feasible; pollution that cannot be prevented or recycled should be treated in an environmentally safe manner whenever feasible; and disposal or other release into the environment should be employed only as a last resort and should be conducted in an environmentally safe manner.

The role of the government in encouraging this policy is one of providing a "carrot" as opposed to the "stick" of direct end-pipe regulations. The federal government is providing states matching funds under the act for programs to promote the use of source reduction techniques for business. A clearinghouse has been established to compile the data generated by the grants and to serve as a center for source reduction technology transfer.

Despite the voluntary nature of actions under this act, pollution prevention is becoming an important concept in business today. Chemical companies, for example, are beginning to see waste as avoidable and inefficient and are looking for ways to change their production processes to reduce the amount of waste they create.

Examples abound of firms that are joining the pollution prevention bandwagon. For example, DuPont, America's largest producer of chemicals, voluntarily cut its greenhouse gas emissions by more than 50 percent of their 1991 levels. As a result, DuPont has saved 6 dollars for each ton of carbon equivalent emissions prevented.[15] Similarly, BP initiated an internal carbon trading system

---

[15] Paul Hawkins et al., Natural Capitalism 258–259 (2001).

Linking Law & Business

Marketing and Management

In your marketing or management class, you may have learned about environmental sustainability, which is a management approach that focuses on sustaining the environment and still generating profits for a firm. As firms advance toward environmental sustainability, there are four levels that companies examine to gauge their firms' progress.

The first and most basic level is pollution prevention. As we've already discussed in the previous section, this involves the prevention or reduction of waste before it is created. Companies that are highlighting pollution prevention often use "green marketing" plans by developing environmentally friendly packaging, better pollution controls, and ecologically safer products.

The second level in environmental sustainability is product stewardship, which extends the focus from production creation to the entire product life cycle. In this level, firms often implement design for environment (DFE) policies that consider future consequences of the firm's products. Consequently, measures are taken by firms to find more efficient ways of recovering, reusing, or recycling their products.

The third level is new environmental technologies. Because some companies that already have progressed in pollution prevention and product stewardship are limited by available technologies, new technologies are sometimes needed to meet their environmental goals.

The fourth level of environmental sustainability is sustainability vision, in which organizations develop a guide for their firms' future methods of environmental responsibility. This vision provides a framework for pollution control, product stewardship, and environmental technology.

By focusing on these four levels of environmental sustainability, there is a greater likelihood that firms using this management approach will promote the goals of environmentalists, which hopefully will result in a greener and safer planet. Additionally, these organizations will potentially be at less risk of litigation for unsafe practices and will, therefore, maintain a more positive image with the general public.

Source: P. Kotler and G. Armstrong, *Principles of Marketing* (Upper Saddle River, N.J.: Prentice Hall, 2004), pp. 462–464.

---

that finds low-cost reductions in greenhouse gas emissions. The internal system has not only yielded a 20 percent reduction in greenhouse gases but also saved $650 million in increased efficiency. Currently, BP is exploring ways to further cut emissions and save money.[16]

Whatever the cause of this new emphasis on pollution prevention—whether it is the increasing cost of waste disposal, a fear of stricter direct regulations, public pressure for firms to be "greener," or the federal government's new emphasis on pollution prevention—firms are changing their attitudes toward the environment. Whether this trend toward voluntary source reduction will continue remains to be seen. Certainly, there is every indication that it will.

---

[16] Rockefeller Brothers Fund, Cutting Greenhouse Gas Emissions Is Possible and Even Profitable (2003).

GLOBAL DIMENSIONS OF ENVIRONMENTAL REGULATION

THE NEED FOR INTERNATIONAL COOPERATION

In most areas of regulation, the United States first enacted national legislation and only later, if at all, considered the worldwide implications of the problem that the law was enacted to resolve. This tendency was not the case with environmental regulation. In fact, the first major piece of environmental legislation, NEPA, addressed the global nature of environmental problems. The act instructed the federal government to recognize the worldwide and long-range character of environmental problems and, when consistent with the foreign policy of the United States, lend appropriate support to initiatives, resolutions, and programs designed to maximize international cooperation in anticipating and preventing a decline in the quality of the world environment.

THE TRANSNATIONAL NATURE OF POLLUTION

International cooperation on environmental matters is essential because environmental problems do not respect national borders. There are three primary means by which environmental problems originating in one area of the globe affect other areas: (1) movement of air in prevailing wind patterns; (2) movement of water through ocean currents, and (3) active and passive migration of numerous species of plants and animals.

Scientists have discovered that air tends to circulate within one of three regional areas, or belts, that circle the globe north and south of the equator. For example, between the latitudes 30° and 60° north (N) of the equator, the prevailing air currents are the westerly winds. Thus, the air between these latitudes circulates in a westerly direction all around the globe, remaining primarily within those latitudes.

The United States and China both have much of their land masses within these two latitudes. As a result, pollutants emitted into the air in the United States may be carried by these westerly winds to China, just as pollutants emitted into the air anywhere between 30°N and 60°N of the equator anywhere in the world may ultimately end up in the air above the United States. Consequently, the United States could have extremely strict air pollution laws, yet still have polluted air as a result of other countries' emissions. Likewise, our failure to enact adequate air pollution control laws can adversely affect air quality in other countries. Canada, for instance, attributes some of its pollution problems to the United States' failure to enact stricter control on sulfur dioxide emissions.

A similar situation exists with respect to the flow of water, except that the regions are not as clearly defined. All ocean currents ultimately connect with one another, so a pollutant discharged into any body of water that flows into an ocean may end up having a negative impact on water quality hundreds of miles away from the country in which it was dumped.

The migration of plants and animals also spreads pollutants. Many animals, such as geese, whales, salmon, seals, and whooping cranes, travel across national borders seasonally. If an animal ingests a hazardous chemical in one country, travels to another country, and is eaten by an animal in that country, that pollutant has now been inserted into the food web in the second country.

THE GLOBAL COMMONS

Another closely related reason that international cooperation on environmental matters is necessary is that many of the planet's resources, such as the oceans, are within no country's borders and are, therefore, available for everyone's use. For this reason, these resources are often called the *global commons*. Because everyone has access to them, they are susceptible to exploitation and overuse. Cooperation to protect these global resources is the only way to preserve them.

PRIMARY RESPONSES OF THE UNITED STATES

The United States has played a role in establishing global environmental policies in four primary ways: (1) research, (2) conferences, (3) treaties, and (4) economic aid. It is important to recognize that these responses have not been extremely successful, nor has there been a major commitment of U.S. resources to the resolution of transnational environmental problems.

Research. Research, the results of which are shared with other nations, is our typical response to international environmental issues. For example, in response to international concerns about changes in environmental conditions, the U.S. government sponsors research in universities and in federal laboratories by various governmental agencies. Some critics argue that we need to commit more money to research. Others claim that we use research as an excuse for not acting. Many environmentalists view a "commitment to research" as a stalling technique to prevent the imposition of needed controls. These environmentalists point out that conclusive scientific evidence on many matters is not likely to be available before irreparable harm has been done.

Conferences. Countries often have conferences to discuss specific transnational environmental problems. Many are arranged through the United Nations. The first such conference was the United Nations Conference on the Human Environment, held in Stockholm in 1972. Similarly, in 1992, delegates from over 120 nations met in Rio de Janeiro for the United Nations Conference on Environment and Development, commonly referred to as the Rio Earth Summit. Marking the 10-year anniversary of the Rio Earth Summit, more than 100 heads of state from around the world gathered for the Johannesburg Earth Summit during the summer of 2002 to discuss global climate change and sustainable development. These conferences serve primarily to promote an understanding of the global implications of environmental problems. Often these conferences lead to the negotiation of treaties designed to help resolve environmental problems. For example, Agenda 21 is a plan for sustainable development, covering a diverse range of issues, including hazardous waste, ocean pollution, and human health. Perhaps most important is a plan to aid Third World nations in the cleanup of pollution and prevention of deforestation. Agenda 21 was signed by 171 countries at the Rio Earth Summit. Agenda 21 was revisited at the Johannesburg Earth Summit where methods of better implementation were discussed. Today, Agenda 21 remains an important plan for international progress on some of the most significant international issues of the twenty-first century.

Treaties. Treaties are written agreements between two or more nations that specify how particular issues are to be resolved. The process of accepting a treaty varies from country to country. In the United States, a treaty must be negotiated and signed by a representative of the executive branch, generally the president. Then it must be approved by two-thirds of the U.S. Senate. A treaty's implementation then generally requires the passage of federal legislation that translates the objectives of the treaty into laws.

The United States has entered into numerous bilateral (signed by only two nations) and multilateral (signed by more than two nations) treaties, sometimes called conventions, in this area. One of the more successful multilateral treaties the United States has signed is the Montreal Protocol. Originally signed by 24 nations and the European Community on September 16, 1987, the Montreal Protocol on Substances That Deplete the Ozone Layer ultimately led to an elimination of the production of ozone-depleting chlorofluorocarbons (CFCs) by January 1, 1996. A series of summits concerning the problem of ozone depletion has taken place since that initial meeting, and nations continue to amend the treaty to restrict production of more ozone-destroying compounds as our understanding of these chemicals grows.

One of the problems with treaties, however, is that they are unenforceable when the signatories decide no longer to obey them. Many include clauses that allow a nation to withdraw from a contract or to cease abiding by particular terms after giving notice of its intent to the other parties to the treaty.

For example, despite the success of the Montreal Protocol, the United States has backed out of a number of environmental treaties since 2001. Most notable, however, is the U.S. refusal to join Japan, the European Union, Canada, China, and 119 other countries in ratifying the Kyoto Protocol. In 2002, the Bush administration signaled that it would not be party to the important treaty that could significantly reduce greenhouse gas emissions to 1990 levels. But in 2004, Russia signed the Protocol, allowing it to come into force without participation of the United States.

More recently, other methods have been used to foster international environmental action. Trade agreements have started to incorporate provisions regarding environmental protection. The North American Free Trade Agreement (NAFTA), for example, included a side agreement on the environment. Although it has been called the most environmentally sensitive trade agreement ever, there is concern that this agreement may ultimately result in a lessening of environmental protection.

In the preamble to NAFTA, the treaty does cite "sustainable development" as a goal. However, there are no specific provisions to ensure attainment of, or even progress toward, that goal. In the body of the agreement, parties have the right to establish a level of environmental protection each deems appropriate, as long as it is based on a "legitimate" objective. The ambiguity of the term *legitimate* causes concern for some environmentalists.

Aid. A final way in which the United States affects environmental policy transnationally is by the judicious use of foreign aid, either financing pollution control projects or giving economic aid for a particular project only when certain environmentally sound conditions have been met. Some aid is also given in the form of technical assistance and training. For example, the U.S. Soil Conservation Service (SCS) provides technical assistance in soil and water conservation to many Latin American and African countries. The SCS also teaches conservation techniques to students from these countries.

As the foregoing demonstrates, environmental problems are not simply a national affair. They are global in nature, and cooperation will be needed to alleviate them.

SUMMARY

There are many ways a nation can protect its environment. Some of these methods include tort law, subsidies, discharge permits, emission charges, and direct regulation. Beginning in 1970, with the passage of the National Environmental Policy Act (NEPA), our nation began a course of environmental protection based primarily on specific direct regulations.

The Federal Water Pollution Control Act established a discharge permit system designed to make the waterways fishable and swimmable. The Safe Drinking Water Act sets standards to make our drinking water safe. The Clean Air Act, as amended several times, establishes the National Ambient Air Quality Standards, standards designed to ensure that conventional air pollutants do not pose a risk to human health or the environment. This act also establishes standards for toxic air pollutants.

Hazardous wastes and toxic substances are primarily regulated by four pieces of legislation. The Resource Conservation and Recovery Act sets standards for waste disposal sites and establishes the manifest system for the tracking of hazardous wastes from creation to disposal. CERCLA, as amended by SARA, provided funding and a mechanism for cleaning up hazardous waste sites. The Toxic Substances Control Act provided a mechanism for testing new chemicals to ensure that they do not pose unreasonable risks before being used in commerce. Finally, FIFRA established a procedure for the regulation of pesticides through a registration system.

The newest trend in the environmental area is toward pollution prevention. This trend is encouraged by the Pollution Prevention Control Act of 1990.

Despite the comprehensive system of environmental laws that we have created, solving environmental problems requires cooperation among all nations. Four ways the United States tries to work to solve these problems on a global scale are through shared research, conferences, treaties, and aid.

REVIEW QUESTIONS

21-1 Explain the common-law methods of resolving pollution problems and evaluate their effectiveness.

21-2 Explain the circumstances under which an environmental impact statement must be filed and describe the statement's required content.

21-3 Explain how emission charges and discharge permits could be used to help control pollution.

21-4 Present the arguments of those who would abolish the use of the EIS. How would you evaluate those criticisms?

21-5 Describe the structure of the amended Federal Water Pollution Control Act, and explain how each element of the act is designed to further the goals of the FWPCA.

21-6 Compare the structure of the FWPCA with that of the Clean Air Act.

REVIEW PROBLEMS

21-7 The defendant operated a mining company. Because of improper drainage techniques used by the defendant, drainage of pollutants from his mining operation contaminated the private water supplies of the plaintiff property owners located downstream from him. What legal theories would the plaintiffs use to sue the defendant? Would the plaintiffs be likely to win their lawsuit? Why or why not?

21-8 The lead industry challenged the EPA's establishment of a primary air quality standard for lead that incorporated an "adequate margin of safety." In setting the standard, the EPA had not considered the feasibility or the cost of meeting the standards. Must the EPA take such factors into consideration in setting primary air quality standards?

21-9 Ohio's SIP was submitted to the EPA. Approval of a portion of the plan was denied because it was not adequate to ensure the attainment and maintenance of the primary standard for photochemical oxidants in the Cincinnati area. The EPA supplemented the Ohio plan with a provision requiring a vehicle inspection and registration procedure for the Cincinnati area. Cincinnati set up the requisite inspection facilities but refused to withhold registration from those vehicles failing the inspection. The EPA sought an injunction ordering Ohio to implement "as written" the inspection and registration procedure described in the plan. Was the injunction granted?

21-10 The Idaho EPA, in developing its SIP, determined that the maximum sulfur dioxide emissions that could be captured from zinc smelters with the currently available technology was 72 percent. The state consequently adopted that standard for zinc smelters under the SIP. The federal EPA refused to accept that part of the SIP and promulgated an 82 percent standard. Did the federal EPA have authority to make such a change in the SIP?

21-11 Kantrell Corporation uses about 50 gallons a day of a highly corrosive acid as a cleaning agent in its production process. It collects the used acid and funnels it through a pipe out into a pond located entirely on company property that was dug to serve as a place in which to dispose of the acid and other wastes that could not be incinerated or recycled. Is Kantrell violating any federal environmental regulations?

21-12 The defendant operated a plant that had refined coal tar for 55 years. It had disposed of its wastes on the site. After the plant closed, the land was purchased by a municipal housing authority. The wastes buried on the site leaked into the groundwater, contaminating the drinking water of nearby cities. The state and the municipalities spent considerable sums of money cleaning up the site. The U.S. government joined the suit, seeking to hold the defendant liable under CERCLA. Was the defendant responsible even though he no longer owned the dump site?

CASE PROBLEMS

21-13 L.A. Moore bought property from Texaco in 1955 that was adjacent to his own property. Upon his death in 1976, the property went to his son, Tommy Moore. Both Tommy and his father knew that Texaco had housed on the land some barrels that had been used for oil storage. These barrels were removed in 1954. The younger Moore sued Texaco when he discovered in 1997 that soil and groundwater on the property were contaminated. Moore sued for several different claims, including nuisance, for which he claimed Texaco owed him damages and abatement. The nuisance claim was both a public and a private nuisance claim. The district court denied both of Moore's nuisance claims, and the court of appeals

affirmed. What possible reasons do you think the court would have for denying the nuisance claims? *Moore v. Texaco, Inc.*, 244 F.3d 1229 (2001)

21-14 The Talent Irrigation District (TID) in Oregon provides irrigation to its members through a series of irrigation canals. In order to remove aquatic weeds and vegetation, TID applies Magnacide H, a very toxic chemical. In 1996, after TID applied the chemical, the Oregon Department of Fish and Wildlife found over 90,000 dead fish in a nearby creek. An earlier fish kill had occurred in 1983 after the application of the same chemical. Two nonprofit agencies brought suit against TID under the Clean Water Act in 1998 because TID did not have, nor had it ever applied for, a National Pollution Discharge Elimination System (NPDES) permit. The district court ruled in favor of TID because Magnacide H was regulated and controlled by FIFRA, and the label affixed under FIFRA regulations did not mention that an NPDES permit was required. The court of appeals agreed to hear the case. Did it reverse or affirm the district court decision? Why? *Headwaters, Inc., and Oregon Natural Resources Council Action v. Talent Irrigation District*, 243 F.3d 526 (2001)

21-15 The Buckey Reclamation Landfill was declared a Superfund sight in 1983 and Consolidation Coal was found liable for its cleanup expense. Under CERCLA, Consolidation Coal sought a declaration of liability and equitable allocation of expense cost to Nevill Chemical for admittedly dumping 472,000 gallons of waste sludge into the landfill in the late 1970s. The chemical company appealed the lower court's decision that under CERCLA it was liable for a portion of the cleanup costs, arguing that the waste sludge caused no harm. Was Nevill Chemical sucessful in removing its liability from the Superfund cleanup? Why was it or was it not successful? *United States v. Consolidation Coal Co.* 345 F.3d 409 (2003)

21-16 Several railroad companies operated in Columbus, Ohio, in the 1800s. Sometime during their operation, a box filled with creosote and benzene was buried near a railroad depot. Subsequently, the railroad companies' successor, American Premier Underwriters, Inc. (APU), received over $5 million for the land from the City of Columbus when the city exercised eminent domain in 1973. In October 1989, the Franklin County Convention Facilities Authority (CFA) became interested in the land and performed environmental assessments to determine the quality of the property. After the testing, CFA subleased the property from the city with the intention of building a facility on it.

In October 1990, a contractor was digging to create a storm sewer line when he split open the creosote-and-benzene filled box. A strong odor was emitted and an environmental consultant was immediately notified and came to the property. The Ohio EPA was also notified, and later CFA notified the city. The remedial action chosen by CFA was to remove and transport the contamination. A contractor performed the action, for which CFA paid. During the remedial action, it was discovered that the creosote had migrated 45 feet and surrounded a sewer line. The appropriate barrier was

erected. CFA then commenced an action against APU to recover the costs of the cleanup under CERCLA. Although CFA is not a state, CFA could still recover under CERCLA if its cleanup was performed in a manner consistent with the National Oil and Hazardous Substances Pollution Contingency Plan.

The district court found that CFA had performed a CERCLA-quality cleanup, found APU to be the only responsible party, and assessed 100 percent of the cleanup costs to APU. APU appealed the decision on many counts but particularly the finding that CFA was not a potentially responsible party. How do you think the court of appeals ruled on the issue of whether CFA was a potentially responsible party? *Franklin County Convention Facilities Authority v. American Premier Underwriters, Inc., et al.*, 240 F.3d 534 (2001)

21-17 The environmnetal group Bluewater Network sought review of the EPA's emission standards for snowmobiles under the Clean Air Act and NAAQ standards. The proposed regulations of carbon monoxide (CO), hydrocarbons (HC), and nitrogen oxides (NOx) required that snowmobile engines meet progressivly stringent emission standards in three succesive phases. However, Bluewater argued that the standards were excessivly lenient. Furthermore, Bluewater disagreed with the EPA's ruling that pollution prevention technologies could not be applied to all new snowmobiles by 2012.

Arguing in the opposite direction, the International Snowmobile Manufacurers Association (ISMA) challenged the EPA's authority to implement the regulations of CO, HC, and NOx. Did the EPA exceed its authority in regulating CO, HC, and NOx emissions from snowmobiles? Or did the EPA not go far enough in the creation of stringent emission standards? *Bluewater Network v. EPA*, 370 F.3d 1 (2004)

21-18 RGM Corporation argued that the wetlands on its property were not subject to the protections and regulations of the Clean Water Act because the wetlands did not extend to a navagable, or intracoastal, waterway. The federal government argued that its jursidiction did extend into the wetland owned by RGM because the ordinarily high watermark caused the water to flow toward navagable waters, thus allowing for Clean Water Act protections. Did the court find that the Clean Water Act grants jurisdiction to RGM's wetland? How would you decide? *United States v. RGM Corp.*, 222 F. Supp.2d 780 (2002)

ASSIGNMENT ON THE INTERNET

Environmental protection is often a slow and arduous process because many enforcement efforts end up in the court system. Using Internet sites such as LexisNexis or www.law.cornell.edu/topics/environmental.html find a recent court case involving a Superfund cleanup site.

What was disputed in the case? What reasons and/or laws were cited in the court's decision? How does the information in this chapter better assist you in understanding the court's decision? Who was found responsible for the cleanup of the site, if cleanup was done? Finally, do you agree with the ethical norms that underlie the court's decision? Why or why not?

 ## ON THE INTERNET

www.epa.gov The EPA home page is a source of valuable information about the main agency responsible for protecting the environment.

www.eis.noaa.gov/esdim This is the site of the National Environmental Information Services, which contains frequently requested documents on environmental quality.

www.whitehouse.gov/ceq Here is the home page of the Council on Environmental Quality.

sedac.ciesin.columbia.edu/entri/index.jsp This site provides environmental treaties and resource indicators.

www.epa.gov/superfund Information about the EPA's Superfund program can be found at this site.

www.nrdc.org The National Resource Defense Council works to prevent negative externalities that harm the environment.

www.law.cornell.edu/topics/environmental.html This site provides important information and links to environmental laws and recent court decisions.

www.eenews.net/sr_nsr.htm This site provides information and updates about New Source Review.

22

RULES GOVERNING
THE ISSUANCE AND TRADING
OF SECURITIES

- INTRODUCTION TO THE REGULATION OF SECURITIES
- THE SARBANES-OXLEY ACT OF 2002
- THE SECURITIES ACT OF 1933
- THE SECURITIES EXCHANGE ACT OF 1934
- REGULATION OF INVESTMENT COMPANIES
- STATE SECURITIES LAWS
- E-COMMERCE, ONLINE SECURITIES DISCLOSURE, AND FRAUD REGULATION
- GLOBAL DIMENSIONS OF RULES GOVERNING THE ISSUANCE AND TRADING OF SECURITIES

In Chapter 16, we said that the corporation was the dominant form of business organization in the United States—and also the most regulated. Two of the most strongly regulated aspects of corporate business are the issuance and trading of securities. Corporate securities—stocks and bonds—are, of course, used to raise capital for the corporation. They are also used by individuals and institutional investors to accumulate wealth. In the case of individuals, this wealth is often passed on to heirs, who use it to accumulate more wealth. Thus, securities provide a means for one generation in a family to "do better" than the preceding generation. Securities also provide a means for financing pension funds and insurance plans through institutional investment.

Securities holders are powerful determinants of trends in business: If an individual company, industry, or segment of the economy is not growing and paying a good rate of return, investors will switch their funds to another company, industry, or segment in expectation of better returns. Securities holders (or their proxies) elect the board of directors of a corporation, who, in turn, select the officers who manage the daily operations of a corporation. Finally, securities holders' ability to bring lawsuits helps keep officers and directors honest in their use of investors' funds.

Both because of their importance to the operation of our free enterprise society and because of the ease with which they can be manipulated, securities have been regulated by governments for nearly a century. This chapter examines chiefly the role of the federal government in regulating securities. We introduce the subject with a brief history of securities regulation that contains a summary of the most important federal legislation. Then we

Critical Thinking About the Law

Because securities can be easily manipulated by issuers, federal and state governments have strongly regulated the issuance and trading of securities. Studying the following case and answering some critical thinking questions about it will help you better appreciate the need for regulation of securities.

Jessica received a phone call from a man claiming to represent Buy-It-Here, a corporation that was relocating to Jessica's town. The man stated that the corporation was planning to issue new securities, and he was extending this offer to residents in Jessica's town. He claimed that Buy-It-Here would easily double its profits within six months. The man said that if Jessica would send $3,000, he would buy stock in Buy-It-Here for Jessica. Jessica sent the money; two weeks later she discovered that Buy-It-Here was in the process of filing for bankruptcy.

1. This case is an example of the need for government regulation. We want the government to protect citizens from cases such as Jessica's buying stock in a bankrupt company. If we want governmental protection from potentially shady businesses, what ethical norm are we emphasizing?

    Clue: Put yourself in Jessica's place. Why would you want governmental protection? Now match your answer to an ethical norm listed in Chapter 1. Think about which ethical norm businesses would emphasize.

2. Jessica wants to sue Buy-It-Here for misrepresentation. Before she brings her case, what additional information do you think Jessica should discover?

    Clue: What additional information do you want to know about the case? Without having extensive knowledge about securities, you can identify areas in which you might need more information about Jessica's case. For example, pay close attention to the role of the telephone caller.

3. Jessica did some research about securities cases in her state. She discovered a case in which a woman named Andrea Stevenson had purchased $100,000 in stock from a stockbroker. The company went bankrupt three months later. The stockbroker had known that the company had potential financial problems but had said nothing to Andrea. The jury in this case found in favor of Andrea. Jessica wants to use Andrea's case as an analogy in her lawsuit. Do you think that Andrea's case is an appropriate analogy?

    Clue: What are the similarities between the cases? How are the cases different? Are these differences so significant that they overwhelm the similarities?

turn to the creation, function, and structure of the **Securities and Exchange Commission**, one of the most powerful regulatory bodies in the U.S. government. In the second section, we examine the provisions of the Sarbanes-Oxley Act of 2002 and the Securities Act of 1933 that govern the issuance of securities, paying special attention to the registration requirements for both securities and transactions and the allowable exemptions from those requirements. The Securities Exchange Act of 1934 that governs trading in securities is then discussed. We next examine the Investment Company Act, state securities, and online securities disclosure and fraud regulation. We end with a discussion of the global dimensions of the 1933 and 1934 securities acts as well as the Foreign Corrupt Practices Act, as amended in 1988, and finally the Convention on Combating Bribery of Foreign Officials in International Business Transactions.

INTRODUCTION TO THE REGULATION OF SECURITIES

Securities and Exchange Commission (SEC) The federal administrative agency charged with overall responsibility for the regulation of securities, including ensuring that investors receive "full and fair" disclosure of all material facts with regard to any public offering of securities. It has wide enforcement powers to protect investors against price manipulation, insider trading, and other dishonest dealings.

Securities have no value in and of themselves. They are not like most goods produced or consumed (e.g., television sets or toys), which are easily regulated in terms of their hazards or merchantability. Because they are paper, they can be produced in unlimited numbers and, thus, can easily be manipulated by their issuers.

The first attempt to regulate securities in the United States was made by the state of Kansas in 1912. When other states followed the Kansas legislature's example, corporations played off one state against another by limiting their securities sales to states that had less stringent regulations. Despite the corporations' ability to thwart state efforts at regulation rather easily, there was strong resistance to the idea of federal regulation in Congress. It was not until after the collapse of the stock market in 1929 and the free fall of stock prices on the New York Stock Exchange—when the Dow Jones Industrial Average registered an 89 percent decline between 1929 and 1933—that Congress finally acted.

SUMMARY OF FEDERAL SECURITIES LEGISLATION

The following legislation, enacted by Congress since 1933, provides the framework for the federal regulation of securities. It is also important to note that this legislation is the basis ("enabling act") for rule making by the Securities and Exchange Commission (SEC). Congressional legislation is emphasized here, but it is important to know that SEC rule making may be equally significant in the long term. (You will remember that we discussed rule making for federal agencies in Chapter 17.)

- The *Securities Act of 1933* (also known as the Securities Act or the 1933 Act) regulates the initial offering of securities by public corporations by prohibiting an offer or sale of securities not registered with the Securities and Exchange Commission. The 1933 Act sets forth certain exemptions from the registration process as well as penalties for violations of the act. This act is examined in detail in this chapter. Both the 1933 and 1934 Acts were amended by Congress and the SEC rule-making process, much of which is summarized in the following pages.

- The *Securities Exchange Act of 1934* (also known as the Exchange Act) regulates the trading in securities once they are issued. It requires brokers and dealers who trade in securities to register with the Securities and Exchange Commission, the regulatory body created to enforce both the 1933 and 1934 Acts. The Exchange Act is also examined in detail in this chapter.

- The *Public Utility Holding Company Act of 1935* requires public utility and holding companies to register with the SEC and to disclose their financial organization, structure, and operating process.

- The *Trust Indenture Act of 1939* regulates the public issuance of bonds and other debt securities in excess of $5 million. This act imposes standards for trustees to follow to ensure that bondholders are protected.

- The *Investment Company Act (ICA) of 1940*, as amended in 1970 and 1975, gives the SEC authority to regulate the structure and operation of public investment companies that invest in and trade in securities. A company is an "investment company" under this act if it invests or trades in securities and if more than 40 percent of its assets are "investment securities" (which are all corporate securities and securities invested in subsidiaries). Accompanying legislation, entitled the *Investment Advisers Act of 1940*, authorizes the SEC to regulate persons and firms that give investment advice to clients. This act requires the registration of all such individuals or firms and contains antifraud provisions that seek to protect broker–dealers' clients.

- The *Securities Investor Protection Act (SIPA) of 1970* established the non-profit Securities Investor Protection Corporation (SIPC) and gave it authority to supervise the liquidation of brokerage firms that are in financial trouble, as well as to protect investors from losses up to $500,000 due to the financial failure of a brokerage firm. The SIPC does not have the monitoring and "bailout" functions that the Federal Deposit Insurance Corporation (FDIC) has in banking; it only supervises the liquidation of an already financially troubled brokerage firm through an appointed trustee.

- Chapter 11 of the *Bankruptcy Reform Act of 1978* gives the SEC the authority to render advice when certain debtor corporations have filed for reorganization.

- The *Foreign Corrupt Practices Act (FCPA) of 1977*, as amended in 1988, prohibits the direct or indirect giving of "anything of value" to a foreign official for the purpose of influencing that official's actions. The FCPA sets out an intent or "knowing" standard of liability for corporate management. It requires all companies (whether doing business abroad or not) to set up a system of internal controls that will provide reasonable assurance that the company's records "accurately and fairly reflect" its transactions. The FCPA is discussed in the last section of this chapter.

- The *International Securities Enforcement Cooperation Act (ISECA) of 1990* clarifies the SEC's authority to provide securities regulators of other governments with documents and information and exempts from Freedom of Information Act disclosure requirements all documents given to the SEC by foreign regulators. The ISECA also authorizes the SEC to impose administrative sanctions on securities buyers and dealers who have engaged in illegal activities in foreign countries. Finally, it authorizes the SEC to investigate violations of the securities law set out in the act that occur in foreign countries. The ISECA is also discussed in the last section of the chapter.

- The *Market Reform Act of 1990* authorizes the SEC to regulate trading practices during periods of extreme volatility. For example, the SEC can take such emergency action as suspending trading when computer-program–driven trading forces the Dow Jones Industrial Average to rise or fall sharply within a short time period.

- The *Securities Enforcement Remedies and Penney Reform Act of 1991* (the 1991 Remedies Act) gives the SEC powerful new means for policing the securities industry: cease-and-desist powers and the power to impose substantial monetary penalties in administrative proceedings. The 1991 Remedies Act also gives the SEC and the federal courts the following powers over anyone who violates federal securities law:

  1. The imposition of monetary penalties by a federal court for a violation of the securities law on petition by the SEC.

  2. The power of the federal courts to bar anyone who has violated the fraud provisions of the federal securities laws from ever serving as an officer or director of a publicly held firm.

  3. The power of the SEC to issue permanent cease-and-desist orders against "any person who is violating, has violated, or is about to violate" any provision of a federal securities law.

  This act arms the SEC with some of the most sweeping enforcement powers ever given to a single administrative agency other than criminal enforcement agencies such as the Justice Department.

- The *Private Securities Litigation Reform Act of 1995* provides a safe harbor from liability for companies that make statements to the public and investors about risk factors that may occur in the future.

- *Securities Litigation Uniform Standards Act of 1998* sets national standards for securities class action lawsuits involving national trade securities. The act amends the 1933 and 1934 Acts and prohibits any private class action suits in state or federal court alleging (1) any untrue statement or omission in connection with the purchase or sale of a covered security or (2) the defendant used any manipulation or deceptive device in connection with the transaction.

- *Sarbanes-Oxley Act of 2002* amends the 1933 and 1934 Acts. Provisions of this act are discussed in detail in this chapter. The act includes provisions dealing with corporate governance, financial regulation, criminal penalties, and corporate responsibility.

For your convenience, all the federal securities legislation is summarized in Table 22-1.

THE SECURITIES AND EXCHANGE COMMISSION (SEC)

Creation and Function. The **Securities and Exchange Commission (SEC)** was created under the Securities Exchange Act of 1934 for the purpose of ensuring investors "full and fair" disclosure of all material facts with regard to any public offering of securities. The SEC is not charged with evaluating the worth of a public offering of securities by a corporation (for example, determining

TABLE 22-1

SUMMARY OF THE MAJOR FEDERAL SECURITIES LEGISLATION

Federal Securities Legislation	*Purpose*
Securities Act of 1933	SEC regulates the initial public offering of securities.
Securities Exchange Act of 1934	SEC regulates the trading in securities.
Public Utility Holding Company Act of 1935	SEC regulates public utility and holding companies through registering and disclosure processes.
Trust Indenture Act of 1939	SEC regulates the public issuance of bonds and other debt securities.
Investment Company Act of 1940	SEC regulates structure and operation of public investment companies.
Securities Investor Protection Act of 1970	Securities Investor Protection Corporation supervises the liquidation of financially troubled brokerage firms.
Bankruptcy Reform Act of 1978	SEC has authority to advise debtor corporations that have filed for reorganization.
Foreign Corrupt Practices Act of 1977	Prohibits the payment of anything of value to influence foreign officials' actions.
International Securities Enforcement Corporation Act of 1990	SEC has authority to provide securities regulators of other governments with information on alleged violators of securities law in the United States and abroad.
Market Reform Act of 1990	SEC regulates trading practices during periods of extreme volatility.
Securities Enforcement Remedies and Penney Reform Act of 1991	SEC regulates securities industry through cease-and-desist powers and threat of substantial monetary penalties.
Private Securities Litigation Reform Act of 1995	SEC provides a safe harbor from liability for companies that make statements to the public or investors about risk factors that may occur in the future.
Securities Litigation Uniform Standards Act of 1998	Sets national standards for securities class action lawsuits involving nationally traded securities. The act amends the 1933 and 1934 Acts and prohibits any private class action suit in state or federal court alleging (1) any untrue statement or omission in connection with the purchase or sale of a covered security or (2) the defendant used manipulation or deceptive device in connection with the transaction.
Sarbanes-Oxley Act of 2002	Amends the 1933 and 1934 Acts and other federal statutes. Provisions of this act are discussed in detail in the chapter. The act includes provisions dealing with corporate governance, financial regulation, criminal penalties, and corporate responsibility.

whether the offering is speculative or not); it is concerned only with whether potential investors are provided with adequate information to make investment decisions. To this end, the commission was given the power to set up and enforce proper registration regulations for securities as well as to prevent fraud in the registration and trading of securities.

Structure. Exhibit 22-1 lays out the structure of the SEC. It has five commissioners (inclusive of the chairman) appointed by the president with the advice and consent of the Senate; each serves for a period of five years, and no more than three commissioners can be of the same political party. The commission, based in Washington, D.C., has nine regional offices across the United States. There are five divisions: Corporation Finance, Market Regulation,

EXHIBIT 22-1 THE SECURITIES AND EXCHANGE COMMISSION

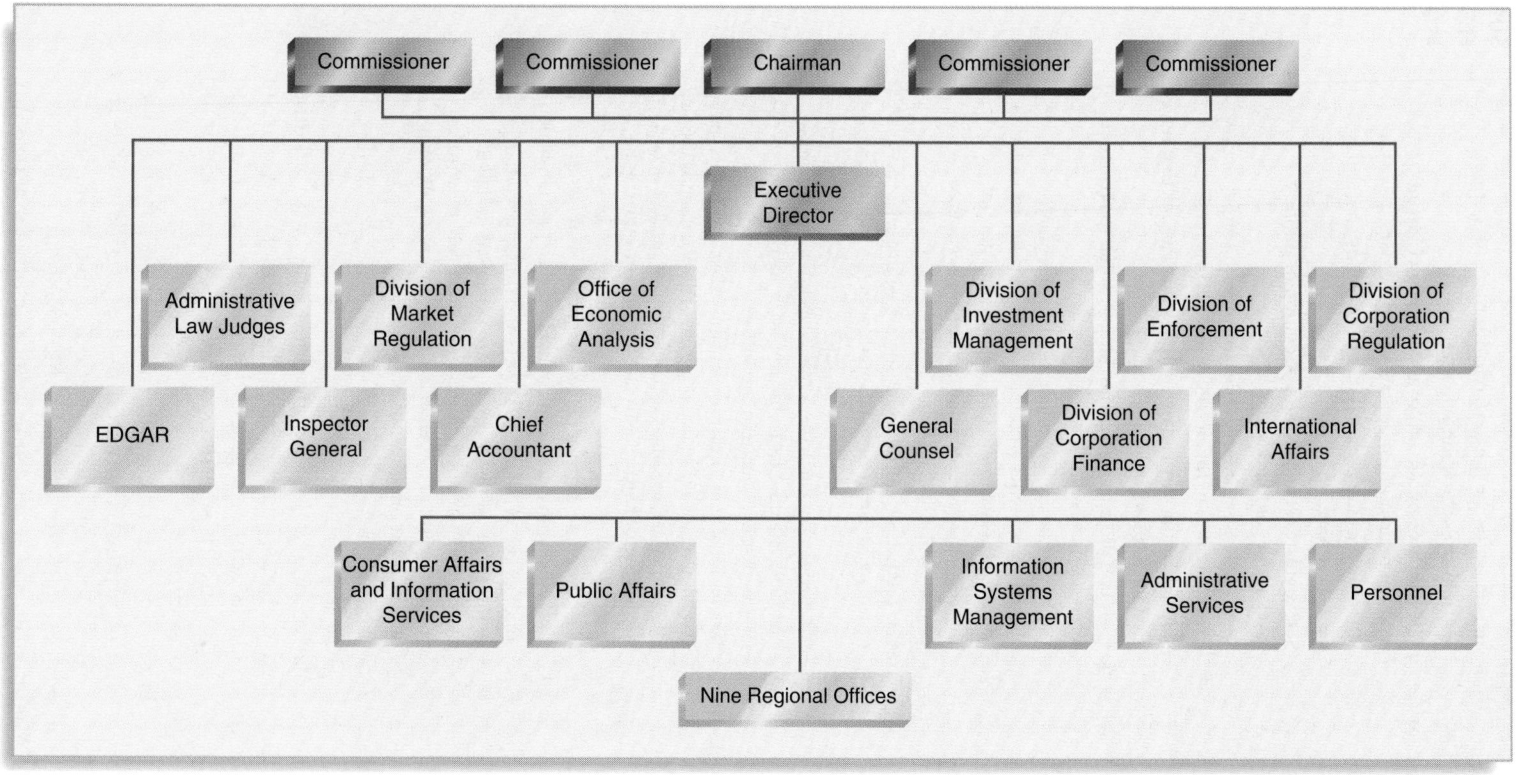

Enforcement, Corporate Regulation, and Investment Management. (Note in Exhibit 22-1 that five major offices—Consumer Affairs, Public Affairs, etc.—also serve the commission, along with an executive director.)

Division of Corporation Finance. This division is responsible for establishing and overseeing adherence to standards of financial reporting and disclosure for all companies that fall under SEC jurisdiction as well as for setting and administering the disclosure requirements prescribed by the 1933 and the 1934 securities acts, the Public Utility Holding Company Act, and the Investment Company Act. The Division of Corporation Finance reviews all registration statements, prospectuses, and quarterly and annual reports of corporations as well as their proxy statements. Its importance in offering informal advisory opinions to issuers (corporations about to make a public offering of stock) cannot be overemphasized. Accountants, lawyers, financial officers, and underwriters all rely heavily on this division's advice.

Division of Market Regulation. This is the SEC division that regulates the national security exchanges (such as the New York Stock Exchange) as well as broker–dealers registered under the Investment Advisers Act of 1940. Through ongoing surveillance of both the exchanges and broker–dealers, the Division of Market Regulation seeks to discourage manipulation or fraud in the issuance, sale, or purchase of securities. It can recommend to the full commission the suspension of an exchange for up to one year as well as the suspension or permanent prohibition of a broker or dealer because of certain types of conduct. In addition, the division provides valuable informal advice to investors, issuers, and others on securities statutes that come within the SEC's jurisdiction.

Division of Enforcement. This division is responsible for the review and supervision of all enforcement activities recommended by the SEC's other divisions and regional offices. It also supervises investigations and the initiation of injunctive actions.

Division of Corporation Regulation. This division administers the Public Utility Holding Company Act of 1935 and advises federal bankruptcy courts in proceedings brought under Chapter 11 of the Bankruptcy Reform Act of 1978.

Division of Investment Management. This is the SEC division that administers the Investment Company Act of 1940 and the Investment Advisers Act of 1940. All investigations arising under these acts dealing with issuers and dealers are carried out by this division.

THE SARBANES-OXLEY ACT OF 2002

Following financial and accounting scandals involving Martha Stewart Living, Inc., Tyco International, Inc., Enron Corporation, and others, Congress passed a bipartisan measure in 2002 sponsored by Senator Paul Sarbanes (D, Md.) and Representative Michael Oxley (R, Ohio) and signed into law by President Bush.[1] The act requires a new approach to corporate governance. Chief executive officers (CEOs) and Chief Financial Officers (CFOs) must now certify that statements and reports are accurate under pain of imprisonment if intent to mislead can be shown (Exhibit 22-2). A new entity, the Public Company Accounting Oversight

---

[1] H. R. 3762. The act became effective on August 29, 2002. Pub. L. 107–204. (Codified as Exchange Act Section 4), 15 U.S.C. Section 78(d)–3.

EXHIBIT 22-2

STATEMENT UNDER OATH OF PRINCIPAL EXECUTIVE OFFICER AND PRINCIPAL FINANCIAL OFFICER REGARDING FACTS AND CIRCUMSTANCES RELATING TO EXCHANGE ACT FILINGS

- [Name of principal executive officer or principal financial officer], state and attest that:
- To the best of my knowledge, based upon a review of the covered reports of [company name], and, except as corrected or supplemented in a subsequent covered report:
- no covered report contained an untrue statement of a material fact as of the end of the period covered by such report (or in the case of a report on Form 8-K or definitive proxy materials, as of the date on which it was filed; and
- no covered report omitted to state a material fact necessary to make the statements in the covered report, in light of the circumstances under which they were made, not misleading as of the end of the period covered by such report for in the case of a report on Form 8-K or definitive proxy materials, as of the date on which it was filed)

Board, was established to regulate accounting firms. New expansive powers for the SEC involving private civil actions as well as administrative actions are now available. Some provisions of Sarbanes-Oxley are outlined next. The SEC, using its rule-making power, has begun to implement some of these provisions.

CORPORATE ACCOUNTABILITY

The act requires CEOs and CFOs to certify financial reports. Officers must forfeit profits and bonuses if earnings are restated by a company due to securities fraud. Companies are required to immediately disclose material changes in their financial condition.

NEW ACCOUNTING REGULATIONS

A five-member board is established with legislative and disciplinary power. A majority of the board is independent from publicly held accounting companies. The board will be funded by publicly held companies overseen by the SEC.

The act prohibits auditors (accounting firms) from offering nine types of consulting services to corporate clients retained by them.

CRIMINAL PENALTIES

- The maximum penalty is raised to 25 years for securities fraud.
- For destroying, altering records, or fabricating such records a new crime is created under this act that provides a maximum penalty of 20 years.
- Penalties are increased for CEOs or CFOs who knowingly certify a report that does not meet the requirements of this act to $1 million in fines and up to five years in prison. If officers "willfully" certify a report, the penalty may be up to $5 million in fines and 20 years in prison or both.
- Under this act, penalties for mail and wire fraud are raised to 20 years and for defrauding pension funds up to 10 years.

Other Sarbanes-Oxley Provisions include:

- Lengthening the statue of limitations for securities fraud to five years or two years from discovery.
- Protection for whistle-blowers who report wrongdoing to employers or participate in a government investigation involving a potential securities violation.

- Prevents officials who are facing court judgments based on fraud charges from using bankruptcy laws to escape liability.
- Certain loans to directors and officers are prohibited from public and private companies that are filing initial public offerings. Arranging, receiving, or maintaining personal loans, except consumer or housing loans, is forbidden under this act.

THE SECURITIES ACT OF 1933

In the depths of the Great Depression, Congress enacted this first piece of federal legislation regulating securities. Its major purpose, as we have said, was to ensure full disclosure on new issues of securities.

DEFINITION OF A SECURITY

When most people use the word *securities*, they mean stocks or bonds that are held personally or as part of a group in a pension fund or a mutual fund. However, Congress, the SEC, and the courts have gone far beyond this simple meaning in defining securities. Section 2(1) of the 1933 Act defines the term **security** as

> *any note, stock, treasury stock, bond, debenture, evidence of indebtedness, certificate of interest or participation in any profit sharing agreement, collateral trust certificate, reorganization certificate or subscription, transferable share, investment contract, voting trust certificate, certificate of deposit for a security, fractional undivided interest in oil, gas or other mineral rights, or, in general, any interest or instrument commonly known as a security. ...*

The words "or, in general, any interest or instrument commonly known as a security" have led to various interpretations by the SEC and the courts of what constitutes a security. In the landmark case *SEC v. Howey*,[2] the Supreme Court sought to discover the economic realities behind the façade or form of a transaction and to set out specific criteria that could be used by the courts in defining a security. The Court in that case held that the sale of rows of orange trees to the public with a service contract, under which the Howey Company cultivated, harvested, and marketed the oranges, constituted a security within the meaning of Section 2(1) of the 1933 Act. Its decision was based on three elements or characteristics: (1) There existed a contract or scheme whereby an individual invested money in a common enterprise; (2) the investors had reasonable expectations of profits; and (3) the profits were derived solely from the efforts of persons other than the investors. These criteria are examined in detail here because they have been the basis of considerable litigation.

Common Enterprise. The first element of the **Howey test** has been interpreted by most courts as requiring investors to share in a single pool of assets so that the fortunes of a single investor are dependent on those of the other investors. For example, commodities accounts involving commodities brokers' discretion have been held to be "securities" on the ground that "the fortunes of all investors are inextricably tied" to the success of the trading enterprise.

Reasonable Expectations of Profit. The second element of the Howey test requires that the investor enter the transaction with a clear expectation of

security A stock or bond or any other instrument of interest that represents an investment in a common enterprise with reasonable expectations of profits that are derived solely from the efforts of those other than the investor.

Howey test The three-part test used to determine whether an instrument or contract is a security for purposes of federal securities laws: (1) The investment is in a common enterprise and (2) there is an expectation of profit that is (3) derived from efforts of others.

---

[2] 328 U.S. 293 (1946).

making a profit on the money invested. The U.S. Supreme Court has held that neither an interest in a noncontributory, compulsory pension plan nor stock purchases by residents in a low-rent cooperative constitute "securities" within the definition of *Howey*. In the case involving the pension plan,[3] the Court stated that the employee expected funds for his pension to come primarily from contributions made by the employer rather than from returns on the assets of the pension plan fund. Similarly, in the low-rent housing case,[4] the Court decided that shares purchased solely to acquire a low-cost place to live were not bought with a reasonable expectation of profit.

Profits Derived Solely from the Efforts of Others. The third element of the Howey test requires that profits come "solely" from the efforts of people other than the investors. The word *solely* was interpreted to mean that the investors can exert "some efforts" in bringing other investors into a pyramid sales scheme but that the "undeniably significant ones" must be the efforts of management, not of the investors.

CASE 22-1

SEC v. Alpha Telecom, Inc.
U.S. District Court (N.D. District, Ore)
187 F.Supp 2d 1250 (2002)

Plaintiff, Securities and Exchange Commission, sued Alpha Telecom, Inc., and Paul Rubera, its founder, for violations of the 1933 Securities Act. The defendant, Rubera and Alpha Telecom, Inc., argued that its pay phone program did not involve a sale of securities as defined by statutory and case law. Alpha began to install phones in 1997 in Grant Pass, Oregon, using a "Level Four Service Agreement," which required the plaintiff to perform several tasks. Alpha selected the location for a phone, installed it, obtained licenses, maintained and cleaned each, paid the bills, and collected the revenue. Buyers of the phones were guaranteed 14 percent in the agreement. The pay phone program was promoted and marketed through an Alpha subsidiary, American Telecommunication Company (ATC), from July 1998 to June 2001. Revenue and expenses totaled $21,698 and $21,798, respectively. Alpha paid investors $17.9 million despite its losses by virtue of loans from ATC. Alpha filed for bankruptcy in August 2001.

Justice Panner

An investment contract involves: (1) an investment of money; (2) in a common enterprise; (3) with the expectation of profits to be derived from the efforts of others.

The first element is met. The investors make cash investments with the expectation of receiving profits.

The second element of the test can be satisfied by the existence of either vertical commonality or horizontal commonality. Vertical commonality is the dependence of the investors' fortunes on the success or expertise of the promoter. Horizontal commonality is the pooling of investor funds and interests.

Vertical commonality clearly exists. Investors relied on the expertise of Alpha to negotiate and lease sites for the phones, to establish service lines for the phones, and to make all business decisions related to the operation of the phones. Alpha also serviced and maintained the phones, which was important to these investors who had no expertise in the workings of telephones and no desire to maintain or service the phones.

Horizontal commonality also exists. ATC loaned money to Alpha. [I]t was clearly used, at least in part, to make payments to existing investors. ATC's only source of revenue was money from new investors. As a result, new investor money was being used to pay returns to existing investors. Other evidence of horizontal commonality exists in that Alpha did not pay its investors

---

[3] *International Brotherhood of Teamsters, Chauffeurs, Warehousers, and Helpers of America v. Daniel,* 439 U.S. 551 (1979).

[4] *United Housing Foundation, Inc. v. SEC,* 423 U.S. 884 (1975).

according to the revenue generated by individual pay phones. Investors would receive their 14 percent return regardless of whether their particular phone actually generated that much money.

The issue for (the third) element is whether the efforts made by those other than the investor are the undeniably significant ones, those essential managerial efforts which affect the failure or success of the enterprise.

[N]inety percent of investors chose Alpha as the service provider. ... [T]hese investors had no expertise or interest in the operation of pay telephones. Alpha was ultimately responsible for those essential managerial efforts [that] affect the failure or success of the enterprise, and the investors retained no control over the business.

The federal district court ruled *in favor* of Plaintiff, SEC.

REGISTRATION OF SECURITIES UNDER THE 1933 ACT

Purpose and Goals. The 1933 Act requires the registration of nonexempt securities, as defined by Section 2(1), for the purpose of full disclosure so that potential investors can make informed decisions on whether to buy a proposed public offering of stock. As we noted earlier in the chapter, the 1933 Act does not authorize the SEC or any other agency to decide whether or not the offering is meritorious and should be sold to the public.

Registration Statement and Process. Section 5 of the 1933 Act requires that, to serve the goals of disclosure, a registration statement consist of two parts—the prospectus and a "Part II" information statement—to be filed with the SEC before any security can be sold to the public. The **prospectus** (Exhibit 22-3) provides (1) material information about the business and property of the issuer; (2) the purpose of the offering; (3) the use to be made of the funds garnered by the offering and the risks involved for investors; (4) the managerial experience, history, and remuneration of the principals; and (5) financial statements certified by public accountants attesting to the firm's financial health. The prospectus must be given to every prospective buyer of the securities. Part II is a longer, more detailed statement than the prospectus. It is not given to prospective buyers but is open for public inspection at the SEC.

During the registration process, the SEC bans public statements by the issuers, other than those contained in the registration statement, until the effective date of registration. There are three important stages in this process: the prefiling, waiting, and posteffective periods. They are summarized in Table 22-2.

Proposed rules by the SEC as of October 26, 2004, will revamp the entire securities offering process. These rules will allow brokers to promote securities sales before registration becomes effective. New technology will help simplify the registration process. Readers will note that this section will have many changes when the proposed rules are finalized. Following the publication of this text, changes may be made after further comments by interested parties.

Prefiling Period. Section 5(c) of the 1933 Act prohibits any offer to sell or buy securities before a registration statement is filed. The key question here is what constitutes an "offer." Section 2(3) of the act exempts from the definition any preliminary agreements or negotiations between the issuer and the underwriters or among the underwriters themselves. **Underwriters** are investment banking firms that purchase a securities issue from the issuing corporation with a view to eventually selling the securities to brokerage houses, which, in turn, sell them to the public. These underwriters—such as Goldman Sachs, Kidder Peabody, or First Boston—may arrange for distribution of the public offering of securities, but they cannot make

prospectus The first part of the registration statement the SEC requires from issuers of new securities. It contains material information about the business and its management, the offering itself, the use to be made of the funds obtained, and certain financial statements.

underwriter Investment banking firm that agrees to purchase a securities issue from the issuer, usually on a fixed date at a fixed price, with a view to eventually selling the securities to brokers, who, in turn, sell them to the public.

EXHIBIT 22-3

RULES GOVERNING THE ISSUANCE AND TRADING OF SECURITIES

PROPECTUS
March 1, 1998

INVESTMENT OBJECTIVE:
LONG-TERM CAPITAL APPRECIATION

The Links Fund invests primarily in common stocks and securities convertible into common stocks, but may also invest in other securities that are suited to the Fund's investment objective.

INVESTMENT OBJECTIVE:
LONG-TERM CAPITAL APPRECIATION

The Links International Fund invests primarily in a diversified portfolio of international securities.

NO LOAD — NO SALES CHARGE

NO 12b-1 FEES

Minimum Investment	Ticker Symbols
Initial purchase—$1,000	The Links Fund—LNX
($500 for an IRA)	The Links International Fund—LNIX
Subsequent investments—$100	

The Funds may invest to a limited extent in high-yield, high-risk bonds. See "Risk Factors."

This prospectus contains information you should know before investing. Please retain it for future reference. A Statement of Additional Information regarding the Funds dated the date of this prospectus has been filed with the Securities and Exchange Commission and (together with any supplement to it) is incorporated by reference. The Statement of Additional Information may be obtained at no charge by writing or telephoning the Trust at its address or telephone number shown inside the back cover.

THESE SECURITIES HAVE NOT BEEN APPROVED OR DISAPPROVED BY THE SECURITIES AND EXCHANGE COMMISSION OR ANY STATE SECURITIES COMMISSION, NOR HAS THE SECURITIES AND EXCHANGE COMMISSION OR ANY STATE SECURITIES COMMISSION PASSED UPON THE ACCURACY OR ADEQUACY OF THIS PROSPECTUS. ANY REPRESENTATION TO THE CONTRARY IS A CRIMINAL OFFENSE.

red herring A preliminary prospectus that contains most of the information that will appear in the final prospectus, except for the price of the securities. The "red herring" prospectus may be distributed to potential buyers during the waiting period, but no sales may be finalized during this period.

offerings or sales to dealers or the public at this time. During the prefiling period, the SEC regulations also forbid sales efforts in the form of speeches or advertising by the issuer that seek to "hype" the offering or the issuer's business. However, a press release setting forth the details of the proposed offering and the issuer's name, without mentioning the underwriters, is generally permitted.

Waiting Period. In the interim between the filing and the time when registration becomes effective, SEC rules allow oral offers but not sales. The SEC examines the prospectus for completeness during this period. SEC rules permit the publication of a written preliminary, or **red herring**, prospectus that summarizes the registration but disavows in red print (hence, its name) any attempt to offer or sell securities. Notices of underwriters containing certain information about the proposed issue are also allowed to appear in newspapers during this period, but such notices must be bordered in black and specify that they are not offers to sell or solicitations to buy securities.

Stage	Prohibitions
1. Prefiling period	No offer to sell or buy securities may be made before a registration statement is filed.
2. Waiting period	SEC rules allow oral offers during this period but no sales. A "red herring" prospectus that disavows any attempt either to offer or sell securities may be published.
3. Posteffective period	Registration generally becomes effective 20 days after the registration statement is filed, though effective registration may be accelerated or postponed by the SEC. Offer and sale of securities are now permitted.

TABLE 22-2

STAGES IN THE SECURITIES REGISTRATION PROCESS

Posteffective Period. The third stage in the process is called the posteffective period because the registration statement usually becomes effective 20 days after it is filed, although sometimes the commission accelerates or postpones registration for some reason. Underwriters and lenders can begin to offer and sell securities after the 20 days or upon commission approval, whichever comes first.

Under Section 8 of the 1933 Act, the SEC may issue a "refusal order" or "stop order," which prevents a registration statement from becoming effective or suspends its effectiveness, if the staff discovers a misstatement or omission of a material fact in the statement. Stop orders are reserved for the most serious cases. In general, the issuer is forewarned by the SEC in informal "letters of comment" or "deficiency" before a stop order is put out, so they have the opportunity to make the necessary revisions. The commission may shorten the usual 20-day period between registration and effectiveness if the issuer is willing to make modifications requested by the SEC staff. This procedure, in fact, is the present trend.

The 1933 Act requires that a prospectus be issued upon every sale of a security in interstate commerce except sales by anyone not an "issuer, underwriter or dealer." If a prospectus is delivered more than nine months after the effective date of registration, it must be updated so that the information is not more than 16 months old. The burden is on the dealer to update all material information about the issuer that is not in the prospectus. Dealers who fail to do so risk civil liability under Sections 12(1) and 12(2) of the 1933 Act.

In the following landmark case, the U.S. Supreme Court defined the reach of Section 12(2). When reading the edited Court decision, you should note its reliance on legislative history in arriving at a conclusion.

CASE 22-2

Arthur Gustafson et al. v. Alloyd Company, Inc., et al.
United States Supreme Court
513 U.S. 561 (1995)

Alloyd Shareholders (plaintiff-respondent) sued Gustafson and others (defendant-petitioners) under Section 12(2) of the Securities Act of 1993 for rescission of a previous agreement with regard to its stock purchase of Alloyd Company made from Gustafson. Plaintiffs purchased substantially all of the stock of Alloyd from the defendants in a private contractual arrangement. Under the contract, if a year-end audit and financial statements revealed variances between estimated and actual increased value, the disappointed party would receive an adjustment as a result of the audit. The plaintiffs (shareholders of Alloyd) were entitled to recover an adjustment but instead sought a rescission (cancellation) of the whole contract under Section 12(2) of the 1993 Act. This section gives buyers the right of rescission against sellers who make material misstatements or omissions "by means of a prospectus." The district court granted the defendant Gustafson's motion for summary judgment, holding that Section 12(2) claims can arise only out of initial stock offerings and not from a private sale agreement. The court of appeals reversed in favor of the plaintiff, vacating the summary judgment. The court claimed that the definition of prospectus included "communication," which, therefore, includes all written communication included in the offering of a security for sale and, thus, a 12(2) right of action for rescission applies to private sale agreements. The defendants, Gustafson et al., appealed.

Justice Kennedy

Under Section 12(2) of the Securities Act of 1933, buyers have an express cause of action for rescission against sellers who make material misstatements or omissions "by means of a prospectus." The question presented is whether this right of rescission extends to a private, secondary transaction, on the theory that recitations in the purchase agreement are part of a "prospectus."

The rescission claim against Gustafson is based upon Section 12(2) of the 1933 Act. In relevant part, the section provides that any person who

> *offers or sells a security (whether or not exempted by the provisions of section 77c of this title, other than paragraph (2) of subsection (a) of said section), by the use of any means or instruments of transportation or communication in interstate commerce or of the mails, by means of a prospectus or oral communication, which includes an untrue statement of a material fact or omits to state a material fact necessary in order to make the statements, in the light of the circumstances under which they were made, not misleading (the purchaser not knowing of such untruth or omission), and who shall not sustain the burden of proof that he did not know, and in the exercise of reasonable care could not have known, of such untruth or omission, "shall be liable to the person purchasing such security from him, who may sue either at law or in equity in any court of competent jurisdiction, to recover the consideration paid for such security with interest thereon, less the amount of any income received thereon, upon the tender of such security, or for damages if he no longer owns the security."*

As this case reaches us, we must assume that the stock purchase agreement contained material misstatements of fact made by the sellers and that Gustafson would not sustain its burden of proving due care. On these assumptions, Alloyd would have a right to obtain rescission if those misstatements were made "by means of a prospectus or oral communication." The parties (and the court of appeals) agree that the phrase "oral communication" is restricted to oral communications that relate to the prospectus. The determinative question, then, is whether the contract between Alloyd and Gustafson is a "prospectus" as the term is used in the 1933 Act.

It is understandable that Congress would provide buyers with a right to rescind, without proof of fraud or reliance, as to misstatements contained in a document prepared with care, following well established procedures relating to investigations with due diligence, and in the context of a public offering by an issuer or its controlling shareholders. It is not plausible to infer that Congress created this extensive liability for every casual communication between buyer and seller in the secondary market. It is often difficult, if not altogether impractical, for those engaged in casual communications not to omit some fact that would, if included, qualify the accuracy of a statement. Under Alloyd's view any casual communication between buyer and seller in the aftermarket could give rise to an action for rescission, with no evidence of fraud on the part of the seller or reliance on the part of the buyer. In many instances buyers in practical effect would have an option to rescind, impairing the stability of past transactions where neither fraud nor detrimental reliance on misstatements or omissions occurred. We find no basis for interpreting the statute to reach so far.

Nothing in the legislative history, moreover, suggests Congress intended to create two types of prospectuses: a formal and less formal one. The Act proceeds by definitions more stable and precise. The legislative history confirms what the text of the Act dictates: Section 10's requirements govern all prospectuses defined by Section 2(10). In discussing Section 10, the House Report stated:

> Section 10 of the bill requires that any "prospectus" used in connection with the sale of any securities, if it is more than a mere announcement of the name and price of the issue offered and an offer of full details upon request, must include a substantial portion of the information required in the "registration statement."

"Prospectus" is defined in section 2(1) [now Section 2(10)] to include "any prospectus, notice, circular, advertisement, letter, or other communication offering any security for sale."

The purpose of these sections is to secure for potential buyers the means of understanding the intricacies of the transaction into which they are invited.

In sum, the word "prospectus" is a term of art referring to a document that describes a public offering of securities by an issuer or controlling shareholder. Here the contract of sale, and its recitations, were not held out to the public and were not a prospectus as the term is used in the 1933 Act.

Reversed in favor of Defendant, Gustafson.

Shelf Registration. Traditionally, the marketing of securities has taken place through underwriters who buy or offer to buy securities and then employ dealers across the United States to sell them to the general public. The SEC, with Rule 415, has established a procedure, called **shelf registration**, that allows a large corporation to file a registration statement for securities that it may wish to sell over a period of time rather than immediately. Once the securities are registered, the corporation can place them on the "shelf" for future sale and not have to register them again. It can then sell these securities when it needs capital and when the marketplace indicators are favorable. A company that files a shelf registration statement must file periodic amendments with the SEC if any fundamental changes occur in its activities that would be material to the average prudent investor's decision to invest in its stock.

shelf registration
Procedure whereby large corporations can file a registration statement for securities it wishes to sell over a period of time rather than immediately.

SECURITIES AND TRANSACTIONS EXEMPT FROM REGISTRATION UNDER THE 1933 ACT

Section 5 of the 1933 Act requires registrations of any sale by any person of any security unless specifically exempted by the 1933 Act. The cost of the registration process, in terms of hiring lawyers, accountants, underwriters, and other financial experts, makes it appealing for a firm to put a transaction together in such a way as not to fall within the definition of a security. If that is impossible, firms often attempt to meet the requirements of one of the following four classes of exemptions to the registration process (summarized in Table 22-3).

Private Placement Exemptions. Section 4(2) of the 1933 Act exempts from registration transactions by an issuer that do not involve any public offering. Behind this exemption is the theory that institutional investors have the sophisticated knowledge necessary to evaluate the information contained in a private placement and, thus, unlike the average investor, do not need to be protected by the registration process set out in the 1933 Act. The private placement exemption is often used in stock option plans, in which a corporation issues securities to its own employees for the purpose of increasing productivity or retaining top-level managers. Because various courts had different views on what factual situations constituted a private placement exemption, the SEC published Rule 146, which seeks to clarify the criteria used by the commission in allowing this exemption:

1. The number of purchasers of the company's (issuer's) securities should not exceed 35. If a single purchaser buys more than $150,000, that purchaser will not be counted among the 35.

2. Each purchaser must have access to the same kind of information that would be available if the issuer had registered the securities.

3. The issuer can sell only to purchasers who it has reason to believe are capable of evaluating the risks and benefits of investment and are able to bear those risks or to purchasers who have the services of a representative with the knowledge and experience to evaluate the risks for them.

4. The issuer may not advertise the securities or solicit public customers.

5. The issuer must take precautions to prevent the resale of securities issued under a private placement exemption.

Intrastate Offering Exemption. Section 3 of the 1933 Act provides an exemption for any "security which is part of an issue offered or sold to persons

TABLE 22-3

EXEMPTIONS FROM THE REGISTRATION PROCESS UNDER THE 1933 SECURITIES ACT

Exemption	*Definition*
Private placement	Transactions by an issuing company not involving any public offering. Usually the transaction involves sophisticated investors with knowledge enough to evaluate information given them (e.g., stock option plans for top-level management).
Intrastate offering	Any security or part of an offering offered or sold to persons resident within a single state or territory.
Small business	Section 3(b) of the 1933 Act allows the SEC to exempt offerings not exceeding $5 million. Regulations A and D promulgated by the SEC define the type of investors and the amount of securities that are exempt within a certain time period.
Other offering exemptions	By virtue of the 1933 Act, exemptions are allowed for transactions by any person other than an issuer, underwriter, or dealer. Also government securities are exempt (federal, state, or municipal bonds). Also exempt are securities issued by banks, charitable organizations, savings and loans institutions, and common carriers under the jurisdiction of the Interstate Commerce Commission.

resident within a single state or territory, where the issuer of such security is a resident and doing business within, or, if a corporation, incorporated by, or doing business within such a state." To qualify for this exemption, an issuer must meet the strictly interpreted "doing-business-within-a-state" requirement: The issuer must be a resident of the state and "do business" solely with (i.e., offer securities to) people who live within the state.

Courts have interpreted Section 3 very strictly. One federal court ruled that a company incorporated in the state of California and making an offering of common stock solely to residents of California did not qualify for the intrastate exemption because it advertised in the *Los Angeles Times*, a newspaper sold in the mails to residents of other states. Another factor in the court's decision in this case was that 20 percent of the proceeds from the securities sale were to be used to refurbish a hotel in Las Vegas, Nevada.[5]

After that decision, the SEC issued Rule 147, which sets standards for the intrastate exemption by defining important terms in Section 3 of the 1933 Act. For example, an issuer is "doing business within" the state if (1) it receives at least 80 percent of its gross revenue from within the state; (2) at least 80 percent of its assets are within the state; (3) it intends to use 80 percent of the net proceeds of the offering within the state; and (4) its principal office is located in the state. Rule 147 is also concerned with whether the offering has "come to rest" within a state or whether it is the beginning of an interstate distribution. An offering is considered "intrastate" only if no resales are made to nonresidents of the state for at least nine months after the initial distribution of securities is completed.

Small Business Exemptions. Section 3(b) of the 1933 Act authorizes the SEC, by use of its rule-making power, to exempt offerings not exceeding $5 million when it finds registration not necessary. Under this authority, the commission has promulgated Regulations A and D.

Regulation A exempts small public offerings made by the issuer—defined as offerings not exceeding $1.5 million over a 12-month period. The issuer must file an

---

[5] *SEC v. Trustee Showboat*, 157 F. Supp. 824 (S.D. Calif. 1957).

"offerings" and a "notification circular" with an SEC regional office 10 days before each proposed offering. The circular contains information similar to that required for a 1933 Act registration prospectus but in less detail, and the accompanying financial statements may be unaudited. It should be noted that for these small business offerings, the SEC staff follows the same "letter of comment" procedure associated with registration statements; thus, a Regulation A filing may be delayed. Regulation A circulars do not give rise to civil liability under Section 11 of the 1933 Act (discussed later in this chapter), but they do make an issuer liable under Section 12(2) for misstatements or omissions (also discussed later in this chapter). The advantages of this regulation for small businesses are that the preparation of forms is simpler and less costly and the SEC staff can usually act more quickly.

Regulation D, which includes Rules 501–506, attempts to implement Section 3 of the 1933 Act. Rule 501 defines an accredited investor as a bank; an insurance or investment company; an employee benefit plan; a business development company; a charitable or educational institution (with assets of $5 million or more); any director, officer, or general partner of an issuer; any person with a net worth of $1 million or more; or any person with an annual income of more than $200,000. This definition is important because an accredited investor, as defined by Rule 501, is not likely to need the protection of the 1933 Act's registration process.

Rule 504 allows any **noninvestment company** to sell up to $1 billion worth of securities in a 12-month period to any number of purchasers, accredited or nonaccredited, without furnishing any information to the purchaser. However, this $1 billion maximum is reduced by the amount of securities sold under any other exemption.

noninvestment company A company whose primary business is not in investing or trading in securities.

Rule 505 allows any private noninvestment company to sell up to $5 million of securities in a 12-month period to any number of accredited investors (as previously defined) and to up to 35 nonaccredited purchasers. Sales to nonaccredited purchasers are subject to certain restrictions concerning the manner of offering— for example, no public advertising is allowed—and resale of the securities.

Rule 506 allows an issuer to sell an unlimited number of securities to any number of accredited investors and to up to 35 nonaccredited purchasers. However, the issuer must have reason to believe that each nonaccredited purchaser or representative has enough knowledge or experience in business to be able to evaluate the merits and risks of the prospective investment. Again, there are certain resale restrictions attached to offerings made under this rule as well as a prohibition against advertising. Rule 506 seeks to clarify Section 4(2) of the 1933 Act, dealing with private placement exemptions, already discussed.

Other Offering Exemptions. Section 4(2) of the 1933 Act allows exemptions for "transactions by any person other than an issuer, underwriter or dealer." Since Sections 4(3) and 4(4) allow qualified exemptions for dealers and brokers, the issuer and the underwriters become the only ones not exempted. SEC Rules 144 and 144a define the conditions under which a person is not an underwriter and is not involved in selling securities.

Exempt Securities. Government securities issued or regulated by agencies other than the SEC are exempt from the 1933 Act. For example, debt issued by or guaranteed by federal, state, or local governments as well as securities issued by banks, religious and charitable organizations, savings and loan associations, and common carriers under the Interstate Commerce Commission are exempt. These securities usually fall under the jurisdiction of other federal agencies, such as the Federal Reserve System or the Federal Home Loan Board, or of state or local agencies.

The collapse of the Penn Central Railroad in 1970 and the default of the cities of Cleveland and New York on municipal bonds led Congress and the SEC to reexamine certain exemptions with a view to eliminating them. In fact, the Railroad Revitalization Act of 1976 eliminated the 1933 Act exemption for securities issued by railroads (other than trust certificates for certain equipment), and 1975 amendments to the securities acts now require firms that deal solely in state and local government securities to register with the commission and to adhere to rules laid down by the Municipal Securities Rulemaking Board.

RESALE RESTRICTIONS

Restrictions are placed on the resale of securities issued for investment purposes pursuant to intrastate, private placement, or small business exemptions.

- Rule 147 states that securities sold pursuant to an intrastate offering exemption (above) cannot be sold to residents for nine months.
- Rule 144 states that securities sold pursuant to private placement or small business exemption must be held one year from the date the securities are lost.

INTEGRATION

Often a company will seek to obtain a private placement or small business exemption by dividing a large issuance of securities into several small units. Under its integration and aggregation rules, the SEC prohibits this action by integrating (putting together) two exempt offerings that are similar and are made at nearly the same time by the same issuing company. The SEC integrates and aggregates two or more otherwise exempt offerings when:

1. The offerings are part of a unitary plan of financing by the issuing company.
2. The offerings concern the same class of securities.
3. The offerings are made for the same general purpose and at about the same level of pricing.

The SEC has also adopted a "safe harbor rule," which, in effect, states that any offering made at least six months before or six months after another offering will not be integrated with that offering.

LIABILITY, REMEDIES, AND DEFENSES UNDER THE 1933 SECURITIES ACT

Private Remedies. The 1933 Act provides remedies for individuals who have been victims of (1) misrepresentations in a registration statement, (2) an issuer's failure to file a registration statement with the SEC, or (3) misrepresentation or fraud in the sale of securities. Each is examined here along with some affirmative defenses.

Misrepresentations in a Registration Statement. These are untruths or omissions for which Section 11 of the 1933 Act imposes liability. Section 11 allows a right of action to "any person acquiring such a security" who can show (1) a material misstatement or omission in a registration statement and (2) monetary damages. The term *material* is defined by SEC Rule 405 as pertaining to matters "of which an average prudent investor ought reasonably to be informed before purchasing the security registered." In addition, the issuer's omission of such facts as might cause investors to change their minds about investing in a particular security are considered material omissions for the purposes of Section 11. These facts include an impending bankruptcy, new government regulations that may be costly to the company, and the impending conviction and sentencing of the company's top executives for numerous violations of the Foreign Corrupt Practices Act of 1977 (discussed later in this chapter).

Three affirmative defenses are available to defendants:

1. The purchaser (plaintiff) knew of the omission or untruth.

2. The decline in value of the security resulted from causes other than the misstatement or omission in the registration statement.

3. The statement was prepared with the due diligence expected of each defendant.

Whereas others associated with the company can raise the **due diligence defense**, the issuing company itself cannot. Section 11(a) is very specific about what other individuals may be held jointly or severally liable in addition to the issuing company:

1. Every person who signed the registration statement. (Section 16 of the 1933 Act requires signing by the issuer, the issuing company's chief executive officer, the company's financial and accounting officers, and a majority of the company's board of directors.)

2. All directors.

3. Accountants, appraisers, engineers, and other experts who consented to being named as having prepared all or part of the registration statement.

4. Every underwriter of the securities.

It should be noted that there are two exceptions to Section 11 liability:

1. An expert is liable only for the misstatements or omissions in the portion of the registration statement that the expert prepared or certified.

2. An underwriter is liable only for the aggregate public offering portion of the securities it underwrote.

Section 11 liability has made such a strong impact that today virtually all professionals and experts involved in the preparation of a registration statement make precise agreements concerning the assignment of responsibility for that statement. Failure to grasp the import of Section 11 and related sections of the 1933 and 1934 Acts can lead to loss of reputation and employment by businesspersons and professionals. The first case brought under Section 11[6] sent tremors through Wall Street, the accounting profession, and outside directors. In that case, the court evaluated each defendant's plea of due diligence on the basis of each individual's relationship to the corporation and expected knowledge of registration requirements.

Failure to File a Registration Statement. Failure to file a registration statement with the SEC when selling a nonexempt security is the second basis for a private action by the purchaser for rescission (cancellation of the sale). Section 12(1) of the 1933 Act provides that any person who sells a security in violation of Section 5 (which you recall from our discussion of the registration statement) is liable to the purchaser to refund the full purchase price. A purchaser whose investment has decreased in value may recover the full purchase price without

due diligence defense An affirmative defense raised in lawsuits charging misrepresentation in a registration statement. It is based on the defendant's claim to have had reasonable grounds to believe that all statements in the registration statement were true and no omission of material fact had been made. This defense is not available to the issuer of the security.

---

[6] *Escott v. Barchris Construction Corp.*, 283 F. Supp. 643 (S.D.N.Y. 1968).

showing a misstatement or fraud if the seller is unable to meet the conditions of one of the exemptions we discussed earlier. In short, a business that fails to file a registration statement because of a mistaken assumption that it has qualified for one of the exemptions could be making a very expensive mistake.

Misrepresentation or Fraud in the Sale of a Security. A third basis for a private action is misrepresentation in the sale of a security as defined by Section 12(2) of the 1933 Act, which holds liable any person who offers or sells securities by means of any written or oral statement that misstates a material fact or omits a material fact that is necessary to make the statement truthful. Unlike Section 11, Section 12(2) is applicable whether or not the security is subject to the registration provisions of the 1933 Act, provided there is use of the mails or other facilities in interstate commerce. The persons liable are only those from whom the purchaser bought the security. For example, under Section 12(2), a purchaser who bought the security from an underwriter, a dealer, or a broker cannot sue the issuer unless able to show that the issuer was "a substantial factor in causing the transaction to take place." A further requirement is that the purchaser must prove the sale was made "by means of" the misleading communications. The defense usually raised by sellers in such suits is that they did not know and, using reasonable care, could not have known of the untruth or omission at the time the statement was made. (See *Gustafson v. Alloyd*, 22–2, set out earlier in this chapter.)

Fraud in the sale of a security is covered by Section 17(a) of the 1933 Act, which imposes criminal, and possibly civil, liability on anyone who aids and abets any fraud in connection with the offer or sale of a security. Although Section 17(a) is clearly a basis for criminal liability, an implied right of private action by a purchaser to recover against an individual is still in doubt because of the recent trend of Supreme Court decisions in this area. The Court has refused to infer a private right of action under the antifraud provisions of both the 1933 Act and the 1934 Exchange Act on the ground that it has not been shown that Congress intended such a right. Still, a few lower courts continue to recognize an implied private right of action under Section 17.

Governmental Remedies. When a staff investigation uncovers evidence of a violation of the securities laws, the SEC can (1) take administrative action, (2) take injunctive action, or (3) recommend a criminal prosecution to the Justice Department.

Administrative Action. Upon receiving information of a possible violation of the 1933 Act, the SEC staff undertakes an informal inquiry. This involves interviewing witnesses but generally does not involve issuing subpoenas. If the staff uncovers evidence of a possible violation of a securities act, it asks the full commission for a formal order of investigation. A formal investigation is usually conducted in private under SEC rules. A witness compelled to testify or to produce evidence can be represented by counsel, but no other witness or counsel may be present during the testimony. A witness can be denied a copy of the transcript of his or her own testimony for good cause, although the witness is allowed to inspect the transcript.

Witnesses at a private SEC investigation do not enjoy the ordinary exercise of Fourth, Fifth, and Sixth Amendment rights. For example, Fourth Amendment rights are limited because the securities industry is subject to pervasive government regulation, and those going into it know so in advance. Fifth Amendment rights are limited because the production of records related to a business may be compelled despite a claim of self-incrimination. (See the sections on the Fourth and Fifth Amendments in Chapter 5.) As for the Sixth Amendment, in a private investigation, the SEC is not required to notify the targets of the investigation, nor do such targets have a right to appear before the staff or the full commission to defend themselves against charges. The wide scope of SEC powers in these nonpublic investigations was reinforced when the U.S. Supreme Court upheld a lower court's decision to deny injunctive relief with regard to subpoenas directed at plaintiffs in an SEC private investigation.[7]

An administrative proceeding may be ordered by the full commission if the SEC staff uncovers evidence of a violation of the securities laws. This proceeding before an administrative law judge can be brought only against a person or firm that is registered with the commission (an investment company, a dealer, or a broker). The ALJ has the power to impose sanctions, including censure, revocation of registration, and limitations on the person's or the firm's activities or practice before the commission.

In addition, after a hearing, the full commission may issue a stop order to suspend a registration statement found to contain a material misstatement or omission. If the statement is later amended, the stop order will be lifted. As we mentioned earlier in the chapter, stop orders are usually reserved for the most serious cases. **Letters of deficiency** are the more frequent method used by the SEC to obtain corrections in registration statements. The remedies available under the 1991 Remedies Act, discussed earlier in the chapter under "Summary of Federal Securities Legislation," apply here as well.

Injunctive Action. The SEC may commence an injunctive action when there is a "reasonable likelihood of further violation in the future" or when a defendant is considered a "continuing menace" to the public. For example, under the 1933 Act, the SEC may go to court to seek an injunction to prevent a party from using the interstate mails to sell a nonexempt security. Violation of an injunctive order may give rise to a contempt citation. Also, parties under such an order are disqualified from receiving an exemption under Regulation A (the small business exemption). Again, the remedies available under the 1991 Remedies Act apply here.

Criminal Penalties. Willful violations of the securities acts and the rules and regulations made pursuant to those acts are subject to criminal penalties. Anyone convicted of willfully omitting a material fact or making an untrue statement in connection with the offering or sale of a security can be fined up to $1 million for each offense or imprisoned for up to five years or both. The commission does not prosecute criminal cases itself but refers them to the Justice Department.

letter of deficiency
Informal letter issued by the SEC indicating what corrections need to be made in a registration statement for it to become effective.

THE SECURITIES EXCHANGE ACT OF 1934

One year after passing the Securities Act of 1933, Congress crafted this second extremely important piece of securities legislation to come out of the Great Depression. More comprehensive than the 1933 Act, it had two major purposes: to regulate trading in securities and to establish the Securities and Exchange Commission to oversee all securities regulations and bar the kind of large market manipulations that had characterized the 1920s and previous boom periods.

REGISTRATION OF SECURITIES ISSUERS, BROKERS, AND DEALERS

Registration of Securities Issuers. Section 12 of the Securities Exchange Act requires every issuer of debt and equity securities to register with both the SEC

---

[7] *SEC v. Jerry T. O'brien, Inc., et al.,* 467 U.S. 735 (1984).

and the national exchange on which its securities are to be traded. Congress extended this requirement to all corporations that (1) have assets of more than $5 million, (2) have a class of equity securities with more than 500 shareholders, and (3) are involved in interstate commerce. Registration becomes effective within 60 days after filing, unless the SEC accelerates the process.

The commission has devised forms to ensure that potential investors will have updated information on all registrants whose securities are being traded on the national exchanges. Thus, registrants are required to file annual reports (Form 10-K; Exhibit 22-4) and quarterly reports (Form 10-Q; Exhibit 22-5) as well as SEC-requested current reports (Form 8-K). This last form must be filed within 15 days of the request, which is usually brought about by a perceived material change in the corporation's position (e.g., a potential merger or bankruptcy) that the commission's staff believes a prudent investor should know about.

In a proposed Codification of the Federal Securities Law (CFSL), the American Law Institute has sought to streamline the registration process under the 1933 and 1934 Acts by requiring single issuance registration under the 1933 Act and an annual company "offering statement" for securities traded on a national exchange under the 1934 Act. At present, Section 22 of the Exchange Act makes a registering company liable for civil damages to securities purchasers who can show that they relied on a misleading statement contained in any of the SEC-required reports.

Registration of Brokers and Dealers. Brokers and dealers are required to register with the SEC under the Exchange Act unless exempted. A **dealer**, as defined by the 1934 Act, is a "person engaged in the business of buying and selling securities for his own account," whereas a **broker** is a person engaged in the business of "effectuating transactions in securities for the account of others." We use the convenient term *broker–dealer* throughout to refer to all those who trade in securities, and the specific term *broker* or *dealer* when only one type of trader is meant.

Broker–dealers must meet a financial responsibility standard that is based on a net capital formula; a minimum capital of $25,000 is required in most cases. Brokers are obliged to segregate customer funds and securities.

dealer A person engaged in the business of buying and selling securities for his or her own account.

broker A person engaged in the business of buying and selling securities for others' accounts.

Analysts or "Cheerleaders"? Conflicts of Interest

In July 2001, Merrill Lynch barred its stock analysts from investing in stock that they researched in order to prevent a potential conflict of interest. This was a reaction to several events:

- Individuals and members of Congress had lost confidence in analysts, particularly in an economy and market that had been in a turndown for 18 months. Never before had so many individual investors actually been invested in stocks and bonds and seen their paper wealth grow and then fall. The "party" appeared to be over for a time.

- Federal investigators were alleging the manipulation of Internet stock initial public offerings (IPOs) and the taking of kickbacks by investment bankers in July 2001.

- The same trading companies that had investment banking divisions that were floating new issuances of securities hired securities analysts to rank the securities of companies they were raising money for. The individual investor had begun to realize that there existed no "Chinese Wall" between stock analysts and investment bankers in the same brokerage firm. In fact, some companies gave stock analysts bonuses when they helped encourage investment banking business by giving stocks high ratings. For example, bullish ratings were so meaningless that "sell" ratings were less than 2 percent of all ratings shown, based on one study. In many cases stocks fell as much as 90 percent from their high before analysts removed "buy" ratings.* This could be called "cheerleading."

- Money managers who ran large mutual funds with money from IRAs, Keoghs, 401(k)s, and 403(b)s became skeptical of analysts as their investors, who tended to be passive in nature and dependent on them and on analysts, saw their retirement funds dwindling. Confidence in the money managers was lost by these investors.

While this assessment appeared gloomy, many investors argued that analysts should be encouraged to own stocks in the companies they do research in, believing that they should "put their money where their mouth is." Some argued that the very purpose of the securities laws is full disclosure, and that all analysts should be forced to disclose what holdings they have and to advise investors when they have a potential conflict of interest.

*"Stock Analysts Get Overall Rap for Deceiving Investors," *USA Today*, July 5, 2001, p. 10A.

Critical Thinking About the Law

1. There are any number of reasons why it might be a good idea for analysts to own stock in companies they are evaluating for clients. Can you suggest a couple of those reasons?

   Clue: Place yourself in the role of someone who is calling the analyst for advice. What are the advantages of your knowing that the analyst herself owns the stock she is recommending?

2. Now that you have spent some time thinking about the issue, surely you have some questions about the extent of the problem. What additional information would you need before you could be more confident about your position on this issue?

   Clue: Just how serious is this problem? Don't we need some evidence that the problem is one that is affecting many people or at least a few people in a major way?

The Securities Investor Protection Act (SIPA) provides a basis for indemnifying the customers of a brokerage firm that becomes insolvent: All registered brokers must contribute to a SIPA fund managed by the Securities Investor Protection Corporation (SIPC), a nonprofit corporation whose functions are to liquidate an insolvent brokerage firm and to protect customer investments up to a maximum of $500,000. Upon application to the SEC, SIPC can borrow up to $1 billion from the U.S. Treasury to supplement the fund when necessary.

Under Section 15(b) of the Exchange Act, which contains the antifraud provisions, the SEC may revoke or suspend a broker–dealer's registration or may censure a broker–dealer. (Municipal securities dealers and investment advisers are subject to similar penalties.) In general, the commission takes such actions against broker–dealers either for putting enhancement of their personal worth ahead of their professional obligation to their customers—conflict of interest—or for trading

EXHIBIT 22-4

ANNUAL REPORT FORM 10-K

Source: Securities Exchange Commission, Washington, D.C. Names, dates, company, and data are purely fictitious.

SECURITIES AND EXCHANGE COMMISSION
Washington, D.C. 20549

FORM 10-K
ANNUAL REPORT

PURSUANT TO SECTION 13 OR 15(d) OF THE SECURITIES EXCHANGE ACT OF 1934

Kubasek and Brennan, Inc.
(Exact name of registrant as specified in its charter)

Delaware
(State or other jurisdiction of incorporation or organization)
15999 McCutheonville Road
Pemberville, Ohio
(Address of principal executive officers)

(I.R.S. Employer Identification Number)
43450
(Zip Code)

(419) 654-4128
(Registrant's telephone number)
Securities registered pursuant to Section 12(b) of the Act:

Title of each class	Name of each exchange on which registered
Common Stock - Par Value $1 Per Share	New York Stock Exchange
	Pacific Coast Stock Exchange

Securities registered pursuant to Section 12(g) of the Act
4% Convertible Subordinated Debentures
(Title of class)
9 1/2% Sinking Fund Debentures originally
(Title of class)

Indicate by check mark whether the registrant (1) has filed all reports required to be filed by Section 13 or 15(d) of the Securities Exchange Act of 1934 during the preceding 12 months and (2) has been subject to such filing requirements for the past 90 days.
Yes X   No·

Indicate by check mark whether the registrant has filed all documents and reports required to be filed by Sections 12, 13 or 15(d) of the Securities Exchange Act of 1934 subsequent to the distribution of securities under a plan confirmed by a court.
Yes X   No·

The aggregate market value of Common Stock, Par Value $1 Per Share, held by non-affiliates (based upon the closing sale price of the New York Stock Exchange) was approximately $38,998,000.
As of August 31, 2000, there were 7,799,584 shares of Common Stock Par Value $1 Per Share, outstanding.

DOCUMENTS INCORPORATED BY REFERENCE

Portions of the definitive Proxy Statement for the Annual meeting of Stockholders are incorporated by reference into Part III.

SECURITIES AND EXCHANGE COMMISSION
Washington, D.C. 20549
FORM 10-Q
QUARTERLY REPORT UNDER SECTION 13 OR 15(d)
OF THE SECURITIES EXCHANGE ACT OF 1934

For Quarter Ended

Kubasek-Brennan, Inc.
(Exact name of registrant as specified in its charter)

DELAWARE
(State or other jurisdiction of
incorporation or organization)

_____
(I.R.S. Employer
Identification Number)

Kubasek-Brennan, Inc.
(address of principal executive officers and Zip code)

Registrant's telephone number, including area code (419) 654-4128

Indicate by check mark whether the registrant (1) has filed all reports required to be filed by Section 13 or 15(d) of the Securities Exchange Act of 1934 during the preceding 12 months (or for such shorter period that the registrant was required to file such reports), and (2) has been subject to such filing requirements for the past 90 days.
Yes _X_   No ___

Indicate the number of shares outstanding of each of the issuer's classes of common stock, as of the latest practicable date.

Class	Outstanding
Common Stock, par value 66-2/3¢ per share	7,020,531

KUBASEK-BRENNAN, INC.
INDEX

EXHIBIT 22-5

QUARTERLY REPORT FORM 10-Q

Source: Securities and Exchange Commission, Washington, D.C. The names, company, and data are purely fictitious.

in or recommending certain securities without having reliable information about the company. Broker–dealers are liable to both government and private action for failing to disclose conflicts of interest. When even the potential for such a conflict exists, a broker must supply a customer with written confirmation of each transaction, including full disclosure of whom the broker is representing in the transaction.

> **Fair Disclosure Rule: Chilling Effect of SEC Rule Making or "Leveling the Playing Field"?**
>
> Monday, October 23, 2000, was an important day for securities analysts. Regulation FD (Fair Disclosure) became effective. This new rule required companies to publicize all potentially market-moving data at the time that the data are available. No longer could such data be made available to certain analysts in a securities firm before being given to the public at large. Analysts traditionally followed one industry and were in frequent contact by phone or e-mail with its chief financial officers, investor relations officials, and often CEOs. By gaining bits of information from several companies in an industry, they were able to provide earning forecasts and then determine "buy," "sell," and "hold" ratings for the trading company they were employed by.
>
> For example, Hallie Frobose, an analyst for 17 years for Brennan and Kubasek Company, may have concentrated on companies that were involved in lumber and forest products. By making telephone calls in the pre–Regulation FD days, she could obtain financial factors off the record for hundreds of variables that might affect earnings expectations for a major company (e.g., Lumber Pacific). By constructing a model with all the important variables, and checking them with officers of the lumber company, recommendations could be made to Brennan and Kubasek's large investors. Not so for Hallie or her company following October, 2000.
>
> Regulation FD is now having a "chilling effect" on analysts and contacts they once had with corporate managers and has led to a decrease in the predictability of earnings reports like those of Hallie's. Market inefficiency is a result in the eyes of many.
>
> Those favoring Regulation FD argue the major purpose of our securities laws is full disclosure and that both large and small investors should have access to the same data, resulting in a "level playing field."

SECURITIES MARKETS

We defined a *security* earlier in this chapter as a stock or bond or any other instrument or interest that represents an investment in a common enterprise with reasonable expectations of profits derived solely from the efforts of people other than the investors. A security can also be considered a form of currency that, once issued, can be traded for other securities on what is called a securities market. We are concerned here with the markets for stocks and how they are regulated under the Exchange Act.

There are generally two types of markets in stocks: exchange and over-the-counter (OTC) markets. The **exchange market** provides for the buying and selling of securities within a physical facility such as the New York Stock Exchange (NYSE) or regional exchanges such as the Boston, Detroit, Midwest (Chicago), Pacific Coast (Los Angeles and San Francisco), and Philadelphia exchanges. These exchanges traditionally prescribed not only the number and the qualifications of their broker–members but also the commissions they could charge. In 1975, commissions were deregulated by the SEC and, since then, bro-

exchange market A securities market that provides a physical facility for the buying and selling of stocks and prescribes the number and qualifications of its broker–members. These brokers buy and sell stocks through the exchange's registered specialist, who are dealers on the floor of the exchange.

kers have been free to set the commissions they charge their customers. Brokers do not trade directly on an exchange market but rather transmit a customer's order to a registered specialist in a stock, who buys and sells that security for his or her own account on the floor of the exchange.

The **OTC (over-the-counter) market** has no physical facility—computers and telephones link OTC members—and no qualifications for membership. Its commissions have always been determined by the law of supply and demand. OTC firms serve as dealers or market makers in stocks and deal directly with the public.

over-the-counter (OTC) market A securities market that has no physical facility and no membership qualifications and whose broker–dealers are market makers who buy and sell stocks directly from the public.

Today the National Association of Securities Dealers (NASD) and the exchanges help the SEC to regulate the securities market. In enacting the Securities Exchange Act in 1934, Congress recognized that the stock exchanges had been regulating their members for 140 years and did not seek to dismantle their self-regulatory mechanisms. Rather, it superimposed the SEC on already existing self-regulatory bodies by requiring every "national securities exchange" to register with the SEC. Under Section 6(b) of the Exchange Act, an exchange cannot be registered unless the SEC determines that its rules are designed "to prevent fraudulent and manipulative acts and practices" and to discipline its members for any violations of its rules or the securities laws. Both the New York Stock Exchange—the most important exchange market in the nation—and the NASD have promulgated rules relating to stock transactions and qualifications for those participating in such transactions. In general, these rules are enforced by the self-regulating bodies.

To clarify the SEC's supreme role, Congress amended the Exchange Act in 1975 to give the SEC explicit authority over all self-regulatory organizations (SROs). Any exchange or OTC rule change now requires advance approval from the SEC. The commission also has reviewing power over all disciplinary actions taken by the SROs. Moreover, as we mentioned earlier, the 1975 amendments eliminated the power of exchanges to fix minimum commission rates.

Two legal questions have arisen concerning Congress's delegation of power to the SROs to adopt rules that have the force of law: (1) Can an exchange be held liable for damages resulting from its failure to enforce a rule it has adopted? and (2) Are SRO members who violate one of the organization's rules liable to a person injured by the violation? The courts have generally said yes to the first question and are split on the second.

Grasso at the Big Board: Success or Failure?

Richard Grasso resigned from the New York Stock Exchange (NYSE, or Big Board) as chairman on September 17, 2003, after it was disclosed by the *Wall Street Journal* that over a 36-year period he had built up a $139.5 million retirement pay package. NYSE's board of directors, floor traders, institutional investors, and politicians called for his resignation and a return of part of the moneys he had earned. The attorney general of the State of New York filed suit seeking a return in excess of $100 million. Grasso filed a counterclaim for $50 million against the attorney general, the Big Board, and the new chairman of the New York Stock Exchange. The countersuit, filed in July 2004, claimed that Grasso's contract was breached and his reputation besmirched (or defamed). The chairman of the SEC, which oversees the work of the NYSE, asked for a corporate governance overhaul. All this happened in the midst of a $1.4 billion settlement with Wall Street firms and analysts' apparent conflict of interest.[1] (See "Analysts or Cheerleaders?" in this chapter)"

Grasso had increased new stock listings on the NYSE and brought technological improvements to the Big Board in his role as a market CEO in order to allow it to compete with the NASDAQ. A conflict of interest may have lain in his second role as "chief regulator," using the power delegated to the NYSE by the SEC. His pay was set by a board of directors made up of CEOs of firms that the NYSE regulated. This apparent conflict of interest became more controversial after a proposal to make the NYSE itself a publicly traded corporation was first backed and then opposed by Grasso.[2]

Grasso was paid a CEO market salary rather than that of a regulator. His pay exceeded that of CEOs who were on the board of the NYSE. Some NYSE members saw another conflict of interest in that they were asked to pay $80 million in new fees for technology advances while the board of directors of the NYSE voted Grasso a pay package of $30 million for the year 2001 alone.[3]

---

[1] S. Labaton, "10 Wall Street Firms Settle with U.S. in Analysts Inquiry," *Wall Street Journal*, April 29, 2003, p. 1.
[2] L. Dugan, "NYSE Feels Heat from Inside and Outside," *Wall Street Journal*, September 8, 2003, p. 1C-1.
[3] *Id.*

PROXY SOLICITATIONS

Procedural and Substantive Rules. Section 14 of the Exchange Act and the accompanying SEC regulations set forth the ground rules governing proxy solicitations by inside management, dissident shareholders, and potential acquirers of a company. You will remember from our discussion in Chapter 16 that proxies are documents by which the shareholders of a publicly registered company designate another individual or institution to vote their shares at a shareholders' meeting. They are often used by inside management to defeat proposals by dissident shareholders or to prevent a takeover by a "hostile" company. The real significance of the proxy solicitation process, however, is that it may result in materially changing the direction of the corporation without its owners' (the shareholders') awareness. Because very few individual shareholders (under 1 percent) attend annual shareholders' meetings, proxy voting is management's major instrument for electing the directors and setting the policy it wants.

Against this background, Congress enacted Section 14 of the Exchange Act—the section known as the Williams Act—making it unlawful for a company to solicit proxies in "contravention of such rules and regulations as the Commission [SEC] may prescribe as necessary or appropriate in the public interest or for the protection of investors." With this broad statutory authority, the SEC has promulgated rules and regulations that require all companies registered under the Securities Act to file proxy statements with the commission ten days before mailing them to shareholders. During this ten-day period, the SEC staff comments on the statements and sometimes asks for changes, usually because it believes all material information has not been included. Under its Rule 22, the commission requires proxy statements to carry several items of information, ranging from a notice on the revocability of proxies to a notification of the interest that the soliciting individuals or institutions have in the subject matter to be voted on. The purpose of this procedure is to make sure that shareholders have full disclosure on a matter before they agree to any grant of their proxy. The SEC also requires companies to send shareholders a form on which they can mark their approval or disapproval of the subject matter to be voted on. If a proxy is solicited for electing new directors, the shareholders must receive an annual report of the corporation as well.

Shareholder Proposals. If a shareholder of a registered issuing company wishes to place an item on the agenda, Rule 14(a)(8) requires that management be notified in a timely way before a regular shareholder meeting or a special meeting. Once notified, management must include the proposal (200 words or fewer) in the proxy statement it sends to all the shareholders. Management may also include its own view on the proposal. Shareholder proposals in recent years have included prohibitions against discrimination, pollution, dumping of wastes, "golden parachutes," "poison pills," and "greenmail" (the last three topics are discussed later in this section under the heading "Remedies and Defensive Strategies"). In a sense, proxy solicitation became a form of "shareholder democracy"—one that corporate management felt was getting out of hand. After vigorous debate by all interested groups, the SEC amended Rule 14(a) in 1983 to allow management to exclude a shareholder proposal if:

1. Under the particular state law governing the corporation, the proposal would be unlawful if agreed to by the directors.
2. It involves a personal grievance.
3. It is related to ordinary operational business functions.
4. It is a matter not significantly related to the company's business. (The commission has defined this criterion as matters accounting for less than 5 percent of the assets, earnings, and sales of a company.)
5. The stockholder making the proposal has not owned more than $1,000 worth of stock or 1 percent of the shares outstanding for a period of one year or more. (Several shareholders may accumulate shares to meet this criterion.)
6. The shareholder proposal received less than 5 percent of the votes when submitted in a previous year. Furthermore, shareholders are limited to one proposal per annual company meeting.

If management excludes a proposal, it must explain why, and the shareholder may then appeal to the SEC. The SEC staff decides whether the proposal should be placed on the agenda for the next annual meeting.

Proxy Contests. Proxy contests normally come about when an insurgent group of shareholders seeks to elect its own slate of candidates to the board of directors to replace management's slate. Both insurgent shareholders and management may seek shareholder proxies in this contest.

The SEC has set out specific rules governing disclosure by insurgents and management and the rights of each. An information statement must be filed by the insurgents disclosing all participants in their group and the background of each, including past employment and any criminal history. When soliciting shareholder votes, insurgents must provide their own proxy statement, as must management. Insurgents have the right to obtain the company's shareholder list so they can mail their proxy statement directly to the shareholders. Alternatively, management must mail the insurgents' proxy request to the shareholders along with its own proxy statement, with the extra costs of the mailing borne by the insurgents.

Both criminal and civil liability attach to a company that sends a misleading proxy statement to its shareholders. The civil liability is based on a negligence standard (preponderance of evidence). The SEC may, through injunctive relief, prevent the solicitation of proxies or may declare an election of directors, based on misleading proxies, to be invalid. Under the Insider Trader Sanctions Act of 1984 (discussed later in this chapter), the commission may also institute criminal and administrative proceedings against a company. Furthermore, persons who rely on a misleading proxy statement to buy or sell securities have the right to institute a private action, as do insurgent shareholders in a proxy fight.

TENDER OFFERS AND TAKEOVER BIDS

A series of hostile takeovers in the 1990s, and creative defensive strategies used by management of some targeted companies, renewed concerned parties' interest in the regulation of tender offers and takeover bids.

tender offer A public offer by an individual or corporation made directly to the shareholders of another corporation in an effort to acquire the targeted corporation at a specific price.

In a takeover bid, the acquiring company or individual, using a public **tender offer**, seeks to purchase a controlling interest (51 percent) in another company—the target company—which would lead to a takeover of that company's board of directors and management. The acquiring company makes this public offer in such national newspapers as the *Wall Street Journal* or the *New York Times* to company shareholders, requesting that they tender their shares for cash or for the acquiring company's securities, or for both, usually at a price exceeding that quoted for the shares on a national exchange. Because of abuses in the 1960s, when shareholders frequently were given only a short time to make up their minds and, thus, could not properly evaluate tender offers, Congress enacted legislation to give shareholders more information and a longer period to make a decision. This legislation became Sections 13 and 14 of the Securities Exchange Act.

Rules Governing Tender Offers. Sections 13 and 14 of the Exchange Act together constitute the regulatory framework for tender offers. Section 13 requires any person (or group) that acquires more than 5 percent of any class of registered securities to file within ten days a statement with both the issuer (the target company) and the SEC. This statement must set forth (1) the background of the acquiring person or group, (2) the source of the funds used to acquire the 5 percent, (3) the purpose(s) of the acquisition of the stock, (4) the number of shares presently owned, (5) any relevant contracts with the target company, and (6) plans of the person or group for the targeted company.

Section 14 provides that no one may make a tender offer that results in ownership of more than 5 percent of a class of registered securities unless that person or group files with the SEC, and also with each offeree, a statement containing information similar to that required by Section 13. It also restricts the terms of the offer, particularly the right of withdrawal by the offerer and extensions or changes in the offer.

hostile bid A tender offer that is opposed by the management of the target company.

The SEC has issued detailed rules concerning Section 14. For example, even if the offer is a **hostile bid**—meaning the management of the target company opposes it—the target company must either mail the tender offer to all shareholders or promptly forward a list of the shareholders to the tender offerer. Management must also, within ten days of receiving a tender offer, state whether it opposes or favors it or lacks enough information to make a judgment. SEC rules also compel management to file a form called Schedule 14-9. Schedule 14-9 requires top managers to (1) disclose whether they intend to hold their shares in the company or tender them to the offerer; (2) describe any agreements they may have made with the tender offerer; and (3) disclose, if the tender offer is hostile, whether they have engaged in any negotiations with a friendly or "white knight" company.

Section 14 of the 1934 Act and SEC rules require that a tender offer be open for at least 20 days so shareholders will have a reasonable amount of time to consider it. The SEC has also set out certain withdrawal rights for shareholders who have tendered their shares.

REMEDIES AND DEFENSIVE STRATEGIES

Remedies. Section 14(e) (known as the Williams Act) makes it a criminal offense to make an untrue or misleading statement or to engage in fraudulent acts or deceptive practices in connection with a tender offer. The emphasis here is on intent to deceive. Shareholders of a targeted company can bring civil actions under Section 14(e) for violations of Sections 13(d) and 14(b) if they can show they have been injured because they relied on fraudulent statements in the tender offer. In addition, under the Insider Trader Sanctions Act (discussed later in this section under "Securities Fraud"), the SEC may start administrative proceedings against violators, which is a much quicker remedy than going to court.

In the landmark case that follows, in which the U.S. Supreme Court interpreted the meaning of Section 14(e) of the Securities Act, note the Court's concern over the correct interpretation of the word *manipulative*, which is the basis for causes of actions brought under this section.

CASE 22-3

Barbara Schreiber v. Burlington Northern, Inc.
United States Supreme Court
472 U.S. 1 (1985)

Petitioner Schreiber, on behalf of herself and other shareholders of El Paso Gas Company, sued respondent Burlington Northern, claiming that the company had violated Section 14(e) of the Securities Exchange Act of 1934. In December 1982, Burlington issued a hostile tender offer for El Paso Gas Company. Burlington did not accept the shares tendered by a majority of shareholders of El Paso but instead rescinded the December offer and substituted another offer for El Paso in January. The rescission of the first tender offer resulted in a smaller payment per share to El Paso shareholders who retendered after the January offer. The petitioners claimed that Burlington's withdrawal of the December tender offer and the substitution of the January offer were a "manipulative" distortion of the market for El Paso stock and a violation of Section 14(e). Respondent argued that "manipulative" acts under 14(e) require misrepresentation or nondisclosure and that no such acts had taken place in this case. Therefore, respondent moved for dismissal of the case based on a failure to state a cause of action. The federal district court granted the motion for dismissal. The court of appeals affirmed. Schreiber appealed to the U.S. Supreme Court.

Chief Justice Burger

We are asked in this case to interpret Section 14(e) of the Securities Exchange Act. The starting point is the language of the statute. Section 14(e) provides:

It shall be unlawful for any person to make any untrue statement of a material fact or omit to state any material fact necessary in order to make the statements made, in the light of the circumstances under which they are made, not misleading, or to engage in any fraudulent, deceptive or manipulative acts or practices, in connection with any tender offer or request or invitation for tenders, or any solicitation of security holders in opposition to or in favor of any such offer, request, or invitation. The Commission shall, for the purposes of this subsection, by rules and regulations define, and prescribe means reasonably designed to prevent, such acts and practices as are fraudulent, deceptive, or manipulative.

Our conclusion that "manipulative" acts under Section 14(e) require misrepresentation or nondisclosure is buttressed by the purpose and legislative history of the provision. Section

14(e) was originally added to the Securities Exchange Act as part of the Williams Act.

It is clear that Congress relied primarily on disclosure to implement the purpose of the Williams Act. Senator Williams, the bill's Senate sponsor, stated in the debate:

> *Today, the public shareholder in deciding whether to accept or reject a tender offer possesses limited information. No matter what he does, he acts without adequate knowledge to enable him to decide rationally what is the best course of action. This is precisely the dilemma which our securities laws are designed to prevent.*

The expressed legislative intent was to preserve a neutral setting in which the contenders could fully present their arguments. To implement this objective, the Williams Act added Sections 13(d), 13(e), 14(e), and 14(f) to the Securities Exchange Act. Some relate to disclosure; Sections 13(d), 14(d), and 14(f) all add specific registration and disclosure provisions. Others—Sections 13(e) and 14(d)—require or prohibit certain acts so that investors will possess additional time within which to take advantage of the disclosed information.

To adopt the reading of the term "manipulative" urged by petitioner would not only be unwarranted in light of the legislative purpose but would be at odds with it. Inviting judges to read the term "manipulative" with their own sense of what constitutes "unfair" or "artificial" conduct would inject uncertainty into the tender offer process. An essential piece of information—whether the court would deem the fully disclosed actions of one side or the other to be "manipulative"—would not be available until after the tender offer had closed. This uncertainty would directly contradict the expressed Congressional desire to give investors full information.

Congress's consistent emphasis on disclosure persuades us that it intended takeover contests to be addressed to shareholders. In pursuit of this goal, Congress, consistent with the core mechanism of the Securities Exchange Act, created sweeping disclosure requirements and narrow substantive safeguards. The same Congress that placed such emphasis on shareholder choice would not at the same time have required judges to oversee tender offers for substantive fairness.

We hold that the term "manipulative" as used in Section 14(e) requires misrepresentation or nondisclosure. It connotes "conduct designed to deceive or defraud investors by controlling or artificially affecting the price of securities." *Ernst Ernst v. Hochfelder*, 425 U.S., at 199. Without misrepresentation or nondisclosure, Section 14(e) has not been violated.

Applying that definition to this case, we hold that the actions of respondents were not manipulative. The amended complaint fails to allege that the cancellation of the first tender offer was accompanied by any misrepresentation, nondisclosure, or deception.

Affirmed in favor of Defendant, Burlington Northern.

Critical Thinking About the Law

Sometimes ambiguity is present in the court's own reasoning; a judge might argue that a "reasonable" person would not be offended by sexual advances made by a fellow employee. At other times, the court must interpret ambiguity in congressional legislation to make a legal judgment.

Case 22-3 deals with the second of those judicial confrontations with ambiguity. It is important to be aware not only of the Court's interpretation of an ambiguity but also of the evidence it selects in supporting that interpretation. The very fact that an important term is ambiguous means that there might be other legitimate interpretations; thus, in judging whether you agree with the particular interpretation at hand, you must evaluate the evidence presented for it. It is also important to recognize the primary ethical norm that informed the Court's interpretation. The following questions address those considerations.

1. **What legislative ambiguity was the Court dealing with in Case 22-3?**

    Clue: The meaning of this term is the central issue of the case.

2. **Specifically, to what evidence did the Court refer to support its own interpretation of the ambiguity?**

    Clue: Reread the paragraph immediately following the quotation from Section 14(e).

3. **In supporting its strict interpretation of legislative ambiguity, the Court stated that Congress intended to leave issues of fairness up to shareholders and not judges, making full disclosure the most important consideration. In this prioritization of the liberty (of shareholders) over potentially more just outcomes (allowing judges to decide fairness), one might argue that the primary ethical norm of liberty drove the Court's reasoning. What other primary ethical norm is implicit in this prioritization?**

    Clue: Consider the primary ethical norm that would be damaged if judges decided fairness (especially with the inevitable increase in court cases).

Defensive Strategies. The business judgment rule, which we discussed in Chapter 16, is based primarily on the 50 states' case law and the Revised Model Business Corporations Act. It has traditionally allowed wide latitude to managements of targeted companies, as long as they act in good faith in the best interests of the shareholders, do not waste the corporate assets, and do not enter into conflict-of-interest situations.

Here is a list of defensive strategies that managements of targeted companies have used to repel hostile takeovers in recent years.

- Awarding large compensation packages ("golden parachutes") to target-company management when a takeover is rumored.
- Issuing new classes of securities before or during a takeover battle that require a tender offerer to pay much more than the market price for the stock ("poison pill").
- Buying out a "hostile" shareholder at a price far above the current market price of the target company's stock in exchange for the hostile shareholder's agreement not to buy more shares for a period of time ("greenmail"). Congress has eliminated this defense by legislation.
- Writing supermajority requirements for merger approval into the bylaws and corporation articles ("porcupine provisions").
- Issuing treasury shares (stock that was repurchased by the issuing corporation) to friendly parties.
- Moving to states with strong antitakeover ("shark repellent") laws.
- Bankrupting the company ("scorched-earth" policy).
- Prevailing upon another company or individual (a "white knight") to buy out the hostile bidder to prevent the undesirable takeover.

SECURITIES FRAUD

The courts have had a difficult time defining securities fraud. An appellate court once stated: "Fraud is infinite, and were a Court of Equity once to lay down rules, how far they would go, and no further, in extending their relief against it, or to define strictly the species or evidence of it, the jurisdiction would be cramped, and perpetually eluded by new schemes which the fertility of man's invention would contrive." This is the philosophical position that has been adopted by the SEC: There cannot be a law against every type of fraud imaginable. Instead, the SEC staff has sought to use Section 10(b) of the Securities Act broadly, going beyond its exact language to develop a "fraud-on-the-market" theory that does not require the investor-plaintiff ever to have relied on false documents or specific acts but only on the integrity of the market and a fair stock price.

Section 10(b) of the Securities Exchange Act. One of the purposes of the Securities Exchange Act of 1934 was to ensure the full disclosure of all material information to potential investors. Full disclosure enables the market mechanism to operate efficiently and ensures that consumers are provided with a fair price for securities. Section 10(b) prohibits the use of the mails or other facilities (e.g., truck or car and satellite or data transmission) in interstate commerce "in connection with the purchase or sale of any security, any manipulative or deceptive device or contrivance in contravention of such rules and regulations as the Commission may prescribe as necessary or appropriate in the public interest or for the protection of investors." This board statutory language signals a congressional intent to cover all possible forms of fraud. To that end,

> *it shall be unlawful for any person, directly or indirectly, by the use of any means or instrumentality of interstate commerce, or of the mails, or of any facility of any national securities exchange, (1) to employ any device, scheme, or artifice to defraud, (2) to make any untrue statement of a material fact necessary in order to make the statements made, in the light of circumstances under which they were made, not misleading or (3) to engage in any act, practice, or course of business which operates or would operate as a fraud or deceit upon any person, in connection with the purchase or sale of any security.*

A private party's standing to sue under Section 10(b) and associated SEC Rule 10(b)-5 has been upheld in cases in which manipulative or deceptive acts were committed in connection with the purchase or sale of securities. The question of standing that the Supreme Court answers in the following case is whether civil liability under Rule 10(b)-5 extends also to those who aid and abet violators.

CASE 22-4

Central Bank of Denver, N.A. v. First Interstate Bank of Denver, N.A., and Jack K. Naber
United States Supreme Court
114 S.Ct. 1439 (1994)

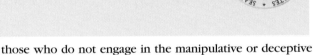

After a default on certain bonds it had purchased, plaintiff First Interstate Bank of Denver (Interstate) sued Central Bank of Denver (Central Bank), the public building authority, the bonds' underwriter, and the land developer. Interstate alleged that defendant Central Bank was secondarily liable under Rule 10(b)-5 for its conduct in aiding and abetting the other defendants' fraud. Because the other defendants were primarily liable, Central Bank moved for a summary judgment, claiming that a private plaintiff does not have standing to bring an aiding-and-abetting suit under Rule l0(b)-5. The federal district court granted summary judgment for Central Bank. The Tenth Circuit Court of Appeals reversed in favor of the plaintiff, setting forth three elements that must be present in such a Section l0(b) suit: (1) a primary violation of Section l0(b); (2) recklessness by the aider and abettor as to the primary violation; and (3) substantial assistance given to the primary violator by the aider and abettor. The defendant appealed.

Justice Kennedy

As we have interpreted it, Section l0(b) of the Securities Exchange Act of 1934 imposes private civil liability on those who commit a manipulative or deceptive act in connection with the purchase or sale of securities. In this case, we must answer a question reserved in two earlier decisions: whether private civil liability under Section l0(b) extends as well to

those who do not engage in the manipulative or deceptive practice but who aid and abet the violation.

We reach the uncontroversial conclusion, accepted even by those courts recognizing a Section 10(b) aiding and abetting cause of action, that the text of the 1934 Act does not itself reach those who aid and abet a Section 10(b) violation. Unlike those courts, however, we think that conclusion resolves the case. It is inconsistent with settled methodology in Section 10(b) cases to extend liability beyond the scope of conduct prohibited by the statutory text. To be sure, aiding and abetting a wrongdoer ought to be actionable in certain instances. The issue, however, is not whether imposing private civil liability on aiders and abettors is good policy but whether aiding and abetting is covered by the statute.

As in earlier cases considering conduct prohibited by Section 10(b), we again conclude that the statute prohibits only the making of a material misstatement (or omission) or the commission of a manipulative act. The proscription does not include giving aid to a person who commits a manipulative or deceptive act. We cannot amend the statute to create liability for acts that are not themselves manipulative or deceptive within the meaning of the statute.

From the fact that Congress did not attach private aiding and abetting liability to any of the express causes of action in the securities Acts, we can infer that Congress likely would not have attached aiding and abetting liability to Section 10(b) had it provided a private Section 10(b) cause of action. There is no reason to think that Congress would have attached aiding and abetting liability only to Section 10(b) and not to any of the express private rights of action in the Act. In *Blue Chip Stamps*, we noted that it would be "anomalous to impute to Congress an intention to expand the plaintiff class for a judicially implied cause of action beyond the bounds it delineated for comparable express causes of action." Here, it would be just as anomalous to impute to Congress an intention in effect to expand the defendant class for 10(b)-5 actions beyond the bounds delineated for comparable express causes of action.

Our reasoning is confirmed by the fact that respondents' argument would impose 10(b)-5 aiding and abetting liability when at least one element critical for recovery under 10(b)-5 is absent: reliance. A plaintiff must show reliance on the defendant's misstatement or omission to recover under 10(b)-5. Were we to allow the aiding and abetting action proposed in this case, the defendant could be liable without any showing that the plaintiff relied upon the aider and abettor's statements or actions. Allowing plaintiffs to circumvent the reliance requirement would disregard the careful limits on 10(b)-5 recovery mandated by our earlier cases.

Because the text of Section 10(b) does not prohibit aiding and abetting, we hold that a private plaintiff may not maintain an aiding and abetting suit under Section 10(b). The absence of Section 10(b) aiding and abetting liability does not mean that secondary actors in the securities markets are always free from liability under the securities Acts. Any person or entity, including a lawyer, accountant, or bank, who employs a manipulative device or makes a material misstatement (or omission) on which a purchaser or seller of securities relies may be liable as a primary violator under 10(b)-5, assuming all of the requirements for primary liability under Rule 10(b)-5 are met. In any complex securities fraud, moreover, there are likely to be multiple violators; in this case, for example, respondents named four defendants as primary violators.

Respondents concede that Central Bank did not commit a manipulative or deceptive act within the meaning of Section 10(b). Instead, in the words of the complaint, Central Bank was "secondarily liable under Section 10(b) for its conduct in aiding and abetting the fraud." Because of our conclusion that there is no private aiding and abetting liability under Section 10(b), Central Bank may not be held liable as an aider and abettor.

Reversed in favor of Defendant, Central Bank.

Critical Thinking About the Law

The significance of how we formulate issues cannot be overstated. The answers that we find are to a large extent molded by the questions that we ask. Suppose that you are a business manager who is responsible for employee evaluations. Suppose further that in evaluating each employee, you can ask but one of two questions: Does the employee work quickly? or Does the employee do quality work? For each employee, you will probably get very divergent answers depending on which question you ask. One employee may work very quickly but often has to redo assignments. Another employee may work more slowly, perhaps even to the point of missing deadlines, but still do superior work. Thus, the issue you formulate—that is, the question you ask—will be the decisive factor in determining which of these two employees you evaluate more favorably. Of course, in a normal evaluation process, you would likely pose both questions; however, for the sake of highlighting the importance of issue formulation, this either–or example is illuminating.

What a court decides is the issue of a case is crucial to the legal outcome of that case. Consequently, we will explore this function of the Court in the questions that follow.

1. **What issue did the Court seek to resolve in Case 22-4?**

   Clue: Reread the first paragraph of the decision.

2. **The lower court, in finding in favor of the plaintiff, based its judgment on a set of criteria. How did Justice Kennedy's formulation of the issue affect the significance of those criteria?**

   Clue: You want to focus on the fact that the two courts handed down opposite opinions.

3. **What key fact in the Securities Act's legislative history helped bolster the Supreme Court's decision that aiding and abetting liability did not properly come under the purview of the act?**

   Clue: Reread the fourth paragraph of Case 22-4, paying particular attention to private causes of action.

TABLE 22-4

SECURITIES FRAUD UNDER SECTION 10(B) OF THE SECURITIES EXCHANGE ACT OF 1934

Activity	*Definition*
Insider trading	The use of nonpublic information received from a corporate source by an individual(s) who has a fiduciary obligation to shareholders and potential investors and who benefits from trading on such information.
Misstatement of corporation	Any report, release, financial statement, or any other statement that is released by an officer, director, or employee of a corporation in connection with the purchase or sale of a security that shows an intent to mislead shareholders or potential investors.
Corporate mismanagement	Any transaction involving the purchase or sale of a security in which there is fraud based on an action of management. The plaintiff must be either a purchaser or a seller of securities in such transaction.

The use of Section 10(b) and Rule 10(b)-5 has been controversial in three major areas of securities fraud: insider trading, misstatements by corporate management, and mismanagement of a corporation (Table 22-4). After exploring each of these areas in turn, we will say something about a new concept that shareholder suits based on fraud have been invoking: "fraud-on-the-market" theory.

insider trading The use of material, nonpublic information received from a corporate source by someone who has a fiduciary obligation to shareholders and potential investors and who benefits from trading on such information.

Insider Trading and Section 10(b) of the Securities Act. Insider trading is the use of material, nonpublic information received from a corporate source by an individual who has a fiduciary obligation to shareholders and potential investors and who benefits from trading on such information. Insiders have been found by the courts to be (1) officers and directors of a corporation, (2) partners in investment banking and brokerage firms, (3) attorneys in a retained law firm, (4) underwriters and broker–dealers, (5) financial reporters, and (6) in a unique case, an employee of a financial printing firm that printed documents for a tender offer. (See Exhibit 22-6 for a look at Wall Street's army of insiders, from the general to the grunts.)

"Holy Toledo": Securities Fraud May Be Easy

On April 29, 1999, Martin Frankel, a high school graduate and a native of Toledo, Ohio, absconded with a reputed $335 million. A string of eight insurance companies in several southern states had provided Mr. Frankel with large sums of money to invest, in his capacity as founder of "Thunor Trust." The con was uncovered when the Franklin American Corporation, owner of these insurance companies, introduced Mr. Frankel as a prominent bond trader on April 28, 1999. After failing to attend a meeting with regulators, Mr. Frankel wired $334.6 million of Franklin American's money to a foreign bank account. Additionally, he burned all the documents at his Greenwich, Connecticut, mansion, creating a suspicious fire that led to a police search. He then fled to Europe, ending up in jail in Germany. After a period of six months, he was extradited to the United States and was convicted of fraud charges after pleading guilty. Five states are seeking roughly $215 million which Mr. Frankel is charged with stealing. Approximately $9 million was received at an auction of 822 diamonds seized from Mr. Frankel. On December 10, 2004, he was sentenced to a federal prison for 16 years, 6 months.

Unlike convicted felons Ivan Boesky and Michael Milken, Frankel was not a high-profile individual. The use of aliases and the pretension of being a multimillionaire were all that was required. The fact that he used state-regulated insurance companies in this case may have helped the scheme. The SEC and the Justice Department were not involved until he had fled the country.

Sources: L. Mergener, "Frankel Gets 16 Years for Fraud," _The Blade_, December 11, 2004, p. 1; A. Cowan, "Onetime Fugitive Gets 17 Years for Looting Insurers," _New York Times_, December 11, 2004, PB–3.

The expansion of targets in insider trading cases, from management and corporate directors to a _Wall Street Journal_ reporter and a printer employee, has resulted from the SEC enforcement staff's determination that in order to provide full disclosure in the marketplace for potential investors, it had to extend its jurisdiction over tippers (insiders) and tippees (those who receive tips from insiders). In the following case, the SEC staff was able to convince the U.S. Supreme Court that a misappropriation theory could be the basis for liability for insider trading. This theory holds that if an individual misappropriates information and trades on it for personal gain, that individual should be held liable for securities fraud.

THE INSIDERS

As part of their jobs, hundreds of people help to arrange mergers and buybacks that will push up stock prices once the deals become public. The process often begins in the executive suite, when chairpeople talk merger and bring in their top associates.
- Vice chairpeople
- General counsel
- Board of directors

INVESTMENT BANKERS

Any company involved in a merger hires a Wall Street bank, with its numerous specialists.
- Financial experts
- Research analysts
- Merger and acquisition teams

THE SUPPORTING CAST
- Law firms
- Public relations advisers
- Banks, bond dealers, lenders

ON THE EDGE

Many others get insider information from the key players. These are the friends and relatives of the deal makers. Arbitragers, who speculate on mergers, can end up as well informed as the key players through constant sleuthing.
- Proxy solicitors
- Printers
- Assistants

EXHIBIT 22-6

INSIDER TRADERS

Source: "Wall Street's Army of Insiders," reprinted from the _New York Times_, May 18, 1986, p. F1. Copyright © 1986 by The New York Times Company. Reprinted by permission.

CASE 22-5

United States v. James O'Hagan
United States Supreme Court
117 S. Ct. 2199 (1997)

After Grand Metropolitan PLC (Grand Met) retained the law firm of Dorsey & Whitney to represent it regarding a potential tender offer for the Pillsbury Company's common stock, respondent O'Hagan, a Dorsey & Whitney partner who did no work on the representation, began purchasing call options for Pillsbury stock, as well as shares of the stock. After Dorsey & Whitney had withdrawn from the representation, Grand Met publicly announced its tender offer, the price of Pillsbury stock rose dramatically, and O'Hagan sold his call options and stock at a profit of more than $4.3 million. A Securities and Exchange Commission (SEC) investigation culminated in a 57-count indictment alleging, *inter alia*, that O'Hagan had defrauded his law firm and its client, Grand Met, by misappropriating for his own trading purposes material, nonpublic information regarding the tender offer. The indictment charged O'Hagan with securities fraud in violation of Section 10(b) of the Securities Exchange Act of 1934 and SEC Rule 10(b)-5, with fraudulent trading in connection with a tender offer in violation of Section 14(e) of the Exchange Act and SEC Rule 14(e)-3(a), and with violations of the federal mail fraud and money-laundering statutes. A jury convicted O'Hagan on all counts, and he was sentenced to prison. The Eighth Circuit Court reversed all of the convictions, holding that Section 10(b) and Rule 10(b)-5 liability may not be grounded on the "misappropriation theory" of securities fraud on which the prosecution relied; that Rule 14(e)-3(a) exceeds the SEC's Section 14(e) rule-making authority because the rule contains no breach-of-fiduciary-duty requirement; and that the mail fraud and money-laundering convictions rested on violations of the securities laws, so could not stand once the securities fraud convictions were reversed.

Justice Ginsberg

This case concerns the interpretation and enforcement of Section 10(b) and Section 14(e) of the Securities Exchange Act of 1934, and rules made by the Securities and Exchange Commission pursuant to these provisions, Rule 10(b)-5 and Rule 14(e)-3(a). Two prime questions are presented. The first relates to the misappropriation of material, nonpublic information for securities trading; the second concerns fraudulent practices in the tender offer setting. In particular, we address and resolve these issues: (1) Is a person who trades in securities for personal profit, using confidential information misappropriated in breach of a fiduciary duty to the source of the information, guilty of violating Section 10(b) and Rule 10(b)-5? (2) Did the Commission exceed its rule-making authority by adopting Rule 14(e)-3(a), which proscribes trading on undisclosed information in the tender

offer setting, even in the absence of a duty to disclose? Our answer to the first question is yes, and to the second question, viewed in the context of this case, no.

A person who trades in securities for personal profit, using confidential information, misappropriated in breach of a fiduciary duty to the source of the information, may be held liable for violating Section 10(b) and Rule 10(b)-5.

(a) Section 10(b) proscribes (1) using any "deceptive device" (2) "in connection with the purchase or sale of any security," in contravention of SEC rules. The Commission adopted Rule 10(b)-5 pursuant to its Section 10(b) rule-making authority; liability under Rule 10(b)-5 does not extend beyond conduct encompassed by Section 10(b)'s prohibition. Under the "traditional" or "classical theory" of insider trading liability, a violation of Section 10(b) and Rule 10(b)-5 occurs when a corporate insider trades in his corporation's securities on the basis of material, confidential information he has obtained by reason of his position. Such trading qualifies as a "deceptive device" because there is a relationship of trust and confidence between the corporation's shareholders and the insider that gives rise to a duty to disclose or abstain from trading. Under the complementary "misappropriation theory" urged by the Government here, a corporate "outsider" violates Section 10(b) and Rule 10(b)-5 when he misappropriates confidential information for securities trading purposes, in breach of a fiduciary duty owed to the source of the information, rather than to the persons with whom he trades.

Misappropriation, as just defined, is the proper subject of a Section 10(b) charge because it meets the statutory requirement that there be "deceptive" conduct "in connection with" a securities transaction. First, misappropriators deal in deception: A fiduciary who pretends loyalty to the principal while secretly converting the principal's information for personal gain dupes or defrauds the principal. A company's confidential information qualifies as property to which the company has a right of exclusive use; the undisclosed misappropriation of such information constitutes fraud akin to embezzlement. Deception through nondisclosure is central to liability under the misappropriation theory. The theory is thus consistent with a decision underscoring that Section 10(b) is not an all-purpose breach of fiduciary duty ban, but trains on conduct that is manipulative or deceptive. Conversely, full disclosure forecloses liability. Because the deception essential to the theory involves feigning fidelity to the information's source, if the fiduciary discloses to the source that he plans to trade on the information, there is no "deceptive device" and thus no Section 10(b) violation. Second, Section 10(b)'s requirement that the misappropriator's deceptive use of information be "in connection with the purchase or sale of (a) security" is satisfied by the misappropriation theory because the fiduciary's fraud is consummated, not when he obtains the confidential information, but when, without disclosure to his principal, he uses the information in purchasing or selling securities. The transaction and the breach of duty coincide, even though the person or entity defrauded is not the other party to the trade, but is, instead, the source of the nonpublic information. Because undisclosed trading on the basis of misappropriated, nonpublic information both deceives the source of the information and harms members of the investing public, the misappropriation theory is tuned to an animating purpose of the Exchange Act: to ensure honest markets, thereby promoting investor confidence. It would make scant sense to hold a lawyer-turned-trader like O'Hagan a Section 10(b) violator if he works for a law firm representing the target of a tender offer, but not if he works for a firm representing the bidder.

The statute's text requires no such result. The Eighth Circuit erred in holding that the misappropriation theory is inconsistent with Section 10(b). First, that court understood the theory to require neither misrepresentation nor nondisclosure; as this Court explains, however, deceptive nondisclosure is essential to Section 10(b) liability under the theory. Concretely, it was O'Hagan's failure to disclose his personal trading to Grand Met and Dorsey, in breach of his duty to do so, that made his conduct "deceptive" under Section 10(b). Second, the Eighth Circuit misread this Court's precedents when it ruled that only a breach of a duty to parties to a securities transaction, or, at the most, to other market participants such as investors, is sufficient to give rise to Section 10(b) liability.

Vital to this Court's decision that criminal liability may be sustained under the misappropriation theory is the Exchange Act's requirement that the Government prove that a person "willfully" violated Rule 10(b)-5 in order to establish a criminal violation, and the Act's provision that a defendant may not be imprisoned for such a violation if he proves that he had no knowledge of the Rule. The requirement of culpable intent weakens O'Hagan's charge that the misappropriation theory is too indefinite to permit the imposition of criminal liability. The Eighth Circuit may address on remand O'Hagan's other challenges to his Section 10(b) and Rule 10(b)-5 convictions.

As relevant to this case, the SEC did not exceed its rule-making authority under Section 14(e) by adopting Rule 14(e)-3(a) without requiring a showing that the trading at issue entailed a breach of fiduciary duty. Section 14(e) prohibits "fraudulent ... acts ... in connection with any tender offer,"

and authorizes the SEC to "define, and prescribe means reasonably designed to prevent such acts." Adopted under that statutory authorization, Rule 14(e)-3(a) forbids any person to trade on the basis of material, nonpublic information that concerns a tender offer and that the person knows or should know has been acquired from an insider of the offeror or issuer, or someone working on their behalf, unless within a reasonable time before any purchase or sale such information and its source are publicly disclosed. Rule 14(e)-3(a) imposes a duty to disclose or abstain from trading whether or not the trader owes a fiduciary duty to respect the confidentiality of the information. In invalidating Rule 14(e)-3(a), the Eighth Circuit reasoned, *inter alia*, that Section 14(e) empowers the SEC to identify and regulate "fraudulent" acts, but not to create its own definition of "fraud"; that, under *Schreiber v. Burlington Northern, Inc.*, 472 U.S. 1, 7–8, Section 10(b) interpretations guide construction of Section 14(e); and that, under *Chiarella*, *supra*, at 228, a failure to disclose information can be "fraudulent" for Section 10(b) purposes only when there is a duty to speak arising out of a fiduciary or similar relationship of trust and confidence. This Court need not resolve whether the SEC's Section 14(e) fraud-defining authority is broader than its like authority under Section 10(b), for Rule 14(e)-3(a), as applied to cases of this genre, qualifies under Section 14(e) as a "means reasonably designed to prevent" fraudulent trading on material, nonpublic information in the tender offer contest. A prophylactic measure properly encompasses more than the core activity prohibited. Under Section 14(e), the SEC may prohibit acts not themselves fraudulent under the common law or Section 10(b), if the prohibition is reasonably designed to prevent acts and practices that are fraudulent. See *Schreiber*, *supra*, at 11 n. 11. In this case, the SEC's assessment is none of these. It is a fair assumption that trading on the basis of material, nonpublic information will often involve a breach of a duty of confidentiality to the bidder or target company or their representatives. The SEC, cognizant of proof problems that could enable sophisticated traders to escape responsibility for such trading, placed in Rule 14(e)-3(a) a "disclose or abstain from trading" command that does not require specific proof of a breach of fiduciary duty. Insofar as it serves to prevent the type of misappropriation charged against O'Hagan, the Rule is therefore a proper exercise of the SEC's prophylactic power under Section 14(e). This Court declines to consider in the first instance O'Hagan's alternate arguments that Rule 14(e)-3(a)'s prohibition of preoffer trading conflicts with Section 14(e) and violates due process. The Eighth Circuit may address on remand any such argument that O'Hagan has preserved.

Reversed and remanded in favor of Plaintiff, United States.

Misstatements of Corporations and Section 10(b). The second area of controversy to which Section 10(b) applies involves statements by corporate executives. Any report, release, or financial statement or any other statement that

Linking Law & Business

Economics

Efficient Markets

In microeconomics, you learned that the law of supply and demand brings about equilibrium price levels, assuming a free flow of information and mobility of resources. These factors will bring about efficient markets.

Microeconomics presents an important link to securities law. When plaintiffs argue a fraud-on-the-market theory, they are arguing that there is a distortion or omission of information and, thus, the purchase or sale of the security is subject to fraud and a violation of securities law. As noted in the *O'Hagan* case, the United States Supreme Court has accepted this theory (right or wrong depending on your view).

scienter Knowledge that a representation is false.

sets forth material information (information that would affect the judgment of the average prudent investor) falls within Section 10(b).

Whereas Sections 13 and 14 of the Exchange Act, which we discussed earlier, apply only to reports, proxy statements, and other documents filed by a company registered with the SEC and a national exchange, Rule 10(b)-5 applies to any statement made by any issuer, registered or not. To be considered a securities fraud, corporate misstatements must meet two requirements: (1) They must be issued "in connection with the purchase or sale of any security," and (2) there must be a showing of **scienter** (intent). As you read the landmark case set out here, you should try to determine how closely the defendants met those requirements.

CASE 22-6

Securities and Exchange Commission v. Texas Gulf Sulphur Company
United States Court of Appeals
401 F.2d 833 (2d Cir. 1968)

The SEC (plaintiff) brought an action against the Texas Gulf Sulphur Company (TGS) and 13 of its directors, officers, and employees (defendants) for violation of Section 10(b) of the Exchange Act and SEC Rule 10(b)-5, seeking an injunction against further misleading press releases and requesting rescission of defendants' purchases and stock options. On June 6, 1963, TGS had acquired an option to buy 160 acres of land in Timmons, Ontario. On November 11, 1963, preliminary drilling indicated there would be major copper and zinc finds. TGS acquired the land and resumed drilling on March 31, 1964, and by April 8, it was evident that there were substantial copper and zinc deposits. On April 9, Toronto and New York newspapers reported that TGS had discovered "one of the largest copper deposits in America." On April 12, TGS's management said that the

rumors of a major find were without factual basis. At 10 A.M. on April 14, the board of directors authorized the issuance of a statement confirming the copper and zinc finds and announcing the discovery of silver deposits as well. On April 20, the New York Stock Exchange announced that it "was barring stop orders [orders to brokers to buy a stock if its price rises to a certain level to lock in profits in case of a sharp rally in that stock] in Texas Gulf Sulphur" because of the extreme volatility in the trading of the stock.

Approximately one month later, rumors circulated about insider trading. It was later found that when drilling began on November 12, 1963, TGS's directors, officers, and employees owned only 1,135 shares of stock in the company and had no calls (options to purchase shares at a fixed price). By March 31, 1964, when drilling resumed, insiders (tippers) and their tippees had acquired an additional 7,100 shares and 12,300 calls. On February 20, 1964, TGS had issued stock options to three officers and two other employees as part of a compensation package. From April 9, 1964, to April 14, 1964, when the confirmatory press release was issued, ten insiders and their tippees made estimated profits of $273,892 on the purchase of their shares or calls of TGS stock. The federal district court dismissed charges against all but two defendants. Those defendants, Clayton and Crawford, appealed, and the SEC appealed from that part of the district court decision that had dismissed the complaint against TGS and the nine other individual defendants.

Judge Waterman

Rule 10(b)-5 was promulgated pursuant to the grant of authority given the SEC by Congress in Section 10(b) of the Securities Exchange Act of 1934. By that Act Congress proposed to prevent inequitable and unfair practices and to ensure fairness in securities transactions generally, whether conducted face-to-face, over the counter, or on exchanges. The Act and the Rule apply to the transactions here, all of which were consummated on exchanges.

The essence of the Rule is that anyone who, trading for his own account in the securities of a corporation, has "access, directly or indirectly, to information intended to be available only for a corporate purpose and not for the personal benefit of anyone" may not take "advantage of such information knowing it is unavailable to those with whom he is dealing," i.e., the investing public. Insiders, as directors or management officers, are, of course, by this Rule, precluded from so unfairly dealing, but the Rule is also applicable to one possessing the information who may not be strictly termed an "insider" within the means of Sec. 10(b) of the Act. Thus, anyone in possession of material inside information must either disclose it to the investing public, or, if he is disabled from disclosing it in order to protect a corporate confidence, or he chooses not to do so, must abstain from trading in or recommending the securities concerned while such insider information remains undisclosed. So, it is here no justification for insider activity that disclosure was forbidden by the legitimate corporate objective of acquiring options to purchase the land surrounding the exploration site; if the information was, as the SEC contends, material, its possessors should have kept out of the market until disclosure was accomplished.

As we stated in *List v. Fashion Park, Inc.*, "The basic test of materiality is whether a reasonable man would attach importance in determining his choice of action in the transaction in question." This, of course, encompasses any fact "which in reasonable and objective contemplation might affect the value of the corporation's stock or securities." Such a fact is a material fact and must be effectively disclosed to the investing public prior to the commencement of insider trading in the corporation's securities. The speculators and chartists of Wall and Bay Streets are also "reasonable" investors entitled to the same legal protection afforded conservative traders. Thus, material facts include not only information disclosing the earnings and distributions of a company but also those facts which affect the probable future of the company and those which may affect the desire of investors to buy, sell, or hold the company's securities.

The core of Rule 10(b)-5 is the implementation of the Congressional purpose that all investors should have equal access to the rewards of participation in securities transactions. It was the intent of Congress that all members of the investing public should be subject to identical market risks—which market risks include, of course, the risk that one's evaluative capacity or one's capital available to put at risk may exceed another's capacity or capital. The insiders here were not trading on an equal footing with the outside investors. They alone were in a position to evaluate the probability and magnitude of what seemed from the outset to be a major ore strike; they alone could invest safely, secure in the expectation that the price of TGS stock would rise substantially in the event such a major strike should materialize, but would decline little, if at all, in the event of failure, for the public, ignorant at the outset of the favorable probabilities, would likewise be unaware of the unproductive exploration, and the additional exploration costs would not significantly affect TGS market prices. Such inequities based upon unequal access to knowledge should not be shrugged off as inevitable in our way of life, or, in view of the congressional concern in the area, remain uncorrected.

We hold, therefore, that all transactions in TGS stock or calls by individuals apprised of the drilling results of K-55-1 were made in violation of Rule 10(b)-5.

Reversed and remanded in favor of Plaintiff, SEC.

Corporate Mismanagement and Section 10(b). The third controversial area of securities fraud under Section 10(b) is corporate mismanagement. Suits alleging corporate mismanagement and fraud brought by minority shareholders in class action or derivative suits must prove three elements: (1) that the transaction being attacked (e.g., the sale of a controlling stock interest in a corporation at a premium) involves the purchase or sale of securities, (2) that the alleged fraud is in connection with a purchase or sale, and (3) that the plaintiff is either a purchaser or a seller of securities in the transaction involved. The *Hochfelder* case, referred to in the *Schreiber* case, is an example of fraud perpetrated on shareholders by management. Other cases alleging fraud dealing with reorganizations and mergers have been brought, but since the mid-1970s, the Supreme Court has been reluctant to allow cases brought under Section 10(b) to preempt state laws and, thus, has made plaintiffs meet all three elements in an exacting manner.

Fraud-on-the-Market Theory and Section 10(b). The Supreme Court has attached stringent criteria to all private-party actions brought under Section 10(b)-5 and SEC Rule 10(b)-5. Defrauded investors generally need to show that their losses resulted from specific conduct of the company or its employees or agents and that they had relied on specific misstatements, omissions, or fraudulent actions in making investment decisions. Shareholders have more recently used an efficient-market concept as the basis for suits claiming fraud. That is, they have alleged that they relied on the integrity of an efficient market to assimilate all information about a company and to reflect this information in a fair price for securities. The plaintiff in such a suit argues that when a company makes fraudulent disclosures or omissions, it distorts the information flow to the market and, thus, fixes the price of the company's securities too high, in violation of Section 10(b) and Rule 10(b)-5. This fraud-on-the-market theory assumes that the market price reflects all known material information. In a landmark decision (*United States v. O'Hagan*, presented earlier in this chapter) the U.S. Supreme Court upheld this theory.

LIABILITY AND REMEDIES UNDER THE 1934 EXCHANGE ACT

Criminal Penalties. Violations of Section 10(b) and Rule 10(6) may lead individuals to be fined up to $5 million and imprisoned up to 20 years or both under the Sarbanes-Oxley Act discussed earlier in this chapter. A partnership or corporation may be fined $25 million for a proven willful violation. The violator may be imprisoned for 25 years, plus a fine. The SEC must refer all criminal action to the Justice Department.

SEC Action. Under the Insider Trading Sanctions Act of 1984[8] and the Insider Trading and Securities Enforcement Act of 1988 the SEC may sue civilly anyone violating or aiding or abetting, a violation of the 1934 Act or an SEC rule by purchasing or selling a security while in possession of material nonpublic information. Violations must occur on or through a national securities exchange or from or through a broker or dealer. If held liable, the court may triple (treble) the profits that are gained illegally.

The Insider Trading and Securities Fraud Enforcement Act of 1988 enlarged the class of people who may be subject to civil liability for insider trading. Also, bonus payments can be given to anyone providing information leading to the prosecution of insider trading violations.[9]

Private Actions. Private parties may sue violators under Rule 10-5 and Section 10(b). Such potential violators include accountants, attorneys, and others who aid and abet violations of Section 10(6). As noted later in this chapter, a corporation can bring an action to recover short-swing profits under Section 16(b). Under Section 10(6) a private plaintiff may seek rescission of a securities

---

[8] 15 U.S.C. Section 78u(d)(2)(A).
[9] 15 U.S.C. Section 78u-1.

contract or recover damages for breach disgorgements of illegal profits gained. In the excerpted case that follows the United States Supreme Court emphasizes the role of a private plaintiff in securities fraud violation.

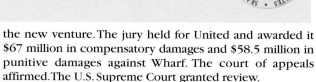

CASE 22-7

The Wharf (Holdings) Limited v. United International Holdings, Inc.
U.S. Supreme Court
121 S.et.1776 (2001)

United International Holding, Inc., sued the Wharf (Holdings) Limited in federal district court for securities fraud for violating Section 10(b) and Rule 10(6)-5 of the 1934 Exchange Act.

The Wharf (Holdings) Limited is a Hong Kong firm that was interested in obtaining a license to operate a cable television system in Hong Kong. In 1991, the Hong Kong government announced that it would accept bids for the award of an exclusive license to operate a cable television system in Hong Kong. Wharf decided to find a business partner with cable system experience. Wharf located United International Holdings, Inc., a Colorado-based company with substantial experience in operating cable television systems. Wharf orally agreed to grant United an option to buy 10 percent of the stock of the new Hong Kong cable system if Wharf was awarded the license.

In May 1993, Hong Kong awarded the cable franchise to Wharf. When United raised $66 million and tried to exercise its option to invest 10 percent in the new cable company, Wharf refused to permit United to buy any of the new company's stock. Documents and other evidence showed that at the time Wharf granted United the oral 10 percent stock option, it had not intended to ever sell United any stock in the new venture. The jury held for United and awarded it $67 million in compensatory damages and $58.5 million in punitive damages against Wharf. The court of appeals affirmed. The U.S. Supreme Court granted review.

Justice Breyer

Wharf points out that its agreement to grant United an option to purchase shares in the cable system was an oral agreement. And it says that Section 10(b) does not cover oral contracts of sale. There is no convincing reason to interpret the Act to exclude oral contracts as a class. The Act itself says that it applies to "any contract" for the purchase or sale of a security. Oral contracts for the sale of securities are sufficiently common that the Uniform Commercial Code and statutes of frauds in every State now consider them enforceable. To sell an option while secretly intending not to permit the option's exercise is misleading, because a buyer normally presumes good faith. Since Wharf did not intend to honor the option, the option was, unbeknownst to United, valueless.

Affirmed for Plaintiff, United.

SHORT-SWING PROFITS

Purpose and Coverage. Section 16(b) of the Exchange Act seeks to further the goal of complete disclosure of trading by insiders by requiring directors, officers, and owners of more than 10 percent of a class of stock of a registered company to file regular reports with the SEC and the exchanges the stock trades on. Directors and officers must file an initial statement of their holdings in the company when they take office, and the others must file when they come to own more than 10 percent. A follow-up statement is due monthly if they change their holdings in any manner. Any profits made by a director or officer or a 10 percent beneficial owner as a result of buying and selling the securities within a six-month period—known as **short-swing profits**—are presumed to be based on insider information. A plaintiff does not have to show that these insiders had access to, relied on, or took advantage of the insider information. In 1991, the SEC adopted new rules relating to Section 16 that (1) created a new form (Form 5) that must be filed by all insiders within 45 days of the end of the issuer's calendar year; (2) waive liability for insiders for transactions that occur within six months of becoming an insider;

short-swing profits Profits made by directors, officers, or owners of 10 percent of the securities of a corporation as a result of buying and selling the securities within a six-month period.

(3) make the acquisition of a derivative security (e.g., warrant) fall under Section 16; and (4) define an officer under Section 16 as people who have a policy function (e.g., chief executive officer, president, and vice president). Now those company officers who handle day-to-day operations do not fall under Section 16. **Liability.** Suits based on short-swing profits seek to force the insiders to return the profits to the corporation. Only the issuers—meaning the directors and officers of the corporation—and the shareholders have standing to sue. Officers and directors generally do not sue other officers and directors, so virtually all suits are brought by other shareholders. However, the expense of such litigation makes use of this enforcement action infrequent.

REGULATION OF INVESTMENT COMPANIES

With the growth of investment companies (e.g., hedge funds and mutual funds) and mutual funding, professionals are now managing huge portfolios. The Investment Company Act of 1940 provided for SEC regulation. It was expanded and amended in 1970, 1975, and 1995. The 1995 National Securities Market Improvement Act limited regulation of investment companies to the SEC and did away with most of the states' authority.

All investment companies must register with the SEC and file yearly reports. All company assets must be held in a bank or with a stock exchange member and be handled according to SEC procedures.

REFORMS OF MUTUAL FUNDS UNDER THE 1940 INVESTMENT COMPANY ACT

Several new and proposed SEC rules have come forward in light of abuses uncovered in 2003 by the commission and the attorney general of New York. Mutual fund companies such as Alliance Capital, Strong Capital, and Pilgrim Baxter (PBGH)[10] were accused of insider trading when rapid trading ("market timing") was allowed contrary to oral or written company policy. Additionally, mutual fund companies were allowing postclosing (4 P.M. EST) trading for select investors in violation of SEC regulations. Settlements took place with state and federal authorities amounting to millions of dollars.

A list of reforms has been enacted by the SEC:

- Requirement of an independent chairperson of each fund has been adopted. The new rule requires 75 percent of each fund's directors be independent. The question remains as to what the requirements are for "independence".

- Customers must sign a statement just before a sale, which would reveal any "soft dollar" costs charged to a fund that were previously hidden.

- A fund will have to reveal its conduct if it steers stock traders to a certain brokerage in exchange for rebates to buy the firm's investment research ("soft dollar").

- A proposal under discussion would modify the manner in which funds estimate their daily net asset value (NAV).

---

[10] R. Abelson and R. Allas, "Pilgrim Baxter Founders Accused of Fraud," *New York Times*, November 21, 2003, p. C11.

Reforms for Mutual Funds

Proposal	Status
Independent chairman and independent directors (75 percent) required	Adopted
Disclosure of hidden fees at point of sale	Adopted
Ban on hidden deals with brokers who sell funds	Adopted
Compliance officer required, and a code of ethics	Adopted

For each of these proposals and rules, it should be noted that there will be a cost to the shareholder of the mutual fund affected. For example, the independent director must be paid, and the premiums on liability insurance for independent directors (D&O) must be included in the cost of shares of the fund. These costs will be passed on to the consumer–shareholder in some form.

STATE SECURITIES LAWS

State securities laws are often referred to as "blue sky" laws. They regulate securities purchased and sold in intrastate commerce. Securities are regulated (concurrently) by both state and federal laws. State laws require that securities be registered (or qualified) with both federal and state authorities. There is usually a state official or office so designated. State disclosure requirements and antifraud provisions are similar to each other and their federal counterparts, for example, Securities Exchange Act of 1934, SEC Rule 10(b), and Section 10(b).

The Uniform Securities Act has been adopted in part by some states in order to bring uniformity to state security laws. The 1995 National Securities Market Improvement Act limited regulation of investment companies to the SEC and did away with some state authority.

E-COMMERCE, ONLINE SECURITIES DISCLOSURE, AND FRAUD REGULATION

MARKETPLACE OF SECURITIES

The Internet is now used daily to register securities. Online initial public offering (IPOs) are a frequent occurrence that has brought efficiency (in economic terms) to the marketplace of securities. Small companies in particular use the Internet to avoid paying commissions to brokers or underwriters. Regulation A, discussed in this chapter, allows a simple method of registration.

In addition to using the Internet to provide information (e.g., 10-K) to the SEC as required by the 1933 and 1934 Acts, as well as others, potential investors receive information more rapidly and are willing to take advantage of this to purchase or sell securities. Online filings of many documents with the SEC are now routine matters for most large corporations, which benefit by the additional time given to them that did not exist when "snail mail" was used.

Furthermore, investors and companies can take advantage of the Electronic Data Gathering Analysis and Retrieval (EDGAR) database, which includes proxy statements, annual corporate reports, and a multitude of documents that are filed with the commission. All of this allows the SEC to accomplish its goal of full disclosure.

E-COMMERCE AND FRAUD IN THE MARKETPLACE

The SEC continues to deal with fraud in the marketplace via the Internet. Chat rooms have become a place in the cyberworld that are locations for violation of the 1933 and 1934 Securities Acts. Often a stock price is "pumped up" as a result of information obtained in chat rooms. After it is "pumped," it will be "dumped" quickly. The SEC has been tracing such actions that seek to manipulate stock prices in violation of the 1934 Exchange Act. As noted in our discussion of the Sarbanes-Oxley Act, penalties can be costly, not only in dollar terms, but also in possible prison time.

GLOBAL DIMENSION OF RULES GOVERNING THE ISSUANCE AND TRADING OF SECURITIES

The growing internationalization of money and securities markets has made it important to understand the transnational reach of U.S. securities regulations. Both the 1933 Act and the Exchange Act speak of the use of "facilities or instrumentation in interstate commerce." Interstate commerce is defined in the 1933 Act to include "commerce between any foreign country and the United States."

This section of the chapter is divided into two parts: (1) legislation prohibiting certain forms of bribery and money laundering overseas by United States–based corporations and (2) legislation governing foreign securities sold in the United States. You will notice throughout our discussion that provisions of the 1933 Act and the 1934 Exchange Act overlap.

LEGISLATION PROHIBITING BRIBERY AND MONEY LAUNDERING OVERSEAS

The Foreign Corrupt Practices Act (FCPA) of 1977 as Amended in 1988. In the course of investigating illegal corporate payments made to President Nixon's 1972 reelection campaign, the SEC staff came across information showing that hundreds of corporations had also made questionable payments to foreign political parties, heads of state, and individuals to obtain business that they would not otherwise have gained. The companies argued that these payments were not illegal under U.S. law, and besides, they were necessary to compete with foreign state-owned and -operated enterprises and with state-subsidized multinationals. The SEC, however, considered this information material under both the 1933 and 1934 securities acts because it affected the integrity of management and the records of the corporations involved. In 1974 and 1975, the SEC allowed approximately 435 companies to enter into consent orders whereby the companies did not admit to making illegal payments but agreed to report such payments in the future to the SEC. The SEC also urged Congress to enact legislation prohibiting bribery overseas by U.S. corporations.

The Foreign Corrupt Practices Act of 1977 (FCPA), as amended in 1988, does just that. It applies both to companies registered under the securities acts of 1933 and 1934 and to all other domestic concerns, whether they do business abroad or not. Its antibribery provisions prohibit all domestic firms from offering or authorizing a "corrupt" payment to a foreign official, a foreign political party, or a foreign political candidate to induce the recipient to act, or to refrain from acting, so that a U.S. corporation can obtain business it would not ordinarily get without the payment. The standard of criminal conduct to which corporate officials and employees are held is "knowing." If such a payment is known to violate the FCPA, the corporation can be fined up to $2 million, and its officers, directors, stockholders, employees, and U.S. agents can be fined up to $100,000 and be imprisoned for up to five years. The FCPA prohibits not just the payment of a bribe but also the "offer" or "promise" of "anything of value," even if the offer or promise is never consummated. "Facilitating or expediting payments" to ensure routine governmental action is not prohibited. Also, under the 1988 amendments, liability can be avoided if the defendant proves that the payments were legal in the foreign country where they were made.

The FCPA's accounting provisions, enacted as amendments to Section 13(b) of the Exchange Act, apply only to registered nonexempt companies. They require that companies make and keep records and accounts in "reasonable detail" that "accurately and fairly" reflect transactions. Also, companies are required to maintain systems that provide "reasonable assurance" that transactions have been recorded in accordance with generally accepted accounting principles.

The FCPA is jointly enforced by the Justice Department and the SEC. The SEC can investigate and bring civil charges under the act's bribery provisions, but it refers criminal cases to the Justice Department for prosecution. The Justice Department can bring both civil and criminal charges against alleged violators of the FCPA. The SEC is charged with the enforcement of the accounting provisions and can bring both civil actions and administrative proceedings.

Convention on Combating Bribery of Foreign Officials in International Business Transactions (CCBFOIBT). In 1977, the U.S. Foreign Corrupt Practices Act was enacted. It was amended in 1988 to water down the original act. Twenty years later, the CCBFOIBT was signed in December 1997 by 34 countries after debate by the Organization for Economic Cooperation and Development (OECD). Signatories will be required to criminalize bribery of foreign officials, eliminate the tax deductibility of bribes, and subject companies to wider disclosure. Russia (an observer) and China are not signatories; the 34 signatories include the United States, Canada, Japan, and Germany. The treaty creates one loophole: "grease payments." It is acknowledged that these facilitating payments are the cost of doing business and can be paid to low-level officials.

The major change for the United States will be the need to amend the FCPA to cover foreign subsidiaries of U.S. companies whose activities have a nexus with interstate or foreign commerce. Under current U.S. law, such subsidiaries are not subject to the FCPA.

The International Securities Enforcement Cooperation Act (ISECA) of 1990. After it was found that many insider traders in the United States were holding secret accounts in Switzerland, the SEC in June 1982 entered into a memorandum of understanding with the Swiss government that established a procedure for processing SEC requests for information about Swiss bank clients suspected of insider trading. As reports of overseas "money laundering" of profits made from insider trading in the United States mounted throughout the late 1980s, the SEC encouraged Congress to clarify the commission's authority to act, not only against those who were sheltering their profits from illegal insider trading in foreign countries but also against others who were violating U.S. securities laws abroad.

In 1990, Congress passed the International Securities Enforcement Cooperation Act (ISECA). The most important provisions of this act are as follows:

1. It provides for giving foreign regulators U.S. government documents and information needed to trace laundered money and those suspected of doing the laundering.

2. It exempts from the Freedom of Information Act (FOIA) disclosure requirements documents given to the SEC by foreign regulators. Without this exemption, foreign regulators would be reluctant to provide U.S. regulators with information, and alleged violators could obtain information too easily.

3. It gives the SEC authority to impose administrative sanctions on buyers and dealers who engage in activities that are illegal under U.S. law while they are in foreign countries.

4. It authorizes the SEC to investigate violations of all U.S. securities laws that occur in foreign countries.

LEGISLATION GOVERNING FOREIGN SECURITIES SOLD IN THE UNITED STATES

Schedule B of the Securities Act of 1933 sets forth disclosure requirements for initial offerings by foreign issuers of stock on U.S. exchanges. Foreign issuers are entitled to some of the same exemptions in this area as domestic issuers, except that exemptions under Regulation A are granted only to U.S. and Canadian issuers. Also, the SEC has special registration forms for initial foreign offerings. In Section 12(g)(3) of the Exchange Act, Congress gave the SEC power to exempt foreign issuers whose securities are traded on U.S. exchanges or the OTC markets from certain registration requirements if the commission believed such action would be in the public interest. Under SEC Rule 12(g)(3)-2, the securities of a foreign issuer are exempt from annual and current reports if the issuer or its government furnishes the SEC with annual information material to investors that is made public in the issuer's own country. In 1983, the commission published a list of exemptions for foreign-issued securities and adopted regulations that generally require foreign securities that are registered under the Exchange Act to be quoted also on the National Association of Securities Dealers Authorized Quotations (NASDAQ).

SUMMARY

The Securities and Exchange Commission (SEC) is the federal agency responsible for overseeing the securities markets and enforcing federal securities legislation.

Several pieces of legislation provide the framework for the federal regulation of securities issuance and trading, but the most important are the Securities Act of 1933 and the Securities Exchange Act of 1934, and the most recent addition with the Sarbanes-Oxley Act, which amends both the 1933 and 1934 acts, and other pieces of federal legislation.

The Securities Act of 1933 seeks to ensure that investors receive full and fair disclosure of all material information about a new stock issue. It prescribes a three-stage registration process for new securities: prefiling, filing, and postfiling. Several types of securities are exempt from registration, principally private placements, intrastate offerings, and small business offerings.

The Securities Exchange Act of 1934 governs six areas of securities trading: the registration of securities issuers and broker–dealers, securities markets, proxy solicitations, tender offers and takeover bids, securities fraud, and short-swing profits. Provisions of the act dealing with securities fraud include insider trading, misstatements by corporate management, and mismanagement of a corporation.

The more recent reforms adopted, or under consideration, by the SEC with regard to the mutual funds industry may have long-lasting implications. The e-commerce world has made online investing via the Internet a common occurrence. The SEC, with the help of EDGAR, has sought to modernize, assisting both investors and issuing companies.

The increasing internationalization of securities markets has led Congress and the SEC to extend the reach of U.S. securities regulations through specific agreements with foreign governments and through provisions of the Foreign Corrupt Practices Act and the International Securities Enforcement Cooperation Act.

REVIEW QUESTIONS

22-1 Describe the differences between the national exchanges (e.g., the New York Stock Exchange) and the over-the-counter markets (OTC).

22-2 Explain what is meant by shelf registration of securities.

22-3 Under the proxy rules, when may the management of a registered issuing company exclude a shareholder proposal from the agenda of an annual meeting?

22-4 What criteria are used by the courts to determine whether an instrument or transaction will be called a security?

22-5 Which securities must be registered under the 1933 Act? Explain.

22-6 Which securities are exempt from registration under the 1933 Act? Explain.

REVIEW PROBLEMS

22-7 Livingston had worked for Merrill Lynch for 20 years as a securities sales representative ("account executive"). In January 1972, he and 47 other account executives were given the honorary title of "vice president" because of their outstanding sales records. None of their duties were changed, however, and they never attended a meeting of the board of directors. In November and December 1972, Livingston sold and repurchased the same number of shares of Merrill Lynch, making a profit of $14,836.37. Merrill Lynch sued Livingston for recovery of the profits, claiming that he had violated Section 16(b) of the Securities and Exchange Act of 1934. Livingston denied such charges. Who won this case, and why?

22-8 Daniel had been a member of the Teamsters Union and an employee of the same trucking firm for 23 years.

The company had signed a collective bargaining agreement with the union that contained a pension plan. Under the plan, an employee had to work for 20 continuous years for the company. Daniel had not worked for 20 continuous years because he had had a single short break in his employment. He claimed that the pension plan constituted a "security" under the 1933 and 1934 Securities Acts, and he sued the union for fraud under Section 10(b) of the 1934 Act and SEC Rule 10(b)-5. The union denied that the pension plan qualified as a security. Who won this case, and why?

22-9 Panzirer read an article in the *Wall Street Journal* stating that buying stock in a specific company would be a wise investment. She purchased stock in that company. The company later went bankrupt and Panzirer lost her investment. She sued the company's officers, directors, and independent accountants under SEC Rule 10(b)-5, claiming that, although she had never read the company's annual report, she satisfied the reliance requirement for fraud because she had relied on the "integrity of the marketplace," and a "fraud on the market" had been committed by the company. Who won this case, and why?

22-10 Schlitz Brewing Company failed to disclose on its registration statement, as well as in its periodic reports to the SEC, certain kickback payments that it was making to retailers to encourage them to sell Schlitz products, as well as the fact that the company had been convicted of violating a Spanish tax law. The SEC claimed that the failure to include such information was a violation of the antifraud provisions of the 1933 and 1934 Acts because it was material. Schlitz claimed that the information was not material because the kickbacks represented only $3 million, a tiny sum compared with the company's $1 billion in revenues. Was the information material, and was its omission, thus, a violation of Section 10(b) of the 1934 Act and SEC Rule 10(b)-5? Explain.

22-11 International Mining Exchange and a person named Parker sold a "Gold Tax Shelter Investment Program." Anyone who wished to invest had to write a check payable to an individual designated by International Mining and sign certain papers. Investors acquired a leasehold interest in a gold mine with proven reserves, and they agreed to allow International Mining to arrange for sale options to purchase the gold that would be mined. In effect, investors received the right to profits from the gold mined plus a tax deduction based on the cost of developing the mine. The SEC claimed that this transaction involved "securities" and, thus, was not exempt from registration under the 1933 Act. International Mining claimed that this transaction was not within the definition of a security. What was the result? Explain.

22-12 Continental, a manufacturer of cigarettes, sold to a group of 38 investors bonds with warrants attached to purchase common stock. The sales took place in a high-pressure atmosphere in a room with phones ringing and apparent new orders coming in. Each investor signed an agreement that she or he had received written information about the corporation, and each testified to having access to additional information if requested. The SEC brought an action claiming that Continental was in violation of the registration provisions of the 1933 Act for selling unregistered nonexempt securities. Continental argued that it qualified for a private placement exemption. What was the result? Explain.

CASE PROBLEMS

22-13 On November 8, 1990, the *Wall Street Journal* reported rumors of a possible merger of AT&T and NCR. AT&T declined to comment on the rumors. That same day, Charles Brumfield, vice president of labor relations for AT&T, called his friend Joseph Cusimano and told him that he believed the contents of the newspaper article were true. Cusimano made a series of trades in NCR securities on November 9, 12, and 15 through 20. The AT&T board authorized the acquisition of NCR on November 14 and publicly announced its interest on December 2. Did either Brumfield or Cusimano violate Section 10(b) and Rule 10b–5? On what theory? Was Brumfield's information nonpublic and material? *United States v. Cusimano*, 123 F.3d 83 (2d Cir. 1997), cert. denied, 552 U.S. 1133 (1998)

22-14 Life Partners, Inc. (LPI), facilitates the sale of life insurance policies that are owned by persons suffering from AIDS to investors at a discount. The investors pay LPI, and LPI pays the policyholder. Typically, the policyholder, in turn, assigns the policy to LPI. On the policy-holder's death, LPI receives the proceeds of the policy and pays the investor. In this way, the terminally ill sellers secure much-needed income in the final years of life. The SEC sought to enjoin LPI from engaging in further transactions on the ground that the investment contracts were securities, which LPI had failed to register with the SEC in violation of securities laws. Do the investment contracts meet the definition of a security discussed in this chapter? *SEC v. Life Partners, Inc.*, 87 F.3d 536 (D.C. Cir. 1996)

22-15 Louis Ferraro was the chairman and president of Anacomp, Inc. In June 1988, Ferraro told his good friend Michael Maio that Anacomp was negotiating a tender offer for stock in Xidex Corporation. Maio passed on the information to Patricia Ladavac, a friend of both Ferraro and Maio. Maio and Ladavac immediately purchased shares in Xidex stock. On the day that the tender offer was announced—an announcement that caused the price of Xidex shares to increase—Maio and Ladavac sold their Xidex stock and made substantial profits. The SEC brought an action against the three individuals, alleging that they had violated, among other laws, SEC Rule 10(b). Explain. *SEC v. Maio*, 51 F.3d 123 (7th Cir. 1995)

22-16 In 1997, Scott and Sabrina Levine formed Friendly Power Co. (FPC) and Friendly Power Franchise Co. (FPCFranchise). FPC obtained a license to operate as a utility company in California. Each operator paid for a "franchise"—a geographic area, determined by such factors as the number of households and competition from other utilities. In exchange for 50 percent of FPC's net profits on sales to residential customers in its territory, each franchise was required to maintain a 5 percent market share of power customers in that territory. Franchises were sold to telemarketing firms, which solicited customers. The telemarketers sold interests in each franchise to between 50 and 94 "partners," each of whom invested money. FPC began supplying electricity to its customers in May 1998. Less than three months later, the Securities and Exchange Commission filed a suit in a federal district court against the Levines and others, alleging that the "franchises" were unregistered securities offered for sale to the public in violation of the Securities Act of 1933. Who won? Why? *SEC v. Friendly Power Co., LLC*, 49 F.Supp.2d 363 (S.D. Fla. 1999)

22-17 2TheMart, Inc., was conceived in January 1999 to launch an auction Web site to compete with eBay, Inc. On January 19, 2TheMart announced that its Web site was in its "final development" stages and expected to be active by the end of July as a "preeminent" auction site and that the company had "retained the services of leading Web site design and architecture consultants to design and construct" the site. Based on the announcement, investors rushed to buy 2TheMart's stock, causing a rapid increase in the price. On February 3, 2TheMart entered into an agreement with IBM to take preliminary steps to plan the site. Three weeks later, 2TheMart announced that the site was "currently in final development." On June 1, 2TheMart signed a contract with IBM to design, build, and test the site, with a target delivery date of October 8. When 2TheMart's site did not debut as announced, Mary Harrington and others who had bought the stock filed a suit in a federal district court against the firm's officers, alleging violations of the Securities Exchange Act of 1934. The defendants responded, in part, that any alleged misrepresentations were not material and asked the court to dismiss the suit. Who won? Why? *In re 2TheMark.com, Inc. Securities Litigation*, 114 F.Supp.2d 955 (C.D. Ca. 2000)

ASSIGNMENT ON THE INTERNET

The Securities and Exchange Commission brings civil lawsuits against individuals who are accused of violating one or more securities laws, regulations, or rules. Using the Internet, visit the Securities and Exchange Commission's litigation Web site (**www.sec.gov/litigation.shtml**) and read a brief

or press release of a recent case. What rule or regulation was violated? What did the individual do to violate the rule or regulation? Finally, how does examining the reasoning of a court's decision about securities law help you to better understand the chapter you just read?

 ## ON THE INTERNET

securities.stanford.edu The Securities Action Clearinghouse provides a wealth of information about federal securities litigation, including cases, statutes, reports, and settlements.

www.sec.gov/index.htm This is the home page of the Securities and Exchange Commission.

www.nasaa.org From this page, find out about the North American Securities Administration Association, an organization devoted to investor protection.

www.seclaw.com/secrules.htm This site provides securities statutes, rules, and regulations at both state and federal levels.

www.law.cornell.edu/topics/securities.html This site contains a basic overview of securities law as well as recent judicial decision about securities law.

www.findlaw.com/01topics/34securities/publications.html This site contains numerous links to securities law and securities fraud information.

23

ANTITRUST LAWS

- **INTRODUCTION TO ANTITRUST LAW**
- **ENFORCEMENT OF AND EXEMPTIONS FROM THE ANTITRUST LAWS**
- **THE SHERMAN ACT OF 1890**
- **THE CLAYTON ACT OF 1914**
- **OTHER ANTITRUST STATUTES**
- **GLOBAL DIMENSIONS OF ANTITRUST STATUTES**

There is disagreement in many areas of public law between those who believe that business conduct should be disciplined through government regulation and those who favor the marketplace and economic-efficiency criteria as the sole instruments of business discipline. Nowhere is this struggle sharper than in the area of antitrust law.

American attitudes toward government restraints in the area of contracts originated in the English common law, which traditionally upheld the freedom of the individual to contract. U.S. courts generally refused to interfere with commercial agreements: Price-fixing and horizontal and vertical territorial divisions of markets were considered part of the business environment and, hence, legal. This laissez-faire approach was accepted up to the second half of the nineteenth century, when the economic might of huge monopolies stirred Congress to enact the Interstate Commerce Act of 1887 and the Sherman Act of 1890. With the advance of technology these statutes as interpreted by the courts provide for major differences of opinion based on the goals of antitrust as adopted by writers/enforcers and others involved in the judicial and political systems.

The chapter begins with an introduction to the meaning of antitrust and a summary of the federal antitrust statutes. Then it discusses enforcement of the antitrust laws and exemptions made to those laws. Next it examines the types of business conduct that are forbidden by the Sherman Act as well as the Clayton Act, the Federal Trade Commission Act, and the Bank Merger Act of 1966. Because these acts have affected, directly and indirectly, almost every business and political institution in American society, and carry criminal and/or civil penalties, much of the chapter focuses on dissecting them. Finally, it examines the global dimensions of antitrust policy.

INTRODUCTION TO ANTITRUST LAW

A DEFINITION OF ANTITRUST

Trusts were originally business arrangements in which owners of stocks in several companies placed their securities in the hands of trustees, who controlled and managed the companies. The securities owners, in return, received certificates that gave each a specified share of the earnings of the jointly managed companies. The trust device itself was not—and is not today—illegal. However, in the late 1880s

> **trust** A business arrangement in which owners of stocks in several companies place their securities with trustees, who jointly manage the companies and pay out a specific share of their earnings to the securities holders.

Critical Thinking About the Law

Antitrust law is full of controversial cases. Should the government restrict businesses? To what extent? Should we prevent businesses from creating monopolies? These questions are addressed in a variety of laws regarding antitrust policy. A recent case (see pp. 719, Case 23-4) of an antitrust action by the government involves Microsoft. Microsoft was charged with unfair monopolistic practices. The government claimed that Microsoft unfairly restricted its competitors by forcing computer manufacturers to ship the Microsoft Internet Explorer along with Windows 95. Answering the following questions about Microsoft can help you think critically about antitrust law.

1. Before you can critically evaluate claims, you need to identify the reasons and conclusion. To get in the habit of paying attention to reasons, try to generate reasons for and against governmental intervention in Microsoft's practices.

    Clue: Reread the introduction. Why would Microsoft want to be free of governmental intervention? Why would the government want to regulate Microsoft?

2. Your roommate makes the following statement: "Businesses have to comply with far too many regulations. They should just be free to make their own rules. Businesses that aren't fair to the public will not be successful. The government shouldn't regulate Microsoft." How would you respond to your roommate?

    Clue: Even though you have not yet read this chapter, you can evaluate your roommate's statement. Do you see any problems with this statement?

3. Microsoft argues that the Internet Explorer is simply part of Windows. Furthermore, Microsoft claims that it is serving its customers by including the Internet Explorer. Customers don't have to worry about finding an additional World Wide Web browser. Thus, the government is essentially hurting the public by regulating Microsoft. Are you persuaded by Microsoft's argument?

    Clue: What information might be missing from Microsoft's argument? What more would you like to know about the World Wide Web industry?

and 1890s, trusts were used by a few companies to buy up or drive out of business many small companies in a single industry. Standard Oil Company, for example, used this process to monopolize the oil industry. Unscrupulous methods of competition—such as bribery, setting up bogus companies, and harassing small companies with lawsuits—were used by large trusts to gain monopolistic profits. Magazine and newspaper exposures of scandalous transactions involving trusts shook the public's confidence in unregulated markets. Against this background, the Sherman Act was enacted in 1890. Because it was aimed at monopolies that called themselves trusts, it was called an antitrust statute.

LAW AND ECONOMICS: SETTING AND ENFORCING ANTITRUST POLICY

The formulation and enforcement of antitrust policy have been substantially affected by the disciplines of law and economics. And there is a strong difference of opinion about antitrust law between lawyers and economists who favor some government regulation of business and those who want to see deregulation or, more radically, no regulation at all. These two approaches to antitrust policy are known, respectively, as the Harvard School and the Chicago School after the universities where many of their proponents have taught and written.

Chicago School
An approach to antitrust policy that is based solely on the goal of economic efficiency, or the maximization of consumer welfare.

The **Chicago School** (a market or efficiency approach to antitrust policy) argues that antitrust decisions should be based solely on the criterion of economic efficiency—that is, the maximization of consumer welfare, which may be defined as improving the allocation of scarce resources without in some way decreasing productive efficiencies. In our discussion of antitrust goals very shortly, you will find that one of those goals is the "promotion of the maximization of consumer welfare using market principles and efficiency criteria." But the Chicago School argues that unless efficiency is the sole criterion for antitrust policy making, consumers will not be able to obtain goods at the lowest price possible and United States–based multinationals will not be able to compete with foreign multinationals. Adherents of the Chicago School would like to see antitrust statutes enforced less strictly, especially in the areas of vertical price and territorial restraints, and would decriminalize many antitrust offenses. Finally, proponents of this approach believe that bigness in U.S. business is far from bad, considering that competitive foreign firms are big and are sometimes aided by their governments as well. You will see the Chicago approach at work when you come to read the *GTE Sylvania* case later in this chapter.

Harvard School
An approach to antitrust policy that is based on the desirability of preserving competition to prevent the accumulation of economic and political power, the dislocation of labor, and market inefficiency.

The **Harvard School** (a structural approach to antitrust policy) favors the preservation of an economy characterized by many buyers and sellers, with little domination by any one. Adherents of this approach condemn the accumulation of economic power because they believe that it leads to substantial political power at the federal, state, and local levels as politicians are "bought" by the holders of economic power. The resulting concentration of economic and political power allows a small elite to dominate society and to dictate the closing of plants, downsizing, and the loss of jobs from a community. The Harvard School's position on the creation and enforcement of antitrust policy is embodied in all four of the antitrust goals we next discuss.

Try not to choose sides on this issue until you have read and critically analyzed this chapter. But it is important that you understand from the outset of your study of antitrust policy that the political, economic, and judicial systems of this country are profoundly affected by these two opposing schools of thought (Table 23-1). Also, it might be interesting to see how the courts have adopted some criteria belonging to both schools.

Chicago School	Harvard School
1. Sole criterion for formulating antitrust policy is efficiency: the maximization of consumer welfare.	**1.** Several criteria, including (a) preservation of many buyers and sellers in the economy, (b) prevention of concentration of political and economic power, (c) preservation of local control of business and prevention of dislocation of labor markets, and (d) efficiency of markets.
2. Decriminalize many offenses, including vertical restraints of trade and monopolies.	**2.** Enforce the antitrust statutes rigorously and increase the criminal penalties in most areas of antitrust.
3. Encourage joint ventures between U.S. and foreign multinationals without requiring government approval.	**3.** Allow joint ventures but retain strict oversight by the Justice Department and Federal Trade Commission to prevent worldwide concentration and division of global markets by multinationals.

TABLE 23-1

CHICAGO AND HARVARD SCHOOLS' APPROACHES TO ANTITRUST POLICY

GOALS OF THE ANTITRUST STATUTES

A century of debate by lawyers, economists, and others has not produced a real consensus on the goals of the antitrust statutes. Nonetheless, these four goals can be derived from the study of antitrust legislation and case law:

1. *The preservation of small businesses and an economy characterized by many sellers competing with one another.* Proponents of this goal would break up large corporations such as General Motors (GM), International Business Machines (IBM), and Microsoft.

2. *The prevention of concentration of political and economic power in the hands of a few sellers in each industry.* Proponents of this goal argue that there is a direct correlation between large corporations, economic power, and control of the political process. They point to 1980, 1984, and 2000 postpresidential election analyses indicating that well-financed political action committees (PACs) controlled by big businesses had a tremendous effect on the elections' outcomes.

3. *The preservation of local control of business and protection against the effects of labor dislocation.* The advocates of this antitrust goal argue that when large companies are allowed to merge, fix prices, and participate in joint ventures, jobs are lost and plants are shut down in some areas. The consequences are a dislocation of labor and a decline in local and state economies as their tax bases shrink because people are moving elsewhere in pursuit of jobs.

4. *The promotion of the maximization of consumer welfare using market principles and efficiency criteria.* Advocates of this goal define consumer welfare as an improvement in the allocation of resources without an impairment to productive efficiency. In effect, the proponents of this goal argue that, by encouraging the allocation of resources in an efficient manner, antitrust enforcement can make sure that consumers will be provided goods at the lowest possible prices.

Some of these goals conflict.[1] For example, the Harvard School proponents of goal 1 (preserving small businesses) are criticized by adherents of the Chicago School, who favor only goal 4 (consumer welfare maximization), because they believe that large firms are needed to manufacture goods at the lowest cost per unit. They point out that until Henry Ford introduced the assembly-line production of automobiles, few people could afford cars. Many small businesses are economically inefficient, they say, and attempts to preserve them through antitrust policy will be underwritten by consumers in the form of higher prices. The Chicago School also insists that if U.S. manufacturers are not allowed to merge and participate in joint ventures, they will be unable to compete with large foreign multinationals and foreign companies owned or subsidized by their governments. One of the reasons the Justice Department moved to dismiss an antitrust suit against the International Business Machines Corporation in 1982 was that the computer market had become international in character since the original government complaint against IBM in 1972. If IBM had been broken up, it would not have been able to compete with large foreign multinationals either in the United States or in other countries.

A summary of the federal antitrust statutes is provided in Table 23-2.

TABLE 23-2

SUMMARY OF FEDERAL ANTITRUST LAWS

Act	*Provisions*
Sherman Act of 1890 Section 1	Makes illegal every contract, combination, or conspiracy in restraint of trade; felony offense punishable by fine up to $100 million per corporation and up to $1 million per individual; a person may be imprisoned up to ten years, fined, or both.
Section 2	Forbids monopolizing, attempts to monopolize, or conspiracies to monopolize; penalties are the same as for Section 1.
Clayton Act of 1914 Section 2	Forbids discrimination in price between different purchasers of goods of like grade and quality where the effect may be to lessen competition or to tend to create a monopoly in any line of commerce, or to injure, destroy, or prevent competition with the seller, the buyer, or either's customers.
Section 3	Forbids selling or leasing goods on the condition that the buyer or lessee shall not use or deal in goods sold or leased by the seller's or lessor's competitor, where the effect of such an agreement may be substantially to lessen competition or to tend to create a monopoly. In effect, this section outlaws exclusive dealing and tying arrangements.
Section 7	Forbids unlawful selling of corporate assets or stock mergers when the effect may be substantially to lessen competition or to tend to create a monopoly.
Federal Trade Commission Act of 1914	Forbids unfair methods of competition in commerce and unfair or deceptive acts in commerce.

---

[1] To examine four conflicting opinions on the goals of antitrust, see T. Calvani, "Consumer Welfare Is Prime Objective of Antitrust," *Legal Times*, December 24–31, 1984, p. 14; B. Brennan, "A Legal-Economic Dichotomy: Contribution to Failure in Regulatory Policy," *American Business, Law Journal* 4 (1976), p. 52; W. Cann Jr., "The New Merger Guidelines: Is the Justice Department Enforcing the Law?" *American Business, Law Journal* 21 (1983), pp. 1, 2–13; R. Bork, *The Antitrust Paradox* (New York: Basic Books, 1978), pp. 6, 90–91, 104, 108.

ENFORCEMENT OF AND EXEMPTIONS FROM THE ANTITRUST LAWS

ENFORCEMENT

Enforcement of the antitrust laws is carried out in both the public and the private sectors. The Department of Justice and the Federal Trade Commission (FTC) (see Table 23-3) are primarily responsible for enforcement in the public sector, whereas any individual or business entity in the private sector that establishes that it has been directly injured by illegal business conduct may bring an action under the federal statutes outlined here as well as under state antitrust statutes. Table 23-3 shows which parties have enforcement powers for the three major federal antitrust statutes.

Public Enforcement. The Antitrust Division of the Justice Department exclusively enforces the Sherman Act and has concurrent jurisdiction with the Federal Trade Commission to enforce the Clayton Act. The FTC has exclusive jurisdiction to enforce the Federal Trade Commission Act (FTCA).

Usually, the Justice Department files civil suits in a federal district court. The remedy requested is ordinarily an injunction to prevent a particular action from occurring, along with a specific order requiring the business to change its conduct or operation. Most of the time, the defending parties, because of the cost of litigation and the attendant bad publicity, choose not to fight the case and instead agree to enter into a consent decree (consent order) with the Justice Department, which binds them to stop the activity complained of (e.g., attempting to manipulate a market). As you know from our discussion of administrative agencies in Chapter 17, entering into a consent order does not involve admitting to any liability. The federal district court must approve the consent order.

For serious violations of the Sherman Act (e.g., price-fixing among competitors), the Justice Department may bring a criminal action. A corporation convicted of criminal conduct under the act faces a fine of up to $100 million for each offense; individual officers and employees who are convicted face a maximum $1 million fine for each offense, or up to ten years in jail, or both. *Nolo contendere* pleas are often negotiated between the Justice Department and corporate or individual criminal defendants. This plea of no contest subjects the defendant to a lesser punishment than would result from conviction at a trial. Though technically not an admission of guilt, a *nolo contendere* plea is treated as such by a judge. Like a consent decree, it must be approved by the court.

Both consent decrees in a civil action and *nolo contendere* pleas in a criminal action are often entered into by defendants to avoid the cost of litigation and

TABLE 23-3 PARTIES THAT ENFORCE THE FEDERAL ANTITRUST LAW

	Sherman Act	*Clayton Act*	*Federal Trade Commission Act*
Justice Department	Civil and criminal enforcement powers	Civil enforcement power	No power to enforce
Federal Trade Commission	No power to enforce	Civil enforcement power	Civil enforcement power
Private parties	Power to enforce civil litigation	Power to enforce civil litigation	No power to enforce

publicity. Another advantage of these decrees and pleas for defendants is that they cannot be used as a basis for shareholder-derivative or indemnity suits. For the Justice Department, such decrees and pleas save time and taxpayers' money.

In December 1997, at the urging of the Justice Department, a federal judge issued a temporary restraining order to prevent Microsoft from allegedly violating a 1995 court order by forcing computer makers to install its Internet browser software along with its Windows 95 operating system. Several days later the federal court issued a contempt order advising that the company was making a mockery of the court's order. Microsoft appealed in January 1998. Violation of antitrust laws was at issue. On another front, 18 states have brought a separate antitrust action (later joined with the federal government), which has wider implications than the mere tying of a browser system to Windows 95. In this case, the 18 state attorneys general seek to show an effort by Microsoft to eliminate competition under the Clayton Act, Section 7, and to fix prices under Section 1 of the Sherman Act as well as several other anticompetitive practices to be studied in this chapter. This action by the states is a continuation of their joint efforts to pursue cases against the tobacco companies, telemarketing advertisers, and environmental violators, all under the name of consumer protection. For elected attorneys general, these are popular cases to be grouped.[2] Parts of the most recent *Microsoft* litigation are set forth in this chapter (see pp. 712 and 714).

The Federal Trade Commission can bring only civil actions, which are usually argued before an administrative law judge. The ALJ makes findings of fact and recommends action to the full five-member commission, which may issue a cease-and-desist order. The defendant has the option of appealing such an order to a U.S. Court of Appeals, and further to the Supreme Court. But usually such cease-and-desist orders are negotiated by the parties before a hearing by the ALJ and are approved by the commission. Failure to abide by a cease-and-desist order carries a penalty of $10,000 a day for each day the defendant is not in compliance.

Private Enforcement. Section 4 of the Clayton Act says that

> *any person who shall be injured in his person or in his business or property by reason of anything forbidden in the antitrust laws may sue [and] ... shall recover threefold the damages by him sustained and the cost of suit including a reasonable attorney's fee.*

This section provides the incentive for private enforcement of our antitrust laws because it requires the court to triple the amount of damages awarded to a plaintiff by a jury or by a judge. It also awards reasonable attorney's fees to the plaintiff's attorney.

Private-action suits can be brought by individuals or businesses against perceived violators of the antitrust laws. In recent years, approximately 90 percent of all antitrust claims were brought by private-party plaintiffs. Moreover, when a small company, such as Microwave Communication, Inc. (MCI), sues a large company, such as American Telephone and Telegraph (AT&T), for antitrust violations, victory has the double advantage of enhancing its cash flow and showing bond-rating agencies and investors that it is a viable entity able to take on a big company.

Individuals in a class action suit and state attorneys general in parens patriae actions on behalf of their citizenry can also bring suits. In a **class action suit**, one member of a group of plaintiffs injured by an antitrust violation (e.g., price-fixing,

class action suit A lawsuit brought by a member of a group of persons on behalf of all members of the group.

---

[2] See J. Marttott, "13 States Planning Broader Suits Against Microsoft," *New York Times*, April 30, 1988.

which results in higher prices for direct purchasers) institutes an action on behalf of the group. This kind of suit is particularly useful when the amount of each individual claim is small. Similar to class actions are **parens patriae suits**, which are usually brought by a state attorney general on behalf of purchasers and taxpayers in a state (previously discussed with action pending against Microsoft and actions against tobacco companies by attorney generals of several states).

parens patriae suit A lawsuit brought by a state attorney general on behalf of the citizenry of that state.

CASE 23-1

Paper Systems, Inc. v. Nippon Paper Industries
U.S. Court of Appeals,
281 F.3d 629 (Seventh Cir. 2002)

Paper Systems (Plaintiff) and two other buyers of thermal fax paper sued Nippon and other producers in federal district court alleging antitrust violations of the Sherman Act. Four defendants reached a settlement with the plaintiffs, and the lower court dismissed the suit against Nippon. Plaintiffs are appealing the dismissal.

Justice Easterbrook

The rule of joint and several liability is … each member of a conspiracy is liable for all damages caused by the conspiracy's entire output.

If Nippon Paper was among those conspirators, then it is responsible for the *entire* overcharge of *all five manufacturers*—and any direct purchaser from any conspirator can collect its own portion of damages (that is, the damages attributable to its direct purchases) from any conspirator. This makes it impossible to dismiss Nippon Paper outright.

The difficulty of tracing overcharges through the chain of distribution is unimportant; duplicative recovery has been blocked at the outset.

A simple example makes the point. Suppose that five vertically integrated manufacturers sell directly to consumers at $12 per unit, and that this price is an overcharge attributable to a cartel; the competitive price would have been $10 per unit. Each manufacturer sells 100 units per year, so the total overcharge is $1,000 ($2 on each of 500 units) and treble damages under the Sherman Act are $3,000. Given joint and several liability, each of the five conspirators is liable to pay the whole $3,000—though no consumer can recover more than $6 per unit purchased. Now suppose further that

one of the five manufacturers gets out of the distribution business and sells its output to a wholesaler for $10 per unit: the wholesaler resells the product for $12 per unit. It is hard to see why this should change the total damages any conspirator must pay under the antitrust laws. [I]t changes who may collect damages (the wholesaler, as direct purchaser, owns the right to collect damages on 100 units each year) but not how much each [member of the cartel] owes in the aggregate. Yet Nippon Paper's position is that the use of a wholesaler has a profound effect; it reduces that manufacturer's total exposure from $3,000 to $600 (treble the $2 overcharge on 100 units sold to the wholesaler)—and then only if the wholesaler sues. [The courts reject] just such a proposal. [I]f one direct purchaser wholesaler declines to sue, then the total damages the five example manufacturers owe jointly and severally cannot exceed what is recoverable by direct purchasers that do litigate (in our example, for $2,400). Every participant in the conspiracy remains liable for damages on every sale to every direct purchaser from any of the manufacturers.

The U.S. Court of Appeals reversed the lower court, and remanded the case to the federal district court (lower court) to determine whether Nippon in fact was a member of a cartel. If so, it was jointly and severally liable for any overcharges to Paper Systems and other buyers of the thermal paper to the extent such damages are attributable to each direct buyer's purchase. Nippon and other defendants are liable for overcharges.

Reversed and remanded in favor of Plaintiff, Paper Systems, Inc.

EXEMPTIONS

Several activities and industries are fully or partially exempt from the antitrust statutes (Table 23-4). These exemptions are based on federally enacted statutes or case law of the courts. When exemptions are granted by statute, they are

TABLE 23-4

SELECT ACTIVITIES EXEMPT UNDER U.S. ANTITRUST LAW

Activity	Basis for Exemption and Examples
Regulated industries	Transportation, electric, gas, and telephone.
Labor union activities	Collective bargaining.
Intrastate activities	Intrastate telephone calls are regulated by state public utility commissions.
Agricultural activities	Farmers may belong to cooperatives that legally set prices.
Baseball	The U.S. Supreme Court declared baseball a sport, not a trade. No other professional sport has been exempted by the Congress or courts.
Activities falling within the "State Action" doctrine	In *Parker v. Brown* [317 U.S. 341 (1943)] the U.S. Supreme Court held a state marketing program that was clearly anticompetitive to be exempt from the federal antitrust statutes because it obtained its authority from a "clearly articulated legislative command of the state." The Court looks at the degree of involvement before exempting any activity under this doctrine.
Cities', towns', and villages' activities	The *Local Government Antitrust Act of 1984* prohibits monetary recovery under the federal antitrust laws from any of these local subdivisions or from local officials, agents, or employees.
Export activities	The *Webb-Pommerce Trade Act of 1918* and the *Export Trading Act of 1982* made the formation of selling cooperatives of U.S. exporters exempt. Also, the *Joint Venture Trading Act of 1983* exempted certain joint ventures of competing companies when seeking to compete with foreign companies that are private and/or state controlled. Approval of the Justice Department is required. The *Shipping Act of 1984* allows shipping lines to enter into joint ventures and to participate in international shipping conferences that set worldwide rates and divide routes and shipments.
Oil marketing	Interstate Oil Compact of 1935 allows states to set quotas on oil to the market in interstate commerce.
Joint efforts by businesses to seek government action	Such actions are exempt unless it is an attempt to make anticompetitive use of governmental processes. See *Eastern R. R. v. Noer Main Freight*, 365 U.S. 127 (1961).

largely the result of successful lobbying of Congress by an industry. Soft-drink franchisers, for example, lobbied successfully in 1980 to obtain a limited exemption from the antitrust statutes, and shipping lines received a similar exemption in 1984.

THE SHERMAN ACT OF 1890

The Sherman Act of 1890 is intended to prevent control of markets by any one powerful entity. In other words, it is designed to thwart anticompetitive behavior. Sections 1 and 2 of the act, covered here, profoundly affect decisions and behaviors of business managers. As we shall see, the Sherman Act is also an important tool to protect consumers from a number of activities that will be discussed here.

SECTION 1: COMBINATIONS AND RESTRAINTS OF TRADE

Section 1 of the Sherman Act reads:

> *Every contract, combination in the form of trust or otherwise, or conspiracy, in restraint of trade or commerce among the several States, or with foreign nations, is declared to be illegal. Every person who shall make any contract or engage in any combination or conspiracy hereby declared to be illegal shall be deemed guilty of a felony, and, on conviction thereof shall be punished by fine not exceeding one million dollars if a corporation, or, if any other person, one hundred thousand dollars or by imprisonment not exceeding three years, or by both.*

The **Sherman Act** requires three elements for a violation: (1) a combination, contract, or conspiracy; (2) a restraint of trade that is unreasonable; and (3) a restraint that is involved in interstate, as opposed to intrastate, commerce. We examined the third element in Chapter 5, when we discussed the effects of the Commerce Clause on business. Here we will analyze the first two elements.

Combination, Contract, or Conspiracy. The Sherman Act requires a contract, combination, or conspiracy, so more than one person must be involved (one cannot make a contract, or conspire, or combine with oneself). Just as an offeror and an offeree are necessary parties to a contract, there must be coconspirators in a conspiracy. In other words, there must be concerted action (action taken together) by two or more individuals or business entities. In antitrust language, there must be an "agreement," or **collusion**. Such an agreement can be expressed in writing or orally, or it can be implied, as established by circumstantial evidence such as trends toward uniformity in pricing in an industry and opportunities to conspire.

It is in cases of implied agreements established by circumstantial evidence that the courts deal with two major problems: (1) whether there can be an intra-enterprise conspiracy that violates the Sherman Act and (2) what actions constitute conscious parallelism as opposed to price-fixing. **Conscious parallelism** exists when identical actions (usually price increases) are taken independently and nearly simultaneously by two or more leading companies in an industry and, thus, have the apparent effect of having arisen from a conspiracy.

The courts' solution to the first problem has generally been that there can be no conspiracy between two divisions, departments, or subsidiaries of the same corporation. In answer to the second problem, the courts have generally held that if there is supportable evidence of conscious parallelism, as opposed to an expressed or implied agreement among competitors, no antitrust violation exists.

Restraints of Trade. The second element required to prove a violation of Section 1 of the Sherman Act is that there be a **restraint of trade** and that this restraint be "unreasonable" as defined by the courts. In enacting the Sherman Act, Congress gave no indication of whether it meant all restraints or just some.

Rule-of-Reason Standard. Taking its direction from the English courts, the U.S. Supreme Court adopted a **rule-of-reason standard**. Over time, the Court has followed certain indices, laid out by Justice Louis D. Brandeis in 1918, to determine whether a specific business activity is an unreasonable restraint of trade:

1. The nature and purpose of the restraint.
2. The scope of the restraint.
3. Its effect on the business and on competitors.
4. Its intent.

Sherman Act Makes illegal every combination, contract, or conspiracy that is an unreasonable restraint of trade when this concerted action involves interstate commerce.

collusion Concerted action by two or more individuals or business entities in violation of the Sherman Act.

conscious parallelism Identical actions (usually price increases) that are taken independently but nearly simultaneously by two or more leading companies in an industry.

restraint of trade Action that interferes with the economic law of supply and demand.

rule-of-reason standard A legal standard that holds that only unreasonable restraints of trade violate Section 1 of the Sherman Act. If the court determines an action's anticompetitive effects outweigh its procompetitive effects, the restraint is unreasonable.

When using a rule-of-reason standard, the U.S. Supreme Court terms a restraint reasonable and, thus, legal if it has a procompetitive purpose and its effect does not go beyond that purpose. A restraint is unreasonable and unlawful if it allows the parties to substitute themselves and their judgment for the laws of supply and demand. Restraints that are judged by a rule-of-reason standard and, therefore, may be in violation of Section 1 of the Sherman Act (as seen in the *Microsoft* litigation in this chapter), include some tying arrangements, activities of trade and athletic associations, some exclusive-dealing arrangements, nonprice vertical restraints, and some franchising arrangements. Most of these are discussed later.

Per Se Standard. Over time, the courts have judged certain business activities and arrangements facially so anticompetitive in nature that they have seen no need to listen to any procompetitive economic justifications. This **per se standard** favors the plaintiff because all that has to be proved is that the restraint (e.g., price-fixing) took place; the only defense is that the activity did not occur. However, since the present Supreme Court began looking at the economic impact of previous per se rulings, the number of restraints of trade in this category has fallen. Restraints that are judged by the per se standard and, therefore, are automatically in violation of Section 1 of the Sherman Act include horizontal and vertical price-fixing, some tying arrangements, some divisions of markets, and group boycotts. Table 23-5 compares the types of activities that come under each of those standards.

We discuss the various activities that are considered restraints of trade under two headings: horizontal restraints and vertical restraints.

Horizontal Restraints. Horizontal restraints of trade are those that take place between competitors at the same level of the marketing structure. Three types of activities are considered horizontal restraints: horizontal price-fixing, horizontal divisions of markets, and horizontal boycotts.

Horizontal Price-Fixing. Suppose that competitors X, Y, and Z are the only manufacturers of a certain heat tape used in the construction of office buildings. They agree to take turns bidding on certain jobs, thus eliminating competition and holding up prices. From the viewpoint of these companies, this is a way to make high profits, stay in business, and keep their employees working. However, the Supreme Court views such **horizontal price-fixing** as per se illegal restraints because it interferes with the price mechanism—that is, the law of supply and demand—which requires that competing sellers make decisions about prices on their own without agreement or collusion, either expressed or implied. Besides direct price-fixing agreements, the Court has struck down such indirect price-fixing arrangements as minimum fee schedules for lawyers and

per se standard A legal standard that is applicable to restraints of trade that are inherently anticompetitive. Because such restraints are automatically in violation of Section 1 of the Sherman Act, courts do not balance procompetitive and anticompetitive effects in such cases.

horizontal restraint of trade Restraint of trade that occurs between competitors at the same level of the marketing structure.

horizontal price-fixing Collusion between two or more competitors to, directly or indirectly, set prices for a product or service.

TABLE 23-5

SHERMAN ACT SECTION 1 ACTIVITIES JUDGED BY THE PER SE STANDARD AND THE RULE-OF-REASON STANDARD

Per Se Standard	*Rule-of-Reason Standard*
Price-fixing—both horizontal and vertical agreements	Restrictive convenant in a sale or employment
Group boycotts	Location and resale restraints by manufacturer on some tying arrangements
Some tying arrangements	Exchange of information
Some divisions of markets	Joint research and development ventures; some horizontal price tampering based on unique nature of industry

engineers, exchanges of price information among groups of competitors, and agreements between competitors about terms of credit when these become part of the overall price structure in an industry.

The case that follows illustrates an agreement among professional competitors that affected prices (i.e., price-fixing).

CASE 23-2

Federal Trade Commission v. Superior Court Trial Lawyer's Association
United States Supreme Court,
493 U.S. 411 (1991)

In the District of Columbia, lawyers in private practice are appointed to represent indigent defendants in less serious felony and misdemeanor cases. These private attorneys are paid pursuant to the District's Criminal Justice Act (CJA), which in 1982 provided for fees of $30 per hour for court time and $20 per hour for out-of-court time. Most appointments went to approximately 100 lawyers called "CJA regulars," who handled more than 25,000 cases in 1982. These lawyers derived almost all of their income from representing indigents.

The CJA regulars belonged to the Superior Court Trial Lawyers Association (SCTLA), which was a professional organization and not a labor union. Beginning in 1982, SCTLA unsuccessfully tried to persuade the District to increase CJA rates. In August 1983, about 100 CJA lawyers resolved not to accept any new cases after September 6, 1983, if legislation providing for an increase in fees was not passed by that date. When the legislation was not enacted, on September 6 most CJA regulars refused to accept new assignments. As anticipated, their action had a severe impact on the District's criminal justice system. Within ten days, the District's criminal justice system was on the brink of collapse. At the last minute the District offered to pay CJA lawyers $45 per hour out of court and $55 in court time. The CJAs accepted.

Justice Stevens
Prior to the boycott CJA lawyers were in competition with one another, each deciding independently whether and how often to offer to provide services to the District at CJA rates. The agreement among the CJA lawyers was designed to obtain higher prices for their services and was implemented by a concerted refusal to serve the only customer in the market for the particular services that CJA regulars offered. This constriction of supply is the essence of price-fixing.

The horizontal arrangement among these competitors was unquestionably a "naked restraint" on price and output. The social justifications preferred for respondents' restraint of trade thus do not make it any less unlawful. The statutory policy underlying the Sherman Act precludes inquiry into the question whether competition is good or bad. No matter how altruistic the motives of respondents may have been, it is undisputed that their immediate objective was to increase the price that they would be paid for their services. The per se rules are, of course, the product of judicial interpretations of the Sherman Act, but the rules nevertheless have the same force and effect as any other statutory commands.

Affirmed in favor of Plaintiff, FTC.

How "per se" is the per se rule in the area of price-fixing? For example, it is clear that certain forms of price-fixing are per se legal by statute. Before deregulation of long-distance phone service in the early 1980s, prices for this service were set by the Federal Communications Commission and, therefore, were exempt from the Sherman Act. Similarly, before deregulation of the trucking industry, trucking rates were set by the Interstate Commerce Commission and, therefore, were exempt. In contrast, organizations of engineers, lawyers, and doctors have been found guilty of per se illegal price-fixing when they set minimum or maximum schedules of rates or recommend certain minimum prices. There is no "bright line" in this area of antitrust law showing which pricing activities will be judged per se illegal in the future.

Critical Thinking About the Law

Primary ethical norms not only underlie judges' reasoning, but they also influence Congress's reasoning when it creates statutory law. In a given area of regulation, Congress emphasizes certain ethical norms over others when enacting a new statute. When a case is brought to trial that involves these statutes, the court has the opportunity to affirm Congress's regulatory measures and the ethical norms contained therein. The court also may find exceptions to the regulations, or at some point declare such regulations unconstitutional. A court's response to Congress's statutory legislation reflects in part the extent to which the court agrees with the primary ethical norms implicit within Congress's reasons for creating the statutes. The following questions, pertaining to Case 23-2 urge you to think about the relevance of primary ethical norms in statutory law and a court's application of those laws.

1. The Supreme Court references the Sherman Act as the relevant statute in this case. Which primary ethical norm underlies Congress's objectives in making this legislation?

   Clue: Reread the section in this chapter entitled "Goals of the Antitrust Statutes" (p. 695).

2. Which ethical norm would have led to a reversal in the Court's decision in Case 23-2?

   Clue: This norm would have involved the Court's placing greater worth on the interests of the defendants over the interests of the plaintiff.

---

horizontal division of markets Collusion between two or more competitors to divide markets, customers, or product lines among themselves.

Horizontal Division of Markets. Territorial division, customer allocation, and product-line division of markets between competitors have traditionally been deemed illegal per se. The **horizontal division of markets** is considered particularly dangerous to a free-market economy because it eliminates all forms of competition, in contrast to price-fixing, which eliminates only price competition. "Naked" horizontal agreements to divide markets, customers, or product lines have had no redeeming value in the eyes of the courts.

More recently, however, it has been argued that price-fixing and division-of-market agreements that are part of cooperative productive activity (as opposed to "naked" restraints) are economically efficient and, therefore, desirable. Thus, the advocates of these "more-than-naked horizontal agreements" contend that a rule-of-reason standard should guide the courts.

An example of price-fixing and division of markets that has been long accepted is a law partnership. Lawyers who would ordinarily compete with each other eliminate competition by signing a partnership agreement that restricts work output to their specialization (market division) and that provides for an agreement on fees to be charged by partners and their associates (price-fixing). In effect, an integrated economic unit fixes prices and divides markets (output) internally so that the partnership may operate more efficiently in competing externally with other law firms.

horizontal boycott
A concerted refusal by a trade association to deal with members that do not follow the association's regulations.

Horizontal Boycotts. Trade associations frequently promulgate rules among their memberships that amount to concerted refusals to deal with members that do not follow the association's regulations. This activity constitutes a **horizontal boycott** and is per se illegal because it takes away the freedom of other members to interact with the boycotted members and, in many instances, lessens the ability of a boycotted member to compete.

Many professional associations have rules that contain sanctions for violations, ranging from reprimands to suspension or expulsion from the association.

In this era of deregulation and, thus, indirect encouragement of industry self-regulation, certain antitrust cases have become extremely important. If an industry's own rules are arbitrary and capricious or lacking in due process, the courts will generally not uphold them under the rule of reason. For example, when the New York Stock Exchange, without a hearing, ordered all exchange members to withdraw wire connection with a nonmember broker, the Supreme Court held that "concerted termination of trade relations, which would ordinarily constitute an illegal boycott, might be exempt from the antitrust law as a result of the duty of self-regulation imposed on the Exchange [by Congress and the Securities and Exchange Commission], but only if fair procedures were followed, including notice and hearing."[3] In another case,[4] however, the Court found no unreasonable restraint of trade arising out of the program established by the National Sanitation Foundation (NSF) for testing production of and issuing a seal of approval for products that complied with the NSF's promulgated standards, which were strictly enforced among manufacturers. The Court has indicated that when an alleged boycott of an unapproved manufacturer takes place, the plaintiff must show either that it was discriminated against vis-à-vis its competitors or that it was subjected to anticompetitive conduct.

Clearly, self-regulatory associations will continue to be watched carefully by the courts for due process and reasonable conduct. In July 1985, the Supreme Court ruled that a wholesale purchasing cooperative's expulsion of a member without notice, a hearing, or an opportunity to challenge the decision could not be conclusively presumed to be a per se violation of Section 1 of the Sherman Act.[5] The Court remanded the case to the federal district court, directing that a rule-of-reason approach be used to determine whether the cooperative had the market power to exclude competitors and whether the expulsion of a member was likely to have an anticompetitive effect.

In the case of noncommercial refusals to deal, it is clear that the per se rule will not be applied by the courts. For example, when the National Organization of Women (NOW) organized a boycott of convention facilities in all states that had refused to endorse the proposed Equal Rights Amendment to the U.S. Constitution, Missouri sued NOW, claiming that the organization was in violation of Section 1 of the Sherman Act. The circuit court of appeals stated that the Sherman Act was nonapplicable in this case because the boycott had a noncommercial goal—to influence legislation in the political arena.[6] The court had used the rule-of-reason standard to determine whether the group's purpose was truly noncommercial in nature.

A conflict between constitutional principles—such as the right to free speech and to petition one's government under the First Amendment of the Constitution—and enforcement of the Sherman Act against boycotts or refusals to deal must often be resolved by the courts. Usually, as in the *NOW* case, constitutional principles have prevailed when noncommercial groups have been involved. The *NYNEX* case is an important illustration of whether an individual buyer's decision to buy from one supplier rather than another constitutes a group boycott. Also at issue is whether the per se rule should apply here or the rule of reason.

---

[3] See *Silver v. New York Stock Exchange*, 373 U.S. 341 (1965).

[4] *Eliason Corp. v. National Sanitation Foundation*, 614 F.2d 126 (1980).

[5] *Northwest Wholesale Stationers, Inc. v. Pacific Stationery and Printing Co.*, U.S. 284 (1985).

[6] *Missouori v. NOW, Inc.*, 620 F.2d 1301 (8th Cir. 1980), cert. denied 449 U.S. 8412 (1981).

CASE 23-3

NYNEX Corporation v. Discon, Inc.
United States Supreme Court,
525 U.S. 128 (1998)

NYNEX Corporation owns New York Telephone Company (NYTel), which provides telephone service to most of New York. NYTel has a monopoly on phone service in the areas that it serves. NYNEX also owns NYNEX Material Enterprises. Material Enterprises obtains removal services for NYTel. These services consist of salvaging and disposing of obsolete equipment. Material Enterprises, which had been using the services of Discon, Inc. (plaintiff), switched its business to AT&T Technologies, Inc., which supplied the removal services at inflated prices. Material Enterprises charged the inflated prices to NYTel, which passed the charges on to its customers. Material Enterprises later received secret rebates of the excessive charges from AT&T. When the scheme was uncovered, NYTel agreed to refund over $35 million to its customers. Discon, Inc., filed a suit in federal district court against NYNEX and others, alleging, among other things, that as part of their scheme, the defendants had conspired to eliminate Discon from the market in favor of AT&T, because Discon had refused to participate in the rebate scheme. Discon contended that this was an illegal group boycott. The defendants filed a motion to dismiss, which the court granted. Discon appealed to the U.S. Court of Appeals for the Second Circuit, which reversed the lower court's judgment and held that the treatment of Discon could be an illegal group boycott. The defendants appealed.

Justice Breyer

The specific legal question before us is whether an agreement by a buyer to purchase goods or services from one supplier rather than another should apply the per se rule if it finds no legitimate business reason for that purchasing decision. We conclude no boycott-related per se rule applied and that the plaintiff here must allege and prove harm, not just to a single competitor, but to the competitive process.

Our conclusion rests in large part upon precedent, for precedent limits the per se rule in the boycott context to cases involving horizontal agreements among direct competitors.

In a previous case this Court held that a "vertical restraint is not illegal per se unless it includes some agreement on price or price levels." This precedent makes the per se rule inapplicable, for the case before us concerns only a vertical agreement and a vertical restraint, a restraint that takes the form of depriving a supplier of a potential customer.

Nor have we found any special feature of this case that could distinguish it from the precedents. We concede Discon's claim that the petitioners' behavior hurt consumers by raising telephone service rates. But that consumer injury naturally flowed not so much from a less competitive market for removal of services, as from the exercise of market power that is lawfully in the hands of a monopolist, namely, New York Telephone.

To apply the per se rule here—where the buyer's decision, though not made for competitive reasons, composes part of a regulatory fraud—would transform cases involving business behavior that is improper for various reasons, say, cases involving nepotism or person pique, into treble-damages antitrust cases. And that per se rule would discourage firms from changing suppliers—even where the competitive process itself does not suffer harm.

The freedom to switch suppliers lies close to the heart of the competitive process that the antitrust laws seek to encourage. At the same time, other laws, for example, "unfair competition" laws, business tort laws, or regulatory laws, provide remedies for various competitive practices thought to be offensive to proper standards of business morality. Thus, this Court has refused to apply per se reasoning in cases involving that kind of activity.

Vacated the Court of Appeals decision *and remanded* for further proceedings.

---

vertical restraint of trade
Restraint that occurs between individuals or corporations at different levels of the marketing structure.

Vertical Restraints. Those restraints agreed to between individuals or corporations at different levels of the manufacturing and distribution process are called **vertical restraints of trade**. For example, manufacturers and retailers, as well as franchisors and franchisees, are often involved in the following types of vertical restraints: resale-price maintenance (price-fixing), territorial and customer restrictions, tying agreements, and exclusive-dealing contracts. Although the latter two restraints involve violations of Section 3 of the Clayton Act, the courts have also condemned such actions under Section 1 of the Sherman Act.

Critical Thinking About the Law

Judges are rarely required to view cases without guidance. They can more clearly respond to the facts of cases when there are legal precedents from which they can make subsequent decisions. Case 23-3 is no exception. The Court clearly states that the basis for its decision rests primarily on precedent; Justice Breyer relates the facts of the precedent with the facts of the present case. However, simply because an analogy is drawn does not necessarily ensure the appropriateness of the analogy, as some facts may significantly differ between both cases.

The next two questions will help you think critically about legal analogies.

1. What precedent does the Court cite as the basis for its decision?

   Clue: Reread the paragraph in Case 23-3, in which the Court discusses a previous decision.

2. Why does the Court believe that this precedent is relevant in this case? Also, the Court provides an exception when citing the precedent. What missing information would be highly relevant to any assessment of whether the Court gave appropriate consideration to this exception?

   Clue: Find the paragraphs in which the Court discusses the applicability of the per se rule in this case. With regard to missing information, what additional evidence would help us decide, even though there was a vertical agreement, whether there was an additional agreement that would make the per se standard applicable in Case 23-3?

As we examine these vertical restraints, we would like you to focus on two policy implications for business managers:

1. What effect do court decisions have on intrabrand competition (retailers competing with one another in selling the same manufacturer's brand) and interbrand competition (competition between different manufacturers of a similar product when sold at the retail level)?

2. Are the courts moving in the direction of judging such restraints by a per se or a rule-of-reason standard?

Vertical Price-Fixing (Resale Price-Maintenance). When a manufacturer sells to a retailer, the company may attempt to specify what price it expects the retailer to charge for the product or, at least, a minimum price. **Vertical price-fixing** agreements of this type have been traditionally judged per se illegal by the courts if a "contract, combination, or conspiracy" exists under Section 1 of the Sherman Act. This has been true regardless of whether the manufacturer coerced the retailer into entering the agreement (by refusing to supply the product) or the retailer entered the agreement voluntarily.

vertical price-fixing
Stipulation by a manufacturer to a retailer to whom it sells products what price the retailer must charge for those products.

The courts' major concern in this area has been whether the retailer made the pricing decision independently or by agreement with the manufacturer. For example, many manufacturers offer suggested prices to their retailers in the form of price lists. The question often before the court is what type of surveillance the manufacturer uses to coerce an initial agreement or to gain compliance. If the prices are truly suggested, how many times has the retailer deviated from such prices, and what has been the response of the manufacturer? The courts have scrutinized manufacturers' responses carefully, particularly when there is evidence of a manufacturer's refusal to deal. The courts have generally agreed that a manufacturer, on its own initiative, can announce in advance an intention not to deal with an individual retailer who does not sell the manufacturer's product at a specific price. No agreement is involved in these unilateral cases. However, the court will infer an agreement, and thus per se illegal price-fixing, if the manufacturer refuses to deal with a retailer who fails to adhere to a resale then reinstates the retailer when it agrees to conform. In the case that follows the issue is whether a setting of a maximum resale price was a per se violation of the Sherman Act.

CASE 23-4

State Oil Company v. Khan
United States Supreme Court,
522 U.S. 3 (1997)

Barkot U. Khan (plaintiff) and his corporation entered into an agreement with State Oil Company to lease and operate a gas station and convenience store owned by State Oil. The agreement provided that Khan would obtain his station's gasoline supply from State Oil. The agreement also provided that Khan could charge any price for the gasoline he sold to the station's customers, but if the price charged was higher than State Oil's "suggested retail price," the excess was to be rebated to State Oil. Khan could also choose to sell gasoline for less than State Oil's suggested retail price. After operating the station under these terms for about one year, Khan lost the station back to State Oil for falling behind in lease payments. Khan sued State Oil, alleging that the maximum resale price required by State Oil was a per se violation of Section 1 of the Sherman Act. The district court entered summary judgment for State Oil. The court of appeals reversed and held that the maximum resale price set by State Oil was a per se violation of Section 1. The court of appeals cited a previous U.S. Supreme Court Case—*Albrecht v. Herald Co.*, 390 U.S. 145 (1968)—that held that the setting of maximum resale prices also was a per se violation of Section 1. State Oil appealed.

Justice O'Connor

Although the Sherman Act, by its terms, prohibits every agreement in restraint of trade, this Court has long recognized that Congress intended to outlaw only unreasonable restraints. As a consequence, most antitrust claims are analyzed under a rule of reason, according to which the finder of fact must decide whether the questioned practice imposes an unreasonable restraint on competition, taking into account a variety of factors, including specific

information about the relevant business, its condition before and after the restraint was imposed, and the restraint's history, nature, and effect. Some types of restraints, however, have such predictable and pernicious anticompetitive effect, and such limited potential for procompetitive benefit, that they are deemed unlawful per se.

We find it difficult to maintain that vertically imposed maximum prices could harm consumers or competition to the extent necessary to justify their per se invalidation. *Albrecht* reflected the Court's fear that maximum price fixing could be used to disguise arrangements to fix minimum prices, which remain illegal per se.

Although we have acknowledged the possibility that maximum pricing might mask minimum pricing, we believe that such conduct can be appropriately recognized and punished under the rule of reason. Indeed, both courts and antitrust scholars noted that *Albrecht's* rule may actually harm consumers and manufacturers. After reconsidering *Albrecht's* rationale and the substantial criticism the decision has received, we conclude that there is insufficient economic justification for per se invalidation of vertical maximum price fixing.

In overruling *Albrecht*, we of course do not hold that all vertical maximum price fixing is per se lawful. Instead, vertical maximum price fixing, like the majority of commercial arrangements subject to the antitrust laws, should be evaluated under the rule of reason. In our view, rule-of-reason analysis will effectively identify those situations in which vertical maximum price fixing amounts to anticompetitive conduct.

Remanded to trial court for new trial based on rule of reason.

Vertical Territorial and Customer Restraints. The restraints used by a manufacturer to limit the territory in which a retailer may sell the company's product and to restrict the number of retailer-owned stores as well as the customers a retailer can serve in a location are classified as **nonprice vertical restraints**.

Linking Law & Business

Economics

We will learn in this chapter that Section 2 of the Sherman Act of 1890 attempted to deal with monopolies (cartels) or attempts to monopolize and conspiracies to monopolize by using criminal and civil sanctions. Additionally, when seeking to enforce Section 1 of the act, emphasis has been placed on agreements to fix prices (a legal issue) rather than the effect of the seller's conduct on price and output (an economic issue). Smoothly functioning cartels have historically failed to produce witnesses to written or oral agreements.

Some characteristics that indicate a tendency toward price-fixing are shown by use of economic analysis. You may remember some of these from your economics courses.

1. *When there is one seller.* For example, there are fewer costs of coordinating activities.
2. *The homogeneity of a product.* The monopoly or cartel can't easily change the quality of the product because it will be obvious.
3. *The elasticity of demand with respect to price.* Other matters being equal, the less elastic demand is, the larger will be the profits that a monopoly price will generate, and the greater the incentive to monopolize.
4. *The condition of entry for other entrants is important.* If entry can take place rapidly and there will not be higher longer-run costs, the profit of cartelization will be small.

Think about these tendencies toward price-fixing and monopolization when reading cases in the chapter.

Source: George J. Stigler, "The Economic Effects of Antitrust Laws", *Organization of Industry*, 259 (1968).

Lawyers, economists, and scholars in many disciplines have studied non-price vertical restraints in great depth. Those urging that a rule-of-reason standard be applied to such territorial restraints argue that they encourage economic efficiencies and, thus, provide for spirited interbrand competition.

Vertical restraints allow a manufacturer to concentrate its advertising and distributional programs on one or two retailers in a location, making it better able to compete at the retail level with different brand manufacturers of the same product. Customer restrictions are also beneficial in this view because they enable a manufacturer to give better service and to cut out the costs of distributors' and retailers' services. For example, a manufacturer may reserve certain large commercial customers for itself, selling directly to them in large quantities and disallowing retailer involvement with them. Those arguing that a per se standard should be applied to vertical territorial restraints suggest that not only is intrabrand competition enhanced by this approach but also that customers are better able to compare the prices charged by different retailers selling the same brand. They argue that the elimination of intrabrand competition reduces the number of sellers of a leading brand in a market and increases overall market concentration in the product.

In the following landmark opinion, the U.S. Supreme Court changed the standard for judging vertical territorial and customer restrictions from per se to rule-of-reason standard. This was just ten years after it had gone in the opposite direction in another case.[7]

nonprice vertical restraint Restraint used by a manufacturer to limit the territory in which a retailer may sell the manufacturer's products and the number of stores the retailer can operate, as well as the customers the retailer can serve, in a location.

---
[7] *United States v. Schwinn and Co.*, 388 U.S. 365 (1967).

CASE 23-5

Continental TV, Inc. v. GTE Sylvania
United States Supreme Court,
433 U.S. 36 (1977)

Before 1962, GTE Sylvania (plaintiff-respondent) found that it was losing market share to other television manufacturers, so it adopted a plan that placed both territorial and customer restrictions on its retailers and phased out its wholesale distributors. Sylvania limited the number of retailers selling its product in each area and designated the location within each area where the stores could be located. When Sylvania was unhappy with its sales in San Francisco, it established another retailer besides Continental (defendant-appellant) to carry the product. Continental protested, canceled a large order of Sylvania televisions, and ordered a competitor's product. Continental then requested permission to open another store in Sacramento. Sylvania opposed such an opening, claiming that it would be in violation of Continental's franchise agreement. When Continental advised Sylvania that nevertheless it was going to open in the new location, Sylvania cut Continental's credit line, and Continental, in turn, withheld all payments on inventory owed to the manufacturer's credit company. Sylvania terminated the franchise and sued for the money owed and the Sylvania merchandise in the hands of the defendant. Continental filed a cross-claim, alleging that Sylvania had violated Section 1 of the Sherman Act with its restriction on the location of the retailers that could sell its product. The district court found in favor of Continental on the cross-claim. The U.S. Court of Appeals reversed for Sylvania. Continental appealed to the U.S. Supreme Court.

Justice Powell

The Court [in *Schwinn* (1967)] proceeded to articulate the following "bright line" per se rule of illegality for vertical restrictions. "Under the Sherman Act, it is unreasonable for a manufacturer to seek to restrict and confine areas or persons with whom an article may be treated after the manufacturer has parted with dominion over it." But the Court expressly stated that the rule of reason governs when "the manufacturer retains title, dominion, and risk with respect to the product and the position and function of the dealer in question are, in fact, indistinguishable from those of an agent or salesman of the manufacturer."

In the present case, it is undisputed that title to the televisions passed from Sylvania to Continental. Thus, the *Schwinn* per se rule applies unless Sylvania's restriction on locations falls outside *Schwinn*'s prohibition against a manufacturer attempting to restrict a "retailer's freedom as to where and to whom it will resell the products."

Sylvania argues that if *Schwinn* cannot be distinguished, it should be reconsidered. Although *Schwinn* is supported

by the principle of *stare decisis*, we are convinced that the need for clarification in this area justified reconsideration. Since its announcement, *Schwinn* has been the subject of continuing controversy and confusion, both in the scholarly journals and in the federal courts. The great weight of scholarly opinion has been critical of the decision, and a number of the federal courts confronted with analogous vertical restrictions have sought to limit its reach. In our view, the experience of the past 10 years should be brought to bear on this subject of considerable commercial importance.

In essence, the issue before us is whether *Schwinn*'s per se rule can be justified under the demanding standards of *Northern Pac. R. Co.* (1958). The Court's refusal to endorse a per se standard in *White Motor Co.* (1963) was based on its uncertainty as to whether vertical restrictions satisfied those standards. Addressing this question for the first time, the Court stated:

> We need to know more than we do about the actual impact of these arrangements on competition to decide whether they have such a "pernicious effect on competition and lack … any redeeming virtue" and therefore should be classified as per se violations of the Sherman Act.

Only four years later the Court in *Schwinn* announced its sweeping per se rule without even a reference to *Northern Pac. R. Co.* and with no explanation of its sudden change in position.

The question remains whether the per se rule stated in *Schwinn* should be expanded to include nonsale transactions or abandoned in favor of a return to the rule of reason. We have found no persuasive support for expanding the rule. As noted above, the *Schwinn* Court recognized the undesirability of "prohibit[ing] all vertical restrictions of territory and all franchising. …" And even Continental does not urge us to hold that all such restrictions are per se illegal.

We revert to the standard articulated in *Northern Pac. R. Co.*, and reiterated in *White Motor*, for determining whether vertical restriction must be "conclusively presumed to be unreasonable and therefore illegal without elaborate inquiry as to the precise harm they have caused or the business excuse for their use." Such restrictions, in varying forms, are widely used in our free market economy. As indicated above, there is substantial scholarly and judicial authority supporting their economic utility. There is relatively little authority to the contrary. Certainly, there has been no showing in this case, either generally or with respect to Sylvania's agreements, that vertical restrictions have or are likely to have a "pernicious effect on competition" or that they "lack … any redeeming virtue." Accordingly, we conclude that the per se rule stated in *Schwinn* must be overruled. In so holding we do not foreclose the possibility that particular applications of vertical restrictions might justify per se prohibition under *Northern Pac. R. Co.* But we do make clear that departure from the rule of reason standard must be based upon demon-strable economic effect rather than—as in *Schwinn*—upon formalistic line drawing.

In sum, we conclude that the appropriate decision is to return to the rule of reason that governed vertical restrictions prior to *Schwinn*.

Affirmed in favor of Plaintiff, Sylvania.

Critical Thinking About the Law

The Supreme Court decision in Case 23-5 had a significant impact on the vertical territorial and consumer restraint standard, as the Supreme Court overturned the standard of the *Schwinn* case. The Supreme Court's decision, however, is not arbitrary. The justices attempted to provide sound reasoning for their decision to move away from the precedent established in *Schwinn*. But before we can evaluate the soundness of the Supreme Court's argument, we must first find the argument. The following questions highlight the crucial steps prior to evaluation of an argument: finding the issue, conclusion, and reasons.

1. State the issue in Case 23-5 in question form. What is the Court's conclusion?

   Clue: Remember that the issue is the primary question that a court is addressing. The conclusion is the court's response to the issue.

2. What reasons does the Court provide for its conclusion?

   Clue: In Case 23-5, the reasons answer the question "Why did the Court overturn the *Schwinn* per se standard?"

Tying Arrangements. As discussed previously under the enforcement section of this chapter (and the *Microsoft* case), a tying arrangement is one in which a single party agrees to sell a product or service (tying product, e.g., Windows 95) on condition that the other party agrees to buy a second (tied) product service (e.g., Internet browser). For example, if a company owns a patent on a tabulating machine (tying product), it will attempt to get its customers to buy only tabulating cards produced by it (tied product); or if a franchisor owns a trademark symbol such as golden arches (tied product), it will seek to get its franchisees to use only products with the designated trademark symbol on them or products approved or manufactured by the franchisor (tying products). As noted in Table 23-2, tying arrangements are violations of Section 3 of the Clayton Act; however, that section of the act applies only to tying arrangements involving tangible commodities. Therefore, actions are frequently brought under Section 1 of the Sherman Act when either the tying or tied products involve services or real property.

Tying arrangements have generally been adjudged per se illegal if the man-ufacturer of the tying product has a monopoly on the tying product either by virtue of a patent or as a result of a natural monopoly situation. If the tying arrangement does not exist in a monopoly situation, it may still be an illegal ver-tical restraint of trade if the following three conditions are present:

1. The manufacturer or seller of the tying product has sufficient economic power to lessen competition in the market of the tied product. For example, if the owner (A) of a patent on salt-dispensing machines (tying product) leases the machines only to companies or individuals (B) who agree to buy salt (tied

product) from A, such an agreement may be considered per se illegal because it limits the sellers of the tied product (salt) from competing vigorously in the salt market. However, if there are similar salt-dispensing-machine manufacturers and lessors that the lessees (B) can buy from, it is clear that A will not be able to lessen competition in the salt market.

2. A substantial amount of interstate commerce is affected. If the manufacturer and lessor of the salt machines, through a tying agreement, has little impact on the market of the tied product (salt), the courts will not consider this agreement to be per se illegal and, using a rule-of-reason approach, will dismiss the case.

3. Two separate products or services are involved. Some franchisors have argued successfully that their trademark (e.g., the golden arches) and their products and services (building, equipment, service contract) are one and the same package rather than separate products and, thus, no tying arrangement exists.

Chronology of Events and Litigation in Selective *Microsoft* Cases

October 1998	Justice Department and 18 states file suits against Microsoft under federal and state antitrust laws.
October 19, 1998	Arguments before Judge Penfield Jackson open in district court in Washington, D.C.
November 5, 1999	Judge Jackson makes a preliminary finding that Microsoft harmed consumers by exploiting its monopoly position in operating systems to limit competition under Section 2 of the Sherman Act.
November 20, 1999	Judge Jackson names Richard Posner, antitrust expert and Chief Judge of the Seventh Circuit Court of Appeals, to bring the parties together for some settlement talks.
March/April 1, 2000	Microsoft offers a settlement proposal, which is rejected by the government, and talks are ended.
April 14, 2000	Judge Jackson finds that Microsoft violated the antitrust laws.
June 8, 2000	Judge Jackson orders that Microsoft be broken up and agrees to restrictions sought by plaintiffs. The company's stock falls $15.37 to $90.875, losing $80 billion of its market value.
June 20, 2000	Judge Jackson certifies the case for immediate review by the U.S. Supreme Court and stays the breakup order pending action. Eighteen states join on appeal.
September 26, 2000	In 8–1 ruling, the U.S. Supreme Court denies an expedited review and sends the case back to the U.S. Court of Appeals of the D.C. Circuit, the same court that ruled favorably for Microsoft in 1998.
February 27, 2001	Oral argument before the U.S. Court of Appeals by plaintiffs and Microsoft.
June 28, 2001	The D.C. Court of Appeals rules favorably for plaintiffs on the monopolization issue (Section 1 of the Sherman Act), denies a Microsoft violation of Section 2, and agrees that Microsoft violated Section 1 as tying arrangements. The court of appeals vacates in full the final judgment of the district court embodying the remedial order and remands the case for reassignment to a different judge from a pool of federal district judges.
July 13, 2001	Plaintiffs file a motion with the U.S. Court of Appeals to accelerate the selection of a new judge and the proceedings in general upon remand.
July 18, 2001	Defendant files a motion with the U.S. Court of Appeals to reconsider its ruling that Microsoft sought to limit competition and Windows operating system software and its Internet browser from "commingling."
July 22–September 15, 2001	Microsoft, Justice Department, and 18 states continue to hold talks with regard to a settlement.

August 3, 2001	The U.S. Court of Appeals refuses to reconsider its ruling that Microsoft illegally blended its software with its operating system.
August 12, 2001	Microsoft and other PC makers argue over desktop icons; while Microsoft announced Windows XP, a new version of its operating system would be available October 1. It indicates that it would integrate Internet shopping, music, and instant message services into the new system.
August 17, 2001	The U.S. Court of Appeals rejects an appeal from Microsoft to delay the selection of a new federal district court judge to consider appropriate penalties until the U.S. Supreme Court returns in October 2001 and decides whether the whole case should be thrown out based on District Court Judge Penfield Jackson's inappropriate conduct.
August 24, 2001	Judge Colleen Kellar-Kotelly is selected randomly from a pool of federal district court judges.
August 29, 2001	Judge Kellar-Kotelly orders all governments and Microsoft lawyers to confer jointly and prepare a report outlining the remaining issues and procedures to resolve them within a two-week period.
August 30, 2001	The European Commission, the executive body of the European Union, announces it is expanding their probe into complaints that Microsoft illegally thwarted competition for audiovisual software by bundling its Media Player with its Windows operating system. Microsoft is sent a "statement of objections." The company had two months to reply and a hearing would follow.
September 6, 2001	Justice Department drops the charge that Microsoft's bundling or tying of software to Windows was illegal. Furthermore, the Justice Department would not seek to break up Microsoft. It would seek curbs on other Microsoft behavior in the marketplace.
September 28, 2001	Citing terror attacks in New York, Washington, D.C., and near Pittsburgh (on September 11, 2001), Judge Colleen Kellar-Kotelly orders around-the-clock negotiations to settle the case by November.
October 25, 2001	Microsoft releases latest operating system XP: 18 states and the District of Columbia hire lawyers to pursue action against Microsoft.
November 2, 2001	Microsoft and the Justice Department reach a proposed settlement of the antitrust case.
November 6, 2001	Nine of the 18 states and the District of Columbia refuse to sign the settlement, alleging that the proposed agreement has too many loopholes and does not promote competition. The states refusing to sign are California, Massachusetts, Utah, Connecticut, Florida, Iowa, Kansas, Minnesota, and West Virginia. Many of these states are home to Microsoft's biggest rivals and others who have complained about Microsoft's aggressive marketing tactics. Other states agreeing with the Justice Department and Microsoft ware New York, Michigan, Illinois, Ohio, Kentucky, Louisiana, Maryland, North Carolina, and Wisconsin.
December 21, 2001	Microsoft moves for a four-month delay of new proceedings on the proposed settlement, claiming the nine states (and the District of Columbia) are seeking an expansion of the case beyond the remedies ordered by the U.S. Court of Appeals on June 28, 2001.
December 31, 2001	Nine states (and the District of Columbia) oppose Microsoft's request, stating that consumers and competitors will suffer injury if the proceedings are delayed.
January 7, 2002	Federal Judge Colleen Kellar-Kotelly rejects Microsoft's request for a four-month delay of the trial to determine penalties for Microsoft antitrust violations.
March 15, 2002	Trial on tougher sanctions begins in the U.S. District Court; Judge Kellar-Kotelly presiding.

November 1, 2002	Judge Kellar-Kotelly approves Microsoft's settlement with the Justice Department rejecting tougher sanctions requested by some states and competitors of Microsoft. Some minor changes made.
October 29, 2003	Microsoft settles suit with five states and the District of Columbia in the amount of $200 million.
March 24, 2004	The European Union Commission fines Microsoft $612.7 million for abusing its market power. Microsoft is ordered to disclose codes from its Windows operating system and offer other PC makers a second version of Windows that doesn't include Media Player.
June 9, 2004	Microsoft appeals EU Commission's decision to the European Court of First Instance claiming that the regulator's decision would undermine innovation.
June 30, 2004	Microsoft pays its fine of $612.7 million imposed by the European Commission on March 24, 2004. The money will be held in an escrow account pending an appeal.
July 1, 2004	U.S. Circuit Court of Appeals for the District of Columbia rejects arguments by Massachusetts and competitors that the agreement of Microsoft with the Justice Department didn't effectively curb the company's monopoly power.
October 28, 2004	Microsoft settled suits with five states for several million dollars. It also settled a suit with Time Warner One's AOL unit for $750 million Sun Microsystems a competitor was paid $1.6 billion to settle an antitrust suit.
November 1, 2004	Microsoft in settlement of a suit with competitor Novell, paid $536 million. It also announced a truce with Computer and Communication Industry Association (CCIA), a trade group, which participated in legal action against the company in the United States and Europe. As part of the settlement Microsoft paid all legal expenses, and joined CCIA paying a $65,000 membership fee.

The following case concerns a tying arrangement involving integrated computer hardware and software within a natural monopoly situation. Look carefully at the court's concern over the per se rule and the rule of reason in this edited opinion.

CASE 23-6

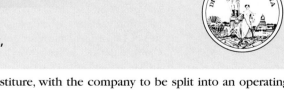

United States v. Microsoft Corporation
U.S. Court of Appeals for the District of Columbia Circuit,
253 F3d.34 (D.C. Cir. 2001)

The United States and 18 state attorney generals (plaintiffs) brought this action against the Microsoft Corporation (defendant) charging (1) a monopoly in the market for Intel-compatible PC operating systems in violation of Section 2 of the Sherman Act; (2) attempt to gain a monopoly in the market for Internet browsers in violation of Section 2; and (3) the illegal tie-in of separate products, Windows and Internet Explorer ("IE") in violation of Section 1. Microsoft denied all three charges. The district court issued a judgment favorable to the plaintiffs on all three charges. To remedy the Sherman Act violations, the lower court issued a final judgment requiring Microsoft to submit a proposed plan of divestiture, with the company to be split into an operating systems business and an applications business. A number of interim restrictions on Microsoft's conduct were also set out in the district court in final judgment. The U.S. Supreme Court turned down an expedited appeal from the U.S. District Court and the plaintiffs, returning the case to the U.S. Court of Appeals for the District of Columbia. Defendant Microsoft now appealed to the court of appeals.

Per Curiam
The District Court concluded that Microsoft's contractual and technological bundling of the IE web browser (the

"tied" product) with its Windows operating system ("OS") (the "tying" product) resulted in a tying arrangement that was per se unlawful. We hold that the rule of reason, rather than per se analysis, should govern the legality of tying arrangements involving platform software products. The Supreme Court has warned that it is only after considerable experience with certain business relationships that courts classify them as per se violations. While every "business relationship" will in some sense have unique features, some represent entire, novel categories of dealings. As we shall explain, the arrangement before us is an example of the latter, offering the first up-close look at the technological integration of added functionality into software that serves as a platform for third-party applications. There being no close parallel in prior antitrust cases, simplistic application of per se tying rules carries a serious risk of harm. Accordingly, we vacate the District Court's finding of a per se tying violation and remand the case. Plaintiffs may on remand pursue their tying claim under the rule of reason.

The facts underlying the tying allegation substantially overlap with those set forth later in this chapter. There are four elements to a per se tying violation: (1) the tying and tied goods are two separate products; (2) the defendant has market power in the tying product market; (3) the defendant affords consumers no choice but to purchase the tied product from it; and (4) the tying arrangement forecloses a substantial volume of commerce.

Microsoft does not dispute that it bound Windows and IE in the four ways the District Court cited. Instead it argues that Windows (the tying good) and IE browsers (the tied good) are not "separate products," and that it did not substantially foreclose competing browsers from the tied product market (Microsoft also contends that it does not have monopoly power in the tying product market, but, for reasons given in Section A, we uphold the District Court's finding to the contrary).

We first address the separate-products inquiry. Our purpose is to highlight the poor fit between the separate-products test and the facts of this case. We then offer further reasons for carving an exception to the per se rule when the tying product is platform software. In the final section we discuss the District Court's inquiry if plaintiffs pursue a rule of reason claim on remand.

A. Separate-Products Inquiry Under the Per Se Test

The requirement that a practice involve two separate products before being condemned as an illegal tie started as a purely linguistic requirement: unless products are separate, one cannot be "tied" to the other.

Direct competition on the merits of the tied product is foreclosed when the tying product either is sold only in a bundle with the tied product, or though offered separately, is sold at a bundled price, so that the buyer pays the same price whether he takes the tied product or not. In both cases, a consumer buying the tying product becomes entitled to the tied product; he will therefore likely be unwilling to buy a competitor's version of the tied product even

if, making his own price/quality assessment, that is what he would prefer.

But not all ties are bad. Bundling obviously saves distribution and consumer transaction costs. Phillip E. Arreda, Antitrust Law Section 1703G2, at 51-52 (1991). This is likely to be true, to take some examples from the computer industry, with the integration of math co-processors and memory into microprocessor chips and the inclusion of spell checkers in word processors.

We now turn to the separate-products inquiry before us. The District Court found that many consumers, if given the option, would choose their browser separately from the OS (noting that "corporate consumers ... prefer to standardize on the same browser across different [OS]" at the workplace). Turning to industry custom, the court found that, although all major OS vendors bundled browsers with their OSs, these companies either sold versions without a browser, or allowed OEMs or end-users either not to install the bundled browser or in any event to "uninstall" it. The court did not discuss the record evidence as to whether OS vendors other than Microsoft sold at a bundled price, with no discount for a browserless OS, perhaps because the record evidence on the issue was in conflict.

Microsoft does not dispute that many consumers demand alternative browsers. But on industry custom Microsoft contends that no other firm requires non-removal because no other firm has invested the resources to integrate web browsing as deeply into its OS as Microsoft has.

Microsoft contends not only that its integration of IE into Windows is innovative and beneficial but also that it requires non-removal of IE. In our discussion of monopoly maintenance we find that these claims fail the efficiency balancing applicable in that context. But the separate-products analysis is supposed to perform its function as a proxy without embarking on any direct analysis of efficiency. Accordingly, Microsoft's implicit argument—that in this case looking to a competitive fringe is inadequate to evaluate fully its potentially innovative technological integration, that such a comparison is between apples and oranges—poses a legitimate objection to the operation of the separate-products test for the per se rule.

In light of the monopoly maintenance section, obviously, we do not find that Microsoft's integration is welfare-enhancing or that it should be absolved of tying liability. Rather, we heed Microsoft's warning that the separate-products element of the per se rule may not give newly integrated products a fair shake.

B. Per Se Analysis Inappropriate for This Case

Supreme Court cases on tying dealt with arrangements whereby the sale or lease of a patented product was conditioned on the purchase of certain unpatented products from the patentee. In none of these cases was the tied good physically and technologically integrated with the tying good. Nor did the defendants ever argue that their tie improved the value of the tying product to users and to makers of complementary goods. In those cases where the defendant claimed that use of the tied good made the tying good more valuable to users, the Court ruled that the same result could be achieved via quality standards for substitutes of the tied good.

Here Microsoft argues the IE and Windows are an integrated physical product and that the bundling of IE APIs with Windows makes the latter a better applications platform for third-party software. It is unclear how the benefits from IE APIs could be achieved by quality standards for different browser manufacturers. We do not pass judgment on Microsoft's claims regarding the benefits from integration of its APIs. We merely note that these and other novel, purported efficiencies suggest that judicial "experience" provides little basis for believing that, "because of their pernicious effect on competition and lack of any redeeming virtue," a software firm's decision to sell multiple functionalities as a package should be "conclusively presumed to be unreasonable and therefore illegal without elaborate inquiry as to the precise harm they have caused or the business excuse for their use."

While the paucity of cases examining software bundling suggests a high risk that per se analysis may produce inaccurate results, the nature of the platform software market affirmatively suggests that per se rules might stunt valuable innovation. We have in mind two reasons.

First, as we explained in the previous section, the separate-products test is a poor proxy for net efficiency from newly integrated products. Under per se analysis the first firm to merge previously distinct functionalities (e.g., the inclusion of starter motors in automobiles) or to eliminate entirely the need for a second function (e.g., the invention of the stain-resistant carpet) risks being condemned as having tied two separate products because at the moment of integration there will appear to be a robust "distinct" market for the tied product. See 10 Areeda et al., Antitrust Law 1746, at

224. Rule of reason analysis, however, affords the first mover an opportunity to demonstrate that an efficiency gain from its "tie" adequately offsets any distortion of consumer choice.

Second, because of the pervasively innovative character of platform software markets, tying in such markets may produce efficiencies that courts have not previously encountered and thus the Supreme Court had not factored into the per se rule as originally conceived.

Our judgment regarding the comparative merits of the per se rule and the rule of reason is confined to the tying arrangement before us, where the tying product is software whose major purpose is to serve as a platform for third-party applications and the tied product is complementary software functionality. While our reasoning may at times appear to have broader force, we do not have the confidence to speak to facts outside the record, which contains scant discussion of software integration generally. Microsoft's primary justification for bundling IE APIs is that their inclusion with Windows increases the value of third-party software (and Windows) to consumers. Because this claim applies with distinct force when the tying product is platform software, we have no present basis for finding the per se rule is applicable to software markets generally. Nor should we be interpreted as setting a precedent for switching to the rule of reason every time a court identifies an efficiency justification for a tying arrangement. Our reading of the record suggests merely that integration of new functionality into platform software is a common practice and the wooden application of per se rules in this litigation may cause a cloud over platform innovation in the market for PCs, network computers, and information appliances.

Remanded to the district court, applying the rule of reason as to tying arrangements.

Exclusive-Dealing Contracts. Agreements between manufacturers and retailers (dealers), or between franchisors and franchisees, requiring the second party to sell and promote only the brand of goods supplied by the first party are known

exclusive-dealing contract
Agreement in which one party requires another party to sell and promote only the brand of goods supplied by the first party.

as **exclusive-dealing contracts**. For example, the Standard Oil Company of California had exclusive-dealing contracts with independent stations in seven western states that required the stations to buy all their oil and other petroleum products from the company. Sales under that exclusive-dealing contract involved approximately 7 percent of all sales of such products in the seven states. Using a comparative substantiability test (one comparing the effect of such agreements on competing sellers of petroleum products in the geographic area), the U.S. Supreme Court found a violation of Section 3 of the Clayton Act.[8]

Since that case, the Court has generally followed a rule-of-reason approach in cases that involve exclusive-dealing agreements. Such agreements are found to be illegal when they foreclose a substantial portion of a relevant market. The Court has found that legitimate business reasons for exclusive-dealing contracts exist in certain industries. For example, it ruled that an exclusive-dealing con-

---

[8] *Standard Oil Co. of California v. United States,* 337 U.S. 293 (1949).

tract between an electrical utility and a coal supplier extending 20 years was lawful because it had procompetitive effects.[9] The contract assured the utility and its customers a regular supply of coal at a reasonably fixed rate and allowed the coal company to better plan its production and employment needs over a long period; in turn, it was allowed to offer the utility a lower price.

SECTION 2: MONOPOLIES

Section 2 of the Sherman Act reads:

> *Every person who shall monopolize, or attempt to monopolize, or combine or conspire with any other person or persons to monopolize any part of trade or commerce among the several states, or with foreign nations, shall be deemed guilty of a felony, and on conviction thereof shall be punished by a fine not exceeding one million dollars if a corporation or, if any other person, one hundred thousand dollars, or by imprisonment not exceeding three years, or by both.*

Section 2, therefore, prohibits monopolization, attempts to monopolize, and conspiracies to monopolize. Each of these prohibitions is examined in this section. In reading this material, keep the following four factors in mind:

1. One of the purposes of antitrust law, as we stated earlier in this chapter, is to promote a competitive model. Such a model traditionally assumes the existence of many buyers and sellers who have equal access to information about the marketplace and labor that is mobile.

2. In framing Section 2 of the Sherman Act, Congress was vague about what it meant by a **monopoly**. Therefore, it has been up to the courts to define the concept case by case, sometimes with the aid of economic analysis.

3. Some claim that U.S. corporations need to be large in order to compete with state-owned and state-supported foreign multinationals.

4. Large companies that have attained their monopolistic position through innovation and research, leading to patents, may be forced in some cases to share the results of their efforts with competitors in order to avoid bringing down on themselves a Section 2 enforcement and possible penalties of fines or imprisonment or both.

monopoly An economic market situation in which a single business has the power to fix the price of goods or services.

Monopolization. The U.S. Supreme Court has developed three criteria, or steps, to determine whether a firm has attained a monopolistic position and is misusing its power in violation of Section 2 of the Sherman Act:

1. It determines the relevant product and geographic markets within which the alleged monopolist operates.

2. It determines whether the defendant has overwhelming power in the relevant markets.

3. It examines whether there is an intent on the part of the alleged monopolist to monopolize.

Relevant Product and Geographic Markets. Markets are divided into product and geographic markets. How the courts determine the boundaries of those markets helps decide what market share a company has and, thus, its market power.

The courts have generally defined the relevant product market as that in which the company alleged to be a monopolist can raise or lower prices with

---

[9] *Tampa Electric Co. v. Nashville Coal Co.*, 365 U.S. 320 (1961).

cross-elasticity of demand, or substitutability If an increase in the price of one product leads consumers to purchase another product, the two products are substitutable and there is said to be cross-elasticity of demand.

relative independence of the forces of supply and demand. In a monopoly situation, the courts look to the concept of **cross-elasticity of demand, or substitutability**.

Cross-elasticity of demand measures the impact that upward and downward changes in price have on the demand for the product. If cross-elasticity of demand is positive, an increase in price of the alleged monopolistic product will result in consumers' switching to a substitute product. For example, in a landmark case,[10] the government charged the DuPont Company with monopolizing the cellophane industry because it produced 75 percent of all the cellophane sold in the United States. DuPont argued that cellophane was not the correct product market because there were many substitutes for cellophane; rather, flexible packaging materials was the correct product market to consider in this case. If the court agreed, DuPont would not be a monopolist because cellophane constituted only 25 percent of the flexible packaging materials market. The U.S. Supreme Court did rule in favor of DuPont, on the basis of the availability of substitutes and the high elasticity of demand for cellophane. The Court noted that a slight increase in the price of cellophane caused many customers to switch to other flexible wrapping materials, which showed there was a positive cross-elasticity of demand and that DuPont lacked monopoly status.

The courts generally have defined the geographic market as the area where the defendant's firm competes head-on with others in the previously determined relevant product market. Usually, geographic markets are stipulated (agreed to) by the plaintiff and the defendant as regional, national, or international. However, an exception occurred in a leading monopoly case decided by the Supreme Court.[11] In this case, the parties argued over whether the products that were sold were at a regional market level (Grinnell) or at a national level (United States). The products in which Grinnell had ownership interests included tires, sprinklers, plumbing supplies, and burglary systems, together called accredited central station protection services.

Overwhelming Power in the Market. Once the relevant markets have been determined, the alleged monopolist's market power to control prices and to exclude fringe competition is significant. The courts are interested in whether the defendant has overwhelming market power, not absolute power, because there are usually small competitors who produce poor substitutes. The courts will ask: Do the pricing and output of the alleged monopolist control the conduct of the few competitors in the industry?

In order to answer that question, the courts have traditionally looked at five factors: market share, the size of other firms in the industry or market, the pricing structure of the market, entry barriers, and the unique nature of the industry. In the case of *Aspen Skiing Company v. Aspen Highlands Skiing Corporation*,[12] the U.S. Supreme Court stated that in viewing market power, it would look not only at the market share that the alleged monopolist held but also at whether the power was acquired and maintained through predatory conduct that would be illegal or as a result of a superior product, business acumen, or historical accident. This approach is fair because a corporation attaining monopoly power through innovation and research could easily be punished instead of rewarded if market share were the sole measure of overwhelming market power. A company would

---

[10] *United States v. DuPont Co.*, 351 U.S. 3717 (1956).

[11] *United States v. Grinnell Co.*, 384 U.S. 563 (1966).

[12] 388 U.S. 365 (1967).

then have little incentive to compete to gain a market share in excess of 50 percent because if it did gain that much (or perhaps even less), it would risk being charged a monopolist under Section 2 of the Sherman Act.

Intent to Monopolize. After defining the relevant product and geographic markets and determining whether the company has overwhelming market power, the courts must decide if the company has a general intent to monopolize the market. This step is significant because having overwhelming power by virtue of being "big" in the market is not enough to make a firm liable for a Section 2 violation. The courts will look at specific conduct that tends to show "intent," such as attempts to exclude competitors or to raise barriers to entry. They particularly look at the foreseeable consequences of an alleged monopolist's actions: Would these actions naturally lead to a monopoly position? For example, the Aluminum Company of America (ALCOA) anticipated every demand increase and expanded its output in the aluminum industry. It was, thus, able to exclude competitors from the aluminum ingot market by lowering prices. These generally would be good business practices if ALCOA had not been judged to have overwhelming market power in the relevant product market. The courts draw a fine line between a monopoly gained by innovation, patents, and business acumen and one attained by conduct whose foreseeable consequence is the reinforcement of a monopoly position. The first position is gained in a passive manner, the second in an active manner that shows intent to monopolize. Note carefully the court's analysis that is outlined in the case that follows.

CASE 23-7

United States v. Microsoft Corporation
U.S. Court of Appeals for the District of Columbia Circuit,
253 F3d.34 (D.C. Cir. 2001)

(The authors recommend a close reading of the facts as earlier set out in this text—U.S. v. Microsoft, p. 712–714—as well as the box entitled "Chronology of Events and Litigation in Selective Microsoft Cases.")

Section 2 of the Sherman Act makes it unlawful for a firm to "monopolize." The offense of monopolization has two elements: (1) the possession of monopoly power in the relevant market and (2) the willful acquisition or maintenance of that power as distinguished from growth or development as a consequence of a superior product, business acumen, or historic accident.

The district court found that Microsoft possesses monopoly power in the market for Intel-compatible PC operating systems. Focusing primarily on Microsoft's efforts to suppress Netscape Navigator's threat to its operating systems monopoly, the court also found that Microsoft maintained its power not through competition on the merits, but through unlawful means. Microsoft challenges both conclusions. We defer to the District Court's finding of fact, setting them aside only if clearly erroneous.

We begin by considering whether Microsoft possesses monopoly power and finding that it does, we turn to the question whether it maintained this power through anticompetitive means. Agreeing with the District Court that the company behaved anticompetitively and that these actions contributed to the maintenance of its monopoly power we affirm the court's finding of liability for monopolization.

A. Monopoly Power

While merely possessing monopoly power is not itself an antitrust violation, it is a necessary element of a monopolization charge. The Supreme Court defines monopoly power as the power to control prices or exclude competition. More precisely, a firm is a monopolist if it can profitably raise prices substantially above the competitive level where evidence that a firm has in fact probably done so, the existence of monopoly power is clear. Because such direct proof is only rarely available courts more typically examine market structure in search of circumstantial evidence of monopoly power. Under this structural approach monopoly power may be inferred from a firm's possession of a dominant share of a relevant market that is protected by entry barriers.

"Entry barriers" are factors (such as certain regulatory requirements) that prevent new rivals from timely responding to an increase in price above the competitive level.

The District Court considered these structural factors and concluded that Microsoft possesses monopoly power in a relevant market. Defining the market as Intel-compatible PC operating systems, the District Court found that Microsoft has a greater than 95% share. It also found the company's market position protected by a substantial entry barrier.

Microsoft argues that the District Court incorrectly defined the relevant market. It also claims that there is no barrier to entry in that market. Alternatively, Microsoft argues that because the software industry is uniquely dynamic, direct proof, rather than circumstantial evidence, more appropriately indicates whether it possesses monopoly power. Rejecting each argument, we uphold the District Court's finding of monopoly power in its entirety.

1 Market Structure

a. Market definition

The relevant market must include all products "reasonably interchangeable by consumers for the same purposes." In this case, the District Court defined the market as "the licensing of all Intel-compatible PC operating systems worldwide," finding that there are "currently no products—and . . . there are not likely to be any in the near future—that a significant percentage of computer users worldwide could substitute for [these operating systems] without incurring substantial costs." Calling this market definition "far too narrow," Microsoft argues that the District Court improperly excluded three types of products: non–Intel-compatible operating systems (primarily Apple's Macintosh operating system, Mac OS), operating systems for non-PC.

Microsoft does not argue that the District Court findings do not support its conclusion that information appliances and portal Web sites are outside the relevant market.

This brings us to Microsoft's main challenge to the District Court's market definition: the exclusion of middleware. Microsoft argues that, because middleware could usurp the operating system's platform function and might eventually take over other operating system functions (for instance, by controlling peripherals), the District Court erred in excluding Navigator and Java from the relevant market. The District Court found, however, that neither Navigator, Java, nor any other middleware product could now, or would soon, expose enough APIs to serve as a platform for popular applications, much less take over all operating system functions. Again, Microsoft fails to

challenge these findings, instead simply asserting middleware's "potential" as a competitor. The test of reasonable interchangeability, however, required the District Court to consider only substitutes that constrain pricing in the reasonably foreseeable future, and only products that can enter the market relatively short time can perform this function. Because market definition is meant to identify products "reasonably interchangeable by consumers," and because middleware is not now interchangeable with Windows, the District Court had good reason for excluding middleware from the relevant market.

b. Market power

Having thus properly defined the relevant market, the District Court found that Windows accounts for a greater than 95% share. The court also found that even if Mac OS were included, Microsoft's share would exceed 80%. Microsoft challenges neither finding, nor does it argue that such a market share is non-predominant.

Instead, Microsoft claims that even a predominant market share does not by itself indicate monopoly power. Although the "existence of [monopoly] power ordinarily may be inferred from the predominant share of the market," we agree with Microsoft that because of the possibility of competition from new entrants, looking to current market share alone can be "misleading." In this case, however, the District Court was not misled. Considering the possibility of new rivals, the court focused not only on Microsoft's present market share, but also on the structural barrier that protects the company's future position. That barrier—the "applications barrier to entry"—stems from two characteristics of the software market: (1) most consumers prefer operating systems for which a large number of applications have already been written; and (2) most developers prefer to write for operating systems that already have a substantial consumer base.

2. Direct Proof

a. Having sustained the District Court's conclusion that circumstantial evidence proves that Microsoft possesses monopoly power, we turn to Microsoft's alternative argument that it does not behave like a monopolist. Claiming that software competition is uniquely "dynamic," the company suggests a new rule: that monopoly power in the software industry should be proven directly, that is, by examining a company's actual behavior to determine if it reveals the existence of monopoly power. According to Microsoft, not only does no such proof of its power exist, but record evidence demonstrates the absence of monopoly power. The company claims that it invests heavily in research and development and charges a low price for Windows, a small percentage

CHAPTER 23 • Antitrust Laws

of the price of an Intel-compatible PC system and less than the price of its rivals.

Microsoft's argument fails because, even assuming that the software market is uniquely dynamic in the long term, the District Court correctly applied the structural approach to determine if the company faces competition in the short term.

Structural market power analyses are meant to determine whether potential substitutes constrain a firm's ability to raise prices above the competitive level; only threats that are likely to materialize in the relatively near future perform this function to any significant degree. The District Court expressly considered and rejected Microsoft's claims that innovations such as handheld devices and portal Web sites would soon expand the relevant market beyond Intel-compatible PC operating systems. Because the company does not challenge these findings, we have no reason to believe that prompt substitutes are available. The structural approach, as applied by the District Court, is thus capable of fulfilling its purpose even in a changing market. Microsoft cites no case, nor are we aware of one, requiring direct evidence to show monopoly power in any market. We decline to adopt such a rule now.

B. Anticompetitive Conduct

As discussed above, having a monopoly does not by itself violate Section 2. A firm violates Section 2 only when it acquires or maintains, or attempts to acquire or maintain, a monopoly by engaging in exclusionary conduct "as distinguished from growth or development as a consequence of a superior product, business acumen, or historic accident." *Grinnell*, 384 U.S. at 571; see also *United States v. Aluminum Co. of Am.*, 148 F.2d 416, 430 (2d Cir. 1945) ... ("The successful competitor, having been urged to compete, must not be turned upon when he wins.").

In this case, after concluding that Microsoft had monopoly power, the District Court held that Microsoft had violated Section 2 by engaging in a variety of exclusionary acts (not including predatory pricing), to maintain its monopoly by preventing the effective distribution and use of products that might threaten that monopoly. Specifically, the District Court held Microsoft liable for: (1) the way in which it integrated IE into Windows; (2) its various dealings with Original Equipment Manufacturers ("OEMs"), Internet Access Providers ("IAP"), Internet Content Providers ("ICPs"), Independent Software Vendors ("ISVs"), and Apple Computer; (3) its efforts to contain and to subvert Java technologies; and (4) its course of conduct as a whole.

Upon appeal, Microsoft argues that it did not engage in any exclusionary conduct. Whether any particular act of a monopolist is exclusionary, rather than merely a form of vigorous competition, can be difficult to discern: the means of illicit exclusion, like the means of legitimate

competition, are myriad. The challenge for an antitrust court lies in stating a general rule for distinguishing between exclusionary acts, which reduce social welfare, and competitive acts, which increase it. From a century of case law on monopolization under Section 2, however, several principles do emerge. First, to be condemned as exclusionary, a monopolist's act must have an "anticompetitive effect." In contrast, harm to one or more competitors will not suffice. "The [Sherman Act] directs itself not against conduct which is competitive, even severely so, but against conduct which unfairly tends to destroy competition itself."

Second, the plaintiff, on whom the burden of proof of course rests, overruled on grounds must demonstrate that the monopolist's conduct indeed has the requisite anticompetitive effect. For a case brought by a private plaintiff, the plaintiff must show that its injury is of the type that the statute was intended to cover.

1. Licenses Issued to Original Equipment Manufacturers
The District Court condemned a number of provisions in Microsoft's agreements licensing Windows to OEMs, because it found that Microsoft's imposition of those provisions (like many of Microsoft's other actions at issue in this case) serves to reduce usage share of Netscape's browser and, hence, protect Microsoft's operating system monopoly. The reason market share in the browser market affects market power in the operating system market is complex, and warrants some explanation.

Browser usage share is important because, as we explained in Section II.A above, a browser (or any middleware product, for that matter) must have a critical mass of users in order to attract software developers to write applications relying upon the APIs it exposes, and away from the APIs exposed by Windows. Applications written to a particular browser's APIs, however, would run on any computer with that browser, regardless of the underlying operating system. The overwhelming majority of consumers will only use a PC operating system for which there already exists a large and varied set of applications. ...

If a consumer could have access to the applications he desired—regardless of the operating system he uses—simply by installing a particular browser on his computer, then he would no longer feel compelled to select Windows in order to have access to those applications; he could select an operating system other than Windows based solely upon its quality and price. In other words, the market for operating systems would be competitive.

Therefore, Microsoft's efforts to gain market share in one market (browsers) served to meet the threat to Microsoft's monopoly in another market (operating systems) by keeping rival browsers from gaining the critical mass of users necessary to attract developer attention away from Windows as the platform for software development. Plaintiffs also argue that Microsoft's actions injured competition in the browser market—an argument we will examine below in relation to their specific claims that Microsoft attempted to monopolize the browser market and unlawfully tied its browser to its operating system so as to foreclose competition in the market.

a. Anticompetitive effect of the license restrictions

The restrictions Microsoft places upon Original Equipment Manufacturers are of particular importance in determining browser usage share because having an OEM pre-install a browser on a computer is one of the two most cost-effective methods by far of distributing browsing software. (The other is bundling the browser with internet access software distributed by an IAP.) The District Court found that the restrictions Microsoft imposed in licensing Windows to OEMs prevented many OEMs from distributing browsers other than IE. In particular, the District Court condemned the license provisions prohibiting the OEMS from: (1) removing any desktop icons, folders, or "Start" menu entries; (2) altering the initial boot sequence; and (3) otherwise altering the appearance of the Windows desktop.

The District Court concluded that the first license restriction—the prohibition upon the removal of desktop icons, folders, and Start menu entries—thwarts the distribution of a rival browser by preventing OEMs from removing visible means of user access to IE. The OEMs cannot practically install a second browser in addition to IE, the court found, partly because "[p]re-installing more than one product in a given category ... can significantly increase an OEM's support costs, for the redundancy can lead to confusion among novice users." That is, a certain number of novice computer users, seeing two browser icons, will wonder which to use when and will call the OEM's support line. Support calls are extremely expensive and, in the highly competitive original equipment market, firms have a strong incentive to minimize costs.

The second license provision at issue prohibits OEMs from modifying the initial boot sequence—the process that occurs the first time a consumer turns on the computer. Prior to the imposition of that restriction, "among the programs that many OEMs inserted into the boot sequence were Internet sign-up procedures that encouraged users to choose from a list of IAPs assembled by the OEM. Microsoft's prohibition on any alteration of the boot sequence thus prevents OEMs from using that process to promote the services of IAPs, many of which—at least at the time Microsoft imposed the restriction—used Navigator.

Microsoft does not deny that the prohibition on modifying the boot sequence has the effect of decreasing competition against IE by preventing OEMs from promoting rivals' browsers. Because this prohibition has a substantial effect in protecting Microsoft's market power, and does so through a means other than competition on the merits, it is anticompetitive. Again the question whether the provision is nonetheless justified awaits later treatment.

Finally, Microsoft imposes several additional provisions that, like the prohibition on removal of icons, prevent OEMs from making various alterations to the desktop: Microsoft prohibits OEMs from causing any user interface other than the Windows desktop to launch automatically, from adding icons or folders different in size or shape from those supplied by Microsoft, and from using the "Active Desktop" feature to promote third-party brands. These restrictions impose significant costs upon the OEMs; prior to Microsoft's prohibiting the practice, many OEMs would change the appearance of the desktop in ways they found beneficial. The anti-competitive effect of the license restrictions is, as Microsoft itself recognizes, that OEMs are not able to promote rival browsers, which keeps developers focused upon the APIs in Windows.

In sum, we hold that with the exception of the one restriction prohibiting automatically launched alternative interfaces, all the OEM license restrictions at issue represent uses of Microsoft's market power to protect its monopoly, unredeemed by any legitimate justification. The restrictions therefore violate Section 2 of the Sherman Act.

2. Integration of IE and Windows

Although Microsoft's license restrictions have a significant effect in closing rival browsers out of one of the two primary channels of distribution, the District Court found that "Microsoft's executives believed ... its contractual restrictions placed on OEMs would not be sufficient in themselves to reverse the direction of Navigator's usage share." Consequently, in late 1995 or early 1996, Microsoft set out to bind [IE] more tightly to Windows 95 as a technical matter.

Technologically binding IE to Windows, the District Court found, both prevented OEMs from pre-installing other browsers and deterred consumers from using them. In particular, having the IE software code as an irremovable part of Windows meant that pre-installing a second browser would "increase an OEM's product testing costs," because an OEM must test and train its support staff to answer calls related to every software product reinstalled on the machine; moreover, pre-installing a browser in addition to IE would to many OEMs be "a questionable use of the scarce and valuable space on a PC's hard drive."

Although the District Court, in its Conclusions of Law, broadly condemned Microsoft's decision to bind "Internet Explorer to Windows with … technological shackles, its findings of fact in support of that conclusion center upon three specific actions Microsoft took to weld IE to Windows: excluding IE from the "Add/Remove Programs" utility; designing Windows so as in certain circumstances to override the user's choice of a default browser other than IE; and commingling code related to browsing and other code in the same files, so that any attempt to delete the files containing IE would, at the same time, cripple the operating system. As with the license restrictions, we consider first whether the suspect actions had an anticompetitive effect, and then whether Microsoft has provided a procompetitive justification for them.

a. Anticompetitive effect of integration

As a general rule, courts are properly very skeptical about claims that competition has been harmed by a dominant firm's product design changes. In a competitive market, firms routinely innovate in the hope of appealing to consumers, sometimes in the process making their products incompatible with those of rivals; the imposition of liability when a monopolist does the same thing will inevitably deter a certain amount of innovation. This is all the more true in a market, such as this one, in which the product itself is rapidly changing. Judicial deference to product innovation, however, does not mean that a monopolist's product design decisions are per se lawful.

The District Court first condemned as anticompetitive Microsoft's decision to exclude IE from the "Add/Remove Programs" utility in Windows 98. Microsoft had included IE in the Add/Remove Programs utility in Windows 95, but when it modified Windows 95 to produce Windows 98, it took IE out of the Add/Remove Programs utility. This change reduces the usage share of rival browsers not by making Microsoft's own browser more attractive to consumers but, rather, by discouraging OEMs from distributing rival products. Because Microsoft's conduct, through something other than competition on the merits, has the effect of significantly reducing usage of rivals' products and hence protecting its own operating system monopoly, it is anticompetitive; we defer for the moment the question whether it is nonetheless justified.

Second, the District Court found that Microsoft designed Windows 98 "so that using Navigator on Windows 98 would have unpleasant consequences for users" by, in some circumstances, overriding the user's choice of a browser other than IE as his or her default browser. Plaintiffs argue that this override harms the competitive process by deterring consumers from using a browser other than IE even though they might

prefer to do so, thereby reducing rival browsers' usage share and, hence, the ability of rival browsers to draw developer attention away from the APIs exposed by Windows. Microsoft does not deny, of course, that overriding the user's preference prevents some people from using other browsers. Because the override reduces rivals' usage share and protects Microsoft's monopoly, it too is anticompetitive.

Finally, the District Court condemned Microsoft's decision to bind IE to Windows 98 "by placing code specific to Web browsing in the same files as code that provided operating system functions." Putting code supplying browsing functionality into a file with code supplying operating system functionality "ensure[s] that the deletion of any file containing browsing-specific routines would also delete vital operating system routines and thus cripple Windows. … " As noted above, preventing an OEM from removing IE deters it from installing a second browser because doing so increases the OEM's product testing and support costs; by contract, had OEMs been able to remove IE, they might have chosen to pre-install Navigator alone.

Microsoft denies, as a factual matter, that it commingled browsing and nonbrowsing code, and it maintains the District Court's findings to the contrary are clearly erroneous.

In view of the contradictory testimony in the record, some of which supports the District Court's finding that Microsoft commingled browsing and non-browsing code, we cannot conclude that the finding was clearly erroneous. Accordingly, we reject Microsoft's argument that we should vacate [findings] as it relates to the commingling of code, and we conclude that such commingling has an anticompetitive effect; as noted above, the commingling deters OEMs from pre-installing rival browsers, thereby reducing the rivals' usage share and, hence, developers' interest in rivals' APIs as an alternative to the API set exposed by Microsoft's operating system.

3. Agreements with Internet Access Providers

The District Court also condemned as exclusionary Microsoft's agreements with various IAPs. The IAPs include both Internet Service Providers, which offer consumers Internet access, and Online Services ("OLSs") such as America Online ("AOL"), which offer proprietary content in addition to Internet access and other services. The District Court deemed Microsoft's agreements with the IAPs unlawful because: Microsoft licensed [IE] and the [IE] Access Kit to hundreds of IAPs for no charge. Then, Microsoft extended valuable promotion treatment to the ten most important IAPs in exchange for their commitment to promote and distribute [IE] and to exile Navigator from the desktop. Finally, in exchange for efforts to upgrade existing subscribers to client software that came bundled with [IE] instead of Navigator, Microsoft granted rebates—and in some cases made outright payments—to those same IAPs.

The District Court condemned Microsoft's actions in (1) offering IE free of charge to IAPs and (2) offering IAPs a bounty for each customer the IAP signs up for service using the IE browser. In effect, the court concluded that Microsoft is acting to preserve its monopoly by offering IE to IAPs at an attractive price. Similarly, the District Court held Microsoft liable for (3) developing the IE Access Kit ("IEAK"), a software package that allows an IAP to "create a distinctive identity for its service in as little as a few hours by customizing the [IE] title bar, icon, start and search pages," and (4) offering the IEAK to IAPs free of charge, on the ground that those acts, too, helped Microsoft preserve its monopoly. Finally, the District Court found that (5) Microsoft agreed to provide easy access to IAPs' services from the Windows desktop in return for the IAPs' agreement to promote IE exclusively and to keep shipments of Internet access software using Navigator under a specific percentage, typically 25%.

By ensuring that the "majority" of all IAP subscribers are offered IE either as the default browser or as the only browser, Microsoft's deals with the IAPs clearly have a significant effect in preserving its monopoly; they help keep usage of Navigator below the critical level necessary for Navigator or any other rival to pose a real threat to Microsoft's monopoly.

Plaintiffs having demonstrated a harm to competition, the burden falls upon Microsoft to defend its exclusive dealing contracts with IAPs by providing a procompetitive justification for them. Significantly, Microsoft's only explanation for its exclusive dealing is that it wants to keep developers focused upon its APIs—which is to say, it wants to preserve its power in the operating system market. That is not an unlawful end, but neither is it a procompetitive justification for the specific means here in question, namely exclusive dealing contracts with IAPs. Accordingly, we affirm the District Court's decision holding that Microsoft's exclusive contracts with IAPs are exclusionary devices, in violation of Section 2 of the Sherman Act.

4. Dealings with Internet Content Providers, Independent Software Vendors, and Apple Computer

The District Court held that Microsoft engages in exclusionary conduct in its dealings with ICPs, which develop Web sites; ISVs, which develop software; and Apple, which is both an OEM and a software developer. The District Court condemned Microsoft's deals with ICPs and ISVs, stating: "By granting ICPs and ISVs free licenses to bundle [IE] with their offerings, and by exchanging other valuable inducements for their agreement to distribute, promote[,] and rely on [IE] rather than Navigator, Microsoft directly induced developers to focus on its own APIs rather than ones exposed by Navigator."

Microsoft offers no procompetitive justification for the exclusive dealing arrangement. It makes only the irrelevant claim that the IE-for-Mac Office deal is part of a multifaceted set of agreements between itself and Apple … [which] does not mean it has any procompetitive justification. Accordingly, we hold that the exclusive deal with Apple is exclusionary, in violation of Section 2 of the Sherman Act.

5. Java

Java, a set of technologies developed by Sun Microsystems, is another type of middleware posing a potential threat to Windows' position as the ubiquitous platform for software development. The Java technologies include: (1) a programming language; (2) a set of programs written in that language, called the "java class libraries," which expose APIs; (3) a compiler, which translates code written by a developer into "bytecode"; and (4) a Java Virtual Machine ("JVM"), which translates bytecode into instructions to the operating system. Programs calling upon the Java APIs will run on any machine with a "Java runtime environment," that is, Java class libraries and a JVM.

In May 1995 Netscape agreed with Sun to distribute a copy of the Java runtime environment with every copy of Navigator, and "Navigator quickly became the principal vehicle by which Sun placed copies of its Java runtime environment on the PC systems of Windows users." Microsoft, too, agreed to promote the Java technologies—or so it seemed. For at the same time, Microsoft took steps "to maximize the difficulty with which applications written in Java could be ported from Windows to other platforms, and vice versa." Specifically, the District Court found that Microsoft took four steps to exclude Java from developing as a viable cross-platform threat: (a) designing a JVM incompatible with the one developed by Sun; (b) entering into contracts, the so-called "First Wave Agreements," requiring major ISVs to promote Microsoft's JVM exclusively; (c) deceiving Java developers about the Windows-specific nature of the tools it distributed to them; and (d) coercing Intel to stop aiding Sun in improving the Java technologies.

[Authors' note: While reversing the district court imposition of liability for Microsoft development and promotion of its JVM (item (a) above), the court of appeals held that items (b) through (d) above were in violation of Section 2 of the Sherman Act.]

c. Causation

As a final parry, Microsoft urges this court to reverse on the monopoly maintenance claim, because plaintiffs never established a causal link between Microsoft's anticompetitive conduct, in particular its foreclosure of Netscape's and Java's distribution channels, and the maintenance of Microsoft's operating system monopoly. This is the flip side of Microsoft's earlier argument that the District Court should have included middleware in the relevant market. According to Microsoft, the District Court cannot simultaneously find that middleware is not a reasonable substitute and that Microsoft's exclusionary conduct contributed to the maintenance of monopoly power in the operating system market. Microsoft claims that the first finding depended on the court's view that middleware does not pose a serious threat to Windows, while the second finding required the court to find that Navigator and Java would have developed into serious enough cross-platform threats to erode the applications barrier to entry. We disagree.

We may infer causation when exclusionary conduct is aimed at producers of nascent competitive technologies as well as when it is aimed at producers of established substitutes. Admittedly, in the former case there is added uncertainty, inasmuch as nascent threats are merely potential substitutes. But the underlying proof problem is the same—neither plaintiffs nor the court can confidently reconstruct a product's hypothetical development in a world absent the defendant's exclusionary conduct. Microsoft (has) no defense to liability for its unlawful actions undertaken to maintain its monopoly in the operating system market.

Remedies

On remand, the District Court must reconsider whether the use of the structural remedy of divestiture is appropriate with respect to Microsoft, which argues that it is a unitary company. By and large, cases upon which plaintiffs rely in arguing for the split of Microsoft have involved the dissolution of entities formed by mergers and acquisitions. On the contrary, the Supreme Court has clarified that divestiture has traditionally been the remedy for Sherman Act violations whose heart is intercorporate combination and control, and that complete divestiture is particularly appropriate where asset or stock acquisitions violate the antitrust laws.

One apparent reason why courts have not ordered the dissolution of unitary companies is logistical difficulty. If the court on remand is unconvinced of the causal connection between Microsoft's exclusionary conduct and the company's position in the OS market, it may well conclude that divestiture is not an appropriate remedy.

While we do not undertake to dictate to the District Court the precise form that relief should take on remand, we note again that it should be tailored to fit the wrong creating the occasion for the remedy. In sum, we vacate the District Court's remedies decree for three reasons. First, the District Court failed to hold an evidentiary hearing despite the presence of remedies-specific factual disputes. Second, the court did not provide adequate reasons for its decreed remedies. Finally, we have drastically altered the scope of Microsoft's liability, and it is for the District Court in the first instance to determine the propriety of a specific remedy for the limited ground of liability which we have upheld.

Affirmed in part and reversed in part, and remanded,
vacating final judgment of District Court.

Comment

As of August 2001, the plaintiffs have urged the court of appeals to expedite a hearing before the district court. A judge was chosen from a pool of members of the District of Columbia District Court, excluding Judge Jackson. In the eyes of the court of appeals, he violated ethical restrictions by discussing the case in public (with reporters in chambers) while the trial was proceeding. Canon 3A(6) of the Code of Conduct for United States Judges requires federal judges to "avoid public comments on the merits of … pending or impending" cases. The court of appeals indicated that Judge Jackson violated the canon by talking about the case with reporters while it was ongoing. It called this conduct "deliberate, repeated, egregious, and flagrant." See Chronology on pages 712–714 from October 1998 to November 1, 2004.

Attempt to Monopolize. Section 2 of the Sherman Act forbids not only monopolization but also even attempts to monopolize because the drafters of the section were concerned about the damage that efforts to attain a monopoly could inflict on an industry even if such efforts failed. So great was their concern, in fact, that the penalties are the same for both monopolization and attempts to monopolize. Case law indicates that after determining the relevant geographic and product markets, the courts look for one or some combination of three factors when a firm is charged with an attempt to monopolize: specific intent, predatory conduct, and a dangerous probability of success. We will discuss the first two; the third is self-explanatory.

Specific intent is shown by bringing forth evidence that a firm has engaged in predatory or anticompetitive conduct aimed at a stated or potential competitor.

Predatory conduct includes (1) stealing trade secrets, (2) interfering unlawfully in requirement contracts that third parties have with other competitors, and

predatory pricing Pricing below the average or marginal cost in order to drive out competition.

(3) attempting to destroy the reputation of a competitor through defamatory actions. Recently, the courts have added **predatory pricing**—pricing below average variable cost (or, in some cases, below average total cost)—to this list on the ground that when a company is pricing below average variable cost, it is not seeking to maximize profits but is intending to drive a competitor out of business.

THE CLAYTON ACT OF 1914

Clayton Act Prohibits price discrimination, tying, and exclusive-dealing arrangements, and corporate mergers that substantially lessen competition or tend to create a monopoly in interstate commerce.

The Clayton Act was enacted in 1914 after a major debate in the presidential campaign of 1912. The Supreme Court had ruled in 1911 that only restraints that were unreasonable by their nature or in their effect could be declared unlawful under the Sherman Act. This ruling left much room for interpretation by federal judges as well as by Justice Department prosecutors. Democratic candidate Woodrow Wilson argued during the presidential campaign that the Supreme Court was hostile to the antitrust laws and that businesspeople needed guidance as to what specific practices were illegal. He urged the creation of an agency to investigate trade practices and to advise businesspeople about which actions were lawful and which were not. Upon election, Wilson proposed a bill that, after great debate and compromise in Congress, was enacted into law as the **Clayton Act** of 1914. It declared the following acts to be illegal under certain circumstances:

1. Price discrimination (Section 2).
2. Tying arrangements and exclusive-dealing contracts (Section 3).
3. Corporate mergers and acquisitions that tend to lessen competition or to create a monopoly (Section 7).
4. Interlocking directorates (Section 8).

At the same time, Congress passed the Federal Trade Commission Act of 1914, setting up the Federal Trade Commission (FTC) and giving it authority to police these and other "unfair or deceptive acts or practices affecting interstate commerce."

SECTION 2: PRICE DISCRIMINATION

Section 2 of the Clayton Act (as amended in 1936 by the Robinson–Patman Act) prohibits each of the business activities set out in Table 23-6. As you read the table, pay attention to all the italicized words because they have been the source of litigation and acceptable defenses to that litigation.

Section 2(a) of the Clayton Act prohibits discrimination in price by seller between two purchasers of a commodity of like grade and quality, in interstate commerce, and resulting in injury to competition. Each of these elements must be proved by a plaintiff in any action brought under Section 2(a). Let us dissect these elements one by one.

price discrimination A price differential that is below the average variable cost for the seller; considered predatory and, therefore, illegal under the Clayton Act.

- *Price.* Section 2(a) forbids direct or indirect discrimination in price. **Price discrimination** is deemed by most courts and scholars to be a price differential that is below the average variable cost for the seller and, thus, is "predatory" and illegal. An example of indirect price discrimination would be a seller's giving a preferred buyer a 60-day option to purchase a product at the present price, while giving another purchaser only a 30-day option. The courts have ruled that this situation constitutes price discrimination under Section 2(a).

TABLE 23-6 SUMMARY OF PROVISIONS OF THE CLAYTON ACT AS AMENDED BY THE ROBINSON–PATMAN ACT

Section	Action(s) Prohibited	Defense
2(a)	Discrimination in price by seller between two purchasers of a *commodity of like grade and quality* where effect may be to *substantially lessen competition* or tend to create a monopoly.	Cost *justification* or a good faith attempt to *meet equally low prices of competitors.*
2(c)	Fictitious brokerage payments (or discounts where services not rendered).	None.
2(d)	Payments for promotions or allowances for promotional services by seller unless made available to all buyers on *proportionately equal terms.*	*Meeting competition.*
2(e)	Promotional services by seller unless provided to all buyers on *proportionately equal terms.*	*Meeting competition* for seller.
2(f)	*Inducing* to discriminate in price or knowingly receiving the benefits of such discrimination.	*Cost justification.*

- *Sales.* There must be two actual sales (not leases or consignments) by a single seller that are close in time. Say that seller A offers to sell to B a widget for $1.00 and then sells the widget to C for $.95. If B charges price discrimination, that claim will not be upheld because there was no sale between A and B but merely an offer to sell. A sale exists only when there is an enforceable contract.

- *Commodities.* Commodities are movable or tangible properties (e.g., milk or bicycle tires). Services and other intangibles are not covered by Section 2(a).

- *Like Grade and Quality.* The commodities must be of similar grade and quality; they need not be exactly the same. For example, price differences in milk cartons that are slightly different in size do fall under Section 2(a) jurisdiction. However, differences in price between car tires and bicycle tires are differences in prices of commodities of different grade and quality, so they do not fall under Section 2(a) jurisdiction.

- *Interstate Commerce.* The sales must occur in interstate commerce. If the two sales by a single seller to two purchasers take place in intrastate commerce, the Clayton Act, being a federal statute, does not apply.

- *Competitive Injury.* Finally, the plaintiff must show that the price discrimination caused competitive injury, which under the Clayton Act is price discrimination that either substantially lessens competition, tends to create a monopoly, or injures, destroys, or prevents competition with the person or firm that knowingly receives the benefits of discrimination.

Injury to competition includes:

1. **Primary-line injury** (at the seller level), which occurs when a seller cuts prices in one geographic area in order to drive out a local competitor.

2. **Secondary-line injury** (at the buyer level), which occurs when competitors of one of the buyers are injured because the seller sold to that one buyer at a lower price than he sold to the others. The buyer who received the lower wholesale price can then undersell the other buyers, which may substantially lessen competition.

1. **Tertiary-line injury** (at the retailer level), which occurs when a discriminatory price is passed along from a secondary-line buyer to a retailer. Retailers who get the benefit of a seller's lower price to a buyer will be able to undersell their competitors.

primary-line injury A form of price discrimination in which a seller attempts to put a local competitive firm out of business by lowering its prices only in the region where the local firm sells its products.

secondary-line injury A form of price discrimination in which a seller offers a discriminatory price to one buyer but not to another buyer.

tertiary-line injury A form of price discrimination in which a discriminatory price is passed along from a secondary-line party to a favored party at the next level of distribution.

The Meeting-the-Competition Defense. Section 2(b) of the Clayton Act allows a seller to discriminate in price if able to show that the lower price "was made in good faith to meet an equally low price of a competitor." The seller can discriminate to meet the competition but not to "bury" or "beat" the competition. The breadth of the meeting-the-competition defense has long been debated.

SECTION 3: TYING ARRANGEMENTS AND EXCLUSIVE-DEALING CONTRACTS

Section 3 of the Clayton Act reads:

> *That it shall be unlawful for any person engaged in commerce, in the course of such commerce, to lease or make a sale or contract for sale of goods, wares, merchandise, machinery, supplies, or other commodities, whether patented or unpatented for use, consumption or resale within the United States or any territory thereof or the District of Columbia or any insular possession or other place under the jurisdiction of the United States, or fix a price charged therefore, or discount from or rebate upon, such price, on the condition, agreement or understanding that the lessee or purchaser thereof shall not use or deal in the goods, wares, merchandise, machinery, supplies, or other commodities of a competitor or competitors of the lessor or seller, where the effect of such lease, sale, or contact for sale or such condition, agreement or understanding may be to substantially lessen competition or tend to create a monopoly in any line of commerce.*

This is the section of the act that courts have generally relied on in cases concerning tying arrangements and exclusive-dealing contracts. Tying arrangements and exclusive-dealing contracts may not be per se illegal in a particular instance, despite past treatment of them as per se illegal in other instances by the courts.

SECTION 7: MERGERS AND ACQUISITIONS

Section 7 of the Clayton Act reads:

> *That no corporation engaged in commerce shall acquire, directly or indirectly, the whole or any part of the stock or other share capital and no corporation subject to the jurisdiction of the Federal Trade Commission shall acquire the whole or any part of the assets of another corporation engaged also in commerce, where in any line of commerce in any section of the country, the effect of such acquisition may be substantially to lessen competition, or to tend to create a monopoly.*

The purpose of Section 7 of the Clayton Act, as amended in 1950, is to prohibit anticompetitive mergers and acquisitions that tend to lessen competition at their incipiency—that is, in the words of Justice Brennan, "to arrest apprehended consequences of intercorporate relationships before those relationships [can] work their evil, which may be at or any time after the acquisition."[13]

merger One company's acquisition of another company's assets or stock in such a way that the second company is absorbed by the first.

The language of the statute has led to controversy and considerable litigation, especially since the business world went on a **merger** binge in the early 1980s. There were more than 2,000 mergers each year from 1983 through 1986, and some of this country's largest corporations were involved in the deal making. For example, in 1984, Chevron purchased Gulf Oil for $13.2 billion, and Texaco bought Getty for $10.1 billion. The emphasis in 1983 and 1984 was on large oil company acquisitions, but 1985 and 1986 saw acquisitions by companies in the manufacturing, technology, and service areas of the economy as well. Although

---

[13] *United States v. E.I. du Pont de Nemours & Co.*, 353 U.S. 586 (1957).

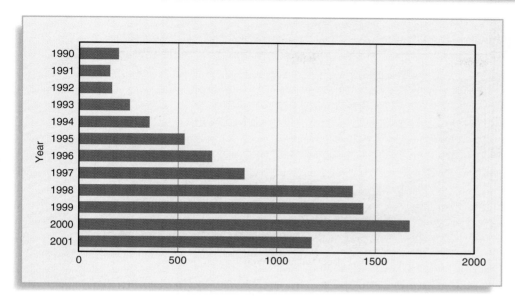

EXHIBIT 23-1

MERGER ACTIVITY

Source: M. Wiedenbaum, *Business and Government in the Global Marketplace,* 7th ed. (Upper Saddle River, N.J.; Prentice Hall, 2004), p. 134.

the 1980s is the decade associated with big deal making, the merger frenzy continued into the 1990s and decreased in numbers in 2001 (see Exhibit 23-1).

Reasons for the Increase in Mergers. Mergers are a method of external growth as opposed to internal corporate expansion. They may take place for one or any combination of the following reasons:

1. *Undervalued assets.* It is cheaper for a company such as General Motors (GM) to buy Electronic Data Systems (EDS) and Hughes Aircraft in order to obtain computer capabilities, a computer transmission network, and telecommunications capabilities than to borrow money and expand internally in those areas. In the opinion of GM and its investment banking advisers, both EDS and Hughes Aircraft were undervalued stocks in the marketplace and, therefore, a "good buy."

2. *Diversification.* During a recession (e.g., 1981–1983), when stocks are generally underpriced, companies may seek to diversify—that is, to reduce their risks in one industry's business cycle by investing in another industry. U.S. Steel's acquisition of Marathon Oil Company was an attempt at diversification by a steel company hit hard by recession and foreign imports.

3. *Tax credits for research and development.* Between the middle of 1981 and the end of 1985, the Internal Revenue Code allowed a 25 percent tax credit for increases in research capabilities acquired through mergers.

4. *Economies of scale.* A merger often brings about greater efficiency and lower unit costs, particularly in research and development and in manufacturing.

5. *The philosophy that "bigness" is not "bad."* This flexible approach to mergers was embodied in the Justice Department's Merger Guidelines, which are examined later in this chapter.

Criteria for Determining the Legality of Mergers under Section 7. The U.S. Supreme Court, the lower federal courts, the Justice Department, and the Federal Trade Commission use the following criteria, or steps, to decide on the legality of a merger:

EXHIBIT 23-2
LARGEST ANNOUNCED MERGERS IN THE SECOND QUARTER

Source: Wall Street Journal, July 1, 2004 p. C-13.

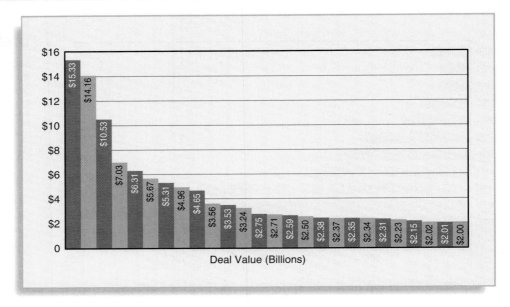

Deal Value (Billions)

ACQUIRER	TARGET	DATE (2004) ANNOUNCED	DEAL VALUE (BILLIONS)	STATUS
Revival Acquisitions	Marks & Spencer	May 27	$15.33	Pending
Wachovia	SouthTrust Corp	June 21	14.16	Pending
Citizens Financial	Charter One Financial	May 4	10.53	Pending
SunTrust Banks	Nat'l Commerce Financial	May 9	7.03	Pending
Westfield Holdings	Westfield Trust	April 22	6.31	Pending
Westfield Holdings	Westfield America Trust	April 22	5.67	Pending
MGM Mirage	Mandalay Resort	June 4	5.31	Pending
UnitedHealth	Oxford Health Plans	April 26	4.96	Pending
Lend Lease Corp.	General Property Trust	June 2	4.65	Pending
Simon Property Group	Chelsea Property Group	June 21	3.56	Pending
Kohlberg Kravis Roberts	PanAmSat Corp.	April 20	3.53	Pending
May Department Stores	Marshall Field	June 9	3.24	Pending
UCB SA	Celltech Group	May 18	2.75	Pending
Rockwood Specialties	Dynamit Nobel	April 19	2.71	Pending
Kerr-McGee	Westport Resources	April 7	2.59	Completed
T-Mobile USA	GSM Network	May 25	2.50	Pending
Jean Coutu Group	JC Penney (Eckerd)	April 5	2.38	Pending
Investor Group	LeasePlan Corp.	April 21	2.37	Pending
CCE Holdings	CrossCountry Energy	June 22	2.35	Pending
EnCana	Tom Brown	April 15	2.34	Part Complete
Coeur D'alene Mines	Wheaton River Minerals	May 27	2.31	Pending
NuCoastal	CrossCountry Energy	May 21	2.23	Pending
CVS	JC Penney (Eckerd Texas & Florida)	April 5	2.15	Pending
Investor Group	DDI Pocket	June 21	2.02	Pending
National Grid Transco	Crown Castle UK	June 25	2.01	Pending
Investor Group	Loews Cineplex Entertainment	June 2	2.00	Pending

1. Relevant product and geographic markets.

2. Probable impact of the merger on competition in the relevant product and geographic markets.

Relevant Product and Geographic Markets. We said in our discussion of monopolies that how courts determine the boundaries of the product and geographic markets helps them decide what market share a company has and, hence, its market power. The same holds true when the courts are ruling on mergers: The market share of the new, combined company will have a strong bearing on the court's decision on the legality of the merger.

The primary criterion the courts use in determining the relevant product market is, again, substitutability or cross-elasticity of demand for a product. Other factors used are (1) public recognition of the product market, (2) distinct customer prices, (3) the product's sensitivity to price changes, (4) whether unique facilities are necessary for production, and (5) peculiar product characteristics.

When identifying the geographic market, what the courts are interested in is where the merging companies compete. The courts may decide that this geographic market includes all cities with a population of over 10,000, or they may judge this market to be regional, national, or international.

Probable Impact on Competition. The courts have traditionally gauged a merger's impact on competition by examining such factors as:

1. Market foreclosure, resulting from the merger of a customer and its supplier, so that competing customers may be foreclosed from the market if the supplier's goods are in demand and that demand exceeds supply.

2. Potential elimination of competition from a market if two competing firms merge.

3. Entrenchment of a smaller firm in a market if a large firm with "deep pockets" acquires it and supplies the capital the small firm needs to eliminate competitors.

4. Trends in the market revealing a high rate of concentration, as measured by percentage of the market that the leading four to six competitors in an industry have.

5. Postmerger evidence revealing anticompetitive effects on a market.

Types of Mergers. The courts have distinguished among horizontal, vertical, and conglomerate mergers because each type has a potentially different impact on competition. **Horizontal mergers** involve the acquisition of one firm by another that is at the same competitive level in the distribution system. This type of merger usually leads to the elimination of a competitor. For example, in 1984, Chevron's purchase of the Gulf Oil Corporation eliminated one oil company at the seller's level in the industry. **Vertical mergers** involve the acquisition of one firm by another that is at a different level in the distribution system. For example, if a shoe manufacturer acquires a company that has many retail shoe outlets, the merger is termed vertical because one company is at the manufacturing level and the other is at the retailing level of the distribution system. **Conglomerate mergers** involve the acquisition by one firm of another that produces products or services that are not directly related to those of the acquiring firm. For example, the acquisition by GM (an automobile company) of EDS (a technology company) merged two companies that did not produce directly related products and services.

Horizontal Mergers. In the 1960s and early 1970s, whenever a merger would result in what was labeled undue concentration in a particular market, there was a presumption of illegality. In a landmark case,[14] the Supreme Court termed a postacquisition market share of 30 percent or more prima facie illegal. In another equally important case involving the merger of two retail grocery store chains,[15] the Court, perceiving a trend toward fewer competitors in the

> **horizontal merger**
> A merger between two or more companies producing the same or a similar product and competing for sales in the same geographic market.
>
> **vertical merger** A merger that integrates two firms that have a supplier–customer relationship.
>
> **conglomerate merger**
> A merger in which the businesses of the acquiring and the acquired firm are totally unrelated.

---

[14] *United States v. Philadelphia National Bank*, 374 U.S. 321 (1963).

[15] *United States v. Vons Grocery*, 384 U.S. 270 (1966).

retail-store market, held a postacquisition share of 8.9 percent presumptively illegal. In both cases, the Court's initial determination of the relevant product and geographic markets and the percentage of market shares the merged company would have became determinative of the result.

Vertical Mergers. Vertical mergers are termed *backward* when a retailer attempts to acquire a supplier and *forward* when a supplier attempts to acquire a retailer. In vertical merger cases, unlike in horizontal merger cases, the courts have tended not to put great emphasis on market share percentage. Instead, they have generally examined the potential for foreclosing competition in the relevant market. For example, if a retailer acquires a supplier of widgets, will other widget suppliers be foreclosed from selling to the retailer? What impact will that foreclosure have on the widget market? The courts also look at the trend in the supplier's market toward concentration, barriers to entry, and the financial health of the acquired firm.

Conglomerate Mergers. As with horizontal and vertical mergers, the courts, using a case-by-case approach, have developed criteria that they look at in conglomerate merger situations to determine whether Section 7 of the Clayton Act has been violated. Because conglomerate mergers result in the combining of firms in different fields that are not competing with each other, the courts have found for the plaintiffs when it can be shown that the acquiring firm was already planning to move into the field and did not move into it only because it had "acquired" its way in; in effect, the conglomerate merger had prevented a company that was a potential entrant from entering and increasing the number of competitors.

Defenses to Section 7 Complaints. In cases brought under Section 7 of the Clayton Act, defendants have met complaints by private plaintiffs, as well as those filed by the Justice Department or the FTC, by asserting the following defenses.

1. *The merger does not have a substantial effect on interstate commerce.* In order for the Clayton Act to be applicable, the merger must be shown to have a substantial effect on interstate commerce, for the federal government may act—and a federal statute may be applied—only if interstate activity, as opposed to intrastate activity, is involved. As we noted in Chapter 5, however, activities involving interstate commerce have been broadly interpreted under the Commerce Clause of the Constitution by the federal courts.

2. *The merger does not have the probability of substantially lessening competition or tending to create a monopoly.* Since the 1980s, firms have argued that mergers are procompetitive and beneficial to the economy and the nation because they improve economic efficiency and enable United States–based companies to compete with state-subsidized and state-owned foreign multinationals.

3. *One of the companies to the merger is failing.* This defense must meet three criteria: (a) The failing company had little hope of survival without the merger; (b) the acquiring company is the only one interested in purchasing the failing company or, if there are several interested purchasers, it is the least threat to competition in the relevant market; and (c) all possible methods of saving the failing company have been tried and have been unsuccessful.

4. *The merger is solely for investment purposes.* Section 7 does not apply to a corporation's purchase of stock in another company "solely for investment purposes," so long as the acquiring corporation does not use its stock purchase for "voting or otherwise to bring about, or attempting to bring about,

the substantial lessening of competition." The courts look on this defense skeptically, especially when purchases of a company's stock by another company exceed 5 percent of the shares outstanding.

Enforcement. The Justice Department, the Federal Trade Commission, and private individuals and corporations can all enforce Section 7. The Justice Department divides authority with the FTC on the basis of areas of historical interest as well as according to the expertise of the staff of each agency.

When the Clayton Act was enacted, it provided no criminal punishment for violators but merely allowed the Justice Department to obtain injunctions to prevent further violations. Recall that Sections 1 and 2 of the Sherman Act do provide for criminal sanctions, and that Section 4 of the Clayton Act (see page 698, *Private Enforcement*) allows individuals to sue on their own behalf and to obtain triple damages, court costs, and attorneys' fees if they can show injury based on violations of either the Sherman Act or the Clayton Act. The Clayton Act also allows individuals to obtain injunctions. Furthermore, if a business is found guilty of violating the Sherman Act in a suit brought by the Justice Department, this finding is prima facie evidence of a violation when a private party sues for treble damages under the Clayton Act. That is, the private party need not prove a violation of the antitrust statutes over again but merely introduces into evidence a copy of the court order that found the defendant guilty of a Sherman Act violation.

Merger Guidelines. The Justice Department has sought to put the business community on notice about what it views as violations of Section 7, and when it is most likely to bring an enforcement action, by issuing Merger Guidelines. These guidelines do not constitute law; they serve only an advisory function. They can be changed by each new administration to fit preordained political goals. The Federal Trade Commission generally follows the Justice Department's Merger Guidelines.

The first guidelines, issued in 1968, were based essentially on market share analysis. In 1982, the guidelines were substantially revised to reflect the courts' growing emphasis on economic analysis that goes beyond the traditional postacquisition market share criterion. The **Hertindahl–Hirschman Index (HHI)** is now used to determine whether the Justice Department will challenge a horizontal merger. This index is calculated by adding the squares of the market shares of a firm in the relevant product and geographic markets. For example, if two firms each control 50 percent of the relevant market, the HHI is equal to 502 + 502, or 5,000. The smaller the HHI, the less concentrated the market, and the less likely the Justice Department is to challenge the merger. A postmerger HHI below 1,000 is unlikely to be challenged, and a postmerger HHI between 1,000 and 1,800 will probably be challenged only if the merger produces an increase in the HHI of more than 100 points. Whether a postmerger HHI of more than 1,800 will be challenged depends on whether a leading firm is involved, the ease of entry into the relevant market, the nature of the product, market performance, and certain other factors the department regards as relevant in a particular case.

In general, the Justice Department did not challenge vertical mergers in 1982–1992 unless they facilitated collusion or raised barriers to entry. Usually, the HHI has to exceed 1,800 in order to gain the department's attention. No mention is made of conglomerate mergers in the 1982 Merger Guidelines.

In 1984, the Merger Guidelines were revised again to set out changes and clarifications. One important difference was that the guidelines allowed the Justice Department to take into consideration foreign competition in determining

Hertindahl–Hirschman Index (HHI) An index calculated by adding the squares of the shares of the relevant market held by each firm in a horizontal merger to determine the competitive effects of the merger. In using the HHI to decide whether to challenge a merger, the Justice Department considers both the level of the postmerger HHI and the increase in the HHI caused by the merger.

whether to bring an enforcement action. This revision was prompted by the Commerce Department, which was concerned about the ability of large United States–based corporations to compete with foreign multinationals. When a foreign firm imports into a relevant U.S. product and geographic market in a particular merger case, its impact on that market will be considered by the FTC and the Justice Department when deciding whether to challenge the merger.

A new political administration in Washington in 1993 produced new guidelines with a five-step approach to challenging horizontal mergers:

> **STEP 1** Before challenging a merger, the Antitrust Division of the Justice Department will determine whether the merger significantly increases market concentration. The definition of market participation was broadened to include all current producers and potential entrants. The 1982 HHI remains the measuring stick.
>
> **STEP 2** Next the division will determine the potential adverse competitive effect of a merger. The focus here was changed from the potential for postmerger collusion to the potential for "coordinated interaction among participants."
>
> **STEP 3** The division will then look at whether entry into the market is so easy that prices will not profitably increase after the proposed merger.
>
> **STEP 4** The 1993 Merger Guidelines omit the previous guidelines' requirement that the merging companies present clear and convincing evidence for these efficiencies of scale.
>
> **STEP 5** Finally, the division will determine whether one of the merging companies is a "failing" firm or company division that would leave the market unless allowed to merge with the stronger company. Under the 1993 Merger Guidelines, the "failing" company defense will be limited to firms in liquidation; Chapter 11 reorganization under the bankruptcy laws will not be enough to meet the guidelines.

Since 2001 the Justice Department and the Federal Trade Commission as part of a new administration have sought to negotiate with parties seeking to merge or to enter into acquisitions. A market-oriented policy based on efficiency standards has become significant in determining whether a proposed merger will tend to create a monopoly under Section 7. Often parties may have to agree to divest themselves of companies they own in order to obtain approval of a proposed merger. In the accompanying box outlining two possible mergers in the gaming industry, it is expected that some properties owned by the acquiring parties will be subject to divestment in order to gain government agencies' approval.

In October 2004, the Justice Department set forth some 'guiding principles' emphasizing structural remedies, involving divestiture of assets, rather than remedies that control conduct, in all antitrust enforcement merger and acquisition activities.

Two companies, Harrah's and MGM, sought the acquisition of properties belonging to Caesars Entertainment, Inc., and Mandalay, respectively, in Las Vegas in June and July 2004. These two major companies would then dominate what is known as the Las Vegas Strip (See Exhibit 23-3).

As the popularity of gambling increased in the 1990s and early 2000s, Las Vegas became a tourist and convention center. While growth was slowing in 11 states that allowed gambling in traditional casino forms by the year 2000, there were alternative gambling locations in such places as indian reservations; slot machines at racetracks, online gambling on the internet worldwide, and new places such as Macao where Las Vegas casinos began operating In 2004. These alternatives, and the search by state governments for additional revenues, led to attempts to acquire properties by Harrah's and MGM.

For Harrah's, the largest of all casinos owners, there was a need to funnel its customers from its riverboat and other properties throughout the United States, to the "gambling mecca" of Las Vegas and its acquired properties of Caesars Entertainment. Loyalty from its customers in the "heartland" and Atlantic City, and its huge customer database would assist it in this effort.[1]

MGM was seeking to become the sole "high roller" on the Las Vegas Strip with its possible acquisition of Mandalay properties. Harrah's, fearing this possibility, realized it needed to acquire properties before it was not a contender on the Strip where it held one large property (Harrah's) and the Rio casino just off the Strip. A favorable tax environment and few government restrictions in Nevada made capital investment in gambling easier.

When the Justice Department and the FTC examined these proposed mergers, the important issue was to determine the relevant geographic market. What would be the effect of these acquisitions on the gaming market? Was there a tendency toward monopoly and a lessening of competition in the gaming industry? Were there political implications for these acquisitions? What cultural and moral implications were involved? What information is needed for the readers of this text to make these decisions? (See Chapter 1 of this text, particularly the steps outlined for critical thinking.)

---

[1] See C. Woodward and M. Krantz, "Latest Vegas Marriage," *USA Today*, July 16, 2004, pp. B-1, 2.

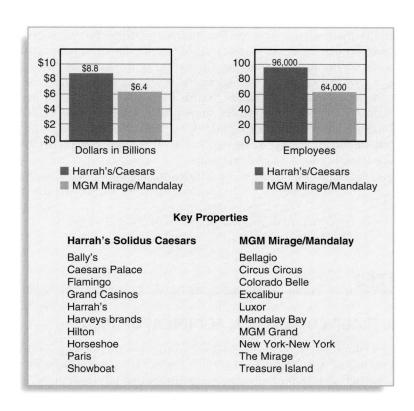

EXHIBIT 23-3

CASINO GIANTS

Source: Adapted from *Wall Street Journal*, July 15, 2004, p. 2.

premerger notification requirement The legislatively mandated requirement that certain types of firms notify the FTC and the Justice Department 30 days before finalizing a merger so that these agencies can investigate and challenge any mergers they find anticompetitive.

Premerger Notification. The Hart–Scott Robinson Act of 1976, which amended Section 7 of the Clayton Act, introduced a **premerger notification requirement** into the area of mergers. If the acquiring company has sales of $100 million or more, if the acquired firm has sales of $10 million or more, and if either affects interstate commerce, both firms must file notice of the pending merger with the Justice Department and the Federal Trade Commission 30 days before the merger is finalized. This notice enables the department and the FTC to assess the probable competitive impact of the merger before it takes place.

Remedies. When parties decide to go ahead with a merger despite being advised that an enforcement action will be brought, the Justice Department and the FTC have three basic civil remedies available: civil injunctions, cease-and-desist orders, and divestiture. However, the Antitrust Division of the Justice Department has tried to avoid using these remedies. Instead, it has sought compromise. Thus, at times it has succeeded in getting the acquiring firm to agree to a divestiture of some subsidiaries of the postmerged firm. At other times it has prevailed on the acquiring firm to agree that the postmerged firm will refrain from some form of business conduct—for example, that it will not compete in certain geographic areas for a period of years.

Individuals and corporations may also bring private civil actions for triple damages against a firm that violates Section 7 of the Clayton Act. These private actions, which far outnumber government antitrust cases, are important for preserving a competitive business environment.

SECTION 8: INTERLOCKING DIRECTORATES

Section 8 prohibits an individual from becoming a director in two or more corporations if any of them has capital, surplus, and individual profits aggregating more than $51 million or is engaged in interstate commerce, or if any of them were or are competitors, or where agreements to eliminate competition between such corporations would be a violation of the antitrust law.

With the growing number of conglomerates and the rise of the "professional" director who sits on many companies' boards for a fee, this long dormant section of the Clayton Act has been the basis of some private civil litigation in recent years. The trend toward diversification by many large firms has resulted in overlapping areas of competition in many corporations, so there are potential violations of Section 8 for outside directors of these firms.

It should be noted that Section 8 excludes from its coverage banks, banking associations, trust companies, and common carriers subject to the Interstate Commerce Act of 1887. Directors of corporations in those industries, therefore, do not have to be concerned about a potential Section 8 violation.

OTHER ANTITRUST STATUTES

FEDERAL TRADE COMMISSION ACT (FTCA) OF 1914

The outburst of reform that produced the Clayton Act also produced the Federal Trade Commission Act (FTCA), which prohibits "unfair methods of competition." This broad, sweeping language, and the courts' interpretation of it, allow the Federal Trade Commission to bring antitrust enforcement actions against business conduct prohibited by the Sherman and Clayton Acts. Where prosecution may be difficult because of the level of proof required under those acts, the FTC may bring a civil action under the FTCA. Also, business conduct that may not quite reach the level of prohibition under either the Sherman or the Clayton Act may be actionable under the "unfair" competition language of the FTCA.

The following case illustrates the reach of this statute.

CASE 23-8

California Dental Association v. Federal Trade Commission
United States Supreme Court,
526 U.S. 756 (1999)

The California Dental Association (CDA) (defendant) is a nonprofit association of local dentists' organizations to which about 75 percent of California's dentists belong. The CDA provides insurance arrangements and other benefits for its members and engages in lobbying, litigation, marketing, and public relations on the members' behalf.

The CDA's members agree to abide by the association's Code of Ethics, which, among other things, prohibits false or misleading advertising. The CDA has issued interpretive advisory opinions and guidelines relating to advertising. These guidelines included restrictions on two types of truthful, nondeceptive advertising: price advertising, particularly discounted fees, and advertising relating to the quality of dental services.

The Federal Trade Commission (FTC) filed a complaint with an administrative law judge (ALJ), alleging that the CDA violated Section 5 of the Federal Trade Commission Act in applying its guidelines to restrict the price and quality advertising. The ALJ found that the CDA violated Section 5. On appeal, the FTC upheld this finding, as did the U.S. Court of Appeals for the Ninth Circuit.

Justice Souter

Even on the view that bars [prohibitions] on truthful and verifiable price and quality advertising are prima facie anticompetitive and place the burden of procompetitive justification on those who agree to adopt them, the very issue at the threshold of this case is whether professional price and quality advertising is sufficiently verifiable in theory and in fact to fall within such a general rule. ... [I]t seems to us that the CDA's advertising restrictions might plausibly be thought to have a net procompetitive effect, or possibly no effect at all on competition. The restrictions on ... advertising are, at least on their face, designed to avoid false or deceptive advertising in a market characterized by striking disparities between the information available to the professional and the patient. In a market for professional services, in which advertising is relatively rare and the comparability of service packages not easily established, the difficulty for customers or potential competitors to get and verify information about the price and availability of services magnifies the dangers to competition associated with misleading advertising. What is more, the quality of professional services tends to resist either calibration or monitoring by individual patients or clients, partly because of the specialized knowledge required to evaluate the services, and partly because of the difficulty in determining whether, and the degree to which, an outcome is attributable to the quality of services (like a poor job of tooth-filling) or to something else (like a very tough walnut). Patients' attachments to particular professionals, the rationality of which is difficult to assess, complicate the picture even further. The existence of such significant challenges to informed decision-making by the customer for professional services immediately suggests that advertising restrictions arguably protecting patients from misleading or irrelevant advertising call for more than cursory treatment as obviously comparable to classic horizontal agreements to limit output or price competition.

Judgment for the Defendants. *Vacated and remanded* to Court of Appeals.

BANK MERGER ACT OF 1966

The Bank Merger Act of 1966 requires that all bank mergers be approved in advance by the banking agency having jurisdiction—that is, the Federal Reserve Board, the Federal Deposit Insurance Corporation (FDIC), or the Comptroller of

Critical Thinking About the Law

One of the central ideas of critical thinking is that the quality of anyone's conclusion, including that of Justice Souter, is related closely to the quality of the evidence used to support that particular conclusion. Although Justice Souter is not making the final decision in Case 23-8, what he did is certainly supportive of the efforts of the CDA to continue its current restrictions on its members. Evaluating evidence is often made easier by asking, what kinds of evidence would have been ideal.

1. To form his argument, Justice Souter makes a number of assertions. Name two claims he made in Case 23-8 that need additional evidence for us to have confidence in their accuracy.

   Clue: Find places where Justice Souter makes factual claims but offers no evidence beyond his statement to support their validity.

2. To demonstrate to yourself that evidence is necessary for us to believe someone, locate two assertions made by Justice Souter in Case 23-8 that have no evidence supporting them. Write two statements that say the opposite of what Justice Souter said. Do your statements assist the plaintiff in this case?

   Clue: If your statements were true, would the CDA's restrictions on advertising be more likely to harm consumers than if Justice Souter's statements were true?

the Currency. The agency with jurisdiction must obtain a report "on the competitive factors involved" from the U.S. attorney general, and from the other two agencies as well, before making a decision.

Even if the agency approves the merger, the Justice Department may bring a suit within 30 days. This action automatically stays the merger, and a federal district court must then review all issues concerning the merger de novo (newly, or from the beginning). If not challenged by the U.S. attorney general within 30 days, a bank merger is still subject to liability under Section 2 of the Sherman Act if it is shown to have resulted in a monopoly. Acquisitions by bank holding companies are subject to the same antitrust standards that are applied to other industries.

The Bank Merger Act has become more significant in light of a 1985 decision of the U.S. Supreme Court approving regional banking and acquisitions by banks across state lines, where state legislatures have given prior approval. Furthermore, major bank, insurance, and brokerage companies (e.g., Travelers and Citicorp) have merged, and large banks have merged with each other (e.g., Bank One and National Bank of Chicago).

GLOBAL DIMENSIONS OF ANTITRUST STATUTES

TRANSNATIONAL REACH OF U.S. ANTITRUST LEGISLATION

Sections 1 and 2 of the Sherman Act explicitly apply to "trade or commerce . . . with foreign nations," so they obviously have transnational reach. In contrast, Sections 2 and 3 of the Clayton Act, because they apply to price discrimination, tying arrangements, and exclusive-dealing contracts for commodities sold for "use, consumption, or resale within the United States," have no transnational reach. However, Section 5 of the Federal Trade Commission Act is given express

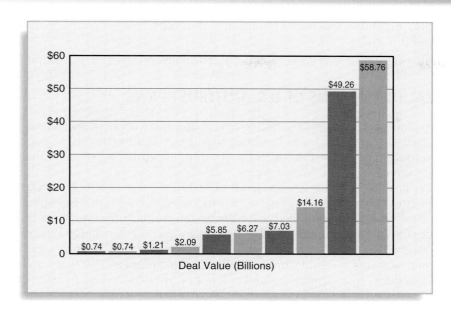

EXHIBIT 23-4

LEADING COMMERCIAL BANKING DEALS IN 2004

Source: Wall Street Journal, June 23, 2004, p. C-4.

Leading Commercial Banking Deals in 2004

ACQUIRING COMPANY	TARGET COMPANY	DEAL VALUE (BILLIONS)
J. P. Morgan Chase & Co. (NY)	Bank One (Chicago, Ill)	**$58.76**
Wachovia (Charlotte, NC)	SouthTrust (Birmingham, AL)	14.16
SunTrust Banks (Atlanta, GA)	Nat'l Commerce Financial (Tenn)	7.03
North Fork Bancorp (Melville, NY)	GreenPoint Financial (NY)	6.27
Regions Financial (AL)	Union Planters (Memphis, Tenn)	5.85
National City (OH)	Provident Financial Group (LA, CA)	2.09
BancWest (Honolulu, HI)	Community First Bankshares (ND)	1.21

transnational reach by Section 4 of the Export Trading Act (Webb–Pomerence Export Act), which extends the meaning of "unfair methods of competition" to practices in export trade against other competitors engaged in such trade even though acts constituting unfair methods of competition "are done without the territorial jurisdiction of the United States." The courts, using a case-by-case approach, have interpreted the language of these statutes so as to establish principles of law that guide companies and their management in determining whether certain activities are illegal because of their transnational impact.

In 1994, Congress passed the Antitrust Enforcement Assistance Act of 1994, which gave the Department of Justice authority to negotiate "mutual assistance" agreements with foreign antitrust enforcers. Also in 1994, the Justice Department and the FTC issued guidelines, based on current statutory and case law, that tell foreign and U.S. companies when either of the agencies is likely to act against alleged anticompetitive action in international trade. The following kinds of behavior may be investigated under the guidelines:

1. A merger of foreign companies that have significant sales in the United States.

2. Conduct by foreign companies that has a direct, substantial, and reasonably foreseeable effect on commerce within the United States or on U.S. companies' export business.

3. Anticompetitive schemes by importers that have a significant impact on the United States.

4. Anticompetitive actions by foreign firms selling to the U.S. government.

GLOBAL DIMENSIONS OF U.S. ANTITRUST LAWS

The general principle guiding the courts in the application of the Sherman Act (and other U.S. antitrust laws) has been that if U.S. or foreign private companies enter into an agreement forbidden by Section 1, and that agreement affects the foreign commerce of the United States, then the U.S. courts have jurisdiction. The question arises: How much commerce must be affected before U.S. courts will assume jurisdiction? The Department of Justice's guidelines on its foreign antitrust enforcement policy announced a jurisdictional standard that requires business practices to have a "substantial and foreseeable effect on the foreign commerce of the United States." An example would be an agreement by U.S. corporations selling roller bearings to divide up markets in Latin America. The department has stated that this country's antitrust laws will not be applied to certain business practices if they have no "direct or intended effect," and most commentators agree that trivial restraints affecting the foreign commerce of the United States are likely not to be prosecuted. (The *Assignment on the Internet* (p. 743) seeks to encourage the reader to deal with some of the issues raised here.)

U.S. appellate courts have held that U.S. courts do have jurisdiction over business conduct by a foreign corporation that is based on a decision by the corporation's government to replace a competitive economic model with a state-regulated model. State-regulated models encourage price-fixing and collaboration among competitors, especially when a government actually prohibits competition between firms. The courts of the United States do not evaluate the lawfulness of acts of foreign sovereigns performed within their own territories, even if the foreign commerce of the United States is affected by those acts, because the act-of-state doctrine forbids them to. Under this doctrine (discussed in Chapter 3), when the illegal conduct is that of a foreign government (as opposed to that of foreign individuals), the courts are not permitted to examine and decide the merits of any claim alleged. This approach applies to any case in which a statute, a decree, an order, or a resolution of a foreign government or governments is alleged to be unlawful under U.S. law. For instance, when the International Association of Machinists brought a suit claiming that an agreement by member states of the Organization of Petroleum Exporting Countries (OPEC) to increase the price of crude oil through taxes and price setting was in violation of Sections 1 and 2 of the Sherman Act, the federal district court dismissed the case for lack of jurisdiction based on the act-of-state doctrine.

ENFORCEMENT

A court decision condemning certain business practices prohibited by U.S. antitrust laws—such as price-fixing, allocation of markets, or boycotts—may give a plaintiff satisfaction but no equitable relief. For example, if a U.S. corporation enters into a price-fixing agreement with a foreign corporation to determine the price of uranium worldwide, the foreign corporation may be made a defendant in a U.S. court and the plaintiff may win the case. But can the foreign defendant be forced to pay triple damages? Usually not, unless it has assets in the United States that can be seized or there is a treaty of friendship and commerce between the United States and the foreign corporation's home country providing for the implementation of judicial decrees of U.S. courts in that country's courts. The second possibility is limited by the fact that there are very few treaties containing those terms. The first possibility is more promising because many foreign corporations have assets, such as bank accounts, in the United States. The plaintiff can get a decree freezing those assets until the corporation pays the court-ordered damages because Section 6 of the Sherman Act provides forfeiture of property to enforce an antitrust decree.

In the OPEC case referred to earlier, a group of foreign governments colluded to fix prices, but the crude oil was extracted, transported, and sold by U.S. oil corporations. Would it have been appropriate for the plaintiffs in that case to obtain a court decree ordering the seizure of the assets of the oil companies on the ground that they were coconspirators in the price-fixings? Would OPEC have cared about U.S. oil companies' assets? If it did care, would it have ceased selling oil to the United States? The answer to that question would probably depend on the supply and demand of oil on the world market.

SUMMARY

A history and summary of sections of the Sherman Act, Clayton Act, Federal Trade Commission Act, and Bank Merger Act are included in this chapter. We have sought to examine the policy implications of the acts for business managers and consumers (e.g., the *Microsoft* case). We have also examined the international dimensions of U.S. antitrust statutes in light of multinationals coming to the United States, as well as the impact of the U.S. antitrust statutes on those doing business in other countries. We have called this the transnational reach of antitrust legislation. Enforcement by the U.S. federal courts in both cases has become more frequent.

REVIEW QUESTIONS

23-1 Who is responsible for the enforcement of the antitrust statutes?

23-2 What industries and activities are exempt from the antitrust law?

23-3 Explain the difference between horizontal and vertical restraints under Section 1 of the Sherman act.

23-4 List and define three types of mergers.

23-5 Describe the approach the Justice Department takes to horizontal mergers under current Merger Guidelines.

REVIEW PROBLEMS

23-6 Ronwin was an unsuccessful candidate for admission to the Arizona State Bar. Under Arizona Supreme Court rules, a Committee on Examinations and Admissions appointed by the court was authorized to examine the applicants on specified subjects, to grade the exam on a formula submitted to the court before the exam, and then to submit its recommendation to the court. A rejected applicant could seek review of the state supreme court's decision. After he was rejected by both the committee and the state supreme court, Ronwin appealed to the U.S. Supreme Court, claiming that the committee had violated Section 1 of the Sherman Act by artificially reducing the number of attorneys in the state. He argued that the committee had set the grading scale with reference to the number of new attorneys it thought was desirable in Arizona, as opposed to a "suitable" level of competence. Defendants argued that they were immune from antitrust liability under the act-of-state doctrine. Who won this case, and why?

23-7 Topco is a cooperative association of 25 small and medium-sized regional supermarket chains that operate in 33 states. In order to compete with large supermarket chains, Topco buys and distributes for its members quality merchandise under private labels. Each member of the cooperative has to sign an agreement promising to sell Topco-brand products only in a certain designated territory. The government sued Topco, claiming it was horizontally dividing markets in violation of Section 1 of the Sherman Act. The defendant argued that this territorial restriction was necessary to compete with large chains. Who won this case, and why?

23-8 Falstaff Brewing Company was the fourth-largest brewer in the United States, with 5.9 percent of the national market. Falstaff acquired a local New England brewery, Narragansett, in order to penetrate the New

England market. Narragansett had 20 percent of that market. The Justice Department filed suit against Falstaff under Section 7 of the Clayton Act. What was the result? Explain.

23-9 Alcoa was the leading producer of aluminum conductors in the United States, with 27.8 percent of the market. Alcoa acquired Rome Electric, which had 1.3 percent of the market. Rome ranked ninth among all companies in the aluminum conductor market. The Justice Department sued, claiming a violation of Section 7 of the Clayton Act and asking for a divestiture by Alcoa. What was the result? Explain.

23-10 Ford Motor acquired Autolite, an independent manufacturer of spark plugs that accounted for 15 percent of national sales of spark plugs. GM, through its AC brand, accounted for another 30 percent of national sales. After Ford's acquisition of Autolite, Champion was the only independent manufacturer of spark plugs remaining in the market. Its market share declined from 50 percent to 33 percent after the acquisition. The Justice Department sued Ford for being in violation of Section 7, and the federal district court ruled in favor of the United States. The court ordered Ford to do the following: (1) divest itself of Autolite; (2) stop manufacturing spark plugs for ten years; and (3) purchase 50 percent of its requirements from Autolite for five years. Ford appealed. Who won, and why?

CASE PROBLEMS

23-11 The National Collegiate Athletic Association (NCAA) coordinates the intercollegiate athletic programs of its members by issuing rules and setting standards. The NCAA set up a Cost Reduction Committee to consider ways to cut the costs of intercollegiate athletics while maintaining competition. The committee proposed a rule to restrict the annual compensation of certain coaches to $16,000. The NCAA adopted the rule. Basketball coaches affected by the rule filed a suit in a federal district court against the NCAA, alleging a violation of Section 1 of the Sherman Antitrust Act. Is this a per se violation of the Sherman Act or should it be evaluated based on the rule of reason? If it is subject to the rule of reason, is it an illegal restraint of trade? Explain. *Law v. National Collegiate Athletic Association*, 134 F.3d 1010 (10th Cir. 1998)

23-12 High fructose corn syrup (HFCS) is a sweetener made from corn and used in food products. There are two grades, HFCS 42 and HFCS 55. The five principal HFCS makers, including Archer Daniels Midland Co.

(ADM), account for 90 percent of the sales. In 1988, ADM announced that it was raising its price for HFCS 42 to 90 percent of the price of HFCS 55. It cost only 65 percent as much to manufacture HFCS 42, but the other makers followed suit. Over the next seven years, the makers sometimes bought HFCS from each other even when they could have produced the amount at a lower cost, and many sales to other customrs were made at prices below the list prices. After Wilson, head of ADM's corn processing division was imprisoned for antitrust violations with regard to other ADM products, HFCS buyers filed a suit in a federal district court against the makers, alleging a per se violation of the Sherman Act and seeking billions of dollars in damages. How should the court rule? Discuss. *In re High Fructose Corn Syrup Antitrust Litigation*, 295 F.3d 651 (7th Cir. 2002)

23-13 Snuff is a smokeless tobacco product sold in small round cans from racks, which include point-of-sale (POS) ads. POS ads are critical because tobacco advertising is restricted and the number of people who use smokeless tobacco products is relatively small. In the snuff market in the United States, there are only four competitors, including U.S. Tobacco Co., and its affiliates (USTC) and Conwood Co. In 1990, USTC, which held 87 percent of the market, began to convince major retailers, including Wal-Mart Stores, Inc., to use USTC's "exclusive racks" to display its products and those of all other snuff makers. USTC agents would then destroy competitors' racks. USTC also began to provide retailers with false sales data to convince them to maintain its poor-selling items and crop competitors' less expensive products. Conwood's Wal-Mart market share fell from 12 percent to 6.5 percent. In stores in which USTC did not have rack exclusivity, however, Conwood's market share increased to 25 percent. Conwood filed a suit in a federal district court against USTC, alleging in part that USTC used its monopoly power to exclude competitors from the moist snuff market. Who won? *Conwood Co., L.P. v. U.S. Tobacco Co.*, 290 F.3d 768 (6th Cir. 2002)

23-14 Certified registered nurse anesthetists (CRNAs) sued a hospital and its doctors, claiming a violation of Section 1 of the Sherman Act, based on the hospital's staffing decision to terminate its contract with the CRNAs and instead use a group of physician anesthesiologists, a competitor, that would provide anesthesia services for the hospital at lower cost. The district court dismissed the case. Was that the correct decision? *BCB Anesthesia Care v. Passavant Memorial Area Hospital*, 36 F.3d 664 (7th Cir. 1994)

23-15 Compcare, an HMO (health maintenance organization), sued Marshfield Clinic for monopolizing the HMO market. HMOs charge their members fixed annual fees. The HMO negotiates with each physician it has under contract the amount it will pay for each medical procedure performed. The idea is that HMOs can bargain with physicians for lower fees and then pass the savings on to HMO members. Compcare objected that Marshfield Clinic signed up so many physicians that there were too few physicians left in the region for Compcare to use. Marshfield defended by pointing out that all of its HMO physicians remained free to treat patients from other HMOs. What was the result? *Blue Cross & Blue Shield United of Wisconsin v. Marshfield Clinic*, 65 F.3d 1406 (7th Cir. 1995)

ASSIGNMENT ON THE INTERNET

This chapter introduces you to antitrust law in the United States and the global dimensions of those laws. A Supreme Court decision, *Hoffman-LaRoche Ltd. v. Empagran S.A.*, clarified the reach of the Foreign Trade Antitrust Improvement Act. Use the Internet to read a brief summary of the case at the following site:

www.oyez.org/oyez/resource/case/1746. What was the specific issue the court addressed? Do you agree with the Court's reasoning? Why? (See page 740)

Finally, use the Internet to search for commentary on the case. What do other legal scholars have to say about the Court's decision?

 ## ON THE INTERNET

www.findlaw.com/01topics/01antitrust/mail_usenet.html This is a site where you can begin your search for legal resources related to antitrust law and policy.

www.stolaf.edu/people/becker/antitrust The Antitrust Case Browser, located at this address, provides a collection of U.S. Supreme Court case summaries dealing with violations of antitrust statutes.

www.law.cornell.edu/topics/antitrust.html The Legal Information Institute provides an overview to antitrust law as well as links to recent antitrust court decisions.

www.usdoj.gov/atr This is the Department of Justice Antitrust Division.

www.antitrustinstitute.org/index.cfm The American Antitrust Institute home page contains news and information about antitrust enforcement.

www.ftc.gov/ftc/antitrust.htm This is the Federal Trade Commission's Antitrust Web site, which contains numerous links to current antitrust issues.

24

LAWS OF DEBTOR–CREDITOR RELATIONS AND CONSUMER PROTECTION

 **DEBTOR–CREDITOR RELATIONS**

 **THE EVOLUTION OF CONSUMER LAW**

FEDERAL REGULATION OF BUSINESS TRADE PRACTICES AND CONSUMER–BUSINESS RELATIONSHIPS

FEDERAL LAWS REGULATING CONSUMER CREDIT AND BUSINESS DEBT-COLLECTION PRACTICES

STATE CONSUMER LEGISLATION

 **GLOBAL DIMENSIONS OF CONSUMER PROTECTION LAW**

I n Chapters 10 and 11 covering contract law, we offered you a view of private law and how it governs the relationship between two individuals or corporations that buy and sell items. When you went to the bookstore to buy this textbook, you entered into a legally binding contract. The bookstore made an *offer*, and you, as buyer, accepted that offer. Your *acceptance* was signified by your picking out the book and paying for it at the cash register. Assuming there was consideration, mutual assent, competent parties, and a legal object (and we are convinced that this text is a legal object), you entered into an enforceable contract. Before taking this course, you probably never thought of the act of buying a textbook as a legally binding transaction. Most consumers do not. They generally see it as an exchange of money for something that they want or are required to buy.

Because consumers do not think of buying a product as a formal legal transaction, they are usually unaware of the legal implications of an exchange of money for a product or service until they have problems. The post-transaction business–consumer relationship then becomes the basis for angry exchanges, hurt feelings—and sometimes litigation. If both business managers and consumers had some knowledge of the requirements of contract law, as well as federal, state, and local statutes governing consumer transactions, there would be less friction between these two important parties in our economy (and fewer disputes over the types of product and service liabilities we discussed in Chapter 13).

In this chapter, we describe debtor–creditor relationships and the evolution of consumer law through legislation and case law. Then we examine the major federal legislation governing such trade practices as advertising, labeling, and the issuance of warranties on products. Federal laws pertaining to the credit arrangements entered into by consumers and the debt-collection practices of businesses are explained. We also touch on state laws governing consumer transactions. The chapter ends with an examination of the global dimensions of consumer protection laws.

Critical Thinking About the Law

You have already thought about the law and contracts. But you probably never realized that you enter into a legally enforceable contract when you buy a product. If the principles of a contract apply to consumer behavior, why is it necessary to have federal and state agencies that regulate business and trade practices? In other words, why can't we rely on contract law to deal with consumer problems? Why create additional agencies to protect consumers?

These agencies often serve as watchdogs for consumers. Some agencies prevent unfair advertising; others monitor credit arrangements. You can use the following critical thinking questions to improve your thinking about consumer protection law.

1. You are the CEO of one of the largest corporations in the United States. You discover that one of your competitors is falsely representing the quality of one of your products. You decide to sue that competitor for deceptive advertising. You are thankful that you have a course of action through the legal system. What ethical norm seems to influence your thinking?

   Clue: While looking at the list of ethical norms, think about which norm promotes protection.

2. Your competitor receives the notification that her corporation is being sued for deceptive advertising. Your competitor is outraged, primarily because she believes that the government should not regulate advertising behavior. What ethical norm seems to dominate her thinking?

   Clue: Again, examine the list of ethical norms.

3. Advertisers typically have 30 seconds to convey a convincing message to consumers. Therefore, they must use quite persuasive language in a brief amount of time. Think about cases in which companies are sued for deceptive advertising. Why might ambiguity be a particularly important aspect of a case involving deceptive advertising?

   Clue: How might the ambiguity of a word serve as a defense for a business accused of deceptive advertising?

DEBTOR–CREDITOR RELATIONS

In this section we will briefly describe the rights and remedies for creditors and debtors. Both the case law of federal and state courts and federal and state statutory law play a significant role. The U.S. economy has more and more become a credit-based economy. One can use a Visa or MasterCard to purchase everything from a home and automobile to clothes and a computer. When these transactions take place, a creditor and a debtor are created. We will define the **creditor** as the lender in the transaction (e.g., the bank that issues the credit card) and the **debtor** as the borrower (e.g., the business or individual who uses the credit card).

RIGHTS AND REMEDIES FOR CREDITORS

The following rights and remedies are most commonly used by creditors to enforce their rights. They include liens, garnishments, creditor's composition agreements, mortgage foreclosures, and debtor's assignment of assets for the credits.

Liens. A **lien** is a claim on debtor's property that must be satisfied before any creditor can make a claim. We have both statutory liens—mechanic's liens—and common-law liens, which include an artisan and innkeeper's lien.

A **mechanic's lien** is placed on the real property of a debtor when the latter does not pay for the work done by the creditor. In effect a debtor–creditor relationship is created in which the real property becomes the security interest for the debt owed. For example, when a contractor adds a room onto the house of the debtor, and payment is not paid, the contractor becomes a lienholder for the property after a period of time (usually 60–120 days), and foreclosure may take place. Notice of foreclosure must be given to the debtor in advance.

An **artisan's lien** is created by common law that enables a creditor to recover payment from a debtor on labor and services provided on the latter's personal property. For example, Andrew leaves a lawnmower at Jake's repair shop. Jake repairs the lawnmower, but Andrew never picks up his personal property. After a period of time, Jake can attach the lawnmower.

Once a debt is due and the creditor brings legal action, the debtor's property may be seized by virtue of a judicial lien. Types of judicial liens include attachment, writ of execution, and garnishment.

Attachment involves a court-ordered judgment allowing a local officer of the court (e.g., sheriff) to seize property of a debtor. On the motion of the creditor, this order of seizure may take place after all procedures have been followed according to state law. This is usually a prejudgment remedy, but not always. If at trial the creditor prevails, the court will order the seized property to be sold in order to satisfy the judgment rendered.

If the debtor refuses to pay the creditor or cannot pay, usually a clerk of the court will direct the sheriff, in a **writ of execution**, to seize any of the debtor's real or personal property (nonexempt) within the court's jurisdiction. Any excess after the sale will be returned to the debtor.

A creditor may ask for a **garnishment** order of the court, usually directed at wages owed by an employer or a bank where the debtor has any account. This can be either a post- or a prejudgment remedy. The latter requires a hearing.

---

creditor The lender in the transaction.

debtor The borrower in the transaction.

lien A claim on a debtor's property that must be satisfied before any creditor can make a claim.

mechanic's lien A lien placed on the real property of a debtor when the latter does not pay for the work done by the creditor.

artisan's lien A lien that enables a creditor to recover payment from a debtor on labor and services provided on the debtor's personal property, for example, fixing a lawnmower.

attachment A court-ordered judgment allowing a local officer of the court to seize property of a debtor.

writ of execution An order by a clerk of the court directing the sheriff to seize any of the nonexempt real or personal property of a debtor who refuses to or cannot pay a creditor.

garnishment An order of the court granted to a creditor to seize wages or bank accounts of a debtor.

Both federal and state laws limit the amount of money that a debtor's take-home pay may be garnished for.[1] The courts have been faced with the question of whether an employee's wages, including tips, received directly from a customer can be included in a garnishment order.

CASE 24-1

Shanks v. Lowe
Court of Appeals of Maryland
774 A. 3d 411 (2001)

Laura Shanks, plaintiff, sued Susan Lowe, defendant, and won a judgment at the trial court level. The plaintiff served a garnishment order on Kibby's Restaurant and Lounge for the amount of $6,000 (the judgment) and costs associated with the case. The garnishment order sought to attach the defendant's wages. Under Maryland statutes one of two amounts were exempt, whichever was greater: (1) $154.50 multiplied by the number of weeks in which wages due were earned or (2) 75 percent of disposable wages. Kibby, the employer, stated in response that the defendant Lowe's gross wage averaged $95 per week, and her disposable income per week was approximately $35–$40, which was less than the allowable exemption of $154.50. Kibby stated that Lowe earned tips that were included in her wages for tax purposes but were not wages for garnishment purposes because the customers of the restaurant paid them directly to Lowe (they were never in possession of Kibby). The court dismissed the garnishment. The plaintiff, Shanks, appealed to a state intermediate appellate court, which affirmed the dismissal of the garnishment order. Shanks appealed to the highest state court, the Maryland Court of Appeals.

Justice Weiner

The issue before us is whether tips earned by a waitress constitute "wages" for purposes of the Maryland wage garnishment law. Principally at issue is whether tips fall within the definition of "wages" in [Maryland Code Section] 15-601(c): "all monetary remuneration paid to any employee for his employment."

Maryland Code requires each employer in Maryland to pay its employees the minimum wage required by the Federal Fair Labor Standards Act. The term "wage" is defined as "all compensation that is due to an employee for employment." Section 3-419 takes specific account of tips and, as to any employee who regularly receives more than $30/month in tips, that an employer may include, "as part of the wage of an employee to whom this section applies," an amount that the employer sets to represent the tips of the employee, up to $2.77/hour. This is consistent with the Federal law, which defines a "tipped employee" as an employee engaged in an occupation in which he or she customarily and regularly receives more than $30/month in tips and, in relevant part, calculates the required minimum wage for such an employee as the actual cash wage paid by the employer plus an additional amount on account of tips equal to the difference between that actual cash wage and the minimum wage. Thus, for purposes of the State and Federal minimum wage laws, tips are regarded as part of wages.

Tips are included within the meaning of wages for purposes of the unemployment insurance and workers' compensation laws, each of which provide benefits based on the employee's wages. Were Ms. [Lowe] to file a claim for either unemployment insurance or workers' compensation benefits, any benefits to which she might be entitled would be determined on the basis of the aggregate amounts she received from both Kibby's and its customers.

These statutes illustrate a consistent view by the General Assembly that, in using terms such as "wage" or "wages," it intended to include all forms of remuneration, whether or not paid directly by the employer, except to the extent specifically excluded. When it desired to limit the scope of a statute to the remuneration paid in the form of a salary or other periodic payment by an employer, it made that intent clear.

Reversed and remanded to the lower court in favor of Plaintiff, Shanks.

---

[1] Consumer Credit Protection Act of 1968 15 U.S.C. Section (60) *et seq* allows debtor to retain 75 percent of a debtor's disposable weekly income per week, or the sum equivalent to 30 hours paid at federal minimum wage, whichever is greater.

=== **Critical Thinking About the Law** ===

Because important ambiguity is prevalent in most court cases, careful legal reasoning calls for precise definitions, especially when a court's decision depends on the definition of a particular word or phrase. Case 24-1 provides one illustration in which the outcome of the case depended on the definition of one word. The following questions encourage you to evaluate the evidence the court provides in support of its chosen definition.

1. To reiterate the first step in any critical evaluation, what is the issue of Case 24-1?

   Clue: The court explicitly states the issue in the first paragraph of its opinion.

2. What reasons does the court provide to prefer its chosen definition?

   Clue: Ask yourself *why* the court preferred this definition and conclusion.

Mortgage Foreclosure. Creditors called mortgage holders (mortgagees) have a right to foreclose on real property when a debtor (mortgagor) defaults. There are statutes in each of the 50 states calling for the process of foreclosure. In general, a court-ordered sale of the property takes place when the debtor receives notice and cannot pay. After the cost of foreclosure and the mortgage debt has been satisfied, the mortgagor (debtor) may receive the surplus.

suretyship A contract between a third party and a creditor that allows the third party to pay the debt of the debtor; the surety is primarily liable.

guaranty Similar to a suretyship except that the third person is secondarily liable (i.e., required to pay only after the debtor has defaulted).

Suretyship and Guaranty Contracts. A contract of **suretyship** allows a third person to pay the debt of another (debtor) which is owed to a creditor in the event the debtor does not pay. The suretyship creates an express contract with the creditor, and the surety is primarily liable. In Chapter 10 on the law of contracts, we discussed this matter under third-party beneficiary contracts.

A **guaranty** contract is similar to a suretyship arrangement except the third person is secondarily liable to the creditor. The guarantor is required to pay the debtor's obligation only after the debtor has defaulted and usually only after the creditor has made an attempt to collect. In Chapter 10, we discussed primary and secondary liability under the Statute of Frauds, which requires that a guaranty contract be in writing. The case of primary liability is the main exception to that requirement.

RIGHTS AND REMEDIES FOR DEBTORS

Debtors are protected by the law as well as creditors. For example, property is exempt from creditors' actions. Federal and state consumer protection statutes will be discussed at length in this chapter. We will also discuss bankruptcy laws as they apply to debtors and creditors.

Exemptions to Attachments. We have indicated that creditors can attach, or levy, real and personal property. In order to protect debtors, certain exemptions are made. The best-known exemption for debtors is the *homestead exemption*. Historically, people have been allowed to retain their home up to a specified dollar amount or in the entirety. The purpose is to prevent a person from losing his or her home if forced into bankruptcy or faced with an unsecured creditor. For example, Texas and California offer by far the most generous homestead exemption in bankruptcy proceedings. Many people move to one of these states when faced with bankruptcy.

Some personal property is exempt depending on state statutory law. Some examples include household furniture, a vehicle to get to work with, equipment used in a trade, and animals used on a farm.

THE BANKRUPTCY REFORM ACT (BRA) OF 1978

Goals. The Bankruptcy Reform Act of 1978 (as amended many times most recently in 2005) is intended to protect consumer-debtors in need of assistance after "falling on hard times." Congress sought to give consumer-debtors, whether individuals or companies, a "fresh start" without being dragged down by past debts. (See Table 24-1.)

Provisions. The Bankruptcy Reform Act (BRA) provides two forms of relief for consumer-debtors: (1) liquidation under Chapter 7, and (2) a wage earner's plan set out in Chapter 13 of the act. Chapter 11 of the act is designed primarily for the reorganization of a financially unsound business, though it can also be used by individuals. Chapter 12 deals specifically with family farms.

Chapter 7. Under *Chapter 7* (straight bankruptcy) a debtor turns all assets over to a trustee. The trustee sells the nonexempt assets and distributes the proceeds to creditors. The remaining debts are discharged.

Exemptions under Chapter 7. Although a trustee takes control of debtor's property, under the Bankruptcy Code, certain exemptions are permitted individual debtors. Dollar amounts for the following exemptions are adjusted under the federal code every three years, based on the consumer price index:

1. Up to $17,423 in equity in the debtor's residence and burial plot. This is referred to as the "homestead exemption."
2. Interest in a motor vehicle up to $2,775.
3. Interest, up to $450 for a particular item, in household goods and furnishings, wearing apparel, appliances, books, animals, crops, and musical instruments (the aggregate total of all items is limited, however, to $9,300).
4. Interest in jewelry up to $1,150.
5. Interest in any other property up to $925, plus any unused part of the $17,425 homestead exemption up to $8,725.
6. Interest in any tools of the debtor's trade up to $1,750.
7. Any unmatured life insurance contracts owned by the debtor.
8. Certain interests in accrued dividends and interest under life insurance contracts owned by the debtor.

TABLE 24-1 TYPES OF BANKRUPTCY PROCEEDINGS

Chapter	Chapter 7	Chapter 11	Chapter 12	Chapter 13
Purpose	Liquidation	Reorganization	Adjustment	Adjustment
Eligible Debtors	Most debtors	Most debtors, including railroads	Family farmer who meets certain debt limitations	Individual with regular income who meets certain debt limitations
Type of Petition	Voluntary or involuntary	Voluntary or involuntary	Voluntary	Voluntary

9. Professionally prescribed health aids.

10. The right to receive Social Security and certain welfare benefits, alimony and support, and certain pension benefits.

11. Right to receive certain personal injury and other awards up to $17,425.

Individual states have the power to pass legislation that precludes debtors from using federal exemptions within the state. Thus, only state, not federal, exemptions may be used. A majority of states do this. Other states may choose federal or state law exemptions.

Chapter 13. Under *Chapter 13* of the BRA (the wage earner's plan), a portion of the consumer-debtor's earnings is paid into the court for distribution to creditors over three years or, with court approval, over five years. Both wage earners and individuals engaged in business whose unsecured debts are not in excess of $290,525 and who have secured debts not in excess of $871,550 may qualify under Chapter 13. Only voluntary petitions for bankruptcy may be filed under this chapter. Creditors cannot force petitioners into bankruptcy. Often creditors agree to a composition plan, whereby each creditor receives a percentage of what the debtor owes in exch ange for releasing the debtor from the debt.

Bankruptcy Reform:

The Bankruptcy Abuse Prevention and Consumer Protection Act of 2004 was reintroduced into the House and Senate and, discussed in the House–Senate Joint Conference Committee. As of this writing in 2005, readers may find some the material outlined here to have become law.

The legislation was a result of increased bankruptcy filings from 300,000 in 1980 to approximately 1.2 million in 2004. The business lobby, representing business interests, in Washington D.C., saw this as an attempt to avoid debts by many using the bankruptcy laws. This legislation forces debtors to pay as much as possible instead of having their debts discharged under Chapter 7. It provides a "means test." In most states if your income falls below $50,000 you automatically qualify for Chapter 7. In effect if debtors can afford to repay a certain percentage of their debt owed (over a five-year period), they will not be able to file under Chapter 7, and may have to accept a Chapter 13 repayment plan. In addition, financial counseling will be required before filing for bankruptcy.

Other provisions are a result of negotiations between business lobbying groups (creditors) who favor a stricter bankruptcy law and those representing consumer groups (debtors).

New provisions include:

- making credit card companies more fully disclose finance charges and payment schedule.

- preventing parents from avoiding child support payments by using the bankruptcy laws, as well as advoiding alimony, and repayment of student loans.

- providing more protection for family farmers.

- preventing those in at least six states from taking advantage of the homestead exemption provision of the present act, which allows any debtor to build a house of any value and shield any equity in his or her home. Some limits are now placed on the exemption ($125,000) if a home is not owned for at least 40 months.

- legislation will be effective six months from the date of execution (signing) by the President.

Chapter 11. *Chapter 11* of the BRA is generally aimed at financially troubled businesses, but individuals (with the exception of stockbrokers) are also eligible. Its purpose is to allow a business to reorganize and to continue to function while it is arranging for the discharge of its debts. Note the contrast to Chapter 7, which discharges debts by selling off all assets; you can see why Chapter 11 is more advantageous for individuals who qualify. Reorganization under Chapter 11 may be voluntary or involuntary. The court, after receiving the debtor's petition and ordering relief, appoints committees representing stockholders in the business as well as creditors. If these groups can agree to a fair and reasonable plan that satisfies their constituencies, the court will order its implementation. If some creditors or stockholders disagree on the plan, the court will still order it if the judge finds it fair and reasonable under the circumstances.

A "test track" Chapter 11 for small businesses, whose liabilities do not exceed $2 million and who do not own or manage real property, exists. This allows a bankruptcy proceeding without the appointment of a creditors' committee, saving time and costs.

Chapter 12. Any family farmer (one whose total debt does not exceed 50 percent farm dependent and is at least 80 percent farm related) or any partnership or corporation owned by a family farm whose debt does not exceed $1.5 million is eligible for a special form of bankruptcy protection. The farmer-debtor must file a reorganization plan within 90 days of an order for relief.

The provision most important to the farmer is that mortgage loans can be rewritten to the fair value of the property, in case where such value has gone below the fair value of the loan.

1984 Amendments. The 1984 amendments to the Bankruptcy Reform Act provide that (1) consumer-debtors who owe largely consumer-oriented debts and are petitioning for Chapter 7 bankruptcy must be advised of the availability of the more advantageous Chapter 13; (2) a Chapter 7 petition may be dismissed by a bankruptcy court if the petitioner has previously abused the bankruptcy process; and (3) consumer-debtors who purchase a large number of goods before filing in order to take advantage of exemptions will find it difficult to get those debts discharged.

THE EVOLUTION OF CONSUMER LAW

As Adam Smith's laissez-faire philosophy with its revolt against government intervention in the economy gained popularity in the eighteenth and nineteenth centuries, the **freedom-to-contract doctrine** evolved through case law out of our state court systems. The courts said that, assuming parties were legally competent, they should be allowed to enter into whatever contracts they wished. Neither the courts nor any other public authority should intervene except in cases of fraud, undue influence, duress, or some other illegality. Governed by this doctrine, the U.S. courts throughout the nineteenth century generally

freedom-to-contract doctrine Parties who are legally competent are allowed to enter into whatever contracts they wish.

refused to interfere in contractual relations merely because one party was more economically powerful or better able to drive a hard bargain. In effect, they upheld the principle of caveat emptor (let the buyer beware).

Since the 1930s, state courts (and some federal courts) have curtailed the traditional freedom to contract by establishing rules of public policy and doctrines of unconscionability and fundamental breach that allow the courts to interfere in contractual relationships, especially when the seller is in the stronger economic position and a consumer has no other source to buy from. The doctrine of freedom to contract has also been limited by the implied warranty doctrine, as well as by the courts' relaxation of strict privity relationships between manufacturers and consumers. (These aspects of contract and product and service liability law were discussed in Chapters 10 and 13.)

Then the consumer rights revolution that started in the 1960s inspired major pieces of consumer legislation at the local, state, and federal levels. Although this chapter deals largely with federal consumer legislation, you should keep three matters in mind as consumer law moves into the twenty-first century.

1. Consumer law includes both statutory and case law. Case law at the state level began the consumer revolution by curtailing the freedom-to-contract doctrine.

2. Statutory law passed by Congress has served as a model for state and local consumer legislation. State and local enforcers of consumer legislation are very important, however, because they are closer geographically to the questionable transaction.

3. Privately funded foundations and legal aid societies do research and play a major role in enforcing consumer legislation at all levels of government.

Linking Law & Business

Economics

In previous chapters we have studied the role of business organizations (Chapter 16), and here we study the interaction between consumers and government (federal, state, and local). The role of government in this chapter has been one of an actor and a referee between consumers and the business community.

As an *actor* the government at all levels consumes about 20 percent of the nation's total output and employs 21 million individuals. State and local governments employ over 18 million people and spend $1 trillion a year.[1]

In its role as *referee*, we have seen that rules (laws) have been set out over a period of time that may interfere in classical economics theory (or marketplace economics). The laws of supply and demand may not function when competition is affected by consumer legislation such as the Fair Credit Reporting Act (FCRA), the Fair Credit Billing Act (FCBA), and the Equal Credit Opportunity Act (ECOA). These rules or laws may be based on political as opposed to economic decisions. Prior to these forms of legislation in the 1960s and 1970s consumers were told that *caveat emptor* (consumer beware) was the golden rule. Government's role as referee has become prominent. A debate exists among economists, political scientists, and legal scholars as to what role, if any, the government should play as a referee between consumers and business organizations.[2]

---

[1] D. Colander, *Microeconomics*, 5th ed. (New York: McGraw-Hill, 2003), pp. 66, 67.
[2] R. Posner, *Economic Analysis of Law*, 6th ed. (New York: Aspen/Littlebrown, 2003), Ch. 2.

FEDERAL REGULATION OF BUSINESS TRADE PRACTICES AND CONSUMER–BUSINESS RELATIONSHIPS

THE FEDERAL TRADE COMMISSION: FUNCTIONS, STRUCTURE, AND ENFORCEMENT POWERS

Functions. The Federal Trade Commission (FTC) has been discussed throughout this book. It was created by the Federal Trade Commission Act (FTCA) expressly to enforce Section 5 of the act, which forbids "unfair methods of competition." Section 5 was originally intended to be used to regulate anticompetitive business practices not reached by the Sherman Act. In 1938, it was amended by the *Wheeler–Lea Act* to prohibit "unfair or deceptive acts or practices." From then on, even if a business practice did not violate the Sherman or Clayton antitrust statutes, the FTC could use the broad "unfair or deceptive" language of Section 5 to protect consumers against misleading advertising and labeling of goods as well as against other anticompetitive conduct by business. Thus, the FTC became the leading federal consumer-protection agency.

Since 1938, Congress has passed several statutes delegating further administrative and enforcement authority to the FTC. Among them are the *Fair Packaging and Labeling Act*, the Lanham Act, the *Magnuson–Moss Warranty–Federal Trade Improvement Act*, the *Telemarketing and Consumer Fraud and Abuse Prevention Act*, important sections of the *Consumer Credit Protection Act*, the *Bankruptcy Reform Act*, Hobby Protection Act, the Wool Products Labeling Act, the Hart–Scott–Rodino Antitrust Improvement Act; and the Food, Drugs, and Cosmetics Act. Those that are italicized are described in this chapter.

Structure and Enforcement Powers. In Chapter 17, we used the Federal Trade Commission in our example of the adjudicative process for federal administrative agencies, and we presented a diagram of the agency's structure in Exhibit 17-4. Before you read any further here, you may want to turn back to that exhibit (page 483) to get a quick picture of how the agency is organized.

The commission is composed of a chairperson and four commissioners, who are nominated by the president and confirmed by the Senate. No more than three commissioners may come from the same political party.

The FTC's Bureau of Competition is responsible for the investigation of complaints of "unfair or deceptive practices" under Section 5 of the FTCA. If the bureau finds merit in the complaint and cannot get the offending party either to voluntarily stop the deceptive or unfair practice or to enter into a consent order, it issues a formal complaint, which leads to a hearing before an administrative law judge.

The FTC has other enforcement weapons at its disposal. It may assess fines, obtain injunctive orders, order corrective advertising (as it did in the *Warner Lambert* case excerpted in Chapter 17), order rescissions of contracts and refunds to consumers, and obtain court orders forcing sellers to pay damages to consumers.

DECEPTIVE AND UNFAIR ADVERTISING

Deceptive Advertising. In passing the 1938 Wheeler–Lea Act amending Section 5 of the FTCA, Congress made it clear that it wished to give the commission the power "to cover every form of advertising deception over which it would be humanly practicable to exercise government control." Through their interpretation of the "unfair or deceptive" language of Section 5 over the years, the commission and the courts have evolved a three-part standard whereby the FTC staff must show:

1. There is a misrepresentation or omission in the advertising likely to mislead consumers.

2. Consumers are acting reasonably under the circumstances.

3. The misrepresentation or omission is material. Neither intent to deceive nor reliance on the advertising need be shown.

We look at three types of deceptive advertising in this section: (1) that involving prices, (2) that involving product quality and quantity, and (3) testimonials by well-known sports, entertainment, and business figures. False price comparisons are one form of deceptive price advertising. Another is offers of a "free" item to a customer who buys one at a "regular" price, when, in fact, the "regular" price covers the cost of the "free" good. The classic deceptive price advertising is the "bait and switch" tactic, or advertising one product at a low price to entice customers into the store and then switching their attention to a higher-priced product. The following case is a classic "bait and switch" example.

CASE 24-2

Tashoff v. FTC
United States Circuit Court of Appeals 4
37 F.2d 707 (D.C. Cir. 1980)

The FTC charged Leon Tashoff (defendant-appellant) with falsely advertising its discount eyeglasses and with several other unfair and deceptive practices. Tashoff owned the New York Jewelry Company (NYJC), which was located in a low-income neighborhood. The administrative law judge (formerly called a hearing examiner) dismissed the charges against Tashoff. The full commission disagreed with the administrative law judge, found the defendant guilty of unfair and deceptive practices under Section 5 of the Federal Trade Commission Act, and issued a cease-and-desist order. Tashoff appealed to the District of Columbia Circuit Court of Appeals.

Judge Bazelon

The Commission first found that NYJC employed a "bait and switch" maneuver with respect to sales of eyeglasses. The evidence showed that NYJC advertised eyeglasses "from $7.50 complete," including "lenses, frames and case." The newspaper advertisements, but not the radio advertisements, mentioned a "moderate examining fee." During this period NYJC offered free eye examinations by a sign posted in its store, and through cards it mailed out and distributed on the street. The NYJC claimed that it offered $7.50 eyeglasses only to persons with their own prescriptions. But we have no doubt that the record amply sup-

ports the Commission's finding that the advertising campaign taken as a whole offered complete eyeglass service for $7.50.

That much shows "bait." There was no direct evidence of "switch"—no direct evidence, that is, that NYJC disparaged or discouraged the purchase of the $7.50 eyeglasses, or that the glasses were unavailable on demand, or unsuited for their purpose. The evidence on which the Commission rested its finding was a stipulation that out of 1,400 pairs of eyeglasses sold each year by NYJC, less than 10 were sold for $7.50 with or without a prescription. NYJC claims that this evidence does not support the finding. We disagree.

It seems plain to us that the Commission drew a permissible inference of "switch" from the evidence of bait, advertising and minimal sales of the advertised product. At best only nine sales—64/100 of one percent of NYJC's eyeglass sales—were made at $7.50. The record leaves unexplained why NYJC's customers, presumably anxious to purchase eyeglasses at $7.50 found them unavailable. Further, NYJC continued to advertise the $7.50 glasses for a year and a half despite the scarcity of sales, a fact which tends to support a finding of a purpose to bring customers into the store for other reasons. This evidence, we think, was sufficient to shift the burden of coming forward to the respondent. NYJC offered no evidence to negate the inference of "switch." The relevant facts are in NYJC's possession and it was in the best position to show, if it could be shown at all, that $7.50 glasses were actually available in the store. Yet the most NYJC could produce was its sales manager's denial that the $7.50 glasses were disparaged.

Affirmed in favor of Plaintiff, FTC.

Critical Thinking About the Law

The facts of a case are an essential ingredient in the court's reasoning. They are the building blocks of the story the court constructs to persuade us of the appropriateness of its decision.

Facts are closely related to, but do not by themselves constitute, reasons. They become reasons only when the court interprets them as having meaning significant to the case. You want to recognize that different interpretations can have different consequences for the court's decision. For example, that a toothpaste company advertised that two out of three dentists prefer its brand will have different implications as a "fact" in a false advertising case, depending on the court's acceptance of this statistic's truthfulness.

In Case 24-2, the court finds that NYJC's practices were a "bait and switch" maneuver. The evidence for the "switch" is indirect and depends to a great extent on an interpretation of the meaning of certain facts. Consequently, the questions that follow will focus on this part of the court's reasoning.

1. What key fact does the court cite in stating that the commission "drew a permissible inference of 'switch'"?

   Clue: This fact is the same evidence on which the commission based its ruling.

2. What missing information would be useful in evaluating the court's interpretation of this fact?

   Clue: Think of information that would help you to decide what kind of impact NYJC's advertising claim had on its sales. A low impact might suggest that NYJC was not using the "bait and switch" tactic.

Secondly, advertising about *product quality and quantity* is often found to be *deceptive* under Section 5 of the Federal Trade Commission Act. For example, when a car sales representative tells a customer, "This car is the best-running car that has ever been sold," is this mere **puffery**, or is it deception? This kind of hype is usually considered an acceptable form of puffery. However, had the sales representative said, "This car will run at least 50,000 miles without a change of oil," the claim would cross the line into the territory of deception.

The FTC staff does not have to show that a claim is expressly deceptive; it is sufficient to show that deception is implicit. Also, the FTC must present evidence that there is no basis for the claim made by the advertiser. When an advertiser claims a certain quality in a product on the basis of what "studies show," it must possess reasonable substantiation of its claim. The commission will consider the cost of substantiation, the consequences of a false claim, the nature of the product, and what experts believe constitutes reasonable substantiation before deciding whether the advertising was deceptive.

Years ago, American Home Products, manufacturers of Anacin, advertised that its drug had a unique painkilling formula that was superior to the formulas of all other drugs containing analgesics. The FTC staff charged that this claim was deceptive because there was insufficient substantiation to show that Anacin was either unique or superior to other nonprescription drugs containing the

puffery An exaggerated recommendation made in a sales talk to promote the product.

same ingredients (aspirin and caffeine).[2] The full commission and the court of appeals agreed after examining the evidence presented by American Home Products. In a similar case in 1984, the FTC filed a complaint against General Nutrition (GN), charging it with deceptive advertising for claiming, purportedly on the basis of a National Academy of Science report, that consumption of its dietary supplement Healthy Greens was related to reduced rates of cancer in humans. General Nutrition entered into a consent order in which it agreed to cease such advertising.[3]

testimonial A statement by a public figure professing the merits of some product or service.

The third form of deceptive advertising discussed here is **testimonials** by public figures (e.g., athletes and entertainers) endorsing a product. The FTC guidelines require that such figures actually use the product they are touting and prefer it to competitive products. The FTC's Bureau of Consumer Protection also monitors claims by public figures that they have superior knowledge of a product. For example, singer Pat Boone represented Acne Stain as a cure for acne when there was no scientific basis for the claim; he also failed to disclose a financial interest he had in Acne Stain. After the FTC filed a complaint against him, Boone agreed to enter into a consent order.[4]

Unfair Advertising. Section 5 of the Federal Trade Commission Act also forbids "unfair" advertising. The FTC guidelines consider advertising to be unfair if consumers cannot reasonably avoid injury, the injury is harmful in its net effect, or it causes substantiated harm to a consumer. In 1975, the commission promulgated a rule for public comment that forbade all children's television advertising. This action came about after complaints by groups that advertising by cereal and toy companies on Saturday morning television programs was addressed to a select age group that could not weigh the advertising rationally; thus, the advertising was "unfair." In 1980, Congress terminated the FTC rule-making proceedings dealing with children's advertising for political reasons and, for good measure, forbade the FTC to initiate rule-making proceedings of any type based on the concept of "unfairness." The commission may still challenge individual acts or practices as unfair under Section 5 of the FTCA in an adjudicatory context.

Private Party Suits and Deceptive Advertising. A company may sue a competitor under the *Lanham Act* of 1947 (see the discussion in Chapter 14 about trademarks), which forbids "false description or representation." Parties bringing actions based on violations of this act may request an injunction or corrective advertising. For example, McDonald's and Wendy's, in separate cases, accused Burger King of falsely portraying its hamburgers as superior to rivals' burgers on the basis of an alleged taste test. In their suits, McDonald's and Wendy's questioned the scientific basis of Burger King's survey and its analysis of the results. Both cases were settled out of court.[5]

The FTC and Deceptive Labeling and Packaging. Under the *Fair Packaging and Labeling Act (FPLA)*, the Department of Health and Human Services (DHHS) promulgates rules governing the labeling and packaging of products.

---

[2] *American Home Products v. FTC*, 695 F.2d 681 (3rd Cir. 1982).

[3] "General Nutrition Inc. Prohibited Trade Practices," *Federal Register* 54, March 6, 1989, p. 9198.

[4] *In re Cooga Mooga, Inc., and Charles E. Boorea*, 92 F.T.C. 310 (1978).

[5] *McDonald's v. Burger King*, 82/2005 (S.D. Fla. 1982); *Wendy's International Inc. v. Burger King*, C-2-82-1179 (S.D. Ohio 1982).

The department has issued rules governing the packaging of foods, drugs, and cosmetics—all of which the FTC has enforcement jurisdiction over. The FPLA and the enacted rules require that such product packaging contain the name and address of the manufacturer or distributor; the net quantity, which must be placed in a conspicuous location on the package front; and an accurate description of all contents. The purpose of the FPLA is to allow consumers to compare prices on the basis of some uniform measure of content.

CONSUMER LEGISLATION

Franchising Relationships. Misrepresentation by franchisors of the potential profits to be made by franchisees is a violation of Section 5 of the Federal Trade Commission Act, which prohibits "unfair" methods of competition as well as "unfair and deceptive trade practices." To combat blatant fraud involved in franchising (discussed in Chapter 16), the FTC in 1979 promulgated rules governing franchise systems.

In its *1979 Franchising Rule*, the commission defines a franchise as a commercial operation in which the franchisee pays a minimum fee of $500 to use the trademark of, or to sell goods and services supplied by, a franchisor that exercises significant control over, or promises significant aid to, the franchisee's business operation. The fee must be paid within six months after the business is begun. For example, McDonald's franchisees receive the trademark (the "golden arches") in return for an initial fee and a percentage of revenues that go to the McDonald's Corporation (the franchisor). McDonald's, in its franchising agreement, specifies the products that must be bought from McDonald's, the quality of food to be served, the store hours, cleanliness standards, and grounds for termination of the franchising agreement.

The FTC rule governing franchising requires each franchisor to provide a disclosure document to prospective franchisees that tells such pertinent information as the names and addresses of the officers of the franchisor, any felony convictions, involvement in any bankruptcy proceedings, all restrictions on a franchisee's territories or the customers it may sell to, and any training or financing the franchisor makes available to franchisees. If a franchisor suggests a potential level of sales, income, or profits, all materials that form the basis of those predictions must be made available to prospective franchisees and the FTC.

Violations of the FTC Franchising Rule may lead to a fine of up to $10,000. The FTC can bring a civil action for damages on behalf of franchisees in federal district court as well as administrative enforcement actions before an administrative law judge.

Consumer Warranties. The FTC is also in charge of enforcing the Magnuson–Moss Warranty Act–Federal Trade Improvement Act of 1975, which applies to manufacturers and sellers of consumer products that make an express written warranty. You recall from our discussion of product and service liability law in Chapter 13 that an express warranty is a guarantee or promise by the seller or manufacturer that goods (products) meet certain standards of performance. Note that the act does not cover oral warranties, whether express or implied. "Consumer products," as defined by the act, are goods that are normally purchased for personal, family, or household use. The courts have interpreted this definition liberally.

The purpose of the Magnuson–Moss Warranty Act is to prevent sellers and manufacturers from passing on confusing and misleading information to consumers. To that end, the act requires that all conditions of a warranty be clearly and conspicuously disclosed for any product sold in interstate commerce that costs more than $10. Furthermore, consumers must be told what to do if a product is defective.

Before this act was passed, a consumer purchasing a video recorder, for instance, could not be sure whether the "limited warranty" covered all labor and parts or only some labor and parts. Thus, after sending the video recorder back to the manufacturer or authorized dealer for repairs, the consumer might discover that the warranty covered a $50 part but not $150 in labor costs—a rather nasty surprise.

Full or Limited Warranties. All written warranties of consumer products that cost more than $10 must be designated as "full" or "limited." A **full warranty** means the manufacturer or dealer must fix the product or the warranty is breached and there are grounds for a breach-of-warranty suit. If efforts to fix the product fail, the consumer must be given a choice of refund or replacement free of charge. A manufacturer or supplier that gives only a **limited warranty** on its product can restrict the duration of implied warranties if the limit is designated conspicuously on the product. In effect, a limited warranty is any warranty that does not meet the conditions of a full warranty.

Second buyers and bailees as well as bystanders are covered by the act and pertinent FTC regulations. Also, manufacturers or sellers cannot limit the time period within which implied warranties of the product are effective. Finally, damages to the consumer cannot be limited unless the limits are expressly stated on the face of the product.

Remedies. The Magnuson–Moss Warranty Act gives an individual consumer, or a class of consumers, the right to bring a private action for a breach of a written (remember, not an oral) warranty. Consumers who bring such actions can recover the costs of the suit, including attorneys' fees, if they win. However, before they file suit, they must give the manufacturer or seller a reasonable opportunity to "cure" the breach of warranty by replacing or fixing the product.

Telemarketing Legislation. Restricts the activities of telemarketers and bans certain interstate telephone sales practices altogether. Some of the prohibited practices are:

- Calling a person's residence at any time other than between 8 A.M. and 8 P.M.

- Claiming an affiliation with a governmental agency at any level when such an affiliation does not exist.

- Claiming an ability to improve a consumer's credit records or to obtain loans for a person regardless of that person's credit history.

- Not telling the receiver of the calls that it is a sales call.

- Claiming an ability to recover goods or money lost by a consumer.

Each violation of these regulations is punishable by a fine of up to $10,000. Exempted are insurers, franchisers, online services, stocks and bonds salespeople regulated by the SEC, and not-for-profit organizations.

The FTC's regulations are an outgrowth of a federal statute, the *Telemarketing and Consumer Fraud and Abuse Prevention Act of 1994.* Congress passed this statute after holding hearings that revealed that some telemarketing firms ("budget shops") used imaginary sweepstakes and other schemes to bilk $40 billion a year from consumers (particularly the elderly) and small businesses.

full warranty Under the Magnuson–Moss Warranty Act, a written protection for buyers that guarantees free repair of a defective product. If the product can't be fixed, the consumer must be given a choice of a refund or a replacement free of charge.

limited warranty Under the Magnuson–Moss Warranty Act, any written warranty that does not meet the conditions of a full warranty.

The statute and the FTC regulations were made enforceable in the federal courts by the 50 state attorneys general as well as by the FTC. This broad scope was intended to put an end to the situation in which telemarketers who engaged in fraud moved quickly from one state to another without being caught because state attorneys general did not have the authority to pursue them under federal law. Moreover, state law often did not provide for suitable punishment when such telemarketers were caught.

Technology and the Legal Environment

E-Commerce: Junk Telephone Calls, Junk Faxes, "Do Not Call" and Antispam Legislation

The Telephone Company Protection Act of 1991 restricts automated devices that dial up thousands of calls an hour to play recorded advertising messages without prior written consent of the called party. The act exempts emergency calls, calls made to businesses, and calls made to or by nonprofit organizations. Personal calls are not covered by the act. The Federal Communications Commission enforces the act. In a court of appeals decision, the law was upheld as valid restriction on commercial speech. (*Moser v. Federal Communications Commission*, 46 F.3d 970 [9th Cir. 1995]).

Another provision of the 1991 act bans unsolicited faxes that contain advertisements. Junk faxes were outlawed to prevent owners of fax machines from having to pay for paper as a receiver. Private and political faxes are exempt. The act has a damage maximum of $500 in damages for each violation. A class action suit against Hooters of America in a federal district court in Georgia brought about a jury verdict of $12 million. A local businessman, Sam Nicholson (and 1,320 other people), sued.

Some have argued that we need to learn to push the "delete" button instead of requesting more legislation. Public response to unwanted (unsolicited) advertising has led to legislation and an increasing number of cases. Advertisers blame the trial lawyers and fax or telephone marketers. In the *Hooters* case, 42 reams of paper with Hooters' advertisements in the form of coupons were introduced into evidence.

The "Do Not Call" Registry, which allows consumers to sign up with the Federal Trade Commission (FTC) in order to eliminate some calls coming from "pitch men" or telemarketers, has now some 50 million registers since it became effective in October 2003.

There are many exceptions allowed under this statute, for example, calls from people conducting surveys or raising funds for charities or politicians. Calls are allowed from people where consumers have "established relationships," for example, firms that consumers pay bills to or obtain a delivery service from. There are possibilities that some businesses may attempt to exploit this law by using questionnaires, raffle entries, or coupons in order to establish a "relationship." States now have "baby" "Do Not Call" laws. Such legislation covers intrastate telemarketing calls.

As junk telephone calls led to congressional actions, the advent of "spam" or "junk" e-mail has brought about reactions from consumers who use the Internet. Yahoo!, and other Internet service providers are also opposed to the overwhelming amount of spam they are forced to carry.

The FTC has brought a small number of enforcement actions under the *Controlling the Assault of Non-Solicited Pornography and Marketing Act (CAN-SPAM Act)* of 2003 which was to slow the quantity of unsolicited e-mails. The law bars senders of commercial e-mail from using fictitious identities and requires them to provide ways for recipients to remove themselves from mailing lists. The difficulty in these cases is largely based on gaining jurisdiction over defendants who are elusive.

Spam now accounts for 85 percent of all e-mail traffic by some industry estimates. The cost to U.S. business may be as high as $2,000 per employee in wasted productivity according to one analysis by Nuclous Research, a technology research firm. Compliance with the CAN-SPAM Act has dwindled to 1 percent based on a study of a quarter million e-mail messages by MX Logic,

Inc., a software company that produces spam-blocking programs.[1]

At the state level several states have enacted anti-spam statutes. See, for example, *State v. Heckel*, 24 P. 3d 4004 (WA, 2001), where the State of Washington's Supreme Court upheld an antispam statute that prohibits false and misleading e-mail messages. The FTC has joined with *19* agencies from *15* countries to combat un-solicited e-mail or spam in an Action Plan for Enforcement as of October 2004.

---

[1] H. Witt, "The Spam King," *Toledo Blade* (Knight-Ryder), August 7, 2004, p. D-1. D. Nasaw, "Federal Law Fails to Lessen Flow of Junk E-Mail," *Wall Street Journal*, August 10, 2004, p. D-2.

FEDERAL LAWS REGULATING CONSUMER CREDIT AND BUSINESS DEBT-COLLECTION PRACTICES

Consumer credit means buyer power, which translates into demand for products, which, in turn, increases the supply of products produced by manufacturers. In short, this nation's economy runs on credit. With Americans owing over $1.5 trillion and businesses and banks mailing out thousands of credit card applications almost daily, it is imperative that both business managers and consumers understand the rules governing credit arrangements.

Until 1969, when Congress passed the Consumer Credit Protection Act, most consumer protection was left to the states. There were many abuses in the issuance and reporting of credit terms. Often consumer-debtors were ignorant of the annual percentage rates they were being charged, which made it impossible for them to shop around and compare rates. The Consumer Credit Protection Act (CCPA) of 1969 was designed to give consumers a fair shake in all areas of credit. We examine here several important sections of this comprehensive act under their popular titles: the Truth-in-Lending Act; the Electronic Fund Transfer Act; the Fair Credit Reporting Act; the Equal Credit Opportunity Act; the Fair Credit Billing Act; the Fair Debt Collection Practices Act; and the Consumer Leasing Act (Exhibit 24-1).

TRUTH-IN-LENDING ACT

Goals. The Truth-in-Lending Act of 1969 (TILA), as amended in 1982, seeks to make creditors disclose all terms of a credit arrangement before they enter into an agreement with a consumer-debtor. It also, by virtue of mandating uniform terms and standards, seeks to give consumers a basis for comparative shopping. The ability of consumers to shop around for the lowest interest rates or finance charges promotes competition in the consumer-credit market.

Scope. The TILA applies to creditors that regularly extend credit for less than $25,000 to natural persons for personal and family purposes. Corporations and persons applying for more than $25,000 in credit (except for buying a home) are not covered by the act. To be covered by the act, creditors must regularly extend credit (e.g., banks, finance companies, retail stores, credit card issuers, or savings and loans), demand payment in more than four installments, or assess a finance charge.

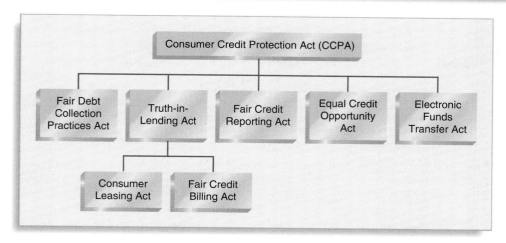

EXHIBIT 24-1

SIGNIFICANT SECTIONS OF THE CONSUMER CREDIT PROTECTION ACT

Provisions. The TILA is a complex, detailed, and costly act for both management (creditors) and consumers (debtors). Six important provisions of the TILA deal with general disclosure, finance charges, the annual percentage rate, the right to cancel a contract, open- and closed-end credit transactions, and credit advertising.

General Disclosure. The general disclosure provisions of the TILA require all qualified creditors to disclose all terms clearly and conspicuously in meaningful sequence and to furnish the consumer with a copy of the disclosure requirements. Additional information, so long as it is not confusing, may be incorporated into the disclosure statement. Exhibit 24-2 is an example of a Truth-in-Lending disclosure statement.

Finance Charges. The finance charge provisions of the TILA—as well as the Federal Reserve Board's **Regulation Z**, which implements some provisions of the act—require a system of disclosing charges so that consumers can compare credit costs using uniform standards. A finance charge includes any dollar charges that make up the cost of credit to the consumer. These may be interest rates; service, carrying, or transaction charges; charges for mandatory credit life insurance on an installment loan in the event of the death of the debtor; loan fees; "points" when buying a home; and appraisal fees.

Annual Percentage Rate. The **annual percentage rate (APR)**—the effective annual rate of interest being charged by the creditor—must be disclosed in a meaningful and sequential way to all consumers of credit. Annual percentage rates differ according to the compounding period being used by the creditor, so this disclosure requirement makes it easy for consumers to see exactly what interest rate they are paying and to do some comparison shopping. The Federal Reserve Board publishes Regulation Z Annual Percentage Tables. If creditors use these tables and follow their instructions, there is a legal presumption of correctness.

Right to Cancel. The right to cancel a contract applies only to home loans. A consumer has a right to cancel such a loan three days after entering the contract. The three days begin after the proper truth-in-lending disclosures have been made, usually at the closing by a bank employee. Because so many documents are being signed at this time, the disclosure statement is sometimes overlooked by both the bank employee and the borrower. TILA was amended in 1995 to prevent borrowers from rescinding loans for minor clerical errors in closing documents. The following case concerns a suit by a consumer seeking relief under the TILA.

Regulation Z A group of rules, set forth by the Federal Reserve Board, to implement some provisions of the Truth-in-Lending Act, requiring lenders to disclose certain information to borrowers.

annual percentage rate (APR) The effective annual rate of interest being charged a consumer by a creditor, which depends on the compounding period the creditor is using.

EXHIBIT 24-2

A DISCLOSURE STATEMENT THAT CONFORMS TO THE TRUTH-IN-LENDING ACT

Application#:
Loan#:

Borrowers

John Jones
15980 Main Street
Pemberville, OH

Property

15980 Main Street
Pemberville, OH

Itemization of Amount Financed

$	Total amount financed	$
$	TAX SERVICE FEE	
$	Interim interest	
$	MI premium	
$	MI renewal reserves	
$	Total prepaid finance charges	$
$	1992 COUNTY TAXES	
$	Appraisal fee	
$	Credit report	
$	Hazard insurance reserves	
$	County tax reserves	
$	Settlement or closing fee	
$	Document preparation	
$	Title insurance	
$	Recording fees	
$	State tax/stamps	
$	SEPTIC INSPECTION	
$	Proc/underwriting fee	
$	Total amount paid to others	

LOAN AMOUNT $

THE FIRST PAYMENT
FOR YOUR ADVANCE 7/23

FOR: $200,000
AT: 7.65%

WHICH WILL PAY OFF IN 84 PAYMENTS

IS BROKEN DOWN AS FOLLOWS:

PRINCIPAL &/OR INTEREST $

Mortgage Insurance

Taxes

Insurance

Other

TOTAL OF PAYMENT $

ANNUAL PERCENTAGE RATE	FINANCE CHARGE	Amount Financed	Total of Payments
The cost of your credit as a yearly rate.	The dollar amount the credit will cost you. $	The amount of credit provided to you or on your behalf.	The amount you will have paid after you have made all payments as scheduled.

Your Payment Schedule Will Be:

THIS LOAN MUST EITHER BE PAID IN FULL AT MATURITY OF MODIFIED TO A MARKET LEVEL FIXED RATE OVER THE REMAINING 30 YEAR TERM. YOU MUST REPAY THE ENTIRE PRINCIPAL BALANCE OF THE LOAN AND UNPAID INTEREST THEN DUE IF YOU DO NOT QUALIFY FOR THE CONDITIONAL MODIFICATION AND EXTENSION FEATURE AS SPECIFIED IN THE NOTE ADDENDUM AND MORTGAGE RIDER. THE LENDER IS UNDER NO OBLIGATION TO REFINANCE THE LOAN IF QUALIFICATION CONDITIONS ARE NOT MET. YOU WILL, THEREFORE, BE REQUIRED TO MAKE PAYMENT OUT OF OTHER ASSETS YOU MAY OWN, OR YOU WILL HAVE TO FIND A LENDER, WHICH MAY BE THE LENDER YOU HAVE THIS LOAN WITH, WILLING TO LEND YOU THE MONEY. IF YOU REFINANCE THIS LOAN AT MATURITY YOU MAY HAVE TO PAY SOME OR ALL OF THE CLOSING COSTS NORMALLY ASSOCIATED WITH A NEW LENDER EVEN IF YOU OBTAIN REFINANCING FROM THE LENDER.

Security Interest: You are giving a security interest in the property located at

Late Charge: If payment is 15 days late, you will be charged 5.0000% of the payment.
Prepayment: If you pay off early, you will not have to pay a penalty.
    If you pay off early, you will not be entitled to a refund of part of the finance charge.
Assumption: Someone buying your home cannot assume the remainder of the mortgage on the original terms.
This Obligation: WILL have a demand feature.

Insurance: You may obtain property insurance from anyone you want that is acceptable to Lender. See your contract documents for any additional information about nonpayment, default, any required repayment in full before the scheduled date, prepayment refunds and penalties.

I (We) hereby acknowledge receiving a completed copy of this disclosure.   Date: ___/___/___

_____

Nancy Kubasek

CASE 24-3

Purtle v. Eldridge Auto Sales, Inc.
U.S. Court of Appeals
91 F.3d 797 (6th Cir. 1998)

Renee Purtle bought a 1986 Chevrolet Blazer from Eldridge Auto Sales, Inc. To finance the purchase through Eldridge, Purtle filled out a credit application on which she misrepresented her employment status. Based on the misrepresentation, Eldridge extended credit. In the credit contract, Eldridge did not disclose the finance charge, the annual percentage rate, or the total sales price or use the term "amount financed," as the TILA and its regulations require. Purtle defaulted on the loan, and Eldridge repossessed the vehicle. Purtle filed a suit in a federal district court against Eldridge, alleging violations of the TILA. The court awarded Purtle $1,000 in damages, plus attorneys' fees and costs. Eldridge appealed, arguing in part that Purtle was not entitled to damages because she had committed fraud on her credit application.

Justice Forester

[T]he TILA imposes mandatory disclosure requirements on those who extend credit to consumers. In the event that a creditor fails to disclose any of the credit terms required under the TILA and its regulations, a consumer may bring a civil action against the creditor. If a violation is proven, the consumer may recover twice the amount of the finance charge (but not less than $100.00 nor more than $1,000.00). The purpose of the statutory recovery is "to encourage lawsuits by individual consumers as a means of enforcing creditor compliance with the Act." The TILA also permits recovery of reasonable attorneys' fees and costs.

[O]nce a court finds a violation of the TILA, no matter how technical, the court has no discretion as to the imposition of civil liability. Based on the unambiguous statutory language, it is clear that the district court appropriately awarded Purtle the statutory penalty set out above.

The Court of Appeals affirmed the lower court ruling and the lender was forced to pay damages despite the plaintiff's fraud.

Open- and Closed-End Credit Transactions. Regulation Z distinguishes between open-end credit and closed-end credit; each has separate disclosure requirements. An **open-end credit** transaction (e.g., MasterCard or a revolving charge account in a retail store such as Sears) is one that extends credit for an indefinite time period and gives the debtor the option to pay in full or in installments. The initial statement to the debtor with such an account must include such items as the elements of any finance charge and the conditions under which it will be imposed, the APR as estimated at the time of extending credit, if and when overcharges will be imposed, and the minimum payment for each periodic statement.

A **closed-end credit** transaction (e.g., a personal consumer loan, a student loan, or a car loan) is extended by the creditor for a limited time period. All conditions of the loan, including the total amount financed, the number of payments, and the due dates, have to be agreed on before the loan is extended. For this type of credit transaction, Regulation Z requires creditors to disclose the total finance charges, the APR, the total number of payments due, any security interest, and any prepayment penalties or rebates to the consumer if payment is made ahead of time.

Credit Advertising. The TILA governs all advertising or "commercial messages" to the public that "aid, promote, or assist" in the extension of consumer credit. Thus, many television and radio commercials, newspaper ads, direct mail, postings in a store, and all announcements of a "blue ribbon" extension of credit to customers in a store must meet certain disclosure requirements. These include the amount of the down payment, the conditions of repayment, and the finance charges, expressed in annual percentage terms.

open-end credit Credit extended on an account for an indefinite time period so that the debtor can keep charging on the account, up to a certain amount, while paying the outstanding balance either in full or in installment payments.

closed-end credit A credit arrangement in which credit is extended for a specific period of time, and the exact number of payments and the total amount due have been agreed upon between the borrower and the creditor.

Critical Thinking About the Law

Asymmetric information refers to situations in which one party possesses more information than another party. Unequal information often exists in buyer–seller relationships. For example, most used-car salespeople have greater knowledge about the quality of cars that they are selling than is possessed by prospective buyers of those cars. Asymmetric information in buyer–seller relationships generally places a seller in a more advantageous position relative to a buyer. Similarly, asymmetric information exists in creditor–debtor relationships, in the sense that creditors typically have more knowledge about the credit arrangements they offer, while also having a better understanding of how those terms compare with other creditors' terms. The debtor-consumer, on the other hand, usually does not possess as much information as a creditor and is, therefore, in a less favorable position. To remedy this disparity of information between creditors and debtors, Congress created several acts, including the Truth-in-Lending Act (TILA). The following questions urge you to consider the primary ethical norms influencing congressional legislation affecting creditor–debtor relationships.

Please refer to Case 24-3 and consider the following questions.

1. **What reasons might a legislator provide to support TILA?**

    Clue: Reread the section prior to the case about the goals of TILA.

2. **In the *Purtle* case, what primary ethical norms guided the court's reasoning?**

    Clue: Consider why the court held the plaintiff's interests over the defendant's interests, even though both sides engaged in wrongdoing.

Remedies. The Federal Trade Commission and seven other federal agencies are responsible for enforcement of the Truth-in-Lending Act. All these agencies have at their disposal uniform corrective actions that can be brought on behalf of a consumer-debtor.

First, a consumer can be reimbursed for a creditor's overcharging and for billing errors with regard to finance charges. Second, if the creditor has exhibited a pattern of negligence, misleading statements, or an intentional failure to disclose, the case may be referred to the Justice Department for criminal action. Conviction in such cases can bring a fine of up to $5,000, or imprisonment up to one year, or both.

Private parties are the major enforcers of the TILA. A private party who brings suit must show, first, that the transaction affected interstate commerce and, second, that the creditor failed to comply with the TILA or Regulation Z. Private parties (usually consumer-debtors) do not have to show that they were injured by the failure to disclose. Moreover, the creditor's noncompliance need only be slight. Damages recovered are usually actual damages plus a penalty of twice the finance charges imposed in connection with the transaction. "Reasonable attorney fees," as determined by the court, can also be collected.

Class actions brought on behalf of consumer-debtors are also permissible under the TILA. Usually, these are brought by legal aid societies or other nonprofit groups against creditors with a history of blatantly unscrupulous dealings with consumers.

THE ELECTRONIC FUND TRANSFER ACT

Goals. In 1978 Congress amended the TILA and enacted the Electronic Fund Transfer Act (EFTA) to regulate financial institutions that offer electronic fund transfers involving an account held by a customer. The Federal Reserve Board was empowered to enforce the provisions of the act and adopted Regulation E to further interpret the act. Types of consumer electronic funds include automated teller machines (ATMs), point-of-sale terminals (e.g., debit cards), pay-by-phone systems, and direct deposit and withdrawals.

Provisions. Consumer rights established by the EFTA apply in the following areas:

1. *Unsolicited cards.* Banks can send unsolicited EFTA cards to a consumer only if the card is not valid for use when received.

2. *Errors in billing.* Customers have 60 days from the receipt of a bank statement to notify the bank of its error. The bank has 10 days to investigate. The bank can recredit the customer account to gain 45 more days to investigate.

3. *Lost or stolen debit cards.* If the bank is notified within two days from the time a card is lost, the customer can be liable for only $50 for unauthorized use. Liability increases to $300 up to 60 days, and more than $500 after 60 days when no notice is given.

4. *Transactions.* A bank has to provide written evidence of a transaction made through a computer terminal.

5. *Statements.* Banks must provide a monthly statement to an EFTA customer at the end of a month in which a transaction is made. If no transactions are made, a quarterly statement must be provided.

The EFTA covers only transactions involving accounts held by natural persons for personal, family, or household purposes. Many fund transfers fall outside the EFTA. An attempt to create a uniform body of law in the 50 states took place in 1989 with the creation of Article 4A of the UCC. Article 4A and the EFTA are mutually exclusive. Article 4A does not apply to regulate any part of an electronic fund transfer that is subject to the EFTA.

Remedies. Under the EFTA, a financial institution is liable to any customer for all damages caused by its failure to make an electronic transfer in a timely manner and when instructed to do so by the customer. The institution is liable for damages caused by its failure to credit a deposit of funds and failure to stop a preauthorized transfer from a customer's account.

If an act of God or other circumstance beyond its control or a technical malfunction takes place, the financial institution is not liable.

A Plastic Society

With credit cards consumers can spend more money more quickly than what they really have when using cash. Consumer debt is at an estimated $838 billion. Card issuers obtain anywhere from 1–5 percent commission on each transaction.[1] The necessity for the Electronic Fund Transfer Act (discussed here) is shown by the fact that credit cards are omnipresent and susceptible to theft.

Technological advances may limit the use of cards in the future. With an increase in online shoppers, the credit industry is looking forward to using silicon wafers embedded in your computer keyboard, which would read a fingerprint and match it online with a bank copy. The bank would then authorize the sale. Could the "plastic society" be changing?

---

[1] See J. Sapsford, "As Cash Wanes, America Becomes a Plastic Nation," *Wall Street Journal*, July 23, 2004, p. A-1, 6.

THE FAIR CREDIT REPORTING ACT

Goals. The Fair Credit Reporting Act (FCRA) was enacted by Congress in 1970 as an amendment to the Consumer Credit Protection Act to ensure that credit information obtained by credit agencies would remain confidential. Individual privacy is a major concern in an era in which three major credit bureaus (TRW, TransUnion, and Equifax) hold files on a majority of U.S. citizens. At the same time, Congress wanted to force the agencies to adopt reasonable procedures to allow lenders, such as banks and finance corporations, to have access to information they needed to make decisions on whether to lend money.

The FCRA sought especially to correct three common abuses by credit agencies: the failure to set uniform standards for keeping information confidential, the retention of irrelevant and sometimes inaccurate information in their files, and the failure to respond to consumer requests for information.

Provisions. These are the most important provisions of the FCRA:
1. The creditor or lender must give notice to a consumer whenever that consumer has been unfavorably affected by an adverse credit report from a consumer reporting agency. A consumer reporting agency is defined as any entity that "regularly engages in the practice of assembling or evaluating consumer credit or other information on consumers for the purpose of furnishing consumer reports to third parties." If a company infrequently furnishes information to a third party or collects it for internal use only, it does not fall within the FCRA.

2. The consumer may go to the credit agency that issued the adverse report and be "informed of the nature and substance" of the information on file. A written request for information by a consumer must also be honored.

3. Credit reporting agencies are required to keep files up-to-date and to delete inaccuracies. If these inaccuracies have been passed on to lenders, the agencies are also required to notify them of their error. Agencies cannot retain stale information and must follow reasonable procedures to update information dealing with bankruptcies, tax liens, criminal records, and bad debts. If a credit transaction involves $50,000 or more, these agency actions are not necessary in issuing a credit report.

4. If consumers do not agree with what is in their file, or with what has been reported by the credit agency to a lender, they can file a written report of 100 words or fewer, giving their side of the dispute.

5. A consumer credit agency may issue credit information reports to (a) a court in response to a court order; (b) the consumer to whom the report relates (upon written request); (c) a person or entity who the agency has reason to believe will use the information in connection with making a credit transaction, obtaining employment, licensing, or obtaining personal or family insurance; and (d) anyone having a legitimate business need for the information in order to carry on a business transaction with a consumer.

6. In 1997 the act was amended to restrict the use of credit reports by employers. An employer must notify a job applicant or current employee that a report may be used and must obtain the applicant's consent prior to requesting an individual credit report from a credit bureau. Additionally, before refusing to hire or terminating or denying a promotion, the employer must provide an individual with a "pre-adverse action disclosure," which

must contain the credit report of the individual and a copy of the FTC's "A Summary of Your Rights Under the Fair Credit Reporting Act."

The following case illustrates the application of the 1997 amendment to the Fair Disclosure Act, which restricts the use of a credit report.

CASE 24-4

Phillips v. Grendahl
United States Court of Appeals, 3
12 F.3d 357, Eighth Circuit, 2002

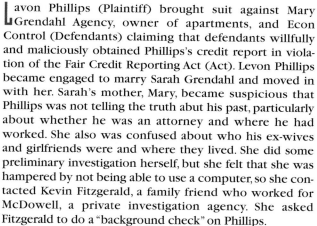

Lavon Phillips (Plaintiff) brought suit against Mary Grendahl Agency, owner of apartments, and Econ Control (Defendants) claiming that defendants willfully and maliciously obtained Phillips's credit report in violation of the Fair Credit Reporting Act (Act). Levon Phillips became engaged to marry Sarah Grendahl and moved in with her. Sarah's mother, Mary, became suspicious that Phillips was not telling the truth abut his past, particularly about whether he was an attorney and where he had worked. She also was confused about who his ex-wives and girlfriends were and where they lived. She did some preliminary investigation herself, but she felt that she was hampered by not being able to use a computer, so she contacted Kevin Fitzgerald, a family friend who worked for McDowell, a private investigation agency. She asked Fitzgerald to do a "background check" on Phillips.

Fitzgerald searched public records in Minnesota and Alabama, where Phillips had lived earlier, and discovered one suit against Phillips for delinquent child support in Alabama, a suit to establish child support for two children in Minnesota, and one misdemeanor conviction for writing dishonored checks. Fitzgerald then supplied the social security information to Econ Control and asked for "Finder's Reports" on Phillips. Fitzgerald testified that he believed that Finder's Reports were not consumer reports and, therefore, that they were not subject to the Fair Credit Reporting Act.

Econ Control was in the business of furnishing credit reports, Finder's Reports, and credit scoring for credit grantors and for private investigators. Econ Control then obtained a consumer report from Computer Science Corporation on Phillips and passed it onto McDowell. Fitzgerald met with Mary Grendahl and gave her the results of his investigation, including the Finder's Report. Someone wrote on the copy of the Finder's Report on Phillips: "Credit Inquiry Reports and Employment Trace."

Phillips learned that Sarah Grendahl's family had investigated his past when Laura Grendahl, Sarah's sister, telephoned Sarah about nine months after the investigation.

The trial court entered summary judgment for the defendants. Plaintiff appealed.

Justice Gibson

The Fair Credit Reporting Act, prohibits the disclosure of consumer credit reports by consumer credit reporting agencies, except in response to the following kinds of requests: (1) court order or subpoena, (2) request by governmental agencies involved in setting or enforcing child support awards, (3) request authorized in writing by the consumer about whom the report is made; or (4) request by a person whom the reporting agency has reason to believe intends to use the consumer report for one of a number of specific, permissible business reasons.

Phillips pursues two theories under the Fair Credit Reporting Act—that the defendants obtained a consumer report on him by use of false pretenses, and that they obtained a consumer report for an impermissible purpose.

The Fair Credit Reporting Act was amended in 1998 to add to section a provision that forbids using or obtaining a consumer report unless the report was obtained for a permitted purpose. Moreover section received new language imposing civil liability against natural persons for "obtaining a consumer report under false pretenses or knowingly without a permissible purpose." Thus, the civil liability provisions now explicitly cover the act of obtaining a consumer report without a permissible purpose, which formerly was included only by incorporating the criminal liability statute.

Here there is evidence that the defendants believed their conduct to be covered by the Fair Credit Reporting Act. There is evidence that each of the defendants had some experience dealing with credit reports and knew that such reports can only be obtained legally under certain circumstances. Since Phillips evidence raises a fact issue as to whether Mary Grendahl Agency knowingly obtained a consumer report on him with conscious disregard of his legal rights, it is sufficient to make a submissible case.

The court of appeals *reversed and remanded* in favor of Plaintiff, Phillips.

Remedies. The FTC may bring actions in the federal courts to obtain cease-and-desist orders against credit agencies and users of information, or it may seek to obtain administrative enforcement orders from an administrative law judge. Violations of the FCRA are considered "unfair or deceptive practices" under Section 5 of the Federal Trade Commission Act. Seven other government entities can also enforce the FCRA: the Federal Reserve Board, the Comptroller of the Currency, the Federal Home Loan Bank Board, the National Credit Union, the Interstate Commerce Commission, and the Secretary of Agriculture.

Identity Theft and Credit Ratings

Identity theft may be defined as the use of another's name to obtain some illegal gain through financial instruments held or owned by another. Often this includes stolen credit cards, social security number, computer codes, telephone numbers, etc.

The Fair and Accurate Credit Transaction Act of 2003[1] (FACTA) (which amends the Fair Credit Reporting Act) seeks to combat identity theft by allowing consumers to place fraud alerts in their credit files, and to block information from being placed in a file if caused by identity theft or fraud. Additionally, FACTA provides the FTC, and other federal regulatory agencies, with rule-making authority to combat identity theft which agencies have lacked before. Also, the FTC may receive reports and studies on identity theft by non-governmental national credit agencies, and other private sector firms, and consumers may receive the same.

FACTA provides that the FTC and other agencies may study the effect of credit scores, collected by credit agencies, and their effect on the affordability of financial products such as mortgages and insurance. Consumers may now have access to their individual credit reports once a year free of charge from one of three national non-governmental credit agencies (Equifax, Experian, TransUnion). In applying for mortgages, insurance, loans, and other financial tools, credit reports will be helpful.

[1] Pub. L. N. 108–159 (2003); 15 U.S.C: Section 168.

Criminal liability is incurred by a person who "knowingly and willfully obtains information on a consumer from a consumer reporting agency under false pretenses." Anyone convicted of this charge is subject to a fine up to $5,000 and possible imprisonment for a maximum of one year.

Civil liability is incurred by a credit agency for any user of credit agency information (e.g., a bank) if a consumer, in a private action, can show that the agency willfully violated the FCRA through repetitive errors. For such violations, the court may assess punitive and actual damages, court costs, and attorneys' fees. A consumer who is able to show negligence on the part of the credit agency or user will obtain actual damages, court costs, and reasonable attorneys' fees.

EQUAL CREDIT OPPORTUNITY ACT

Goals. When Congress enacted the Equal Credit Opportunity Act (ECOA) in 1974, it was trying to eliminate all forms of discrimination in granting credit, including those based on race, sex, color, religion, national origin, marital status, receipt of public assistance—and exercise of one's rights under the act. The Federal Reserve Board, which is charged with implementing ECOA's regulations, may exempt any "classes of transactions not primarily for household or family purposes." Thus, most commercial transactions are exempt from the act.

Provisions. The ECOA and *Regulation B*, promulgated by the Federal Reserve Board, provide that:

1. A creditor may not request information from a credit applicant about a spouse or a former spouse, the applicant's marital status, any alimony and child support received, gender, childbearing, race, color, religion, or national origin.

2. A creditor must notify the applicant of what action has been taken on the application within 30 days of receiving it. The notification must contain (a) a statement of the action taken and, if the application is denied, either a statement of the reasons for the denial or a disclosure of the applicant's right to receive a statement of such reasons; (b) a statement of the basic provisions of the ECOA; and (c) the name and address of the relevant administrative agency that deals with compliance by creditors. There is a two-year statute of limitations to bring a suit under the ECOA. However, this sometimes does not apply when the act is used as a defense. For example, there is a conflict among state and federal court decisions in cases in which the wife is illegally required under ECOA to cosign a loan guarantee for her husband's business. When the bank later brings suit to collect on the promissory note that has been defaulted on by the husband, the wife raises the defense of a violation of the act even though the two-year statute of limitations has run out. Other ECOA violations besides requiring a spouse to cosign include (a) asking for information about an applicant's spouse or former spouse when not relevant; (b) taking race, sex, or national origin into account when making a credit decision; (c) requiring certain types of life insurance before issuing a loan; (d) basing a credit decision on the area in which the applicant lives; and (e) asking about an applicant's intent to have children.

Remedies. The FTC and other agencies can bring administrative actions on behalf of consumers before an administrative law judge as well as civil injunctive actions in the federal district courts. In addition, if a creditor violates the ECOA, individuals who feel they have been injured under the act can bring an action in federal district court for actual and punitive damages. Punitive damages may not exceed $10,000 for an individual successful plaintiff, but they may go as high as $500,000 for successful class action plaintiffs. Plaintiffs may also ask for injunctive relief to prohibit future discriminatory actions by the creditor.

THE FAIR CREDIT BILLING ACT

Goals. Congress enacted the Fair Credit Billing Act (FCBA) as an amendment to the TILA in 1974 in order to eliminate inaccurate and unfair billing practices, as well as to limit the liability of consumer creditors for the unauthorized use of their credit cards.

Provisions. The FCBA provisions cover (1) issuers of credit cards, (2) creditors who extend credit in more than four monthly installments, and (3) creditors who assess finance charges. The following provisions of the act establish a procedure for correcting billing errors:

1. All creditors must notify consumer-debtors of their rights and duties when an account is opened and every six months thereafter. They must notify debtors on the billing statement where they are to inquire when they notice a billing error.

2. Consumer-debtors who believe their billing statement contains an error must notify the creditor in writing within 60 days, identifying themselves, their account number, the item, and the amount in dispute. Within 30 days, the creditor must notify the debtor that it has received notice of the alleged billing error. Within 90 days, or two billing cycles, the creditor must notify the consumer-debtor of the outcome of its investigation. During this period, the creditor cannot take any action to collect the debt in dispute. It may continue to send billing statements listing the disputed item, but these statements must give notice to the consumer that the item in dispute does not have to be paid.

3. If after investigation the creditor finds that there was a billing error, it must correct the error and notify the consumer. If it finds no error, it must notify the consumer-debtor and substantiate its reason. A bad credit report cannot be filed until ten days after the substantiation has been sent out.

If a faulty product is purchased on credit, the consumer can withhold payment until the dispute is settled, provided he or she notifies the creditor immediately after finding the fault in the product. The creditor is then obligated to attempt to negotiate the dispute between the seller of the product and the consumer-debtor.

Remedies. Individual consumer-debtors, as well as government agencies, can bring actions against creditors who violate the FCBA. The only penalty set forth in the act is that creditors forfeit their right to collect up to $50 on each item in dispute on each periodic statement. This amount includes interest and finance charges on the amount in dispute.

THE FAIR DEBT COLLECTION PRACTICES ACT

Goals. The purpose of the Fair Debt Collection Practices Act is to prevent harassment by creditors or debt collectors of consumer-debtors at their place of work or at home. The act defines debt collectors as those who are in the business of collecting debts from others. In 1987, attorneys who regularly perform debt activities were brought under the provisions of the FDCPA. See *Heinz v. Jenkins*, U.S. Supreme Court, 513 U.S. 1109 (1995).

Approximately 5,000 debt-collection agencies seek about $5 billion in debts from some 8 million consumers annually. Many use sophisticated WATTS telephone lines and computers. They are paid a 20 to 50 percent commission on what they collect, so they often are quite aggressive in their collection methods—as well as successful. So successful that in the 1980s the federal government turned over many outstanding federal loans (including student loans) to these private collection agencies.

States are exempt from FDCPA enforcement within their boundaries if they have laws meeting the FDCPA requirements. Actually, state laws are often more vigorously enforced than the federal law.

Provisions. The FDCPA prohibits the following activities by debt collectors who are covered by the act:

1. They may not contact a third party (other than the debtor's family and lawyer) except to find out where the debtor is. The idea behind this provision is that the debtor's name should not be ruined among friends, acquaintances, or employers.

2. They may not contact a debtor during "inconvenient" hours. This provision seeks to prevent creditors from harassing a debtor in the middle of the night. "Inconvenient hours" are considered to be from 9:00 P.M. to 8:00 A.M. for a debtor whose workday is normally 8:00 A.M. to 5:00 P.M. If the credit collection agency knows that the debtor is represented by a lawyer, it may not contact the debtor at all.

3. They cannot contact a debtor in an abusive, deceptive, or unfair way. For example, posing as a lawyer or police officer is forbidden.

4. The act requires a debt collector, within five days of the initial communication with a consumer, to provide the consumer with a written notice that includes (1) the amount of the debt; (2) the name of the current creditor; and (3) a statement informing the consumer that he or she can request verification of the alleged debt. The consumer can recover damages from the collection agency for violations of the act.

The following case illustrates the importance of language in interpreting a statute.

CASE 24-5

Miller v. McCalla, Raymer Padrick and Clark, L.L.C.
U.S. Court of Appeals
214 F.3d 872 (7th Circuit, 2000)

Miller (plaintiff) sued McCalla (defendant) for violation of the Fair Debt Collection Practices Act (Act) for failing to state "the amount of the debt" in the dunning letter it (defendant) sent. Plaintiff argued that the relevant time for determining debt is when it first arises, not when collection begins. Defendants replied that they did state the amount of the debt.

Lower court granted summary judgment for defendants. Plaintiff appealed.

Justice Posner

The defendants [argue] that since the Act under which the plaintiff is suing governs debt collection, the relevant time is when the attempt at collection is made. Oddly, there are no reported appellate decisions on the issue, though it was assumed that the relevant time is when the loan is made, not when collection is attempted.

The language of the statute favors this interpretation. "Debt" is defined as "any obligation or alleged obligation of a consumer to pay money arising out of a transaction in which the money, property, insurance, or services which are the subject of the transaction are primarily for personal family, or household purposes."

So the Act is applicable and we move to the question whether the defendants violated the statutory duty to state the amount of the loan. The dunning letter said that the "unpaid principal balance" of the loan was $178,844.65, but added that "this amount does not include accrued but unpaid interest, unpaid late charges, escrow advances or other charges for preservation and protection of the lender's interest in the property, as authorized by your loan agreement. The amount to reinstate or pay off your loan changes daily. You may call our office for complete reinstatement and payoff figures." An 800 number is given.

The statement does not comply with the Act (again we can find no case on the question). The unpaid principal balance is not the debt; it is only a part of the debt; the Act requires statement of the debt.

We hold that the following statement satisfies the debt collector's duty to state the amount of the debt in cases like this where the amount varies from day to day: "As of the date of this letter, you owe $_____ [the exact amount due]. Because of interest, late charges, and other charges that may vary from day to day, the amount due on the day you pay may be greater. Hence, if you pay the amount shown above, an adjustment may be necessary after we receive your check, in which event we will inform you before depositing the check for collection. For further information, write the undersigned or call 1-800-[phone number]." A debt collector who uses this form will not violate the "amount of the debt" provision, provided, of course, that the information he furnishes is accurate and he does not obscure it by adding confusing other information (or misinformation). Of course we do not hold that a debt collector must use this form of words to avoid violating the statute; but if he does, and (to repeat an essential qualification) does not add other words that confuse the message, he will as a matter of law have discharged his duty to state clearly the amount due. No reasonable person could conclude that the statement that we have drafted does not inform the debtor of the amount due.

Reversed and remanded to the lower court in favor of Plaintiff, Miller.

Remedies. A violation of the FDCPA is considered a violation of Section 5 of the FTCA. The FTC and individual debtors may both bring actions. The FTC may issue cease-and-desist orders and levy fines after an internal administrative agency proceeding.

Individual debtors may bring civil actions to recover actual damages, including those for embarrassment and mental distress. An additional $1,000 may be assessed for each violation for malicious damages. Attorneys' fees are recoverable by debtors who win their suits and also in the event that the creditor brings an action against the debtor and it is found to be "harassing."

THE CONSUMER LEASING ACT (CLA) OF 1988

Goals. Congress enacted the Consumer Leasing Act in 1988 as an amendment to the Truth-in-Lending Act for the express purpose of providing meaningful disclosure to consumers who lease goods. Before the CLA was passed, the lease terms for consumer goods were often so complex that the average consumer could not understand them.

Provisions. The CLA applies to leases of "consumer goods," which are defined as a "lease of personal property" for "person, family, or household" use. The lease period must be more than four months, and the dollar value of the lease obligation cannot exceed $25,000. The CLA defines a "lessor" as any natural person or legal entity (corporation, partnership, franchise, or individual proprietorship) that regularly engages in or arranges for leasing as a normal part of business. Apartment leases and leases between neighbors are not covered by the act.

When a lease falls under the CLA's definition, the creditor-lessor must provide the following information for the consumer-lessee in the lease agreement:

1. The date and name of the lessor and the lessee.
2. A description of the personal property being leased, plus an itemization of all financing charges, the date of lease payments, and any expressed warranties regarding the leased property.
3. The responsibility of consumer-lessee and the lessor-creditor for attorney's fees in the case of a suit by either party, insurance coverage, and the terms and conditions for terminating and transferring the lease.

Remedies. Violations of the Consumer Leasing Act are subject to the same penalties as violations of the Truth-in-Lending Act, discussed previously.

E-Commerce and Consumer Protection

The Federal Trade Commission has indicated that more than 160,000 Internet-related fraud complaints were received in 2003 with estimated losses of nearly $200 million.[1] About 50 percent of the complaints involved online auctions. Despite these numbers, very few cases are actually filed in courts or with administrative agencies because fraud on the Internet is often practiced by people in foreign countries. Jurisdiction over these cases has become important. Additionally, the staffs of local, state, and federal officials combined have too few enforcers. Also, there is a fear of disclosing some suspects because it may assist other alleged criminals in evading law enforcement authorities.

Government regulators at all levels have sought to keep up with scammers who use a "phishing" technique. E-mails are sent to Internet users asking for passwords and other information, disguising the messages as official communications from companies such as eBay and many others. In eBay's case, this method is used to swipe the identities of users, in particular eBay sellers who have built a reputation for honesty.[2] This identity scam allows those seeking to defraud others to obtain thousands of potential targets.

The FTC (and other federal and state agencies) has become a referee for business and consumer transactions on the Internet. Everything from airline tickets to books to pianos may be purchased on the Web. As this activity increases so does the likelihood of techniques involving fraud. As discussed in this chapter, deceptive advertising never ceases as part of transactions involving business and consumer. "Junk" faxes, telephone calls, and spam lead to cases of fraud. The best weapon for consumer protection may be an educated consumer working with business and government agencies.

At the state level consumer protection statutes have been amended to cover Internet transactions. Often the most effective consumer protection may be initiated at local levels. The Internet complaint process has become an important tool.

---

[1] N. Wingfield, "Problem for Cops on ᴇBᴀʏ Bᴇᴀᴛ," *Wall Street Journal*, August 8, p. A-1, 8.

[2] *Id.*

STATE CONSUMER LEGISLATION

It has often been argued that state, city, county, and private agencies (e.g., the Better Business Bureau) are closer geographically to the problems that the average consumer encounters and, thus, are more effective at resolving them than are federal agencies, particularly when relatively small amounts of money are involved. In this section, we examine some consumer-oriented legislation applied in the states. Though it is often overlooked in treatments of consumer protection law, it is important because it touches the lives of many Americans daily.

UNIFORM CONSUMER CREDIT CODE

The *Uniform Consumer Credit Code (UCCC)* was drafted by the National Conference of Commissioners on State Laws in 1968 and was revised in 1974 and 1982. The commissioners' aim was to replace the patchwork of differing state consumer laws with a uniform state law in the area of consumer credit.

The UCCC takes a disclosure approach to consumer credit similar to that of the federal legislation discussed in this chapter. It regulates interest and finance rates, sets out creditors' remedies, and prohibits fine-print clauses. (It incorporates the TILA by reference.) Like the FTC regulations, the UCCC gives the consumer three days to cancel a sale when it is made as a result of home solicitations. So far, only ten states have enacted the UCCC. Only a few states have adopted the UCCC and each of them has altered the state statute as written.

UNFAIR AND DECEPTIVE PRACTICES STATUTES

All states and the District of Columbia have statutes forbidding deceptive acts and practices in a way similar to Section 5 of the Federal Trade Commission Act. So closely are they modeled on the act, in fact, that these statutes are often called baby FTC laws.

State attorney general offices typically have consumer fraud divisions that investigate consumer fraud and false advertising and that seek injunctions, fines, or restitution in state courts. Often notice of investigation by a state attorney general's office is sufficient to discourage the continuation of a practice such as false advertising. Furthermore, private consumer actions, as well as class actions, are permitted under most state statutes. Usually, consumers may obtain actual and punitive damages as well as court costs and attorney's fees.

Attempts to combat consumer fraud at the state level range from mandatory disclosure statutes requiring merchants to set out all terms and conditions in a financing agreement to laws requiring "cooling-off" periods that allow consumers a set number of days to cancel a purchase sold by a door-to-door salesperson. One class of state consumer laws, the "lemon laws," gives consumers warranty and refund rights on used cars when a material defect can be shown. Mandatory seat-belt-use laws and license-suspension statutes are also consumer oriented in that they protect buyers and drivers of automobiles.

ARBITRATION OF DISPUTES

State attorneys general have recently been encouraging private groups, such as the Better Business Bureau, to play a role in exposing fraudulent sales tactics and in arbitrating disputes. One excellent example in this area is a formal agreement between General Motors (GM) and the Better Business Bureau that allows consumers to bring their complaints about car engines to the bureau. General Motors has agreed to be bound by the bureau's decisions, although consumers have the right to go to court if they disagree with a decision.

GLOBAL DIMENSIONS OF CONSUMER PROTECTION LAW

As companies have become multinational, there has become a need to look at varying national consumer protection laws and how they differ. For example, in advertising, a company such as Coca-Cola seeks to standardize its advertising for purposes of reducing costs and improving quality and appeal to internationally mobile consumers. However, one of the factors that prevents complete standardization of advertising is legality. Differing national views on consumer protection, competitive protection, and standards of morality and nationalism prevent a multinational company from delivering the same advertising message in each nation where it sells goods.

In the area of consumer protection, countries differ on the amount of deception in advertising permitted. For example, the United Kingdom and the United States allow competing companies to advertise in a comparative way (for example, Burger King and McDonald's). In contrast, the Philippines prohibits this form of advertising. In the United States we are concerned with sexism in advertising, as well as advertising of tobacco. Most countries in Europe, Asia, and Latin America have few, if any, prohibitions in those areas.

In 1984, the European Union's Commission adopted what was termed a "Misleading Advertising Directive." Similar to Section 5 of the Federal Trade Commission Act, the directive called on member states of the European Union to prohibit misleading advertising by statute and to create means to enforce such laws. Similar to the U.S. laws, the directive requires that courts and agencies within member states be given the power to require companies to substantiate claims made in advertisements. Member nations have gradually enacted legislation that fits the cultural mores it is to be applied to.

In Mexico, the Federal Consumer Protection Act of 1975 (FCPA) was modeled in large part after several U.S. statutes. Some provisions dealing with advertising include the "principle of truthfulness" between customers and merchants. Labeling instructions must be clear as to content. There must be warnings on all advertised products, as well as truthfulness in advertising on radio and television. In addition to advertising, the FCPA covers areas such as warranties, consumer credit disclosure, and unconscionable clauses in contracts. Both private parties and the Federal Attorney General for Consumer Affairs may bring actions in courts of law. With the advent of NAFTA, the FCPA has become more important as the United States, Canada, and Mexico seek to bring some uniformity to their consumer protection laws.

SUMMARY

Consumer law began in the 1930s in case law and evolved quickly during the consumer rights movement of the 1960s and 1970s. Federal regulation of business and trade practices is highly dependent on the Federal Trade Commission, which is the watchdog agency charged with enforcing Section 5 of the Federal Trade Commission Act, forbidding unfair or deceptive business practices and unfair methods of competition. Prohibited trade practices include deceptive and unfair advertising, misrepresentation by franchisors, deceptive or confusing warranties, and deceptive telemarketing practices.

Federal laws regulating consumer credit all come under the comprehensive Consumer Credit Protection Act. Important parts of this umbrella act are the Truth-in-Lending Act, which forces creditors to disclose all terms of a credit arrangement to consumer-debtors before they sign the agreement; the Fair Credit Reporting Act, which seeks to ensure that credit agencies keep accurate, confidential records; the Equal Credit Opportunity Act; the Fair Credit Billing Act; the Fair Debt Collection Practices Act; and the Consumer Leasing Act. The Bankruptcy Reform Act is intended to help debtors who have fallen on hard times.

State consumer legislation is important because state and local agencies are often closer to consumers' problems than federal agencies are and, therefore, they are more effective.

As indicated in this chapter, as international business grows, it is important to look at consumer protection laws around the world so that multinational companies are aware of their rights and duties.

REVIEW QUESTIONS

24-1 What is meant by the freedom-to-contract doctrine?

24-2 List the enforcement weapons the Federal Trade Commission has to use against a corporation or an individual who violates Section 5 of the Federal Trade Commission Act.

24-3 With which general types of deceptive advertising is the Federal Trade Commission most concerned?

24-4 What must franchisors disclose to prospective franchisees under the Federal Trade Commission rule governing franchising?

24-5 What must be disclosed by a consumer credit reporting agency under the Fair Credit Reporting Act?

24-6 What enforcement weapon does the FTC use against parties who violate the Equal Credit Opportunity Act? Explain.

REVIEW PROBLEMS

24-7 Robert Martin allowed a business associate, E. L. McBride, to use his American Express Card in a joint business venture in which they were involved. He orally authorized McBride to use the card and to charge anything up to $500. Martin received a statement from American Express three months later; the amount due on his account was $5,300. Martin refused to pay, claiming that he had not signed the invoices and, therefore, was liable, under the Truth-in-Lending Act, only up to $50 for "unauthorized use" of the card. American Express claimed that McBride was an "authorized" user and sued for the full balance of the account. Who won this case, and why?

24-8 Joe T. Morris received from the Credit Bureau of Cincinnati a bad credit rating based on a bankruptcy filing of his wife that had occurred before their marriage and two unpaid delinquent department-store accounts that were also his wife's. (The delinquent accounts had ended up in his file by accident.) He was denied credit in several instances. After he reported the error to the credit bureau, the bureau corrected his record, but by mistake it opened another account using the name "Joseph T. Morris" with the same inaccurate information. Once again, Morris was denied credit. He sued under the Fair Credit Reporting Act, requesting compensatory and punitive damages. Who won? Explain.

24-9 When Jerry Markham and Marcia Harris became engaged, they found a house that they wanted to buy

and jointly applied for a mortgage to Colonial Mortgage Service Company, an agent of Illinois Federal Savings and Loan Association. Three days before the closing date for the purchase of the house, the loan committee of Illinois Federal rejected the couple's loan application, claiming that their separate incomes were not sufficient to meet the bank's criteria for "loan and job tenure." Markham and Harris sued, claiming a violation of the Equal Credit Opportunity Act, which forbids discrimination based on marital status when the creditworthiness of individuals is evaluated. Who won this case, and why?

24-10 Campbell Soup ran ads on television showing solid ingredients at the top of a bowl of soup in a "mock-up" display. The company placed marbles at the bottom of the bowl to force the solid ingredients to the top. The FTC claimed that this was a violation of Section 5 of the Federal Trade Commission Act in that it was deceptive advertising. Who won? Explain.

24-11 Tropicana Products, Inc., in a television advertisement, had Bruce Jenner, U.S. Olympic decathlon champion, squeezing an orange. As the juice went into a Tropicana carton, he said, "It's pure, pasteurized juice as it comes from the orange." The voiceover then stated, "It's the only leading brand not made with concentrate and water." Coca-Cola, owner of Minute Maid, sued Tropicana for false advertising under the Lanham Act. It claimed that the juice was not freshly squeezed juice but was often heated and frozen before packaging. Who won this case, and why?

24-12 Millstone applied for a new automobile insurance policy after he moved from Washington, D.C., to St. Louis. He was told that a background investigation would be conducted in connection with the application. One week later he was notified that the policy would not be granted because of a report that the insurance company had received from Investigative Reports, a credit bureau. After repeated efforts to obtain his file, Millstone was informed by Investigative Reports that his former neighbors in Washington considered him a "hippie," a drug user, and a possible political dissident. Investigative Reports refused to discuss the matter further. Has Investigative Reports fulfilled its obligations to Millstone? Explain.

CASE PROBLEMS

24-13 At a Circle-K store, Alan Snow paid for merchandise with his personal check in the amount of $23.12. Circle-K deposited the check at its bank, but the check was dishonored because of insufficient funds. Circle-K sent the returned check to its attorney, Jesse L. Riddle, P.C., for collection. In a letter to Snow, Riddle wrote that "the check amount, along with a service fee of $15, must be paid within seven (7) days of this notice. If it is not paid, [a] suit [will] be filed." Snow paid the check and then filed a suit in a federal district court against Riddle. Snow alleged in part that Riddle's letter violated the FDCPA (Fair Debt Collection Practices Act) because it did not contain a "validation notice." Riddle filed a motion to dismiss on the ground that the FDCPA does not cover a dishonored check. Does the check constitute a "debt" under the FDCPA or is it an "extension of credit"? Who won? Explain. *Snow v. Riddle*, 143 F.3d 1350 (1998)

24-14 Kevin Miller bought a house in Atlanta in 1992 and took out a mortgage. He lived in the house until 1995, when he accepted a job in Chicago; from then on, he rented the house to others. He received a dunning (a demand for payment) letter from one of the defendant law firms on behalf of the mortgagee in 1997. By this time, the plaintiff was renting the property to strangers and, thus, was making a business use of the property. The plaintiff claimed that the defendants violated the Fair Debt Collection Practices Act by failing to state "the amount of the debt" in the dunning letter of which he complains. Who won under the FDCPA? Explain. *Miller v. McCalla* et al., 214 F.3d 872 (2000)

24-15 In 1990, Greg Henson sold his 1980 Chevrolet Camaro Z-28 to his brother, Jeff Henson. To purchase the car, Jeff secured a loan with Cosco Federal Credit Union (Cosco). Soon thereafter, the car was stolen and Jeff stopped making payments on his loan from Cosco. At the time, Cosco was unsure whether Greg retained an interest in the car, so Cosco sued both Jeff and Greg for possession of the car. The trial court rendered a default judgment against Jeff and ruled that Greg had no longer any interest in the car. However, the clerk erroneously noted in the judgment docket that the money judgment had been rendered against Greg as well as against Jeff. However, the official record of judgments and orders correctly reflected that only Jeff was affected by the money judgment. Two credit agencies, CSC Credit Services (CSC) and TransUnion Corporation (TransUnion) relied on the state court judgment docket and indicated in Greg's credit report that he owed the money judgment. Greg and his wife, Mary Henson, allege that they then "contacted Trans [Union] twice, in writing, to correct this horrible injustice." When TransUnion did not respond, the Hensons brought this action alleging violations of the Federal Credit Reporting Act (FCRA). The district court, noting that to state a claim under FCRA a consumer must allege that a credit reporting agency prepared a credit report containing inaccurate information, granted the defendants' motions to dismiss. Who won on appeal? Explain. *Henson v. CSC Credit Services*, 29 F.3d 280 (2000)

24-16 CrossCheck, Inc., provides check authorization services to retail merchants. When a customer presents a check, the merchant contacts CrossCheck, which estimates the probability that the check will clear the bank. If the check is within an acceptable statistical range, CrossCheck notifies the merchant. If the check is dishonored, the merchant sends it to CrossCheck, which pays it. CrossCheck then attempts to redeposit the check. If this fails, CrossCheck takes further steps to collect the amount. William Winterstein took his truck to C&P Auto Service Center, Inc., for a tune-up and paid for the service with a check. C&P contacted

CrossCheck and, on its recommendation, accepted the check. When the check was dishonored, C&P mailed it to CrossCheck, which reimbursed C&P and sent a letter to Winterstein, requesting payment. Winterstein filed a suit in a federal district court against CrossCheck, asserting that the letter violated the Fair Debt Collection Practices Act. CrossCheck filed a motion for summary judgment. Who won? Explain. *Winterstein v. CrossCheck, Inc.*, 149 F.Supp.2d 466 (N.D. Ill. 2001)

24-17 Source One Associates, Inc., is based in Poughquag, New York. Peter Easton, Source One's president, is responsible for its daily operations. Between 1995 and 1997, Source One received requests from persons in Massachusetts seeking financial information about individuals and businesses. To obtain this information, Easton first obtained the targeted individuals' credit reports through Equifax Consumer Information Services by claiming the reports would be used only in connection with credit transactions involving the consumers. From the reports, Easton identified financial institutions at which individuals held accounts and then called the institutions to learn the account balances by impersonating either officers of the institutions or the account holders. The information was then provided to Source One's customers for a fee. Easton did not know why the customers wanted the information. The Commonwealth of Massachusetts filed a suit in a Massachusetts state court against Source One and Easton, alleging violations of the Fair Credit Reporting Act (FCRA). Did the defendants violate the FCRA? Explain. *Commonwealth v. Source One Associates, Inc.* 763 N.E.2d 42 (2002)

ASSIGNMENT ON THE INTERNET

As e-commerce continues to grow in the United States and abroad, new consumer protection laws are needed. Now that you know something about current consumer protection laws in the United States, use the Internet to research recent developments in consumer protection for transactions through cyberspace. Make a list of recommendations for new regulations or rules that you would like to see enacted. What ethical norms are implicit in your recommendations?

 ## ON THE INTERNET

www.lectlaw.com//tcos.html Here is a law library site that is a good place from which to begin your research about consumer protection issues.

www.law.cornell.edu/topics/debtor_creditor.html The Legal Information Institute provides an overview to debtor–creditor law as well as links to recent debtor–creditor law decisions.

www.ct.gov/dcp/site/default.asp The Connecticut State Department of Consumer Protection Web site provides citizens of that state with consumer information. Many states offer some form of consumer protection.

www.ftc.gov/ftc/consumer.htm The Federal Trade Commission maintains a Web site with consumer information.

library.lp.findlaw.com/bankruptcy.html This site contains information about bankruptcy law and links to related issues.

www.nclc.org This site is the National Consumer Law Center, which provides a wealth of information on the topic.

THE CONSTITUTION OF THE UNITED STATES

PREAMBLE

We the People of the United States, in Order to form a more perfect Union, establish Justice, insure domestic Tranquility, provide for the common defence, promote the general Welfare, and secure the Blessings of Liberty to ourselves and our Posterity, do ordain and establish this Constitution for the United States of America.

ARTICLE I

Section 1. All legislative Powers herein granted shall be vested in a Congress of the United States, which shall consist of a Senate and a House of Representatives.

Section 2. [1] The House of Representatives shall be composed of Members chosen every second Year by the People of the several States, and the Electors in each State shall have the Qualifications requisite for Electors of the most numerous Branch of the State Legislature.

[2] No Person shall be a Representative who shall not have attained to the Age of twenty five Years, and been seven Years a Citizen of the United States, and who shall not, when elected, be an Inhabitant of that State in which he shall be chosen.

[3] Representatives and direct Taxes shall be apportioned among the several States which may be included within this Union, according to their respective Numbers, which shall be determined by adding to the whole Number of free Persons, including those bound to Service for a Term of Years, and excluding Indians not taxed, three fifths of all other Persons. The actual Enumeration shall be made within three Years after the first Meeting of the Congress of the United States, and within every subsequent Term of ten Years, in such Manner as they shall by Law direct. The Number of Representatives shall not exceed one for every thirty Thousand, but each State shall have at Least one Representative; and until such enumeration shall be made, the State of New Hampshire shall be entitled to choose three, Massachoosetts eight, Rhode Island and Providence Plantations one, Connecticut five, New York six, New Jersey four, Pennsylvania eight, Delaware one, Maryland six, Virginia ten, North Carolina five, South Carolina five, and Georgia three.

[4] When vacancies happen in the Representation from any State, the Executive Authority thereof shall issue Writs of Election to fill such Vacancies.

[5] The House of Representatives shall choose their Speaker and other Officers and shall have the sole Power of Impeachment.

Section 3. [1] The Senate of the United States shall be composed of two Senators from each State, chosen by the Legislature thereof, for six Years; and each Senator shall have one vote.

[2] Immediately after they shall be assembled in Consequence of the first Election, they shall be divided as equally as may be into three Classes. The Seats of the Senators of the first Class shall be vacated at the Expiration of the Second Year, of the second Class at the Expiration of the fourth Year, and of the third Class at the Expiration of the sixth Year, so that one third may be chosen every second Year; and if Vacancies happen by Resignation, or otherwise, during the Recess of the Legislature of any State, the Executive thereof may make temporary Appointments until the next Meeting of the Legislature, which shall then fill such Vacancies.

[3] No Person shall be a Senator who shall not have attained to the Age of thirty Years, and been nine Years a Citizen of the United States, and who shall not, when elected, be an Inhabitant of that State for which he shall be chosen.

[4] The Vice President of the United States shall be President of the Senate, but shall have no Vote, unless they be equally divided.

[5] The Senate shall choose their other Officers, and also a President pro tempore, in the Absence of the Vice President, or when he shall exercise the Office of President of the United States.

[6] The Senate shall have the sole Power to try all Impeachments. When sitting for that Purpose, they shall be on Oath or Affirmation. When the President of the United States is tried, the Chief Justice shall preside: And no Person shall be convicted without the Concurrence of two thirds of the Members present.

[7] Judgment in Cases of Impeachment shall not extend further than to removal from Office, and disqualification to hold and enjoy any Office of honor, Trust, or Profit under the United States: but the Party convicted shall nevertheless be liable and subject to Indictment, Trial, Judgment, and Punishment, according to Law.

Section 4. [1] The Times, Places and Manner of holding Elections for Senators and Representatives, shall be prescribed in each State by the Legislature thereof; but the Congress may at any time by Law make or alter such Regulations, except as to the Places of choosing Senators.

[2] The Congress shall assemble at least once in every Year, and such Meeting shall be on the first Monday in December, unless they shall by Law appoint a different Day.

Section 5. [1] Each House shall be the Judge of the Elections, Returns, and Qualifications of its own Members, and a Majority of each shall constitute a Quorum to do Business, but a smaller Number may adjourn from day to day, and may be authorized to compel the

Attendance of absent Members, in such Manner, and under such Penalties as each House may provide.

[2] Each House may determine the Rules of its Proceedings, punish its Members for Disorderly Behavior, and, with the Concurrence of two thirds, expel a Member.

[3] Each House shall keep a Journal of its Proceedings, and from time to time publish the same, excepting such Parts as may in their Judgment require Secrecy; and the Yeas and Nays of the Members of either House on any question shall, at the Desire of one fifth of those Present, be entered on the Journal.

[4] Neither House, during the Session of Congress, shall, without the Consent of the other, adjourn for more than three days, nor to any other Place than that in which the two Houses shall be sitting.

Section 6. [1] The Senators and Representatives shall receive a Compensation for their Services, to be ascertained by Law, and paid out of the Treasury of the United States. They shall in all Cases, except Treason, Felony and Breach of the Peace, be privileged from Arrest during their Attendance at the Session of their respective Houses, and in going to and returning from the same; and for any speech or Debate in either House, they shall not be questioned in any other Place.

[2] No Senator or Representative shall, during the Time for which he was elected, be appointed to any civil Office under the Authority of the United States, which shall have been created, or the Emoluments whereof shall have been increased during such time and no Person holding any Office under the United States, shall be a Member of either House during his Continuance in Office.

Section 7. [1] All Bills for raising Revenue shall originate in the House of Representatives; but the Senate may propose or concur with Amendments as on other Bills.

[2] Every Bill which shall have passed the House of Representatives and the Senate, shall, before it become a Law, be presented to the President of the United States; If he approve he shall sign it, but if not he shall return it, with his Objections to the House in which it shall have originated, who shall enter the Objections at large on their Journal, and proceed to reconsider it. If after such Reconsideration two thirds of that House shall agree to pass the Bill, it shall be sent together with the Objections, to the other House, by which it shall likewise be reconsidered, and if approved by two thirds of that House, it shall become a Law. But in all such Cases the Votes of both Houses shall be determined by Yeas and Nays, and the Names of the Persons voting for and against the Bill shall be entered on the Journal of each House respectively. If any Bill shall not be returned by the President within ten Days (Sundays excepted) after it shall have been presented to him, the Same shall be a Law, in like Manner as if he had signed it, unless the Congress by their Adjournment prevent its Return in which Case it shall not be a Law.

[3] Every Order, Resolution, or Vote, to Which the Concurrence of the Senate and House of Representatives may be necessary (except on a question of Adjournment) shall be presented to the President of the United States; and before the Same shall take Effect, shall be approved by him, or being disapproved by him, shall be repassed by two thirds of the Senate and House of Representatives, according to the Rules and Limitations prescribed in the Case of a Bill.

Section 8. [1] The Congress shall have Power To lay and collect Taxes, Duties, Imposts and Excises, to pay the Debts and provide for the common Defence and general Welfare of the United States; but all Duties, Imposts and Excises shall be uniform throughout the United States;

[2] To borrow money on the credit of the United States;

[3] To regulate Commerce with foreign Nations, and among the several States, and with the Indian Tribes;

[4] To establish an uniform Rule of Naturalization, and uniform Laws on the subject of Bankruptcies throughout the United States;

[5] To coin Money, regulate the Value thereof, and of foreign Coin, and fix the Standard of Weights and Measures;

[6] To provide for the Punishment of counterfeiting the Securities and current Coin of the United States;

[7] To Establish Post Offices and Post Roads;

[8] To promote the Progress of Science and useful Arts, by securing for limited Times to Authors and Inventors the exclusive Right to their respective Writings and Discoveries;

[9] To constitute Tribunals inferior to the supreme Court;

[10] To define and punish Piracies and Felonies committed on the high Seas, and Offenses against the Law of Nations;

[11] To declare War, grant Letters of Marque and Reprisal, and make Rules concerning Captures on Land and Water;

[12] To raise and support Armies, but no Appropriation of Money to that Use shall be for a longer Term than two Years;

[13] To provide and maintain a Navy;

[14] To make Rules for the Government and Regulation of the land and naval Forces;

[15] To provide for calling forth the Militia to execute the Laws of the Union, suppress Insurrections and repel Invasions;

[16] To provide for organizing, arming, and disciplining, the Militia, and for governing such Part of them as may be employed in the Service of the United States, reserving to the States respectively, the Appointment of the Officers, and the Authority of training the Militia according to the discipline prescribed by Congress;

[17] To exercise exclusive Legislation in all Cases whatsoever, over such District (not exceeding ten Miles square) as may, by Cession of particular States, and the Acceptance of Congress, become the Seat of the Government of the United States, and to exercise like Authority over all Places purchased by the consent of the Legislature of the State in which the Same shall be, for the Erection of Forts, Magazines, Arsenals, dock-Yards, and other needful Buildings; — And

[18] To make all Laws which shall be necessary and proper for carrying into Execution the foregoing Powers, and all other Powers vested by this Constitution in the Government of the United States, or in any department or Officer thereof.

Section 9. [1] The Migration or Importation of Such Persons as any of the States now existing shall think proper to admit, shall not be prohibited by the Congress prior to the Year one thousand eight hundred and eight, but a Tax or duty may be imposed on such Importation, not exceeding ten dollars for each Person.

[2] The privilege of the Writ of Habeas Corpus shall not be suspended, unless when in Cases of Rebellion or Invasion the public Safety may require it.

[3] No Bill of Attainder or ex post facto law shall be passed.

[4] No Capitation, or other direct, Tax shall be laid, unless in Proportion to the Census or Enumeration herein before directed to be taken.

[5] No Tax or Duty shall be laid on articles exported from any State.

[6] No Preference shall be given by any Regulation of Commerce or Revenue to the Ports of one State over those of another: nor shall Vessels bound to, or from, one State be obliged to enter, clear, or pay Duties in another.

[7] No money shall be drawn from the Treasury, but in Consequence of Appropriations made by Law; and a regular Statement and Account of the Receipts and Expenditures of all public Money shall be published from time to time.

[8] No Title of Nobility shall be granted by the United States: And no Person holding any Office of Profit or Trust under them, shall, without the Consent of the Congress, accept of any present, Emolument, Office, or Title, of any kind whatever, from any King, Prince, or foreign State.

Section 10. [1] No State shall enter into any Treaty, Alliance, or Confederation; grant Letters of Marque and Reprisal; coin Money; emit Bills of Credit; make any Thing but gold and silver Coin a Tender in Payment of Debts; pass any Bill of Attainder, ex post facto Law, or Law impairing the Obligation of Contracts, or grant any Title of Nobility.

[2] No State shall, without the Consent of the Congress, lay any Imposts or Duties on Imports or Exports, except what may be absolutely necesarry for executing its inspection Laws: and the net Produce of all Duties and Imposts, laid by any States on Imports or Exports, shall be for the Use of the Treasury of the United States; and all such Laws shall be subject to the Revision and Control of the Congress.

[3] No State shall, without the Consent of Congress, lay any Duty of Tonnage, keep Troops, or Ships of War in time of Peace, enter into any Agreement or Compact with another State, or with a foreign Power, or engage in War, unless actually invaded, or in such imminent Danger as will not admit of delay.

ARTICLE II

Section 1. [1] The executive Power shall be vested in a President of the United States of America. He shall hold his Office during the Term of four Years, and, together with the Vice President, chosen for the same Term, be elected, as follows:

[2] Each State shall appoint, in such Manner as the Legislature thereof may direct, a Number of Electors, equal to the whole Number of Senators and Representative to which the State may be entitled in the Congress; but no Senator or Representative, or Person holding an Office of Trust or Profit under the United States, shall be appointed as Elector.

[3] The Electors shall meet in their respective States, and vote by Ballot for two Persons, of whom one at least shall not be an Inhabitant of the same State with themselves. And they shall make a List of all the Persons voted for, and of the Number of Votes for each; which List they shall sign and certify, and transmit sealed to the Seat of the Government of the United States, directed to the President of the Senate. The President of the Senate shall, in the Presence of the Senate and House of Representatives, open all the Certificates, and the Votes shall then be counted. The Person having the greatest Number of Votes shall be the President, if such Number be a Majority of the whole Number of Electors appointed; and if there be more than one who have such Majority, and have an equal Number of Votes, then the House of Representatives shall immediately choose by Ballot one of them for President; and if no Person have a Majority, then from the five highest on the List the said House shall in like Manner choose the President. But in choosing the President, the Votes shall be taken by States the Representation from each State having one Vote; A quorum for this Purpose shall consist of a Member or Members from two thirds of the States, and a Majority of all the States shall be necessary to a Choice. In every Case, after the Choice of the President, the Person having the greater Number of Votes of the Electors shall be the Vice President. But if there should remain two or more who have equal Votes, the Senate shall choose from them by Ballot the Vice President.

[4] The Congress may determine the Time of choosing the Electors, and the Day on which they shall give their Votes; which Day shall be the same throughout the United States.

[5] No person except a natural born Citizen, or a Citizen of the United States, at the time of the Adoption of this constitution, shall be eligible to the Office of President; neither shall any Person be eligible to that Office who shall not have attained to the Age of thirty five Years, and been fourteen Years a Resident within the United States.

[6] In case of the removal of the President from Office, or of his Death, Resignation or Inability to discharge the Powers and Duties of the said Office, the Same shall devolve on the Vice President, and the Congress may by Law provide for the Case of Removal, Death, Resignation or Inability, both of the President and Vice President, declaring what Officer shall then act as President, and such Officer shall act accordingly, until the disability be removed, or a President shall be elected.

[7] The President shall, at stated Times, receive for his Services, a Compensation, which shall neither be increased nor diminished during the Period for which he shall have been elected, and he shall not receive within that Period any other Emolument from the United States, or any of them.

[8] Before he enter on the Execution of his Office, he shall take the following Oath or Affirmation: "I do solemnly swear (or affirm) that I will faithfully execute the Office of President of the United States, and will to the best of my Ability, preserve, protect and defend the Constitution of the United States."

Section 2. [1] The President shall be Commander in Chief of the Army and Navy of the United States, and of the militia of the several States, when called into the actual Service of the United States; he may require the Opinion, in writing, of the principal Officer in each of the Executive Departments, upon any Subject relating to the Duties of their respective Offices, and he shall have Power to grant Reprieves and Pardons for Offenses against the United States, except in Cases of Impeachment.

[2] He shall have Power, by and with the Advice and Consent of the Senate to make Treaties, provided two thirds of the Senators present concur; and he shall nominate, and by and with the Advice and Consent of the Senate, shall appoint Ambassadors, other public Ministers and Consuls, Judges of the supreme Court, and all other Officers of the United States, whose Appointments are not herein otherwise provided for, and which shall be established by Law; but the Congress may by Law vest the Appointment of such inferior Officers, as they think proper, in the President alone, in the Courts of Law, or in the Heads of Departments.

[3] The President shall have Power to fill up all Vacancies that may happen during the Recess of the Senate, by granting Commissions which shall expire at the End of their next Session.

Section 3. He shall from time to time give to the Congress Information of the State of the Union, and recommend to their Consideration such Measures as he shall judge necessary and expedient; he may, on extraordinary Occasions, convene both Houses, or either of them, and in Case of Disagreement between them, with Respect to the Time of Adjournment, he may adjourn them to such Time as he shall think proper; he shall receive Ambassadors and other public Ministers; he shall take Care that the Laws be faithfully executed, and shall Commission all the Officers of the United States.

Section 4. The President, Vice President and all civil Officers of the United States shall be removed from Office on Impeachment for, and Conviction of, Treason, Bribery, or other high Crimes and Misdemeanors.

ARTICLE III

Section 1. The judicial Power of the United States, shall be vested in one supreme Court, and in such inferior Courts as the Congress may from time to time ordain and establish. The Judges, both of the supreme and inferior Courts, shall hold their Offices during good Behaviour, and shall, at stated Times, receive for their Services a Compensation, which shall not be diminished during their Continuance in Office.

Section 2. [1] The judicial Power shall extend to all Cases, in Law and Equity, arising under this Constitution, the Laws of the United States, and Treaties made, or which shall be made, under their Authority; — to all Cases affecting Ambassadors, other public Ministers and Consuls; — to all Cases of admiralty and maritime Jurisdiction; — to Controversies to which the United States shall be a Party; — to Controversies between two or more States; — between a State and Citizens of another State; — between Citizens of different States; — between Citizens of the same State claiming Lands under the Grants of different States, and between a State, or the Citizens thereof, and foreign States, Citizens or Subjects.

[2] In all Cases affecting Ambassadors, other public Ministers and Consuls, and those in which a State shall be a Party, the supreme Court shall have original Jurisdiction. In all the other Cases before

mentioned, the supreme Court shall have appellate Jurisdiction, both as to Law and Fact, with such Exceptions, and under such Regulations as the Congress shall make.

[3] The trial of all Crimes, except in Cases of Impeachment, shall be by Jury; and such Trial shall be held in the State where the said Crimes shall have been committed; but when not committed within any State, the Trial shall be at such Place or Places as the Congress may by Law have directed.

Section 3. [1] Treason against the United States, shall consist only in levying War against them, or, in adhering to their Enemies, giving them Aid and Comfort. No Person shall be convicted of Treason unless on the Testimony of two Witnesses to the same overt Act, or on Confession in open Court.

[2] The Congress shall have Power to declare the Punishment of Treason, but no Attainder of Treason shall work Corruption of Blood, or Forfeiture except during the Life of the Person attainted.

ARTICLE IV

Section 1.   Full Faith and Credit shall be given in each State to the public Acts, Records, and judicial Proceedings of every other State. And the Congress may by general Laws prescribe the Manner in which such Acts, Records and Proceedings shall be proved, and the Effect thereof.

Section 2.   [1] The Citizens of each State shall be entitled to all Privileges and Immunities of Citizens in the Several States.

[2] A Person charged in any State with Treason, Felony, or other Crime, who shall flee from Justice, and be found in another State, shall on demand of the executive Authority of the State from which he fled, be delivered up, to be removed to the State having Jurisdiction of the Crime.

[3] No Person held to Service or Labour in one State, under the Laws thereof, escaping into another, shall, in Consequence of any Law or Regulation therein, be discharged from such Service or Labour, but shall be delivered up on Claim of the Party to whom such Service or Labour may be due.

Section 3.   [1] New States may be admitted by the Congress into this Union; but no new State shall be formed or erected within the Jurisdiction of any other State; nor any State be formed by the Junction of two or more States, or Parts of States, without the Consent of the Legislatures of the States concerned as well as of the Congress.

[2] The Congress shall have Power to dispose of and make all needful Rules and Regulations respecting the Territory or other Property belonging to the United States; and nothing in this Constitution shall be so construed as to Prejudice any Claims of the United States, or of any particular State.

Section 4.   The United States shall guarantee to every State in this Union a Republican Form of Government, and shall protect each of them against Invasion; and on Application of the Legislature, or of the Executive (when the Legislature cannot be convened) against domestic Violence.

ARTICLE V

The Congress, whenever two thirds of both Houses shall deem it necessary, shall propose Amendments to this Constitution, or, on the Application of the Legislatures of two thirds of the several States, shall call a Convention for proposing Amendments, which, in either Case, shall be valid to all Intents and Purposes, as part of this Constitution, when ratified by the Legislatures of three fourths of the several States, or by Conventions in three fourths thereof, as the one or the other Mode of Ratification may be proposed by the Congress; Provided that no Amendment which may be made prior

to the Year One thousand eight hundred and eight shall in any Manner affect the first and fourth Clauses in the Ninth Section of the first Article; and that no State, without its Consent, shall be deprived of its equal Suffrage in the Senate.

ARTICLE VI

[1] All Debts contracted and Engagements entered into, before the Adoption of this Constitution shall be as valid against the United States under this Constitution, as under the Confederation.

[2] This Constitution, and the Laws of the United States which shall be made in Pursuance thereof; and all Treaties made, or which shall be made, under the Authority of the United States, shall be the supreme Law of the Land; and the Judges in every State shall be bound thereby, any Thing in the Constitution or Laws of any State to the Contrary notwithstanding.

[3] The Senators and Representatives before mentioned, and the Members of the several State Legislatures, and all executive and judicial Officers, both of the United States and of the several States, shall be bound by Oath or Affirmation, to support this Constitution; but no religious Test shall ever be required as a Qualification to any Office or public Trust under the United States.

ARTICLE VII

The Ratification of the conventions of nine States shall be sufficient for the Establishment of this Constitution between the States so ratifying the Same.

ARTICLES IN ADDITION TO, AND AMENDMENT OF, THE CONSTITUTION OF THE UNITED STATES OF AMERICA, PROPOSED BY CONGRESS, AND RATIFIED BY THE LEGISLATURES OF THE SEVERAL STATES PURSUANT TO THE FIFTH ARTICLE OF THE ORIGINAL CONSTITUTION.

AMENDMENT I [1791]

Congress shall make no law respecting an establishment of religion, or prohibiting the free exercise thereof; or abridging the freedom of speech, or of the press; or the right of the people peaceably to assemble, and to petition the Government for a redress of grievances.

AMENDMENT II [1791]

A well regulated Militia, being necessary to the security of a free State, the right of the people to keep and bear Arms, shall not be infringed.

AMENDMENT III [1791]

No Soldier shall, in time of peace be quartered in any house, without the consent of the Owner, nor in time of war, but in a manner to be prescribed by law.

AMENDMENT IV [1791]

The right of the people to be secure in their persons, houses, papers, and effects, against unreasonable searches and seizures, shall not be violated, and no Warrants shall issue, but upon probable cause, supported by Oath or affirmation, and particularly describing the place to be searched, and the persons or things to be seized.

AMENDMENT V [1791]

No person shall be held to answer for a capital, or otherwise infamous crime, unless on a presentment or indictment of a Grand Jury, except in cases arising in the land and naval forces, or in the Militia, when in actual service in time of War or public danger; nor shall any person be subject for the same offence to be twice put in jeopardy of life or limb; nor shall be compelled in any criminal case to be a witness against himself, nor be deprived of life, liberty, or property, without due process of law; nor shall private property be taken for public use, without just compensation.

AMENDMENT VI [1791]

In all criminal prosecutions, the accused shall enjoy the right to a speedy and public trial, by an impartial jury of the State and district wherein the crime shall have been committed, which district shall have been previously ascertained by law, and to be informed of the nature and cause of the accusation; to be confronted with the witnesses against him; to have compulsory process for obtaining witnesses in his favor, and to have the Assistance of Counsel for his defence.

AMENDMENT VII [1791]

In Suits at common law, where the value in controversy shall exceed twenty dollars, the right of trial by jury shall be preserved, and no fact tried by jury, shall be otherwise re-examined in any Court of the United States, than according to the rules of the common law.

AMENDMENT VIII [1791]

Excessive bail shall not be required, nor excessive fines imposed, nor cruel and unusual punishments inflicted.

AMENDMENT IX [1791]

The enumeration in the Constitution, of certain rights, shall not be construed to deny or disparage others retained by the people.

AMENDMENT X [1791]

The powers not delegated to the United States by the Constitution, nor prohibited by it to the States, are reserved to the States respectively, or to the people.

AMENDMENT XI [1798]

The Judicial power of the United States shall not be construed to extend to any suit in law or equity, commenced or prosecuted against one of the United States by Citizens of another State, or by Citizens or Subjects of any Foreign State.

AMENDMENT XII [1804]

The Electors shall meet in their respective states and vote by ballot for President and Vice-President, one of whom, at least, shall not be an inhabitant of the same state with themselves; they shall name in their ballots the person voted for as President, and in distinct ballots the person voted for as Vice-President, and they shall make distinct lists of all persons voted for as President, and of all persons voted for as Vice-President, and of the number of votes for each, which lists they shall sign and certify, and transmit sealed to the seat of the government of the United States, directed to the President of the Senate; — The President of the Senate shall, in the presence of the Senate and House of Representatives, open all the certificates and the votes shall then be counted; — The person having the greatest number of votes for President, shall be the President, if such number be a majority of the whole number of Electors appointed; and if no person have such majority, then from the persons having the highest numbers not exceeding three on the list of those voted for as President, the House of Representatives shall choose immediately, by ballot, the President. But in choosing the President, the votes shall be taken by states, the representation from each state having one vote; a quorum for this purpose shall consist of a member or members from two-thirds of the states, and a majority of all the states shall be necessary to a choice. And if the House of Representatives shall not choose a President whenever the right of choice shall devolve upon them before the fourth day of March next following, then the Vice-President shall act as President, as in the case of the death or other constitutional disability of the President. — The person having the greatest number of votes as Vice-President, shall be the Vice-President, if such number be a majority of the whole number of Electors appointed, and if no person have a majority, then from the two highest numbers on the list, the Senate shall choose the Vice-President; a quorum for the purpose shall consist of two-thirds of the whole number of Senators, and a majority of the whole number shall be necessary to a choice. But no person constitutionally ineligible to the office of President shall be eligible to that of Vice-President of the United States.

AMENDMENT XIII [1865]

Section 1. Neither slavery nor involuntary servitude, except as a punishment for crime whereof the party shall have been duly convicted, shall exist within the United States, or any place subject to their jurisdiction.

Section 2. Congress shall have power to enforce this article by appropriate legislation.

AMENDMENT XIV [1868]

Section 1. All persons born or naturalized in the United States, and subject to the jurisdiction thereof, are citizens of the United States and of the State wherein they reside. No State shall make or enforce any law which shall abridge the privileges or immunities of citizens of the United States; nor shall any State deprive any person of life, liberty, or property, without due process of law; nor deny to any person within its jurisdiction the equal protection of the laws.

Section 2. Representatives shall be apportioned among the several States according to their respective numbers, counting the whole number of persons in each State excluding Indians not taxed. But when the right to vote at any election for the choice of electors for President and Vice President of the United States, Representatives in Congress, the Executive and Judicial officers of a State, or the members of the Legislature thereof, is denied to any of the male inhabitants of such State, being twenty-one years of age, and citizens of the United States, or in any way abridged, except for participation in rebellion, or other crime, the basis of representation therein shall be reduced in the proportion which the number of such male citizens shall bear to the whole number of male citizens twenty-one years of age in such State.

Section 3. No person shall be a Senator or Representative in Congress, or elector of President and Vice President, or hold any office, civil or military, under the United States, as a member of any State, who having previously taken an oath, as a member of Congress, or as an officer of the United States, or as a member of any State legislature, or as an executive or judicial officer of any State, to support the

Constitution of the United States, shall have engaged in insurrection or rebellion against the same, or given aid or comfort to the enemies thereof. But Congress may by a vote of two-thirds of each House, remove such disability.

Section 4.   The validity of the public debt of the United States, authorized by law, including debts incurred for payment of pensions and bounties for services in suppressing insurrection or rebellion, shall not be questioned. But neither the United States nor any State shall assume or pay any debt or obligation incurred in aid of insurrection or rebellion against the United States, or any claim for the loss or emancipation of any slave; but all such debts, obligations and claims shall be held illegal and void.

Section 5.   The Congress shall have power to enforce, by appropriate legislation, the provisions of this article.

AMENDMENT XV [1870]

Section 1.   The right of citizens of the United States to vote shall not be denied or abridged by the United States or by any State on account of race, color, or previous condition of servitude.

Section 2.   The Congress shall have power to enforce this article by appropriate legislation.

AMENDMENT XVI [1913]

The Congress shall have power to lay and collect taxes on incomes, from whatever source derived, without apportionment among the several States, and without regard to any census or enumeration.

AMENDMENT XVII [1913]

[1] The Senate of the United States shall be composed of two Senators from each State, elected by the people thereof, for six years and each Senator shall have one vote. The electors in each State shall have the qualifications requisite for electors of the most numerous branch of the State legislatures.

[2] When vacancies happen in the representation of any State in the Senate, the executive authority of such State shall issue writs of election to fill such vacancies: *Provided,* That the legislature of any State may empower the executive thereof to make temporary appointments until the people fill the vacancies by election as the legislature may direct.

[3] This amendment shall not be so construed as to affect the election or term of any Senator chosen before it becomes valid as part of the Constitution.

AMENDMENT XVIII [1919]

Section 1.   After one year from the ratification of this article the manufacture, sale, or transportation of intoxicating liquors within, the importation thereof into, or the exportation thereof from the United States and all territory subject to the jurisdiction thereof for beverage purposes is hereby prohibited.

Section 2.   The Congress and the several States shall have concurrent power to enforce this article by appropriate legislation.

Section 3.   This article shall be inoperative unless it shall have been ratified as an amendment to the Constitution by the legislatures of the several States, as provided in the Constitution, within seven years from the date of the submission hereof to the States by the Congress.

AMENDMENT XIX [1920]

[1] The right of citizens of the United States to vote shall not be denied or abridged by the United States or by any State on account of sex.

[2] Congress shall have power to enforce this article by appropriate legislation.

AMENDMENT XX [1933]

Section 1.   The terms of the President and Vice President shall end at noon on the 20th day of January, and the terms of Senators and Representatives at noon on the 3d day of January, of the years in which such terms would have ended if this article had not been ratified; and the terms of their successors shall then begin.

Section 2.   The Congress shall assemble at least once in every year, and such meeting shall begin at noon on the 3d day of January, unless they shall by law appoint a different day.

Section 3.   If, at the time fixed for the beginning of the term of the President, the President elect shall have died, the Vice President elect shall become President. If the President shall not have been chosen before the time fixed for the beginning of his term, or if the President elect shall have failed to qualify, then the Vice President elect shall act as President until a President shall have qualified; and the Congress may by law provide for the case wherein neither a President elect nor a Vice President elect shall have qualified, declaring who shall then act as President, or the manner in which one who is to act shall be selected, and such person shall act accordingly until a President or Vice President shall have qualified.

Section 4.   The Congress may by law provide for the case of the death of any of the persons from whom the House of Representatives may choose a President whenever the right choice shall have devolved upon them, and for the case of the death of any of the persons from whom the Senate may choose a Vice President whenever the right of choice shall have devolved upon them.

Section 5.   Sections 1 and 2 shall take effect on the 15th day of October following the ratification of this article.

Section 6.   This article shall be inoperative unless it shall have been ratified as an amendment to the Constitution by the legislatures of three-fourths of the several States within seven years from the date of its submission.

AMENDMENT XXI [1933]

Section 1.   The eighteenth article of amendment to the Constitution of the United States is hereby repealed.

Section 2.   The transportation or importation into any State, Territory, or possession of the United States for delivery or use therein of intoxicating liquors, in violation of the laws thereof, is hereby prohibited.

Section 3.   This article shall be inoperative unless it shall have been ratified as an amendment to the Constitution by conventions in the several States, as provided in the Constitution, within seven years from the date of the submission hereof to the States by the Congress.

AMENDMENT XXII [1951]

Section 1.   No person shall be elected to the office of the President more than twice, and no person who has held the office of President, or acted as President, for more than two years of a term to which some other person was elected President shall be elected to the office of President more than once. But this Article shall not apply to any person holding the office of President when this Article was proposed by the Congress, and shall not prevent any person who may be holding the office of President, or acting as President, during the term within which this Article becomes operative from holding the office of President or acting as President during the remainder of such term.

Section 2.   This article shall be inoperative unless it shall have been ratified as an amendment to the Constitution by the legislatures of three-fourths of the several States within seven years from the date of its submission to the States by the Congress.

AMENDMENT XXIII [1961]

Section 1.   The District constituting the seat of Government of the United States shall appoint in such manner as the Congress may direct:

A number of electors of President and Vice President equal to the whole number of Senators and Representatives in Congress to which the District would be entitled if it were a State, but in no event more than the least populous state; they shall be in addition to those appointed by the states, but they shall be considered, for the purposes of the election of President and Vice President, to be electors appointed by a state; and they shall meet in the District and perform such duties as provided by the twelfth article of amendment.

Section 2.   The Congress shall have power to enforce this article by appropriate legislation.

AMENDMENT XXIV [1964]

Section 1.   The right of citizens of the United States to vote in any primary or other election for President or Vice President, for electors for President or Vice President, or for Senator or Representative in Congress, shall not be denied or abridged by the United States, or any State by reason of failure to pay any poll tax or other tax.

Section 2.   The Congress shall have power to enforce this article by appropriate legislation.

AMENDMENT XXV [1967]

Section 1.   In case of the removal of the President from office or of his death or resignation, the Vice President shall become President.

Section 2.   Whenever there is a vacancy in the office of the Vice President, the President shall nominate a Vice President who shall take office upon confirmation by a majority vote of both Houses of Congress.

Section 3.   Whenever the President transmits to the President pro tempore of the Senate and the Speaker of the House of Representatives his written declaration that he is unable to discharge the powers and duties of his office, and until he transmits to them a written declaration to the contrary, such powers and duties shall be discharged by the Vice President as Acting President.

Section 4.   Whenever the Vice President and a majority of either the principal officers of the executive departments or of such other body as Congress may by law provide, transmit to the President pro tempore of the Senate and the Speaker of the House of Representatives their written declaration that the President is unable to discharge the powers and duties of his office, the Vice President shall immediately assume the powers and duties of the office as Acting President.

Thereafter, when the President transmits to the President pro tempore of the Senate and the Speaker of the House of Representatives his written declaration that no inability exists, he shall resume the powers and duties of his office unless the Vice President and a majority of either the principal officers of the executive department or of such other body as Congress may by law provide, transmit within four days to the President pro tempore of the Senate and the Speaker of the House of Representatives their written declaration and the President is unable to discharge the powers and duties of his office. Thereupon Congress shall decide the issue, assembling within forty-eight hours for that purpose if not in session. If the Congress, within twenty-one days after receipt of the latter written declaration, or, if Congress is not in session, within twenty-one days after Congress is required to assemble, determines by two-thirds vote of both Houses that the President is unable to discharge the power and duties of his office, the Vice President shall continue to discharge the same as Acting President; otherwise, the President shall resume the powers and duties of his office.

AMENDMENT XXVI [1971]

Section 1.   The right of citizens of the United States, who are eighteen years of age or older, to vote shall not be denied or abridged by the United States or by any State on account of age.

Section 2.   The Congress shall have power to enforce this article by appropriate legislation.

AMENDMENT XXVII [1996]

No law, varying the compensation for the services of the Senators and Representatives, shall take effect, until an election of Representatives shall have intervened.

APPENDIX B

UNIFORM COMMERCIAL CODE (2000 OFFICIAL TEXT), ARTICLE 2

ARTICLE 2. SALES

Part 1. Short Title, General Construction and Subject Matter

§ 2–101. Short Title.

This Article shall be known and may be cited as Uniform Commercial Code—Sales.

§ 2–102. Scope; Certain Security and Other Transactions Excluded From This Article.

Unless the context otherwise requires, this Article applies to transactions in goods; it does not apply to any transaction which although in the form of an unconditional contract to sell or present sale is intended to operate only as a security transaction nor does this Article impair or repeal any statute regulating sales to consumers, farmers or other specified classes of buyers.

§ 2–103. Definitions and Index of Definitions.

(1) In this Article unless the context otherwise requires
  (a) "Buyer" means a person who buys or contracts to buy goods.
  (b) "Good faith" in the case of a merchant means honesty in fact and the observance of reasonable commercial standards of fair dealing in the trade.
  (c) "Receipt" of goods means taking physical possession of them.
  (d) "Seller" means a person who sells or contracts to sell goods.

(2) Other definitions applying to this Article or to specified Parts thereof, and the sections in which they appear are:

"Acceptance"	Section 2-606.
"Banker's credit"	Section 2-325.
"Between merchants"	Section 2-104.
"Cancellation"	Section 2-106(4).
"Commercial unit"	Section 2-105.
"Confirmed credit"	Section 2-325.
"Conforming to contract"	Section 2-106.
"Contract for sale"	Section 2-106.
"Cover"	Section 2-712.
"Entrusting"	Section 2-403.
"Financing agency"	Section 2-104.
"Future goods"	Section 2-105.
"Goods"	Section 2-105.
"Identification"	Section 2-501.
"Installment contract"	Section 2-612.
"Letter of Credit"	Section 2-325.
"Lot"	Section 2-105.
"Merchant"	Section 2-104.
"Overseas"	Section 2-323.
"Person in position of seller"	Section 2-707.
"Present sale"	Section 2-106.
"Sale"	Section 2-106.
"Sale on approval"	Section 2-326.
"Sale or return"	Section 2-326.
"Termination"	Section 2-106.

(3) The following definitions in other Articles apply to this Article:

"Check"	Section 3-104.
"Consignee"	Section 7-102.
"Consignor"	Section 7-102.
"Consumer goods"	Section 9-102.
"Dishonor"	Section 3-502.
"Draft"	Section 3-104.

(4) In addition Article 1 contains general definitions and principles of construction and interpretation applicable throughout this Article.

§ 2–104. Definitions: "Merchant"; "Between Merchants"; "Financing Agency".

(1) "Merchant" means a person who deals in goods of the kind or otherwise by his occupation holds himself out as having knowledge

or skill peculiar to the practices or goods involved in the transaction or to whom such knowledge or skill may be attributed by his employment of an agent or broker or other intermediary who by his occupation holds himself out as having such knowledge or skill.

(2) "Financing agency" means a bank, finance company or other person who in the ordinary course of business makes advances against goods or documents of title or who by arrangement with either the seller or the buyer intervenes in ordinary course to make or collect payment due or claimed under the contract for sale, as by purchasing or paying the seller's draft or making advances against it or by merely taking it for collection whether or not the documents of title accompany the draft. "Financing agency" includes also a bank or other person who similarly intervenes between persons who are in the position of seller and buyer in respect to the goods (Section 2 – 707).

(3) "Between merchants" means in any transaction with respect to which both parties are chargeable with the knowledge or skill of merchants.

§ 2–105. Definitions: Transferability; "Goods"; "Future" Goods; "Lot"; "Commercial Unit".

(1) "Goods" means all things (including specially manufactured goods) which are movable at the time of identification to the contract for sale other than the money in which the price is to be paid, investment securities (Article 8) and things in action. "Goods" also includes the unborn young of animals and growing crops and other identified things attached to realty as described in the section on goods to be severed from realty (Section 2 - 107).

(2) Goods must be both existing and identified before any interest in them can pass. Goods which are not both existing and identified are "future" goods. A purported present sale of future goods or of any interest therein operates as a contract to sell.

(3) There may be a sale of a part interest in existing identified goods.

(4) An undivided share in an identified bulk of fungible goods is sufficiently identified to be sold although the quantity of the bulk is not determined. Any agreed proportion of such a bulk or any quantity thereof agreed upon by number, weight or other measure may to the extent of the seller's interest in the bulk be sold to the buyer who then becomes an owner in common.

(5) "Lot" means a parcel or a single article which is the subject matter of a separate sale or delivery, whether or not it is sufficient to perform the contract.

(6) "Commercial unit" means such a unit of goods as by commercial usage is a single whole for purposes of sale and division of which materially impairs its character or value on the market or in use. A commercial unit may be a single article (as a machine) or a set of articles (as a suite of furniture or an assortment of sizes) or a quantity (as a bale, gross, or carload) or any other unit treated in use or in the relevant market as a single whole.

§ 2–106. Definitions: "Contract"; "Agreement"; "Contract for Sale"; "Sale"; "Present Sale"; "Conforming" to Contract; "Termination"; "Cancellation".

(1) In this Article unless the context otherwise requires "contract" and "agreement" are limited to those relating to the present or future sale of goods. "Contract for sale" includes both a present sale of goods and a contract to sell goods at a future time. A "sale" consists in the passing of title from the seller to the buyer for a price (Section 2 - 401). A "present sale" means a sale which is accomplished by the making of the contract.

(2) Goods or conduct including any part of a performance are "conforming" or conform to the contract when they are in accordance with the obligations under the contract.

(3) "Termination" occurs when either party pursuant to a power created by agreement or law puts an end to the contract otherwise than for its breach. On "termination" all obligations which are still executory on both sides are discharged but any right based on prior breach or performance survives.

(4) "Cancellation" occurs when either party puts an end to the contract for breach by the other and its effect is the same as that of "termination" except that the cancelling party also retains any remedy for breach of the whole contract or any unperformed balance.

§ 2–107. Goods to Be Severed From Realty: Recording.

(1) A contract for the sale of minerals or the like (including oil and gas) or a structure or its materials to be removed from realty is a contract for the sale of goods within this Article if they are to be severed by the seller but until severance a purported present sale thereof which is not effective as a transfer of an interest in land is effective only as a contract to sell.

(2) A contract for the sale apart from the land of growing crops or other things attached to realty and capable of severance without material harm thereto but not described in subsection (1) or of timber to be cut is a contract for the sale of goods within this Article whether the subject matter is to be severed by the buyer or by the seller even though it forms part of the realty at the time of contracting, and the parties can by identification effect a present sale before severance.

(3) The provisions of this section are subject to any third party rights provided by the law relating to realty records, and the contract for sale may be executed and recorded as a document transferring an interest in land and shall then constitute notice to third parties of the buyer's right under the contract for sale.

Part 2. Form, Formation and Readjustment of Contra

§ 2–201. Formal Requirements; Statute of Frauds.

(1) Except as otherwise provided in this section a contract for the sale of goods for the price of $500 or more is not enforceable by way of action or defense unless there is some writing sufficient to indicate that a contract for sale has been made between the parties and signed by the party against whom enforcement is sought or by his authorized agent or broker. A writing is not insufficient because it omits or incorrectly states a term agreed upon but the contract is not enforceable under this paragraph beyond the quantity of goods shown in such writing.

(2) Between merchants if within a reasonable time a writing in confirmation of the contract and sufficient against the sender is received and the party receiving it has reason to know its contents, it satisfies the requirements of subsection (1) against such party unless written notice of objection to its contents is given within 10 days after it is received.

(3) A contract which does not satisfy the requirements of subsection (1) but which is valid in other respects is enforceable

    (a) if the goods are to be specially manufactured for the buyer and are not suitable for sale to others in the ordinary course of the seller's business and the seller, before notice of repudiation is received and under circumstances which reasonably indicate that the goods are for the buyer, has made either a substantial beginning of their manufacture or commitments for their procurement; or

    (b) if the party against whom enforcement is sought admits in his pleading, testimony or otherwise in court that a contract for sale was made, but the contract is not enforceable under this provision beyond the quantity of goods admitted; or

    (c) with respect to goods for which payment has been made and accepted or which have been received and accepted (Section 2-606).

§ 2–202. Final Written Expression: Parol or Extrinsic Evidence.

Terms with respect to which the confirmatory memoranda of the parties agree or which are otherwise set forth in a writing intended by the parties as a final expression of their agreement with respect to such terms as are included therein may not be contradicted by evidence of any prior agreement or of a contemporaneous oral agreement but may be explained or supplemented

    (a) by course and dealing or usage of trade (Section 1-205) or by course of performance (Section 2-208); and

(b) by evidence of consistent additional terms unless the court finds the writing to have been intended also as a complete and exclusive statement of the terms of the agreement.

§ 2–203. Seals Inoperative.

The affixing of a seal to a writing evidencing a contract for sale or an offer to buy or sell goods does not constitute the writing a sealed instrument and the law with respect to sealed instruments does not apply to such a contract or offer.

§ 2–204. Formation in General.

(1) A contract for sale of goods may be made in any manner sufficient to show agreement, including conduct by both parties which recognizes the existence of such a contract.

(2) An agreement sufficient to constitute a contract for sale may be found even though the moment of its making is undetermined.

(3) Even though one or more terms are left open a contract for sale does not fail for indefiniteness if the parties have intended to make a contract and there is a reasonably certain basis for giving an appropriate remedy.

§ 2–205. Firm Offers.

An offer by a merchant to buy or sell goods in a signed writing which by its terms gives assurance that it will be held open is not revocable, for lack of consideration, during the time stated or if no time is stated for a reasonable time, but in no event may such period of irrevocability exceed three months; but any such term of assurance on a form supplied by the offeree must be separately signed by the offeror.

§ 2–206. Offer and Acceptance in Formation of Contract.

(1) Unless otherwise unambiguously indicated by the language or circumstances

    (a) an offer to make a contract shall be construed as inviting acceptance in any manner and by any medium reasonable in the circumstances;

    (b) an order or other offer to buy goods for prompt or current shipment shall be construed as inviting acceptance either by a prompt promise to ship or by the prompt or current shipment of conforming or non-conforming goods, but such a shipment of non-conforming goods does not constitute an acceptance if the seller seasonably notifies the buyer that the shipment is offered only as an accomodation to the buyer.

(2) Where the beginning of a requested performance is a reasonable mode of acceptance an offeror who is not notified of acceptance within a reasonable time may treat the offer as having lapsed before acceptance.

§ 2–207. Additional Terms in Acceptance or Confirmation.

(1) A definite and seasonable expression of acceptance or a written confirmation which is sent within a reasonable time operates as an acceptance even though it states terms additional to or different from those offered or agreed upon, unless acceptance is expressly made conditional on assent to the additional or different terms.

(2) The additional terms are to be construed as proposals for addition to the contract. Between merchants such terms become part of the contract unless:

    (a) the offer expressly limits acceptance to the terms of the offer;

    (b) they materially alter it; or

    (c) notification of objection to them has already been given or is given within a reasonable time after notice of them is received.

(3) Conduct by both parties which recognizes the existence of a contract is sufficient to establish a contract for sale although the writings of the parties do not otherwise establish a contract. In such case the terms of the particular contract consist of those terms on which the writings of the parties agree, together with any supplementary terms incorporated under any other provisions of this Act.

§ 2–208. Course of Performance or Practical Construction.

(1) Where the contract for sale involves repeated occasions for performance by either party with knowledge of the nature of the performance and opportunity for objection to it by the other, any course of performance accepted or acquiesced in without objection shall be relevant to determine the meaning of the agreement.

(2) The express terms of the agreement and any such course of performance, as well as any course of dealing and usage of trade, shall be construed whenever reasonable as consistent with each other; but when such construction is unreasonable, express terms shall control course of performance and course of performance shall control both course of dealing and usage of trade (Section 1 – 205).

(3) Subject to the provisions of the next section on modification and waiver, such course of performance shall be relevant to show a waiver or modification of any term inconsistent with such course of performance.

§ 2–209. Modification, Rescission and Waiver.

(1) An agreement modifying a contract within this Article needs no consideration to be binding.

(2) A signed agreement which excludes modification or rescission except by a signed writing cannot be otherwise modified or rescinded, but except as between merchants such a requirement on a form supplied by the merchant must be separately signed by the other party.

(3) The requirements of the statute of frauds section of this Article (Section 2 – 201) must be satisfied if the contract as modified is within its provisions.

(4) Although an attempt at modification or rescission does not satisfy the requirements of subsection (2) or (3) it can operate as a waiver.

(5) A party who has made a waiver affecting an executory portion of the contract may retract the waiver by reasonable notification received by the other party that strict performance will be required of any term waived, unless the retraction would be unjust in view of a material change of position in reliance on the waiver.

§ 2–210. Delegation of Performance; Assignment of Rights.

(1) A party may perform his duty through a delegate unless otherwise agreed or unless the other party has a substantial interest in having his original promisor perform or control the acts required by the contract. No delegation of performance relieves the party delegating of any duty to perform or any liability for breach.

(2) Except as otherwise provided in Section 9 – 406, unless otherwise agreed all rights of either seller or buyer can be assigned except where the assignment would materially change the duty of the other party, or increase materially the burden or risk imposed on him by his contract, or impair materially his chance of obtaining return performance. A right to damages for breach of the whole contract or a right arising out of the assignor's due performance of his entire obligation can be assigned despite agreement otherwise.

(3) The creation, attachment, perfection, or enforcement of a security interest in the seller's interest under a contract is not a transfer that materially changes the duty of or increases materially the burden or risk imposed on the buyer or impairs materially the buyer's chance of obtaining return performance within the purview of subsection (2) unless, and then only to the extent that, enforcement actually results in a delegation of material performance of the seller. Even in that event, the creation, attachment, perfection, and enforcement of the security interest remain effective, but (i) the seller is liable to the buyer for damages caused by the delegation to the extent that the damages could not reasonably be prevented by the buyer, and (ii) a court having jurisdiction may grant other appropriate relief, including cancellation of the contract for sale or an injunction against enforcement of the security interest or consummation of the enforcement.

(4) Unless the circumstances indicate the contrary a prohibition of assignment of "the contract" is to be construed as barring only the delegation to the assignee of the assignor's performance.

(5) An assignment of "the contract" or of "all my rights under the contract" or an assignment in similar general terms is an assignment of rights and unless the language or the circumstances (as in an assignment for security) indicate the contrary, it is a delegation of performance of the duties of the assignor and its acceptance by the assignee constitutes a promise by him to perform those duties. This promise is enforceable by either the assignor or the other party to the original contract.

(6) The other party may treat any assignment which delegates performance as creating reasonable grounds for insecurity and may without prejudice to his rights against the assignor demand assurances from the assignee (Section 2-609).

Part 3. *General Obligation and Construction of Contract*

§ 2–301. General Obligations of Parties.

The obligation of the seller is to transfer and deliver and that of the buyer is to accept and pay in accordance with the contract.

§ 2–302. Unconscionable Contract or Clause.

(1) If the court as a matter of law finds the contract or any clause of the contract to have been unconscionable at the time it was made the court may refuse to enforce the contract, or it may enforce the remainder of the contract without the unconscionable clause, or it may so limit the application of any unconscionable clause as to avoid any unconscionable result.

(2) When it is claimed or appears to the court that the contract or any clause thereof may be unconscionable the parties shall be afforded a reasonable opportunity to present evidence as to its commercial setting, purpose and effect to aid the court in making the determination.

§ 2–303. Allocation or Division of Risks.

Where this Article allocates a risk or a burden as between the parties "unless otherwise agreed", the agreement may not only shift the allocation but may also divide the risk or burden.

§ 2–304. Price Payable in Money, Goods, Realty, or Otherwise.

(1) The price can be made payable in money or otherwise. If it is payable in whole or in part in goods each party is a seller of the goods which he is to transfer.

(2) Even though all or part of the price is payable in an interest in realty the transfer of the goods and the seller's obligations with reference to them are subject to this Article, but not the transfer of the interest in realty or the transferor's obligations in connection therewith.

§ 2–305. Open Price Term.

(1) The parties if they so intend can conclude a contract for sale even though the price is not settled. In such a case the price is a reasonable price at the time for delivery if

    (a) nothing is said as to price; or

    (b) the price is left to be agreed by the parties and they fail to agree; or

    (c) the price is to be fixed in terms of some agreed market or other standard as set or recorded by a third person or agency and it is not so set or recorded.

(2) A price to be fixed by the seller or by the buyer means a price for him to fix in good faith.

(3) When a price left to be fixed otherwise than by agreement of the parties fails to be fixed through fault of one party the other may at his option treat the contract as cancelled or himself fix a reasonable price.

(4) Where, however, the parties intend not to be bound unless the price be fixed or agreed and it is not fixed or agreed there is no contract. In such a case the buyer must return any goods already received or if unable so to do must pay their reasonable value at the time of delivery and the seller must return any portion of the price paid on account.

§ 2–306. Output, Requirements and Exclusive Dealings.

(1) A term which measures the quantity by the output of the seller or the requirements of the buyer means such actual output or requirements as may occur in good faith, except that no quantity unreasonably disproportionate to any stated estimate or in the absence of a stated estimate to any normal or otherwise comparable prior output or requirements may be tendered or demanded.

(2) A lawful agreement by either the seller or the buyer for exclusive dealing in the kind of goods concerned imposes unless otherwise agreed an obligation by the seller to use best efforts to supply the goods and by the buyer to use best efforts to promote their sale.

§ 2–307. Delivery in Single Lot or Several Lots.

Unless otherwise agreed all goods called for by a contract for sale must be tendered in a single delivery and payment is due only on such tender but where the circumstances give either party the right to make or demand delivery in lots the price if it can be apportioned may be demanded for each lot.

§ 2–308. Absence of Specified Place for Delivery.

Unless otherwise agreed

    (a) the place for delivery of goods is the seller's place of business or if he has none his residence; but

    (b) in a contract for sale of identified goods which to the knowledge of the parties at the time of contracting are in some other place, that place is the place for their delivery; and

    (c) documents of title may be delivered through customary banking channels.

§ 2–309. Absence of Specific Time Provisions; Notice of Termination.

(1) The time for shipment or delivery or any other action under a contract if not provided in this Article or agreed upon shall be a reasonable time.

(2) Where the contract provides for successive performance but is indefinite in duration it is valid for a reasonable time but unless otherwise agreed may be terminated at any time by either party.

(3) Termination of a contract by one party except on the happening of an agreed event requires that reasonable notification be received by the other party and an agreement dispensing with notification is invalid if its operation would be unconscionable.

§ 2–310. Open Time for Payment or Running of Credit; Authority to Ship Under Reservation.

Unless otherwise agreed

    (a) payment is due at the time and place at which the buyer is to receive the goods even though the place of shipment is the place of delivery; and

    (b) if the seller is authorized to send the goods he may ship them under reservation, and may tender the documents of title, but the buyer may inspect the goods after their arrival before payment is due unless such inspection is inconsistent with the terms of the contract (Section 2-513); and

    (c) if delivery is authorized and made by way of documents of title otherwise than by subsection (b) then payment is due at the time and place at which the buyer is to receive the documents regardless of where the goods are to be received; and

    (d) where the seller is required or authorized to ship the goods on credit the credit period runs from the time of shipment but post-dating the invoice or delaying its dispatch will correspondingly delay the starting of the credit period.

§ 2–311. Options and Cooperation Respecting Performance.

(1) An agreement for sale which is otherwise sufficiently definite (subsection (3) of Section 2-204) to be a contract is not made invalid by the fact that it leaves particulars of performance to be specified by

one of the parties. Any such specification must be made in good faith and within limits set by commercial reasonableness.

(2) Unless otherwise agreed specifications relating to assortment of the goods are at the buyer's option and except as otherwise provided in subsections (1) (c) and (3) of Section 2–319 specifications or arrangements relating to shipment are at the seller's option.

(3) Where such specification would materially affect the other party's performance but is not seasonably made or where one party's cooperation is necessary to the agreed performance of the other but is not seasonably forthcoming, the other party in addition to all other remedies

    (a) is excused for any resulting delay in his own performance; and

    (b) may also either proceed to perform in any reasonable manner or after the time for a material part of his own performance treat the failure to specify or to cooperate as a breach by failure to deliver or accept the goods.

§ 2–312. Warranty of Title and Against Infringement; Buyer's Obligation Against Infringement.

(1) Subject to subsection (2) there is in a contract for sale a warranty by the seller that

    (a) the title conveyed shall be good, and its transfer rightful; and

    (b) the goods shall be delivered free from any security interest or other lien or encumbrance of which the buyer at the time of contracting has no knowledge.

(2) A warranty under subsection (1) will be excluded or modified only by specific language or by circumstances which give the buyer reason to know that the person selling does not claim title in himself or that he is purporting to sell only such right or title as he or a third person may have.

(3) Unless otherwise agreed a seller who is a merchant regularly dealing in goods of the kind warrants that the goods shall be delivered free of the rightful claim of any third person by way of infringement or the like but a buyer who furnishes specifications to the seller must hold the seller harmless against any such claim which arises out of compliance with the specifications.

§ 2–313. Express Warranties by Affirmation, Promise, Description, Sample.

(1) Express warranties by the seller are created as follows:

    (a) Any affirmation of fact or promise made by the seller to the buyer which relates to the goods and becomes part of the basis of the bargain creates an express warranty that the goods shall conform to the affirmation or promise.

    (b) Any description of the goods which is made part of the basis of the bargain creates an express warranty that the goods shall conform to the description.

    (c) Any sample or model which is made part of the basis of the bargain creates an express warranty that the whole of the goods shall conform to the sample or model.

(2) It is not necessary to the creation of an express warranty that the seller use formal words such as "warrant" or "guarantee" or that he have a specific intention to make a warranty, but an affirmation merely of the value of the goods or a statement purporting to be merely the seller's opinion or commendation of the goods does not create a warranty.

§ 2–314. Implied Warranty: Merchantability; Usage of Trade.

(1) Unless excluded or modified (Section 2–316), a warranty that the goods shall be merchantable is implied in a contract for their sale if the seller is a merchant with respect to goods of that kind. Under this section the serving for value of food or drink to be consumed either on the premises or elsewhere is a sale.

(2) Goods to be merchantable must be at least such as

    (a) pass without objection in the trade under the contract description; and

    (b) in the case of fungible goods, are of fair average quality within the description; and

    (c) are fit for the ordinary purposes for which such goods are used; and

    (d) run, within the variations permitted by the agreement, of even kind, quality and quantity within each unit and among all units involved; and

    (e) are adequately contained, packaged, and labeled as the agreement may require; and

    (f) conform to the promises or affirmations of fact made on the container or label if any.

(3) Unless excluded or modified (Section 2–316) other implied warranties may arise from course of dealing or usage of trade.

§ 2–315. Implied Warranty: Fitness for Particular Purpose.

Where the seller at the time of contracting has reason to know any particular purpose for which the goods are required and that the buyer is relying on the seller's skill or judgment to select or furnish suitable goods, there is unless excluded or modified under the next section an implied warranty that the goods shall be fit for such purpose.

§ 2–316. Exclusion or Modification of Warranties.

(1) Words or conduct relevant to the creation of an express warranty and words or conduct tending to negate or limit warranty shall be construed wherever reasonable as consistent with each other, but subject to the provisions of this Article on parol or extrinsic evidence (Section 2–202) negation or limitation is inoperative to the extent that such construction is unreasonable.

(2) Subject to subsection (3), to exclude or modify the implied warranty of merchantability or any part of it the language must mention merchantability and in case of a writing must be conspicuous, and to exclude or modify any implied warranty of fitness the exclusion must be by a writing and conspicuous. Language to exclude all implied warranties of fitness is sufficient if it states, for example, that "There are no warranties which extend beyond the description on the face hereof."

(3) Notwithstanding subsection (2)

    (a) unless the circumstances indicate otherwise, all implied warranties are excluded by expression like "as is", "with all faults" or other language which in common understanding calls the buyer's attention to the exclusion of warranties and makes plain that there is no implied warranty; and

    (b) when the buyer before entering into the contract has examined the goods or the sample or model as fully as he desired or has refused to examine the goods there is no implied warranty with regard to defects which an examination ought in the circumstances to have revealed to him; and

    (c) an implied warranty can also be excluded or modified by course of dealing or course of performance or usage of trade.

(4) Remedies for breach of warranty can be limited in accordance with the provisions of this Article on liquidation or limitation of damages and on contractual modification of remedy (Sections 2–718 and 2–719).

§ 2–317. Cumulation and Conflict of Warranties Express or Implied.

Warranties whether express or implied shall be construed as consistent with each other and as cumulative, but if such construction is unreasonable the intention of the parties shall determine which warranty is dominant. In ascertaining that intention the following rules apply:

    (a) Exact or technical specifications displace an inconsistent sample or model or general language of description.

    (b) A sample from an existing bulk displaces inconsistent general language of description.

(c) Express warranties displace inconsistent implied warranties other than an implied warranty of fitness for a particular purpose.

§ 2–318. Third Party Beneficiaries of Warranties Express or Implied.

Note: *If this Act is introduced in the Congress of the United States this section should be omitted. (States to select one alternative.)*

Alternative A. A seller's warranty whether express or implied extends to any natural person who is in the family or household of his buyer or who is a guest in his home if it is reasonable to expect that such person may use, consume or be affected by the goods and who is injured in person by breach of the warranty. A seller may not exclude or limit the operation of this section.

Alternative B. A seller's warranty whether express or implied extends to any natural person who may reasonably be expected to use, consume or be affected by the goods and who is injured in person by breach of the warranty. A seller may not exclude or limit the operation of this section.

Alternative C. A seller's warranty whether express or implied extends to any person who may reasonably be expected to use, consume or be affected by the goods and who is injured by breach of the warranty. A seller may not exclude or limit the operation of this section with respect to injury to the person of an individual to whom the warranty extends.

§ 2–319. F.O.B. and F.A.S. Terms.

(1) Unless otherwise agreed the term F.O.B. (which means "free on board") at a named place, even though used only in connection with the stated price, is a delivery term under which

(a) when the term is F.O.B. the place of shipment, the seller must at that place ship the goods in the manner provided in this Article (Section 2-504) and bear the expense and risk of putting them into the possession of the carrier; or

(b) when the term is F.O.B. the place of destination, the seller must at his own expense and risk transport the goods to that place and there tender delivery of them in the manner provided in this Article (Section 2-503);

(c) when under either (a) or (b) the term is also F.O.B. vessel, car or other vehicle, the seller must in addition at his own expense and risk load the goods on board. If the term is F.O.B. vessel the buyer must name the vessel and in an appropriate case the seller must comply with the provisions of this Article on the form of bill of lading (Section 2-323).

(2) Unless otherwise agreed the term F.A.S. vessel (which means "free alongside") at a named port, even though used only in connection with the stated price, is a delivery term under which the seller must

(a) at his own expense and risk deliver the goods alongside the vessel in the manner usual in that port or on a dock designated and provided by the buyer; and

(b) obtain and tender a receipt for the goods in exchange for which the carrier is under a duty to issue a bill of lading.

(3) Unless otherwise agreed in any case falling within subsection (1)(a) or (c) or subsection (2) the buyer must seasonably give any needed instructions for making delivery, including when the term is F.A.S. or F.O.B. the loading berth of the vessel and in an appropriate case its name and sailing date. The seller may treat the failure of needed instructions as a failure of cooperation under this Article (Section 2 - 311). He may also at his option move the goods in any reasonable manner preparatory to delivery or shipment.

(4) Under the term F.O.B. vessel or F.A.S. unless otherwise agreed the buyer must make payment against tender of the required documents and the seller may not tender nor the buyer demand delivery of the goods in substitution for the documents.

§ 2–320. C.I.F. and C. & F. Terms.

(1) The term C.I.F. means that the price includes in a lump sum the cost of the goods and the insurance and freight to the named destination. The term C. & F. or C.F. means that the price so includes cost and freight to the named destination.

(2) Unless otherwise agreed and even though used only in connection with the stated price and destination, the term C.I.F. destination or its equivalent requires the seller at his own expense and risk to

(a) put the goods into the possession of a carrier at the port for shipment and obtain a negotiable bill or bills of lading covering the entire transportation to the named destination; and

(b) load the goods and obtain a receipt from the carrier (which may be contained in the bill of lading) showing that the freight has been paid or provided for; and

(c) obtain a policy or certificate of insurance, including any war risk insurance, of a kind and on terms then current at the port of shipment in the usual amount, in the currency of the contract, shown to cover the same goods covered by the bill of lading and providing for payment of loss to the order of the buyer or for the account of whom it may concern; but the seller may add to the price the amount of the premium for any such war risk insurance; and

(d) prepare an invoice of the goods and procure any other documents required to effect shipment or to comply with the contract; and

(e) forward and tender with commercial promptness all the documents in due form and with any indorsement necessary to perfect the buyer's rights.

(3) Unless otherwise agreed the term C. & F. or its equivalent has the same effect and imposes upon the seller the same obligations and risks as a C.I.F. term except the obligation as to insurance.

(4) Under the term C.I.F. or C. & F. unless otherwise agreed the buyer must make payment against tender of the required documents and the seller may not tender nor the buyer demand delivery of the goods in substitution for the documents.

§ 2–321. C.I.F. or C. & F.: "Net Landed Weights"; "Payment on Arrival"; Warranty of Condition on Arrival.

Under a contract containing a term C.I.F. or C. & F.

(1) Where the price is based on or is to be adjusted according to "net landed weights", "delivered weights", "out turn" quantity or quality or the like, unless otherwise agreed the seller must reasonably estimate the price. The payment due on tender of the documents called for by the contract is the amount so estimated, but after final adjustment of the price a settlement must be made with commercial promptness.

(2) An agreement described in subsection (1) or any warranty of quality or condition of the goods on arrival places upon the seller the risk of ordinary deterioration, shrinkage and the like in transportation but has no effect on the place or time of identification to the contract for sale or delivery or on the passing of the risk of loss.

(3) Unless otherwise agreed where the contract provides for payment on or after arrival of the goods the seller must before payment allow such preliminary inspection as is feasible; but if the goods are lost delivery of the documents and payment are due when the goods should have arrived.

§ 2–322. Delivery "Ex-Ship".

(1) Unless otherwise agreed a term for delivery of goods "ex-ship" (which means from the carrying vessel) or in equivalent language is not restricted to a particular ship and requires delivery from a ship which has reached a place at the named port of destination where goods of the kind are usually discharged.

(2) Under such a term unless otherwise agreed

(a) the seller must discharge all liens arising out of the carriage and furnish the buyer with a direction which puts the carrier under a duty to deliver the goods; and

(b) the risk of loss does not pass to the buyer until the goods leave the ship's tackle or are otherwise properly unloaded.

§ 2–323. Form of Bill of Lading Required in Overseas Shipment; "Overseas".

(1) Where the contract contemplates overseas shipment and contains a term C.I.F. or C. & F. or F.O.B. vessel, the seller unless otherwise agreed must obtain a negotiable bill of lading stating that the goods have been loaded on board or, in the case of a term C.I.F. or C. & F., received for shipment.

(2) Where in a case within subsection (1) a bill of lading has been issued in a set of parts, unless otherwise agreed if the documents are not to be sent from abroad the buyer may demand tender of the full set; otherwise only one part of the bill of lading need be tendered. Even if the agreement expressly requires a full set

(a) due tender of a single part is acceptable within the provisions of this Article on cure of improper delivery (subsection (1) of Section 2-508); and

(b) even though the full set is demanded, if the documents are sent from abroad the person tendering an incomplete set may nevertheless require payment upon furnishing an indemnity which the buyer in good faith deems adequate.

(3) A shipment by water or by air or a contract contemplating such shipment is "overseas" insofar as by usage of trade or agreement it is subject to the commercial, financing or shipping practices characteristic of international deep water commerce.

§ 2–324. "No Arrival, No Sale" Term.

Under a term "no arrival, no sale" or terms of like meaning, unless otherwise agreed.

(a) the seller must properly ship conforming goods and if they arrive by any means he must tender them on arrival but he assumes no obligation that the goods will arrive unless he has caused the non-arrival; and

(b) where without fault of the seller the goods are in part lost or have so deteriorated as no longer to conform to the contract or arrive after the contract time, the buyer may proceed as if there had been casualty to identified goods (Section 2-613).

§ 2–325. "Letter of Credit" Term; "Confirmed Credit".

(1) Failure of the buyer seasonably to furnish an agreed letter of credit is a breach of the contract for sale.

(2) The delivery to seller of a proper letter of credit suspends the buyer's obligation to pay. If the letter of credit is dishonored, the seller may on seasonable notification to the buyer require payment directly from him.

(3) Unless otherwise agreed the term "letter of credit" or "banker's credit" in a contract for sale means an irrevocable credit issued by a financing agency of good repute and, where the shipment is overseas, of good international repute. The term "confirmed credit" means that the credit must also carry the direct obligation of such an agency which does business in the seller's financial market.

§ 2–326. Sale on Approval and Sale or Return; Rights of Creditors.

(1) Unless otherwise agreed, if delivered goods may be returned by the buyer even though they conform to the contract, the transaction is

(a) a "sale on approval" if the goods are delivered primarily for use, and

(b) a "sale or return" if the goods are delivered primarily for resale.

(2) Goods held on approval are not subject to the claims of the buyer's creditors until acceptance; goods held on sale or return are subject to such claims while in the buyer's possession.

(3) Any "or return" term of a contract for sale is to be treated as a separate contract for sale within the statute of frauds section of this Article (Section 2-201) and as contradicting the sale aspect of the contract within the provisions of this Article on parol or extrinsic evidence (Section 2-202).

§ 2–327. Special Incidents of Sale on Approval and Sale or Return.

(1) Under a sale on approval unless otherwise agreed

(a) although the goods are identified to the contract the risk of loss and the title do not pass to the buyer until acceptance; and

(b) use of the goods consistent with the purpose of trial is not acceptance but failure seasonably to notify the seller of election to return the goods is acceptance, and if the goods conform to the contract acceptance of any part is acceptance of the whole; and

(c) after due notification of election to return, the return is at the seller's risk and expense but a merchant buyer must follow any reasonable instructions.

(2) Under a sale or return unless otherwise agreed

(a) the option to return extends to the whole or any commercial unit of the goods while in substantially their original condition, but must be exercised seasonably; and

(b) the return is at the buyer's risk and expense.

§ 2–328. Sale by Auction.

(1) In a sale by auction if goods are put up in lots each lot is the subject of a separate sale.

(2) A sale by auction is complete when the auctioneer so announces by the fall of the hammer or in other customary manner. Where a bid is made while the hammer is falling in acceptance of a prior bid the auctioneer may in his discretion reopen the bidding or declare the goods sold under the bid on which the hammer was falling.

(3) Such a sale is with reserve unless the goods are in explicit terms put up without reserve. In an auction with reserve the auctioneer may withdraw the goods at any time until he announces completion of the sale. In an auction without reserve, after the auctioneer calls for bids on an article or lot, that article or lot cannot be withdrawn unless no bid is made within a reasonable time. In either case a bidder may retract his bid until the auctioneer's announcement of completion of the sale, but a bidder's retraction does not revive any previous bid.

(4) If the auctioneer knowingly receives a bid on the seller's behalf or the seller makes or procures such a bid, and notice has not been given that liberty for such bidding is reserved, the buyer may at his option avoid the sale or take the goods at the price of the last good faith bid prior to the completion of the sale. This subsection shall not apply to any bid at a forced sale.

Part 4.   Title, Creditors and Good Faith Purchasers

§ 2–401. Passing of Title; Reservation for Security; Limited Application of This Section.

Each provision of this Article with regard to the rights, obligations and remedies of the seller, the buyer, purchasers or other third parties applies irrespective of title to the goods except where the provision refers to such title. Insofar as situations are not covered by the other provisions of this Article and matters concerning title become material the following rules apply:

(1) Title to goods cannot pass under a contract for sale prior to their identification to the contract (Section 2-501), and unless otherwise explicitly agreed the buyer acquires by their identification a special property as limited by this Act. Any retention or reservation by the seller of the title (property) in goods shipped or delivered to the buyer is limited in effect to a reservation of a security interest. Subject to these provisions and to the provisions of the Article on Secured Transactions (Article 9), title to goods passes from the seller to the

buyer in any manner and on any conditions explicitly agreed on by the parties.

(2) Unless otherwise explicitly agreed title passes to the buyer at the time and place at which the seller completes his performance with reference to the physical delivery of the goods, despite any reservation of a security interest and even though a document of title is to be delivered at a different time or place; and in particular and despite any reservation of a security interest by the bill of lading

    (a) if the contract requires or authorizes the seller to send the goods to the buyer but does not require him to deliver them at destination, title passes to the buyer at the time and place of shipment; but

    (b) if the contract requires delivery at destination, title passes on tender there.

(3) Unless otherwise explicitly agreed where delivery is to be made without moving the goods.

    (a) if the seller is to deliver a document of title, title passes at the time when and the place where he delivers such documents; or

    (b) if the goods are at the time of contracting already identified and no documents are to be delivered, title passes at the time and place of contracting.

(4) A rejection or other refusal by the buyer to receive or retain the goods, whether or not justified, or a justified revocation of acceptance revests title to the goods in the seller. Such revesting occurs by operation of law and is not a "sale".

§ 2–402. Rights of Seller's Creditors Against Sold Goods.

(1) Except as provided in subsections (2) and (3), rights of unsecured creditors of the seller with respect to goods which have been identified to a contract for sale are subject to the buyer's rights to recover the goods under this Article (Sections 2 – 502 and 2 – 716).

(2) A creditor of the seller may treat a sale or an identification of goods to a contract for sale as void if as against him a retention of possession by the seller is fraudulent under any rule of law of the state where the goods are situated, except that retention of possession in good faith and current course of trade by a merchant-seller for a commercially reasonable time after a sale or identification is not fraudulent.

(3) Nothing in this Article shall be deemed to impair the rights of creditors of the seller

    (a) under the provisions of the Article on Secured Transactions (Article 9); or

    (b) where identification to the contract or delivery is made not in current course of trade but in satisfaction of or as security for a pre-existing claim for money, security or the like and is made under circumstances which under any rule of law of the state where the goods are situated would apart from this Article constitute the transaction a fraudulent transfer or voidable preference.

§ 2–403. Power to Transfer; Good Faith Purchase of Goods; "Entrusting".

(1) A purchaser of goods acquires all title which his transferor had or had power to transfer except that a purchaser of a limited interest acquires rights only to the extent of the interest purchased. A person with voidable title has power to transfer a good title to a good faith purchaser for value. When goods have been delivered under a transaction of purchase the purchaser has such power even though

    (a) the transferor was deceived as to the identity of the purchaser, or

    (b) the delivery was in exchange for a check which is later dishonored, or

    (c) it was agreed that the transaction was to be a "cash sale", or

    (d) the delivery was procured through fraud punishable as larcenous under the criminal law.

(2) Any entrusting of possession of goods to a merchant who deals in goods of that kind gives him power to transfer all rights of the entruster to a buyer in ordinary course of business.

(3) "Entrusting" includes any delivery and any acquiescence in retention of possession regardless of any condition expressed between the parties to the delivery or acquiescence and regardless of whether the procurement of the entrusting or the possessor's disposition of the goods have been such as to be larcenous under the criminal law.

(4) The rights of other purchasers of goods and of lien creditors are governed by the Articles on Secured Transactions (Article 9). [Bulk Transfers/Sales (Article 6)* and Documents of Title (Article 7)].

Part 5. Performance

§ 2–501. Insurable Interest in Goods; Manner of Identification of Goods.

(1) The buyer obtains a special property and an insurable interest in goods by identification of existing goods as goods to which the contract refers even though the goods so identified are non-conforming and he has an option to return or reject them. Such identification can be made at any time and in any manner explicitly agreed to by the parties. In the absence of explicit agreement identification occurs.

    (a) when the contract is made if it is for the sale of goods already existing and identified;

    (b) if the contract is for the sale of future goods other than those described in paragraph (c), when goods are shipped, marked or otherwise designated by the seller as goods to which the contract refers;

    (c) when the crops are planted or otherwise become growing crops or the young are conceived if the contract is for the sale of unborn young to be born within twelve months after contracting or for the sale of crops to be harvested within twelve months or the next normal harvest season after contracting, whichever is longer.

(2) The seller retains an insurable interest in goods so long as title to or any security interest in the goods remains in him and where the identification is by the seller alone he may until default or insolvency or notification to the buyer that the identification is final substitute other goods for those identified.

(3) Nothing in this section impairs any insurable interest recognized under any other statute or rule of law.

§ 2–502. Buyer's Right to Goods on Seller's Insolvency.

(1) Subject to subsections (2) and (3) and even though the goods have not been shipped a buyer who has paid a part or all of the price of goods in which he has a special property under the provisions of the immediately preceding section may on making and keeping good a tender of any unpaid portion of their price recover them from the seller if:

    (a) in the case of goods bought for personal, family, or household purposes, the seller repudiates or fails to deliver as required by the contract; or

    (b) in all cases, the seller becomes insolvent within ten days after receipt of the first installment on their price.

(2) The buyer's right to recover the goods under subsection (1)(a) vests upon acquisition of a special property, even if the seller had not then repudiated or failed to deliver.

(3) If the identification creating his special property has been made by the buyer he acquires the right to recover the goods only if they conform to the contract for sale.

§ 2–503. Manner of Seller's Tender of Delivery.

(1) Tender of delivery requires that the seller put and hold conforming goods at the buyer's disposition and give the buyer any notification reasonably necessary to enable him to take delivery. The manner, time and place for tender are determined by the agreement and this Article, and in particular

    (a) tender must be at a reasonable hour, and if it is of goods they must be kept available for the period reasonably necessary to enable the buyer to take possession; but

(b) unless otherwise agreed the buyer must furnish facilities reasonably suited to the receipt of the goods.

(2) Where the case is within the next section respecting shipment tender requires that the seller comply with its provisions.

(3) Where the seller is required to deliver at a particular destination tender requires that he comply with subsection (1) and also in any appropriate case tender documents as described in subsections (4) and (5) of this section.

(4) Where goods are in the possession of a bailee and are to be delivered without being moved

(a) tender requires that the seller either tender a negotiable document of title covering such goods or procure acknowledgment by the bailee of the buyer's right to possession of the goods; but

(b) tender to the buyer of a non-negotiable document of title or of a written direction to the bailee to deliver is sufficient tender unless the buyer seasonably objects, and receipt by the bailee of notification of the buyer's rights fixes those rights as against the bailee and all third persons; but risk of loss of the goods and of any failure by the bailee to honor the non-negotiable document of title or to obey the direction remains on the seller until the buyer has had a reasonable time to present the document or direction, and a refusal by the bailee to honor the document or to obey the direction defeats the tender.

(5) Where the contract requires the seller to deliver documents

(a) he must tender all such documents in correct form, except as provided in this Article with respect to bills of lading in a set (subsection (2) of Section 2-323); and

(b) tender through customary banking channels is sufficient and dishonor of a draft accompanying the documents constitutes non-acceptance or rejection.

§ 2–504. Shipment by Seller.

Where the seller is required or authorized to send the goods to the buyer and the contract does not require him to deliver them at a particular destination, then unless otherwise agreed he must

(a) put the goods in the possession of such a carrier and make such a contract for their transportation as may be reasonable having regard to the nature of the goods and other circumstances of the case; and

(b) obtain and promptly deliver or tender in due form any document necessary to enable the buyer to obtain possession of the goods or otherwise required by the agreement or by usage of trade; and

(c) promptly notify the buyer of the shipment.

Failure to notify the buyer under paragraph (c) or to make a proper contract under paragraph (a) is a ground for rejection only if material delay or loss ensues.

§ 2–505. Seller's Shipment Under Reservation.

(1) Where the seller has identified goods to the contract by or before shipment:

(a) his procurement of a negotiable bill of lading to his own order or otherwise reserves in him a security interest in the goods. His procurement of the bill to the order of a financing agency or of the buyer indicates in addition only the seller's expectation of transferring that interest to the person named.

(b) a non-negotiable bill of lading to himself or his nominee reserves possession of the goods as security but except in a case of conditional delivery (subsection (2) of Section 2-507) a non-negotiable bill of lading naming the buyer as consignee reserves no security interest even though the seller retains possession of the bill of lading.

(2) When shipment by the seller with reservation of a security interest is in violation of the contract for sale it constitutes an improper contract for transportation within the preceding section but impairs neither the rights given to the buyer by shipment and identification of the goods to the contract nor the seller's powers as a holder of a negotiable document.

§ 2–506. Rights of Financing Agency.

(1) A financing agency by paying or purchasing for value a draft which relates to a shipment of goods acquires to the extent of the payment or purchase and in addition to its own rights under the draft and any document of title securing it any rights of the shipper in the goods including the right to stop delivery and the shipper's right to have the draft honored by the buyer.

(2) The right to reimbursement of a financing agency which has in good faith honored or purchased the draft under commitment to or authority from the buyer is not impaired by subsequent discovery of defects with reference to any relevant document which was apparently regular on its face.

§ 2–507. Effect of Seller's Tender; Delivery on Condition.

(1) Tender of delivery is a condition to the buyer's duty to accept the goods and, unless otherwise agreed, to his duty to pay for them. Tender entitles the seller to acceptance of the goods and to payment according to the contract.

(2) Where payment is due and demanded on the delivery to the buyer of goods or documents of title, his right as against the seller to retain or dispose of them is conditional upon his making the payment due.

§ 2–508. Cure by Seller of Improper Tender or Delivery; Replacement.

(1) Where any tender or delivery by the seller is rejected because non-conforming and the time for performance has not yet expired, the seller may seasonably notify the buyer of his intention to cure and may then within the contract time make a conforming delivery.

(2) Where the buyer rejects a non-conforming tender which the seller had reasonable grounds to believe would be acceptable with or without money allowance the seller may if he seasonably notifies the buyer have a further reasonable time to substitute a conforming tender.

§ 2–509. Risk of Loss in the Absence of Breach.

(1) Where the contract requires or authorizes the seller to ship the goods by carrier

(a) if it does not require him to deliver them at a particular destination, the risk of loss passes to the buyer when the goods are duly delivered to the carrier even though the shipment is under reservation (Section 2-505); but

(b) if it does require him to deliver them at a particular destination and the goods are there duly tendered while in the possession of the carrier, the risk of loss passes to the buyer when the goods are there duly so tendered as to enable the buyer to take delivery.

(2) Where the goods are held by a bailee to be delivered without being moved, the risk of loss passes to the buyer

(a) on his receipt of a negotiable document of title covering the goods; or

(b) on acknowledgment by the bailee of the buyer's right to possession of the goods; or

(c) after his receipt of a non-negotiable document of title or other written direction to deliver, as provided in subsection (4)(b) of Section 2-503.

(3) In any case not within subsection (1) or (2), the risk of loss passes to the buyer on his receipt of the goods if the seller is a merchant; otherwise the risk passes to the buyer on tender of delivery.

(4) The provisions of this section are subject to contrary agreement of the parties and to the provisions of this Article on sale on approval (Section 2-327) and on effect of breach on risk of loss (Section 2-510).

§ 2–510. Effect of Breach on Risk of Loss.

(1) Where a tender or delivery of goods so fails to conform to the contract as to give a right of rejection the risk of their loss remains on the seller until cure or acceptance.

(2) Where the buyer rightfully revokes acceptance he may to the extent of any deficiency in his effective insurance coverage treat the risk of loss as having rested on the seller from the beginning.

(3) Where the buyer as to conforming goods already identified to the contract for sale repudiates or is otherwise in breach before risk of their loss has passed to him, the seller may to the extent of any deficiency in his effective insurance coverage treat the risk of loss as resting on the buyer for a commercially reasonable time.

§ 2–511. Tender of Payment by Buyer; Payment by Check.

(1) Unless otherwise agreed tender of payment is a condition to the seller's duty to tender and complete any delivery.

(2) Tender of payment is sufficient when made by any means or in any manner current in the ordinary course of business unless the seller demands payment in legal tender and gives any extension of time reasonably necessary to procure it.

(3) Subject to the provisions of this Act on the effect of an instrument on an obligation (Section 3–310), payment by check is conditional and is defeated as between the parties by dishonor of the check on due presentment.

§ 2–512. Payment by Buyer Before Inspection.

(1) Where the contract requires payment before inspection non-conformity of the goods does not excuse the buyer from so making payment unless

    (a) the non-conformity appears without inspection; or

    (b) despite tender of the required documents the circumstances would justify injunction against honor under this Act (Section 5–109(b)).

(2) Payment pursuant to subsection (1) does not constitute an acceptance of goods or impair the buyer's right to inspect or any of his remedies.

§ 2–513. Buyer's Right to Inspection of Goods.

(1) Unless otherwise agreed and subject to subsection (3), where goods are tendered or delivered or identified to the contract for sale, the buyer has a right before payment or acceptance to inspect them at any reasonable place and time and in any reasonable manner. When the seller is required or authorized to send the goods to the buyer, the inspection may be after their arrival.

(2) Expenses of inspection must be borne by the buyer but may be recovered from the seller if the goods do not conform and are rejected.

(3) Unless otherwise agreed and subject to the provisions of this Article on C.I.F. contracts (subsection (3) of Section 2–321), the buyer is not entitled to inspect the goods before payment of the price when the contract provides

    (a) for delivery "C.O.D." or on other like terms; or

    (b) for payment against documents of title, except where such payment is due only after the goods are to become available for inspection.

(4) A place or method of inspection fixed by the parties is presumed to be exclusive but unless otherwise expressly agreed it does not postpone identification or shift the place for delivery or for passing the risk of loss. If compliance becomes impossible, inspection shall be as provided in this section unless the place or method fixed was clearly intended as an indispensable condition failure of which avoids the contract.

§ 2–514. When Documents Deliverable on Acceptance; When on Payment.

Unless otherwise agreed documents against which a draft is drawn are to be delivered to the drawee on acceptance of the draft if it is payable more than three days after presentment; otherwise, only on payment.

§ 2–515. Preserving Evidence of Goods in Dispute.

In furtherance of the adjustment of any claim or dispute

    (a) either party on reasonable notification to the other and for the purpose of ascertaining the facts and preserving

evidence has the right to inspect, test and sample the goods including such of them as may be in the possession or control of the other; and

    (b) the parties may agree to a third party inspection or survey to determine the conformity or condition of the goods and may agree that the findings shall be binding upon them in any subsequent litigation or adjustment.

Part 6. Breach, Repudiation and Excuse

§ 2–601. Buyer's Rights on Improper Delivery.

Subject to the provisions of this Article on breach in installment contracts (Section 2–612) and unless otherwise agreed under the sections on contractual limitations of remedy (Sections 2–718 and 2–719), if the goods or the tender of delivery fail in any respect to conform to the contract, the buyer may

    (a) reject the whole; or

    (b) accept the whole; or

    (c) accept any commercial unit or units and reject the rest.

§ 2–602. Manner and Effect of Rightful Rejection.

(1) Rejection of goods must be within a reasonable time after their delivery or tender. It is ineffective unless the buyer seasonably notifies the seller.

(2) Subject to the provisions of the two following sections on rejected goods (Sections 2–603 and 2–604),

    (a) after rejection any exercise of ownership by the buyer with respect to any commercial unit is wrongful as against the seller; and

    (b) if the buyer has before rejection taken physical possession of goods in which he does not have a security interest under the provisions of this Article (subsection (3) of Section 2–711), he is under a duty after rejection to hold them with reasonable care at the seller's disposition for a time sufficient to permit the seller to remove them; but

    (c) the buyer has no further obligations with regard to goods rightfully rejected.

(3) The seller's rights with respect to goods wrongfully rejected are governed by the provisions of this Article on Seller's remedies in general (Section 2–703).

§ 2–603. Merchant Buyer's Duties as to Rightfully Rejected Goods.

(1) Subject to any security interest in the buyer (subsection (3) of Section 2–711), when the seller has no agent or place of business at the market of rejection a merchant buyer is under a duty after rejection of goods in his possession or control to follow any reasonable instructions received from the seller with respect to the goods and in the absence of such instructions to make reasonable efforts to sell them for the seller's account if they are perishable or threaten to decline in value speedily. Instructions are not reasonable if on demand indemnity for expenses is not forthcoming.

(2) When the buyer sells goods under subsection (1), he is entitled to reimbursement from the seller or out of the proceeds for reasonable expenses of caring for and selling them, and if the expenses include no selling commission then to such commission as is usual in the trade or if there is none to a reasonable sum not exceeding ten percent on the gross proceeds.

(3) In complying with this section the buyer is held only to good faith and good faith conduct hereunder is neither acceptance nor conversion nor the basis of an action for damages.

§ 2–604. Buyer's Options as to Salvage of Rightfully Rejected Goods.

Subject to the provisions of the immediately preceding section on perishables if the seller gives no instructions within a reasonable time after notification of rejection the buyer may store the rejected goods for the seller's account or reship them to him or resell them for the seller's account with reimbursement as provided in the preceding section. Such action is not acceptance or conversion.

§ 2–605.   Waiver of Buyer's Objections by Failure to Particularize.

(1) The buyer's failure to state in connection with rejection a particular defect which is ascertainable by reasonable inspection precludes him from relying on the unstated defect to justify rejection or to establish breach

    (a) where the seller could have cured it if stated seasonably; or

    (b) between merchants when the seller has after rejection made a request in writing for a full and final written statement of all defects on which the buyer proposes to rely.

(2) Payment against documents made without reservation of rights precludes recovery of the payment for defects apparent on the face of the documents.

§ 2–606.   What Constitutes Acceptance of Goods.

(1) Acceptance of goods occurs when the buyer

    (a) after a reasonable opportunity to inspect the goods signifies to the seller that the goods are conforming or that he will take or retain them in spite of their non-conformity; or

    (b) fails to make an effective rejection (subsection (1) of Section 2-602), but such acceptance does not occur until the buyer has had a reasonable opportunity to inspect them; or

    (c) does any act inconsistent with the seller's ownership; but if such act is wrongful as against the seller it is an acceptance only if ratified by him.

(2) Acceptance of a part of any commercial unit is acceptance of that entire unit.

§ 2–607.   Effect of Acceptance; Notice of Breach; Burden of Establishing Breach After Acceptance; Notice of Claim or Litigation to Person Answerable Over.

(1) The buyer must pay at the contract rate for any goods accepted.

(2) Acceptance of goods by the buyer precludes rejection of the goods accepted and if made with knowledge of a non-conformity cannot be revoked because of it unless the acceptance was on the reasonable assumption that the non-conformity would be seasonably cured but acceptance does not of itself impair any other remedy provided by this Article for non-conformity.

(3) Where a tender has been accepted

    (a) the buyer must within a reasonable time after he discovers or should have discovered any breach notify the seller of breach or be barred from any remedy; and

    (b) if the claim is one for infringement or the like (subsection (3) of Section 2-312) and the buyer is sued as a result of such a breach he must so notify the seller within a reasonable time after he receives notice of the litigation or be barred from any remedy over for liability established by the litigation.

(4) The burden is on the buyer to establish any breach with respect to the goods accepted.

(5) Where the buyer is sued for breach of a warranty or other obligation for which his seller is answerable over

    (a) he may give his seller written notice of the litigation. If the notice states that the seller may come in and defend and that if the seller does not do so he will be bound in any action against him by his buyer by any determination of fact common to the two litigations, then unless the seller after seasonable receipt of the notice does come in and defend he is so bound.

    (b) if the claim is one for infringement or the like (subsection (3) of Section 2-312) the original seller may demand in writing that his buyer turn over to him control of the liti-

gation including settlement or else be barred from any remedy over and if he also agrees to bear all expense and to satisfy any adverse judgment, then unless the buyer after seasonable receipt of the demand does turn over control the buyer is so barred.

(6) The provisions of subsection (3), (4) and (5) apply to any obligation of a buyer to hold the seller harmless against infringement or the like (subsection (3) of Section 2–312).

§ 2–608.   Revocation of Acceptance in Whole or in Part.

(1) The buyer may revoke his acceptance of a lot or commercial unit whose non-conformity substantially impairs its value to him if he has accepted it

    (a) on the reasonable assumption that its non-conformity would be cured and it has not been seasonably cured; or

    (b) without discovery of such non-conformity if his acceptance was reasonably induced either by the difficulty of discovery before acceptance or by the seller's assurances.

(2) Revocation of acceptance must occur within a reasonable time after the buyer discovers or should have discovered the ground for it and before any substantial change in condition of the goods which is not caused by their own defects. It is not effective until the buyer notifies the seller of it.

(3) A buyer who so revokes has the same rights and duties with regard to the goods involved as if he had rejected them.

§ 2–609.   Right to Adequate Assurance of Performance.

(1) A contract for sale imposes an obligation on each party that the other's expectation of receiving due performance will not be impaired. When reasonable grounds for insecurity arise with respect to the performance of either party the other may in writing demand adequate assurance of due performance and until he receives such assurance may if commercially reasonable suspend any performance for which he has not already received the agreed return.

(2) Between merchants the reasonableness of grounds for insecurity and the adequacy of any assurance offered shall be determined according to commercial standards.

(3) Acceptance of any improper delivery or payment does not prejudice the aggrieved party's right to demand adequate assurance of future performance.

(4) After receipt of a justified demand failure to provide within a reasonable time not exceeding thirty days such assurance of due performance as is adequate under the circumstances of the particular case is a repudiation of the contract.

§ 2–610.   Anticipatory Repudiation.

When either party repudiates the contract with respect to a performance not yet due the loss of which will substantially impair the value of the contract to the other, the aggrieved party may

    (a) for a commercially reasonable time await performance by the repudiating party; or

    (b) resort to any remedy for breach (Section 2-703 or Section 2-711), even though he has notified the repudiating party that he would await the latter's performance and has urged retraction; and

    (c) in either case suspend his own performance or proceed in accordance with the provisions of this Article on the seller's right to identify goods to the contract notwithstanding breach or to salvage unfinished goods (Section 2-704).

§ 2–611.   Retraction of Anticipatory Repudiation.

(1) Until the repudiating party's next performance is due he can retract his repudiation unless the aggrieved party has since the repudiation cancelled or materially changed his position or otherwise indicated that he considers the repudiation final.

(2) Retraction may be by any method which clearly indicates to the aggrieved party that the repudiating party intends to perform, but

must include any assurance justifiably demanded under the provisions of this Article (Section 2–609).

(3) Retraction reinstates the repudiating party's rights under the contract with due excuse and allowance to the aggrieved party for any delay occasioned by the repudiation.

§ 2–612. "Installment Contract"; Breach.

(1) An "installment contract" is one which requires or authorizes the delivery of goods in separate lots to be separately accepted, even though the contract contains a clause "each delivery is a separate contract" or its equivalent.

(2) The buyer may reject any installment which is non-conforming if the non-conformity substantially impairs the value of that installment and cannot be cured or if the non-conformity is a defect in the required documents; but if the non-conformity does not fall within subsection (3) and the seller gives adequate assurance of its cure the buyer must accept that installment.

(3) Whenever non-conformity or default with respect to one or more installments substantially impairs the value of the whole contract there is a breach of the whole. But the aggrieved party reinstates the contract if he accepts a non-conforming installment without seasonably notifying of cancellation or if he brings an action with respect only to past installments or demands performance as to future installments.

§ 2–613. Casualty to Identified Goods.

Where the contract requires for its performance goods identified when the contract is made, and the goods suffer casualty without fault of either party before the risk of loss passes to the buyer, or in a proper case under a "no arrival, no sale" term (Section 2-324) then

(a) if the loss is total the contract is avoided; and

(b) if the loss is partial or the goods have so deteriorated as no longer to conform to the contract the buyer may nevertheless demand inspection and at his option either treat the contract as avoided or accept the goods with due allowance from the contract price for the deterioration or the deficiency in quantity but without further right against the seller.

§ 2–614. Substituted Performance.

(1) Where without fault of either party the agreed berthing, loading, or unloading facilities fail or an agreed type of carrier becomes unavailable or the agreed manner of delivery otherwise becomes commercially impracticable but a commercially reasonable substitute is available, such substitute performance must be tendered and accepted.

(2) If the agreed means or manner of payment fails because of domestic or foreign governmental regulation, the seller may withhold or stop delivery unless the buyer provides a means or manner of payment which is commercially a substantial equivalent. If delivery has already been taken, payment by the means or in the manner provided by the regulation discharges the buyers obligation unless the regulation is discriminatory, oppressive or predatory.

§ 2–615. Excuse by Failure of Presupposed Conditions.

Except so far as a seller may have assumed a greater obligation and subject to the preceding section on substituted performance:

(a) Delay in delivery or non-delivery in whole or in part by a seller who complies with paragraphs (b) and (c) is not a breach of his duty under a contract for sale if performance as agreed has been made impracticable by the occurrence of a contingency the non-occurrence of which was a basic assumption on which the contract was made or by compliance in good faith with any applicable foreign or domestic governmental regulation or order whether or not it later proves to be invalid.

(b) Where the causes mentioned in paragraph (a) affect only a part of the seller's capacity to perform, he must allocate production and deliveries among his customers but may

at his option include regular customers not then under contract as well as his own requirements for further manufacture. He may so allocate in any manner which is fair and reasonable.

(c) The seller must notify the buyer seasonably that there will be delay or non-delivery and, when allocation is required under paragraph (b), of the estimated quota thus made available for the buyer.

§ 2–616. Procedure on Notice Claiming Excuse.

(1) Where the buyer receives notification of a material or indefinite delay or an allocation justified under the preceding section he may by written notification to the seller as to any delivery concerned, and where the prospective deficiency substantially impairs the value of the whole contract under the provisions of this Article relating to breach of installment contracts (Section 2-612), then also as to the whole,

(a) terminate and thereby discharge any unexecuted portion of the contract; or

(b) modify the contract by agreeing to take his available quota in substitution.

(2) If after receipt of such notification from the seller the buyer fails so to modify the contract within a reasonable time not exceeding thirty days the contract lapses with respect to any deliveries affected.

(3) The provisions of this section may not be negated by agreement except in so far as the seller has assumed a greater obligation under the preceding section.

Part 7. Remedies

§ 2–701. Remedies for Breach of Collateral Contracts Not Impaired.

Remedies for breach of any obligation or promise collateral or ancillary to a contract for sale or not impaired by the provisions of this Article.

§ 2–702. Seller's Remedies on Discovery of Buyer's Insolvency.

(1) Where the seller discovers the buyer to be insolvent he may refuse delivery except for cash including payment for all goods theretofore delivered under the contract, and stop delivery under this Article (Section 2-705).

(2) Where the seller discovers that the buyer has received goods on credit while insolvent he may reclaim the goods upon demand made within ten days after the receipt, but if misrepresentation of solvency has been made to the particular seller in writing within three months before delivery the ten day limitation does not apply. Except as provided in this subsection the seller may not base a right to reclaim goods on the buyer's fraudulent or innocent misrepresentation of solvency or of intent to pay.

(3) The seller's right to reclaim under subsection (2) is subject to the rights of a buyer in ordinary course or other good faith purchaser under this Article (Section 2-403). Successful reclamation of goods excludes all other remedies with respect to them.

§ 2–703. Seller's Remedies in General.

Where the buyer wrongfully rejects or revokes acceptance of goods or fails to make a payment due on or before delivery or repudiates with respect to a part or the whole, then with respect to any goods directly affected and, if the breach is of the whole contract (Section 2-612), then also with respect to the whole undelivered balance, the aggrieved seller may

(a) withhold delivery of such goods;

(b) stop delivery by any bailee as hereafter provided (Section 2-705);

(c) proceed under the next section respecting goods still unidentified to the contract;

(d) resell and recover damages as hereafter provided (Section 2-706);

(e) recover damages for non-acceptance (Section 2-708) or in a proper case the price (Section 2-709);

(f) cancel.

§ 2-704. Seller's Right to Identify Goods to the Contract Notwithstanding Breach or to Salvage Unfinished Goods.

(1) An aggrieved seller under the preceding section may

(a) identify to the contract conforming goods not already identified if at the time he learned of the breach they are in his possession or control;

(b) treat as the subject of resale goods which have demonstrably been intended for the particular contract even though those goods are unfinished.

(2) Where the goods are unfinished an aggrieved seller may in the exercise of reasonable commercial judgment for the purposes of avoiding loss and of effective realization either complete the manufacture and wholly identify the goods to the contract or cease manufacture and resell for scrap or salvage value or proceed in any other reasonable manner.

§ 2-705. Seller's Stoppage of Delivery in Transit or Otherwise.

(1) The seller may stop delivery of goods in the possession of a carrier or other bailee when he discovers the buyer to be insolvent (Section 2-702) and may stop delivery of carload, truckload, planeload or larger shipments of express or freight when the buyer repudiates or fails to make a payment due before delivery or if for any other reason the seller has a right to withhold or reclaim the goods.

(2) As against such buyer the seller may stop delivery until

(a) receipt of the goods by the buyer; or

(b) acknowledgment to the buyer by any bailee of the goods except a carrier that the bailee holds the goods for the buyer; or

(c) such acknowledgment to the buyer by a carrier by reshipment or as warehouseman; or

(d) negotiation to the buyer of any negotiable document of title covering the goods.

(3) (a) To stop delivery the seller must so notify as to enable the bailee by reasonable diligence to prevent delivery of the goods.

(b) After such notification the bailee must hold and deliver the goods according to the directions of the seller but the seller is liable to the bailee for any ensuing charges or damages.

(c) If a negotiable document of title has been issued for goods the bailee is not obliged to obey a notification to stop until surrender of the document.

(d) A carrier who has issued a non-negotiable bill of lading is not obliged to obey a notification to stop received from a person other than the consignor.

§ 2-706. Seller's Resale Including Contract for Resale.

(1) Under the conditions stated in Section 2-703 on seller's remedies, the seller may resell the goods concerned or the undelivered balance thereof. Where the resale is made in good faith and in a commercially reasonable manner the seller may recover the difference between the resale price and the contract price together with any incidental damages allowed under the provisions of this Article (Section 2-710), but less expenses saved in consequence of the buyer's breach.

(2) Except as otherwise provided in subsection (3) or unless otherwise agreed resale may be at public or private sale including sale by way of one or more contracts to sell or of identification to an existing contract of the seller. Sale may be as a unit or in parcels and at any time and place and on any terms but every aspect of the sale including the method, manner, time, place and terms must be commercially reasonable. The resale must be reasonably identified as referring to the broken contract, but it is not necessary that the goods be in existence

or that any or all of them have been identified to the contract before the breach.

(3) Where the resale is at private sale the seller must give the buyer reasonable notification of his intention to resell.

(4) Where the resale is at public sale

(a) only identified goods can be sold except where there is a recognized market for a public sale of futures in goods of the kind; and

(b) it must be made at a usual place or market for public sale if one is reasonably available and except in the case of goods which are perishable or threaten to decline in value speedily the seller must give the buyer reasonable notice of the time and place of the resale; and

(c) if the goods are not to be within the view of those attending the sale the notification of sale must state the place where the goods are located and provide for their reasonable inspection by prospective bidders; and

(d) the seller may buy.

(5) A purchaser who buys in good faith at a resale takes the goods free of any rights of the original buyer even though the seller fails to comply with one or more of the requirements of this section.

(6) The seller is not accountable to the buyer for any profit made on any resale. A person in the position of a seller (Section 2-707) or a buyer who has rightfully rejected or justifiably revoked acceptance must account for any excess over the amount of his security interest, as hereinafter defined (subsection (3) of Section 2-711).

§ 2-707. "Person in the Position of a Seller".

(1) A "person in the position of a seller" includes as against a principal an agent who has paid or become responsible for the price of goods on behalf of his principal or anyone who otherwise holds a security interest or other right in goods similar to that of a seller.

(2) A person in the position of a seller may as provided in this Article withhold or stop delivery (Section 2-705) and resell (Section 2-706) and recover incidental damages (Section 2-710).

§ 2-708. Seller's Damages for Non-Acceptance or Repudiation.

(1) Subject to subsection (2) and to the provisions of this Article with respect to proof of market price (Section 2-723), the measure of damages for non-acceptance or repudiation by the buyer is the difference between the market price at the time and place for tender and the unpaid contract price together with any incidental damages provided in this Article (Section 2-710), but less expenses saved in consequence of the buyer's breach.

(2) If the measure of damages provided in subsection (1) is inadequate to put the seller in as good a position as performance would have done then the measure of damages is the profit (including reasonable overhead) which the seller would have made from full performance by the buyer, together with any incidental damages provided in this Article (Section 2-710), due allowance for costs reasonably incurred and due credit for payments or proceeds of resale.

§ 2-709. Action for the Price.

(1) When the buyer fails to pay the price as it becomes due the seller may recover, together with any incidental damages under the next section, the price

(a) of goods accepted or of conforming goods lost or damaged within a commercially reasonable time after risk of their loss has passed to the buyer; and

(b) of goods identified to the contract if the seller is unable after reasonable effort to resell them at a reasonable price or the circumstances reasonably indicate that such effort will be unavailing.

(2) Where the seller sues for the price he must hold for the buyer any goods which have been identified to the contract and are still in his control except that if resale becomes possible he may resell them at any time prior to the collection of the judgment. The net proceeds

of any such resale must be credited to the buyer and payment of the judgment entitles him to any goods not resold.

(3) After the buyer has wrongfully rejected or revoked acceptance of the goods or has failed to make a payment due or has repudiated (Section 2–610), a seller who is held not entitled to the price under this section shall nevertheless be awarded damages for non-acceptance under the preceeding section.

§ 2–710. Seller's Incidental Damages.

Incidental damages to an aggrieved seller include any commercially reasonable charges, expenses or commissions incurred in stopping delivery, in the transportation, care and custody of goods after the buyer's breach, in connection with return or resale of the goods or otherwise resulting from the breach.

§ 2–711. Buyer's Remedies in General; Buyer's Security Interest in Rejected Goods.

(1) Where the seller fails to make delivery or repudiates or the buyer rightfully rejects or justifiably revokes acceptance then with respect to any goods involved, and with respect to the whole if the breach goes to the whole contract (Section 2–612), the buyer may cancel and whether or not he has done so may in addition to recovering so much of the price as has been paid

    (a) "cover" and have damages under the next section as to all the goods affected whether or not they have been identified to the contract; or

    (b) recover damages for non-delivery as provided in this Article (Section 2–713).

(2) Where the seller fails to deliver or repudiates the buyer may also

    (a) if the goods have been identified recover them as provided in this Article (Section 2–502); or

    (b) in a proper case obtain specific performance or replevy the goods as provided in this Article (Section 2–716).

(3) On rightful rejection of justifiable revocation of acceptance a buyer has a security interest in goods in his possession or control for any payments made on their price and any expenses reasonably incurred in their inspection, receipt, transportation, care and custody and may hold such goods and resell them in like manner as an aggrieved seller (Section 2–706).

§ 2–712. "Cover"; Buyer's Procurement of Substitute Goods.

(1) After a breach within the preceding section the buyer may "cover" by making in good faith and without unreasonable delay any reasonable purchase of or contract to purchase goods in substitution for those due from the seller.

(2) The buyer may recover from the seller as damages the difference between the cost of cover and the contract price together with any incidental or consequential damages as hereinafter defined (Section 2–715), but less expenses saved in consequence of the seller's breach.

(3) Failure of the buyer to effect cover within this section does not bar him from any other remedy.

§ 2–713. Buyer's Damages for Non-Delivery or Repudiation.

(1) Subject to the provisions of this Article with respect to proof of market price (Section 2–723), the measure of damages for non-delivery or repudiation by the seller is the difference between the market price at the time when the buyer learned of the breach and the contract price together with any incidental and consequential damages provided in this Article (Section 2–715), but less expenses saved in consequence of the seller's breach.

(2) Market price is to be determined as of the place for tender or, in cases of rejection after arrival or revocation of acceptance, as of the place of arrival.

§ 2–714. Buyer's Damages for Breach in Regard to Accepted Goods.

(1) Where the buyer has accepted goods and given notification (subsection (3) of Section 2–607) he may recover as damages for any non-conformity of tender the loss resulting in the ordinary course of events from the seller's breach as determined in any manner which is reasonable.

(2) The measure of damages for breach of warranty is the difference at the time and place of acceptance between the value of the goods accepted and the value they would have had if they had been as warranted, unless special circumstances show proximate damages of a different amount.

(3) In a proper case any incidental and consequential damages under the next section may also be recovered.

§ 2–715. Buyer's Incidental and Consequential Damages.

(1) Incidental damages resulting from the seller's breach include expenses reasonably incurred in inspection, receipt, transportation and care and custody of goods rightfully rejected, any commercially reasonable charges, expenses or commissions in connection with effecting cover and any other reasonable expense incident to the delay or other breach.

(2) Consequential damages resulting from the seller's breach include

    (a) any loss resulting from general or particular requirements and needs of which the seller at the time of contracting had reason to know and which could not reasonably be prevented by cover or otherwise; and

    (b) injury to person or property proximately resulting from any breach of warranty.

§ 2–716. Buyer's Right to Specific Performance or Replevin.

(1) Specific performance may be decreed where the goods are unique or in other proper circumstances.

(2) The decree for specific performance may include such terms and conditions as to payment of the price, damages, or other relief as the court may deem just.

(3) The buyer has a right of replevin for goods identified to the contract if after reasonable effort he is unable to effect cover for such goods or the circumstances reasonably indicate that such effort will be unvailing or if the goods have been shipped under reservation and satisfaction of the security interest in them has been made or tendered. In the case of goods bought for personal, family, or household purposes, the buyer's right of replevin vests upon acquisition of a special property, even if the seller had not then repudiated or failed to deliver.

§ 2–717. Deduction of Damages From the Price.

The buyer on notifying the seller of his intention to do so may deduct all or any part of the damages resulting from any breach of the contract from any part of the price still due under the same contract.

§ 2–718. Liquidation or Limitation of Damages; Deposits.

(1) Damages for breach by either party may be liquidated in the agreement but only at an amount which is reasonable in the light of the anticipated or actual harm caused by the breach, the difficulties of proof of loss, and the inconvenience of nonfeasibility of otherwise obtaining an adequate remedy. A team fixing unreasonably large liquidated damages is void as a penalty.

(2) Where the seller justifiably withholds delivery of goods because of the buyer's breach, the buyer is entitled to restitution of any amount by which the sum of his payments exceeds

    (a) the amount to which the seller is entitled by virtue of terms liquidating the seller's damages in accordance with subsection (1), or

    (b) in the absence of such terms, twenty percent of the value of the total performance for which the buyer is obligated under the contract or $500, whichever is smaller.

(3) The buyer's right to restitution under subsection (2) is subject to offset to the extent that the seller establishes

    (a) a right to recover damages under the provisions of this Article other than subsection (1), and

    (b) the amount or value of any benefits received by the buyer directly or indirectly by reason of the contract.

(4) Where a seller has received payment in goods their reasonable value or the proceeds of their resale shall be treated as payments for the purposes of subsection (2); but if the seller has notice of the buyer's breach before reselling goods received in part performance, his resale is subject to the conditions laid down in this Article on resale by an aggrieved seller (Section 2-706).

§ 2–719. Contractual Modification or Limitation of Remedy.

(1) Subject to the provisions of subsections (2) and (3) of this section and of the preceding section on liquidation and limitation of damages,

>> (a) the agreement may provide for remedies in addition to or in substitution for those provided in this Article and may limit or alter the measure of damages recoverable under this Article, as by limiting the buyer's remedies to return of the goods and repayment of the price or to repair and replacement of non-conforming goods or parts; and

>> (b) resort to a remedy as provided is optional unless the remedy is expressly agreed to be exclusive, in which case it is the sole remedy.

(2) Where circumstances cause an exclusive or limited remedy to fail of its essential purpose, remedy may be had as provided in this Act.

(3) Consequential damages may be limited or excluded unless the limitation or exclusion is unconscionable. Limitation of consequential damages for injury to the person in the case of consumer goods is prima facie unconscionable but limitation of damages where the loss is commercial is not.

§ 2–720. Effect of "Cancellation" or "Rescission" on Claims for Antecedent Breach.

Unless the contrary intention clearly appears, expressions of "cancellation" or "rescission" of the contract or the like shall not be construed as a renunciation or discharge of any claim in damages for an antecedent breach.

§ 2–721. Remedies for Fraud.

Remedies for material misrepresentation or fraud include all remedies available under this Article for non-fraudulent breach. Neither rescission or a claim for rescission of the contract for sale nor rejection or return of the goods shall bar or be deemed inconsistent with a claim for damages or other remedy.

§ 2–722. Who Can Sue Third Parties for Injury to Goods.

Where a third party so deals with goods which have been identified to a contract for sale as to cause actionable injury to a party to that contract

>> (a) a right of action against the third party is in either party to the contract for sale who has title to or a security interest or a special property or an insurable interest in the goods; and if the goods have been destroyed or converted a right of action is also in the party who either bore the risk of loss under the contract for sale or has since the injury assumed that risk as against the other,

>> (b) if at the time of the injury the party plaintiff did not bear the risk of loss as against the other party to the contract

for sale and there is no arrangement between them for disposition of the recovery, his suit or settlement is, subject to his own interest, as a fiduciary for the other party to the contract;

>> (c) either party may with the consent of the other sue for the benefit of whom it may concern.

§ 2–723. Proof of Market Price: Time and Place.

(1) If an action based on anticipatory repudiation comes to trial before the time for performance with respect to some or all of the goods, any damages based on market price (Section 2-708 or Section 2-713) shall be determined according to the price of such goods prevailing at the time when the aggrieved party learned of the repudiation.

(2) If evidence of a price prevailing at the times or places described in this Article is not readily available the price prevailing within any reasonable time before or after the time described or at any other place which in commercial judgment or under usage of trade would serve as a reasonable substitute for the one described may be used, making any proper allowance for the cost of transporting the goods to or from such other place.

(3) Evidence of a relevant price prevailing at a time or place other than the one described in this Article offered by one party is not admissible unless and until he has given the other party such notice as the court finds sufficient to prevent unfair surprise.

§ 2–724. Admissibility of Market Quotations.

Whenever the prevailing price or value of any goods regularly bought and sold in any established commodity market is in issue, reports in official publications or trade journals or in newspapers or periodicals of general circulation published as the reports of such market shall be admissible in evidence. The circumstances of the preparation of such a report may be shown to affect its weight but not its admissibility.

§ 2–725. Statute of Limitations in Contracts for Sale.

(1) An action for breach of any contract for sale must be commenced within four years after the cause of action has accrued. By the original agreement the parties may reduce the period of limitation to not less than one year but may not extend it.

(2) A cause of action accrues when the breach occurs, regardless of the aggrieved party's lack of knowledge of the breach. A breach of warranty occurs when tender of delivery is made, except that where a warranty explicitly extends to future performance of the goods and discovery of the breach must await the time of such performance the cause of action accrues when the breach is or should have been discovered.

(3) Where an action commenced within the time limited by subsection (1) is so terminated as to leave available a remedy by another action for the same breach such other action may be commenced after the expiration of the time limited and within six months after the termination of the first action unless the termination resulted from voluntary discontinuance or from dismissal for failure or neglect to prosecute.

(4) This section does not alter the law on tolling of the statute of limitations nor does it apply to causes of action which have accrued before this Act becomes effective.

GLOSSARY

24-hour rule Prohibits both union representatives and employers from making speeches to "captive audiences" of employees within 24 hours of a representative election.

absolute privilege The right to make any statement, true or false, about someone and not be held liable for defamation.

acid rain Precipitation with a high acidic content (pH level of less than 5) caused by atmospheric pollutants.

act-of-state doctrine States that each sovereign nation is bound to respect the independence of every other sovereign national and that the courts of one nation will not sit in judgment on the acts of the courts of another nation.

actual authority Includes expressed authority as well as implied authority, or that authority customarily given to an agent in an industry, trade, or profession.

administrative agency Any body that is created by the legislative branch to carry out specific duties.

administrative law Any rule (statute or regulation) that directly or indirectly affects an administrative agency.

administrative law judge (ALJ) A judge, selected on the basis of a merit exam, who is assigned to a specific administrative agency.

Administrative Procedure Act (APA) Establishes the standards and procedures federal administrative agencies must follow in their rule-making and adjudicative functions.

adversarial system System of litigation in which the judge hears evidence and arguments presented by both sides in a case and then makes an objective decision based on the facts and the law as presented by each side.

adverse possession Acquiring ownership of realty by openly treating it as one's own, with neither protest nor permission from the real owner, for a statutorily established period of time.

affirm Term used for an appellate court's decision to uphold the decision of a lower court in a case that has been appealed.

affirmative action plans Programs adopted by employers to increase the representation of women and minorities in their workforces.

Age Discrimination in Employment Act of 1967 (ADEA) Prohibits employers from refusing to hire, discharging, or discriminating against people in terms of conditions of employment on the basis of age.

agency A fiduciary relationship between two persons in which one (the agent) acts on behalf of, and is subject to the control of, the other (the principal).

agency by estoppel (apparent authority) An agency relationship in which the principal is estopped from denying that someone is the principal's agent after leading a third party to believe the person is an agent.

agency by implied authority Agency relationship in which customs and circumstances, rather than a detailed formal agreement, determine the agent's authority.

agency by ratification Agency relationship in which an unauthorized agent commits the principal to an agreement and the principal later accepts the unauthorized agreement, thus ratifying the agency relationship.

alternative dispute resolution (ADR) Resolving legal disputes through methods other than litigation, such as negotiation and settlement, arbitration, mediation, private trials, minitrials, summary jury trials, and early neutral case evaluation.

ambiguous Susceptible to two or more possible interpretations.

Americans with Disabilities Act of 1991 (ADA) Requires that employers make reasonable accommodations to the known disabilities of an otherwise qualified job applicant or employee with a disability, unless the necessary accommodation would impose an undue burden on the employer's business.

analogy A comparison based on the assumption that if two things are alike in some respect, they must be alike in other respects.

annual percentage rate (APR) The effective annual rate of interest being charged a consumer by a creditor, which depends on the compounding period the creditor is using.

appellate jurisdiction The power to review a previously made decision by the trial court.

appropriate bargaining unit May be an entire plant, a single department, or all employees of a single employer, as long as there is a mutuality of interest among the proposed members of the unit.

appropriation A privacy tort that consists of using a person's name or likeness for commercial gain without the person's permission.

arbitration A dispute-resolution method whereby the disputing parties submit their disagreement to a mutually agreed-upon neutral decision maker or one provided for by statute.

arbitration A dispute-resolution method whereby the disputant parties submit their disagreement to a mutually agreed upon neutral decision maker or one provided for by statute.

arraignment Formal appearance of the defendant in court to answer the indictment by entering a plea of guilty or not guilty.

arrest To seize and hold under the authority of the law.

artisan's lien A lien that enables a creditor to recover payment from a debtor on labor and services provided on the debtor's personal property, for example, fixing a lawnmower.

assault Intentional placing of a person in fear or apprehension of an immediate, offensive bodily contact.

assignment The present transfer of an existing right.

assumption of the risk A defense to negligence based on showing that the plaintiff voluntarily and unreasonably encountered a known risk and that the harm that the plaintiff suffered was the harm that was risked.

attachment A court-ordered judgment allowing a local officer of the court to seize property of a debtor.

attorney-client privilege Provides that information furnished by a client to an attorney in confidence, in conjunction with a legal matter, may not be revealed by the attorney without the client's permission.

autonomous/semiautonomous work group A team of workers, led by either a supervisor appointed by management or a worker elected by the team, that determines for itself how it will accomplish the work task it is given to perform. Those groups with full authority over all subtasks, scheduling of overtime, and hiring of new team members are autonomous; those with less authority are semiautonomous.

award The arbitrator's decision.

bail An amount of money the defendant pays to the court upon release from custody as security that he or she will return for trial.

bailment A relationship in which one person (the bailor) transfers possession of personal property to another (the bailee) to be used in an agreed-on manner for an agreed-on period of time.

battery Intentional unwanted and offensive bodily contact.

bilateral contract The exchange of one promise for another promise.

bilateral investment treaty Treaty between two parties to outline conditions for investment in either country.

binding arbitration clause A provision in a contract mandating that all disputes arising under the contract be settled by arbitration.

bonds Long-term loans secured by a lien or mortgage on corporate assets.

boycott A refusal to deal with, purchase goods from, or work for a business.

bribery The offering, giving, soliciting, or receiving of money or any object of value for the purpose of influencing the judgment or conduct of a person in a position of trust, especially a government official.

broker A person engaged in the business of buying and selling securities for others' accounts.

business ethics The study of what makes up good and bad conduct as related to business activities and values.

business judgment rule A rule that says corporate officers and directors are not liable for honest mistakes of business judgment.

capital structure The percentage of each type of capital—debt, preferred stock, and common equity—used by the corporation.

case law Law resulting from judicial interpretations of constitutions and statutes.

Chicago School An approach to antitrust policy that is based solely on the goal of economic efficiency, or the maximization of consumer welfare.

civil law Law governing litigation between two private parties.

Civil Rights Act of 1866 Guarantees that all persons in the United States have the same right to make and enforce contracts and have the full and equal benefit of the law.

Civil Rights Act of 1871 Prohibits discrimination by state and local governments.

class action suit A lawsuit brought by a member of a group of persons on behalf of all members of the group.

Clayton Act Prohibits price discrimination, tying, and exclusive-dealing arrangements, and corporate mergers that substantially lessen competition or tend to create a monopoly in interstate commerce.

closed-end credit A credit arrangement in which credit is extended for a specific period of time, and the exact number of payments and the total amount due have been agreed upon between the borrower and the creditor.

closely held corporation A corporation whose stock is not traded on the national securities exchanges but is privately held by a small group of people.

collective bargaining Negotiations between an employer and a union over, primarily, wages, hours, and terms and conditions of employment.

collusion Concerted action by two or more individuals or business entities in violation of the Sherman Act.

Commerce Clause Empowers Congress to regulate commerce with foreign nations, with Indian tribes, and among the states; found in Article I.

commercial impracticability Situation that makes performance of a contract unreasonably expensive, injurious, or costly to a party.

common stock A class of stock that entitles its owner to vote for the corporation's board of directors, to receive dividends, and to participate in the net assets upon liquidation of the corporation.

comparative negligence A defense that allocates recovery based on percentage of fault allocated to plaintiff and defendant; available in either pure or modified form.

compensatory damages Monetary damages awarded for a breach of contract that results in higher costs or lost profits for the injured party.

competency A person's ability to understand the nature of the transaction and the consequences of entering into it at the time the contract was entered into.

complaint The initial pleading in a case that states the names of the parties to the action, the basis for the court's subject matter jurisdiction, the facts on which the party's claim is based, and the relief that the party is seeking.

complete performance Completion of all the terms of the contract.

conclusion A position or stance on an issue; the goal toward which reasoning moves.

concurrent jurisdiction Applies to cases that may be heard in either the federal or the state court system.

condemnation The process whereby the government acquires the ownership of private property for a public use over the protest of the owner.

condition precedent A particular event that must take place to give rise to a duty of performance of a contract.

condition subsequent A particular event that, when following the execution of a contract, terminates it.

conditional estate The right to own and possess the land, subject to a condition whose happening (or non-happening) will terminate the estate.

conditional privilege The right to make a false statement about someone and not be held liable for defamation provided the statement was made without malice.

conflict of interest A conflict that occurs when a corporate officer or director enters into a transaction with the corporation in which he or she has a personal interest.

conglomerate merger A merger in which the businesses of the acquiring and the acquired firm are totally unrelated.

conscious parallelism Identical actions (usually price increases) that are taken independently but nearly simultaneously by two or more leading companies in an industry.

consent order An agreement by a business to stop an activity an administrative agency alleges to be unlawful and to accept the remedy the agency imposes; no admission of guilt is necessary.

consideration A bargained-for exchange of promises in which a legal detriment is suffered by the promisee.

contingency fee Agent's compensation that consists of a percentage of the amount the agent secured for the principal in a business transaction.

contract A legally enforceable exchange of promises or an exchange of a promise for an act.

contributory copyright infringement The act of presenting material on a Web site that encourages site users to violate copyright laws.

contributory negligence A defense to negligence that consists of proving the plaintiff did not exercise the ordinary degree of care to protect against an unreasonable risk of harm and that this failure contributed to causing the plaintiff's harm.

conversion Intentional permanent removal of property from the rightful owner's possession and control.

cooperative A not-for-profit organization formed by individuals to market products.

co-ownership Ownership of land by multiple persons or business organizations; all tenants have an equal right to occupy all of the property.

copyright The exclusive legal right to reproduce, publish, and sell the fixed form of expression of an original creative idea.

corporate opportunity doctrine A doctrine, established by case law, that says corporate officers, directors, and agents cannot take personal advantage of an opportunity that in all fairness should have belonged to the corporation.

corporation An entity formed and authorized by state law to act as a single person and to raise capital by issuing stock to investors who are the owners of the corporation.

counterclaim Defendant's statement of facts showing cause for action against the plaintiff and a request for appropriate relief.

creditor The lender in the transaction.

creditor-beneficiary contract One in which the promisee obtains a promise from the promisor to fulfill a legal obligation of the promisee to a third party.

criminal fraud Intentional use of some sort of misrepresentation to gain an advantage over another party.

criminal law Composed of federal and state statutes prohibiting wrongful conduct ranging from murder to fraud.

critical thinking skills The ability to understand the structure of an argument and apply a set of evaluative criteria to assess its merits.

cross-elasticity of demand, or substitutability If an increase in the price of one product leads consumers to purchase another product, the two products are substitutable and there is said to be cross-elasticity of demand.

cross-licensing An illegal practice in which two patent holders license each other to use their patented objects only on condition that neither will license anyone else to use those patented objects without the other's consent.

culture The learned norms of a society that are based on values, beliefs, and attitudes.

cybersquatters or cyberpirates Individuals or businesses that intentionally obtain a domain name registration for a company's trademark so that it can sell the domain name back to the trademark owner.

dealer A person engaged in the business of buying and selling securities for his or her own account.

debentures Unsecured long-term corporate loans.

debtor The borrower in the transaction.

deed Instrument of conveyance of property.

defamation Intentional publication (communication to a third party) of a false statement that is harmful to the plaintiff's reputation.

defendant Party against whom an action is being brought.

denial-of-service attack A crime that occurs when hackers clog a Web site's equipment by sending it too many requests for information.

deposition Pretrial testimony by witnesses who are examined under oath.

disclaimer Disavowal of the liability for breach of warranty by the manufacturer or seller of a good in advance of the sale of the good.

disclosed principal One whose identity is known by the third party when the latter enters into an agreement negotiated by the agent.

discovery The pretrial gathering of information from each other by the parties.

disparagement Intentionally defaming a business product or service.

disparate impact cases Discrimination cases in which the employer's facially neutral policy or practice has a discriminatory effect on employees that belong to a protected class.

disparate treatment cases Discrimination cases in which the employer treats one employee less favorably than another because of that employee's color, race, religion, sex, or national origin.

domain name Text names matched to particular Internet protocols or addresses.

donative intent Intent to transfer ownership to another at the time the donor makes actual or constructive delivery of the gift to the donee.

donee-beneficiary contract One in which the promisee obtains a promise from the promisor to make a gift to a third party.

due diligence defense An affirmative defense raised in lawsuits charging misrepresentation in a registration statement. It is based on the defendant's claim to have had reasonable grounds to believe that all statements in the registration statement were true and no omission of material fact had been made. This defense is not available to the issuer of the security.

Due Process Clause Provides that no one can be deprived of life, liberty, or property without "due process of law"; found in Fifth Amendment.

duress Any wrongful act or threat that prevents a party from exercising free will when executing a contract.

duress defense An affirmative defense claiming that the defendant was forced to commit the wrongful act by threat of immediate bodily harm or loss of life.

early neutral case evaluation When parties explain their respective positions to a neutral third party who then evaluates the strengths and weaknesses of the case. This evaluation then guides the parties in reaching a settlement.

easement An irrevocable right to use some portion of another's land for a specific purpose.

economic strike A nonviolent work stoppage for the purpose of obtaining better terms and conditions of employment under a collective bargaining agreement.

effluent limitations Maximum allowable amounts of pollutants that can be discharged from a point source within a given time period.

embezzlement The wrongful conversion of the property of another by one who is lawfully in possession of that property.

eminent domain The constitutional right of the government to take privately owned real property for a public purpose in exchange for a just compensation to the owner.

employer-employee relationship One in which an agent (employee) who works for pay and is subject to the control of the principal (employer) may enter into contractual relationships on the latter's behalf.

employer-independent contractor relationship One in which the agent (independent contractor) is hired by the principal (employer) to do a specific job but is not controlled with respect to physical conduct or details of work performance.

employment-at-will doctrine A contract of employment for an indeterminate term is terminable at will by either the employer or the employee; the traditional "American rule" governing employer-employee relations.

enabling legislation Legislation that grants lawful power to an administrative agency to issue rules, investigate potential violations of rules or statutes, and adjudicate disputes.

entrapment An affirmative defense claiming that the idea for the crime did not originate with the defendant but was put into the defendant's mind by a police officer or other government official.

Environmental Impact Statement (EIS) A statement that must be prepared for every major federal activity that would significantly affect the quality of the human environment.

Environmental Protection Agency (EPA) The federal agency charged with responsibility for conducting an integrated, coordinated attack on all forms of pollution of the environment.

Equal Pay Act of 1963 Prohibits wage discrimination based on sex.

equitable remedies Nonmonetary damages awarded for breach of contract when monetary damages would be inadequate or impracticable.

estoppel A legal bar to either alleging or denying a fact because of one's own previous words or actions to the contrary.

ethical norms Standards of conduct that we consider good or virtuous.

ethics The study of what makes up good and bad conduct inclusive of related actions and values.

exchange market A securities market that provides a physical facility for the buying and selling of stocks and prescribes the number and qualifications of its broker-members. These brokers buy and sell stocks through the exchange's registered specialist, who are dealers on the floor of the exchange.

exclusive federal jurisdiction Applies to cases that may be heard only in the federal court system.

exclusive-dealing contract Agreement in which one party requires another party to sell and promote only the brand of goods supplied by the first party.

executed contract One for which all the terms have been performed.

executive administrative agency An agency located within a department of the executive branch of government; heads and appointed members serve at the pleasure of the president.

executive exemption Exemption to the ADEA that allows mandatory retirement of executives at age 65.

executive power The power delegated by Congress to an administrative agency to investigate whether the rules enacted by the agency have been properly followed by businesses and individuals.

express contract An exchange of oral or written promises between parties that are enforceable in a court of law.

express warranty A warranty that is clearly stated by the seller or manufacturer.

expressed agency (agency by agreement) Agency relationship formed through oral or written agreement.

expressed authority Authority that arises from specific statements made by the principal (employer) to the agent (employee).

expropriation The taking of private property by a host country government for political or economic reasons.

fair use doctrine A legal doctrine providing that a copyrighted work may be reproduced for purposes of "criticism, comment, news reporting, teaching (including multiple copies for classroom use), scholarship, and research."

false imprisonment The intentional restraint or confinement, by force or threat of force, of a person against that person's will and without justification.

false light A privacy tort that consists of intentionally taking actions that would lead observers to make false assumptions about the person.

Family and Medical Leave Act (FMLA) A law designed to guarantee that workers facing a medical catastrophe or certain specified family responsibilities will be able to take needed time off from work without pay but without losing medical benefits or their job.

federal preemption In an area in which federal regulation is pervasive, state legislation cannot stand.

federal supremacy Principle that states that any state or local law that directly conflicts with the federal Constitution, laws, or treaties is void.

federalism A system of government in which power is divided between a central authority and constituent political units.

fee simple absolute The right to own and possess the land against all others, without conditions.

felony A serious crime that is punishable by death or imprisonment in a penitentiary.

Fifth Amendment Protects individuals against self-incrimination and double jeopardy and guarantees them the right to trial by jury; protects both individuals and businesses through the Due Process Clause and the Takings Clause.

First Amendment Guarantees freedom of speech, press, and religion and the right to peacefully assemble and to petition the government for redress of grievances.

first appearance Appearance of the defendant before a magistrate, who determines whether there was probable cause for the arrest.

fixture An item that is initially a piece of personal property but is later attached permanently to the realty and is treated as part of the realty.

foreign subsidiary A company that is wholly or partially owned and controlled by a company based in another country.

Fourteenth Amendment Applies the entire Bill of Rights, excepting parts of the Fifth Amendment, to the states.

Fourth Amendment Protects the right of individuals to be secure in their persons, homes, and personal property by prohibiting the government from conducting unreasonable searches of individuals and seizing their property.

franchising A commercial agreement between a party that owns a trade name or trademark (the franchisor) and a party that sells or distributes goods or services using that trade name or trademark (the franchisee).

fraud Misrepresentation of a material fact made with intent to deceive the other party to a contract, who reasonably relied on the misrepresentation and was injured as a result. See also *criminal fraud*.

freedom-to-contract doctrine Parties who are legally competent are allowed to enter into whatever contracts they wish.

full warranty Under the Magnuson-Moss Warranty Act, a written protection for buyers that guarantees free repair of a defective product. If the product can't be fixed, the consumer must be given a choice of a refund or a replacement free of charge.

future interest The present right to possess and own the land in the future.

garnishment An order of the court granted to a creditor to seize wages or bank accounts of a debtor.

general partnership A partnership in which management responsibilities and profits are divided (usually equally) among the partners, and all partners have unlimited personal liability for the partnership's debts.

general warranty deed A deed that promises that the grantor owns the land and has the right to convey it and that the land has no encumbrances other than those stated in the deed.

genuine assent Assent to a contract that is free of fraud, duress, undue influence, and mutual mistake.

good-faith bargaining Following procedural standards laid out in Section 8 of the NLRA; failure to bargain in good faith, by either the employer or the union, is an unfair labor practice.

grand jury A group of 12 to 23 citizens convened in private to decide whether enough evidence exists to try the defendant for a felony.

guaranty Similar to a suretyship except that the third person is secondarily liable (i.e., required to pay only after the debtor has defaulted).

Harvard School An approach to antitrust policy that is based on the desirability of preserving competition to prevent the accumulation of economic and political power, the dislocation of labor, and market inefficiency.

hazardous waste Any waste material that is ignitable, corrosive, reactive, or toxic when ingested or absorbed.

hedging Exporting companies contract with a bank that guarantees the exporter a fixed number of U.S. dollars in exchange for payment of the goods it receives in a foreign currency. The exporting company pays a fee to the bank. The fee is based on the risk the bank is taking that the foreign currency will fluctuate.

Hertindahl-Hirschman Index (HHI) An index calculated by adding the squares of the shares of the relevant market held by each firm in a horizontal merger to determine the competitive effects of the merger. In using the HHI to decide whether to challenge a merger, the Justice Department considers both the level of the postmerger HHI and the increase in the HHI caused by the merger.

horizontal boycott A concerted refusal by a trade association to deal with members that do not follow the association's regulations.

horizontal division of markets Collusion between two or more competitors to divide markets, customers, or product lines among themselves.

horizontal merger A merger between two or more companies producing the same or a similar product and competing for sales in the same geographic market.

horizontal price-fixing Collusion between two or more competitors to, directly or indirectly, set prices for a product or service.

horizontal restraint of trade Restraint of trade that occurs between competitors at the same level of the marketing structure.

hostile bid A tender offer that is opposed by the management of the target company.

Howey test The three-part test used to determine whether an instrument or contract is a security for purposes of federal securities laws: (1) The investment is in a common enterprise and (2) there is an expectation of profit that is (3) derived from efforts of others.

identity theft A form of fraud in which an individual assumes someone else's identity information as his or her own.

implied contract One that is established by the conduct of a party rather than by the party's written or spoken words.

implied covenant of good faith and fair dealing An exception to the employment-at-will doctrine that is based on the theory that every employment contract, even an unwritten one, contains the implicit understanding that the parties will deal fairly with each other.

implied warranty A warranty that automatically arises out of a transaction.

implied warranty of fitness for a particular purpose A warranty that arises when the seller tells the consumer a good is fit for a specific use.

implied warranty of merchantability A warranty that a good is reasonably fit for ordinary use.

impossibility of performance Situation in which the party cannot legally or physically perform the contract.

in personam jurisdiction (jurisdiction over the person) The power of a court to render a decision that affects the legal rights of a specific person.

in rem jurisdiction The power of a court to render a decision that affects property directly rather than the owner of the property.

indemnity Obligation of the principal to reimburse the agent for any losses the agent incurs while acting on the principal's behalf.

independent administrative agency An agency whose appointed heads and members serve for fixed terms and cannot be removed by the president except for reasons defined by Congress.

indictment A formal written accusation in a felony case.

information A formal written accusation in a misdemeanor case.

informational picketing Picketing designed to truthfully inform the public of a labor dispute.

injunction Temporary or permanent court order preventing a party to a contract from doing something.

insanity defense An affirmative defense claiming that the defendant's mental condition precluded understanding the wrongful nature of the act he or she committed or distinguishing wrong from right in general.

insider trading The use of material, nonpublic information to purchase or sell securities in violation of a duty the person owes to the company whose stock the person is trading.

insider trading The use of material, nonpublic information received from a corporate source by someone who has a fiduciary obligation to shareholders and potential investors and who benefits from trading on such information.

intangible property Personal property that does not have a physical form and is usually evidenced in writings (e.g., an insurance policy).

intentional infliction of emotional distress Intentionally engaging in outrageous conduct that is likely to cause extreme emotional pain to the person toward whom the conduct is directed.

intentional interference with a contract Knowingly and successfully taking action for the purpose of enticing a third party to breach a valid contract with the plaintiff.

intentional tort A civil wrong that involves taking some purposeful action that the defendant knew, or should have known, would harm the person, property, or economic interests of the plaintiff.

interactivity The extent to which a Web site involves two-way communication between the site and user.

international franchising A contractual agreement whereby a company (licensor) permits another company (licensee) to market its trademarked goods or services in a particular nation.

international licensing A contractual agreement by which a company (licensor) makes its intellectual property available to a foreign individual or company (licensee) for payment.

international trade The export of goods and services from a country and the import of goods and services into a country.

invasion of privacy A privacy tort that consists of encroaching on the solitude, seclusion, or personal affairs of someone who has the right to expect privacy.

joint stock company A partnership agreement in which members of the company own shares that are transferable, but all goods are held in the name of the members, who assume partnership liability.

joint tenancy Form of co-ownership of real property in which all owners have equal shares in the property, may sell their shares without the consent of the other owners, and may have their interest attached by creditors.

joint venture Relationship between two or more persons or corporations, or an association between a foreign multinational and an agency of the host government or a host country national, set up for a specific business undertaking or a limited time period.

joint/several liability The legal principle that makes two or more people liable for a judgment, either as individuals or in any proportional combination. Under this principle, a person who is partially responsible for a tort can end up being completely liable for damages.

judicial activism A judicial philosophy that says the courts need to take an active role in encouraging political, economic, and social change.

judicial power The power delegated by Congress to an administrative agency to adjudicate cases through an administrative proceeding; includes the power to issue a complaint, hold a hearing by an administrative law judge, and issue either an initial decision or a recommended decision to a head(s) of an agency.

judicial restraint A judicial philosophy that says courts should refrain from determining the constitutionality of a legislative act unless absolutely necessary and that social, political, and economic change should come out of the political process.

jurisdiction The power of a court to hear a case and render a binding decision.

jurisdictional picketing Picketing by one union to protest an assignment of jobs to another union's members.

jurisprudence The science or philosophy of law; law in its most generalized form.

keywording Occurs when advertisers pay to have their advertisements displayed when a computer user types in certain keywords.

labor-management committee A forum in which workers communicate directly with upper management. May be illegal under the NLRA if the committee has an impact on working conditions, unless all workers in a bargaining unit or a plant participate or the employees on the committee are carrying out a traditional management function.

Landrum-Griffith Act Governs the internal operation of labor unions.

larceny The secretive and wrongful taking and carrying away of the personal property of another with the intent to permanently deprive the rightful owner of its use or possession.

lease The contract that transfers possessory interest in a property from the owner (lessor) to the tenant (lessee).

leasehold The right to possess property for an agreed-upon period of time stated in a lease.

legal acceptance An acceptance that shows objective intent to enter into the contract, that is communicated by proper means to the offeror, and that mirrors the terms of the offer.

legal object Contract subject matter that is lawful under statutory and case law.

legal offer An offer that shows objective intent to enter into the contract, is definite, and is communicated to the offeree.

legislative power The power delegated by Congress to an administrative agency to make rules that must be adhered to by individuals and businesses regulated by the agency; these rules have the force of law.

letter of deficiency Informal letter issued by the SEC indicating what corrections need to be made in a registration statement for it to become effective.

libel Publication of a defamatory statement in permanent form.

license A temporary, revocable right to be on someone else's property.

lien A claim on a debtor's property that must be satisfied before any creditor can make a claim.

life estate The right to own and possess the land until one dies.

limited liability company (LLC) A hybrid corporation-partnership, such as the Subchapter S corporation, but with far fewer restrictions.

limited partnership A partnership that has one general partner, who is responsible for managing the business, and one or more limited partners, who invest in the partnership but do not participate in its management and whose liability is limited to the amount of capital they contribute.

limited warranty Under the Magnuson-Moss Warranty Act, any written warranty that does not meet the conditions of a full warranty.

liquidated damages Monetary damages for nonperformance that are stipulated in a clause in the contract.

litigation A dispute-resolution process that involves going through the judicial system; a lawsuit.

long-arm statute A statute authorizing a court to obtain jurisdiction over an out-of-state defendant when that party has sufficient minimum contacts with a state.

malpractice suits Service liability suits brought against professionals, usually based on a theory of negligence, breach of contract or fraud.

mandatory subjects of collective bargaining Subjects over which the parties must bargain, including rates of pay, wages, hours of employment, and other terms and conditions of employment.

manifest program A program that attempts to see that hazardous wastes are properly transported to disposal facilities licensed by the EPA so that the agency will have an accurate record (manifest) of the location and amount of all hazardous wastes.

market share theory A theory of recovery in liability cases according to which damages are apportioned among all the manufacturers of a product based on their market share at the time the plaintiff's cause of action arose.

mechanic's lien A lien placed on the real property of a debtor when the latter does not pay for the work done by the creditor.

mediation An alternative dispute-resolution method in which the disputant parties select a neutral party to help them reconcile their differences by facilitating communication and suggesting ways to solve their problems.

merger One company's acquisition of another company's assets or stock in such a way that the second company is absorbed by the first.

mineral rights The legal ability to dig or mine the minerals from the earth below the surface of one's land.

minitrial An alternative dispute-resolution method in which lawyers for each side present the case for their side at a proceeding referred by a neutral adviser, but settlement authority usually resides with senior executives of the disputing corporations.

Miranda rights Certain legal rights—such as the right to remain silent to avoid self-incrimination and the right to an attorney—that a suspect must be immediately informed of upon arrest.

misappropriation Use of an unsolicited idea for a product, service, or marketing method without compensating the originator of the idea.

misdemeanor A crime that is less serious than a felony and is punishable by fine or imprisonment in a local jail.

mistake Error as to material fact. A bilateral mistake is one made by both parties; a unilateral mistake is one made by only one party to the contract.

mistake-of-fact defense An affirmative defense claiming that a mistake made by the defendant vitiates criminal intent.

mock jury Group of individuals, demographically matched to the actual jurors in a case, in front of whom lawyers practice their arguments before presenting their case to the actual jury.

modify Term used for an appellate court's decision that, although the lower court's decision was correct, it granted an inappropriate remedy that needs to be changed.

monetary damages Dollar sums awarded for a breach of contract; "legal" remedies.

monopoly An economic market situation in which a single business has the power to fix the price of goods or services.

motion to dismiss Defendant's application to the court to put the case out of judicial consideration because even if the plaintiff's factual allegations are true, the plaintiff is not entitled to relief.

multinational (transnational) corporation A corporation whose production, distribution, ownership, and management span several nations.

national ambient air quality standards (NAAQSs) A two-tiered set of standards developed for the chief conventional air pollutants: primary standards, designed to protect public health; and secondary standards, designed to protect public welfare.

National Institute for Occupational Safety and Health (NIOSH) A research facility established by the OSH Act to identify occupational health and safety problems, develop controls to prevent occupational accidents and diseases, and disseminate its findings, particularly to OSHA.

National Labor Relations Board (NLRB) The administrative agency set up to interpret and enforce the Wagner Act (NLRA).

negligence Failure to live up to the standard of care that a reasonable person would meet to protect others from an unreasonable risk of harm.

negligence per se Legal doctrine that says when a statute has been enacted to prevent a certain type of harm and the defendant violates that statute, causing that type of harm to befall the plaintiff, the plaintiff may use proof of the violation as proof of negligence.

negligent tort A civil wrong that involves a failure to meet the standard of care a reasonable person would meet and, because of that failure, harm to another resulted.

negotiation and settlement An alternative dispute-resolution method in which the disputant parties come together informally to try to resolve their differences.

nolo contendere A plea of no contest that subjects the defendant to punishment but is not an admission of guilt.

nominal damages Monetary damages of a very small amount (e.g., $1) awarded to a party that is injured by a breach of contract but cannot show real damages.

noninvestment company A company whose primary business is not in investing or trading in securities.

nonprice vertical restraint Restraint used by a manufacturer to limit the territory in which a retailer may sell the manufacturer's products and the number of stores the retailer can operate, as well as the customers the retailer can serve, in a location.

norm A standard of conduct.

notes Short-term loans.

nuisance An unreasonable interference with someone else's use and enjoyment of his or her land.

Occupational Safety and Health Act (OSH Act) A regulatory act designed to provide a workplace free from recognized hazards that are likely to cause death or serious harm to employees.

Occupational Safety and Health Administration (OSHA) The agency responsible, under the OSH Act, for setting and enforcing standards for occupational health and safety.

Occupational Safety and Health Review Commission (OSHRC) An independent body that reviews OSHA citations, penalties, and abatement periods that are contested by an employer.

open-end credit Credit extended on an account for an indefinite time period so that the debtor can keep charging on the account, up to a certain amount, while paying the outstanding balance either in full or in installment payments.

organizational (recognitional) picketing Picketing designed to force the employer to recognize and bargain with an uncertified union.

original jurisdiction The power to initially hear and decide (try) a case.

over-the-counter (OTC) market A securities market that has no physical facility and no membership qualifications and whose broker-dealers are market makers who buy and sell stocks directly from the public.

par value The nominal or face value of a stock or bond.

parens patriae suit A lawsuit brought by a state attorney general on behalf of the citizenry of that state.

parol evidence rule When parties have executed a written agreement that is complete on its face, oral agreements made prior to, or at the same time as, the written agreement that vary, alter, or contradict it are invalid.

partially disclosed principal One whose identity is not known to the third party at the time of the agreement, though the third party does know the agent represents a principal.

partnership A voluntary association of two or more persons formed to carry on a business as co-owners for profit.

patent Grants the holder the exclusive right to produce, sell, and use a product, process, invention, machine, or asexually reproduced plant for 20 years.

patent Protects a product, process, invention, machine, or plant produced by asexual reproduction.

patent infringement Occurs when someone uses, sells, or manufactures the patented invention without the patent holder's permission.

per se standard A legal standard that is applicable to restraints of trade that are inherently anticompetitive. Because such restraints are automatically in violation of Section 1 of the Sherman Act, courts do not balance procompetitive and anticompetitive effects in such cases.

permissive subjects of collective bargaining Subjects that are not primarily about conditions of emploment and, therefore, need not be bargained over.

personal property All property that is not real property; may be tangible or intangible.

pesticides Any substance designed to prevent, destroy, repel, or mitigate any pest or to be used as a plant regulator or defoliant.

petit jury A jury of 12 citizens impaneled to decide on the facts at issue in a criminal case and to pronounce the defendant guilty or not guilty.

petty crime A minor crime punishable, under federal statutes, by fine or incarceration of no more than six months.

picketing The stationing of individuals outside an employer's place of business to inform passersby of the fact of a labor dispute.

plaintiff Party on whose behalf the complaint is filed.

plea bargaining The negotiation of an agreement between the defendant's attorney and the prosecutor whereby the defendant pleads guilty to a certain charge or charges in exchange for the prosecution reducing the charges.

pleadings Papers filed by a party in court and then served on the opponent in a civil lawsuit.

point sources Distinct places from which pollutants are discharged into water, such as paper mills, electric utility plants, sewage treatment facilities, and factories.

police power The state's retained authority to pass laws to protect the health, safety, and welfare of the community.

power of attorney An agency agreement used to give an agent authority to sign legal documents on behalf of the principal.

predatory pricing Pricing below the average or marginal cost in order to drive out competition.

preferred stock A class of stock that entitles its owner to special preferences relating to either dividends or the distribution of assets.

premerger notification requirement The legislatively mandated requirement that certain types of firms notify the FTC and the Justice Department 30 days before finalizing a merger so that these agencies can investigate and challenge any mergers they find anticompetitive.

preponderance of evidence A legal standard whereby a bare majority (51 percent) of the evidence is sufficient to justify a ruling.

price discrimination A price differential that is below the average variable cost for the seller; considered predatory and, therefore, illegal under the Clayton Act.

primary ethical norms The four norms that provide the major ethical direction for the laws governing business behavior: freedom, stability, justice, and efficiency.

primary-line injury A form of price discrimination in which a seller attempts to put a local competitive firm out of business by lowering its prices only in the region where the local firm sells its products.

principal-agent relationship One in which the principal gives the agent expressed or actual authority to act on the former's behalf.

private international law Law that governs the relationships between private parties involved in international transactions. Includes international business law.

private law Law dealing with the enforcement of private duties.

private trial An alternative dispute-resolution method in which cases are tried, usually in private, by a referee who is selected by the disputants and empowered by statute to enter a binding judgment.

probable cause The reasonable inference from the available facts and circumstances that the suspect committed the crime.

procedural due process Procedural steps to which individuals are entitled before losing their life, liberty, or property.

procedural rule A rule that governs the internal processes of an administrative agency.

professional corporation A corporation organized by doctors, dentists, lawyers, accountants, or other professionals specified in state statutes.

property A bundle of rights, in relation to others, to possess, use, and dispose of a tangible or intangible object.

prospectus The first part of the registration statement the SEC requires from issuers of new securities. It contains material information about the business and its management, the offering itself, the use to be made of the funds obtained, and certain financial statements.

proxy A document by which shareholders or a publicly held company can transfer their rights to vote at a shareholders' meeting to a second party.

public disclosure of private facts A privacy tort that consists of unwarranted disclosure of a private fact about a person.

public international law Law that governs the relationships between nation-states.

public law Law dealing with the relationship of government to individual citizens.

public policy exception An exception to the employment-at-will doctrine that makes it unlawful to dismiss an employee for taking certain actions in the public interest.

publicly held corporation A corporation whose stock is traded on at least one national securities exchange.

puffery An exaggerated recommendation made in a sales talk to promote the product.

punitive damages Monetary damages awarded in excess of compensatory damages for the sole purpose of deferring similar conduct in the future.

quality circle A small group of workers that voluntarily meets on a regular basis, under the leadership of a supervisor, to discuss work problems and recommend solutions to management.

quasi-contract A court-imposed agreement to prevent the unjust enrichment of one party when the parties had not really agreed to an enforceable contract.

quitclaim deed A deed that simply transfers to the grantee the interest that the grantor owns in the property.

Racketeer Influenced Corrupt Organizations Act (RICO) Prohibits persons employed by or associated with an enterprise from engaging in a pattern of racketeering activity, which is broadly defined to include almost all white-collar crimes as well as acts of violence.

real property Land and everything permanently attached to it.

reason An explanation or justification provided as support for a conclusion.

red herring A preliminary prospectus that contains most of the information that will appear in the final prospectus, except for the price of the securities. The "red herring" prospectus may be distributed to potential buyers during the waiting period, but no sales may be finalized during this period.

reformation Correction of terms in an agreement so that they reflect the true understanding of the parties.

Regulation Z A group of rules, set forth by the Federal Reserve Board, to implement some provisions of the Truth-in-Lending Act, requiring lenders to disclose certain information to borrowers.

Rehabilitation Act of 1973 Prohibits discrimination in employment against otherwise qualified persons who have a handicap. Applies only to the federal government, employers who have contracts with the federal government, and parties who administer programs receiving federal financial assistance.

remand Term used for an appellate court's decision that an error was committed that may have affected the outcome of the case and that therefore the case must be returned to the lower court.

res ipsa loquitur Legal doctrine that allows a judge or a jury to infer negligence on the basis of the fact that accidents of the type that happened to the plaintiff generally do not occur in the absence of negligence on the part of the someone in the defendant's position.

rescission Cancellation of a contract.

respondeat superior Legal doctrine imposing liability on a principal for torts committed by an agent who is employed by the principal and subject to the principal's control.

restraint of trade Action that interferes with the economic law of supply and demand.

restrictive covenants Promises by the owner, generally included in the deed, to use or not to use the land in particular ways.

reverse Term used for an appellate court's decision that the lower court's decision was incorrect and cannot be allowed to stand.

reverse discrimination Discrimination in favor of members of groups that have been previously discriminated against; claim usually raised by white males.

rule-of-reason standard A legal standard that holds that only unreasonable restraints of trade violate Section 1 of the Sherman Act. If the court determines an action's anticompetitive effects outweigh its procompetitive effects, the restraint is unreasonable.

rules of civil procedure The rules governing proceedings in a civil case; federal rules of procedure apply in all federal courts, and state rules apply in state courts.

scienter Knowledge that a representation is false.

secondary boycott A boycott against one employer to force it to cease doing business with another employer with whom the union has a dispute.

secondary-line injury A form of price discrimination in which a seller offers a discriminatory price to one buyer but not to another buyer.

Securities and Exchange Commission (SEC) The federal administrative agency charged with overall responsibility for the regulation of securities, including ensuring that investors receive "full and fair" disclosure of all material facts with regard to any public offering of securities. It has wide enforcement powers to protect investors against price manipulation, insider trading, and other dishonest dealings.

security A stock or bond or any other instrument of interest that represents an investment in a common enterprise with reasonable expectations of profits that are derived solely from the efforts of those other than the investor.

separation of powers Constitutional doctrine whereby the legislative branch enacts laws and appropriates funds, the executive branch sees that the laws are faithfully executed, and the judicial branch interprets the laws.

service Providing the defendant with a summons and a copy of the complaint.

sexual harassment Unwelcome sexual advances, requests for sexual favors, and other verbal or physical conduct of a sexual nature that explicitly or implicitly makes submission a term or condition of employment or that creates an intimidating, hostile, or offensive environment.

shadow jury Group of individuals, demographically matched to the actual jurors in a case, that sits in the courtroom during a trial and then "deliberates" at the end of each day so that lawyers have continuous feedback of how their case is going.

shelf registration Procedure whereby large corporations can file a registration statement for securities it wishes to sell over a period of time rather than immediately.

Sherman Act Makes illegal every combination, contract, or conspiracy that is an unreasonable restraint of trade when this concerted action involves interstate commerce.

short-swing profits Profits made by directors, officers, or owners of 10 percent of the securities of a corporation as a result of buying and selling the securities within a six-month period.

sick building syndrome Indoor air pollution caused by the absence of fresh air in overly insulated new buildings and by the emission of harmful substances found in many building materials and office furnishings.

slander Spoken defamatory statement.

social responsibility Concern of business entities about profit and nonprofit activities and their unintended impact on others directly or indirectly involved.

sole proprietorship A business owned by one person, who has sole control over management and profits.

sovereign immunity doctrine States that a government expropriating foreign-owned private property is immune from the jurisdiction of courts in the owner's country.

spam Unsolicited commercial or "junk" e-mail.

specific performance A court order compelling a party to perform in such a way as to meet the terms of the contract.

standing The legal status necessary to file a lawsuit.

state court jurisdiction Applies to cases that may be heard only in the state court system.

state implementation plan (SIP) A plan, required of every state, that explains how the state will meet federal air pollution standards.

state-of-the-art defense A product liability defense based on adherence to existing technologically feasible standards at the time the product was manufactured.

statute of limitations A statute that bars actions arising more than a specified number of years after the cause of the action arises.

statute of repose A statute that bars actions arising more than a specified number of years after the product was purchased.

statutory law Law made by the legislative branch of government.

stock The capital that a corporation raises through the sale of shares that entitle their holders to certain rights of ownership.

stock option A stock warrant issued to employees; cannot be traded.

stock warrant A document authorizing its holder to purchase a stated number of shares of stock at a stated price, usually for a stated period of time; may be freely traded.

strict liability offense An offense for which no state of mind is required.

strict liability tort A civil wrong that involves taking action that is so inherently dangerous under the circumstances of its performance that no amount of due care can make it safe.

strike A temporary concerted withdrawal of labor.

Subchapter S corporation A business that is organized like a corporation but, under Internal Revenue Code Subchapter S, is treated like a partnership for tax purposes so long as it abides by certain restrictions pertaining to stock, shareholders, and affiliations.

subject matter jurisdiction The power of a court to render a decision in a particular type of case.

submission agreement Separate agreement providing that a specific dispute be resolved through arbitration.

substantial performance Completion of nearly all the terms of the contract plus an honest effort to complete the rest of the terms coupled with no willful departure from any of the terms.

substantive due process Requirement that laws depriving individuals of liberty or property be fair.

substantive rule A rule that creates, defines, or regulates the legal rights of administrative agencies and the parties they regulate.

summary jury trial An alternative dispute-resolution method that consists of an abbreviated trial, a nonbinding jury verdict, and a settlement conference.

summons Order by a court to appear before it at a certain time and place.

Superfund A fund authorized by CERCLA to cover the costs of cleaning up hazardous waste disposal sites whose owners cannot be found or are unwilling or unable to pay for the cleanup.

Supremacy Clause Provides that the U.S. Constitution and all laws and treaties of the United States constitute the supreme law of the land; found in Article V.

suretyship A contract between a third party and a creditor that allows the third party to pay the debt of the debtor; the surety is primarily liable.

syndicate An investment group that privately agrees to come together for the purpose of financing a large commercial project that none of the syndicate members could finance alone.

Taft-Hartley Act Bars unions from engaging in specified unfair labor practices, makes collective bargaining agreements enforceable in U.S. district courts, and provides a civil damages remedy for parties injured by certain prohibited union activities.

Takings Clause Provides that if the government takes private property for public use, it must pay the owner just compensation; found in Fifth Amendment.

tangible property Personal property that is material and movable (e.g., furniture).

technology driven standards Standards that take account of existing levels of technology and require the best control system possible given the limits of that technology.

technology forcing standards Standards of pollution control set primarily on the basis of health considerations, with the assumption that once regulators have set the standards, industry will be forced to develop the technology to meet them.

tenancy by the entirety Form of co-ownership of real property, allowed only to married couples, in which one owner cannot sell without the consent of the other and the creditors of only one owner cannot attach the property.

tenancy in common Form of co-ownership of real property in which owners may have equal or unequal shares of the property, may sell their shares without the consent of the other owners, and may have their interest attached by creditors.

tender offer A public offer by an individual or corporation made directly to the shareholders of another corporation in an effort to acquire the targeted corporation at a specific price.

tertiary-line injury A form of price discrimination in which a discriminatory price is passed along from a secondary-line party to a favored party at the next level of distribution.

testimonial A statement by a public figure professing the merits of some product or service.

title Ownership of property.

Title VII The statute that prohibits discrimination in hiring, firing, or other terms and conditions of employment on the basis of race, color, religion, sex, or national origin.

tort An injury to another's person or property; a civil wrong.

toxic substance Any chemical or mixture whose manufacture, processing, distribution, use, or disposal presents an unreasonable risk of harm to human health or the environment.

trade dress The overall appearance and image of a product that has acquired secondary meaning.

trade secret A process, product, method of operation, or compilation of information used in a business that is not known to the public and that may bestow a competitive advantage on the business.

trademark A distinctive mark, word, design, picture, or arrangement used by the producer of a product that tends to cause consumers to identify the product with the producer.

trespass to personalty Intentionally exercising dominion and control over another's personal property.

trespass to realty (trespass to real property) Intentionally entering the land of another or causing an object to be placed on the land of another without the landowner's permission.

trust A business arrangement in which owners of stocks in several companies place their securities with trustees, who jointly manage the companies and pay out a specific share of their earnings to the securities holders.

tying arrangement A restraint of trade wherein the seller permits a buyer to purchase one product or service only if the buyer agrees to purchase a second product or service. For example, a patent holder issues a license to use a patented object on condition that the licensee agree to also buy nonpatented products from the patent holder.

Ultamares Doctrine Rule making accountants liable only to those in a privity-of-contract relationship with the accountant.

underwriter Investment banking firm that agrees to purchase a securities issue from the issuer, usually on a fixed date at a fixed price, with a view to eventually selling the securities to brokers, who, in turn, sell them to the public.

undisclosed principal One whose identity and existence are both unknown to the third party.

undue influence Mental coercion exerted by one party over the other party to the contract.

unfair competition Entering into business for the sole purpose of causing a loss of business to another firm.

unfair labor practice strike A nonviolent work stoppage for the purpose of protesting an employer's commission of an unfair labor practice.

unilateral contract An exchange of a promise for an act.

valid contract One that meets all legal requirements for a fully enforceable contract.

variance Permission given to a landowner to use a piece of his or her land in a manner prohibited by the zoning laws; generally granted to prevent undue hardship.

venue County of the trial court; prescribed by state statute.

vertical merger A merger that integrates two firms that have a supplier-customer relationship.

vertical price-fixing Stipulation by a manufacturer to a retailer to whom it sells products what price the retailer must charge for those products.

vertical restraint of trade Restraint that occurs between individuals or corporations at different levels of the marketing structure.

virus A computer program that destroys, damages, rearranges, or replaces computer data.

void contract One that at its formation has an illegal object of serious defects.

voidable contract One that gives one of the parties the option of withdrawing.

voir dire Process whereby the judge and/or the attorneys question potential jurors to determine whether they will be able to render an unbiased opinion in the case.

Wagner Act (NLRA) Guarantees the rights of workers to organize and bargain collectively and forbids employers from engaging in specified unfair labor practices. Also called National Labor Relations Act.

warehousing An act of bad faith that occurs when an individual or business registers domain names in the hope that the name can be sold to a business.

warranty A guarantee or binding promise that goods (products) meet certain standards of performance.

water rights The legal ability to use water flowing across or underneath one's property.

white-collar crime A crime committed in a commercial context by a member of the professional-managerial class.

winding-up The process of completing all unfinished transactions, paying off outstanding debts, distributing assets, and dividing remaining profits after a partnership has been terminated or dissolved.

workers' compensation laws State laws that provide financial compensation to covered employees or their dependents when employees are injured on the job.

work-product doctrine Provides that formal and informal documents prepared by an attorney in conjunction with a client's case are privileged and may not be revealed by the attorney without the client's permission.

worm A program that travels from one computer to another but does not attach itself to the operating system of the computer it "infects." It differs from a "virus," which is also a migrating program, but one that attaches itself to the operating system of any computer it enters and can infect any other computer that uses files from the infected computer.

writ of execution An order by a clerk of the court directing the sheriff to seize any of the nonexempt real or personal property of a debtor who refuses to or cannot pay a creditor.

zoning Government restrictions on the use of private property in order to ensure the orderly growth and development of a community and to protect the health, safety, and welfare of citizens.

B

Baby FTC laws, 774
Bail, 169
Bailee, 394
Bailments, 394
Bailor, 394
"Bait and switch" technique, 753-755
Balint, K., 182
Bank Merger Act of 1966, 737-738, 741
Bankruptcy Reform Act of 1978, 643, 645,
 647, 753
 bankruptcy proceedings, types of, 749
 Chapter 7 bankruptcy:
 defined, 749
 exemptions under, 749-750
 Chapter 11 bankruptcy, 749, 751
 Chapter 12 bankruptcy, 749, 751
 Chapter 13 bankruptcy, 749-750
 1984 amendments, 751
 reform, 750
Barbara Schreiber v. Burlington Northern,
 Inc., 671-672
Bargained-for exchange of promises, 272
Bates v. State Bar of Arizona, 216-218
Batson v. Kentucky, 60, 63
Battery, 318
Bay Garden Manor Condominium
 Association v. James Marks, 365
Baycol, 343
BCB Anesthesia Care v. Passavant
 Memorial Area Hospital, 743
Beachem v. Unemployment Compensation
 Board of Review, 497-498
Beattie v. Beattie, 34
Becker, J., 455
Benedict v. McNeil Consumer Products Co.,
 342
Berleman, H., 196
Berne Convention of 1886, 406-407, 408
Best Practicable Control Technology
 (BPCT), 617
Better Business Bureaus (BBBs), 89
Bhopal, India, gas leak accident, 204-205,
 207, 222
Bias v. Advantage International, Inc.,
 423-424
Bicultural, 580
Bicultural stress, 580
Biculturalism, 580
Bilateral contract, 265
Bilateral investment treaties (BITs), 240
Bilateral mistake, 275
Bill of Rights, 134
Binding arbitration clause, 78
Blackground Records, 331
Blakely v. Washington, 181-182
Blue Cross & Blue Shield United of
 Wisconsin v. Marshfield Clinic, 743
Bluewater Network v. EPA, 638

BMW of North America, Inc. v. Ira Gore, Jr.,
 311-314
Board of directors, role of, 448-449
Board rules, 539
Bochan v. LaFontaine, 71
Bodily contact, use of term, 318
Boesky, Ivan, 677
Bona fide occupational qualification
 (BFOQ), 577-578, 590
Bond v. United States, 136-137
Bonds, 442, 640
Booking, 168-169
Boomer et al. v. Atlantic Cement Company,
 607-609
Bork, R., 696
Bourne v. Walt Disney Co., 34
Boycotts, 554
Bramble Bush, The (Llewellyn), 23
Bramson, M., 165
Braswell v. United States, 133
Breach of contract:
 breach of sales contract (goods), remedies
 for, 299-300
 equitable remedies for, 296-298
 remedies for, 293-300
 compensatory damages, 294
 liquidated damages, 295-296
 monetary damages, 294
 nominal damages, 294
 punitive damages, 294
Breach-of-warranty actions, defenses to,
 351
Brennan, B., 209, 696
Brennan-Kubasek Corporation, articles of
 incorporation of, 443
Brian Kato Kaelin v. Globe
 Communications Corp., 337
Bribery, 183
Broker-dealers, 662-666
Brokers, 662
Brown University and International
 Union, United Automobile,
 Aerospace and Agricultural
 Implement Workers of America, UAW
 AFL-CIO, Petitioner, 548-549
Brown v. Abbott Laboratories, 362
Brown v. Legal Foundation of Washington,
 136
Browner, Carol, 612
Broz v. Cellular Information Systems, Inc.,
 466
Bubba's Bar-B-Q Oven v. The Holland
 Company, 400
Burden of proof, 170-171
Business associations:
 global dimensions of, 462-463
 and law, 433-468
 specialized forms of, 459-460
 cooperative, 460
 franchising, 461-462

joint stock company, 460
joint venture, 460
syndicate, 460
Business debt-collection practices, federal
 laws regulating, 760-773
Business ethics, *See also* Ethics
 defined, 206-208
 ethical workplace, 207
Business judgment rule, 452
Business managers, 4
Business organization:
 common forms of, 434-455
 corporation, 435, 438-455
 factors influencing a business manager's
 choice of, 458-459
 partnership, 435-438
 sole proprietorship, 434-435, 458
Business trade practices:
 consumer legislation, 757-760
 consumer warranties, 757-758
 franchising relationships, 757
 deceptive advertising, 753-755
 "bait and switch" technique, 753-755
 deceptive labeling and packaging,
 756-757
 false price/nlcomparisons, 754
 private party suits, 756
 and product quality/quantity, 755-756
 puffery, 755
 testimonials, 756
 unfair advertising, 756
 federal regulation of, 753-760
 telemarketing legislation, 758-759

C

Cairns, H., 21
California and Hawaiian Sugar Company
 v. Sun Ship, Inc., 296-297
California Dental Association v. Federal
 Trade Commission, 737
California Federal Savings and Loan
 Association et al. v. Department of
 Fair Employment and Housing et
 al., 581
Calvani, T., 696
Cann, W. Jr., 696
Capital structure, corporations, 446
Carbon monoxide, 619
Carefirst of Maryland, Inc. v. Carefirst
 Pregnancy Centers, Inc., 41
Carl Sagan v. Apple Computer Co., 319
Carr v. Reno, 593
Case law, 30
 and legal object, 278
Castle v. United States, 285
Causation, 330
Cause:
 actual, 330